EIGHTH EDITION

Consumer Behavior

Buying, Having, and Being

Michael R. Solomon

**Saint Joseph's University and
The University of Manchester (U.K.)**

PEARSON

Prentice
Hall

Pearson Education International

Executive Editor: Melissa Sabella
Vice President/Editorial Director: Sally Yagan
Editor in Chief: David Parker
Product Development Manager: Ashley Santora
Project Manager, Editorial: Melissa Pellerano
Marketing Manager: Anne Fahlgren
Marketing Assistant: Susan Osterlitz
Senior Managing Editor: Judy Leale
Project Manager, Production: Kelly Warsak
Manager, Rights and Permissions: Charles Morris
Senior Operations Supervisor: Arnold Vila
Creative Director: Leslie Osher
Senior Art Director: Janet Slowik
Interior Design: Karen Quigley
Illustration (Interior): S4Carlisle Publishing Services
Director, Image Resource Center: Melinda Patelli
Manager, Rights and Permissions: Zina Arabia
Manager, Visual Research: Beth Brenzel
Manager, Cover Visual Research & Permissions: Karen Sanatar
Image Permission Coordinator: Craig Jones
Photo Researcher: Kathy Ringrose
Composition: S4Carlisle Publishing Services
Full-Service Project Management: Heather Willison/S4Carlisle Publishing Services
Printer/Binder: Quebecor World Color
Cover Printer: Phoenix Color Corp.
Typeface: 9.5/12 Utopia

Credits and acknowledgments borrowed from other sources and reproduced, with permission, in this textbook appear on appropriate page within text.

If you purchased this book within the United States or Canada you should be aware that it has been wrongfully imported without the approval of the Publisher or the Author.

Pearson Education LTD.
Pearson Education Singapore, Pte. Ltd
Pearson Education Canada, Inc.
Pearson Education–Japan

Pearson Education Australia PTY, Limited
Pearson Education North Asia Ltd
Pearson Educación de Mexico, S.A. de C.V.
Pearson Education Malaysia, Pte. Ltd.
Pearson Education Upper Saddle River, New Jersey

10 9 8 7 6 5 4 3 2 1
ISBN-13: 978-0-13-515336-9
ISBN-10:   0-13-515336-0

Brief Contents

Contents

Chapter 6: Personality and Lifestyles 242

Chapter 7: Attitudes 280

Chapter 8: Attitude Change and Interactive Communications 312

Chapter 12: Organizational and Household Decision Making 470

■ SECTION 4

CONSUMERS AND SUBCULTURES 507

Chapter 13: Income and Social Class 508

Chapter 14: Ethnic, Racial, and Religious Subcultures 542

Chapter 15: Age Subcultures 572

About the Author

Michael R. Solomon, Ph.D., is Professor of Marketing and Director of the Center for Consumer Research in the Haub School of Business at Saint Joseph's University in Philadelphia. He also is Professor of Consumer Behaviour at the Manchester School of Business, The University of Manchester, United Kingdom. Prior to joining the Saint Joseph's faculty in fall 2006, he was the Human Sciences Professor of Consumer Behavior at Auburn University. Before moving to Auburn in 1995, he was Chair of the Department of Marketing in the School of Business at Rutgers University, New Brunswick, New Jersey. Professor Solomon began his academic career in the Graduate School of Business Administration at New York University, where he also served as Associate Director of NYU's Institute of Retail Management. He earned B.A. degrees in psychology and sociology *magna cum laude* at Brandeis University in 1977, and a Ph.D. in social psychology at The University of North Carolina at Chapel Hill in 1981. He was awarded the Fulbright/FLAD Chair in Market Globalization by the U.S. Fulbright Commission and the government of Portugal, and in fall 1996 he served as Distinguished Lecturer in Marketing at The Technical University of Lisbon.

Professor Solomon's primary research interests include consumer behavior and lifestyle issues; branding strategy; the symbolic aspects of products; the psychology of fashion, decoration, and image; services marketing; marketing in virtual worlds, and the development of visually oriented online research methodologies. He has published numerous articles on these and related topics in academic journals, and he has delivered invited lectures on these subjects in the United Kingdom, Scandinavia, Australia, and Latin America. His research has been funded by the American Academy of Advertising, the American Marketing Association, the U.S. Department of Agriculture, the International Council of Shopping Centers, and the U.S. Department of Commerce. Three research projects are currently funded by major multiyear grants from the National Textile Center and U.S. Department of Commerce. He currently sits on the editorial boards of the *Journal of Consumer Behaviour,* the *Journal of Retailing,* and *The European Business Review,* and he recently completed an elected six-year term on the Board of Governors of the Academy of Marketing Science. Professor Solomon has been recognized as one of the fifteen most widely cited scholars in the academic behavioral sciences/fashion literature, and as one of the ten most productive scholars in the field of advertising and marketing communications.

Professor Solomon is a frequent contributor to mass media. His feature articles have appeared in such magazines as *Psychology Today, Gentleman's Quarterly,* and *Savvy.* He has been quoted in numerous national magazines and newspapers, including *Allure, Elle, Glamour, Mademoiselle, Mirabella, Newsweek, the New York Times, Self, USA Today,* and the *Wall Street Journal.* He frequently appears on television and speaks on radio to comment on consumer behavior issues, including *The Today Show, Good Morning America,* CNBC, *Channel One, Inside Edition, Newsweek on the Air,* the Wall Street Journal Radio Network, the Entrepreneur Sales and Marketing Show, the WOR Radio Network, and National Public Radio. He acts as consultant to numerous companies on consumer behavior and marketing strategy issues and often speaks to business groups throughout the United States and overseas. In addition to this text, Professor Solomon is co-author of the widely used textbook *Marketing: Real People, Real Choices.* He has three children, Amanda, Zachary, and Alexandra and a son-in-law Orly. He lives in Philadelphia with his wife Gail and their "other child"—a pug named Kelbie Rae.

Preface

I love to people-watch, don't you? People shopping, people flirting, people consuming. Consumer behavior is the study of people and the products that help to shape their identities. Because I'm a consumer myself, I have a selfish interest in learning more about how this process works—and so do you.

In many courses, students are merely passive observers; they learn about topics that affect them indirectly, if at all. Not everyone is a plasma physicist, a medieval French scholar, or a marketing professional. But we are all consumers. Many of the topics in this book have both professional and personal relevance to the reader, regardless of whether he or she is a student, professor, or businessperson. Nearly everyone can relate to the trials and tribulations of last-minute shopping; primping for a big night out; agonizing over an expensive purchase; fantasizing about a week in the Caribbean; celebrating a holiday, or commemorating a landmark event, such as graduating, getting a driver's license, or (dreaming about) winning the lottery.

In this edition, I have tried to introduce you to the latest and best thinking by some very bright scientists who develop models and studies of consumer behavior. But that's not enough. Consumer behavior is an applied science, so we must never lose sight of the role of "horse sense" when we try to apply our findings to life in the real world. That's why you'll find a lot of practical examples to back up these fancy theories.

What Makes This Book Different: Buying, Having, and Being

As this book's subtitle suggests, my vision of consumer behavior goes well beyond studying the act of *buying*—*having* and *being* are just as important, if not more so. Consumer behavior is more than buying things; it also embraces the study of how having (or not having) things affects our lives and how our possessions influence the way we feel about ourselves and about each other—our state of being. I developed the *Wheel of Consumer Behavior* that appears at the beginning of text sections to underscore the complex—and often inseparable—interrelationships between the individual consumer and his or her social realities.

In addition to understanding why people buy things, we also try to appreciate how products, services, and consumption activities contribute to the broader social world we experience. Whether we are shopping, cooking, cleaning, playing basketball, hanging out at the beach, or even looking at ourselves in the mirror, the marketing system touches our lives. As if these experiences aren't complex enough, the task of understanding the consumer multiplies geometrically when we take a multicultural perspective.

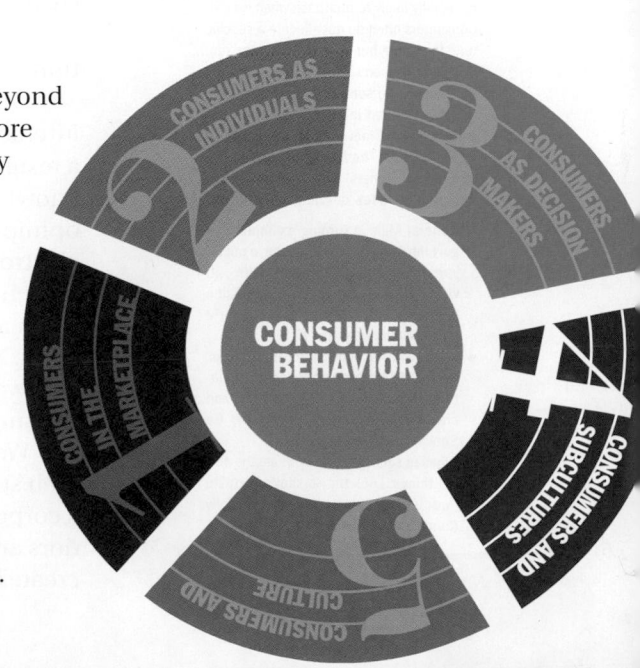

We'll explore these ideas with intriguing and current examples as we show how the consumer behavior discipline relates to your daily life. Throughout the eighth edition, you'll find up-to-the-minute discussions of topics such as social networking, twittering and consumer-generated content, sustainability and carbon footprints, virtual identity and online avatars, Übersexuals, the long tail, brand sluts, machinimas, being spaces, shopmobbing, microloans, fortress brands, and plinking™. If you can't identify all of these terms, I can suggest a textbook you should read immediatcly!

Going Global

The American experience is important, but it's far from the whole story. This book also considers the many other consumers around the world whose diverse experiences with buying, having, and being we must understand. That's why you'll find numerous examples of marketing and consumer practices relating to consumers and companies outside the United States throughout the book. You'll find a list of those examples, with specific page references, on the inside back cover of this book. If we didn't know it before the tragic events of September 11, 2001, we certainly know it now: Americans also are global citizens, and it's vital that we all appreciate others' perspectives.

Digital Consumer Behavior: A Virtual Community

As more of us go online everyday, there's no doubt the world is changing—and consumer behavior is evolving faster than you can say "World Wide Web." This eighth edition continues to highlight and celebrate the brave new world of digital consumer behavior. Today, consumers and producers come together electronically in ways we have never before experienced. Rapid transmission of information is altering the speed at which new trends develop and the direction in which they travel—especially because the virtual world lets consumers participate in the creation and dissemination of new products.

One of the most exciting aspects of the new digital world is that consumers can interact directly with other people who live around the block or around the world. As a result, the meaning of community is radically redefined. It's no longer enough to acknowledge that consumers like to talk to each other about products. Now we share opinions and get the buzz about new movies, CDs, cars, clothes—you name it—in electronic communities that may include a housewife in Alabama, a disabled senior citizen in Alaska, or a teen loaded with body piercings in Amsterdam. And many of them are meeting up in computer-mediated environments (CMEs) such as Facebook, MySpace, and Second Life. I'm totally fascinated by what goes on in these virtual worlds and you'll see a lot of material in this edition related to these emerging consumer playgrounds.

We have just begun to explore the ramifications for consumer behavior when a Web surfer can project her own picture onto a Web site to get a virtual makeover or a corporate purchasing agent can solicit bids for a new piece of equipment from vendors around the world in minutes. These new ways of interacting in the marketplace create bountiful opportunities for businesspeople and consumers alike. You will find

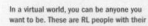

Net Profit

Along with the increase in time poverty, researchers also note a rise in *polychronic activity*, or *multitasking*, where consumers do more than one thing at a time.[19] We're especially likely to multitask when we eat. Consumers often do not allocate a specific time for dining but instead eat on the run. In a poll, 64 percent of respondents said they usually do something else while eating. As one food industry executive commented, "We've moved beyond grazing and into gulping."[20] The food industry is racing to meet consumers' desires to eat on the run. Here are a few on-the-go products:

- General Mills is turning its Yoplait yogurt into a meal with Nouriche, a nonfat yogurt smoothie fortified with 20 vitamins and minerals. A television commercial proclaims, "No time for a meal? Nouriche yourself."
- Kraft Foods launched Nabisco Go-Paks, cupholder-ready contour packages featuring mini versions of its cookies and crackers, similar to the Frito-Lay Go Snacks already on the market.
- Tubes to squeeze on the run are the next big things: Look for Hershey's Portable Pudding in tubes as well as Jolly Rancher Gel Snacks.[21]

illustrations of the changing digital world sprinkled liberally throughout this edition. In addition, each chapter features boxes I call *Net Profit* that point to specific examples of the Net's potential to improve the way business is conducted.

But is the digital world always a rosy place? Unfortunately, just as in the "real world," the answer is no. The potential to exploit consumers, whether by invading their privacy, preying on the curiosity of children, or simply providing false product information, is always there. That's why you'll also find boxes I call *The Tangled Web* that point out some of the abuses of this fascinating new medium. Still, I can't imagine a world without the Web, and I hope you'll enjoy the ways it's changing our field. When it comes to the new virtual world of consumer behavior, you're either on the train or under it.

Consumer Research Is a Big Tent: The Importance of a Balanced Perspective

Like most of you who will read this book, the field of consumer behavior is young, dynamic, and in flux. It is constantly cross-fertilized by perspectives from many different disciplines—the field is a big tent that invites many diverse views to enter. I have tried to express the field's staggering diversity in these pages. Consumer researchers represent virtually every social science discipline, plus a few from the physical sciences and the arts for good measure. From this melting pot comes a healthy "stew" of research perspectives, viewpoints regarding appropriate research methods, and even deeply held beliefs about what are and what are not appropriate issues for consumer researchers to study in the first place.

The book also emphasizes how strategically vital it is to understand consumers. Many (if not most) of the fundamental concepts in marketing emanate from a manager's ability to know people. After all, if we don't understand why people behave as they do, how can we identify their needs? If we can't identify their needs, how can we satisfy their needs? If we can't satisfy people's needs, we don't have a marketing concept, so we might as well fold our big tent and go home!

To illustrate the potential of consumer research to inform marketing strategy, the text contains numerous examples of specific applications of consumer behavior concepts by marketing practitioners as well as examples of windows of opportunity where we could use these concepts (perhaps by alert strategists after taking this course!). The *Marketing Opportunity* boxes you'll find in each chapter highlight the fascinating ways that marketing practitioners translate wisdom they glean from consumer research into actual business activities.

The Good, the Bad, and the Ugly

A strategic focus is great, but this book doesn't assume that everything marketers do is in the best interests of consumers or of their environment. Likewise, as consumers we do many things that are not so positive either. We suffer from addictions, status envy, ethnocentrism, racism, sexism, and many other isms. Regrettably, there are times when marketing activities—deliberately or not—encourage or exploit these human flaws. This book deals with the totality of consumer behavior, warts and all. We'll highlight marketing mistakes or ethically suspect activities in boxes I call *Marketing Pitfall*. In particular, this edition highlights the importance of sustainability and green consumption. We won't have much consumer behavior to study if we deplete all of our natural resources by consuming them irresponsibly. I firmly believe we are on the verge of a tidal wave of environmentalism as people around the

The Tangled Web

The release of several popular video games underscores the concern of some critics who argue that these games play on racial stereotypes, including images of African American youths committing and reveling in violent street crime:

- Grand Theft Auto: San Andreas is set in a city resembling gang[...] es of Los Angeles of th[...] tures a digital cast of A[...] and Hispanic men, som[...] ed hair and scarves ove[...] aiming Uzis from low-ri[...]
- Def Jam Fight for NY fe[...] style characters (one w[...] the rapper Snoop Dogg[...] and pummel one anoth[...] such as the 125th Stre[...] in Harlem.
- 25 to Life is an "urbar[...] that includes a hip-hop[...] lets gamers play the rol[...] cers or criminals, and [...] images of young gun[...] American gangsters.
- Notorious: Die to Drive fe[...] style car combat" with [...] to "rule the streets of f[...] neighborhoods." The ga[...] proclaims, "High-price[...] finest bling, and millic[...] just some of the reward[...] ous few who can surviv[...] gerous game. Once yor[...] there's no going back."[4]

Marketing Opportunity

Exciting new advances in technology promise to automate our routine tasks even more. These new gadgets are part of a trend the industry calls **silent commerce** that enables transactions and information gathering to occur in the background without consumers or managers directly intervening. In Singapore, cars "talk" to the streets on which they drive. Retailers in the United States are testing a system that enables products to inform the store when they're bought so that the store managers can quickly replenish their inventories. In home kitchens later this decade, frozen dinners will automatically give cooking instructions to microwave ovens.[15]

Many of these new *smart products* are possible because the items themselves are imbedded with a tiny plastic **RFID** (*response frequency identification device*) tag that holds a very inexpensive computer chip capable of storing a small amount of information, along with a tiny antenna that lets the chip communicate with a computer network. Researchers predict that in time these tags will be on almost everything, from egg cartons that will alert a store manager when their contents have passed their expiration date to roof tiles on houses that will e-mail a roofing repair company when they fall off. A wine lover can check on the contents of his home wine cellar while browsing the new shipment of cabernets. You'll always know the location of your sunglasses—or maybe even those mysterious socks that always seem to "vanish" in the dryer!

Marketing Pitfall

Labels provide valuable information about the proper way to use products, but sometimes they can be less than clear. Here are some examples of "interesting" labels:[31]

- On a Conair Pro Style 1600 hair dryer: WARNING: Do not use in shower. Never use while sleeping.
- Instructions for folding up a portable baby carriage: Step 1: Remove baby.
- A rest stop on a Wisconsin highway: Do not eat urinal cakes.
- On a bag of Fritos: You could be a winner! No purchase necessary. Details inside.
- On some Swanson frozen dinners: Serving suggestion: Defrost.
- On Tesco's Tiramisu dessert (printed on bottom of box): Do not turn upside down.
- On Marks & Spencer bread pudding: Product will be hot after heating.
- On packaging for a Rowenta iron: Do not iron clothes on body.
- On Nytol sleeping aid: Warning: May cause drowsiness.

globe (including Americans at last!) wake up to the "inconvenient truth" and start to change their ways. The marketers that understand this and change their ways as well will profit, both morally and financially.

On a more cheerful note, marketers create wonderful (or at least unusual) things, such as holidays; comic books; Krispy Kreme donuts; nu-jazz music; Webkinz; and the many stylistic options that beckon to us in the domains of clothing, home design, the arts, and cuisine. I also take pains to acknowledge the sizable impact of marketing on popular culture. Indeed, the final section of this book reflects very recent work in the field that scrutinizes, criticizes, and sometimes celebrates consumers in their everyday worlds. I hope you will enjoy reading about such wonderful things as much as I enjoyed writing about them. Welcome to the fascinating world of consumer behavior!

 ## Consumer Behavior in the Trenches

I'm a huge believer in the value of up-to-date information. Our field changes so rapidly that often yesterday's news is no news at all. True, there are "timeless" studies that demonstrate basic consumer behavior constructs as well today as they did 20 years ago or more (I may even have authored some of them!). Still, I feel a real obligation to present students and their professors with a current view of research, popular culture, and marketing activities whenever I can. For this reason, each time I start to contemplate my next edition, I write to colleagues to ask for copies of papers they have in press that they believe will be important in the future. Their cooperation with my request allows me to include a lot of fresh research examples; in some cases these article will not yet have been published when this book comes out. I've listed those who help me in this endeavor in the Acknowledgments section, which follows.

I've taken this initiative to the next level in this edition with a new feature I call *CB as I See It*. In every chapter you'll find the writing of a "flesh-and-blood" consumer behavior professor sharing his or her perspective as a leading researcher in a particular area of specialization about an appropriate topic. I've let these esteemed colleagues largely speak for themselves so now you can benefit from other voices who chime in on relevant research issues. Again, I've listed these participants in the Acknowledgments section and I'm grateful for their wonderful cooperation—and for letting me share their words—and their photos!—with you.

CB AS I SEE IT

Professor Roland Rust
University of Maryland

As information technology advances, it is easy for companies to build products that are increasingly complicated. We see cell phones that do everything but the laundry, and even old-fashioned appliances such as televisions and cars are becoming so complicated that people can't use them. I recently received a mouse pad that had a radio, calculator, clock, alarm, and even a user's manual. This trend is not going away, so it is important for us to understand how consumers deal with this kind of complexity.

With my co-authors, Debora Thompson and Rebecca Hamilton, I have studied the concept of "feature fatigue." We discovered that consumers actually tend to want and choose products that are too complicated, only to be sorry later. We need to know more about how consumers react to complex products and whether the problem is going away as the generation that grew up with PC's, iPods, and text messages take the lead role in consumption.

Our studies showed that consumers place more weight on product capabilities than on usability before purchase, leading them to buy products with lots of features. After usage, though, the importance of usability increases a great deal, and consumers prefer a smaller number of features. This can have an important impact on customer retention because customers who buy a product with too many features may become frustrated and not repurchase. So the firm is actually better off putting fewer features in the product and counting on better customer retention rates and better word-of-mouth to counteract the perhaps somewhat lower initial sales. This strategy can be phenomenally successful, as we have seen from the success of the Apple iPod.

 ## Topics and Key Terms New to This Edition

Chapter 1

The mystery of Peeps

Social networking and the power of groups

Cult of the amateur

Package size and the j.n.d.

Saccadic eyeball motion

Rich media

Behavioral pricing

Reference price

Chapter 2

Sensory marketing

Multitasking

Portion size and the obesity epidemic

Chapter 3

Lanham Act lawsuits

Spacing effect

Passthoughts

Bitcoms
Food nostalgia
Illusion of truth effect

Chapter 4

Magnetic points in self-actualization
Interactive mobile marketing
Consumer-generated content
Web 2.0
Machinimas
Cross-cultural value differences
Apple iPhone as cult product
Carbon footprint
Greenhouse gas offsets
Sustainability as a core value
Downshifting
Locavores

Chapter 5

Twittering
Impression management
Facebook postings and Reputation
  Defender
Virtual identity, avatars, metaverse,
  CMEs
Interactive mirror
Gyaru-o ("male gals")
Muslim veiling and sex roles
Übersexuals
Japanese beauty ideals
Transition to realistic ideal
Group dieting/pro-ana movement
Buttock augmentation

Chapter 6

Doppelgänger brand image

Chapter 7

Red campaign
Multiple pathway anchoring and
  adjustment (MPAA) model

Chapter 8

Corporate social responsibility (CSR)
Spokescharacters

Chapter 9

Search engines
Men as (deficient) information searchers

Low-literate consumers
Feature creep
Expanded coverage of neuromarketing
Fake blogs
Music Genome Project
The long tail
Zipf's Law
Brand slut

Chapter 10

Cultural queuing differences
Shopping as role playing
Minipreneurs
Being spaces
Pop-up stores
Ideal Web site shopping features
Freegans
Wedding dress trashing

Chapter 11

Antibrand communities
Protest framing theory
Virtual economies
Netnography
Social network sites
Wisdom of crowds
Shopmobbing
Social contagion and obesity

Chapter 12

Crowdsourcing
Wikis
DINKs
Webkinz

Chapter 13

Wal-Mart's price/brand segmentation
Empowerment
Affluent online
Microloans
Cell phone envy

Chapter 14

Onna Otaku microculture
Uncle Ben makeover
Warming process
Hurban
Halal foods

Chapter 15

Multigenerational marketing
Ridicule and teen socialization
Thumb culture/digital natives
Cyberidentities
Nielsen ratings for dorms

Chapter 16

Package myths
Fortress brands
Sacralization of tea in Turkey

Chapter 17

Consumerspace
Voice of the consumer
Plinking™
Diffusion of skateboarding
Consumer style

 # Critical Thinking in Consumer Behavior: Case Study

Learning by doing is an integral part of the classroom experience. In this edition, we've included a Case Study at the end of each chapter along with discussion questions to help students apply the case to the chapter's contents.

Also included in the eighth edition are the following items that will enhance the student learning experience.

- Chapter Objectives at the beginning of each chapter provide an overview of key issues to be covered in the chapter. Each Chapter Summary is then organized around the objectives to help students integrate the material they have read.
- Review at the end of each chapter helps students to study key issues.
- The Consumer Behavior Challenge at the end of each chapter is divided into two sections:
  - **Discuss** poses thoughtful issues that encourage students to consider pragmatic and ethical implications of the material they have read.
  - **Apply** allows students to "get their hands dirty" by conducting miniexperiments and collecting data in the real world to better grasp the application of consumer behavior principles.

 # Supplements

- Instructor's Resource Center (IRC) on CD—The IRC includes the Instructor's Manual, the Test Item File, PowerPoints, the Image Library, and the Video Guide. These resources (except the Image Library) are also available on the IRC online at www.prenhall.com/solomon.

- Instructor's Manual
- Test Item File—The Test Item File supports Association to Advance Collegiate Schools of Business (AACSB) International Accreditation.

- TestGen (only available on the IRC online)
- PowerPoint presentation
- Videos—The eighth edition video package offers segments that take students on location, profiling well-known companies and their marketing strategies. In addition, we include in-depth examinations of the real world of global consumer behavior. These rich and thought-provoking films have been drawn from the archives of the Association for Consumer Research Film Festivals. These festivals are held annually in North America, and in the annual non-North America conference that rotates among Europe, Latin America, and the Asia Pacific region. The video library is available on DVD. Instructors can choose to have the DVD shrinkwrapped with the text. The Video Guide is available on the IRC on CD and online.
- Companion Website (www.prenhall.com/solomon)—Review quizzes and other study aids are available to students and a link is provided for instructors to access password-protected teaching resources at the IRC online.

Acknowledgments

Two bright and competent doctoral students "kept me honest" as they helped me review recent literature. Thanks go to my "right brain" researcher Sarah Scarborough-Wilner at York University and my "left brain" researcher Andrew Wilson at Florida State University. I'm also grateful for the many helpful comments on how to improve the eighth edition my peer reviewers provided. Special thanks go to the following individuals:

Nadia Abgrab Noormohamed, Salve Regina University
Joseph Adamo, Cazenovia College
Sucheta Ahlawat, Kean University
On Amir, University of California, San Diego
Verl Anderson, Dixie State College
Zeynep Arsel, University of Wisconsin
Paul Arsenault, West Chester University of Pennsylvania
April Atwood, University of Washington
P. V. (Sundar) Balakrishnan, University of Washington, Bothell
Mike Ballif, University of Utah
Somjit Barat, University of Texas, Arlington
Fleura Bardhi, Northeastern University
Susan Baxter, Bethune-Cookman University
Sandy Becker, Rutgers University
Jeri Beggs, Illinois State University
Eileen Bennett, Plymouth State University
Ken Bernhardt, Georgia State University
Adriana Boveda, University of Rhode Island
Roy Cabaniss, University of Arkansas, Monticello
Danette Cagnet, Rochester College
Lon Camomile, Colorado State University
Ken Chapman, California State University, Chico
Anindya Chatterjee, Slippery Rock University
Larry Compeau, Clarkson University
Michael Coolsen, Shippensburg University
Robert Cosenza, University of Mississippi
Emily Crawford, Savannah State University
Jacqueline Didier, Southeastern Louisiana University
Timothy Donahue, Chadron State College
Aimee Drolet, UCLA Anderson School
David Dyson, Oral Roberts University
Richard Easley, Baylor University
Susan Emens, Kent State University
Joyce Ezrow, Anne Arundel Community College
Ken Fairweather, LeTourneau University

Lori Feldman, Purdue University, Calumet
Douglas Friedman, Pennsylvania State University, Harrisburg
David Griffith, Austin College
Alice Griswold, Clarke College
Audrey Guskey, Duquesne University
Bonnie Guy, Appalachian State University
Christine Hansvick, Pacific Lutheran University
Dorothy Harpool, Wichita State University
Curtis Haugtvedt, Ohio State University
Richard Heiens, University of South Carolina, Aiken
James Hess, Ivy Tech Community College
Joyce Hicks, Saint Mary's College
Nasim Hosein, Northern State University
Bruce Huhmann, New Mexico State University
Gary Hunter, Illinois State University
Mazen Jaber, Louisiana State University
Tom Jay, Flathead Valley Community College
Michael Kalsher, Rensselaer Polytechnic Institute
Minjeong Kang, University of Minnesota
Martie Kazura, Berea College
Dale Kehr, University of Memphis
George Kelley, Erie Community College
Rodney Kingery, Hawkeye Community College
Rob Kleine, Ohio Northern University
Susan Kleine, Bowling Green State University
Nathan Kling, Monfort College of Business
Stephen Koernig, DePaul University
Shanker Krishnan, Indiana University
Karen Lancendorfer, Western Michigan University
Brian Larson, Widener University
Freddy Lee, California State University, Los Angeles
Olivia Lee, St. Cloud State University
Michael Levin, Texas Tech University
Paul Londrigan, Mott Community College
William Lundstrom, Cleveland State University
Vivek Madupu, University of Minnesota, Duluth
Larry Maes, Davenport University
Denise Makowski, Norfolk State University
Drew Martin, University of Hawaii at Hilo
Deborah McCabe, Arizona State University
Christina McCale, Regis College
Mary Ann McGrath, Loyola University, Chicago
Michael Messina, Gannon University
Ann Mirabito, Baylor University
Shekhar Misra, California State University, Chico
William Motz, Lansing Community College
Avinandan Mukherjee, Montclair State University
JoNel Mundt, Oasis Consulting
James Nall, Gardner-Webb University
John Nebeck, Viterbo University
Christine Page, Skidmore College
Karen Page, University of Pittsburgh
Barnett Parker, Pfeiffer University
H. Lois Patton, Shepherd University
William Pearce, La Roche College
Susan L. Petrella, California State University, Fullerton

Linda Plank, Ferris State University
Jeffery Podoshen, Franklin and Marshall College
Constantine Polychroniouj, University of Cincinnati
Frank Pons, University of San Diego
Sandra Powell, Weber State University
Scott Radford, University of Missouri
P. S. Raju, University of Louisville
Carmen Reagan, Austin Peay State University
Anja Reimer, University of Miami
Michelle Reiss, Spalding University
Pablo Rhi Perez, University of Texas, Brownsville
Kathleen Richard, Madonna University
Scot Roberts, Roger Williams University
Sandra Robertson, Thomas Nelson Community College
Sean Robson, Radford University
Deborah Rogers, St. Mary's University of Minnesota
Abhijit Roy, University of Scranton
Joel Saegert, University of Texas, San Antonio
John Sailors, University of St. Thomas
Allen Schaefer, Missouri State University
Roberta Schultz, Western Michigan University
Lizzie Scoburgh, University of Northwestern Ohio
Kim Serota, Oakland University
Hamed Shamma, George Washington University
Peggy Shields, University of Southern Indiana
Stowe Shoemaker, University of Houston
Lois Smith, University of Wisconsin, Whitewater
Ruth Smith, St. Anselm's College
Marla Stafford, University of Memphis
Ross Steinman, Temple University
Barbara Stewart, University of Houston
Dave Thiessen, Lewis-Clark State College
Judy Thompson, Briar Cliff University
Patrick Tormey, Iona College
Carrie Trimble, Illinois Wesleyan University
Roy R. Twaddle, University of Rhode Island
Fran Ucci, College of DuPage
Elzbieta ("Liz") Valdis Kaczor, Moraine Valley Community College
Kathleen Vohs, University of Minnesota
William Ward, Alfred University
Gary White, Bucks County Community College
James Wilkinson, Asnuntuck Community College
Natalie Wood, Saint Joseph's University
Sarah Wood, University of Wisconsin, Stout
Richard A. Wozniak, Northern Illinois University
David Wright, Abilene Christian University
Lan Wu, California State University, East Bay
Eric Yorkston, Texas Christian University

Eighteen colleagues generously contributed their thoughts to my new *CB as I See It* boxes:

Alan Andreasen, Georgetown University
Russell Belk, York University
Larry Compeau, Clarkson University
Jennifer Edson Escalas, Vanderbilt University

Susan Fournier, Boston University
Kent Grayson, Northwestern University
Morris B. Holbrook, Columbia University
Lynn Kahle, University of Oregon
Albert Muniz, DePaul University
Cele Otnes, University of Illinois at Urbana-Champaign
Connie Pechmann, University of California, Irvine
Lisa Peñaloza, University of Utah and École De Hautes Études Commerciales du Nord (EDHEC)
Joseph Priester, University of Southern California
Greg Rose, University of Washington at Tacoma
Roland Rust, University of Maryland
Hope Schau, University of Arizona
Ann Schlosser, University of Washington
L. J. Shrum, University of Texas at San Antonio

Many other colleagues and friends made significant contributions to this edition. I would like to thank, in particular, the following people who provided me with a sneak peek at their research materials and manuscripts now in press or under review:

Anders Bengtsson, Suffolk University
Ellen Garbarino, Case Western Reserve
Güliz Ger, Bilkent University
Markus Giesler, York University
Morris B. Holbrook, Columbia University
Jack Jacoby, New York University
Jill Klein, INSEAD
Tina Lowrey, University of Texas at San Antonio
Ann McGill, University of Chicago
Connie Pechmann, University of California at Irvine
L. J. Shrum, University of Texas at San Antonio
Stacy Wood, University of South Carolina

Extra special thanks are due to the preparers of the ancillary materials: Mohan K. Menon, University of South Alabama for preparation of the Instructor's Manual; Andrew T. Norman, Drake University, for preparation of the Case Studies; John R. Brooks, Jr., Houston Baptist University, for the preparation of the Test Item File; Susan A. Peterson, Scottsdale Community College for preparation of the PowerPoints; and Michael K. Coolsen, Shippensburg University for preparation of the Internet Study Guide.

I would also like to thank the good people at Prentice Hall who as always have done yeoman service on this edition. A special thanks to David Parker who "babysat" me between editors and to Anne Fahlgren for her support. Of course, Melissa Pellerano and Christine Ietto did most of the heavy lifting, and I couldn't have put all of this together without them. Thanks also to Charles Morris, Marcy Lunetta, Kathy Ringrose, Heather Willison, and Kelly Warsak for their patience with me. Finally, a shout out to Candace Cooney and Matt Early for their local support.

Without the tolerance of my friends and colleagues, I would never have been able to sustain the illusion that I was still an active researcher while I worked on this edition. I am grateful to my department chair, Diane Phillips, and to Dean Joe DiAngelo for supporting their new high-maintenance faculty member. Also, I am grateful to my undergraduate students, who have been a prime source of inspiration, examples, and feedback. The satisfaction I have garnered from teaching them about consumer behavior motivated me to write a book I felt they would like to read.

Last but not least, I would like to thank my family and friends for sticking by me during this revision. They know who they are; their names pop up in chapter vignettes throughout the book. My apologies for "distorting" their characters in the name of poetic license! Special thanks to my two colleagues and buds Basil Englis and Gary Bamossy for all of their support. My gratitude and love go out to my parents, Jackie and Henry, and my in-laws, Marilyn and Phil. My super children, Amanda, Zachary, and Alexandra—and now my high-tech son-in-law Orly—who always made the sun shine on gray days (and of course my pug Kelbie Rae). Finally, thanks above all to the love of my life—Gail, my wonderful wife, best friend, and occasional re-search assistant: I still do it all for you.

M.R.S.
Philadelphia, Pennsylvania
January 2008

Consumer Behavior

Buying, Having, and Being

Consumers in the Marketplace

This introductory section provides an overview of the field of consumer behavior (CB). In Chapter 1, we look at how consumers influence the field of marketing and also at how marketers influence us. We describe the discipline of consumer behavior and some of the different approaches to understanding what makes consumers tick. We also highlight the importance of the study of consumer behavior to such public policy issues as addiction and environmentalism.

■ **CHAPTERS AHEAD**

CHAPTER 1
Consumers Rule

Consumers Rule

Chapter Objectives

When you finish this chapter you should understand why:

- Consumer behavior is a process.
- Consumers use products to help them define their identities in different settings.
- Marketers need to understand the wants and needs of different consumer segments.
- The Web is changing consumer behavior.
- Consumer behavior relates to other issues in our lives.
- Consumer activities can be harmful to individuals and to society.
- Different types of specialists study consumer behavior.
- There are two major perspectives that seek to understand and study consumer behavior.

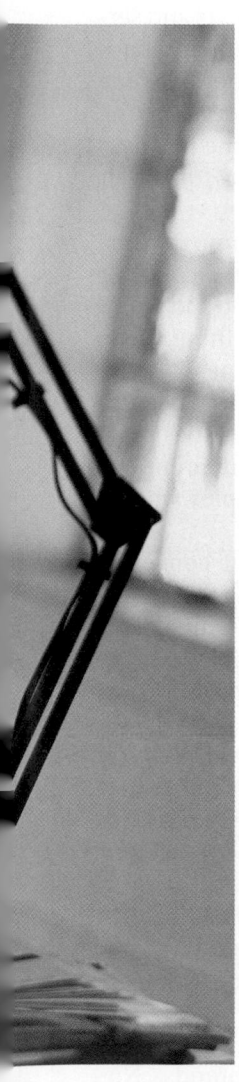

gail has some time to kill before her Accounting class, so she fires up her laptop and surfs the Web. Between studying for her Accounting and Marketing exams she hasn't checked out anything interesting in weeks—even her Facebook friends have been pretty quiet. Enough of the serious stuff, she decides. It's time for some *really* educational surfing.

So, where to go first? Gail figures she'll start at one of the popular women's portals and see what happens. She goes to iVillage.com, where she checks her horoscope (cool! a good day to start a new relationship), scans a few beauty tips, and takes a Great Date quiz (uh-oh, she may need to replace this new guy Byron she's been seeing). Similar stuff is going on at Oxygen.com; its oomph.net social networking site shows the usual bloggers posting on loves gained and loves lost. Then she checks out the new Web site for her sorority at sigmadeltatau.com, which reminds her, "The mission of Sigma Delta Tau is to enrich the college experience of women of similar ideals, to build lasting friendships and to foster personal growth. . . ."[1] Very nice, but she learned all that at Rush. Time to move on. . . .

After an hour of surfing some fascinating e-commerce sites—and vowing to return to some of them to reward herself with a present after exams—Gail decides to get the 411 on what "real people" are doing on the Web. First she checks in on the clubs she belongs to at collegeclub.com—wow, more than 30 people from her campus are logged on right now! Looks like other students are studying as hard as she is! The site's *Campus Culture* link takes her to a story another female student posted, "I was a Hooter's Girl." She reads with a chuckle how she "... undergoes a babelicious transformation so she can serve wings to fat guys."[2] As Gail glances at the clock she realizes she'd better come back to the real world or she'll miss her class. In one final impulse, she logs on to RateMyProfessors.com and posts a nasty comment about her Accounting professor. With a sly smile, Gail throws her laptop in her backpack and heads out to class. She can't wait to sit on the campus shuttle and IM her friends to check out the latest snide comment about Prof. Boring.

 ## Consumer Behavior: People in the Marketplace

This book is about people like Gail—and like YOU. It concerns the products and services they buy and use, and the ways these fit into their lives. This introductory chapter describes some important aspects of the field of consumer behavior and some reasons why it's essential to understand how people interact with the marketing system. For now, though, let's return to one "typical" consumer: Gail, the business major. The preceding vignette allows us to highlight some aspects of consumer behavior that we will cover in the rest of the book.

Gail is a consumer, so let's compare her to other consumers. For some purposes, marketers find it useful to categorize her in terms of her age, gender, income, or occupation. These are some examples of descriptive characteristics of a population, or **demographics**. In other cases, marketers would rather know something about Gail's interests in clothing or music, or the way she spends her leisure time. This sort of information comes under the category of **psychographics**, which refers to aspects of a person's lifestyle and personality. Knowledge of consumer characteristics plays an extremely important role in many marketing applications, such as defining the market for a product or deciding on the appropriate techniques to employ when a company targets a certain group of consumers.

Gail's sorority sisters strongly influence her purchase decisions. The conversations we have with others transmit a lot of product information, as well as recommendations to use or avoid particular brands; this content often is more influential than what we see on television commercials, magazines, billboards, or even MySpace. The growth of the Web has created thousands of online **consumption communities** where members share opinions and recommendations about anything from Barbie dolls to Palm Pilots. Gail forms bonds with fellow group members because they use the same products. There is also pressure on each group member to buy things that will meet with the group's approval. A consumer may pay a steep price in the form of group rejection or embarrassment when she doesn't conform to others' conceptions of what is good or bad, "in" or "out."

As members of a large society, such as the United States, people share certain cultural values, or strongly held beliefs about the way the world should be structured. Members of subcultures, or smaller groups within the culture, also share values; these groups include Hispanics, teens, Midwesterners, or even Lindsay Lohan fan clubs and "Hell's Angels."

While examining Web sites, Gail was exposed to many competing "brands." Numerous sites did not capture her attention at all, whereas she noticed and rejected others because they didn't relate to products, people, or ideas with which she identified or to which she aspired. The use of **market segmentation strategies** means targeting a brand only to specific groups of consumers rather than to everybody—even if it means that other consumers who don't belong to this target market aren't attracted to that product.

Brands often have clearly defined images, or "personalities," that advertising, packaging, branding, and other marketing strategies create. The choice of a favorite Web site is very much a *lifestyle* statement: It says a lot about a person's interests, as well as something about the type of person she would like to be. People often choose a product because they like its image or because they feel its "personality" somehow corresponds to their own. Moreover, a consumer may believe that if she buys and uses the product or service its desirable qualities will "magically" rub off onto her.

When a product, idea, or Web site succeeds in satisfying our specific needs or desires, we may reward it with many years of *brand loyalty*, a bond between product and consumer that is very difficult for competitors to break. Often a change in one's life situation or self-concept is required to weaken this bond.

The appearance, taste, texture, or smell of the item influences our evaluations of products. A good Web site helps people to feel, taste, and smell with their eyes. We may be swayed by the shape and color of a package, as well as by more subtle factors, such as the symbolism in a brand name, in an advertisement, or even in the choice of a cover model for a magazine. These judgments are affected by—and often reflect—how a society feels that people should define themselves at that point in time. If she were asked, Gail might not even be able to say exactly why she considered some Web sites and rejected others. Many product meanings are hidden below the surface of the packaging and advertising; we'll discuss some of the methods marketers and social scientists use to discover or apply these meanings.

As we learned with Gail, our opinions and desires increasingly are shaped by input from around the world, which is becoming a much smaller place as a result of rapid advancements in communications and transportation systems. In today's global culture, consumers often prize products and services that "transport" them to different places and allow them to experience the diversity of other cultures—even if only to watch others brush their teeth on a Webcam.

 # What Is Consumer Behavior?

The field of **consumer behavior** covers a lot of ground: *It is the study of the processes involved when individuals or groups select, purchase, use, or dispose of products, services, ideas, or experiences to satisfy needs and desires.* Consumers take many forms, ranging from an 8-year-old child begging her mother for a Webkinz stuffed animal to an executive in a large corporation deciding on a multimillion-dollar computer system. The items we consume can include anything from canned peas to a massage, democracy, Reggaeton music, or a celebrity such as Aishwarya Rai. Needs and desires to be satisfied range from hunger and thirst to love, status, or even spiritual fulfillment. And, as we'll see throughout this book, people can get passionate about a broad range of products. For example, maybe you are a "sneakerhead" who covets rare models and measures time not by years but by Air Jordan editions. If so, get your kicks at Web sites such as <u>instyleshoes.com</u> and <u>kickz.com</u>.[3]

CONSUMERS ARE ACTORS ON THE MARKETPLACE STAGE

The sociological perspective of **role theory** takes the view that much of consumer behavior resembles actions in a play.[4] As in a play, each consumer has lines, props, and costumes necessary to put on a good performance. Because people act out many different roles, they sometimes alter their consumption decisions depending on the particular "play" they are in at the time. The criteria they use to evaluate products and services in one of their roles may be quite different from those they use in other roles.

■ FIGURE 1.1 STAGES IN THE CONSUMPTION PROCESS

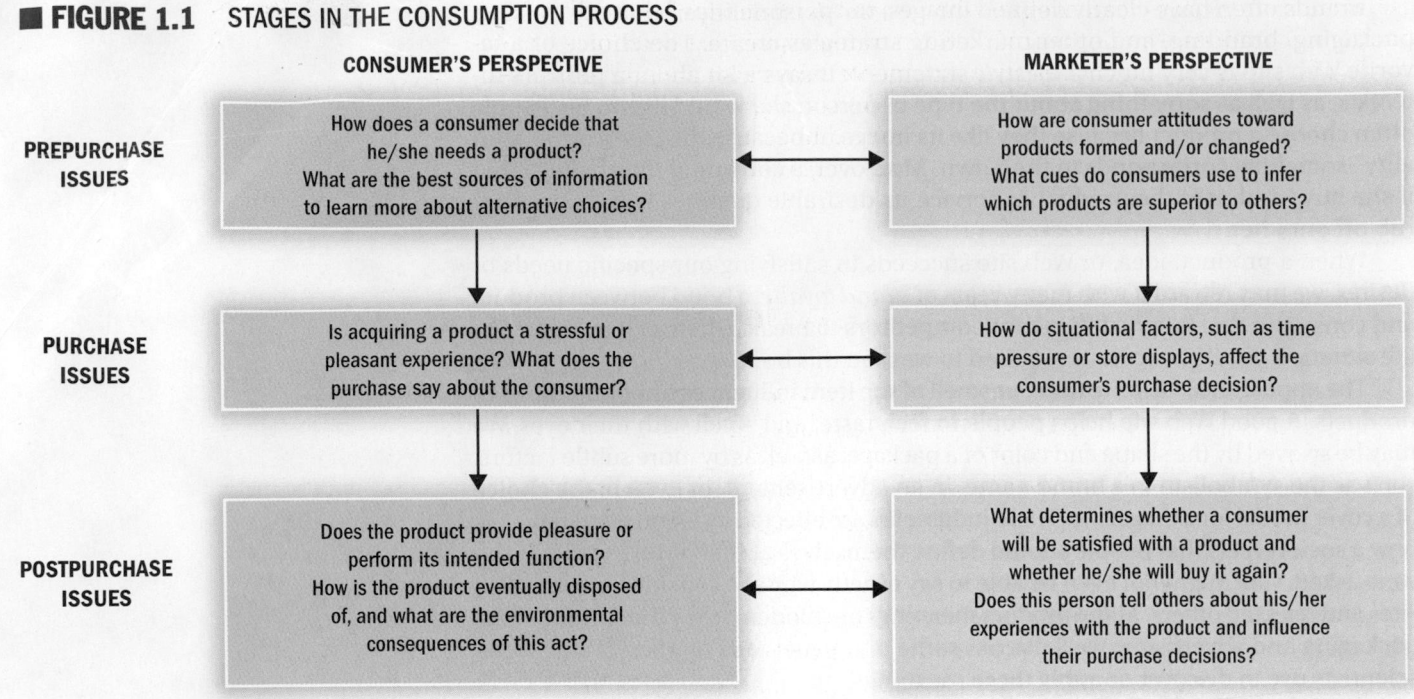

CONSUMER BEHAVIOR IS A PROCESS

In its early stages of development, researchers often referred to the field as *buyer behavior*, reflecting an emphasis on the interaction between consumers and producers at the time of purchase. Most marketers now recognize that consumer behavior is in fact an ongoing process, not merely what happens at the moment a consumer hands over money or a credit card and in turn receives some good or service.

The **exchange**, a transaction in which two or more organizations or people give and receive something of value, is an integral part of marketing.[5] Although exchange remains an important part of consumer behavior, the expanded view emphasizes the entire consumption process, which includes the issues that influence the consumer before, during, and after a purchase. Figure 1.1 illustrates some of the issues that we address during each stage of the consumption process.

CONSUMER BEHAVIOR INVOLVES MANY DIFFERENT ACTORS

We generally think of a **consumer** as a person who identifies a need or desire, makes a purchase, and then disposes of the product during the three stages in the consumption process. In many cases, however, different people are involved in this sequence of events. The purchaser and user of a product might not be the same person, as when a parent picks out clothes for a teenager (and makes selections that can result in "fashion suicide" in the view of the teen). In other cases, another person may act as an *influencer*, providing recommendations for or against certain products without actually buying or using them. A friend's grimace when you try on that new pair of pants may be more influential than anything your mother might say.

Finally, consumers may take the form of organizations or groups. One or several persons may make the decisions involved in purchasing products that many will use, as when a purchasing agent orders the company's office supplies. In other organizational situations, a large group of people may make purchase decisions—for example, company accountants, designers, engineers, sales personnel, and others—all of whom will have a say in the various stages of the consumption process. As we'll see in Chapter 12, one important type of organization is the family, where different family members play pivotal roles in making decisions regarding products and services all will use.

 # Consumers' Impact on Marketing Strategy

Surfing cool Web sites is a lot of fun. But, on the more serious side, why should managers, advertisers, and other marketing professionals bother to learn about consumer behavior?

Very simply, *understanding consumer behavior is good business*. The basic marketing concept states that firms exist to satisfy needs. Marketers can only satisfy these needs to the extent that they understand the people or organizations who will use the products and services they are trying to sell.

Consumer response is the ultimate test of whether a marketing strategy will succeed. Thus, a marketer should incorporate knowledge about consumers into every facet of a successful marketing plan. Data about consumers help organizations to define the market and identify threats to and opportunities for a brand. And, in the wild and wacky world of marketing, nothing is forever: This knowledge also helps to ensure that the product continues to appeal to its core market.

The Sony Walkman is a good example of a successful product that needed to update its image—especially since the company faces fierce competition from the incredibly popular Apple iPod. Although Sony revolutionized the mobile music experience and sold almost 300 million Walkmans in the process, today's teens see portable cassette players as dinosaurs (assuming they've even heard of cassettes!). The company's advertising agency followed 125 teens to see how they use products in their day-to-day lives. Based on this consumer research, Sony relaunched the product with a removable "Memory Stick" instead of a cassette player so it works with MP3 files.[6]

SEGMENTING CONSUMERS

As our society evolves from a mass culture where many consumers share the same preferences to a diverse one where we have almost an infinite number of choices, it's more important than ever to identify distinct market segments and develop specialized messages and products for those groups. McDonald's devotes a third of its U.S. marketing budget to television—compared with two-thirds a few years ago. The company uses that leftover money to sponsor closed-circuit sports programming piped into Hispanic bars and for ads in *Upscale*, a custom-published magazine distributed to barber shops that cater to African American consumers. McDonald's advertises on Foot Locker's in-store video network to reach young men, and it zeroes in on mothers through ads in women's magazines such as *O: The Oprah Magazine* and Web sites such as iVillage.com.[7]

As we'll see later, building loyalty to a brand is a very smart marketing strategy, so sometimes companies define market segments by identifying their most faithful customers or **heavy users**. For example, in the fast-food industry the heavy user (no pun intended) accounts for only one of five customers but for about 60 percent of all visits to fast-food restaurants. In the United States, Taco Bell developed the Chalupa, a deep-fried and higher-calorie version of its Gordita stuffed taco, to appeal to its heavy users. Checkers, a burger chain predominately in the southeastern United States, describes *its* core customer as a single male under age 30 who has a working-class job, loves loud music, doesn't read much, and hangs

Many products help to define our identities. Are you what you drive?

Nothing says more about how you see yourself than the car you choose to drive. And no publication understands this better than Automobile Magazine. It isn't about cars. It's for drivers. And dreamers. Automobile Magazine is where aspiration comes looking for inspiration. Make sure our readers get to see how your brand fits.

WHAT KIND OF CAR ARE YOU?

www.automobilemag.com
PRIMEDIA® Consumer Automotive Group

For advertising information, contact Group Publisher Steve Rousseau at (313) 967-5121 or Steve.Rousseau@primedia.com

out with friends.[8] To attract the same customer, another U.S. restaurant, Hardee's unveiled its Monster Thickburger that weighs in at 1,418 calories—comedian Jay Leno joked that the burger comes in a cardboard box shaped like a coffin.[9] Finally, Burger King aims a lot of its promotions (including its weird but popular King character) to its "Super Fans"—mostly young men who pop into fast-food restaurants 16 times a month on average.[10]

Aside from heavy usage of a product, we use many other dimensions to slice up a larger market. *Demographics* are statistics that measure observable aspects of a population, such as birthrate, age distribution, and income. The U.S. Census Bureau is a major source of demographic data on U.S. families, but many private firms gather additional data on specific population groups as well. The changes and trends demographic studies reveal are of great interest to marketers because they can use the data to locate and predict the size of markets for many products, ranging from

The King appeals to heavy users.

home mortgages to brooms and can openers. Imagine trying to sell baby food to a single male, or an around the world cruise to a couple making $15,000 a year !

SEGMENTATION DIMENSIONS

In this book we explore many of the important demographic variables that make consumers the same or different from others. We also consider other important characteristics that are a bit more subtle, such as differences in consumers' personalities and tastes that we can't objectively measure yet may be tremendously important in influencing product choices. For now, let's summarize a few of the most important demographic dimensions, each of which we'll describe in more detail in later chapters.

Age

Consumers of different *age groups* obviously have very different needs and wants. Although people who belong to the same age group differ in many other ways, they do tend to share a set of values and common cultural experiences that they carry throughout life.[11] In some cases, marketers initially develop a product to attract one age group and then try to broaden its appeal later on. That's what the high-octane energy drink Red Bull is doing. It was aggressively introduced in bars, nightclubs, and gyms to the product's core audience of young people. Over time, the drink became popular in other contexts, and the company began to sponsor the PGA European Tour to broaden its reach to older golfers (who probably aren't up partying all night). It's also handing out free cans to commuters, cab drivers, and car rental agencies to promote the drink as a way to stay alert on the road.[12]

Gender

Differentiating by gender starts at a very early age—even diapers are sold in pink versions for girls and blue for boys. Many products, from fragrances to footwear, target either men or women. An all-female marketing team at Procter & Gamble (P&G), who jokingly call themselves "chicks in charge," introduced Crest Rejuvenating Effects, the first mass-market toothpaste positioned just for women. P&G communicates that this product is feminine by packaging it in a teal tube nestled inside a glimmering "pearlescent" box. The toothpaste is sparkly, teal-toned, and tastes like vanilla and cinnamon.[13]

Family Structure

A person's family and marital status is yet another important demographic variable because this has such a big effect on consumers' spending priorities. Not surprisingly, young bachelors and newlyweds are the most likely to exercise; go to bars, concerts, and movies; and consume alcohol (enjoy it while you can!). Families with young children are big purchasers of health foods and fruit juices, whereas single-parent households and those with older children buy more junk food. Older couples and bachelors are most likely to use home maintenance services.[14]

Social Class and Income

People who belong to the same social class are approximately equal in terms of their incomes and social standing in the community. They work in roughly similar occupations, and they tend to have similar tastes in music, clothing, leisure activities, and art. They also tend to socialize with one another, and they share many ideas and values regarding the way one's life should be lived.[15] The distribution of wealth is of great interest to marketers because it determines which groups have the greatest buying power and market potential.

Race and Ethnicity

African Americans, Hispanic Americans, and Asian Americans are the three fastest-growing ethnic groups in the United States. As U.S. society becomes increasingly multicultural, new opportunities develop to deliver specialized products to racial and ethnic groups and to introduce other groups to these offerings. For example, Reebok introduced its RBK shoe line, championed by popular urban artists such as 50 Cent.

Geography

Many national marketers tailor their offerings to appeal to consumers who live in different parts of the country. For example, in the American South some people are fond of a "good ol' boy" image that leaves others scratching their heads. Although many other parts of the U.S. regard the name "Bubba" as a negative term, businesses in southern states such as South Carolina, Mississippi, and Florida proudly flaunt the name. Bubba Co. is a Charleston, South Carolina-based firm that licenses products such as Bubba-Q-Sauce. In Florida, restaurants, sports bars, nightclubs, and a limousine firm all proudly bear the name Bubba.[16]

Lifestyles: Beyond Demographics

Consumers also have very different lifestyles, even if they share other demographic characteristics such as gender or age. The way we feel about ourselves, the things we value, the things we like to do in our spare time—all of these factors help to determine which products will push our buttons—or even those that make us feel better. Procter & Gamble developed its heartburn medicine Prilosec OTC with an ideal customer in mind based on a lifestyle analysis. Her name is Joanne, and she's a mother over 35 who's more likely to get heartburn from a cup of coffee than from an overdose of pizza and beer. A P&G executive observed, "We know Joanne. We know what she feels. We know what she eats. We know what else she likes to buy in the store."[17]

Marketers are carefully defining customer segments and listening to people in their markets as never before. Many of them now realize that a key to success is building relationships between brands and customers that will last a lifetime. Marketers who believe in this philosophy, called **relationship marketing**, interact with customers on a regular basis and give them reasons to maintain a bond with the company over time.

Another revolution in relationship building is brought to us courtesy of the computer. **Database marketing** involves tracking specific consumers' buying habits very closely and crafting products and messages tailored precisely to people's wants and needs based on this information. Wal-Mart stores massive amounts of information on the 100 million people who visit its stores each week, and the company uses these data to fine-tune its offerings. When the company analyzed how shoppers' buying patterns react when forecasters predict a major hurricane, for example, it discovered that people do a lot more than simply stock up on flashlights. Sales of strawberry Pop-Tarts increase by about 700 percent and the top-selling product of all is—beer. Based on these insights, Wal-Mart loads its trucks with toaster pastries and six-packs to stock local stores when a big storm approaches.[18]

 Marketing's Impact on Consumers

Does marketing imitate life, or vice versa? After the movie *The Wedding Crashers* (2005) became a big hit, hotels, wedding planners, and newlyweds reported an outbreak of uninvited guests who tried to gain access to parties across the United States.[19]

For better or for worse, we all live in a world that the actions of marketers significantly influence. Marketing stimuli surround us as advertisements, stores, and products compete for our attention and our dollars. Marketers filter much of what we learn about the world, whether through the affluence they depict in glamorous magazines or the roles actors play in commercials. These messages begin to reach us very early. At a Florida theme park called Wannado City ("where kids can do what they wannado"), visitors between the ages of 4 and 11 get the chance to try 250 different

We are surrounded by elements of popular culture—the good, the bad, and the ugly. This ad for the Museum of Bad Art reminds us of that.

Some art speaks to you.
Some just belches loudly in your face.

Visit the permanent collection at 580 High Street, Dedham, Massachusetts—617.325.8224—Or on the Web at http://www.glyphs.com/moba—email: moba@world.aol.com   *mo8a   museum of bad art*

grown-up jobs, including home-improvement and broadcasting. Companies sponsor many of these experiences; Publix Super Markets offer a grocery store where kids man cash registers, and a Coca-Cola site lets youngsters control the carbonation level on a bottling line. In Mexico City, at *La Ciudad de los Ninos* (Kiddie City), a slew of marketers promote their brands to the 880,000 guests who visit each year.[20]

Ads show us how we should act with regard to recycling, alcohol consumption, the types of houses and cars we might wish to own—and even how to evaluate others based on the products they buy or don't buy. In many ways we are also "at the mercy" of marketers because we rely on them to sell us products that are safe and that perform as promised, to tell us the truth about what they are selling, and to price and distribute these products fairly.

Popular culture, consisting of the music, movies, sports, books, celebrities, and other forms of entertainment the mass market consumes, is both a product of and an inspiration for marketers. It also affects our lives in more far-reaching ways, ranging from how we acknowledge cultural events such as marriage, death, or holidays to how we view social issues such as global warming, gambling, and addictions. Whether it's the World Cup, Christmas shopping, national elections, newspaper recycling, body piercing, cigarette smoking, in-line skating, or online video games, marketers play a significant role in our view of the world and how we live in it.

This cultural impact is hard to overlook, although many people do not seem to realize how much marketers influence their preferences for movie and musical heroes, the latest fashions in clothing, food, and decorating choices, and even the physical features that they find attractive or ugly in men and women. For example, consider the product icons that companies use to create an identity for their products. Many imaginary creatures and personalities, from the Pillsbury Doughboy to the Jolly Green Giant, at one time or another have been central figures in popular culture. In fact, it is likely that more consumers could recognize such characters than could identify past presidents, business leaders, or artists. Although these figures never really existed, many of us feel as if we "know" them, and they certainly are effective spokescharacters for the products they represent. If you don't believe it, visit the Icon Advertising Museum that is opening in the fall of 2008 in Kansas City.[21]

THE MEANING OF CONSUMPTION

What's the poop on Peeps? Every year, people buy about 1.5 billion of these mostly tasteless marshmallow chicks; about two-thirds of them sell around Easter. They have no nutritional value but they do have a shelf life of 2 years. Maybe that's why not all Peeps get eaten. Devotees use them in decorations, dioramas, online slide shows, and sculptures. Some fans feel challenged to test their physical properties: On more than 200 Peeps Web sites, you can see fetishists skewering, microwaving, hammering, decapitating, and otherwise abusing the spongy confections.[22]

This fascination with a creepy little candy chick illustrates one of the fundamental premises of the modern field of consumer behavior: *People often buy products not for what they do but for what they mean.* This principle does not imply that a product's basic function is unimportant but rather that the roles products play in our lives extend well beyond the tasks they perform. The deeper meanings of a product may help it to stand out from other similar goods and services—all things being equal, people will choose the brand that has an image (or even a personality!) consistent with their underlying needs.

For example, although most people probably couldn't run faster or jump higher if they were wearing Nikes instead of Reeboks, many die-hard loyalists swear by their favorite brand. These archrivals are largely marketed in terms of their images—meanings that have been carefully crafted with the help of legions of rock stars, athletes, slickly produced commercials, and many millions of dollars. So, when you buy a Nike "swoosh" you are doing more than choosing shoes to wear to the mall—you

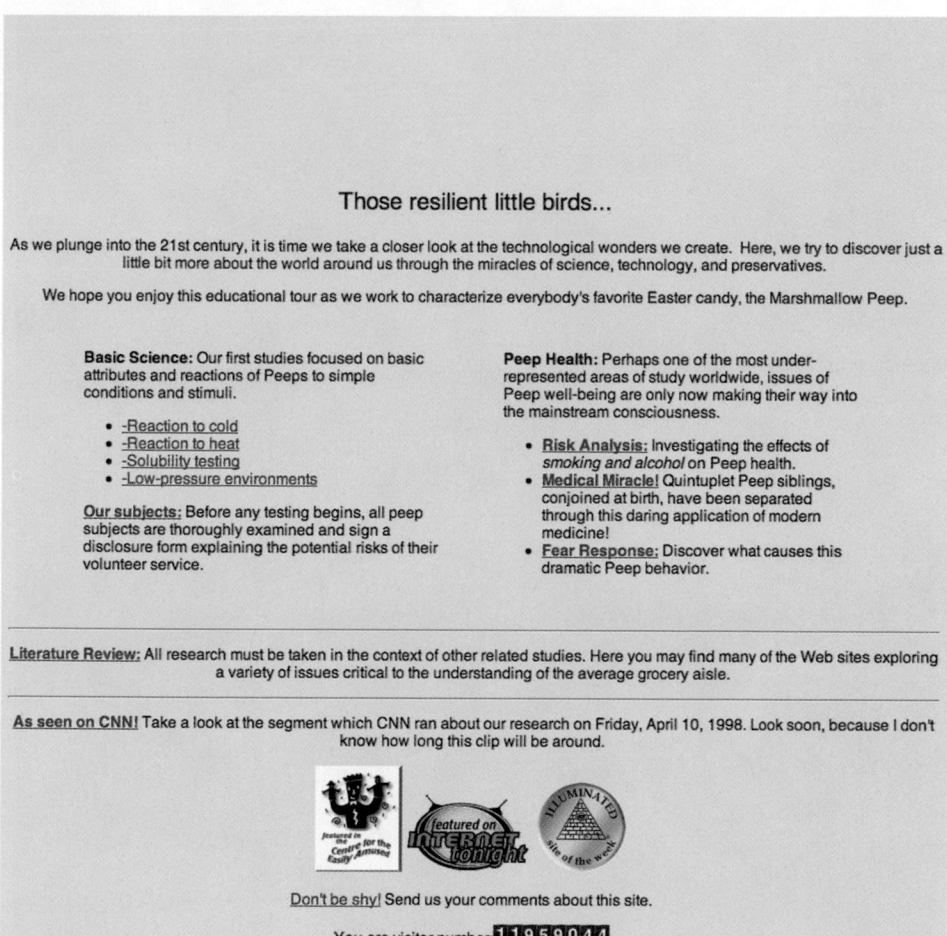

Those resilient little birds...

As we plunge into the 21st century, it is time we take a closer look at the technological wonders we create. Here, we try to discover just a little bit more about the world around us through the miracles of science, technology, and preservatives.

We hope you enjoy this educational tour as we work to characterize everybody's favorite Easter candy, the Marshmallow Peep.

Basic Science: Our first studies focused on basic attributes and reactions of Peeps to simple conditions and stimuli.

- -Reaction to cold
- -Reaction to heat
- -Solubility testing
- -Low-pressure environments

Our subjects: Before any testing begins, all peep subjects are thoroughly examined and sign a disclosure form explaining the potential risks of their volunteer service.

Peep Health: Perhaps one of the most under-represented areas of study worldwide, issues of Peep well-being are only now making their way into the mainstream consciousness.

- **Risk Analysis:** Investigating the effects of *smoking and alcohol* on Peep health.
- **Medical Miracle!** Quintuplet Peep siblings, conjoined at birth, have been separated through this daring application of modern medicine!
- **Fear Response:** Discover what causes this dramatic Peep behavior.

Literature Review: All research must be taken in the context of other related studies. Here you may find many of the Web sites exploring a variety of issues critical to the understanding of the average grocery aisle.

As seen on CNN! Take a look at the segment which CNN ran about our research on Friday, April 10, 1998. Look soon, because I don't know how long this clip will be around.

Don't be shy! Send us your comments about this site.

You are visitor number 11959044

Peeps are objects of devotion—or of abuse—for many consumers.

may also be making a lifestyle statement about the type of person you are or wish you were. For a relatively simple item made of leather and laces, that's quite a feat!

Our allegiances to sneakers, musicians, or even soft drinks help us define our place in modern society, and these choices also help each of us to form bonds with others who share similar preferences. This comment by a participant in a focus group captures the curious bonding that can be caused by consumption choices: "I was at a football party, and I picked up an obscure drink. Somebody else across the room went 'yo!' because he had the same thing. People feel a connection when you're drinking the same thing."[23]

Companies often create product icons to develop an identity for their products. Many made-up creatures and personalities, such as Mr. Clean; Bibendum, the Michelin tire man; and the Pillsbury Doughboy, are widely recognized (and often beloved) figures in popular culture. Bibendum, one of the oldest icons, dates back to the 1890s. He was born at a time when the "machine age" was dawning, so a man constructed of auto parts truly caught the spirit of the times.

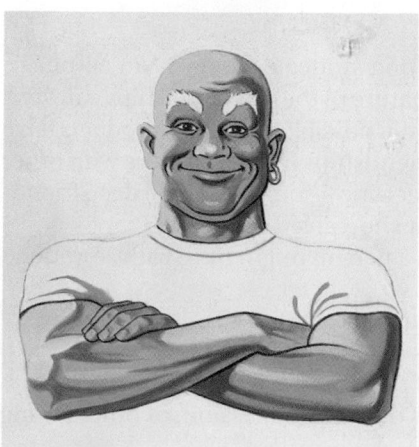

This ad for electronics products by Samsung focuses on pure desire—consuming as experience.

As we have seen, one trademark of marketing strategies today is an emphasis on building relationships with customers. The nature of these relationships can vary, and these bonds help us to understand some of the possible meanings products have to us. Furthermore, researchers find that like friendships and love affairs with other people, our relationships with brands evolve over time—some resemble deep friendships, whereas others are more like exciting but short-lived flings.[24]

Here are some of the types of relationships a person might have with a product:

- **Self-concept attachment**—The product helps to establish the user's identity.
- **Nostalgic attachment**—The product serves as a link with a past self.
- **Interdependence**—The product is a part of the user's daily routine.
- **Love**—The product elicits emotional bonds of warmth, passion, or other strong emotion.[25]

The Global Consumer

The majority of people on Earth live in urban centers—analysts predict that the number of *megacities,* defined as urban centers of 10 million or more, will grow to 26 by 2015.[26] Already, China boasts four shopping centers that are larger than the massive Mall of America in Minnesota, and very soon it will be home to seven of the world's largest malls.[27]

One by-product of sophisticated marketing strategies is the movement toward a **global consumer culture,** one which unites people around the world by their common devotion to brand-name consumer goods, movie stars, celebrities, and leisure activities.[28] Many multinational firms are "household names," widely recognized (though not necessarily liked) by literally billions of people. McDonald's Corp. and Microsoft Corp. are the most visible corporate brands on the planet.[29]

We owe much of this interconnectedness to exciting new developments in technology that allow us to link with companies—and with each other—regardless of our physical locations. Indeed, our old model of sitting in front of a PC to surf the Web soon will disappear like the horse-and-buggy. **U-commerce** is the use of *ubiquitous networks* that will slowly but surely become a part of us, whether in the form of wearable computers or customized advertisements beamed to us on our cell phones ("Hey, you're walking by McDonald's. Come on in for today's burger special.").[30]

Many products already carry a plastic **RFID tag** containing a computer chip and a tiny antenna that lets the chip communicate with a network. Grocery items will tell the store what needs to be restocked and which items are past their expiration dates, and your house will know when you're pulling in the driveway as it turns on the lights and starts your favorite tunes spinning before you walk in the door. Already, IBM has introduced "smart" washers and dryers in some college dorms that let students keep tabs on their laundry from anywhere they can access the Internet—their dorm rooms, the library, or even a cell phone. Students can log onto a Web page to see if any machines are free and receive e-mail or a page when their load is finished.[31]

The rise of global marketing means that even small companies are looking to expand overseas—and this increases the pressure to understand how customers in other countries are the same or different from those in one's own country. In the restaurant industry, for example, Shakey's pizza restaurants are mushrooming in the Philippines, and food from the International House of Pancakes is selling like hotcakes in Tokyo. But menu changes are sometimes called for to please local palates: Schlotzky's in Malaysia offers Smokey Mountain Chicken Crunch with "half-virgin" chicken, and diners at Bob's Big Boy in Thailand snap up Tropical Shrimp, deep fried with "exotic breading." This book will pay special attention to the good and bad aspects of this cultural homogenization.

Virtual Consumption and the Power of Crowds

There's little doubt that the digital revolution is one of the most significant influences on consumer behavior, and the impact of the Web will continue to expand as more and more people around the world log in. Many of us are avid Web surfers, and it's hard to imagine a time when IMing, MP3 files, or BlackBerrys weren't an accepted part of daily life.

Electronic marketing has increased convenience by breaking down many of the barriers caused by time and location. You can shop 24/7 without leaving home, you can read today's newspaper without getting drenched picking up a hard copy in a rainstorm, and you don't have to wait for the 6:00 P.M. news to find out what

This ad from Singapore reminds us that consumers around the world increasingly are modifying their lifestyles as they gain access to modern products.

the weather will be like tomorrow—at home or around the globe. And, with the increasing use of handheld devices and wireless communications, you can get that same information—from stock quotes to the weather—even when you're away from your computer.[32]

And, it's not all about businesses selling to consumers (**B2C e-commerce**). The cyberspace explosion has created a revolution in consumer-to-consumer activity (**C2C e-commerce**): Welcome to the new world of *virtual brand communities.* Just as e-consumers are not limited to local retail outlets in their shopping, they are not limited to their local communities when looking for friends or fellow fans of wine, hip-hop, or skateboarding.

Picture a small group of local collectors who meet once a month at a local diner to discuss their shared interests over coffee. Now multiply that group by thousands, and include people from all over the world who are united by a shared passion for sports memorabilia, Barbie dolls, Harley-Davidson motorcycles, refrigerator magnets, or *MMOGs* (massive multiplayer online games) such as *World of Warcraft*. The Web also provides an easy way for consumers around the world to exchange information about their experiences with products, services, music, restaurants, and movies. The Hollywood Stock Exchange (hsx.com) offers a simulated entertainment stock market where traders predict the 4-week box office take for each film. Amazon.com encourages shoppers to write reviews of books, and just like Gail did you can even rate your professors at RateMyProfessors.com (don't tell your prof about this one; it'll be our secret). The popularity of chat rooms where consumers can go to discuss various topics with like-minded "Netizens" around the world grows every day, as do immersive virtual worlds such as Second Life, Entropia Universe, There.com, and Kaneva. News reports tell us of the sometimes wonderful and sometimes horrific romances that have begun on the Internet as people check out potential mates on sites such as Match.com or Lavalife (in a typical month, 26 million people visit online dating sites!).[33]

Will the Web bring people closer together or drive each of us into our own private virtual worlds? Wired Americans are spending less time with friends and family, less time shopping in stores, and more time working at home after hours. More than one-third of U.S. respondents who have access to the Internet reported that they were online at least 5 hours a week. Also, 60 percent of Internet users said they had reduced their television viewing and one-third said they spent less time reading newspapers.

However, a study by the Pew Internet and American Life Project reported that more than half of users surveyed feel that e-mail actually strengthens family ties. Users reported far more offline social contact than nonusers.[34] These results argue that people are spending more time than ever with others. It's just that they are forming strong relationships over the Internet instead of in person. But the author of the first survey disagrees. As he observes, "If I go home at 6:30 in the evening and spend the whole night sending e-mail and wake up the next morning, I still haven't talked to my wife or kids or friends. When you spend your time on the Internet, you don't hear a human voice and you never get a hug."[35]

A follow-up study found that it works both ways—extroverts tend to make even more friends on the Web, whereas introverts feel even more cut off from the rest of the world. This has been termed the "rich get richer" model of Internet use.[36] So, it seems that just as in the offline world, our new digital reality is both good and bad. Throughout this book, we'll look at some examples of both the pros and cons of virtual consumer behavior in boxes called "Net Profit" and "The Tangled Web."

 # Blurred Boundaries: Marketing and Reality

Marketers and consumers coexist in a complicated, two-way relationship. It's often hard to tell where marketing efforts leave off and "the real world" begins. One result of these blurred boundaries is that we are no longer sure (and perhaps we don't care) where the line separating this fabricated world from reality begins and ends. Sometimes, we gleefully join in the illusion. A story line in a Wonder Woman comic book featured the usual out-of-this-world exploits of a vivacious superhero. But it also included the real-world marriage proposal of the owner of a chain of comic book stores, who persuaded DC Comics to let him woo his beloved in the issue.[37] One shudders to think what he has in mind for the honeymoon!

Marketing messages often borrow imagery from other forms of popular culture to connect with an audience. This line of syrups adapts the "look" of a pulp detective novel.

To what degree do marketers shape the world of popular culture—and even consumers' perceptions of reality? More than many of us believe, and this influence is increasing dramatically as companies experiment with new ways to command our attention. The changes Hasbro recently made to its hugely popular Monopoly board game illustrate the proliferation of brands in our daily lives. Seeking to offer "a representation of America in the twenty-first century," the game now includes tokens styled after name-brand products. Five of the eight tokens in the new Monopoly Here and Now edition are branded, so players can choose to use a Toyota Prius hybrid car, an order of McDonald's French fries, a New Balance running shoe, a cup of Starbucks coffee, or a Motorola Razr cell phone.[38] Skiers journey up Vermont's Stratton Mountain in an Altoids gondola car; those visiting Canada's Whistler Mountain can play in a Nintendo Gamecube terrain park and a Pontiac Race Center, and they are greeted by hosts wearing Evian jackets. Vail's ski resort has a warming hut courtesy of Burton

Snowboards and Mountain Dew.[39] The Triton Hotel in San Francisco features a Häagen-Dazs all-you-can-eat "Sweet Suite" that includes a cabinet filled with Häagen-Dazs pints, scented candles in Häagen-Dazs flavors, a waffle-textured bedspread, and a Häagen-Dazs bathrobe.[40]

And how about marketing messages in the bathroom? One recent invention called the Wizmark gives marketers a new way to get your attention in there as well. The device is billed as an "interactive urinal communicator" that will play a message when liquid activates it.[41]

 ## Marketing Ethics and Public Policy

In business, conflicts often arise between the goal to succeed in the marketplace and the desire to maximize the well-being of consumers by providing them with safe and effective products and services. However, consumers may expect too much from companies and try to exploit these obligations. A case involving the Wendy's fast-food chain made national headlines when a woman claimed she found a finger in her bowl of chili. The restaurants became the butt of jokes (some said they served nail clippers with their food instead of forks), and sales dropped dramatically at the company's franchises, forcing layoffs and reduced hours for many employees—until the woman was arrested for fraud.[42]

Business ethics are rules of conduct that guide actions in the marketplace—the standards against which most people in a culture judge what is right and what is wrong, good or bad. These universal values include honesty, trustworthiness, fairness, respect, justice, integrity, concern for others, accountability, and loyalty. Ethical business is good business. A Conference Board survey of U.S. consumers found the most important criterion when forming opinions about corporations is social responsibility in such areas as labor practices, business ethics, and environmental issues.[43] Consumers think better of products made by firms they feel are behaving ethically.[44]

But just what is ethical behavior? Sometimes it's not so easy to tell. For example, when you download songs from The Pirate Bay, or other file-sharing sites, are you stealing? The film and recording industry thinks you are and is appealing to universities nationwide to help crack down on Internet-based piracy and advocate for tighter controls on file sharing or what it calls "electronic shoplifting."[45]

Of course, notions of right and wrong differ among people, organizations, and cultures. Some businesses believe it is OK for salespeople to pull out all the stops to persuade customers to buy, even if it means giving them false information; other firms feel that anything less than total honesty with customers is terribly wrong. Because each culture has its own set of values, beliefs, and customs, companies around the world define ethical business behaviors quite differently. For example, one study found that because of differences in values (more on this in Chapter 4), Mexican firms are less likely to have formal codes of ethics and they are more likely to bribe public officials than are U.S. or Canadian companies. However, because of different attitudes about work and interpersonal relationships, these companies also are more likely to treat lower-level employees better than do their northern neighbors.[46]

These cultural differences certainly influence whether business practices such as bribery are acceptable. In Japan, it's called *kuroi kiri* (black mist); in Germany, it's *schmiergeld* (grease money), whereas Mexicans refer to *la mordida* (the bite), the French say *pot-de-vin* (jug of wine), and Italians speak of the *bustarella* (little envelope). They're all talking about *baksheesh*, the Middle Eastern term for a "tip" to grease the wheels of a transaction. Giving "gifts" in exchange for getting business from suppliers or customers is common and acceptable in many countries, even though this may be frowned on elsewhere.

The Tangled Web

To what extent should a consumer's personal information be available online? This is one of the most controversial ethical questions today. Scott McNealy, chief executive officer (CEO) of Sun Microsystems, once commented, "You already have zero privacy—get over it." Apparently, many consumers don't agree; they are not happy at the prospect of leaving an electronic trail behind. A poll conducted by the National Consumers League found that consumers are more worried about personal privacy than health care, education, crime, and taxes. People are particularly concerned that businesses or individuals will target their children.[49] Nearly 70 percent of consumers worry about keeping their information private, but according to a Jupiter Media Metrix survey, only 40 percent read privacy policies posted on business Web sites.[50]

How can these thorny ethical issues be solved? Some analysts predict that a market for privacy will emerge; we can ensure some degree of privacy, but it will cost us. Others believe that instead of paying to be left alone, we can actually make money by selling our personal data. As one online executive observed, "Slowly but surely consumers are going to realize that their profile is valuable. For loaning out their identity, they're going to expect something in return."[51]

Bribing foreigners to gain business has been against the law in the United States since 1977 under the Foreign Corrupt Practices Act. The Organization for Economic Cooperation and Development (OECD), to which most industrialized countries belong, also outlaws bribery. More than 800 business experts were asked to identify the countries where this practice is most flagrant. Russian and Chinese companies emerged at the top of the list, and Taiwan and South Korea were close behind. The "cleanest" countries were Australia, Sweden, Switzerland, Austria, and Canada.[47]

Regardless of whether they do it intentionally, some marketers do violate their bonds of trust with consumers. In some cases, these actions are actually illegal, as when a manufacturer deliberately mislabels the contents of a package. Or a retailer may adopt a "bait-and-switch" selling strategy that lures consumers into the store by offering inexpensive products with the sole intent of getting them to switch to higher-priced goods.

In other cases, marketing practices have detrimental effects on society even though they are not explicitly illegal. Some companies erect billboards for alcohol and tobacco products in low-income neighborhoods; others sponsor commercials depicting groups of people in an unfavorable light to get the attention of a target market. Civil rights groups, for example, charge that the marketing of menthol cigarettes by R. J. Reynolds to African Americans is illegal because menthol cigarettes are less safe than regular brands. A company spokeswoman responds, "This links to the bigger issue that minorities require some special protection. We find that offensive, paternalistic, and condescending."[48] Who is right? Throughout this book, we highlight ethical issues related to the practice of marketing. In boxes we call "Marketing Pitfall," we discuss questionable practices by marketers or the possible adverse effects of certain marketing strategies on consumers.

NEEDS AND WANTS:
DO MARKETERS MANIPULATE CONSUMERS?

One of the most common and stinging criticisms of marketing is that companies convince consumers they "need" many material things and that they will be unhappy and inferior people if they do not have these "necessities." The issue is a complex one and is certainly worth considering: Do marketers give people what they want, or do they tell people what they *should* want?

Welcome to Consumerspace

Who controls the market—companies or consumers? This question is even more complicated as new ways of buying, having, and being are invented every day. It seems that the "good old days" of *marketerspace*, a time when companies called the shots and decided what they wanted their customers to know and do, are dead and gone. As we saw with Gail's surfing decisions, many people now feel empowered to choose how, when, or if they will interact with corporations as they construct their own *consumerspace*. In turn, companies need to develop and leverage brand equity in bold new ways to attract the loyalty of these consumer "nomads." People still "need" companies—but in new ways and on their own terms. As we'll see throughout this book, profound changes in consumer behavior are influencing how people search for product information and evaluate alternative brands. In the brave new world of consumerspace, we have the potential to shape our own marketing destinies.[52]

Do Marketers Create Artificial Needs?

The marketing system has come under fire from both ends of the political spectrum. On the one hand, some members of the Religious Right believe that marketers contribute to the moral breakdown of society by presenting images of hedonistic pleasure and encouraging the pursuit of secular humanism at the expense of spirituality and the environment. A coalition of religious groups called the National Religious Partnership for the Environment claimed that gas-guzzling sport utility vehicles (SUVs) are contrary to Christian moral teachings about protecting people and the earth.[53]

On the other hand, some leftists argue that the same deceitful promises of material pleasure function to buy off people who would otherwise be revolutionaries working to change the system.[54] According to this argument, the marketing system creates demand—demand that only its products can satisfy.

A Response. *A **need** is a basic biological motive; a **want** represents one way that society has taught to satisfy the need.* For example, thirst is biologically based; we are taught to want Coca-Cola to satisfy that thirst rather than, say, goat's milk.

This ad was created by the American Association of Advertising Agencies to counter charges that ads create artificial needs.

Thus, the need is already there; marketers simply recommend ways to satisfy it. A basic objective of marketing is to create awareness that needs exist, not to create needs.

Are Advertising and Marketing Necessary?

The social critic Vance Packard wrote more than 50 years ago, "Large-scale efforts are being made, often with impressive success, to channel our unthinking habits, our purchasing decisions, and our thought processes by the use of insights gleaned from psychiatry and the social sciences."[55] The economist John Kenneth Galbraith charged that radio and television are important tools to accomplish this manipulation of the masses. Because consumers don't need to be literate to use these media, repetitive and compelling communications can reach almost everyone. This criticism may even be more relevant to online communications, where a simple click delivers a world of information to us.

Many feel that marketers arbitrarily link products to desirable social attributes, fostering a materialistic society in which we are measured by what we own. One influential critic even argued that the problem is that we are not materialistic enough—that is, we do not sufficiently value goods for the utilitarian functions they deliver but instead focus on the irrational value of goods for what they symbolize. According to this view, for example, "Beer would be enough for us, without the additional promise that in drinking it we show ourselves to be manly, young at heart, or neighborly. A washing machine would be a useful machine to wash clothes, rather than an indication that we are forward-looking or an object of envy to our neighbors."[56]

A Response. *Products are designed to meet existing needs, and advertising only helps to communicate their availability.*[57] According to the **economics of information** perspective, advertising is an important source of consumer information.[58] This view emphasizes the economic cost of the time spent searching for products. Accordingly, advertising is a service for which consumers are willing to pay because the information it provides reduces search time.

This Brazilian ad employs a novel message to encourage eye exams.

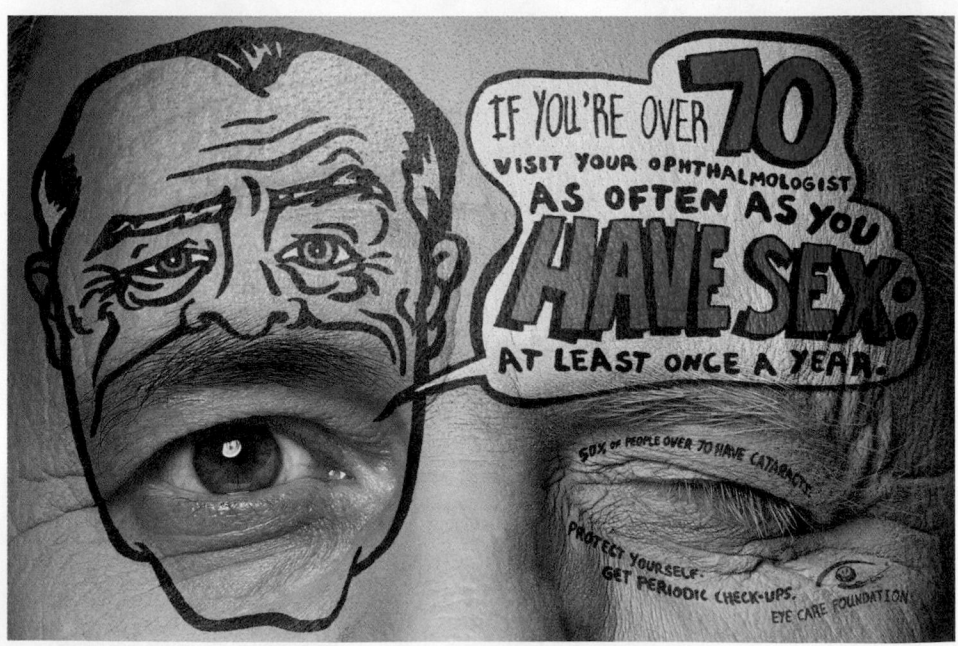

Do Marketers Promise Miracles?

Through advertising, consumers are led to believe that products have magical properties; products will do special and mysterious things for consumers in a way that will transform their lives. Consumers will be beautiful, have power over others' feelings, be successful, and be relieved of all ills. In this respect, advertising functions as mythology does in primitive societies: It provides simple, anxiety-reducing answers to complex problems.

A Response. *Advertisers simply do not know enough about people to manipulate them.* Consider that the failure rate for new products ranges from 40 to 80 percent. Although people think that advertisers have an endless source of magical tricks and scientific techniques to manipulate them, in reality the industry is successful when it tries to sell good products and unsuccessful when selling poor ones.[59]

PUBLIC POLICY AND CONSUMERISM

Concern for the welfare of consumers has been an issue since at least the beginning of the twentieth century, and activists continue to voice concerns about a range of issues such as child labor, exploitative advertising, and genetically engineered food.[60]

Partly as a result of consumers' efforts in the United States, the U.S. government established many federal agencies to oversee consumer-related activities. These include the Department of Agriculture, the Federal Trade Commission, the Food and Drug Administration, the Securities and Exchange Commission, and the Environmental Protection Agency. After Upton Sinclair's 1906 book *The Jungle* exposed the awful conditions in the Chicago meatpacking industry, the U.S. Congress was prompted to pass important pieces of legislation—the Pure Food and Drug Act in 1906 and the Federal Meat Inspection Act a year later—to protect American consumers. A summary of some important consumer legislation enacted in the United States since that time appears in Table 1.1. You can find other information about consumer-related issues at consumerreports.org and cpsc.gov (The Consumer Product Safety Commission).

Consumer Activism: America™?

"Absolut Impotence." So reads a parody vodka ad that Adbusters, a nonprofit organization that advocates for "the new social activist movement of the information age," created. The editor of the group's magazine argues that America is no longer a country, but rather a multitrillion-dollar brand subverted by corporate agendas. He claims that America™ is no different from McDonald's, Marlboro, or General Motors.[61]

Adbusters sponsors numerous initiatives, including Buy Nothing Day and TV Turnoff Week, intended to discourage rampant commercialism. These efforts, along with biting ads and commercials that lampoon advertising messages, are examples of **culture jamming;** a strategy to disrupt efforts by the corporate world to dominate our cultural landscape. The movement believes "culture jamming" will change the way information flows; the way institutions wield power; the way TV stations are run; and the way the food, fashion, automobile, sports, music, and culture industries set their agendas.[62] The *Culture Jammers Manifesto* proclaims opposition to the "mind-polluters": "On the rubble of the old culture, we will build a new one with non-commercial heart and soul."[63] To protest against what the organization claims are Nike's unfair labor practices, Adbusters sells its own Blackspot sneakers. They are made from hemp in a Portuguese factory where workers receive pay higher than the country's minimum wage and where many employees belong to a union.[64]

TABLE 1.1
SAMPLE OF U.S. LEGISLATION INTENDED TO ENHANCE CONSUMERS' WELFARE

Year	Act	Purpose
1951	Fur Products Labeling Act	Regulates the branding, advertising, and shipment of fur products.
1953	Flammable Fabrics Act	Prohibits the transportation of flammable fabrics across state lines.
1958	National Traffic and Safety Act	Creates safety standards for cars and tires.
1958	Automobile Information Disclosure Act	Requires automobile manufacturers to post suggested retail prices on new cars.
1966	Fair Packaging and Labeling Act	Regulates packaging and labeling of consumer products. (Manufacturers must provide information about package contents and origin.)
1966	Child Protection Act	Prohibits sale of dangerous toys and other items.
1967	Federal Cigarette Labeling and Advertising Act	Requires cigarette packages to carry a warning label from the Surgeon General.
1968	Truth-in-Lending Act	Requires lenders to divulge the true costs of a credit transaction.
1969	National Environmental Policy Act	Established a national environmental policy and created the Council on Environmental Quality to monitor the effects of products on the environment.
1972	Consumer Products Safety Act	Established the Consumer Product Safety Commission to identify unsafe products, establish safety standards, recall defective products, and ban dangerous products.
1975	Consumer Goods Pricing Act	Bans the use of price maintenance agreements among manufacturers and resellers.
1975	Magnuson-Moss Warranty-Improvement Act	Creates disclosure standards for consumer product warranties and allows the Federal Trade Commission to set policy regarding unfair or deceptive practices.
1990	The Nutrition Labeling and Education Act	Reaffirms the legal basis for the Food and Drug Administration's new rules on food labeling and establishes a timetable for the implementation of those rules. Regulations covering health claims became effective May 8, 1993. Those pertaining to nutrition labeling and nutrient content claims went into effect May 8, 1994.
1998	Internet Tax Freedom Act	Established a moratorium on special taxation of the Internet, including taxation of access fees paid to America Online and other Internet Service Providers. An extension of the moratorium is being considered.

Although some in corporate America may dismiss these extreme sentiments as the ravings of a lunatic fringe, they deserve to be taken seriously. The recent scandals involving such corporate icons as Enron, Martha Stewart, Arthur Andersen, World-Com, and Merrill Lynch have fueled a growing bonfire of mistrust and skepticism among the consuming public. Time will tell if these backlashes against companies will die down or continue to grow as new scandals continue to come to light. Clearly, we need to take dramatic steps to restore public confidence as the business page of the newspaper starts to read like the crime blotter.

A few examples of coordinated consumer protest movements include the following:

● **The American Legacy Foundation**—created The Truth (funded by settlements from lawsuits involving tobacco companies) to ". . . alert everyone to the lies and hidden practices of the cigarette companies, while giving people the tools to have a voice in changing that." This project develops marketing communications directed to adolescents and other at-risk populations to disseminate information about nicotine addiction, how tobacco products are advertised, and what these products do to the body.[65]

- **Save the Redwoods/Boycott the GAP (SRBG)**—is an organization that specifically targets the GAP chain of stores. The group protests such policies as the alleged use of sweatshop labor on the island of Saipan, which produces some of the store's clothing.[66] In one highly visible demonstration staged in several cities, called "We'd Rather Wear Nothing Than Wear GAP!" activists stripped naked to underscore their message.

- **The Organic Consumers Association (OCA)**—in 2006 launched a boycott in the U.S. against two big-name distributors of organic dairy products—Horizon and Aurora—claiming, "All of Aurora's and much of Horizon's 'organic' milk is coming from factory farm feedlots where the cows have been brought in from conventional farms and have little or no access to pasture." The OCA later expanded its boycott to include such retail chains as Costco, Publix, Safeway, Giant, and Wild Oats because it claims they sell "bogus organic milk from Aurora."[67]

Consumerism and Consumer Research

President John F. Kennedy ushered in the modern era of consumerism in the United States with his "Declaration of Consumer Rights" in 1962. These include the right to safety, the right to be informed, the right to redress, and the right to choice. The 1960s and 1970s were a time of consumer activism as consumers began to organize to demand better-quality products (and to boycott companies that did not provide them).

The publication of books such as Rachel Carson's *The Silent Spring* in 1962, which attacked the irresponsible use of pesticides, and Ralph Nader's *Unsafe at*

Social marketing encourages responsible behavior. This Belgian ad promotes the use of condoms.

Advertising promotes guidelines for appropriate behavior. This ad from Shanghai says: "Who will fall in love with Shanghai beauties like this? Please refrain from picking your nose in public."

Any Speed in 1965, which exposed safety defects in General Motors' Corvair automobile, prompted these movements. Many consumers have a vigorous interest in consumer-related issues ranging from environmental concerns such as global warming and climate change, toxic waste, and so on, to excessive violence and sex on television or in the lyrics of popular rock and rap songs. Recent controversies surrounding American "shock-jocks" such as Don Imus who use the public airwaves to hurl insults about racial or religious groups illustrate that people take these issues very seriously.

The field of consumer behavior can play an important role in improving our lives as consumers.[68] **Social marketing** strategies use techniques marketers normally use to sell beer or detergent to encourage positive behaviors such as increased literacy and to discourage negative activities such as drunk driving.[69] Many researchers play a role in formulating or evaluating public policies such as ensuring that products are labeled accurately, that people can comprehend important information in advertising messages, or that children are not exploited by program-length toy commercials masquerading as television shows.

In addition, **green marketing** is gaining in popularity. Firms that adopt this philosophy choose to protect or enhance the natural environment as they go about their business activities. Some have focused their efforts on reducing wasteful packaging, as when Procter & Gamble introduced refillable containers for Downy fabric softener.[70] We'll discuss this important trend in more detail in Chapter 4.

CB AS I SEE IT

Professor Alan Andreasen
Georgetown University

Much of the consumer behavior research and scholarship that has emerged since Kotler and Levy's 1969 article urging the broadening of marketing has focused on specific conventional challenges in the social sector—charitable and blood donations, smoking, or problems of the poor in inner-city neighborhoods. Many of these topics have reflected current social problems—such as obesity in the twenty-first century—or policy concerns—such as the effectiveness of (or need for)

regulation or commerce. Although interest in social topics has had its ups and downs, the recent growth of social marketing has significantly accelerated interest.

At the moment, I see three broad classes of problems that deserve greater attention. First, we need to understand differences across generically different kinds of consumer behavior. Both social and commercial marketers have behavioral goals—sales or some socially desirable behavior. But the latter comprises unusual types of behavioral challenges: stopping behavior (child abuse, drug use), changing behavior (healthier eating and regularly exercising), and continuing behavior without marketer intervention (sticking to a medical regimen, exercising, giving up sweets). How do these challenges differ in terms of underlying dynamics and explanatory factors? Are they different from commercial sales or building brand loyalty? There needs to be a focus on cross-sector transfer of concepts and tools.

A second challenge involves creating opportunities, including opportunities for a person to engage in desirable behaviors—this is more than simply motivation. It is clear how to do this commercially, but how do we establish conditions for, say, a motivated, poor, obese child to eat better and exercise more if the child attends a school with no playgrounds and fat-laden school lunches? If marketing is all about changing behavior, can our consumer behavior concepts and tools be applied to influencing school principals or city legislators to increase food and exercise options?

Third, how do we handle ethical challenges in the social world? We argue that marketing must be consumer driven. But what if the target audience is poor and illiterate and doesn't appreciate pharmacology or how one increases one's income? What consumer behavior models are available to help us develop programs and goals that really meet the needs of the poor or illiterate—rather than what we Western "experts" think they need?

 ## The Dark Side of Consumer Behavior

The profit motive sometimes motivates companies to offer products that some consider controversial at best and potentially harmful or objectionable. A computer game called *JFK Reloaded* a Scottish company developed raised a stir when it led some people to question the limits to which marketers will go: The game invited competitors to get behind Lee Harvey Oswald's sniper rifle and re-create the former president's assassination.[71] More recently, the U.K. banned *Manhunt 2,* which Rockstar Games released for play on the Wii and PlayStation 2 consoles. Game players assume the role of an escaped mental institution patient who goes on a killing spree as he fights his way to freedom. It's the first game the British banned since it outlawed sales of *Carmageddon,* a game in which players rack up points by driving vehicles over pedestrians.[72]

Despite the best efforts of researchers, government regulators, and concerned industry people, sometimes consumers' worst enemies are themselves. We often think of individuals as rational decision makers, calmly doing their best to obtain products and services that will maximize the health and well-being of themselves, their families, and their society. In reality, however, consumers' desires, choices, and actions often result in negative consequences to individuals and the society in which they live.

This ad from Singapore discourages young people from using ketamine, an animal tranquilizer.

Some of these actions are relatively harmless, but others have more onerous consequences. Some harmful consumer behaviors such as excessive drinking or cigarette smoking stem from social pressures, and the cultural value many of us place on money encourages activities such as shoplifting or insurance fraud. Exposure to unattainable ideals of beauty and success can create dissatisfaction with ourselves. We will touch on many of these issues later in the book, but for now let's review some dimensions of "the dark side" of consumer behavior.

CONSUMER TERRORISM

The terrorist attacks of 2001 were a wake-up call to the free-enterprise system. They revealed the vulnerability of nonmilitary targets and reminded us that disruptions of our financial, electronic, and supply networks can potentially be more damaging to our way of life than the fallout from a conventional battlefield. These incursions may be deliberate or not—economic shockwaves of "mad cow" disease in Europe are still reverberating in the beef industry.[73] Assessments by the Rand Corporation and other analysts point to the susceptibility of the nation's food supply as a potential target of **bioterrorism**.[74]

Even prior to the anthrax scares of 2001, toxic substances placed in products threatened to hold the marketplace hostage. This tactic first drew public attention in

Greenpeace practices social marketing in Spain.

the United States in 1982 when seven people died after taking Tylenol pills laced with cyanide. A decade later, Pepsi weathered its own crisis when more than 50 reports of syringes found in Diet Pepsi cans surfaced in 23 states. In that case, Pepsi pulled off a PR *coup de grace* by convincing the public that the syringes could not have been introduced during the manufacturing process. The company even showed an in-store surveillance video that caught a customer slipping a syringe into a Diet Pepsi can while the cashier's head was turned.[75] Pepsi's aggressive actions underscore the importance of responding to such a crisis head-on and quickly.

More recently, a publicity campaign for a late-night cartoon show backfired when it aroused fears of a terrorist attack and temporarily shut down the city of Boston. The "guerrilla marketing" effort consisted of 1-foot-tall blinking electronic signs with hanging wires and batteries that marketers used to promote the Cartoon Network TV show *Aqua Teen Hunger Force* (a surreal series about a talking milkshake, a box of fries, and a meatball). The signs were placed on bridges and in other high-profile spots in several U.S. cities. Most depicted a boxy, cartoon character making an obscene finger gesture. Bomb squads and other police personnel required to investigate the mysterious boxes cost the city of Boston more than $500,000—and a lot of frayed nerves.[76]

ADDICTIVE CONSUMPTION

Although most people equate addiction with drugs, consumers can use virtually any product or service to relieve (at least temporarily) some problem or satisfy some need to the point that reliance on it becomes extreme. It seems we can become dependent on almost anything—there is even a ChapStick Addicts support group with 250 active members! **Consumer addiction** is a physiological or psychological dependency on products or services. These problems of course include alcoholism, drug addiction, and nicotine addiction—and many companies profit from addictive products or by selling solutions for them.

Even technology can be addicting—as anyone with a BlackBerry can attest. Internet addiction already is a big problem in South Korea, which has the largest high-speed Internet market penetration in the world. More than half of all Korean

This ad for a bar in Spain makes light of alcohol abuse.

households have high-speed Internet connections and the exploding Web culture has "hooked" a huge number of young people on online gaming (80 percent of South Koreans under 25 play these games). Thailand has even imposed a curfew: It fines teens the government catches prowling virtual streets after 10:00 P.M. In Korea, some gamers reportedly have died of exhaustion as a result of overplaying.[77] Many of the gamers hang out in "PC bangs," which are coffeehouses and lounges featuring rows and rows of computers. Critics say the gaming industry is creating millions of zombified addicts who are dropping out of school and (offline) group activities, becoming uncommunicative and even violent because of the electronic games they play. South Korea is a group-oriented society where socializing in bunches is the preferred form of interaction. Critics also claim that the PC bangs are turning into pickup joints, where teenagers swap pictures electronically and decide whether to meet. Reversing the usual pattern in a male-dominated society, the girls tend to be in charge—they send aggressive messages to boys and provide clues to help the boys determine in which bang they are playing and where they are sitting.

COMPULSIVE CONSUMPTION

Some consumers take the expression "born to shop" quite literally. They shop because they are compelled to do so rather than because shopping is a pleasurable or functional task. **Compulsive consumption** refers to repetitive shopping, often excessive, as an antidote to tension, anxiety, depression, or boredom.[78] "Shopaholics" turn to shopping much the way addicted people turn to drugs or alcohol.[79] One man diagnosed with compulsive shopping disorder (CSD) bought more than 2,000 wrenches and never used any of them. Therapists report that women clinically diagnosed with CSD outnumber men by four to one. They speculate that women are attracted to items such as clothes and cosmetics as a way of enhancing their interpersonal relationships, whereas men tend to focus on gadgetry, tools, and guns to achieve a sense of power.

   One out of 20 U.S. adults is unable to control buying goods that he or she did not really want or need. Some researchers say compulsive shopping may

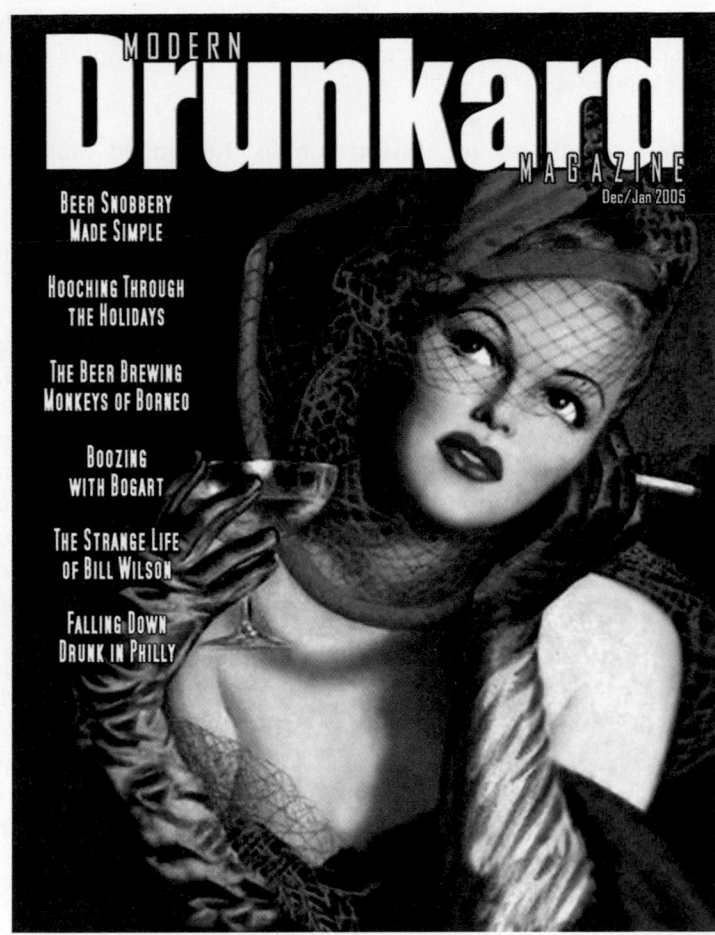

Modern Drunkard magazine targets avid boozers.

be related to low self-esteem. It affects an estimated 2 to 16 percent of the adult U.S. population.[80]

In some cases, like a drug addict the consumer has little or no control over his or her consumption. Whether it is alcohol, cigarettes, chocolate, diet colas, or even ChapStick, the products control the consumer. Even the act of shopping itself is an addicting experience for some people. Three common elements characterize many negative or destructive consumer behaviors: [81]

1 The behavior is not done by choice.
2 The gratification derived from the behavior is short-lived.
3 The person experiences strong feelings of regret or guilt afterward.

Gambling is an example of a consumption addiction that touches every segment of consumer society. Whether it takes the form of casino gambling, playing the "slots," betting on sports events with friends or through a bookie, or even buying lottery tickets, excessive gambling can be quite destructive. Taken to extremes, gambling can result in lowered self-esteem, debt, divorce, and neglected children. According to one psychologist, gamblers exhibit a classic addictive cycle: They experience a "high" while in action and depression when they stop gambling, which leads them back to the thrill of the action. Unlike drug addicts, however, money is the substance that hard-core gamblers abuse.

CONSUMED CONSUMERS

Consumed consumers are people who are used or exploited, willingly or not, for commercial gain in the marketplace. The situations in which consumers themselves

Marketing Pitfall

General Motors (GM) received harsh criticism from mental health advocates after it aired a commercial during the 2007 U.S. Super Bowl that showed a quality-obsessed robot jumping off a bridge in a dream sequence after messing up on the job. The ad opens with the machine dropping a screw while working on a GM assembly line. The robot is kicked out of the plant and finds work waving a "Condos for Sale" sign and holding up a speaker at a fast-food joint as it sadly watches shiny new GM cars drive by. As the Eric Carmen song "All By Myself" plays in the background, the despondent robot leaps off a bridge into the water below. The American Foundation for Suicide Prevention said it started getting complaints the day after the ad aired.[86]

become commodities can range from traveling road shows that feature dwarfs and midgets to the selling of body parts and babies. Some examples of consumed consumers are as follows:

● **Prostitutes**—Expenditures on prostitution in the United States alone are estimated at $20 billion annually. These revenues are equivalent to those in the domestic shoe industry.[82]

● **Organ, blood, and hair donors**—By one estimate, you could make about $46 million if you donated every reusable part of your body (do not try this at home).[83] In the United States, millions of people sell their blood. A lively market also exists for organs (e.g., kidneys), and some women sell their hair to be made into wigs. Bidding for a human kidney on eBay went to more than $5.7 million before the company ended the auction (it's illegal to sell human organs on-line—at least so far). The seller wrote, "You can choose either kidney . . . Of course only one for sale, as I need the other one to live. Serious bids only."[84]

● **Babies for sale**—Several thousand surrogate mothers have been paid to be medically impregnated and carry babies to term for infertile couples. A fertile woman between the ages of 18 and 25 can "donate" one egg every 3 months and rake in $7,000 each time. Over 8 years, that's 32 eggs for a total of $224,000.[85]

Commercial sperm banks have become big business, and the market is international in scope as many countries rely on imports. The head of one of the largest companies boasts, "We think we can be the McDonald's of sperm." This company markets three grades of sperm including an "extra" grade, which contains twice as many sperm as the average grade. The company can deliver to almost any customer in the world within 72 hours with its special freezing techniques in which the sperm travel in liquid nitrogen tanks.

ILLEGAL ACTIVITIES

A survey the McCann-Erickson advertising agency conducted revealed the following tidbits:[87]

● Ninety-one percent of people say they lie regularly. One in three fibs about his or her weight, one in four about income, and 21 percent lie about their age. Nine percent even lie about their natural hair color.

● Four out of ten Americans have tried to pad an insurance bill to cover the deductible.

● Nineteen percent say they've snuck into a theater to avoid paying admission.

● More than three out of five people say they've taken credit for making something from scratch when they have done no such thing. According to Pillsbury's CEO, this ". . . behavior is so prevalent that we've named a category after it—speed scratch."

Many consumer behaviors are not only self-destructive or socially damaging but they are illegal as well. Analysts estimate the cost of crimes consumers commit against business at more than $40 billion per year.

Consumer Theft and Fraud

Who among us has never received an e-mail offering us fabulous riches if we help to recover a lost fortune from a Nigerian bank account? Of course, the only money changing hands will be yours if you fall for the pitch from a so-called *advance fee fraud artist*. These con men have successfully fooled many victims out of hundreds of millions of dollars. However, a small but intrepid group of "counterscammers" sometimes give these crooks a taste of their own medicine by pretending to fall for a scam and humiliating the perpetrator. One common strategy is to trick the con artist into posing for pictures holding a self-mocking sign and then posting these photos on Internet sites. Both online and offline, fraud is rampant.

Stealing from stores is the most common; Someone commits a retail theft every 5 seconds. **Shrinkage** is the industry term for inventory and cash losses from shoplifting and employee theft. This is a massive problem for businesses that gets passed on to consumers in the form of higher prices (about 40 percent of the losses can be attributed to employees rather than shoppers). U.S. shopping malls spend $6 million annually on security, and a family of four spends about $300 extra per year because of markups to cover shrinkage.[88]

Indeed, shoplifting is America's fastest-growing crime. A comprehensive retail study found that shoplifting is a year-round problem that costs U.S. retailers $9 billion annually. The most frequently stolen products are tobacco products, athletic shoes, logo and brand-name apparel, designer jeans, and undergarments. The average theft amount per incident is $58.43, up from $20.36 in a 1995 survey.[89] The problem is equally worrisome in Europe; retailers there catch well over 1 million shoplifters every year. The United Kingdom has the highest rate of shrinkage (as a percent of annual sales), followed by Norway, Greece, and France. Switzerland and Austria have the lowest rates.[90]

The large majority of shoplifting is not done by professional thieves or by people who genuinely need the stolen items.[91] About 2 million Americans are charged with shoplifting each year, but analysts estimate that for every arrest, 18 unreported incidents occur.[92] About three-quarters of those caught are middle- or high-income people who shoplift for the thrill of it or as a substitute for affection. Shoplifting is also common among adolescents. Research evidence indicates that teen shoplifting is influenced by factors such as having friends who also shoplift. It is also more likely to occur if the adolescent does not believe that this behavior is morally wrong.[93]

And what about shoppers who commit fraud when they abuse stores' exchange and return policies? Some big companies such as Guess, Staples, and Sports Authority are using new software that lets them track a shopper's track record of bringing items back. They are trying to crack down on "serial wardrobers" who buy an outfit, wear it once, and return it; customers who change price tags on items, then return one item for the higher amount; and shoppers who use fake or old receipts when making a return. The U.S. retail industry loses approximately $16 billion a year to these and other forms of fraudulent behavior. Retail analysts estimate that about 9 percent of all returns are fraudulent.[94]

Anticonsumption

Some types of destructive consumer behavior are **anticonsumption**, events in which people deliberately deface or mutilate products and services. Some of these actions are relatively harmless, as when a person goes online at <u>dogdoo.com</u> to send a bag of dog manure to a lucky recipient. This site even lets customers calibrate the size of the "gift" by choosing among three "Poo Poo Packages": Econo-Poop (20-pound dog), Poo Poo Special (50-pound dog), and the ultimate in payback, the Poo Poo Grande (110-pound dog).[95] The moral: Smell your packages before opening.

Anticonsumption can range from relatively mild acts like spray-painting graffiti on buildings and subways to serious incidences of product tampering or even the release of computer viruses that can bring large corporations to their knees. It can also take the form of political protest in which activists alter or destroy billboards and other advertisements that promote what they feel to be unhealthy or unethical acts. For example, some members of the clergy in areas heavily populated by minorities have organized rallies to protest the proliferation of cigarette and alcohol advertising in their neighborhoods; these protests sometimes include the defacement of billboards promoting alcohol or cigarettes.

Consumer Behavior as a Field of Study

By now it should be clear that the field of consumer behavior encompasses many things, from the simple purchase of a carton of milk to the selection of a complex networked computer system; from the decision to donate money to a charity to devious plans to rip off a company.

There's an awful lot to understand, and many ways to go about it. Although people have certainly been consumers for a long time, it is only recently that consumption per se has been the object of formal study. In fact, although many business schools now require that marketing majors take a consumer behavior course, most colleges did not even offer such a course until the 1970s.

INTERDISCIPLINARY INFLUENCES ON THE STUDY OF CONSUMER BEHAVIOR

Many different perspectives shape the young field of consumer behavior. Indeed, it is hard to think of a field that is more interdisciplinary. You can find people with training in a very wide range of disciplines—from psychophysiology to literature—doing consumer research. Universities, manufacturers, museums, advertising agencies, and governments employ consumer researchers. Several professional groups, such as the Association for Consumer Research and the Society for Consumer Psychology, have been formed since the mid-1970s.

To gain an idea of the diversity of interests of people who do consumer research, consider the list of professional associations that sponsor the field's major journal, the *Journal of Consumer Research*: the American Association of Family and Consumer Sciences, the American Statistical Association, the Association for Consumer Research, the Society for Consumer Psychology, the International Communication Association, the American Sociological Association, the Institute of Management Sciences, the American Anthropological Association, the American Marketing Association, the Society for Personality and Social Psychology, the American Association for Public Opinion Research, and the American Economic Association. That's a pretty mixed bag.

So, with all of these researchers from diverse backgrounds interested in consumer behavior, which is the "correct" discipline to look into these issues? You might remember a children's story about the blind men and the elephant. The gist of the story is that each man touched a different part of the animal and, as a result, the descriptions each gave of the elephant were quite different. This analogy applies to consumer research as well. Depending on the training and interests of the researchers studying it, they will approach the same consumer phenomenon in different ways and at different levels. Table 1.2 illustrates how a "simple" topic such as magazine usage can be approached in many different ways.

Figure 1.2 provides a glimpse of some of the disciplines working in the field and the level at which each approaches research issues. We can roughly characterize them in terms of their focus on micro versus macro consumer behavior topics. The fields closer to the top of the pyramid concentrate on the individual consumer (micro issues), and those toward the base are more interested in the aggregate activities that occur among larger groups of people, such as consumption patterns members of a culture or subculture share (macro issues). As we make our way through this book, we'll focus on the issues at the top (micro) and then make our way to the bottom of the pyramid by the end of the course. Hang in there!

TABLE 1.2
INTERDISCIPLINARY RESEARCH ISSUES IN CONSUMER BEHAVIOR

Disciplinary Focus	Magazine Usage Sample Research Issues
Experimental Psychology: product role in perception, learning, and memory processes	How specific aspects of magazines, such as their design or layout, are recognized and interpreted; which parts of a magazine are most likely to be read
Clinical Psychology: product role in psychological adjustment	How magazines affect readers' body images (e.g., do thin models make the average woman feel overweight?)
Microeconomics/Human Ecology: product role in allocation of individual or family resources	Factors influencing the amount of money spent on magazines in a household
Social Psychology: product role in the behavior of individuals as members of social groups	Ways that ads in a magazine affect readers' attitudes toward the products depicted; how peer pressure influences a person's readership decisions
Sociology: product role in social institutions and group relationships	Pattern by which magazine preferences spread through a social group (e.g., a sorority)
Macroeconomics: product role in consumers' relations with the marketplace	Effects of the price of fashion magazines and expense of items advertised during periods of high unemployment
Semiotics/Literary Criticism: product role in the verbal and visual communication of meaning	Ways in which underlying messages communicated by models and ads in a magazine are interpreted
Demography: product role in the measurable characteristics of a population	Effects of age, income, and marital status of a magazine's readers
History: product role in societal changes over time	Ways in which our culture's depictions of "femininity" in magazines have changed over time
Cultural Anthropology: product role in a society's beliefs and practices	Ways in which fashions and models in a magazine affect readers' definitions of masculine versus feminine behavior (e.g., the role of working women, sexual taboos)

THE ISSUE OF STRATEGIC FOCUS

Many regard the field of consumer behavior as an applied social science. They argue that the value of the knowledge we generate should be judged in terms of its ability to improve the effectiveness of marketing practice. However, other researchers argue that consumer behavior should not have a strategic focus at all; the field should not be a "handmaiden to business." It should instead focus on the understanding of consumption for its own sake rather than marketers applying this knowledge to making a profit.[96] Most consumer researchers do not hold this rather extreme view, but it has encouraged many to expand the scope of their work beyond the field's traditional focus on the purchase of consumer goods such as food, appliances, and cars to embrace social problems such as homelessness or preserving the environment. Certainly, it has led to some fiery debates among people working in the field!

■ **FIGURE 1.2** THE PYRAMID OF CONSUMER BEHAVIOR

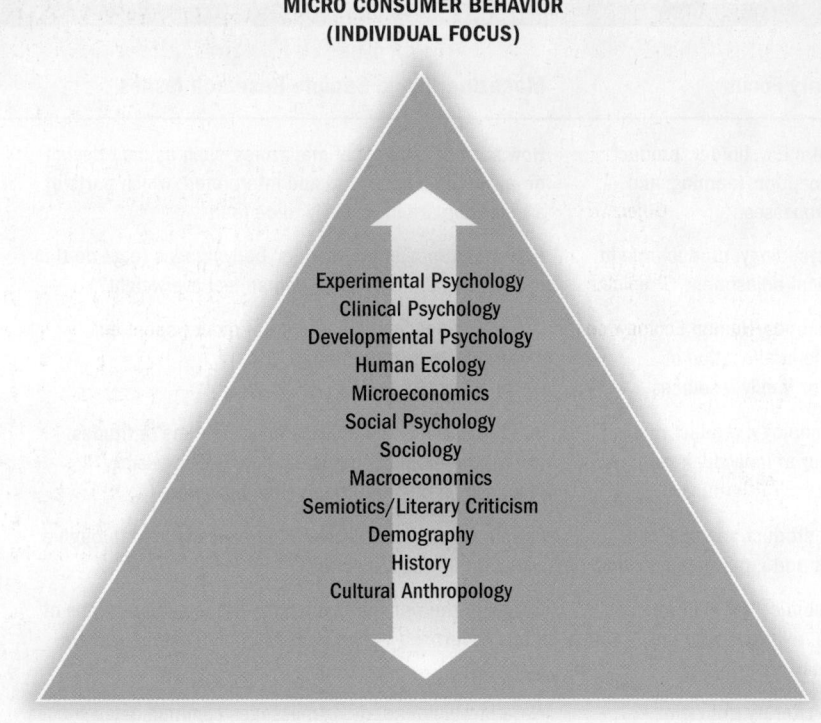

MICRO CONSUMER BEHAVIOR
(INDIVIDUAL FOCUS)

Experimental Psychology
Clinical Psychology
Developmental Psychology
Human Ecology
Microeconomics
Social Psychology
Sociology
Macroeconomics
Semiotics/Literary Criticism
Demography
History
Cultural Anthropology

MACRO CONSUMER BEHAVIOR
(SOCIAL FOCUS)

THE ISSUE OF TWO PERSPECTIVES ON CONSUMER RESEARCH

One general way we can classify consumer research is in terms of the fundamental assumptions the researchers make about what they are studying and how to study it. We call a set of beliefs that guide our understanding of the world a **paradigm**. As in other fields of study, a paradigm dominates the discipline of consumer behavior, but some believe it is in the middle of a *paradigm shift*, which occurs when a competing paradigm challenges the dominant set of assumptions.

The basic set of assumptions underlying the dominant paradigm at this point in time is **positivism** (or sometimes *modernism*). This perspective has significantly influenced Western art and science since the late sixteenth century. It emphasizes that human reason is supreme and that there is a single, objective truth that science can discover. Positivism encourages us to stress the function of objects, to celebrate technology, and to regard the world as a rational, ordered place with a clearly defined past, present, and future.

The newer paradigm of **interpretivism** (or *postmodernism*) questions these assumptions.[97] Proponents of this perspective argue that our society emphasizes science and technology too much, and they feel that this ordered, rational view of behavior denies the complex social and cultural world in which we really live. Others feel that positivism puts too much emphasis on material well-being and that its logical outlook is directed by an ideology that stresses the homogenous views of a culture dominated by (dead) white males.

TABLE 1.3
POSITIVIST VERSUS INTERPRETIVIST APPROACHES TO CONSUMER BEHAVIOR

Assumptions	Positivist Approach	Interpretivist Approach
Nature of reality	Objective, tangible Single	Socially constructed Multiple
Goal	Prediction	Understanding
Knowledge generated	Time-free Context independent	Time-bound Context dependent
View of causality	Existence of real causes	Multiple, simultaneous shaping events
Research relationship	Separation between researcher and subject	Interactive, cooperative with researcher being part of phenomenon under study

Source: Adapted from Laurel A. Hudson and Julie L. Ozanne, "Alternative Ways of Seeking Knowledge in Consumer Research," *Journal of Consumer Research* 14 (March 1988): 508–21. Reprinted with the permission of the University of Chicago Press. Copyright © 1988 JCR, Inc.

Interpretivists instead stress the importance of symbolic, subjective experience, and the idea that meaning is in the mind of the person—that is, we each construct our own meanings based on our unique and shared cultural experiences, so there are no right or wrong answers. In this view, the world in which we live is composed of a **pastiche**, or mixture of images.[98] This perspective rebukes the value we assign to products because they help us to create order; instead it focuses on regarding consumption as offering a set of diverse experiences. Table 1.3 summarizes the major differences between these two perspectives on consumer research.

We can illustrate an interpretative framework to understand marketing communications by referring to an analysis of one of the best-known and longest-running (1959–1978) advertising campaigns of all time: the work the advertising agency Doyle Dane Bernbach (DDB) did for the Volkswagen Beetle. This campaign, widely noted for its self-mocking wit, found many ways to turn the Beetle's homeliness, smallness, and lack of power into positive attributes at a time when most car ads were emphasizing just the opposite.

An interpretative analysis of these messages used concepts from literature, psychology, and anthropology to ground the appeal of this approach within a broader cultural context. Analysts linked the image DDB created for the humble car to other examples of what scholars of comedy call the "Little Man" pattern. This is a type of comedic character that is related to a clown or a trickster, a social outcast who is able to poke holes in the stuffiness and rigidity of bureaucracy and conformity. Other examples of the "Little Man" character include Hawkeye in the TV sitcom *M.A.S.H.*, the comedian Woody Allen, and Charlie Chaplin. When one looks at the cultural meaning of marketing messages this way, it is perhaps no coincidence that IBM chose the Charlie Chaplin character some years later to help it "soften" its stuffy, intimidating image as it tried to convince consumers that its new personal computer products were user-friendly.

Taking It from Here: The Plan of the Book

This book covers many facets of consumer behavior, and in the chapters to come we will highlight many of the research perspectives we briefly described in this one. The plan of the book is simple: It goes from micro to macro. Think of it as a sort of photograph album of consumer behavior: Each chapter provides a "snapshot" of consumers, but the lens used to take each picture gets successively wider. The book begins with issues related to the individual consumer and expands its focus until it eventually considers the behaviors of large groups of people in their social settings. As Figure 1.3 shows, we can depict the topics we will cover as a "wheel of consumer behavior."

Section II, "Consumers as Individuals," considers the consumer at his or her most micro level. It examines how the individual receives information from his or her immediate environment and how this material is learned, stored in memory, and used to form and modify individual attitudes—both about products and about oneself. Section III, "Consumers as Decision Makers," explores the ways in which consumers use the information they have acquired to make decisions about consumption activities, both as individuals and as group members. Section IV, "Consumers and Subcultures," further expands the focus by considering how the consumer functions as part of a larger social structure. This structure includes the influence of different social groups with which the consumer belongs and identifies, including social class, ethnic groups, and age groups. Finally, Section V, "Consumers and Culture," completes the picture as it examines marketing's impact on mass culture. These effects include the relationship of marketing to the expression of cultural values and lifestyles; how products and services are related to rituals and cultural myths; and the interface between marketing efforts and the creation of art, music, and other forms of popular culture that are so much a part of our daily lives.

■ **FIGURE 1.3** THE WHEEL OF CONSUMER BEHAVIOR

- Cultural Influences on Consumer Behavior
- The Creation and Diffusion of Consumer Culture

- Perception
- Learning and Memory
- Values and Motivation
- The Self and Sex Roles
- Personality and Lifestyles
- Attitudes
- Attitude Change and Interactive Communications

- Individual Decision Making
- Organizational and Housing Decision Making
- Buying and Disposing
- Group Influence and Opinion Leadership

- Income and Social Class
- Ethnic, Racial, and Religious Subcultures
- Age Subcultures

CHAPTER SUMMARY

Now that you have finished reading this chapter you should understand why:

Consumer behavior is a process.

● Consumer behavior is the study of the processes involved when individuals or groups select, purchase, use, or dispose of products, services, ideas, or experiences to satisfy needs and desires.

Consumers use products to help them define their identities in different settings.

● A consumer may purchase, use, and dispose of a product, but different people may perform these functions. In addition, we can think of consumers as role players who need different products to help them play their various parts.

Marketers need to understand the wants and needs of different consumer segments.

● Market segmentation is an important aspect of consumer behavior. Consumers can be segmented according to many dimensions, including product usage, demographics (the objective aspects of a population, such as age and sex), and psychographics (psychological and lifestyle characteristics). Emerging developments, such as the new emphasis on relationship marketing and the practice of database marketing, mean that marketers are much more attuned to the wants and needs of different consumer groups. This is especially important as people are empowered to construct their own consumerspace— accessing product information where and when they want it and initiating contact with companies on the Internet instead of passively receiving marketing communications.

The Web is changing consumer behavior.

● The Web is transforming the way consumers interact with companies and with each other. Online commerce allows us to locate obscure products from around the world, and consumption communities provide forums for people to share opinions and product recommendations. Potential problems accompany these benefits, including the loss of privacy and the deterioration of traditional social interactions as people log more time online.

Consumer behavior relates to other issues in our lives.

● Marketing activities exert an enormous impact on individuals. Consumer behavior is relevant to our understanding of both public policy issues (e.g., ethical marketing practices) and the dynamics of popular culture.

Consumer activities can be harmful to individuals and to society.

● Although textbooks often paint a picture of the consumer as a rational, informed decision maker, in reality many consumer activities are harmful to individuals or to society. The "dark side" of consumer behavior includes terrorism, addiction, the use of people as products (consumed consumers), and theft or vandalism (anticonsumption).

Different types of specialists study consumer behavior.

● The field of consumer behavior is interdisciplinary; it is composed of researchers from many different fields who share an interest in how people interact with the marketplace. These disciplines can be categorized by the degree to which their focus is micro (the individual consumer) or macro (the consumer as a member of groups or of the larger society).

There are two major perspectives that seek to understand and study consumer behavior.

● There are many perspectives on consumer behavior, but we can roughly divide research orientations into two approaches: The positivist perspective emphasizes the objectivity of science and the consumer as a rational decision maker. The interpretivist perspective, in contrast, stresses the subjective meaning of the consumer's individual experience and the idea that any behavior is subject to multiple interpretations rather than to one single explanation.

KEY TERMS

Anticonsumption, 61
B2C e-commerce, 44
Bioterrorism, 56
Business ethics, 47
C2C e-commerce, 44
Compulsive consumption, 58
Consumed consumers, 59
Consumer, 34
Consumer addiction, 57
Consumer behavior, 33
Consumption communities, 32
Culture jamming, 51

Database marketing, 39
Demographics, 32
Economics of information, 50
Exchange, 34
Global consumer culture, 43
Green marketing, 54
Heavy users, 35
Interpretivism, 64
Market segmentation strategies, 32
Need, 49
Paradigm, 64

Pastiche, 65
Popular culture, 40
Positivism, 64
Psychographics, 32
Relationship marketing, 39
RFID tag, 43
Role theory, 33
Shrinkage, 61
Social marketing, 54
U-commerce, 43
Want, 49

REVIEW QUESTIONS

1 Provide a definition of consumer behavior.

2 What are demographics? Give three examples of demographic characteristics.

3 What is the difference between a culture and a subculture?

4 Define market segmentation.

5 What is role theory, and how does it help us to understand consumer behavior?

6 What do we mean by an exchange?

7 Why is it important for businesses to learn about their heavy users?

8 What is database marketing? Give an example of a company that uses this technique.

9 What is popular culture, and how does this concept relate to marketing and consumer behavior?

10 This chapter states "people often buy products not for what they do but for what they mean." Explain the meaning of this statement and provide an example.

11 Describe two types of relationships a consumer can have with a product.

12 What is meant by the term "global consumer culture"?

13 What is the difference between C2C and B2C e-commerce?

14 The economics of information perspective argues that advertising is important. Why?

15 Provide two examples of important legislation that relate to American consumers.

16 Define social marketing and give an example of this technique.

17 Define consumer addiction and give two examples.

18 What is an example of a consumed consumer?

19 What is shrinkage, and why is it a problem?

20 Define anticonsumption, and provide two examples of it.

21 Name two different disciplines that study consumer behavior. How would their approaches to the same issue differ?

22 What are the major differences between the positivist and interpretivist paradigms in consumer research?

CONSUMER BEHAVIOR CHALLENGE

■ DISCUSS

1 This chapter states that people play different roles and that their consumption behaviors may differ depending on the particular role they are playing. State whether you agree or disagree with this perspective, giving examples from your personal life. Try to construct a "stage set" for a role you play—specify the props, costumes, and script that you use to play a role (e.g., job interviewee, conscientious student, party animal).

2 An American company introduced a teddy bear for Valentine's Day called "Crazy for You." This toy aroused the ire of mental health advocates because a straitjacket restrains the cuddly bear's paws and the stuffed animal comes with institutional commitment papers. Supporters of the company's decision to keep selling the bear say opponents are too "politically correct."[99] What do you think?

3 This chapter discussed a computer game called *JFK Reloaded,* which lets players reenact President Kennedy's assassination. Have the game's developers gone too far, or is any historical event "fair game" to be adapted into an entertainment vehicle?

4 Some researchers believe that the field of consumer behavior should be a pure rather than an applied science. That is, research issues should be framed in terms of their scientific interest rather than their applicability to immediate marketing problems. Give your views on this issue.

5 Name some products or services that your social group uses a lot. State whether you agree or disagree with the notion that these products help to form group bonds, supporting your argument with examples from your list of products used by the group.

6 Although demographic information on large numbers of consumers is used in many marketing contexts, some people believe that the sale of data on customers' incomes, buying habits, and so on constitutes an invasion of privacy and should be stopped. Is Big Brother watching? Comment on this issue from both a consumer's and a marketer's point of view.

7 List the three stages in the consumption process. Describe the issues that you considered in each of these stages when you made a recent important purchase.

8 What aspects of consumer behavior would interest a financial planner? A university administrator? A graphic arts designer? A social worker in a government agency? A nursing instructor?

9 Critics of targeted marketing strategies argue that this practice is discriminatory and unfair, especially if such a strategy encourages a group of people to buy a product that may be injurious to them or that they cannot afford. For example, community leaders in largely minority U.S. neighborhoods have staged protests against billboards promoting beer or cigarettes in these areas. However, the Association of National Advertisers argues that banning targeted marketing constitutes censorship and thus is a violation of the First Amendment. What are your views regarding this issue?

10 Do marketers have the ability to control our desires or the power to create needs? Is this situation changing as the Internet creates new ways to interact with companies? If so, how?

11 An entrepreneur made international news when he set up a Web site to auction the egg cells of fashion models to the highest bidder (minimum bid: $15,000). The site was targeted to people who wanted to have very attractive babies because they believed this would maximize their chances of succeeding in our society. Is the buying and selling of humans just another example of consumer behavior at work? Do you agree that this service is simply a more efficient way to maximize the chance of having happy, successful children? Should this kind of marketing activity be allowed? Would you sell your eggs or sperm on a Web site?

12 A recent book bemoans the new wave of consumer-generated content, labeling it "the cult of the amateur." It compares the social networking phenomenon to the old story about the monkeys: If you put an infinite number of monkeys in a room with an infinite number of typewriters, eventually they will (by hitting keys randomly) reproduce all the major works of literature. In other words, the large majority of user-generated content is at about the same level and the future of professionally produced, quality work is in doubt.[100] Do you agree or disagree with this assertion?

■ APPLY

13 To what degree will consumers trade lower prices for less privacy? Car owners now can let insurance companies monitor their driving using a new technology in exchange for lower rates. U.S. customers who sign up for Progressive's TripSense program get a device the size of a Tic Tac box to plug into their cars. The device will track speed and how many miles are driven at what times of day. Every few months, customers unplug the device from the car, plug it into a computer, download the data, and send them to the company. Depending on results, discounts will range from 5 to 25 percent. In Great Britain, a major insurer is testing a program called Pay as You Drive. Volunteers will get a device the size of a Palm computer installed in their cars. The gadget will use global positioning satellite technology to track where the car goes, constantly sending information back to the insurance company. Cars that spend more time in safer areas will qualify for bigger discounts.[101] Of course, the potential downside to these efforts is that the insurance companies may be able to collect data on where you have driven, how long you stayed in one location, and so on. Conduct a poll of 10 drivers of various ages where you describe these programs and ask respondents if they would participate in order to receive a discount on their insurance premiums. What reasons do they give pro and con? Do you find any differences in attitudes based on demographic characteristics such as age or gender?

14 While you're talking to car owners, probe to see what (if any) relationships they have with their vehicles. Do these feelings correspond to the types of consumer/product attachments we discussed in this chapter? How are these relationships acted on (hint: see if any of the respondents have nicknames for their cars, or if they "decorate" them with personal items)?

15 Many college students "share" music by downloading clips from the Internet. Interview at least five people who have downloaded at least one song or movie without paying for it. Do they feel they are stealing? What explanations do they offer for this behavior? Try to identify any common themes as a result of these interviews. If you were devising an ad campaign to discourage free downloading, how might you use what you have learned to craft a convincing message?

Case Study

MEXORYL

There's a new drug that is gaining a great deal of popularity in the United States. It won't get you high or help to produce muscle mass. But it will provide what some consider an even bigger rush: the prevention of wrinkles and skin cancer.

The Paris-based skin-care giant L'Oréal makes Mexoryl SX t as an ingredient to be used in sunscreen. While this product has been available in Europe and in Canada for more than a decade, the Food and Drug Administration has only recently approved the chemical for use in the United States. In fact, this is the first time that the FDA has approved a new sunscreen filter since 1988.

So what's the big deal? Aren't all sunscreens created equal? Not according to modern research. UV rays come in two varieties, UVA and UVB. UVB rays are the ones that burn the skin. But UVA rays penetrate the outer layer of skin where they break down skin proteins, damage cells and DNA, decrease the skin's immunity, and generate harmful free radicals. This in turn leads to wrinkles, sagging skin, brown spots, yellow discoloration, and various types of skin cancer.

To add to these harmful effects, UVA light is virtually inescapable. According to Dr. Katie Rodan, an associate clinical dermatologist at Stanford University, "It's present in the same amount from sunup to sundown, 365 days a year, totally independent of climate conditions." It not only penetrates car windows and T-shirts, but it also reaches the skin during fog, rain, and even blizzards.

Most U.S. market sunscreens contain only UVB blockers, that the familiar SPF ratings measure. These products help to prevent burning and associated damage to the skin. The types of UVA blockers that have been available for U.S. consumption (namely zinc oxide, titanium dioxide, and avobenzone) are not nearly as effective as Mexoryl, and most sunscreens don't contain them. Dermatologists have proclaimed Mexoryl one of the most effective filters of all wavelengths of ultraviolet light. To add to this strength, Mexoryl does not decompose when exposed to sunlight like UVB and other UVA filters.

Most U.S. consumers do not know the difference between UVA and UVB rays, and therein lies the problem. People apply sunscreens with UVB blockers and assume that if their skin doesn't burn they are protected. As a result, people spend more time in the sun and more time exposed to harmful UVA rays. Scientists believe that this is one of the primary reasons that skin cancer rates have tripled between 1980 and 2003.

With Mexoryl's approval, L'Oréal should enjoy a big competitive advantage because it's the only company that owns the rights to it. Competitors such as Neutrogena and Johnson & Johnson have made big improvements to other UVA blockers like Avobenzone. But even with such improvements, none come close to the effectiveness of Mexoryl. As of yet, Mexoryl is only available in two L'Oréal products. Will this new wonder drug catch on and dominate the sunscreen category? Only time will tell.

DISCUSSION QUESTIONS

1 What factors will likely have the greatest effect on any possible changes in consumer perception and acceptance of UVA blocking sunscreens?

2 Considering the implications of a product like Mexoryl on human health, what obligations does L'Oréal have to educate the public? To make it available in all its sunscreen products? To license it for use by other manufacturers? What obligations to consumers do companies like Neutrogena and Johnson & Johnson have?

3 What aspects of consumer behavior does L'Oréal need to understand to improve its chances of success with Mexoryl? How can it go about obtaining that knowledge?

Sources: Herman Valli, "New Sunscreen Formulas Add to Our Daily Defense Against the Sun's Damaging Rays," *Los Angeles Times* (June 17, 2007): P11.

Jennifer Barrett, "Fighting Crow's Feet and Cancer," *Newsweek* (June 27, 2005): 38.

Laurel Naversen Geraghty, "Psst! This Stuff Keeps You Young, but It's Illegal," *New York Times* (June 9, 2005): G3.

NOTES

1. Quoted at www.sigmadeltatau.net, accessed August 12, 2007.
2. Quoted at www.collegeclub.com/article/view/36;jsessionid=F04A1EFCB751386226EB3EC9C0C595CE, accessed August 12, 2007.
3. Olivia Ma, "Sneaker Freaks," *Newsweek* (August 16, 2004): 69.
4. Erving Goffman, *The Presentation of Self in Everyday Life* (Garden City, NY: Doubleday, 1959); George H. Mead, *Mind, Self, and Society* (Chicago: University of Chicago Press, 1934); Michael R. Solomon, "The Role of Products as Social Stimuli: A Symbolic Interactionism Perspective," *Journal of Consumer Research* 10 (December 1983): 319–29.
5. Michael R. Solomon and Elnora W. Stuart, *Marketing: Real People, Real Choices*, 2nd ed. (Upper Saddle River, NJ: Prentice Hall, 2000): 5–6.
6. Evan Ramstad, "Walkman's Plan for Reeling in the Ears of Wired Youths," *Wall Street Journal Interactive Edition* (May 18, 2000).
7. Anthony Bianco, "The Vanishing Mass Market," *BusinessWeek* (July 12, 2004): 61–67.
8. Jennifer Ordonez, "Cash Cows: Burger Joints Call Them 'Heavy Users'—But Not to Their Faces," *Wall Street Journal Interactive Edition* (January 12, 2000).
9. Steven Gray, "At Fast-Food Chains, Era of the Giant Burger (Plus Bacon) Is Here," *The Wall Street Journal Online* (January 27, 2005).
10. Allison Fass, "Kingdom Seeks Magic," *Forbes* (October 2006): 68–70.
11. Natalie Perkins, "Zeroing in on Consumer Values," *Advertising Age* (March 22, 1993): 23.
12. Hannah Karp, "Red Bull Aims at an Older Crowd," *Wall Street Journal* (June 7, 2004): B3.
13. Jack Neff, "Crest Spinoff Targets Women," *Advertising Age* (June 3, 2002): 1.
14. Charles M. Schaninger and William D. Danko, "A Conceptual and Empirical Comparison of Alternative Household Life Cycle Models," *Journal of Consumer Research* 19 (March 1993): 580–94; Robert E. Wilkes, "Household Life-Cycle Stages, Transitions, and Product Expenditures," *Journal of Consumer Research* 22 (June 1995): 27–42.
15. Richard P. Coleman, "The Continuing Significance of Social Class to Marketing," *Journal of Consumer Research* 10 (December 1983): 265–80.
16. Motoko Rich, "Region's Marketers Hop on the Bubba Bandwagon," *Wall Street Journal Interactive Edition* (May 19, 1999).
17. Sarah Ellison, "Prilosec OTC Blitz by P&G Represents New Drug Foray," *Wall Street Journal on the Web* (September 12, 2003).
18. Constance L. Hayes, "What Wal-Mart Knows About Customers' Habits," *New York Times on the Web* (November 14, 2004).
19. Mylene Mangalindan, "Hollywood's 'Wedding Crashers' Inspires the Invitationless," *Wall Street Journal* (December 28, 2005): B1.
20. www.wannadocity.com/, accessed June 11, 2007; Allison Fass, "Where Child Labor Is Child's Play," *Forbes* (September 20, 2004): 205–6.
21. www.advertisingiconmuseum.com, accessed June 11, 2007.
22. Thomas Vinciguerra, "Soft, Chewy and Taking Over the World," *New York Times* (July 5, 2006): Sec. 4, p. 2.
23. Quoted in "Bringing Meaning to Brands," *American Demographics* (June 1997): 34.
24. Jennifer Aaker, Susan Fournier, and S. Adam Brasel, "When Good Brands Do Bad," *Journal of Consumer Research* 31 (2004): 1–16.
25. Susan Fournier, "Consumers and Their Brands. Developing Relationship Theory in Consumer Research," *Journal of Consumer Research* 24 (March 1998): 343–73.
26. Brad Edmondson, "The Dawn of the Megacity," *Marketing Tools* (March 1999): 64.
27. David Barbosa, "China, New Land of Shoppers, Builds Malls on Gigantic Scale," *New York Times Online* (May 25, 2005).
28. For a discussion of this trend, see Russell W. Belk, "Hyperreality and Globalization: Culture in the Age of Ronald McDonald," *Journal of International Consumer Marketing* 8 (1995): 23–38.
29. Ronald Alsop, "Best-Known Companies Aren't Always Best Liked," *Wall Street Journal* (November 15, 2004): B4.
30. Richard T. Watson, Leyland F. Pitt, Pierre Berthon, and George M. Zinkhan, "U-Commerce: Expanding the Universe of Marketing," *Journal of the Academy of Marketing Science* 30 (2002): 333–47.
31. "I.B.M. Unveils 'Smart' Laundry," *New York Times on the Web* (August 30, 2002).
32. Some material in this section was adapted from Michael R. Solomon and Elnora W. Stuart, *Welcome to Marketing.Com: The Brave New World of E-Commerce* (Upper Saddle River, NJ: Prentice Hall, 2000).
33. Patricia Winters Lauro, "Marketing Battle for Online Dating," *New York Times on the Web* (January 27, 2003).
34. Rebecca Fairley Raney, "Study Finds Internet of Social Benefit to Users," *New York Times on the Web* (May 11, 2000).
35. John Markoff, "Portrait of a Newer, Lonelier Crowd Is Captured in an Internet Survey," *New York Times on the Web* (February 16, 2000).
36. Lisa Guernsey, "Professor Who Once Found Isolation Online Has a Change of Heart," *New York Times on the Web* (July 26, 2001).
37. Charles Sheehan, "Upcoming Comic Features Real-Life Marriage Proposal," *Montgomery Advertiser* (February 24, 2002).
38. Stuart Elliott, "Would You Like Fries with That Monopoly Game?" *New York Times Online* (September 12, 2006).
39. Paul Tolme, "Sponsoring the Slopes," *Newsweek* (December 8, 2003): 10.
40. "Hotel Offers All-You-Can-Eat Häagen-Dazs Suite," *Marketing Daily*, www.mediapost.com, accessed June 20, 2007.
41. Jonathan Miller, "And Now, a Few Words from the Urinal," *New York Times* (September 30, 2004): E5.
42. "Woman in Wendy's Finger Case Is Arrested," *New York Times on the Web* (April 22, 2005).
43. Reported in *American Demographics* (December 1999): 18.
44. Valerie S. Folkes and Michael A. Kamins, "Effects of Information About Firms' Ethical and Unethical Actions on Consumers' Attitudes," *Journal of Consumer Psychology* 8 (1999): 243–59.
45. "Media Want Colleges to Fight Piracy," *New York Times on the Web* (October 11, 2002).
46. Jacqueline N. Hood and Jeanne M. Logsdon, "Business Ethics in the NAFTA Countries: A Cross-Cultural Comparison," *Journal of Business Research* 55 (2002): 883–90.
47. Barbara Crossette, "Russia and China Called Top Business Bribers," *New York Times on the Web* (May 17, 2002). For more details about the survey see www.transparency.org.

48. Quoted in Ira Teinowitz, "Lawsuit: Menthol Smokes Illegally Targeted to Blacks," *Advertising Age* (November 2, 1998): 16.

49. Pamela Paul, "Mixed Signals," *American Demographics* (July 2001): 44.

50. R. Harris, "Most Customers Using Internet Fail to Read Retailers' Privacy Policies," *Ventura County Star* (June 6, 2002).

51. Quoted in Jennifer Lach, "The New Gatekeepers," *American Demographics* (June 1999): 41–42.

52. Michael R. Solomon, *Conquering Consumerspace: Marketing Strategies for a Branded World* (New York: AMACOM, 2003).

53. Jeffrey Ball, "Religious Leaders to Discuss SUVs with GM, Ford Officials," *Wall Street Journal Interactive Edition* (November 19, 2002); Danny Hakim, "The S.U.V. Is a Beast, and It's Hairy, Too," *New York Times on the Web* (February 2, 2005).

54. William Leiss, Stephen Kline, and Sut Jhally, *Social Communication in Advertising: Persons, Products, and Images of Well-Being* (Toronto: Methuen, 1986); Jerry Mander, *Four Arguments for the Elimination of Television* (New York: William Morrow, 1977).

55. Packard (1957); quoted in Leiss et al., *Social Communication*, 11.

56. Raymond Williams, *Problems in Materialism and Culture: Selected Essays* (London: Verso, 1980).

57. Leiss et al., *Social Communication*.

58. George Stigler, "The Economics of Information," *Journal of Political Economy* (1961): 69.

59. Leiss et al., *Social Communication*, 11.

60. Robert V. Kozinets and Jay M. Handelman, "Adversaries of Consumption: Consumer Movements, Activism, and Ideology," *Journal of Consumer Research* 31 (December 2004): 691–704.

61. Adbusters Media Foundation, "Adbusters" (Vancouver, British Columbia) (June 27, 2002), available from http://secure.adbusters.org/orders/culturejam.

62. Adbusters Media Foundation, "Adbusters" (Vancouver, British Columbia) (June 27, 2002), available from http://adbusters.org/information/network.

63. www.nikesweatshop.net, accessed June 29, 2002.

64. Nat Ives, "Anti-Ad Group Tries Advertising," *New York Times on the Web* (September 21, 2004).

65. The Truth.com, "About Truth," cited March 15, 2002, available from www.thetruth.com.

66. www.gapsucks.org , accessed June 12, 2007; "We'd Rather Wear Nothing Than Wear GAP!" available from www.newstarget.com/019806.html.

67. "Horizon Milk, Wild Oats Named in Consumer Boycott of "False" Organic Products" (July 28, 2006) NewsTarget, www.newstarget.com/019806.html, accessed June 12, 2007.

68. For consumer research and discussions related to public policy issues, see Paul N. Bloom and Stephen A. Greyser, "The Maturing of Consumerism," *Harvard Business Review* (November–December 1981): 130–39; George S. Day, "Assessing the Effect of Information Disclosure Requirements," *Journal of Marketing* (April 1976): 42–52; Dennis E. Garrett, "The Effectiveness of Marketing Policy Boycotts: Environmental Opposition to Marketing," *Journal of Marketing* 51 (January 1987): 44–53; Michael Houston and Michael Rothschild, "Policy-Related Experiments on Information Provision: A Normative Model and Explication," *Journal of Marketing Research* 17 (November 1980): 432–49; Jacob Jacoby, Wayne D. Hoyer, and David A. Sheluga, *Misperception of Televised Communications* (New York: American Association of Advertising Agencies, 1980); Gene R. Laczniak and Patrick E. Murphy, *Marketing Ethics: Guidelines for Managers* (Lexington, MA: Lexington Books, 1985); 117–23; Lynn Phillips and Bobby Calder, "Evaluating Consumer Protection Laws: Promising Methods," *Journal of Consumer Affairs* 14 (Summer 1980): 9–36; Donald P. Robin and Eric Reidenbach, "Social Responsibility, Ethics, and Marketing Strategy: Closing the Gap Between Concept and Application," *Journal of Marketing* 51 (January 1987): 44–58; Howard Schutz and Marianne Casey, "Consumer Perceptions of Advertising as Misleading," *Journal of Consumer Affairs* 15 (Winter 1981): 340–57; Darlene Brannigan Smith and Paul N. Bloom, "Is Consumerism Dead or Alive? Some New Evidence," in Thomas C. Kinnear, ed., *Advances in Consumer Research* 11 (1984): 369–73.

69. Cf. Philip Kotler and Alan R. Andreasen, *Strategic Marketing for Nonprofit Organizations*, 4th ed. (Upper Saddle River, NJ: Prentice Hall, 1991); Jeff B. Murray and Julie L. Ozanne, "The Critical Imagination: Emancipatory Interests in Consumer Research," *Journal of Consumer Research* 18 (September 1991): 192–244; William D. Wells, "Discovery-Oriented Consumer Research," *Journal of Consumer Research* 19 (March 1993): 489–504.

70. "Concerned Consumers Push for Environmentally Friendly Packaging," *Boxboard Containers* (April 1993): 4.

71. Tom Zeller, Jr., "A Sure-to-Be-Controversial Game Fulfills That Expectation Fully," *New York Times on the Web* (November 29, 2004).

72. Associated Press, "U.K. Bans Sales of 'Manhunt 2' Game," *Wall Street Journal Online Edition* (June 19, 2007).

73. "Japan Calls for Tighter Food Security Against Mad Cow Disease," *Xinhua News Agency* (May 20, 2002), cited June 29, 2002, available from www.xinhuanet.com/English.

74. Kenneth E. Nusbaum, James C. Wright, and Michael R. Solomon, "Attitudes of Food Animal Veterinarians to Continuing Education in Agriterrorism," paper presented at the 53rd Annual Meeting of the Animal Disease Research Workers in Southern States, University of Florida (February 2001).

75. Betty Mohr, "The Pepsi Challenge: Managing a Crisis," *Prepared Foods* (March 1994): 13.

76. "Boston Officials Livid over Ad Stunt," *New York Times Online* (February 1, 2007).

77. Synthetic Worlds Initiative at Indiana University http://swi.indiana.edu/ardenworld.htm, accessed July 17, 2007.

78. Derek N. Hassay and Malcolm C. Smith, "Compulsive Buying: An Examination of the Consumption Motive," *Psychology & Marketing* 13 (December 1996): 741–52.

79. Thomas C. O'Guinn and Ronald J. Faber, "Compulsive Buying: A Phenomenological Explanation," *Journal of Consumer Research* 16 (September 1989): 154.

80. Curtis L. Taylor, "Guys Who Buy, Buy, Buy," *Newsday* (October 6, 2006); Jim Thornton, "Buy Now, Pay Later," *Men's Health* (December, 2004): 109–12.

81. Georgia Witkin, "The Shopping Fix," *Health* (May 1988): 73; see also Arch G. Woodside and Randolph J. Trappey III, "Compulsive Consumption of a Consumer Service: An Exploratory Study of Chronic Horse Race Track Gambling Behavior," working paper #90-MKTG-04, A. B. Freeman School of Business, Tulane University, 1990; Rajan Nataraajan and Brent G. Goff, "Manifestations of Compulsiveness in the Consumer-Marketplace Domain," *Psychology & Marketing* 9 (January 1992): 31–44; Joann Ellison Rodgers, "Addiction: A Whole New View," *Psychology Today* (September–October 1994): 32.

82. Helen Reynolds, *The Economics of Prostitution* (Springfield, IL: Thomas, 1986).

83. Patrick Di Justo, "How to Sell Your Body for $46 Million," *Wired* (August 2003): 47.

84. Amy Harmon, "Illegal Kidney Auction Pops Up on eBay's Site," *New York Times on the Web* (September 3, 1999).

85. Di Justo, "How to Sell Your Body for $46 Million," 47.

86. "GM Will Edit Robot Super Bowl Ad," *Wall Street Journal Electronic Edition* (February 9, 2007).

87. "Advertisers Face Up to the New Morality: Making the Pitch," *Bloomberg* (July 8, 1997).

88. "Shoplifting: Bess Myerson's Arrest Highlights a Multibillion-Dollar Problem That Many Stores Won't Talk About," *Life* (August 1988): 32.

89. "New Survey Shows Shoplifting Is a Year-Round Problem," *Business Wire* (April 12, 1998).

90. "Customer Not King, but Thief," *Marketing News* (December 9, 2002): 4.

91. Catherine A. Cole, "Deterrence and Consumer Fraud," *Journal of Retailing* 65 (Spring 1989): 107–20; Stephen J. Grove, Scott J. Vitell, and David Strutton, "Non-Normative Consumer Behavior and the Techniques of Neutralization," in Terry Childers et al., eds., *Marketing Theory and Practice,* 1989 AMA Winter Educators' Conference (Chicago: American Marketing Association, 1989): 131–35.

92. Mark Curnutte, "The Scope of the Shoplifting Problems," *Gannett News Service* (November 29, 1997).

93. Anthony D. Cox, Dena Cox, Ronald D. Anderson, and George P. Moschis, "Social Influences on Adolescent Shoplifting–Theory, Evidence, and Implications for the Retail Industry," *Journal of Retailing* 69 (Summer 1993): 234–46.

94. Stephanie Kang, "New Return Policy: Retailers Say 'No' to Serial Exchangers," *Wall Street Journal* (November 29, 2004): B1.

95. www.dogdoo.com, accessed June 12, 2007.

96. Morris B. Holbrook, "The Consumer Researcher Visits Radio City: Dancing in the Dark," in Elizabeth C. Hirschman and Morris B. Holbrook, eds., *Advances in Consumer Research* 12 (Provo, UT: Association for Consumer Research, 1985): 28–31.

97. For a recent overview, see Eric J. Arnould and Craig J. Thompson, "Consumer Culture Theory (CCT): Twenty Years of Research," *Journal of Consumer Research* 31 (March 2005): 868–82.

98. Alladi Venkatesh, "Postmodernism, Poststructuralism and Marketing," paper presented at the American Marketing Association Winter Theory Conference, San Antonio, February 1992; see also Stella Proctor, Ioanna Papasolomou-Doukakis, and Tony Proctor, "What Are Television Advertisements Really Trying to Tell Us? A Postmodern Perspective," *Journal of Consumer Behavior* 1 (February 2002): 246–55; A. Fuat Firat and Alladi Venkatesh, "The Making of Postmodern Consumption," in Russell W. Belk and Nikhilesh Dholakia, eds., *Consumption and Marketing: Macro Dimensions* (Boston: PWS-Kent, 1993).

99. Pam Belluck, "Toy's Message of Affection Draws Anger and Publicity," *New York Times on the Web* (January 22, 2005).

100. Andrew Keen, *The Cult of the Amateur: How Today's Internet Is Killing Our Culture*, (New York: Currency 2007).

101. Kevin Maney, "Drivers Let Big Brother in to Get a Break," *Ethics* (August 9, 2004): 1B.

FRANCESCOBIASIA
HANDBAGS

Consumers as Individuals

In this section, we focus on the internal dynamics of consumers. Although "no man is an island," each of us is to some degree a self-contained receptor of information about the outside world. Advertising messages, products, and other people constantly confront us—not to mention personal thoughts about ourselves that make us happy or sad. Each chapter in this section considers a different aspect of the individual that is "invisible" to others—but of vital importance to ourselves.

Chapter 2 describes the process of perception, where we absorb and interpret information about products and other people from the outside world. Chapter 3 focuses on the way we mentally store this information and how it adds to our existing knowledge about the world during the learning process. Chapter 4 discusses our reasons or motivations to absorb this information and how our cultural values influence what we do.

Chapter 5 explores how our views about ourselves—particularly our sexuality and our physical appearance—affect what we do, want, and buy. Chapter 6 goes on to consider how people's individual personalities influence these decisions and how the choices we make in terms of products, services, and leisure activities help to define our lifestyles.

Chapters 7 and 8 discuss how marketers form and change our attitudes—our evaluations of all these products and messages— and how we as individual consumers engage in an ongoing dialogue with the marketplace.

■ CHAPTERS AHEAD

Perception

Chapter Objectives

When you finish reading this chapter you will understand why:

- Perception is a three-stage process that translates raw stimuli into meaning.

- Products and commercial messages often appeal to our senses, but we won't be influenced by most of them.

- The design of a product today is a key driver of its success or failure.

- Subliminal advertising is a controversial—but largely ineffective—way to talk to consumers.

- We interpret the stimuli to which we do pay attention according to learned patterns and expectations.

- The field of semiotics helps us to understand how marketers use symbols to create meaning.

the European vacation has been wonderful, and this stop in Lisbon is no exception. Still, after 2 weeks of eating his way through some of the Continent's finest pastry shops and restaurants, Gary's getting a bit of a craving for his family's favorite snack—a good old American box of Oreos and an ice-cold carton of milk. Unbeknownst to his wife, Janeen, he had stashed away some cookies "just in case"—this was the time to break them out.

Now, all he needs is the milk. On an impulse, Gary decides to surprise Janeen with a midafternoon treat. He sneaks out of the hotel room while she's napping and finds the nearest *grosa*. When he heads to the small refrigerated section, though, he's puzzled—no milk here. Undaunted, Gary asks the clerk, *"Leite, por favor?"* The clerk quickly smiles and points to a rack in the middle of the store piled with little white square boxes. No, that can't be right—Gary resolves to work on his Portuguese. He repeats the question, and again he gets the same answer.

Finally, he investigates and sure enough he sees the boxes with labels saying they contain something called ultra heat treated (UHT) milk. Nasty! Who in the world would drink milk out of a little box that's been sitting on a warm shelf for who knows how long? Gary dejectedly returns to the hotel, his snack time fantasies crumbling like so many stale cookies.

Introduction

Gary would be surprised to learn that many people in the world drink milk out of a box every day. UHT is pasteurized milk that has been heated until the bacteria causing spoilage are destroyed, and it can last for 5 to 6 months without refrigeration if its aseptic container is unopened.

Shelf-stable milk is particularly popular in Europe, where refrigerator space in homes is smaller and stores tend to carry less inventory than in the United States. Seven out of ten Europeans drink it routinely. Manufacturers are trying to crack the U.S. market as well, though analysts are dubious about their prospects. To begin with, milk consumption in the United States is declining steadily as teenagers choose soft drinks instead. Indeed, the U.S. Milk Industry Foundation pumped $44 million into an advertising campaign to promote milk drinking ("Got Milk?").

But enticing Americans to drink milk out of a box is even harder. In focus groups, U.S. consumers say they have trouble believing the milk is not spoiled or unsafe. In addition, they consider the square, quart-sized boxes more suitable for dry food. Many schools and fast-food chains already buy UHT milk because of its long shelf life.[1] Still, although Americans may not think twice about drinking a McFlurry from McDonald's made with shelf-stable milk, it's going to be a long, uphill battle to change their perceptions about the proper accompaniment to a bagful of Oreos.

Whether it's the taste of Oreos, the sight of an Obsession perfume ad, or the sound of the music group Outkast, we live in a world overflowing with sensations. Wherever we turn, we are bombarded by a symphony of colors, sounds, and odors. Some of the "notes" in this symphony occur naturally, such as the loud barking of a dog, the shades of the evening sky, or the heady smell of a rose bush. Others come from people: The person sitting next to you in class might sport tinted blonde hair, bright pink pants, and enough nasty perfume to make your eyes water.

Marketers certainly contribute to this commotion. Consumers are never far from advertisements, product packages, radio and television commercials, and billboards—all clamoring for our attention. Sometimes we go out of our way to experience "unusual" sensations, whether they are thrills from bungee jumping; playing virtual reality games; or going to theme parks such as Universal Studios in California, which offers "Fear Factor Live" attractions that ask vacationers to swallow gross things or perform stomach-churning stunts.[2]

American reality shows such as *Fear Factor* attract people who want to test the limits of their sensations. On a popular Peruvian TV show called *Laura en America*, contestants show just what people are capable of experiencing (with the right incentive): For $20, two women stripped to their underwear and had buckets of slime and toads poured over their bodies. For the same amount, three men raced to gobble down bowls of large tree grubs from the Amazon jungle. For $30, a woman licked the armpits of a sweaty bodybuilder who had not bathed for 2 days.[3] And you thought college fraternity stunts were out there?

Game-show contestants or not, each of us copes with the bombardment of sensations by paying attention to some stimuli and tuning out others. The messages to which we *do* choose to pay attention often wind up differing from what the sponsors intended, as we each put our personal "spin" on things by adopting meanings consistent with our own unique experiences, biases, and desires. This chapter focuses on the process of perception, in which the consumer absorbs sensations and then uses these to interpret the surrounding world.

Sensation refers to the immediate response of our sensory receptors (eyes, ears, nose, mouth, fingers) to basic stimuli such as light, color, sound, odor, and texture. **Perception** is the process by which people select, organize, and interpret these sensations. The study of perception, then, focuses on what we *add* to these raw sensations in order to give them meaning.

■ FIGURE 2.1   AN OVERVIEW OF THE PERCEPTUAL PROCESS

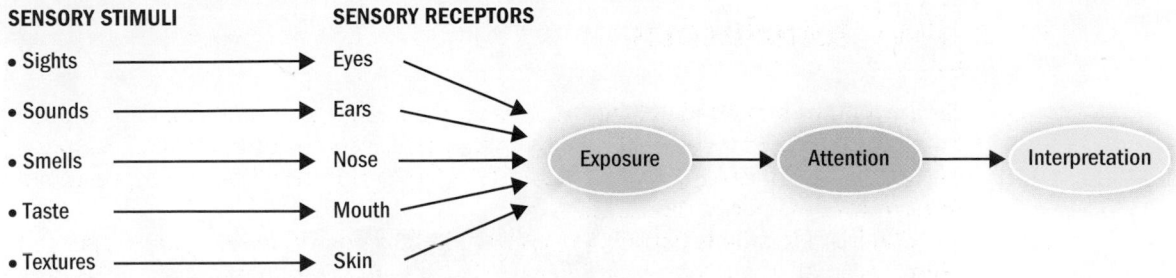

Gary's encounter with milk in a box illustrates the perceptual process. He has learned to equate the cold temperature of refrigerated milk with freshness, so he experienced a negative physical reaction when confronted with a product that contradicted his expectations. Gary's evaluation was affected by factors such as the design of the package, the brand name, and even the section in the grocery store in which the milk was displayed. These expectations are largely affected by a consumer's cultural background. Europeans do not necessarily have the same perceptions of milk as Americans, and as a result their reactions to the product are quite different from those of Americans.

Like computers, we undergo stages of *information processing* in which we input and store stimuli. Unlike computers, though, we do not passively process whatever information happens to be present. In the first place, we notice only a very small number of the stimuli in our environment. Of those we do notice, we attend to an even smaller number. And we might not process the stimuli that do enter consciousness objectively. Each individual interprets the meaning of a stimulus to be consistent with his or her own unique biases, needs, and experiences. As Figure 2.1 shows, these three stages of exposure, attention, and interpretation make up the process of perception. Before considering each of these stages, let's step back and look at the sensory systems that provide sensations to us in the first place.

 Sensory Systems

We can receive external stimuli, or *sensory inputs,* on a number of channels. We may see a billboard, hear a jingle, feel the softness of a cashmere sweater, taste a new flavor of ice cream, or smell a leather jacket. The inputs our five senses detect are the raw data that begin the perceptual process. For example, sensory data emanating from the external environment (e.g., hearing a tune on the radio) can generate internal sensory experiences when the song triggers a young man's memory of his first dance and brings to mind the smell of his date's perfume or the feel of her hair on his cheek.

The unique sensory quality of a product can play an important role in helping it to stand out from the competition, especially if the brand creates a unique association with the sensation. The Owens-Corning Fiberglass Corporation was the first company to trademark a color when it used bright pink for its insulation material; it adopted the Pink Panther cartoon character as its spokescharacter. Harley-Davidson actually tried to trademark the distinctive sound made by a "hog" revving up.[4] These responses are an important part of **hedonic consumption,** the multisensory, fantasy, and emotional aspects of consumers' interactions with products.[5]

This Italian ad for a yoga school plays with our sensory systems.

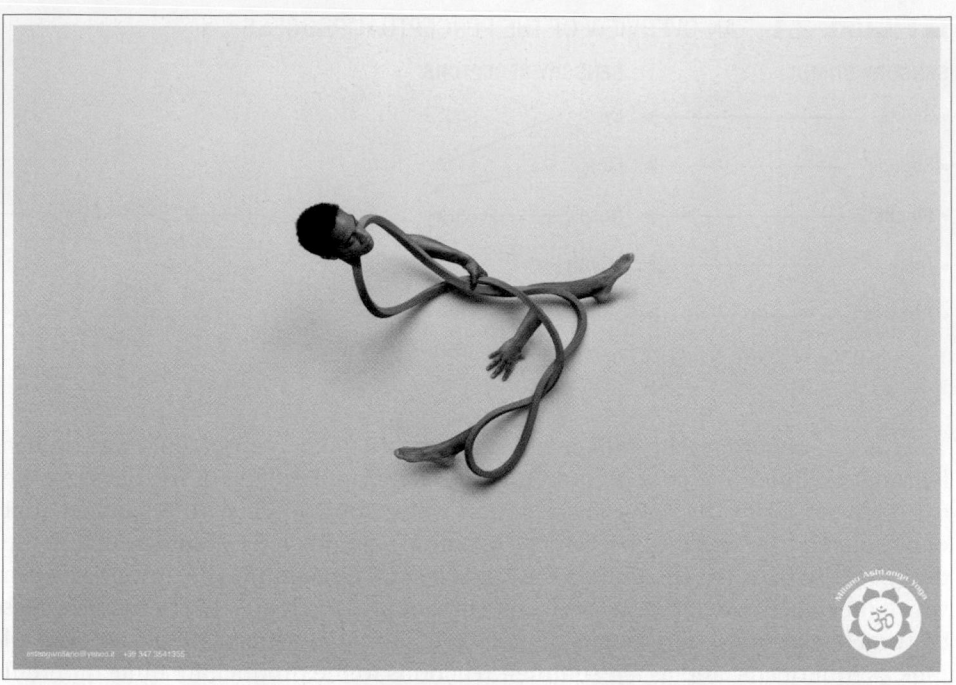

HEDONIC CONSUMPTION AND THE DESIGN ECONOMY

In recent years, the sensory experiences we receive from products and services have become an even larger priority when we choose among competing options. As manufacturing costs go down and the amount of "stuff" that people accumulate goes up, consumers increasingly want to buy things that will give them hedonic value in addition to simply doing what they're designed to do. A Dilbert comic strip poked fun at this trend when it featured a product designer who declared: "Quality is yesterday's news. Today we focus on the emotional impact of the product." Fun aside, the new focus on emotional experience is consistent with psychological research that finds that people prefer additional experiences to additional possessions as their incomes rise.[6]

In this environment, form *is* function. Two young entrepreneurs named Adam Lowry and Eric Ryan discovered that basic truth when they quit their day jobs to develop a line of house-cleaning products they called Method. Cleaning products—what a yawn, right?

But, think again: For years companies such as Procter & Gamble have plodded along, peddling boring boxes of soap powder to generations of housewives who suffered in silence, scrubbing and buffing, yearning for the daily respite of martini time. Lowry and Ryan gambled that they could offer an alternative—cleaners in exotic scents such as cucumber, lavender, and ylang-ylang that come in aesthetically pleasing bottles. The bet paid off. Within 2 years, the partners were cleaning up, taking in more than $2 million in revenue. Shortly thereafter, they hit it big when the U.S. retailer Target contracted to sell Method products in its stores.[7]

There's a method to Target's madness. Design is no longer the province of upper-crust sophisticates who never got close enough to a cleaning product to be revolted by it. The red-hot store chain has helped to make designers such as Karim Rashid, Michael Graves, Philippe Starck, Todd Oldham, and Isaac Mizrahi household names. Mass-market consumers are thirsting for great design, and they're rewarding those companies that give it to them with their enthusiastic patronage and loyalty. From razor blades such as the Gillette Sensor to computers such as the Apple, and even to the lowly trash can, design *is* substance.

Ironically, even staid old P&G is starting to get the idea. Although it's a bit like turning a battleship, Procter & Gamble now recognizes the importance of integrating

This Finnish ad emphasizes the sensual reasons to visit the city of Helsinki.

design into every product initiative. In the "good old days" (that is, a couple of years ago), design was basically an afterthought. Marketing meant appealing to customers in terms of efficiency rather than aesthetics. Now, its CEO wants P&G to focus on what he calls "the first moment of truth"—winning consumers in the store with packaging and displays. As a result, P&G now has a vice president (VP) of design, strategy, and innovation who reports directly to the CEO. Her philosophy sums it up: "Competitive advantage comes not just from patents, but also from incorporating design into products, much like Apple, Sony or Dell."[8]

SENSORY MARKETING: HARNESSING PERCEPTION FOR COMPETITIVE ADVANTAGE

Guests at Omni luxury hotels are in for a host of new experiences. When they visit the hotel chain's Web site to reserve a room, they will hear the sound of soft chimes

See-Food Diets—How Your Eyes Make You Lose and Gain Weight

Our eyes play tricks on us, and these perceptions can have calorie consequences.[14] When pouring or eating foods from larger boxes, these boxes suggest it is appropriate or "acceptable" to eat more than from smaller ones—and we do! One study gave Chicago moviegoers free medium-size or large-size popcorn buckets and showed that those given the larger buckets ate 45 percent more.[15] Even when 14-day-old popcorn was used, people still ate 32 percent more, even though they said they hated the popcorn.[16] The same thing happens at parties. Master of business administration (MBA) students at a Champaign, Illinois, Super Bowl party were offered Chex Mix from either huge gallon-size bowls or from twice as many half-gallon bowls. Those dishing from the gallon-size bowls took and ate 53 percent more.[17]

What's weird is that we also use our eyes to tell us we're full and not our stomachs. That's what gets us in trouble. In the "Bottomless Bowl" study, college students who ate from soup bowls that secretly refilled themselves from underneath the table ate 73 percent more soup than those eating from the normal bowls.[18] The kicker is that they estimated they ate the same amount and they even rated themselves as no more full. They used their eyes to tell them whether they had eaten enough. Because there was still food in their bowls, they believed they were not yet full.

playing. On entering the lobby, they'll be hit with the scent of lemongrass and green tea and view elaborate floral displays. In their rooms, they will find eucalyptus bath salts and Sensation Bars; minibars stocked with items such as mojito-flavored jelly beans and miniature Zen gardens. In a joint promotion with Starbucks, guests will find small scented stickers on the front pages of their free copies of *USA Today* newspaper; a blackberry aroma suggests they start their day at the hotel with a cup of Starbucks coffee "paired with a fresh muffin."[9]

Welcome to the new era of **sensory marketing,** where companies pay extra attention to the impact of sensations on our product experiences. From hotels to carmakers to brewers, they recognize that our senses help us to decide which products appeal to us—and which ones stand out from a host of similar offerings in the marketplace. In this section, we'll take a closer look at how some smart marketers use our sensory systems to create a competitive advantage.

VISION

Marketers rely heavily on visual elements in advertising, store design, and packaging. They communicate meanings on the *visual channel* through a product's color, size, and styling. Philips gives its electronics a younger feel by making them thinner and more colorful. Its audio products used to be all silver, but now each component comes in four colors, including electric green.[10]

Colors may even influence our emotions more directly. Evidence suggests that some colors (particularly red) create feelings of arousal and stimulate appetite, and others (such as blue) create more relaxing feelings. Advertisements of products presented against a backdrop of blue are better liked than when shown against a red background, and cross-cultural research indicates a consistent preference for blue whether people live in Canada or Hong Kong.[11] American Express chose to name its new card Blue after research showed the color evokes positive feelings about the future. Its advertising agency named blue the color of the new millennium because people associate it with sky and water, "providing a sense of limitlessness and peace."[12]

Some reactions to color come from learned associations. In Western countries, black is the color of mourning, whereas in some Eastern countries, notably Japan, white plays this role. In addition, we associate the color black with power. Teams in both the National Football League and the National Hockey League who wear black uniforms are among the most aggressive; they consistently rank near the top of their leagues in penalties during the season.[13]

Other reactions are a result of biological and cultural differences. Women are drawn toward brighter tones and they are more sensitive to subtle shadings and patterns. Some scientists attribute this to biology because females see color better than males do and men are 16 times more likely to be color blind. Age also influences our responsiveness to color. As we get older, our eyes mature and our vision takes on a yellow cast. Colors look duller to older people, so they prefer white and other bright tones. This helps to explain why mature consumers are much more likely to choose a white car—Lexus, which sells heavily in this market, makes 60 percent of its vehicles in white.

The trend toward brighter and more complex colors also reflects the increasingly multicultural makeup of the United States. For example, Hispanics tend to prefer brighter colors as a reflection of the intense lighting conditions in Latin America; strong colors keep their character in strong sunlight.[23] That's why Procter & Gamble uses brighter colors in makeup it sells in Latin countries.[24]

Scientists and philosophers have been talking about the meanings of colors since the time of Socrates in the fifth century B.C., but it took Sir Isaac Newton in the early seventeenth century to shine light through a prism and reveal the color spectrum. Even then, Newton's observations weren't totally scientific; he identified seven major colors to be consistent with the number of planets known at that time, as well as the seven notes of the diatonic scale.

We now know that perceptions of a color depend on both its physical wavelength and how the mind responds to that stimulus. Yellow is in the middle of wavelengths detectable by the human eye so it is the brightest and attracts attention. The U.S. phone directory, the Yellow Pages, originally were colored yellow to heighten the attention level of bored telephone operators.[25] However, our culture and even our language affect the colors we see. For example, the Welsh language has no words that correspond with green, blue, gray, or brown in English, but it uses other colors that English-speakers don't (including one that covers part of green, part of gray, and the whole of our blue). Hungarian has two words for what we call red; Navajo has a single word for blue and green, but two words for black.[26]

Because colors elicit such strong emotional reactions, obviously the choice of a palette is a key issue in package design. These choices used to be made casually.

BLACK CAKE
White is for virgins.

Jan 30 – Feb 10
SAN FRANCISCO BALLET
Helgi Tomasson, Artistic Director

Stephen Legate and Lucia Lacarra photographed by Stan Musilek.

■ **FIGURE 2.2**
THE VERTICAL-HORIZONTAL ILLUSION: WHICH LINE IS LONGER?

These visual illusions also influence how much we pour and drink. Take drinking glasses. As Figure 2.2 shows, when we pour into a glass, we tend to focus on the height of the liquid we are pouring and not the width.[19] If we are given two glasses that both hold 24 ounces, for instance, we will tend to pour more than 30 percent more into the shorter, wider glass than into the taller glass because we focus on the height and don't account for the width. This illusion tricks even the pros. When 48 Philadelphia bartenders were asked to pour a "shot" of alcohol into either a wide tumbler or a tall highball glass, even they overpoured 27 percent more gin, whiskey, and vodka in the wide glasses than in the tall ones.[20]

Our eyes continue to trick us even when it comes to variety. When we see an assortment of foods, such as at Thanksgiving dinner or at an all-you-can-eat buffet, this abundance suggests it's appropriate to eat more. College students who were given bowls of M&Ms that had 10 colors of M&Ms ate 26 percent more than those given the same size bowls with seven colors—even though all M&Ms taste the same. Also, students who were given six different flavors of jelly beans took and ate 85 percent more when they were mixed up than when they were neatly organized by flavor.[21] The bottom line: When it comes to how much we eat and drink, our eyes often have more to say than our stomachs.[22]

In Western culture the color black is often associated with sophistication while white connotes innocence.

For example, Campbell's Soup made its familiar can in red and white because a company executive liked the football uniforms at Cornell University!

Today, however, color choices are a serious business. These decisions help to "color" our expectations of what's inside the package. When introducing a white cheese as a "sister product" to an existing blue "Castello" cheese, a Danish company launched it in a red package under the name of Castello Bianco. They chose this color to provide maximum visibility on store shelves. Although taste tests were very positive, sales were disappointing. A subsequent analysis of consumer interpretations showed that the red packaging and the name gave the consumers wrong associations with the product type and its degree of sweetness. Danish consumers had trouble associating the color red with the white cheese. Also, the name "Bianco" connoted a sweetness that was incompatible with the actual taste of the product. The company relaunched it in a white package and named it "White Castello." Almost immediately, sales more than doubled.[27]

Some color combinations come to be so strongly associated with a corporation that they become known as the company's **trade dress,** and the company may even be granted exclusive use of these colors. For example, Eastman Kodak has successfully protected its trade dress of yellow, black, and red in court. As a rule, however, judges grant trade dress protection only when consumers might be confused about what they are buying because of similar coloration of a competitor's packages.[28]

Of course, our color preferences also are strongly influenced by fashion trends, so it's no surprise that we tend to encounter a "hot" color on clothing and in home designs in one season that something else replaces the next season (as when the *fashionistas* proclaim: "Brown is the new black!"). These styles do not happen by accident; most people don't know (but now you do) that a handful of firms produce *color forecasts* that manufacturers and retailers buy so they can be sure they are stocking up on the next hot hue. For example, Pantone, Inc. (one of these color arbiters), named chili pepper the color of 2007. Citing its boldness and energy, these experts proclaimed that "Whether expressing danger, celebration, love or passion, red will not be ignored . . . in 2007, there is an awareness of the melding of diverse cultural influences, and chili pepper is a reflection of exotic tastes both on the tongue and to the eye. Nothing reflects the spirit of adventure more than the color red. At the same time, chili pepper speaks to a certain level of confidence and taste."[29]

SMELL

Odors can stir emotions or create a calming feeling. They can invoke memories or relieve stress. One study found that consumers who viewed ads for either flowers or chocolate and who also were exposed to flowery or chocolaty odors spent more time processing the product information and were more likely to try different alternatives within each product category.[30] Many consumers control the odors in their environments and this growing interest has spawned a lot of new products since Glade marketed the first air freshener to suburban families in 1956. Today, younger people are at the forefront of scented air as they take advantage of plug-ins, fragrance fans, diffusers, and potpourri. Sensing a growing market, Procter & Gamble introduced Febreze air products in 2004 and appealed to twentysomethings by making air freshener products seem cool—Scentstories is a Febreze dispenser P&G designed to look like a CD player, complete with "stop" and "play" buttons that radiate scents rather than music.[31]

Some of our responses to scents result from early associations that call up good or bad feelings, and that explains why businesses are exploring connections among smell, memory, and mood.[32] Researchers for Folgers found that for many people the smell of coffee summons up childhood memories of their mothers cooking breakfast, so the aroma reminds them of home. The company turned this insight into a commercial in which a young man in an army uniform arrives home early one morning. He goes to the kitchen, opens a Folgers' package, and the aroma wafts upstairs. His mother opens her eyes, smiles, and exclaims, "He's home!"[33]

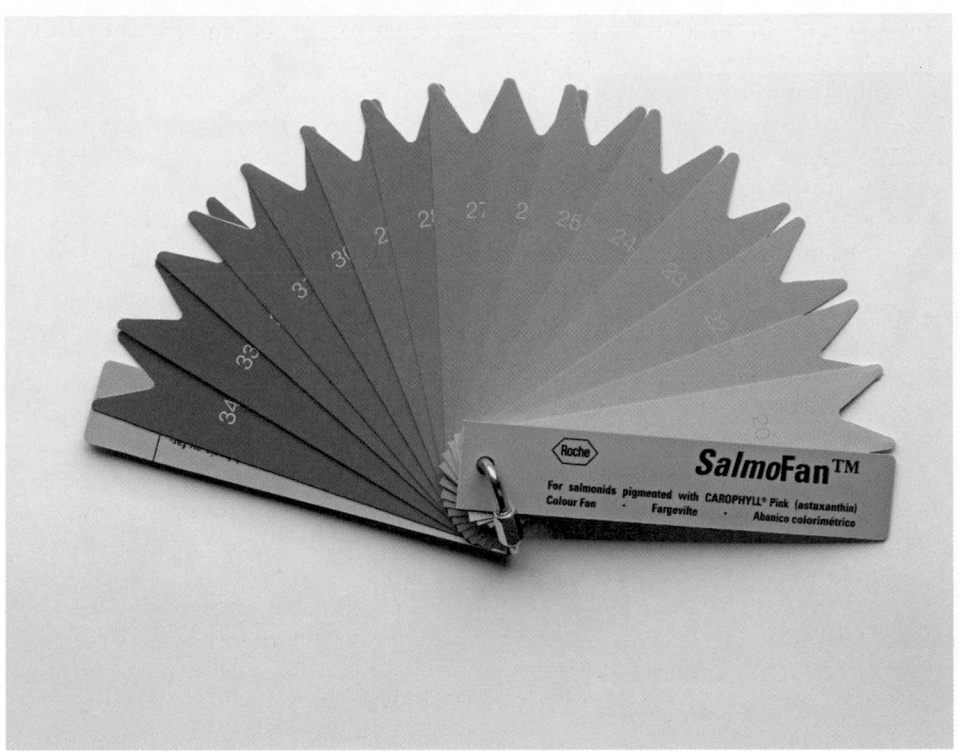

Consumers often learn to associate the qualities of a product with colors. Salmon aficionados expect the fish to have a pinkish hue. Unfortunately, the flesh of farmed salmon—which don't eat the krill that colors the wild ones—is gray. So clever fish farmers use the SalmoFan™—a reference that, like paint chips, lets them pick a color. By adding the right mixture of chemicals to the salmon pens, they can harvest any color fish they choose.

We process fragrance cues in the *limbic system,* the most primitive part of the brain and the place where we experience immediate emotions. One study even found that the scent of fresh cinnamon buns induced sexual arousal in a sample of male students![34] In another study, women sniffed T-shirts that men had worn for 2 days (wonder how much they paid them to do that?) and reported which ones they preferred. The women were most attracted to the odor of men who are genetically similar to themselves, though not *too* similar. The researchers claimed the findings were evidence that we are "wired" to select compatible mates, but not those so similar as to cause inbreeding problems.[35]

Something fishy? This Indonesian ad for Harpist socks that suppress odor claims: "It would not happen with Harpist."

An Indian ad for Tide detergent: "Now with surprising fragrances."

As scientists continue to discover the powerful effects of smell on behavior, marketers are coming up with ingenious ways to exploit these connections. Ad companies spend about $80 million per year on scent marketing; the Scent Marketing Institute estimates that number will reach more that $500 million by 2016.[36] This form of *sensory marketing* is taking interesting turns as manufacturers find new ways to put scents into products, including men's suits, lingerie, detergents, and aircraft cabins. Here are a few recent smelly strategies:

● One hundred gas stations in California are trying technology that wafts a coffee aroma at the pump in a bid to tempt its pay-and-go customers into the store for a cup to go.

● Kraft Foods sponsored a special holiday issue of *People* magazine. Five of its ads in the issue allow readers to rub a spot to experience the smell of a product being advertised, such as Chips Ahoy and Philadelphia Cream Cheese.

● Mars has recently used scent technology to spread the aroma of chocolate around its M&M's World retail outlets, and it put Pedigree dog-food-scented stickers in front of supermarkets and pet stores.

● A company called ScenAndrea that describes itself as a "multisensory communications" vendor is putting 8,000 scent-delivery systems called Smellavision in stores, including the North American retailer Kroger and Wal-Mart.[37]

● In the United States, in the summer of 2007, Kentucky Fried Chicken (KFC) launched its new $2.99 Deals in several office buildings by strategically placing a plate of chicken, a side item and a biscuit in mail carts that pass out interoffice mail. A spokesperson notes that "Mailroom staffers were all fed first so that they would have the strength to deal with the employees clamoring for the KFC." Perhaps the next time you get a letter that's still soggy with gravy you'll know why.[38]

● To promote the drama series *Cane*, which is set in South Florida where a Cuban-American family runs the Duque rum and sugar business, editions of *Rolling Stone* included Peel 'n Taste® flavor strips that deliver the (nonalcoholic) taste of a fictional Duque Rum mojito cocktail.[39]

HEARING

We're bombarded with the sound of voices and music (some good, some painful) all the time—but now advertisers can be more selective about just who hears what they have to say. A TV commercial for a horror film called *The Messengers* targeted to teenagers included a high-pitched noise that most adults were unable to hear. As people age, many develop *aging ear,* which is a loss of the ability to hear higher-frequency sounds. And some teens have figured out on their own that their parents don't have the same range of hearing the teens do (probably as a result of years of listening to heavy metal music before the kids came along). Some teens download a special ring tone off the Internet to alert them while they're sitting in class to incoming text messages without their teachers knowing about them. Ironically, this tone is a spin-off of technology that was originally meant to *repel* teenagers. A Welsh security company developed what it called the "Mosquito" to help shopkeepers disperse young people loitering in front of their stores while leaving adults unaffected.[41] In this case aging ear comes in handy; grownups couldn't hear the high, whining buzz that sent kids running.

Many aspects of sound (at least the ones we *can* hear) affect people's feelings and behaviors. By decomposing brand names into individual sounds, or *phonemes,* one study showed how even these cues affect consumer evaluations and convey unique meanings about inherent properties of the product. For instance, English-speaking consumers infer that brands containing the vowel sound of short [i] are lighter than brands containing the vowel sound of short [a].[42]

The Muzak Corporation estimates that 80 million people hear its recordings every day. This so-called "functional music" is played in stores, shopping malls, and offices to either relax or stimulate consumers. Research shows that workers tend to slow down during midmorning and midafternoon, so Muzak uses a system it calls "stimulus progression" that increases the tempo during those slack times. Muzak links its system to reductions in absenteeism among factory workers, and the company even claims that the milk and egg output of cows and chickens increases under its influence.[43] Think what it might do for your term papers!

TOUCH

Although scientists have done relatively little research on the effects of tactile stimulation on consumer behavior, common observation tells us that this sensory channel is important. Consider the classic, contoured Coca-Cola bottle. The bottle was designed approximately 90 years ago to satisfy the request of a U.S. bottler for a soft-drink container that people could identify even in the dark.

Sensations that reach the skin, whether from a luxurious massage or the bite of a winter wind, stimulate or relax us. Researchers even have shown that touch can influence sales interactions. In one study, diners whom waitstaff touched gave bigger tips, and the same researchers reported that food demonstrators in a supermarket who lightly touched customers had better luck in getting shoppers to try a new snack product and to redeem coupons for the brand.[44] Britain's Asda grocery chain removed the wrapping from several brands of toilet tissue in its stores so that shoppers could feel and compare textures. The result, the retailer says, was soaring sales for its own in-store brand, resulting in a 50 percent increase in shelf space for the line.[45]

Some anthropologists view touch much like a primal language, one we learn well before writing and speech. Indeed, researchers are starting to identify the important role the *haptic* (touch) sense plays in consumer behavior. Haptic senses appear to moderate the relationship between product experience and judgment confidence, confirming the commonsense notion that we're more sure about what we perceive when we can touch it (a major problem for those who sell products online).[46] Individuals who score high on a "Need for Touch" (NFT) scale are especially influenced

Marketing Pitfall

The California Milk Processor Board (the "Got Milk?" people) had to remove cookie-scented advertisements at five San Francisco bus stops after several groups complained about the smell. The idea was to get passersby thinking about cookies, which would then lead to thoughts of milk. Unfortunately, not everyone got the message; the campaign managed to offend antifragrance anti-allergy and anti-obesity groups simultaneously. Moo.[40]

by this dimension. Those with a high need for touch respond positively to such statements as:

- When walking through stores, I can't help touching all kinds of products.
- Touching products can be fun.
- I feel more comfortable purchasing a product after physically examining it.[47]

The Japanese take this idea a step farther when they practice what they call **Kansei engineering,** a philosophy that translates customers' feelings into design elements. In one application of this practice, the designers of the Mazda Miata focused on young drivers who saw the car as an extension of their body, a sensation they call "horse and rider as one." After extensive research they discovered that making the stick shift exactly 9.5 cm long conveys the optimal feeling of sportiness and control.[48] Similar thinking went into the driver's seat of the Chrysler 300C, which is designed to make you feel a bit taller. In auto-industry speak, the car has a higher *H-point*, which refers to the location of the seated driver's hip. The change is prompted by the popularity of SUVs, pickups, and minivans that make drivers feel they are riding high on the highway. Ford calls its version "Command Seating" to reinforce the feeling of power it wants drivers to feel as they look down on all those little vehicles buzzing around below them.[49]

Fragrance and cosmetics containers in particular tend to speak to consumers via their tactile appeal. Most modern perfume bottles still are made of glass because when women handle an elegantly sculpted glass container they experience a sense of luxury that more modern materials can't provide. For example, when Nina Ricci introduced L'Air du Temps perfume in 1948, the fragrance came in a Lalique crystal bottle with a stopper capped by a pair of crystal lovebirds. The bottle's elegance assured consumers who were not regular buyers of fragrances that this one was of high quality—why would anyone put anything less in such a nice container? In contrast, Calvin Klein's abstract bottle for its Euphoria fragrance is more futuristic and the container looks like it's made of metal—but a touch still reassures that it is in fact still made of glass. The importance of the haptic dimension explains why people still buy most high-end fragrances in stores rather than online.[50]

We also link the perceived richness or quality of the material in clothing, bedding, or upholstery to its "feel," whether rough or smooth, flexible or inflexible. We equate

TABLE 2.1
TACTILE-QUALITY ASSOCIATIONS

Perception	Male	Female	
High class	Wool	Silk	Fine
Low class	Denim	Cotton	↕
	Heavy ←	→ Light	Coarse

a smooth fabric, such as silk, with luxury, whereas we consider denim to be considered practical and durable. Table 2.1 summarizes some of these tactile-quality associations. Fabrics composed of scarce materials or that require a high degree of processing to achieve their smoothness or fineness tend to be more expensive and thus we assume they are of a higher class. Similarly, we assume lighter, more delicate textures are feminine. Men often value a feeling of roughness, whereas women seek smoothness.

TASTE

Our taste receptors obviously contribute to our experience of many products. So-called "flavor houses" keep busy developing new concoctions to please the changing palates of consumers. Scientists are right behind them as they develop new devices to test these flavors. Alpha M.O.S. sells a sophisticated electronic tongue for tasting

Marketing Opportunity

When players walk past a crack in a wall in the computer game *Broken Sword,* they feel a draft of air in the real world. When a virtual plane flies by, a set of fans next to the monitor generates a breeze to make them feel like they're on the runway. Philips' amBX system includes a wrist pad that rumbles and lamps that flash to simulate thunder and lighting. As games get more realistic, manufacturers push the sensory envelope to let players experience them with all their senses. Some companies sell subwoofer devices that attach to the base of a chair to give gamers a sonic bump in the tailbone when they get blown up in a game. The Ultimate Game Chair has 12 vibrating built-in motors—seven in the back, five in the seat—and a pair of speakers at the top. If a grenade goes off nearby in a video game, the chair gives the player a corresponding jolt to the back. Now if they can just simulate how that day-old pizza tastes.[51]

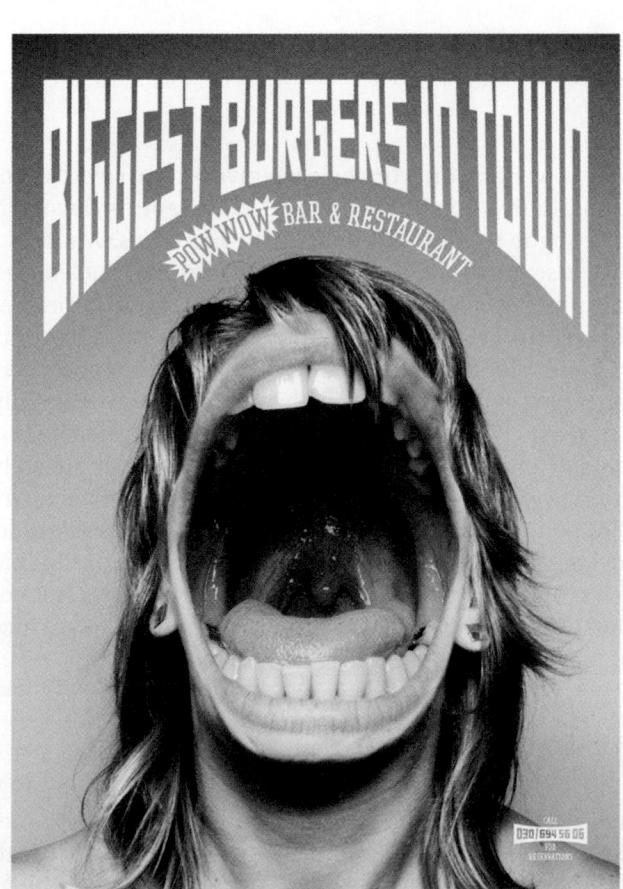

This German ad reminds us that sometimes we bite off more than we can chew.

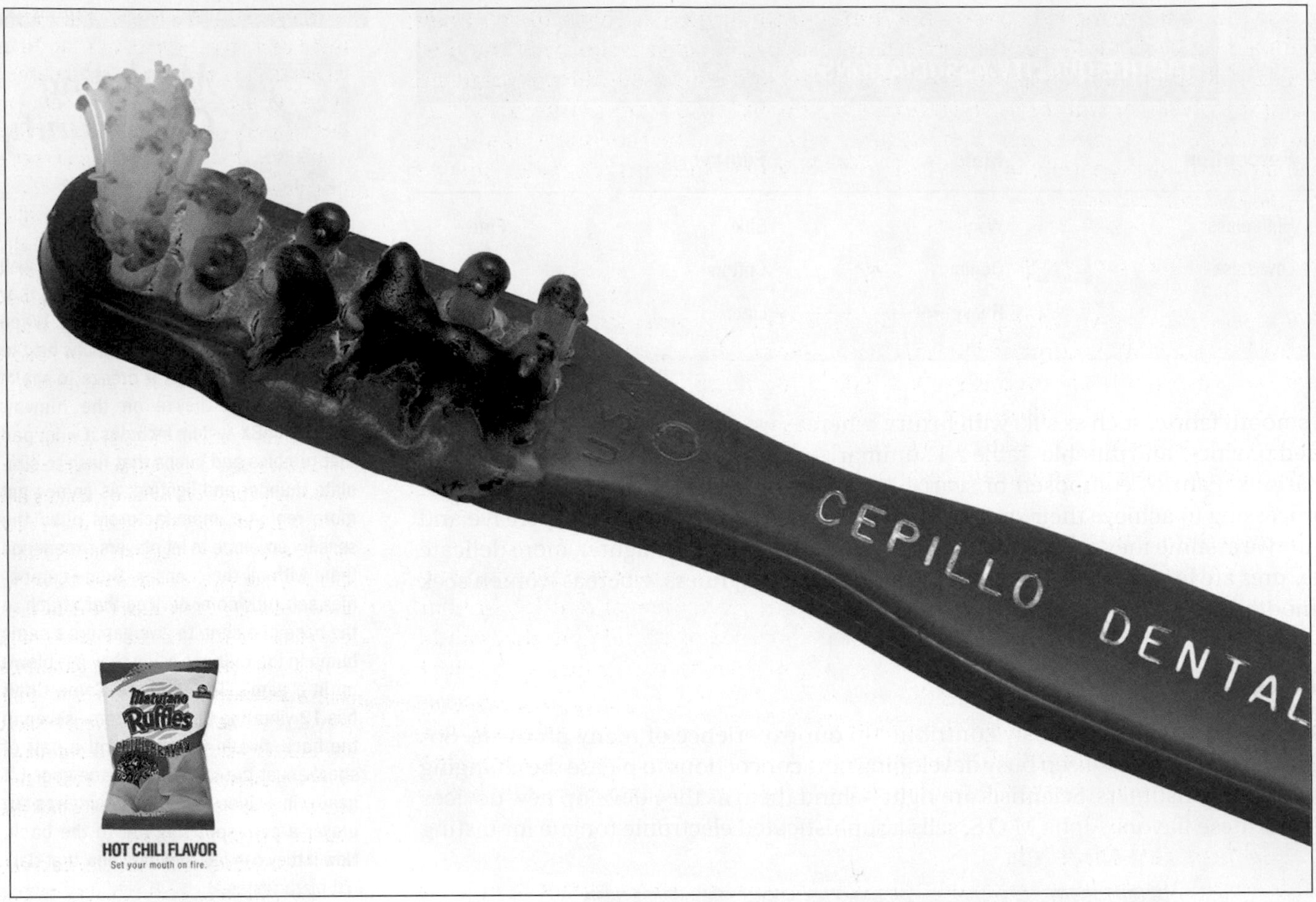

This Spanish ad for a hot chili-flavored chip uses a novel visual image to communicate the ferocity of the product's flavor.

Marketing Pitfall

It's no secret that Americans are getting fatter. Americans are eating about 12 percent more calories a day than they did in the mid-1980s, according to government statistics. The percentage of Americans who are overweight increased to 66 percent from 47 percent in the late 1970s.

One reason for this tremendous "growth" may be that they've become used to perceiving enormous portion sizes as "normal." They seem to be experiencing "portion inflation"; some menu items at fast-food restaurants are now two to five times larger than those of the 1950s.

and the company is working on what its executives call an electronic mouth, complete with artificial saliva, to chew food and to dissect its flavor. Coca-Cola and PepsiCo use the tongue to test the quality of corn syrups, whereas Bristol-Myers Squibb and Roche use the device to devise medicines that don't taste bitter.[52]

Changes in our culture also determine the tastes we find desirable. For example, consumers' greater appreciation of different ethnic dishes has contributed to increased desires for spicy foods, so the quest for the ultimate pepper sauce is a hot taste trend. More than 50 stores in the United States now specialize in supplying fiery concoctions with names such as Sting and Linger, Hell in a Jar, and Religious Experience (comes in Original, Hot, and Wrath).[53] Some of these sauces are so hot that stores ask customers to sign waivers of legal liability before they will sell them. Purists measure the "heat" of peppers in units called Scovilles. In 1912, Wilbur Scoville asked a five-person panel to see how much sugar water it would take to eliminate the hotness of a pepper. How's this for a hot tip: It takes 1,981 gallons of sweetened water to neutralize a teaspoon of Da' Bomb, which is advertised as the hottest sauce ever made.[54]

Exposure

Exposure occurs when a stimulus comes within the range of someone's sensory receptors. Consumers concentrate on some stimuli, are unaware of others, and even go out of their way to ignore some messages. We are capable of noticing stimuli that come within range for even a very short time—*if* we so choose. That's the reasoning behind Cadillac's ads for cars that can go from zero to 60 miles an hour in less than 5 seconds. Rather than using the traditional 30 seconds to get out this message, the company ran 5-second commercials to make its point.[55] However, getting a message noticed in such a short time (or even in a longer one) is no mean feat. Before we consider what else people may choose not to perceive, let's consider what they *are* capable of perceiving.

SENSORY THRESHOLDS

If you have ever blown a dog whistle and watched pets respond to a sound you cannot hear, you won't be surprised to learn that there are some stimuli that people simply are not capable of perceiving. Some of us are better able to pick up sensory information than those whose sensory channels may be impaired by disabilities or age. **Psychophysics** is the science that focuses on how the physical environment is integrated into our personal, subjective world.

The Absolute Threshold

When we define the lowest intensity of a stimulus that can be registered on a sensory channel, we speak of its *threshold*. It sounds like a great name for a rock band, but the **absolute threshold** refers to the minimum amount of stimulation that can be detected on a given sensory channel. The sound emitted by a dog whistle is too high to be detected by human ears, so this stimulus is beyond our auditory absolute threshold. The absolute threshold is an important consideration in designing marketing stimuli. A highway billboard might have the most entertaining copy ever written, but this genius is wasted if the print is too small for passing motorists to see it.

The Differential Threshold

Differential threshold refers to the ability of a sensory system to detect changes or differences between two stimuli. The minimum difference we can detect between two stimuli is the **j.n.d.** (just noticeable difference).

The issue of when and if consumers will notice a difference between two stimuli is relevant to many marketing situations. Sometimes a marketer may want to ensure that consumers notice a change, as when a retailer offers merchandise at a discount. In other situations, the marketer may want to downplay the fact that it has made a change, such as when a store raises a price or a manufacturer reduces the size of a package (see the *CB As I See It* box on reference prices).

A consumer's ability to detect a difference between two stimuli is relative. A whispered conversation that might be unintelligible on a noisy street can suddenly become public and embarrassingly loud in a quiet library. It is the *relative difference* between the decibel level of the conversation and its surroundings, rather than the absolute loudness of the conversation itself, that determines whether the stimulus will register.

In the nineteenth century, a psychophysicist named Ernst Weber found that the amount of change required for the perceiver to notice a change is systematically related to the intensity of the original stimulus. The stronger the initial stimulus, the greater a change must be for us to notice it. This relationship is known as **Weber's Law,** which this equation summarizes:

$$K = \frac{\Delta i}{I}$$

where

K = a constant (this varies across the senses)
Δi = the minimal change in intensity of the stimulus required to produce a j.n.d.
I = the intensity of the stimulus where the change occurs

Burger King (BK) is one of the chains that's been most aggressively "upsizing" its menu. In recent years, it's introduced a Triple Whopper, the BK Stacker with four beef patties, and an Enormous Omelet sandwich with sausage, bacon, and cheese on a bun. Then there's its Meat 'Normous breakfast sandwich, which BK describes as "A full pound of sausage, bacon and ham...." McDonald's is catching up quickly; even though Mickey D's is scoring a hit with weight-conscious moms by adding salads to its menu, it has also introduced the Angus Third Pounder—weighing in at 860 calories. [56]

Customers associate huge quantities of food with value, a proposition that makes reducing portions difficult. Restaurants also point out that even when consumers say they want smaller portions or healthier choices, they often do not order those options. Indeed, in 2004 when the Ruby Tuesday chain reduced the size of some of its entrees and started printing nutritional information on the menu, customers complained and the restaurants went back to the original sizes after only 5 months, A company executive explained, "Even if they don't eat everything on the plate, they like that it's a generous portion."

Although larger portions may be a better value, they also make us eat more than if the portions are smaller. In one study, for example, consumers who were given 50 percent more of a pasta dish ate 43 percent more than those with a smaller portion. Researchers found similar increases when they offered bigger portions of potato chips, deli sandwiches, popcorn, and soup.

Still, changes may be coming. Industry research finds that the majority of adults believe that portion sizes in casual dining restaurants are too big. T.G.I. Friday's recently introduced "Right Size" portions that are about two-thirds the size of the usual serving—focus groups told them that diners would feel cheated if the portions were shrunk to half their current size. After release of the documentary *Super Size Me* in which the filmmaker ate only McDonald's food for a month (and paid the consequences), McDonald's and Wendy's dropped their "Supersize" and "Biggie" menus amid a flood of negative publicity. (A new study finds that Wendy's simply renamed its "Biggie" drink, at 32 ounces, a medium, and a large drink now contains 42 ounces.)[57]

CB AS I SEE IT

Professor Larry Compeau
Clarkson University

Surveys consistently show that consumers consider price the most important factor when they buy, but marketers too often view price merely as an economic variable—that is, the amount of money the consumer must sacrifice to obtain the product. Years of recent research, however, show us that consumers regard price more than simply as the cost of a product.[58] To truly understand price, we need to think of it as an information stimulus, like color, aroma, and other more traditional stimuli we interpret. How consumers respond to and use price in their perceptual processes has been the focus of recent research. This research considers price as an information cue that is perceived and interpreted (attaching meaning to it). We call this area of research *behavioral pricing.*

One stream of behavioral pricing research looks at price as an information cue we use to judge a product.[59] You've certainly heard the old adage "You get what you pay for," which may or may not be true depending on the circumstances. Nonetheless, when consumers don't have other information on which they can rely, they often use price as an indicator of quality (more on this in Chapter 9). In this sense, price is an important information source consumers use to help them decide among product options.

In another stream of research, we expand the scope to consider the broader context and other information marketers often present along with the actual selling price.[60] We refer to the pieces of information that surround the actual selling price as *semantic cues* because the consumer's interpretation or judgment of the selling price depends on how he or she interprets this information (semantics!).

When we conceptualize price as an information cue or stimulus, then we must also accept the fact that price is subject to the same types of perceptual processes that lead to different judgments depending on the context. A common strategy sellers use in providing contextual information for consumers is to present a *reference price* along with the selling price.

This refers to a price against which buyers compare the actual selling price. Marketers usually present it in price advertisements, on price tickets, or even on store displays. For example, how often have you seen an advertisement that states a selling price without some other "reference price" next to it showing the "regular price," "original price," "compare-at price," or "MSLP" (manufacturer's suggested list price)? It's pretty rare. When an item goes on sale and the old price and the new price are available to ascertain the savings, this price information is informative and helps the consumer.

A reference price communicates the value of the deal to the buyer. But if a seller knows that consumers rely on semantic cues to assess the deal, the seller can alter the cue information to enhance the deal's attractiveness:

Which is the better deal on an LCD television?

Product A: 47 inch, 1080p, high definition—regular price: $2,499; sale price: $1,499

Product B: 47 inch, 1080p, high definition—regular price: $1,799; sale price: $1,499

Like most consumers, you probably picked product A. Why? To make your decision, you used the reference prices. Getting a $2,500 television for $1,500 is a better deal than getting an $1,800 television for $1,500—you save more, and you get a better television, right? What if the televisions are identical? If the seller of product A deliberately exaggerates the regular price of $2,499, then the information may not be as informative as it is deceptive. Using higher reference prices, sellers can get consumers to increase their perceptions of the value of the deal, when in fact the deal is not better.[61] When this happens, consumers are more likely to purchase that item and less likely to shop around.[62] As a result, there is the potential for harm to consumers.

Important public policy implications (i.e., government rules and regulations) arise based on research on reference pricing.[63] We must consider how to protect consumers from deceptive practices, such as exaggerating reference prices, and this research plays a critical role in determining if deception occurs and what can be done about it. Many state and federal laws, along with guidelines from the Better Business Bureau, have specific regulations regarding the use of reference prices to avoid harming consumers, but a litany of court cases demonstrates that the research is critical to inform these laws and regulations and their interpretation by the courts.[64] Perception theory then is a critical base on which we can build a sophisticated understanding of how consumers use price. We then use this knowledge to protect consumers and enhance overall consumer welfare.

For example, consider how Weber's Law might work with respect to a product that has had its price decreased for a special sale. A rule of thumb some retailers use is that a markdown should be at least 20 percent for the reduction to make an impact on shoppers. If this is the case, a pair of socks that retails for $10 should be put on sale for $8 (a $2 discount) for shoppers to realize a difference. However, a sports coat selling for $100 would not benefit from a "mere" $2 discount—a retailer would have to mark it down to $80 to achieve the same impact.

Weber's Law, ironically, is a challenge to green marketers who are trying to reduce the sizes of packages by producing concentrated (and more earth-friendly)

Over the last 125 years, Campbell's Soup gradually modified its label. In 1999 the company decided to retire the label and consumers rushed to hoard the classic Campbell's Soup cans. The new cans feature photos of actual soup in the bowl but the design retains the distinctive red-and-white colors and unique script to avert a consumer backlash.

This Canadian beer ad pokes fun at subliminal advertising.

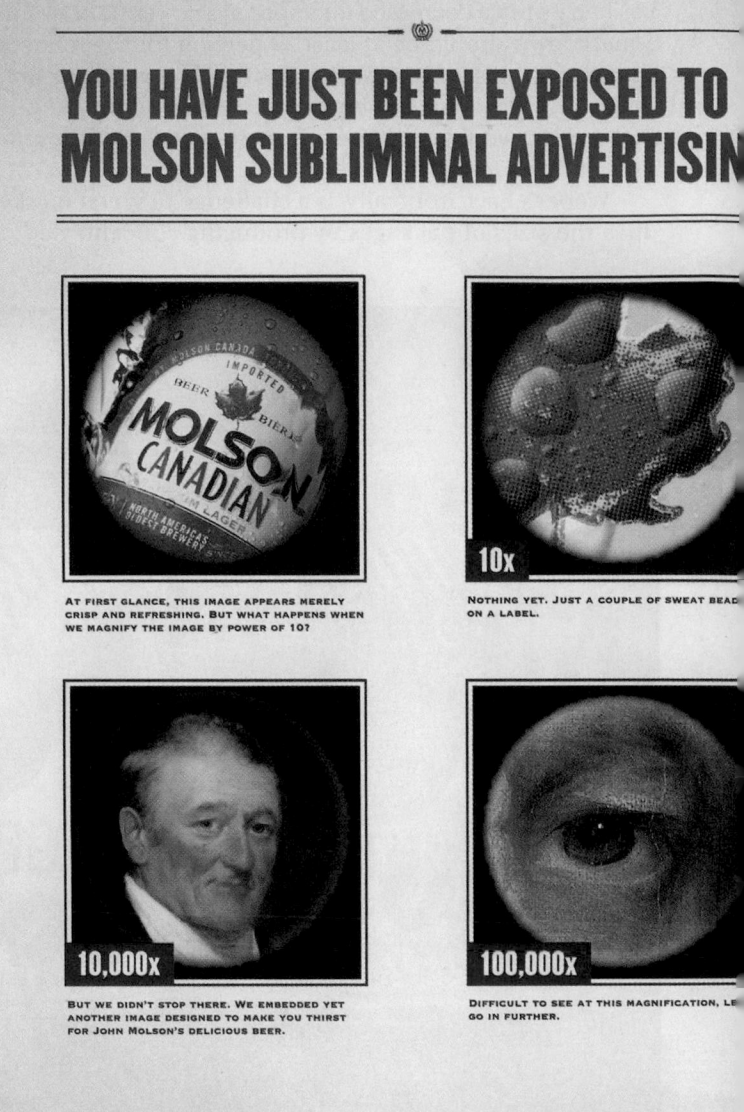

YOU HAVE JUST BEEN EXPOSED TO MOLSON SUBLIMINAL ADVERTISIN

AT FIRST GLANCE, THIS IMAGE APPEARS MERELY CRISP AND REFRESHING. BUT WHAT HAPPENS WHEN WE MAGNIFY THE IMAGE BY POWER OF 10?

10x

NOTHING YET. JUST A COUPLE OF SWEAT BEAD ON A LABEL.

10,000x

BUT WE DIDN'T STOP THERE. WE EMBEDDED YET ANOTHER IMAGE DESIGNED TO MAKE YOU THIRST FOR JOHN MOLSON'S DELICIOUS BEER.

100,000x

DIFFICULT TO SEE AT THIS MAGNIFICATION, LE GO IN FURTHER.

versions of their products. So some makers of laundry detergent brands have to convince their customers to pay the same price for about half the detergent. Also, because of pressure from powerful retailers such as Wal-Mart that want to fit more bottles on their shelves, the size of detergent bottles is shrinking significantly. Procter & Gamble, Unilever, and Henkel all maintain that their new concentrated versions will allow people to wash the same number of loads with half the detergent. One perceptual trick they're using to try to convince consumers of this is the redesign of the bottle cap: Both P&G and Church & Dwight are using a cap with a broader base and shorter sides to persuade consumers that they need a smaller amount.[65]

SUBLIMINAL PERCEPTION

Most marketers are concerned with creating messages above consumers' thresholds so they will be noticed. Ironically, a good number of consumers appear to believe marketers design many advertising messages so the consumers perceive them unconsciously, or *below* the threshold of recognition. Another word for threshold is *limen* (just remember "the secret of Sprite"), and we term stimuli that fall below the

MAY NOT BE AWARE OF IT, BUT RIGHT NOW YOUR SUBCONSCIOUS IS JONESING FOR A COLD, CRISP MOLSON. WHY?
USE WE SLIPPED THROUGH THE BACK DOOR OF YOUR BRAIN AND PLANTED A FEW VISUAL CUES DEEP IN YOUR MIND.
F THE IMAGES BELOW SEEM STRANGELY FAMILIAR?

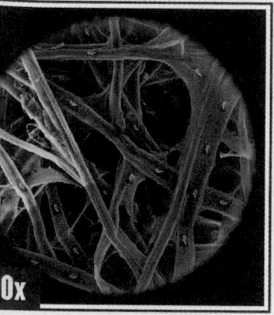

IFIED AT 100X HOWEVER, WE BEGIN TO
OMETHING.

AN IMAGE OF JOHN MOLSON PRINTED ON THE PAPER
FIBER OF THE BEER LABEL. THOUGH MINUTE, YOUR
BRAIN PICKED UP ON THIS SUBLIMINAL CUE TO A
219-YEAR HERITAGE OF BREWING GREAT-TASTING BEER.

ERE IT IS! AN IMAGE OF PEOPLE SOCIALIZING
AN ICE-COLD MOLSON.

A MICROSCOPIC REMINDER THAT MOLSON HAS BEEN
BRINGING FRIENDS TOGETHER SINCE 1786. SHOULD
YOU SUDDENLY AWAKEN IN A CROWDED BAR ORDERING
A ROUND OF MOLSON FOR EVERYONE, WE DID THAT.
AND YOU'RE WELCOME.

limen *subliminal*. **Subliminal perception** occurs when the stimulus is below the level of the consumer's awareness.

Subliminal perception is a topic that has captivated the public for more than 50 years, despite the fact that there is virtually no proof that this process has *any* effect on consumer behavior. A survey of American consumers found that almost two-thirds believe in the existence of subliminal advertising, and more than one-half are convinced that this technique can get them to buy things they do not really want. [66] Most recently, ABC rejected a Kentucky Fried Chicken (KFC) commercial that invited viewers to slowly replay the ad to find a secret message, citing the network's long-standing policy against subliminal advertising. KFC argued that the ad wasn't subliminal at all because the company was telling viewers about the message and how to find it. The network wasn't convinced.[67]

Like this KFC ad, most examples of subliminal advertising that people have "discovered" are not subliminal at all—on the contrary, the images are quite apparent. Remember, if you can see it or hear it, it's not subliminal; the stimulus is above the level of conscious awareness. Nonetheless, the continuing controversy about subliminal persuasion has been important in shaping the public's beliefs about advertisers' and marketers' abilities to manipulate consumers against their will.

Subliminal Techniques

Marketers supposedly send *subliminal messages* on both visual and aural channels. **Embeds** are tiny figures that are inserted into magazine advertising by using high-speed photography or airbrushing. These hidden figures, usually of a sexual nature, supposedly exert strong but unconscious influences on innocent readers. Some limited evidence hints at the possibility that embeds can alter the moods of men who are exposed to sexually suggestive images presented subliminally, but the effect (if any) is very subtle—and may even work in the opposite direction by creating negative feelings among viewers.[68] To date, the only real impact of this interest in hidden messages is to sell more copies of "exposés" written by a few authors and to make some consumers (and students taking a consumer behavior class) look a bit more closely at print ads—perhaps seeing whatever their imaginations lead them to see.

The possible effects of messages hidden on sound recordings also fascinate many consumers. We can see one attempt to capitalize on subliminal auditory perception techniques in the growing market for self-help audios. CDs and tapes, which typically feature the sounds of crashing waves or other natural sounds, supposedly contain subliminal messages to help listeners stop smoking, lose weight, gain confidence, and so on. Despite the rapid growth of this market, there is little evidence that subliminal stimuli transmitted on the auditory channel can bring about desired changes in behavior.[69]

Does Subliminal Perception Work? Evaluating the Evidence

Some research by clinical psychologists suggests that people can be influenced by subliminal messages under very specific conditions, though it is doubtful that these techniques would be of much use in most marketing contexts. Effective messages must be very specifically tailored to individuals rather than the mass messages required by advertising for the general public.[70] They should also be as close to the liminal threshold as possible. Here are other discouraging factors:

- There are wide individual differences in threshold levels. In order for a message to avoid conscious detection by consumers who have low thresholds, it would have to be so weak that it would not reach those who have high thresholds.
- Advertisers lack control over consumers' distance and position from a screen. In a movie theater, for example, only a small portion of the audience would be in exactly the right seats to be exposed to a subliminal message.
- The viewer must be paying absolute attention to the stimulus. People watching a television program or a movie typically shift their attention periodically and might not even be looking when the stimulus is presented.
- Even if the desired effect is induced, it operates only at a very general level. For example, a message might increase a person's thirst but not necessarily for a specific drink. Because basic drives are affected, marketers could find that after all the bother and expense of creating a subliminal message, demand for competitors' products increases as well!

Clearly, there are better ways to get our attention—let's see how.

 # Attention

As you sit in a lecture, you might find your mind wandering (yes, even you!). One minute you are concentrating on the professor's words, and the next you catch yourself daydreaming about the upcoming weekend. Suddenly, you tune back in as you hear your name being spoken. Fortunately, it's a false alarm—the professor has called on another "victim" who has the same first name. But, she's got your attention now.

Attention refers to the extent to which processing activity is devoted to a particular stimulus. As you know from sitting through both interesting and "less interesting" lectures, this allocation can vary depending on both the characteristics of the stimulus (i.e., the lecture itself) and the recipient (i.e., your mental state at the time).

Although we live in an "information society," we can have too much of a good thing. Consumers often are in a state of **sensory overload,** where they are exposed to far more information than they can process. In our society, much of this bombardment comes from commercial sources, and the competition for our attention is steadily increasing. The average adult is exposed to about 3,500 pieces of advertising information every single day—up from about 560 per day 30 years ago.

That's why marketers must worry constantly about whether consumers are paying attention to their messages—so they are constantly trying to devise new ways to measure how effective they are. For example, a company called PreTesting recently introduced a system called eMotion that uses a PC-connected camera to measure the *saccadic motion* of viewers' eyes—the subtle eyeball vibrations that increase when we see something of interest. PreTesting follows up its eye measurements with an interview to determine how much the viewers remembered. Then a proprietary algorithm gives advertising executives instant feedback on how well the spot worked.[71]

Getting the attention of young people in particular is a challenge—as your professor probably knows! By one estimate, 80 percent of teens today engage in **multitasking,** where they process information from more than one medium at a time as they attend to their cell phones, TVs, instant messages, and so on.[72] One study observed 400 people for a day and found that 96 percent of them were multitasking about a third of the time they were using media.[73] Marketing researchers are struggling to understand this new condition as they try to figure out how to reach people who are doing many things at once.

As we'll also see in later chapters, marketers are constantly searching for ways to break through the clutter and grab people's attention—at times with mixed results:

- Networks are trying to engage viewers during commercial breaks by wedging original content into the blocks of advertising time so that viewers will anticipate seeing something fun if they sit through a few ads. Fox Broadcasting recently televised a series of clips about an animated character named Oleg, a New York cab driver, who popped up in 8-second vignettes during commercial breaks in series such as *24.* In a Greek accent, Oleg urged viewers to visit Fox's Web site. In one clip, Oleg sang about himself to the Barry Manilow tune "Copacabana." In others, he drove around celebrities such as Tom Cruise and Rosie O'Donnell. Although Oleg generated more than 100,000 Web site hits on some nights, some viewers complained that he was an ethnic stereotype and others couldn't understand what he was saying—so Oleg is history. But, it was a good idea in principle.[74]
- The CW television network runs *content wraps,* which mix sponsors' products into program snippets. Sometimes these wraps involve the cast of the shows in which the commercials appear. This is hardly a new strategy, however; so-called "cast commercials" were common in the days of *I Love Lucy, The Beverly Hillbillies,* and even *The Flintstones.*
- In the online world, advertisers are trying more tricks to get visitors to watch their messages. One of the most popular today is called **rich media,** in which elements of the ad surprise you with movement: LowerMyBills.com is notorious for its endless loops of silhouetted dancers and surprised office workers, whereas other ads spring into action when you move the cursor over them. Other rich media are online versions of familiar TV commercials that sit frozen on the Web site until you click them. *Teaser ads,* much like those you see on TV that give you a taste of the story but make you return later for the rest, also are turning up on Web sites. Yahoo! often uses this technique. For example, you might see a headline on its home page announcing that DNA tests have revealed the father of Anne Nicole Smith's baby (something we all needed to know . . .); you have to click on the link to find out that it was Larry Birkhead. More importantly for Yahoo!, by getting your attention this way the company sells two pages of ads rather than only one.[75]

- Of course, a sure-fire way to grab our attention is to do something outrageous, or at least unusual, in a public place. To promote a new class at the New York Health and Racquet Club, six men and women stood outside the city's Grand Central Terminal flashing their underwear at strangers. The garments featured the club's logo and "Booty Call," the name of the class.
- A London agency projected the image of a naked woman (a contender to win a contest to select the 100 Sexiest Women in the UK) onto the Houses of Parliament in London for 10 minutes one Sunday evening.
- Sometimes these stunts backfire (but is there such a thing as bad publicity?): IBM had to pay fines after spray painting "peace, love, and Linux" graphics on sidewalks in Chicago and San Francisco.[76]

Because the brain's capacity to process information is limited, consumers are very selective about what they pay attention to. The process of **perceptual selection** means that people attend to only a small portion of the stimuli to which they are exposed. Consumers practice a form of "psychic economy," picking and choosing among stimuli to avoid being overwhelmed. How do they choose? Both personal and stimulus factors help to decide.

PERSONAL SELECTION FACTORS

The actions of a Colorado judge illustrate how powerful our own tastes can be in determining what we want to see and hear. He requires young people convicted of violating the city's noise ordinance to listen to music they don't like—including a heavy dose of such "favorites" as Wayne Newton, Dean Martin, and bagpipe recordings.[77] What, no Britney Spears? **Experience,** which is the result of acquiring and processing stimulation over time, is one factor that determines how much exposure to a particular stimulus a person accepts. **Perceptual filters** based on our past experiences influence what we decide to process.

Perceptual vigilance is one such factor. Consumers are more likely to be aware of stimuli that relate to their current needs. A consumer who rarely notices car ads will become very much aware of them when she or he is in the market for a new car. A newspaper ad for a fast-food restaurant that would otherwise go unnoticed becomes significant when one sneaks a glance at the paper in the middle of a five o'clock class. A campaign by Mini USA relies on the idea that we're more likely to pay attention to messages that single us out personally. Mini Cooper owners can view customized messages when they drive by digital signs the company calls "talking" billboards. Each board is programmed to identify approaching Mini drivers through a coded signal from a radio chip embedded in their key fob. The messages are personal, based on questionnaires that owners filled out: "Mary, moving at the speed of justice," if Mary is a lawyer. The signs also urge Mini owners to treat themselves to the car customization features they've put on a wish list ("You've earned your spoiler") and wish them a happy birthday on the appropriate day. Because more than a third of Mini owners name their cars, the messages will sometimes refer to the car by name.[78] Digital technology has great potential to capture our attention—but then again we need to hope that it doesn't do it *too* well: Driving safety researchers warn that—much like cell phones in cars—these boards absorb too much of our attention and may well be another dangerous distraction for drivers.[79]

The flip side of perceptual vigilance is **perceptual defense.** This means that people see what they want to see—and don't see what they don't want to see. If a stimulus is threatening to us in some way, we may not process it—or we may distort its meaning so that it's more acceptable. For example, a heavy smoker may block out images of cancer-scarred lungs because these vivid reminders hit a bit too close to home.

Still another factor is **adaptation,** the degree to which consumers continue to notice a stimulus over time. The process of adaptation occurs when consumers no longer pay attention to a stimulus because it is so familiar. A consumer can "habituate" and require increasingly stronger "doses" of a stimulus to notice it. A commuter en route to work might read a billboard message when it is first installed, but after a few days, it simply becomes part of the passing scenery. Several factors can lead to adaptation:

- **Intensity**—Less-intense stimuli (e.g., soft sounds or dim colors) habituate because they have less sensory impact.
- **Duration**—Stimuli that require relatively lengthy exposure in order to be processed habituate because they require a long attention span.
- **Discrimination**—Simple stimuli habituate because they do not require attention to detail.
- **Exposure**—Frequently encountered stimuli habituate as the rate of exposure increases.
- **Relevance**—Stimuli that are irrelevant or unimportant habituate because they fail to attract attention.

STIMULUS SELECTION FACTORS

In addition to the receiver's mind-set, characteristics of the stimulus itself play an important role in determining what gets noticed and what gets ignored. Marketers need to understand these factors so they can create messages and packages that will have a better chance of cutting through the clutter. This idea even applies to getting animals' attention: A British ad agency created a TV commercial aimed at felines that used fish and mouse images and sounds to attract catty consumers. In trials, 60 percent of cats showed some form of response to the ad, from twitching their ears to tapping the television screen.[80] That's a better track record than some "people commercials" have shown!

In general, we are more likely to notice stimuli that differ from others around them (remember Weber's Law). A message can create **contrast** in several ways:

- **Size**—The size of the stimulus itself in contrast to the competition helps to determine if it will command attention. Readership of a magazine ad increases in proportion to the size of the ad.[81]
- **Color**—As we've seen, color is a powerful way to draw attention to a product or to give it a distinct identity. For example, Black & Decker developed a line of tools called DeWalt targeted to the residential construction industry. B&D colored the new line yellow instead of black, which made it stand out against other "dull" tools.[82]
- **Position**—Not surprisingly, we stand a better chance of noticing stimuli that are in places we're more likely to look. That's why the competition is so heated among suppliers to have their products displayed in stores at eye level. In magazines, ads that are placed toward the front of the issue, preferably on the right-hand side, also win out in the race for readers' attention. (Hint: The next time you read a magazine, notice which pages you're more likely to spend time looking at.)[83] A study that tracked consumers' eye movements as they scanned telephone directories also illustrates the importance of a message's position. Consumers scanned listings in alphabetical order, and they noticed 93 percent of quarter-page display ads but only 26 percent of plain listings. Their eyes were drawn to color ads first, and these were viewed longer than black-and-white ones. In addition, subjects spent 54 percent more time viewing ads for businesses they ended up choosing, which illustrates the influence of attention on subsequent product choice.[84]
- **Novelty**—Stimuli that appear in unexpected ways or places tend to grab our attention. One solution is to put ads in unconventional places, where there will be less competition for attention. These places include the backs of shopping carts, walls of tunnels, floors of sports stadiums, and yes, even public restrooms.[85] A promotion to introduce Vanilla Coke in Europe illustrates how effective novelty can be. Coke put big wooden boxes in shopping malls and told

people to stick their heads in them. The brave souls who complied were rewarded with a bottle of the stuff. This request tied into TV commercials for the new product that tell viewers to "Reward your curiosity."[86]

Interpretation

Interpretation refers to the meaning that we assign to sensory stimuli. Just as people differ in terms of the stimuli that they perceive, the meanings we assign to these stimuli vary as well. Two people can see or hear the same event, but their interpretation of it can be as different as night and day, depending on what they had expected the stimulus to be. For example, Vernor's ginger ale did poorly in a taste test against leading ginger ales. When the research team introduced it instead as a new type of soft drink with a tangier taste, it won handily. The drink tasted good, but it didn't jibe with people's expectations of what a ginger ale should taste like.[87] Another, more recent study powerfully illustrates the power of expectations: Kids ages 3 to 5 who ate McDonald's French fries served in a McDonald's bag overwhelmingly thought they tasted better than those who ate the same fries out of a plain white bag. Even carrots tasted better when they came out of a McDonald's bag – more than half the kids preferred them to the same carrots served in a plain package! Ronald would be proud.[88]

The meaning we assign to a stimulus depends on the **schema,** or set of beliefs, to which we assign it. That helps to explain why Gary was so revolted at the thought

Advertisers know that consumers often will relate an ad to a preexisting schema in order to make sense of it. This Singaporean ad for Toyota evokes a car schema even though the materials used in the picture are chairs and couches one might find inside a house.

Toyota Spacio

A popular British retailer called French Connection relies on the priming process to evoke a response to its advertising by using an acronym that closely resembles another word.

of warm milk. In a process we call **priming,** certain properties of a stimulus evoke a schema. This in turn leads us to compare the stimulus to other similar ones we encountered in the past.

Identifying and evoking the correct schema is crucial to many marketing decisions because this determines what criteria consumers will use to evaluate the product, package, or message. Extra Strength Maalox Whip Antacid flopped even though a spray can is a pretty effective way to deliver the product. But to consumers aerosol whips mean dessert toppings, not medication.[89] However, when a college cafeteria gave menu items descriptive labels (e.g., Red Beans with Rice versus Traditional Cajun Red Beans with Rice, Chocolate Pudding versus Satin Chocolate Pudding) so that diners had more information about each option and were able to better categorize them, sales increased by more than 25 percent.[90]

STIMULUS ORGANIZATION

One factor that determines how we will interpret a stimulus is the relationship we assume it has with other events, sensations, or images in memory. When RJR Nabisco introduced a version of Teddy Grahams (a children's product) for adults, it used understated packaging colors to reinforce the idea that the new product was for grown-ups. But sales were disappointing. Nabisco changed the box to bright yellow to convey the idea that this was a fun snack, and buyers' more positive association between a bright primary color and taste prompted adults to start buying the cookies.[91]

Our brains tend to relate incoming sensations to others already in memory, based on some fundamental organizational principles. These principles derive from *Gestalt psychology,* a school of thought that maintains that people interpret meaning from the *totality* of a set of stimuli rather than from any individual stimulus. The German word **Gestalt** roughly means whole, pattern, or configuration, and we summarize this term as "the whole is greater than the sum of its parts." A piecemeal perspective that analyzes each component of the stimulus separately can't capture the total effect. The *Gestalt* perspective provides several principles relating to the way our brains organize stimuli:

- The **closure principle** states that people tend to perceive an incomplete picture as complete. That is, we tend to fill in the blanks based on our prior experience. This principle explains why most of us have no trouble reading a neon sign even if several of its letters are burned out. The principle of closure is also at work when we hear only part of a jingle or theme. Marketing strategies that use the closure principle encourage audience participation, which increases the chance that people will attend to the message.
- The **principle of similarity** tells us that consumers tend to group together objects that share similar physical characteristics. Green Giant relied on this principle when the company redesigned the packaging for its line of frozen vegetables. It created a "sea of green" look to unify all of its different offerings.
- The **figure-ground principle** states that one part of a stimulus will dominate (the *figure*), and other parts recede into the background (the *ground*). This concept is easy to understand if one thinks literally of a photograph with a clear and sharply focused object (the figure) in the center. The figure is dominant, and the eye goes straight to it. The parts of the configuration a person will perceive as figure or ground can vary depending on the individual consumer as well as other factors. Similarly, marketing messages that use the figure-ground principle can make a stimulus the focal point of the message or merely the context that surrounds the focus.

The Australian postal service uses a unique application of the figure-ground principle.

(e.g., the Ford Mustang has a galloping horse on the hood). An **index** is a sign that is connected to a product because they share some property (e.g., the pine tree on some of Procter & Gamble's Spic and Span cleanser products conveys the shared property of fresh scent). A **symbol** is a sign that relates to a product by either conventional or agreed-on associations (e.g., the lion in Dreyfus Fund ads provides the conventional association with fearlessness and strength that it carries [or hopes to carry] over to the company's approach to investments).

A lot of time, thought, and money go into creating brand names and logos that will clearly communicate a product's image (even when a name such as Exxon is generated by a computer!). The Nissan Xterra combines the word *terrain* with the letter *X*, which many young people associate with extreme sports, to give the brand name a cutting-edge, off-road feel.

The choice of a logo is even more difficult when the brand has to travel across cultures. For example, as Chinese business becomes more global, companies are refashioning ancient Chinese pictograms into new corporate logos that resonate with both the East and the West. Chinese pictograms really are icons because the ancient symbols were once graphic depictions of the words they signify. For example, China Telecom's logo features two interlocking letter *C*'s that together form the Chinese character for China but also represent the concept of "customer" and "competition," the firm's new focus. In addition, though, the symbol also resembles the horns of an ox, a hard-working animal. The software company Oracle redesigned its logo for the Chinese market by adding three Chinese characters that signify the literal translation of the word *oracle*: "writing on a tortoise shell." The expression dates back to ancient China when prophecies were scrawled on bones. The California firm was enthusiastic about the translation because it conveyed Oracle's core competency—data storage.[98]

Hyperreality

One of the hallmarks of modern advertising is that it creates a condition of **hyperreality.** This refers to the process of making real what is initially simulation or "hype." Advertisers create new relationships between objects and interpretants by inventing new connections between products and benefits, such as equating Marlboro cigarettes with the American frontier spirit.[99]

Over time, the true relationship between the symbol and reality is no longer possible to discern in a hyperreal environment. The "artificial" associations between product symbols and the real world may take on lives of their own. Consider, for example, the region of Switzerland that tourism marketers renamed "Heidiland" in honor of the supposed "birthplace" of the imaginary Swiss girl. In the town of Maienfeld, Heidi attractions flourish. A Heidi trail leads to a Heidi refreshment stand and then to a man there who poses full-time as Heidi's grandfather. Initially, officials refused to permit "Welcome to Heidiland" highway signs because Swiss law allows only real place names. The volume of tourists making pilgrimages to the "home" of this mythical character apparently changed their minds.[100] In our hyperreal world, Heidi lives.

In the age of hyperreality, fictional characters and, yes, even made-up products can cross over from make-believe to the real world. That explains why the exploits of the "Taster's Choice couple," a flirtatious man and woman featured in a long-running advertising campaign, became the subjects of a romance novel in the United Kingdom or why a publisher can sell a cookbook featuring the favorite recipes of Aunt Bea (the fictional character in the classic TV sitcom *The Andy Griffith Show*).

In the cult hit movie *Office Space* (1999), a weird character named Milton devotes his workdays to guarding his red Swingline stapler against pilfering by covetous co-workers. Swingline was swamped with orders for the red stapler as a result. There was a slight problem: The company didn't make bright-red staplers; the Swingline in the movie was custom painted by a prop designer. When real-life Miltons found out they couldn't buy one from the manufacturer, they simply made their own, creating a thriving market on eBay for Swinglines spray-painted red. Lo and behold, 3 years after the red-stapler buzz began, Swingline began selling a "Rio Red" stapler. "Staple and be heard!" the Swingline Web site (swingline.com) exalts. "WHAM-cubicles! WHAM-dress code! WHAM WHAM WHAM!"[101]

PERCEPTUAL POSITIONING

As we've seen, we often interpret a product stimulus in light of what we already know about a product category and the characteristics of existing brands. Our perception of a brand comprises both its functional attributes (e.g., its features, its price, and so on) and its symbolic attributes (its image and what we think it says about us when we use it). We'll look more closely at issues such as brand image in later chapters, but for now it's important to keep in mind that (as we stated in the previous chapter) our evaluation of a product typically is the result of what it means rather than what it does. This meaning—as consumers perceive it—constitutes the product's market position, and it may have more to do with our expectations of product performance as communicated by its color, packaging, or styling than with the product itself.

How does a marketer determine where a product actually stands in the minds of consumers? One technique is to ask them what attributes are important to them and how they feel competitors rate on these attributes. We can use this information to construct a **perceptual map,** a vivid way to paint a picture of where products or brands are "located" in consumers' minds. GRW Advertising created a perceptual map for HMV music stores, a British company. The agency wanted to know more about how its target market, frequent buyers of CDs, perceived the different stores they might patronize. GRW plotted perceptions of such attributes of competitors as selection, price, service, and hipness on an imaginary street map. Based on this research, the firm determined that HMV's strengths were service, selection, and the stores' abilities to cater to local tastes because store managers can order their own stock. It used this map as part of its strategic decision to specialize in music products as opposed to competing by offering other items the competition sells, such as video games, fragrances, and computer CD-ROMs.[102]

This decision became part of HMG's **positioning strategy,** which is a fundamental component of a company's marketing efforts as it uses elements of the marketing mix (i.e., product design, price, distribution, and marketing communications) to influence the consumer's interpretation of its meaning in the marketplace relative to its competitors. For example, although consumers' preferences for the taste of one product over another are important, this functional attribute is only one component of product evaluation.

Coca-Cola found this out the hard way when it committed its famous New Coke marketing blunder in the 1980s. Consumers preferred New Coke to Pepsi in *blind taste tests* (in which researchers did not identify the products) by an average of 55 to 45 percent in 17 markets, yet New Coke ran into problems when it replaced the older version. Consumers' impassioned protests and letter-writing campaigns eventually forced the company to bring back "Classic Coke." Why the reversal? People do not buy a cola for taste alone; they are buying intangibles such as brand image as well.[103] Coca-Cola's unique position as part of an American, fun-loving lifestyle is based on years of marketing efforts that involve a lot more than its literal taste.

Marketers can use many dimensions to carve out a brand's position in the marketplace. These include the following:[104]

- **Lifestyle**—Grey Poupon mustard is a "higher-class" condiment.
- **Price leadership**—L'Oréal's Noisôme brand face cream is sold in upscale beauty shops, whereas its Plenitude brand is available for one-sixth the price in discount stores—even though both are based on the same chemical formula.[105]

- **Attributes**—Bounty paper towels are "the quicker picker upper."
- **Product class**—The Mazda Miata is a sporty convertible.
- **Competitors**—Northwestern Insurance is "the quiet company."
- **Occasions**—Wrigley's gum is an alternative at times when smoking is not permitted.
- **Users**—Levi's Dockers are targeted primarily to men in their 20s to 40s.
- **Quality**—At Ford, "Quality is job 1."

CHAPTER SUMMARY

Now that you have finished reading this chapter you should understand why:

Perception is a three-stage process that translates raw stimuli into meaning.

- Perception is the process by which physical sensations, such as sights, sounds, and smells, are selected, organized, and interpreted. The eventual interpretation of a stimulus allows it to be assigned meaning. A perceptual map is a widely used marketing tool that evaluates the relative standing of competing brands along relevant dimensions.

Products and commercial messages often appeal to our senses, but we won't be influenced by most of them.

- Marketing stimuli have important sensory qualities. We rely on colors, odors, sounds, tastes, and even the "feel" of products when evaluating them. Not all sensations successfully make their way through the perceptual process. Many stimuli compete for our attention, and the majority are not noticed or accurately comprehended. People have different thresholds of perception. A stimulus must be presented at a certain level of intensity before our sensory detectors can detect it. In addition, a consumer's ability to detect whether two stimuli are different (the differential threshold) is an important issue in many marketing contexts, such as package design, the size of a product, or its price.

The design of a product today is a key driver of its success or failure.

- In recent years the sensory experiences we receive from products and services have become a high priority when choosing among competing options. Consumers increasingly want to buy things that will give them hedonic value in addition to functional value. They often believe that most brands perform similarly, so they weigh a product's aesthetic qualities heavily when choosing among competing options.

Subliminal advertising is a controversial—but largely ineffective—way to talk to consumers.

- A lot of controversy has been sparked by so-called subliminal persuasion and related techniques in which people are exposed to visual and aural messages below the sensory threshold. Although evidence that subliminal persuasion is effective is virtually nonexistent, many consumers continue to believe that advertisers use this technique.

  Some of the factors that determine which stimuli (above the threshold level) do get perceived include the amount of exposure to the stimulus, how much attention it generates, and how it is interpreted. In an increasingly crowded stimulus environment, advertising clutter occurs when too many marketing-related messages compete for attention.

We interpret the stimuli to which we do pay attention according to learned patterns and expectations.

● We don't attend to a stimulus in isolation. We classify and organize it according to principles of perceptual organization. A *Gestalt*, or overall pattern, guides these principles. Specific grouping principles include closure, similarity, and figure-ground relationships. The final step in the process of perception is interpretation. Symbols help us make sense of the world by providing us with an interpretation of a stimulus that others often share. The degree to which the symbolism is consistent with our previous experience affects the meaning we assign to related objects.

The field of semiotics helps us to understand how marketers use symbols to create meaning.

● Marketers try to communicate with consumers by creating relationships between their products or services and desired attributes. A semiotic analysis involves the correspondence between stimuli and the meaning of signs. The intended meaning may be literal (e.g., an icon such as a street sign with a picture of children playing). Or it may be indexical if it relies on shared characteristics (e.g., the red in a stop sign means danger). Meaning also can be conveyed by a symbol in which an image is given meaning by convention or by agreement of members of a society (e.g., stop signs are octagonal, whereas yield signs are triangular). Marketer-created associations often take on lives of their own as consumers begin to believe that hype is, in fact, real. We call this condition hyperreality.

KEY TERMS

Absolute threshold, 91
Adaptation, 98
Attention, 96
Closure principle, 101
Contrast, 99
Differential threshold, 91
Embeds, 96
Experience, 98
Exposure, 90
Figure-ground principle, 102
Gestalt, 101
Hedonic consumption, 79
Hyperreality, 105
Icon, 103

Index, 105
Interpretant, 103
Interpretation, 100
j.n.d., 91
Kansei engineering, 88
Multitasking, 97
Object, 103
Perception, 78
Perceptual defense, 98
Perceptual filters, 98
Perceptual map, 106
Perceptual selection, 98
Perceptual vigilance, 98
Positioning strategy, 106

Priming, 101
Principle of similarity, 102
Psychophysics, 91
Rich media, 97
Schema, 100
Semiotics, 103
Sensation, 78
Sensory marketing, 82
Sensory overload, 97
Sign, 103
Subliminal perception, 95
Symbol, 105
Trade dress, 84
Weber's Law, 91

REVIEW QUESTIONS

1 Define hedonic consumption and provide an example.

2 Does the size of a package influence how much of the contents we eat? Provide an example.

3 How does the sense of touch influence consumers' reactions to products?

4 Identify and describe the three stages of perception.

5 What is the difference between an absolute threshold and a differential threshold?

6 Does subliminal perception work? Why or why not?

7 "Consumers practice a form of 'psychic economy.'" What does this mean?

8 Describe two factors that can lead to stimulus adaptation.

9 Define a "schema" and provide an example of how this concept is relevant to marketing.

10 "The whole is greater than the sum of its parts." Explain this statement.

11 List the three semiotic components of a marketing message, giving an example of each.

12 What do we mean by the concept of hyperreality? Give an example that is not discussed in the chapter.

13 What is a positioning strategy? What are some ways marketers can position their products?

CONSUMER BEHAVIOR CHALLENGE

■ DISCUSS

1 Many studies have shown that our sensory detection abilities decline as we grow older. Discuss the implications of the absolute threshold for marketers attempting to appeal to the elderly.

2 Assuming that some forms of subliminal persuasion may have the desired effect of influencing consumers, do you think the use of these techniques is ethical? Explain your answer.

3 Do you believe that marketers have the right to use any or all public spaces to deliver product messages? Where would you draw the line in terms of places and products that should be off limits?

4 The slogan for the movie *Godzilla* was "Size does matter." Should this be the slogan for America as well? Many marketers seem to believe so. The average serving size for a fountain drink has gone from 12 ounces to 20 ounces. An industry consultant explains that the 32-ounce Big Gulp is so popular because "people like something large in their hands. The larger the better." Hardee's Monster Burger, complete with two beef patties and five pieces of bacon, weighs in at 63 grams of fat and more than 1,000 calories. The standard for TV sets used to be 19 inches; now it's 32 inches and growing. Hulking sport utility vehicles (SUVs) have replaced tiny sports cars as the status vehicle of the new millennium. What's up with our fascination with bigness? Is this a uniquely American preference? Do you believe that "bigger is better"? Is this a sound marketing strategy?

■ APPLY

5 Interview three to five male and three to five female friends about their perceptions of both men's and women's fragrances. Construct a perceptual map for each set of products. Based on your map of perfumes, do you see any areas that are not adequately served by current offerings? What (if any) gender differences did you notice regarding both the relevant dimensions used by raters and the placement of specific brands along these dimensions?

6 Assume that you are a consultant for a marketer who wants to design a package for a new premium chocolate bar targeted to an affluent market. What recommendations would you provide in terms of such package elements as color, symbolism, and graphic design? Give the reasons for your suggestions.

Using magazines archived in the library, track the packaging of a specific brand over time. Find an example of gradual changes in package design that may have been below the j.n.d.

7 Visit a set of Web sites for one type of product (e.g., personal computers, perfumes, laundry detergents, or athletic shoes) and analyze the colors and other design principles employed. Which sites "work" and which don't? Why? Look through a current magazine and select one ad that captures your attention over the others. Explain why this ad attracts you.

8 Find ads that use the techniques of contrast and novelty. Give your opinion of the effectiveness of each ad and whether the technique is likely to be appropriate for the consumers targeted by the ad.

Case Study

THE BRAVE NEW WORLD OF SUBWAY ADVERTISING

What do American Express, Target Stores, Coca-Cola, the Discovery Channel, Cadillac, Minute Maid, the Cartoon Network, Royal Caribbean, and Calvin Klein all have in common? They are all breaking through the clutter of traditional ad spaces to grab the attention of potential customers. And in the process, they are dazzling them right out of the boredom of riding the subway.

Subway advertising has been around nearly as long as the subway itself. But advertising media pioneers Submedia, Sidetrack Technologies, and MotionPoster give the old venue a new twist. By employing an innovative technology similar to that of a childhood flip book, they are lighting up dark subway tunnels and turning them into valuable showcases for major advertisers.

At the core of this new method is a series of lit panels containing static images. The panels occupy 500 to 1,000 feet of space that normally contain only graffiti, grime, and the occasional rat. When viewed from a standstill, they appear as simple still images. But when a subway passes by, they come to life for riders as a 15- to 30-second full-motion commercial.

Having just another place to air a commercial might not seem so appealing to advertisers. But in a media environment where consumers are increasingly bypassing ads (think TiVo), the placement of these ads in subway tunnels presents exceptional possibilities. Advertisers are clamoring for opportunities to break through the typical clutter. And these ads are so unique, most consumers have never seen anything like them. "We think this will catch people so totally by surprise that when they see them, they can't help but watch them," said Dan Hanrahan, Royal Caribbean's senior vice president of marketing and sales.

But the uniqueness of this medium is only part of the formula that gives these advertising agencies the belief that they're creating a revolution. The rest is based on the nature of the subway audience: captive and bored. "Everybody overwhelmingly says it takes away from the boredom of the ride," said Joshua Spodek, founder of New York City-based Submedia. "It's not like it's taking away from a beautiful view, like a billboard as you're driving around a beautiful area in Vermont. A subway tunnel is a semi-industrial environment."

Whether it's because the ads give a bored audience something to do or because this new wave of out-of-home advertisements is truly cutting edge, industry officials claim that the public reaction has been overwhelmingly positive. Transit authorities even claim that customers bombard them with compliments about the ads. Exaggeration? Wishful thinking? Not according to Gabe Grant, a regular rider of Boston's Red

Target Store ad running on Boston's MBTA Red Line tunnel walls.
Source: Courtesy SideTrack Technologies, Inc.

Line. "Wow. They do think of everything. I'm pretty psyched about that. It's not the most exciting ride without it."

Comments like this make it easy to believe the claims of underground advertising agencies. One estimate asserts that more than 80 percent of consumers remember the advertised product while only 20 percent have that same level of recall for televisions ads. This means big ad revenues, and not just for the agencies. Mass transit organizations potentially can realize a big source of secondary income when they lease out this unused real estate.

Currently brightening the tunnels of numerous mass transit systems in North and South America, Asia, and Europe, these advertisements represent something every advertiser dreams of: an ad that people go out of their way to look at. In a world that is becoming increasingly skeptical about too much advertising, this is an express ride to success.

DISCUSSION QUESTIONS

1 Based on the principles of attention the chapter presents, explain why riders receive these new ads so positively.

2 Using the same principles, what should the ads' creators consider to avoid the potential burnout of this medium?

Sources: "Eye-Catching Commercials Go Underground," *Reuters* (June 23, 2006), *www.submediaworld.com.*
Kevin McGran, "Next Subway Stop is TV," *Toronto Star* (September 20, 2004): p. B01.
Naomi Aoki, "Next Stop, Ad Buzz. Wall of Subway Tunnel Is Turned Into a Billboard for Cruise Line," *Boston Globe* (August 18, 2004): C1.

NOTES

1. "Going Organic," *Prepared Foods* (August 2002): 18; Cathy Sivak, "Purposeful Parmalat: Part 1 of 2," *Dairy Field* 182, no. 9 (September 1999): 1; "North Brunswick, NJ-Based Food Company Signs Deal with Online Grocer," *Home News Tribune* (March 21, 2000).
2. Nat Ives, "Putting Some Terror in Family Outings," *New York Times on the Web* (January 17, 2005).
3. Rick Vecchio, "'Reality TV' Peru Style: Trashy Shows Entertain, Distract during Election Year," *Opelika-Auburn News* (March 15, 2000): 15A.
4. Glenn Collins, "Owens-Corning's Blurred Identity," *New York Times* (August 19, 1994): D4.
5. Elizabeth C. Hirschman and Morris B. Holbrook, "Hedonic Consumption: Emerging Concepts, Methods, and Propositions," *Journal of Marketing* 46 (Summer 1982): 92–101.
6. Virginia Postrel, "The New Trend in Spending," *New York Times on the Web* (September 9, 2004).
7. Emily Cadei, "Cleaning Up: S.F. Duo Putting a Shine on its Product Line," *San Francisco Business Times Online Edition* 17, no. 16.
8. Quoted in Jack Neff, "P&G Boosts Design's Role in Marketing," *Advertising Age* 1 no. 2 (February 9, 2004): 52.
9. Stuart Elliott, "Joint Promotion Adds Stickers to Sweet Smell of Marketing" *New York Times. Online Edition* (April 2, 2007).
10. Gabriel Kahn, "Philips Blitzes Asian Market as It Strives to Become Hip," *Wall Street Journal Interactive Edition* (August 1, 2002).
11. Amitava Chattopadhyay, Gerald J. Gorn, and Peter R. Darke, "Roses Are Red and Violets Are Blue—Everywhere? Cultural Universals and Differences in Color Preference among Consumers and Marketing Managers" (unpublished manuscript, University of British Columbia, Fall 1999); Joseph Bellizzi and Robert E. Hite, "Environmental Color, Consumer Feelings, and Purchase Likelihood," *Psychology & Marketing* 9 (1992): 347–63; Ayn E. Crowley, "The Two-Dimensional Impact of Color on Shopping," *Marketing Letters* 4 (January 1993); Gerald J. Gorn, Amitava Chattopadhyay, and Tracey Yi, "Effects of Color as an Executional Cue in an Ad: It's in the Shade," (unpublished manuscript, University of British Columbia, 1994).
12. Adam Bryant, "Plastic Surgery at AmEx," *Newsweek* (October 4, 1999): 55.
13. Mark G. Frank and Thomas Gilovich, "The Dark Side of Self and Social Perception: Black Uniforms and Aggression in Professional Sports," *Journal of Personality and Social Psychology* 54 (1988): 74–85.
14. Brian Wansink, *Mindless Eating: The Hidden Persuaders That Cause Us to Lose and Gain Weight* (New York: Bantam-Dell, 2006).
15. Brian Wansink and SeaBum Park, "At the Movies: How External Cues and Perceived Taste Impact Consumption Volume," *Food Quality and Preference* 12, no. 1 (January 2001): 69–74.
16. Brian Wansink and Junyong Kim (2005), "Bad Popcorn in Big Buckets: Portion Size Can Influence Intake as Much as Taste," *Journal of Nutrition Education and Behavior* 37, no. 5 (September–October): 242–5.
17. Brian Wansink and Matthew M. Cheney, "Super Bowls: Serving Bowl Size and Food Consumption," *Journal of the American Medical Association* 293, no. 14 (April 13): 1727–28.
18. Brian Wansink, James E. Painter, and Jill North, "Bottomless Bowls: Why Visual Cues of Portion Size May Influence Intake," *Obesity Research* 13, no. 1 (January): 93–100.
19. Priya Raghubir and Aradna Krishna, "Vital Dimensions in Volume Perception: Can the Eye Fool the Stomach?" *Journal of Marketing Research* 36 (August 1999): 313–26.
20. Brian Wansink and Koert van Ittersum, "Bottoms Up! The Influence of Elongation and Pouring on Consumption Volume," *Journal of Consumer Research* 30, no. 3 (December 2003): 455–63.
21. Barbara E. Kahn and Brian Wansink, "The Influence of Assortment Structure on Perceived Variety and Consumption Quantities," *Journal of Consumer Research* 30, no. 4 (March 2004): 519–33.
22. This section was contributed by Prof. Brian Wansink of Cornell University and is reprinted here with his kind permission.
23. Pamela Paul, "Color by Numbers," *American Demographics* (February 2002): 31–36.
24. Paulette Thomas, "Cosmetics Makers Offer World's Women an All-American Look with Local Twists," *Wall Street Journal* (May 8, 1995): B1.
25. Marc Gobé, *Emotional Branding: The New Paradigm for Connecting Brands to People* (New York: Allworth Press, 2001).
26. Dirk Olin, "Color Cognition," *New York Times on the Web* (November 30, 2003).
27. "Ny Emballage og Nyt Navn Fordoblede Salget," *Markedsforing* 12 (1992): 24. Adapted from Michael R. Solomon, Gary Bamossy, and Soren Askegaard, *Consumer Behavior: A European Perspective*, 2nd ed. (London: Pearson Education, 2001).
28. Meg Rosen and Frank Alpert, "Protecting Your Business Image: The Supreme Court Rules on Trade Dress," *Journal of Consumer Marketing* 11 (1994): 50–55.
29. Quoted in "Pantone Crowns Color of the Year: Chili Pepper," *Marketing Daily* (January 17, 2007), available from *www.mediapost.com*, accessed January 17, 2007.
30. Deborah J. Mitchell, Barbara E. Kahn, and Susan C. Knasko, "There's Something in the Air: Effects of Congruent or Incongruent Ambient Odor on Consumer Decision-Making," *Journal of Consumer Research* 22 (September 1995): 229–38; for a review of olfactory cues in store environments, see also Eric R. Spangenberg, Ayn E. Crowley, and Pamela W. Henderson, "Improving the Store Environment: Do Olfactory Cues Affect Evaluations and Behaviors?" *Journal of Marketing* 60 (April 1996): 67–80.
31. Thom Forbes, "P&G Noses Its Way into Youthful Air Freshener Market" (January 3, 2007), available from *mediapost.com*, accessed January 3, 2007.
32. Pam Scholder Ellen and Paula Fitzgerald Bone, "Does It Matter If It Smells? Olfactory Stimuli as Advertising Executional Cues," *Journal of Advertising* 27 (Winter 1998): 29–40.
33. Jack Hitt, "Does the Smell of Coffee Brewing Remind You of Your Mother?" *New York Times Magazine* (May 7, 2000): 73–77.
34. Maxine Wilkie, "Scent of a Market," *American Demographics* (August 1995): 40–49.
35. Nicholas Wade, "Scent of a Man Is Linked to a Woman's Selection," *New York Times on the Web* (January 22, 2002).
36. Newman, Kara, "How to Sell with Smell," *Business 2.0* (April 2007): 36.
37. Brian Steinberg, "Ad Play in *People* Magazine Uses Some Scented Spots to Tickle Readers' Fancy," *Wall Street Journal* (November 13, 2006): B5; Stephanie Thompson, "A Push to Make Dollars from Scents," *Advertising Age* (October 2006): 4.
38. Nina M. Lentini, "KFC Targets the Nostrils of Hungry Office Workers" (August 29, 2007), *Marketing Daily*, *www.mediapost.com*, accessed August 29, 2007.
39. Nina M. Lentini, "CBS Raising 'Cane' Profile Among 'Rolling Stone' Readers" (September 6, 2007), *Marketing Daily*, *www.mediapost.com*, accessed September 6, 2007.
40. Jesse McKinley, "City Sours on Cookie-Scented Ads" (December 6, 2006), available from *NewYorkTimes.com*, accessed December 6, 2006.
41. Maria Aspan, "Horror Movie at High Pitch in TV Ad Aimed at Teenagers" *New York Times Online Edition* (February 19, 2007); "Students Find Ring Tone Adults Can't Hear," *New York Times Online Edition* (June 12, 2006).
42. E. Yorkson and G. Menon, "A Sound Idea: Phonetic Effects of Brand Names on Consumer Judgments," *Journal of Consumer Research* 31, no. 1 (2004): 43–51.
43. Otto Friedrich, "Trapped in a Musical Elevator," *Time* (December 10, 1984): 3.
44. Jacob Hornik, "Tactile Stimulation and Consumer Response," *Journal of Consumer Research* 19 (December 1992): 449–58.
45. Sarah Ellison and Erin White, "'Sensory' Marketers Say the Way to Reach Shoppers Is the Nose," *Advertising* (November 24, 2000): 1–3.
46. Douglas Heingartner, "Now Hear This, Quickly," *New York Times on the Web* (October 2, 2003).
47. J. Peck and T. L. Childers (2003), "Individual Differences in Haptic Information Processing: The 'Need for Touch' Scale," *Journal of Consumer Research* 30, no. 3: 430–42.
48. Material adapted from a presentation by Glenn H. Mazur, QFD Institute, 2002.
49. Joseph B. White, "Taller in the Saddle: Higher Driver's Seats in Sedans Are Effort to Appeal to Fans of SUVs and Minivans," *Wall Street Journal on the Web* (August 23, 2004).
50. Randall Frost, "Feeling Your Way in a Global Market," available from *brandchannel.com*, accessed October 18, 2006.
51. Mike Musgrove, "Bringing Senses into Play: Gaming Gadgets Create Whoooshes and Rumbles, *Washington Post* (June 19, 2007): D1.
52. John Tagliabue, "Sniffing and Tasting with Metal and Wire," *New York Times Online* (February 17, 2002).
53. Becky Gaylord, "Bland Food Isn't So Bad—It Hurts Just to Think about This Stuff," *Wall Street Journal* (April 21, 1995): B1.

54. Dan Morse, "From Tabasco to Insane: When You're Hot, It May Not Be Enough," *Wall Street Journal Interactive Edition* (May 15, 2000).

55. Stuart Elliott, "TV Commercials Adjust to a Shorter Attention Span," *New York Times Online* (April 8, 2005).

56. Nina M. Lentini, "McDonald's Tests 'Angus Third Pounder' in California," available from *mediapost.com*, accessed March 27, 2007.

57. Andrew Martin, "Will Diners Still Swallow This?" available from *NewYorkTimes.com*, accessed March 25, 2007.

58. Dhruv Grewal and Larry D. Compeau, "Consumer Responses to Price and Its Contextual Information Cues: A Synthesis of Past Research, a Conceptual Framework, and Avenues for Further Research," *Review of Marketing Research* 3 (2007): 109–31; Kent B. Monroe, *Pricing: Making Profitable Decisions*, 3rd ed. (New York: McGraw-Hill, 2003); Dhruv Grewal, Kent B. Monroe, and R. Krishnan, "The Effects of Price Comparison Advertising on Buyers' Perceptions of Acquisition Value and Transaction Value," *Journal of Marketing* 62 (April 1998): 46–60.

59. William B. Dodds, Kent B. Monroe, and Dhruv Grewal, "Effects of Price, Brand, and Store Information on Buyers' Product Evaluations," *Journal of Marketing Research* 28 (August 1991): 307-19; Merrie Brucks, Valerie Zeithaml, and Gillian Naylor, "Price and Brand Name as Indicators of Quality Dimensions of Consumer Durables," *Journal of the Academy of Marketing Science* 28, no. 3 (2000): 359–74.

60. Dhruv Grewal and Larry D. Compeau, "Comparative Price Advertising: Informative or Deceptive?" *Journal of Public Policy and Marketing* 11 (Spring 1991): 52–62; Larry D. Compeau and Dhruv Grewal, "Comparative Price Advertising: An Integrative Review," *Journal of Public Policy and Marketing* 17 (Fall 1998): 257–73; Larry D. Compeau, Dhruv Grewal, and Joan Lindsey-Mullikin, "An Analysis of Consumers' Interpretations of Semantic Phrases Found in Reference Price Advertisements," *Journal of Consumer Affairs* 38 (Summer 2004): 178–87.

61. Larry D. Compeau and Dhruv Grewal, "Adding Value by Communicating Price Deals Effectively: Does It Matter How You Phrase It?" *Pricing Strategy and Practice: An International Journal* 2, no. 2 (1994): 28–36.

62. Joel E. Urbany, William O. Bearden, and Don C. Weilbaker, "The Effect of Plausible and Exaggerated Reference Prices on Consumer Perceptions and Price Search," *Journal of Consumer Research* 15 (1998): 95–110.

63. Larry D. Compeau and Dhruv Grewal, "Comparative Price Advertising: An Integrative Review," *Journal of Public Policy and Marketing* 17 (Fall 1998): 257–73; Dhruv Grewal and Larry D. Compeau, "Pricing and Public Policy: A Research Agenda and an Overview," *Journal of Public Policy and Marketing* 18 (Spring 1999): 3–10.

64. Larry D. Compeau, Dhruv Grewal, and Diana S. Grewal, "Adjudicating Claims of Deceptive Advertised Reference Prices: The Use of Empirical Evidence," *Journal of Public Policy and Marketing* 13 (Fall 1994): 312–18; Dhruv Grewal and Larry D. Compeau, *Journal of Public Policy and Marketing: Special Issue on Pricing and Public Policy* 18 (Spring 1999), Chicago, IL: American Marketing Association. Also see *www.bbb.org/membership/codeofad.asp#Comparative%20Price* , *www.ftc.gov/bcp/guides/decptprc.htm* for guidelines on use of reference prices.

65. Ellen Byron, "Selling Detergent Bottles' Big Shrink Suds Makers' Challenge: Convince Consumers Less Isn't Really Less," *Wall Street Journal* (May 21, 2007).

66. Michael Lev, "No Hidden Meaning Here: Survey Sees Subliminal Ads," *New York Times* (May 3, 1991): D7.

67. Associated Press, "ABC Rejects KFC Commercial, Citing Subliminal Advertising," *Wall Street Journal* (March 2, 2006).

68. Andrew B. Aylesworth, Ronald C. Goodstein, and Ajay Kalra, "Effect of Archetypal Embeds on Feelings: An Indirect Route to Affecting Attitudes?" *Journal of Advertising* 28, no. 3 (Fall 1999): 73–81.

69. Philip M. Merikle, "Subliminal Auditory Messages: An Evaluation," *Psychology & Marketing* 5, no. 4 (1988): 355–72.

70. Joel Saegert, "Why Marketing Should Quit Giving Subliminal Advertising the Benefit of the Doubt," *Psychology & Marketing* 4 (Summer 1987): 107–20; see also Dennis L. Rosen and Surendra N. Singh, "An Investigation of Subliminal Embed Effect on Multiple Measures of Advertising Effectiveness," *Psychology & Marketing* 9 (March–April 1992): 157–73; for a more recent review, see Kathryn T. Theus, "Subliminal Advertising and the Psychology of Processing Unconscious Stimuli: A Review of Research," *Psychology & Marketing* (May–June 1994): 271–90.

71. Todd Wasserman, "An Eyeball Test for Better Ads," *Business 2.0* (March 2007): 34.

72. Jennifer Pendleton, "Multi-Taskers," *Advertising Age* (March 29, 2004): S8.

73. Sharon Waxman, "At an Industry Media Lab, Close Views of Multitasking," *New York Times* (May 15, 2006).

74. Stuart Elliott, "Trying to Keep the Viewers When the Ads Come On," *New York Times* (May 14, 2007).

75. Lee Gomes, "As Web Ads Grow, Sites Get Trickier about Targeting You," *Wall Street Journal* (May 9, 2007): B1.

76. Lisa Sanders, "Fight for the Streets," *Advertising Age* (May 31, 2004): 58; Nat Ives, "More Demand for Guerilla Marketing," *New York Times on the Web* (June 24, 2004).

77. "Court Orders Bagpipes for Noise Violations," *Montgomery Advertiser* (March 6, 1999): 1A.

78. Barnaby Feder, "Billboards That Know You by Name," *New York Times* (January 29, 2007).

79. Andy Manis, "Digital Billboard Up Ahead: New-Wave Sign or Hazard?" *New York Times*; Louise Story, "A Digital Billboard on the Beltline Highway in Madison, Wis., Displays Different Ads at Different Times," *New York Times* (January 11, 2007).

80. Lucy Howard, "Trying to Fool a Feline," *Newsweek* (February 8, 1999): 8.

81. Roger Barton, *Advertising Media* (New York: McGraw-Hill, 1964).

82. Suzanne Oliver, "New Personality," *Forbes* (August 15, 1994): 114.

83. Adam Finn, "Print Ad Recognition Readership Scores: An Information Processing Perspective," *Journal of Marketing Research* 25 (May 1988): 168–77.

84. Gerald L. Lohse, "Consumer Eye Movement Patterns on Yellow Pages Advertising," *Journal of Advertising* 26 (Spring 1997): 61–73.

85. Michael R. Solomon and Basil G. Englis, "Reality Engineering: Blurring the Boundaries between Marketing and Popular Culture," *Journal of Current Issues and Research in Advertising* 16, no. 2 (Fall 1994): 1–18; Michael McCarthy, "Ads Are Here, There, Everywhere: Agencies Seek Creative Ways to Expand Product Placement," *USA Today* (June 19, 2001): 1B.

86. Erin White and David Pringle, "New Ads for Vanilla Coke Reward Curiosity in Europe," *Wall Street Journal Interactive Edition* (October 30, 2002).

87. Tim Davis, "Taste Tests: Are the Blind Leading the Blind?" *Beverage World* (April 1987): 44.

88. Nicholas Bakalar (August 14, 2007), "If It Says McDonald's, Then It Must Be Good," *New York Times Online Edition*, accessed August 14, 2007.

89. Robert M. McMath, "Image Counts," *American Demographics* (May 1998): 64.

90. Brian Wansink, James Painter, and Koert van Ittersum, "Descriptive Menu Labels' Effect on Sales," *Cornell Hotel and Restaurant Administration Quarterly* (December 2001): 68–72.

91. Anthony Ramirez, "Lessons in the Cracker Market: Nabisco Saved New Graham Snack," *New York Times* (July 5, 1990): D1.

92. Albert H. Hastorf and Hadley Cantril, "They Saw a Game: A Case Study," *Journal of Abnormal and Social Psychology* 49 (1954): 129–34; see also Roberto Friedmann and Mary R. Zimmer, "The Role of Psychological Meaning in Advertising," *Journal of Advertising* (1988): 31–40.

93. Robert M. McMath, "Chock Full of (Pea)nuts," *American Demographics* (April 1997): 60.

94. Benedict Carey, "Knowing the Ingredients Can Change the Taste," *New York Times* (December 12, 2006).

95. See David Mick, "Consumer Research and Semiotics: Exploring the Morphology of Signs, Symbols, and Significance," *Journal of Consumer Research* 13 (September 1986): 196–213.

96. Teresa J. Domzal and Jerome B. Kernan, "Reading Advertising: The What and How of Product Meaning," *Journal of Consumer Marketing* 9 (Summer 1992): 48–64.

97. Ernest Beck, "A Minefield in Maienfeld: 'Heidiland' Is Taking Over," *Wall Street Journal Interactive Edition* (October 2, 1997).

98. Arthur Asa Berger, *Signs in Contemporary Culture: An Introduction to Semiotics* (New York: Longman, 1984); David Mick, "Consumer Research and Semiotics: Exploring the Morphology of Signs, Symbols, and Significance," 196–213; Charles Sanders Peirce, in Charles Hartshorne, Paul Weiss, and Arthur W. Burks, eds., *Collected Papers* (Cambridge, MA: Harvard University Press, 1931–1958); cf. also V. Larsen, D. Luna, and L. A. Peracchio, "Points of View and Pieces of Time: A Taxonomy of Image Attributes," *Journal of Consumer Research* 31, no. 1 (2004): 102–11.

99. Gabriel Kahn, "Chinese Characters Are Gaining New Meaning as Corporate Logos," *Wall Street Journal Interactive Edition* (July 18, 2002).

100. Geoffrey A. Fowler, "Cult Film, 1999's *Office Space*, Transforms Swingline Stapler," *Wall Street Journal Interactive Edition* (July 2, 2002).

101. Jean Baudrillard, *Simulations* (New York: Semiotext(e), 1983); A. Fuat Firat and Alladi Venkatesh, "The Making of Postmodern Consumption," in Russell Belk and Nikhilesh Dholakia, eds., *Consumption and Marketing: Macro Dimensions* (Boston: PWS-Kent, 1993); A. Fuat Firat, "The Consumer in Postmodernity," in Rebecca H. Holman and Michael R. Solomon, eds., *Advances in Consumer Research* 18 (Provo, UT: Association for Consumer Research, 1991): 70–76.

102. Stuart Elliott, "Advertising: A Music Retailer Whistles a New Marketing Tune to Get Heard Above the Cacophony of Competitors," *New York Times* (July 2, 1996): D7; personal communication, GRW Advertising (April 1997).

103. See Tim Davis, "Taste Tests: Are the Blind Leading the Blind?" 43–44; Betsy McKay, "Pepsi to Revive a Cola-War Barb: The Decades-Old Blind Taste Test," *Wall Street Journal Interactive Edition* (March 21, 2000).

104. Adapted from Michael R. Solomon and Elnora W. Stuart, *Marketing: Real People, Real Choices*, 2nd ed. (Upper Saddle River, NJ: Prentice Hall, 2000).

105. William Echikson, "Aiming at High and Low Markets," *Fortune* (March 22, 1993): 89.

Learning and Memory

Chapter Objectives

When you have finished reading this chapter you will understand why:

- It's important for marketers to understand how consumers learn about products and services.
- Conditioning results in learning.
- Learned associations can generalize to other things and why this is important to marketers.
- There is a difference between classical and instrumental conditioning.
- We learn by observing others' behavior.
- Memory systems work.
- The other products we associate with an individual product influence how we will remember it.
- Products help us to retrieve memories from our past.
- Marketers measure our memories about products and ads.

ah, Sunday morning! The sun is shining, the birds are singing, and Joe is feeling groovy! He puts on his vintage Levi's 501 jeans (circa 1968) and his Woodstock T-shirt (the "real" Woodstock, not that fake abomination they put on back in the 1990s, thank you) and saunters down to the kitchen. Joe smiles in anticipation of his morning plans. He's just returned from his college reunion and now it's time to "process" all the people he's seen and the stories he heard about their old antics. Joe cranks up the Lava Lamp, throws a Jefferson Airplane record on the turntable (ah, the sublime joys of vinyl), and sits back on his Barcalounger clutching a huge bowl filled to the brim with his all-time favorite cereal, Cap'n Crunch. Let the memories begin!

Learning

Joe journeys through time with the aid of many products that make him feel good because they remind him of earlier parts of his life. These include a "comfort food" such as the cereal that many grown-ups still like to eat. Perhaps this need for "edible security blankets" helps to explain the appeal of Cereality (cereality.com), a chain of restaurants that specializes in serving cereal-based goodies with toppings such as marshmallows and M&Ms to college students. Employees wearing pajama tops dole out the sugary treats while a TV tuned to the Cartoon Network re-creates the feel of home.

The first store opened across from the University of Pennsylvania's Wharton School after the owner got the idea for the place when he noticed that a business associate on Wall Street kept a stash of Cocoa Puffs in his office. One college student explained the appeal of cereal: "It's some kind of Freudian childhood regression thing. It's a comfort mechanism. I remember eating cereal in the mornings with my dad and brother before kindergarten and first grade." Another student explained that she uses cereal as a buffer against instability in the world, especially following 9/11: "When you're hungry, you just put it in the bowl and put the milk in and go watch TV and everything's OK," she said. "You know how when you're depressed, you eat ice cream? Well, I eat cereal like that." So, in addition to students, it seems that older people like Joe react the same way. That's why new Cereality stores are moving beyond college campuses into the "real world," including a location near the Mercantile Exchange in Chicago, an airport, and a highway toll plaza. Looks like kids aren't the only ones who are "CooCoo for Cocoa Puffs."[1]

Many marketers realize that long-standing, learned connections between products and memories are a potent way to build and keep brand loyalty. Some companies are bringing their old trademark characters out of retirement, including the Campbell's Soup Kids, the Pillsbury Doughboy, Betty Crocker, and Planters' Mr. Peanut.[2] Several familiar faces returned in major advertising campaigns recently, including the Jolly Green Giant (born in 1925); Charlie the Tuna (who first appeared in 1961); and even Charmin's Mr. Whipple, who came out of retirement in 1999.[3] In this chapter, we'll explore how learned associations among feelings, events, and products—and the memories they evoke—are an important aspect of consumer behavior.

Learning is a relatively permanent change in behavior caused by experience. The learner need not have the experience directly; we can also learn by observing events that affect others.[4] We learn even when we don't try: Consumers recognize many brand names and they can hum many product jingles, for example, even for products they themselves do not use. We call this casual, unintentional acquisition of knowledge **incidental learning**.

Learning is an ongoing process. Our knowledge about the world is constantly revised as we are exposed to new stimuli and as we receive ongoing feedback that allows us to modify our behavior when we find ourselves in similar situations at a later time. The concept of learning covers a lot of ground, ranging from a consumer's simple association between a stimulus such as a product logo (e.g., Coca-Cola) and a response (e.g., "refreshing soft drink") to a complex series of cognitive activities (e.g., writing an essay on learning for a consumer behavior exam).

Psychologists who study learning have advanced several theories to explain the learning process. These theories range from those focusing on simple stimulus–response connections (*behavioral theories*) to perspectives that regard consumers as complex-problem solvers who learn abstract rules and concepts by observing others (*cognitive theories*). It's important for marketers to understand these theories as well because basic learning principles are at the heart of many consumer purchase decisions.

Our tastes are formed as a result of a learning process, sometimes with painful results.

Behavioral Learning Theories

Behavioral learning theories assume that learning takes place as the result of responses to external events. Psychologists who subscribe to this viewpoint do not focus on internal thought processes. Instead, they approach the mind as a "black box" and emphasize the observable aspects of behavior, as Figure 3.1 depicts. The observable aspects consist of things that go into the box (the stimuli or events perceived from the outside world) and things that come out of the box (the responses, or reactions to these stimuli).

■ **FIGURE 3.1**
THE CONSUMER AS A "BLACK BOX":
A BEHAVIORIST PERSPECTIVE
ON LEARNING

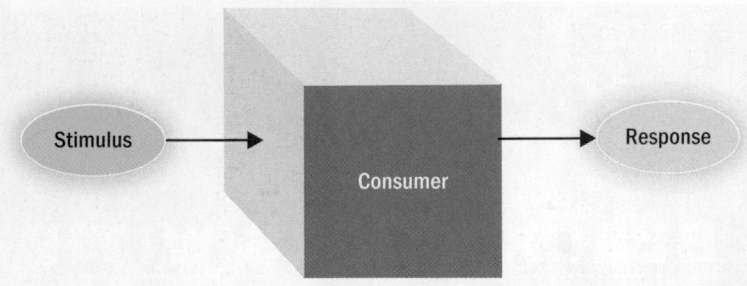

Two major approaches to learning represent this view: *classical conditioning* and *instrumental conditioning*. According to the behavioral learning perspective, the feedback we receive as we go through life shapes our experiences. Similarly, we respond to brand names, scents, jingles, and other marketing stimuli because of the learned connections we form over time. People also learn that actions they take result in rewards and punishments, and this feedback influences the way they will respond in similar situations in the future. Consumers who receive compliments on a product choice will be more likely to buy that brand again, but those who get food poisoning at a new restaurant are not likely to patronize it in the future.

CLASSICAL CONDITIONING

Classical conditioning occurs when a stimulus that elicits a response is paired with another stimulus that initially does not elicit a response on its own. Over time, this second stimulus causes a similar response because we associate it with the first stimulus.

Ivan Pavlov, a Russian physiologist doing research on digestion in animals, first demonstrated this phenomenon in dogs. Pavlov induced classically conditioned learning by pairing a neutral stimulus (a bell) with a stimulus known to cause a salivation response in dogs (he squirted dried meat powder into their mouths). The powder was an **unconditioned stimulus (UCS)** because it was naturally capable of causing the response. Over time, the bell became a **conditioned stimulus (CS)**; it did not initially cause salivation, but the dogs learned to associate the bell with the meat powder and began to salivate at the sound of the bell only. The drooling of these canine consumers because of a sound, now linked to feeding time, was a **conditioned response (CR)**.

This basic form of classical conditioning that Pavlov demonstrated primarily applies to responses the autonomic (e.g., salivation) and nervous (e.g., eye blink) systems control. That is, it focuses on visual and olfactory cues that induce hunger, thirst, sexual arousal, and other basic drives. When these cues are consistently paired with conditioned stimuli, such as brand names, consumers may learn to feel hungry, thirsty, or aroused when later exposed to the brand cues.

Classical conditioning can have similar effects for more complex reactions, too. Even a credit card becomes a conditioned cue that triggers greater spending, especially because it is a stimulus present only in situations in which consumers are spending money. People learn they can make larger purchases with credit cards, and they also leave larger tips than when paying by cash.[5] Small wonder that American Express reminds us, "Don't leave home without it."

Repetition

Conditioning effects are more likely to occur after the conditioned (CS) and unconditioned (UCS) stimuli have been paired a number of times.[6] Repeated exposures increase the strength of stimulus–response associations and prevent the decay of these associations in memory. Some research indicates that the intervals between exposures may influence the effectiveness of this strategy as well as the type of medium used; the

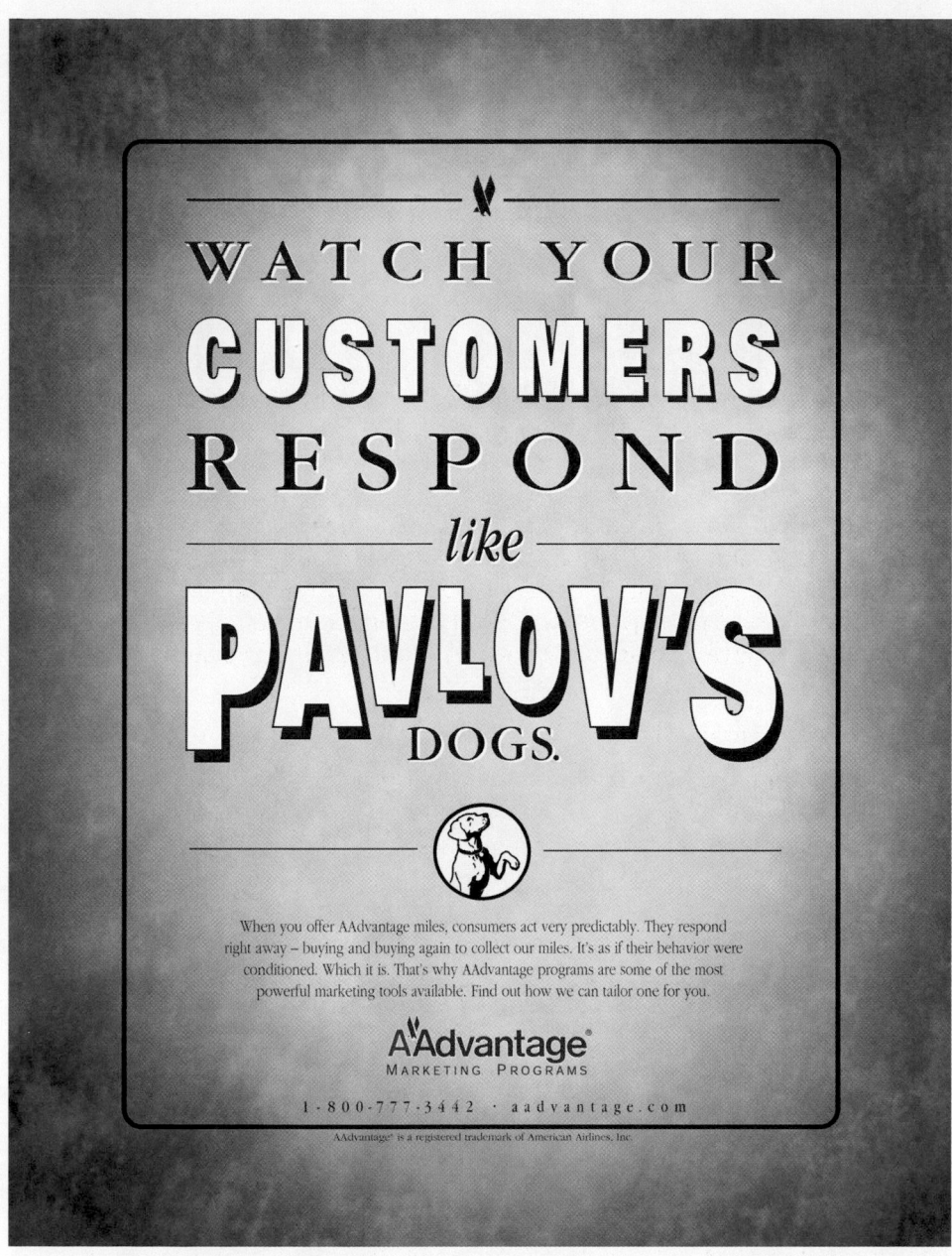

American Airlines uses an obvious reference to classical conditioning effects.

most effective repetition strategy is a combination of spaced exposures that alternate in terms of media that are more and less involving, such as television advertising complemented by print media.[7]

Many classic advertising campaigns consist of product slogans that companies repeat so often they are etched in consumers' minds. Conditioning will not occur or will take longer if the CS is only occasionally paired with the UCS. One result of this lack of association is **extinction**, which occurs when the effects of prior conditioning diminish and finally disappear. This can occur, for example, when a product is overexposed in the marketplace so that its original allure is lost. The Izod Lacoste polo shirt, with its distinctive crocodile crest, is a good example of this effect. When the once-exclusive crocodile started to appear on baby clothes and many other items, it lost its cachet. Other contenders, such as the Ralph Lauren polo player, successfully challenged it as a symbol of casual elegance. Now that Izod is being more careful about where its logo appears, the brand is starting to regain its "cool" in some circles.

Many classic advertising campaigns consist of product slogans that have been repeated so many times that they are etched in consumers' minds. The ad shown here brags about the high awareness of the Chiquita banana jingle (I'm a Chiquita banana, and I'm here to say . . .")

How strong is the Chiquita® name?
How many banana commercials can you sing?

Most people can't remember the TV commercials they saw last night as well as the Chiquita jingle they first heard in 1944.

In the 32 years since, Chiquita has come to be the first name that comes to mind for 9 out of every 10 consumers who buy bananas. Which is another reason why Chiquitas sell better than bananas.

Chiquita bananas today have a brand awareness of 92%. That's 30% higher than the awareness of the next leading brand..."what'sitsname?"

Stimulus Generalization

Stimulus generalization refers to the tendency of stimuli similar to a CS to evoke similar, conditioned responses. For example, Pavlov noticed in subsequent studies that his dogs would sometimes salivate when they heard noises that only resembled a bell, such as keys jangling.

People also react to other, similar stimuli in much the same way they responded to the original stimulus; we call this generalization a **halo effect**. A drugstore's bottle of private brand mouthwash deliberately packaged to resemble Listerine mouthwash may evoke a similar response among consumers, who assume that this "me-too" product shares other characteristics of the original. Indeed, consumers in one study on shampoo brands tended to rate those with similar packages as similar in quality and performance as well.[8] This "piggybacking" strategy can cut both ways: When the quality of the me-too product turns out to be lower than that of the original brand, consumers may exhibit even more positive feelings toward the original. However, if the quality of the two competitors is perceived to be about equal, consumers may conclude the price premium they are paying for the original is not worth it.[9]

In a twist on this principle, some companies now use a strategy they call **masked branding**, where they deliberately *hide* a product's true origin. For example, the giant corporation General Motors distanced itself from its Saturn brand and positioned the carmaker as a small-town business, and Levi Strauss markets its Red Tab line to appeal to young consumers who don't want to be associated with an "old" brand. Blue Moon positions its beer as sophisticated and the label lists the manufacturer as the Blue Moon Brewing Co., although in reality Coors makes it; whereas Miller Brewing Co. created a dummy company called Plank Road Brewery when it launched its Icehouse and Red Dog beers.[10]

Stimulus Discrimination

Stimulus discrimination occurs when a UCS does not follow a stimulus similar to a CS. When this happens, reactions are weakened and will soon disappear. Part of the learning process involves making a response to some stimuli but not to other, similar stimuli. Manufacturers of well-established brands commonly urge consumers not to buy "cheap imitations" because the results will not be what they expect.

MARKETING APPLICATIONS OF CLASSICAL CONDITIONING PRINCIPLES

Behavioral learning principles apply to many consumer phenomena, ranging from creating a distinctive brand image to the perceived linkage between a product and an underlying need. The transfer of meaning from an unconditioned stimulus to a conditioned stimulus explains why "made-up" brand names, such as Marlboro, Coca-Cola, or Reebok, can exert such powerful effects on consumers. The association between the Marlboro man and the cigarette is so strong that in some cases the company no longer even bothers to include the brand name in its ads. When researchers pair *nonsense syllables* (meaningless sets of letters) with such evaluative words as *beauty* or *success*, the meaning transfers to the fake words. This change in the symbolic significance of initially meaningless words shows that fairly simple associations can condition even complex meanings and the learning that results can last a long time.[11] These associations are crucial to many marketing strategies that rely on the creation and perpetuation of **brand equity**, in which a brand has strong positive associations in a consumer's memory and commands a lot of loyalty as a result.[12]

Marketing Applications of Repetition

One advertising researcher argued that any more than three exposures to a marketing communication is wasted. The first exposure creates awareness of the product, the second demonstrates its relevance to the consumer, and the third reminds him or her of the product's benefits.[13] However, even this bare-bones approach implies that repetition is needed to ensure that the consumer is actually exposed to (and processes) the message at least three times. As we saw in Chapter 2, this exposure is by no means guaranteed because people tend to tune out or distort many marketing communications. Marketers attempting to condition an association must ensure that the consumers they have targeted will be exposed to the stimulus a sufficient number of times to make it "stick."

However, it is possible to have too much of a good thing. Consumers can become so used to hearing or seeing a marketing stimulus that they no longer pay attention to it. Varying the way in which the basic message is presented can alleviate this problem of **advertising wear-out**. For example, the U.S. tax preparation firm of H&R Block is famous for its long-standing "Another of the 17 reasons to use H&R Block" campaign.

Marketing Applications of Conditioned Product Associations

Advertisements often pair a product with a positive stimulus to create a desirable association. Various aspects of a marketing message, such as music, humor, or imagery, can affect conditioning. In one study, for example, subjects who viewed a slide of pens paired with either pleasant or unpleasant music were more likely later to select the pen that appeared with the pleasant music.[14]

The order in which the conditioned stimulus and the unconditioned stimulus occur also can affect the likelihood that learning will occur. Generally speaking, a marketer should present the conditioned stimulus prior to the unconditioned stimulus. The opposite sequence of *backward conditioning*, such as playing a jingle (the UCS) and then showing a soft drink (the CS), generally is not effective.[15] Because sequential presentation is desirable for conditioning to occur, classical conditioning is not as effective in static situations, for example, in magazine ads where (in contrast to TV or radio) the marketer cannot control the order in which the reader perceives the CS and the UCS.

Because of the danger of extinction, a classical conditioning strategy may not be as effective for products that consumers frequently encounter because there is no guarantee the CS will accompany them. A bottle of Pepsi paired with the refreshing sound of a carbonated beverage being poured over ice may seem like a good application of conditioning. Unfortunately, people would also see the product in many other contexts in which this sound was absent, which reduces the effectiveness of a conditioning strategy.

By the same reasoning, a marketer is better off choosing a novel tune rather than a popular one to pair with a product because people will also hear the popular song in many situations where the product is absent.[16] Music videos in particular may serve as effective UCSs because they often have an emotional impact on viewers, and this effect may transfer to ads accompanying the video.[17]

Marketing Applications of Stimulus Generalization

The process of stimulus generalization often is central to branding and packaging decisions that try to capitalize on consumers' positive associations with an existing brand or company name. We can clearly appreciate the value of this kind of linkage by looking at universities with winning sports teams where loyal fans snap up merchandise, from clothing to bathroom accessories, emblazoned with the school's name. This business did not even exist 20 years ago when schools were reluctant to commercialize their images. Texas A&M was one of the first schools that even bothered to file for trademark protection, and that was only after someone put the Aggie logo on a line of handguns. Today, it's a different story. Many college administrators crave the revenue they receive from sweatshirts, drink coasters, and even toilet seats emblazoned with school logos. Strategies marketers base on stimulus generalization include the following:

- **Family branding**—Many products capitalize on the reputation of a company name. Companies such as Campbell's, Heinz, and General Electric rely on their positive corporate images to sell different product lines.
- **Product line extension**—Marketers add related products to an established brand. Dole, which we associate with fruit, introduced refrigerated juices and juice bars, whereas Sun Maid went from raisins to raisin bread. The gun manufacturer Smith & Wesson launched its own line of furniture and other home items, whereas makers of the two top diaper brands, Huggies and Pampers, are both introducing lines of toiletries for babies and small children. Starbucks Corp. and Jim Beam Brands recently brought out Starbucks Coffee Liqueur. Meanwhile, Procter & Gamble is cleaning up with its Mr. Clean brand of liquid cleanser, aggressively putting the name on new products such as Mr. Clean Magic Eraser, for removing crayon marks from walls and scuff marks from chair rails, and Mr. Clean Autodry, for leaving a freshly washed car spot-free without hand drying.[20]

- **Licensing**—Companies often "rent" well-known names. This strategy is increasing in popularity as marketers try to link their products and services with popular brands or designers. *Prevention* magazine introduced vitamins and *Runners World* magazine puts its name on jogging suits. *Maxim* magazine, which brought out its own brand of hair color for men, is looking at putting its name on nightclubs and frozen food, and *Vibe* magazine produces a line of Vibe sheets as well as greeting cards featuring quotes from the songs of music celebrities. Even New York City firefighters and police got into the act following 9/11 by licensing such products as Billy Blazes Firefighter dolls by Fisher-Price, bottled water, and fire department computer software games by Activision.[21]

- **Look-alike packaging**—Distinctive packaging designs create strong associations with a particular brand. Companies that make generic or private-label brands and want to communicate a quality image often exploit this linkage by putting their products in similar packages to those of popular brands.[22] How does this strategy affect consumers' perceptions of the original brand? One study found that a negative experience with an imitator brand actually *increased* consumers' evaluations of the original brand, whereas a positive experience with the imitator had the opposite effect of decreasing evaluations of the original brand.[23] Another study found that consumers tend to react positively to "copycat brands" as long as the imitator doesn't make grandiose claims that it can't fulfill.[24]

  Of course, this strategy can make a lot of work for lawyers if the copycat brand gets *too* close to the original. Marketers of distinctive brands work hard to protect their designs and logos, and each year companies file numerous lawsuits in so-called *Lanham Act* cases that hinge on the issue of "consumer confusion"; how likely is it that one company's logo, product design, or package is so similar to another that the typical shopper would mistake one for the other? For example, Levi Strauss has sued almost 100 other apparel manufacturers that it claims have borrowed its trademark pocket design of a pentagon surrounding a drawing of a seagull in flight or its distinctive tab that it sews into its garments' vertical seams.[25]

An emphasis on communicating a product's distinctive attributes vis-à-vis its competitors is an important aspect of *positioning*, where consumers learn to differentiate a brand from its competitors (see Chapter 2). This is not always an easy task, especially in product categories in which the brand names of many of the alternatives look and sound alike. This is an issue today in the automotive industry as carmakers have moved away from giving their models unique names such as DeVille, New Yorker, and so on. More recently luxury brands favor combinations of letters and numbers, such as the BMW X5 and Lexus LS 450. Unfortunately, they're starting to run out of unique combinations they can call their own. Take the letter *M*. Mercedes-Benz uses it for its ML-Class sport utility vehicle (SUV). BMW AG's high-performance models are the M3, M5, and M Roadster, whereas Infiniti calls its performance sedan the M45. Toyota makes a sports car it calls the MR2—although in French this sounds a lot like a common vulgarity so in France the car simply goes by MR Coupe. When Infiniti ran commercials in Canada to announce the arrival of a new M, BMW filed a lawsuit claiming that Infiniti's use of the M in the commercial could cause confusion with BMW's M series. Infiniti also found itself on the other end of a dispute over the letter *Q*. Since 1989, Infiniti has had a sedan called the Q45; according to a Nissan executive, "We liked the shape of the letter. We thought it was unique and had more presence than other letters." More recently, an Audi unit named a new SUV the Q7, taking the letter from its "quattro" all-wheel drive technology. This time it was Nissan that filed the lawsuit (Nissan and Audi eventually settled the case). All told, automakers have used 22 of the alphabet's 26 letters, so stimulus discrimination in this realm is getting harder to achieve (apparently they don't use the remaining letters *O, P, U,* and *Y* because drivers perceive them as being too ordinary for luxury cars).[26]

Companies with a well-established brand image try to encourage stimulus discrimination by promoting the unique attributes of their brand—hence the constant

These semantic combinations are getting harder to find, so some consultants appeal to our more basic instincts by focusing on linkages between the raw sounds of vowels and consonants (*phonemes*) and emotional responses. Studies on sound symbolism show that respondents who speak different languages associate the same sounds with such emotion-laden qualities as sad and insecure, alive and daring. To get at these associations, researchers usually give subjects pairs of nonsense names that differ in only a single phoneme, for example, *paressa* and *taressa*, and ask which sounds faster, more daring, nicer, and so on. They've found that sounds that come to a full stop (/p/, /b/, /t/, /d/) connote slowness, whereas the /f/, /v/, /s/, and /z/ sounds seem faster. Prozac and Amazon convey a sense of speed (of recovery or of delivery). When naming consultants got the assignment to label a new handheld personal digital assistant (PDA,) they first thought of Strawberry because the little keyboard buttons resembled seeds. They liked the "berry" part of the name because they knew that people associated the letter *b* with reliability and a berry communicated smallness compared to other PDAs. But a linguist pointed out that "straw" is a slow syllable and the product needed to have a fast connotation. Voila! The BlackBerry PDA was born.[19]

reminders for American Express Traveler's Checks: "Ask for them by name." However, a brand name that a firm uses so widely that it is no longer distinctive becomes part of the public domain and competitors are free to borrow it—think of well-worn names such as aspirin, cellophane, yo-yo, and escalator.

Another big problem arises when fake products masquerade as the real thing. The International Anticounterfeiting Coalition, an industry group that combats piracy, estimates that trademark counterfeiting robs the United States of $200 billion annually.[27] "A 2005 study found that one-third of all music CDs in the world are pirated versions, and in 31 countries the fake ones outsell the real ones."[28]

As Chinese marketers continue to develop new domestic products, some knock off familiar brand names as well. When executives at Shanghai Automotive Industry Corp. failed in their bid to buy the celebrated Rover brand name for a line of cars they are introducing, they called them Roewe instead. Honda Motor Co. successfully sued a Chinese motorcycle maker for using the name Hongda. More recently, though, a Chinese company called Chery is preparing to export a car to the United States—the company claims the resemblance to Chevy is just a coincidence as its English name derives from the sound of its Chinese name, Qirui, pronounced *che-ray*, which means, "unusually lucky." That argument is a bit harder to make for a wireless e-mail service another Chinese company calls "Redberry."[29]

INSTRUMENTAL CONDITIONING

Instrumental conditioning (or *operant conditioning)* occurs when we learn to perform behaviors that produce positive outcomes and avoid those that yield negative outcomes. We most closely associate this learning process with the psychologist B. F. Skinner, who demonstrated the effects of instrumental conditioning by teaching pigeons and other animals to dance, play Ping-Pong, and perform other activities by systematically rewarding them for desired behaviors.[30]

Whereas responses in classical conditioning are involuntary and fairly simple, we make those in instrumental conditioning deliberately to obtain a goal, and may be more complex. We may learn the desired behavior over a period of time as a **shaping** process rewards our intermediate actions. For example, the owner of a new store may award prizes to shoppers simply for coming in, hoping that over time they will continue to drop in and eventually even buy something.

Also, whereas classical conditioning involves the close pairing of two stimuli, instrumental learning occurs when a learner receives a reward *after* she performs the desired behavior. Learning takes place over time, while the learner attempts and abandons other behaviors that don't get reinforced. A good way to remember the difference is to keep in mind that in instrumental learning the person makes a response because it is *instrumental* in gaining a reward or avoiding a punishment. Over time, consumers come to associate with people who reward them and to choose products that make them feel good or satisfy some need.

Instrumental conditioning occurs in one of three ways:

1 When the environment provides **positive reinforcement** in the form of a reward, this strengthens the response and we learn the appropriate behavior. For example, a woman who gets compliments after wearing Obsession perfume learns that using this product has the desired effect, and she will be more likely to keep buying the product.

2 **Negative reinforcement** also strengthens responses so that we learn the appropriate behavior. A perfume company might run an ad showing a woman sitting home alone on a Saturday night because she did not wear its fragrance. The message this conveys is that she could have avoided this negative outcome if only she had used the perfume.

3 In contrast to situations where we learn to do certain things in order to avoid unpleasantness, **punishment** occurs when unpleasant events follow a response

(such as when our friends ridicule us if we wear a nasty-smelling perfume)—we learn the hard way not to repeat these behaviors.

To help you understand the differences among these mechanisms, keep in mind that reactions from a person's environment to his behavior can be either positive or negative and that marketers can either apply or remove these outcomes (or anticipated outcomes). That is, under conditions of both positive reinforcement and punishment, the person receives a reaction after doing something. In contrast, negative reinforcement occurs when the person avoids a negative outcome—the removal of something negative is pleasurable and hence is rewarding.

Finally, when a person no longer receives a positive outcome, *extinction* is likely to occur, and the learned stimulus–response connection will not be maintained (as when a woman no longer receives compliments on her perfume). Thus, positive and negative reinforcement strengthen the future linkage between a response and an outcome because of the pleasant experience. This tie is weakened under conditions of both punishment and extinction because of the unpleasant experience. Figure 3.2 will help you to "reinforce" the relationships among these four conditions.

Determining the most effective reinforcement schedule to use with consumers is important to marketers because it relates to the amount of effort and resources they must devote to rewarding desired behaviors. Several schedules are possible:

● **Fixed-interval reinforcement**—After a specified time period has passed, the first response you make brings the reward. Under such conditions, people tend to respond slowly right after being reinforced, but their responses get faster as the time for the next reinforcement approaches. For example, consumers may crowd into a store for the last day of its seasonal sale and not reappear until the next one.

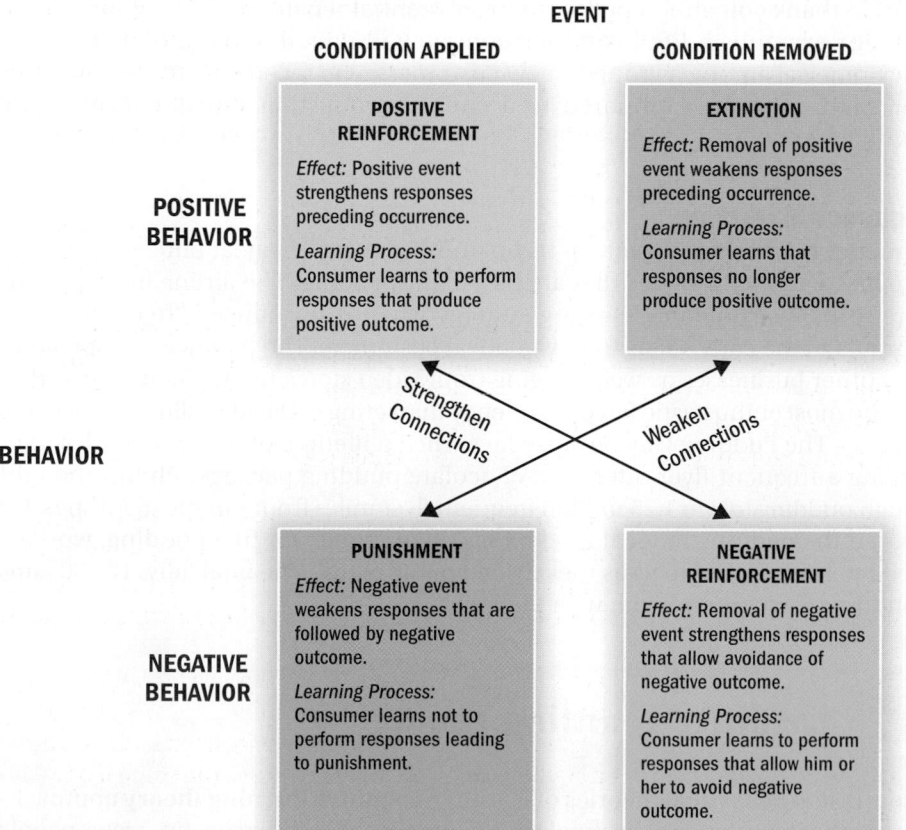

■ **FIGURE 3.2**
TYPES OF REINFORCEMENT

● **Variable-interval reinforcement**—The time that must pass before you get reinforced varies based on some average. Because you don't know exactly when to expect the reinforcement, you have to respond at a consistent rate. This is the logic behind retailers' use of so-called *secret shoppers*, who are people who periodically test for service quality by posing as customers at unannounced times. Because store employees never know exactly when to expect a visit, they must maintain high quality constantly "just in case."

● **Fixed-ratio reinforcement**—Reinforcement occurs only after a fixed number of responses. This schedule motivates you to continue performing the same behavior over and over. For example, you might keep buying groceries at the same store in order to earn a prize after collecting 50 register receipts.

● **Variable-ratio reinforcement**—You get reinforced after a certain number of responses, but you don't know how many responses are required. People in such situations tend to respond at very high and steady rates, and this type of behavior is very difficult to extinguish. This reinforcement schedule is responsible for consumers' attractions to slot machines. They learn that if they keep throwing money into the machine, they will eventually win something (if they don't go broke first).

MARKETING APPLICATIONS OF INSTRUMENTAL CONDITIONING PRINCIPLES

Principles of instrumental conditioning are at work when a marketer rewards or punishes a consumer for a purchase decision. Businesspeople shape behavior by gradually reinforcing the appropriate actions consumers take. For example, a car dealer might encourage a reluctant buyer to simply sit in a floor model, then suggest a test drive, and then try to close the deal.

Marketers have many ways to reinforce consumers' behaviors, ranging from a simple thank you after a purchase to substantial rebates and follow-up phone calls. For example, a life insurance company obtained a much higher rate of policy renewal among a group of new customers who received a thank you letter after each payment, compared to a control group that did not receive any reinforcement.[31]

Frequency Marketing

Frequency marketing is a popular technique that rewards regular purchasers by giving them prizes with values that are based on spending. The airline industry pioneered this instrumental learning strategy when it introduced "frequent flyer" programs in the early 1980s to reward loyal customers. The practice has spread to many other businesses as well, ranging from video stores to fast-food places. Perhaps the most enthusiastic fan of frequency marketing is David Phillips. He became known as The Pudding Guy because he earned a lifetime of free plane rides after noticing a frequent flyer offer on a chocolate pudding package. Phillips bought enough pudding to win 1.25 million frequent flyer miles from American Airlines. He donated the pudding to local food banks; in exchange for free pudding, workers agreed to peel off the labels as they dished out the stuff. The final tally: 12,150 cups of pudding.[32] Whipped cream with that?

 # Cognitive Learning Theory

In contrast to behavioral theories of learning, **cognitive learning theory** approaches stress the importance of internal mental processes. This perspective views people as problem solvers who actively use information from the world around them to

It's natural to want to be rewarded.

master their environments. Supporters of this view also stress the role of creativity and insight during the learning process.

An Ocean Spray commercial for diet cranberry juice illustrates how marketers can harness their knowledge of cognitive theories to tweak marketing messages. The spot features two men, in the role of cranberry growers, standing knee-deep in a bog. A group of women who are exercising joins them. Originally, the ad depicted the women having a party, but a cognitive scientist who worked on the campaign nixed that idea; she argued that the exercise class would send the diet message more quickly, whereas the party scene would confuse viewers who would spend too much time trying to figure out why the group was celebrating. This extra cognitive activity would distract from the ad's message. And, contrary to standard practice in advertising that the actors name the product as early as possible, she decided that the main characters should wait a few seconds before mentioning the new diet product. She reasoned that viewers would need a second or so more time to process the images because of the additional action in the ad (the exercising). In a test of which ads get remembered best, this new version scored in the top 10 percent.[33]

IS LEARNING CONSCIOUS OR NOT?

A lot of controversy surrounds the issue of whether or when people are aware of their learning processes.[34] Whereas behavioral learning theorists emphasize the routine, automatic nature of conditioning, proponents of cognitive learning argue that even these simple effects are based on cognitive factors: They create expectations that a response will follow a stimulus (the formation of expectations requires mental activity). According to this school of thought, conditioning occurs because subjects develop conscious hypotheses and then act on them.

There is some evidence supporting the existence of *nonconscious procedural knowledge.* People apparently do process at least some information in an automatic, passive way, a condition researchers call "mindlessness" (we've all experienced that!).[35] When we meet someone new or encounter a new product, for example, we have a tendency to respond to the stimulus in terms of existing categories we have learned, rather than taking the trouble to formulate new ones. In these cases a *trigger feature*, some stimulus that cues us toward a particular pattern, activates a reaction. For example, men in one study rated a car in an ad as superior on a variety of characteristics if a seductive woman (the trigger feature) was present, despite the fact that the men did not believe the woman's presence actually had an influence on their evaluations.[36]

Another recent study also illustrates this process. Undergraduates who were on their way to participate in a psychology experiment "accidentally" encountered a laboratory assistant who was laden with textbooks, a clipboard, papers and a cup of hot or iced coffee—and asked for a hand with the cup. Guess what? The students who held a cup of iced coffee rated a hypothetical person they later read about as much colder, less social, and more selfish than did their fellow students who had helped out by holding a cup of hot coffee. Other researchers report similar findings; people tidy up more thoroughly when there's a faint tang of cleaning liquid in the air and they act more competitively if there's a briefcase in the room. In each case they change their behavior without being aware of doing so.[37] Indeed, a controversial bestselling book, *Blink: The Power of Thinking without Thinking,* argues that we often make snap judgments that result in superior decisions compared to those we think about a lot because we rely on our "adaptive unconscious" to guide us.[38]

Nonetheless, many modern theorists are beginning to regard some instances of automatic conditioning as cognitive processes, especially where expectations are formed about the linkages between stimuli and responses. Indeed, studies using *masking effects,* which make it difficult for subjects to learn CS/UCS associations, show substantial reductions in conditioning.[39] An adolescent girl may observe that women on television and in real life seem to be rewarded with compliments and attention when they smell nice and wear alluring clothing. She figures out that the probability of these rewards occurring is greater when she wears perfume, so she deliberately wears a popular scent to obtain the reward of social acceptance.

OBSERVATIONAL LEARNING

Observational learning occurs when people watch the actions of others and note the reinforcements they receive for their behaviors—learning occurs as a result of *vicarious* rather than direct experience. This type of learning is a complex process; people store these observations in memory as they accumulate knowledge, perhaps using this information at a later point to guide their own behavior. **Modeling** (not the runway kind) is the process of imitating the behavior of others. For example, a woman shopping for a new kind of perfume may remember the reactions her friend received on wearing a certain brand several months earlier, and she will mimic her friend's behavior with the hope of getting the same feedback.

■ **FIGURE 3.3** THE OBSERVATIONAL LEARNING PROCESS

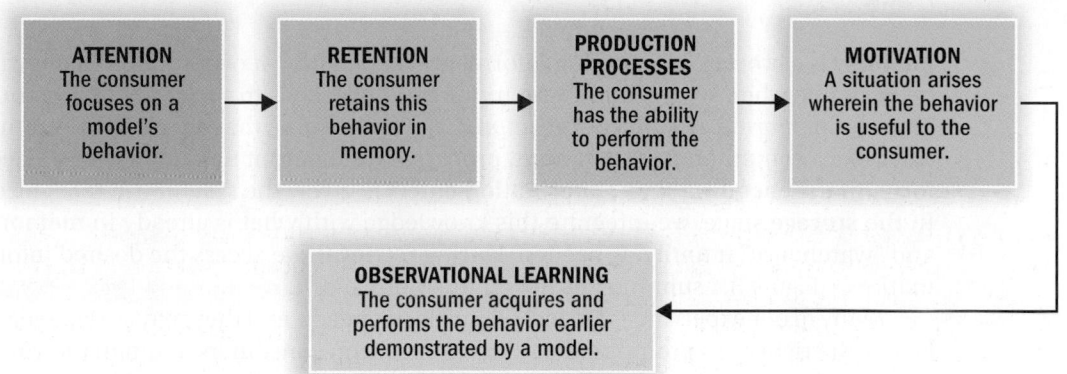

The modeling process is a powerful form of learning, and people's tendencies to imitate others' behaviors can have negative effects. Of particular concern is the potential of television shows and movies to teach violence to children. Children may be exposed to new methods of aggression by models (e.g., cartoon heroes) in the shows they watch. At some later point, when the child becomes angry, he may imitate these behaviors. A classic study demonstrates the effect of modeling on children's actions. Kids who watched an adult stomp on, knock down, and otherwise torture a large inflated "Bobo doll" repeated these behaviors when later left alone in a room with the doll; children who did not witness these acts did not.[40] Unfortunately, the relevance of this study to violent TV shows seems quite clear.

Figure 3.3 shows that in order for observational learning in the form of modeling to occur, four conditions must be met:[41]

1 The consumer's attention must be directed to the appropriate model, whom, for reasons of attractiveness, competence, status, or similarity, he must want to emulate.
2 The consumer must remember what the model says or does.
3 The consumer must convert this information into actions.
4 The consumer must be motivated to perform these actions.

MARKETING APPLICATIONS OF COGNITIVE LEARNING PRINCIPLES

The ability to learn vicariously by observing how others' behaviors are reinforced makes the lives of marketers much easier. Because people do not have to be directly reinforced for their actions, marketers don't necessarily have to actually reward or punish consumers for purchase behaviors (think how expensive or even ethically questionable that might be!). Instead, they can show what happens to desirable models who use or do not use their products, knowing that consumers often will be motivated to imitate these actions at a later time. For example, a perfume commercial might depict a woman surrounded by a throng of admirers who are providing her with positive reinforcement for using the product. Needless to say, this learning process is more practical than providing the same attention to each woman who actually buys the perfume!

Consumers' evaluations of the people they model go beyond simple stimulus–response connections. For example, a celebrity's image elicits more than a simple reflexive response of good or bad.[42] It is a complex combination of many attributes. In general, the degree to which a person emulates someone else depends on that model's level of *social attractiveness*. Attractiveness can be based on several components, including physical appearance, expertise, or similarity to the evaluator (more on this in Chapter 8).

Memory

Memory is a process of acquiring information and storing it over time so that it will be available when we need it. Contemporary approaches to the study of memory employ an *information-processing approach*. They assume that the mind is in some ways like a computer: Data are input, processed, and output for later use in revised form. In the **encoding** stage, information enters in a way the system will recognize. In the **storage** stage, we integrate this knowledge with what is already in memory and "warehouse" it until it is needed. During **retrieval,** we access the desired information.[43] Figure 3.4 summarizes the memory process.

Many of our experiences are locked inside our heads, and they may surface years later if the right cues prompt them. Marketers rely on consumers to retain information they have obtained about products and services, trusting they will apply it to future purchase decisions. During the *consumer decision-making process* (which we will learn about in detail in Chapter 9), we combine this *internal memory* with *external memory*. This includes all of the product details on packages and other marketing stimuli that permit us to identify and evaluate brand alternatives in the marketplace.[44]

The grocery shopping list is a good example of a powerful external memory aid. When consumers use shopping lists, they buy approximately 80 percent of the items on the list. And the likelihood of a shopper purchasing a particular list item is higher if the person who wrote the list also participates in the shopping trip. This means that, if marketers can induce a consumer to plan to purchase an item before she goes shopping, there is a high probability she will buy it. One way to encourage this kind of advance planning is to provide peel-off stickers on packages so that, when the consumer notices the supply is low, she can simply peel off the label and place it directly on a shopping list.[45]

HOW INFORMATION GETS ENCODED

The way we *encode*, or mentally program, information helps to determine how we will represent it in memory. In general, we have a better chance of retaining incoming data we associate with other information already in memory. For example, we tend to remember brand names we link to physical characteristics of a product category (e.g., Coffee-Mate creamer or Sani-Flush toilet bowl cleaner) or that we can easily visualize (e.g., Tide detergent or Ford Mustang cars) compared to more abstract brand names.[46]

Today, one of the biggest memory problems relates to our need to retain the numerous passwords we have to remember to function in our high-tech society. In fact, one in nine consumers keeps his passwords written down in electronic form—making the whole system so insecure that federal regulators require online banks to add more layers of authentication. A company called Cogneto recently introduced a new service aimed at eliminating passwords by substituting what it calls "passthoughts." These are based on how each unique person's memory works. The company's software asks you some personal questions and then it looks at how you answered (How long did you take? Where did your cursor hover while responding?) to create retrieval cues you won't need to actively remember.[47]

■ **FIGURE 3.4** THE MEMORY PROCESS

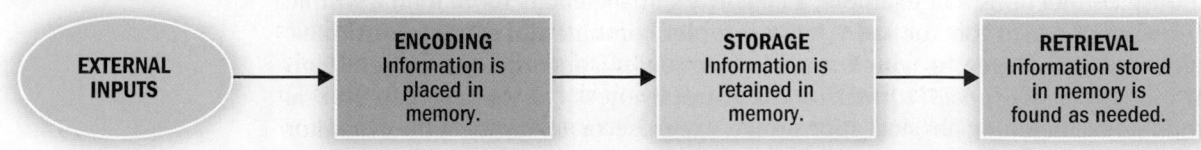

Rocky Road, a classic candy product, uses a brief narrative to remind consumers of its long-lasting value.

Types of Meaning

Sometimes we process a stimulus simply in terms of its *sensory meaning*, such as the literal color or shape of a package. We may experience a feeling of familiarity when, for example, we see an ad for a new snack food we have recently tasted. In many cases, though, we encode meanings at a more abstract level. *Semantic meaning* refers to symbolic associations, such as the idea that rich people drink champagne or that fashionable women have navel piercings. Let's take a closer look at how we might encode these deeper meanings.

Personal Relevance

Episodic memories relate to events that are personally relevant.[48] As a result, a person's motivation to retain these memories will likely be strong. Couples often have "their song," which reminds them of their first date or wedding. We call some especially vivid associations *flashbulb memories* (for example, where were you when you first heard about the attack on The World Trade Center?). And recall of the past may affect future behavior. For example, a college fund-raising campaign can raise more money by evoking pleasant college memories than it can by being neutral or reminding participants of unpleasant ones.

One method of conveying product information is through a **narrative** or story. Much of the social information we acquire gets represented in memory in story form, so constructing ads in the form of a narrative can be a very effective technique for resonating with consumers. Narratives persuade people to construct mental representations of the information that they are viewing. Pictures aid in this construction and allow for a more developed and detailed mental representation.[49] Research supports the idea that we are more likely to positively evaluate and purchase brands when they connect with us like this.[50]

MEMORY SYSTEMS

According to the information-processing perspective, there are three distinct memory systems: *sensory memory*, *short-term memory (STM)*, and *long-term memory (LTM)*. Each plays a role in processing brand-related information. Figure 3.5 summarizes the interrelationships among these memory systems.

Sensory Memory

Sensory memory permits storage of the information we receive from our senses. This storage is very temporary; it lasts a couple of seconds at most. For example, a man walking past a donut shop gets a quick, enticing whiff of something baking inside. Although this sensation lasts only a few seconds, it is sufficient to allow him to consider whether he should investigate further. If he retains this information for further processing, it passes through an **attentional gate** and transfers to short-term memory.

CB AS I SEE IT

Professor Jennifer Edson Escalas
Vanderbilt University

Although a great deal of research in cognitive psychology has examined how people process information, form mental categories, encode and retrieve information, and so forth, only recently has there been an interest in narrative thought. Scholars use the analogy of science and literature to propose two different modes of thought: the rigorous world of logical deduction, called *paradigmatic thought*, and the imprecise world of aesthetic intentions, called *narrative thought* (Bruner, 1986), which is the subject of this discussion. Using narrative thought, we create stories that are coherent accounts of particular experiences that are temporally structured and context sensitive (Baumeister and Newman, 1994). The narrative mode of thought does not necessitate that individuals form elaborate, complex novels in their minds. Rather, under conditions of narrative processing, people think about incoming information as if they were trying to create a story. In day-to-day living, individuals continuously attempt to impose narrative structure on occurrences in order to understand them. Narrative processing helps individuals organize and understand situations, others, and themselves.

An important aspect of narrative thought is its structure, which consists of two important elements: chronology and causality. First, narrative thought organizes events in terms of a temporal dimension; things occur over time. Time is configured in narratives as episodes, whereas time in reality is an undifferentiated, continuous flow. The human perception of events with beginnings, middles, and ends, known as experienced time, is structured time.

Second, narrative thought structures elements into an organized framework that establishes relationships between the story's elements and allows for causal inferencing. Narrative story organization incorporates general knowledge about human goal-oriented action sequences; events are organized according to the causal and intentional relations among them. In stories, actors engage in actions to achieve goals. Because narrative elements are organized through time, causal inferences can be made. What happens in time 1 (for example, the protagonist feels jealous) causes what happens in time 2 (he kills his rival).

My research stream examines the role of narrative processing in response to advertisements, focusing on how narratives persuade consumers. Narrative processing has been shown to affect persuasion through a mechanism called *transportation*, which is defined as "immersion into a text" (Green and Brock, 2000, p. 702; Gerrig, 1994). Whereas "elaboration leads to attitude change via logical consideration and

■ **FIGURE 3.5**   THE MEMORY PROCESS

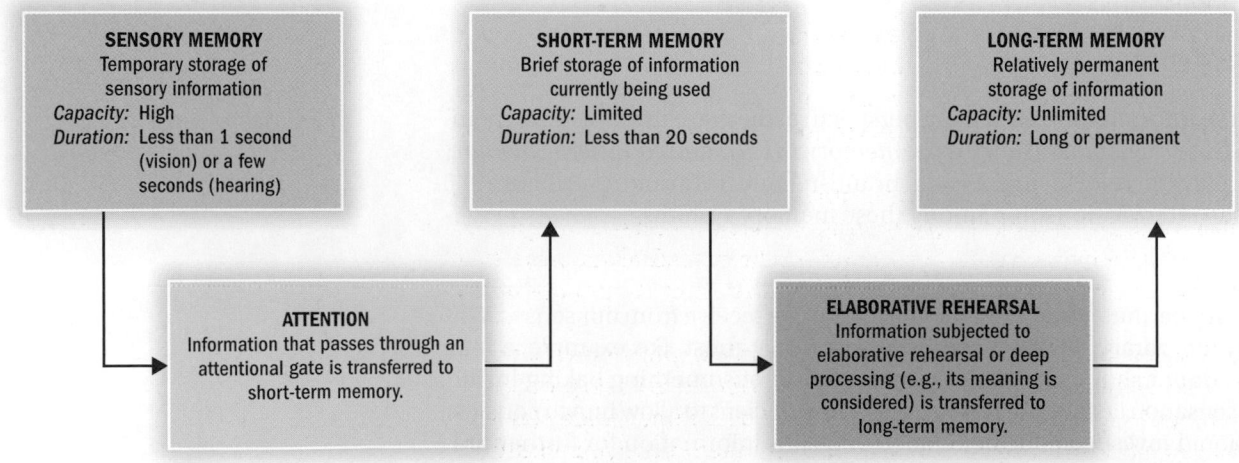

evaluation of arguments," transportation leads to persuasion through reduced negative cognitive responding, realism of experience, and strong affective responses (Green and Brock, 2000, p. 702). Thus, an ad that tells a story does not rely on logical arguments to persuade the viewer to buy the product, but rather narrative ads resonate with the ad viewer, enhance character identification, capture the viewer's attention, and draw him or her into an ad (transporting the viewer into the story). The story format is more persuasive because it creates an emotional response. It has been argued that emotions, such as warm feelings, arise in reaction to people or situations (Aaker, Stayman, and Hagerty, 1986). Narratives provide the characters and situations necessary to evoke positive feelings, which, in turn, spill over onto the brand being advertised.

Because people naturally create meaning in the world based on stories, it is logical to assume that advertising narratives will help create brand meaning for consumers. Narrative research has shown that people are very good at establishing relationships among story elements and extrapolating meaning (Carr, 1986; Polkinghorne, 1991). Thus, a story ad that provides a brand with a series of linkages to certain types of characters, settings, and usage scenarios creates meaning for that brand. Consumers come to understand how and appreciate how the brand is to be used based on an advertising narrative. In this sense, narrative ads can serve as "generic plots" that actually frame or influence subsequent consumption experiences with the brand. The stories present usage scenarios that may serve as templates enabling consumers to evaluate and make sense of their later experiences with the brand. Many consumer behavior researchers have alluded to the power of stories in guiding and constructing subsequent consumption experiences. For example, Puto and Wells (1984) assert that transformational ads can "transform" product usage experiences, and Deighton (1984) argues that advertising suggests a hypothesis for consumers regarding what their consumption experiences will be like. Finally, because people often think of themselves in the form of narratives, narrative thought may create a link between the brand and the self, which contributes to a brand's meaning and value.

Referenced Works

Aaker, D., Stayman, D. M., and Hagerty, M. R. (1986), "Warmth in Advertising: Measurement, Impact, and Sequence Effects," *Journal of Consumer Research, 12*(4):365–81.

Baumeister, R. F., and Newman, L. S. (1994), "How Stories Make Sense of Personal Experiences: Motives that Shape Autobiographical Narratives," *Personality and Social Psychology Bulletin, 20*(6):676–90.

Bruner, J. (1986), *Actual Minds, Possible Worlds* (Cambridge, MA: Harvard University Press).

Carr, D. (1986), *Time, Narrative, and History* (Bloomington: Indiana University Press),

Deighton, J. (1984), "The Interaction of Advertising and Evidence," *Journal of Consumer Research, 11*(3): 763–70.

Gerrig, Richard J. (1994), "Narrative Thought?" *Personality and Social Psychology Bulletin, 20*(6):712–15.

Green, Melanie C., and Brock, Timothy C. (2000), "The Role of Transportation in the Persuasiveness of Public Narratives," *Journal of Personality and Social Psychology, 79*(5):701–21.

Polkinghorne, D. E. (1991), "Narrative and Self-Concept," *Journal of Narrative and Life History, 1*(2 & 3):135–53.

Puto, C. P., and Wells, W. D. (1984), "Informational and Transformational Advertising: The Differential Effects of Time," in Kinnear, T. C., ed.. *Advances in Consumer Research,* 11 (Proto, UT: Association for Consumer Research): 572–76.

Short-Term Memory

Short-term memory (STM) also stores information for a limited period of time, and it has limited capacity. Similar to a computer, we can think about this system as *working memory*; it holds the information we are currently processing. Our memories can store verbal input *acoustically* (in terms of how it sounds) or *semantically* (in terms of what it means).

We store this information by combining small pieces into larger ones in a process we call **chunking**. A chunk is a configuration that is familiar to the person and that he can think about as a unit. For example, a brand name such as Glade can be a chunk that summarizes a great deal of detailed information about the product.

Initially, researchers believed that our STM was capable of processing between five and nine chunks of information at a time—they described this basic property as "the magical number 7+/−2". This is the reason our phone numbers today (at least in the United States) have seven digits.[51] It now appears that three to four chunks is the optimal size for efficient retrieval (we remember seven-digit phone numbers

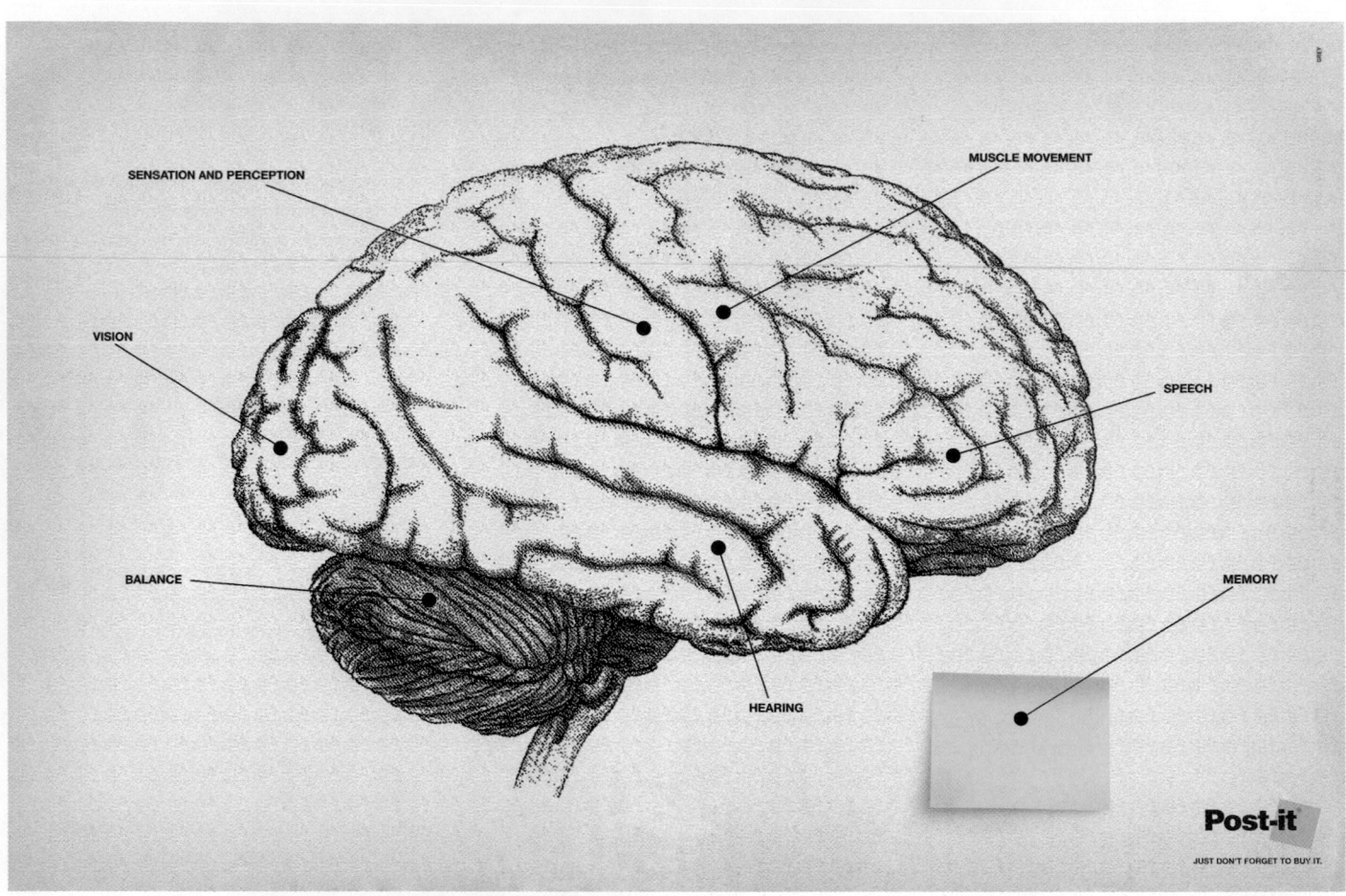

This Brazilian ad illustrates that external memory aids like Post-its can help us to remember many of the details of modern life.

because we chunk the individual digits, so we may remember a three-digit exchange as one piece of information).[52] Phone calls aside, chunking is important to marketers because it helps determine how consumers keep prices in short-term memory when they comparison shop.[53]

Long-Term Memory

Long-term memory (LTM) is the system that allows us to retain information for a long period of time. A cognitive process we call **elaborative rehearsal** allows information to move from short-term memory into long-term memory. This involves thinking about the meaning of a stimulus and relating it to other information already in memory. Marketers sometimes assist in the process by devising catchy slogans or jingles that consumers repeat on their own.

STORING INFORMATION IN MEMORY

Relationships among the types of memory are a source of some controversy. The traditional perspective, known as *multiple-store*, assumes that STM and LTM are separate systems. More recent research has moved away from the distinction between the two types of memory, emphasizing instead the interdependence of the systems. According to this work, depending on the nature of the processing task, different levels of processing occur that activate some aspects of memory rather than others. We call these approaches **activation models of memory**.[54] The more effort it takes to process information (so-called "deep processing"), the more likely it is that information will transfer into long-term memory.

Associative Networks

According to activation models, an incoming piece of information is stored in an **associative network** containing many bits of related information organized based on some set of relationships. We each have organized systems of concepts relating to brands, manufacturers, and stores stored in our memories; the contents, of course, depend on our own unique experiences.

Think of these storage units, or *knowledge structures*, as complex spider webs filled with pieces of data. Incoming information gets put into nodes that are linked with one another. When we view separate pieces of information as similar for some reason, we chunk them together under some more abstract category. Then, we interpret new, incoming information to be consistent with the structure we have created (recall the discussion in Chapter 2 about how prior expectations influence current experiences).[55] This helps explain why we are better able to remember brands or stores that we believe "go together," for example, when Spalding rather than Chanel sponsors a golf tournament. Recent research indicates that people can recall brands that are not as obviously linked (for example, when an unlikely product sponsors an event), but to do so marketers have to work hard to explain the linked relationship.[56]

In the associative network, links form between nodes. For example, a consumer might have a network for "perfumes." Each node represents a concept related to the category. This node can be an attribute, a specific brand, a celebrity the consumer identifies with a specific perfume brand, or even a related product. A network for perfumes might include concepts such as the names Chanel, Obsession, and CKOne, as well as attributes such as sexy and elegant.

When we ask the consumer to list perfumes, this consumer recalls only those brands contained in the appropriate category. This group constitutes her **evoked set**. The task of a new entrant that wants to position itself as a category member (e.g., a new luxury perfume) is to provide cues that facilitate its placement in the appropriate category. Figure 3.6 shows a sample network for perfumes.

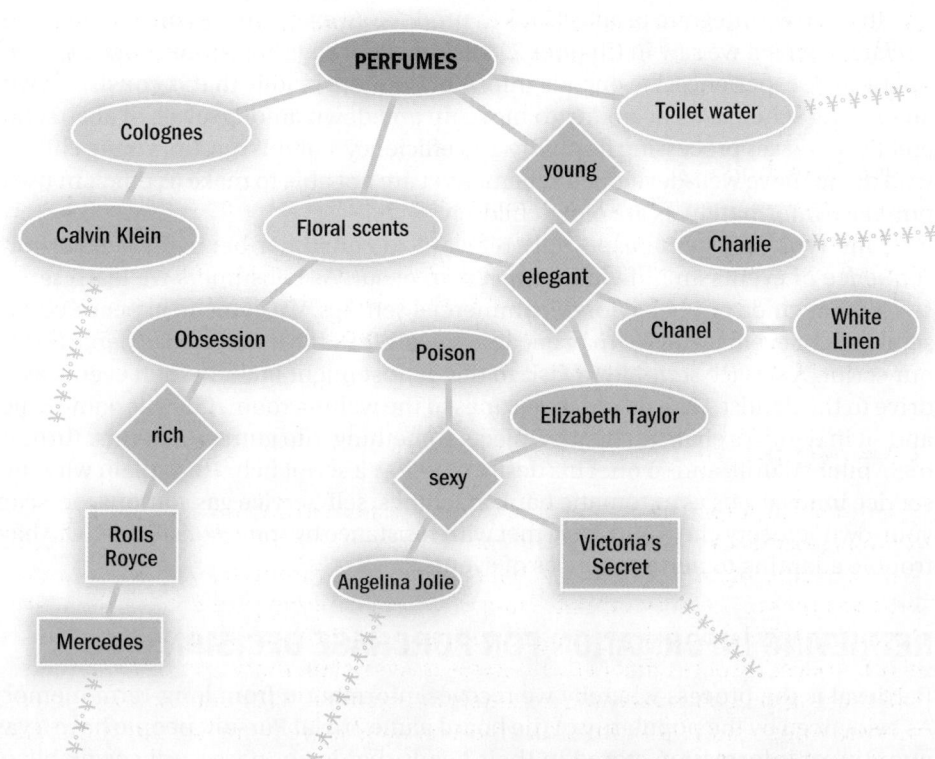

■ FIGURE 3.6

AN ASSOCIATIVE NETWORK FOR PERFUMES

SPREADING ACTIVATION

A marketing message may activate our memory of a brand directly (for example, by showing us a picture of it) or it may do so indirectly by linking to something else that's related to the brand in our knowledge structure. If it activates a node, it will also activate other linked nodes much as tapping a spider's web in one spot sends movement reverberating across the web. Meaning thus spreads across the network, and we recall concepts, such as competing brands and relevant attributes, that we use to form attitudes toward the brand.

This process of **spreading activation** allows us to shift back and forth among levels of meaning. The way we store a piece of information in memory depends on the type of meaning we initially assign to it. This meaning type, in turn, will determine how and when something activates the meaning. For example, we could store the memory trace for an Axe men's fragrance ad in one or more of the following ways:

- **Brand-specific**—Memory is stored in terms of claims the brand makes ("it's macho").
- **Ad-specific**—Memory is stored in terms of the medium or content of the ad itself (a macho-looking guy uses the product).
- **Brand identification**—Memory is stored in terms of the brand name (e.g., "Axe").
- **Product category**—Memory is stored in terms of how the product works or where it should be used (a can of Axe sits in a guy's medicine cabinet).
- **Evaluative reactions**—Memory is stored as positive or negative emotions ("that looks cool").[57]

Levels of Knowledge

Within a knowledge structure we code elements at different levels of abstraction and complexity. *Meaning* concepts (such as "macho") get stored as individual nodes. We may combine these concepts into a larger unit we call a *proposition* (or a *belief*). A proposition links two nodes together to form a more complex meaning, which can serve as a single chunk of information. For example, "Axe is cologne for macho men" is a proposition (not necessarily a correct one!).

In turn, we integrate propositions to produce an even more complex unit called a *schema*, which we saw in Chapter 2. A schema is a cognitive framework we develop through experience. We encode information more readily that is consistent with an existing schema.[58] The ability to move up and down among levels of abstraction greatly increases processing flexibility and efficiency. For this reason, young children who do not have well-developed schemas yet are not able to make as efficient use of purchase information as are older children.[59]

One type of schema especially relevant to consumer behavior is a **script**, a sequence of events an individual expects to occur. As consumers we learn *service scripts* that guide our behavior in commercial settings. We come to expect a certain sequence of events, and we may become uncomfortable if the service departs from our script. A service script for a visit to the dentist might include such events as (1) drive to the dentist, (2) read old magazines in the waiting room, (3) hear name called and sit in dentist's chair, (4) dentist injects something into gums, (5) dentist turns on high-pitched drill, and so on. This desire to follow a script helps to explain why such service innovations as automatic bank machines, self-service gas stations, or "scan-your-own" grocery checkouts have met with resistance by some consumers who have trouble adapting to new sequences of events.[60]

RETRIEVING INFORMATION FOR PURCHASE DECISIONS

Retrieval is the process whereby we recover information from long-term memory. As evidenced by the popularity of the board game Trivial Pursuit, people have a vast quantity of information stored in their heads that is not necessarily available on demand. Although most of the information that enters our long-term memory does not go away, it may be difficult or impossible to retrieve unless the appropriate cues are present.

Factors That Influence Retrieval

Individual cognitive or physiological factors are responsible for some of the differences we see in retrieval ability among people.[61] Some older adults consistently display inferior recall ability for current items, such as prescription drug instructions, although they may recall events that happened to them when they were younger with great clarity.[62] The recent popularity of puzzles, such as Soduku, and centers that offer "mental gymnastics" attests to emerging evidence that we can keep our retrieval abilities sharp by exercising our minds just as we keep our other muscles toned by working out on a regular basis.

Other factors that influence retrieval are situational; they relate to the environment in which the message is delivered. Not surprisingly, recall is enhanced when we pay more attention to the message in the first place. Some evidence indicates that we can retrieve information about a *pioneering brand* (the first brand to enter a market) more easily from memory than we can for *follower brands* because the first product's introduction is likely to be distinctive and, for the time being, no competitors divert our attention.[63] In addition, we are more likely to recall descriptive brand names than those that do not provide adequate cues as to what the product is.[64]

Not surprisingly, the way a marketer presents her message influences the likelihood we'll be able to recall it later. The **spacing effect** describes the tendency for us to recall printed material more effectively when the advertiser repeats the target item periodically rather than presenting it repeatedly in a short time period.[65] The viewing environment of a marketing message also affects recall. For example, commercials we see during baseball games yield the lowest recall scores among sports programs because the activity is stop-and-go rather than continuous. Unlike football or basketball, the pacing of baseball gives many opportunities for attention to wander even during play. Similarly, General Electric found that its commercials fared better in television shows with continuous activity, such as stories or dramas, compared to variety shows or talk shows that are punctuated by a series of acts.[66] Finally, a large-scale analysis of TV commercials found that viewers recall commercials shown first in a series of ads better than those they see last.[67]

Some advertisers today are experimenting with **bitcoms** that try to boost viewers' retention of a set of ads inserted within a TV show (we call this a *commercial pod*). In a typical bitcom, when the pod starts, a stand-up comedian (perhaps an actor in the show itself) performs a small set that leads into the actual ads. This is one way that marketers are trying to integrate a show's contents with commercial messages and increase viewers' involvement with advertising.[68]

Finally, it goes without saying that the nature of the ad itself plays a big role in determining whether it's memorable. One recent study on print advertising reported that we are far more likely to remember spectacular magazine ads, including multipage spreads, three-dimensional pop-ups, scented ads, and ads with audio components. For example, a Pepsi Jazz two-page spread with a three-dimensional pop-up of the opened bottle and a small audio chip that played jazz music from the bottle's opening as well as a scratch-and-sniff tab that let readers smell its black cherry vanilla flavor scored an amazing 100 percent in reader recall.[69] Unfortunately, that kind of multimedia treatment is very expensive; not every ad can mimic a Broadway production!

State-Dependent Retrieval

Is it true that you'll do better on an exam if you study for it in the classroom in which you'll take the test? Perhaps. The process we call **state-dependent retrieval** illustrates that we are better able to access information if our internal state is the same at the time of recall as when we learned the information. So, we are more likely to recall an ad if our mood or level of arousal at the time of exposure is similar to that in the purchase environment. Re-creating the cues that were present when the information was first presented can enhance recall. In America, for example, Life cereal uses a picture of "Mikey" from its commercial on the cereal box, which facilitates recall of brand claims and favorable brand evaluations.[70]

Familiarity and Recall

As a general rule, prior familiarity with an item enhances its recall. Indeed, this is one of the basic goals of marketers who try to create and maintain awareness of their products. The more experience a consumer has with a product, the better use she makes of product information.[71] However, there is a possible fly in the ointment: As we noted earlier in this chapter, some evidence indicates that extreme familiarity can result in inferior learning and recall. When consumers are highly familiar with a brand or an advertisement, they may attend to fewer attributes because they do not believe that any additional effort will yield a gain in knowledge.[72] For example, when researchers expose consumers to a radio ad that repeats the audio track from a television ad they've already seen, they do very little critical, evaluative processing and instead mentally replay the video portion of the ad.[73]

Salience and Recall

The **salience** of a brand refers to its prominence or level of activation in memory. As we noted in Chapter 2, stimuli that stand out in contrast to their environments are more likely to command attention which, in turn, increases the likelihood that we will recall them. Almost any technique that increases the novelty of a stimulus also improves recall (a result we call the **von Restorff Effect**).[74] This explains why unusual advertising or distinctive packaging tends to facilitate brand recall.[75]

Introducing a surprise element in an ad can be particularly effective in aiding recall, even if it is not relevant to the factual information the ad presents.[76] In addition, *mystery ads*, in which the ad doesn't identify the brand until the end, are more effective at building associations in memory between the product category and that brand—especially in the case of relatively unknown brands.[77]

Pictorial versus Verbal Cues: Is a Picture Worth a Thousand Words?

There is some evidence for the superiority of visual memory over verbal memory, but this advantage is unclear because it is more difficult to measure recall of pictures.[78] However, the available data indicate that we are more likely to recognize information presented in picture form at a later time. [79] Certainly, visual aspects of an ad are more likely to grab a consumer's attention. In fact, eye-movement studies indicate that about 90 percent of viewers look at the dominant picture in an ad before they bother to view the copy.[80]

Although pictorial ads may enhance recall, they do not necessarily improve comprehension. One study found that television news items presented with illustrations (still pictures) as a backdrop result in improved recall for details of the news story, even though understanding of the story's content does not improve.[81] Another study confirmed that typically consumers recall ads with visual figures more often and like them better.[82]

WHAT MAKES US FORGET?

Marketers obviously hope that consumers will not forget about their products. However, in a poll of more than 13,000 adults, more than half were unable to remember any specific ad they had seen, heard, or read in the past 30 days.[83] How many can you remember right now? Clearly, forgetting by consumers is a big headache for marketers (not to mention a problem for students when studying for exams!).

Early memory theorists assumed that memories simply fade with the passage of time. In a process of **decay**, the structural changes learning produces in the brain simply go away. Forgetting also occurs as a result of **interference**; as we learn additional information, it displaces the earlier information. Consumers may forget stimulus–response associations if they subsequently learn new responses to the same or similar stimuli; we call this process *retroactive interference*. Or prior learning can interfere with new learning, a process we term *proactive interference*. Because we store pieces of information in memory as nodes linked to one another, we are more likely to retrieve a meaning concept that is connected by a larger number of links. But as we learn new responses, a stimulus loses its effectiveness in retrieving the old response.[84]

These interference effects help to explain problems in remembering brand information. Consumers tend to organize attribute information by brand.[85] Additional attribute information regarding a brand or similar brands may limit the person's ability to recall old brand information. Recall may also be inhibited if the brand name is composed of frequently used words. These words cue competing associations and, as a result, we retain less brand information.[86]

In one study, brand evaluations deteriorated more rapidly when ads for the brand appeared with messages for 12 other brands in the same category than when the ad was shown with ads for 12 dissimilar products.[87] Thus, increasing the salience of a brand impairs the recall of other brands.[88] However, calling a competitor by name can result in poorer recall for one's own brand.[89]

Finally, a phenomenon we call the **part-list cueing effect** allows marketers strategically to use the interference process. When they present only a portion of the items in a category to consumers, they don't recall the omitted items as easily. For example, comparative advertising that mentions only a subset of competitors (preferably those that the marketer is not very worried about) may inhibit recall of the *unmentioned* brands with which the product does not favorably compare.[90]

PRODUCTS AS MEMORY MARKERS

Products and ads can themselves serve as powerful retrieval cues. Indeed, the three types of possessions consumers most value are furniture, visual art, and photos. These objects are most likely to jog memories of the past.[91] Researchers find that valued possessions can evoke thoughts about prior events on several dimensions, including sensory experiences, friends and loved ones, and breaking away from parents or former partners.[92] Food can do the same thing: A recent study looked at how favorite recipes stimulate memories of the past. When the researchers asked informants to list three of their favorite recipes and to talk about these choices, they found that people tended to link them with memories of past events such as childhood memories, family holidays, milestone events (such as dishes they only make on special holidays like corned beef and cabbage on St. Patrick's Day), heirlooms (recipes handed down across generations), and the passing of time (e.g., only eating blueberry cobbler in the summer).[93]

Products are particularly important as markers when our sense of the past is threatened, as for example, when an event, such as divorce, relocation, or graduation challenges a consumer's current identity.[95] Our possessions often have *mnemonic* qualities that serve as a form of external memory by prompting consumers to retrieve episodic memories. For example, family photography allows consumers to create their own retrieval cues, the 11 billion amateur photos we take annually form a kind of external memory bank for our culture. A stimulus is, at times, able to evoke a weakened response even years after we first perceived it. We call this effect **spontaneous recovery**, and this reestablished connection may explain consumers' powerful emotional reactions to songs or pictures they have not been exposed to in quite a long time.

Net Profit

Yearbooks are a favorite way to preserve our memories ("What *was* I thinking with that haircut?"), but traditional albums are giving way to more high-tech solutions such as <u>MyYearbook.com</u>. This Web site allows users to create a profile with separate sections for high school, college, graduate school, and professional life. Students who sign up are linked automatically to others at their school. They can select friends from among their classmates and "autograph" each others' yearbook pages. Users also can vote for the biggest flirt, best athlete, and most popular students. The traditional players in this area, such as Jostens (which sells almost $350 million of yearbooks annually), aren't sure if hard copy albums are obsolete, so they are hedging their bets by offering students a supplemental DVD that lets them add their own music, photos, and videos. One of the sibling cofounders of <u>MyYearbook.com</u> (at age 16!) thinks hard copies are history: "If you think about it, all you're going to do with it is put it on the shelf and never really look at it."[94]

THE MARKETING POWER OF NOSTALGIA

Marketers often resurrect popular characters and stories from days gone by; they hope that consumers' fond memories will motivate them to revisit the past. U.S. consumers had a 1950s revival in the 1970s, and U.S. consumers in the 1980s got a heavy dose of memories from the 1960s. Today, it seems that popular characters only need to be gone for a few years before someone tries to bring them back. That's the case with the Teletubbies, four characters a BBC television show introduced in 1997 that were aimed at children ages 3 and under. Ragdoll, the British company that owns the rights to these lovable (yet strangely creepy) creatures, brought them back with features including a trivia quiz, podcasts, and a Web site at takethetelettubbiestest.com.[96] What emotions do these characters evoke in you? **Nostalgia** describes a bittersweet emotion where we view the past with both sadness and longing.[97] References to "the good old days" are increasingly common, as advertisers call up memories of youth— and hope these feelings will translate to what they're selling today.

Reminisce is a magazine devoted to fans of nostalgia.

The McDonald's fast-food chain is riding a nostalgia wave as the nerdy Ronald McDonald and other icons from the 1960s became hot with young hipsters who are scrambling to score T-shirts emblazoned with the clown or other Mickey D's characters such as Mayor McCheese, the Hamburglar, and Grimace. This peak in nostalgia was no accident, however. The company recently launched a word-of-mouth marketing campaign (much more on this in Chapter 11) to boost its uncool image among fashion-conscious young people. It hired the same company that revived other nostalgia figures, such as Strawberry Shortcake, and for the first time licensed the use of its old ad slogans and characters on merchandise. McDonald's sold retro T-shirts in trendy L.A. boutiques such as Lisa Kline and Intuition. It also started to use pop stars such as Justine Timberlake and Destiny's Child in its ads.[98]

Why do consumers relish nostalgia appeals? According to one consumer analyst, "We are creating a new culture, and we don't know what's going to happen. So we need some warm fuzzies from our past."[99] In the aftermath of September 11, 2001, U.S. consumers seem to crave the comfort of items from the past even more. Marketers such as Ford, GE, S.C. Johnson, and Sears are sponsoring campaigns that celebrate their heritage. Other companies are reviving once-popular products such as Breck shampoo, Sea & Ski sun-care lotion, St. Joseph's aspirin, and the Care Bears; or bringing back themes and characters from old shows to sell new products, as when Old Navy transforms "The Brady Bunch" into "The Rugby Bunch" in America to push its shirts.[100] A **retro brand** is an updated version of a brand from a prior historical period (such as the PT Cruiser we'll talk about in Chapter 17). These products trigger nostalgia, and researchers find that they often inspire consumers to think back to an era where (at least in our memories) life was more stable, simple, or even utopian—they let us "look backward through rose-colored glasses."[101]

Memory and Aesthetic Preferences

In addition to liking ads and products that remind us of our past, those experiences also help to determine what we like now. Consumer researchers created a *nostalgia index* that measures the critical ages during which our preferences are likely to form and endure over time. For example, liking a specific song appears to be related to how old a person was when that song was popular—on average, we are most likely to favor songs that were popular when we were 23.5 years old. Preferences for fashion models peak at age 33 and we tend to like movie stars that were popular when we were 26 or 27 years old. Men but not women also show evidence of nostalgic attachment to cars from their youth.[102]

MEASURING OUR MEMORY FOR MARKETING MESSAGES

Because marketers pay so much money to place their messages in front of consumers, they are naturally concerned that people will actually remember these messages at a later point. It seems that they have good reason to be concerned. In one study, fewer than 40 percent of U.S. television viewers made positive links between commercial messages and the corresponding products, only 65 percent noticed the brand name in a commercial, and only 38 percent recognized a connection to an important point.[103]

Ironically, we may be more likely to remember companies that we don't like—perhaps because of the strong negative emotions they evoke. In a 2007 survey, for example, that assessed both recall of companies and their reputations, 4 of the 10 best-remembered companies also ranked in the bottom 10 of reputation rankings: Halliburton Co., Ford Motor Co., General Motors Corp., and Exxon Mobil Corp. In fact, Halliburton, with the lowest reputation score, scored the highest media recall of all 60 companies in the survey.[104]

Even more sadly, only 7 percent of television viewers can recall the product or company featured in the most recent television commercial they watched. This figure represents less than half the recall rate recorded in 1965. We can explain this drop-off in terms of such factors as the increase of 30- and 15-second commercials

Fossil's product designs evoke memories of earlier, classic styles.

and the practice of airing television commercials in clusters rather than in single-sponsor programs.[105]

Recognition versus Recall

One indicator of good advertising is, of course, the impression it makes on consumers. But how can we define and measure this impact? Two basic measures of impact are **recognition** and **recall**. In the typical *recognition test*, researchers show ads to subjects one at a time and ask if they have seen them before. In contrast, *free recall tests* ask consumers to independently think of what they have seen without being prompted for this information first—obviously, this task requires greater effort on their part. Intermedia Advertising Group is a research firm that measures advertising effectiveness by monitoring the TV-viewing population's ability to remember an ad within 24 hours. The firm assigns a *recall index* to each ad to indicate the strength of the impact it had. In one recent year, whereas ads with well-known celebrities such as Britney Spears, Austin Powers, and Michael Jordan had very high recall rates, three of the top five most-remembered ads starred another (and taller) celebrity: Toys "R" Us spokesanimal Geoffrey the Giraffe![106]

Under some conditions, these two memory measures tend to yield the same results, especially when the researchers try to keep the viewers' interest in the ads constant.[107] Generally, though, recognition scores tend to be more reliable and do not decay over time the way recall scores do.[108] Recognition scores are almost always better than recall scores because recognition is a simpler process and the consumer has more available retrieval cues.

Both types of retrieval play important roles in purchase decisions, however. Recall tends to be more important in situations in which consumers do not have product data at their disposal, so they must rely on memory to generate this information.[109] However, recognition is more likely to be an important factor in a store, where retailers confront consumers with thousands of product options (i.e., external memory is abundantly available) and the task simply may be to recognize a familiar package. Unfortunately, package recognition and familiarity can have negative consequences; consumers may ignore warning labels because they take their messages for granted and don't really notice them.[110]

The Starch Test

The **Starch Test**, a research service founded in 1932, is a widely used commercial measure of advertising recall for magazines. This service provides scores on a number of aspects of consumers' familiarity with an ad, including such categories as "noted," "associated," and "read most." It also scores the impact of the component parts of an overall ad, giving such information as "seen" for major illustrations and "read some" for a major block of copy.[111] Factors such as the size of the ad, location (whether it appears toward the front or the back of the magazine), position (whether it is on the right or left page), and the size of illustrations play important roles in affecting the amount of attention readers give to an ad.

PROBLEMS WITH MEMORY MEASURES

Although measuring an ad's memorability is important, analysts have questioned whether existing measures accurately assess these dimensions for several reasons, which we explore now.

Response Biases

Results we obtain from a measuring instrument are not necessarily based on what we are measuring but rather on something else about the instrument or the respondent. This form of contamination is a **response bias**. For example, people tend to give "yes" responses to questions, regardless of what they are asked. In addition, consumers often are eager to be "good subjects" by pleasing the experimenter. They will try to give the responses for which they think she is looking. In some studies, the rate at which subjects claim they recognize *bogus ads* (ads that have not been seen before) is almost as high as their recognition rate for real ads.[112]

Memory Lapses

People are also prone to unintentionally forgetting information. Typical problems include *omitting* (leaving facts out), *averaging* (the tendency to "normalize" memories by not reporting extreme cases), and *telescoping* (inaccurate recall of time).[113] These distortions call into question the accuracy of product usage databases that rely on consumers to recall their purchase and consumption of food and household items. For example, one study asked people to describe what portion of various foods—small, medium, or large—they ate in a typical meal. However, the researchers used different definitions of "medium." Regardless of the definition they gave, about the same number of people claimed they typically ate "medium" portions.[114] Another study documented the **illusion of truth effect**, where telling people (especially elderly subjects) that a consumer claim is false can make them misremember it as true. Respondents were repeatedly told that a claim was false; after a 3-day delay they were likely to remember it as true. This is because the repetition of the claim increases familiarity with it but respondents don't retain their memories of the context (where the claim was debunked). This effect has potentially important implications, especially for social marketing campaigns that try to educate people about false claims.[115]

Memory for Facts versus Feelings

Although researchers continue to work on techniques that increase the accuracy of memory scores, these improvements do not address the more fundamental issue of whether recall is even necessary for advertising to have an effect. In particular, some critics argue that these measures do not adequately tap the impact of "feeling" ads whose objective is to arouse strong emotions rather than to convey concrete product benefits. Many ad campaigns, including those for Hallmark cards, Chevrolet, and Pepsi, use this approach.[116] In these cases, the marketers hope to create a long-term buildup of positive feelings rather than relying on a one-shot attempt to convince consumers to buy their products.

Also, it is not clear that recall translates into preference. We may recall the benefits touted in an ad but not believe them. Or the ad may be memorable because it is so obnoxious and the product becomes one we "love to hate." The bottom line: Although recall is important, especially for creating brand awareness, it is not necessarily

This advertising agency recognizes that there's often a big difference between knowing something and feeling strongly about it.

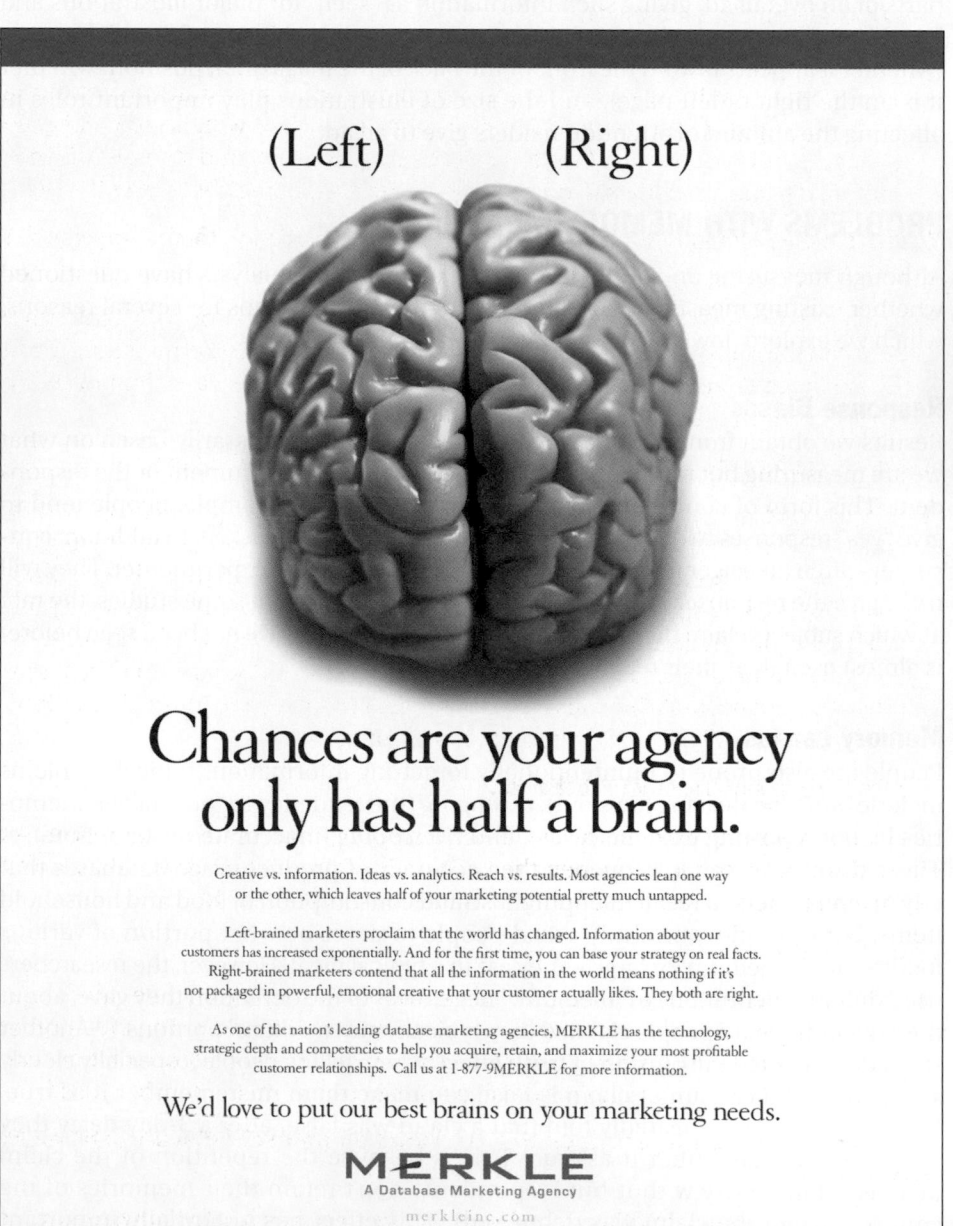

sufficient to alter consumer preferences. To accomplish this, we need more sophisticated attitude-changing strategies. We'll discuss these issues in Chapters 7 and 8.

CHAPTER SUMMARY

Now that you have finished reading this chapter you should understand why:

It's important for marketers to understand how consumers learn about products and services.

● Learning is a change in behavior that experience causes. Learning can occur through simple associations between a stimulus and a response or via a complex series of cognitive activities.

Conditioning results in learning.

● Behavioral learning theories assume that learning occurs as a result of responses to external events. Classical conditioning occurs when a stimulus that naturally elicits a response (an unconditioned stimulus) is paired with another stimulus that does not initially elicit this response. Over time, the second stimulus (the conditioned stimulus) comes to elicit the response even in the absence of the first.

Learned associations can generalize to other things and why this is important to marketers.

● This response can also extend to other, similar stimuli in a process we call stimulus generalization. This process is the basis for such marketing strategies as licensing and family branding, where a consumer's positive associations with a product transfer to other contexts.

There is a difference between classical and instrumental conditioning.

● Operant, or instrumental, conditioning occurs as the person learns to perform behaviors that produce positive outcomes and avoid those that result in negative outcomes. Whereas classical conditioning involves the pairing of two stimuli, instrumental learning occurs when reinforcement occurs following a response to a stimulus. Reinforcement is positive if a reward follows a response. It is negative if the person avoids a negative outcome by not performing a response. Punishment occurs when an unpleasant event follows a response. Extinction of the behavior will occur if reinforcement no longer occurs.

We learn by observing others' behavior.

● Cognitive learning occurs as the result of mental processes. For example, observational learning occurs when the consumer performs a behavior as a result of seeing someone else performing it and being rewarded for it.

Memory systems work.

● Memory is the storage of learned information. The way we encode information when we perceive it determines how we will store it in memory. The memory systems we call sensory memory, short-term memory, and long-term memory each play a role in retaining and processing information from the outside world.

The other products we associate with an individual product influence how we will remember it.

● We don't store information in isolation; we incorporate it into knowledge structure where our brains associate it with other related data. The location of product information in associative networks, and the level of abstraction at which it is coded, help to determine when and how we will activate this information at a later time. Some factors that influence the likelihood of retrieval include the level of familiarity with an item, its salience (or prominence) in memory, and whether the information was presented in pictorial or written form.

Products help us to retrieve memories from our past.

● Products also play a role as memory markers; consumers use them to retrieve memories about past experiences (autobiographical memories), and we often value them because they are able to do this. This function also encourages the use of nostalgia in marketing strategies.

Marketers measure our memories about products and ads.

● We can use either recognition or recall techniques to measure memory for product information. Consumers are more likely to recognize an advertisement if it is presented to them than they are to recall one without being given any cues. However, neither recognition nor recall automatically or reliably translates into product preferences or purchases.

KEY TERMS

Activation models of memory, 134
Advertising wear-out, 121
Associative network, 135
Attentional gate, 131
Behavioral learning theories, 117
Bitcoms, 137
Brand equity, 121
Chunking, 134
Classical conditioning, 118
Cognitive learning theory, 126
Conditioned response (CR), 118
Conditioned stimulus (CS), 118
Decay, 139
Elaborative rehearsal, 134
Encoding, 130
Episodic memories, 131
Evoked set, 135
Extinction, 119
Family branding, 122
Frequency marketing, 126

Halo effect, 120
Illusion of truth effect, 143
Incidental learning, 116
Instrumental conditioning, 124
Interference, 139
Learning, 116
Licensing, 123
Long-term memory (LTM), 134
Look-alike packaging, 123
Masked branding, 121
Memory, 130
Modeling, 128
Narrative, 131
Negative reinforcement, 124
Nostalgia, 140
Observational learning, 128
Part-list cueing effect, 139
Positive reinforcement, 124
Product line extension, 122
Punishment, 124

Recall, 142
Recognition, 142
Response bias, 143
Retrieval, 130
Retro brand, 141
Salience, 138
Script, 136
Sensory memory, 131
Shaping, 124
Short-term memory (STM), 134
Spacing effect, 137
Spontaneous recovery, 139
Spreading activation, 136
Starch Test, 143
State-dependent retrieval, 137
Stimulus discrimination, 121
Stimulus generalization, 120
Storage, 130
Unconditioned stimulus (UCS), 118
Von Restorff Effect, 138

REVIEW QUESTIONS

1 What is the difference between an unconditioned stimulus and a conditioned stimulus?

2 Give an example of a halo effect in marketing.

3 How can marketers use repetition to increase the likelihood that consumers will learn about their brand?

4 Why is it not necessarily a good idea to advertise a product in a commercial where a really popular song is playing in the background?

5 What is the difference between classical conditioning and instrumental conditioning?

6 How do different types of reinforcement enhance learning? How does the strategy of frequency marketing relate to conditioning?

7 What is the major difference between behavioral and cognitive theories of learning?

8 Name the three stages of information processing.

9 What is external memory and why is it important to marketers?

10 Give an example of an episodic memory.

11 Why do phone numbers have seven digits?

12 List the three types of memory, and tell how they work together.

13 How is associative memory like a spider web?

14 How does the likelihood that a person will be willing to use an ATM machine relate to a schema?

15 Why does a pioneering brand have a memory advantage over follower brands?

16 If a consumer is familiar with a product, advertising for it can work by either enhancing or diminishing recall. Why?

17 How does learning new information make it more likely that we'll forget things we've already learned?

18 Define *nostalgia,* and tell why it's such a widely used advertising strategy.

19 Name the two basic measures of memory and describe how they differ from one another.

20 List three problems with measures of memory for advertising.

CONSUMER BEHAVIOR CHALLENGE

■ DISCUSS

1 In his 2005 book, *Blink: The Power of Thinking without Thinking,* author Malcolm Gladwell argues that hallowed marketing research techniques such as focus groups aren't effective because we usually react to products quickly and without much conscious thought, so it's better simply to solicit consumers' first impressions rather than getting them to think at length about why they buy. What's your position on this issue?

2 Some die-hard fans were not pleased when The Rolling Stones sold the tune "Start Me Up" for about $4 million to Microsoft, which wanted the classic song to promote its Windows 95 launch. The Beach Boys sold "Good Vibrations" to Cadbury Schweppes for its Sunkist soft drink, Steppenwolf offered his "Born to Be Wild" to plug the Mercury Cougar, and even Bob Dylan sold "The Times They Are A-Changin'" to Coopers & Lybrand (now called PriceWaterhouseCoopers).[117] Other rock legends have refused to play the commercial game, including Bruce Springsteen, The Grateful Dead, Led Zeppelin, Fleetwood Mac, R.E.M., and U2. According to U2's manager, "Rock 'n roll is the last vestige of independence. It is undignified to put that creative effort and hard work to the disposal of a soft drink or beer or car."[118] Singer Neil Young is especially adamant about not selling out; in his song "This Note's for You," he croons, "Ain't singing for Pepsi, ain't singing for Coke, I don't sing for nobody, makes me look like a joke." What's your take on this issue? How do you react when one of your favorite songs turns up in a commercial? Is this use of nostalgia an effective way to market a product? Why or why not?

■ APPLY

3 Devise a "product jingle memory test." Compile a list of brands that are or have been associated with memorable jingles, such as Chiquita Banana or Alka-Seltzer. Read this list to friends, and see how many jingles they remember. You may be surprised at the level of recall.

4 Identify some important characteristics of a product with a well-known brand name. Based on these attributes, generate a list of possible brand extension or licensing opportunities, as well as some others that would most likely not be accepted by consumers.

5 Collect some pictures of "classic" products that have high nostalgia value. Show these pictures to consumers, and allow them to free associate. Analyze the types of memories that they evoke, and think about how a marketer might employ these associations in a product's promotional strategy.

Case Study

HERSHEY'S VERSUS M&MS: THE WAR OF THE BITE-SIZE MILK CHOCOLATES

What immediately comes to mind when you hear the brand name "M&Ms"? Milk chocolate? Candy coating? A variety of colors? Handy individual-serving-sized bags? The slogan, "Melts in your mouth, not in your hands"? The truth is, the average consumer thinks of many different things. This is no accident. Masterfoods, the makers of M&Ms, has carefully managed the core brand and all of its extensions to ensure that we think lots of good thoughts about its cherished chocolate candy.

Now, what comes to mind when you hear the brand name "Hershey's Kisses"? The trademark shape? The foil wrapper? The paper flag? Since 2005, Hershey's has been doing its best to steal some of M&Ms' tricks for its Kisses brand. When it extended its well-known brand name to Kissables, a miniature candy-coated version of its flagship candy, Hershey's launched a direct assault on the nearly $1 billion M&M franchise.

Kissables are shaped like the familiar Hershey's Kisses. However, the big departure from the core Kisses brand is that they are bite-size and coated in red, blue, yellow, green, and orange hues with similarly colorful bags. What's more, the company expects to develop a variety of extensions for the new product. Don't be surprised to see Kissables in versions that might include minis, megas, and peanut or almond centers among others. Hershey's strategy is to move Kisses beyond home candy dishes into take-along snacks with a variety of sizes and package types that people will munch on at different occasions.

Hershey's has slowly been increasing its efforts to build the Kisses brand with limited edition flavors and varieties. However, annual sales for the brand and all of its varieties are little more than half of the $450 million that M&Ms reaches each year. CEO Rick Lenny has recognized that the foil wrapping on each Kiss might just be holding sales back. He feels that ironically, the brand's signature packaging element for decades may put off some impatient consumers who don't want to take the time to unwrap the candy.

Hershey's sees the Kissables extension as a vehicle to allow the core brand to retain the original attributes that made it famous, while at the same time capitalizing on some of the attributes that have brought success to rival M&Ms. It's no surprise then that Hershey's is focusing on Kissables' take-along convenience which doesn't require the work of peeling off that pesky silver Kisses wrapper.

The war of the bite-size chocolates is on. Hershey's ramped up its media spending for the Kiss and Kissable lines to give M&Ms a run for its money. And Hershey's has something else to bank on. In 2007, it celebrated the 100-year anniversary of the Kiss, driving home its veteran status as the American favorite. In contrast, M&Ms didn't appear until 1941. In fact, the lovable Kiss is even older than sliced bread, which debuted in 1912! Perhaps this is why more than half of Americans surveyed admitted that if they were stranded on an island, they'd rather have a supply of Hershey's Kisses than their favorite book.

DISCUSSION QUESTIONS

1 Discuss how consumers come to know the various attributes of brands such as Hershey's Kisses and M&Ms according to activation models of memory.

2 What are the benefits and dangers that Hershey's faces in extending a blue chip brand such as Kisses?

3 How might Hershey's use a nostalgia campaign to promote Kisses and/or Kissables?

Sources: Tamara El-Khoury, "An Epic Kiss," *St. Petersburg Times* (March 8, 2007): 1E; Mike Beirne, "Hershey Has a Taste for Line Extensions: Kisses, Ice Breakers and York Get Offshoots under CEO Lenny," *Brandweek,* (October 27, 2003); Stephanie Thompson, "Kisses Attempts to Smother M&Ms," *Advertising Age,* (August 1, 2005): 1.

NOTES

1. Nick Summers, "Trix Are for Traders," *Newsweek* (July 4, 2005): 10; Lisa W. Foderaro, "These Days, the College Bowl Is Filled with Milk and Cereal," *New York Times Online Edition* (November 14, 2004).

2. Stuart Elliott, "At 75, Mr. Peanut Is Getting Expanded Role at Planters," *New York Times* (September 23, 1991): D15.

3. Todd Pruzan, "Brand Illusions," *New York Times on the Web* (September 12, 1999).

4. Robert A. Baron, *Psychology: The Essential Science* (Boston: Allyn & Bacon, 1989).

5. Richard A. Feinberg, "Credit Cards as Spending Facilitating Stimuli: A Conditioning Interpretation," *Journal of Consumer Research* 13 (December 1986): 348–56.

6. R. A. Rescorla, "Pavlovian Conditioning: It's Not What You Think It Is," *American Psychologist* 43 (1988): 151–60; Elnora W. Stuart, Terence A. Shimp, and Randall W. Engle, "Classical Conditioning of Consumer Attitudes: Four Experiments in an Advertising Context," *Journal of Consumer Research* 14 (December 1987): 334–39.

7. C. Janiszewski, H. Noel, and A. G. Sawyer, "A Meta-analysis of the Spacing Effect in Verbal Learning: Implications for Research on Advertising Repetition and Consumer Memory," *Journal of Consumer Research* 30, no. 1 (2003): 138–49.

8. James Ward, Barbara Loken, Ivan Ross, and Tedi Hasapopoulous, "The Influence of Physical Similarity of Affect and Attribute Perceptions from National Brands to Private Label Brands," in Terence A. Shimp et al., eds., *American Marketing Educators' Conference* (Chicago: American Marketing Association, 1986), 51–56.

9. Judith Lynne Zaichkowsky and Richard Neil Simpson, "The Effect of Experience with a Brand Imitator on the Original Brand," *Marketing Letters* 7, no. 1 (1996): 31–39.

10. Janice S. Griffiths and Mary Zimmer, "Masked Brands and Consumers' Need for Uniqueness," *American Marketing Association* (Summer 1998): 145–53.

11. Randi Priluck Grossman and Brian D. Till, "The Persistence of Classically Conditioned Brand Attitudes," *Journal of Advertising* 21, no. 1 (1998): 23–31; Chris T. Allen and Thomas J. Madden, "A Closer Look at Classical Conditioning," *Journal of Consumer Research* 12 (December 1985): 301–15; Chester A. Insko and William F. Oakes, "Awareness and the Conditioning of Attitudes," *Journal of Personality and Social Psychology* 4 (November 1966): 487–96; Carolyn K. Staats and Arthur W. Staats, "Meaning Established by Classical Conditioning," *Journal of Experimental Psychology* 54 (July 1957): 74–80.

12. Kevin Lane Keller, "Conceptualizing, Measuring, and Managing Customer-Based Brand Equity," *Journal of Marketing* 57 (January 1993): 1–22.

13. Herbert Krugman, "Low Recall and High Recognition of Advertising," *Journal of Advertising Research* (February–March 1986): 79–80.

14. Gerald J. Gorn, "The Effects of Music in Advertising on Choice Behavior: A Classical Conditioning Approach," *Journal of Marketing* 46 (Winter 1982): 94–101.

15. Noreen Klein, Virginia Tech, personal communication (April 2000); Calvin Bierley, Frances K. McSweeney, and Renee Vannieuwkerk, "Classical Conditioning of Preferences for Stimuli," *Journal of Consumer Research* 12 (December 1985): 316–23; James J. Kellaris and Anthony D. Cox, "The Effects of Background Music in Advertising: A Reassessment," *Journal of Consumer Research* 16 (June 1989): 113–18.

16. Frances K. McSweeney and Calvin Bierley, "Recent Developments in Classical Conditioning," *Journal of Consumer Research* 11 (September 1984): 619–31.

17. Basil G. Englis, "The Reinforcement Properties of Music Videos: 'I Want My . . . I Want My . . . I Want My . . . MTV,'" paper presented at the meetings of the Association for Consumer Research, New Orleans, 1989.

18. Stuart Elliott, "A Name Change at Philip Morris," *New York Times on the Web* (November 19, 2001).

19. Sharon Begley, "StrawBerry Is No BlackBerry: Building Brands Using Sound," *Wall Street Journal Interactive Edition* (August 26, 2002).

20. Anand Natarajan, "Branding: Interiors by Smith & Wesson," *BusinessWeek* (November 10, 2003): 16; James B. Arndorfer, "Starbucks Wakes Up to Liquor Possibilities," *Advertising Age* (November 22, 2004): 4; Claudia Deutsch, "Will Real Men Buy Mr. Clean"? *New York Times on the Web* (September 24, 2003); Jane L. Levere, "Huggies and Pampers Seek to Extend Brands into Toiletries," *New York Times on the Web* (January 18, 2005).

21. Tracie Rozhon, "Read Our Article, and Purchase Our Hair Color While You're at It," *New York Times on the Web* (June 17, 2004); Patricia Winters Lauro, "Fire and Police Try to Market Goods," *New York Times on the Web* (June 10, 2002).

22. "Look-Alikes Mimic Familiar Packages," *New York Times* (August 9, 1986): D1.

23. Zaichkowsky and Simpson, "The Effect of Experience with a Brand Imitator on the Original Brand," 31–39.

24. Luk Warlop and Joseph W. Alba, "Sincere Flattery: Trade-Dress Imitation and Consumer Choice," *Journal of Consumer Psychology* 14, nos. 1 & 2 (2004): 21–27.

25. Jim Wilson, "Levi's Turns to Suing Its Rivals," *New York Times*; Michael Barbaro and Julie Creswell, "Levi's Designers Worked on Jeans at the Company's Headquarters," *New York Times Online Edition* (January 29, 2007).

26. Gina Chon, "Henry Ford's Model A Would Be at Home in Car-Name Game; Using Letters Spells Prestige but Alphabet Has Limits; The Big Fight over MKX," *Wall Street Journal* (April 20, 2006): A1.

27. *www.iacc.org*, accessed November 27, 2002.

28. "One-Third of Music CDs Sold in the World Are Pirated," *Wall Street Journal Interactive Edition* (June 24, 2005).

29. Gordon Fairclough, "From Hongda to Wumart, Brand Names in China Have Familiar, If Off-Key, Ring," *Wall Street Journal* (October 19, 2006): B1.

30. For a comprehensive approach to consumer behavior based on operant conditioning principles, see Gordon R. Foxall, "Behavior Analysis and Consumer Psychology," *Journal of Economic Psychology* 15 (March 1994): 5–91.

31. J. Blaise Bergiel and Christine Trosclair, "Instrumental Learning: Its Application to Customer Satisfaction," *Journal of Consumer Marketing* 2 (Fall 1985): 23–28.

32. Jane Costello, "Do Offers of Free Mileage Sell? The Proof Is in Pudding Guy," *Wall Street Journal Interactive Edition* (January 24, 2000).

33. Suzanne Vranica, "Agencies Don Lab Coats to Reach Consumers, Firms Deploy Scientists Within Creative Groups to Make Messages Stick" *Wall Street Journal Online* (June 4, 2007): B8.

34. Cf. for example E. M. Eisenstein and J. W. Hutchinson, "Action-Based Learning: Goals and Attention in the Acquisition of Market Knowledge," *Journal of Marketing Research* 43, no. 2 (2006): 244–58.

35. Ellen J. Langer, *The Psychology of Control* (Beverly Hills, CA: Sage, 1983).

36. Robert B. Cialdini, *Influence: Science and Practice*, 2nd ed. (New York: William Morrow, 1984); Y. Rottenstreich, S. Sood, and L. Brenner, "Feeling and Thinking in Memory-Based versus Stimulus-Based Choices," *Journal of Consumer Research* 33 no. 4 (2007): 461–69.

37. Benedict Carey, "Who's Minding the Mind,?" *New York Times Online* (July 31, 2007).

38. Malcolm Gladwell, *Blink: The Power of Thinking without Thinking* (New York: Little, Brown, 2005).

39. Chris T. Allen and Thomas J. Madden, "A Closer Look at Classical Conditioning," *Journal of Consumer Research* 12 (December 1985): 301–15; see also Terence A. Shimp, Elnora W. Stuart, and Randall W. Engle, "A Program of Classical Conditioning Experiments Testing Variations in the Conditioned Stimulus and Context," *Journal of Consumer Research* 18 (June 1991): 1–12.

40. Terence A. Shimp, "Neo-Pavlovian Conditioning and Its Implications for Consumer Theory and Research," in Thomas S. Robertson and Harold H. Kassarjian, eds., *Handbook of Consumer Behavior* (Upper Saddle River, NJ: Prentice Hall, 1991).

41. Albert Bandura, *Social Foundations of Thought and Action: A Social Cognitive View* (Upper Saddle River, NJ: Prentice Hall, 1986).

42. Ibid.

43. R. C. Atkinson and I. M. Shiffrin, "Human Memory: A Proposed System and Its Control Processes," in K. W. Spence and J. T. Spence, eds., *The Psychology of Learning and Motivation: Advances in Research and Theory* 2 (New York: Academic Press, 1968): 89–195.

44. James R. Bettman, "Memory Factors in Consumer Choice: A Review," *Journal of Marketing* (Spring 1979): 37–53. For a study that explores the relative impact of internal versus external memory on brand choice, see Joseph W. Alba, Howard Marmorstein, and Amitava Chattopadhyay, "Transitions in Preference over Time: The Effects of Memory on Message Persuasiveness," *Journal of Marketing Research* 29 (1992): 406–16.

45. Lauren G. Block and Vicki G. Morwitz, "Shopping Lists as an External Memory Aid for Grocery Shopping: Influences on List Writing and List Fulfillment," *Journal of Consumer Psychology* 8, no. 4 (1999): 343–75.

46. Kim Robertson, "Recall and Recognition Effects of Brand Name Imagery," *Psychology & Marketing* 4 (Spring 1987): 3–15.

47. Datta, Saheli, "A Mind-Reading Security Check," *Business 2.0* (April 2007): 39.

48. Endel Tulving, "Remembering and Knowing the Past," *American Scientist* 77 (July–August 1989): 361.

49. Rashmi Adaval and Robert S. Wyer, Jr., "The Role of Narratives in Consumer Information Processing," *Journal of Consumer Psychology* 7, no. 3 (1998): 207–46.

50. Jennifer Edson Escalas, "Narrative Processing: Building Consumer Connections to Brands," *Journal of Consumer Psychology* 14, nos. 1 & 2 (2004): 168–80.

51. George A. Miller, "The Magical Number Seven, Plus or Minus Two: Some Limits on Our Capacity for Processing Information," *Psychological Review* 63 (1956): 81–97.

52. James N. MacGregor, "Short-Term Memory Capacity: Limitation or Optimization?" *Psychological Review* 94 (1987): 107–8.

53. M. Vanhuele, G. Laurent,, and X. Dreze, "Consumers' Immediate Memory for Prices," *Journal of Consumer Research* 33, no. 2 (2006): 163–72.

54. See Catherine A. Cole and Michael J. Houston, "Encoding and Media Effects on Consumer Learning Deficiencies in the Elderly," *Journal of Marketing Research* 24 (February 1987): 55–64; A. M. Collins and E. F. Loftus, "A Spreading Activation Theory of Semantic Processing," *Psychological Review* 82 (1975): 407–28; Fergus I. M. Craik and Robert S. Lockhart, "Levels of Processing: A Framework for Memory Research," *Journal of Verbal Learning and Verbal Behavior* 11 (1972): 671–84.

55. Walter A. Henry, "The Effect of Information-Processing Ability on Processing Accuracy," *Journal of Consumer Research* 7 (June 1980): 42–48.

56. T. B. Cornwell, M. S. Humphreys, A. M. Maguire, C. S. Weeks, and C. L. Tellegen, "Sponsorship-Linked Marketing: The Role of Articulation in Memory," *Journal of Consumer Research* 33, no. 3 (2006): 312–21.

57. Kevin Lane Keller, "Memory Factors in Advertising: The Effect of Advertising Retrieval Cues on Brand Evaluations," *Journal of Consumer Research* 14 (December 1987): 316–33. For a discussion of processing operations that occur during brand choice, see Gabriel Biehal and Dipankar Chakravarti, "Consumers' Use of Memory and External Information in Choice: Macro and Micro Perspectives," *Journal of Consumer Research* 12 (March 1986): 382–405.

58. Susan T. Fiske and Shelley E. Taylor, *Social Cognition* (Reading, MA: Addison-Wesley, 1984).

59. Deborah Roedder John and John C. Whitney Jr., "The Development of Consumer Knowledge in Children: A Cognitive Structure Approach," *Journal of Consumer Research* 12 (March 1986): 406–17.

60. Michael R. Solomon, Carol Surprenant, John A. Czepiel, and Evelyn G. Gutman, "A Role Theory Perspective on Dyadic Interactions: The Service Encounter," *Journal of Marketing* 49 (Winter 1985): 99–111.

61. S. Danziger, S. Moran, and V. Rafaely, "The Influence of Ease of Retrieval on Judgment as a Function of Attention to Subjective Experience," *Journal of Consumer Psychology* 16, no. 2 (2006): 191–95.

62. Roger W. Morrell, Denise C. Park, and Leonard W. Poon, "Quality of Instructions on Prescription Drug Labels: Effects on Memory and Comprehension in Young and Old Adults," *The Gerontologist* 29 (1989): 345–54.

63. Frank R. Kardes, Gurumurthy Kalyanaram, Murali Chandrashekaran, and Ronald J. Dornoff, "Brand Retrieval, Consideration Set Composition, Consumer Choice, and the Pioneering Advantage" (unpublished manuscript, the University of Cincinnati, Ohio, 1992).

64. Judith Lynne Zaichkowsky and Padma Vipat, "Inferences from Brand Names," paper presented at the European meeting of the Association for Consumer Research, Amsterdam, June 1992.

65. H. Noel, "The Spacing Effect: Enhancing Memory for Repeated Marketing Stimuli," *Journal of Consumer Psychology* 16 no. 3 (2006): 306–20; for an alternative explanation, see S. L. Appleton-Knapp, R. A. Bjork, and T. D. Wickens, "Examining the Spacing Effect in Advertising: Encoding Variability, Retrieval Processes, and Their Interaction," *Journal of Consumer Research* 32, no. 2 (2005): 266–76.

66. Herbert E. Krugman, "Low Recall and High Recognition of Advertising," *Journal of Advertising Research* (February–March 1986): 79–86.

67. Rik G. M. Pieters and Tammo H. A. Bijmolt, "Consumer Memory for Television Advertising: A Field Study of Duration, Serial Position, and Competition Effects," *Journal of Consumer Research* 23 (March 1997): 362–72.

68. David Goetzl, "Turner: We'll Get Your Brand into Our Programming," *Marketing Daily*, available from *mediapost.com*, accessed March 14, 2007.

69. Erik Sass, "Study Finds Spectacular Print Ads Get Spectacular Recall," available from *www.mediapost.com*, accessed February 23, 2007.

70. Keller, "Memory Factors in Advertising."

71. Eric J. Johnson and J. Edward Russo, "Product Familiarity and Learning New Information," *Journal of Consumer Research* 11 (June 1984): 542–50.

72. Eric J. Johnson and J. Edward Russo, "Product Familiarity and Learning New Information," in Kent Monroe, ed., *Advances in Consumer Research* 8 (Ann Arbor, MI: Association for Consumer Research, 1981): 151–55; John G. Lynch and Thomas K. Srull, "Memory and Attentional Factors in Consumer Choice: Concepts and Research Methods," *Journal of Consumer Research* 9 (June 1982): 18–37.

73. Julie A. Edell and Kevin Lane Keller, "The Information Processing of Coordinated Media Campaigns," *Journal of Marketing Research* 26 (May 1989): 149–64.

74. Lynch and Srull, "Memory and Attentional Factors in Consumer Choice."

75. Joseph W. Alba and Amitava Chattopadhyay, "Salience Effects in Brand Recall," *Journal of Marketing Research* 23 (November 1986): 363–70; Elizabeth C. Hirschman and Michael R. Solomon, "Utilitarian, Aesthetic, and Familiarity Responses to Verbal versus Visual Advertisements," in Thomas C. Kinnear, ed., *Advances in Consumer Research* 11 (Provo, UT: Association for Consumer Research, 1984): 426–31.

76. Susan E. Heckler and Terry L. Childers, "The Role of Expectancy and Relevancy in Memory for Verbal and Visual Information: What Is Incongruency?" *Journal of Consumer Research* 18 (March 1992): 475–92.

77. Russell H. Fazio, Paul M. Herr, and Martha C. Powell, "On the Development and Strength of Category-Brand Associations in Memory: The Case of Mystery Ads," *Journal of Consumer Psychology* 1, no. 1 (1992): 1–13.

78. Hirschman and Solomon, "Utilitarian, Aesthetic, and Familiarity Responses to Verbal versus Visual Advertisements."

79. Terry Childers and Michael Houston, "Conditions for a Picture-Superiority Effect on Consumer Memory," *Journal of Consumer Research* 11 (September 1984): 643–54; Terry Childers, Susan Heckler, and Michael Houston, "Memory for the Visual and Verbal Components of Print Advertisements," *Psychology & Marketing* 3 (Fall 1986): 147–50.

80. Werner Krober-Riel, "Effects of Emotional Pictorial Elements in Ads Analyzed by Means of Eye Movement Monitoring," in Thomas C. Kinnear, ed., *Advances in Consumer Research* 11 (Provo, UT: Association for Consumer Research, 1984): 591–96.

81. Hans-Bernd Brosius, "Influence of Presentation Features and News Context on Learning from Television News," *Journal of Broadcasting & Electronic Media* 33 (Winter 1989): 1–14.

82. Edward F. McQuarrie and David Glen Mick, "Visual and Verbal Rhetorical Figures under Directed Processing versus Incidental Exposure to Advertising," *Journal of Consumer Research* (March 2003): 29, 579–87; cf. also Ann E. Schlosser, "Learning through Virtual Product Experience: The Role of Imagery on True versus False Memories," *Journal of Consumer Research* 33, no. 3 (2006): 377–83.

83. Raymond R. Burke and Thomas K. Srull, "Competitive Interference and Consumer Memory for Advertising," *Journal of Consumer Research* 15 (June 1988): 55–68.

84. Ibid.

85. Johnson and Russo, "Product Familiarity and Learning New Information."

86. Joan Meyers-Levy, "The Influence of Brand Name's Association Set Size and Word Frequency on Brand Memory," *Journal of Consumer Research* 16 (September 1989): 197–208.

87. Michael H. Baumgardner, Michael R. Leippe, David L. Ronis, and Anthony G. Greenwald, "In Search of Reliable Persuasion Effects: II. Associative Interference and Persistence of Persuasion in a Message-Dense Environment," *Journal of Personality and Social Psychology* 45 (September 1983): 524–37.

88. Alba and Chattopadhyay, "Salience Effects in Brand Recall."

89. Margaret Henderson Blair, Allan R. Kuse, David H. Furse, and David W. Stewart, "Advertising in a New and Competitive Environment: Persuading Consumers to Buy," *Business Horizons* 30 (November–December 1987): 20.

90. Lynch and Srull, "Memory and Attentional Factors in Consumer Choice."

91. Russell W. Belk, "Possessions and the Extended Self," *Journal of Consumer Research* 15 (September 1988): 139–68.

92. Morris B. Holbrook and Robert M. Schindler, "Nostalgic Bonding: Exploring the Role of Nostalgia in the Consumption Experience," *Journal of Consumer Behavior* 3, no. 2 (December 2003): 107–27.

93. Stacy Menzel Baker, Holli C. Karrer, and Ann Veeck, "My Favorite Recipes: Recreating Emotions and Memories through Cooking," *Advances in Consumer Research* 32, no. 1 (2005): 304–305.

94. Quoted in Valerie Bauman, "Web Generation Preserves Memories Online," *BusinessWeek on the Web* (June 24, 2006).

95. Russell W. Belk, "The Role of Possessions in Constructing and Maintaining a Sense of Past," in Marvin E. Goldberg, Gerald Gorn, and Richard W. Pollay, eds., *Advances in Consumer Research* 16 (Provo, UT: Association for Consumer Research, 1989): 669–78.

96. Stuart Elliott, "Remember the Teletubbies? The Brand Owner Hopes So," *New York Times Online Edition* (March 26, 2007).

97. Susan L. Holak and William J. Havlena, "Feelings, Fantasies, and Memories: An Examination of the Emotional Components of Nostalgia," *Journal of Business Research* 42 (1998): 217–26.

98. Suzanne Vranica, "McDonald's Chic: Vintage T-Shirts Are Sizzling," *Wall Street Journal* (April 27, 2006): B2.

99. Keith Naughton and Bill Vlasic, "Nostalgia Boom," *BusinessWeek* (March 23, 1998): 59–64.

100. Stuart Elliot, "Ads from the Past with Modern Touches," *New York Times on the Web* (September 9, 2002); Julia Cosgrove, "Listen Up, Sucka, the 80s Are Back," *BusinessWeek* (August 5, 2002): 16.

101. Stephen Brown, Robert V. Kozinets, and John F. Sherry, "Teaching Old Brands New Tricks: Retro Branding and the Revival of Brand Meaning," *Journal of Marketing* 67 (July 2003): 19–33.

102. Robert M. Schindler and Morris B. Holbrook, "Nostalgia for Early Experience as a Determinant of Consumer Preferences," *Psychology & Marketing* 20, no. 4 (April 2003): 275–302; Morris B. Holbrook and Robert M. Schindler, "Some Exploratory Findings on the Development of Musical Tastes," *Journal of Consumer Research* 16 (June 1989): 119–24; Morris B. Holbrook and Robert M. Schindler, "Market Segmentation Based on Age and Attitude toward the Past: Concepts, Methods, and Findings Concerning Nostalgic Influences on Consumer Tastes," *Journal of Business Research* 37 (September 1996)1: 27–40.

103. "Only 38% of T.V. Audience Links Brands with Ads," *Marketing News* (January 6, 1984): 10.

104. Ronald Alsop, "How Boss's Deeds Buff A Firm's Reputation ," *Wall Street Journal Online Edition* (January 31, 2007).

105. "Terminal Television," *American Demographics* (January 1987): 15.

106. Vanessa O'Connell, "Toys 'R' Us Spokesanimal Makes Lasting Impression: Giraffe Tops List of Television Ads Viewers Found the Most Memorable," *Wall Street Journal Interactive Edition* (January 2, 2003).

107. Richard P. Bagozzi and Alvin J. Silk, "Recall, Recognition, and the Measurement of Memory for Print Advertisements," *Marketing Science* 2 (1983): 95–134.

108. Adam Finn, "Print Ad Recognition Readership Scores: An Information Processing Perspective," *Journal of Marketing Research* 25 (May 1988): 168–77.

109. James R. Bettman, "Memory Factors in Consumer Choice: A Review," *Journal of Marketing* (Spring 1979): 37–53.

110. Mark A. Deturck and Gerald M. Goldhaber, "Effectiveness of Product Warning Labels: Effects of Consumers' Information Processing Objectives," *Journal of Consumer Affairs* 23, no. 1 (1989): 111–25.

111. Adam Finn, "Print Ad Recognition Readership Scores: An Information Processing Perspective," *Journal of Marketing Research* 25 (May 1988): 168–77.

112. Surendra N. Singh and Gilbert A. Churchill, Jr., "Response-Bias-Free Recognition Tests to Measure Advertising Effects," *Journal of Advertising Research* (June–July 1987): 23–36.

113. William A. Cook, "Telescoping and Memory's Other Tricks," *Journal of Advertising Research* 27 (February–March 1987): 5–8.

114. "On a Diet? Don't Trust Your Memory," *Psychology Today* (October 1989): 12.

115. I. Skurnik, C. Yoon, D. C. Park, and N. Schwarz, "How Warnings about False Claims Become Recommendations," *Journal of Consumer Research* 31, no. 4 (2005): 713–24.

116. Hubert A. Zielske and Walter A. Henry, "Remembering and Forgetting Television Ads," *Journal of Advertising Research* 20 (April 1980): 7–13; Cara Greenberg, "Future Worth: Before It's Hot, Grab It," *New York Times* (1992): C1; S. K. List, "More Than Fun and Games," *American Demographics* (August 1992): 44.

117. Thomas F. Jones, "Our Musical Heritage Is Being Raided," *San Francisco Examiner* (May 23, 1997).

118. Kevin Goldman, "A Few Rockers Refuse to Turn Tunes into Ads," *New York Times* (August 25, 1995): B1.

Motivation and Values

Chapter Objectives

When you have finished reading this chapter you will understand why:

● It's important for marketers to recognize that products can satisfy a range of consumer needs.

● The way we evaluate and choose a product depends on our degree of involvement with the product, the marketing message, and/or the purchase situation.

● Our deeply held cultural values dictate the types of products and services we seek out or avoid.

● Consumers vary in the importance they attach to worldly possessions, and this orientation in turn has an impact on their priorities and behaviors.

as Basil scans the menu at the trendy health-food restaurant Paula has dragged him to, he reflects on what a man will give up for love. Now that Paula has become a die-hard vegetarian, she's slowly but surely working on him to forsake those juicy steaks and burgers for healthier fare. He can't even hide from tofu and other delights at school; the dining facility in his dorm just started offering "veggie" alternatives to its usual assortment of greasy "mystery meats" and other delicacies he has come to love.

Paula is totally into it; she claims that eating this way not only cuts out unwanted fat but also is good for the environment. Just his luck to fall head-over-heels for a "tree-hugger." As Basil gamely tries to decide between the stuffed artichokes with red pepper vinaigrette and the grilled marinated zucchini, fantasies of a sizzling 14-ounce T-bone dance before his eyes.

Introduction

Paula certainly is not alone in believing that eating green is good for the body, the soul, and the planet. In the United States, for example, about 7 percent of the general population is vegetarian, and women and younger people are even more likely to adopt a meatless diet. An additional 10 to 20 percent of consumers are interested in vegetarian options in addition to their normal fare of dead animals. And, more and more people are taking the next step and adopting a vegan lifestyle. Vegetarianism refers only to one's diet, while *veganism* links to a set of ethical beliefs about cruelty to animals. In addition to objecting to hunting or fishing, adherents protest cruel animal training, the degrading use of animals in circuses, zoos, rodeos and races and they also oppose the testing of drugs and cosmetics on animals.[1] Although the proportion of consumers who are vegetarian or vegan is quite small compared to those of us who still like to pound down a Quarter Pounder, big companies are taking notice of this growing interest in vegetarian and cruelty-free products. Colgate recently purchased a controlling interest in Tom's of Maine and Dean Foods, (America's largest processor of dairy foods) bought Silk and its parent company White Wave. PETA (People for the Ethical Treatment of Animals) offers resources to promote an animal-friendly lifestyle, including an Online Vegetarian Starter Kit for kids.[2] The beef industry fights back with its high-profile advertising campaign— "Beef It's What's for Dinner" and a Web site to promote meat consumption (beefitswhatsfordinner.com).[3] It's obvious our menu choices have deep-seated consequences.

The forces that drive people to buy and use products are generally straightforward, for example, when a person chooses what to have for lunch. As hard-core vegetarians demonstrate, however, even the basic food products we consume also relate to wide-ranging beliefs regarding what we think is appropriate or desirable. In some cases, these emotional responses create a deep commitment to the product. Sometimes people are not even fully aware of the forces that drive them toward some products and away from others. Often a person's values—his or her priorities and beliefs about the world—influence these choices.

To understand motivation is to understand why consumers do what they do. Why do some people choose to bungee jump off a bridge or compete on reality shows, whereas others spend their leisure time playing chess or gardening? Whether it is to quench a thirst, kill boredom, or attain some deep spiritual experience, we do everything for a reason, even if we can't articulate what that reason is. Marketing students are taught from Day 1 that the goal of marketing is to satisfy consumers' needs. However, this insight is useless unless we can discover what those needs are and why they exist. A beer commercial once asked, "Why ask why?" In this chapter, we'll find out.

 The Motivation Process

Motivation refers to the processes that lead people to behave as they do. It occurs when a need is aroused that the consumer wishes to satisfy. The need creates a state of tension that drives the consumer to attempt to reduce or eliminate it. This need may be *utilitarian* (i.e., a desire to achieve some functional or practical benefit, as when a person loads up on green vegetables for nutritional reasons) or it may be *hedonic* (i.e., an experiential need, involving emotional responses or fantasies, as when Basil thinks longingly about a juicy steak). The desired end state is the consumer's **goal**. Marketers try to create products and services that will provide the desired benefits and permit the consumer to reduce this tension.

A want is a manifestion of a need. This ad from Singapore reminds us that consumer society tempts us with wants.

Whether the need is utilitarian or hedonic, the magnitude of the tension it creates determines the urgency the consumer feels to reduce it. We call this degree of arousal a **drive**. We can satisfy a basic need in any number of ways, and the specific path a person chooses is influenced both by her unique set of experiences and by the values instilled by her culture.

These personal and cultural factors combine to create a **want,** which is one manifestation of a need. For example, hunger is a basic need that all of us must satisfy; the lack of food creates a tension state that we can reduce by the intake of cheeseburgers, double-fudge Oreo cookies, raw fish, or bean sprouts. The specific route to drive reduction is culturally and individually determined. When a person attains the goal, this reduces the tension and the motivation recedes (for the time being). We describe motivation in terms of its *strength*, or the pull it exerts on the consumer, and its *direction*, or the particular way the consumer attempts to reduce it.

 ## Motivational Strength

The degree to which a person is willing to expend energy to reach one goal as opposed to another reflects his or her underlying motivation to attain that goal. Psychologists have advanced many theories to explain why people behave the way they do. Most share the basic idea that people have some finite amount of energy that must be directed toward certain goals.

BIOLOGICAL VERSUS LEARNED NEEDS

Early work on motivation ascribed behavior to *instinct*, the innate patterns of behavior that are universal in a species. This view is now largely discredited. For one thing, the existence of an instinct is difficult to prove or disprove because we infer the instinct from the behavior it is supposed to explain (we call this type of circular explanation a *tautology*).[4] It is like saying that a consumer buys products that are status symbols because he is motivated to attain status—hardly a satisfying explanation.

This ad for exercise equipment shows an ideal body (as dictated by contemporary Western culture), and suggests a solution (purchase of the equipment) to attain it.

Drive Theory

Drive theory focuses on biological needs that produce unpleasant states of arousal (e.g., your stomach grumbles during a morning class). The arousal this tension causes motivates us to reduce it. Some researchers feel this need to reduce arousal is a basic mechanism that governs much of our behavior.

In a marketing context, tension refers to the unpleasant state that exists if a person's consumption needs are not fulfilled. A person may be grumpy if he hasn't eaten, or he may be dejected or angry if he cannot afford that new car he wants. This state activates goal-oriented behavior, which attempts to reduce or eliminate this unpleasant state and return to a balanced one we refer to as **homeostasis**.

Conceived, designed & released by PUBLINET ADVERTISING & PUBLICITY LLC, Dubai, UAE.

This ad from the United Arab Emirates appeals to our basic drive to reduce hunger.

If a behavior reduces the drive, we'll naturally tend to repeat it. (We discussed this process of *reinforcement* in Chapter 3). Your motivation to leave class early to grab a snack would be greater if you hadn't eaten in 24 hours than if you had eaten only 2 hours earlier. If you did sneak out and got indigestion afterward, say, from wolfing down a package of crisps, you would be less likely to repeat this behavior the next time you want a snack. One's degree of motivation, then, depends on the distance between one's present state and the goal.

Drive theory runs into difficulties when it tries to explain some facets of human behavior that run counter to its predictions. People often do things that increase a drive state rather than decrease it. For example, people may *delay gratification*. If you know you are going out for a lavish dinner, you might decide to forego a snack earlier in the day even though you are hungry at that time.

Expectancy Theory

Most current explanations of motivation focus on cognitive factors rather than biological ones to understand what drives behavior. **Expectancy theory** suggests that expectations of achieving desirable outcomes—positive incentives—rather than being pushed from within motivate our behavior. We choose one product over another because we expect this choice to have more positive consequences for us. Thus, we use the term *drive* here loosely to refer to both physical and cognitive processes.

Motivational Direction

Motives have direction as well as strength. They are goal oriented in that they drive us to satisfy a specific need. We can reach most goals by a number of routes, and the objective of a company is to convince consumers that the alternative it offers provides the best chance to attain the goal. For example, a consumer who decides that she needs a pair of jeans to help her reach her goal of being admired by others can choose among Levi's, Wranglers, True Religion, Diesel, Seven, and many other alternatives, each of which promises to deliver certain benefits.

Delay of gratification can increase a drive rather than reduce it.

Rethink What's Possible. Think you're still years from an upgrade in wheels? Well, the all-new MAZDA3*s* will give you plenty of reasons to rethink. For starters, there's a powerful 160-hp, 2.3-liter DOHC engine and 17-inch alloy wheels. For stoppers, sophisticated 4-wheel disc brakes with available ABS and Electronic Brakeforce Distribution. You can even add available options like the DVD-based navigation system and Xenon headlights. But the best part is what *we've* added: the immediate gratification that comes from driving a Mazda.

*MSRP excludes $520 destination, tax, title and license fees.

www.MazdaUSA.com

 # Needs versus Wants

The specific way we choose to satisfy a need depends on our unique history, learning experiences, and cultural environment. For example, two classmates may feel their stomachs rumbling during a lunchtime lecture. If neither person has eaten since the night before, the strength of their respective needs (hunger) would be about the same. However, the ways each person goes about satisfying this need might be quite different. The first person may be a vegetarian like Paula who fantasizes about gulping down a big handful of trail mix, whereas the second person may be a meat hound like Basil who gets turned on by the prospect of a greasy cheeseburger and french fries.

TYPES OF NEEDS

People are born with a need for certain elements necessary to maintain life, such as food, water, air, and shelter. These are *biogenic needs*. People have many other needs, however, that are not innate. We acquire *psychogenic needs* as we become members of a specific culture. These include the needs for status, power, and affiliation. Psychogenic needs reflect the priorities of a culture, and their effect on behavior will vary from environment to environment. For example, a U.S. consumer may be driven to devote a good chunk of his income to products that permit him to display his individuality, whereas his Japanese counterpart may work equally hard to ensure that he does not stand out from his group.

We also can be motivated to satisfy either utilitarian or hedonic needs. When we focus on a *utilitarian need* we emphasize the objective, tangible attributes of products, such as kilometers per liter in a car; the amount of fat, calories, and protein in a cheeseburger; or the durability of a pair of blue jeans. *Hedonic needs* are subjective and experiential; here we might look to a product to meet our needs for excitement, self-confidence, or fantasy—perhaps to escape the mundane or routine aspects of life.[5] Of course, we can also be motivated to purchase a product because it provides *both* types of benefits. For example, a woman (perhaps a politically incorrect one) might buy a mink coat because of the luxurious image it portrays and because it also happens to keep her warm through the long, cold winter.

MOTIVATIONAL CONFLICTS

A goal has *valence*, which means that it can be positive or negative. We direct our behavior toward goals we value positively; we are motivated to *approach* the goal and to seek out products that will help us to reach it. However, we are not always motivated by the desire to approach a goal. As we saw in the previous chapter's discussion of negative reinforcement, sometimes we're also motivated to *avoid* a negative outcome. We structure purchases or consumption activities to reduce the chances of attaining this end result. For example, many consumers work hard to avoid rejection by their peers, a negative goal. They will stay away from products that they associate with social disapproval. Products such as deodorants and mouthwash frequently rely on consumers' negative motivation by depicting the onerous social consequences of underarm odor or bad breath.

Because a purchase decision can involve more than one source of motivation, consumers often find themselves in situations in which different motives, both positive and negative, conflict with one another.[6] Marketers attempt to satisfy consumers' needs by providing possible solutions to these dilemmas. As Figure 4.1 shows, there are three general types of conflicts we should understand. Let's review each kind.

Approach–Approach Conflict

A person has an **approach–approach conflict** when she must choose between two desirable alternatives. A student might be torn between going home for the holidays and going on a skiing trip with friends. Or she might have to choose between two

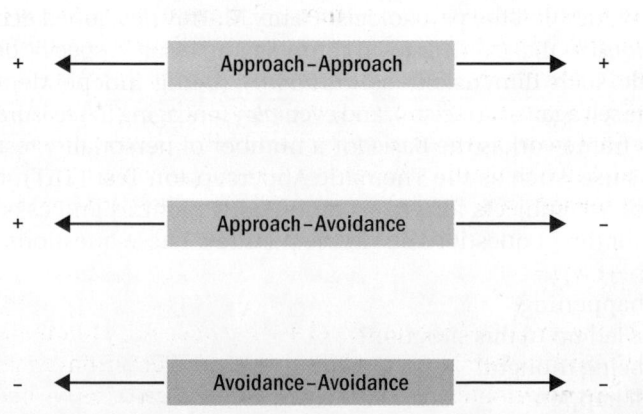

■ FIGURE 4.1
TYPES OF MOTIVATIONAL CONFLICTS

CDs at the store. The **theory of cognitive dissonance** is based on the premise that people have a need for order and consistency in their lives and that a state of *dissonance* (tension) exists when beliefs or behaviors conflict with one another. We resolve the conflict that arises when choosing between two alternatives through a process of *cognitive dissonance reduction*, where we look for a way to reduce this inconsistency (or dissonance), thus eliminating unpleasant tension.

Dissonance often occurs when a consumer must choose between two products, both of which usually possess good and bad qualities. By choosing one product and not the other, the person gets the bad qualities of the chosen product and loses out on the good qualities of the unchosen one. This loss creates an unpleasant, dissonant state that the person seeks to reduce. We tend to convince ourselves, after the fact, that the choice we made was the smart one by finding additional reasons to support the alternative we did choose—perhaps by "discovering" flaws with the option we did not choose (sometimes we call this "rationalization"). A marketer can resolve an approach–approach conflict by bundling several benefits together. For example, the American beer brand Miller Lite's claim that it is "less filling" *and* "tastes great" allows the drinker to "have his beer and drink it too."

Approach–Avoidance Conflict

Many of the products and services we desire have negative consequences attached to them as well. We may feel guilty or ostentatious when buying a status-laden product such as a fur coat, or we might feel like a glutton when we crave a tempting package of crisps. An **approach–avoidance conflict** exists when we desire a goal but wish to avoid it at the same time.

Some solutions to these conflicts include the proliferation of fake furs, which eliminate guilt about harming animals to make a fashion statement, and the success of diet foods, such as those Weight Watchers (weight-watchers.com) sells, which promise good food without the calories. Many marketers try to help consumers overcome guilt by convincing them that they deserve these luxuries (e.g., when the model for L'Oréal cosmetics exclaims, "Because I'm worth it!").

Avoidance–Avoidance Conflict

Sometimes we find ourselves "caught between a rock and a hard place." We may face a choice with two undesirable alternatives, for instance, the option of either spending more money on an old car or buying a new one. Marketers frequently address an **avoidance–avoidance conflict** with messages that stress the unforeseen benefits of choosing one option (e.g., by emphasizing special credit plans to ease the pain of car payments).

CLASSIFYING CONSUMER NEEDS

Psychologists have worked hard to classify human needs. Some defined a universal inventory of needs that they could trace systematically to explain virtually all behavior. One such inventory that the psychologist Henry Murray developed delineates a set of 20 *psychogenic needs* that (sometimes in combination) result in specific behaviors. These needs include such dimensions as *autonomy* (being independent), *defendance* (defending the self against criticism), and even *play* (engaging in pleasurable activities).[7]

Murray's framework is the basis for a number of personality tests modern day psychologists use, such as the Thematic Apperception Test (TAT). In the TAT, the analyst shows test subjects four to six ambiguous pictures and asks them to write answers to four direct questions about the pictures. These questions are as follows:

1 What is happening?
2 What has led up to this situation?
3 What is being thought?
4 What will happen?

The researcher then analyzes each answer for references to certain needs. The theory behind the test is that people will freely project their own subconscious needs onto the neutral stimulus. By getting responses to the pictures, the analyst is really getting at the person's true needs for achievement or affiliation or whatever other need may be dominant. Murray believed that everyone has the same basic set of needs but that individuals differ in their priority rankings of these needs.[8]

Specific Needs and Buying Behavior

Other motivational approaches focus on specific needs and their ramifications for behavior. For example, individuals with a high *need for achievement* strongly value personal accomplishment.[9] They place a premium on products and services that signify success because these consumption items provide feedback about the realization of their goals. These consumers are good prospects for products that provide evidence of their achievement. One study of working women found that those who were high in achievement motivation were more likely to choose clothing they considered businesslike and less likely to be interested in apparel that accentuated their femininity.[10] Some other important needs that are relevant to consumer behavior include the following:

- **Need for affiliation**—(to be in the company of other people):[11] The need for affiliation is relevant to products and services for people in groups, such as participating in team sports, frequenting bars, and going to shopping malls, and it serves to alleviate loneliness.
- **Need for power**—(to control one's environment):[12] Many products and services allow consumers to feel that they have mastery over their surroundings. These products range from "hopped-up" muscle cars and loud boom boxes (large portable radios that impose one's musical tastes on others) to luxury resorts that promise to respond to every whim of their pampered guests.
- **Need for uniqueness**—(to assert one's individual identity):[13] Products can satisfy the need for uniqueness by pledging to accentuate a consumer's distinctive qualities. For example, Cachet perfume claims to be "as individual as you are."

Maslow's Hierarchy of Needs

The psychologist Abraham Maslow proposed one influential approach to motivation. He originally developed this approach to understand personal growth and the attainment of "peak experiences"; marketers later adapted it to understand consumer motivations.[14] Maslow formulated a hierarchy of biogenic and psychogenic needs that specifies certain levels of motives. This *hierarchical* structure implies that the order of development is fixed—that is, we must attain a certain level before we activate a need for the next, higher one. Marketers embraced this perspective because it (indirectly) specifies certain types of product benefits people might be looking for, depending on the different stages they are in in their development or on their environmental conditions.[15]

Figure 4.2 summarizes this model. At each level, different priorities exist in terms of the product benefits for which a consumer is looking. Ideally, an individual progresses up the hierarchy until her dominant motivation is a focus on "ultimate" goals, such as justice and beauty. Unfortunately, this state is difficult to achieve (at least on a regular basis); most of us have to be satisfied with occasional glimpses, or *peak experiences*. One study of men aged 49 to 60 found these respondents engaged in three types of activities to attain self-fulfillment: (1) *sport and physical activity*, (2) *community and charity*, and (3) *building and renovating*. Regardless of whether these activities were related to their professional work, these so-called *magnetic points* gradually took the place of those that were not as fulfilling.[16]

The basic lesson of Maslow's hierarchy is that one must first satisfy basic needs before progressing up the ladder (a starving man is not interested in status symbols, friendship, or self-fulfillment). That implies that consumers value different product

■ FIGURE 4.2 MASLOW'S HIERARCHY

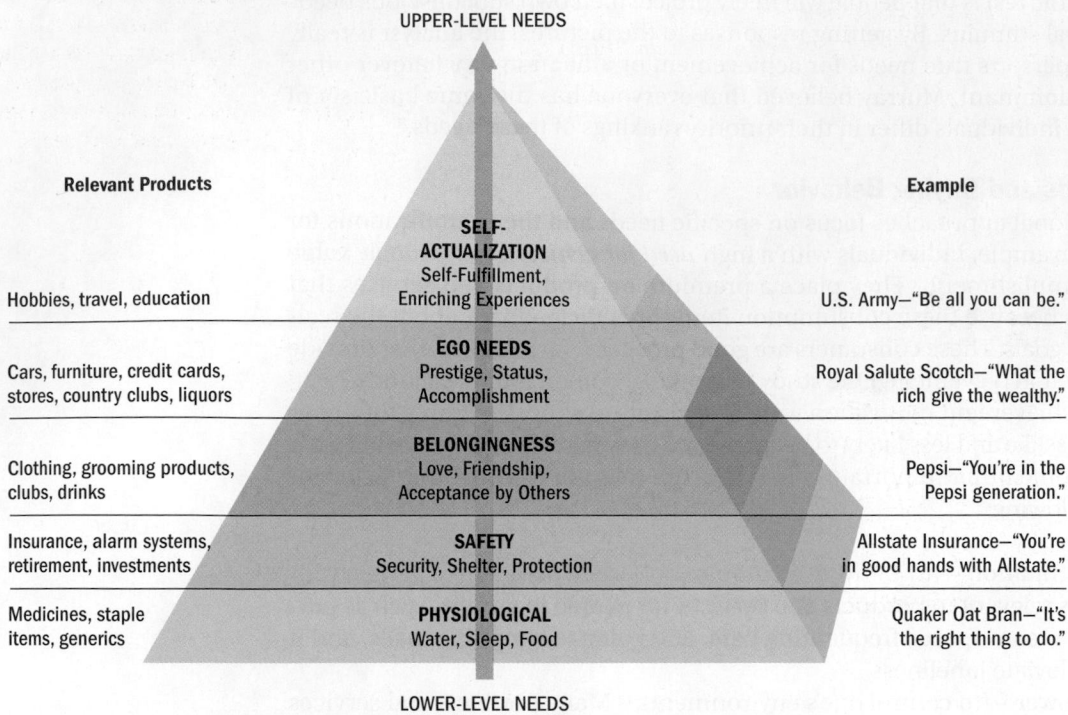

UPPER-LEVEL NEEDS

Relevant Products		Example
	SELF-ACTUALIZATION Self-Fulfillment,	
Hobbies, travel, education	Enriching Experiences	U.S. Army—"Be all you can be."
	EGO NEEDS	
Cars, furniture, credit cards, stores, country clubs, liquors	Prestige, Status, Accomplishment	Royal Salute Scotch—"What the rich give the wealthy."
	BELONGINGNESS	
Clothing, grooming products, clubs, drinks	Love, Friendship, Acceptance by Others	Pepsi—"You're in the Pepsi generation."
Insurance, alarm systems, retirement, investments	**SAFETY** Security, Shelter, Protection	Allstate Insurance—"You're in good hands with Allstate."
Medicines, staple items, generics	**PHYSIOLOGICAL** Water, Sleep, Food	Quaker Oat Bran—"It's the right thing to do."

LOWER-LEVEL NEEDS

attributes depending on what is currently available to them. For example, consumers in the former Eastern bloc are now bombarded with images of luxury goods, yet may still have trouble obtaining basic necessities. In one study, Romanian students named the products they hoped to acquire. Their wish lists included not only the expected items such as sports cars and the latest model televisions but also staples such as water, soap, furniture, and food.[17]

Marketers' application of this hierarchy has been somewhat simplistic, especially as the same product or activity can satisfy a number of different needs. For example, one study found that gardening could satisfy needs at every level of the hierarchy:[18]

● **Physiological**—"I like to work in the soil."
● **Safety**—"I feel safe in the garden."
● **Social**—"I can share my produce with others."
● **Esteem**—"I can create something of beauty."
● **Self-actualization**—"My garden gives me a sense of peace."

Another problem with taking Maslow's hierarchy too literally is that it is culture-bound; its assumptions may apply only to Western culture. People in other cultures (or, for that matter, even some in Western cultures as well) may question the order of the levels it specifies. A religious person who has taken a vow of celibacy would not necessarily agree that physiological needs must be satisfied before self-fulfillment can occur.

Similarly, many Asian cultures value the welfare of the group (belongingness needs) more highly than needs of the individual (esteem needs). The point is that this hierarchy, although marketers widely apply it, is helpful primarily because it reminds us that consumers may have different need priorities in different consumption situations and at different stages in their lives—not because it *exactly* specifies a consumer's progression up the ladder of needs.

A study that compared Dutch and American students' conceptions of paradise asked respondents to construct collages that expressed their vision of an ideal life. This Dutch collage emphasizes higher-order needs relating to interpersonal harmony and environmental awareness.

 ## Consumer Involvement

Do consumers form strong relationships with products and services? If you don't believe so, consider these events:

- A consumer in Brighton, England, loves a local restaurant called the All in One so much that he had its name and phone number tattooed on his forehead. The owner remarked, "Whenever he comes in, he'll go straight to the front of the queue."[19]
- *Lucky* is a magazine devoted to shopping for shoes and other fashion accessories. The centerfold of the first issue featured rows of makeup sponges. The editor observed, "It's the same way that you might look at a golf magazine and see a spread of nine irons. *Lucky* is addressing one interest in women's lives, in a really obsessive, specific way."[20]
- After being jilted by his girlfriend, a Tennessee man tried to marry his car. His plan was thwarted, however, after he listed his fiancée's birthplace as Detroit, her father as Henry Ford, and her blood type as 10W40. Under Tennessee law, only a man and a woman can legally wed.[21] So much for that exciting honeymoon at the carwash.

Clearly, we can get pretty attached to products. Our motivation to attain a goal increases our desire to acquire the products or services we believe will satisfy it. However, not everyone is motivated to the same extent—one person might be convinced he can't live without the latest Apple iPhone, whereas another is perfectly happy with his 3-year-old LG.

Involvement is "a person's perceived relevance of the object based on their inherent needs, values, and interests."[22] We use the word *object* in the generic sense to refer to a product (or a brand), an advertisement, or a purchase situation. Consumers can find involvement in all these *objects*. Figure 4.3 shows that because involvement is a motivational construct, different antecedents can trigger it. These factors can be something about the person, something about the object, or something about the situation.

■ **FIGURE 4.3** CONCEPTUALIZING INVOLVEMENT

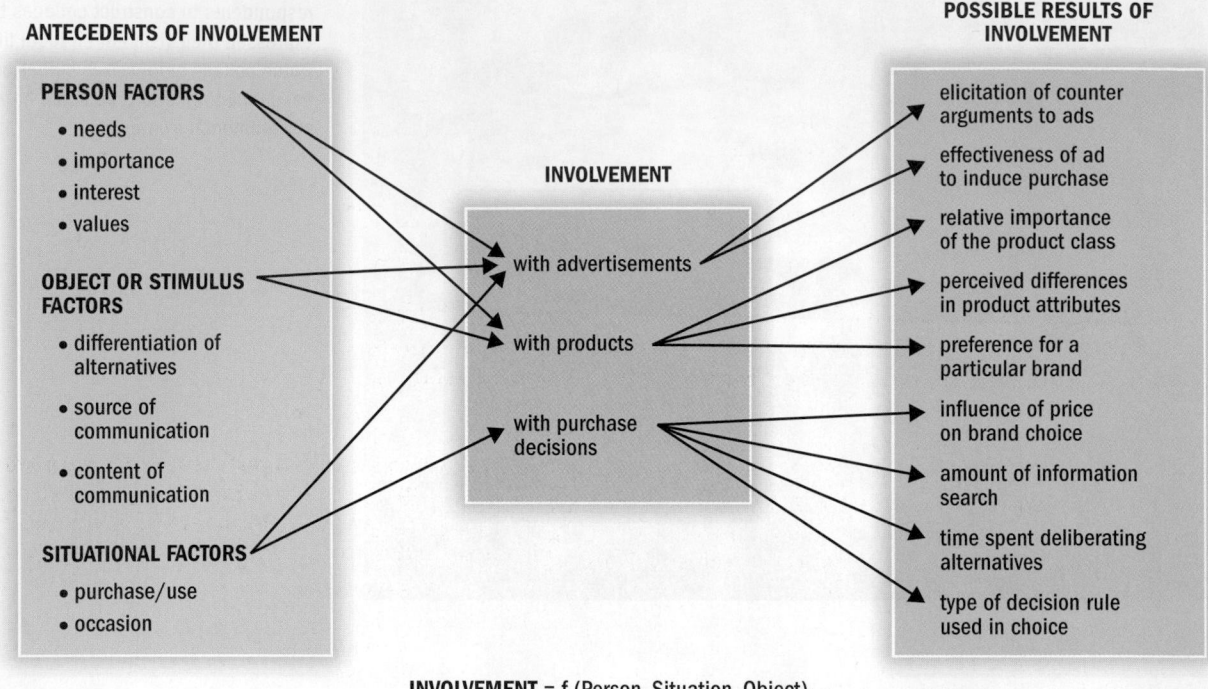

INVOLVEMENT = f (Person, Situation, Object)

The level of involvement may be influenced by one or more of these three factors. Interactions among persons, situation, and object factors are likely to occur.

Involvement reflects how motivated we are to process information.[23] To the degree that you feel knowing more about a product will help you to achieve some goal, you'll be motivated to pay attention to information about it. And as our involvement with a product increases, we devote more attention to ads related to the product, we exert more cognitive effort to understand these ads, and we focus more attention on the product-related information in the ads.[24]

LEVELS OF INVOLVEMENT: FROM INERTIA TO PASSION

The type of information processing that occurs depends on the consumer's level of involvement. It can range from *simple processing*, where she considers only the basic features of a message all the way to *elaboration* where she links this information to her preexisting knowledge system.[25]

Inertia

Think of a person's degree of involvement as a continuum, ranging from absolute lack of interest in a marketing stimulus at one end to obsession at the other. **Inertia** describes consumption at the low end of involvement, where we make decisions out of habit because we lack the motivation to consider alternatives. At the high end of involvement, we can expect to find the type of passionate intensity we reserve for people and objects that carry great meaning for us. For example, the passion of some consumers for famous people (those living, such as Oprah Winfrey, or—supposedly—dead, such as Elvis Presley) demonstrates the high end of the involvement continuum.

When consumers are truly involved with a product, an ad, or a Web site, they enter a **flow state**. This state is the Holy Grail of Web designers who want to create sites that are so entrancing the surfer loses all track of time as he becomes engrossed in the site's contents (and hopefully buys stuff in the process!). Flow is an optimal experience the following characterizes:

● A sense of playfulness
● A feeling of being in control
● Concentration and highly focused attention
● Mental enjoyment of the activity for its own sake
● A distorted sense of time
● A match between the challenge at hand and one's skills.[26]

Cult Products

In June 2007, a momentous event shook the modern world: Apple started selling its iPhone. Thousands of adoring iCultists (including the mayor of Philadelphia) around the country waited in front of Apple stores for days to be one of the first to buy the

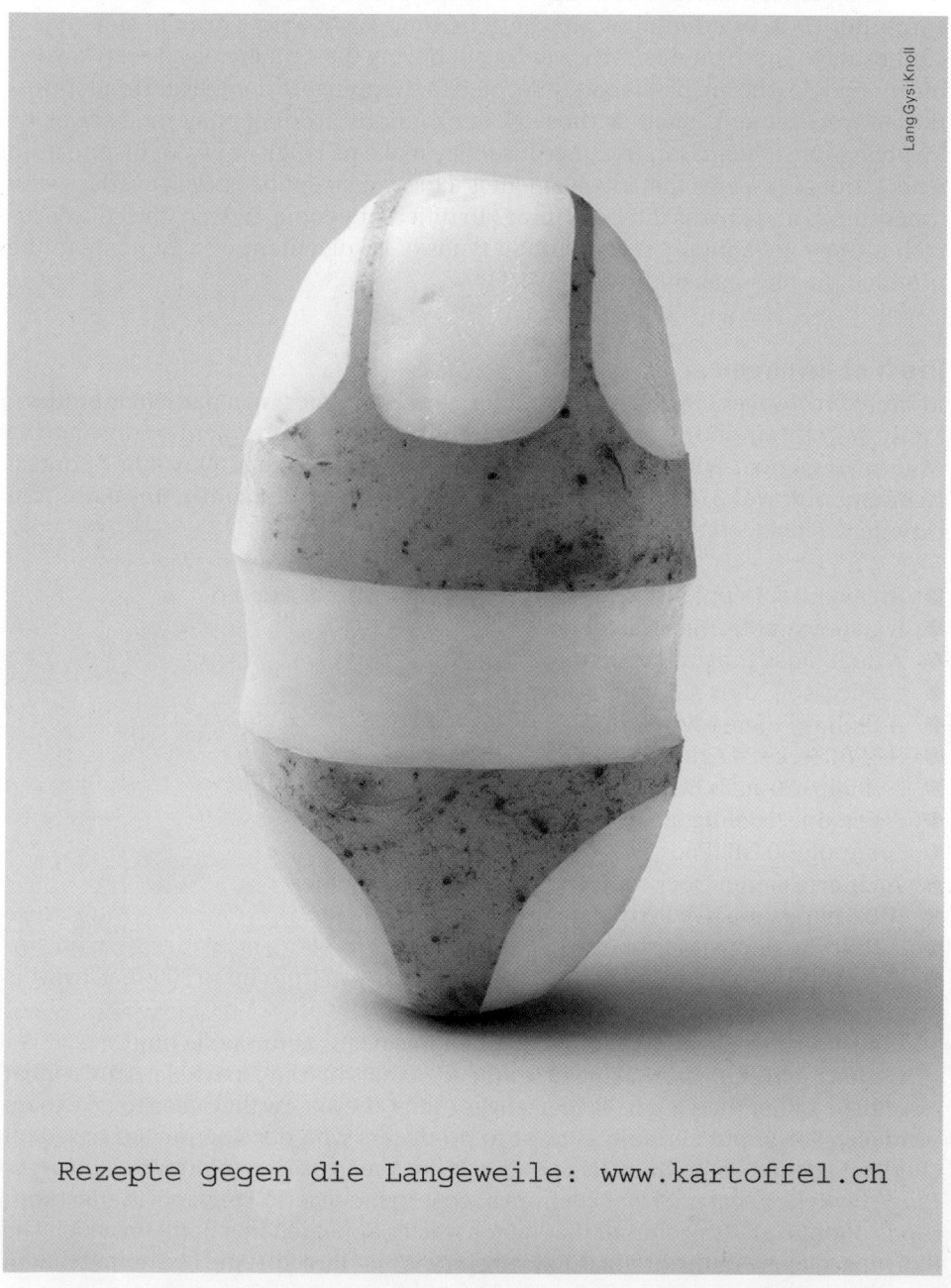

Lang Gysi Knoll

Rezepte gegen die Langeweile: www.kartoffel.ch

The Swiss Potato Board is trying to increase involvement with its product. The ad reads, "Recipes against boredom."

device—even though they could order the phone online and have it delivered in 3 days. Somehow that was too long to wait for a cell phone with a touchscreen. As one loyal consumer admitted, "If Apple made sliced bread, yeah, I'd buy it."[27]

Cult products command fierce consumer loyalty, devotion, and maybe even worship by consumers who are very highly involved with a brand. These items take many forms, from Apple computers and Harley-Davidson motorcycles to Krispy Kreme donuts, Jones Soda, and Webkinz, not to mention consumers' devotion to recording artists and sports teams.[28] What else explains the willingness of many women (like Carrie on the TV show *Sex and the City*) to shell out up to $3,400 for a pair of Manolo Blahnik designer shoes?

THE MANY FACES OF INVOLVEMENT

Involvement can take many forms. It can be cognitive, as when a "Webhead" is motivated to learn all he can about the latest specs of a new multimedia personal computer (PC), or emotional, as when the thought of a new Armani suit gives a clotheshorse goose bumps.[29] The very act of buying the Armani may be very involving for people who are passionately devoted to shopping. To complicate matters further, advertisements such as those Nike or Adidas produce may themselves be involving for some reason (e.g., because they make us laugh or cry, or inspire us to work harder). It seems that involvement is a fuzzy concept because it overlaps with other things and means different things to different people. Indeed, the consensus is that there are actually several broad types of involvement we can relate to the product, the message, or the perceiver.[30]

Product Involvement

Product involvement refers to a consumer's level of interest in a particular product. Many sales promotions aim to increase this type of involvement—consider the American woman who recently won Roto-Rooter's "Pimped-Out John" contest (winning out over 318,000 other entries). Her prizes to maximize her bathroom experience included the following:[31]

- An Avanti 4.3-cubic-foot compact refrigerator with a beer tap
- A Gateway eMachines Notebook
- A dual-sided magnification mirror
- A Microsoft Xbox 360 core system
- A Philips Progressive-Scan DVD player
- A TiVo Series2 Digital Video Recorder
- A Philips 20-inch LCD Flat-Panel TV
- A personal cooling fan
- An Apple 30 GB iPod
- An iCarta Stereo Dock for iPod with bath tissue holder
- A Baseline Resistive Pedal Exerciser
- A Roto-Rooter Service button
- A megaphone so anyone in the house can hear you from up to 300-feet away!

Talk about satisfying utilitarian and hedonic needs at the same time!

Smart marketers are waking up to the idea that their most avid fans are a great resource—rather than ignoring their suggestions, they know they need to take them seriously. This input certainly is clear to producers who develop movies based on cherished comic book characters or other stories such as Harry Potter or *Lord of the Rings*. Liv Tyler's character was cut from a scene in the second *Rings* movie after thousands of online fans protested that her character appeared in a battle in which she didn't participate in the original Tolkien story. When director Ang Lee hinted that in

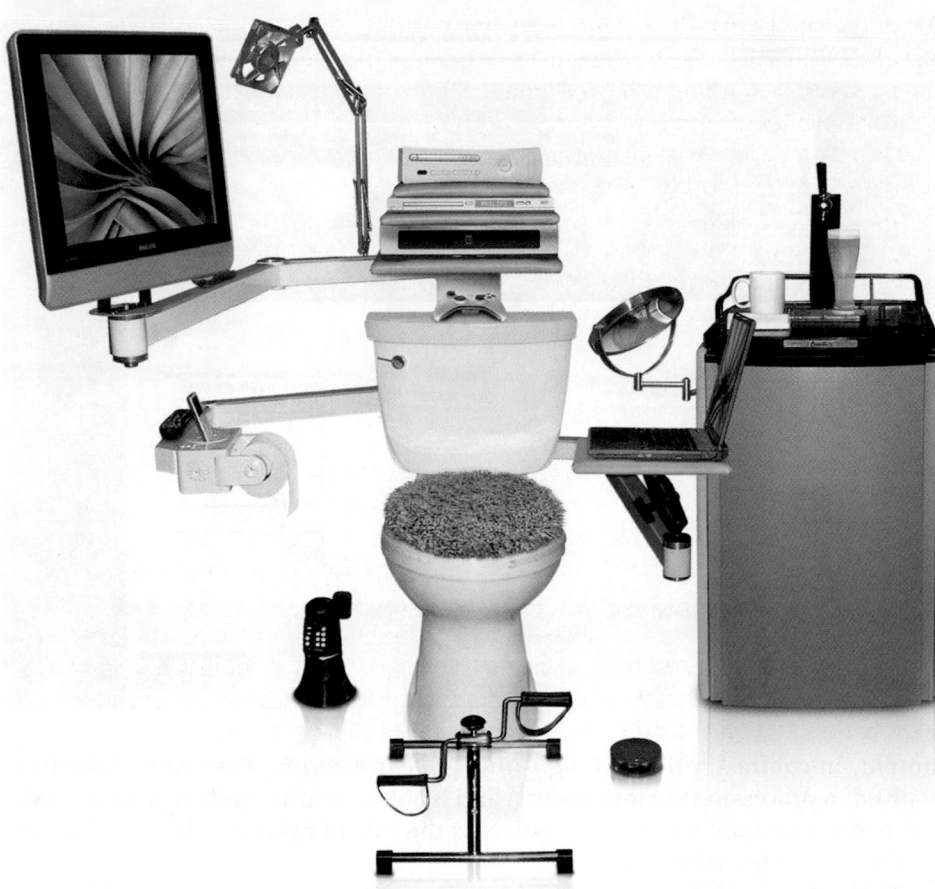

The winner of Roto-Rooter's "Pimped-Out John" Contest satisfies both utilitarian and hedonic needs at the same sitting.

his movie version *The Hulk* might not wear his trademark purple pants—or any pants at all—devotees of the comic character bombarded the Web with protests and threats of a boycott. Guess what? When the movie was released, The Hulk was indeed sporting his familiar attire.[32]

Perhaps the most powerful way to enhance product involvement is to invite consumers to play a role in designing or personalizing what they buy. **Mass customization** is the personalization of products and services for individual customers at a mass-production price.[33] Improved manufacturing techniques in many industries are allowing companies to produce made-to-order products for many customers at a time. Customers love it—today about 40 percent of the online retailer Lands' End shoppers choose a customized garment rather than the standard-sized equivalent, even though these items cost at least $20 more and take about 3 to 4 weeks to arrive. At Nike.com, buyers can specify a unique palette of colors or even words that will appear on their shoes. Masterfoods is letting candy lovers go online to choose 1 of 13 colors and add a personal slogan that will appear on one side of M&Ms candy shells. Even the U.S. Postal Service is getting into the act by offering personalized stamps featuring (almost) any image you would like.[34]

Message–Response Involvement

Vigilante marketing, where freelancers and fans film their own commercials for favorite products and post them on Web sites, is hot. In one unauthorized spot, an iPod Mini zips around to the song "Tiny Machine" by the Darling Buds (more on this craze in a bit).[35] This devotion to creating a commercial is an extreme example of *message–response involvement* (also called *advertising involvement*), which refers to the consumer's interest in processing marketing communications.[36]

Television is a *low-involvement medium* because it requires a passive viewer who exerts relatively little control (remote-control "zipping" notwithstanding) over

Loyal users can log in and hang out at the Jones Soda Web site.

content. In contrast, print is a *high-involvement medium*. The reader is actively involved in processing the information and is able to pause and reflect on what she has read before moving on.[37] We'll discuss the role of message characteristics in changing attitudes in Chapter 8.

Marketers are experimenting with novel ways to increase consumers' involvement with different message formats. Procter & Gamble created a new medium by printing trivia questions and answers on its Pringles snack chips using ink made of blue or red food coloring, whereas a company called Speaking Roses International patented a technology to laser-print words, images, or logos on flower petals.[38] Snapple's attempt to promote a new line of frozen treats in a novel way got sticky during a recent summer when a 25-foot, 17.5-ton giant popsicle the company was erecting in downtown Manhattan toppled over, flooding a city square with kiwi-strawberry goo that sent pedestrians scrambling for higher ground![39]

The quest to heighten message involvement is fueling the rapid growth of **interactive mobile marketing**, where consumers participate in real-time promotional campaigns via their trusty cell phones, usually by text-messaging entries to on-air TV contests. These strategies are very popular in the U.K., for example, where revenue from phone and text-messaging services for TV programs brings in almost a half billion dollars a year. The U.S. market is starting to catch up Americans sent 9.8 billion text messages in December 2005, up from 4.8 billion a year earlier. Although a handful of U.S. TV shows, such as *American Idol*, have been inviting viewers to vote on contestants using their cell phones for years, this wasn't a popular strategy until recently. There was little money to be made because consumers generally paid only about 10 cents per message and the cell phone companies typically kept most of the revenue. The United States particularly has been slow in adopting text voting because programmers have to deal with several time zones and several different wireless network technologies, whereas in many other countries there is only one time zone and one dominant wireless network technology. Also a few major cell phone operators wouldn't let marketers use their networks because of concerns about network overload. However, this all changed in 2006 when the leading wireless operators agreed on "consumer best practices guidelines" for text-message voting on TV shows. The guidelines now allow programmers to charge as much as 99 cents a message as long as viewers are aware of the cost. And programmers no longer run the risk of frustrating audience members who have the wrong cell phone service now that all major operators are participating. Later that year, viewers sent more than 500,000 text-message votes within 2 days during the reality show *Big Brother*. *American Idol* still reigns supreme in this category; 64 million viewers sent text messages to vote for or chat with contestants in one season, up from only 7.5 million in 2003.[40]

Purchase Situation Involvement

Purchase situation involvement refers to differences in motivation when people buy the same product but in different contexts. For example, when you want to impress someone, you may try to buy a brand with a certain image that you think reflects good taste. When you have to buy a gift for someone in an obligatory situation, such as a wedding gift for a cousin you do not really like, you may not care what image the gift portrays. Again, some smart retailers are waking up to the value of increasing purchase situation involvement when they appeal to hedonic shoppers who are looking to be entertained or otherwise engaged in addition to simply "buying stuff."[41] We'll learn more about how they're doing this via the creation of themed retailing venues and other strategies in Chapter 10.

MEASURING AND ENHANCING INVOLVEMENT

Measuring involvement is important for many marketing applications. For example, research evidence indicates that a viewer who is more involved with a television show will respond more positively to commercials he sees during that show and that these spots will have a greater chance of influencing his purchase intentions.[42] Table 4.1 shows one of the most widely used scales researchers use to assess people's extent of involvement.

French researchers devised another scale to measure the antecedents of product involvement. Recognizing that consumers can be involved with a product because it is a risky purchase and its use reflects on or affects the self, they advocate the development of an *involvement profile* containing five components:[43]

TABLE 4.1
MEASURING INVOLVEMENT

To Me [Object to Be Judged] Is

1. important	_:_:_:_:_:_:_	unimportant*
2. boring	_:_:_:_:_:_:_	interesting
3. relevant	_:_:_:_:_:_:_	irrelevant*
4. exciting	_:_:_:_:_:_:_	unexciting*
5. means nothing	_:_:_:_:_:_:_	means a lot to me
6. appealing	_:_:_:_:_:_:_	unappealing*
7. fascinating	_:_:_:_:_:_:_	mundane*
8. worthless	_:_:_:_:_:_:_	valuable
9. involving	_:_:_:_:_:_:_	uninvolving*
10. not needed	_:_:_:_:_:_:_	needed

Note: Totaling the 10 items gives a score from a low of 10 to a high of 70.

* Indicates item is reverse scored. For example, a score of 7 for item no. 1 (important/unimportant) would actually be scored as 1.

Source: Judith Lynne Zaichkowsky, "The Personal Involvement Inventory: Reduction, Revision, and Application to Advertising," *Journal of Advertising* 23, no. 4 (December 1994): 59–70. Copyright © 1994 by American Academy of Advertising. Reprinted with permission of M.E. Sharpe, Inc. All rights reserved. Not for reproduction.

1 The personal interest a consumer has in a product category, its personal meaning or importance;

2 The perceived importance of the potential negative consequences associated with a poor choice of the product (risk importance);

3 The probability of making a bad purchase;

4 The pleasure value of the product category;

5 The sign value of the product category (how closely it's related to the self).

These researchers asked a sample of homemakers to rate a set of 14 product categories on each of the facets of involvement. Table 4.2 shows the results. These data indicate that no single component captures consumer involvement. For example, consumers see the purchase of a durable product, such as a vacuum cleaner, as risky because one might get stuck with a bad choice for many years. However, the vacuum cleaner does not provide pleasure (hedonic value), and it is not high in sign value (i.e., its use is not related to the person's self-concept). In contrast, chocolate is high in pleasure value, but people don't see it as risky or closely related to the self. Dresses and bras, however, appear to be involving for a combination of reasons. Note also that involvement with a product class may vary across cultures. Although this sample of French consumers rated champagne high in both sign value and personal value, the ability of champagne to provide pleasure or to be central to self-definition might not transfer to other countries (e.g., Islamic cultures). Measures such as this are useful to marketers who want to segment their customers in terms of the types of benefits they hope to receive from brands; for example, a yogurt manufacturer might find that even though its

TABLE 4.2
INVOLVEMENT PROFILES FOR A SET OF FRENCH CONSUMER PRODUCTS

	Importance of Negative Consequences	Subjective Probability of Mispurchase	Pleasure Value	Sign Value
Dresses	121	112	147	181
Bras	117	115	106	130
Washing machines	118	109	106	111
TV sets	112	100	122	95
Vacuum cleaners	110	112	70	78
Irons	103	95	72	76
Champagne	109	120	125	125
Oil	89	97	65	92
Yogurt	86	83	106	78
Chocolate	80	89	123	75
Shampoo	96	103	90	81
Toothpaste	95	95	94	105
Facial soap	82	90	114	118
Detergents	79	82	56	63

Average product score = 100.
Note the first two antecedents of personal importance and importance of negative consequences are combined in these data.
Source: Reprinted with permission from Journal of Marketing Research, published by the American Marketing Association, Giles Laurant and Jean-Noel Kapterer, "Measuring Consumer Involvement Profiles" Feb. 1985, vol. 22, p. 45. Copyright © 1985 American Marketing Association. Used with permission.

product is low in sign value for one group of consumers, it might highly relate to the self-concept of another market segment, such as health-food enthusiasts or avid dieters. The company could adapt its strategy to account for the motivation of different segments to process information about the product.

Although consumers differ in their levels of involvement with respect to a product message, marketers do not have to simply sit back and hope for the best. By being aware of some basic factors that increase or decrease attention, they can take steps to increase the likelihood that product information will get through. A marketer can boost consumers' motivations to process relevant information by using one or more of the following techniques:[44]

- **Appeal to the consumers' hedonic needs**—For example, ads using sensory appeals generate higher levels of attention.[45]
- **Use novel stimuli, such as unusual cinematography, sudden silences, or unexpected movements, in commercials**—When a British firm called Egg Banking introduced a credit card to the French market, its ad agency created unusual commercials to make people question their assumptions. One ad stated, "Cats always land on their paws," and then two researchers in white lab coats dropped a kitten off a rooftop—never to see it again (animal rights activists were not amused).[46]
- **Use prominent stimuli, such as loud music and fast action, to capture attention in commercials**—In print formats, larger ads increase attention. Also, viewers look longer at colored pictures than at black and white ones.
- **Include celebrity endorsers to generate higher interest in commercials**—(We'll discuss this strategy in Chapter 8.)
- **Build bonds with consumers by maintaining ongoing relationships with them**—Charmin brand bathroom tissue set up public toilets in New York's Times Square that thousands of grateful visitors used—thousands more people (evidently with time on their hands) visited the brand's Web site to view the display.[47]

CONSUMER-GENERATED CONTENT

Have you checked out one of those crazy Mentos/Diet Coke videos yet? At least 800 of them flooded the Internet after people discovered that when you drop the quarter-size candies into bottles of Diet Coke you get a geyser that shoots 20 feet into the air. Needless to say, Mentos got a gusher of free publicity out of the deal too.[48]

Consumer-generated content, where everyday people voice their opinions about products, brands, and companies on blogs, podcasts, and social networking sites such as Facebook and MySpace, and even film their own commercials that thousands view on sites such as YouTube, probably is the biggest marketing phenomenon of the past few years (even bigger than the iPhone or Paris Hilton's jail stay!). This important trend helps to define the era of so-called **Web 2.0,** the rebirth of the Internet as a social, interactive medium from its original roots as a form of one-way transmission from producers to consumers.

Although many marketers find this change threatening because it forces them to "share" ownership of their brands with users, this new form of user participation is here to stay. The reality is that companies no longer can rely solely on a "push method" to inform their customers about their products; now they need to encourage a vibrant two-way dialogue that allows consumers to contribute their evaluations of products within their respective Web communities. Consumers embrace this trend for several reasons: The technology is readily available and inexpensive to use. Internet access allows any surfer to become (somewhat of) an expert on anything in a matter of hours, and people trust their peers' opinions more than they do those of big companies (more on this in Chapter 11).[49] So marketers need to accept this new reality—even when they don't necessarily like what customers have to say about their brands. When it comes to consumer-generated content, they're either on the train or under it! Here are a few of the many consumer-generated campaigns we've seen recently:[50]

- At MasterCard's <u>priceless.com</u> Web site consumers can write advertising copy for two filmed commercials by contributing four lines of dialogue, ending with the kicker, "Priceless."
- A Converse campaign that allowed customers to send in homemade commercials to <u>conversegallery.com</u> attracted about 1,500 submissions. Converse ran several of them on television.
- Kao Corp., which makes Ban deodorant, asked young women to create ads that talk to fellow teens who worry about underarm odor. Readers of teen magazines submitted images and filled in the blanks in the company's "Ban It" slogan. One typical submission shows four girls in similar jeans and tank tops with their backs to the camera; the headline reads: "Ban Uniformity."
- The video game *Sims 2* from Electronic Arts (EA) capitalized on video gamers' fondness for making short films based on scenes from games (called **machinimas**) to promote its Sims 2 game. EA brought 15 gamers to its headquarters to make the films, which became the basis of TV, online, and print ads.
- The CNN news network created <u>CNN.com/exchange</u>, where citizen journalists can submit photos, graphics, audio, and video that others can view.
- PepsiCo sponsored a Creative Challenge in China that invited consumers to develop the next Pepsi TV commercial starring Asian pop-music superstar Jay Chou. Pepsi got almost 27,000 scripts in 6 weeks. To help promote the contest, China's Back Dorm Boys, a pair of lip-syncing "net celebrities" Pepsi sponsored, acted out scripts in their dorm room. In the United States, Pepsi offered consumers a chance to design a new can for the beverage; the winning design will appear on 500 million Pepsi cans.
- Lucasfilm made clips of *Star Wars* available to fans on the Internet to *mash up* (remix) them at will in celebration of the thirtieth anniversary of the epic's release. Working with an easy-to-use editing program, fans can cut, add to, and retool the clips. Then they can post their creations to blogs or social networking sites such as <u>MySpace</u>.
- Now that TV spin-offs from the *Star Trek* series have ended, bereft Trekkies are filling the void by banding together to make their own episodes. Up to two dozen of these fan-made *Star Trek* projects are in various stages of completion, depending what you count as a full-fledged production. You can view a Scottish production at <u>www.ussintrepid.org.uk</u>. A Los Angeles group has filmed more than 40 episodes, some of which explore gay themes the original didn't get near (check out <u>www.hiddenfrontier.com</u>), A Texas-based group resurrected a ship whose crew was turned into salt in an episode of the original series (<u>www.starshipexeter.com</u>).
- California State University, Fresno, sponsored a campus competition to create video clips posted to <u>YouTube</u> that appeal to potential applicants as well as stir feelings of pride among students, alumni, and members of the faculty and staff.
- The Nokia concept Lounge invited designers in Europe to share ideas for the next new cool phone, whereas a Nespresso contest yielded coffee-drinking ideas such as the Nespresso InCar coffee machine and the Nespresso Chipcard that, on being inserted into a vending machine, communicates with a central database to brew a personalized cup of coffee.
- The *L-Word* Fanisode competition asked viewers to create an episode of the hit television show by assembling a full script, scene by scene. The grand prizewinner got a script-writing session with the show's creator in addition to cash.
- Danish Vores Øl ("Our Beer") claims to be the world's first open-source brew. The brewer publishes the recipe under a *Creative Commons* license, meaning that anyone can use Vores Øl's name. As long as home brewers publish the recipe under the same license, they're free to make money from their versions of the brand.
- Honda U.K. is sponsoring a new blog network, <u>2TalkAbout.com</u>, that lets audiences publish their views on well-known brands, as well as respond to other

people's views. Although the online community is completely independent from Honda, Honda engineers and associates regularly log on to contribute and respond to feedback to give users direct access to the brand.

 ## Values

A **value** is a belief that some condition is preferable to its opposite. For example, it's safe to assume that most people prefer freedom to slavery. Others avidly pursue products and services that will make them look younger rather than older. A person's set of values plays a very important role in consumption activities. Consumers purchase many products and services because they believe these products will help to attain a value-related goal.

Pleasanty surprise of groping
探索的惊喜

Marketing Pitfall

Chevrolet learned the hard way about the downside of giving control over its brands to consumers. The carmaker introduced a Web site allowing visitors to take existing video clips and music, insert their own words, and create customized 30-second commercials for the 2007 Chevrolet Tahoe. The idea was to generate interest in the Tahoe by encouraging satisfied drivers to circulate videos on the Web of themselves. Sure enough, plenty of videos circulated— but many of the messages for the gas-hungry SUV weren't exactly flattering. One ad used a sweeping view of the Tahoe driving through a desert. "Our planet's oil is almost gone," it said. "You don't need G.P.S. to see where this road leads." Another commercial asked, "Like this snowy wilderness? Better get your fill of it now. Then say hello to global warming."

A spokeswoman for Chevrolet said, "We anticipated that there would be critical submissions. You do turn over your brand to the public, and we knew that we were going to get some bad with the good. But it's part of playing in this space."[51]

Recognizing that the values of visitors from around the world may sometimes differ, the Chinese government is preparing its citizens for the Olympics in Beijing with aggressive campaigns to curtail behaviors including groping and spitting in public. Sometimes the language can be a little "awkward."

Two people can believe in the same behaviors (e.g., vegetarianism), but their underlying *belief systems* may be quite different (e.g., animal activism versus health concerns). The extent to which people share a belief system is a function of individual, social, and cultural forces. Advocates of a belief system often seek out others with similar beliefs so that social networks overlap, and as a result, believers tend to be exposed to information that supports their beliefs (e.g., "tree-huggers" rarely hang out with loggers).[52]

CORE VALUES

More than 8.2 million women in 50 countries read versions of *Cosmopolitan* in 28 different languages—even though due to local norms about modesty some of them have to hide the magazine from their husbands! Adapting the *Cosmo* credo of "Fun, Fearless Female" in all these places gets a bit tricky. Different cultures emphasize varying belief systems that define what it means to be female, feminine, or appealing—and what is considered appropriate to see in print on these matters. Publishers of the Chinese version aren't even permitted to mention sex at all, so articles about uplifting cleavage are replaced by uplifting stories about youthful dedication. Ironically, there isn't much down-and-dirty material in the Swedish edition either—but for the opposite reason: The culture is so open about this topic that it doesn't grab readers' attention the way it would in the United States.[53]

In India, you won't come across any *Cosmo* articles about sexual positions. And *Playboy* recently announced plans to publish a magazine in India—but without nudes. The magazine views the country as a promising, new market with values similar to those of people in the United States in the 1950s when *Playboy* was first published: India is on the verge of a sexual revolution but it's not quite there yet. In a sharp departure even from fairly recent times, today pollsters report that in India one-quarter of urban, unmarried women have sex; one-third read erotic literature; and half go on dates. And there is a small but growing class of young, urban Indian men with disposable incomes who are eager to learn about the good life. However, as one Indian analyst observed, "In urban India, the concept of single men living alone is quite new. Here, most men, until they're married, live at home. Once you're married, your wife wonders what you're reading."[54]

Every culture has a set of values that it imparts to its members.[55] People in one culture might feel that being a unique individual is preferable to subordinating one's identity to the group, whereas another culture may emphasize the virtues of group membership. A study by Wirthlin Worldwide found that the most important values to Asian executives are hard work, respect for learning, and honesty. In contrast, North American businesspeople emphasize the values of personal freedom, self-reliance, and freedom of expression.[56]

These differences in values often explain why marketing efforts that are a big hit in one country can flop in another. For example, a hugely successful advertisement in Japan promoted breast cancer awareness by showing an attractive woman in a sundress drawing stares from men on the street as a voice-over says, "If only women paid as much attention to their breasts as men do." The same ad flopped in France because the use of humor to talk about a serious disease offended the French.[57]

Values regarding issues such as sexuality are important in the United States also. A recent flap over a condom commercial illustrates how these beliefs can touch a nerve (in fact, it was only recently that we started to see prophylactic advertising on TV at all!). In the Trojan spot, women in a bar find themselves sitting next to pigs. One magically turns into a handsome suitor after it buys a condom from a vending machine. The tag line reads, "Evolve. Use a condom every time." The CBS and Fox networks rejected the ad and some local NBC affiliates refused to run it. A blogger noted the ambiguity of our values about this sensitive issue: "I'm offended by the reality that television is so hypersexualized and glorifies sexual excess and promiscuity, and

One consequence of differences in values across cultures is that images consumers in one market consider acceptable may be beyond the pale for people in others. This laxative ad from Thailand illustrates that effect.

then runs screaming into the megachurch and drops to its knees when someone wants to run an advertisement that urges people to be responsible about their sexual expression."[58]

Or take the core value of cleanliness—everyone wants to be clean, but some societies are more fastidious than others and won't accept products and services that they think cut corners. Italian women on average spend 21 hours a week on household chores other than cooking—compared with only 4 hours for Americans according to Procter & Gamble's research. The Italian women wash kitchen and bathroom floors at least four times a week, Americans only once. Italian women typically iron nearly all their wash, even socks and sheets, and they buy more cleaning supplies than women elsewhere do.

So they should be ideal customers for cleaning products, right? That's what Unilever thought when it launched its all-purpose Cif spray cleaner there, but it flopped. Similarly, P&G's best-selling Swiffer wet mop bombed big time. Both companies underestimated this market's desire for products that are tough cleaners, not timesavers. Only about 30 percent of Italian households have dishwashers because many women don't trust machines to get dishes as clean as they can get them by hand, manufacturers say. Many of those who have machines tend to thoroughly rinse the dishes before loading them in the machines. The explanation for this value: After World War II, Italy remained a poor country until well into the 1960s, so labor-saving devices, such as washing machines, that had become popular in wealthy countries arrived late. Italian women joined the workforce later than many other European women and in smaller numbers. Young Italian women increasingly work outside the home, but they still spend nearly as much time as their mothers did on housework.

When Unilever did research to determine why Italians didn't take to Cif, they found that these women weren't convinced that a mere spray would do the job on tough kitchen grease or that one product would adequately clean different surfaces (it turns out that 72 percent of Italians own more than eight different cleaning products). The company reformulated the product and reintroduced it with different varieties instead of as an all-in-one. It also made the bottles 50 percent bigger because Italians clean so frequently and changed its advertising to emphasize the products' cleaning strength rather than convenience. P&G also reintroduced its Swiffer, this time adding beeswax and a Swiffer duster that is now a bestseller. It sold 5 million boxes in the first 8 months, twice the company's forecasts.[59]

In many cases, of course, values are universal. Who does not desire health, wisdom, or world peace? What sets cultures apart is the *relative importance*, or ranking, of these universal values. This set of rankings constitutes a culture's **value system**.[60] For example, one study found that North Americans have more favorable attitudes toward advertising messages that focus on self-reliance, self-improvement, and the achievement of personal goals as opposed to themes stressing family integrity, collective goals, and the feeling of harmony with others. Korean consumers exhibited the reverse pattern.[61]

We characterize every culture in terms of its members' endorsement of a value system. Every individual may not endorse these values equally, and in some cases, values may even seem to contradict one another (e.g., Americans appear to value both conformity and individuality, and seek to find some accommodation between the two). Nonetheless, it is usually possible to identify a general set of **core values** that uniquely define a culture. Core values such as freedom, youthfulness, achievement, materialism, and activity characterize American culture.

In contrast, most Japanese are happy to trade off a bit of independence for security and a feeling of safety—especially when it comes to their children. It's common for communities to post guards along school routes and for parents to place global positioning system (GPS) devices and safety buzzers in their kids' backpacks. Numerous indoor parks in Japan are highly secure environments designed to ease parents' minds. At a typical one called the Fantasy Kids Resort, there are uniformed monitors, security cameras, and antibacterial sand. Visitors spray their stroller wheels with antiseptic soap, and guards require identification from visitors before admitting them.[62]

How do we determine what a culture values? We term the process of learning the beliefs and behaviors endorsed by one's own culture **enculturation**. In contrast, we call the process of learning the value system and behaviors of another culture (often a priority for those who wish to understand consumers and markets in foreign countries) **acculturation** (more on this in Chapter 14). *Socialization agents*, including parents, friends, and teachers, impart these beliefs to us.

Another important type of agent is the media; we learn a lot about a culture's priorities by looking at the values advertising communicates. For example, sales strategies differ significantly between the United States and China. U.S. commercials are more likely to present facts about products and suggestions from credible authorities, whereas Chinese advertisers tend to focus more on emotional appeals without bothering too much to substantiate their claims. U.S. ads tend to be youth oriented, whereas Chinese ads are more likely to stress the wisdom of older people.[63]

HOW VALUES LINK TO CONSUMER BEHAVIOR

Despite their importance, values haven't been as helpful in understanding consumer behavior as we might expect. One reason is that broad-based concepts such as freedom, security, or inner harmony are more likely to affect general purchasing patterns than to differentiate between brands within a product category. This is why some researchers distinguish among broad-based *cultural values* such as security or happiness, *consumption-specific values* such as convenient shopping or prompt service, and *product-specific values* such as ease of use or durability, which affect the relative importance people in different cultures place on possessions.[64]

A recent study of product-specific values looked in depth at Australians who engage in extreme sports such as surfing, snowboarding, and skateboarding. The researchers identified four dominant values that drove brand choice: freedom, belongingness, excellence, and connection. For example, one female surfer they studied embraced the value of belongingness. She expressed this value by wearing popular brands of surfing apparel even when these major brands had lost their local

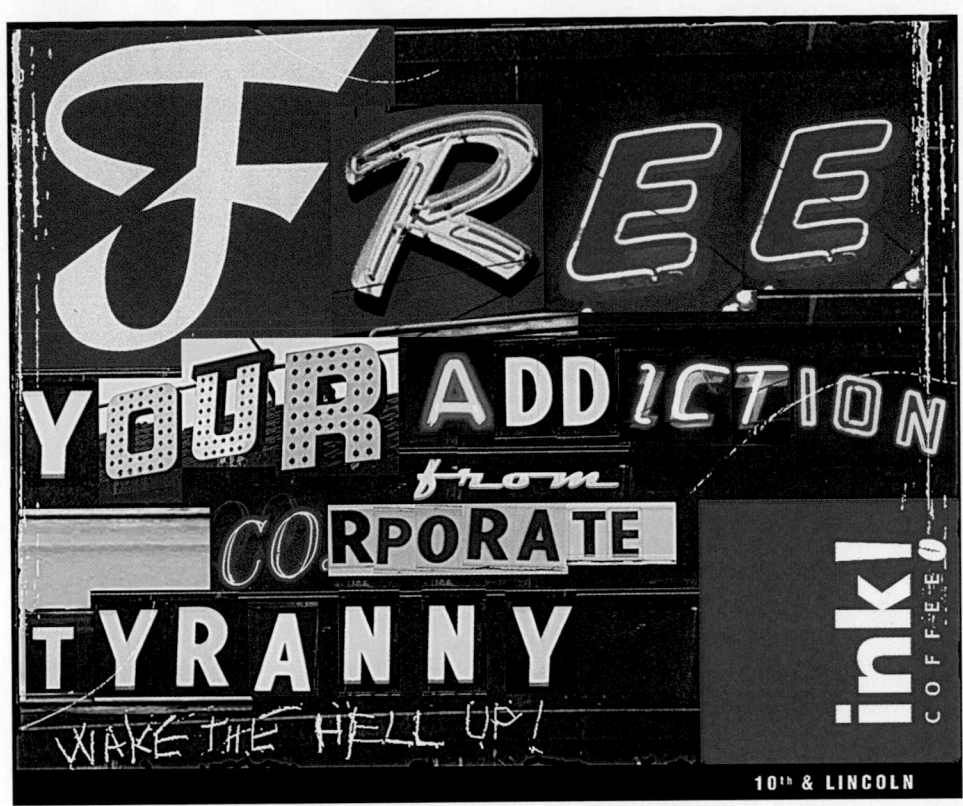

The positive value we place on the activities of large corporations is changing among some consumers who prefer to go "anti-corporate." This ad for a coffee shop in Boulder, Colorado, reflects that sentiment.

roots by going mainstream. In contrast, another surfer in the study valued connection; he expressed this by selecting only locally made brands and going out of his way to support local surfing events.[65]

Some aspects of brand image such as sophistication tend to be common across cultures, but others are more likely to be relevant in specific places. The Japanese tend to value peacefulness, whereas Spaniards emphasize passion, and the value of ruggedness appeals to Americans.[66] Because values drive much of consumer behavior (at least in a very general sense), we might say that virtually *all* consumer research ultimately is related to identifying and measuring values. In this section we'll describe some specific attempts by researchers to measure cultural values and apply this knowledge to marketing strategy.

The Rokeach Value Survey

The psychologist Milton Rokeach identified a set of **terminal values**, or desired end states, that apply to many different cultures. The *Rokeach Value Survey* also includes a set of **instrumental values**, or actions we need to take to achieve these terminal values.[67] Table 4.3 lists these two sets of values.

Some evidence indicates that differences in these global values do translate into product-specific preferences and differences in media usage. Nonetheless, marketing researchers have not widely used the Rokeach Value Survey.[68] One reason is that our society is evolving into smaller and smaller sets of *consumption microcultures* within a larger culture, each with its own set of core values (more on this in Chapter 13). For example, in the United States, a sizeable number of people are strong believers in natural health practices and alternative medicine. This focus on wellness instead of mainstream medical approaches to sickness influences many of their behaviors, from food choices to the use of alternative medical practitioners, as well as their opinions on political and social issues.[69] Indeed, U.S. value structures shift a bit as one moves around the country: Researchers find that people in the Mountain region, for example, are relatively more concerned with environmental mastery, whereas those

TABLE 4.3	
TERMINAL AND INSTRUMENTAL VALUES	

Instrumental Values	Terminal Values
Ambitious	A comfortable life
Broad-minded	An exciting life
Capable	A sense of accomplishment
Cheerful	A world of peace
Clean	A world of beauty
Courageous	Equality
Forgiving	Family security
Helpful	Freedom
Honest	Happiness
Imaginative	Inner harmony
Independent	Mature love
Intellectual	National security
Logical	Pleasure
Loving	Salvation
Obedient	Self-respect
Polite	Social recognition
Responsible	True friendship
Self-controlled	Wisdom

Source: Richard W. Pollay, "Measuring the Cultural Values Manifest in Advertising," *Current Issues and Research in Advertising* (1983): 71–92. Reprinted by permission, CtC Press. All rights reserved.

in the West South Central region focus on personal growth and feeling cheerful and happy; people in the West North Central area emphasize feeling calmness, peacefulness, and satisfaction; and those in the East South Central area are more concerned with contributing to others' well-being.[70]

The List of Values (LOV)

The **List of Values (LOV) Scale** isolates values with more direct marketing applications. This instrument identifies nine consumer segments based on the values members endorse and relates each value to differences in consumption behaviors. These segments include consumers who place priorities on such values as a sense of belonging, excitement, warm relationships with others, and security. For example, in the United States people who endorse the sense-of-belonging value are older, are more likely to read *Reader's Digest* and *TV Guide*, drink and entertain more, and prefer group activities more than people who do not endorse this value as highly. In contrast, those who endorse the value of excitement are younger and prefer *Rolling Stone* magazine.[71]

The Means–End Chain Model

Another research approach that incorporates values is the *means–end chain model*. This approach assumes that people link very specific product attributes (indirectly)

CB AS I SEE IT

Professor Lynn Kahle
The University of Oregon

Three-year-olds often pester adults by repeatedly asking, "Why?" Even after getting a clear answer to a question, they often continue to try to satisfy their enormous curiosity by following up with another "Why?" Some consumer researchers have this 3-year-old level of insatiable curiosity, bugging consumers with a series of "why" questions. The outcome of applying the 3-year-olds' strategy to consumer research results in an interesting discovery: Consumers often follow a predictable pattern with their responses.

When you first ask a consumer why he or she selected a particular product, the answer links the purchase to a product or service attribute. For example, if you ask, "Why did you buy that toothpaste?" a consumer might respond by pointing

to a specific attribute: "I bought it because it has fluoride." If you follow up with another why question, the next answer will probably point to a consequence of that attribute. "Why did you want a toothpaste with fluoride?" The consumer answers, "Fluoride fights cavities." Often additional "why" questions will lead to an answer of a social value. "Why did you want a toothpaste that would fight cavities?" "I want a toothpaste that will give me a healthy mouth. To accomplish all that I want in life, I need to be healthy." If you continue with the 3-year-olds' game beyond the value answer, you risk the consumer throwing a 3-year-olds' temper tantrum. Consumers usually believe that they have completed the chain of reasons for a purchase when they articulate the value behind the purchase decision.

Based on this research, it is clear that consumers often believe the core reason for their consumption decisions are based in their values. Research has also shown that ads and persuasive messages that link values to brands increase the attractiveness of those brands to people who share those values. If you want to sell a computer to a person

who values "a sense of accomplishment," you might emphasize how well it runs software that aides accomplishment, such as the latest accounting or organizing tools. If you want to sell the same computer to someone who values "fun and enjoyment in life" above all else, you might emphasize the entertaining video games and Web sites that are available on the computer.

My colleagues and I continue to research how values and lifestyle relate to consumer choices. Consumers often reveal their values in their lifestyle choices, ranging from sports to religion, and these attempts to realize values influence the choices they make as consumers. How does the correspondence between consumer values and brands occur? We hope to understand better how this process works by asking consumers the "why" questions without actually causing temper tantrums.

Source: For more information, see Lynn R. Kahle and Guang-Xin Xie, "Social Values in Consumer Psychology," in Curt Haugvedt, Paul. Herr, and Frank Kardes, eds., *Handbook of Consumer Psychology* (Mahwah, NJ: Lawrence Erlbaum, in press).

to terminal values: We choose among alternative means to attain some end state we value (such as freedom or safety). Thus, we value products to the extent that they provide the means to some end we desire. A technique researchers call **laddering** uncovers consumers' associations between specific attributes and these general consequences. Using this approach, they help consumers climb up the "ladder" of abstraction that connects functional product attributes with desired end states.[72] Based on consumer feedback, then they create *hierarchical value maps* that show how specific product attributes get linked to end states.

Figure 4.4 shows three different hierarchical value maps from a study of consumers' perceptions of cooking oils in three European countries.[73] The laddering technique illustrates how different product/values links can be across cultures. For Danish people, health is the most important end state. The British also focus on health, but saving money and avoiding waste are more important for them than for people elsewhere. And unlike the other two countries, French people link oil (especially olive oil) to their cultural identity.

■ FIGURE 4.4 HIERARCHICAL VALUE MAPS FOR VEGETABLE OIL IN THREE COUNTRIES

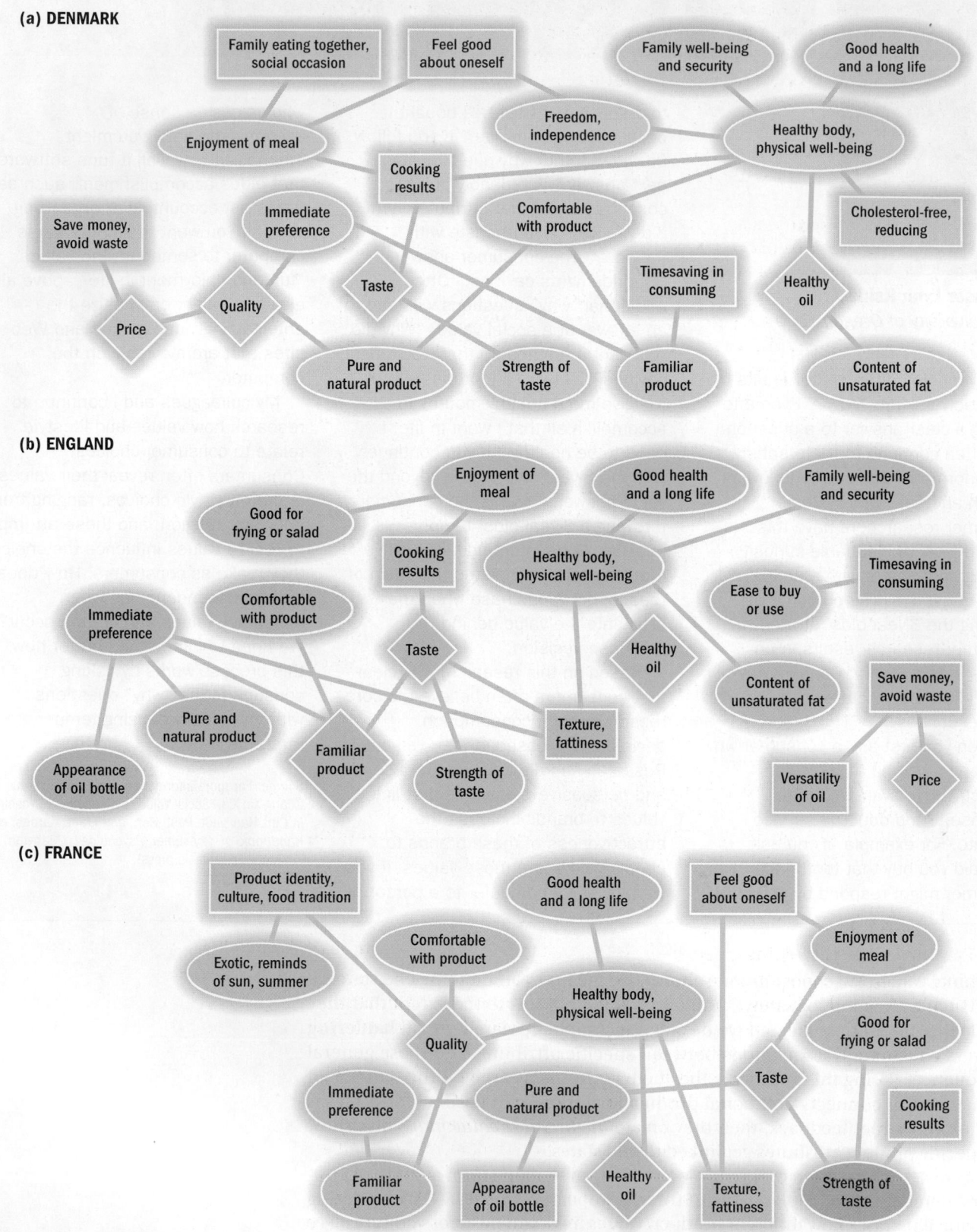

(a) DENMARK

(b) ENGLAND

(c) FRANCE

Source: N. A. Nielsen, T. Bech-Larsen, and K. G. Grunert, "Consumer Purchase Motives and Product Perceptions: A Laddering Study on Vegetable Oil in Three Countries," *Food Quality and Preference* 9(6) (1998): 455–66. © 1998 Elsevier. Used with permission.

Syndicated Surveys

A number of companies track changes in values through large-scale surveys. They sell the results of these studies to marketers, who often also pay a fee to receive regular updates on changes and trends. This approach originated in the mid-1960s, when Playtex was concerned about sagging girdle sales (pun intended). The company commissioned the market research firm of Yankelovich, Skelly & White to see why sales had dropped. Their research linked the decline to a shift in values regarding appearance and naturalness. Playtex went on to design lighter, less restrictive garments, whereas Yankelovich went on to track the impact of these types of changes in a range of industries.

Gradually, the firm developed the idea of one big study to track U.S. attitudes. In 1970, it introduced the Yankelovich *Monitor*™, which is based on 2-hour interviews with 4,000 respondents.[74] This survey attempts to pick up changes in values; for example, it reported a movement among American consumers toward simplification and away from hype as people try to streamline their hectic lives and reduce their concerns about gaining the approval of others through their purchases. **Voluntary simplifiers** believe that once we satisfy our basic material needs, additional income does not add to happiness. Instead of adding yet another car to the collection in the garage, simplifiers are into community building, public service, and spiritual pursuits (think about the self-actualization level we saw in Maslow's hierarchy earlier in the chapter).[75] Members range from senior citizens who downsize their homes to young, mobile professionals who don't want to be tied down to their possessions. These sentiments snowballed after the tragedy of September 11, 2001, when many people became more reflective and less materialistic. In the months that followed, stories abounded of successful careerists who gave it all up to spend time with their families.

Today, many other syndicated surveys also track changes in values. Advertising agencies operate some of these so that they can stay on top of important cultural trends and help shape the messages they craft for clients. These services include VALS2™ (more on this in Chapter 6), GlobalScan (operated by the advertising agency Backer Spielvogel Bates), New Wave (the Ogilvy & Mather advertising agency), and the Lifestyles Study the DDB World Communications Group conducts.

The *New World Teen Study* surveyed more than 27,000 teenagers in 44 countries and identified six values segments that characterize young people from Cairo to Caracas. Companies such as Coca-Cola and Royal Phillips Electronics use the results of this massive segmentation exercise to develop ads that appeal to youth around the world. Table 4.4 summarizes some of the findings from this study.

SUSTAINABILITY: A NEW AMERICAN CORE VALUE?

Are U.S. consumers finally going green—for real? In a 2007 survey, fully 8 in 10 consumers said they believe it's important to buy green brands and products from green companies, and that they'll pay more to do so. The U.S. consumer's focus on personal health is merging with a growing interest in global health. Some analysts call this new value **conscientious consumerism**.[76]

Who is driving this change? Marketers point to a segment of consumers who practice *LOHAS*—an acronym for "lifestyles of health and sustainability." This label refers to people who worry about the environment, want products to be produced in a sustainable way, and spend money to advance what they see as their personal development and potential. These so-called "Lohasians" (others refer to this segment as *cultural creatives)* represent a great market for products such as organic foods, energy-efficient appliances, and hybrid cars, as well as alternative medicine, yoga tapes, and ecotourism. One organization that tracks this group estimates they make up about 16 percent of the adults in the United States, or 35 million people; it values the market for socially conscious products at more than $200 billion.[77]

TABLE 4.4
NEW WORLD TEEN STUDY

Segment	Key Countries	Driving Principles	Overview	Marketing Approach
Thrills and Chills	Germany, England, Lithuania, Greece, Netherlands, South Africa, United States, Belgium, Canada, Turkey, France, Poland, Japan, Italy, Denmark, Argentina, and Norway	Fun, friends, irreverance, and sensation	Stereotype of the devil-may-care, trying-to-become-independent hedonist. For the most part, they come from affluent or middle-class parents, live mainly in developed countries, and have allowance money to spend.	Respond to sensory stimulation. Tend to get bored easily so stale advertising messages will escape their notice. They want action ads with bells and whistles, humor, novelty, color, and sound. Edgier than their peers. Constantly seek out the new. First ones to hear of the newest technology or the hippest Web site. Experimenting is second nature. Wear all sorts of body rings and wear their hair in different shades.
Resigned	Denmark, Sweden, Korea, Japan, Norway, Germany, Belgium, Netherlands, Argentina, Canada, Turkey, England, Spain, France, and Taiwan	Friends, fun, family, and low expectations	Resemble the thrills-and-chills teens, often decorating their bodies with rings and dye. However, they are alienated from society and very pessimistic about their chances for economic success. The punk rockers of the world, who sometimes take drugs and drink to excess. Respond to heavy metal and grunge music that emphasizes the negative and angry side of society.	Do not have as much discretionary income to spend as teens in other segments. Infrequent consumers save for some fast-food, low-ticket clothes items, tobacco, and alcohol. They are drawn to irony and to ads that make fun of the pompousness of society.
World Savers	Hungary, Philippines, Venezuela, Brazil, Spain, Colombia, Belgium, Argentina, Russia, Singapore, France, Poland, Ukraine, Italy, South Africa, Mexico, and England	Environment, humanism, fun, and friends	A long list of do-good global and local causes that spark their interest. The intelligentsia in most countries who do well in school. They are the class and club leaders who join many organizations. They attend the same parties as the thrills-and-chills kids. But, they are more into romance, relationships, and strong friendships. Eagerly attend concerts, operas, and plays. They exhibit a *joie de vivre* about life and enjoy dancing or drinking at bars and cafes with friends. They love the outdoors as well, including camping, hiking, and other sports activities.	Attracted by honest and sincere messages that tell the truth. Offended by any ad that puts people down or makes fun of another group. Piggyback a promotion with a worthwhile cause.
Quiet Achievers	Thailand, China, Hong Kong, Ukraine, Korea, Lithuania, Russia, and Peru	Success, anonymity, anti-individualism, and social optimism	Value anonymity and prefer to rest in the shadows. They are the least rebellious of all the groups, avoid the limelight and do not ever want to stand out in the crowd. These are the bookish and straight kids who study long hours, are fiercely ambitious and highly goal-directed. Their top priority is to make good grades in school and use higher education to further their career advancement. Most of the quiet achievers live in Asia, especially Thailand and China.	Love to purchase stuff. Part of the reward for working diligently is being able to buy products. Their parents will defer to their children's needs when it comes to computers and other technological products that will aid in homework. This group is also keen on music; they are inner directed and adept at creating their own good times. Prefer ads that address the benefits of a product. They are embarrassed by ads that display rampant

Segment	Key Countries	Driving Principles	Overview	Marketing Approach
			But these somewhat stereotypical studious types also exist in the United States, where they are sometimes regarded as being techies or nerds.	sexuality. And they do not respond to the sarcastic or the irreverent.
Boot-strappers	Nigeria, Mexico, United States, India, Chile, Puerto Rico, Peru, Venezuela, Colombia, and South Africa	Achievement, individualism, optimism, determination, and power	Most dreamy and childlike of the six segments. They live sheltered and ordered lives that seem bereft of many forms of typical teen fun and wild adult-emulating teen behavior. Spend a lot of time at home, doing homework and helping around the house. Eager for power; they are the politicians in every high school who covet the class offices. They view the use of authority as a means for securing rewards, and they are constantly seeking out recognition. Geographically many of these teens come from emerging nations such as Nigeria and India. In the United States, bootstrappers represent one in every four teens. Moreover, they represent 40% of young African Americans. A major error of U.S. marketers is to misread the size and purchasing power of this ambitious African American segment.	Young yuppies in training. They want premium brands and luxury goods. Bootstrappers are also on the lookout for goods and services that will help them get ahead. They want to dress for success, have access to technology and software, and stay plugged into the world of media and culture to give them a competitive edge. They are attracted by messages that portray aspirations and possibilities for products and their users.
Upholders	Vietnam, Indonesia, Taiwan, China, Italy, Peru, Venezuela, Puerto Rico, India, Philippines, and Singapore	Family, custom, tradition, and respect for individuals	Traditions act as a rigid guideline, and these teens would be hard-pressed to rebel or confront authority. They are content to rest comfortably in the mainstream of life, remaining unnoticed. The girls seek mostly to get married and have families. The boys perceive that they are fated to have jobs similar to their fathers'. Predominate in Asian countries, such as Indonesia and Vietnam that value old traditions and extended family relationships. Teens in these countries are helpful around the home and protective of their siblings. Moreover, many upholders are in Catholic countries where the Church and tradition guide schooling, attitudes, and values.	Advertisers and marketers have had success selling to upholders using youthful, almost childlike communication and fun messages. These are teens that still watch cartoons and are avid media consumers. They are highly involved in both watching and playing sports, particularly basketball and soccer. More than any other group, they plan to live in their country of birth throughout adulthood. Essentially upholders are homebodies. They are deeply rooted in family and community and they like to make purchase decisions that are safe and conform to their parents' values. Brands that take a leadership stance will attract upholders for their risk-free quality value and reliability.

Source: Adapted from "The Six Value Segments of Global Youth," *Brandweek* 11, no. 21 (May 22, 2000), 38, based on data initially presented in *The $100 Billion Allowance: How to Get Your Share of the Global Teen Market* by Elissa Moses (New York: John Wiley & Sons, 2000).

Marketing Pitfall

Strongly held values can make life very difficult for marketers who sell personal-care products. This is the case with tampons; 70 percent of U.S. women use them, but only 100 million out of a potential market of 1.7 billion eligible women around the world do. Resistance to using this product posed a major problem for Tambrands. The company makes only one product, so it needs to sell tampons in as many countries as possible to continue growing. But Tambrands has trouble selling its feminine hygiene products in some cultures such as Brazil, where many young women fear they will lose their virginity if they use a tampon. A commercial it showed there featured an actress who says in a reassuring voice, "Of course, you're not going to lose your virginity."

Prior to launching a new global advertising campaign for Tampax in 26 countries, the firm's advertising agency conducted research and divided the world into three clusters based on residents' resistance to using tampons. Resistance was so intense in Muslim countries that the agency didn't even try to sell there!

In cluster 1 (including the United States, the United Kingdom, and Australia), women felt comfortable with the idea and offered little resistance. The agency developed a *teaser ad* to encourage more frequency of use: "Should I sleep with it, or not?"

Marketers and retailers are responding with thousands of new ecofriendly products and programs. Colgate bought a big stake in the natural toothpaste brand Tom's of Maine, and L'Oreal acquired The Body Shop. Kellogg's introduced organic versions of some of its bestselling cereals such as Rice Krispies. Kraft launched a 30 percent Rainforest Alliance-certified blend of Yuban coffee. We're seeing a significant increase in products with better-for-you positioning, but new products that take an ethical stance also are driving this trend, whether the claim links to fair-trade, sustainability, or ecological friendliness.

Whereas in the past it was sufficient for companies to offer recyclable products, this new movement is creating a whole new vocabulary as consumers begin to "vote with their forks" by demanding food, fragrances, and other items that are made without genetically modified ingredients (GMOs); hormone-free, that don't involve animal clones or animal testing, that are locally grown, and that are cage-free, just to name a few of consumers' concerns and requirements. Indeed, between 2005 and 2006 grocery sales of products making ethical claims grew by 17 percent to nearly $33 billion and they are continuing to climb as more people get on the ecofriendly bandwagon—the food industry predicts sales of $57 billion by 2011.[78]

Although Lohasians have been fueling demand for ecofriendly products for several years, the big news today is that conscientious consumerism now is spreading to the mass market as well. In fact, even Wal-Mart is making the effort to go green. The world's largest retailer developed a survey called the "Live Better Index" that allows it to monitor customers' feelings about ecofriendly products. The first wave of research polled more than 2,500 Americans on five products: compact fluorescent lightbulbs (CFLs), organic milk, concentrated/reduced-packaging liquid laundry detergents, extended-life paper products and organic baby food. In this survey, 62 percent of respondents said they would buy more ecofriendly products if there were no price difference. Nearly half (47 percent) said they completely agree that buying environmentally friendly products makes them feel like smart consumers, and 68 percent agree that "even the small act of recycling at home has an impact on the environment."[79]

As mainstream marketers recognize this change, they are starting to alter their practices to satisfy Americans' desires for healthy and earth-friendly products. Here are some recent examples:

- Wendy's eliminated most artery-clogging trans fats from its menu. The country's third-largest burger chain now sells french fries and chicken sandwiches and strips that either have no trans fats or have only a fraction of what they previously had. Its hamburgers still contain small amounts of the substance, which occur naturally in beef and dairy products.[80]

- Home Depot, the nation's second-largest retailer, introduced an Eco Options label for almost 3,000 products, such as fluorescent lightbulbs that conserve electricity and natural insect killers that promote energy conservation, sustainable forestry, and clean water. The company expects products it certifies under this program to represent 12 percent of its total sales by 2009.[81]

- H&M is selling clothes made from organic cotton fabrics to fashion-conscious shoppers. Gap introduced an organic cotton T-shirt for men in more than 500 of its stores.[82]

- Procter & Gamble Co. reduced the size of its packaging for its liquid detergent. It's switching to a double concentrate formula to serve its $4 billion North American liquid detergent market. Its competitor Unilever launched its concentrated liquid detergent "Small and Mighty" in the United States in 2005, which it estimates reduces packaging by more than 40 percent, water usage by about 60 percent, and shipping volumes by 60 percent.[83]

- Scotts' Organic Choice brand is part of the giant gardening company's move toward less dependence on synthetically created chemicals, which include the main components in its distinctive blue Miracle-Gro plant food. The company plans to gradually introduce more gardening soil, fertilizer, and bug killer made with natural ingredients, including animal manure and Sri Lankan coconut husks.[84]

● Airplanes are notorious for their huge carbon footprints (i.e., the pollutants they expel into the atmosphere), but even the aerospace industry is going green. European plane maker Airbus calls its massive A380 superjumbo "the gentle green giant" because, with 550 people onboard, it burns less fuel per passenger than a small car. Its promotional materials show a silhouette of the largest commercial jetliner ever made set against images of dolphins, rain forests, and fishing boats on a misty pond. An Airbus spokesman introduced the behemoth at a 2007 air show with the claim that Airbus is ". . . saving the planet, one A380 at a time."[85]

Not content to wait for companies to change their practices, everyday consumers also are taking action. Many are joining numerous organizations such as Slow Food to advocate for lifestyle changes. One such movement called "Local First" stresses the value of buying locally made products. This group (some members call themselves "locavores") values small community businesses, but it also formed as a reaction to waste that results from people importing things they need from long distances. For example, one proponent of this movement calculates that the average U.S. meal travels 1,500 miles before it lands on our dinner plates. This cause already is affecting the grocery industry; the U.S. Department of Agriculture reports that the number of farmers markets grew from 1,755 in 1994 to 4,388 in 2006. At the Sunflower Market stores in Columbus, Ohio, you'll find old-style, half-gallon glass milk containers from a local dairy among dozens of other locally sourced products. The popular Whole Foods chain recently tightened up its definition of local, using the label only if products traveled less than 7 hours from farm to store. The chain is offering $10 million in low-interest loans annually to local farmers and has opened up its parking lots on Sundays to farmers looking to sell direct to its customers.[86]

Still other consumers are rebelling against the huge market for bottled water. They object to the fact that some brands come from as far away as Fiji. These imports contribute to the creation of pollution because of the tanker ships that cart them halfway around the world and the waste millions of discarded plastic bottles creates. In the summer of 2007, San Francisco's mayor decreed that city government would not use city money to buy bottled water for its employees. Despite owning a pristine reservoir in the Sierra Nevada that produces some of the country's best-tasting tap water, the city spends nearly $500,000 a year on bottled water—now other major cities are looking into banning these imports as well.[87]

The environmental effect of an object seemingly as innocent as a plastic water bottle points to the concern many now have about the size of the **carbon footprint**. As Figure 4.5 shows, this measures, in units of carbon dioxide, the impact human activities have on the environment in terms of the amount of greenhouse gases they produce. The average American is responsible for 9.44 tons of CO_2 per year![88] A carbon footprint comes from the sum of two parts, the direct, or primary, footprint and the indirect, or secondary, footprint:

1 The *primary footprint* is a measure of our direct emissions of CO_2 from the burning of fossil fuels, including domestic energy consumption and transportation (e.g., cars and planes).
2 The *secondary footprint* is a measure of the indirect CO_2 emissions from the whole lifecycle of products we use, from their manufacture to their eventual breakdown.[89]

Thousands of consumers use services such as Climate Clean and TerraPass that sell them *greenhouse gas (GHG) offsets*. These businesses enable individuals and businesses to reduce their GHG emissions by offsetting, reducing, or displacing the GHG to another place, typically where it is more economical to do so. GHG offsets typically

---

In cluster 2 (including France, Israel, and South Africa), about 50 percent of women use the product, but some concerns about the loss of virginity remain. To counteract these objections, the agency obtained endorsements from gynecologists within each country.

In cluster 3 (including Brazil, China, and Russia), Tambrands encountered the greatest resistance. To try to make inroads in these countries, the researchers found that the first priority is simply to explain how to use the product without making women feel squeamish—a challenge they still are trying to puzzle out. If they do— and that's a big if—Tambrands will have changed the consumer behavior of millions of women and added huge new markets to its customer base in the process.[93]

This product category also illustrates how values about even "sensitive" products such as tampons can evolve over time. A start-up company called Dittie L.L.C. hopes to compete against the big manufacturers by transforming a feminine hygiene product into a stylish accessory. The company's founder recalls, "I was in the feminine protection aisle, trying to sort through the endless sea of products, and I was floored when it hit me— not one box had an ounce of style. Where was the fun, the feminine flair? Kotex looked like Dr. Scholl's Wart Remover, Tampax looked like Lactaid and Playtex looked like Benadryl." Each of Dittie's color-coded hygiene products features sophisticated illustrations of modern women of different ethnicities striking confident poses. Product wrappers carry messages such as, "I'm proud of my body and every nook and cranny!"[94]

■ **FIGURE 4.5**
CARBON FOOTPRINT BREAKDOWN

■ **FIGURE 4.5**
CARBON FOOTPRINT BREAKDOWN

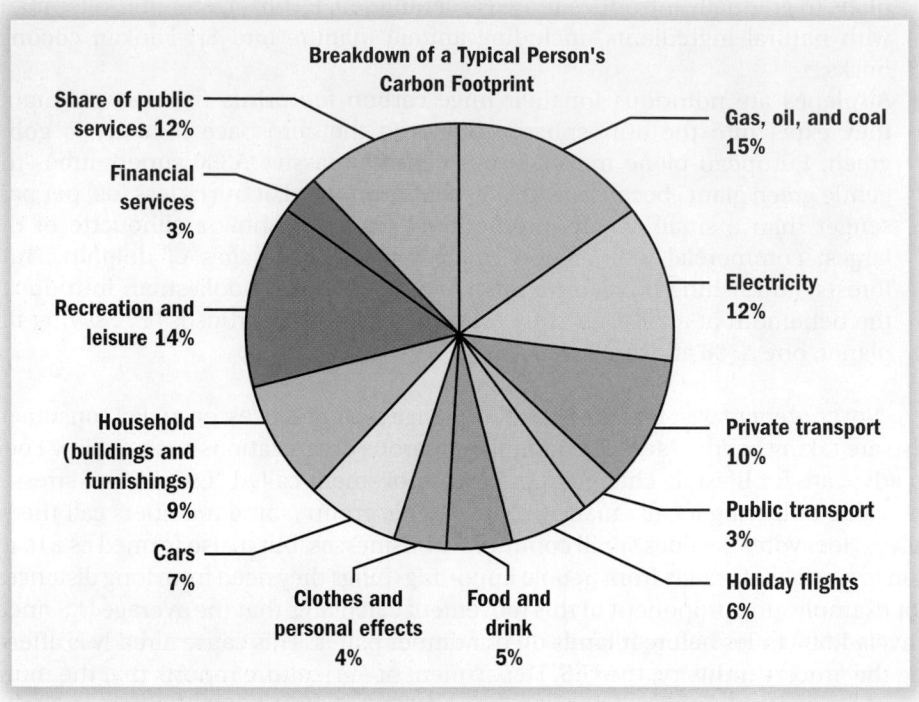

Breakdown of a Typical Person's Carbon Footprint

Share of public services 12%

Financial services 3%

Recreation and leisure 14%

Household (buildings and furnishings) 9%

Cars 7%

Clothes and personal effects 4%

Food and drink 5%

Holiday flights 6%

Public transport 3%

Private transport 10%

Electricity 12%

Gas, oil, and coal 15%

include using renewable energy, energy efficiency, and methane capture that reduce the emission of gases scientists tell us contribute to global warming. For example, if your company flies you to another city for a business trip, it might purchase an "offset" equal to the amount of emissions the airplane created to get you there.[90] In one extreme case that drew the attention of many admirers, a Manhattanite calling himself *No Impact Man* used himself and his family as a living experiment—and blogged about it. As he wrote on his Web site:

> The way I see it, waiting for the senators and the CEOs to change the way we treat the world is taking too long. Polar bears are already drowning because the polar ice is melting. . . . I can't stand my so-called liberal self sitting around not doing anything about it anymore. The question is: What would it be like if I took the situation (or at least my tiny part of it) into my own hands? I'm finding out. For one year, my wife, my 2-year-old daughter, my dog and I, while living in the middle of New York City, are attempting to live without making any net impact on the environment. In other words, no trash, no carbon emissions, no toxins in the water, no elevators, no subway, no products in packaging, no plastics, no air conditioning, no TV, no toilets. . . .[91]

MATERIALISM: "HE WHO DIES WITH THE MOST TOYS, WINS"

No Impact Man sets a great example, but most of us probably wouldn't jump at the chance to live without our creature comforts (apparently his wife isn't too thrilled either). Our possessions play a central role in our lives and our desire to accumulate them shapes our value systems. **Materialism** refers to the importance people attach to worldly possessions.[92] We sometimes take the bounty of products and services for granted, until we remember how recent this abundance is. For example, in 1950, two of five U.S. homes did not have a telephone, and in 1940, half of all households still did not possess complete indoor plumbing.

During World War II, members of "cargo cults" in the South Pacific literally worshiped cargo salvaged from crashed aircraft or washed ashore from ships. These people believed that their ancestors piloted the ships and planes passing near their islands so they tried to attract them to their villages. They went so far as to construct fake planes from straw in hopes of luring the real ones![95]

Climate Clean is one of several services that lets consumers calculate their carbon footprint and then purchase "offsets" to compensate for the amount of personal pollution their activities create.

We may not worship products to that extent, but many of us certainly work hard to attain our vision of the good life, which abounds in material comforts. Most young people can't imagine a life without cell phones, MP3 players, and other creature comforts. In fact, we can think of marketing as a system that provides certain standards of living to consumers. To some extent, then, our lifestyles are influenced by the standards of living we have come to expect and desire—either by personal experience or as a result of the affluent characters we see on TV and in movies.[96] Materialistic values tend to emphasize the well-being of the individual versus the group, which may conflict with family or religious values. That conflict may help to explain why people with highly material values tend to be less happy.[97]

Not only do we like our creature comforts but many people also tend to gauge the worth of themselves and others in terms of how much they own (see Chapter 13). The popular American bumper sticker, "He Who Dies with the Most Toys, Wins," is a comment on this philosophy. Of course, Americans are not alone; many people around the world crave the good life. In Africa, the Winners Church has branches in 32 countries. This sect is one of several booming Pentecostal churches whose leaders attract followers by preaching what they call a Prosperity Theology: Success comes to those who pray, and believers celebrate wealth.[98]

Of course, not all of us are materialists and indeed large numbers of consumers are trying to reduce their reliance on possessions by **downshifting**. Like the voluntary simplifiers we discussed earlier, this means learning to get by with less, avoiding the use of credit cards, and in extreme cases, as we'll see shortly, living totally "off the grid" without using commercial services. One of the most famous downshifters is the so-called Ditch Monkey, a dapper young lawyer who created quite a stir in the U.K. when he spent a year living in a ditch on the outskirts of London (and of course blogging about his experience). He explained, "I want to make people think about how much they consume that is not necessary. I am trying to prove it is possible to do everything you normally do, maintaining a full existence, while cutting back. I have realized [sic] I can lead my life without television, carpets, sofa, electricity, chairs, tables, a fridge and a freezer." After getting over her initial surprise at this abrupt lifestyle change, his girlfriend eventually grew proud of the statement he was making. However, she notes (in typically understated British fashion) that the move shocked her parents: "They were a bit disappointed he wasn't a home owner and were certainly perplexed."[99]

Materialists are more likely to value possessions for their status and appearance-related meanings, whereas those who do not emphasize this value tend to prize products that connect them to other people or that provide them with pleasure in using them.[100]

As a result, high materialists prefer products likely to be publicly consumed and to be more expensive. A study that compared specific items that low versus high materialists value found that people low on the materialism value cherished items such as a mother's wedding gown, picture albums, a rocking chair from childhood, or a garden, whereas those who scored high preferred things such as jewelry, china, or a vacation home.[101]

As we saw in our discussion of the *LOHAS* value segment earlier in this chapter, U.S. society is struggling to reconcile desires for material goods with the need for environmental consciousness and spirituality. This shift is blurring some of the expected boundaries between "traditional" and "progressive" segments. As one analyst noted, for example, even conservative small towns now often feature "new age" stores and services where people of all ages shop. Retailers that used to be considered "Bohemian" now are mainstream; grocers such as Fresh Fields sell Mayan Fungus soap and vegetarian dog biscuits to a hodgepodge of consumers. Big corporations such as Apple and The Gap use countercultural figures such as Gandhi and Jack Kerouac in their advertising, and Ben & Jerry's boasts of its unconventional corporate philosophy. It's become hard to separate establishment from antiestablishment as Bohemian attitudes of the hippie 1960s have merged with the bourgeois attitudes of the yuppie 1980s to form a new culture that is a synthesis of the two. The people who dominate our culture (this analyst calls them "BoBos," or *Bourgeois Bohemians*) now are richer and more worldly than hippies but more spiritual than yuppies.[102] As we noted earlier, even core values do change over time; stay tuned to see how our always-evolving culture continues to put a fresh spin on materialism and other values.

The disenchantment among some people with a culture big corporations dominate shows up in events that promote uniqueness and anticorporate statements. Probably the most prominent movement is the annual Burning Man project. This is a week-long annual antimarket event, where thousands of people gather at Black Rock Desert in Nevada to proclaim their emancipation from corporate America. The highlight of the festival involves the burning of a huge wooden figure of a man, which symbolizes freedom from market domination. Ironically, some critics point out that even this high-profile, antimarket event is being commercialized as it becomes more popular each year![103] Although the event is supposed to run on what participants call a "gift economy" where no U.S. currency changes hands, the 2007 event broke

Participants at the anti-corporate Burning Man Festival find novel ways to express their individuality.

with tradition by allowing green energy companies to exhibit products. Ironically, it turns out that this huge countercultural event uses huge amounts of fossil fuel (lots of gas to burn that man)—the group wants to offset the 28,000 tons of carbon it estimates that it generates.[104]

CHAPTER SUMMARY

Now that you have finished reading this chapter you should understand why:

It's important for marketers to recognize that products can satisfy a range of consumer needs.

- Marketers try to satisfy consumer needs, but the reasons people purchase any product can vary widely. The identification of consumer motives is an important step in ensuring that a product will satisfy appropriate needs. Traditional approaches to consumer behavior have focused on the abilities of products to satisfy rational needs (utilitarian motives), but hedonic motives (e.g., the need for exploration or for fun) also play a key role in many purchase decisions.

- As Maslow's hierarchy of needs demonstrates, the same product can satisfy different needs, depending on the consumer's state at the time. In addition to his objective situation (e.g., have basic physiological needs already been satisfied?), we must also consider the consumer's degree of involvement with the product.

The way we evaluate and choose a product depends on our degree of involvement with the product, the marketing message, and/or the purchase situation.

- Product involvement can range from very low, where purchase decisions are made via inertia, to very high, where consumers form very strong bonds with what they buy. In addition to considering the degree to which consumers are involved with a product, marketing strategists also need to assess their extent of involvement with marketing messages and with the purchase situation.

Our deeply held cultural values dictate the types of products and services we seek out or avoid.

- Underlying values often drive consumer motivations. Products thus take on meaning because they are seen as being instrumental in helping the person to achieve some goal that is linked to a value, such as individuality or freedom. A set of core values characterizes each culture, to which many of its members adhere.

Consumers vary in the importance they attach to worldly possessions, and this orientation in turn has an impact on their priorities and behaviors.

- *Materialism* refers to the importance people attach to worldly possessions. Although we describe many Americans as materialists, there are indications of a value shift within a sizable portion of the population—and this accompanies much greater interest in environmentally sustainable products and services.

KEY TERMS

Acculturation, 176
Approach–approach conflict, 159
Approach–avoidance conflict, 160
Avoidance–avoidance conflict, 160
Carbon footprint, 185

Conscientious consumerism, 181
Consumer-generated content, 171
Core values, 176
Cult products, 166
Downshifting, 187

Drive, 155
Drive theory, 156
Enculturation, 176
Expectancy theory, 157
Flow state, 164

REVIEW QUESTIONS

1 What is motivation, and how is this idea relevant to consumer behavior?

2 Describe three types of motivational conflicts, citing an example of each from current marketing campaigns.

3 Explain the difference between a need and a want.

4 What is cognitive dissonance?

5 Name the levels in Maslow's hierarchy of needs, and give an example of a marketing appeal that is focused at each level.

6 What is consumer involvement? How does this concept relate to motivation?

7 Why would marketers want their customers to enter into a flow state when shopping for their products?

8 List three types of consumer involvement, giving an example of each type.

9 What are some strategies marketers can use to increase consumers' involvement with their products?

10 What are values, and why should marketers care?

11 What is the difference between enculturation and acculturation?

12 What is LOHAS, and why are people who follow this lifestyle important?

13 Describe at least two alternative techniques marketing researchers have used to measure values.

14 What is materialism and why is it relevant to marketing?

CONSUMER BEHAVIOR CHALLENGE

■ DISCUSS

1 "College students' concerns about the environment and vegetarianism are simply a passing fad; a way to look 'cool.'" Do you agree?

2 Some market analysts see a shift in values among young people. They claim that this generation has not had a lot of stability in their lives. They are fed up with superficial relationships and are yearning for a return to tradition. This change is reflected in attitudes toward marriage and family. One survey of 22- to 24-year-old women found that 82 percent thought motherhood was the most important job in the world. *Bride's* magazine reports a swing toward traditional weddings—80 percent of brides today are tossing their garters, and Daddy walks 78 percent of them down the aisle.[105] So, what's your take on this? Are young people indeed returning to the values of their parents (or even their grandparents)? How have these changes influenced your perspective on marriage and family?

3 How (if at all) do you think consumers have changed as a result of 9/11? Are these changes long-term or will we start to revert back to our pre-2001 mind-set?

4 Core values evolve over time. What do you think are the three to five core values that best describe Americans today?

■ APPLY

5 Devise separate promotional strategies for an article of clothing, each of which stresses one of the levels of Maslow's hierarchy of needs.

6 Collect a sample of ads that appeals to consumers' values. What value is being communicated in each ad, and how is this done? Is this an effective approach to designing a marketing communication?

7 Describe how a man's level of involvement with his car would affect how different marketing stimuli influence him. How might you design a strategy for a line of car batteries for a segment of low-involvement consumers, and how would this strategy differ from your attempts to reach a segment of men who are very involved in working on their cars?

8 Interview members of a celebrity fan club. Describe their level of involvement with the "product" and devise some marketing strategies to reach this group.

CAMPBELL'S SOUP ON THE GO

Traditional companies such as Campbell's are constantly trying to come up with new product offerings that will appeal to the ever-changing nature of consumer markets. While Campbell's maintains its position as the market leader for canned, condensed soups, it has found the size of that market shrinking in recent years. But thanks to Carl Johnson, chief strategy officer of Campbell Soup Co., the company is introducing new products that are propelling a surprising turnaround at a $7 billion company that has long struggled for growth.

Lifestyle changes in today's world have given rise to shopper classifications known to industry insiders as "grab and go," "immediate consumption," and "cook and carry." Given the activities that people are engaged in today, they are less and less likely to sit down at home and eat a prepared meal. One might think that opening a can of soup, pouring it in a dish, and heating it in a microwave would not be too much work for the average consumer in today's world. However, the fact that traditional canned soups are not seeing the growth they once enjoyed is a good illustration of just how fickle consumers can be.

Among Campbell's new product offerings is the Soup at Hand line. Sometimes, the success of a new product can be as simple as changing the container of the old product. So, rather than a traditional can, Soup at Hand soups come in single-serving, contoured, high-density polyethylene containers. Easily removable pull-ring metal tops make the soups instantly microwavable right in their containers. A plastic sipping cap, similar to those found on fancy lattes, fits neatly on top and allows for hot soup to be carried and sipped without spilling. And of course, this new container fits in any cup holder found in your average car.

Among other new offerings from various packaged foods companies, Soup at Hand soups are finding a place in convenience stores. "Campbell's recognizes changing consumer shopping behaviors and the role of the convenience store channel in targeting the 'on-the-go' consumer," says George Loesch, Campbell's vice president of national sales for convenience stores. "Products like Campbell's Soup at Hand and Chunky Soup in microwaveable bowls have made it more convenient for consumers to enjoy microwaveable soup that can be eaten any time, anywhere."

So, are Soup at Hand soups as good as traditional vegetable beef or chicken noodle? That will be up to the consumer to decide. However, certain modifications had to be made to the products in order to work with the new packaging. For example, in order for soup to seep safely through the small opening of the plastic sipping cap, Campbell's has made textural compromises. Chicken and beef are downsized to pellets. Noodles are round and small. Even the broth is different, having a slight gluey texture.

Campbell's is experiencing a resurgence based on lines of on-the-go products that might have flopped 10 or 20 years ago; today, they're just what the customer ordered.

DISCUSSION QUESTIONS

1 What consumer needs are driving the success of products like Campbell's Soup at Hand? Consider both biological and learned needs.

2 Are some needs more powerful than others? Illustrate this by discussing the needs that customers might be sacrificing in order to satisfy other needs.

Sources: Kate Bertrand, "Convenience Stores Support a Speed-to-Mouth Lifestyle," *BrandPackaging* (March 2005): 6; Stephanie Thompson, "Souping Up a Classic," *Advertising Age* (May 2, 2005):1.

NOTES

1. www.afa-online.org/vegan.html, accessed August 12, 2007.
2. www.petakids.com/save_animals.htm, accessed August 12, 2007
3. beefitswhatsfordinner.com, accessed August 12, 2007.
4. Robert A. Baron, *Psychology: The Essential Science* (Boston: Allyn & Bacon, 1989).
5. Russell W. Belk, Guliz Ger, and Søren Askegaard, "The Fire of Desire: A Multisited Inquiry into Consumer Passion," *Journal of Consumer Research* 30 (2003): 326–51.
6. Thomas Kramer and Song-Oh Yoon, "Approach-Avoidance Motivation and the Use of Affect as Information," *Journal of Consumer Psychology* 17, no. 2 (2007): 128–38.
7. See Paul T. Costa and Robert R. McCrae, "From Catalog to Classification: Murray's Needs and the Five-Factor Model," *Journal of Personality and Social Psychology* 55 (1988): 258–65; Calvin S. Hall and Gardner Lindzey, *Theories of Personality*, 2nd ed. (New York: Wiley, 1970); James U. McNeal and Stephen W. McDaniel, "An Analysis of Need-Appeals in Television Advertising," *Journal of the Academy of Marketing Science* 12 (Spring 1984): 176–90.
8. Michael R. Solomon, Judith L. Zaichkowsky, and Rosemary Polegato, *Consumer Behaviour: Buying, Having, and Being—Canadian Edition* (Scarborough, Ontario: Prentice Hall Canada, 1999).
9. See David C. McClelland, *Studies in Motivation* (New York: Appleton-Century-Crofts, 1955).
10. Mary Kay Ericksen and M. Joseph Sirgy, "Achievement Motivation and Clothing Preferences of White-Collar Working Women," in Michael R. Solomon, ed., *The Psychology of Fashion* (Lexington, MA: Lexington Books, 1985), 357–69.
11. See Stanley Schachter, *The Psychology of Affiliation* (Stanford, CA: Stanford University Press, 1959).
12. Eugene M. Fodor and Terry Smith, "The Power Motive as an Influence on Group Decision Making," *Journal of Personality and Social Psychology* 42 (1982): 178–85.
13. C. R. Snyder and Howard L. Fromkin, *Uniqueness: The Human Pursuit of Difference* (New York: Plenum, 1980).
14. Abraham H. Maslow, *Motivation and Personality*, 2nd ed. (New York: Harper & Row, 1970).

15. A more recent integrative view of consumer goal structures and goal-determination processes proposes six discrete levels of goals wherein higher-level (versus lower-level) goals are more abstract, more inclusive, and less mutable. In descending order of abstraction, these goal levels are life themes and values, life projects, current concerns, consumption intentions, benefits sought, and feature preferences. See Cynthia Huffman, S. Ratneshwar, and David Glen Mick, "Consumer Goal Structures and Goal-Determination Processes: An Integrative Framework," in S. Ratneshwar, David Glen Mick, and Cynthia Huffman, eds., *The Why of Consumption* (London: Routledge, 2000): 9–35.

16. Paul Henry, "Magnetic Points for Lifestyle Shaping: The Contribution of Self-Fulfillment, Aspirations and Capabilities," *Qualitative Market Research* 9 no. 2 (2006): 170.

17. Russell W. Belk, "Romanian Consumer Desires and Feelings of Deservingness," in Lavinia Stan, ed., *Romania in Transition* (Hanover, NH: Dartmouth Press, 1997): 191–208, quoted on p. 193.

18. Study conducted in the Horticulture Department at Kansas State University, cited in "Survey Tells Why Gardening's Good," *Vancouver Sun* (April 12, 1997): B12; see also Paul Hewer and Douglas Brownlie, "Constructing 'Hortiporn': On the Aesthetics of Stylized Exteriors," *Advances in Consumer Research* 33 no. 1 (2006).

19. "Forehead Advertisement Pays Off," *Montgomery Advertiser* (May 4, 2000): 7A.

20. Alex Kuczynski, "A New Magazine Celebrates the Rites of Shopping," *New York Times on the Web* (May 8, 2000).

21. "Man Wants to Marry His Car," *Montgomery Advertiser* (March 7, 1999): 11A.

22. Judith Lynne Zaichkowsky, "Measuring the Involvement Construct in Marketing," *Journal of Consumer Research* 12 (December 1985): 341–52

23. Andrew Mitchell, "Involvement: A Potentially Important Mediator of Consumer Behavior," in William L. Wilkie, ed., *Advances in Consumer Research* 6 (Provo, UT: Association for Consumer Research, 1979): 191–96.

24. Richard L. Celsi and Jerry C. Olson, "The Role of Involvement in Attention and Comprehension Processes," *Journal of Consumer Research* 15 (September 1988): 210–24.

25. Anthony G. Greenwald and Clark Leavitt, "Audience Involvement in Advertising: Four Levels," *Journal of Consumer Research* 11 (June 1984): 581–92.

26. Mihaly Csikszentmihalyi, *Flow: The Psychology of Optimal Experience* (New York: HarperCollins, 1991); Donna L. Hoffman and Thomas P. Novak, "Marketing in Hypermedia Computer-Mediated Environments: Conceptual Foundations," *Journal of Marketing* (July 1996): 50–68.

27. Jeremy W. Peters, "Gave Up Sleep and Maybe a First-Born, but at Least I Have an iPhone," *New York Times Online* (June 30, 2007).

28. Robert W. Pimentel and Kristy E. Reynolds, "A Model for Consumer Devotion: Affective Commitment with Proactive Sustaining Behaviors," *Academy of Marketing Science Review* no. 5 (2004), available from www.amsreview.org/articles/pimentel05-2004.pdf.

29. Judith Lynne Zaichkowsky, "The Emotional Side of Product Involvement," in Paul Anderson and Melanie Wallendorf, eds., *Advances in Consumer Research* 14 (Provo, UT: Association for Consumer Research): 32–35.

30. For a discussion of interrelationships between situational and enduring involvement, see Marsha L. Richins, Peter H. Bloch, and Edward F. McQuarrie, "How Enduring and Situational Involvement Combine to Create Involvement Responses," *Journal of Consumer Psychology* 1, no. 2 (1992): 143–53. For more information on the involvement construct, see "Special Issue on Involvement," *Psychology & Marketing* 10, no. 4 (July–August 1993).

31. "A Woman Wins Roto-Rooter's Tricked Out Toilet," PROMO, April 3, 2007, available from www.promomagazine.com/news/woman_wins_roto_rooters_toilet_043007/index.html; www.designnews.com/blog/1080000108/post/650006865.html, accessed June 27, 2007.

32. Scott Bowles, "Fans Use Their Muscle to Shape the Movie," *USA Today* (June 20, 2003): 2A.

33. Joseph B. Pine, II, and James H. Gilmore, *Markets of One—Creating Customer-Unique Value through Mass Customization* (Boston: Harvard Business School Press, 2000); www.managingchange.com/masscust/overview.htm, accessed May 30, 2005.

34. Julie Schlosser, "Cashing in on the New World of Me," *Fortune* (December 13, 2004): 244–50.

35. Nat Ives, "Advertising: Unauthorized Campaigns Used by Unauthorized Creators Become a Trend," *New York Times on the Web* (December 23, 3004).

36. Rajeev Batra and Michael L. Ray, "Operationalizing Involvement as Depth and Quality of Cognitive Responses," in Alice Tybout and Richard Bagozzi, eds., *Advances in Consumer Research* 10 (Ann Arbor, MI: Association for Consumer Research, 1983): 309–13.

37. Herbert E. Krugman, "The Impact of Television Advertising: Learning without Involvement," *Public Opinion Quarterly* 29 (Fall 1965): 349–56.

38. "Read My Chips? Pringles Has Plans to Print Jokes, Trivia on Its Potatoes," *Wall Street Journal on the Web* (May 20, 2004): C13; David Serchuk, "A Rose with Another Name," *Forbes* (December 27, 2004): 52.

39. "Bystanders Flee Giant Popsicle," *Montgomery Advertiser* (June 23, 2005).

40. Li Yuan, "Television's New Joy of Text Shows with Vote by Messaging Are on the Rise as Programmers Try to Make Live TV Matter," *Wall Street Journal* (July 20, 2006): B1.

41. Mark J. Arnold and Kristy E. Reynolds, "Hedonic Shopping Motivations," *Journal of Retailing* 79 (2003): 77–95.

42. Kevin J. Clancy, "CPMs Must Bow to 'Involvement' Measurement," *Advertising Age* (January 20, 1992): 26.

43. Gilles Laurent and Jean-Noël Kapferer, "Measuring Consumer Involvement Profiles," *Journal of Marketing Research* 22 (February 1985): 41–53. This scale was validated on an American sample as well; see William C. Rodgers and Kenneth C. Schneider, "An Empirical Evaluation of the Kapferer–Laurent Consumer Involvement Profile Scale," *Psychology & Marketing* 10 (July–August 1993): 333–45. For an English translation of this scale, see Jean-Noël Kapferer and Gilles Laurent, "Further Evidence on the Consumer Involvement Profile: Five Antecedents of Involvement," *Psychology & Marketing* 10 (July–August 1993): 347–56; Robin A. Coulter, Linda L. Price, and Lawrence Feick, "Rethinking the Origins of Involvement and Brand Commitment: Insights from Postsocialist Central Europe," *Journal of Consumer Research* 30 (September 2003): 151–69.

44. David W. Stewart and David H. Furse, "Analysis of the Impact of Executional Factors in Advertising Performance," *Journal of Advertising Research* 24 (1984): 23–26; Deborah J. MacInnis, Christine Moorman, and Bernard J. Jaworski, "Enhancing and Measuring Consumers' Motivation, Opportunity, and Ability to Process Brand Information from Ads," *Journal of Marketing* 55 (October 1991): 332–53.

45. Morris B. Holbrook and Elizabeth C. Hirschman, "The Experiential Aspects of Consumption: Consumer Fantasies, Feelings, and Fun," *Journal of Consumer Research* 9 (September 1982): 132–40.

46. Elaine Sciolino, "Disproving Notions, Raising a Fury," *New York Times on the Web* (January 21, 2003).

47. Louise Story, "Times Sq. Ads Spread Via Tourists' Cameras," *New York Times Online* (December 11, 2006).

48. Suzanne Vranica and Chad Terhune, "Mixing Diet Coke and Mentos Makes a Gusher of Publicity," *Wall Street Journal* (June 12, 2006): B1.

49. Scott Donaton, "How to Thrive in New World of User-Created Content: Let Go" *Advertising Age* 77, no. 18 (May 2006): 38; "Interactive: User-Generated—Cheap, but Is It Safe to Let Go?" *Marketing Week* (May 2006): 40–41; Todd Wasserman, "Intelligence Gathering" *Brandweek*, 47, no. 25 (June 2006): S8–S18.

50. Julie Bosman, "Chevy Tries a Write-Your-Own-Ad Approach, and the Potshots Fly," *New York Times Online* (April 4, 2006); Suzanne Vranica, "Marketers' New Idea: Get the Consumer to Design the Ads," *Wall Street Journal* (December 14, 2005): B1; William M. Bulkeley, "CNN Posts User-Generated Content—Got a Better Letter Opener? Staples Solicits Inventive Ideas from the Public for Products It Can Brand, Sell Exclusively," *Wall Street Journal* (July 13, 2006): B1; Norman Madden, "Forget Creatives: Pepsi has Chinese Consumers," *The World* (November 2006): 48; Nina M. Lentini, "Pepsi to Let One Consumer Design 500 Million Cans," (April 5, 2007), *Marketing Daily*, available from mediapost.com; Sarah McBride, "Make-It-Yourself 'Star Wars' Lucasfilm Will Post Clips from Film Saga on the Web, Inviting Fans to Edit at Will," *Wall Street Journal* (May 24, 2007): B1; Stuart Elliott, "Forget Spartacus, I Am Fresno State," *New York Times Online* (May 22, 2007); "May 2006 Trend Briefing," available from www.trendwatching.com/briefing/, accessed June 27, 2007; Danny Hakim, "Star Trek' Fans, Deprived of a Show, Recreate the Franchise on Digital Video," *New York Times Online* (June 18, 2006).

51. Julie Bosman, "Chevy Tries a Write-Your-Own-Ad Approach, and the Potshots Fly," *New York Times Online* (April 4, 2006).

52. Ajay K. Sirsi, James C. Ward, and Peter H. Reingen, "Microcultural Analysis of Variation in Sharing of Causal Reasoning about Behavior," *Journal of Consumer Research* 22 (March 1996): 345–72.

53. David Carr, "Romance in *Cosmo*'s World Is Translated in Many Ways," *New York Times on the Web* (May 26, 2002).

54. Anand Giridharadas, "*Playboy* Makes Move in India, but without the Centerfold," *New York Times Online* (January 2, 2006).

55. Richard W. Pollay, "Measuring the Cultural Values Manifest in Advertising," *Current Issues and Research in Advertising* 6, no. 1 (1983): 71–92.

56. Paul M. Sherer, "North American and Asian Executives Have Contrasting Values, Study Finds," *Wall Street Journal* (March 8, 1996). For a recent study that assessed how "biculturals" who are influenced by two different sets of values reconcile these, cf. Loraine G. Lau-Gesk, "Activating Culture through Persuasion Appeals: An Examination of the Bicultural Consumer," *Journal of Consumer Psychology* 13, no. 3 (2003): 301–15.

57. Sarah Ellison, "Sexy-Ad Reel Shows What Tickles in Tokyo Can Fade Fast in France," *Wall Street Journal Interactive Edition* (March 31, 2000).

58. Quoted in Andrew Adam Newman, "With Condoms in Particular, Local Stations Can Say No," *New York Times on the Web* (July 16, 2007).

59. Deborah Ball, "Women in Italy Like to Clean but Shun the Quick and Easy: Convenience Doesn't Sell When Bathrooms Average Four Scrubbings a Week," *Wall Street Journal* (April 25, 2006): A1.

60. Milton Rokeach, *The Nature of Human Values* (New York: Free Press, 1973).

61. Sang-Pil Han and Sharon Shavitt, "Persuasion and Culture: Advertising Appeals in Individualistic and Collectivistic Societies," *Journal of Experimental Social Psychology* 30 (1994): 326–50.

62. Chisaki Watanabe, "Japanese Parents Embrace Ultra-secure Children's Park," *Phiadelphia Inquirer Online* (September 4, 2006): A2.

63. Carolyn A. Lin, "Cultural Values Reflected in Chinese and American Television Advertising," *Journal of Advertising* 30 (Winter 2001): 83–94.

64. Donald E. Vinson, Jerome E. Scott, and Lawrence R. Lamont, "The Role of Personal Values in Marketing and Consumer Behavior," *Journal of Marketing* 41 (April 1977): 44–50; John Watson, Steven Lysonski, Tamara Gillan, and Leslie Raymore, "Cultural Values and Important Possessions: A Cross-Cultural Analysis," *Journal of Business Research* 55 (2002): 923–31.

65. Pascale Quester, Michael Beverland, and Francis Farrelly, "Brand-Personal Values Fit and Brand Meanings: Exploring the Role Individual Values Play in Ongoing Brand Loyalty in Extreme Sports Subcultures," *Advances in Consumer Research* 33, no. 1 (2006): 21–28.

66. Jennifer Aaker, Veronica Benet-Martinez, and Jordi Garolera, "Consumption Symbols as Carriers of Culture: A Study of Japanese and Spanish Brand Personality Constructs," *Journal of Personality and Social Psychology* (2001).

67. Milton Rokeach, *Understanding Human Values* (New York: Free Press, 1979); see also J. Michael Munson and Edward McQuarrie, "Shortening the Rokeach Value Survey for Use in Consumer Research," in Michael J. Houston, ed., *Advances in Consumer Research* 15 (Provo, UT: Association for Consumer Research, 1988): 381–86.

68. B. W. Becker and P. E. Conner, "Personal Values of the Heavy User of Mass Media," *Journal of Advertising Research* 21 (1981): 37–43; Scott Vinson and Lamont Vinson, "The Role of Personal Values in Marketing and Consumer Behavior," 44–50.

69. Craig J. Thompson and Maura Troester, "Consumer Value Systems in the Age of Postmodern Fragmentation: The Case of the Natural Health Microculture," *Journal of Consumer Research* 28 (March 2002): 550–71.

70. Victoria C. Plaut and Hazel Rose Markus, "Place Matters: Consensual Features and Regional Variation in American Well-Being and Self," *Journal of Personality and Social Psychology* 83 (2002): 160–84.

71. Sharon E. Beatty, Lynn R. Kahle, Pamela Homer, and Shekhar Misra, "Alternative Measurement Approaches to Consumer Values: The List of Values and the Rokeach Value Survey," *Psychology & Marketing* 2 (1985): 181–200; Lynn R. Kahle and Patricia Kennedy, "Using the List of Values (LOV) to Understand Consumers," *Journal of Consumer Marketing* 2 (Fall 1988): 49–56; Lynn Kahle, Basil Poulos, and Ajay Sukhdial, "Changes in Social Values in the United States during the Past Decade," *Journal of Advertising Research* 28 (February–March 1988): 35–41; see also Wagner A. Kamakura and Jose Alfonso Mazzon, "Value Segmentation: A Model for the Measurement of Values and Value Systems," *Journal of Consumer Research* 18 (September 1991): 28; Jagdish N. Sheth, Bruce I. Newman, and Barbara L. Gross, *Consumption Values and Market Choices: Theory and Applications* (Cincinnati: South-Western Publishing Co., 1991).

72. Thomas J. Reynolds and Jonathan Gutman, "Laddering Theory, Method, Analysis, and Interpretation," *Journal of Advertising Research* (February–March 1988): 11–34; Beth Walker, Richard Celsi, and Jerry Olson, "Exploring the Structural Characteristics of Consumers' Knowledge," in Melanie Wallendorf and Paul Anderson, eds., *Advances in Consumer Research* 14 (Provo, UT: Association for Consumer Research, 1986): 17–21; Veludo-de-Oliveira, Tania Modesto, Ana Akemi Ikeda, and Marcos Cortez Campomar, "Laddering in the Practice of Marketing Research: Barriers and Solutions," *Qualitative Market Research: An International Journal* 9, no. 3 (2006): 297–306. For a recent critique of this technique, cf. Elin Brandi Sørenson and Søren Askegaard, "Laddering: How (Not) to Do Things with Words," *Qualitative Market Research: An International Journal* 10, no. 1 (2007): 63–77.

73. This example was adapted from Michael R. Solomon, Gary Bamossy, and Søren Askegaard, *Consumer Behaviour: A European Perspective*, 2nd ed. (London: Pearson Education Limited, 2002).

74. "25 Years of Attitude," *Marketing Tools* (November–December 1995): 38–39.

75. Amitai Etzioni, "The Good Society: Goals beyond Money," *The Futurist* 35, no. 4 (2001) 68–69; D. Elgin, *Voluntary Simplicity: Toward a Way of Life That Is Outwardly Simple, Inwardly Rich* (New York: Quill, 1993); *Ascribe Higher Education News Service*, "PNA Trend in Consumer Behavior Called 'Voluntary Simplicity' Poses Challenges for Marketers" (December 6, 2001); Caroline Bekin, Marylyn Carrigan, and Isabelle Szmigin, "Defying

76. Emily Burg, "Whole Foods Is Consumers' Favorite Green Brand," *Marketing Daily*, available from mediapost.com, accessed May 10, 2007.

77. www.lohas.com/about.htm, accessed June 30, 2007.

78. Adrienne W. Fawcett, "Conscientious Consumerism Drives Record New Product Launches in 2006," available from NewYorkTimes.com/magazine, accessed January 24, 2007.

79. Sarah Mahoney, "Wal-Mart: The Average Joe Is Greener Than You Think," *Marketing Daily*, available from mediapost.com, accessed April 19, 2007.

80. Richard Gibson, "Wendy's Moves to Eliminate Most Trans Fats from Menu," *Wall Street Journal* (June 9, 2006): A13.

81. Michael Barbaro, "Home Depot to Display an Environmental Label," *New York Times Online* (April 17, 2007).

82. Sarah Mahoney, "Putting Green n Vogue: Organic Clothes Get Hot," *Marketing Daily*, available from www.mediapost.com, accessed April 17, 2007.

83. P&G Going Green Liquid Detergents Will Come in Smaller Packaging with Double Concentrate as the Company Moves to Become Enviro-friendly, According to a Published Report, available from CNNMoney.com, accessed May 2, 2007.

84. Emily Lambert, "Marketing, Organic Miracle," *Forbes* (September 4, 2006): 68.

85. Quoted in Lynn Lunsford and Daniel Michaels, "On Paris's Jet Runways, Green Is the New Gray," *Wall Street Journal Online Edition* (June 22, 2007).

86. Mya Frazier, "Farmstands vs. Big Brands: With Consumers Interested in Locally Produced Goods, Marketers Scramble to Get in on a Movement Going Mainstream" available from advertisingage.com, accessed June 5, 2007.

87. Cecilia M. Vega, "Mayor to Cut Off Flow of City Money for Bottled Water," available from http://sfgate.com/cgi-bin/article.cgi?f=/c/a/2007/06/22/BAGE8QJVIL1.DTL, accessed June 22, 2007.

88. green.yahoo.com/index.php?q=action, accessed June 30, 2007.

89. www.carbonfootprint.com/carbon_footprint.html, accessed June 30, 2007.

90. www.climateclean.net/, accessed June 30, 2007; www.terrapass.com/, accessed June 30, 2007.

91. Quoted from http://noimpactman.typepad.com/blog/2007/02/the_no_impact_e.html, accessed June 30, 2007.

92. Susan Schultz Kleine and Stacy Menzel Baker, "An Integrative Review of Material Possession Attachment," *Academy of Marketing Science Review* no. 1 (2004).

93. Yumiko Ono, "Tambrands Ads Try to Scale Cultural, Religious Obstacles," *Wall Street Journal Interactive Edition* (March 17, 1997).

94. Courtney Kane, "Marketing a New Feminine Hygiene Product," *New York Times on the Web* (May 11, 2004).

95. Russell W. Belk, "Possessions and the Extended Self," *Journal of Consumer Research* 15 (September 1988): 139–68; Melanie Wallendorf and Eric J. Arnould, "'My Favorite Things': A Cross-Cultural Inquiry into Object Attachment, Possessiveness, and Social Linkage," *Journal of Consumer Research* 14 (March 1988): 531–47.

96. L. J. Shrum, James E. Burroughs, and Aric Rindfleisch, "Television's Cultivation of Material Values," *Journal of Consumer Research*, in press.

97. James E. Burroughs and Aric Rindfleisch, "Materialism and Well-Being: A Conflicting Values Perspective," *Journal of Consumer Research* 29 (December 2002): 348–70.

98. Norimitsu Onishi, "Africans Fill Churches That Celebrate Wealth," *New York Times on the Web* (March 13, 2002).

99. Quoted in Anushka Asthana, "The Man Who Wakes Up in a Ditch. . . Then Goes to Work at Sotheby's," *The Observer* (September 4, 2005), available at http://observer.guardian.co.uk/uk_news/story/0,6903,1562293,00.html, accessed June 30, 2007; cf. also www.organicfood.co.uk/inspiration/downshifting and www.handbag.com/careers/careerchange/downshifting/ June 30, 2007.

100. Marsha L. Richins, "Special Possessions and the Expression of Material Values," *Journal of Consumer Research* 21 (December 1994): 522–33.

101. Ibid.

102. David Brooks, "Why BoBos Rule," *Newsweek* (April 3, 2000): 62–64.

103. Robert V. Kozinets, "Can Consumers Escape the Market? Emancipatory Illuminations from Burning Man," *Journal of Consumer Research* 29 (June 2002): 20–38; see also Douglas B. Holt, "Why Do Brands Cause Trouble? A Dialectical Theory of Consumer Culture and Branding," *Journal of Consumer Research* 29 (June 2002): 70–90.

104. Chris Taylor, "Burning Man Grows Up" *Business 2.0* (June 28 2007), available from http://money.cnn.com/magazines/business2/business2_archive/2007/07/01/100117064/, accessed June 30, 2007.

105. Helene Stapinski, "Y Not Love?" *American Demographics* (February 1999): 62–68.

Market Sovereignty: Voluntary Simplicity at New Consumption Communities," *Qualitative Market Research* 8, no. 4 (2005): 413.

The Self

Chapter Objectives

When you have finished reading this chapter you will understand why:

- The self-concept strongly influences consumer behavior.
- Products often play a pivotal role in defining the self-concept.
- Sex-role identity is different from gender, and society's expectations of masculinity and femininity help to determine the products we buy to be consistent with these expectations.
- The way we think about our bodies (and the way our culture tells us we should think) is a key component of self-esteem.
- Our desire to live up to cultural expectations of appearance can be harmful.
- Every culture dictates certain types of body decoration or mutilation that help to identify its members.

Lisa is trying to concentrate on the report her client expects by 5:00 P.M. She has always worked hard to maintain this important account for the firm, but today she is distracted, thinking about her date with Eric last night. Although things seemed to go OK, she couldn't shake the feeling that Eric regarded her more as a friend than as a potential romantic partner?

Leafing through *Glamour* and *Cosmopolitan* during her lunch hour, Lisa is struck by all of the articles about ways to become more attractive by dieting, exercising, and wearing sexy clothes. She begins to feel depressed as she looks at the svelte models in the many advertisements for perfumes, apparel, and makeup. Each woman is more glamorous and beautiful than the last. She could swear that some of them must have had assorted "adjustments"—women simply don't look that way in real life. Then again, it's unlikely that Eric could ever be mistaken for Brad Pitt on the street.

In her down mood, though, Lisa actually entertains the thought that maybe she should look into cosmetic surgery. Even though she's never considered herself unattractive, maybe a new nose or removing that mole on her cheek would make her feel better about herself. Who knows, she might look so good she'll get up the nerve to submit a photo to that Web site <u>www.hotornot.com</u> that everyone's talking about. On second thought, though, is Eric even worth it?

Perspectives on the Self

Lisa is not alone in feeling that her physical appearance and possessions affect her "value" as a person. Consumers' insecurities about their appearance are rampant. We buy many products, from cars to cologne, because we want to highlight or hide some aspect of the self. In this chapter, we'll focus on how consumers' feelings about themselves shape their consumption practices, particularly as they strive to fulfill their society's expectations about how a male or female should look and act.

DOES THE SELF EXIST?

Justin Kan doesn't go anywhere without a video camera strapped to his baseball cap, constantly beaming live video to his Web site, justin.tv. The company this 2005 Yale graduate founded with some friends hopes to use the *all-Kan-all-the-time* show to fine-tune a platform for letting anyone broadcast his life on the Web. Similarly, a new service called Kyte (kyte.tv) is a "me TV" that uploads photos and videos you take on your phone and broadcasts them to a group of friends who subscribe to your channel.[1] New Line Cinema hired street teams to go to 80 bars or events such as the Super Bowl across the country with a confession booth and a video camera so that people could confess their obsessions and post them on a Web site to promote the movie *The Number 23*. One woman owned up to being infatuated with the singer Justin Timberlake and another revealed that she used to put Visine eye drops in the beers of customers when she was a bartender![2] Don't have video access but still feel a need to let your peeps know exactly what you're doing 24/7? Just *twitter* them by using the increasingly popular text-messaging service at twitter.com.[3]

The growth of social networking services such as these enables everyone to focus on himself or herself and share their lives with anyone who's interested (why they are is another story!). Although it seems natural to think about each consumer as having a self that's simply waiting for its 15 minutes of fame (as the pop icon Andy Warhol once predicted), the idea that each single human life is unique rather than a part of a group only developed in late medieval times (between the eleventh and fifteenth centuries).

Justin TV is all Justin, all the time.

Furthermore, the emphasis on the unique nature of the self is much greater in Western societies.[4] Many Eastern cultures stress the importance of a *collective self,* where a person derives her identity in large measure from a social group. Both Eastern and Western cultures see the self as divided into an inner, private self and an outer, public self. But where they differ is in terms of which part is seen as the "real you"—the West tends to subscribe to an independent understanding of the self, which emphasizes the inherent separateness of each individual.

Non-Western cultures, in contrast, tend to focus on an interdependent self where we define our identities largely by the relationships we have with others.[5] For example, a Confucian perspective stresses the importance of "face"—others' perceptions of the self and maintaining one's desired status in their eyes. One dimension of face is *mien-tzu*—reputation achieved through success and ostentation. Some Asian cultures developed explicit rules about the specific garments and even colors that certain social classes and occupations were allowed to display. These traditions live on today in Japanese style manuals that provide very detailed instructions for dressing and for addressing people of differing status.[6]

That orientation is a bit at odds with such Western conventions as "casual Friday," which encourages employees to express their unique selves (at least short of muscle shirts and flip flops). To further illustrate these cross-cultural differences, a Roper Starch Worldwide survey compared consumers in 30 countries to see which were the most and least vain. Women living in Venezuela were the chart toppers; 65 percent said they thought about their appearance all the time.[7] Other high-scoring countries included Russia and Mexico. The lowest scorers lived in the Philippines and in Saudi Arabia, where only 28 percent of consumers surveyed agreed with this statement.

SELF-CONCEPT

The **self-concept** summarizes the beliefs a person holds about his own attributes and how he evaluates the self on these qualities. Although your overall self-concept may be positive, there certainly are parts of it you evaluate more positively than others. For example, Lisa feels better about her professional identity than she does about her feminine identity.

The self-concept is a very complex structure. We describe attributes of self-concept along such dimensions as *content* (e.g., facial attractiveness versus mental aptitude), *positivity* (i.e., self-esteem), *intensity and stability* over time, and *accuracy* (i.e., the degree to which one's self-assessment corresponds to reality).[8] As we'll see later in this chapter, consumers' self-assessments can be quite distorted, especially with regard to their physical appearance.

SELF-ESTEEM

Self-esteem refers to the positivity of a person's self-concept. People with low self-esteem expect that they will not perform very well, and they will try to avoid embarrassment, failure, or rejection. In developing a new line of snack cakes, for example, Sara Lee found that consumers low in self-esteem preferred portion-controlled snack items because they felt they lacked self-control.[9]

Alberto-Culver uses a self-esteem appeal to promote a new product that reflects our changing society: Soft & Beautiful Just for Me Texture Softener, an alternative to hair pressing or relaxing. It's targeted to white mothers who don't know how to care for the hair of their multiracial children who have "hair texture" issues. The self-esteem portion of the campaign, dubbed "Love Yourself. Love Your Hair," includes a Web site, <u>texturesoftener.com</u> that offers "conversation starters" to help parents find ways to talk to their daughters about self-image.[10]

Marketing communications can influence a consumer's self-esteem. Exposure to ads such as the ones Lisa was checking out can trigger a process of *social*

The Tangled Web

Millions of people have posted photos at Hot or Not (<u>www.hotornot.com</u>), a hot Web site two engineers founded where visitors rate each picture on a scale from 1 to 10. One of the site's creators remembers, "Basically, we were sitting around drinking beers in the middle of the afternoon when a comment Jim made about a woman he had seen at a party made us think, wouldn't it be cool if there was a Web site where you could tell if a girl was a perfect 10?"

The phenomenal success of the site spawned hundreds of copycats, many of them not exactly the PG-rated environment this site offers. Some of the photos people send in aren't what you would call flattering (especially the ones submitted as jokes on unsuspecting friends); one possible explanation is the psychological concept of *self-handicapping* where we set ourselves up for failure so that in case ratings are low we can blame the picture rather than ourselves. Another is that the world is crowded with people so hungry for attention that they will submit to any number of indignities to have others look at them. What do you think?[11]

comparison, where the person tries to evaluate herself by comparing it to the people these artificial images depict.[12] This is a basic human tendency, and many marketers tap into our need for benchmarks by supplying idealized images of happy, attractive people who just happen to be using their products. A recent ad campaign for Clearasil is a good example. In one typical ad, two teenaged boys enter a kitchen where a 40-ish mother is mixing something in a bowl. When her son leaves the room, his friend hits on Mom. The ad's tagline: "Clearasil may cause confidence."

A study that illustrates the social comparison process showed that female college students tend to compare their physical appearance with models in advertising. Furthermore, study participants who were exposed to beautiful women in advertisements afterward expressed lowered satisfaction with their own appearance, as compared to other participants who did not view ads with attractive models.[13] Another study demonstrated that young women alter their perceptions of their own body shapes and sizes after they watch as little as 30 minutes of TV programming.[14] Researchers report similar findings for men.[15]

Self-esteem advertising attempts to change our attitudes toward products by stimulating positive feelings about one's self. One strategy is to challenge the consumer's self-esteem and then show a linkage to a product that provides a remedy. For example, the Marine Corps uses this strategy with its theme "If you have what it takes. . . ." Another strategy is outright flattery, as when Virginia Slims cigarette ads proclaim, "You've come a long way, baby."

REAL AND IDEAL SELVES

In South Korean shopping malls, teenage girls line up at photo machines that provide high-tech makeovers with options including glamour lighting, a hair-blowing breeze, and virtual plastic surgery. At the Beauty Plus booth, for example, the fashion model wannabees can digitally trim jaw lines, puff up lips, eliminate blemishes, and give themselves Western-style eyelids (this is the most popular option at booths in Seoul).[16]

When a consumer compares some aspect of himself to an ideal, this judgment influences his self-esteem. He might ask, "Am I as good-looking as I would like to be?" or "Do I make as much money as I should?" The **ideal self** is a person's conception of how he or she would like to be, whereas the **actual self** refers to our more realistic appraisal of the qualities we have and don't have. We choose some products because we think they are consistent with our actual self, whereas we buy others to help us to reach more of an ideal standard. And we often engage in a process of **impression management** where we work hard to "manage" what others think of us by strategically choosing clothing and other cues that will put us in a good light.[17]

Today, this process is very apparent when people exaggerate their positive qualities on their MySpace, Xanga, or Facebook pages. And those who post photos of their actual selves in unflattering situations (that must have been a pretty wild party . . .) are learning to regret their actions as potential employers start to check out their pages before they look at their resumes. Some are turning to services such as Reputation Defender that scour the Internet to remove embarrassing postings before the boss (or Mom) sees them.[18]

FANTASY: BRIDGING THE GAP BETWEEN THE SELVES

Most people experience a discrepancy between their real and ideal selves, but for some consumers this gap is especially large. These people are especially good targets for marketing communications that employ *fantasy appeals.*[19] A **fantasy** or daydream is a self-induced shift in consciousness, which is sometimes a way of compensating for a lack of external stimulation or of escaping from problems in the real world.[20] Many products and services are successful because they appeal to consumers'

This Dutch ad underscores the process of impression management.

fantasies. These marketing strategies allow us to extend our vision of ourselves by placing us in unfamiliar, exciting situations or by permitting us to "try on" interesting or provocative roles. And with today's technology, such as *Cosmopolitan*'s online makeover (virtualmakeover.com), consumers can experiment with different looks before actually taking the plunge in the real world.

MULTIPLE SELVES

In a way, each of us really is a number of different people—your mother probably would not recognize the "you" that emerges at a party at 4:00 in the morning! We have as many selves as we do different social roles. Depending on the situation, we act differently, use different products and services, and even vary in terms of how much we *like* the aspect of ourselves that is on display. A person may require a different set of products to play each of her roles: She may choose a sedate, understated perfume when she is being her professional self but splash on something more provocative on Saturday night as she becomes her *femme fatale* self.

As we saw in Chapter 1, the dramaturgical perspective on consumer behavior views people as actors who play different roles. We each play many roles, and each has its own script, props, and costumes.[21] We can think of the self as having different components, or *role identities,* and only some of these are active at any given time. Some identities (e.g., husband, boss, student) are more central to the self than others, but other identities (e.g., stamp collector, dancer, or advocate for the homeless) may be dominant in specific situations.[22] Strategically, this means a marketer may want to take steps to ensure the appropriate role identity is active before pitching products needed to play a particular role. One obvious way to do that is to place advertising messages in contexts where people are likely to be well aware of that role identity—for example, by promoting fitness and energy products at a marathon.

VIRTUAL IDENTITY

The thousands of personal Web sites people create to make statements about themselves relate to the motivation to project a version of the self (perhaps an idealized one) into popular culture. A study investigated why consumers create personal

Web sites and how those Web space strategies compare to the self-presentation strategies we use in real life. The authors found that events such as a graduation or promotion trigger many of these personal sites; other prominent causes include a desire for personal growth (mastering of technology, search for a job, etc.), or *advocacy* (homage to a favorite artist or product). The creators choose every element of the site carefully, selecting images and text that symbolize something about their self-identity, and many of them digitize their physical selves as part of their self-presentation. Also the sites often reveal intimate aspects of the self that people wouldn't necessarily share in real life (RL).[23]

In the influential cyberpunk novel *Snow Crash,* author Neal Stephenson envisioned a virtual world, called the *Metaverse,* as a successor to the Internet. In the Metaverse, everyday people take on glamorous identities in a three-dimensional immersive digital world. The book's main character delivers pizza in RL, but in the Metaverse, he's a warrior prince and champion sword fighter.[24] The hugely popular *Matrix* movie trilogy paints a similar (though more sinister) picture of a world that blurs the lines between physical and digital reality.

Today these fictional depictions come to life as we witness the tremendous growth of real-time, interactive virtual worlds that allow people to assume **virtual identities** in cyberspace. More than 9 million people worldwide belong to the virtual world of *Second Life,* more than 8 million play the online game *World of Warcraft,* and one-third of Korean adults belong to *CyWorld*. Add to that the millions more who play *The Sims Online* or who visit other computer-mediated environments (CMEs) such as *Webkinz, There, Whyville, Entropia Universe,* MTV's Virtual Laguna Beach (www.mtv.com/ontv/dyn/laguna_beach/vlb.jhtml) and so on and you're looking at a lot of serious role-playing.

On these sites people assume visual identities, or **avatars,** ranging from realistic versions of themselves to tricked-out versions with "exaggerated" physical

In a virtual world, you can be anyone you want to be. These are RL people with their avatars.

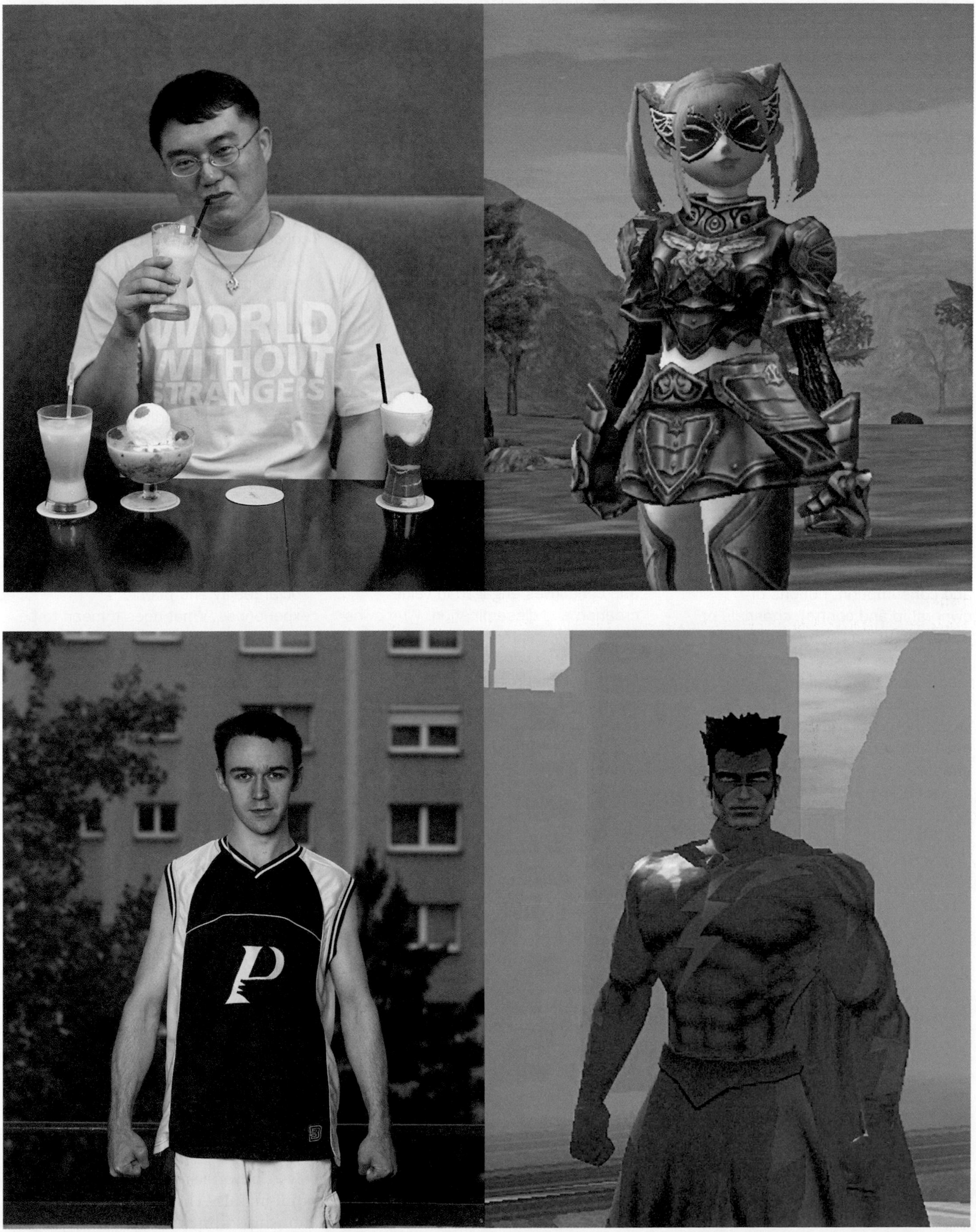
WORLD
WITHOUT
STRANGERS

CB AS I SEE IT

Professor Hope Schau
The University of Arizona

How does technology impact marketplace relationships? This question is at the center of my ongoing research efforts. How people use technology is of great significance to the study of social phenomena in general and of markets in particular. Technology impacts marketplace relationships as ideas of production and consumption, notions of ownership and control, channels of product and service distribution, modes of social interaction, and media of self-presentation morph with technological advancements. As Guttenberg's printing press is said to have enabled and supported nationalism, technology is a force of social change. The availability of and

access to global telecommunications has revolutionized the manner in which people engage in marketplace relationships, the power they wield in the market, and the manner in which they conspicuously communicate through active referencing of commercial brands. Personal Web spaces, such as personal homepages, blogs, virtual photo albums, and vlogs (video logs); social network Web spaces, such as MySpace and Facebook; and online dissemination spaces, such as YouTube, are changing the way individuals interact with brands, firms, and other individuals. They are enabling brand communities to flourish as people with like interests find each other across time ad space. They are rewriting our theories of production as individuals and collectives engaged in value creation and dissemination. Who owns what? Who creates value when? Who disseminates value to whom? These are the questions emerging today.

I explore self-presentation in personal Web space and the way people use commercial language (like brand names) to create and communicate identities. Online, in the

absence of corporeality, people actively use brands as a shorthand to convey complex meanings to known and unknown others. I delve into the realm of brand communities and collective consumption. Here, identities are imagined, formed, maintained, and communicated; collectives emerge and spread; new modes of value are created, shared, and exchanged using technology. Why do consumers enthusiastically (and for free) promote brands and companies voluntarily? With new software that can be used to create and disseminate consumer-generated, brand-related content, there is a growing trend toward vigilante marketing and consumer-generated marketing communications. I examine the role of technology to redefine social reality and people's experiences. What does it mean to be "old" in a world that relies on virtual technologies? How can technology mobilize people and create more fruitful life possibilities?

Is there a dark side of technology as Orwell imagined? Absolutely, but I'll leave that for others to explore. I seek positive realities.

characteristics or winged dragons or superheroes. Researchers are just starting to investigate how these online selves will influence consumer behavior and how the identities we choose in CMEs relate to our RL (or "meat-world") identities. Already we know that when people take on avatar forms, they tend to interact with other avatars much as their meat-world selves interact with other RL people. For example, just as in the RL, males in *Second Life* leave more space between them when talking to other males versus females and they are less likely to maintain eye contact than females are. And when avatars get very close to one another, they tend to look away from each other—the norms of the RL are creeping into the virtual world.[25]

SYMBOLIC INTERACTIONISM

If each person potentially has many social selves, how does each develop and how do we decide which self to "activate" at any point in time? The sociological tradition of **symbolic interactionism** stresses that relationships with other people play a large part in forming the self.[26] According to this perspective, people exist in a symbolic environment, and we assign meaning to any situation or object by interpreting the symbols in this environment. As members of society, we learn to agree on shared meanings. Thus, we "know" that a red light means stop, the "golden arches" means fast food, and "blondes have more fun." That's important to understand consumer behavior because it implies that our possessions play a key role as we evaluate ourselves and decide "who we are."[27]

Each of us, then, interprets our identity, and this assessment continually evolves as we encounter new situations and people. In symbolic interactionist terms, we *negotiate* these meanings over time. Essentially, each of us poses the question, "Who am I in this situation?" Those around us greatly influence how we answer this query, and we ask, "Whom do *other people* think I am?" We tend to pattern our behavior on the perceived expectations of others as a form of *self-fulfilling prophecy*. By acting the way we assume others expect us to act, we often wind up confirming these perceptions.

THE LOOKING-GLASS SELF

Some stores are testing a new interactive mirror that doubles as a high-resolution digital screen. When you choose an article of clothing, the mirror superimposes it on your reflection so that you can see how it would look on you. A camera relays live images of you modeling your virtual outfit to an Internet site where your friends can log to instant message (IM) you to tell you what they think; their comments pop up on the side of the mirror for you to read. They can also select virtual items for you to try on that will be reflected in the "magic" mirror.[28]

Sociologists call the process of imagining the reactions of others toward us "taking the role of the other," or the **looking-glass self.**[29] According to this view, our desire to define ourselves operates as a sort of psychological sonar: We take readings of our own identity by "bouncing" signals off others and trying to project the impression they have of us. The looking-glass image we receive will be different, depending on whose views we consider.

Like the distorted mirrors in a funhouse, our appraisal of who we are varies depending on whose perspective we are considering and how accurately we predict their evaluations of us. A confident career woman, such as Lisa, may sit morosely at

A few stores are testing a virtual mirror that superimposes garments on your body - while your friends chime in from around the Web.

Source: Andrea Mohin/The New York Times.

a nightclub, imagining that others see her as an unattractive woman with little sex appeal (regardless of whether these perceptions are true). A *self-fulfilling prophecy* may operate here because these "signals" may influence Lisa's actual behavior. If she doesn't believe she's attractive, she may choose dowdy clothing that actually does make her less attractive. However, her self-confidence in a professional setting may cause her to assume that others hold her "executive self" in even higher regard than they actually do (we've all known people like that!).

SELF-CONSCIOUSNESS

There are times when people seem to be painfully aware of themselves. If you have ever walked into a class in the middle of a lecture and you were convinced that all eyes were on you, you can understand this feeling of *self-consciousness*. In contrast, consumers sometimes behave with shockingly little self-consciousness. For example, we may behave in a stadium, a riot, or at a fraternity party in ways we would never do if we were highly conscious of our behavior.[30]

Some people seem to be more sensitive in general to the image they communicate to others. However, we all know people who act as if they're oblivious to the impression they are making. A heightened concern about the nature of one's public "image" also results in more concern about the social appropriateness of products and consumption activities.

Researchers use several techniques to measure this tendency. Consumers who score high on a scale of *public self-consciousness*, for example, are also more interested in clothing and are heavier users of cosmetics than those who score lower.[31] Similarly, high *self-monitors* are more attuned to how they present themselves in their social environments, and their estimates of how others will perceive their product choices influence what they choose to buy.[32] A scale to measure self-monitoring asks consumers how much they agree with statements such as "I guess I put on a show to impress or entertain others" or "I would probably make a good actor." Perhaps not surprisingly, publicly visible types, such as college football players and fashion models, tend to score higher on these dimensions.[33]

CONSUMPTION AND SELF-CONCEPT

Identity marketing is a promotional strategy where consumers alter some aspects of their selves to advertise for a branded product:[34]

● A British marketing firm paid five people to legally change their names for one year to "Turok," the hero of a video game series about a time-traveling Native American who slays bionically enhanced dinosaurs.
● The Internet Underground Music Archive (IUMA) paid a Kansas couple $5,000 to name their baby boy Iuma.
● The Casa Sanchez restaurant in San Francisco gives free lunches for life to anyone who gets its logo tattooed on their body.
● The Great Northern Brewing Company, which brews Black Star Beer, recently held its second annual Black Star Beer Tattoo Contest, giving away a Harley-Davidson to whoever showed up with the biggest tattoo of its "yahoo-in cowboy" company logo.
● The Daytona Cubs baseball team awards free season tickets for life to anyone who will tattoo the Cubs logo on their body.
● According to the International Trademark Association, the Harley tattoo is still the most widespread corporate logo tattoo in North America, but other contenders include Nike, Adidas, Budweiser, Corona, Apple computers, Ford, Chevy, and Volkswagen.

BMW 3 SERIES CONVERTIBLE. THE WORLD IS LOOKING AT YOU.

This Italian ad reminds us of the power of self-consciousness: "The world is looking at you."

PRODUCTS THAT SHAPE THE SELF: YOU ARE WHAT YOU CONSUME

Recall that the reflected self helps shape self-concept, which implies that people see themselves as they imagine others see them. Because what others see includes a person's clothing, jewelry, furniture, car, and so on, it stands to reason that these products also help to determine the perceived self. A consumer's possessions place him or her into a social role, which helps to answer the question, "Who am I now?"

People use an individual's consumption behaviors to help them judge that person's social identity. In addition to considering a person's clothes and grooming habits, we make inferences about personality based on a person's choice of leisure activities (e.g., squash versus bowling), food preferences (e.g., tofu and beans versus steak and potatoes), cars, home decorating choices, and so on. When researchers show people pictures of someone's living room, for example, they are able to make surprisingly accurate guesses about the occupant's personality.[35] In the same way that a consumer's use of products influences others' perceptions, the same products can help to determine his own self-concept and social identity.[36]

A consumer exhibits attachment to an object to the extent that he uses it to maintain a self-concept.[37] Objects act as a sort of security blanket by reinforcing our identities, especially in unfamiliar situations. For example, students who decorate their dorm rooms with personal items are less likely to drop out of college. This coping process may protect the self from being diluted in a strange environment.[38] When a pair of researchers asked children of various ages to create "who am I?" collages where respondents chose pictures that represented their selves, they found that the extent to which kids used photos of branded merchandise in their collages increased in number and sophistication between middle childhood and early adolescence. These linkages changed from concrete relationships (e.g., "I own it") to more sophisticated, abstract relationships (e.g., "It is like me").[39]

Our use of consumption information to define the self is especially important when we have yet to totally form a social identity, such as when we find ourselves playing a new role in life. Think, for example, of the insecurity many of us felt when we first started college or reentered the dating market after leaving a really long relationship. **Symbolic self-completion theory** suggests that people who have an incomplete self-definition tend to complete this identity by acquiring and displaying symbols they associate with that role.[40] Adolescent boys, for example, may use "macho" products such as cars and cigarettes to bolster their developing masculinity; these items act as a "social crutch" during a period of uncertainty about their new identity as adult males. As we mature into a role, we actually rely less on the products people associate with it: For example, when kids start to skateboard they often invest in pro skateboard "decks" with graphics and branding that cost between $40 and $70 even without the "trucks" (wheels and axles). But—to the chagrin of the skateboard industry—as they get more serious about boarding, many think it's just fine to buy "blank decks," the plain wood boards that cost only $15 to $30.[41]

The contribution of possessions to self-identity is perhaps most apparent when we lose these treasured objects. One of the first acts of institutions such as prisons or the military that want to repress individuality and encourage group identity is to confiscate personal possessions.[42] Victims of burglaries and natural disasters commonly report feelings of alienation, depression, or of being "violated." One consumer's comment after she was robbed is typical: "It's the next worse thing to being bereaved; it's like being raped."[43] Burglary victims exhibit a diminished sense of community, lowered feelings of privacy, and less pride in their houses' appearance than do their neighbors.[44]

A study of postdisaster conditions, where consumers may have lost literally everything but the clothes on their backs following a fire, hurricane, flood, or earthquake, highlights the dramatic impact of product loss. Some people are reluctant to undergo the process of re-creating their identities by acquiring new possessions. Interviews with disaster victims reveal that some hesitate to invest the self in new possessions and so become more detached about what they buy. This comment from a woman in her 50s is representative of this attitude: "I had so much love tied up in my things. I can't go through that kind of loss again. What I'm buying now won't be as important to me."[45]

SELF/PRODUCT CONGRUENCE

Because many consumption activities are related to self-definition, it is not surprising to learn that consumers demonstrate consistency between their values (see Chapter 4) and the things they buy.[46] **Self-image congruence models** suggest that we choose products when their attributes match some aspect of the self.[47] These models assume a process of *cognitive matching* between product attributes and the consumer's self-image.[48]

A recent exploration of the conflicts Muslim women who choose to wear headscarves experience illustrates how even a simple piece of cloth reflects a person's aesthetic, political, and moral dimensions.[49] The Turkish women in the study expressed the tension they felt in their ongoing struggle to reconcile ambiguous religious principles that simultaneously call for modesty and beauty. Society sends Muslim women contradictory messages in modern-day Turkey. Although the Koran denounces waste, many of the companies that produce religious headscarves introduce new designs each season and, as styles and tastes change, the women are encouraged to purchase more scarves than necessary. Moreover, the authors point out that a wearer communicates her fashion sense by the fabrics she selects and by the way she drapes and ties her scarf. In addition, veiling sends contradictory images about the proper sex roles of men and women. On the one hand, women who cover their heads by choice feel a sense of empowerment. On the other, the notion that Islamic law exhorts women to cover themselves lest they threaten men's self-restraint and honor is a persistent sign that men exert control over women's bodies and restrict their freedom. As a compromise solution Nike designed a uniform for observant women in Somalia who want to play sports without abandoning the traditional *hijab* (a robe that wraps around the head and loosely drapes over the entire body). The company streamlined the garment so that volleyball players could move but still keep their bodies covered.[50]

Although results are somewhat mixed, the ideal self appears to be more relevant than the actual self as a comparison standard for highly expressive social products such as perfume. In contrast, the actual self is more relevant for everyday, functional products. These standards are also likely to vary by usage situation.[51] For example, a consumer might want a functional, reliable car to commute to work every day and a flashier model with more "zing" when going out on a date in the evening.

Research tends to support the idea of congruence between product usage and self-image. One of the earliest studies to examine this process found that car owners' ratings of themselves tended to match their perceptions of their cars: Pontiac drivers saw themselves as more active and flashy than did Volkswagen drivers.[52] Indeed, a recent German study found that observers were able to match photos of male and female drivers to pictures of the cars they drove almost 70 percent of the time.[53] Researchers have also reported congruity between consumers and their most preferred brands of beer, soap, toothpaste, and cigarettes relative to their least preferred brands, as well as between consumers' self-images and their favorite stores.[54] Some specific attributes useful to describe matches between consumers and products include rugged/delicate, excitable/calm, rational/emotional, and formal/informal.[55]

Although these findings make some intuitive sense, we cannot blithely assume that consumers will always buy products whose characteristics match their own. It is not clear that consumers really see aspects of themselves in down-to-earth, functional products that don't have very complex or humanlike images. It is one thing to consider a brand personality for an expressive, image-oriented product, such as perfume, and quite another to impute human characteristics to a toaster.

Another problem is the old "chicken-and-egg" question: Do people buy products because the products are seen as similar to the self, or do people assume that these products must be similar to themselves because they have bought them? The similarity between a person's self-image and the images of products he purchases does tend to increase over the time he owns the product, so we can't rule out this explanation.

THE EXTENDED SELF

A college student named John Freyer sold all his possessions on eBay to see if our "stuff" really defines who we are. His treasures included an open box of taco shells, half a bottle of mouthwash, and his sideburns packaged in a plastic bag (yes, it seems people will buy just about anything!). Those who bought any of the artifacts he listed for sale registered them on a Web site called allmylifeforsale.com. Freyer then undertook a decidedly nonspiritual odyssey as he set out to "visit" all of his possessions in their new homes around the world—including a bag of PorkyO's BBQ Pork Skins that wound up in Japan.[56]

As we noted earlier, many of the props and settings consumers use to define their social roles become parts of their selves. Those external objects that we consider a

Marketing Pitfall

Are you what you drive? If your ride is an SUV, maybe you'd better hope not. The hugely popular vehicles are coming under fire for being selfish gas-guzzlers that suck up a huge share of scarce resources and intimidate other drivers—and as gas prices continue to rise some people are rethinking their choices. Even religious groups are organizing protests, arguing that SUVs are contrary to moral teachings about protecting people and the earth. The tagline for one set of ads reads, "What Would Jesus Drive?"[58]

A book called *High and Mighty* goes even further. The author, a *New York Times* reporter who covers the auto industry, claims that the SUV is the car of choice for the nation's most self-centered people. He reports that automakers' research on the types of people who are likely buyers finds they tend to be "insecure and vain. They are frequently nervous about their marriages and uncomfortable about parenthood. They often lack confidence in their driving skills. Above all, they are apt to be self-centered and self-absorbed, with little interest in their neighbors and communities. . . . They tend to like fine restaurants a lot more than off-road driving, seldom go to church and have limited interest in doing volunteer work to help others." And the automakers are doing their part to cater to drivers who want to play out their aggressive instincts on the road. For example, designers deliberately made the Dodge Durango look like a savage jungle cat, with vertical bars across the grille to represent teeth and big jawlike fenders.[59]

part of us comprise the **extended self.** In some cultures, people literally incorporate objects into the self—they lick new possessions, take the names of conquered enemies (or in some cases eat them), or bury the dead with their possessions.[57]

We don't usually go that far, but some people do cherish possessions as if they were a part of them. Consider shoes, for example: You don't have to be Carrie of *Sex and the City* fame to acknowledge that many people feel a strong bond to their footwear. One study found that people commonly view their shoes as magical emblems of self, Cinderella-like vehicles for self-transformation. Based on data collected from consumers, the researcher concluded that (like their sister Carrie) women tend to be more attuned to the symbolic implications of shoes than men. A common theme that emerged was that a pair of shoes obtained when younger—whether a first pair of

This Italian ad demonstrates that our favorite products are part of the extended self.

FRANCESCO**BIASIA**
HANDBAGS

leather shoes, a first pair of high heels, or a first pair of cowboy boots—had a big impact even later in life. These experiences were similar to those that occur in such well-known fairy tales and stories as Dorothy's red shoes in *The Wizard of Oz* (1939), Karen's magical red shoes in Hans Christian Anderson's *The Red Shoes* (1845), and Cinderella's glass slippers.[60]

In addition to shoes, of course, many material objects ranging from personal possessions and pets to national monuments or landmarks help to form a consumer's identity. Just about everyone can name a valued possession that has a lot of the self "wrapped up" in it, whether it is a beloved photograph, a trophy, an old shirt, a car, or a cat. Indeed, usually we can construct a pretty accurate "biography" of someone simply by cataloging the items on display in his bedroom or office.

The extended self helps to explain why to the Japanese it's a deal killer if you mishandle a business card. Japanese businesspeople view a card as an extension of their self and they expect the recipient to treat it respectfully. If you bend the card or make it do double duty as a toothpick, you are insulting the card's owner big time. Arriving in Japan without an ample stock of business cards is akin to arriving barefoot. There is an elaborate etiquette connected to giving and receiving cards. This should be done solemnly and you need to study the card intently rather than shoving it into your coat pocket to file later.[61]

We describe four levels of the extended self, ranging from very personal objects to places and things that allow people to feel as though they are rooted in their larger social environments:[62]

1 **Individual level:** Consumers include many of their personal possessions in self-definition. These products can include jewelry, cars, clothing, and so on. The saying "You are what you wear" reflects the belief that one's things are a part of one's identity.
2 **Family level:** This part of the extended self includes a consumer's residence and the furnishings in it. We can think of the house as a symbolic body for the family, and the place where we live often is a central aspect of who we are.
3 **Community level:** It is common for consumers to describe themselves in terms of the neighborhood or town from which they come. For farm families or other residents with close ties to a community, this sense of belonging is particularly important.
4 **Group level:** We regard our attachments to certain social groups as a part of the self—we'll consider some of these consumer *subcultures* in later chapters. A consumer also may feel that landmarks, monuments, or sports teams are a part of the extended self.

 Sex Roles

Sexual identity is a very important component of a consumer's self-concept. People often conform to their culture's expectations about how those of their gender should act, dress, or speak. Of course, these guidelines change over time, and they differ radically across societies. It's unclear to what extent gender differences are innate versus culturally shaped—but they're certainly evident in many consumption situations.

Consider the gender differences market researchers observe when they compare the food preferences of men to those of women. Women eat more fruit; men are more likely to eat meat. As one food writer put it, "Boy food doesn't grow. It is - hunted or killed."[63] The sexes also differ sharply in the quantities of food they eat: When researchers at Hershey discovered that women eat smaller amounts of candy, they created a white chocolate confection called Hugs, one of the most successful food introductions of all time. However, a man in a Burger King Whopper ad ditches his date at a fancy restaurant, complaining that he is "too hungry to settle for chick food." Pumped up on Whoppers, a swelling mob of men shake their fists, punch one another, toss a van off a bridge, and sing, "I will eat this meat until my innie turns into an outie," and "I am hungry. I am incorrigible. I am man."[64]

GENDER DIFFERENCES IN SOCIALIZATION

Can the smell of burning rubber and gasoline light the fires of love? In the United States, Harlequin, a major publisher of romance novels with a predominantly female readership, is partnering with male-dominated NASCAR (National Association for Stock Car Auto Racing) to turn out car racing-themed stories. In one, the heroine is an ex-kindergarten teacher who falls in love with a real NASCAR driver named Lance Cooper after he hits her with his car (subtle, right?); she winds up driving his racing team's motor coach from race to race. In a typical passage, the novel describes a kiss: "It wasn't gentle, it wasn't passive, it was a kiss that instantly proved the two of them were like high-octane fuel, their flesh sparking off each other. . . ."[65] Yet another case of boy meets girl, boy runs over girl.

A society communicates its assumptions about the proper roles of men and women by stressing ideal behaviors for each gender. Many commercial sources, in addition to parents and friends, provide lessons in *gender socialization* for both girls and boys:

- Mattel is partnering with U.S. cosmetics manufacturer Bonne Bell in 2008 to market a line of cosmetics to young girls aged 6 to 9. The popular Bratz doll line already licenses its name to a cosmetics line also aiming for this age group.
- ESPN Zone in Chicago is a male preserve that lets boys be boys and men be . . . boys. Customers perceive the venue as a safe haven where buddies can watch men's sports and establish camaraderie with other men.[66]
- Sony created a TV ad for its Bravia line of liquid-crystal-display (LCD) televisions that offers different endings to men and women. The spot shows a man and a woman gazing through a storefront window at a Bravia LCD. Unaware of each other, the two simultaneously whisper: "Nice picture." Suddenly, two buttons appear on the screen that read: "Ending for Men" and "Ending for Women." The male ending is either a funny clip from a sports show or a cartoon spoof of a martial-arts movie. Women see either a 1950s-era musical centered on shoes or a tear-jerker about a female doctor who saves the life of an orphan.[67]

As these examples illustrate, manufacturers and retailers tend to reinforce a society's expectations regarding the "correct" way for boys and girls, men and women, to look and act. Even countries that are physically close to each other may send very different messages. In comparing Malaysian and Singaporean commercials, for example, researchers found that Malaysian males tend to dominate ads for technical products, whereas females dominate the Singaporean ones, which suggests that in Singapore people accept women to a greater degree when they assume professional roles. To support this argument, they also found that men are portrayed more often in high-level business or professional roles in Malaysia, whereas in Singapore both genders were portrayed equally.[68]

Many societies expect males to pursue **agentic goals,** which stress self-assertion and mastery. However, they teach females to value **communal goals,** such as affiliation and the fostering of harmonious relations.[69] One study even found that people perceived a male voice emanating from a computer to be more accurate and authoritative than a female voice reading the very same words. And participants valued computer-generated words of praise to a greater extent when the voice was male![70] Similarly, an analysis of TV commercials aimed at children in the United States and Australia found that they depict boys as more knowledgeable, active, aggressive, and instrumental.[71]

These differences in orientation show up early in our development. When Mattel decided to develop Ello, a new brand of building toy for girls, its designers began by watching the play patterns of 5- to 10-year-olds. The toy features interconnecting plastic squares, balls, triangles, squiggles, flowers, and sticks, in pastel colors and with rounded corners that let users snap pieces together to create houses, people, jewelry, and picture frames. As one of the developers observed, "boys enjoy stacking blocks and working towards a goal, such as finishing a building. Their play is more physically active, and they like to create conflict between characters. Girls don't like repetitive stacking. They prefer to create relationships between characters, building communities and decorative spaces."[72]

Gender versus Sexual Identity

Gender-role identity is a state of mind as well as body. A person's biological gender (i.e., male or female) does not totally determine whether he or she will exhibit **sex-typed traits,** characteristics we stereotypically associate with one gender or the other. A consumer's subjective feelings about his or her sexuality are crucial as well.[73]

Unlike maleness and femaleness, masculinity and femininity are not biological characteristics. A behavior one culture considers to be masculine might get a different response in another. For example, the norm in the United States is that male friends avoid touching each other (except in "safe" situations such as on the football field). In some Latin and European cultures, however, it is common for men to hug and kiss one another as a form of greeting.

Each society determines what "real" men and women should and should not do and it communicates these expectations. For example, as part of a campaign to sell

This ad for Bijan illustrates how sex-role identities are culturally bound by contrasting the expectations of how women should appear in two different countries.

a new shaver to China's growing ranks of young urban professional men, Philips Electronics developed an Internet campaign featuring a trio of slinky secret agents who dispense tips on shaving, romance, and success. The young women, collectively called "My Secret Weapon," are modeled on *Charlie's Angels:* Black-clad Jennifer helps with career networking, sultry Angelina dishes out romantic tips, and martini-sipping party girl Victoria offers guidance on social matters. According to the company's marketing research, many single Chinese men don't get this kind of advice at home, so Philips is trying to satisfy a need for guidance—and hopefully sell a bunch of shavers in the process.[74]

SEX-TYPED PRODUCTS

A popular book once proclaimed, *Real Men Don't Eat Quiche.* Many products (in addition to quiche) also are "sex typed." They take on masculine or feminine attributes, and consumers associate them with one gender or another.[75] Marketers often encourage the sex typing of products such as Princess telephones, boys' and girls' bicycles, or Luvs color-coded diapers. A vodka brand called Thor's Hammer illustrates this stereotyping. The booze comes in a short, squat bottle and the company's vice president of marketing describes it as "bold and broad and solid. This is a man's kind of vodka . . . it's not your frosted . . . girly-man vodka." Thor was the Norse god of thunder, and the company claims the name has no connection to the slang phrase "getting hammered," which can happen if you drink too much of the stuff.[76]

ANDROGYNY

Androgyny refers to the possession of both masculine and feminine traits.[77] Researchers make a distinction between *sex-typed people*, who are stereotypically masculine or feminine, and *androgynous people*, whose orientation isn't as clearly defined. People who don't neatly fit into one gender category or another may create uncertainly among others who aren't sure how to relate to them. A recent study demonstrated that sex-role assumptions travel into cyberspace as well. The researchers asked each volunteer to interact with another respondent via a chat room. They showed subjects an avatar representing the other person, with images ranging from "an obviously female" blonde to one with no clear gender to a strong-jawed male. The subjects rated their partners as less "credible" when they saw an androgynous avatar than when they saw one with sex-typed facial characteristics.[78]

Of course, the "normality" of sex-typed behaviors varies across cultures. For example, although acceptance of homosexuality varies in Asian cultures, it doesn't occur to most Asians to assume that a man with some feminine qualities is gay. A recent survey of Korean consumers found that more than 66 percent of men and 57 percent of women younger than age 40 were living self-described "androgynous" lifestyles—with men having more traditionally female traits and women having more traditionally male ones than they might have years ago. But the respondents didn't link that with sexual orientation. Although the Koreans nickname males with feminine interests "flower men," they don't consider this to be a derogatory term.[79] In Japan, men that people call *gyaru-o* ("male gals") are common on city streets. Tanned and meticulously dressed (and usually heterosexual), these fops cruise Tokyo's stylish boutiques.[80]

Differences in sex-role orientation can influence how we respond to marketing stimuli, at least under some circumstances.[81] For example, females are more likely to undergo more elaborate processing of message content, so they tend to be more sensitive to specific pieces of information when forming a judgment, whereas males are more influenced by overall themes.[82] In addition, women with relatively strong masculine components in their sex-role identity prefer ad portrayals that include nontraditional women.[83] Some research indicates that sex-typed people are more

A typical gyaru-o in Tokyo.

sensitive to the sex-role depictions of characters in advertising, although women appear to be more sensitive generally to gender-role relationships than men are.

In one study, subjects read two versions of a beer advertisement couched in either masculine or feminine terms. The masculine version contained phrases such as "X beer has the strong aggressive flavor that really asserts itself with good food and good company," and the feminine version made claims such as "Brewed with tender care, X beer is a full-bodied beer that goes down smooth and gentle." People who rated themselves as highly masculine or highly feminine preferred the version that was described in (respectively) very masculine or feminine terms.[84] Sex-typed people in general are more concerned with ensuring that their behavior is consistent with their culture's definition of gender appropriateness.

Researchers developed a scale to identify "nontraditional males" (NTMs) who exhibit stereotypically female tendencies. The scale included statements such as these:

- I enjoy looking through fashion magazines.
- In our family, I take care of the checkbook and pay the bills.
- I am concerned about getting enough calcium in my diet.

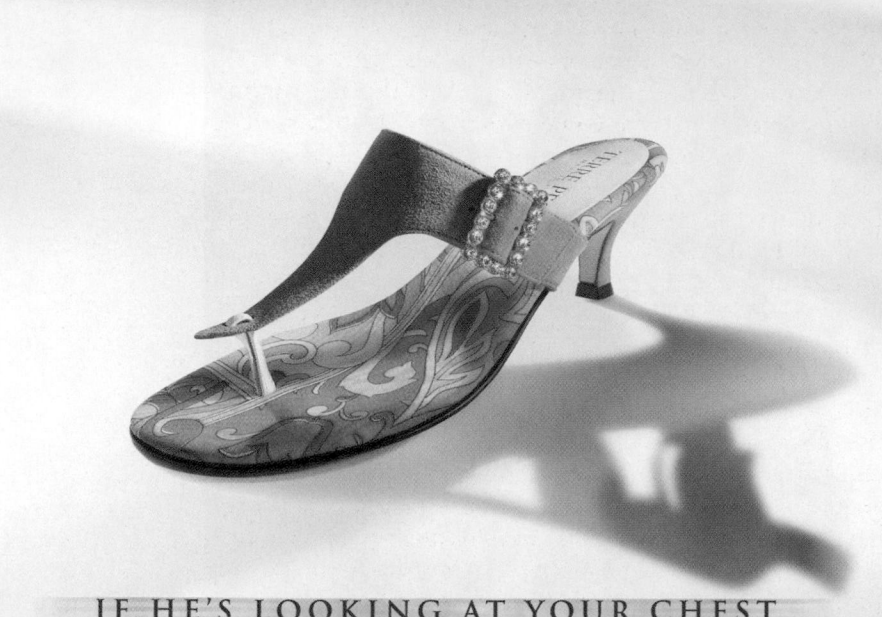

IF HE'S LOOKING AT YOUR CHEST,
HE'S NOT BOWING DOWN FAR ENOUGH.

BETSY FISHER

Feed the fetish

1224 Connecticut Avenue, NW, Washington, DC 20036 | M 10-7 T 10-7 W 10-7 Th 10-9 F 10-9 Sa 10-6 Su 12-4

Advertising often reflects society's attitudes regarding how men should regard women and vice versa.

- I am good at fixing mechanical things.
- I would do better than average in a fistfight.

Not too surprisingly, strong differences emerged between men who rated the statements along traditional sex-role lines versus those who had nontraditional orientations. When asked how they would others to see them, NTMs were more likely than traditional males (TMs) to say that they would like to be considered stylish, sophisticated, up to date, and trendsetting. They were also more likely to say that they would like to be seen as sensitive, spiritual, affectionate, organized, and thrifty but less likely to say they would like to be seen as "outdoorsy."[85]

FEMALE SEX ROLES

In the 1949 movie *Adam's Rib*, Katherine Hepburn played a stylish and competent lawyer. This film was one of the first to show that a woman can have a successful career and still be happily married. Today, the evolution of a new managerial class of women has forced marketers to change their traditional assumptions about women as they target this growing market. For example, Suzuki is going out of its way to appeal to the growing number of women in India who are achieving financial independence and buying their own cars. Its Zen Estilo (*Estilo* means "style" in Spanish) model comes in eight colors, including "purple fusion," "virgin blue" and "sparkling olive."[86]

And in the West, in general, younger women's views of themselves are quite different from those of their mothers who fought the good fight for feminism years ago.

To some extent they may take for granted that they have certain rights for which their mothers had to fight. After all, they have grown up with female role models who are strong leaders; they participate to a much greater degree in organized sports; and they spend a lot of time on the Internet where factors such as gender, race, and social status tend to disappear. In one study, only 34 percent of girls aged 13 to 20 labeled themselves as feminists—even though they strongly endorsed the principles of the feminist movement. Ninety-seven percent of the same group of respondents believe a woman should receive the same pay for the same work a man does; 92 percent agree that a woman's lifestyle choices should not be limited by her gender; and 89 percent say a woman can be successful without either a man or children. But 56 percent also believe that "a man should always open the door for a woman."[87]

These changes have forced marketers to reexamine their strategies. For example, most sporting goods manufacturers have long sold products for women, but this often meant simply creating an inferior version of the male product and slapping a pink label on it. Then the companies discovered that many women were buying products intended for boys because they wanted better quality, so some of them figured out that they needed to take this market segment seriously. Burton Snowboard Company was one of the early learners. When the company started to offer high-quality clothing and gear made specifically for women, female boarders snapped them up. Burton also changed the way it promotes these products. It redesigned its Web site after getting feedback from female riders. Now, models in the women's section are shot from the bottom looking up, which makes them look more empowered. In contrast, the photos in the men's section feature tighter shots of the gear itself, since Burton's research showed that males are more interested in the technical details.[88]

Women consume many products intended to alter their appearance to be in line with cultural expectations.

Love isn't blind. If it were, there would be no such thing as makeup and pushup bras.

Marketing Opportunity

Some U.S. marketers have figured out that products men traditionally love appeal to women as well. In the automotive industry, they are discovering that a growing number of women spend big bucks to add extra horsepower to their cars, along with 17-inch wheels, custom racing seats, and other accessories. Although attributes such as safety, security, and reliability still appeal to women, like men they are increasingly drawn to power, speed, and hot looks. The so-called tuner industry, which includes aftermarket products such as spoilers, Xenon headlights, and turbochargers, is feeling this change—women now buy almost 25 percent of the $2.2 billion in merchandise and services that car freaks purchase each year.[93]

Similarly, the high-tech industry launched a "Technology is a girl's best friend" campaign to entice women to buy more electronics products. This makes sense because the Consumer Electronics Association estimates that about 75 percent of consumer-electronics purchasing decisions involve women. Gateway even managed to get a pink laptop computer prominently placed in the movie *Legally Blonde 2.* Other manufacturers are coming out with products ranging from headphones to cell phone covers in pink and other feminine colors to attract women. Palm's Zire Handheld PDA emphasizes its clear packaging and simple name. Palm's new focus evidently worked: For the first time with any Palm product, more than half of Zire buyers are women.[94]

And women are invading that bastion of maleness we call video games. They make up about 40 percent of the total gaming audience. Some 64 percent of online gamers in the United States are female according to a recent Nielsen study. And in the emerging mobile-game market, women account for 55 percent of players. For example, Buena Vista games targets women aged 18 to 49 with a **PC** game based on *Desperate Housewives.*[95]

Still, it's premature to proclaim the death of traditional sex-role stereotypes. This is certainly true in traditional Islamic countries, such as Saudi Arabia, that require women to be completely covered in public and that prohibit them to work as salespeople in stores open to the public (even if the store sells female intimate apparel).[89] In the United States, a line of collectible scale cars called Fast Women reminds us that traditional sex-role stereotypes are alive and well: The cars come with painted-resin female models that pose on their hoods. The line includes five figures with names such as Candy and Mitzi, clad in different skimpy outfits.[90]

To further complicate matters, sex roles constantly evolve—in a complex society like ours we often encounter contradictory messages about "appropriate" behavior. And, like other fashion phenomena that we'll talk about in Chapter 17, a wave in one direction may set off a ripple in another. We can clearly see this in the messages U.S. girls have been getting from the media for the last several years: It's cool to be slutty. Role models like Paris Hilton, Lindsay Lohan, Britney Spears, and even Bratz dolls convey standards about how far preteens and teens should go in broadcasting their sexuality. Now, as these messages seem to go over the top (at least in the eyes of some concerned parents), we start to see early signs of a backlash. At the Pure Fashion Web site, girls get style tips including skirts and dresses that fall no more than four fingers above the knee and no tank tops without a sweater or jacket over them. Several other sites such as ModestApparelUSA.com, ModestByDesign.com and DressModestly.com advocate a return to styles that leave almost everything to the imagination.[91] Is U.S. culture moving from a celebration of "girls gone wild" to "girls gone mild?" Stay tuned.

As we'll see in the next chapter, it's not realistic to paint a huge group of consumers with the same brush, so we often need to subdivide them into segments that share important characteristics. This logic certainly applies to women, and smart marketers understand that they can't assume all female consumers have been socialized the same way. For example, a research company called Cohorts identifies nine segments of single American women alone. Cohorts describes the three most promising segments as follows:[92]

1 *Megan:* A stylish, tech-savvy student with a median income of $16,000. She reads *Self, Rolling Stone, InStyle,* and *Us Weekly.* She is likely to channel surf when ads come on TV and she wouldn't watch TV at all without cable. Her favorite channels are Oxygen, Nick at Nite, Disney Channel, MTV, VH1, E!, and TBS. She's turned on by what's cool or the latest thing, she's liberal, seizes opportunities, and she spends on a whim.

2 *Allison:* An educated working woman with a median income of $52,000. She reads *Elle, Shape, Cosmopolitan,* and *Entertainment Weekly.* Her favorite channels are Lifetime, Bravo, Cartoon Network, E!, FX, TBS, and TLC. She's into travel and her career, and she prides herself on her sophisticated tastes.

3 *Elizabeth:* An affluent career woman with a median income of $174,000. She reads *Vogue, Harper's Bazaar, People,* and *Martha Stewart Living.* When she takes time to watch TV, she tunes in to networks such as Lifetime, WEtv, Comedy Central, MTV, CNBC, E!, HBO, A&E, Bravo, and AMC. She values foreign travel, fitness, and her career, and she's savvy and spontaneous.

MALE SEX ROLES

Our culture's stereotype of the ideal male is a tough, aggressive, muscular man who enjoys "manly" sports (and *The Man Show* on Comedy Central). Just as for women, however, the true story is more complicated than that. Indeed, scholars of **masculinism** study the male image and the complex cultural meanings of masculinity.[96] Like women, men receive mixed messages about how they are supposed to behave and feel.

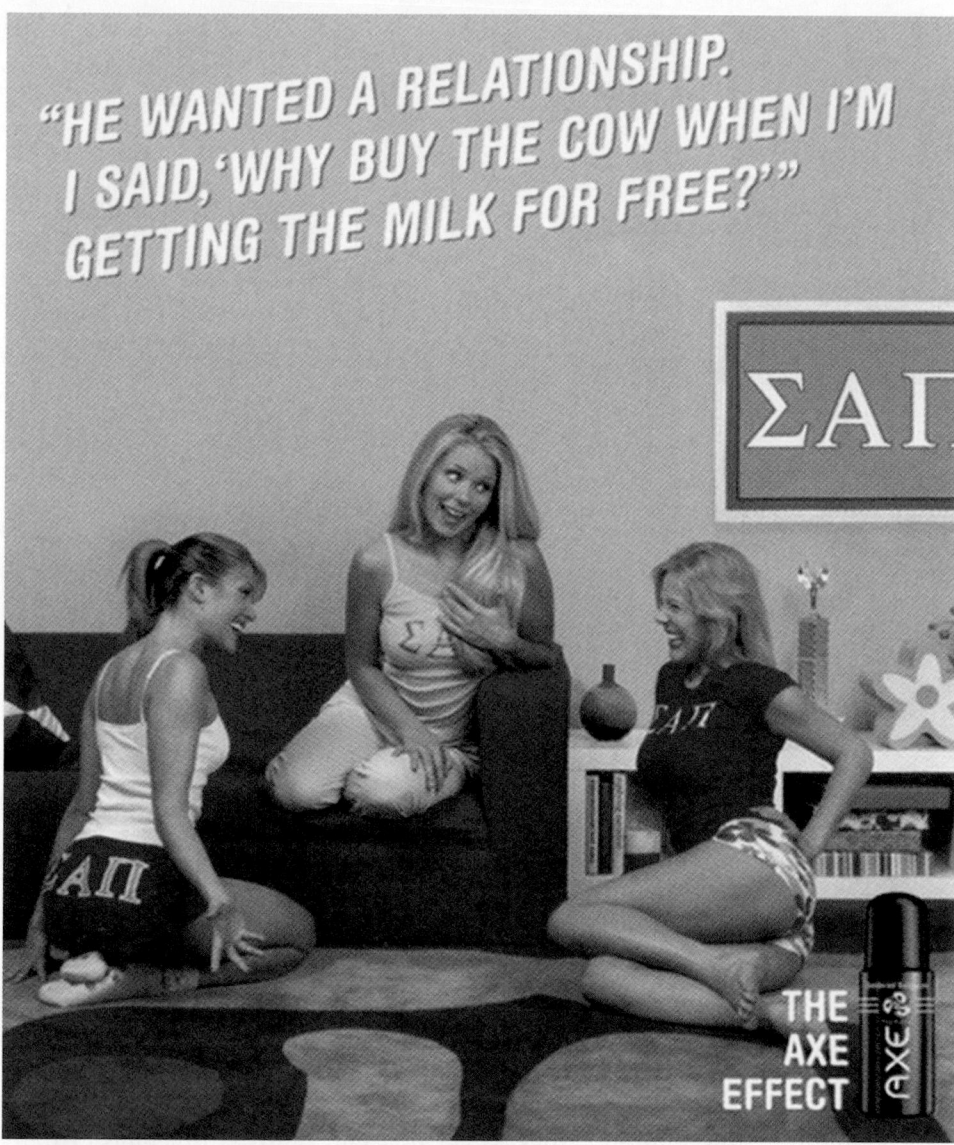

"HE WANTED A RELATIONSHIP. I SAID, 'WHY BUY THE COW WHEN I'M GETTING THE MILK FOR FREE?'"

ΣΑΓ

THE AXE EFFECT

The Axe line of male personal care products puts a twist on an old stereotype by depicting men as sex objects.

Some analysts argue that men are threatened because they don't necessarily recognize themselves in the powerful male stereotypes against which feminists protest.[97] One study examined how American men pursue masculine identities through their everyday consumption. The researchers suggest that men are trying to make sense out of three different models of masculinity that they call *breadwinner*, *rebel*, and *man-of-action hero*, as they figure out just who they are supposed to be. On the one hand, the breadwinner model draws from the American myth of success and celebrates respectability, civic virtues, pursuit of material success, and organized achievement. The rebel model, on the other hand, emphasizes rebellion, independence, adventure, and potency. The man-of-action hero is a synthesis that draws from the better of the other two models.[98]

One consequence of the continual evolution of sex roles is that men are concerned as never before with their appearance. Men spend $7.7 billion on grooming products globally each year. A wave of male cleansers, moisturizers, sunscreens, depilatories, and body sprays is washing up on U.S. shores, largely from European marketers. L'Oréal Paris reports that men's skincare products is now its fastest-growing sector. In Europe, 24 percent of men younger than age 30 use skincare products—and 80 percent of young Korean men do.[99]

This Dutch beer ad communicates
expectations about the male sex role.

This trend influences other product categories as well, for example, men's
jewelry. Once considered a fringe market for rockers, rappers, gay men, and gangsters, mass-market retailers are finding that mainstream guys also seek out titanium pendants, three-diamond rings, silver dog tags, and ID bracelets. Tiffany
expanded its watch and cuff link collections to include a broad range of sporty men's
jewelry after the company outfitted actor Brad Pitt with a silver pendant and cuff
links for the movie *Ocean's Twelve* (2004); men started showing up in stores to ask
for the "Brad Pitt" pieces. Singer Lenny Kravitz and actor Orlando Bloom have been
shot wearing jewelry on magazine covers, and men's jewelry sales (excluding watches)
now make up about 10 percent of the industry's sales.[100]

U.S. men are showing a willingness to use other traditionally feminine products,
such as depilatories, to give them that smooth-torso look. They're even buying vanity products that alter their shape, including Bodyslimmers underwear that holds in
the waist, Super Shaper Briefs that round out the buttocks, and the C-In2 "sling"
brief that provides a lift similar to the Wonder Bra (along with a new version of this
gravity-defying product called the Trophy Shelf). Indeed, whereas women used to
purchase 80 percent of men's underwear for their boyfriends and spouses today
two-thirds of males buy their own—including (according to Jockey, a leading manufacturer) many who think of underwear as an "event purchase," something special
to don on Saturday night.[101]

No doubt one of the biggest marketing buzzwords over the past few years is the
metrosexual, a straight, urban male who is keenly interested in fashion, home
design, gourmet cooking, and personal care. A gay writer named Mark Simpson
actually coined the term way back in a 1994 article when he "outed" British (and now

American) soccer star and pop icon David Beckham as a metrosexual. Simpson noted that Beckham is "almost as famous for wearing sarongs and pink nail polish and panties belonging to his wife, Victoria (aka Posh from the Spice Girls), as he is for his impressive ball skills."[102]

Hype aside, how widespread is the Western metrosexual phenomenon? Although there's no doubt that "everyday guys" are expanding their horizons, many actively resist this label because they don't want others to question their sexual preferences (as we'll see in Chapter 11, this is a great example of a *negative reference group*). Clearly, our cultural definition of masculinity is evolving as men try to redefine sex roles while they stay in a "safety zone" of acceptable behaviors bounded by danger zones of sloppiness at one extreme and effeminate behavior at the other. For example, a man may decide that it's OK to use a moisturizer but draw the line at an eye cream that he considers too feminine.[103] And, much like the "girls gone milder" trend we discussed earlier in the chapter, some cultural observers report the emergence of "retrosexuals;" men who want to emphasize their old-school masculinity by getting plastic surgery to create a more rugged look that includes hairier chests and beards, squarer chins and more angular jaw lines.[104]

Indeed, in many circles the "M word" has become taboo and other (perhaps less threatening) labels are popping up instead. One such label is the **übersexual,** which *The Urban Dictionary* defines as

> metro-sexuality for the noughties (2000–2009). . . . in German it means the best, the greatest, super, or above. Übersexuals are the most attractive (not just physically), most dynamic, and most compelling men of their generations. They are confident, masculine, stylish, and committed to uncompromising quality in all areas of life. Übersexuals also have depth, subtlety and individuality . . . a male who is similar to a metro-sexual but has the traditional manly qualities such as confidence, strength, and class . . . without giving into the negative stereotypes such as chauvinism, emotional unavailability and a brain only filled with sports stats, beer and burgers. Compared with the metrosexual, the übersexual is more into relationships than self. It is a masculinity that combines the best of traditional manliness (strength, honor, character) with positive traits traditionally associated with females such as nurturance, communicativeness, and co-operation. . . .

The current icon of übersexuals is Bono. He's global and socially aware, confident, and compassionate, and he commands a huge base of followers who are fans of his music and his humanitarianism. Other notable übersexuals are Bill Clinton, George Clooney, Jon Stewart, Pierce Brosnan, Donald Trump, and Ewan McGregor.[105]

American Brewer Miller Genuine Draft recently conducted a survey of American men aged 21 to 34 to try to get a handle on these new definitions so that it can position its brand to appeal to them. The company found that, indeed, many "average Joes" are moving on from the days of drinking whatever beer is available and wearing baseball hats backward, but they also don't want to sacrifice their identities as regular guys. They care more about preparing a good meal, meeting friends for a beer, and owning a home than they do about amassing shoes, savoring fine wine, or dining at expensive restaurants. This new man is discerning when it comes to some important everyday and lifestyle decisions but isn't overtly concerned about fitting into cultural molds or trends. Here are some highlights from the survey:

- Fifty-seven percent of men aged 25 to 29 say that if a woman were simply to pop in, they could whip up a full meal in a moment's notice with the items they have in the house.
- Nearly 7 out of 10 men (68 percent) own at least one cookbook, and 47 percent claim to have used a cookbook within the past month.
- Fifty-five percent of those in the 25- to -29-age set say they try to keep their living space as neat as possible as often as they can.

The new Fast Women line of collectible scale cars reminds us that traditional sex-role stereotypes are alive and well.

- Thirty-two percent of men aged 25 to 29 want to find a woman with whom they can enjoy a cold beer, whereas only 15 percent want to find a woman who can get them into the best restaurants in town.
- Including all types of shoes (athletic, work, etc.), nearly half (43 percent) of men surveyed own five pairs or less. Almost one-third (31 percent) of men who preferred wine to beer or liquor own 10 or more pairs of shoes.[106]

GAY, LESBIAN, BISEXUAL, AND TRANSGENDER (GLBT) CONSUMERS

The proportion of the U.S. population that is gay or lesbian is difficult to determine, and efforts to measure this group have been controversial.[107] Estimates among academics and marketing experts range widely from about 4 to 8 percent of the total U.S. population, or between 11 million and 23 million people. The 2000 U.S. Census reported 1.2 million same-sex "unmarried" partners in the United States, and this number excludes single gays and lesbians.[108] The respected research company Yankelovich Partners Inc., which, as we saw in Chapter 4, has tracked consumer values and attitudes since 1971 in its annual *Monitor*™ survey, now includes a question about sexual identity in its instrument and reports that about 6 percent of respondents identify themselves as gay/homosexual/lesbian. This study was virtually the first to use a sample that reflects the population as a whole instead of polling only smaller or biased groups (such as readers of gay publications) whose responses may not be as representative of all consumers.

One barrier to computing an accurate estimate is that some respondents are reluctant to answer questions about their sexual orientations. The anonymity of the Internet has helped a bit—Harris Interactive found that although only about 2 percent of adult respondents identify themselves as "gay or lesbian" in telephone surveys, 4 percent self-identify themselves as such online. Harris has also discovered that how it asks the question influences response rates. When given the option to self-identify as "gay," "lesbian," "bisexual," or "transgendered" (GLBT) (those who have physically changed their sex) as opposed to "gay or lesbian," a full 6 percent respond affirmatively.[109]

These results help to paint a more accurate picture of the potential size and attractiveness of this segment to marketers. To put things in perspective, the U.S. GLBT market is at least as large, if not larger, than the Asian American population (currently at about 12 million people). The GLBT consumer market spends in the range of $250 billion to $350 billion a year. A Simmons study of readers of gay publications found that readers are almost 12 times more likely to hold professional jobs, twice as likely to own a vacation home, and eight times more likely to own a notebook computer compared to heterosexuals.[110]

In the mid-1990s, IKEA, a Swedish furniture retailer with stores in several major U.S. markets, broke new ground by running a TV spot featuring a gay couple that purchased a dining room table at the store.[111] For many American consumers, gay culture is more familiar largely because of the prominence of gay people in popular shows such as *The L Word* and because of decisions by stars such as Ellen DeGeneres and Rosie O'Donnell to openly discuss their sexuality.

Also, although it has been common for years for these companies to run ads in gay publications (often unbeknownst to their straight customers), now major marketers, including American Express, Audi, Cartier, Chili's, Diageo, Marshall Field's, General Motors, Target, Volkswagen, and Wrigley, are using openly gay and lesbian celebrities in campaigns aimed at the wider general audience. They are hiring personalities such as singers k.d. lang and Melissa Etheridge, designers Isaac Mizrahi and Todd Oldham, actor John Cameron Mitchell, and John Amaechi, a former NBA center who is the first professional basketball player to disclose that he is gay.[112] In 2007, Second Life hosted several Gay Pride events on L-Word Island that Altoids' mints sponsored, including a date auction, a gay prom, and two parades that occurred in sync with the real-life Los Angeles, New York, and San Francisco events.[113]

American Express, Stolichnaya vodka, Atlantic Records, and Naya bottled water are among those corporations that run ads in lesbian publications (an ad for American Express Travelers Cheques for Two shows two women's signatures on a check). Acting on research that showed lesbians are four times as likely as the average consumer to own one of their cars, Subaru of America decided to target this market in a big way. And in one of the first mainstream pitches to directly address the controversy over gay marriage, Grand Marnier, a French cognac, launched print ads that read, "Your sister is finally getting remarried. Her fiancée's name is Jill."[115]

BODY IMAGE

A person's physical appearance is a large part of his self-concept. **Body image** refers to a consumer's subjective evaluation of his physical self. As was the case with the overall self-concept, this image is not necessarily accurate. A man may think of himself as being more muscular than he really is, or a woman may feel she appears fatter than is the case. Some marketers exploit consumers' tendencies to distort their body images by preying on insecurities about appearance. They try to create a gap between the real and ideal physical self and consequently motivate a person to purchase products and services he thinks will narrow that gap.

Body cathexis refers to a person's feelings about his or her body. The word *cathexis* refers to the emotional significance of some object or idea; we know that

Marketing Pitfall

Mars, the maker of Snickers, aired a commercial during the 2007 Super Bowl that stirred up a lot of controversy. Eventually, the company agreed to stop airing the ad after organizations such as the Gay and Lesbian Alliance against Defamation protested. The ad shows two mechanics eating from opposite ends of a Snickers candy bar until their lips touch. Shocked and dismayed by this linkup, they rip out their chest hair in a desperate attempt to "do something manly."[114]

A product endorsement by an openly gay professional athlete.

some parts of the body are more central to self-concept than are others. One study of young adults' feelings about their bodies found that the respondents were the most satisfied with their hair and eyes and they had the least positive feelings about their waists. These feelings were also linked to grooming products the respondents said they used. Consumers who were more satisfied with their bodies were more frequent users of such "preening" products as hair conditioner, blow dryers, cologne, facial bronzer, tooth polish, and pumice soap.[116]

IDEALS OF BEAUTY

Our satisfaction with the physical image we present to others depends on how closely we think the image corresponds to the ideal our culture values.[117] An **ideal of beauty** is a particular model, or *exemplar,* of appearance. Ideals of beauty for both men and women may include physical features (e.g., big breasts or small, bulging muscles or not) as well as clothing styles, cosmetics, hairstyles, skin tone (pale versus tan), and body type (petite, athletic, voluptuous, etc).

IS BEAUTY UNIVERSAL?

It's no secret that despite the popular saying "You can't judge a book by its cover" people can and do. Fairly or not, we assume that more attractive people are smarter, more interesting, and more competent—researchers call this the *"what is beautiful is good"* stereotype.[118] By the way, this bias affects both men and women—men with above-average looks earn about 5 percent more than those of average appearance, and those who are below average in appearance make an average of 9 percent less than the norm. Hitting close to home, in one study, researchers collected teaching evaluations for 463 courses taught by 94 faculty members at the University of Texas at Austin, along with some characteristics of the instructors, such as sex and race and whether they were on tenure track. They asked a panel of undergrads to rate photos of the professors in terms of their physical attractiveness. Guess what? Good-looking professors got significantly higher scores—and this effect was even more pronounced for male professors than for females. Fortunately, your consumer behavior professor is no doubt near the top of the scale.[119]

And virtually every culture displays this beauty bias, even though the standards by which people judge what is hot and what is not may differ. Communist China once banned beauty contests as "spiritual pollution," but then again China recently hosted the "Miss World" pageant. The Chinese consider appearance so important that they view plastic surgery as a commercial investment, and it's common for people to take out loans to fund procedures.[120]

Recent research indicates that preferences for some physical features rather than others are "wired in" genetically, and that these preferences tend to be the same among people around the world. When researchers show babies as young as 5 hours old pictures of faces adults rate as beautiful and not so beautiful, they report that the infants spend more time looking at the attractive faces.[121] Specifically, people appear to favor features we associate with good health and youth, attributes we link to reproductive ability and strength. These characteristics include large eyes, high cheekbones, and a narrow jaw. Another cue that people across ethnic and racial groups use to signal sexual desirability is whether the person's features are balanced. People with symmetrical features on average start having sex 3 to 4 years earlier than those with unbalanced features.[122]

Men also are more likely to use a woman's body shape as a sexual cue, and one explanation is because feminine curves provide evidence of reproductive potential. During puberty, a typical female gains almost 35 pounds of "reproductive fat" around the hips and thighs that supply the approximately 80,000 extra calories needed to support a pregnancy. Most fertile women have waist–hip ratios of 0.6 to 0.8, an hourglass shape that also happens to be the one men rank highest. Even though preferences for overall weight change over time, waist–hip ratios tend to stay in this range. Even the superthin model Twiggy (who pioneered the "waif look" decades before Kate Moss) had a ratio of 0.73.

Women, however, favor men with heavy lower faces (an indication of a high concentration of androgens that impart strength), those who are slightly above average in height, and those with prominent brows. A recent study provided evidence that women judge potential mates by how masculine their features are. Respondents viewed a series of male headshots that had been digitally altered to exaggerate or minimize masculine traits. They saw men with square jaws and well-defined brow ridges as good short-term partners, whereas they preferred those with feminine traits, such as rounder faces and fuller lips, for long-term mates. Overwhelmingly, participants said those with more masculine features were likely to be risky and competitive and also more apt to fight, challenge bosses, cheat on spouses, and put less effort into parenting. They assume men with more feminine faces would be good parents and husbands, hard workers, and emotionally supportive mates.[123]

One study found these preferences actually fluctuate during the course of a woman's menstrual cycle: Researchers showed women in Japan and Scotland a series of computer-generated photos of male faces that were systematically altered in terms of such dimensions as the size of the jaw and the prominence of the eyebrow ridge.[124] Women in the study preferred the heavier masculine features when they were ovulating, but these choices shifted during other parts of their monthly cycles. If this is true, these results indicate a "wired-in" preference for strong men who can pass on this trait to offspring.

Another study supplied tantalizing evidence that these preferences, indeed, are triggered physiologically: The researchers found that young college women tended to wear more fashionable or flashier clothing and jewelry when they were ovulating—and they compared this behavior to that of animals who commonly signal when they are fertile via scents or skin color changes. They asked 30 university students to come to their lab where they tested their urine to determine when they were ovulating. The women came back several times over the course of a month and they were photographed twice—once in their fertile phase and another time in their least-fertile phase. Then the researchers asked a separate panel of men and women to look at these pairs of photos (with the faces blacked out) and choose the one in which the person is trying to look more attractive. The judges chose the photograph taken during the women's fertile phases 60 percent of the time, a level well beyond chance.[125]

Of course, the way we "package" these faces still varies enormously, and that's where marketers come in: Advertising and other forms of mass media play a significant role in determining which forms of beauty we consider desirable at any point in time. An ideal of beauty functions as a sort of cultural yardstick. Consumers compare themselves to some standard (often one the fashion media advocates), and they are dissatisfied with their appearance to the extent that they don't match up to it. This may lower their own self-esteem or, in some cases, possibly diminish the effectiveness of an ad because of negative feelings a highly attractive model arouses.[126]

Our language provides phrases to sum up these cultural ideals. We may talk about a "bimbo," a "girl-next-door," or an "ice queen," or we may refer to specific women who have come to embody an ideal, such as J-Lo, Gwyneth Paltrow, or the late Princess Diana.[127] Similar descriptions for men include "jock," "pretty boy," and "bookworm," or a "Brad Pitt type," a "Wesley Snipes type," and so on.

THE WESTERN IDEAL OF BEAUTY

Beauty is about more than aesthetics—we use cues such as skin color and eye shape to make inferences about a person's status, sophistication, and social desirability. People in less powerful cultures tend to adopt the standards of beauty prevalent in dominant cultures. For example, an ad on Malaysian television shows an attractive college student who can't get a second glance from a boy at the next desk. "She's pretty," he says to himself, "but. . . ." Then, she applies Pond's Skin Lightening Moisturizer by Unilever PLC and she reappears looking several shades paler. Now the boy wonders, "Why didn't I notice her before?" In many Asian cultures, people historically equated light skin with wealth and status, and they associated dark skin with the laboring class that toils in the fields. This stereotype persists today: In a survey, 74 percent of men in Malaysia, 68 percent in Hong Kong, and 55 percent in Taiwan said they are more attracted to women with fair complexions. And about a third of the female respondents in each country said they use skin-whitening products. Olay has a product called White Radiance, and L'Oréal sells a line called White Perfect.[128]

As media images of glamorous American (Caucasian) celebrities proliferate around the globe, women who buy into the Western ideal of beauty—big round eyes, tiny waists, large breasts, blond hair, and blue eyes— literally go under the knife to achieve these attributes:

- A few years ago, a model named Cindy Burbridge, who was the local spokeswoman for Lux soap and Omega watches, became the first blue-eyed Miss Thailand. She's one of a generation of racially mixed Thais who now dominate the local fashion and entertainment industries as the public abandons the round face, arched eyebrows, and small mouth of the classical Thai look in favor of a Western ideal. Many buy blue contact lenses to enhance their looks. In a poll to name the sexiest men and the sexiest women in Thailand, seven out of the nine top scorers were of mixed blood.[129] The Thai language reflects the stigma of darker skin. One common insult is *tua dam,* or "black body," and another is *dam tap pet,* or "black like a duck's liver."[130]

- Year after year, winners of the Most Beautiful Girl in Nigeria performed very poorly in the Miss World competition. Local organizers had about given up on the idea that an African woman could win a contest Western beauties dominated. Then, Agbani Darego, the 2001 Most Beautiful Girl, went on to win the Miss World title. She was the first African winner in the contest's 51-year history. However, pride mixed with puzzlement: The new Miss World didn't possess the voluptuous figure African culture prized. In West and Central Africa, big women are revered and many beauty contestants weigh more than 200 pounds. In Niger, women even eat livestock feed or special vitamins to bulk up. The Calabari in southeastern Nigeria send prospective brides to fattening farms, where they are fed huge amounts of food and massaged into rounder shapes. After weeks of this regimen, the bigger brides proudly parade in the village square.[131] As one African explained, "Plumpness means prosperity. Thin represents everything you don't want: poverty, AIDS, and other diseases, misery and hunger." In contrast, Ms. Darego is 6 feet tall and skinny. Older Nigerians did not find the winner especially attractive at all, and some bitingly described her as a white girl in black skin. But younger people feel different. For them, thin is in. In Lagos, fashionable thin girls are called *lepa* and there is even a popular song with this title. A movie called *Lepa Shandi* celebrates the more svelte look; the title means a girl as slim as a 20-naira bill.[132]

- It's good to be a plastic surgeon in Seoul. Many Korean women are lifting their noses, shaving their jaws, and widening their eyes in pursuit of a Western image of beauty. The newest craze is a leg job to reduce the size of thick calves that are common in this country as women seek the slender legs of Western supermodels.[133]

- Japanese retailers are scrambling to stock larger dress sizes to keep up with a new look the fashion industry calls *bonkyu-bon*. This means "big-small-big" and it stands for a change in that culture's body ideal: Japanese women are getting curvier. Today, the average Japanese woman's hips, at 35 inches, are about an inch wider than those of women a generation older. Women in their 20s wear bras at least two sizes larger than those of their mothers, whereas waist sizes have gotten smaller. The government reports that the average 20-year-old is also nearly 3 inches taller than she was in 1950. These changes are the result of a diet that is becoming more Westernized; the traditional meal of fish, vegetables, and tofu is now more likely to consist of red meat, dairy, and decadent desserts such as Krispy Kreme doughnuts and Cold Stone Creamery ice cream. Juicy Couture, known for its figure-hugging terrycloth tracksuits, opened one of its biggest stores in Tokyo, and other department stores feature larger sizes from other American designers. Wacoal Corp., Japan's largest lingerie company, was once known for its superpadded brassieres. Now the company has a new bestseller: the "Love Bra," a cleavage-boosting creation with less padding, aimed at curvier women in their 20s.[134]

IDEALS OF BEAUTY OVER TIME

Although beauty may be only skin deep, throughout history women have worked very hard to attain it. They have starved themselves; painfully bound their feet; inserted plates into their lips; spent countless hours under hair dryers, in front of mirrors, and beneath tanning lights; and opted for breast reduction or enlargement operations to alter their appearance and meet their society's expectations of what a beautiful woman should look like.

In retrospect, we can characterize periods of history by a specific "look," or ideal of beauty. Often these relate to broader cultural happenings, such as today's emphasis on fitness and toned bodies. One study compared measures of the public's favorite actresses with socioeconomic indicators between 1932 and 1995. When market conditions were bad, people preferred actresses with mature features, including small eyes, thin cheeks, and a large chin. When the economy was in good shape, however, the public embraced women with babyish features, such as large eyes and full cheeks.[135]

A look at U.S. history reveals a succession of dominant ideals. For example, in sharp contrast to today's emphasis on health and vigor, in the early 1800s it was fashionable to appear delicate to the point of looking ill. The poet John Keats described the ideal woman of that time as "a milk white lamb that bleats for man's protection." Other past looks include the voluptuous, lusty woman that Lillian Russell made popular; the athletic Gibson Girl of the 1890s; and the small, boyish flapper of the 1920s that the silent movie actress Clara Bow exemplified.[136]

In much of the nineteenth century, the desirable waistline for U.S. women was 18 inches, a circumference that required the use of corsets pulled so tight that they routinely caused headaches, fainting spells, and possibly even the uterine and spinal disorders common among women of the time. Although modern women are not quite as "straight-laced," many still endure such indignities as high heels, body waxing, eyelifts, and liposuction. In addition to the millions women spend on cosmetics, clothing, health clubs, and fashion magazines, these practices remind us that—rightly or wrongly—the desire to conform to current standards of beauty is alive and well.

Our culture communicates these standards—subtly and not so subtly—virtually everywhere we turn: on magazine covers, in department store windows, on TV shows. Feminists argue that fashion dolls, such as the ubiquitous Barbie, reinforce an unnatural ideal of thinness. When we extrapolate the dimensions of these dolls to average female body sizes, indeed they are unnaturally long and thin.[137] If the traditional Barbie doll were a real woman, her dimensions would be 38–18–34! In 1998, Mattel conducted "plastic surgery" on Barbie to give her a less pronounced bust and slimmer hips, but she is still not exactly dumpy.[138] The company now sells an even more realistic Barbie featuring wider hips and a smaller bust (and for the first time Barbie has a belly button).[139]

As we've seen, the ideal body type of Western women changes over time—check out portraits of models from several hundred years ago by Botticelli and others to appreciate by just how much. These changes periodically cause us to redefine *sexual dimorphic markers*—those aspects of the body that distinguish between the sexes. The first part of the 1990s saw the emergence of the controversial "waif" look in which successful models (most notably Kate Moss) were likely to have bodies resembling those of young boys. Using heights and weights from winners of the Miss America pageant, nutrition experts concluded that many beauty queens were in the undernourished range. In the 1920s, contestants had a body mass index in the range now considered normal—20 to 25. Since then, an increasing number of winners have had indexes under 18.5, which is the World Health Organization's standard for undernutrition.[140]

Similarly, a study of almost 50 years of *Playboy* centerfolds shows that the women have become less shapely and more androgynous since Marilyn Monroe graced the first edition with a voluptuous hourglass figure of 37–23–36. However, a magazine spokesman comments, "As time has gone on and women have become more athletic, more in the business world and more inclined to put themselves through fitness regimes, their bodies have changed, and we reflect that as well. But I would think that no one with eyes to see would consider playmates to be androgynous."[141] Fair enough. Indeed, a recent reexamination of centerfold data for the years 1979 to 1999 shows that the trend toward increasing thinness seems to have stabilized and actually may have begun to reverse. Still, although the women shown in the magazine became somewhat heavier over the 21-year period the researchers reviewed, the Playmates remain markedly below weights medical experts consider normal for their age group.[142]

IS THE WESTERN IDEAL GETTING REAL?

Fed up because you don't get mistaken for a svelte supermodel on the street? A provocative campaign by Dove that started in Europe featuring women with imperfect bodies in their underwear may help. One ad reads, "Let's face it, firming the thighs of a size 8 supermodel wouldn't have been much of a challenge." Unilever initiated the campaign after its research showed that many women didn't believe its products worked because the women shown using them were so unrealistic.[143] When the company asked 3,200 women around the world to describe their looks, most summed themselves up as "average" or "natural." Only 2 percent called themselves "beautiful." Marketers of its Dove brand sensed an opportunity, and they set out to reassure women about their insecurities by showing them as they are, wrinkles, freckles, pregnant bellies, and all. Taglines ask "Oversized or Outstanding?"; "Wrinkled or Wonderful?" Dove even has a Web site (campaignforrealbeauty.com) where visitors can view the ads and cast their votes. Dove also sponsored a survey of 1,800 American women to assess how they felt about their looks. Overall, they found that women were satisfied with who they are, and these positive feelings were even stronger in subgroups such as African American and Hispanic women, younger women, and wealthier women. Fifty-two percent of women between the ages of 18 and 39 said that "looking beautiful" describes them very well, whereas 37 percent of women aged 40 and older feel the same. And 75 percent of the women agree that beauty does not come from a woman's looks but from her spirit and love of life. Only 26 percent feel that our society uses reasonable standards to evaluate women's beauty.[144]

Perhaps at least partly because of the success of the Dove campaign, other companies also are turning to ordinary people instead of professional models when they advertise. McDonald's held a casting call for consumers who will appear on its world cup and bag packaging as an extension of its "I'm lovin' it" campaign. Nike and Wal-Mart also have run advertisements with average Janes.[145]

And menswear designers and fashion magazines are starting to choose male models who look more like "regular" guys as they try to broaden the industry's appeal to the mass market. Until recently, most male models have been either superthin and boyish looking or overly muscular. Now, with more men than ever before doing their own clothes shopping, some designers see an opportunity to cater to men who want to dress fashionably but who are turned off by the edgy looks they see in magazines. One industry insider credits celebrities such as actor Ashton Kutcher—a former model himself—and TV shows such as *Entourage* and *Grey's Anatomy* with showing men that guys can be stylish without being too muscular, too thin, or too manicured. He describes this look as "Chiseled without being too pretty."[146]

Despite a modest increase in sales (about 3 percent in the first 6 months of the campaign), Dove learned that the same approach doesn't necessarily fly all around the world. One new body-lotion ad featuring women with scars resonated with European women but got mixed reviews in tests elsewhere. Unilever also decided not

Dove's use of real women in its advertising has contributed to changes in how we think about ideals of beauty.

to use the body-weight theme in Asia or Argentina, where people consider images of heavier women a big turn-off. It's also seeing more potential in selling this "I'm OK just as I am" approach to Middle America than to *fashionistas*. Unilever developed a special Dove campaign for Wal-Mart that ran on the retailer's in-store television network and features real employees. In one spot, a smiling worker named Diana says, "I'll see a picture of myself and I'll say, 'whoa, I'm a big girl.' I like being an Amazon. I feel strong and powerful."[147] As we'll see shortly, these "warts and all" campaigns do seem to reflect cultural changes—especially when it comes to unrealistically skinny fashion models.

We also distinguish among ideals of beauty for men in terms of facial features, musculature, and facial hair—who could confuse Tom Cruise with George Clooney? In fact, one national survey that asked both men and women to comment on male aspects of appearance found that the dominant standard of beauty for men is a strongly masculine, muscled body—though women tend to prefer men with less muscle mass than men themselves strive to attain.[149] Advertisers appear to have the males' ideal in mind—a study of men appearing in advertisements found that most sport the strong and muscular physique of the male stereotype.[150]

Betting that men are becoming every bit as body-conscious as women, manufacturers including Seven for All Mankind, Miss Sixty, and Diesel are introducing figure-enhancing jeans for men in styles that would have been deemed too risky even a few years ago. The new styles feature many of the same touches that designers have brought to women's jeans: low-rise cuts, stretchy fabrics, and bleached-out colors. Chip and Pepper lowered the back pockets on one men's style by several inches to make pear-shaped guys look less . . . pear-like, and Diesel's slim-fitting "Bumix" jeans features a "sexy undercrotch enforcement."[151]

WORKING ON THE BODY

Because many consumers are motivated to match some ideal of appearance, they often go to great lengths to change aspects of their physical selves. From cosmetics to plastic surgery, tanning salons to diet drinks, a multitude of products and services promise to alter aspects of the physical self. It is difficult to overstate the importance of the physical self-concept (and consumers' desires to improve their appearances) to many marketing activities.

FATTISM

As reflected in the expression "you can never be too thin or too rich," it's no secret our society has an obsession with weight. The media continually bombard us with images of thin, happy people. Various surveys report that as early as nursery school age, children prefer drawings of peers in wheelchairs, on crutches, or with facial disfigurements to those of fat children. One survey of girls aged 12 to 19 reported that 55 percent said they see ads "all the time" that make them want to go on a diet.[152]

Although Americans' obsession with thinness is legendary worldwide, the weight loss obsession is spreading—often with help from American media figures. In traditional Fijian culture, for example, the body ideal for females is, to put it delicately, robust. When a woman started to lose weight in Fiji, this was cause for concern and a sign of probable illness. Then, a few years ago the island finally got satellite TV feeds that exposed Fijians for the first time to American TV shows such as s *Melrose Place* and *Beverly Hills 90210* that feature casts of skinny stars. Now, the tables have turned and teenage girls in Fiji are starting to exhibit eating disorders. A study found that teens who watched TV three or more nights per week were 50 percent more likely to feel too fat than were other girls. Participants cited actresses such as Heather Locklear as inspiration for changing their bodies.[153]

Or consider changes now occurring in the Middle East. As in Fiji, Egyptians traditionally preferred somewhat plumper women—and the belly dancing tradition encouraged this. Now, though, weight loss diets are fashionable. The head of Egyptian television announced that overweight female newscasters had 3 months to shed those extra pounds (10 to 20 pounds in most cases) or he would fire them. Egypt's first lady, Suzanne Mubarak, visits schools to promote thinness, and Egyptian advertising increasingly uses skinny, blond, light-skinned models to sell products to customers who don't look anything like them. An entrepreneur named Samia Allouba is Egypt's answer to Jane Fonda. She sells home exercise and diet videos, and her twice-weekly exercise program is beamed to millions of viewers around the Middle East via satellite. Of course, Fonda never had to face the obstacles Allouba does. In deference to Islamic sensibilities, she and female guests exercising on her shows wear only loose-fitting clothes. And, although they are doing aerobic exercises, the women aren't allowed to breathe too heavily.[154]

Jump over to Europe, where the diet brand Slim-Fast recently tackled a common stereotype: British women are the plump ones on the beaches of Europe. The United Kingdom has the highest obesity rate in Europe; nearly one in five of all 15-year-olds are overweight. The company ran ads that rally British women to lose weight or lose face to their sexier Continental counterparts in France, Spain, and Sweden. In one Slim-Fast ad, a French model says, "I love British women. They make me look great." In another spot, a shapely Spanish woman scolds, "Face it, British women, it's not last year's bikini getting smaller."[155]

BODY IMAGE DISTORTIONS

Some people exaggerate the connection between self-esteem and appearance to such an extent that they sacrifice their health to attain what they consider to be a desirable body image. Women in particular tend to pick up messages from the media that the quality of their bodies reflects their self-worth, so it is not surprising that most (though certainly not all) major distortions of body image occur among females.

Marketing Opportunity

The size and shape of the "average" U.S. consumer today is dramatically different from what it was 60 years ago. Nevertheless, apparel companies still develop clothing lines based on a 1941 American military study that set sizing standards based on a small sample of mostly white, young (and presumably physically fit) female soldiers.

Those standards are finally starting to change based on the fact that the typical woman's body is no longer as "petite" as it used to be. The most commonly purchased dress today is a size 14; it was a size 8 in 1985! Slowly but surely, standards are changing as many women reject the unrealistic body ideal of the waif and subscribe to the battle cry: "Big is beautiful!" The popularity of "full-figured" women, such as Oprah, Queen Latifah, and Rosie O'Donnell, and plus-size spokesmodels, such as Emme, also has helped to improve the self-esteem of larger women.

In addition, standards based on this outdated snapshot of U.S. women need to recognize the diversity of today's ethnic population: According to current criteria, fully 78 percent of African American women and 72 percent of Hispanic women are overweight, compared with 58 percent of white women. And non-Caucasian body shapes differ as well—for example, Hispanic Americans and Asian Americans tend to be shorter than their Caucasian counterparts.

The clothing industry can't take the market potential of this segment lightly—women spent about $47 billion on plus-size garments in 2005, accounting for 20 percent of the total apparel market. Now, the apparel industry is sponsoring SizeUSA, an ambitious project to revamp the way we think about body size and shape. This survey uses sophisticated three-dimensional body scanners to measure the complete physical dimensions of 10,000 people representing the entire U.S. population. Once these new standards make their way into designers' lines, today's size 14 might become tomorrow's size 8. What an easy way to lose weight![148]

Marketing Opportunity

Men do not tend to differ in ratings of their current figure, their ideal figure, and the figure they think is most attractive to women. In contrast, women rate both the figure they think is most attractive to men and their ideal figure as much thinner than their actual figure.[157] In one survey, two-thirds of college women admitted resorting to unhealthy behavior to control weight. Advertising messages that convey an image of slimness help to reinforce these activities by arousing insecurities about weight.[158]

Researchers have linked a distorted body image to eating disorders, which are particularly prevalent among young women. People with *anorexia* perceive themselves as being too fat, and they virtually starve themselves in the quest for thinness. This condition often results in *bulimia,* which involves two stages. First, binge eating occurs (usually in private), in which a person may consume more than 5,000 calories at one time. The binge is followed by induced vomiting, abuse of laxatives, fasting, or overly strenuous exercise—a "purging" process that reasserts the woman's sense of control.

Most eating disorders occur among white, upper-middle-class teens and college age women. Victims often have brothers or fathers who are hypercritical of their weight, and these disorders are also associated with a history of sexual abuse.[159] In addition, one's peers can encourage binge eating; groups such as athletic teams, cheerleading squads, and sororities may reinforce this practice. In one study of a college sorority, members' popularity within the group increased the more they binged.[160]

In fact, **group dieting** is a new phenomenon that the Internet fuels. A growing number of blog rings are devoted to excessive weight loss—especially by challenging female college students to lose as much weight as possible before events such as spring break. In one typical post, a woman confessed to eating ". . . one cracker, one strawberry and a little bit of soup" in a 24-hour period, whereas another recounted a lunch of a slice of mango and a stick of gum. These sites, often adorned with photos of ultrathin celebs and slogans such as "Diet Coke Is Life" appeal to followers of an underground movement called *pro-ana* (pro-anorexia) who sometimes identify themselves in public by wearing red bracelets.[161]

Although about 90 percent of teens doctors treat for eating disorders are female, body image disturbances in men may be more widespread than most of us believe. Psychiatrists report increasing cases of *body dysmorphic disorder* (an obsession with perceived flaws in appearance) among young males (the average age of onset is 15). Symptoms of this disorder include excessive checking of mirrors and attempts to camouflage imagined deformities. Eating disorders in males are especially common among jockeys, boxers, and other athletes who must conform to weight requirements.[162]

As with women, media images and products encourage men to attain an unrealistic physique; as we've seen recently in the steroid scandals plaguing major league sports, professional athletes certainly are not immune to this pressure. Consider, for example, that if the dimensions of the original GI Joe action figure were projected onto a real 5-foot,10-inch man, he would have a 32-inch waist, a 44-inch chest, and 12-inch biceps. Or how about the same exercise for the Batman action figure: If this superhero came to life, he would boast a 30-inch waist, 57-inch chest, and 27-inch biceps.[163] Holy steroids, Robin!

COSMETIC SURGERY

Consumers increasingly choose to have cosmetic surgery to change a poor body image or simply to enhance appearance.[165] According to the American Academy of Cosmetic Surgery, U.S. doctors perform nearly 860,000 cosmetic-surgery procedures each year—and men make up more than 150,000 of the patients. Highlighting the growing acceptance of such procedures into the mainstream is the popularity of two television shows: *Nip/Tuck,* a drama about two high-flying Miami plastic surgeons, and *Extreme Makeover,* a reality show on ABC network that features people getting transformed by a series of radical surgeries.[166] As cosmetic surgery becomes increasingly acceptable (even expected in some circles), consumers and the medical profession are expanding the scope of body parts they want to alter. Perhaps spurred by fashions such as low-rise jeans and spandex workout gear that call attention to the derrière, for example, buttock augmentation surgery is gaining in popularity. The operation typically costs about $20,000, so clearly it's not intended for the bottom of the market.[167]

Virtually any body part is fair game for surgical alteration. For example, belly-button reconstruction is a popular form of cosmetic surgery in Japan. The navel is an important part of Japanese culture, and mothers often save a baby's umbilical cord in a wooden box. In Japanese, a "bent navel" is a grouch, and a phrase meaning "give me a break" translates as "yeah, and I brew tea in my bellybutton." A popular insult among children is "Your mother has an outie."[168] Interest in the United States tends to center elsewhere. Popular operations for men include the implantation of silicon pectoral muscles (for the chest) and even calf implants to fill out "chicken legs."[169]

Traveling upward our culture tends to equate breast size with sex appeal. Consumer research an underwear company performed demonstrates the impact of breast size on self-concept. While conducting focus groups on bras, an analyst noted that small-chested women typically reacted with hostility when discussing the subject. The participants would unconsciously cover their chests with their arms as they spoke and complained that the fashion industry ignored them.. To meet this overlooked need, the company introduced a line of A-cup bras called "A-OK" and gave birth to a new market segment.

Some women elect to have breast augmentation procedures because they feel that larger breasts will increase their allure.[170] Although some of these procedures have generated controversy as a result of negative side effects, it is unclear whether potential medical problems will deter large numbers of women from choosing surgical options to enhance their (perceived) femininity. And as Lisa discovered, many companies are promoting nonsurgical alterations by pushing push-up bras that merely create the illusion of larger cleavage. These products offer "cleavage enhancement" that uses a combination of wires and internal pads (the industry calls them "cookies") to create the desired effect.

BODY DECORATION AND MUTILATION

People in every culture adorn or alter their bodies in some way. Decorating the self serves a number of purposes:[171]

- **To separate group members from nonmembers:** Chinook, Native Americans of North America, pressed the head of a newborn between two boards for a year, permanently altering its shape. In our society, teens go out of their way to adopt distinctive hair and clothing styles that will separate them from adults.
- **To place the individual in the social organization:** Many cultures engage in puberty rites during which a boy symbolically becomes a man. Some young men in part of Ghana paint their bodies with white stripes to resemble skeletons to symbolize the death of their child status. In Western cultures, this rite may involve some form of mild self-mutilation or engaging in dangerous activities.
- **To place the person in a gender category:** The Tchikrin, Native Americans of South America, insert a string of beads in a boy's lip to enlarge it. Western women wear lipstick to enhance femininity. At the turn of the twentieth century, small lips were fashionable because they represented women's submissive role at that time.[172] Today, big, red lips are provocative and indicate an aggressive sexuality. Some women, including a number of famous actresses and

Marketing Pitfall

In less than 2 months, 4 young Brazilian women died in widely publicized cases of anorexia, which sparked an international debate about body image and eating disorders. The first to die was a 21-year-old model who stood 5 feet, 8 inches tall but weighed slightly more than 80 pounds when she collapsed at a fashion shoot in Japan. In Spain, the government imposed a controversial ban on extremely thin models as measured by their body mass index, or BMI (a formula that takes into account both height and weight). It requires a BMI greater than 17.4 for female models younger than 18 years old, or 18.5 for models older than 18 years old. For a 5-foot, 9-inch model older than 18, that translates to a weight requirement of 126 pounds. Unilever, in turn, banned the use of so-called "size 0" models in its ads for products ranging from Lux shower gel and Sunsilk shampoo to Slim-Fast diet drinks.[164] Will the current outrage permanently remove waifs from the runway? Perhaps, but then again after waif model Kate Moss was accused of using drugs, major fashion companies dropped her from their campaigns in outrage. Six short months later, she renewed those contracts and signed others.

models, receive collagen injections or lip inserts to create large, pouting lips (insiders in the modeling industry call them "liver lips").[173]

- **To enhance sex-role identification:** We can compare the modern use of high heels, which podiatrists agree are a prime cause of knee and hip problems, backaches, and fatigue, with the traditional Asian practice of foot binding to enhance femininity. As one doctor observed, "When [women] get home, they can't get their high-heeled shoes off fast enough. But every doctor in the world could yell from now until Doomsday, and women would still wear them."[174]

- **To indicate desired social conduct:** The Suya of South America wear ear ornaments to emphasize the importance placed on listening and obedience in their culture. In Western society, some gay men may wear an earring in the left or right ear to signal what role (submissive or dominant) they prefer in a relationship.

Body piercing has become a form of expression for young people the world over.

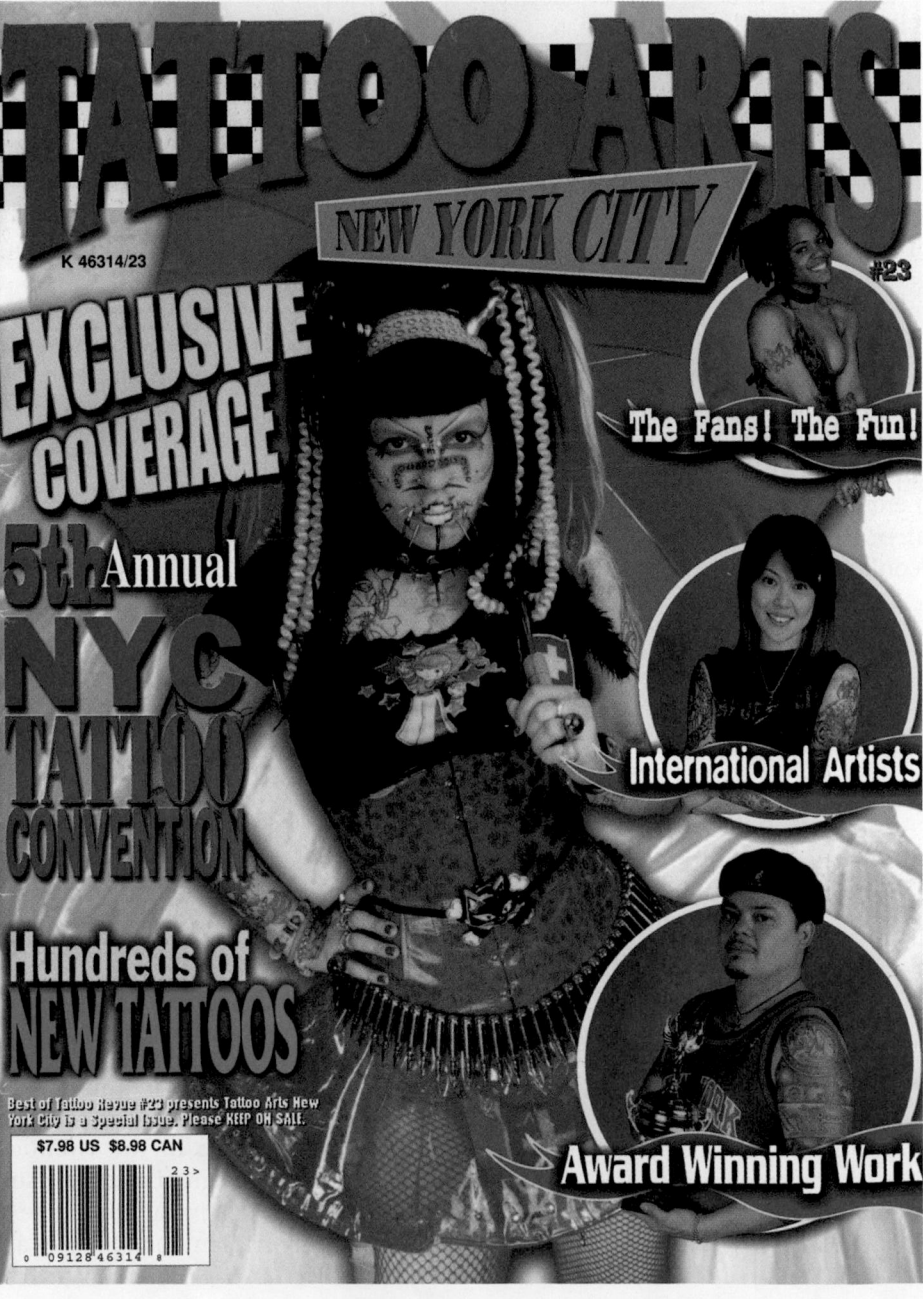

- **To indicate high status or rank:** The Hidates, Native Americans of North America, wear feather ornaments that indicate how many people they have killed. In our society, some people wear glasses with clear lenses, even though they do not have eye problems, to enhance their perceived status.
- **To provide a sense of security:** Consumers often wear lucky charms, amulets, and rabbits' feet to protect them from the "evil eye." Some modern women wear a "mugger whistle" around their necks for a similar reason.

TATTOOS

Tattoos—both temporary and permanent—are a popular form of body adornment.[175] People use this body art to make statements about the self, and these skin designs serve some of the same functions that other kinds of body painting do in primitive cultures. Tattoos (from the Tahitian *ta-tu*) have deep roots in folk art. Until recently, the images were crude and were primarily death symbols (e.g., a skull), animals (especially panthers, eagles, and snakes), pinup women, or military designs. More current influences include science fiction themes, Japanese symbolism, and tribal designs.

Historically, people associated tattoos with social outcasts. For example, authorities in sixth-century Japan tattooed the faces and arms of criminals to identify them, and these markings served the same purpose in nineteenth-century prisons and twentieth-century concentration camps. Marginal groups, such as bikers or Japanese *yakuze* (gang members), often use these emblems to express group identity and solidarity.

Today, a tattoo is a fairly risk-free way of expressing an adventurous side of the self. One recent trend is for middle-aged women to get one in order to commemorate a milestone such as a big birthday, a divorce, or becoming an "empty nester." So now these skin designs are more of a fashion statement than a declaration of rebellion—especially because 10 percent of Americans have one.[176] What are you waiting for?

BODY PIERCING

Decorating the body with various kinds of metallic inserts also has evolved from a practice we associated with some fringe groups to become a popular fashion statement. Historians credit the initial impetus for the mainstreaming of what had been an underground West Coast fad to Aerosmith's 1993 video "Cryin'," in which Alicia Silverstone gets both a navel ring and a tattoo.[178] Piercings can range from a hoop protruding from a navel to scalp implants, where metal posts are inserted in the skull (do not try this at home!). Publications such as *Piercing Fans International Quarterly* are seeing their circulations soar, and Web sites are attracting numerous followers.

Marketing Opportunity

As more people jump on the tattoo bandwagon (the FDA estimates that 17 million Americans have gotten inked), it's inevitable that some of them will regret this decision later (perhaps when they wake up in the morning?). Tattoo removal centers with names such as Dr. Tattoff, Tat2BeGone, and Tattoo MD are meeting the need to deal with so-called "tattoo regret." One industry member estimates that as many as 100,000 Americans undergo tattoo removal each year. Unfortunately, at least for now, it's a lot more complicated to remove a tattoo than to put one on you. A design that cost several hundred dollars could require several thousand dollars and many laser sessions to remove. A special laser device shatters tattoo pigment into particles that the body's lymphatic system clears. Full removal takes an average of eight treatments, spaced at least a month apart, using different lasers for different colored inks.[177] The moral: Before you get a significant other's name etched onto your body, be pretty sure you plan to stay together.

CHAPTER SUMMARY

Now that you have finished reading this chapter you should understand why:

The self-concept strongly influences consumer behavior.

● Consumers' self-concepts are reflections of their attitudes toward themselves. Whether these attitudes are positive or negative, they will help to guide many purchase decisions; we can use products to bolster self-esteem or to "reward" the self.

Products often play a pivotal role in defining the self-concept.

● We choose many products because we think that they are similar to our personalities. The symbolic interactionist perspective of the self implies that each of us actually has many selves, and we require a different set of products as props to play each role. We can view many things other than the body as part of the self. People use valued objects, cars, homes, and even attachments to sports teams or national monuments to define the self, when they incorporate these into the extended self.

Sex-role identity is different from gender, and society's expectations of masculinity and femininity help to determine the products we buy to be consistent with these expectations.

● A person's sex-role identity is a major component of self-definition. Conceptions about masculinity and femininity, largely shaped by society, guide the acquisition of "sex-typed" products and services.

● The media play a key role in teaching us how to behave as "proper" males and females. Advertising and other media play an important role in socializing consumers to be male and female. Although traditional women's roles have often been perpetuated in advertising depictions, this situation is changing somewhat. The media do not always portray men accurately either.

The way we think about our bodies (and the way our culture tells us we should think) is a key component of self-esteem.

● A person's conception of his or her body also provides feedback to self-image. A culture communicates certain ideals of beauty, and consumers go to great lengths to attain these. Many consumer activities involve manipulating the body, whether through dieting, cosmetic surgery, piercing, or tattooing.

Our desire to live up to cultural expectations of appearance can be harmful.

● Sometimes these activities are carried to an extreme, as people try too hard to live up to cultural ideals. One common manifestation is eating disorders, diseases in which women in particular become obsessed with thinness.

Every culture dictates certain types of body decoration or mutilation that help to identify its members.

● Body decoration or mutilation may serve such functions as separating group members from nonmembers, marking the individual's status or rank within a social organization or within a gender category (e.g., homosexual), or even providing a sense of security or good luck.

KEY TERMS

Actual self, 198
Agentic goals, 210
Androgyny, 212
Avatars, 200
Body cathexis, 221
Body image, 221
Communal goals, 210
Extended self, 208

Fantasy, 198
Group dieting, 230
Ideal of beauty, 222
Ideal self, 198
Identity marketing, 204
Impression management, 198
Looking-glass self, 203
Masculinism, 216

Metrosexual, 218
Self-concept, 197
Self-image congruence models, 206
Sex-typed traits, 211
Symbolic interactionism, 202
Symbolic self-completion theory, 206
Übersexual, 219
Virtual identities, 200

REVIEW QUESTIONS

1 How do Eastern and Western cultures differ in terms of how people think about the self?
2 List three dimensions that describe the self-concept.
3 Compare and contrast the real versus the ideal self. List three products for which each type of self is likely to be used as a reference point when a purchase is considered.
4 What does "the looking-glass self" mean?
5 How do feelings about the self influence the specific brands people buy?
6 Define the extended self and provide three examples.

7 What is the difference between agentic and communal goals?
8 Is masculinity/femininity a biological distinction? Why or why not?
9 Give two examples of sex-typed products.
10 What is body cathexis?
11 Have ideals of beauty in the United States changed during the past 50 years? If so, how?
12 What is fattism?
13 How did tattoos originate?

CONSUMER BEHAVIOR CHALLENGE

■ DISCUSS

1 The "metrosexual" is a big buzzword in marketing, but is it real or simply media hype? Do you see men in your age group changing their ideas about acceptable interests for males (e.g., home design, cooking, etc.)?
2 How prevalent is the Western ideal of beauty among your peers? How do you see this ideal evolving now (if at all)?
3 Some historians and social critics say our obsession with thinness is based less on science than on morality. They equate our society's stigmatizing obese people (treating them as "sick," disabled, or weak) with the Salem witch trials or McCarthyism (the paranoid anticommunism movement of the 1950s). These critics argue that the definition of obesity has often arbitrarily shifted throughout history. Indeed, being slightly overweight was once associated with good health (as we've seen, in some parts of the world, it still is) in a time when many of the most troubling illnesses were wasting diseases such as tuberculosis. Plumpness used to be associated with affluence

and the aristocracy (King Louis XIV of France padded his body to look more imposing), whereas today it is associated with the poor and their supposedly bad eating habits.[179] What do you think?
4 Should fast-food restaurants be liable if customers sue them for contributing to their obesity?
5 How might the creation of a self-conscious state be related to consumers who are trying on clothing in dressing rooms? Does the act of preening in front of a mirror change the dynamics by which people evaluate their product choices? Why?
6 Is it ethical for marketers to encourage infatuation with the self?
7 To date, the bulk of advertising targeted to gay consumers has been placed in exclusively gay media. If it were your decision to make, would you consider using mainstream media as well to reach gays, who constitute a significant proportion of the general population? Or, remembering

that members of some targeted segments have serious objections to this practice, especially when the product (e.g., liquor, cigarettes) may be viewed as harmful in some way, should marketers single out gays at all?

8 Some consumer advocates have protested the use of superthin models in advertising, claiming that these women encourage others to starve themselves in order to attain the waif look. Other critics respond that the media's power to shape behavior has been overestimated, and that it is insulting to people to assume that they are unable to separate fantasy from reality. What do you think?

9 Does sex sell? There's certainly enough of it around, whether in print ads, television commercials, or on Web sites. When Victoria's Secret broadcast a provocative fashion show of skimpy lingerie live on the Web (after advertising the show on the Super Bowl), 1.5 million visitors checked out the site before it crashed as a result of an excessive number of hits. Of course, the retailer was taking a risk because, by its own estimate, 90 percent of its sales are to women. Some of them did not like this display of skin. One customer said she did not feel comfortable watching the Super Bowl ad with her boyfriend: "It's not that I'm offended by it; it just makes me feel inferior." Perhaps the appropriate question is not does sex sell, but *should* sex sell? What are your feelings about the blatant use of sex to sell products? Do you think this tactic works better when selling to men than to women? Does exposure to unbelievably attractive men and women models only make the rest of us "normal" folks unhappy and insecure? Under what conditions (if any) should sex be used as a marketing strategy?

■ APPLY

10 Watch a set of ads on TV featuring men and women. Try to imagine the characters with reversed roles (i.e., the male parts played by women and vice versa). Can you see any differences in assumptions about sex-typed behavior?

11 Construct a "consumption biography" of a friend or family member. Make a list of or photograph his or her favorite possessions, and see if you or others can describe this person's personality just from the information provided by this catalog.

12 Interview victims of burglaries, or people who have lost personal property in floods, hurricanes, or other natural disasters. How do they go about reconstructing their possessions, and what effect did the loss appear to have on them?

13 Locate additional examples of self-esteem advertising. Evaluate the probable effectiveness of these appeals—is it true that "Flattery gets you everywhere?"

Case Study

RIDING THE PLUS-SIZE WAVE

For years, Hollywood and the advertising media have perpetuated a stereotypical image of women. As a result, many consumers have the unrealistic expectation that many women are (or should be) poreless, hipless, silken-haired, high-cheekboned, size 0, 20-year-old goddesses. But, is this beauty myth finally changing? Companies like Charming Shoppes Inc., parent to plus-size retailer Lane Bryant, are doing their darnedest to see that it does.

Lane Bryant was founded in 1900 in New York as the first women's apparel retailer devoted exclusively to plus sizes. Recently acquired by Charming Shoppes Inc., from Limited Brands Inc., Lane Bryant is part of a strategic plan to resurrect the retail holding company from the brink of bankruptcy. Now, 77% of Charming Shoppes' revenue comes from sales of plus-size apparel.

And it appears that the future is only going to get brighter. Kat Fay, an analyst at the Mintel research group in Chicago, estimates that the plus-size-clothing sector rang up $32 billion in sales in 2005. That is a 50 percent increase in five years. She also expects that plus-size apparel will continue to grow at a faster rate than other retail categories. This is due in part to a change in American demographics. The average woman today wears a size 14, compared with a size 8 about 15 years ago.

While this shift in demographics bodes well for Lane Bryant, the increase in the plus-size market does not directly translate into an equal increase in sales. Plus-size customers tend to spend less as a percentage of their disposable income on apparel compared with women who are junior and misses sizes. Most analysts attribute this gap to the fact that retailers have not done a good job of making fashionable clothing available to women in this market segment. And, society's bias against large women may exert a damaging impact upon self-esteem, which in turn diminishes the desire to seek out fashion-forward apparel.

Lane Bryant is fighting this tide. With new product lines and promotional campaigns, the company sends the message that it's not only OK to be a plus-size, but that women in this category can be as in-style as anyone. Lane Bryant is therefore focusing on *en vogue* styles previously available only to more modestly sized shoppers. The strategy includes offering larger sizes in the upscale Seven Jean Collection. It also includes an expansion into the lingerie category with its new Cacique brand. In addition to selling the lingerie in Lane Bryant stores, Charming Shoppes is positioning itself as a Victoria's Secret competitor by opening dozens of stand-alone Cacique stores.

Former *American Idol* runner-up Kimberley Locke now lends more credibility to the brand as its new official spokesperson. "On *American Idol,* people noticed that I wasn't a typical Hollywood size 2," she observed. "In today's society, where everyone is so conscious of their size, it's important for women to know that it's OK to be a plus size—and it's nice to have a celebrity associated with that."

Will Lane Bryant's efforts change how society perceives the "typical" woman? Charming Shoppes' recent financial performance seems to indicate that this may be the case. Revenue for 2006 was at just over $3 billion, a 31 percent increase from 2004. And between 2004 and 2007, the company's stock price shot from around $6 to over $14.

Other retailers are also getting in the game. Hot Topic, Gap/Old Navy, Target, Lands' End, J. Jill, Saks Fifth Avenue, and Nordstrom are among national retailers offering or expanding their assortments of plus apparel sizes and increasing promotional efforts for this category. With these industry changes, who knows what images of women the media of the future will celebrate?

DISCUSSION QUESTIONS

1 Explain the success that Lane Bryant is currently experiencing in relation to self-concept, self esteem, and self consciousness. How can the plus-size industry leverage what we know about consumer behavior to address the self-esteem problem?

2 Discuss the real-world changes that appear to be occurring with respect to media images of women. What are the reasons for this?

3 How do you reconcile the greater degree of acceptance of plus-size women with the parallel emphasis our society continues to place on thinness (as evidenced by the billions we spend on diet products, exercise, and so on)?

Sources: Pallavi Gogoi, "The Skinny on Plus-Size Apparel," *Business Week* (March 24, 2006), at www.businessweek.com; Ann Zimmerman, "Retailers' Panty Raid On Victoria's Secret," *Wall Street Journal* (June 20, 2007): B1; Michael Paoletta, "Retailer Snags 'Idol' Singer," *Chicago Sun-Times* (July 12, 2005): Lifestyles, 55; Wendy Tanaka, "Lane Bryant Executive Looks Forward to Being a 'Lifestyle Player for Women,'" *Philadelphia Inquirer,* (August 18, 2005).

NOTES

1. Om Malik, "Reach Out and Twitter Someone," *Business 2.0* (May 2007): 52; www.justin.tv/Justin, accessed July 1, 2007.
2. Louise Story, "Forgive Me, Viewer, for I Have Confessed in a Banner Ad," *New York Times Online* (February 10, 2007).
3. http://twitter.com, accessed July 1, 2007.
4. Harry C. Triandis, "The Self and Social Behavior in Differing Cultural Contexts," *Psychological Review* 96, no. 3 (1989): 506–20; H. Markus and S. Kitayama, "Culture and the Self: Implications for Cognition, Emotion, and Motivation," *Psychological Review* 98 (1991): 224–53.
5. Markus and Kitayama, "Culture and the Self."
6. Nancy Wong and Aaron Ahuvia, "A Cross-Cultural Approach to Materialism and the Self," in Dominique Bouchet, ed., *Cultural Dimensions of International Marketing* (Denmark: Odense University, 1995): 68–89.
7. Lisa M. Keefe, "You're So Vain," *Marketing News* (February 28, 2000): 8.
8. Morris Rosenberg, *Conceiving the Self* (New York: Basic Books, 1979); M. Joseph Sirgy, "Self-Concept in Consumer Behavior: A Critical Review," *Journal of Consumer Research* 9 (December 1982): 287–300; www.mediapost.com, accessed February 15, 2007; Roy F. Baumeister, Dianne M. Tice, and Debra G. Hutton, "Self-Presentational Motivations and Personality Differences in Self-Esteem," *Journal of Personality* 57 (September 1989): 547–75; Ronald J. Faber, "Are Self-Esteem Appeals Appealing?" in Leonard N. Reid, ed., Proceedings of the 1992 Conference of the American Academy of Advertising (1992): 230–35.
9. Emily Yoffe, "You Are What You Buy," *Newsweek* (June 4, 1990): 59.
10. Christine Bittar, "Alberto-Culver Ties Hair Relaxer to Self-Esteem," available from www.mediapost.com, accessed February 15, 2007.
11. Gary Rivlin, "Facing the World with Egos Exposed," *New York Times Online* (June 3, 2004).
12. Michael Hafner, "How Dissimilar Others May Still Resemble the Self: Assimilation and Contrast after Social Comparison," *Journal of Consumer Psychology* 14, nos. 1 & 2 (2004): 187–96.
13. Marsha L. Richins, "Social Comparison and the Idealized Images of Advertising," *Journal of Consumer Research* 18 (June 1991): 71–83; Mary C. Martin and Patricia F. Kennedy, "Advertising and Social Comparison: Consequences for Female Preadolescents and Adolescents," *Psychology & Marketing* 10 (November–December 1993): 513–30.
14. Philip N. Myers, Jr,. and Frank A. Biocca, "The Elastic Body Image: The Effect of Television Advertising and Programming on Body Image Distortions in Young Women," *Journal of Communication* 42 (Summer 1992): 108–33.
15. Charles S. Gulas and Kim McKeage, "Extending Social Comparison: An Examination of the Unintended Consequences of Idealized Advertising Imagery," *Journal of Advertising* 29 (Summer 2000): 17–28.
16. J. C. Herz, "Flash Face-Lift," *Wired* (March 2002): 45.
17. For the seminal treatment of this process, cf. Erving Goffman, *The Presentation of Self in Everyday Life* (New York: Doubleday, 1959).
18. www.reputationdefender.com, accessed July 1, 2007.
19. Harrison G. Gough, Mario Fioravanti, and Renato Lazzari, "Some Implications of Self versus Ideal-Self Congruence on the Revised Adjective Check List," *Journal of Personality and Social Psychology* 44, no. 6 (1983): 1214–20.
20. Steven Jay Lynn and Judith W. Rhue, "Daydream Believers," *Psychology Today* (September 1985): 14.

21. Erving Goffman, *The Presentation of Self in Everyday Life* (Garden City, NY: Doubleday, 1959); Michael R. Solomon, "The Role of Products as Social Stimuli: A Symbolic Interactionism Perspective," *Journal of Consumer Research* 10 (December 1983): 319–29.

22. A. Reed, "Activating the Self-Importance of Consumer Selves: Exploring Identity Salience Effects on Judgments," *Journal of Consumer Research* 31, no. 2 (2004): 286–95.

23. Hope Jensen Schau and Mary Gilly, "We Are What We Post? Self-Presentation in Personal Web Space," *Journal of Consumer Research* 30 (December 2003): 385–404.

24. Neal Stephenson, *Snow Crash* (New York: Bantam Books, 1992).

25. Svensson, Peter, "Study: Virtual Men Are Standoffish Too" *MyFox 21* (February 2007), www.myfoxkccom/myfox/pages/News/Detail, accessed February 22, 2007.

26. George H. Mead, *Mind, Self and Society* (Chicago: University of Chicago Press, 1934).

27. Debra A. Laverie, Robert E. Kleine, and Susan Schultz Kleine, "Reexamination and Extension of Kleine, Kleine, and Kernan's Social Identity Model of Mundane Consumption: The Mediating Role of the Appraisal Process," *Journal of Consumer Research* 28 (March 2002): 659–69.

28. Natasha Singer, "If the Mirror Could Talk (It Can)," *New York Times Online* (March 18, 2007), accessed March 18, 2007.

29. Charles H. Cooley, *Human Nature and the Social Order* (New York: Scribner's, 1902).

30. J. G. Hull and A. S. Levy, "The Organizational Functions of the Self: An Alternative to the Duval and Wicklund Model of Self-Awareness," *Journal of Personality and Social Psychology* 37 (1979): 756–68; Jay G. Hull, Ronald R. Van Treuren, Susan J. Ashford, Pamela Propsom, and Bruce W. Andrus, "Self-Consciousness and the Processing of Self-Relevant Information," *Journal of Personality and Social Psychology* 54, no. 3 (1988): 452–65.

31. Arnold W. Buss, *Self-Consciousness and Social Anxiety* (San Francisco: Freeman, 1980); Lynn Carol Miller and Cathryn Leigh Cox, "Public Self-Consciousness and Makeup Use," *Personality and Social Psychology Bulletin* 8, no. 4 (1982): 748–51; Michael R. Solomon and John Schopler, "Self-Consciousness and Clothing," *Personality and Social Psychology Bulletin* 8, no. 3 (1982): 508–14.

32. Morris B. Holbrook, Michael R. Solomon, and Stephen Bell, "A Re-Examination of Self-Monitoring and Judgments of Furniture Designs," *Home Economics Research Journal* 19 (September 1990): 6–16; Mark Snyder, "Self-Monitoring Processes," in Leonard Berkowitz, ed., *Advances in Experimental Social Psychology* (New York: Academic Press, 1979): 85–128.

33. Mark Snyder and Steve Gangestad, "On the Nature of Self-Monitoring: Matters of Assessment, Matters of Validity," *Journal of Personality and Social Psychology* 51 (1986): 125–39; Timothy R. Graeff, "Image Congruence Effects on Product Evaluations: The Role of Self-Monitoring and Public/Private Consumption," *Psychology & Marketing* 13 (August 1996): 481–99; Timothy R. Graeff, "Image Congruence Effects on Product Evaluations: The Role of Self-Monitoring and Public/Private Consumption," *Psychology & Marketing* 13 (August 1996): 481–99; Richard G. Netemeyer, Scot Burton, and Donald R. Lichtenstein, "Trait Aspects of Vanity: Measurement and Relevance to Consumer Behavior," *Journal of Consumer Research* 21 (March 1995): 612–26.

34. "Video Game Company Tries Human Branding," *New York Times on the Web* (August 12, 2002); Angela Orend-Cunningham, "Corporate Logo Tattoos: Literal Corporate Branding?" *Consumers, Commodities & Consumption,* American Sociological Association 5, no. 1 (December 2003).

35. Jack L. Nasar, "Symbolic Meanings of House Styles," *Environment and Behavior* 21 (May 1989): 235–57; E. K. Sadalla, B. Verschure, and J. Burroughs, "Identity Symbolism in Housing," *Environment and Behavior* 19 (1987): 579–87.

36. Solomon, "The Role of Products as Social Stimuli," 319–28; Robert E. Kleine III, Susan Schultz-Kleine, and Jerome B. Kernan, "Mundane Consumption and the Self: A Social-Identity Perspective," *Journal of Consumer Psychology* 2, no. 3 (1993): 209–35; Newell D. Wright, C. B. Claiborne, and M. Joseph Sirgy, "The Effects of Product Symbolism on Consumer Self-Concept," in John F. Sherry Jr. and Brian Sternthal, eds., *Advances in Consumer Research* 19 (Provo, UT: Association for Consumer Research, 1992): 311–18; Susan Fournier, "A Person-Based Relationship Framework for Strategic Brand Management" (doctoral dissertation, University of Florida, 1994).

37. A. Dwayne Ball and Lori H. Tasaki, "The Role and Measurement of Attachment in Consumer Behavior," *Journal of Consumer Psychology* 1, no. 2 (1992): 155–72.

38. William B. Hansen and Irwin Altman, "Decorating Personal Places: A Descriptive Analysis," *Environment and Behavior* 8 (December 1976): 491–504.

39. Lan Nguyen Chaplin and Deborah Roedder John, "The Development of Self-Brand Connections in Children and Adolescents," *Journal of Consumer Research* 32 (June 2005): 119–29.

40. R. A. Wicklund and P. M. Gollwitzer, *Symbolic Self-Completion* (Hillsdale, NJ: Erlbaum, 1982).

41. Paul Glader, "Avid Boarders Bypass Branded Gear; The $15 "Blank Decks' Work Just Fine—A Marketing Challenge for Industry," *Wall Street Journal* (July 27, 2007): B1.

42. Erving Goffman, *Asylums* (New York: Doubleday, 1961).

43. Floyd Rudmin, "Property Crime Victimization Impact on Self, on Attachment, and on Territorial Dominance," *CPA Highlights, Victims of Crime Supplement* 9, no. 2 (1987): 4–7.

44. Barbara B. Brown, "House and Block as Territory," paper presented at the Conference of the Association for Consumer Research, San Francisco, 1982.

45. Shay Sayre and David Horne, "I Shop, Therefore I Am: The Role of Possessions for Self-Definition," in Shay Sayre and David Horne, eds., *Earth, Wind, and Fire and Water: Perspectives on Natural Disaster* (Pasadena, CA: Open Door Publishers, 1996), 353–70; cf. also Jill G. Klein and Laura Huang, "After All Is Lost: Meeting the Material Needs of Adolescent Disaster Survivors," *Journal of Public Policy and Marketing* 26, no. 1 (Spring 2007): 1–12.

46. Deborah A. Prentice, "Psychological Correspondence of Possessions, Attitudes, and Values," *Journal of Personality and Social Psychology* 53, no. 6 (1987): 993–1002.

47. Jennifer L. Aaker, "The Malleable Self: The Role of Self-Expression in Persuasion," *Journal of Marketing Research* 36 (February 1999); 45–57; Sak Onkvisit and John Shaw, "Self-Concept and Image Congruence: Some Research and Managerial Implications," *Journal of Consumer Marketing* 4 (Winter 1987): 13–24. For a related treatment of congruence between advertising appeals and self-concept, see George M. Zinkhan and Jae W. Hong, "Self-Concept and Advertising Effectiveness: A Conceptual Model of Congruency, Conspicuousness, and Response Mode," in Rebecca H. Holman and Michael R. Solomon, eds., *Advances in Consumer Research* 18 (Provo, UT: Association for Consumer Research, 1991): 348–54.

48. C. B. Claiborne and M. Joseph Sirgy, "Self-Image Congruence as a Model of Consumer Attitude Formation and Behavior: A Conceptual Review and Guide for Further Research," paper presented at the Academy of Marketing Science Conference, New Orleans, 1990.

49. Sandikci, Özlem and Güliz Ger (date?) "Aesthetics, Ethics and Politics of the Turkish Headscarf," in . . . requested again; I will forward as soon as I get it!

50. Marc Lacey, "Where Showing Skin Doesn't Sell, a New Style Is a Hit," *New York Times Online* (March 20, 2006).

51. Jennifer L. Aaker, "The Malleable Self: The Role of Self-Expression in Persuasion," *Journal of Marketing Research* 36 (February 1999): 45–57.

52. A. L. E. Birdwell, "A Study of Influence of Image Congruence on Consumer Choice," *Journal of Business* 41 (January 1964): 76–88; Edward L. Grubb and Gregg Hupp, "Perception of Self, Generalized Stereotypes, and Brand Selection," *Journal of Marketing Research* 5 (February 1986): 58–63.

53. Benedict Carey, "With That Saucy Swagger, She Must Drive a Porsche," *New York Times Online* (June 13, 2006).

54. Ira J. Dolich, "Congruence Relationship between Self-Image and Product Brands," *Journal of Marketing Research* 6 (February 1969): 80–84; Danny N. Bellenger, Earle Steinberg, and Wilbur W. Stanton, "The Congruence of Store Image and Self Image as It Relates to Store Loyalty," *Journal of Retailing* 52, no. 1 (1976): 17–32; Ronald J. Dornoff and Ronald L. Tatham, "Congruence between Personal Image and Store Image," *Journal of the Market Research Society* 14, no. 1 (1972): 45–52.

55. Naresh K. Malhotra, "A Scale to Measure Self-Concepts, Person Concepts, and Product Concepts," *Journal of Marketing Research* 18 (November 1981): 456–64.

56. Leslie Walker, "More Than the Sum of His Stuff," *Washington Post* (August 11, 2001): E1.

57. Ernest Beaglehole, *Property: A Study in Social Psychology* (New York: Macmillan, 1932).

58. Jeffrey Ball, "Religious Leaders to Discuss SUVs with GM, Ford Officials," *Wall Street Journal Interactive Edition* (September 17, 2002).

59. David R. Shoonmaker, "Book Review: High and Mighty: SUVs—The World's Most Dangerous Vehicles and How They Got That Way," *American Scientist* (January–February 2003): 69; Keith Bradsher, "High and Mighty: SUVs—The World's Most Dangerous Vehicles and How They Got That Way" (New York: Public Affairs, 2002).

60. Russell W. Belk, "Shoes and Self," *Advances in Consumer Research* (2003): 27–33.

61. James Brooke, "Learning to Avoid a Deal-Killing *Faux Pas* in Japan," *New York Times on the Web* (September 17, 2002).

62. Russell W. Belk, "Possessions and the Extended Self," *Journal of Consumer Research* 15 (September 1988): 139–68.

63. Diane Goldner, "What Men and Women Really Want . . . to Eat," *New York Times* (March 2, 1994): C1 (2).

64. Nina M. Lentini, "McDonald's Tests 'Angus Third Pounder' in California," available from www.mediapost.com, accessed March 27, 2007.

65. Charles McGrath, "In Harlequin-NASCAR Romance, Hearts Race," *New York Times Online* (February 19, 2007).

66. John F. Sherry, Jr., Robert V. Kozinets, Adam Duhachek, Benet DeBerry-Spence, Krittinee Nuttavuthisit, and Diana Storm, "Gendered Behavior in a Male Preserve: Role Playing at ESPN Zone Chicago," *Journal of Consumer Psychology* 14, nos. 1 & 2 (2004): 151–58.

67. Suzanne Vranica, "Sony Tries to Lure DVR Ad-Skippers," *Wall Street Journal* (September 20, 2006): A20.

68. Thomas Tsu Wee Tan, Lee Boon Ling, and Eleanor Phua Cheay Theng, "Gender-Role Portrayals in Malaysian and Singaporean Television Commercials: An International Advertising Perspective," *Journal of Business Research* 55 (2002): 853–61.

69. Joan Meyers-Levy, "The Influence of Sex Roles on Judgment," *Journal of Consumer Research* 14 (March 1988): 522–30.

70. Anne Eisenberg, "Mars and Venus, on the Net: Gender Stereotypes Prevail," *New York Times Online* (October 12, 2000).

71. Beverly A. Browne, "Gender Stereotypes in Advertising on Children's Television in the 1990s: A Cross-National Analysis," *Journal of Advertising* 27 (Spring 1998): 83–97.

72. Lisa Bannon, "Mattel Sees Untapped Market for Blocks: Little Girls," *Wall Street Journal* (June 6, 2002): B1.

73. Eileen Fischer and Stephen J. Arnold, "Sex, Gender Identity, Gender Role Attitudes, and Consumer Behavior," *Psychology & Marketing* 11 (March–April 1994): 163–82.

74. Jonathan Cheng, "Shaver's Cutting-Edge China Campaign Trio of Women Dispense Grooming Tips for Guys in Philips Web Effort," *Wall Street Journal* (May 4, 2007): B3.

75. Clifford Nass, Youngme Moon, and Nancy Green, "Are Machines Gender Neutral? Gender-Stereotypic Responses to Computers with Voices," *Journal of Applied Social Psychology* 27, no. 10 (1997): 864–76; Kathleen Debevec and Easwar Iyer, "Sex Roles and Consumer Perceptions of Promotions, Products, and Self: What Do We Know and Where Should We Be Headed," in Richard J. Lutz, ed., *Advances in Consumer Research* 13 (Provo, UT: Association for Consumer Research, 1986): 210–14; Joseph A. Bellizzi and Laura Milner, "Gender Positioning of a Traditionally Male-Dominant Product," *Journal of Advertising Research* (June–July 1991): 72–79.

76. Hillary Chura, "Barton's New High-End Vodka Exudes a 'Macho Personality,'" *Advertising Age* (May 1, 2000): 8; www.thorshammervodka.com, accessed July 1, 2007.

77. Sandra L. Bem, "The Measurement of Psychological Androgyny," *Journal of Consulting and Clinical Psychology* 42 (1974): 155–62; Deborah E. S. Frable, "Sex Typing and Gender Ideology: Two Facets of the Individual's Gender Psychology That Go Together," *Journal of Personality and Social Psychology* 56, no. 1 (1989): 95–108.

78. "Gender-Bending Avatars Suffer Lack of Trust," *SAWF News*, available from http://news.sawf.org/Lifestyle/39848.aspx, accessed July 11, 2007.

79. Geoffrey A. Fowler, "Asia's Lipstick Lads," *Wall Street Journal Online* (May 27, 2005).

80. Matt Alt and Hiroko Yoda, "Big Primpin' in Toyko," *Wired* (May 2007): 46.

81. See D. Bruce Carter and Gary D. Levy, "Cognitive Aspects of Early Sex-Role Development: The Influence of Gender Schemas on Preschoolers' Memories and Preferences for Sex-Typed Toys and Activities," *Child Development* 59 (1988): 782–92; Bernd H. Schmitt, France Le Clerc, and Laurette Dube-Rioux, "Sex Typing and Consumer Behavior: A Test of Gender Schema Theory," *Journal of Consumer Research* 15 (June 1988): 122–27.

82. Carol Gilligan, *In a Different Voice: Psychological Theory and Women's Development* (Cambridge, MA: Harvard University Press, 1982); Joan Meyers-Levy and Durairaj Maheswaran, "Exploring Differences in Males' and Females' Processing Strategies," *Journal of Consumer Research* 18 (June 1991): 63–70.

83. Lynn J. Jaffe and Paul D. Berger, "Impact on Purchase Intent of Sex-Role Identity and Product Positioning," *Psychology & Marketing* (Fall 1988): 259–71; Lynn J. Jaffe, "The Unique Predictive Ability of Sex-Role Identity in Explaining Women's Response to Advertising," *Psychology & Marketing* 11 (September–October 1994): 467–82.

84. Leila T. Worth, Jeanne Smith, and Diane M. Mackie, "Gender Schematicity and Preference for Gender-Typed Products," *Psychology & Marketing* 9 (January 1992): 17–30.

85. Qimei Chen, Shelly Rodgers, and William D. Wells, "Better Than Sex: Identifying Within-Gender Differences Creates More Targeted Segmentation," *Marketing Research* (Winter 2004): 17–22.

86. Eric Bellman, "Suzuki's Stylish Compacts Captivate India's Women," *Wall Street Journal* (May 11, 2007): B1.

87. Rebecca Gardyn, "Granddaughters of Feminism," *American Demographics* (April 2001): 43–47.

88. Ibid.

89. Craig S. Smith, "Underneath, Saudi Women Keep Their Secrets," *New York Times on the Web* (December 3, 2002).

90. Peter Suciu, "Fast Cars? Fast Girls? For Sure," *Newsweek* (March 7, 2005): 10.

91. Jennie Yabroff, "Girls Going Mild(er): A New 'Modesty Movement' Aims to Teach Young Women They Don't Have to be Bad, or Semiclad," *Newsweek* (July 23, 2007), http://boards.youthnoise.com/eve/forums/a/tpc/f/573295355/m/38310644, accessed July 18, 2007.

92. Adapted from www.cohorts.com/meet_the_cohorts.html, accessed June 1, 2007.

93. Fara Warner, "Detroit Discovers That Women Like Power, Too," *New York Times on the Web* (August 10, 2003).

94. Kimberly Palmer, "Tech Companies Try Wooing Women with Girlie Marketing Simplicity and Products in 'Feminine' Colors Are Pushed, but Some Find It Condescending," *Wall Street Journal* (August 26, 2003).

95. Tiffany Myers, "She Noms," *Advertising Age* (October 2006): 5–10.

96. Barbara B. Stern, "Masculinism(s) and the Male Image: What Does It Mean to Be a Man?" in Tom Reichert and Jacqueline Lambiase, eds., *Sex in Advertising: Multi-disciplinary Perspectives on the Erotic Appeal* (Mahwah, NJ: Erlbaum, 2003).

97. Ibid, 215–28.

98. Douglas B. Holt and Craig J. Thompson, "Man-of-Action Heroes: The Pursuit of Heroic Masculinity in Everyday Consumption," *Journal of Consumer Research* 31 (September): 425–40.

99. Vivian Manning-Schaffel, "Metrosexuals: A Well-Groomed Market?" www.brandchannel.com, accessed May 22, 2006.

100. Teri Agins, "Men Say Bling It On—Retailers Court Modern Guys with Baubles All Their Own; Brad Pitt Gives Tiffany a Lift," *Wall Street Journal* (November 30, 2005): B1.

101. Ramin Setoodeh, "Retail: Need a Lift," *Newsweek* (February 2007): 12.

102. "Defining Metro Sexuality" *Metrosource* (September/October/November 2003).

103. Rinallo, Diego, "Metro/Fashion/Tribes of Men: Negotiating the Boundaries of Men's Legitimate Consumption" in B. Cova, R. Kozinets, and A. Shankar, eds., *Consumer Tribes: Theory, Practice and Prospects* (Oxford: Elsevier/Butterworth-Heinemann, 2007); Susan Kaiser, Michael R. Solomon, Janet Hethorn, Basil Englis, Van Dyk Lewis, and Wi-Suk Kwon, "Menswear, Fashion, and Subjectivity," paper presented in Special Session: Susan Kaiser, Michael Solomon, Janet Hethorn, and Basil Englis (Chairs), "What Do Men Want? Media Representations, Subjectivity, and Consumption," at the ACR Gender Conference, Edinburgh, Scotland, June 2006.

104. Catharine Skipp and Arian Campo-Flores, "Looks: A Manly Comeback," *Newsweek* (August 20, 2007), www.msnbc.msn.com/id/20218432/site/newsweek, accessed August 17, 2007.

105. www.urbandictionary.com/define.php?term=ubersexual, accessed July 2, 2007.

106. "National Poll Reveals the Emergence of a 'New Man,'" available from www.Millerbrewing.com, accessed April 15, 2006.

107. Projections of the incidence of homosexuality in the general population often are influenced by assumptions of the researchers, as well as the methodology they employ (e.g., self-report, behavioral measures, fantasy measures). For a discussion of these factors, see Edward O. Laumann, John H. Gagnon, Robert T. Michael, and Stuart Michaels, *The Social Organization of Homosexuality* (Chicago: University of Chicago Press, 1994).

108. Lee Condon, "By the Numbers (Census 2000)," *The Advocate: The National Gay and Lesbian Newsmagazine* (September 25, 2001): 37.

109. R. Gardyn, "A Market Kept in the Closet," *American Demographics* (November 2001): 37–43.

110. For a recent academic study of this subculture, cf. Steven M. Kates, "The Dynamics of Brand Legitimacy: An Interpretive Study in the Gay Men's Community," *Journal of Consumer Research* 31 (September 2004): 455–64.

111. Kate Fitzgerald, "IKEA Dares to Reveal Gays Buy Tables, Too," *Advertising Age* (March 28, 1994); Cyndee Miller, "Top Marketers Take Bolder Approach in Targeting Gays," *Marketing News* (July 4, 1994): 1; Michael Wilke, "Big Advertisers Join Move to Embrace Gay Market," *Advertising Age* (August 4, 1997): 1.

112. Stuart Elliott, "Gay Athletes Slowly Enter the Endorsement Arena," *New York Times Online* (March 12, 2007); Stuart Elliott, "More Gay Celebrities in Ads," *New York Times on the Web* (March 10, 2004).

113. "Web Game 'Second Life' Holds Gay Pride," available from www.gaynz.com, accessed June 14, 2007.

114. "Controversial Snickers Ad Prompts GLAAD to Ask for Meeting with NFL," *Wall Street Journal* (February 7, 2007): B3.

115. Ellen Byron, "Cognac and a Splash of Controversy," *Wall Street Journal* (April 29, 2004): B5.

116. Dennis W. Rook, "Body Cathexis and Market Segmentation," in Michael R. Solomon, ed., *The Psychology of Fashion* (Lexington, MA: Lexington Books, 1985), 233–41; for research that examines how body image influences the likelihood of using virtual models, cf. Ellen C. Garbarino and José Antonio Rosa, "Body Esteem, Body Image Discrepancy and Body Boundary Aberration as Influencers of the Perceived Accuracy of Virtual Models," working paper, Weatherhead School of Management, Case Western Reserve University (2006).

117. Carrie Goerne, "Marketing to the Disabled: New Workplace Law Stirs Interest in Largely Untapped Market," *Marketing News* 3 (September 14, 1992): 1; "Retailers Find a Market, and Models, in Disabled," *New York Times* (August 6, 1992): D4.

118. Karen K. Dion, "What Is Beautiful Is Good," *Journal of Personality and Social Psychology* 24 (December 1972): 285–90.

119. Hal R. Varian, "The Hunk Differential," *New York Times Online* (August 28, 2003).

120. "Saving Face," *The Economist* (July 10, 2004): 55.

121. Emily Flynn, "Beauty: Babes Spot Babes," *Newsweek* (September 20, 2004): 10.

122. Ibid.

123. Abigail W. Leonard, "How Women Pick Mates vs. Flings," *LiveScience* (January 2, 2007). www.livescience.com/health/070102_facial_features.html

124. Corky Siemaszko, "Depends on the Day: Women's Sex Drive a Very Cyclical Thing," *New York Daily News* (June 24, 1999): 3.

125. http://science.netscape.com/story/2006/10/10/fertile-women-dress-to-impress/, accessed February 1, 2007.

126. Amanda B. Bower, "Highly Attractive Models in Advertising and the Women Who Loathe Them: The Implications of Negative Affect for Spokesperson Effectiveness," *Journal of Advertising* 30 (Fall 2001): 51–63.

127. Basil G. Englis, Michael R. Solomon, and Richard D. Ashmore, "Beauty before the Eyes of Beholders: The Cultural Encoding of Beauty Types in Magazine Advertising and Music Television," *Journal of Advertising* 23 (June 1994): 49–64; Michael R. Solomon, Richard Ashmore, and Laura Longo, "The Beauty Match-Up Hypothesis: Congruence between Types of Beauty and Product Images in Advertising," *Journal of Advertising* 21 (December 1992): 23–34.

128. Thomas Fuller, "A Vision of Pale Beauty Carries Risks for Asia's Women," *International Herald Tribune Online* (May 14, 2006).

129. Seth Mydans, "Oh Blue-Eyed Thais, Flaunt Your Western Genes!" *New York Times on the Web* (August 29, 2002).

130. Thomas Fuller, "A Vision of Pale Beauty Carries Risks for Asia's Women."

131. Norimitsu Onishi, "Globalization of Beauty Makes Slimness Trendy," *New York Times on the Web* (October 3, 2002).

132. Ellen Knickermeyer, "Full-Figured Females Favored," *Opelika-Auburn News* (August 7, 2001).

133. Michael Schuman, "Some Korean Women Are Taking Great Strides to Show a Little Leg," *Wall Street Journal Interactive Edition* (February 21, 2001).

134. Amy Chozick, "Developing Nation: Japanese Clothiers Update Their Lines Changes in Diet Produce Curvier Bodies in Women; The 'Love Bra' Catches Fire," *Wall Street Journal* (May 7, 2007): A1.

135. Abraham Tesser and Terry Pettijohn, II, reported in "And the Winner Is . . . Wall Street," *Psychology Today* (March–April 1998): 12.

136. Lois W. Banner, *American Beauty* (Chicago: University of Chicago Press, 1980); for a philosophical perspective, see Barry Vacker and Wayne R. Key, "Beauty and the Beholder: The Pursuit of Beauty through Commodities," *Psychology & Marketing* 10 (November–December 1993): 471–94.

137. Elaine L. Pedersen and Nancy L. Markee, "Fashion Dolls: Communicators of Ideals of Beauty and Fashion," paper presented at the International Conference on Marketing Meaning, Indianapolis, IN, 1989; Dalma Heyn, "Body Hate," *Ms.* (August 1989): 34; Mary C. Martin and James W. Gentry, "Assessing the Internalization of Physical Attractiveness Norms," Proceedings of the American Marketing Association Summer Educators' Conference (Summer 1994): 59–65.

138. Lisa Bannon, "Barbie Is Getting Body Work, and Mattel Says She'll Be 'Rad,'" *Wall Street Journal Interactive Edition* (November 17, 1997).

139. Lisa Bannon, "Will New Clothes, Bellybutton Create 'Turn Around' Barbie," *Wall Street Journal Interactive Edition* (February 17, 2000).

140. "Report Delivers Skinny on Miss America," *Montgomery Advertiser* (March 22, 2000): 5A.

141. "Study: Playboy Models Losing Hourglass Figures" CNN.com (December 20, 2002).

142. Anthony H. Ahrensa, Sarah F. Etua, James J. Graya, James E. Mosimanna, Mia Foley Sypecka, and Claire V. Wisemanb, "Cultural Representations of Thinness in Women, Redux: *Playboy* Magazine's Depiction of Beauty from 1979 to 1999," *Body Image* (September 2006): 229–235.

143. Erin White, "Dove 'Firms' with Zaftig Models: Unilever Brand Launches European Ads Employing Non-Supermodel Bodies," *Wall Street Journal* (April 21, 2004): B3.

144. "The Dove Report: Challenging Beauty," *Unilever* 2004, available from www.dove.com/real_beauty/article.asp?id=430.

145. Laura Petrecca, "More Ads Star Regular People," *USA Today Online* (3 April, 2006).

146. Ray A. Smith, "Male Models Get a New Look as Fashion Targets Regular Guys," *Wall Street Journal* (February 2, 2007): B1.

147. Shelly Branch and Deborah Ball, "Does Reality Sell Beauty? To Appeal to More Women, Advertisers Adjust the Pitch; Suds Fly over Dove Campaign," *Wall Street Journal* (May 19, 2005): B1.

148. Rebecca Gardyn, "The Shape of Things to Come," *American Demographics* (July/August 2003): 25–49.

149. Jill Neimark, "The Beefcaking of America," *Psychology Today* (November–December 1994): 32.

150. Richard H. Kolbe and Paul J. Albanese, "Man to Man: A Content Analysis of Sole-Male Images in Male-Audience Magazines," *Journal of Advertising* 25 (Winter 1996): 1–20.

151. Hannah Karp, "Jeans Makers Launch New Styles to Flatter the Male Figure," *Wall Street Journal* (June 25, 2004): B1.

152. David Goetzl, "Teen Girls Pan Ad Images of Women," *Advertising Age* (September 13, 1999): 32; Carey Goldberg, "Citing Intolerance, Obese People Take Steps to Press Cause," *New York Times on the Web* (November 5, 2000).

153. "Fat-Phobia in the Fijis: TV-Thin Is In," *Newsweek* (May 31, 1999): 70.

154. Amy Dockser Marcus, "With an Etiquette of Overeating, It's Not Easy Being Lean in Egypt," *Wall Street Journal Interactive Edition* (March 4, 1998).

155. Erin White and Deborah Ball, "Slim-Fast Pounds Home Tough Talk Ads Aimed at U.K. Women," *Wall Street Journal* (May 28, 2004): B3.

156. "Retailer Has Big Plans for Big Customers: LivingXL Sells Lifestyle Products for an Increasingly Obese America," available from www.MSNBC.com, accessed May 30, 2007.

157. Debra A. Zellner, Debra F. Harner, and Robbie I. Adler, "Effects of Eating Abnormalities and Gender on Perceptions of Desirable Body Shape," *Journal of Abnormal Psychology* 98 (February 1989): 93–96.

158. Robin T. Peterson, "Bulimia and Anorexia in an Advertising Context," *Journal of Business Ethics* 6 (1987): 495–504.

159. Jane E. Brody, "Personal Health," *New York Times* (February 22, 1990): B9.

160. Christian S. Crandall, "Social Contagion of Binge Eating," *Journal of Personality and Social Psychology* 55 (1988): 588–98.

161. Alex Williams, "Before Spring Break, the Anorexic Challenge," *New York Times Online* (April 2, 2006).

162. Judy Folkenberg, "Bulimia: Not for Women Only," *Psychology Today* (March 1984): 10.

163. Stephen S. Hall, "The Bully in the Mirror," *New York Times Magazine* (downloaded August 22, 1999); Natalie Angier, "Drugs, Sports, Body Image and G.I. Joe," *New York Times* (December 22, 1998): D1.

164. Caroline Muspratt, "Unilever Bans 'Size Zero' Models in Ads," available from www.telegraph.co.uk, accessed May 9, 2007; Larry Rohter, "Burst of High-Profile Anorexia Deaths Unsettles Brazil," *New York Times on the Web* (December 30, 2006); Eric Wilson, "Doctors Fault Designers' Stance over Thin Models," *New York Times Online* (January 9, 2007).

165. John W. Schouten, "Selves in Transition: Symbolic Consumption in Personal Rites of Passage and Identity Reconstruction," *Journal of Consumer Research* 17 (March 1991): 412–25.

166. Janet Whitman, "Extreme Makeovers Blur Line between Medicine and Cosmetics," *Wall Street Journal on the Web* (January 7, 2004).

167. Natasha Singer, "How to Stuff a Wild Bikini Bottom," *New York Times Online* (March 2, 2006).

168. Jane E. Brody, "Notions of Beauty Transcend Culture, New Study Suggests," *New York Times* (March 21, 1994): A14; Norihiko Shirouzu, "Reconstruction Boom in Tokyo: Perfecting Imperfect Belly-Buttons," *Wall Street Journal* (October 4, 1995): B1.

169. Emily Yoffe, "Valley of the Silicon Dolls," *Newsweek* (November 26, 1990): 72.

170. Jerry Adler, "New Bodies for Sale," *Newsweek* (May 27, 1985): 64.

171. Ruth P. Rubinstein, "Color, Circumcision, Tattoos, and Scars," in Michael R. Solomon, ed., *The Psychology of Fashion* (Lexington, MA: Lexington Books, 1985), 243–54; Peter H. Bloch and Marsha L. Richins, "You Look 'Mahvelous': The Pursuit of Beauty and Marketing Concept," *Psychology & Marketing* 9 (January 1992): 3–16.

172. Sondra Farganis, "Lip Service: The Evolution of Pouting, Pursing, and Painting Lips Red," *Health* (November 1988): 48–51.

173. Michael Gross, "Those Lips, Those Eyebrows; New Face of 1989 (New Look of Fashion Models)," *New York Times Magazine* (February 13, 1989): 24.

174. "High Heels: Ecstasy's Worth the Agony," *New York Post* (December 31, 1981).

175. Dannie Kjeldgaard and Anders Bengtsson (2005), "Consuming the Fashion Tattoo," *Advances in Consumer Research* 32, eds. Geeta Menon and Akshay R. Rao (Duluth, MN : Association for Consumer Research): 172–177.

176. Elizabeth Hayt, "Over-40 Rebels with a Cause: Tattoos," *New York Times* (December 22, 2002): sec. 9: 2.

177. Natasha Singer, "Erasing Tattoos, Out of Regret or for a New Canvas," available from www.nytimes.com, accessed June 17, 2007.

178. www.pathfinder.com:80/altculture/aentries/p/piercing.html, accessed August 22, 1997.

179. Dinitia Smith, "Demonizing Fat in the War on Weight," *New York Times Online* (May 1, 2004).

Personality and Lifestyles

CHAPTER 6

Chapter Objectives

When you have finished reading this chapter you will understand why:

● A consumer's personality influences the way he responds to marketing stimuli, but efforts to use this information in marketing contexts meet with mixed results.

● Consumers' lifestyles are key to many marketing strategies.

● Psychographics go beyond simple demographics to help marketers understand and reach different consumer segments.

● Identifying patterns of consumption can be superior to knowledge of individual purchases when a marketer crafts a lifestyle marketing strategy.

ackie and Hank, executives in a high-powered Los Angeles advertising agency, are exchanging ideas about how they are going to spend the big bonus everyone in the firm is getting for landing the Gauntlet body-jewelry account. They can't help but snicker at their friend Susan in accounting, who avidly surfs the Internet for information about a state-of-the-art home theater system she plans to install in her condo. What a couch potato! Hank, who fancies himself a bit of a thrill seeker, plans to blow his bonus on a wild trip to Colorado, where a week of outrageous bungee jumping awaits him (assuming he lives to tell about it, but that uncertainty is half the fun). Jackie replies, "Been there, done that . . . Believe it or not, I'm staying put right here—heading over to Santa Monica to catch some waves." Seems that the surfing bug has bitten her since she started leafing through *Wahine Surfing*, a magazine for the growing number of women taking up the sport.[1]

Jackie and Hank are sometimes amazed at how different they are from Susan, who's content to spend her downtime watching sappy old movies or actually reading books. All three make about the same salary, and Jackie and Susan were sorority sisters at USC. How can their tastes be so different? Oh well, they figure, that's why they make chocolate and vanilla.

Personality

Jackie and Hank are typical of many people who search for new (and even risky) ways to spend their leisure time. This desire translates into big business for the "adventure travel" industry, which specializes in providing white-knuckle experiences. Sports such as bungee jumping, white-water rafting, sky diving, mountain biking, and other physically stimulating activities now account for about one-fifth of the U.S. leisure travel market.[2] In the old days, the California beach culture relegated women to the status of land-locked "Gidgets" who sat on shore while their boyfriends rode the big one. Now (spurred by the female surfers in the movie *Blue Crush*), it's women who fuel the sport's resurgence in popularity. Roxy rides the wave with its collections of women's surf apparel including the Roxy Girl and Teenie Wahine lines.[3]

Just what does make Jackie and Hank so different from their more sedate friend Susan? One answer may lie in the concept of **personality,** which refers to a person's unique psychological makeup and how it consistently influences the way a person responds to her environment.

Do all people *have* personalities? Certainly we can wonder about some we meet! Actually, some psychologists argue that the concept of personality may not be valid. Many studies find that people do not seem to exhibit stable personalities. Because people don't necessarily behave the same way in all situations, they argue that this is merely a convenient way to categorize people.

Intuitively, this argument is a bit hard to accept because we tend to see others in a limited range of situations, and so they *do* appear to act consistently. However, we each know that *we* are not all *that* consistent; we may be wild and crazy at times and serious and responsible at others. Although certainly not all psychologists have abandoned the idea of personality, many now recognize that a person's underlying characteristics are but one part of the puzzle, and situational factors often play a very large role in determining behavior.[4] Still, some aspects of personality continue to be included in marketing strategies. We usually employ these dimensions in conjunction with a person's choices of leisure activities, political outlooks, aesthetic tastes, and other individual factors to segment consumers in terms of *lifestyles,* a process we'll focus on more fully later in this chapter.

CONSUMER BEHAVIOR ON THE COUCH: FREUDIAN THEORY

Sigmund Freud proposed the idea that much of one's adult personality stems from a fundamental conflict between a person's desire to gratify her physical needs and the necessity to function as a responsible member of society. This struggle is carried out in the mind among three systems. (Note: These systems do *not* refer to physical parts of the brain.) Let's quickly review each.

FREUDIAN SYSTEMS

The **id** is totally about immediate gratification—it is the "party animal" of the mind. It operates according to the **pleasure principle;** our basic desire to maximize pleasure and avoid pain guides our behavior. The id is selfish and illogical. It directs a person's psychic energy toward pleasurable acts without regard for any consequences.

The **superego** is the counterweight to the id. This system is essentially the person's conscience. It internalizes society's rules (especially as parents teach them to us) and works to prevent the id from seeking selfish gratification. Finally, the **ego** is the system that mediates between the id and the superego. It is, in a way, a referee in the fight between temptation and virtue. The ego tries to balance these opposing forces according to the **reality principle,** which means it finds ways to

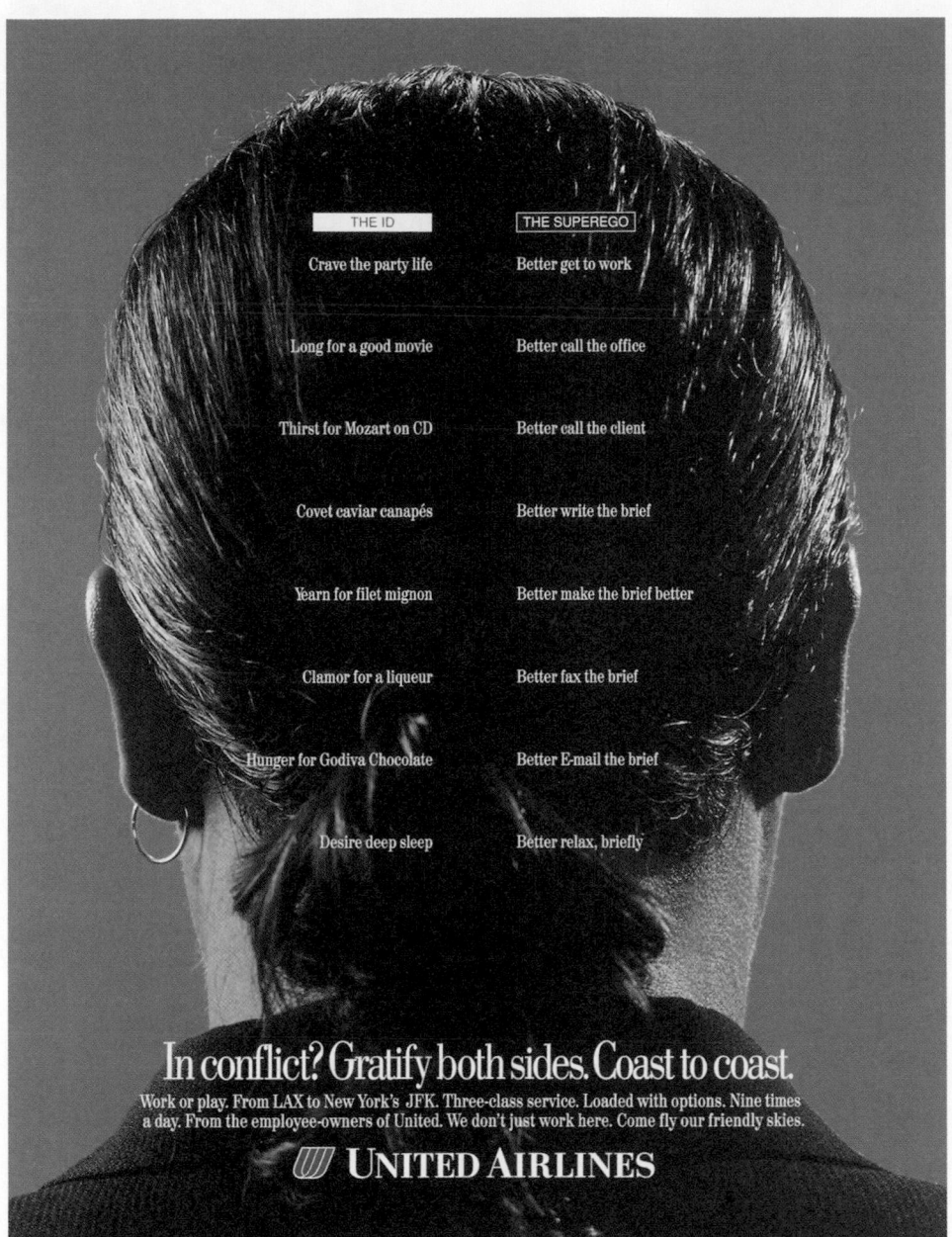

This ad focuses on the conflict between the desire for hedonic gratification (represented by the id) versus the need to engage in rational, task-oriented activities (represented by the superego).

gratify the id that the outside world will find acceptable. These conflicts occur on an unconscious level, so the person is not necessarily aware of the underlying reasons for his behavior.

Consumer researchers have adapted some of Freud's ideas. In particular, his work highlights the potential importance of unconscious motives underlying our purchases. The implication is that consumers cannot necessarily tell us their true motivation for choosing a product, even if we can devise a sensitive way to ask them directly. The Freudian perspective also hints at the possibility that the ego relies on the symbolism in products to compromise between the demands of the id and the prohibitions of the superego. The person channels her unacceptable desire into acceptable outlets by using products that signify these underlying desires. This is the connection between product symbolism and motivation: The product stands for, or represents, a consumer's true goal, which is socially unacceptable or unattainable. By acquiring the product, the person is able to vicariously experience the forbidden fruit.

Sometimes a Cigar *Is* Just a Cigar

Most Freudian applications in marketing relate to the products' sexual symbolism. For example, some analysts have speculated that owning a sports car is a substitute for sexual gratification (especially for men going through a "midlife crisis"). Indeed, some people do seem inordinately attached to their cars and may spend many hours lovingly washing and polishing them. An Infiniti ad reinforces the belief that cars symbolically satisfy consumers' sexual needs in addition to their functional ones by describing one model as "what happens when you cross sheet metal and desire." Other approaches focus on male-oriented symbolism—so-called *phallic symbols*— that appeals to women. Although Freud joked "sometimes a cigar is just a cigar," many popular applications of Freud's ideas revolve around the use of objects that resemble sex organs (e.g., cigars, trees, or swords for male sex organs; tunnels for female sex organs). This focus stems from Freud's analysis of dreams, which he interpreted as communicating repressed desires through symbols.

Motivational Research

In the 1950s, **motivational research** borrowed Freudian ideas to understand the deeper meanings of products and advertisements. This approach adapted psycho-analytical (Freudian) interpretations with a heavy emphasis on unconscious motives. It basically assumed that we channel socially unacceptable needs into acceptable outlets—including product substitutes.

This form of research relies on *depth interviews* with individual consumers. Instead of asking many consumers a few general questions about product usage and combining these responses with those of many other consumers in a representative statistical sample, motivational research involves relatively few consumers but probes deeply into each person's purchase motivations. A depth interview might take several hours, and it's based on the assumption that the respondent cannot immediately articulate his *latent* or underlying motives. A carefully trained interviewer can derive these only after extensive questioning and interpretation.

Ernest Dichter, a psychoanalyst who trained in Vienna in the early part of the twentieth century, pioneered this work. Dichter conducted in-depth interview studies on more than 230 different products, and actual marketing campaigns incorporated many of his findings.[5] For example, Esso (now Exxon in the United States) for many years reminded consumers to "Put a Tiger in Your Tank" after Dichter found that people responded well to this powerful animal symbolism containing vaguely sexual undertones. Table 6.1 provides a summary of major consumption motivations he identified.

Critics attacked motivational research for two opposing reasons—some claim it doesn't work and others accuse it of working *too* well. On the one hand, some people reacted much the same way that they had to subliminal perception studies (see Chapter 2). They attacked this perspective for giving advertisers the power to manipulate consumers.[6] On the other hand, many consumer researchers felt the research lacked sufficient rigor and validity because the interpretations are so subjective.[7] Because the analyst bases his conclusions on his own judgment after interviewing a small number of people, some scientists are dubious about the degree to which a marketer can generalize them to a larger market. In addition, because the original motivational researchers were heavily influenced by orthodox Freudian theory, their interpretations usually involved sexual themes. This emphasis tends to overlook other plausible causes for behavior. Still, motivational research had great appeal to at least some marketers for several reasons, including these:

● Motivational research is less expensive to conduct than large-scale, quantitative survey data collection because interviewing and data-processing costs are relatively minimal.
● The knowledge a company derives from motivational research may help it develop marketing communications that appeal to deep-seated needs and thus provide a more powerful hook to reel in consumers. Even if they are not necessarily valid for

TABLE 6.1	
A MOTIVATIONAL RESEARCHER IDENTIFIES CONSUMPTION MOTIVES	

Motive	Associated Products
Power-masculinity-virility	Power: Sugary products and large breakfasts (to charge oneself up), bowling, electric trains, hot rods, power tools Masculinity-virility: Coffee, red meat, heavy shoes, toy guns, buying fur coats for women, shaving with a razor
Security	Ice cream (to feel like a loved child again), full drawer of neatly ironed shirts, real plaster walls (to feel sheltered), home baking, hospital care
Eroticism	Sweets (to lick), gloves (to be removed by woman as a form of undressing), a man lighting a woman's cigarette (to create a tension-filled moment culminating in pressure, then relaxation)
Moral purity-cleanliness	White bread, cotton fabrics (to connote chastity), harsh household cleaning chemicals (to make housewives feel moral after using), bathing (to be equated with Pontius Pilate, who washed blood from his hands), oatmeal (sacrifice, virtue)
Social acceptance	Companionship: Ice cream (to share fun), coffee Love and affection: Toys (to express love for children), sugar and honey (to express terms of affection) Acceptance: Soap, beauty products
Individuality	Gourmet foods, foreign cars, cigarette holders, vodka, perfume, fountain pens
Status	Scotch: ulcers, heart attacks, indigestion (to show one has a high-stress, important job!), carpets (to show one does not live on bare earth like peasants)
Femininity	Cakes and cookies, dolls, silk, tea, household curios
Reward	Cigarettes, candy, alcohol, ice cream, cookies
Mastery over environment	Kitchen appliances, boats, sporting goods, cigarette lighters
Disalienation (a desire to feel connectedness to things)	Home decorating, skiing, morning radio broadcasts (to feel "in touch" with the world)
Magic-mystery	Soups (having healing powers), paints (change the mood of a room), carbonated drinks (magical effervescent property), vodka (romantic history), unwrapping of gifts

Source: Adapted from Jeffrey F. Durgee, "Interpreting Dichter's Interpretations: An Analysis of Consumption Symbolism," in *The Handbook of Consumer Motivation, Marketing and Semiotics: Selected Papers from the Copenhagen Symposium*, eds. Hanne Hartvig-Larsen, David Glen Mick, and Christian Alstead (Copenhagen, 1991).

all consumers in a target market, these insights still can be valuable to an advertiser who wants to create copy that will resonate with customers.

● Some of the findings seem intuitively plausible after the fact. For example, motivational studies concluded that we associate coffee with companionship, that we avoid prunes because they remind us of old age, and that men fondly equate the first car they owned as an adolescent with the onset of their sexual freedom.

Other interpretations were hard for some researchers to swallow, such as the observation that to a woman baking a cake symbolizes giving birth, or that men are reluctant to give blood because they feel this act drains their vital fluids. However, we do sometimes say a pregnant woman has "a bun in the oven," and Pillsbury claims, "nothing says lovin' like something from the oven." Motivational researcher Dichter did find for the American Red Cross that men (but not women) tend to drastically overestimate the amount of blood they give during a donation. The Red Cross counteracted their fear of losing their virility by symbolically equating the act of giving blood with fertilization: "Give the gift of life." Despite its drawbacks, some ad agencies today still use some forms of motivational research. Consumer researchers can enhance its validity, however, when they use it as an exploratory technique that gives them insights when they design more rigorous research approaches.

NEO-FREUDIAN THEORIES

Freud's work had a huge influence on subsequent theories of personality. Although he opened the door to the realization that explanations for behavior may lurk beneath the surface, many of his colleagues and students felt that an individual's personality is more influenced by how he handles relationships with others than by how he resolves sexual conflicts. We call these theorists *neo-Freudian* (meaning following from or being influenced by Freud).

Karen Horney

One of the most prominent neo-Freudians was Karen Horney. This pioneering psychotherapist described people as moving toward others *(compliant)*, away from others *(detached)*, or against others *(aggressive)*.[8] Indeed, one early study found that compliant people are more likely to gravitate toward name brand products, detached types are more likely to be tea drinkers, and males the researchers classified as aggressive preferred brands with a strong masculine orientation (e.g., Old Spice deodorant).[9] Other well-known neo-Freudians include Alfred Adler, who proposed that people are motivated to overcome feelings of inferiority relative to others, and Harry Stack Sullivan, who focused on how personality evolves to reduce anxiety in social relationships.[10]

Carl Jung

Carl Jung was also a disciple of Freud (and Freud was grooming him to be his successor). However, Jung was unable to accept Freud's emphasis on sexual aspects of personality, and this was a contributing factor in the eventual dissolution of their relationship. Jung went on to develop his own method of psychotherapy, which is called *analytical psychology*.

Jung believed that the cumulative experiences of past generations shape who we are today. He proposed that we each share a *collective unconscious*, a storehouse of memories we inherit from our ancestors. For example, Jung would argue that many people are afraid of the dark because their distant ancestors had good reason to fear it. These shared memories create **archetypes,** or universally recognized ideas and behavior patterns. Archetypes involve themes, such as birth, death, or the devil, that appear frequently in myths, stories, and dreams.

Jung's ideas may seem a bit far-fetched, but advertising messages in fact do often include archetypes. For example, some of the archetypes Jung and his followers identified include the "old wise man" and the "earth mother."[11] These images appear frequently in marketing messages that use characters such as wizards, revered teachers, or even Mother Nature. Our culture's current infatuation with stories such as *Harry Potter* and *The Lord of the Rings* speaks to the power of these images.

Young & Rubicam (Y&R), a major advertising agency, uses the archetype approach in its BrandAsset® Archetypes model that Figure 6.1 depicts. The model proposes healthy relationships among Archetypes as well as unhealthy ones. Researchers at the agency use the model to identify whether a brand has a sick personality. A healthy personality is one in which the Archetypes overwhelm their corresponding Shadows; a sick personality results when one or more Shadows prevail. When a brand's Shadows dominate, it is necessary to take action to guide the brand to a healthier personality, much like one would try to counsel a psychologically ill person. The agency feels that this approach has numerous advantages:

1 Because Archetypes are grounded in the human psyche across all cultures and points in time, it is easy to understand a brand's personality—oftentimes multinationally—using such a structure.

2 Archetypes telegraph instantly to those responsible for brand communication; indeed, the best of this group already incorporates these notions into how they think of the brand: The model helps the rest of them "catch up."

■ FIGURE 6.1 BRANDASSET VALUATOR® ARCHETYPES

Characteristics

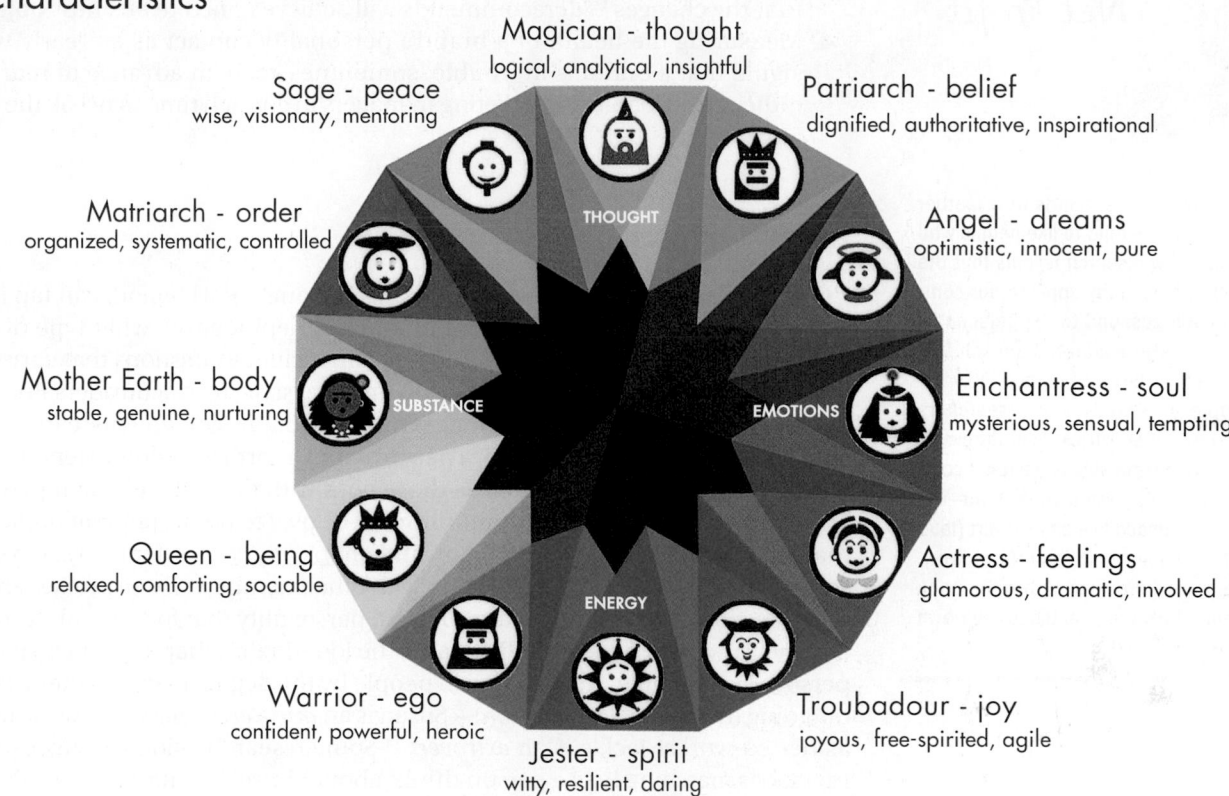

Magician - thought
logical, analytical, insightful

Sage - peace
wise, visionary, mentoring

Patriarch - belief
dignified, authoritative, inspirational

Matriarch - order
organized, systematic, controlled

Angel - dreams
optimistic, innocent, pure

Mother Earth - body
stable, genuine, nurturing

Enchantress - soul
mysterious, sensual, tempting

THOUGHT

SUBSTANCE

EMOTIONS

ENERGY

Queen - being
relaxed, comforting, sociable

Actress - feelings
glamorous, dramatic, involved

Warrior - ego
confident, powerful, heroic

Jester - spirit
witty, resilient, daring

Troubadour - joy
joyous, free-spirited, agile

Shadow Characteristics

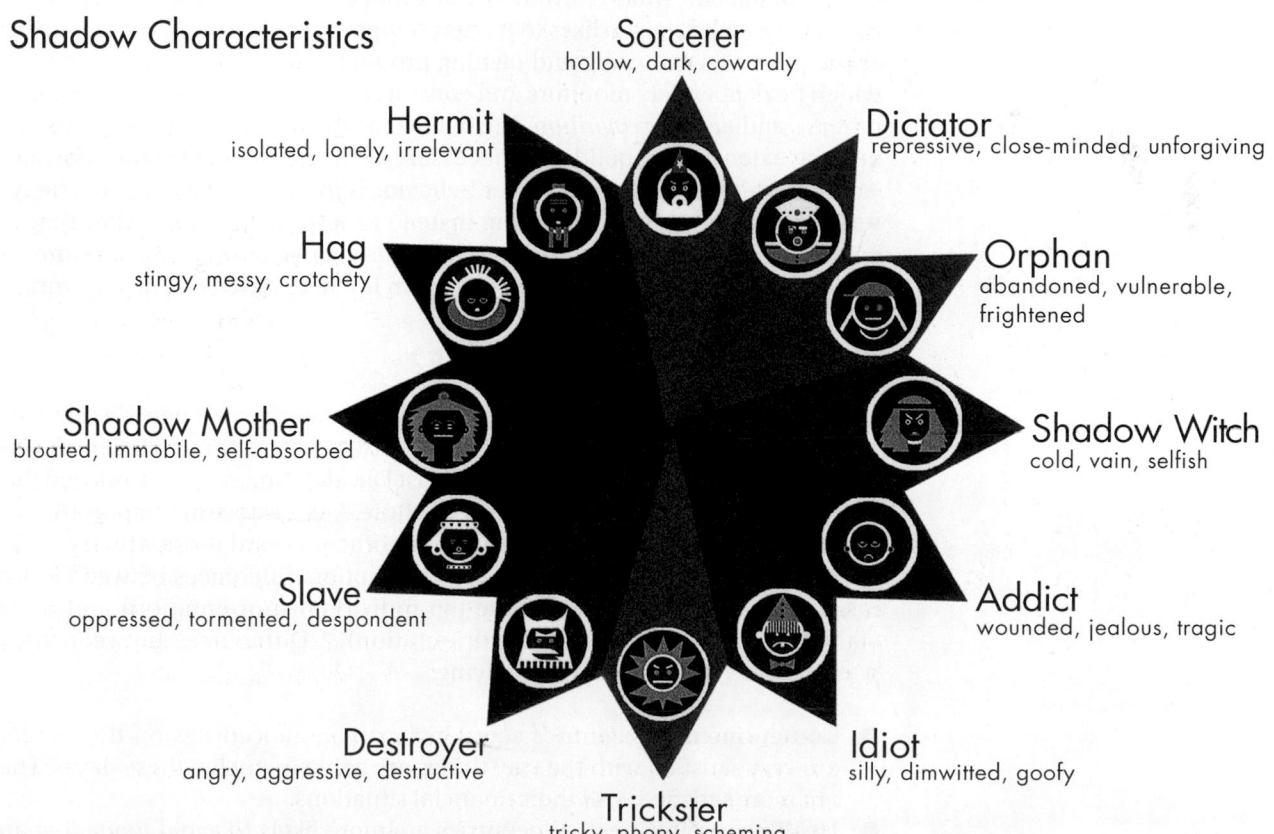

Sorcerer
hollow, dark, cowardly

Hermit
isolated, lonely, irrelevant

Dictator
repressive, close-minded, unforgiving

Hag
stingy, messy, crotchety

Orphan
abandoned, vulnerable, frightened

Shadow Mother
bloated, immobile, self-absorbed

Shadow Witch
cold, vain, selfish

Slave
oppressed, tormented, despondent

Addict
wounded, jealous, tragic

Destroyer
angry, aggressive, destructive

Idiot
silly, dimwitted, goofy

Trickster
tricky, phony, scheming

Source: BrandAsset ® Consulting: A Young & Rubicam Brands Company

Net Profit

3 Linking measures of BrandAsset® Archetypes to more objective brand perception measures provides strong evidence to assure marketing decision makers that the changes Y&R recommends will achieve concrete business objectives.

4 Measuring the health of a brand's personality can act as an "early warning" signal that a brand is in trouble, sometimes years in advance of marketplace indicators. This alerts marketing managers in enough time to tweak the brand as appropriate.[12]

TRAIT THEORY

Customers at Robinson Department Stores in Bangkok, Thailand, can tap into "Life Code," a computer analysis system that helps them identify what type of clothing fashion is best for them. The Life Code system includes questions that correlate personality and individual preferences with dressing style. It alsoconsiders Buddhist beliefs by interpreting fashion preferences from the four basic elements: earth, water, air, and fire. According to this system, a person with an earth element prefers clothes with basic and timeless design, whereas those born with the water element prefer bright and lively colors and a sweet, youthful look.[13] Closer to home, popular online matchmaking services such as match.com and eharmony.com offer to create your "personality profile" and then hook you up with other members whose profiles are similar.

These are examples of an approach to personality that focuses on the quantitative measurement of **personality traits,** the identifiable characteristics that define a person. For example, we distinguish people by the degree to which they are socially outgoing (the trait of *extroversion*)—Susan is an *introvert* (quiet and reserved), whereas her co-worker Jackie is an *extrovert*.[14] Some research evidence suggests that ad messages matching how a person thinks about himself are more persuasive.[15]

Some specific traits relevant to consumer behavior include: *innovativeness* (the degree to which a person likes to try new things), *materialism* (the amount of emphasis he places on acquiring and owning products), *self-consciousness* (the degree to which he deliberately monitors and controls the image of the self that he projects to others), and *need for cognition* (the degree to which a he likes to think about things and, by extension, expends the necessary effort to process brand information).[16] Another trait relevant to consumer behavior is *frugality*. Frugal people deny short-term purchasing whims, choosing instead to resourcefully use what they already own. For example, this personality type tends to favor cost-saving measures such as timing showers and bringing leftovers from home to have for lunch at work.[17]

ARE YOU AN INNIE OR AN OUTIE?

One trait dimensions that interests many consumer researchers distinguishes between those of us who consume to please others versus those who aren't very concerned about what others think. Sociologist David Reisman first introduced the terms *inner-directed* and *outer-directed* to our culture.[18] As we'll see in Chapter 16, some cultures tend to stress individualism, whereas others reward those who try to fit in.

Some recent research examines consumption differences between individuals researchers classify as **idiocentric** (an individualist orientation) and those they classify as **allocentric** (a group orientation).[19] Differences between these two personality types include the following:

● **Contentment:** Idiocentrics score higher than allocentrics on the statement "I am very satisfied with the way things are going in my life these days." They also are more satisfied with their financial situations.

● **Health consciousness:** Allocentrics are more likely to avoid foods that are high in cholesterol, have a high salt content, have additives in them, or have a high amount of fat.

- **Food preparation:** The kitchen is an allocentric's favorite room, and these types spend more time preparing meals than do idiocentrics.
- **Workaholics:** Idiocentrics are more likely to say they work very hard most of the time, and they stay late at work more than do allocentrics.
- **Travel and entertainment:** Idiocentrics are more interested in other cultures and traveling than are allocentrics. They also are more likely to go to movies, art galleries, and museums. Compared to idiocentrics, allocentrics visit the public library more often and read more books. Allocentrics report working on crafts projects such as needlework and model building. However, idiocentric individuals are more likely to collect stamps and rocks, work on do-it-yourself projects, and take photos.[21]

PROBLEMS WITH TRAIT THEORY IN CONSUMER RESEARCH

Because consumer researchers categorize large numbers of consumers according to whether they exhibit various traits, we can apply this approach when we want to segment markets. If a car manufacturer, for example, determines that drivers who fit a given trait profile prefer a car with certain features, it can use this information to great advantage. The notion that consumers buy products that are extensions of their personalities makes intuitive sense. As we'll see shortly, many marketing managers endorse this idea as they try to create *brand personalities* that will appeal to different types of consumers.

Unfortunately, the use of standard personality trait measurements to predict product choices has met with mixed success at best. In general, marketing researchers simply have not been able to predict consumers' behaviors on the basis of measured personality traits. These are some logical explanations for these equivocal results:[22]

- Many of the scales are not sufficiently valid or reliable; they do not adequately measure what they are supposed to measure, and their results may not be stable over time.
- Psychologists typically develop personality tests for specific populations (e.g., people who are mentally ill); marketers then "borrow" them to apply to a more general population where they have questionable relevance.
- Often marketers don't administer the tests under the appropriate conditions; people who are not properly trained may give them in a classroom or at a kitchen table.
- The researchers often make changes in the instruments to adapt them to their own situations, in the process deleting or adding items and renaming variables. These *ad hoc* changes dilute the validity of the measures and also reduce researchers' ability to compare results across consumer samples.
- Many trait scales measure gross, overall tendencies (e.g., emotional stability or introversion); marketers then use these results to make predictions about purchases of specific brands.
- In many cases, marketers ask consumers to respond to a large number of scales with no advance thought about how they will relate these measures to consumer behavior. The researchers then use a "shotgun approach," following up on anything that happens to look interesting.

Although marketing researchers largely abandoned the use of personality measures after many studies failed to yield meaningful results, some researchers have not given up on the early promise of this line of work. More recent efforts (mainly in Europe) have tried to benefit from past mistakes. Researchers are using more specific measures of personality traits that they have reason to believe are relevant to economic behavior. They are trying to increase the validity of these measures, primarily by using multiple measures of behavior rather than relying on the common practice

Marketing Pitfall

It looks like the marketers who came up with the logo for the 2012 Olympic Games in London won't be winning any gold medals. The British tabloids have been less than kind; one paper described the design as a "toileting monkey." An antilogo group got 50,000 people to sign a petition demanding that the design be changed. Some marketing experts feel that this outcry is a good thing because most young Britons are very blasé about the prospect of the Olympics taking place in their backyard so this will get their blood pumping.[30]

The controversial 2012 Olympics logo.

of trying to predict purchasing responses from a single item on a personality test. In addition, these researchers toned down their expectations of what personality traits can tell them about consumers. They now recognize that traits are only part of the solution and that personality data must be incorporated with information about people's social and economic conditions in order to be useful.[23] As a result, some more recent research has had better success at relating personality traits to such consumer behaviors as alcohol consumption among young men or shoppers' willingness to try new, healthier food products.[24]

BRAND PERSONALITY

In 1886, a momentous event occurred in marketing history—the Quaker Oats man first appeared on boxes of hot cereal. Quakers had a reputation in nineteenth-century America for being shrewd but fair, and peddlers sometimes dressed as members of this religious group to cash in on their credibility. When the cereal company decided to "borrow" this imagery for its packaging, this signaled the recognition that its customers might make the same association.[25]

Today thousands of brands also borrow personality traits of individuals or groups to convey an image they want customers to form of them. A **brand personality** is the set of traits people attribute to a product as if it were a person. Many of the most recognizable figures in popular culture are spokescharacters for long-standing brands, such as the Jolly Green Giant, the Keebler Elves, Mr. Peanut, or Charlie the Tuna. Research clearly demonstrates that consumers in different cultures are able to identify the common brands in their culture in terms of distinct personality dimensions, and this occurs for many kinds of products and services, from packaged goods to nonprofit organizations.[26]

Forging a successful brand personality often is key to building brand loyalty, but it's not as easy as it looks. One reason is that many consumers (particularly younger ones) have a very sensitive "BS detector" that alerts them when a brand isn't living up to its claims or is somehow inauthentic. When this happens, the strategy may backfire as consumers rebel. They may create Web sites to attack the brand or post parodies that make fun of it on <u>YouTube</u>. One set of researchers terms this phenomenon a **Doppelgänger brand image** (one that looks like the original but is in fact a critique of it). For example, many consumers were immensely loyal to the Snapple brand until Quaker purchased it. These loyalists felt that Quaker had stripped the brand of its offbeat, grassroots sensibility; one notoriously offensive disc jockey renamed it "Crapple" on his radio show.[27]

Our feelings about a brand's personality are part of brand equity, which refers to the extent to which a consumer holds strong, favorable, and unique associations with a brand in memory—and the extent to which she or he is willing to pay more for the branded version of a product than for a nonbranded (generic) version.[28] Building strong brands is good business—if you don't believe it consider that, in a study of 760 *Fortune* 1,000 companies after the stock market took a nosedive in October of 1997, the 20 strongest corporate brands (e.g., Microsoft, GE) actually gained in market value whereas the 20 weakest lost an average of $1 billion each.[29]

So how do people think about brands? Advertisers are keenly interested in this question, and several ad agencies have conducted extensive consumer research to help them understand how consumers will relate to a brand before they roll out campaigns. DDB Worldwide does a global study called "Brand Capital" of 14,000 consumers; Leo Burnett's "Brand Stock" project involves 28,000 interviews. WPP Group has "BrandZ" and Young & Rubicam uses its BrandAsset Valuator®. DDB's worldwide brand planning director observes, "We're not marketing just to isolated individuals. We're marketing to society. How I feel about a brand is directly related to and affected by how others feel about that brand."[31] Table 6.2 shows some of the things a marketer can do to influence consumers' perceptions of a brand's personality.

TABLE 6.2
BRAND BEHAVIORS AND POSSIBLE PERSONALITY TRAIT INFERENCES

Brand Action	Trait Inference
Brand is repositioned several times or changes its slogan repeatedly	Flighty, schizophrenic
Brand uses continuing character in its advertising	Familiar, comfortable
Brand charges a high price and uses exclusive distribution	Snobbish, sophisticated
Brand frequently available on deal	Cheap, uncultured
Brand offers many line extensions	Versatile, adaptable
Brand sponsors show on PBS or uses recycled materials	Helpful, supportive
Brand features easy-to-use packaging or speaks at consumer's level in advertising	Warm, approachable
Brand offers seasonal clearance sale	Planful, practical
Brand offers five-year warranty or free customer hotline	Reliable, dependable

Source: Adapted from Susan Fournier, "A Consumer-Brand Relationship Framework for Strategic Brand Management," unpublished doctoral dissertation, University of Florida, 1994, Table 2.2, p. 24.

We use some personality dimensions to compare and contrast the perceived characteristics of brands in various product categories including the following:[32]

- Old-fashioned, wholesome, traditional
- Surprising, lively, "with it"
- Serious, intelligent, efficient
- Glamorous, romantic, sexy
- Rugged, outdoorsy, tough, athletic

An advertising agency wrote the following memo to help it figure out how to portray one of its clients. Based on this description of the "client," can you guess who he is? "He is creative . . . unpredictable . . . an imp. . . . He not only walks and talks, but has the ability to sing, blush, wink, and work with little devices like pointers. . . . He can also play musical instruments. . . . His walking motion is characterized as a 'swagger.' . . . He is made of dough and has mass."[33] Of course, we all know today that packaging and other physical cues create a "personality" for a product (in this case, the Pillsbury Doughboy).

Indeed, consumers appear to have little trouble assigning personality qualities to all sorts of inanimate products, from personal care products to more mundane, functional ones—even kitchen appliances. Whirlpool's research showed that people saw its products as more feminine than they saw competing brands. When respondents were asked to imagine the appliance as a person, many of them pictured a modern, family-oriented woman living in the suburbs—attractive but not flashy. In contrast, they envisioned the company's Kitchen Aid brand as a modern professional woman who was glamorous, wealthy, and enjoyed classical music and the theater.[34]

A product that creates and communicates a distinctive brand personality stands out from its competition and inspires years of loyalty. However, personality analysis helps marketers identify a brand's weaknesses that have little to do with its functional qualities: Adidas asked kids in focus groups to imagine that the brand came to life and was at a party, and to tell what they would expect the brand to be doing there. The kids responded that Adidas would be hanging around the keg with its pals, talking about girls. Unfortunately, they also said Nike would *be with* the girls!"[35] These results reminded Adidas' brand managers they had some work to do. We compare this process to **animism,** the common cultural practice whereby people give inanimate objects qualities that make them somehow alive.[36]

We tend to *anthropomorphize* objects, which happens when we give them human characteristics. We may think about a cartoon character or mythical creation as if it were a person and even assume it has human feelings. Again, think about familiar spokescharacters such as Charlie the Tuna, the Keebler Elves, or the Michelin Man, or consider the frustration some people feel when they come to believe their computer is smarter than they are or may even be, "conspiring" to make them crazy! In research for its client Sprint Business Services, Grey Advertising found that when American customers imagined long-distance carriers as animals, they envisioned AT&T as a lion, MCI as a snake, and Sprint as a puma. Grey used these results to position Sprint as a company that could "help you do more business" rather than taking the more aggressive approach of its competitors.[37]

As we saw in Chapter 2, a brand's positioning strategy is a statement about what that brand wants to be in the eyes of its customers—especially relative to the competition. Marketers typically think in these terms (even if they haven't read this book); they routinely describe their brands and the competition as if they were people. For example, here's how the marketing director for Philips Electronics in Asia sums up the problem he faces in updating his brand so that it's seen as hip and young by Chinese consumers: "To put it bluntly, we are received well by middle-aged gentlemen. . . . But a brand like Sony is seen as younger, more arrogant, with a space-age personality."[38]

In a sense, then, a brand personality is a statement about the brand's market position. Understanding this is crucial to marketing strategy, especially if consumers don't see the brand the way its makers intend them to and they must attempt to *reposition* the product (i.e., give it a personality makeover). That's the problem Volvo now faces; its cars are renowned for safety but drivers don't exactly see them as

The Zaltman Metaphor Elicitation Technique (ZMET) is one tool used to assess the strategic aspects of brand personality and is based on the premise that brands are expressed in terms of metaphors; that is, a representation of one thing in terms of another. These associations often are nonverbal, so the ZMET approach is based on a nonverbal representation of brands. Participants collect a minimum of twelve images representing their thoughts and feelings about a topic, and are interviewed in depth about the images and their feelings. Eventually, digital imaging techniques are used to create a collage summarizing these thoughts and feelings, and the person tells a story about the image created. This collage was created by a young woman to express her feelings about Tide detergent. It includes such images as a sunrise to represent freshness and a teddy bear that stands for the soft and comfortable way her laundry feels when she's done. However, the facial expressions also give a clue about her "fondness" for doing laundry!

exciting or sexy. A safe and solid brand personality makes it hard to sell a racy convertible like the C70 model, so a British ad tries to change that perception with the tagline, "Lust, envy, jealousy. The dangers of a Volvo." Just as with people, however, you can only go so far to convince others that your personality has changed. Volvo has been trying to jazz up its image for years, but for the most part consumers aren't buying it. In an earlier attempt in the United Kingdom, the company paired action images like a Volvo pulling a helicopter off a cliff with the headline "Safe Sex"—but market research showed people didn't believe the new image. As one brand consultant observed, "You get the sort of feeling you get when you see your grandparents trying to dance the latest dance. Slightly amused and embarrassed."[39]

Lifestyles and Psychographics

Jackie, Hank, and Susan strongly resemble one another demographically. They all were raised in middle-class households, have similar educational backgrounds, are about the same age, and work for the same company. However, as their leisure choices show, it would be a big mistake to assume that their consumption choices are similar as well. Each person chooses products, services, and activities that help define a unique *lifestyle*. This section first explores how marketers approach the issue of lifestyle and then how they use information about these consumption choices to tailor products and communications to individual lifestyle segments.

LIFESTYLE: WHO WE ARE, WHAT WE DO

In traditional societies, class, caste, village, or family largely dictate a person's consumption options. In a modern consumer society, however, people are freer to select the set of products, services, and activities that define themselves and, in turn, create a social identity they communicate to others. One's choice of goods and services indeed makes a statement about who one is and about the types of people with whom one desires to identify—and even those whom we wish to avoid.

Lifestyle defines a pattern of consumption that reflects a person's choices on how to spend her time and money. In an economic sense, your lifestyle represents the way you elect to allocate income, both in terms of relative allocations to different products and services, and to specific alternatives within these categories.[40] Other somewhat similar distinctions describe consumers in terms of their broad patterns of consumption, such as those differentiating people by those who devote a high proportion of total expenditures to food, or advanced technology, or to such information-intensive goods as entertainment and education.[41]

A *lifestyle marketing perspective* recognizes that people sort themselves into groups on the basis of the things they like to do, how they like to spend their leisure time, and how they choose to spend their disposable income.[42] The growing number of niche magazines that cater to specialized interests reflects the rainbow of choices available to us in today's society. In one recent year, *WWF Magazine* (World Wrestling Federation) gained 913,000 readers and *4 Wheel & Off Road* gained 749,000, whereas mainstream *Reader's Digest* lost more than 3 million readers and *People* lost more than 2 million.[43]

These finely tuned choices in turn create opportunities for market segmentation strategies that recognize the potency of a consumer's chosen lifestyle in determining both the types of products purchased and the specific brands most likely to appeal to a certain lifestyle segment. For example, the popularity of wrestling (or at least watching it) in the United States is creating other lifestyle marketing opportunities: The WWE (World Wrestling Entertainment) is lending its name to the Socko Energy line of beverages that Wal-Mart sells. The drinks include "WWE Slammin' Citrus Powered by Socko" and "WWE Raw Attitude Powered by Socko" and, in turn, Bliss

CB AS I SEE IT

Professor Susan Fournier
Boston University

Consumer research has a long tradition in the concept of cocreation: the processes by which consumers create brand and product meanings in order to make sense of and align consumer goods and services within their lives. Changes in the cultural context are well aligned with this theoretical shift, with numerous developments in technology that fuel consumers' ability to create and share original content for a brand. The ascendancy of empowered consumers as brand-content creators is a marketplace reality that transforms the discipline of brand marketing at its core.

Practitioners have been quick to recognize the likely power of citizen marketing that takes the form of advertising message creation—so-called "homebrew ads," "folk ads," VCAMs (viewer-contributed advertising messages), or more generally, "open source" brands. Mass-market manufacturers Frito-Lay, Unilever, and Chevrolet aired consumer-generated ads (CGAs) on the 2007 Super Bowl and Academy Awards. Still, Chevrolet's Spring 2006 campaign as a CGA first-mover was cause for concern when invited consumers created anti-Chevy ads showcasing Tahoe's destructive role in the environment. Heinz's June 2007 advertising creation contest primarily generated parodies that mocked the brand. More troubling perhaps is the evolution of video-sharing sites such as YouTube.com that serve as organizing platforms for counterconsumption activities. So-called "antiads" have as their subjects not only brands and individual companies but also entire industries. Indeed, a June 2007 headline in *Advertising Age* proclaimed: "Big Pharma Doesn't Like How It Looks on YouTube."

Based on marketplace reactions to these campaigns and others, firms have recently become more cognizant of the risk–reward trade-offs involved with CGAs.

CGA involves a role reversal of sorts in the process of advertising creation and consumption. Consumers—whom advertisers once viewed as receivers of company-created messages, or, more recently, as active translators and cocreators of the meanings that these messages contain—now serve a new function as self-motivated originators of advertising content. Firm roles, too, are shifted. They are now becoming facilitators of the creation and dissemination of consumer-created messages as they filter and select CGAs. Although potentially attractive and beneficial to business, these marketplace shifts bring new concerns and questions. Does a CGA present a fundamentally different advertising paradigm, or does it persuade in much the same way that conventional company-sponsored advertising does? Do CGAs possess the benefits of authenticity, credibility,

Beverages, which makes the beverages, will sponsor WWE pay-per-view matches. Now that's opening a can of lifestyle marketing Whoop-ass.[44]

LIFESTYLES AS GROUP IDENTITIES

Economic approaches are useful to track changes in broad societal priorities, but they do not begin to embrace the symbolic nuances that separate lifestyle groups. Lifestyle is more than the allocation of discretionary income. It is a statement about who one is in society and who one is *not*. Group identities, whether of hobbyists, athletes, or drug users, gel around forms of expressive symbolism. Social scientists describe such self-definitions using a number of terms, including *lifestyle, taste public, consumer group, symbolic community,* and *status culture.*[45]

Many people in similar social and economic circumstances may follow the same general consumption pattern. Still, each person also provides a unique "twist" to the pattern that allows him to inject some individuality into a lifestyle. For example, a "typical" college student (if there is such a thing) may dress much like his friends, and insight that managers assume they hold? How can a firm best design a CGA campaign to control the risk–reward tradeoff? Without a solid base of research, the rules of engagement in the new terrain of consumer-created content remain unknown.

We are undertaking research to better understand the phenomenon of consumer-generated brand messages. Do consumer-created ads exert their effects through similar processes that drive traditional brand communications? What are the characteristics of brands and industries that emerge as targets of vigilante ads? Does format matter, as with short documentaries or on-camera interviews such as those noted for the pharmaceutical industry? How should marketers react to the reality of organized video-graphed protests of their industries and brands?

We currently have two empirical investigations of viewer's responses to the CGA phenomenon in the field: (1) an experiment to contrast the effects of advertisements we identify either as created by consumers or

companies and (2) a qualitative analysis of posted viewer responses to milestone CGAs (e.g., those appear during the Super Bowl and Academy Awards in 2007) to probe persuasion processes in a natural viewing environment. What have we found so far? CGAs are far more persuasive than company ads; viewers are more involved and they process more message claims. When we analyze what people say about the ads, we find that consumers view them as more authentic. Viewers tend to talk about these ads among themselves. These conversations created a multifaceted engagement experience consisting of viewer involvement, ad involvement, creator involvement, brand involvement, contest process involvement, emotional engagement, and cognitive elaboration of the messaging.

Other research in progress builds on the reciprocating relationships that are created between consumers and the brands that they use. Now that we feel comfortable asserting that consumers form relationships with brands, we need to ask: What *kinds* of relationships do they form?

Do they approach brand relationships with different *styles* of relating or attachment? and How exactly do consumer-brand relationships *develop* and change over time? I have one study in the field that explores the phenomenology of abusive relationships with brands, master–slave engagements, adversaries, flings, and secret affairs. This research is exciting in that it accepts and appreciates the fact that not only are most consumer-brand relationships not of the desired "marital commitment" variety but also that a majority in fact are negative in emotional tone. Ironically, we also find lots of cases where the consumer feels she or he has one type of relationship, whereas the firm thinks the relationship is of another variety. The extreme case here involves consumers who feel they are the "firm's best customers," whereas the firm wants to "fire" these resource-hungry persons who want more and more from the company. The brand-relationship paradigm is an exciting one with many interesting questions left to be explored.

hang out in the same places, and like the same foods yet still indulge a passion for marathon running, stamp collecting, or acid jazz that makes him unique.

And lifestyles are not set in stone. Unlike the deep-seated values we discussed in Chapter 4, people's tastes and preferences evolve over time. In fact, down the road we may laugh at consumption patterns we follow now. If you don't believe that, simply think back to what you and your friends were wearing 5 or 10 years ago—where *did* you find those clothes? Because people's attitudes regarding physical fitness, social activism, sex roles for men and women, the importance of home life and family, and so on do change, it is vital for marketers to continually monitor the social landscape to try to anticipate where these changes will lead.

One emerging lifestyle segment is the "Urban Consumer"; analysts claim it's 20 million strong in the United States. They say that U.S. hip-hop and street culture strongly shape the outlook of this 18- to-34-year-old segment with $90 billion in purchasing power—even though about 4 in 10 of urban consumers are white. Many marketers try to attract urban consumers; even mainstream Wal-Mart created a marketing alliance with BET to sell urban-oriented music and movie releases it brands as "BET Official."[46] Urban consumers tend to be materialistic (remember Chapter 4); members crave high-end cars, upscale clothing and accessories, shoes and sneakers, technology, entertainment, cell phones, PDAs, and computers. They disdain entertainers and

An energy drink links itself to a lifestyle statement.

businesspeople they deem one dimensional or limited. One analyst commented, "If you're just a rapper, they're not impressed by that anymore. You have to be a producer, own a record label, have your own line of clothes." Whereas their heroes include Jay Z, P Diddy, and J-Lo, the celebrity they *most* admire is . . . Bill Gates.[47]

PRODUCTS ARE THE BUILDING BLOCKS OF LIFESTYLES

Nike makes a lot of shoes and athletic apparel, but now the company wants to play an even bigger role in defining your lifestyle. It commissioned original workout music for its "Nike + Original Run" series you can buy at Apple's iTunes Music Store. It teamed up with Apple to offer the Nike + shoes that feature a built-in pocket under the insole for the Nike + iPod sensor that lets you track your run and set goals while listening to your favorite tunes. It's releasing other CDs featuring music and voice-over coaching in activities such as yoga, dance, and weight training.[50] At the running clubs its retail stores sponsor, Nike's staff keeps track of members' performances and hails members who have logged more than 100 miles. Of course, Nike is not the only forward-thinking marketer that's figured out the value of integrating the products they sell with their customers' lifestyles:

● At the Whole Foods supermarket in Seattle, shoppers take part in a "singles" night the first Friday of every month. The store's marketing staff organizes a wine tasting or sets out snacks in a room used to stage cooking classes. Customers can opt to wear a red or blue ribbon to indicate whether they are looking for a male or a female partner.

● The outdoor retailer REI offers training in kayaking and mountain biking at its stores; PetSmart and Petco provide training classes for pet owners; and Cabela's, a hunting store, offers classes on "trout tactics" and gun cleaning.[51]

● Versace is branching out into upscale lifestyle products, such as a half-million-dollar Lamborghini Murciélago with a black-and-white leather interior; a helicopter with a Versace-designed cabin; luggage with pieces starting at about

Hummer links the brand to the *feng shui* lifestyle trend of aligning architectural design with natural forces.

The White Aryan Resistance is one of many hate groups with an active presence on the World Wide Web.

The Tangled Web

The Web's power to unite thousands or even millions of people who share attitudes or consumption preferences is a mixed blessing. Many groups spreading a gospel of hate use the Internet to reach fellow believers and to recruit new ones. These include Muslim extremists, skinheads, and black separatist organizations. As the man who founded the White Aryan Resistance group boasted, "[Now that we are online] our reach is much, much farther."[48] Web sites that recruit new soliders for Muslim *jihad* are reaching farther as well. There are literally thousands of *jihadi* Web sites, and when authorities shut one down it often reappears under a different URL. Many of the sites contain up-to-date information about the *jihad* in Iraq and Afghanistan, in addition to other theaters of operations. Analysts say the most effective recruiting materials are video clips and photos of civilians being killed by bombs and of footage showing ambushes of U.S. soldiers. Other postings provide detailed instructions on how to make bombs and explosive substances. These videos also demonstrate the vulnerabilities of U.S. soldiers, attracting more aspiring *mujahideen* to the *jihad* as they show that defeating U.S. forces is possible. Many discussions result in willing recruits posting their e-mail addresses and imploring actual *jihadi* operators to contact them and guide them toward the path of *jihad*.[49]

The recreational-vehicle ad shown here demonstrates how a market segment is defined by a particular allocation of time and money to leisure activity. The ad's claim that the caravan dealer has the product that "says you're you!" implies that dedicated caravanners derive a significant portion of their self-identities from the activities associated with this lifestyle.

$4,000; and its aerodynamically styled "Jet Seat," a leather chair in a high-tech ceramic frame that goes for about $50,000.[52]

- Dockers's khaki pants at one time were the uniform of the dot-com era. When they fell out of favor, Levi Strauss first tried to sell its Dockers division but couldn't find a buyer. So the company decided to expand the label to what it calls a lifestyle brand that includes shirts, sweaters, blazers, and women's clothing. Dockers began to market its men's apparel specifically for four lifestyle occasions—work, weekend wear, dressing up, and golf—and changed the name to Dockers San Francisco to emphasize the lifestyle component and the brand's roots.[53]

- As book sales sag, publishers are looking beyond traditional bookstores as they try to embed their products into consumers' lifestyles. They are pushing books in butcher shops, carwashes, cookware stores, cheese shops, and hardware stores. Delis are selling Italian cookbooks (in plastic bags to be sure salami grease doesn't ruin them), glossy fashion books are moving well at upscale clothing boutiques, and Restoration Hardware sells design titles.[54]

These are smart moves, especially when marketers encourage a sense of *community* among product users (think of the reasons you faithfully check your Facebook account). We often choose a product precisely because we associate it with a certain lifestyle. For this reason, lifestyle-marketing strategies attempt to position a product by fitting it into an existing pattern of consumption and to create a brand personality that is relevant to a variety of products and situations.

Because a goal of lifestyle marketing is to allow consumers to pursue their chosen ways to enjoy their lives and express their social identities, a key aspect of this

■ **FIGURE 6.2**
LINKING PRODUCTS TO LIFESTYLES

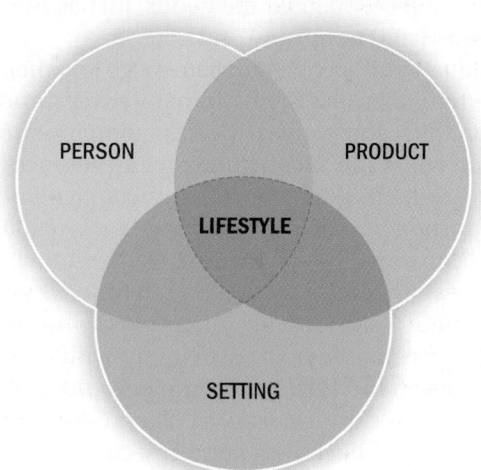

strategy is to focus on product usage in desirable social settings. The desire to associate a product with a social situation is a long-standing one for advertisers, whether they include the product in a round of golf, a family barbecue, or a night at a glamorous club surrounded by the hip-hop elite.[55] Thus, people, products, and settings combine to express a *consumption style,* as Figure 6.2 diagrams.

We can get a clearer picture of how people use products to define lifestyles when we see how they make choices in a variety of product categories. A lifestyle marketing perspective implies that we must look at *patterns of behavior* to understand consumers. As one study noted, "All goods carry meaning, but none by itself. . . . The

Interior designers rely on consumption constellations when choosing items to furnish a room. A decorating style involves integrating products from many different categories—such as appliances, furnishings, knick-knacks, and even artwork—into a unified whole that conveys a certain "look."

Monogram, by GE. It solves the riddle of how to integrate the appliances into custom kitchen design.

No matter what design theme you choose, the one thing you don't have to worry about nowadays is how the appliances will look.

The Monogram line of built-in appliances now offers such an array of models that you have virtually infinite choice and options.

This year we add the first 36" built-in refrigerator that is trimless and completely cabinet friendly. The decorative door panels accept custom handles, so they co-ordinate with the pulls on your cabinets. Because there is no bottom air vent, the base of the cabinet can now extend across the bottom of the refrigerator. No other built-in refrigerator integrates so beautifully.

Monogram now offers a built-in convection wall oven that provides new technology for faster cooking and sleek flush design.

Our Component Cooktops continue to be the only ones that can be installed perpendicular or horizontal to the counter edge to form clusters in gas, electric, updraft and downdraft. And there's also a 5-burner gas cooktop.

The remarkable idea of getting everything from your dishwasher to your microwave from *one* manufacturer also simplifies the complex process of shopping and delivery. And when you buy Monogram, you buy the assurance of the appliance industry's most extensive network of factory service professionals.

Going one step further is the extraordinary GE Answer Center service on duty 24 hours a day *every* day of the year at 800.626.2000. We're there to help in any way. If you would like a brochure that tells you more about Monogram, and if you would like to know where you can see the line, please call.

Monogram, from GE. A synonym for the best in built-in appliances.

Monogram.

meaning is in the relations between all the goods, just as music is in the relations marked out by the sounds and not in any one note."[56]

Indeed, many products and services do seem to "go together," usually because the same types of people tend to select them. In many cases, products do not seem to "make sense" if they are unaccompanied by companion products (e.g., fast food and paper plates, or a suit and tie) or are incongruous in the presence of others (e.g., a Chippendale chair in a high-tech office or Lucky Strike cigarettes with a solid gold lighter).

Therefore, an important part of lifestyle marketing is to identify the set of products and services that consumers seem to link together into a specific lifestyle. And research evidence suggests that even a relatively unattractive product becomes more appealing when consumers link it with other, liked products.[57] Marketers who pursue **co-branding strategies** where they team up with other companies to promote their products understand this. For example, Wendy's and Procter & Gamble joined forces to offer Wendy's Custom Bean, a Folgers Gourmet Selection coffee that the restaurant chain says will become a centerpiece of its new breakfast menu.[58] Some marketers even match up their spokescharacters in ads; the Pillsbury Doughboy appeared in a commercial with the Sprint Guy to pitch cellphones, the lonely Maytag repairman was in an ad for the Chevrolet Impala, and the Taco Bell chihuahua showed up in a commercial for Geico insurance.[59]

Product complementarity occurs when the symbolic meanings of different products relate to one another.[60] Consumers use these sets of products we call a **consumption constellation** to define, communicate, and perform social roles.[61] For example, we defined the American "yuppie" of the 1980s by such products as a Rolex watch, a BMW automobile, a Gucci briefcase, a squash racket, fresh pesto, white wine, and brie cheese. We find somewhat similar constellations for "Sloane Rangers" in the United Kingdom and "Bon Chic Bon Genres" in France. Although people today take pains to avoid being classified as yuppies, this social role had a major influence on defining cultural values and consumption priorities in the 1980s.[62] What consumption constellation might characterize you and your friends today?

PSYCHOGRAPHICS

In 1998, Cadillac introduced its Escalade sport utility vehicle. Critics scoffed at the bizarre pairing of this old-line luxury brand with a truck, but consumers quickly associated the vehicle with the hip-hop lifestyle. Artists such as Jennifer Lopez, Outkast, and Jay-Z referred to it in songs, and Jermaine Dupri proclaimed, "gotta have me an Escalade." Three years later, Cadillac went even further when it rolled out its 18-foot Escalade EXT pickup with a sticker price of $50,000.

The Escalade brand manager describes the target customer for luxury pickups as a slightly earthier version of the SUV buyer. She says that although the two drivers may own $2 million homes next door to each other, the typical luxury SUV driver is about 50, has an MBA from Harvard, belongs to a golf club, maintains connections with his college friends, and works hard at keeping up with the Joneses. In contrast, the luxury pickup driver is roughly 5 years younger. He might have inherited his father's construction business, and he's been working since he was 18 years old. He may or may not have attended college, and unlike the SUV driver, he is absolutely still connected to his high school friends.[63]

As this example shows, marketers often find it useful to develop products that appeal to different lifestyle groups—simply knowing a person's income doesn't predict whether he will drive a Cadillac Escalade SUV, pickup, or a Cadillac El Dorado sedan. As Jackie's, Hank's, and Susan's choices demonstrated, consumers can share the same demographic characteristics and still be very different people. For this reason, marketers need a way to "breathe life" into demographic data to really identify, understand, and target consumer segments that will share a set of preferences for their products and services.

Earlier in this chapter we discussed some of the differences in consumers' personalities that play a role in determining product choices. When marketers combine

NORESUND
estructura de cama
€119,00

DORMITORIOS COMO TÚ.

Redecora tu vida

IKEA

IKEA ALCORCÓN: A-5 Salida 17, dirección Móstoles-Pinto. IKEA S. S. DE LOS REYES: N-1 Salida 19, dirección Burgos. IKEA SEVILLA (Castilleja de la Cuesta): A-49, dirección Huelva, Km 2

As this Spanish ad implies, psychographic analyses allow marketers to match up consumers with products and styles that reflect their identities.

personality variables with knowledge of lifestyle preferences, they have a powerful lens they can focus on consumer segments. Adidas, for example, describes different types of shoe buyers in terms of lifestyles so that it can address the needs of segments such as gearheads (hard-core, older runners who want high-performance shoes), popgirls (teeny-boppers who hang out at the mall and wear Skechers), and fastidious eclectus (Bohemian, cutting-edge types who want hip, distinctive products).[64]

We call this approach psychographics, which involves the "use of psychological, sociological, and anthropological factors . . . to determine how the market is segmented by the propensity of groups within the market—and their reasons—to make a particular decision about a product, person, ideology, or otherwise hold an attitude or use a medium."[65]

Psychographics can help a marketer fine-tune its offerings to meet the needs of different segments. For example, the Best Buy consumer electronics chain recently decided to revamp its stores according to the types of customers they serve. The company identified five prototypical customers:

1 "Jill," a busy suburban mom who wants to talk about how electronics can help her family.

TABLE 6.3
THE PERSONALITIES OF SOUP EATERS

Lifestyle	Personality
Active Lifestyle (Vegetable) · I am outdoorsy · I am physically fit · I am a workaholic · I am socially active	**Mentally Alert (Clam Chowder)** · I am intellectual · I am sophisticated · I am creative · I am detail oriented · I am witty · I am nutrition conscious
Family Spirited (Chicken Noodle) · I am family-oriented · I am a churchgoer · I am pretty traditional	**Social (Chili)** · I am fun at parties · I am outgoing · I am not shy · I am spontaneous · I am a trendsetter
Homebody (Tomato) · I enjoy spending time alone · I am a homebody · I am a good cook · I am a pet lover	**Athletic (Cream Soups)** · I am athletic · I am competitive · I am adventurous
Intellectually Stimulated Pastimes (French Onion) · I am a technology whiz · I am a world traveler · I am a book lover	**Carefree (Minestrone)** · I am down-to-earth · I am affectionate · I am fun loving · I am optimistic

Source: Brian Wansink and S. Park, "Accounting for Taste: Prototypes that Predict Preference," *Journal of Database Marketing*, 2000, 308–320, as described in Norman Bradburn, Seymour Sudman and Brian Wansink, *Asking Questions* (New York: Jossey-Bass, 2004).

2 "Buzz," a focused, active younger male who is interested in buying (and showing off) the latest gadgets.
3 "Ray," a family man who likes his technology practical.
4 "BB4B" (short for Best Buy for Business), a small employer.
5 "Barry," an affluent professional male who's likely to drop tens of thousands of dollars on a home theater system and who is an action-movie enthusiast.

The chain plans to identify the two most dominant customer types who patronize each of its outlets and plan accordingly. Store clerks receive hours of training to help them pick out the most likely category in which to pigeonhole a customer. They are told to label a customer who says his family has a regular "movie night," as a "Ray" or "Jill" and to steer him or her toward home-theater equipment. Stores catering to the "Jill" segment will feature play areas for kids. Instead of a booming bass beat, the soundtrack playing in the background will be instrumental and children's music.[66]

It is possible to identify distinct psychographic segments even for mundane products—like soup. A major soup company did this after noticing that different types of people preferred different varieties.[67] To verify their hunches, company researchers interviewed "experts"—waitresses at diners—and asked them questions such as, "If the soup of the day is chicken noodle, what kind of person would order that soup?" After getting responses that did indicate differences (e.g., the waitresses reported that chicken noodle fanciers seemed to be most friendly and upbeat, whereas tomato soup fans often talked about a pet and were likely to read a paperback if eating alone), the company conducted in-depth interviews with self-proclaimed fanatics of each flavor and then administered a survey to about 1,000 North American adults. Table 6.3 summarizes some of their findings.

THE ROOTS OF PSYCHOGRAPHICS

Marketers first developed psychographic research in the 1960s and 1970s to address the shortcomings of two other types of consumer research: motivational research and quantitative survey research. Motivational research, which involves intensive, one-to-one interviews and projective tests, yields a lot of information about a few people. As we've seen, though, this information is often idiosyncratic and may not be very reliable. At the other extreme, quantitative survey research, or large-scale demographic surveys, yields only a little information about a lot of people. As some researchers observed, "The marketing manager who wanted to know why people ate the competitor's corn-flakes was told '32 percent of the respondents said taste, 21 percent said flavor, 15 percent said texture, 10 percent said price, and 22 percent said don't know or no answer.'"[68]

Marketers use many psychographic variables to segment consumers, but all of these dimensions go beyond surface characteristics to understand consumers' motivations for purchasing and using products. Demographics allow us to describe *who* buys, but psychographics tells us *why* they do. A classic example involves a very popular Canadian advertising campaign for Molson Export beer that included insights from psychographic findings. The company's research showed that Molson's target customers tended to be like boys who never grew up, who were uncertain about the future, and who were intimidated by women's newfound freedoms. Accordingly, the ads featured a group of men, "Fred and the boys," whose get-togethers emphasize male companionship, protection against change, and the reassuring message that the beer "keeps on tasting great."[69]

DOING A PSYCHOGRAPHIC ANALYSIS

Some early attempts at lifestyle segmentation "borrowed" standard psychological scales (that psychologists use to measure pathology or personality disturbances) and related test scores to product usage. As we saw earlier in the chapter, such efforts were largely disappointing. These tests were never intended to be related to every-day consumption activities, so they didn't do much to explain people's purchases. The technique is more effective when the marketers include variables that are more closely related to actual consumer behaviors. If you want to understand purchases of household cleaning products, you are better off asking people about their attitudes toward household cleanliness than testing for personality disorders!

Psychographic studies take several different forms:

- *A lifestyle profile* looks for items that differentiate between users and nonusers of a product.
- *A product-specific profile* identifies a target group and then profiles these consumers on product-relevant dimensions.
- *A general lifestyle segmentation* places a large sample of respondents into homogenous groups based on similarities of their overall preferences.
- *A product-specific segmentation* tailors questions to a product category. For example, if a researcher wants to conduct research for a stomach medicine, she might rephrase the item, "I worry too much" as, "I get stomach problems if I worry too much." This allows her to more finely discriminate among users of competing brands.[70]

AIOs

Most contemporary psychographic research attempts to group consumers according to some combination of three categories of variables—activities, interests, and

Marketing Pitfall

Target Corp. decided to cancel a survey that would have let the retailer compare the psyches of its customer to those of rival Wal-Mart shoppers. Some people complained to the company that items were too personal and inappropriate, including statements such as "My partner is likely to reject me at some point unless I am better (smarter, better looking, etc.) than any other potential mate" and "I could disappear from the face of the earth and no one would notice."[73]

TABLE 6.4
LIFESTYLE DIMENSIONS

Activities	Interests	Opinions	Demographics
Work	Family	Themselves	Age
Hobbies	Home	Social issues	Education
Social events	Job	Politics	Income
Vacation	Community	Business	Occupation
Entertainment	Recreation	Economics	Family size
Club membership	Fashion	Education	Dwelling
Community	Food	Products	Geography
Shopping	Media	Future	City size
Sports	Achievements	Culture	Stage in life cycle

Source: William D. Wells and Douglas J. Tigert, "Activities, Interests, and Opinions," *Journal of Advertising Research* 11 (August 1971): 27–35. © 1971 by The Advertising Research Foundation. Used with permission.

opinions—that we call **AIOs**. Using data from large samples, marketers create profiles of customers who resemble each other in terms of their activities and patterns of product usage.[71] Table 6.4 lists commonly used AIO dimensions.

To group consumers into AIO categories, researchers give respondents a long list of statements and ask them to indicate how much they agree with each one. Thus, we can "boil down" a person's lifestyle by discovering how he spends his time, what he finds interesting and important, and how he views himself and the world around him.

Typically, the first step in conducting a psychographic analysis is to determine which lifestyle segments yield the bulk of customers for a particular product. According to a very general rule of thumb that marketers call the **80/20 rule**—only 20 percent of a product's users account for 80 percent of the volume of product a company sells. Researchers attempt to determine who uses the brand and try to isolate heavy, moderate, and light users. They also look for patterns of usage and attitudes toward the product. In many cases, only a few lifestyle segments account for the majority of brand users.[72] Marketers primarily target these heavy users, even though they may constitute a relatively small number of total users.

After marketers identify and understand their heavy users, they consider more specifically how these customers relate to the brand. Heavy users may have quite different reasons for using the product; often we can further subdivide them in terms of the *benefits* they derive from using the product or service. For instance, marketers at the beginning of the walking-shoe craze assumed that all purchasers were basically burned-out joggers. Subsequent psychographic research showed that there were actually several different groups of "walkers," ranging from those who walk to get to work to those who walk for fun. This realization resulted in shoes that manufacturers aimed at different segments, from Footjoy Joy-Walkers to Nike Healthwalkers.

USES OF PSYCHOGRAPHIC SEGMENTATION

Marketers use psychographic segmentation in a variety of ways:

- **To define the target market:** This information allows the marketer to go beyond simple demographic or product usage descriptions (e.g., middle-aged men or frequent users).

- **To create a new view of the market:** Sometimes marketers create their strategies with a "typical" customer in mind. This stereotype may not be correct because the actual customer may not match these assumptions. For example, marketers of a face cream for women were surprised to find that older, widowed women were their heavy users rather than the younger, sociable women to whom they were pitching their appeals.
- **To position the product:** Psychographic information can allow the marketer to emphasize features of the product that fit in with a person's lifestyle. A company that wants to target people whose lifestyle profiles show a high need to be around other people might focus on its product's ability to help meet this social need.
- **To better communicate product attributes:** Psychographic information can offer very useful input to advertising creatives who must communicate something about the product. The artist or copywriter obtains a much richer mental image of the target consumer than she can simply by looking at dry statistics. For example, research U.S. brewer, Schlitz beer conducted found that heavy beer drinkers tended to feel that life's pleasures were few and far between. In response the brewer developed commercials with the tagline, "You only go around once, so reach for all the gusto you can."[74]
- **To develop overall strategy:** Understanding how a product fits, or does not fit, into consumers' lifestyles allows the marketer to identify new product opportunities, chart media strategies, and create environments most consistent and harmonious with these consumption patterns.
- **To market social and political issues:** Psychographic segmentation can be an important tool in political campaigns and policymakers also can employ the technique to find commonalities among consumers who engage in destructive behaviors, such as drug use or excessive gambling. A psychographic study of U.S. men aged 18 to 24 who drink and drive highlights the potential for this perspective to help in the eradication of harmful behaviors. Researchers divided this segment into four groups: "good timers," "well adjusted," "nerds," and "problem kids." They found that one group in particular—"good timers"—is more likely to believe that it is fun to be drunk, that the chances of having an accident while driving drunk are low, and that drinking increases one's appeal to the opposite sex. Because the study showed that this group is also the most likely to drink at rock concerts and parties, is most likely to watch MTV, and tends to listen to album-oriented rock radio stations, reaching "good timers" with a prevention campaign became easier.[75]

Ma
Pitf

908

When the R. J. Reynolds Company made plans to introduce a new brand of cigarettes called "Dakota" in several test markets, the tobacco company found out the hard way that a psychographic approach can be controversial. The marketing plan that an outside consulting firm submitted in the early 1990s to the company, specifically targeted the cigarette to 18- to 24-year-old women with high school educations or less, who work in entry-level factory or service jobs. This segment is one of the few remaining consumer groups in the United States that exhibits an increase in smoking rates, so from a purely financial point of view it clearly has market potential.

The strategy appealed to a lifestyle segment the consulting firm called the "Virile Female" whom it claimed has this psychographic profile: Her favorite pastimes are cruising, partying, and going to hot rod shows and tractor pulls with her boyfriend, and her favorite TV shows are evening soap operas. Her chief aspirations are to get married in her early 20s and to spend time with her boyfriend, doing whatever he does. This psychographic strategy resulted in a flood of unfavorable publicity as critics charged the company was trying to persuade more young women to take up the habit.[76]

PSYCHOGRAPHIC SEGMENTATION TYPOLOGIES

Marketers are constantly on the prowl for new insights that will allow them to identify and reach groups of consumers who are united by common lifestyles. To meet this need, many research companies and advertising agencies develop their own *segmentation typologies*. Respondents answer a battery of questions that allow the researchers to cluster them into a set of distinct lifestyle groups. The questions usually include a mixture of AIOs plus other items relating to feelings about specific brands, favorite celebrities, and media preferences. Companies that want to learn more about their customers and potential customers then buy one or more of these systems for their own use.

At least at a superficial level, many of these typologies are fairly similar to one another; they usually divide the population into roughly five to eight segments. Researchers give each cluster a descriptive name, and clients receive a profile of "typical" members. Unfortunately, it is often difficult to compare or evaluate different typologies because the methods and data that analysts use to devise these systems frequently are *proprietary*, that is, the company owns the information and does not share its findings with outsiders. Let's review a few typical approaches to classifying consumers in terms of lifestyles.

VALS2™

One well-known segmentation system is **The Values and Lifestyles System (VALS™),** that SRI International developed. SRI built the original VALS™ system on consumers' extent of agreement with various social issues such as abortion rights. After about 10 years, SRI discovered that the social issues it used to categorize consumers were not as predictive of consumer behavior as they once had been. SRI searched for a more powerful way to segment consumers, and the company discovered that certain lifestyle indicators such as "I like a lot of excitement in my life" were better predictors of purchase behavior than the degree to which a person agreed or disagreed with a social value.

The current VALS2™ system uses a battery of 39 items (35 psychological and 4 demographic) to divide U.S. adults into groups, each with distinctive characteristics. As Figure 6.3 shows, the typology arranges groups vertically by their resources (including such factors as income, education, energy levels, and eagerness to buy) and horizontally by self-orientation.

Three self-orientations comprise the horizontal dimension. Consumers with an *Ideals* orientation rely on a belief system to make purchase decisions, and they are not concerned with the views of others. People with an *Achievement* orientation are more competitive; they take into account what their peers will think about their decisions and how these choices will reflect upon them. Finally, those with a

■ **FIGURE 6.3**
VALS2™
Source: SRI International.

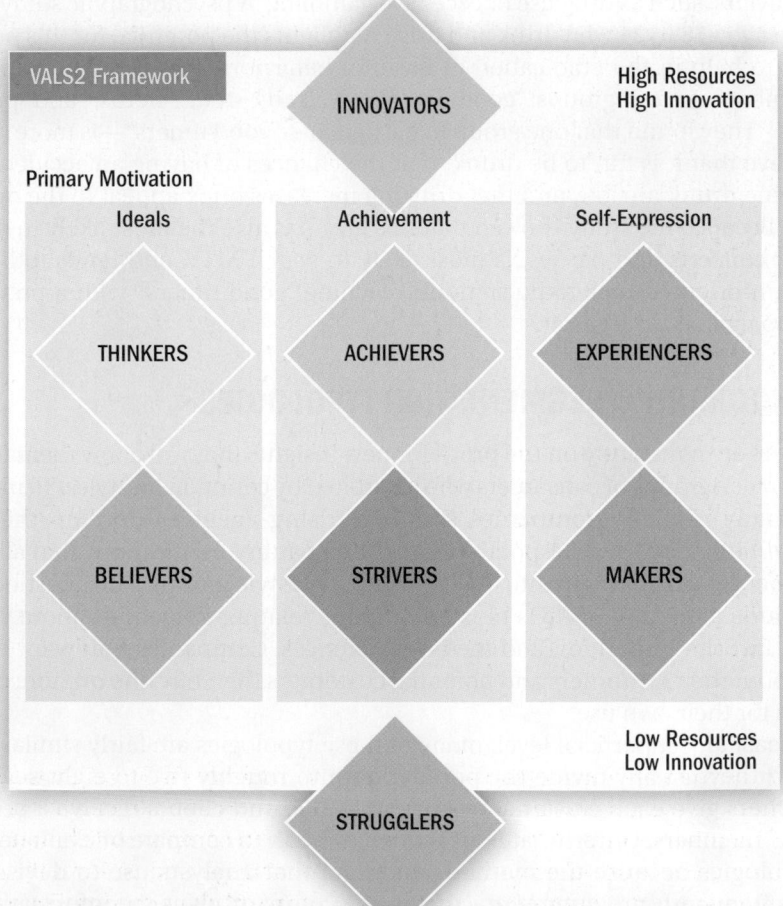

Self-Expression orientation are more concerned with the emotional aspects of purchases and the satisfaction they will personally receive from products and services.

Innovators, the top VALS2™ group, are successful consumers with many resources. This group is concerned with social issues and is open to change. The next three groups also have sufficient resources but differ in their outlooks on life:[77]

- *Thinkers* are satisfied, reflective, and comfortable.
- *Achievers* are career oriented and prefer predictability to risk or self-discovery.
- *Experiencers* are impulsive, young, and enjoy offbeat or risky experiences.

The next four groups have fewer resources:

- *Believers* have strong principles and favor proven brands.
- *Strivers* are similar to Achievers but have fewer resources. They are very concerned about the approval of others.
- *Makers* are action oriented and tend to focus their energies on self-sufficiency. They will often be found working on their cars, canning their own vegetables, or building their own houses.
- *Strugglers* are at the bottom of the economic ladder. They are most concerned with meeting the needs of the moment and have limited ability to acquire anything beyond the basic goods needed for survival.

The VALS2™ system has been a useful way to understand people like Jackie and Hank. SRI estimates that 12 percent of American adults are thrill seekers, who tend to fall into the system's Experiencer category and who are likely to agree with statements such as, "I like a lot of excitement in my life" and "I like to try new things." Experiencers like to break the rules, and extreme sports such as sky surfing or bungee jumping attract them. Not too surprisingly, fully one-third of consumers aged 18 to 34 belong in this category, so it has attracted the interest of many marketers who are trying to appeal to younger people. For example, VALS2™ helped Isuzu market its Rodeo sport utility vehicle by focusing on Experiencers, many of whom believe it is fun to break rules in ways that do not endanger others. Isuzu positioned the Rodeo as a vehicle that lets a driver do just that. It created advertising to support this idea by showing kids jumping in mud puddles, running with scissors, and coloring outside the lines.[78] Isuzu sales increased significantly after this campaign. If you want to see what VALS type you are, go to sric-bi.com/VALS/presurvey.shtml.

Global MOSAIC

The British firm Experian developed Global MOSAIC. This system analyzes consumers in 19 countries including Australia, South Africa, and Peru. Experian boiled down 631 different MOSAIC types to come up with 14 common lifestyles, classifying 800 million people who produce roughly 80 percent of the world's GDP. This allows marketers to identify consumers who share similar tastes around the world. An Experian executive explained, "The yuppie on the Upper East Side of New York has more in common with a yuppie in Stockholm than a downscale person in Brooklyn."

RISC

Since 1978, the Paris-based organization Research Institute on Social Change (RISC) has conducted international measurements of lifestyles and sociocultural change in more than 40 countries.[79] Its long-term measurement of the social climate around the world makes it possible to anticipate future change and to identify signs of change in one country before it eventually spreads to other countries. For example, concern for the environment appeared in Sweden in the early 1970s, then in

Germany in the late 1970s, in France in the beginning of the 1980s, and in Spain in the early 1990s.

RISC asks a battery of questions to identify people's values and attitudes about a wide range of issues. It combines the answers to measure 40 "trends" such as "spirituality" or "blurring of the sexes." Based on statistical analysis of the respondents' score on each trend, each individual is located in a virtual space described by three axes. RISC then divides the population into 10 segments referring to their position in this virtual space. The three axes are as follows:

1 **Exploration/stability:** The vertical axis separates people motivated by change, creativity, volatility, and openness from people motivated by stability, familiarity, tradition, and structure.
2 **Social/individual:** The horizontal axis distinguishes people oriented toward collective needs from people oriented more toward satisfaction of individual needs.
3 **Global/local:** The third axis indicates a distance between people who are comfortable with unfamiliar environments, multiple loose connections, and large-scale networking from people preferring close-knit relationships and a desire for the elements of life to be connected in a predictable manner.

GEODEMOGRAPHY

Geodemography refers to analytical techniques that combine data on consumer expenditures and other socioeconomic factors with geographic information about the areas in which people live, in order to identify consumers who share common consumption patterns. Researchers base this approach on the common assumption that "birds of a feather flock together"; people who have similar needs and tastes also tend to live near one another, so it should be possible to locate "pockets" of like-minded people who marketers can reach more economically by direct mail and other methods. For example, a marketer who wants to reach white, single consumers who are college educated and tend to be fiscally conservative may find that it is more efficient to mail catalogs to zip codes 20770 (Greenbelt, MD) and 90277 (Redondo Beach, CA) than to adjoining areas in either Maryland or California, where there are fewer consumers who exhibit these characteristics.

Geodemography is based on the assumption that "birds of a feather flock together." A frat house next to an all-girls' school says one of them needs to relocate, according to the moving company that created this ad.

Our food preferences say a lot about our lifestyles and values.

FOOD CULTURES

Are you what you eat? One of the most obvious lifestyle domains that our place of residence influences is food. Many marketers regionalize their offerings to appeal to different tastes, as for example, when Campbell's Soup puts a stronger dose of jalapeño pepper in its nacho cheese soup in the Southwest. In Philadelphia, a serving of Philadelphia cream cheese contains 14 percent more calories than the same size serving in Milan. A jar of Hellmann's mayonnaise you purchase in London will have half the saturated fat of the one you buy in Chicago. And a Kellogg's All-Bran bar you buy in the United States has nearly three times the sodium as one for sale across the border in Mexico.

Our food preferences say a lot about us, and many of our likes and dislikes are learned responses to dishes that people who matter to us value—or don't value. Saudis consider sheep eyeballs a delicacy, whereas the Chinese prize a good snake dish. People in Spain and Portugal consume 10 times the amount of fresh fish as those in Austria or the United Kingdom, and the consumption of pork in Denmark is about 10 times that of France. Not surprisingly, the Irish eat a lot of potatoes but not as many as the Greeks. In contrast, Italians avoid the tuber; instead they consume approximately four times more pasta per person than the Swiss, who are the second most avid spaghetti eaters.[80]

A **food culture** is a pattern of food and beverage consumption that reflects the values of a social group. Because these patterns vary so dramatically, food companies often find it rough going when they try to standardize their recipes. Sometimes these preferences are based on tastes and traditions, but in other cases people in other countries differ in terms of their focus on health. In China, Cadbury Schweppes PLC makes its Cadbury milk chocolate less milky and less sweet compared with that in the United Kingdom to suit the low-dairy diet of most Chinese consumers, whereas Kraft adds calcium to the Ritz crackers it sells in China to underscore the Chinese government's focus on promoting the need for consumers to get more calcium. Unilever actually had to reduce the size of its Magnum chocolate-covered ice cream bars sold in China because consumers there were more health conscious than Europeans and resisted the bigger bar.

As Figure 6.4 shows, a large-scale analysis of food cultures in 15 European countries revealed 12 distinct food cultures, many of which parallel national or linguistic borders. For example, the study characterized the French/French-Swiss, Wallonian, and Italian cultures by the importance of the sensory pleasure and high consumption of red wine; the Germanic cluster of countries exhibit a high degree of health consciousness; the Portuguese and Greek food cultures show relatively traditional eating patterns with a fascination for new "global" food; the Norwegian and Danish food cultures are unique in their openness to convenience products (and, for the Danes, also for the love of beer); and it distinguishes the British and Irish by their extraordinary desire for sweets and tea.[81]

■ FIGURE 6.4
EUROPEAN FOOD CULTURES

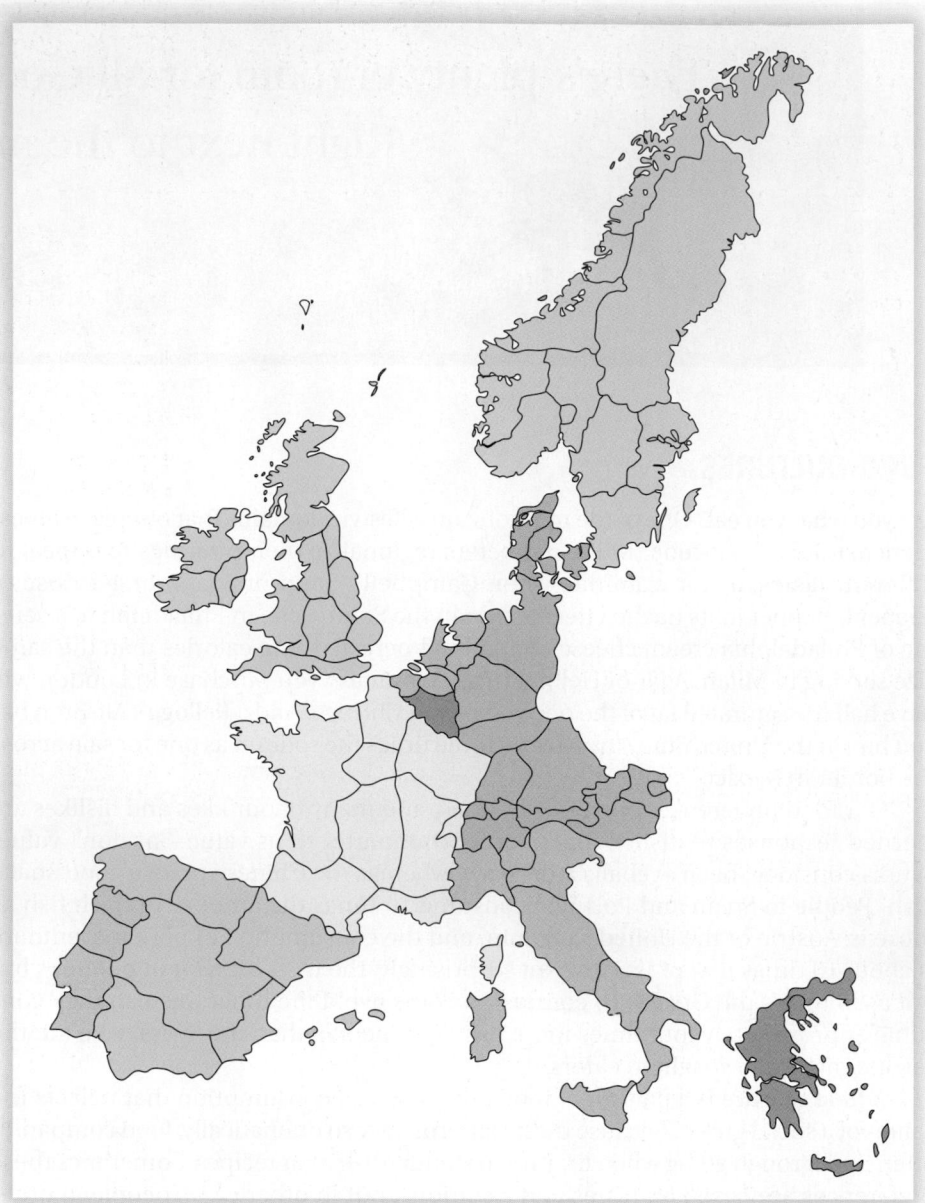

PRIZM

One popular clustering technique is the **PRIZM NE** system by Claritas, Inc. (PRIZM stands for Potential Rating Index by Zip Market). This system classifies every U.S. zip code into 1 of 66 categories, ranging from the most affluent "Blue-Blood Estates" to the least well-off "Public Assistance."[82] It terms a resident of Southern California "Money & Brains" if she lives in Encino (zip code 91316), whereas someone living in Sherman Oaks (zip code 91423) is a "Young Influential."[83] Claritas updated the system from its original set of 40 clusters to reflect the growing ethnic and economic diversity of the United States; some new clusters include "American Dreams," "Kids & Cul-de-Sacs," and "Young Literati."[84]

Residents of different clusters display marked differences in their consumption of products, from annuities to Ziploc bags. The system also ranks these groupings by income, home value, and occupation (i.e., a rough index of social class) on a ZQ (Zip Quality) scale. Table 6.5 provides an idea of how dramatically different the consumption patterns of two clusters can be. This table compares

TABLE 6.5
A COMPARISON OF TWO PRIZM CLUSTERS

Furs & Station Wagons (ZQ3)		Tobacco Roads (ZQ38)	
New money, parents in 40s and 50s		Racially mixed farm towns in the South	
Newly built subdivisions with tennis courts, swimming pools, gardens		Small downtowns with thrift shops, diners, and laundromats; shanty-type homes without indoor plumbing	
Sample neighborhoods:		Sample neighborhoods:	
Plano, TX (75075)		Belzoni, MI (39038)	
Dunwoody, GA (30338)		Warrenton, NC (27589)	
Needham, MA (02192)		Gates, VA (27937)	
High Usage	**Low Usage**	**High Usage**	**Low Usage**
Country clubs	Motorcycles	Travel by bus	Knitting
Wine by the case	Laxatives	Asthma relief remedies	Live theater
Lawn furniture	Nonfilter cigarettes	Malt liquors	Smoke detectors
Gourmet magazine	Chewing tobacco	*Grit* magazine	*Ms.* magazine
BMW 5 Series	*Hunting* magazine	Pregnancy tests	Ferraris
Rye bread	Chevrolet Chevettes	Pontiac Bonnevilles	Whole-wheat bread
Natural cold cereal	Canned stews	Shortening	Mexican foods

Note: Usage rates as indexed to average consumption across all 40 clusters.
Source: "A Comparison of Two Prizm Clusters" from *The Clustering of America* by Michael J. Weiss. Copyright © 1988 by Michael J. Weiss. Reprinted by permission of the Sagalyn Literacy Agency.

consumption data for "Furs & Station Wagons," the third-highest-ranking cluster, with "Tobacco Roads," the third-lowest.

Although consumers in two very different clusters may purchase a product at an equivalent rate, these similarities end when we take other purchases into account. These differences highlight the importance of going beyond simple product-category purchase data and demographics to really understand a market (remember the earlier discussion of product complementarity). For example, people in "Urban Gold Coast," "Money & Brains," and "Blue-Blood Estates" communities buy a lot of high-quality binoculars, but so do those in the "Grain Belt," "New Homesteaders," and "Agri-Business" clusters. The difference is that the former groups use the binoculars to watch birds and other wildlife, whereas the latter use them to help line up the animals in their gun sights. Furthermore, whereas the bird watchers do a lot of foreign travel, listen to classical music, and host cocktail parties, the bird hunters travel by bus, like country music, and belong to veterans' clubs.

Behavioral Targeting

The latest and hottest extension of lifestyle marketing is **behavioral targeting**, which refers to presenting people with advertisements based on their Internet use. In other words, with today's technology it's become fairly easy for marketers to tailor the ads you see to Web sites you've visited. Some critics feel this is a mixed blessing because it implies that big companies are tracking where we go and keeping this information.

Indeed, there are important privacy issues still to be resolved, but interestingly many consumers seem more than happy to trade off some of their personal information in exchange for information they consider more useful to them. A 2006 survey on this issue reported that 57 percent of the consumers it polled say they are willing to provide demographic information in exchange for a personalized online experience. And three-quarters of those involved in an online social network felt that this process would improve their experience because it would serve to introduce them to others who share their tastes and interests. However, a majority still express concern

Marketing Pitfall

How much are you willing to give up in exchange for free phone service? A start-up company called Pudding Media is betting you'll let it eavesdrop on your calls. In late 2007 the firm introduced a service like Skype that provides phone service through the Internet. The difference is that it will use voice recognition software to monitor what you're talking about and push ads to your computer screen based on your conversation. So, as you and your friend debate which movie you want to see this weekend, you might see a movie ad magically appear on your monitor.

Does this intrude on your privacy? The company won't keep recordings or logs of the content of any phone calls and the targeted ads will only arrive during the call itself. The firm's founder claims that the young consumers Pudding targets are less concerned with maintaining privacy than are older people and they won't mind being monitored if it means getting access to more information about the products they discuss. Do you agree?[89]

about the security of their personal data online.[85] Pro or con, it's clear that behavioral targeting is starting to take off in a big way:

- Microsoft combines personal data from the 263 million users of its free Hotmail e-mail service—the biggest in the world—with information it gains from monitoring their searches. When you sign up for Hotmail, the service asks you for personal information including your age, occupation, and address (though you're not required to answer). If you use Microsoft's search engine it calls Live Search, the company keeps a record of the words you search for and the results you clicked on. Microsoft's behavioral targeting system will allow its advertising clients to send different ads to each person surfing the Web. For instance, if a 25-year-old financial analyst living in a big city is comparing prices of cars online, BMW could send her an ad for a Mini Cooper. But it could send a 45-year-old suburban businessman with children who is doing the same search an ad for the X5 SUV.[86]

- The Fox network offers to produce *tweakable ads*—spots it can digitally alter so they contain elements relevant to particular viewers at the time they watch them. By changing voice-overs, scripts, graphic elements, or other images, for instance, advertisers can make an ad appeal to teens in one instance and seniors in another.

- Claria released its PersonalWeb service that allows people to download a piece of tracking software and receive a home page filled with news stories and other information tailored to their interests. If a man, for example, downloaded the software for and surfed through stories about a college basketball tournament and car reviews, his PersonalWeb home page would reflect those interests the next time he clicked on it. It might also include ads from car companies and from stores selling merchandise for his favorite college team.

- Starwood Hotels & Resorts Worldwide Inc. uses a behavioral targeting campaign to promote spas at its hotels. The hospitality company works with an online media company to deliver ads to people who have browsed travel articles on the Internet or surfed the Web site of a Starwood-branded hotel, such as Westin or Sheraton. An internal survey showed that the campaign was rated the highest among all of the company's efforts to raise awareness about the spas.

- Blockbuster.com uses software that recommends video to a customer based on attributes the flick shares with other movies she has already ordered. This results in some suggestions that may not be immediately obvious. For example, someone who watched "Crash" might receive a recommendation for "Little Miss Sunshine" because both involve dysfunctional social groups, dynamic pacing and an interdependent ensemble cast. Blockbuster says the service has increased its average customer's "to watch list" by almost 50%.[87]

- MySpace uses personal details users put on their profile pages and blogs to sell highly targeted advertising in 10 broad categories such as finance, autos, fashion, and music. Facebook is hard at work on a similar system, and it hopes to use sophisticated software to decide how receptive a user will be to an ad based not only on his personal information but that of his frends—even if he hasn't explicitly expressed interest in that topic.[88]

CHAPTER SUMMARY

Now that you have finished reading this chapter you should understand why:

A consumer's personality influences the way he responds to marketing stimuli, but efforts to use this information in marketing contexts meet with mixed results.

- The concept of *personality* refers to a person's unique psychological makeup and how it consistently influences the way a person responds to her environment.

Marketing strategies based on personality differences have met with mixed success, partly because of the way researchers have measured and applied these differences in *personality traits* to consumption contexts. Some analysts try to understand underlying differences in small samples of consumers by employing techniques based on Freudian psychology and variations of this perspective, whereas others have tried to assess these dimensions more objectively in large samples using sophisticated, quantitative techniques.

Consumers' lifestyles are key to many marketing strategies.

- A consumer's *lifestyle* refers to the ways she chooses to spend time and money and how her consumption choices reflect these values and tastes. Lifestyle research is useful to track societal consumption preferences and also to position specific products and services to different segments. Marketers segment based on lifestyle differences, often grouping consumers in terms of their AIOs (activities, interests, and opinions).

Psychographics go beyond simple demographics in helping marketers understand and reach different consumer segments.

- *Psychographic* techniques classify consumers in terms of psychological, subjective variables in addition to observable characteristics (demographics). Marketers have developed a variety of systems, such as VALS, to identify consumer "types" and to differentiate them in terms of their brand or product preferences, media usage, leisure time activities, and attitudes toward broad issues such as politics and religion.

Identifying patterns of consumption can be superior to knowledge of individual purchases when crafting a lifestyle marketing strategy.

- We associate interrelated sets of products and activities with social roles to form *consumption constellations*. People often purchase a product or service because they associate it with a *constellation* that, in turn, they link to a lifestyle they find desirable. *Geodemography* involves a set of techniques that use geographical and demographic data to identify clusters of consumers with similar psychographic characteristics.

KEY TERMS

80/20 rule, 266	Doppelgänger brand image, 252	Personality traits, 250
AIOs, 266	Ego, 244	Pleasure principle, 244
Allocentric, 250	Food culture, 271	PRIZM NE, 272
Animism, 254	Geodemography, 270	Product complementarity, 262
Archetypes, 248	Id, 244	Reality principle, 244
Behavioral targeting, 273	Idiocentric, 250	Superego, 244
Brand personality, 252	Lifestyle, 255	The Values and Lifestyles System
Co-branding strategies, 262	Motivational research, 246	(VALS2), 268
Consumption constellation, 262	Personality, 244	

REVIEW QUESTIONS

1 Describe the id, ego, and superego and tell how they work together according to Freudian theory.

2 What is motivational research? Give an example of a marketing study that used this approach.

3 Describe three personality traits relevant to marketers.

4 Contrast idiocentrics and allocentrics.

5 List three problems with applying trait theory to marketing contexts.

6 Define a brand personality and give two examples.

7 How does lifestyle differ from income?

8 What is the basic philosophy behind a lifestyle marketing strategy?

9 Define psychographics, and describe three ways marketers can use it.

10 What are three specific kinds of AIOs?

11 What is VALS2™, and how do marketers use it?

12 Alcohol drinkers vary sharply in terms of the number of drinks they may consume, from those who occasionally have one at a cocktail party to regular imbibers. Explain how the 80/20 rule applies to this product category.

CONSUMER BEHAVIOR CHALLENGE

■ DISCUSS

1 What consumption constellation might characterize you and your friends today?

2 Geodemographic techniques assume that people who live in the same neighborhood have other things in common as well. Why do they make this assumption, and how accurate is it?

3 Behavioral targeting techniques give marketers access to a wide range of information about a consumer by telling them what Web sites he visits. Do you believe this "knowledge power" presents any ethical problems with regard to consumers' privacy? Should the government regulate access to such information? Should consumers have the right to limit access to these data?

4 Should organizations or individuals be allowed to create Web sites that advocate potentially harmful practices? Should hate groups such as al Qaeda be allowed to recruit members online? Why or why not?

■ APPLY

5 Construct a brand personality inventory for three different brands within a product category. Ask a small number of consumers to rate each brand on about 10 different personality dimensions. What differences can you identify? Do these "personalities" relate to the advertising and packaging strategies used to differentiate these products?

6 Compile a set of recent ads that attempt to link consumption of a product with a specific lifestyle. How does a marketer usually accomplish this goal?

7 Political campaigns may use psychographic analyses. Conduct research on the marketing strategies a candidate used in a recent, major election. How did the campaign segment voters in terms of values? Can you find evidence that the campaign's communications strategies used this information?

8 Construct separate advertising executions for a cosmetics product that targets the Believer, Achiever, Experiencer, and Maker VALS2™ types. How would the basic appeal differ for each group?

New "types" (or more often, updated versions of old types) emerge from popular culture on a regular basis, whether they are shredders, tuners, or geeks. In recent years, for example, some analysts identify the resurrection of the *hipster*. One source describes a person who follows this lifestyle as someone with a "complicated" hairstyle (dyed black or white-blonde) who reads *Nylon* magazine; listens to indie rock; majored in art or writing; drinks Pabst Blue Ribbon beer; wears tight black pants, scarves, and ironic T-shirts; and is addicted to coffee and cigarettes—and denies being a hipster![90] How valid is this lifestyle type in your area? Can you identify people who belong to it or to a similar group?

9 Using media that targets college students, construct a consumption constellation for this social role. What set of products, activities, and interests tend to appear in advertisements depicting "typical" college students? How realistic is this constellation?

10 Extreme sports. You Tube. Blogging. Veganism. Can you predict what will be "hot" in the near future? Identify a lifestyle trend that is just surfacing in your universe. Describe this trend in detail, and justify your prediction. What specific styles or products are part of this trend?

Case Study

THE MAGIC OF IPOD

MP3 players are all the rage. It's no surprise then that the list of manufacturers offering these pint-sized musical powerhouses continues to grow: Microsoft, Samsung, Creative, Sony, Toshiba . . . all have their own versions. And yet Apple, with its line of iPods, continues to dominate this segment. As of April 2007, the company had sold 100 million iPod units. According to Apple's projections, it should surpass Sony's magical sales mark of 309 million Walkman/Discman players by the year 2009, less than eight years after the first iPod went on sale. Apple's share of the MP3 player market continues to hold at around 70 percent.

Why does Apple still run over the competition? One could say that it is because the iPods are technologically superior. And yet new offerings from other companies offer more features at lower prices. Perhaps iPod's commanding lead is due to greater flexibility and compatibility with online music services? That's not likely either, since devices from other companies are compatible with various online music stores, while the iPod only works with Apple's iTunes Store.

The hysteria surrounding the iPod hints that the answer to this question perhaps isn't so rational. Whether they intended to or not, the folks at Apple have created a product that has achieved cult status. The Apple version of the MP3 player is instantly recognizable. It sports a svelte design with rounded edges, circles as control buttons, and distinctive white earbud headphones. No one will mistake an iPod for some other brand. Danika Cleary, a senior marketing manager for Apple, guesses that this artsy look and feel have been a factor in its success. She explains, "Users kind of covet it, in a way. We've seen people caress them."

Caress them? As though they are alive? Maybe that explains why some people even dress their iPods. Devoted users fit their tiny round music boxes with everything from socks and mohair slipcovers to "hoodie" sweatshirts and stick-on tattoos. It's not just enough to have the product anymore. Accessorizing the iPod has become a major trend fueled by a cottage industry of companies that make over 400 supporting products. Style items make up a big chunk of that total. You can even buy iPod cases from Louis Vuitton or Dior Homme for $265—more than several iPod models cost.

From dressing an iPod in Louis Vuitton apparel, it may not be so big a step to believing that the device has its own tiny little mind. Maybe that's why some of us actually name their iPods. That's right, somewhere out there, there are iPods answering to "Steve," "Jaime," and "Gerald." One household with two units has named them "Bert" and "Ernie." "People attribute all sorts of personalities to their iPods," says Cleary. "I've heard many stories of people who think their iPods have certain preferences in music."

If iPods have assumed these brand personalities, then we shouldn't be surprised when they become part of social networks. *Pod-poaching* (swapping iPods with friends, co-workers, and other acquaintances) has become quite popular, especially in New York and Los Angeles. There is one group of 10 employees who work at the Treasury Board. Each Friday, they convene in a boardroom and randomly swap their iPods for the weekend in order to check out each other's tunes and playlists. This practice even occurs between total strangers (when people call it "podjacking").

Apple has indeed achieved something almost all brands can only aspire to. It has a product with a brand image so strong that competitors find it almost impossible to gain ground. But beyond that, Apple has achieved something it may have never anticipated. The company created a product that is having culture-shifting effects and is changing the way people listen to music. And with Apple's addition of the iPhone and iTouch to the iPod line, it may just end up changing the way that we do a lot of other things as well.

DISCUSSION QUESTIONS

1 Describe the brand personality of the iPod. Compare this personality to other high-tech brands, such as Nokia cellphones.

2 According to the information in this case, do iPod users seem to have a unique lifestyle? Describe it. Discuss the changes that iPod has had on music-listening lifestyle in general.

Sources: Nick Wingfield, "Apple Price Cut on New iPhone Shakes Investors," *Wall Street Journal* (September 6, 2007): A1; Mike Musgrove, "Apple's iPod Still Calls the Tune," *Washington Post* (May 30, 2007): D8; James Hebert, "Passionate Owners of Apple's Digital Music Player Snap up a Plethora of Accessories," *San Diego Union-Tribune* (March 7, 2005): D1; Julie Oliver, "The Joy Unit's Faithful: Most Shuffle. Some Swap. All Feel a Happy Glow When They use Their Oh-So-Stylish, High-Capacity Digital Music Players," *Ottawa Citizen*, (October 28, 2004): F3.

NOTES

1. www.wahinesurfing.com, accessed August 15, 2007.
2. For an interesting ethnographic account of skydiving as a voluntary high-risk consumption activity, see Richard L. Celsi, Randall L. Rose, and Thomas W. Leigh, "An Exploration of High-Risk Leisure Consumption Through Skydiving," *Journal of Consumer Research* 20 (June 1993): 1–23.
3. www.roxy.com/collections/07/summer/index.aspx, accessed August 15, 2007.
4. See J. Aronoff and J. P. Wilson, *Personality in the Social Process* (Hillsdale, NJ: Erlbaum, 1985); Walter Mischel, *Personality and Assessment* (New York: Wiley, 1968).
5. Ernest Dichter, *A Strategy of Desire* (Garden City, NY: Doubleday, 1960); Ernest Dichter, *The Handbook of Consumer Motivations* (New York: McGraw-Hill, 1964); Jeffrey J. Durgee, "Interpreting Dichter's Interpretations: An Analysis of Consumption Symbolism," in *The Handbook of Consumer Motivations* (unpublished manuscript, Rensselaer Polytechnic Institute, Troy, New York, 1989); Pierre Martineau, *Motivation in Advertising* (New York: McGraw-Hill, 1957).
6. Vance Packard, *The Hidden Persuaders* (New York: D. McKay, 1957).
7. Harold Kassarjian, "Personality and Consumer Behavior: A Review," *Journal of Marketing Research* 8 (November 1971): 409–18.
8. Karen Horney, *Neurosis and Human Growth* (New York: Norton, 1950).
9. Joel B. Cohen, "An Interpersonal Orientation to the Study of Consumer Behavior," *Journal of Marketing Research* 6 (August 1967): 270–78; Pradeep K. Tyagi, "Validation of the CAD Instrument: A Replication," in Richard P. Bagozzi and Alice M. Tybout, eds., *Advances in Consumer Research* 10 (Ann Arbor, MI: Association for Consumer Research, 1983): 112–14.
10. For a comprehensive review of classic perspectives on personality theory, see Calvin S. Hall and Gardner Lindzey, *Theories of Personality*, 2nd ed. (New York: Wiley, 1970).
11. See Carl G. Jung, "The Archetypes and the Collective Unconscious," in H. Read, M. Fordham, and G. Adler, eds., *Collected Works*, vol. 9, part 1 (Princeton, NJ: Princeton University Press, 1959).
12. This material was contributed by Rebecca H. Holman, senior vice president and director, Consumer Knowledge Structures, The Knowledge Group, Young & Rubicam Brands, July 2005.
13. Jarunee Taemsamran and Charoen Kittikanya, "Unlocking the 'Life Code,'" *Bangkok Post* (December 31, 2002): 6.
14. For a recent application of trait theory, cf. Adam Duhachek and Dawn Iacobucci, "Consumer Personality and Coping: Testing Rival Theories of Process," *Journal of Consumer Psychology* 15, no. 1, (2005): 52–63.
15. S. Christian Wheeler, Richard E. Petty, and George Y. Bizer, "Self-Schema Matching and Attitude Change: Situational and Dispositional Determinants of Message Elaboration," *Journal of Consumer Research* 31 (March, 2005): 787–97.
16. Linda L. Price and Nancy Ridgway, "Development of a Scale to Measure Innovativeness," in Richard P. Bagozzi and Alice M. Tybout, eds., *Advances in Consumer Research* 10 (Ann Arbor, MI: Association for Consumer Research, 1983): 679–84; Russell W. Belk, "Three Scales to Measure Constructs Related to Materialism: Reliability, Validity, and Relationships to Measures of Happiness," in Thomas C. Kinnear, ed., *Advances in Consumer Research* 11 (Ann Arbor, MI: Association for Consumer Research, 1984): 291; Mark Snyder, "Self-Monitoring Processes," in Leonard Berkowitz, ed., *Advances in Experimental Social Psychology* (New York: Academic Press, 1979), 85–128; Gordon R. Foxall and Ronald E. Goldsmith, "Personality and Consumer Research: Another Look," *Journal of the Market Research Society* 30, no. 2 (1988): 111–25; Ronald E. Goldsmith and Charles F. Hofacker, "Measuring Consumer Innovativeness," *Journal of the Academy of Marketing Science* 19, no. 3 (1991): 209–21; Curtis P. Haugtvedt, Richard E. Petty, and John T. Cacioppo, "Need for Cognition and Advertising: Understanding the Role of Personality Variables in Consumer Behavior," *Journal of Consumer Psychology* 1, no. 3 (1992): 239–60.
17. John L. Lastovicka, Lance A. Bettencourt, Renee Shaw Hughner, and Ronald J. Kuntze, "Lifestyle of the Tight and Frugal: Theory and Measurement," *Journal of Consumer Research* 26 (June 1999): 85–98.
18. David Reisman, *The Lonely Crowd: A Study of the Changing American Character* (New Haven, CT: Yale University Press, 1969).
19. Kelly Tepper Tian, William O. Bearden, and Gary L. Hunter, "Consumers' Need for Uniqueness: Scale Development and Validation," *Journal of Consumer Research* 28 (June 2001): 50–66.
20. Bennett Courtney, "Robotic Voices Designed to Manipulate," *Psychology Today* (January–February 2002): 20.
21. Mohan J. Dutta-Bergman and William D. Wells, "The Values and Lifestyles of Idiocentrics and Allocentrics in an Individualist Culture: A Descriptive Approach," *Journal of Consumer Psychology* 12 (March 2002): 231–42.
22. Jacob Jacoby, "Personality and Consumer Behavior: How Not to Find Relationships," in *Purdue Papers in Consumer Psychology*, no. 102 (Lafayette, IN: Purdue University, 1969); Harold H. Kassarjian and Mary Jane Sheffet, "Personality and Consumer Behavior: An Update," in Harold H. Kassarjian and Thomas S. Robertson, eds., *Perspectives in Consumer Behavior*, 4th ed. (Glenview, IL: Scott, Foresman, 1991): 291–353; John Lastovicka and Erich Joachimsthaler, "Improving the Detection of Personality Behavior Relationships in Consumer Research," *Journal of Consumer Research* 14 (March 1988): 583–87. For an approach that ties the notion of personality more directly to marketing issues, see Jennifer L. Aaker, "Dimensions of Brand Personality," *Journal of Marketing Research* 34 (August 1997): 347–57.
23. See Girish N. Punj and David W. Stewart, "An Interaction Framework of Consumer Decision-Making," *Journal of Consumer Research* 10 (September 1983): 181–96.
24. J. F. Allsopp, "The Distribution of On-Licence Beer and Cider Consumption and Its Personality Determinants among Young Men," *European Journal of Marketing* 20, no. 3 (1986): 44–62; Gordon R. Foxall and Ronald E. Goldsmith, "Personality and Consumer Research: Another Look," *Journal of the Market Research Society* 30, no. 2 (April 1988): 111–25.
25. Thomas Hine, "Why We Buy: The Silent Persuasion of Boxes, Bottles, Cans, and Tubes," *Worth* (May 1995): 78–83.
26. Yongjun Sung and Spencer F. Tinkham, "Brand Personality Structures in the United States and Korea: Common and Culture-Specific Factors," *Journal of Consumer Psychology* 15, no. 4 (2005): 334–50; Beverly T. Venable, Gregory M. Rose, Victoria D. Bush, and Faye W. Gilbert, "The Role of Brand Personality in Charitable Giving: An Assessment and Validation, *Journal of the Academy of Marketing Science* 33 (July 2005): 295–312.
27. Craig J. Thompson, Aric Rindfleisch, and Zeynep Arsel, "Emotional Branding and the Strategic Value of the Doppelganger Brand Image," *Journal of Marketing* 70, no. 1 (2006): 50.
28. Kevin L. Keller, "Conceptualization, Measuring, and Managing Customer-Based Brand Equity," *Journal of Marketing* 57 (January 1993): 1–22.
29. Linda Keslar, "What's in a Name?" *Individual Investor* (April 1999): 101–2.
30. Eric Pfanner, "Mocking an Olympics Logo, but Loving the Attention," available from www.nytimes.com, accessed June 12, 2007.
31. Kathryn Kranhold, "Agencies Beef Up Brand Research to Identify Consumer Preferences," *Wall Street Journal Interactive Edition* (March 9, 2000).
32. Aaker, "Dimensions of Brand Personality."
33. Bradley Johnson, "They All Have Half-Baked Ideas," *Advertising Age* (May 12, 1997): 8.
34. Tim Triplett, "Brand Personality Must Be Managed or It Will Assume a Life of Its Own," *Marketing News* (May 9, 1994): 9.
35. Seth Stevenson, "How to Beat Nike," *New York Times on the Web* (January 5, 2003).
36. Susan Fournier, "Consumers and Their Brands: Developing Relationship Theory in Consumer Research," *Journal of Consumer Research* 24, no. 4 (March 1998): 343–73.
37. Rebecca Piirto Heath, "The Frontiers of Psychographics," *American Demographics* (July 1996): 38–43.
38. Gabriel Kahn, "Philips Blitzes Asian Market as It Strives to Become Hip," *Wall Street Journal Online* (August 1, 2002).
39. Erin White, "Volvo Sheds Safe Image for New, Dangerous Ads," *Wall Street Journal Online* (June 14, 2002).
40. Benjamin D. Zablocki and Rosabeth Moss Kanter, "The Differentiation of Life-Styles," *Annual Review of Sociology* (1976): 269–97.
41. Mary Twe Douglas and Baron C. Isherwood, *The World of Goods* (New York: Basic Books, 1979).
42. Zablocki and Kanter, "The Differentiation of Life-Styles."
43. "The Niche's the Thing," *American Demographics* (February 2000): 22.
44. Karl Greenberg, "World Wrestling Brands Bliss Beverages, Launching Integrated Marketing Effort," *Marketing Daily*, available from www.mediapost.com, accessed May 16, 2007.
45. Richard A. Peterson, "Revitalizing the Culture Concept," *Annual Review of Sociology* 5 (1979): 137–66.

46. "BET Alliance Targets Urban Consumer, *DSN Retailing Today* (September 12, 2005), available from http://findarticles.com/p/articles/mi_m0FNP/is_17_44/ai_n15627850, accessed July 6, 2007.

47. Erik Sass, "Goodbye, Urban Consumer. Hello, Urban Hustler," *Marketing Daily*, available from www.mediapost.com, accessed June 5, 2007.

48. "Hate Group Web Sites on the Rise," CNN.com (February 23, 1999); www.resist.com/, accessed June 3, 2005.

49. Abdul Hameed Bakier, "Islamist Websites Succeed in Recruiting Muslims for *Jihad*," *The Jamestown Foundation*, Volume 3, Issue 46 (November 28, 2006), available from http://jamestown.org/terrorism/news/article.php?articleid=2370219, accessed July 7, 2007.

50. Stephanie Kang and Ethan Smith, "Music for Runners, Volume 2: Nike Releases Second Recording," *Wall Street Journal* (October 23, 2006): B6; http://nikeplus.nike.com/nikeplus/#tutorials, accessed July 6, 2007.

51. Jonathan Birchall, "Just Do It, Marketers Say: Nike, Petsmart and Other Companies Are Trying to Sell their Brands by Inviting Consumers to Take Part in Activities Linked to the Product or Service," *LA Times* (April 30, 2007), available from www.latimes.com/business/la-ft-brands30apr30, accessed April 30, 2007.

52. Stacy Meichtry "At Versace, Fashion Is So Last Century: CEO Moves Past Clothes, Emphasizes Lifestyle Goods; Donatella Takes a Step Back," *Wall Street Journal* (June 4, 2007): B1.

53. Ray A. Smith, "At Levi Strauss, Dockers Are In—Rise in Sales Is Bright Spot, as Company Tries to Mend Its Jeans," *Wall Street Journal* (February 14, 2007): A14.

54. Julie Bosman, "Selling Literature to Go with Your Lifestyle," *New York Times on the Web* (November 2, 2006).

55. William Leiss, Stephen Kline, and Sut Jhally, *Social Communication in Advertising* (Toronto: Methuen, 1986).

56. Douglas and Isherwood, *The World of Goods*, quoted on pp. 72–73.

57. Christopher K. Hsee and France Leclerc, "Will Products Look More Attractive When Presented Separately or Together?" *Journal of Consumer Research* 25 (September 1998): 175–86.

58. Nina M. Lentini, "Wendy's, P&G Couple to Offer Folgers Coffee for Breakfast," *Marketing Daily*, available from www.mediapost.com, accessed May 21, 2007.

59. Brian Steinberg, "Whose Ad Is This Anyway? Agencies Use Brand Icons to Promote Other Products; Cheaper Than Zeta-Jones," *Wall Street Journal on the Web* (December 4, 2003).

60. Michael R. Solomon, "The Role of Products as Social Stimuli: A Symbolic Interactionism Perspective," *Journal of Consumer Research* 10 (December 1983): 319–29.

61. Michael R. Solomon and Henry Assael, "The Forest or the Trees? A *Gestalt* Approach to Symbolic Consumption," in Jean Umiker-Sebeok, ed., *Marketing and Semiotics: New Directions in the Study of Signs for Sale* (Berlin: Mouton de Gruyter, 1988), 189–218; Michael R. Solomon, "Mapping Product Constellations: A Social Categorization Approach to Symbolic Consumption," *Psychology & Marketing* 5, no. 3 (1988): 233–58; see also Stephen C. Cosmas, "Life Styles and Consumption Patterns," *Journal of Consumer Research* 8, no. 4 (March 1982): 453–55.

62. Russell W. Belk, "Yuppies as Arbiters of the Emerging Consumption Style," in Richard J. Lutz, ed., *Advances in Consumer Research* 13 (Provo, UT: Association for Consumer Research, 1986): 514–19.

63. Danny Hakim, "Cadillac, Too, Shifting Focus to Trucks," *New York Times on the Web* (December 21, 2001).

64. Seth Stevenson, "How to Beat Nike," *New York Times on the Web* (January 5, 2003).

65. See Lewis Alpert and Ronald Gatty, "Product Positioning by Behavioral Life Styles," *Journal of Marketing* 33 (April 1969): 65–69; Emanuel H. Demby, "Psychographics Revisited: The Birth of a Technique," *Marketing News* (January 2, 1989): 21; William D. Wells, "Backward Segmentation," in Johan Arndt, ed., *Insights into Consumer Behavior* (Boston: Allyn & Bacon, 1968): 85–100.

66. Gary McWilliams, "Analyzing Customers, Best Buy Decides Not All Are Welcome; Retailer Aims to Outsmart Dogged Bargain-Hunters, and Coddle Big Spenders Looking for 'Barrys' and 'Jills'", *Wall Street Journal* (November 8, 2004): A1; Joshua Freed, "Best Buy Stores Adapting to Help Customers They Serve," *Montgomery Advertiser* (May 23, 2004): 31.

67. Brian Wansink and S. Park, "Accounting for Taste: Prototypes that Predict Preference," *Journal of Database Marketing* (2000): 308–20, as described in Norman Bradburn, Seymour Sudman, and Brian Wansink, eds., *Asking Questions* (New York: Jossey-Bass, 2004).

68. William D. Wells and Douglas J. Tigert, "Activities, Interests, and Opinions," *Journal of Advertising Research* 11 (August 1971): 27.

69. Ian Pearson, "Social Studies: Psychographics in Advertising," *Canadian Business* (December 1985): 67.

70. Piirto Heath, "Psychographics: 'Q'est-ce que c'est'?"]

71. Alfred S. Boote, "Psychographics: Mind over Matter," *American Demographics* (April 1980): 26–29; William D. Wells, "Psychographics: A Critical Review," *Journal of Marketing Research* 12 (May 1975): 196–213.

72. Joseph T. Plummer, "The Concept and Application of Life Style Segmentation," *Journal of Marketing* 38 (January 1974): 33–37.

73. Doris Hajewski, "Halted Poll Hits Close to Home: Target Ends Survey That Asks Shoppers Personal Questions," *Milwaukee Journal Sentinel Online* (June 11, 2007), available from www.jsonline.com/story/index.aspx?id=617780, accessed June 11, 2007.

74. Berkeley Rice, "The Selling of Lifestyles," *Psychology Today* (March 1988): 46.

75. John L. Lastovicka, John P. Murry, Erich A. Joachimsthaler, Gurav Bhalla, and Jim Scheurich, "A Lifestyle Typology to Model Young Male Drinking and Driving," *Journal of Consumer Research* 14 (September 1987): 257–63.

76. Anthony Ramirez, "New Cigarettes Raising Issue of Target Market," *New York Times* (February 18, 1990): 28.

77. Martha Farnsworth Riche, "VALS 2," *American Demographics* (July 1989): 25. Additional information provided by William D. Guns, Director, Business Intelligence Center, SRI Consulting, Inc., personal communication, May 1997.

78. Rebecca Piirto Heath, "You Can Buy a Thrill: Chasing the Ultimate Rush," *American Demographics* (June 1997): 47–51.

79. Some of this section is adapted from material presented in Michael R. Solomon, Gary Bamossy, and Søren Askegaard, *Consumer Behaviour: A European Perspective*, 2nd ed. (London: Prentice Hall Europe, 2002).

80. "Euromonitor," *European Marketing Data and Statistics* (1997): 328–31.

81. Deborah Ball, Sarah Ellison, Janet Adamy, and Geoffrey A. Fowler, "Recipes without Borders? Big Food Marketers Adjust Levels of Fat and Sodium to Fit Regulations, Tastes," *Wall Street Journal* (August 18, 2004): B1; Søren Askegaard and Tage Koed Madsen, "The Local and the Global: Patterns of Homogeneity and Heterogeneity in European Food Cultures," *International Business Review* 7, 6, (1999): 549–68; Michael R. Solomon, Suzanne C. Beckmann, and Basil G. Englis, "Exploring and Understanding of Cultural Meaning Systems: Visualizing the Underlying Meaning Structure of Brands," presented at a conference, Branding: Activating & Engaging Cultural Meaning Systems, Innsbruck, Austria, May 2003.

82. Michael J. Weiss, *The Clustering of America* (New York: Harper & Row, 1988).

83. Bob Minzesheimer, "You Are What You Zip," *Los Angeles Times* (November 1984): 175.

84. Christina Del Valle, "They Know Where You Live and How You Buy," *BusinessWeek* (February 7, 1994): 89; www.claritas.com, accessed June 3, 2005.

85. "Consumers Willing to Trade Off Privacy for Electronic Personalization," available from www.mediapost.com, accessed January 23, 2007.

86. Aaron O. Patrick, "Microsoft Ad Push Is All about You: 'Behavioral Targeting' Aims to Use Customer Preferences to Hone Marketing Pitches," *Wall Street Journal* (December 26, 2006): B3; Brian Steinberg, "Next Up on Fox: Ads That Can Change Pitch," *Wall Street Journal* (April 21, 2005): B1; Bob Tedeschi, "Every Click You Make, They'll Be Watching You," *New York Times Online* (April 3, 2006); David Kesmodel, "Marketers Push Online Ads Based on Your Surfing Habits," *Wall Street Journal on the Web* (April 5, 2005).

87. Sarah McBride and Vauhini Vara, "We Know What You Ought to Be Watching This Summer," *Wall Street Journal* (July 31, 2007): D1

88. Associated Press, "MySpace Launches Targeted Ad Program," *New York Times Online* (September 18, 2007), accessed September 18, 2007; Vauhini Vara, "Facebook Gets Personal with Ad Targeting Plan," *Wall Street Journal* (August 23, 2007): B1.

89. Louise Story, "Company Will Monitor Phone Calls to Tailor Ads," *New York Times Online* (September 24, 2007), accessed September 24, 2007.

90. Robert Lanham,. *The Hipster Handbook* (New York: Anchor, 2003); www.urbandictionary.com/define.php?term=hipster, accessed July 5, 2007.

Attitudes

CHAPTER 7

Chapter Objectives

When you finish this chapter you should understand why:

- It's important for consumer researchers to understand the nature and power of attitudes.

- Attitudes are more complex than they first appear.

- We form attitudes in several ways.

- A need to maintain consistency among all of our attitudinal components motivates us to alter one or more of them.

- We use attitude models to identify specific components and combine them to predict a consumer's overall attitude toward a product or brand.

t's a lazy Tuesday night, and Jan, Terri, and Nancy are hanging out at Nancy's apartment doing some channel surfing. Jan clicks to ESPN and the three friends see that the U.S. Women's Open is on. Jan has been a golf fan for as long as she can remember and Annika Sorenstam is one of her role models. Nancy's a teacher, so she enjoys the emotional contests in the Open, where up-and-comers such as Cristie KerrMichelle Wie and Jeong Jang slug it out on the greens.[1] Terri however, doesn't know a bunker shot from a birdie. Golf doesn't really ring her chimes—but as long as she gets to hang out with her girlfriends, she doesn't really care if they watch golf or SpongeBob SquarePants.

The Power of Attitudes

Jan is just the kind of fan golfing executives hope will turn women's golf into an ongoing source of sports fanaticism. Although avid golfer Mary Queen of Scots popularized the game in the 1500s, today the golf industry is still waking up to the potential of attracting more women to the sport, even though there's an old saying that golf is actually an acronym for Gentlemen Only, Ladies Forbidden. The recent flap at the Master's Tournament in Augusta, Georgia, which is a club that doesn't admit women hosts, didn't help matters. Still, many golf destinations, such as Pinehurst in North Carolina, work hard to cater to women when they add kid-friendly family packages, spruce up their golfing apparel collections, and add spa facilities for women who would rather retreat to the clubhouse for a soothing facial than drink beer in the bar.[2] To score big in sports, it's all a question of attitudes.

People use the term *attitude* widely. Someone might ask you, "What is your attitude toward abortion?" A parent might scold, "Young man, I don't like your attitude." Some bars even euphemistically refer to happy hour as "an attitude adjustment period." For our purposes, though, an **attitude** is a lasting, general evaluation of people (including oneself), objects, advertisements, or issues.[3] We call anything toward which one has an attitude an **attitude object** (A_o).

An attitude is lasting because it tends to endure over time. It is general because it applies to more than a momentary event, such as hearing a loud noise, though you might, over time, develop a negative attitude toward all loud noises. Consumers have attitudes toward a wide range of attitude objects, from very product-specific behaviors (e.g., using Crest toothpaste rather than Colgate) to more general, consumption-related behaviors (e.g., how often you should brush your teeth). Attitudes help to determine whom you choose to date, what music you listen to, whether you will recycle aluminum cans, or whether you choose to become a consumer researcher for a living.

In this chapter we'll consider the contents of an attitude, how we form attitudes, and how we measure them. We will also review some of the surprisingly complex relationships between attitudes and behavior. In the next chapter, we'll take a closer look at how marketers can change these attitudes.

 The Functions of Attitudes

Psychologist Daniel Katz developed the **functional theory of attitudes** to explain how attitudes facilitate social behavior.[4] According to this pragmatic approach, attitudes exist *because* they serve some function for the person. That is, they are determined by a person's motives. Consumers who expect that they will need to deal with similar situations at a future time will be more likely to start forming attitudes in anticipation of this event.[5] Two people can each have an attitude toward some object for very different reasons. As a result, it can be helpful for a marketer to know *why* an attitude is held before attempting to change it. The following are attitude functions that Katz identified:

● **Utilitarian function:** The utilitarian function relates to the basic principles of reward and punishment. We develop some attitudes toward products simply on the basis of whether these products provide pleasure or pain. If a person likes the taste of a cheeseburger, that person will develop a positive attitude toward cheeseburgers. Ads that stress straightforward product benefits (e.g., you should drink Diet Coke "just for the taste of it") appeal to the utilitarian function.

● **Value-expressive function:** Attitudes that perform a value-expressive function express the consumer's central values or self-concept. A person forms a product attitude not because of its objective benefits, but because of what the product says about him as a person (e.g., "What sort of man reads *Playboy*?"). Value-expressive attitudes are highly relevant to the lifestyle analyses we discussed in Chapter 6, which consider how consumers cultivate a cluster of activities, interests, and opinions to express a particular social identity.

- **Ego-defensive function:** Attitudes we form to protect ourselves either from external threats or internal feelings perform an ego-defensive function. An early marketing study indicated that housewives in the 1950s resisted the use of instant coffee because it threatened their conception of themselves as capable homemakers.[6] Products that promise to help a man project a "macho" image (e.g., Marlboro cigarettes) may be appealing to his insecurities about his masculinity. Another example is deodorant campaigns that stress the dire, embarrassing consequences of being caught with underarm odor in public.
- **Knowledge function:** We form some attitudes because of need for order, structure, or meaning. This need is often present when a person is in an ambiguous situation or is confronted with a new product (e.g., "Bayer wants you to know about pain relievers").

An attitude can serve more than one function, but in many cases a particular one will be dominant. By identifying the dominant function a product serves for consumers—what *benefits* it provides—marketers can emphasize these benefits in their communications and packaging. Ads relevant to the function prompt more favorable thoughts about what is being marketed and can result in a heightened preference for both the ad and the product.

One study determined that for most people coffee serves more of a utilitarian function than a value-expressive function. As a consequence, subjects responded more positively to copy for a (fictitious) coffee that read, "The delicious, hearty flavor and aroma of Sterling Blend coffee comes from a blend of the freshest coffee beans" (utilitarian appeal) than they did to "The coffee you drink says something about the type of person you are. It can reveal your rare, discriminating taste" (value-expressive function).[7] However, it's worth noting that clever marketers can change these priorities, as Starbucks certainly has for many coffee drinkers.

As we saw in the experiences of the three women watching a golf tournament, the importance of an attitude object may differ quite a bit for different people. Understanding the attitude's centrality to an individual and to others who share similar characteristics can be useful to marketers who are trying to devise strategies that will appeal to different customer segments. A study of football game attendance illustrates that varying levels of commitment result in different fan "profiles."[8] The study identified three distinct clusters of fans:[9]

1 One cluster consisted of the real die-hard fans like Jan who were highly committed to their team and who displayed an enduring love of the game. To reach these fans, the researchers recommend that sports marketers should focus on providing them with greater sports knowledge and relate their attendance to their personal goals and values.

2 A second cluster was like Nancy—their attitudes were based on the unique, self-expressive experience provided by the game. They enjoy the stimulation of cheering for a favorite player and the drama of the competition itself. They are more likely to be "brand switchers" who are fair-weather fans, shifting allegiances when the home team no longer provides the thrills they need. This segment can be appealed to by publicizing aspects of the visiting teams, such as advertising the appearance of stars who are likely to give the fans a game they will remember.

3 A third cluster was like Terri—they were looking for camaraderie above all. These consumers attend games primarily to take part in small-group activities that accompany the event. Marketers could appeal to this cluster by providing improved peripheral benefits, such as making it easier for groups to meet at the stadium and improving parking.

Sports fans can be divided into clusters based on the type and intensity of attitudes they have toward the game and their team. In which cluster would you guess these fans belong?

THE ABC MODEL OF ATTITUDES

An attitude has three components: affect, behavior, and cognition. **Affect** is how a consumer *feels* about an attitude object. **Behavior** refers to his intentions to *take action* about it (but, as we will discuss at a later point, an intention does not always result in an actual behavior). **Cognition** is what he *believes* to be true about the attitude object. You can remember these three components of an attitude as the **ABC model of attitudes**.

The ABC model emphasizes the interrelationships among knowing, feeling, and doing. We can't determine consumers' attitudes toward a product simply by identifying their beliefs about it. For example, a researcher may find that shoppers "know" a particular camcorder has an 8:1 power zoom lens, auto focus, and a flying erase head, but simply knowing this doesn't indicate whether they feel these attributes are good, bad, or irrelevant, or whether they would actually buy the camcorder.

All three components of an attitude are important, but their relative importance varies depending on a consumer's level of motivation with regard to the attitude object, whether they are light or heavy users, and so on.[9]

The differences in athletic interests among the three women in Nancy's apartment illustrate how a person combines these elements in different ways to create an attitude. Attitude researchers developed the concept of a **hierarchy of effects** to explain the relative impact of the three components. Each hierarchy specifies that a fixed sequence of steps occurs en route to an attitude. Figure 7.1 summarizes these three different hierarchies.

The Standard Learning Hierarchy

Jan's positive attitude toward women's golf closely resembles the process by which we construct most attitudes. In this sequence, a person like Jan approaches a product decision as a problem-solving process. First, she forms beliefs about a product by

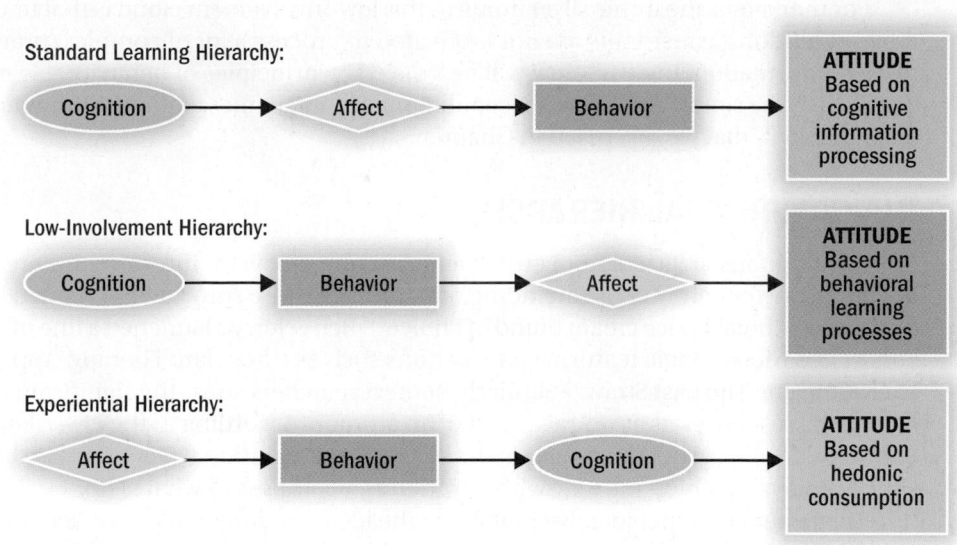

Standard Learning Hierarchy:

Cognition → Affect → Behavior → **ATTITUDE** Based on cognitive information processing

Low-Involvement Hierarchy:

Cognition → Behavior → Affect → **ATTITUDE** Based on behavioral learning processes

Experiential Hierarchy:

Affect → Behavior → Cognition → **ATTITUDE** Based on hedonic consumption

accumulating knowledge (*beliefs*) regarding relevant attributes. Next, she evaluates these beliefs and forms a feeling about the product (*affect*).[10] Over time, Jan assembled information about the sport, began to recognize the players, and learned which were superior to others. Finally, based on this evaluation, she engages in a relevant behavior, such as buying the product or supporting a particular team by wearing its jersey. This careful choice process often results in the type of loyalty Jan displays; she "bonds" with the product over time and it's hard to persuade her to experiment with other brands. The *standard learning hierarchy* assumes that a consumer is highly involved in making a purchase decision.[11] The person is motivated to seek out a lot of information, carefully weigh alternatives, and come to a thoughtful decision.

THE LOW-INVOLVEMENT HIERARCHY

In contrast to Jan, Nancy's interest in the attitude object (women's golf) is at best lukewarm. She is not particularly knowledgeable about the sport, and she may have an emotional response to an exciting game but not to a specific team. Nancy is typical of a consumer who forms an attitude via the *low-involvement hierarchy of effects*. In this sequence, initially she does not have a strong preference for one brand over another, but instead she acts on the basis of limited knowledge and then she forms an evaluation only *after* she has bought the product.[12] The attitude is likely to come about through behavioral learning; good or bad experiences reinforce her initial choice. Nancy will probably be more likely to tune in to future tournaments if they continue to come down to the wire like the Women's Open she was watching.

The possibility that consumers simply don't care enough about many decisions to carefully assemble a set of product beliefs and then evaluate them is important. This implies that all of our concern about influencing beliefs and carefully communicating information about product attributes often may be wasted. Consumers aren't necessarily going to pay attention anyway; they are more likely to respond to simple stimulus–response connections when they make purchase decisions. For example, a consumer choosing among paper towels might remember that "Bounty is the quicker picker-upper" rather than bothering to systematically compare all of the brands on the shelf.

The notion of consumers' low involvement is a bitter pill for some marketers to swallow. Who wants to admit that what they market is not very important or involving? A brand manager for, say, a brand of bubble gum or cat food may find it hard to believe that consumers don't put that much thought into purchasing her product because she herself spends many of her waking (and perhaps sleeping) hours thinking about it.

For marketers, the ironic silver lining to this low-involvement cloud is that under these conditions, consumers are not motivated to process a lot of complex, brand-related information. Instead, they will be swayed by principles of behavioral learning, such as the simple responses that conditioned brand names or point-of-purchase displays elicit, that we discussed in Chapter 3.

THE EXPERIENTIAL HIERARCHY

After getting tons of letters from customers describing how their favorite ice cream flavors relate to their moods (including one from an entire sorority that named the brand as its "breakup ice cream brand of choice"), Ben & Jerry's launched a line of flavors called Mood Magic featuring concoctions such as Chocolate Therapy, Apple-y Ever After, and The Last Straw.[13] Similarly, some researchers stress the significance of emotional responses as a central aspect of an attitude. According to the *experiential hierarchy of effects*, consumers act on the basis of their emotional reactions. So, Terri simply enjoys watching the telly with her friends, regardless of what is on.

The experiential perspective highlights the idea that intangible product attributes, such as package design, advertising, brand names, and the nature of the setting in which the experience occurs, can help shape our attitudes toward a brand. We may base these reactions on hedonic motivations, such as whether using the product is exciting (like the Nintendo Wii). Even the emotions the communicator expresses have an impact. A smile is infectious; in a process we term *emotional contagion*, messages happy people deliver enhance our attitude toward the product.[14] Numerous studies indicate that the mood a person is in when she is exposed to a marketing message influences how she will process the ad, the likelihood that she will remember the information she sees, and how she will feel about the advertised item and related products in the future.[15]

One important debate about the experiential hierarchy concerns the independence of cognition and affect. On the one hand, the *cognitive-affective* model argues that an affective judgment is but the last step in a series of cognitive processes. Earlier steps include the sensory registration of stimuli and retrieving meaningful information from memory to categorize these stimuli.[16]

On the other hand, the *independence hypothesis* takes the position that affect and cognition involve two separate, partially independent systems; affective responses do not always require prior cognitions.[17] A number one song may possess the same attributes as many other songs (e.g., dominant bass guitar, raspy vocals, persistent downbeat), but beliefs about these attributes cannot explain why one song becomes a classic, whereas another that shares the same characteristics winds up in the bargain bin at the local record store (but note that the Music Genome Project [pandora.com], which catalogs song dimensions you like and suggests new music to you on that basis, assumes the opposite!).[18] The independence hypothesis does not eliminate the role of cognition in experience. It simply balances this traditional, rational emphasis on calculated decision making by paying more attention to the impact of aesthetic, subjective experience. This type of holistic processing is more likely to occur when consumers perceive the product as primarily expressive or as delivering sensory pleasure rather than utilitarian benefits.[19]

PRODUCT ATTITUDES DON'T TELL THE WHOLE STORY

Marketers who want to understand consumers' attitudes have to contend with an even more complex issue: In decision-making situations, people form attitudes toward objects other than the product itself that also influence the brands they choose. One additional factor they must consider is the attitude toward the act of buying in general—as we'll see later in this chapter, sometimes people simply are reluctant, embarrassed, or just plain too lazy to expend the effort to actually obtain a desired product or service.

ATTITUDE TOWARD THE ADVERTISEMENT

Our evaluation of a product's advertising influences how we feel about the product itself. Indeed, at times we judge a product solely by how an ad depicts it—we don't hesitate to form attitudes toward products we've never even seen in person, much less used.

One special type of attitude object, then, is the marketing message itself. We define the **attitude toward the advertisement (A_{ad})** as a predisposition to respond in a favorable or unfavorable manner to a particular advertising stimulus during a particular exposure occasion. Determinants of A_{ad} include a person's attitude toward the advertiser, how he evaluates the specific ad execution he sees or hears, the mood the ad evokes, and the degree to which the ad affects his level of physiological arousal.[21] A viewer's feelings about the context in which an ad appears can also influence his brand attitudes. For example, if you see a commercial during one of your favorite TV programs, it's quite possible this pairing will boost your attitude toward the advertised brand.[22] The effects that A_{ad} demonstrates emphasizes the potential importance of an ad's entertainment value in the purchase process.[23] If consumers are not able to view an ad again, both belief and attitude confidence about that ad rapidly diminish. This research underscores the need to *pulse,* or frequently repeat advertisements.[24]

ADS HAVE FEELINGS TOO

The feelings an ad generates can directly affect a product attitude, especially if the brand is unfamiliar to you.[25] Commercials can evoke a wide range of emotional responses, from disgust to happiness. These feelings are influenced both by the way the ad appears (i.e., the specific advertising *execution*) and by the consumer's guesses about the advertiser's motives. For example, many advertisers who are trying to craft messages for adolescents and young adults encounter problems because this age group, having grown up in a "marketing society," tends to be skeptical about attempts to get them to buy things.[26] These reactions can in turn influence memory for advertising content.[27]

Researchers identify three key emotional dimensions in commercials: pleasure, arousal, and intimidation.[28] Specific types of feelings an ad generates include the following:[29]

> *Upbeat feelings:* amused, delighted, playful
>
> *Warm feelings:* affectionate, contemplative, hopeful
>
> *Negative feelings:* critical, defiant, offended

 # Forming Attitudes

We all have lots of attitudes, and we don't usually question how we got them. Certainly, you're not born with the conviction that, say, Pepsi is better than Coke, or that alternative music liberates the soul. From where do these attitudes come?

We form an attitude in several different ways, depending on the particular hierarchy of effects that is operating. As we saw in Chapter 3, we can learn about a brand based on classical conditioning, when a marketer repeatedly pairs an attitude object such as the Pepsi name with a catchy jingle ("You're in the Pepsi Generation"). Or an attitude can be formed as the result of instrumental conditioning, when the marketer reinforces consumption of the attitude object (e.g., you take a swig of Pepsi and it quenches your thirst). Or this learning can result from a very complex cognitive process. For example, a teenager may come to model the behavior of friends and media endorsers, such as Beyoncé, who drink Pepsi because they believe that this will allow them to fit in with the desirable lifestyle Pepsi commercials portray.

ALL ATTITUDES ARE NOT CREATED EQUAL

It's important to distinguish among types of attitudes because not all are formed in the same way.[30] For example, a highly brand-loyal consumer such as Jan, the golf fan, has an enduring, deeply held positive attitude toward an attitude object, and it would be difficult to weaken this involvement. However, another woman, such as Nancy, may be a more fickle consumer: She may have a mildly positive attitude toward a product but be quite willing to abandon it when something better comes along. In this section, we'll consider the differences between strongly and weakly held attitudes and briefly review some of the major theoretical perspectives researchers use to explain how attitudes form and relate to other pre-existing attitudes we hold.

LEVELS OF COMMITMENT TO AN ATTITUDE

Consumers vary in their *commitment* to an attitude; the degree of commitment relates to their level of involvement with the attitude object (see Chapter 4).[31] Consumers are more likely to consider brands that engender strong positive attitudes.[32] Let's look at three (increasing) levels of commitment:

- **Compliance**—At the lowest level of involvement, *compliance*, a person forms an attitude because it helps in gaining rewards or avoiding punishments from others. This attitude is very superficial; it is likely to change when others no

CB AS I SEE IT

Professor Joseph Priester
The University of Southern California

Attitudes have played a central role in understanding human behavior since the very beginning of the scientific study of psychology. At the most basic, attitudes are the extent to which one likes or dislikes some object. That object could include a product, a brand, or a service, or it could include a person, a place, an idea, or an ideology. How better to understand what a person is likely to do than to know that person's attitude? How better to change a

person's behavior than by persuasion (that is, to change that person's attitude)?

What I personally find so interesting about the study of attitudes and persuasion is how it has grown, changed, and come into play in so many different areas over time: The hallmark of attitudes and persuasion has been its theoretical evolution. Starting in the 1970s, researchers addressed the questions of when and why attitudes guide behavior, introducing the notion of attitude strength (some attitudes simply are stronger than others). Current issues on attitudes range from such questions as how the confidence one has in one's thoughts influences whether attitudes will guide behavior (a metacognitive attitude perspective) to how a person can possess attitudes of which he or she is unaware (an implicit attitude perspective).

My own research has focused on using attitudes and persuasion to help understand other findings in consumer behavior. For example, the idea that people make choices based on a limited consideration set has long held great appeal. My contribution was to understand how attitudes and attitude strength influence what products are included in a consideration set. I have also spent a great deal of time considering those times when people feel both positive and negative toward an object—attitudinal ambivalence. Ambivalence has quickly become a topic in considering attitudes that is receiving a great deal of attention in both psychology and consumer behavior. As the study of consumer behavior continues to grow, be sure that attitudes and persuasion will continue to be at the center of many interesting and intriguing questions.

Purex
FOR THE TOUGHEST STAINS

Advertisers often need to resort to ceative imagery to capture consumers' attention and build awareness for their clients.

Marketing Pitfall

A high-profile, well-meaning attempt to appeal to deeply held attitudes has had mixed success and aroused some controversy in the process. The (Product) Red campaign that encourages consumers to buy special "Red" versions of products by marketing powerhouses such as The Gap, Apple, and Motorola to benefit the cause of African poverty hasn't produced the results its sponsors, including Bono and Oprah Winfrey, hoped for. By some estimates, the marketing outlay to promote the campaign was as high as $100 million. The amount Red raised to combat poverty: $45 million as of September 2007. This out-of-whack ratio concerns nonprofit watchdogs, cause-marketing experts, and advertising executives because it may spur a backlash against similar cause-marketing efforts that allow corporate partners to profit even they donate money. They wonder if *fashionistas* decked out in Red T-shirts and iPods really are the best way to save a child dying of AIDS in Africa. At buylesscrap.org, which encourages people to give directly to the Global Fund instead of shopping for tragedy, the message is, "Shopping is not a solution. Buy less. Give more." According to one nonprofit marketing expert, "The Red campaign can be a good start or it can be a colossal waste of money, and it all depends on whether this edgy, innovative campaign inspires young people to be better citizens or just gives them an excuse to feel good about themselves while they buy an overpriced item they don't really need."[33]

longer monitor the person's behavior or when another option becomes available. A person may drink Pepsi because the cafeteria sells it, and it is too much trouble to go elsewhere for a Coca-Cola.

- **Identification**—A process of *identification* occurs when a person forms an attitude to conform to another person's or group's expectations. Advertising that depicts the social consequences of choosing some products over others is relying on the tendency of consumers to imitate the behavior of desirable models (more on this in Chapter 11).
- **Internalization**—At a high level of involvement, a consumer *internalizes* deep-seated attitudes and they become part of her value system. These attitudes are very difficult to change because they are so important to the individual. For example, many consumers had strong attitudes toward Coca-Cola and reacted quite negatively when the company attempted to switch to the New Coke formula in the 1980s. This allegiance to Coke was obviously more than a minor preference for these people; the brand had become intertwined with their social identities and took on patriotic and nostalgic properties.

This ad for New York's famous Smith & Wollensky restaurant emphasizes that marketers and others associated with a product or service are often more involved with it than are their customers.

Steak is our life. All we ask is that you make it your lunch.

Smith & Wollensky.
The quintessential New York City steakhouse.
49th St. & 3rd Ave. (212) 753-1530.

Winner of The *Wine Spectator's* 1987 Grand Award.

Marketing Pitfall

In a study of irritating advertising, researchers examined more than 500 primetime network commercials that had registered negative reactions by consumers. The most irritating commercials were for feminine hygiene products, hemorrhoid medication or laxatives, and women's underwear. The researchers identify the following factors as prime offenders:

- The commercial shows a sensitive product (e.g., hemorrhoid medicine) and emphasizes its usage.
- The situation is contrived or overdramatized.
- A person is put down in terms of appearance, knowledge, or sophistication.
- An important relationship, such as a marriage, is threatened.
- There is a graphic demonstration of physical discomfort.
- The commercial created uncomfortable tension because of an argument or an antagonistic character.
- It portrays an unattractive or unsympathetic character.
- It includes a sexually suggestive scene.
- The commercial suffers from poor casting or execution.[34]

THE CONSISTENCY PRINCIPLE

Have you ever heard someone say, "Pepsi is my favorite soft drink. It tastes terrible," or "I love my boyfriend. He's the biggest idiot I've ever met?" Probably not (at least until the couple gets married!); these beliefs or evaluations aren't consistent. According to the **principle of cognitive consistency**, we value harmony among our thoughts, feelings, and behaviors, and a need to maintain uniformity among these elements motivates us. This desire means that, if necessary, we'll change our thoughts, feelings, or behaviors to make them consistent with other experiences. That boyfriend may slip up and act like an idiot occasionally, but usually his girlfriend (eventually) will find a way to forgive him. The consistency principle is an important reminder that we don't form our attitudes in a vacuum. Instead, a big factor is how well they fit with other, related attitudes we already hold.

COGNITIVE DISSONANCE AND HARMONY AMONG ATTITUDES

The theory of cognitive dissonance states that when a person is confronted with inconsistencies among attitudes or behaviors, he will take some action to resolve this "dissonance," perhaps by changing an attitude or modifying a behavior. The theory has important ramifications for attitudes because situations often confront us where there is some conflict between attitudes and behaviors.[35]

Smokers often reduce cognitive dissonance by modifying or minimizing their beliefs about the negative effects of their behavior.

According to the theory, our motivation to reduce the negative feelings of dissonance makes us find a way for our beliefs and feelings to fit together. The theory focuses on situations in which two cognitive elements clash. A *cognitive element* can be something a person believes about himself, a behavior he performs, or an observation about his surroundings. For example, the two cognitive elements "I know smoking cigarettes causes cancer" and "I smoke cigarettes" are *dissonant* with one another. This psychological inconsistency creates a feeling of discomfort that the smoker tries to reduce. The magnitude of dissonance depends on both the importance and number of dissonant elements.[36] In other words, we're more likely to observe dissonance in high-involvement situations where there is more pressure to reduce inconsistencies. We reduce dissonance when we eliminate, add, or change elements. For example, a person can stop smoking (*eliminating*), or remember Great-Aunt Sophie who smoked until the day she died at age 90 (*adding*). Alternatively, he might question the research that links cancer and smoking (*changing*), perhaps by believing industry-sponsored studies that try to refute this connection.

Dissonance theory can help to explain why evaluations of a product tend to increase after we buy the product. The cognitive element, "I made a stupid decision," is dissonant with the element, "I am not a stupid person," so we tend to find even more reasons to like something after it becomes ours. A classic study at a horse race demonstrated this *postpurchase dissonance*. Bettors evaluated their chosen horse more highly and were more confident of its success *after* they had placed a bet than before. Because the bettor financially commits to the choice, she reduces dissonance by increasing the attractiveness of the chosen alternative relative to the unchosen ones.[37] One implication of this phenomenon is that consumers actively seek support for their decisions so they can justify them; therefore, marketers should supply their customers with additional reinforcement after they purchase to bolster these decisions.

SELF-PERCEPTION THEORY

Do we always change our attitudes to be in line with our behavior because we're motivated to reduce cognitive dissonance? **Self-perception theory** provides an alternative explanation of dissonance effects.[38] It assumes that we observe our own behavior

In one demonstration of postpurchase dissonance, bettors tend to be more confident about their chances of winning after they place their bets than beforehand.

to determine just what our attitudes are, much as we assume that we know what another person's attitude is by watching what he does. The theory states that we maintain consistency by inferring that we must have a positive attitude toward an object if we have bought or consumed it (assuming that we freely made this choice). Thus, Jan might say to herself, "I guess I must be into sports pretty big time. I sure choose to watch them a lot."

Self-perception theory is relevant to the *low-involvement hierarchy* because it involves situations where a person initially performs a behavior in the absence of a strong internal attitude. After the fact, the cognitive and affective components of attitude fall into line. Thus, if you buy a product out of habit, this creates a positive attitude toward it after the fact—why would you buy it if you didn't like it?

Self-perception theory helps to explain the effectiveness of a strategy salespeople call the **foot-in-the-door technique**; they know that a consumer is more likely to comply with a big request if he has already agreed to a smaller one.[39] The name for this technique comes from the practice of door-to-door selling; salespeople learn to plant their foot in a door so the prospect (hopefully) doesn't slam it on them. A good salesperson knows that she is more likely to get an order if she can persuade the customer to open the door and talk. By agreeing to do so, the customer signals that he's willing to listen to the salesperson's pitch. Placing an order is consistent with the self-perception that "I'm the kind of person who is willing to buy something from a salesperson who knocks on my door."

This technique is especially useful to induce people to answer surveys or donate money to charity (e.g., "I'm the kind of person who gives money to a telephone solicitor").[40] Other variations on this strategy include the *low-ball technique*, where the salesperson asks the customer for a small favor and then informs him that it will be more costly than he first thought, or the *door-in-the-face technique*, where the salesperson first asks the customer to do something extreme (he usually refuses) and then he asks the prospect to do something smaller instead. In each of these cases, people tend to go along with the smaller request, possibly because they feel guilty about denying the larger one.[41]

This Brazilian ad uses a variation of the door-in-the-face technique by presenting an extreme request for organ donation and then reassuring us that it's not necessary.

SOCIAL JUDGMENT THEORY

Social judgment theory also assumes that people assimilate new information about attitude objects in light of what they already know or feel.[42] The initial attitude acts as a frame of reference, and we categorize new information in terms of this existing standard. Just as our decision that a box is heavy depends in part on the weight of other boxes we lift, we develop a subjective standard when we make judgments about attitude objects.

Door-to-door salespeople know that their chances of making a sale go up considerably if they can first persuade the potential customer to let them in the door.

One important aspect of the theory is that people differ in terms of the information they will find acceptable or unacceptable. They form **latitudes of acceptance and rejection** around an attitude standard. They will evaluate ideas falling within a latitude favorably, but they are more likely to reject those falling outside of this zone. Because Jan already had a favorable attitude toward the concept of women playing professional golf, she is likely to be receptive to ads such as Nike's that promote female athletic participation. If she were opposed to these activities, she probably wouldn't consider these messages.

People tend to perceive messages within their latitude of acceptance as more consistent with their position than they actually are. We call this exaggeration an *assimilation effect.*

However, we tend to see messages that fall in our latitude of rejection as even more unacceptable than they actually are, which results in an exaggeration we call a *contrast effect.*[43] As a person becomes more involved with an attitude object, her latitude of acceptance gets smaller. In other words, the consumer accepts fewer ideas farther from her own position and she tends to oppose even mildly divergent positions. Discriminating buyers have a smaller latitude of acceptance (e.g., "choosy mothers choose 'Brand X' peanut butter"). However, relatively uninvolved consumers consider a wider range of alternatives. They are less likely to be brand loyal and are more likely to switch brands.[44]

BALANCE THEORY

Have you ever heard the expression, "Any friend of Joe's is a friend of mine?" How about "My enemy's enemy is my friend?" **Balance theory** considers how a person perceives relations among different attitude objects, and how he alters his attitudes so that these remain consistent (or "balanced").[45] This perspective involves relations (always from the perceiver's subjective point of view) among three elements, so we call the resulting attitude structures *triads.* Each triad contains (1) a person and his perceptions of (2) an attitude object and (3) some other person or object. The theory specifies that we want relations among elements in a triad to be harmonious. If they are unbalanced, this creates tension that we are motivated to reduce by changing our perceptions in order to restore balance.

We link elements together in one of two ways: They can have either a *unit relation* where we think that a person is somehow connected to an attitude object (something like a belief), or they can have a *sentiment relation*, where a person expresses liking or disliking for an attitude object. You might perceive that a dating couple has a positive sentiment relation. On getting married, they will have a positive unit relation. If they get divorced, they sever the unit relation.

To see how balance theory might work, consider the following scenario:

● Alex would like to date Larry, who is in her consumer behavior class. In balance theory terms, Alex has a positive sentiment relation with Larry.
● One day, Larry shows up in class wearing an earring. Larry has a positive unit relation with the earring.
● Alex is turned off by men who wear earrings. She has a negative sentiment relation with men's earrings.

According to balance theory, Alex faces an unbalanced triad. As Figure 7.2 shows, she will experience pressure to restore balance by altering some aspect of the triad. How can she do this? She could decide that she does not like Larry after all. Or her liking for Larry could prompt her to decide that earrings on men are pretty cool after all. She might even try to negate the unit relation between Larry and the earring by deciding that he must be wearing it as part of a fraternity initiation (thus reducing the free-choice element). Finally, she could choose to "leave the field" by accepting a date with Larry's roommate Brent who doesn't wear an earring (but who has an awesome tattoo). Note that although the theory does not specify which of these routes Alex will choose, it does predict that she will change one or more of her perceptions to achieve balance. Although this example is an oversimplified

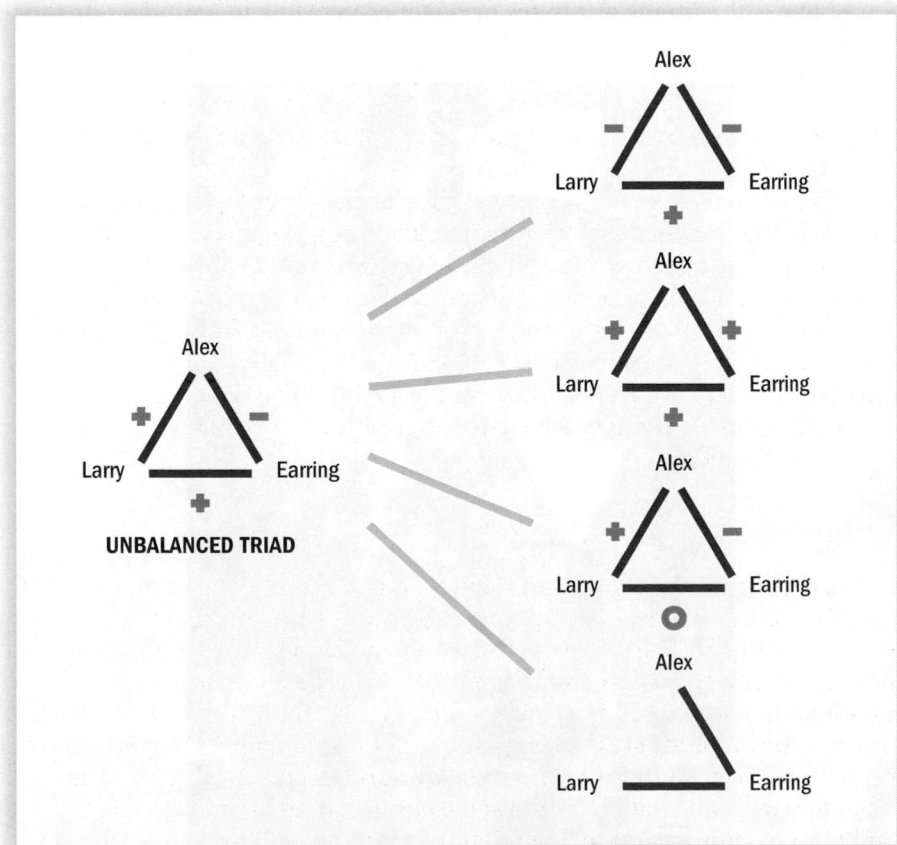

UNBALANCED TRIAD

■ **FIGURE 7.2**
ALTERNATIVES ROUTES TO
RESTORING BALANCE IN A TRIAD

Marketing Opportunity

Consumers often like to publicize their connections with successful people or organizations (no matter how shaky the connection) to enhance their own standing. In balance theory terms, they try to create a unit relation with an attitude object they value. Researchers call this tactic "basking in reflected glory."

A series of studies at Arizona State University (ASU) showed how students' desires to identify with a winning image—in this case, ASU's American-style football team—influenced their consumption behaviors. After the team played a game each weekend, observers recorded the incidence of school-related items, such as ASU T-shirts and caps, students walking around campus wore. The researchers correlated the frequency of these behaviors to the team's performance. If the team won on Saturday, students were more likely to show off their school affiliation (basking in reflected glory) the following Monday than if the team had lost. And the bigger the point spread, the more likely they were to see students sporting a sea of ASU logos.

representation of most attitude processes, it helps to explain a number of consumer behavior phenomena.

Balance theory reminds us that when we have balanced perceptions our attitudes also are likely to be stable. However, when we experience inconsistencies we also are more likely to change our attitudes. Balance theory also helps explain why consumers like to be linked to positively valued objects. Forming a unit relation with a popular product (e.g., buying and wearing fashionable clothing, driving a flashy car, or even being part of a rap singer's posse) may improve the chances that other people will include you as a positive sentiment relation in their triads.

This "balancing act" is at the heart of celebrity endorsements, in which marketers hope that the star's popularity will transfer to the product or when a nonprofit organization gets a celebrity to discourage harmful behaviors.[48] We will consider this strategy at length in the next chapter. For now, it pays to remember that creating a unit relation between a product and a star can backfire if the public's opinion of the celebrity endorser shifts from positive to negative. This happened when Pepsi pulled an ad featuring Madonna after she released a controversial music video involving religion and sex and when celebrity bad girl Paris Hilton got busted. The strategy can also cause trouble if people question the star–product unit relation: This happened when singer Michael Jackson, who also did promotions for Pepsi, subsequently confessed that he does not drink soda at all.

 ## Attitude Models

When market researchers want to assess consumers' attitudes toward beer brands, they might simply go to a bar and ask a bunch of guys, "How do you feel about Budweiser?" However, as we saw earlier, attitudes can be a lot more complex than that. One problem is that many attributes or qualities may link to a product or service

College merchandise helps students and fans alike to "bask in reflected glory."

and, depending on the individual, some of these will be more or less important ("Less filling!" "Tastes great!"). Another problem is that when a person decides to take action toward an attitude object, his behavior is influenced by other factors such as whether he feels that his family or friends would approve. Therefore, *attitude models* try to specify the different elements that might work together to influence people's evaluations of attitude objects.

MULTIATTRIBUTE ATTITUDE MODELS

A simple response does not always tell us everything we need to know, either about *why* the consumer feels a certain way toward a product or about what marketers can do to change his attitude. Our beliefs (accurate or not) about a product often are key to how we evaluate it. Warner-Lambert discovered this while doing research for its Fresh Burst Listerine mouthwash. A research firm paid 37 families to allow it to set up cameras in their bathrooms and watch their daily routines (maybe they should have just checked out YouTube). Participants who bought both Fresh Burst and rival Scope said they used mouthwash to make their breath smell good. But Scope users swished around the liquid and then spit it out, while Listerine users kept the product in their mouths for a long time (one respondent held the stuff in until he got in the car and finally spit it out in a sewer a block away!). These findings told Listerine the brand still hadn't shaken its medicine-like image.[49]

Because attitudes are so complex, marketing researchers may use **multiattribute attitude models** to understand them. This type of model assumes that a consumer's attitude toward an attitude object (A_o) depends on the beliefs she has about several of its attributes. When we use a multiattribute model, we assume that we can identify these specific beliefs and combine them to derive a measure of the consumer's overall attitude. We'll describe how these models work by using the example of a consumer evaluating a complex attitude object that should be very familiar to you: a college.

Basic multiattribute models specify three elements.[50]

● *Attributes* are characteristics of the A_o. A researcher would try to identify the attributes that most consumers would use when they evaluate the A_o. For example, one of a college's attributes is its scholarly reputation.
● *Beliefs* are cognitions about the specific A_o (usually relative to others like it). A belief measure assesses the extent to which the consumer perceives that a brand possesses a particular attribute. For example, a student might believe that the University of North Carolina is strong academically.
● *Importance weights* reflect the relative priority of an attribute to the consumer. Although people might consider an A_o on a number of attributes, some are likely to be more important than others (i.e., they will give them greater weight). Furthermore, these weights are likely to differ across consumers. In the case of colleges and universities, for example, one student might stress research opportunities, whereas another might assign greater weight to athletic programs.

The Fishbein Model

The most influential multiattribute model is called the *Fishbein model*, named after its primary developer.[51] The model measures three components of attitude:

1 *Salient beliefs* people have about an A_o (i.e., those beliefs about the object a person considers during evaluation).
2 *Object-attribute linkages*, or the probability that a particular object has an important attribute.
3 *Evaluation* of each of the important attributes.

Note, however, that the model makes some assumptions that may not always be warranted. It assumes that we have been able to adequately specify all of the

The desire to bask in reflected glory by buying products we associate with a valued attitude object creates numerous marketing opportunities. America's Major League Soccer (MLS) certainly understands this; it's now the only major American team sports league other than NASCAR racing cars to allow advertising on the front of team jerseys (this is common in Europe, Asia, and Latin America). Forming a logical unit relation, Red Bull was quick to act by purchasing ads on jerseys of the New York Red Bulls. Still, the league intends to police the types of unit relations teams can form. The MLS commissioner noted, "We don't want the local bail-bonds company on the front of the Columbus crew jersey."[46]

At the college level, many schools in addition to ASU reap huge revenues by licensing their school's name and logo. Schools with strong athletic programs, such as Michigan, Penn State, and Auburn, clean up by selling millions of dollars worth of merchandise (everything from T-shirts to toilet seats). Yale was a relative latecomer to this game, but the director of licensing explained the decision to profit from the use of the school's name and the likeness of bulldog mascot Handsome Dan: "We recognize that our name means a lot—even to people who didn't go here. Plus, this way we can crack down on the Naked Coed Lacrosse shirts out there with Yale on them."[47]

relevant attributes that, for example, a student uses in evaluating her choices about which college to attend. The model also assumes that the student will go through the process (formally or informally) of identifying a set of relevant attributes, weighing them, and summing them. Although this particular decision is likely to be highly involving, it is still possible she will instead form an attitude according to an overall affective response (a process researchers term *affect referral*).

By combining these three elements, we compute a consumer's overall attitude toward an object (we'll see later how researchers have modified this basic equation to increase its accuracy). The basic formula is:

$$A_{ijk} = \Sigma \beta_{ijk} I_{ik}$$

where

i = attribute

j = brand

k = consumer

I = the importance weight given attribute i by consumer k

β = consumer k's belief regarding the extent to which brand j possesses attribute i

A = a particular consumer's (k's) attitude score for brand j

We obtain the overall attitude score (A) by multiplying a consumer's rating of each attribute for all of the brands she considered by the importance rating for that attribute.

To see how this basic multiattribute model might work, let's suppose we want to predict which college a high school senior is likely to attend. After months of waiting anxiously, Saundra gets accepted to four schools. Because she must now decide among these, we would first like to know which attributes Saundra will consider when she forms an attitude toward each school. We can then ask Saundra to assign a rating regarding how well each school performs on each attribute and also determine the relative importance of the attributes to her.

By summing scores on each attribute (after weighting each by its relative importance), we compute an overall attitude score for each school. Table 7.1 shows these

A prospective student's attitude toward a college is influenced by the attributes she considers to be important and the extent to which she feels that school possesses those attitudes.

TABLE 7.1
THE BASIC MULTIATTRIBUTE MODEL: SAUNDRA'S COLLEGE DECISION

Attribute(*i*)	Importance(*I*)	Beliefs(*B*)			
		Smith	Princeton	Rutgers	Northland
Academic reputation	6	8	9	6	3
All women	7	9	3	3	3
Cost	4	2	2	6	9
Proximity to home	3	2	2	6	9
Athletics	1	1	2	5	1
Party atmosphere	2	1	3	7	9
Library facilities	5	7	9	7	2
Attitude score		163	142	153	131

Note: These hypothetical ratings are scored from 1 to 10, and higher numbers indicate "better" standing on an attribute. For a negative attribute (e.g., cost) higher scores indicate that the school is believed to have "less" of that attribute (i.e., to be cheaper).

hypothetical ratings. Based on this analysis, it seems that Saundra has the most favorable attitude toward Smith. She is clearly someone who would like to attend a college for women with a solid academic reputation rather than a school that offers a strong athletic program or a party atmosphere.

Marketing Applications of the Multiattribute Model

Suppose you were the director of marketing for Northland College, another school Saundra was considering. How might you use the data from this analysis to improve your image?

Capitalize on Relative Advantage. If prospective students view one brand as superior on a particular attribute, a marketer needs to convince consumers such as Saundra that this particular attribute is important. For example, although Saundra rates Northland's social atmosphere highly, she does not believe this attribute is a valued aspect for a college. As Northland's marketing director, you might emphasize the importance of an active social life, varied experiences, or even the development of future business contacts that a student forges when she makes strong college friendships.

Strengthen Perceived Product/Attribute Linkages. A marketer may discover that consumers do not equate his brand with a certain attribute. Advertising campaigns often address this problem when they stress a specific quality to consumers (e.g., "new and improved"). Saundra apparently does not think much of Northland's academic quality, athletic programs, or library facilities. You might develop an informational campaign to improve these perceptions (e.g., "little known facts about Northland").

Add a New Attribute. Product marketers frequently try to distinguish themselves from their competitors by adding a product feature. Northland College might try to emphasize some unique aspect, such as a hands-on internship program for business majors that takes advantage of ties to the local community.

Influence Competitors' Ratings. Finally, you might try to decrease your competitors' higher ratings by using a *comparative advertising* strategy. In this case, you might publish an ad that lists the tuition rates of a number of area schools with which Northland compares favorably and emphasize the value for the money its students get.

DO ATTITUDES PREDICT BEHAVIOR?

Consumer researchers have used multiattribute models for many years, but they are plagued by a major problem: In many cases, a person's attitude doesn't predict her behavior. In a classic demonstration of "do as I say, not as I do," many studies report a very low correlation between a person's reported attitude toward something and her actual behavior toward it. Some researchers are so discouraged that they question whether attitudes are of any use at all in understanding behavior.[52]

This questionable linkage between attitudes and behavior is a big headache for advertisers: Consumers can love a commercial yet still not buy the product. For example, one of the most popular U.S. TV commercials in recent years featured basketball player Shaquille O'Neal for Pepsi. Although the company spent $67 million on this spot and other similar ones in a single year, sales of Pepsi-Cola fell by close to 2 percent, even as sales of archrival Coca-Cola increased by 8 percent during the same period.[53]

THE EXTENDED FISHBEIN MODEL

In response, researchers tinkered with the Fishbein model to improve its predictive ability. They call the newer version the **theory of reasoned action**.[54] This model contains several important additions to the original, and although the model is still not perfect, it does a better job of prediction.[55] Let's look at some of the modifications to this model.

Intentions versus Behavior

Like the motivations we discussed in Chapter 4, attitudes have both direction and strength. A person may like or dislike an attitude object with varying degrees of confidence or conviction. It is helpful to distinguish between firmly held attitudes and those that are more superficial, especially because a person who holds an attitude with greater conviction is more likely to act on it.[56] One study on environmental issues and marketing activities found, for example, that people who express greater conviction in their feelings regarding environmentally responsible behaviors such as recycling show greater consistency between attitudes and behavioral intentions.[57]

However, as the old expression goes, "the road to hell is paved with good intentions." Many factors might interfere with performing the intended behavior. Say you save up to buy a new Apple iPhone. Although you have every intention of buying it, stuff happens: You might lose your job, get mugged on the way to the Apple store, or arrive at the store only to find they've run out of the item. It is not surprising, then, that in some instances researchers find that instead of knowing our intentions, our past purchase behavior does a better job of predicting our future behavior (this is one of the foundations of direct marketing techniques that identify likely customers based on their purchase histories).[58] The theory of reasoned action aims to measure *behavioral intentions*, recognizing that certain uncontrollable factors (such as that mugger) limit our ability to predict the future with 100 percent accuracy.

Social Pressure

Perhaps most importantly, the theory acknowledges the power of other people to influence what we do. Much as we may hate to admit it, what we think others would *like* us to do may override our own preferences. Some research approaches try to assess the extent to which people's "public" attitudes and purchase decisions might be different from what they would do in private. For example, one firm uses a technique it calls "engineered theatre." Researchers go to the actual site where people use a product, such as a bar. They arrange for the bartender to "mistakenly" serve the wrong drink and then observe the consumer's "naked response" to the new brand and her reaction to consuming the brand in a social context.[59]

Returning to Saundra's college choice, you can see in Table 7.1 that she was very positive about going to a predominantly female school. However, if she felt that this choice would be unpopular (perhaps her friends would think she was crazy), she might ignore or downgrade this preference when she made her decision. Researchers added a new element, the **subjective norm (SN)**, to account for the effects of what we believe other people think we should do. They measure SN using two factors: (1) the intensity of a *normative belief (NB)* that others believe an action should be taken or not taken and (2) the *motivation to comply (MC)* with that belief (i.e., the degree to which the consumer takes others' anticipated reactions into account when she evaluates a purchase).

Attitude toward Buying

The newer model also measures **attitude toward the act of buying (A_{act})**, rather than only the attitude toward the product itself. In other words, it focuses on the perceived consequences of a purchase. Knowing how someone feels about buying or using an object turns out to be more valid than merely knowing the consumer's evaluation of the object itself.[60]

To understand this distinction, consider a marketing researcher who wants to measure college students' attitudes toward safe sex and wearing condoms. Although many college students she interviews would probably report a positive attitude toward condoms use, can she conclude from these responses that they will all buy and use them? She might get more accurate results simply by asking the same students how likely they are to *buy* condoms. A person might have a positive A_o toward condoms, but A_{act} might be negative because of the embarrassment or the hassle involved.

Obstacles to Predicting Behavior in the Theory of Reasoned Action

Despite improvements to the Fishbein model, problems arise when researchers misapply it. Like our discussion about measuring personality traits in Chapter 6, sometimes researchers use the model in ways it was not intended or where certain assumptions about human behavior may not be warranted.[61] Other obstacles to predicting behavior include the following:

- The model deals with predicting actual behavior (e.g., taking a diet pill), not with the *outcomes* of behavior that some studies assess (e.g., losing weight).
- Some outcomes are beyond the consumer's control, such as when the purchase requires the cooperation of other people. For instance, a woman might *want* to get a mortgage, but this intention will be worthless if she cannot find a banker to give her one.
- The basic assumption that behavior is intentional may be invalid in a variety of cases, including impulsive acts, sudden changes in one's situation, novelty seeking, or even simple repeat buying. One study found that such unexpected events as having guests, changes in the weather, or reading articles about the healthfulness of certain foods significantly affected actual behaviors.[62]
- Measures of attitude often do not really correspond to the behavior they are supposed to predict, either in terms of the A_o or when the act will occur. One common problem is a difference in the level of abstraction researchers employ. For example, knowing a person's attitude toward sports cars may not predict whether she will purchase a BMW Z4. It is very important to match the level of specificity between the attitude and the behavioral intention.
- A similar problem relates to the *time frame* of the attitude measure. In general, the longer the time between the attitude measurement and the behavior it is supposed to assess, the weaker the relationship will be. For example,

The likelihood of socially desirable behaviors like recycling may be influenced by our *subjective norms*—the belief that others would approve or disapprove of the behavior.

predictability improves greatly if we ask a consumer the likelihood that she would buy a house in the next week as opposed to within the next 5 years.

- We form stronger and more predictive attitudes through direct, personal experience with an A_o than those we form indirectly through advertising.[63] According to the *attitude accessibility perspective,* behavior is a function of the person's immediate perceptions of the A_o, in the context of the situation in which it is encountered. An attitude will guide the evaluation of the object but *only* if it is activated from memory when the person encounters the object. These findings underscore the importance of strategies that induce trials (e.g., by widespread product sampling to encourage the consumer to try the product at home, by taste tests, test drives, etc.) as well as those that maximize exposure to marketing communications.[64]

In addition, most researchers have applied the theory of reasoned action in Western settings. Certain assumptions inherent in the model may not necessarily apply to consumers from other cultures. Several cultural roadblocks diminish the universality of the theory of reasoned action:

- The model tries to predict the performance of a voluntary act. Across cultures, however, many consumer activities, ranging from taking exams and entering military service to receiving an inoculation or even choosing a marriage partner, are not necessarily voluntary.
- The relative impact of subjective norms may vary across cultures. For example, Asian cultures tend to value conformity and "face saving," so it is possible that subjective norms that involve the anticipated reactions of others to the choice will have an even greater impact on behavior for many Asian consumers. Indeed, a recent study conducted among voters in Singapore was able to predict voting for political candidates from their voting intentions, which in turn were influenced by such factors as voters' attitudes toward the candidate, attitudes

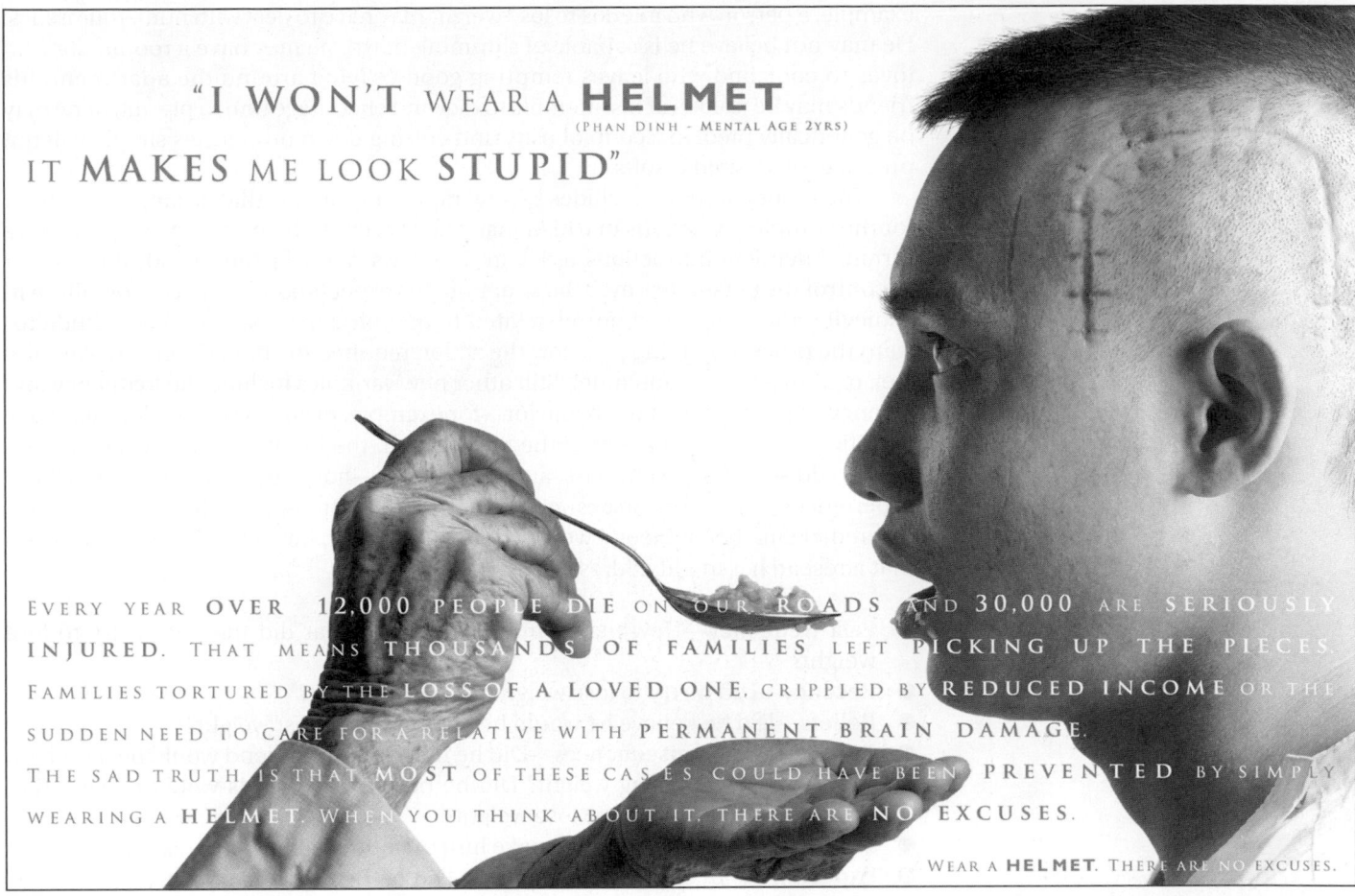

"I WON'T WEAR A **HELMET**
(PHAN DINH - MENTAL AGE 2YRS)

IT **MAKES** ME LOOK **STUPID**"

EVERY YEAR OVER 12,000 PEOPLE DIE ON OUR ROADS AND 30,000 ARE SERIOUSLY INJURED. THAT MEANS THOUSANDS OF FAMILIES LEFT PICKING UP THE PIECES. FAMILIES TORTURED BY THE LOSS OF A LOVED ONE, CRIPPLED BY REDUCED INCOME OR THE SUDDEN NEED TO CARE FOR A RELATIVE WITH PERMANENT BRAIN DAMAGE. THE SAD TRUTH IS THAT MOST OF THESE CASES COULD HAVE BEEN PREVENTED BY SIMPLY WEARING A HELMET. WHEN YOU THINK ABOUT IT, THERE ARE NO EXCUSES.

WEAR A **HELMET**. THERE ARE NO EXCUSES.

This Vietnamese ad employs social pressure (the subjective norm) to address people's attitudes toward wearing helmets.

toward the political party, and subjective norms—which in Singapore includes an emphasis on harmonious and close ties among members of the society.

- The model measures behavioral intentions and thus presupposes that consumers are actively thinking ahead and planning future behaviors. The intention concept assumes that consumers have a linear time sense; they think in terms of past, present, and future. As we'll discuss in Chapter 10, not all cultures subscribe to this perspective on time.
- A consumer who forms an intention is (implicitly) claiming that he is in control of his actions. Some cultures (e.g., Muslim peoples) tend to be fatalistic and do not necessarily believe in the concept of free will. Indeed, one study comparing students from the United States, Jordan, and Thailand found evidence for cultural differences in assumptions about fatalism and control over the future.[65]

Trying to Consume

Other theorists have proposed different perspectives on the attitude–behavior connection. For example, a recent model its authors call the **multiple pathway anchoring and adjustment (MPAA) model** emphasizes multiple pathways to attitude formation, including outside-in (object-centered) and inside-out (person-centered) pathways.[66]

Another perspective tries to address some of these problems by focusing instead on consumers' goals and what they believe they have to do to attain them. The **theory of trying** states that the criterion of behavior in the reasoned action model should be replaced with *trying* to reach a goal.[67] This perspective recognizes that additional factors might intervene between intent and performance—both personal and environmental barriers might prevent the individual from attaining the goal. For example, a person who intends to lose weight may have to deal with numerous issues: He may not believe he is capable of slimming down, he may have a roommate who loves to cook and who leaves tempting goodies lying around the apartment, his friends may be jealous of his attempts to diet and encourage him to pig out, or he may be genetically predisposed to obesity and cutting down on calories simply will not produce the desired results.

The theory of trying includes several new components that attempt to account for the complex situations in which many factors either help or hurt our chances of turning intentions into actions, as Figure 7.3 shows. These factors include the amount of control the person has over the situation, his expectations of success or failure in achieving the goal, social norms related to attaining the goal, and his attitude toward the process of trying (i.e., how the action required to attain the goal makes him feel, regardless of the outcome). Still other new variables include the frequency and recency of past trying of the behavior—for example, even if a person does not have specific plans to go on a diet in the next month, the frequency with which he has tried to do so in the recent past (and the success—however fleeting—he may have experienced) would be the best predictor of future attempts to shed some pounds. To predict whether someone would try to lose weight, here are a few sample issues that a researcher might address:

● **Past frequency**—How many times in the past year did the person try to lose weight?
● **Recency**—Did he try to lose weight in the past week?
● **Beliefs**—Did he believe he would be healthier if he lost weight?
● **Evaluations of consequences**—Did he believe his girlfriend would be happier if he succeeded in losing weight? Did he believe his friends would make fun of him if he tried but failed to lose weight?
● **The process**—Would the diet make him uncomfortable or depressed?
● **Expectations of success and failure**—Did he believe it likely that he would be able to lose weight if he tried?

■ **FIGURE 7.3** THEORY OF TRYING (TT)

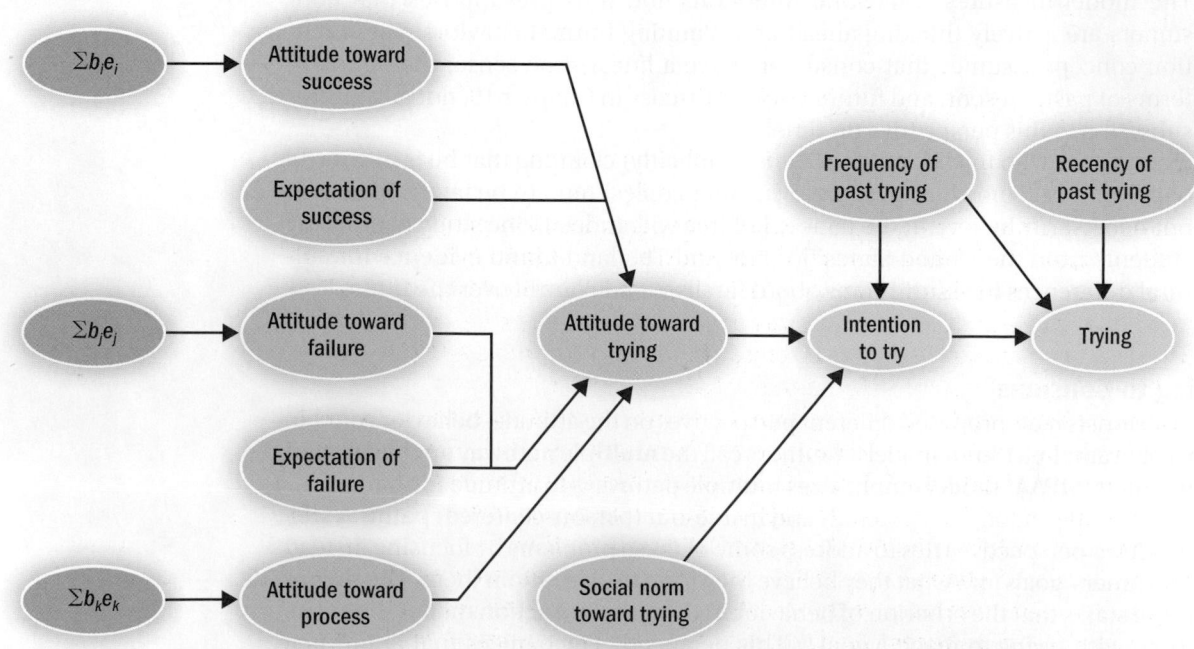

- **Subjective norms toward trying**—Would the people who are important to him approve of his efforts to lose weight?

TRACKING ATTITUDES OVER TIME

An attitude survey is like a snapshot taken at a single point in time. It may tell us a lot about a brand's position at that moment, but it does not permit many inferences about progress the brand has made over time or any predictions about possible future changes in consumer attitudes. To accomplish that, researchers develop an *attitude-tracking* program. This technique, which involves collecting attitudinal data at periodic intervals, helps researchers to sharpen their predictions because they can analyze attitude trends over an extended period.

Attitude tracking is more like a movie than a snapshot. For example, a longitudinal survey the Food Marketing Institute conducted of consumers' attitudes toward food content during the past decade illustrates how priorities can shift in a fairly short time.[68] Concerns about fat and cholesterol content rose dramatically during this period, whereas a focus on nutritional issues such as interest in sugar content decreased. Today, many people focus on their carb intake instead.

ATTITUDE TRACKING STUDIES

Attitude tracking involves administering an attitude survey at regular intervals. Preferably, researchers use the identical methodology each time so that they can reliably compare results. Several syndicated services, such as the Gallup Poll or the Yankelovich Monitor™, track consumer attitudes over time (see Chapter 4).

Attitude tracking is extremely valuable for many strategic decisions. For example, one firm monitored changes in consumer attitudes toward one-stop financial centers. Although a large number of consumers were warm to the idea when it first came out, the number of people who liked the concept did not increase over time despite the millions of dollars the company invested in advertising to promote the centers. This finding indicated some problems with the way they were presenting the concept to consumers, and the company decided to "go back to the drawing board," eventually coming up with a new way to communicate the advantages of this service.

CHANGES TO LOOK FOR OVER TIME

Some of the dimensions of attitude tracking include the following:

- **Changes in different age groups**—Attitudes tend to change as people age (a *lifecycle effect*). In addition, *cohort effects* occur, whereby members of a particular generation tend to share certain outlooks (e.g., the yuppie). Also, we may observe historical effects as large groups of people are affected by profound cultural changes (such as the Great Depression, the terrorist attacks of 2001, or the wreckage of Mississippi and Louisiana by Katrina in 2005).
- **Scenarios about the future**—Researchers frequently track consumers in terms of their future plans and confidence in the economy. These measures can provide valuable data about future behavior and yield insights for public policy. For example, Americans tend to overestimate how much they will earn after retirement, which is a potentially dangerous miscalculation.
- **Identification of change agents**—Social phenomena can alter people's attitudes toward basic consumption activities over time, as when consumers' willingness to buy fur changes. A movie such as Al Gore's *An Inconvenient Truth* can add fuel to the fire of a social movement such as sustainability. Or a consumer's

likelihood of desiring a divorce may be affected by such *facilitators* as changes in the legal system that make this action easier, or by *inhibitors*, such as the prevalence of AIDS and the value of two paychecks in today's economy.[69]

CHAPTER SUMMARY

Now that you have finished reading this chapter you should understand why:

It's important for consumer researchers to understand the nature and power of attitudes.

● An *attitude* is a predisposition to evaluate an object or product positively or negatively. We form attitudes toward products and services that often determine whether we will purchase them or not.

Attitudes are more complex than they first appear.

● Three components make up an attitude: beliefs, affect, and behavioral intentions.

We form attitudes in several ways.

● Attitude researchers traditionally assumed that we learn attitudes in a fixed sequence: First we form beliefs (*cognitions*) about an attitude object, then we evaluate that object (*affect*), and then we take some action (*behavior*). Depending on the consumer's level of involvement and the circumstances, though, his attitudes can result from other hierarchies of effects as well. A key to attitude formation is the function the attitude holds for the consumer (e.g., is it utilitarian or ego defensive?).

A need to maintain consistency among all of our attitudinal components motivates us to alter one or more of them.

● One organizing principle of attitude formation is the importance of consistency among attitudinal components—that is, we alter some parts of an attitude to be in line with others. Such theoretical approaches to attitudes as *cognitive dissonance theory, self-perception theory*, and *balance theory* stress the vital role off our need for consistency.

We use attitude models to identify specific components and combine them to predict a consumer's overall attitude toward a product or brand.

● Multiattribute attitude models underscore the complexity of attitudes; they specify that we identify and combine a set of beliefs and evaluations to predict an overall attitude. Researchers have integrated factors such as subjective norms and the specificity of attitude scales into attitude measures to improve predictability.

KEY TERMS

ABC model of attitudes, 284
Affect, 284
Attitude, 282
Attitude object (A_o), 282
Attitude toward the act of buying
    (A_{act}), 301
Attitude toward the advertisement
    (A_{ad}), 287
Balance theory, 294

Behavior, 284
Cognition, 284
Foot-in-the-door technique, 292
Functional theory of attitudes, 282
Hierarchy of effects, 284
Latitudes of acceptance and
    rejection, 294
Multiattribute attitude
    models, 297

Multiple pathway anchoring and
    adjustment (MPAA) model, 303
Principle of cognitive
    consistency, 290
Self-perception theory, 291
Social judgment theory, 293
Subjective norm (SN), 301
Theory of reasoned action, 300
Theory of trying, 303

REVIEW QUESTIONS

1 How can an attitude play an ego-defensive function?

2 Describe the ABC model of attitudes.

3 List the three hierarchies of attitudes, and describe the major differences among them.

4 How do emotions (affect) and cognitions (beliefs) relate to attitude formation?

5 Other than the direct attitude we might have about a product, what is another type of attitude that might influence the likelihood that we will buy it?

6 How do levels of commitment to an attitude influence the likelihood that it will become part of the way we think about a product in the long term?

7 We sometimes enhance our attitude toward a product after we buy it. How does the theory of cognitive dissonance explain this change?

8 What is the foot-in-the-door technique? How does self-perception theory relate to this effect?

9 What are latitudes of acceptance and rejection? How does a consumer's level of involvement with a product affect his latitude of acceptance?

10 According to balance theory, how can we tell if a triad is balanced or unbalanced? How can consumers restore balance to an unbalanced triad?

11 What is basking in reflected glory, and how does it create marketing opportunities?

12 Describe a multiattribute attitude model, listing its key components.

13 "Do as I say, not as I do." How does this statement relate to attitude models?

14 What is a subjective norm, and how does it influence our attitudes?

15 What are three obstacles to predicting behavior even if we know a person's attitudes?

16 Describe the theory of reasoned action. Why might it not be equally valuable when we apply it to non-Western cultures?

17 What is the value of attitude tracking? What issues do researchers need to consider when doing this?

CONSUMER BEHAVIOR CHALLENGE

■ DISCUSS

1 Students bask in reflected glory when they take credit for victories their teams earn over other colleges. Should students who simply watch the games rather than play them take credit for their team's performance?

2 Contrast the hierarchies of effects the chapter outlines. How should marketers' strategic decisions related to the marketing mix change depending on which hierarchy its target consumers use?

   More than 500 universities have signed up commercial companies to run campus Web sites and e-mail services. These agreements provide Web services to colleges at little or no cost. But these actions have aroused controversy because major companies pay to place advertising on the sites. That gives marketers the opportunity to influence the attitudes of thousands of students who are involuntarily exposed to product messages. One professor complained, "We're throwing our freshmen to the wolves. The University has become a shill for the corporate community." But university administrators argue that they could not provide the services by themselves—students expect to be able to fill out financial aid forms and register for classes online. Colleges that do not offer such services may lose their ability to attract students.[65] How do you feel about this situation? Do you agree that you're being "thrown to the wolves"? Should companies be able to buy access to your eyeballs from the school you pay to attend?

■ APPLY

3 Think of a behavior someone does that is inconsistent with his or her attitudes (e.g., attitudes toward cholesterol, drug use, or even buying things to make him or her stand out or attain status). Ask the person to elaborate on why he or she does the behavior, and try to identify the way the person has resolved dissonant elements.

4 Devise an attitude survey for a set of competing automobiles. Identify areas of competitive advantage or disadvantage for each model you include.

5 Construct a multiattribute model for a set of local restaurants. Based on your findings, suggest how restaurant managers can improve an establishment's image via the strategies described in this chapter.

WAL-MART

It probably comes as no surprise to hear that Wal-Mart is the biggest retailer in the world. But did you know that it is the biggest company in the world? With over 7,000 stores world-wide, Wal-Mart's 2006 revenue of $351 billion was more than 2.5 times larger than the combined revenue of its closest competitors, Target, JCPenny, and Kmart/Sears. What's more, the annual revenue of this behemoth is bigger than the combined revenues of IBM, Dell, Microsoft, and Cisco, some of the largest companies in the world.

Each year, over 80% of Americans make at least one purchase at Wal-Mart. The stores sell over 30% of all household staples American consumers buy, and this percentage is growing. And, this dominance is not exclusive to the United States. Wal-Mart operates over 2,800 stores in 13 countries outside the United States and is also the largest retailer in Canada and Mexico. How has this company, with humble roots in Arkansas, achieved success of such proportions?

Some might say Wal-Mart succeeds because it gives customers what they want. "Low price" is more than just a slogan at Wal-Mart. One study shows that on average, Wal-Mart offers products at prices 14% below its rivals. In addition, Wal-Mart is constantly adding more and more products as it tries to be the ultimate one-stop shop. And finally, it offers the convenience of numerous stores and extended (often 24-hour) operations. Ninety percent of Americans live within range of at least one Wal-Mart store. That number will only increase as the company plans to continue opening one new U.S. store every day for at least the next five years.

Due to its sheer size, Wal-Mart's actions significantly affect the overall economy. Because of the constant attention that Wal-Mart gives to cutting costs, analysts estimate that the company directly saves U.S. consumers billions of dollars each year. But that figure doesn't even include the effects of Wal-Mart's dominance on the overall market. As other retailers have become more efficient, demanded price reductions from suppliers, and passed savings on to consumers, the overall "Wal-Mart factor" stretches to well over $100 billion. In addition, McKinsey estimates that one-eighth of the U.S. productivity gains in the late 1990s came from Wal-Mart's relentless drive for efficiency, and that the discounter has been at least partly responsible for the extraordinarily low inflation rate of recent years. On top of all this, Wal-Mart employs nearly 2 million people worldwide and is the largest private employer in the United States.

It should be easy to see why Wal-Mart is one of the most admired corporations. And yet, it is also one of the most hated. Each year, the super-retailer garners more and more opposition from competing retailers, vendors, organized labor, community activists, and cultural and political progressives. Ironically, some revile it for the same reasons others love it.

As the country's largest private employer, activists generally blame Wal-Mart for driving down retail wages and benefits. Its hard line on costs forces many manufacturers to move production overseas at the expense of American jobs. Indeed, analysts estimate that approximately 70 percent of Wal-Mart merchandise comes from China, accounting for roughly 10% of all Chinese imports to the United States. It has a reputation for strong-arming suppliers, squeezing every last cent out of their profits and even dictating product specifications. And for every Supercenter that Wal-Mart opens, two competing supermarkets will close, not to mention smaller stores that will go out of business. It's hard to calculate how this dominance may have contributed to the demise of "mom-and-pop" stores and to traditional downtown shopping districts.

For the time being, Wal-Mart shows no signs of slowing down. However, it will be interesting to see if the controversial tactics that led to its success will contribute to its decline.

DISCUSSION QUESTIONS

1 Use a multiattribute model to show how individuals may develop either a positive or a negative attitude toward Wal-Mart.

2 Explain why a consumer's behavior might be inconsistent with her attitude toward Wal-Mart. How might a consumer try to resolve this inconsistency?

Sources: Anthony Bianco, "Wal-Mart's Midlife Crisis," *BusinessWeek* (April 30, 2007), p 46; Anthony Bianco and Wendy Zellner, "Is Wal-Mart Too Powerful?" *BusinessWeek* (October 6, 2003), p 100; Steve Maich, "Why Wal-Mart Is Good for Canada," *Canada News Wire* (July 18, 2005).

NOTES

1. www.lpga.com, accessed August 15, 2007; Damon Hack, "In Women's Golf, Teenagers and Teddy Bears," *New York Times* (July 3, 2005): 1 (2).

2. Jennifer Mario, "Ladies, What Has the Golf Industry Done for Us Lately?" TravelGolf.com, available from www.travelgolf.com/departments/clubhouse/mario-womens-golf-column-1133.htm (May 16, 2005), accessed July 6, 2005.

3. Robert A. Baron and Donn Byrne, *Social Psychology: Understanding Human Interaction*, 5th ed. (Boston: Allyn & Bacon, 1987).

4. Daniel Katz, "The Functional Approach to the Study of Attitudes," *Public Opinion Quarterly* 24 (Summer 1960): 163–204, Richard J. Lutz, "Changing Brand Attitudes through Modification of Cognitive Structure," *Journal of Consumer Research* 1 (March 1975): 49–59.

5. Russell H. Fazio, T.N. Lenn, and E.A. Effrein, "Spontaneous Attitude Formation," *Social Cognition* 2 (1984): 214–34.

6. Sharon Shavitt, "The Role of Attitude Objects in Attitude Functions," *Journal of Experimental Social Psychology* 26 (1990): 124–48; see also J.S. Johar and M. Joseph Sirgy, "Value Expressive versus Utilitarian Advertising Appeals: When and Why to Use Which Appeal," *Journal of Advertising* 20 (September 1991): 23–34.

7. Lynn R. Kahle, Kennth M. Kambara, and Gregory M. Rose, "A Functional Model of Fan Attendance Motivations for College Football," *Sports Marketing Quarterly* 5, no. 4 (1996): 51–60; for the original work that focused on the issue of levels of attitudinal commitment, see H.C. Kelman, "Compliance, Identification, and Internalization: Three Processes of Attitude Change," *Journal of Conflict Resolution* 2 (1958): 51–60.

8. Robert D. Jewell and H. Rao Unnava, "Exploring Differences in Attitudes between Light and Heavy Brand Users," *Journal of Consumer Psychology* 14, nos. 1 & 2 (2004): 75–80.

9. For a study that found evidence of simultaneous causation of beliefs and attitudes, see Gary M. Erickson, Johny K. Johansson, and Paul Chao, "Image Variables in Multi-Attribute Product Evaluations: Country-of-Origin Effects," *Journal of Consumer Research* 11 (September 1984): 694–99.

10. Michael Ray, "Marketing Communications and the Hierarchy-of-Effects," in P. Clarke, ed., *New Models for Mass Communications* (Beverly Hills, CA: Sage, 1973), 147–76.

11. Herbert Krugman, "The Impact of Television Advertising: Learning without Involvement," *Public Opinion Quarterly* 29 (Fall 1965): 349–56; Robert Lavidge and Gary Steiner, "A Model for Predictive Measurements of Advertising Effectiveness," *Journal of Marketing* 25 (October 1961): 59–62.

12. Stephanie Thompson, "Bad Breakup? There, There, B&J Know Just How You Feel," *Advertising Age* (January 24, 2005): 8.

13. Daniel J. Howard and Charles Gengler, "Emotional Contagion Effects on Product Attitudes," *Journal of Consumer Research* 28 (September 2001): 189–201.

14. For some recent studies, see Andrew B. Aylesworth and Scott B. MacKenzie, "Context Is Key: The Effect of Program-Induced Mood on Thoughts about the Ad," *Journal of Advertising* 27 (Summer 1998): 17; Angela Y. Lee and Brian Sternthal, "The Effects of Positive Mood on Memory," *Journal of Consumer Research* 26 (September 1999): 115–28; Michael J. Barone, Paul W. Miniard, and Jean B. Romeo, "The Influence of Positive Mood on Brand Extension Evaluations," *Journal of Consumer Research* 26 (March 2000): 386–401. For a study that compared the effectiveness of emotional appeals across cultures, see Jennifer L. Aaker and Patti Williams, "Empathy versus Pride: The Influence of Emotional Appeals across Cultures," *Journal of Consumer Research* 25 (December 1998): 241–61. For research that relates mood (depression) to acceptance of health-related messages, see Punam Anand Keller, Isaac M. Lipkus, and Barbara K. Rimer, "Depressive Realism and Health Risk Accuracy: The Negative Consequences of Positive Mood," *Journal of Consumer Research* 29 (June 2002): 57–69.

15. Punam Anand, Morris B. Holbrook, and Debra Stephens, "The Formation of Affective Judgments: The Cognitive–Affective Model versus the Independence Hypothesis," *Journal of Consumer Research* 15 (December 1988): 386–91; Richard S. Lazarus, "Thoughts on the Relations between Emotion and Cognition," *American Psychologist* 37, no. 9 (1982): 1019–24.

16. Robert B. Zajonc, "Feeling and Thinking: Preferences Need No Inferences," *American Psychologist* 35, no. 2 (1980): 151–75.

17. www.pandora.com, accessed July 6, 2007.

18. Banwari Mittal, "The Role of Affective Choice Mode in the Consumer Purchase of Expressive Products," *Journal of Economic Psychology* 4, no. 9 (1988): 499–524.

19. Cf. http://affect.media.mit.edu, accessed June 3, 2005; Patricia Winters Lauro, "Advertisers Want to Know What People Really Think," *New York Times on the Web* (April 13, 2000); Ian Austen, "Soon: Computers That Know You Hate Them," *New York Times on the Web* (January 6, 2000).

20. Scot Burton and Donald R. Lichtenstein, "The Effect of Ad Claims and Ad Context on Attitude toward the Advertisement," *Journal of Advertising* 17, no. 1 (1988): 3–11; Karen A. Machleit and R. Dale Wilson, "Emotional Feelings and Attitude toward the Advertisement: The Roles of Brand Familiarity and Repetition," *Journal of Advertising* 17, no. 3 (1988): 27–35; Scott B. Mackenzie and Richard J. Lutz, "An Empirical Examination of the Structural Antecedents of Attitude toward the Ad in an Advertising Pretesting Context," *Journal of Marketing* 53 (April 1989): 48–65; Scott B. Mackenzie, Richard J. Lutz, and George E. Belch, "The Role of Attitude toward the Ad as a Mediator of Advertising Effectiveness: A Test of Competing Explanations," *Journal of Marketing Research* 23 (May 1986): 130–43; Darrel D. Muehling and Russell N. Laczniak, "Advertising's Immediate and Delayed Influence on Brand Attitudes: Considerations across Message-Involvement Levels," *Journal of Advertising* 17, no. 4 (1988): 23–34; Mark A. Pavelchak, Meryl P. Gardner, and V. Carter Broach, "Effect of Ad Pacing and Optimal Level of Arousal on Attitude toward the Ad," in Rebecca H. Holman and Michael R. Solomon, eds., *Advances in Consumer Research* 18 (Provo, UT: Association for Consumer Research, 1991): 94–99. Some research evidence indicates that a separate attitude is also formed regarding the brand name itself; see George M. Zinkhan and Claude R. Martin, Jr., "New Brand Names and Inferential Beliefs: Some Insights on Naming New Products," *Journal of Business Research* 15 (1987): 157–72.

21. John P. Murry, Jr., John L. Lastovicka, and Surendra N. Singh, "Feeling and Liking Responses to Television Programs: An Examination of Two Explanations for Media-Context Effects," *Journal of Consumer Research* 18 (March 1992): 441–51.

22. Barbara Stern and Judith Lynne Zaichkowsky, "The Impact of 'Entertaining' Advertising on Consumer Responses," *Australian Marketing Researcher* 14 (August 1991): 68–80.

23. H. Shanker Krishnan and Robert E. Smith, "The Relative Endurance of Attitudes, Confidence, and Attitude Behavior Consistency: The Role of Information Source and Delay," *Journal of Consumer Psychology* 7, no. 3 (1998): 273–98.

24. Alexander Fedorikhin and Catherine A. Cole, "Mood Effects on Attitudes, Perceived Risk and Choice: Moderators and Mediators," *Journal of Consumer Psychology* 14, nos. 1 & 2 (2004): 2–12.

25. For a study on the impact of skepticism on advertising issues, see David M. Boush, Marian Friestad, and Gregory M. Rose, "Adolescent Skepticism toward TV Advertising and Knowledge of Advertiser Tactics," *Journal of Consumer Research* 21 (June 1994): 167–75.

26. Basil G. Englis, "Consumer Emotional Reactions to Television Advertising and Their Effects on Message Recall," in S. Agres, J. A. Edell, and T. M. Dubitsky, eds., *Emotion in Advertising: Theoretical and Practical Explorations* (Westport, CT: Quorum Books, 1990), 231–54.

27. Morris B. Holbrook and Rajeev Batra, "Assessing the Role of Emotions as Mediators of Consumer Responses to Advertising," *Journal of Consumer Research* 14 (December 1987): 404–20.

28. Marian Burke and Julie Edell, "Ad Reactions over Time: Capturing Changes in the Real World," *Journal of Consumer Research* 13 (June 1986): 114–18.

29. Herbert Kelman, "Compliance, Identification, and Internalization: Three Processes of Attitude Change," *Journal of Conflict Resolution* 2 (1958): 51–60.

30. See Sharon E. Beatty and Lynn R. Kahle, "Alternative Hierarchies of the Attitude–Behavior Relationship: The Impact of Brand Commitment and Habit," *Journal of the Academy of Marketing Science* 16 (Summer 1988): 1–10.

31. J. R. Priester, D. Nayakankuppan, M. A. Fleming, and J. Godek, "The A(2)SC(2) Model: The Influence of Attitudes and Attitude Strength on Consideration Set Choice," *Journal of Consumer Research* 30, no. 4 (2004): 574–87.

32. Quoted in Mya Frazier, "Costly Red Campaign Reaps Meager $18 Million; Bono & Co. Spend up to $100 Million on Marketing, Incur Watchdogs' Wrath" *Advertising Age* (March 05, 2007), available from http://adage.com/article?article_id=115287; "Ad Notes: Dollars Flow into (Red)," *Wall Street Journal Online* (September 24, 2007), accessed September 24, 2007.

33. David A. Aaker and Donald E. Bruzzone, "Causes of Irritation in Advertising," *Journal of Marketing* 49 (Spring 1985): 47–57.

34. Leon Festinger, *A Theory of Cognitive Dissonance* (Stanford, CA: Stanford University Press, 1957).

35. Chester A. Insko and John Schopler, *Experimental Social Psychology* (New York: Academic Press, 1972).

36. Robert E. Knox and James A. Inkster, "Postdecision Dissonance at Post Time," *Journal of Personality and Social Psychology* 8, no. 4 (1968): 319–23.

37. Daryl J. Bem, "Self-Perception Theory," in Leonard Berkowitz, ed., *Advances in Experimental Social Psychology* (New York: Academic Press, 1972), 1–62.

38. Jonathan L. Freedman and Scott C. Fraser, "Compliance without Pressure: The Foot-in-the-Door Technique," *Journal of Personality and Social Psychology* 4 (August 1966): 195–202. For further consideration of possible explanations for this effect, see William DeJong, "An Examination of Self-Perception Mediation of the Foot-in-the-Door Effect," *Journal of Personality and Social Psychology* 37 (December 1979): 221–31; Alice M. Tybout, Brian Sternthal, and Bobby J. Calder, "Information Availability as a Determinant of Multiple-Request Effectiveness," *Journal of Marketing Research* 20 (August 1988): 280–90.

39. David H. Furse, David W. Stewart, and David L. Rados, "Effects of Foot-in-the-Door, Cash Incentives and Follow-ups on Survey Response," *Journal of Marketing Research* 18 (November 1981): 473–78; Carol A. Scott, "The Effects of Trial and Incentives on Repeat Purchase Behavior," *Journal of Marketing Research* 13 (August 1976): 263–69.

40. R. B. Cialdini, J. E. Vincent, S. K. Lewis, J. Catalan, D. Wheeler, and B. L. Darby, "Reciprocal Concessions Procedure for Inducing Compliance: The Door-in-the-Face Effect," *Journal of Personality and Social Psychology* 31 (1975): 200–15.

41. Muzafer Sherif and Carl I. Hovland, *Social Judgment: Assimilation and Contrast Effects in Communication and Attitude Change* (New Haven, CT: Yale University Press, 1961).

42. See Joan Meyers-Levy and Brian Sternthal, "A Two-Factor Explanation of Assimilation and Contrast Effects," *Journal of Marketing Research* 30 (August 1993): 359–68.

43. Mark B. Traylor, "Product Involvement and Brand Commitment," *Journal of Advertising Research* (December 1981): 51–56.

44. Fritz Heider, *The Psychology of Interpersonal Relations* (New York: Wiley, 1958).

45. Quoted in Jon Weinbach, "Ad Score! Major League Soccer Teams Will Sell Ad Space on Players' Jerseys," *Wall Street Journal* (September 28, 2006): B1.

46. R. B. Cialdini, R. J. Borden, A. Thorne, M. R. Walker, S. Freeman, and L. R. Sloan, "Basking in Reflected Glory: Three (Football) Field Studies," *Journal of Personality and Social Psychology* 34 (1976): 366–75; "Boola Boola, Moola Moola," *Sports Illustrated* (February 16, 1998): 28.

47. Debra Z. Basil and Paul M. Herr, "Attitudinal Balance and Cause-Related Marketing: An Empirical Application of Balance Theory," *Journal of Consumer Psychology* 16, no. 4, (2006): 391–403.

48. Leslie Kaufman, "Enough Talk," *Newsweek* (August 18, 1997): 48–49.

49. William L. Wilkie, *Consumer Behavior* (New York: Wiley, 1986).

50. M. Fishbein, "An Investigation of the Relationships between Beliefs about an Object and the Attitude toward That Object," *Human Relations* 16 (1983): 233–40.

51. Allan Wicker, "Attitudes versus Actions: The Relationship of Verbal and Overt Behavioral Responses to Attitude Objects," *Journal of Social Issues* 25 (Autumn 1969): 65.

52. Laura Bird, "Loved the Ad. May (or May Not) Buy the Product," *Wall Street Journal* (April 7, 1994): B1.

53. Icek Ajzen and Martin Fishbein, "Attitude–Behavior Relations: A Theoretical Analysis and Review of Empirical Research," *Psychological Bulletin* 84 (September 1977): 888–918.

54. Morris B. Holbrook and William J. Havlena, "Assessing the Real-to-Artificial Generalizability of Multi-Attribute Attitude Models in Tests of New Product Designs," *Journal of Marketing Research* 25 (February 1988): 25–35; Terence A. Shimp and Alican Kavas, "The Theory of Reasoned Action Applied to Coupon Usage," *Journal of Consumer Research* 11 (December 1984): 795–809.

55. R. P. Abelson, "Conviction," *American Psychologist* 43 (1988): 267–75; R. E. Petty and J. A. Krosnick, *Attitude Strength: Antecedents and Consequences* (Mahwah, NJ: Erlbaum, 1995); Ida E. Berger and Linda F. Alwitt, "Attitude Conviction: A Self-Reflective Measure of Attitude Strength," *Journal of Social Behavior and Personality* 11, no. 3 (1996): 557–72.

56. Berger and Alwitt, "Attitude Conviction: A Self-Reflective Measure of Attitude Strength."

57. Richard P. Bagozzi, Hans Baumgartner, and Youjae Yi, "Coupon Usage and the Theory of Reasoned Action," in Rebecca H. Holman and Michael R. Solomon, eds., *Advances in Consumer Research* 18 (Provo, UT: Association for Consumer Research, 1991): 24–27; Edward F. McQuarrie, "An Alternative to Purchase Intentions: The Role of Prior Behavior in Consumer Expenditure on Computers," *Journal of the Market Research Society* 30 (October 1988): 407–37; Arch G. Woodside and William O. Bearden, "Longitudinal Analysis of Consumer Attitude, Intention, and Behavior toward Beer Brand Choice," in William D. Perrault, Jr., ed., *Advances in Consumer Research* 4 (Ann Arbor, MI: Association for Consumer Research, 1977): 349–56.

58. Andy Greenfield, "The Naked Truth (Studying Consumer Behavior)," *Brandweek* (October 13, 1997): 22.

59. Michael J. Ryan and Edward H. Bonfield, "The Fishbein Extended Model and Consumer Behavior," *Journal of Consumer Research* 2 (1975): 118–36.

60. Blair H. Sheppard, Jon Hartwick, and Paul R. Warshaw, "The Theory of Reasoned Action: A Meta-Analysis of Past Research with Recommendations for Modifications and Future Research," *Journal of Consumer Research* 15 (December 1988): 325–43.

61. Joseph A. Cote, James McCullough, and Michael Reilly, "Effects of Unexpected Situations on Behavior–Intention Differences: A Garbology Analysis," *Journal of Consumer Research* 12 (September 1985): 188–94.

62. Russell H. Fazio, Martha C. Powell, and Carol J. Williams, "The Role of Attitude Accessibility in the Attitude-to-Behavior Process," *Journal of Consumer Research* 16 (December 1989): 280–88; Robert E. Smith and William R. Swinyard, "Attitude–Behavior Consistency: The Impact of Product Trial versus Advertising," *Journal of Marketing Research* 20 (August 1983): 257–67.

63. For a recent similar application, cf. N. T. Tavassoli and G. J. Fitzsimons, G. J.,Spoken and Typed Expressions of Repeated Attitudes: Matching Response Modes Leads to Attitude Retrieval versus Construction, *Journal of Consumer Research* 33, no. 2 (2006): 179-87.

64. Kulwant Singh, Siew Meng Leong, Chin Tiong Tan, and Kwei Cheong Wong, "A Theory of Reasoned Action Perspective of Voting Behavior: Model and Empirical Test," *Psychology & Marketing* 12, no. 1 (January 1995): 37–51; Joseph A. Cote and Patriya S. Tansuhaj, "Culture Bound Assumptions in Behavior Intention Models," in Thom Srull, ed., *Advances in Consumer Research* 16 (Provo, UT: Association for Consumer Research, 1989): 105–9.

65. Joel B. Cohen and Americus Reed, "A Multiple Pathway Anchoring and Adjustment (MPAA) Model of Attitude Generation and Recruitment," *Journal of Consumer Research* 33 (June 2006): 1–15.

66. Richard P. Bagozzi and Paul R. Warshaw, "Trying to Consume," *Journal of Consumer Research* 17 (September 1990): 127–40.

67. Barbara Presley Noble, "After Years of Deregulation, a New Push to Inform the Public," *New York Times* (October 27, 1991): F5.

68. Matthew Greenwald and John P. Katosh, "How to Track Changes in Attitudes," *American Demographics* (August 1987): 46.

69. Lisa Guernsey, "Welcome to College. Now Meet Our Sponsor," *New York Times on the Web* (August 17, 1999).

Attitude Change
and Interactive Communications

CHAPTER 8

Chapter Objectives

When you finish this chapter you should understand why:

● The communications model identifies several important components for marketers when they try to change consumers' attitudes toward products and services.

● The consumer who processes such a message is not necessarily the passive receiver of information marketers once believed him to be.

● Several factors influence a message source's effectiveness.

● The way a marketer structures his message determines how persuasive it will be.

● Audience characteristics help to determine whether the nature of the source or the message itself will be relatively more effective.

natalie is sorting through today's mail: bill, ad, bill, fund-raising letter from political candidate, offer for another credit card.

Aha! Here it is; the envelope she's been waiting for: an invitation to a posh cocktail party at her friend Tracy's ad agency. This will be her chance to see and be seen, to mingle, network, and maybe even land a job offer. But what to wear? Somehow her industrial grunge clothes don't seem appropriate for the new life she imagines as an account executive. Natalie needs help, so she does what comes naturally. First, she instant messages (IMs) some of her friends to let them know about the event; then she fires up her computer to check out what the *fashionistas* roaming the blogosphere recommend this season. Browsing through <u>shoppingblog.com</u>, she quickly learns there's a return to simple and elegant. Say goodbye to the many-layered look— today it's menswear-inspired (Katherine Hepburn, with wide soft pants, vests), or retro glamour from the 1940s (cinched waists, pencil skirts, ultra-feminine).[1] On the other hand, she might make a real entrance if she shows up in a wild graphic print by Diane von Furstenberg or Sass & Bide that <u>shoppingthetrend.com</u> is raving about.[2] Natalie quickly copies some snapshots from a bunch of Web sites and e-mails them to her buddies to get their votes. It's fun to get input from "real people" in addition to fashion industry snobs.

Changing Attitudes Through Communication

BUY NOW! Ad marketers constantly bombard us with messages imploring us to change our attitudes—and of course buy their products. These persuasion attempts can range from logical arguments to graphic pictures, from peers who try to intimidate us to celebrities who try to charm us. In this chapter we'll review some of the factors that help to determine the effectiveness of marketing communications. Our focus will be on some basic aspects of communication that specifically help to determine how and if consumers will form new attitudes or modify existing ones. **Persuasion** involves an active attempt to change attitudes. This is of course job number one for many marketing communications. We'll learn more about how marketers try to accomplish this throughout this chapter, but for now we can set the stage by listing some basic psychological principles that influence people to change their minds or comply with a request:[3]

- **Reciprocity:** We are more likely to give if first we receive. That's why including money in a mail survey questionnaire increases the response rate by an average of 65 percent over surveys that come without financial incentives in the envelope.
- **Scarcity:** Like people, items are more attractive when they aren't available. In one study, researchers asked people to rate the quality of chocolate chip cookies. Participants who only got two cookies liked them better than did those who got one of the same kind of cookie. That helps explain why we tend to value "limited edition" items.
- **Authority:** We believe an authoritative source much more readily than one that is less authoritative. That explains why the American public's opinion on an issue can shift by as much as 2 percent when the *New York Times* (but not the *National Enquirer*) runs an article about it.
- **Consistency:** As we saw in the previous chapter, people try not to contradict themselves in terms of what they say and do about an issue. In one study, students at an Israeli university who solicited donations to help disabled people doubled the amount they normally collected in a neighborhood by first asking the residents to sign a petition supporting this cause 2 weeks before actually asking for the donations.
- **Liking:** We agree with those we like or admire. In one study, good-looking fund-raisers raised almost twice as much as other volunteers who were not as attractive.
- **Consensus:** We consider what others do before we decide what to do. People are more likely to donate to a charity if they first see a list of the names of their neighbors who have already done so.

DECISIONS, DECISIONS:
TACTICAL COMMUNICATIONS OPTIONS

Suppose a car company wants to create an advertising campaign for a new ragtop it's targeting to young drivers. As it plans this campaign, the automaker must develop a message that will arouse desire for the car. To craft persuasive messages that might persuade someone to buy this car instead of the many others available, we must answer several questions:

- Who will we show driving the car in the ad? A Formula 1 driver? A career woman? A hip-hop star? The source of a message helps determine whether consumers will accept it.
- How should we construct the message? Should it emphasize the negative consequences of being left out when others are driving cool cars and you're still

tooling around in your old clunker? Should it directly compare the car with others already on the market, or maybe present a fantasy in which a tough-minded female executive meets a dashing stranger while she's cruising down the highway?

- What media should we use? Should the ad run in a magazine? Should we air it on TV? Sell the product door-to-door? Post the material on a Web site? Convince bloggers to write about it? If we do produce a print ad, should we run it in the pages of *Vogue*? *Interiors*? *Car and Driver*? Sometimes *where* you say something is as important as *what* you say. Ideally, we should match the medium's attributes with those of what we're selling. For example, advertising in magazines with high prestige is more effective when we want to communicate messages about overall product image and quality, whereas specialized expert magazines will do a better job when we want to convey factual information.[4]
- What characteristics of the target market might lead them to accept the ad? If targeted users are frustrated in their daily lives, they might be more receptive to a fantasy appeal. If they're status oriented, maybe a commercial should show bystanders swooning with admiration as the car cruises by.

 ## The Elements of Communication

Marketers traditionally rely on the **communications model** that you see in Figure 8.1. This model specifies the elements they need to control in order to communicate with their customers. One of these is a source, where the communication originates. Another is the message itself. There are many ways to say something, and the structure of the message has a significant effect on how we perceive it. We must transmit the message via a medium, which could be TV, radio, magazines, billboards, personal contact, or even a matchbook cover. One or more *receivers* (such as Natalie) interpret the message in light of their own experiences. Finally, the source receives *feedback* so that the marketer can use receivers' reactions to modify aspects of the message as necessary.

 ## An Updated View: Interactive Communications

Although Natalie managed to ignore most of the "junk mail" that arrived at her door, she didn't avoid marketing messages—instead she chose which ones she wanted to

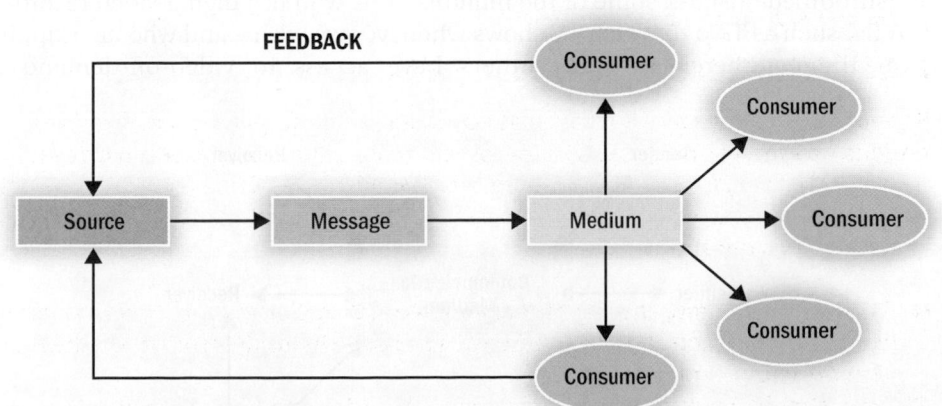

FIGURE 8.1
THE TRADITIONAL COMMUNICATIONS MODEL

Marketing Opportunity

Highly involved consumers who want to share their opinions with manufacturers are an invaluable (and often free) form of input to marketing decisions. Consider these recent examples:

- The beauty division of the NPD Group, which tracks retail purchases, noticed that a product intended to reduce stretch marks called StriVectin-SD was selling exceptionally well at department store beauty counters. The firm found that about 75 percent of buyers actually were using it on their faces as a wrinkle fighter. Taking heed of this new use for the product, its manufacturer unveiled a new advertising slogan, "Better than Botox?"

- Customers have a hand in creating virtually every component of Jones Soda. The company gets suggestions for off-beat flavors (including chocolate fudge and green apple), wacky names (Whoop Ass and MF Grape), and neon colors. Fans submit photos that Jones pastes on its labels. Even the "Deep Thoughts" quotes you'll see underneath the bottle caps ("76.4% of all statistics are meaningless") come straight from Jones enthusiasts.

- General Motors summoned 481 people to a building on an empty fairground in Southern California to critique six early renderings of the Hummer SUV. As they reacted to sketches of the exterior and

see. The traditional communications model is not entirely wrong, but it also doesn't tell the whole story—especially in today's dynamic world of interactivity where consumers have many more choices available to them and greater control over which messages they *choose* to process.[5]

In fact, the popular strategy we call **permission marketing** acknowledges that a marketer will be much more successful when he communicates with consumers who have already agreed to listen to him—consumers who "opt out" of listening to the message probably weren't good prospects in the first place.[6] However, those who say they are interested in learning more are likely to be receptive to marketing communications they have chosen to see or hear. As the permission marketing concept reminds us, we don't have to simply sit there and take it. We have a voice in deciding what messages we choose to see and when—and we exercise that option more and more.

Social scientists developed the traditional model to understand mass communications in which a source transmits information to many receivers at one time—typically via a *broadcast* medium such as television. This perspective essentially views advertising as the process of transferring information to the buyer before a sale. It regards a message as perishable—the marketer repeats the same message to a large audience and then the message "vanishes" when a new campaign takes its place. As we'll see, that model doesn't work as well now that we can *narrowcast*, or finely tune our messages to very small groups of receivers (sometimes even one person at a time).

 ## Who's in Charge of the Remote?

Quick, check your Facebook account. Exciting technological and social developments make us rethink the picture of passive consumers as people increasingly play more proactive roles in communications. In other words, they are to a greater extent becoming *partners*—rather than couch potatoes—in the communications process. Their input is helping to shape the messages they and others like them receive, and furthermore, they may seek out these messages rather than sit home and wait to see them on TV or in the paper. Figure 8.2 illustrates this updated approach to interactive communications.

One of the early instigators of this communications revolution was the humble handheld remote control device. As VCRs (remember them?) began to be commonplace in homes, suddenly consumers had more input into what they wanted to watch—and when. No longer did the TV networks decide when we could watch our favorite shows, and we didn't have to miss the new episode of *Dallas* because it was on at the same time as the football game.

Since that time, of course, our ability to control our media environment has mushroomed. Just ask some of the millions of us who use digital video recorders (DVRs) such as TiVo to watch TV shows whenever we wish—and who are skipping over the commercials.[7] Many others have access to video-on-demand or

■ **FIGURE 8.2**
AN UPDATED COMMUNICATIONS
MODEL

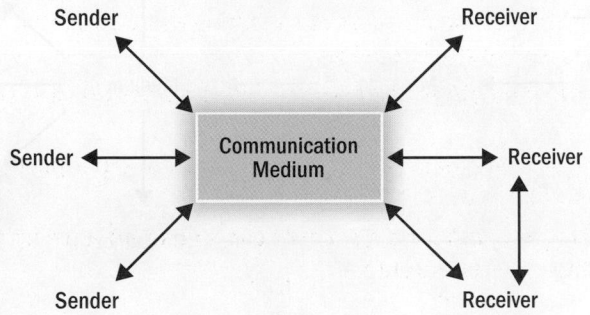

pay-per-view TV. Home-shopping networks encourage us to call in and discuss our passion for cubic zirconium jewelry live on the air. Caller ID devices and answering machines allow us to decide if we will accept a phone call during dinner and to know if a telemarketer is lurking on the other end before we pick up the phone. A bit of Web surfing allows us to identify kindred spirits around the globe, to request information about products, and even to provide suggestions to product designers and market researchers.

 # New Message Formats

An array of new ways to transmit information in both text and picture form offers marketers exciting alternatives to traditional advertising on TV, billboards, magazines, and so on.[8] **M-commerce** (mobile commerce), where marketers promote their goods and services via wireless devices, including cell phones, PDAs, and iPods, is red-hot. In Europe and Asia, consumers already rely on their cell phones to connect them to the world in ways we are only starting to realize in the United States. In Asia, tiny cell phone screens have become electronic wallets that buy Cokes from vending machines and devices that dole out McDonald's coupons on the phone screen. Among the Chinese, cell phones have become such important status symbols that relatives at funeral rites burn paper cell phone effigies so the dead will have their mobiles in the afterlife.

American companies are taking note of this deep attachment and they are talking to their Asian customers via cell also. In Japan, customers of Procter & Gamble's Whisper brand of feminine hygiene products signed up 80,000 women to receive messages about their "happy cycle." A typical message reads: "Your skin gets even more sensitive and dry, especially during this period. . . . Try not to use new skin-care products." Already, TV companies are using video-enabled cell phones to promote their prime-time lineups by sending teasers of new shows. To promote its Britney Spears cologne, Curious, to teens, Elizabeth Arden mounted a $5 million campaign that began with banner ads on teen Internet sites posing questions such as "Do you dare?" Those curious enough to give their phone numbers—27,000 during 7 weeks—received a voice message from Britney herself discussing the campaign's TV spot that was running on Viacom's MTV. In only 5 weeks, Curious became the number-one-selling fragrance in the United States.

Do you blog? The other media format that's getting a lot of attention is **blogging**, where people post messages to the Web in diary form. Blogging started as a grassroots movement where individuals shared their thoughts on a range of topics from the mundane to the profound. This phenomenon hasn't slowed down yet; people post about 40,000 new blogs every day. In fact, as of late 2007 almost half of all Americans had visited the blogosphere and this number jumps to over 3/4 of 18-to-24-year-olds. There's a lot of blogs to choose from—just about a billion at last count.[9]

New forms of blogging itself continue to develop such as the following:

Moblogging: You can post a message to a blog while you're on the go, from a camera phone or handheld device.

Video blogging (vlogging): You can post video diaries on sites such as YouTube.

Podcasting: You can create your own radio show that people can listen to either on their computers or iPods.

RSS (really simple syndication): People can sign up to have updates sent automatically to their computers.

interior, four GM designers listened from behind a curtain, scrawling changes on paper. As a result of drivers' suggestions, designers shrunk the vehicle's grille to make the Hummer look more solid—and less jeeplike. Headlights are flatter to help the sedan-size vehicle seem more imposing. The doors have some detailing to appear less nondescript and flat.

- Dannon USA went to consumers when its reduced-fat Light 'n Fit yogurts were not selling well. The company e-mailed 40,000 men and women and asked them to click on a link to help create a new product and get a shot at winning $10,000. They evaluated a series of yogurt containers with different combinations of name, package design, nutritional labeling, and size. By the end of the project, researchers decided that the yogurt should be called Carb Control, come in a red container, be sold in a four-pack of 4-ounce cups, and that the label should appeal to dieters by highlighting the claims of "80 percent less sugar" and "3 grams of carbs."

- Taco Bell also recruited its customers to help create a hot-selling burrito—one the fast-food chain hoped would be a healthy version that would also taste good. Respondents chose from among 10 categories of fixings, including 3 kinds of chicken and 11 sauces, and watched as an animated program assembled and cooked their concoctions. But instead of coming up with a low-cal item, most people clamored for a three-cheese soaked "indulgent" burrito and said they were willing to pay extra to get it.[11]

Flogs (fake blogs): Companies create flogs to generate buzz. For example, McDonald's created a flog to accompany its Super Bowl ad about the mock discovery of a French fry shaped like American President Abraham Lincoln.[10]

Twittering: Thousands "twitter" their friends (see Chapter 5) as they share moment-by-moment reports on what they're doing at <u>twitter.com</u>.

 # The Source

Regardless of whether we receive a message by "snail mail" (netheads' slang for the postal service) or e-mail, common sense tells us that if different people say or write the very same words, the message can affect us differently. Researchers have studied *source effects* for more than 50 years. By attributing the same message to different sources and measuring the degree of attitude change that occurs after listeners hear it, we can determine which characteristics of a communicator cause attitude change.[12]

Under most conditions, the source of a message can have a big impact on the likelihood that receivers will accept it. Choosing a source to maximize attitude change taps into several dimensions. Marketers can choose a spokesperson because she is an expert, attractive, famous, or even a "typical" consumer who is both likable and trustworthy. *Credibility* and *attractiveness* are two particularly important source characteristics (i.e., how much we either believe or like the communicator).[13]

How do marketing specialists decide whether to stress credibility or attractiveness when choosing a message source? There should be a match between the needs of the recipient and the potential rewards the source offers. When this match occurs, the recipient is more motivated to process the message. An attractive source, for example, is more effective for receivers who tend to be sensitive about social acceptance and others' opinions, whereas a credible, expert source is more powerful when she speaks to internally oriented people.[14] However, even a credible source's trustworthiness evaporates if she endorses too many products.[15]

The choice may also depend on the type of product. A positive source can reduce risk and increase message acceptance overall, but particular types of sources are more effective at reducing different kinds of risk. Experts are effective at changing attitudes toward utilitarian products that have high performance risk, such as vacuums, because they are complex and may not work as we expect. Celebrities are more effective when they focus on products such as jewelry and furniture that have high social risk, where the user is more concerned about the impression others have of him. Finally, "typical" consumers, who are appealing sources because of their similarity to the recipient, tend to be most effective when they provide real-life endorsements for everyday products that are low risk, such as cookies.[16]

SOURCE CREDIBILITY

Source credibility refers to a communicator's expertise, objectivity, or trustworthiness. This dimension relates to consumers' beliefs that this person is competent and that she is willing to provide the necessary information to adequately evaluate competing products. Sincerity is particularly important when a company tries to publicize its *corporate social responsibility (CSR)* activities that benefit the community in some way. When consumers believe it's genuinely doing good things, a company's image can skyrocket. But this effort can backfire if people question the organization's motivations (e.g., if they think the firm is spending more to talk about its good deeds than actually to do them).[17] Not too surprisingly, people who see deceptive advertising experience a feeling of distrust that carries over to other messages from that source and even to other sources because they are more likely to assume that advertising in general is not very credible—a true case of poisoning the well for other marketers![18]

A credible source is particularly persuasive when the consumer has not yet learned much about a product or formed an opinion of it.[19] The decision to pay an expert or a celebrity to tout a product can be a very costly one. However, typically the investment is worth it simply because market analysts use the announcement of an endorsement contract to evaluate a firm's potential profitability, thereby affecting its expected return. On average, then, the impact of endorsements on stock returns appears to be so positive that it offsets the cost of hiring the spokesperson.[20]

THE SLEEPER EFFECT

Although in general more positive sources tend to increase attitude change, there are exceptions to this rule. Sometimes we can think a source is obnoxious, yet still it is effective. A case in point is Mr. Whipple, the irritating but well-known TV character who scolds toilet paper shoppers, "Please don't squeeze the Charmin!" In some instances the differences in attitude change between positive sources and less positive sources become erased over time. After a while, people appear to "forget" about the negative source and wind up changing their attitudes anyway. We call this process the **sleeper effect**.[22]

Researchers debate the explanation for the sleeper effect. Initially, some proposed the *dissociative cue hypothesis,* which states that over time we disassociate the message and the source in our minds. The message remains on its own in memory, causing the delayed attitude change.[23] The rival *availability-valence hypothesis* emphasizes the selectivity of memory based on limited capacity.[24] If the associations we link to the negative source are less available than those we link to the message information, the residual impact of the message enhances persuasion. Consistent with this view, researchers have been able to demonstrate the sleeper effect only when the message had stronger associations in a person's memory than did the source.[25]

Net Profit

Flying in the face of conventional wisdom that says the source of a message is crucial, a popular strategy for online advertising is to disguise the source or even to make one up. At the hugely successful Subservient Chicken site (subservientchicken.com), visitors can make a man in a chicken suit obey their whims—and you have to look hard to figure out that Burger King sponsors the site. The comeclean.com site asks visitors to type in their confessions. These appear on a hand over a sink, where they are washed away with soap (made by Method, the soapmaker that sponsors the site) that you can buy at an online gift shop. Visitors can also peek at previous visitors' anonymous confessions like this one: "I haven't changed my sheets in about a month or two."[21]

Many products are personified by make-believe characters.

CB AS I SEE IT

Professor Ann Schlosser
The University of Washington

It is increasingly common for consumers to go online to gather product information not only from marketers but also from other consumers. Consumer product reviews—or reviews provided by consumers based on their own product experiences—are available online at portals such as Yahoo.com and Citysearch.com as well as shopping sites such as Amazon.com. There are also Web sites such as Epinions.com that are devoted to providing consumer product reviews. In fact, Epinions.com states that it provides "unbiased reviews by real people." Yet, are online consumer reviews really unbiased? Do consumers view them as such?

One might expect that consumers would have little incentive to lie online when posting their product reviews. They can be anonymous, and there are few incentives to write an overly favorable (or unfavorable) review. However, I have found that consumers do strategically edit their online reviews in order to create favorable impressions of being discerning consumers. For example, I found that even when individuals had a positive experience watching a movie, if they learned that another person judged the movie unfavorably, then they posted a less favorable movie rating than they otherwise would.

Another important area to understand is how consumers use such reviews. For instance, do consumers believe that these reviews are unbiased? Might consumers question the credibility, and thus the persuadability, of online reviews? And if they do, on what basis do they base their judgments? I have found that consumers do not blindly trust online reviews but instead assess the content of a review to determine whether the reviewer is credible.[32] Credibility perceptions and thus the persuasiveness of the posted reviews depend in part on (1) whether the reasons that reviewers (or the source) provide when evaluating the product support their product ratings and (2) whether the content of the review supports the readers' (or recipients') general attitudes toward such products. For instance, mentioning both the pros and cons of a product was most credible and persuasive when the reviewer gave the product a moderately rather than extremely favorable rating (e.g., four rather than five stars). Yet mentioning both the pros and cons of a product (e.g., a specific martial arts film) were less credible and persuasive when the reader generally likes such products (e.g., likes martial arts films in general).

BUILDING CREDIBILITY

A message's credibility increases if receivers think the source's qualifications are relevant to the product she endorses. This linkage can overcome other objections people may have to the endorser or the product. Ronald Biggs, whose claim to fame was his 1963 role in The Great Train Robbery in the United Kingdom, successfully served as a spokesman in Brazil for a company that makes door locks—a topic about which he is presumably knowledgeable![26]

It's important to note that what is credible to one consumer segment may be a turnoff to another. Indeed, rebellious or even deviant celebrities may be attractive to some simply for that reason. Tommy Hilfiger cultivated a rebellious, street-smart image by using rapper Snoop Doggy Dogg (who was acquitted of murder charges) to help launch his clothing line and Coolio, a former crack addict and thief, as a runway model.[27] Parents may not be thrilled by these message sources—but isn't that the point?

A consumer's beliefs about a product's attributes will weaken if he perceives that the source is biased.[28] *Knowledge bias* implies that a source's knowledge about a topic is not accurate. *Reporting bias* occurs when a source has the required knowledge but his willingness to convey it accurately is compromised—as when a racket manufacturer pays a star tennis player to use its products exclusively. The source's credentials might be appropriate, but the fact that consumers see the expert as a

Websites like Epinions.com bring consumers more directly into the communications loop as they provide a way for them to give direct feedback to companies.

"hired gun" compromises believability. In one instance, critics jumped on Microsoft when it offered to pay "travel costs" for professors if they presented papers at conferences and mentioned how Microsoft programs helped them in their work.[29]

Concerns are growing in the advertising world about the public's skepticism regarding celebrities who endorse products for money. It doesn't help matters when Britney Spears appears in lavish commercials for Pepsi-Cola but gets caught on camera drinking Coca-Cola, or when Shaquille O'Neal at various times pledges his fast-food allegiance to Burger King, McDonald's, *and* Taco Bell. Tiger Woods promoted Rolex's Tudor watches for 5 years, but then he abruptly switched to Swiss rival Tag Heuer. Although Tiger explained the defection simply by noting that "My tastes have changed," it's possible that the estimated $2 million he got for this new endorsement was a factor.[30] A research firm that tracks celebrities' credibility reported in its 2006 survey that more than a third of respondents who knew of home improvement guru Ty Pennington said they would be more likely to buy a product he endorsed. However, only 4 percent said they trusted Paris Hilton (and this was before she got busted!).[31]

HYPE VERSUS BUZZ: THE CORPORATE PARADOX

Obviously, many marketers spend lavishly to create marketing messages that they hope will convince hordes of customers they are the best. There's the rub—in many cases they may be trying too hard! Let's call this the **corporate paradox**—the more involved a company appears to be in the dissemination of news about its products, the less credible it becomes.[33] As we'll see in Chapter 11, consumer *word of mouth* typically is the most convincing kind of message. As Table 8.1 shows, **buzz** is word of

TABLE 8.1
HYPE VERSUS BUZZ

Hype	⟺	Buzz
Advertising		Word-of-Mouth
Overt		Covert
Corporate		Grass-Roots
Fake		Authentic
Skepticism		Credibility

mouth that consumers think is authentic and truly customer generated. In contrast, we tend to dismiss **hype** as inauthentic—corporate propaganda a company with an axe to grind has planted. So the challenge to marketers is to get the word out there without looking like they are working at it. That's why Coca-Cola decided to promote its newly redesigned can, which resembles the trendy Red Bull brand, by placing it in select Manhattan nightclubs and boutiques. Marketing strategists reasoned that young trendsetters would be more likely to tune in to the brand's new look if they "discovered" it in chic watering holes than learning about it in a bells-and-whistles ad campaign.[34]

The now-famous movie *Blair Witch Project* (1999), which led many viewers to believe the fictional treatment was in fact a real documentary, demonstrated the power of a brand that seems as if it's not one. Some marketers are trying to borrow the veneer of buzz by mounting "stealth" campaigns that seem as if their company had nothing to do with them. *Buzz building* has become the new mantra at many companies that recognize the power of underground word of mouth.[35] Indeed, a bit of a cottage industry has sprung up as some firms begin to specialize in the corporate shill business by planting comments on Web sites made to look as if they originated from actual consumers. Consider these examples:

- Building on the success of its resurrected Buddy Lee icon, Lee Apparel commissioned 15 Web sites devoted to the diminutive doll that looked "horrible, as if fans created them," according to an employee of the company that created the sites. The goal was to make it look as if people were spontaneously turning on to the Buddy Lee phenomenon.[36]
- Dodge's Ram truck made a splash with a Web site that fans supposedly generated to organize drag races in several cities. The site features amateurishly shot footage of a drag race and contains no reference to the Dodge connection, just a shot of the Ram's grille. In this footage, the races were staged so that only Ram trucks emerged victorious. To enhance the "outlaw" image of drag racing, the company sent bogus letters to editors of local newspapers protesting the rise in street racing and mentioning the Dodge Ram's involvement in particular. Supposedly, the guerrilla campaign was so hush-hush even the top brass at the car company were kept in the dark.[37]
- When RCA records wanted to create a buzz around singer Christina Aguilera, it hired a team of young people to swarm the Web and chat about her on popular teen sites such as alloy.com, bolt.com and gurl.com. Posing as fans, they posted entries raving about her new material. Just before one of her albums debuted, RCA also hired a direct-marketing company to e-mail electronic postcards filled with song snippets and biographical information to 50,000 Web addresses.[38] The album quickly went to number one on the charts.

As powerful as these tactics are, they have the potential to poison the well in a big way. Web surfers, already skeptical about what they see and hear, may get to the point where they assume every "authentic" site they find is really a corporate front. Until then, however, buzz building online is going strong.

SOURCE ATTRACTIVENESS

Source attractiveness refers to the social value recipients attribute to a communicator. This value relates to the person's physical appearance, personality, social status, or similarity to the receiver (we like to listen to people who are like us). Former boxer George Foreman made endorsement history when he became the first celebrity to sell his name in perpetuity; the company went on to sell more than 10 million of George Foreman's Lean Mean Fat Reducing Grilling Machines. In exchange for $137.5 million, Foreman agreed never to endorse rival cookware, although he is still free to pitch other products.[39] That's a lot of low-fat burgers! Now, former U.S. National Football League coach Mike Ditka, who coached the Chicago Bears, is blitzing the wine cellar with his collection of vino labels including "Da Coach Pinot Grigio" and "Mike Ditka's Kick Ass Red."[40]

"WHAT IS BEAUTIFUL IS GOOD"

Almost everywhere we turn, beautiful people are trying to persuade us to buy or do something. As Chapter 5 showed us, our society places a very high premium on physical attractiveness. We assume that people who are good looking are smarter, cooler, and happier than other less attractive people. This is an example of a *halo effect*, which occurs when we assume that persons who rank high on one dimension excel on others as well. We can explain this effect in terms of the consistency principle we discussed in Chapter 7, which states that people are more comfortable when all of their judgments about a person correspond. Clearly, beauty sells—so how does this happen?[41]

One explanation is that physical attractiveness is a cue that facilitates or modifies information processing by directing consumers' attention to relevant marketing stimuli. Some evidence indicates that consumers pay more attention to ads that contain attractive models, though not necessarily to the ad copy.[42] In other words, we may be more likely to notice an ad with a beautiful person in it, but we won't necessarily read it. We may enjoy looking at a handsome person, but these positive feelings do not necessarily affect product attitudes or purchase intentions.[43]

Under the right circumstances, however, beauty can indeed be a source of information—especially when the advertised product actually (or so the marketer claims) enhances attractiveness or sexuality.[44] The *social adaptation perspective* assumes that the perceiver will weight information more heavily if he feels it is instrumental in forming an attitude. As we saw in Chapter 2, we filter out irrelevant information to minimize cognitive effort. So in these situations, a hot endorser provides appropriate information and this becomes a central, task-relevant cue. For example, attractiveness affects attitudes toward ads about perfume or cologne (where attractiveness is relevant) but not toward coffee ads (where attractiveness is not relevant).[45]

STAR POWER: CELEBRITIES AS COMMUNICATIONS SOURCES

About 20 percent of U.S. ads feature celebrities, up from close to 10 percent only a decade ago. Indeed, many celebrities used to avoid making commercials for fear that hawking products would cheapen their image. Sometimes they made ads in other countries (especially in Japan—check out japander.com to see some of your favorites pitching all sorts of things) and stipulated that these couldn't be aired back home—but with widespread Internet access now, dozens of these spots, featuring actors such as Arnold Schwarzenegger, George Clooney, and Jennifer Aniston, have found their way

Marketing Pitfall

Dead celebrities are hot. From Einstein to Elvis and Gene Kelly to Orville Redenbacher, they keep popping up posthumously pitching everything from cars to cola. But when the London office of Saatchi & Saatchi featured images of Kurt Cobain and other dead rock stars in ads for Dr. Martens footwear, the agency and its client got burned. Courtney Love (Cobain's widow) saw an ad showing the former lead singer of the band Nirvana sitting on a cloud in the sky and wearing a pair of Docs. She was not happy, and when she posted her objections at the AdCritic Web site, others joined in the cause. The uproar got so heated that Airwair International, the British company that makes Dr. Martens cancelled its contract with the agency. This slipup reportedly cost Saatchi almost $10 million.[48]

online. In many cases, they are plugging their own product lines as retailers try to compete with cheap-chic stores such as H&M and Zara: Celebrities with thriving clothing collections include J-Lo, Gwen Stefani, Mary-Kate and Ashley Olsen, Sean "P. Diddy" Combs, Nelly, and even Donald Trump (let's just hope The Donald doesn't go into hair products).[46]

As (hopefully) our discussion about the consistency principle illustrates, these messages tend to be much more effective when there's a logical connection between the star and the product. Victoria's Secret signed none other than Bob Dylan to pitch its Angels line of lingerie, whose ads include models cavorting in the background to a remixed version of Dylan's 1997 song *Love Sick*. This is an antiestablishment folk singer who once wrote lyrics such as "Advertising signs that con you/Into thinking you're the one/That can do what's never been done/That can win what's never been won. . . ."[47]

Why do stars command this kind of money? One study found that compared to "ordinary" faces, our brains pay more attention to famous faces and more efficiently process information about these images.[49] Celebrities increase awareness of a firm's advertising and enhance both company image and brand attitudes.[50] A celebrity endorsement strategy can be an effective way to differentiate among similar products. This is especially important when consumers do not perceive many actual differences among competitors, as often occurs when brands are in the mature stage of the product life cycle.

Star power works because celebrities embody *cultural meanings*—they symbolize important categories such as status and social class (a "working-class hero," such as Kevin James of *King of Queens*), gender (a "ladies man," such as Leonardo diCaprio), age (the boyish Michael J. Fox), and even personality types (the nerdy but earnest Hiro on *Heroes*). Ideally, the advertiser decides what meanings the product should convey (that is, how it should position the item in the marketplace) and then chooses a celebrity who embodies a similar meaning. The product's meaning thus moves from the manufacturer to the consumer, using the star as a vehicle.[51] In fact, a new E-Score service specifically looks at hundreds of fictional characters to find out what traits the audience associates with movie and TV personalities. It finds that *Grey Anatomy*'s Dr. O'Malley is the most sincere (Supernanny also scores high on this dimension). Gabrielle Solis on *Desperate Housewives* is sexy and a trendsetter, Rory Gilmore of *The Gilmore Girls* is highly believable, and Shrek's sidekick Donkey is the most appealing to younger viewers.[52]

Singer/actress J-Lo or Beyoncé? Athlete David Beckham or Alan Shearer see http://www.timesonline.co.uk/tol/sport/article1031165.ece? With all those famous people out there, how does a firm decide who should be the source of its marketing messages? For celebrity campaigns to be effective, the endorser must have a clear and popular image. In addition, the celebrity's image and that of the product he or she endorses should be similar—researchers refer to this as the **match-up hypothesis**.[53]

A market research company developed one widely used measure called the *Q Score* (*Q* stands for quality) to decide whether a celebrity will make a good endorser. This rating considers two factors: consumers' level of familiarity with a name and the number of respondents who indicate that a person, program, or character is a favorite. The company evaluates approximately 1,500 celebrities (more than 400 are athletes) each year. Although the Q Score is a reasonably good indicator of celebrities with popular reputations, it doesn't work as well when applied to people such as the American professional player Allen Iverson, whose trash-talking, edgy image might be popular among some consumer segments but not others.[54]

NONHUMAN ENDORSERS

Celebrities can be effective endorsers, but there are drawbacks to using them. As we previously noted, their motives may be suspect if they plug products that don't fit their images or if consumers begin to believe the celebrities never met a product they didn't like (for a fee). They may be involved in a scandal or upset customers, for example, in the United States, when the Milk Processor Education Program suspended "Got Milk?" ads featuring actresses Mary-Kate and Ashley Olsen after Mary-Kate entered a treatment facility for an undisclosed health issue.

For these reasons, some marketers seek alternative sources, including cartoon characters and mascots. After all, as the marketing director for a company that manufactures costumed characters for sports teams and businesses points out, "You don't have to worry about your mascot checking into rehab."[55] And researchers report that spokescharacters, such as the Pillsbury Doughboy, Chester the Cheetah, and the Snuggle Bear, do, in fact, boost viewers' recall of claims that ads make and also yield higher brand attitude.[56]

The Toronto-based clothing company Roots Canada Ltd. employs a "Buddy the Beaver" mascot to promote its outlets. Roots' director of communications observed, "A lot of our stores are in shopping malls. Malls are crowded. People don't pay attention. But it's hard to ignore a 7-foot-tall beaver."[57] Some advertisers are reaching into their vaults and reviving popular characters such as Morris the Cat for 9 Lives cat food and E.B. the Energizer bunny, whereas others are creating new characters such as the popular Aflac duck.[58] Following are some other recent "resurrections":[59]

- The lonely Maytag repairman is more active and outgoing than the former "Old Lonely" character.
- Colonel Sanders has shed his white suit jacket for a red cook's apron as the company he founded unveils a worldwide redesign of its KFC restaurants.
- The Brawny Man stars in an online series where he shows eight real-life husbands the finer points of manliness, domestic chores, and ballroom dancing. He teaches guys to throw hatchets, run deep in the woods while carrying a boulder, and clean filthy windows with super-strong paper towels.
- The public is voting on how it wants to update Mr. Peanut's basic look by adding a bow tie, cuff links or a pocket watch.
- The Sun-Maid Raisin Girl was digitally animated in a new TV campaign after 100 years as a frozen portrait on a red box.
- Unilever replaced fading hunk Fabio with a soap opera actor as the new romantic lead for I Can't Believe It's Not Butter.
- The National Federation of Coffee Growers of Colombia recently announced a new "Juan Valdez" to replace the actor who had starred in its advertising since 1969.

As we saw in Chapter 5, an *avatar* is an increasingly popular alternative to flesh-and-blood endorsers. *Avatar* is a Hindu term for a deity that appears in superhuman or animal form. In the computing world, it means a character you can move around inside a visual, graphical world. Consumers who inhabit virtual worlds such as Second Life, Zwinky, There, and Entropia Universe design their avatars to reflect their own unique personalities, desires, and fantasies.

Now, rock bands, soft drink and fast-food companies, and many other big-time marketers are turning to avatars as communications sources—both "in-world" on Second Life and in the real "meat" world. Coca-Cola launched an avatar-populated site for the Hong Kong market where avatars mill around and chat in a Coke-sponsored world. In 2007, Taco Bell hosted an online casting call for fans to create a digital representation of themselves; three of these avatars then starred in a 30-second spot promoting the idea of a "fourthmeal," a late-night snack.[60]

The advantages of using virtual avatars compared to flesh-and-blood models include the ability to change the avatar in real time to suit the needs of the target audience. From an advertising perspective, they are likely to be more cost effective than hiring a real person. From a personal selling and customer service perspective, they can handle multiple customers at one time, they are not geographically limited, and they are operational 24/7, thus freeing up company employees and sales personnel to perform other activities.

A German firm called NoDNA offers its own stable of cybermodels such as Tyra, who is shown here.

 The Message

A major study of more than 1,000 commercials identified factors that determine whether a commercial message will be persuasive. The single most important feature is whether the communication contains a brand-differentiating message. In other words, does the communication stress a unique attribute or benefit of the product?[61] Table 8.2 lists some other good and bad elements.

Characteristics of the message itself help determine its impact on attitudes. These variables include *how* the message is said as well as *what* is said. These are some issues a marketer faces when she creates a message:

- Should she convey the message in words or pictures?
- How often should she repeat the message?
- Should it draw a conclusion or should this be left up to the listener?
- Should it present both sides of an argument?
- Should it explicitly compare the product to competitors?

TABLE 8.2	
POSITIVE AND NEGATIVE EFFECTS OF ELEMENTS IN TELEVISION COMMERCIALS	

Positive Effects	Negative Effects
Showing convenience of use	Extensive information on components, ingredients, or nutrition
Showing new product or improved features	Outdoor setting (message gets lost)
Casting background (i.e., people are incidental to message)	Large number of on-screen characters
Indirect comparison to other products	Graphic displays
Demonstration of the product in use	
Demonstration of tangible results (e.g., bouncy hair)	
An actor playing the role of an ordinary person	
No principal character (i.e., more time is devoted to the product)	

Source: Adapted from David W. Stewart and David H. Furse, "The Effects of Television Advertising Execution on Recall, Comprehension, and Persuasion," *Psychology & Marketing* 2 (Fall 1985): 135–60. Copyright © 1985 by John Wiley & Sons, Inc. Reprinted by permission.

- Should it include a blatant sexual appeal?
- Should it arouse negative emotions such as fear?
- How concrete or vivid should the arguments and imagery be?
- Should it be funny?

SENDING THE MESSAGE

The saying, "One picture is worth a thousand words" captures the idea that visual stimuli can economically deliver a big impact, especially when the communicator wants to influence receivers' emotional responses. For this reason, advertisers often rely on vivid illustrations or photography.[62]

However, a picture is not always as effective at communicating factual information. Ads that contain the same information elicit different reactions when the marketer presents them in visual versus verbal form. The verbal version affects ratings on the utilitarian aspects of a product, whereas the visual version affects aesthetic evaluations. Verbal elements are more effective when an accompanying picture reinforces them, especially if the illustration is *framed* (the message in the picture strongly relates to the copy).[63]

Because it requires more effort to process, a verbal message is most appropriate for high-involvement situations, such as print contexts in which the reader is motivated to really pay attention to the advertising. Verbal material decays more rapidly in memory, so these messages require more frequent exposures to obtain the desired effect. Visual images, in contrast, allow the receiver to *chunk* information at the time of encoding (see Chapter 3). Chunking results in a stronger memory trace that aids retrieval over time.[64]

Visual elements affect brand attitudes in one of two ways. First, the consumer may form inferences about the brand and change his beliefs because of an illustration's imagery. For example, people in a study who saw an ad for a facial tissue accompanied by a photo of a sunset were more likely to believe that the brand came in attractive colors. Second, visual elements may affect brand attitudes more directly; for example, a strong positive or negative reaction will influence the consumer's attitude toward the ad (A_{ad}), which will then affect brand attitudes (A_b). Figure 8.3 illustrates this *dual component model of brand attitudes.*[65]

■ **FIGURE 8.3** DUAL COMPONENT MODEL OF BRAND ATTITUDES

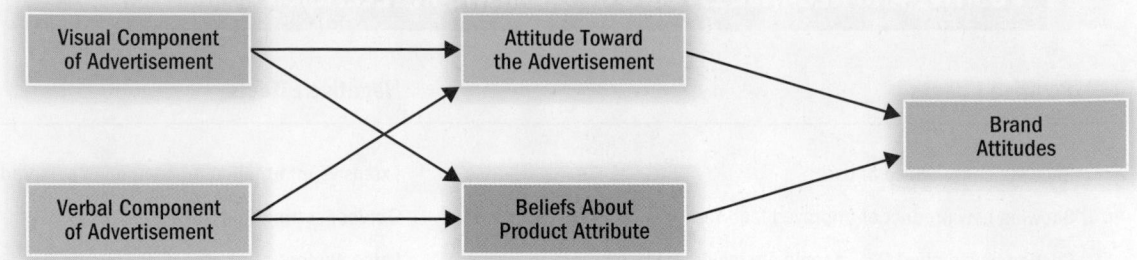

VIVIDNESS

Powerful descriptions or graphics command attention and are more strongly embedded in memory. This may be because they tend to activate mental imagery, whereas abstract stimuli inhibit this process.[66] Of course, this effect can cut both ways: Negative information a marketer presents in a vivid manner may result in more negative evaluations at a later time.[67]

The concrete discussion of a product attribute in ad copy also influences the importance of that attribute because it draws more attention. For example, in a study where participants read two versions of ad copy for a watch, the version that claimed "According to industry sources, three out of every four watch breakdowns are due to water getting into the case," was more effective than the version that simply said, "According to industry sources, many watch breakdowns are due to water getting into the case."[68]

REPETITION

Repetition can be a double-edged sword for marketers. As we noted in Chapter 3, we usually need multiple exposures to a stimulus before learning occurs. Contrary to the saying "familiarity breeds contempt," people tend to like things that are more familiar to them, even if they were not that keen on them initially.[69] Psychologists call this the *mere exposure* phenomenon.

Advertisers find positive effects for repetition even in mature product categories—repeating product information boosts consumers' awareness of the brand, even though the marketers are saying nothing new.[70] However, as we saw in Chapter 2, too

This British clothing ad uses vivid (and perhaps a bit scary?) imagery to communicate.

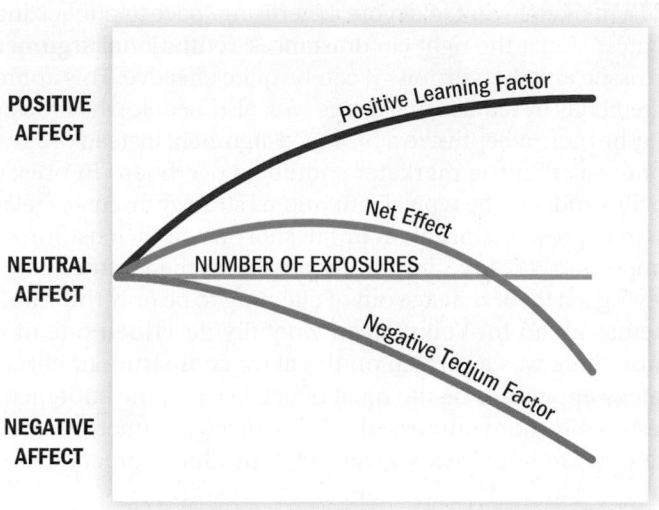

much repetition creates *habituation*, whereby the consumer no longer pays attention to the stimulus because of fatigue or boredom. Excessive exposure can cause advertising wear-out, which can result in negative reactions to an ad after seeing it too much.[71]

The **two-factor theory** explains the fine line between familiarity and boredom; it proposes that two separate psychological processes are operating when we repeatedly show an ad to a viewer. The positive side of repetition is that it increases familiarity and thus reduces uncertainty about the product. The negative side is that over time boredom increases with each exposure. At some point the amount of boredom the viewer experiences begins to exceed the amount of uncertainty reduced, resulting in wear-out. Figure 8.4 depicts this pattern. Its effect is especially pronounced when each exposure is of a fairly long duration (such as a 60-second commercial).[72]

The theory implies that advertisers can overcome this problem by limiting the amount of exposure per repetition (such as using 15-second spots). They can also maintain familiarity but alleviate boredom by slightly varying the content of ads over time; although each spot may be different, campaigns may revolve around a common theme. Recipients who see varied ads about the product absorb more information about product attributes and experience more positive thoughts about the brand than do those who see the same information repeatedly. This additional information also allows the person to resist attempts to change her attitude in the face of a counterattack by a competing brand.[73]

CONSTRUCTING THE ARGUMENT

Many marketing messages are similar to debates or trials; a source presents an argument and tries to convince the receiver to shift her opinion accordingly. As you've no doubt guessed, the *way* we present the argument may be as important as *what* we say.

ONE- VERSUS TWO-SIDED ARGUMENTS

Most messages merely present one or more positive attributes about the product or reasons to buy it. These are *supportive arguments*. An alternative is to use a *two-sided message*, in which the message presents both positive and negative information. Research indicates that two-sided ads can be quite effective, yet marketers rarely use them.[74]

Why would a marketer want to devote advertising space to publicizing a product's negative attributes? Under the right circumstances, **refutational arguments** that first raise a negative issue and then dismiss it can be quite effective. This approach can increase source credibility by reducing *reporting bias*. Also, people who are skeptical about the product may be more receptive to a balanced argument instead of a "whitewash."[75]

This is not to say that the marketer should go overboard in presenting major problems with the product. The typical refutational strategy discusses relatively minor attributes that may present a problem or fall short when the customer compares a product to competitors. Positive, important attributes then refute these drawbacks. For example, Avis got a lot of mileage out of claiming to be only the "No. 2" car rental company, whereas an ad for Volkswagen woefully described one of its cars as a "lemon" because there was a scratch on the glove compartment chrome strip.[76] A two-sided strategy appears to be the most effective when the audience is well educated (and presumably more impressed by a balanced argument).[77] It is also best to use when receivers are not already loyal to the product; "preaching to the choir" about possible drawbacks may raise doubts unnecessarily.

DRAWING CONCLUSIONS

Should the argument draw conclusions, or should the marketer merely present the facts and let the consumer arrive at his own decision? On the one hand, consumers who make their own inferences instead of having them spoon-fed to them will form stronger, more accessible attitudes. On the other hand, leaving the conclusion ambiguous increases the chance that the consumer will not form the desired attitude.

The response to this issue depends on the consumers' motivation to process the ad and the complexity of the arguments. If the message is personally relevant, people will pay attention to it and spontaneously form inferences. However, if the arguments are hard to follow or consumers' motivation to follow them is lacking, it is safer for the ad to draw conclusions.[78]

COMPARATIVE ADVERTISING

In 1971, the U.S. Federal Trade Commission issued guidelines that encouraged advertisers to name competing brands in their ads. The government did this to improve the information available to consumers in ads, and indeed recent evidence indicates that, at least under some conditions, this type of presentation does result in more informed decision making.[79] **Comparative advertising** refers to a strategy in which a message compares two or more recognizable brands and weighs them in terms of one or more specific attributes.[80] A recent Arby's campaign to promote its chicken sandwiches uses this approach: One commercial, set in a fictitious McDonald's boardroom, features a young man trying to convince McDonald's executives to serve a healthier type of chicken by proclaiming, "I propose that McDonald's stops putting phosphates, salt and water into its chicken. Consider replacing your chicken, that is only about 70% chicken, with 100% all-natural chicken." The room erupts with laughter. At the end of the spot, a voice-over chimes in: "Unlike McDonald's, all of Arby's chicken sandwiches are made with 100% all-natural chicken. . . ."[81]

This strategy can cut both ways, especially if the sponsor depicts the competition in a nasty or negative way. Although some comparative ads result in desired attitude changes, they may also be lower in believability and may stir up *source derogation* (i.e., the consumer may doubt the credibility of a biased presentation).[82] Indeed, in some cultures (such as Asia) comparative advertising is rare because people find such a confrontational approach offensive.

Comparative ads do appear to be effective for new products that are trying to build a clear image by positioning themselves vis-à-vis dominant brands in the market (as Arby's, primarily known in the United States and Canada for its roast beef sandwiches, feels it has to do to promote its chicken entrees).[83] These ads work well at generating attention, awareness, favorable attitudes, and purchase intentions—but ironically consumers may not like the ad itself because of its aggressiveness.[84] When the U.S. brewer Michelob slammed beer rival Stella Artois as ordinary and overpriced, its smaller competitor's sales doubled.[85]

But if the aim is to compare the new brand with the market leader in terms of specific product attributes, merely saying it is as good or better than the leader is not sufficient. For example, when study participants read a claim, "Spring has the same fluoride as Crest," they tended to report a positive attitude for the fictitious product, but when they read the more global statement, "Preferred by Europeans in comparison with Crest," this effect didn't occur.[86] And comparative ads are only credible if they don't reach too far by comparing a brand to a competitor that is obviously superior. Not too surprisingly, for example, a survey of new car buyers found that TV commercials comparing a Nissan Altima to a Mercedes were not effective.[87]

TYPES OF MESSAGE APPEALS

A persuasive message can tug at the heartstrings or scare you, make you laugh, make you cry, or leave you yearning to learn more. In this section, we'll review the major alternatives available to communicators.

Emotional versus Rational Appeals

Colgate-Palmolive's successful, new Total brand was the first toothpaste to claim that it fights gingivitis, a benefit that let Colgate inch ahead of Procter & Gamble's Crest for the first time in decades. Colgate initially made a scientific pitch for its new entry as it emphasized Total's germ-fighting abilities. In newer ads, however, former model Brooke Shields cavorts with two children (not hers) as soft music plays in the background. She states, "Having a healthy smile is important to me. Not just as an actress but as a mom."[88]

Similarly, archrival P&G's shampoo ads in China used to follow this formula: Demonstrate the science of how shampoo works, then cue up shots of a smiling woman with nice hair. Now the company is trying a more emotional pitch to capture the hearts of China's new class of young, urban professional women. A campaign for Head & Shoulders shampoo features a woman emerging from an animated cocoon and turning into a butterfly. The "H&S metamorphosis" creates a "new life for hair," the voice-over says. For P&G's Rejoice shampoo, a spot shows a man talking about a woman doing hip-hop and traditional Chinese dancing. It never shows her washing her hair; instead, it's all about a woman being viewed as beautiful through the eyes of a man.[89]

So, which is better: to appeal to the head or to the heart? The answer often depends on the nature of the product and the type of relationship consumers have with it. This issue was at the core of a fierce debate at Polaroid, a company most associated with technological innovation rather than "warm and fuzzy" products. Marketers at the photographic products firm argued strenuously that the company needed to develop new, "fun" products to recapture younger consumers. Engineers were antagonistic about this idea; they felt a "toy" camera would cheapen Polaroid's reputation. In this case, the marketers prevailed and convinced the engineers to create a small instant camera with a cheap lens to produce fuzzy thumbnail-size photos. The I-Zone Instant Pocket camera was born. In a radical move for the company, the ad campaign was based on the theme "being a little bit bad is good." One execution featured a young man who sticks instant pictures on his nipples and then wiggles his chest. Half of the I-Zone's buyers are 13- to 17-year-old girls, and Polaroid reaped revenues of $270 million for the product in 1 year.[90]

Many companies turned to emotional strategies after realizing that consumers do not find many differences among brands, especially those in well-established, mature categories. Ads for products ranging from cars (Lincoln Mercury) to cards (Hallmark) focus instead on emotional aspects. Mercury's capitalization on emotional attachments to old rock songs succeeded in lowering the median age of its consumers for some models by 10 years.[91]

The Crest Pro-Health campaign emphasizes information over emotion as it focuses on the toothpaste's health benefits.

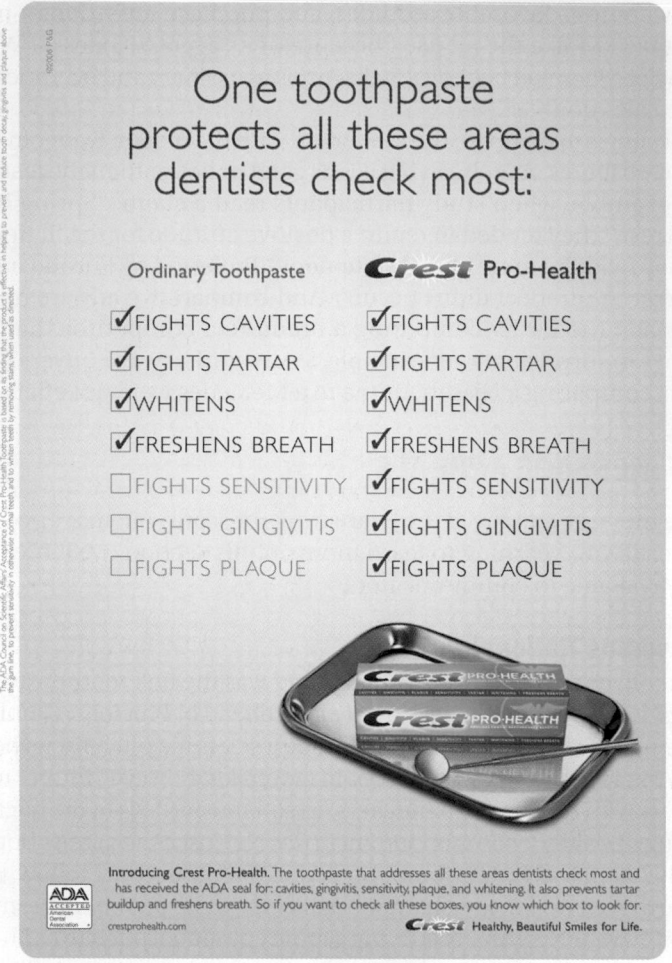

It's hard to gauge the precise effects of rational versus emotional appeals. Although recall of ad content tends to be better for "thinking" ads than for "feeling" ads, conventional measures of advertising effectiveness (e.g., day-after recall) may not be adequate to assess cumulative effects of emotional ads. These open-ended measures are oriented toward cognitive responses, and they may penalize feeling ads because the reactions are not as easy to articulate.[92]

Sex Appeals

A Virgin Atlantic Airways commercial on sex-oriented entertainment channels in hotel rooms spoofs soft-core pornography. To promote Virgin's "Upper Class Suite" service on flights between London and New York, the commercial uses characters with names such as Miles High, Big Ben, and Summer Turbulence. They deliver dialogue replete with double entendres about "your first time" on board and enjoying "several inches more" of legroom.[93] Pfizer aired Viagra commercials in Canada featuring middle-aged men and women talking in a made-up language save for one word. "Viagra spanglecheff?" says a man to a friend at a bowling alley. "Spanglecheff?" his friend asks. "Minky Viagra noni noni boo-boo plats!" the first man replies, with a grin that suggests he's not talking about the weather. The ads end with the slogan, "The International Language of Viagra." There's lots of ways to say the word *sex* without saying it.[94]

Echoing the widely held belief that "sex sells," many marketing communications for products from perfumes to autos feature heavy doses of erotic suggestions that range from subtle hints to blatant displays of skin. Of course, the prevalence of sexual appeals varies from country to country. Even American firms run ads elsewhere that would not go over at home. For example, a "cheeky" ad campaign designed to boost the appeal of American-made Lee jeans among Europeans features a series of bare buttocks. The messages are based on the concept that if bottoms could choose jeans, they would opt for Lee: "Bottoms feel better in Lee Jeans."[95]

Perhaps not surprisingly, female nudity in print ads generates negative feelings and tension among female consumers, whereas men's reactions are more positive.[96] In a case of turnabout being fair play, another study found that males dislike nude males in ads, whereas females responded well to undressed males—but not totally nude ones.[97]

So, does sex work? Although erotic content does appear to draw attention to an ad, its use may actually be counterproductive. In one survey, an overwhelming 61 percent of the respondents said that sexual imagery in a product's ad makes them less likely to buy it.[98] Ironically, a provocative picture can be *too* effective; it can attract so much attention as to hinder processing and recall of the ad's contents. Sexual appeals appear to be ineffective when used merely as a "trick" to grab attention. They do, however, appear to work when the product is *itself* related to sex (e.g., lingerie or Viagra).[99]

A research firm recently explored how American men and women look at sexually themed ads and what effect, if any, what they choose to look at might have on the ads' effectiveness. One part of the study used special software to follow the visual behavior of respondents as they looked at 10 print ads. The ad sample consisted of two U.S. print ads, one sexual and one nonsexual, from each of five product categories. When the participants looked at a sexual ad, men tended to ignore the text, focusing instead on the woman in it, whereas the women participants tended first to explore the ad's text elements. Men said they liked the sexual ads more, liked the products advertised in them more, and would be more likely to buy those products. Women scored the sexual ads lower than the nonsexual ones on all three of those criteria.[100]

Humorous Appeals

A TV commercial for Metamucil caused a bit of a stir in the United States. The spot showed a park service ranger pouring a glass of it down the famous American geyser Old Faithful and announcing that the product keeps the famous geyser "regular." Yellowstone National Park started getting letters from offended viewers such as this one who wrote, "I suppose that in an era when people sell naming rights to sports arenas . . . that some in the National Park Service would see nothing wrong with selling the image of a National Park ranger for the marketing of a product promoting bowel regularity." Park officials also had their own concerns; they didn't want people to think that the geyser needed "help"—or that it's OK to throw things down into it![101]

The use of humor can be tricky, particularly because what is funny to one person may be offensive or incomprehensible to another. Specific cultures may have different senses of humor and use funny material in diverse ways. For example, commercials in the United Kingdom are more likely to use puns and satire than they are in the United States.[102]

Does humor work? Overall, humorous advertisements do get attention. One study found that recognition scores for humorous liquor ads were better than average. However, the verdict is mixed as to whether humor affects recall or product attitudes in a significant way.[103] One function it may serve is to provide a source of *distraction*. A funny ad inhibits *counterarguing* (which is when a consumer thinks of reasons why he doesn't agree with the message), thereby increasing the likelihood of message acceptance.[104]

Humor is more likely to be effective when the ad clearly identifies the brand and the funny material does not "swamp" the message. This danger is similar to one we've already discussed about beautiful models diverting attention from copy points. Subtle humor is usually better, as is humor that does not make fun of the potential consumer. Finally, humor should be appropriate to the product's image. An undertaker or a bank might want to avoid humor, but other products adapt to it quite well. Sales of Sunsweet pitted prunes improved dramatically based on the claim, "Today the pits, tomorrow the wrinkles."[105]

Fear Appeals

Volkswagen's advertising campaign to promote the safety of its Jetta model really got people's attention. The spots depict graphic car crashes from the perspective of the passengers who are chattering away as they drive down the street. Without warning, other vehicles come out of nowhere and brutally smash into their cars. In one spot, viewers can see a passenger's head hitting an airbag. The spots end with shots of stunned passengers, the damaged Jetta, and the slogan: "Safe happens." The ads looked so realistic that consumers called the company asking if any of the actors were hurt. On a Web site, visitors can customize their own accident.[106]

Fear appeals emphasize the negative consequences that can occur unless the consumer changes a behavior or an attitude. Fear appeals are fairly common in advertising, although they are more common in social marketing contexts in which organizations encourage people to convert to healthier lifestyles by quitting smoking, using contraception, relying on a designated driver, or perhaps driving a Jetta.

Does fear work? Most research on this topic indicates that these negative appeals are most effective when the advertiser uses only a moderate threat and when the ad presents a solution to the problem. Otherwise, consumers will tune out the ad because they can do nothing to solve it.[107] This approach also works better when source credibility is high.[108]

When a weak threat is ineffective, there may be insufficient elaboration of the harmful consequences of engaging in the behavior. When a strong threat doesn't work, there may be too much elaboration interfering with the processing of the

This ad for a Dutch insurance company uses a fear appeal.

THERE'S A 24.1% CHANCE THAT YOUR JEWELLERY WILL BE STOLEN DURING A BREAK-IN.
THE HOUSEHOLD INSURANCE FROM REAAL. REALIST IN INSURANCE.

REAAL Verzekeringen

recommended change in behavior—the receiver is too busy thinking of reasons the message doesn't apply to her to pay attention to the offered solution.[109]

A study that manipulated subjects' degree of anxiety about AIDS, for example, found that they evaluated condom ads most positively when a moderate threat was used. In this context, copy that promoted the use of the condom because "Sex is a risky business" (moderate threat) resulted in more attitude change than either a weaker threat that emphasized the product's sensitivity or a strong threat that discussed the certainty of death from AIDS.[110] Similarly, scare tactics have not been as effective as hoped in getting teenagers to decrease their use of alcohol or drugs. Teens simply tune out the message or deny its relevance to them.[111] However, a study of adolescent responses to social versus physical threat appeals in drug prevention messages found that social threat is a more effective strategy.[112]

Some of the research on fear appeals may be confusing a threat (the literal content of a message, such as saying "engage in safe sex or die") with fear (an emotional response to the message). According to this argument, greater fear does result in greater persuasion—but not all threats are equally effective because different people will respond differently to the same threat. Therefore, the strongest threats are not always the most persuasive because they may not have the desired impact on the perceiver. For example, raising the specter of AIDS is about the strongest threat that we can deliver to sexually active kids—but this tactic is only effective if the kids believe they will get the disease. Because many young people (especially those who live in fairly affluent areas) don't believe that "people like them" will be exposed to the AIDS virus, this strong threat may not actually result in a high level of fear.[113] The bottom line is that we need more precise measures of actual fear responses before we can draw definitive conclusions about the impact of fear appeals on consumption decisions.

THE MESSAGE AS ART FORM: METAPHORS BE WITH YOU

Just like book authors, poets, and artists, marketers are storytellers. Their communications take the form of stories because the product benefits they describe are

This Chinese detergent ad uses a handcuff metaphor as it urges the viewer, "Free yourself from the burden of handwash."

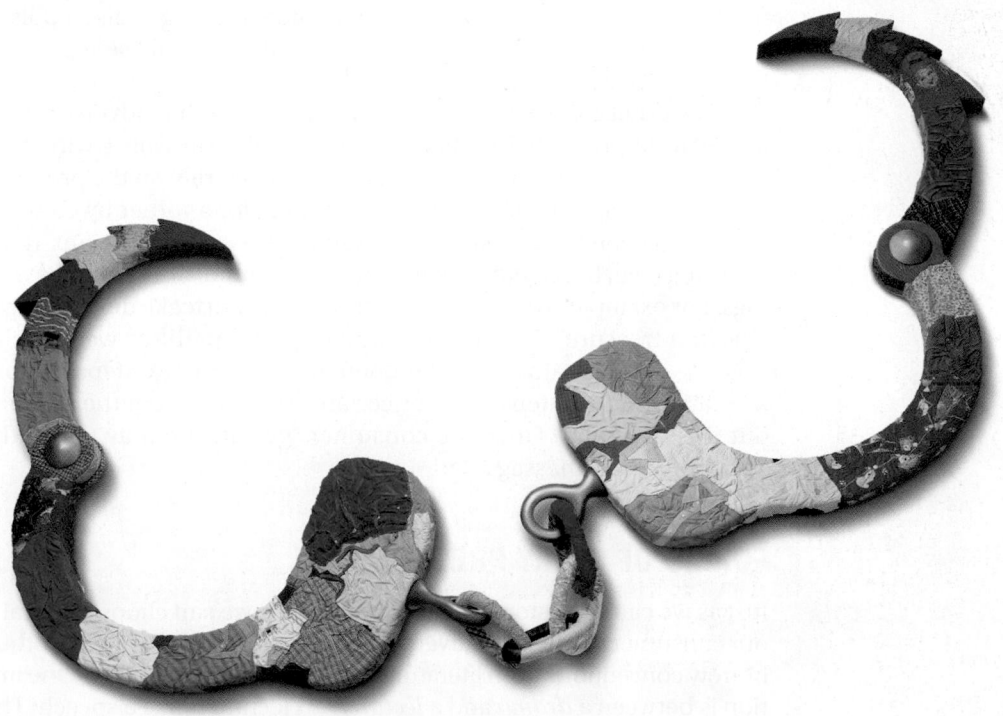

为你解开手洗束缚

TABLE 8.3
SOME EXAMPLES OF ADVERTISING RESONANCE

Product/Headline	Visual
Embassy Suites: "This Year, We're Unwrapping Suites by the Dozen"	Chocolate kisses with hotel names underneath each
Toyota auto parts: "Our Lifetime Guarantee May Come as a Shock"	Man holding a shock absorber
Bucks filter cigarettes: "Herd of These?"	Cigarette pack with a picture of a stag
Bounce fabric softener: "Is There Something Creeping Up Behind You?"	Woman's dress bunched up on her back due to static
Pepsi: "This Year, Hit the Beach Topless"	Pepsi bottle cap lying on the sand
ASICS athletic shoes: "We Believe Women Should Be Running the Country"	Woman jogging in a rural setting

Source: Adapted from Edward F. McQuarrie and David Glen Mick, "On Resonance: A Critical Pluralistic Inquiry into Advertising Rhetoric," *Journal of Consumer Research* 19 (September 1992): 182. Table 1. Reprinted with permission of the University of Chicago Press.

intangible. The storyteller, therefore, must express them in concrete and visible form. Advertising creatives rely (consciously or not) on various literary devices to communicate these meanings. For example, characters such as Mr. Goodwrench, the Jolly Green Giant, and Charlie the Tuna may personify a product or service. Many ads take the form of an **allegory**, a story about an abstract trait or concept for which a person, animal, or vegetable stands.

A **metaphor** places two dissimilar objects into a close relationship such that "A is B," whereas a **simile** compares two objects, "A is like B." A and B, however dissimilar, share some quality that the metaphor highlights. Metaphors allow the marketer to activate meaningful images and apply them to everyday events. In the stock market, "white knights" battle "hostile raiders" using "poison pills"; Tony the Tiger equates cereal with strength; and the Merrill Lynch bull sends the message that the brokerage is "a breed apart."[114]

Resonance is another type of literary device that advertisers use frequently. It is a form of presentation that combines a play on words with a relevant picture. Table 8.3 gives some examples of actual ads that rely on the principle of resonance. Whereas metaphor substitutes one meaning for another by connecting two things that are in some way similar, resonance uses an element that has a double meaning—such as a *pun* where two words sound similar but have different meanings. For example, an ad for a diet strawberry shortcake dessert might bear the copy "berried treasure" so that the brand conveys qualities we associate with buried treasure such as valuable and hidden. Because the text departs from expectations, it creates a state of tension or uncertainty on the part of the viewer until he figures out the word play. Once the consumer "gets it," he may prefer the ad to a more straightforward message.[115]

FORMS OF STORY PRESENTATION

Just as we can tell a story in words or pictures, we can choose several ways to address our consumer audiences. Advertisers structure commercials like other art forms; they borrow conventions from literature and art to communicate.[116] One important distinction is between a *drama* and a *lecture*.[117] A lecture is like a speech: The source speaks directly to the audience to inform them about a product or to persuade them to buy it. Because a lecture clearly implies an attempt at persuasion, the audience will regard it as such. Assuming it motivates listeners, they weigh the merits of the message along with the source's credibility. Cognitive responses like *counterargumentation* occur (e.g., "How much did Coke pay him to say that?"). Consumers accept the appeal if it overcomes objections and is consistent with their beliefs.

In contrast, a drama is similar to a play or movie. Whereas a lecture holds the viewer at arm's length, a drama draws the viewer into the action. The characters indirectly address the audience; they interact with each other about a product or service in an imaginary setting. Dramas attempt to be experiential—to involve the audience emotionally. In *transformational advertising*, the consumer associates the experience of product usage with some subjective sensation—like the feeling you get while watching a silhouetted actor on TV dancing energetically to his iPod.

THE SOURCE VERSUS THE MESSAGE: SELL THE STEAK OR THE SIZZLE?

We've discussed two major components of the communications model: the source and the message. Which aspect has the most impact on persuading consumers to change their attitudes? Should marketers worry more about *what* is said or *how* it's said and *who* says it?

The answer is it depends (surprised?). As we saw in Chapter 4, a consumer's level of involvement determines which cognitive processes will be activated when she receives a message. Research indicates that this level of involvement will determine which aspects of a communication she processes. The situation appears to resemble a traveler who comes to a fork in the road: She chooses one path or the other, and this choice has a significant impact on the factors that will make a difference in persuasion attempts.

THE ELABORATION LIKELIHOOD MODEL

The **elaboration likelihood model (ELM)** assumes that once a consumer receives a message she begins to process it.[118] Depending on the personal relevance of this information, she will follow one of two routes to persuasion. Under conditions of high involvement, she takes the *central route* to persuasion. Under conditions of low involvement, the consumer takes a *peripheral route* instead. Figure 8.5 diagrams this model.

■ **FIGURE 8.5** THE ELABORATION LIKELIHOOD MODEL (ELM) OF PERSUASION

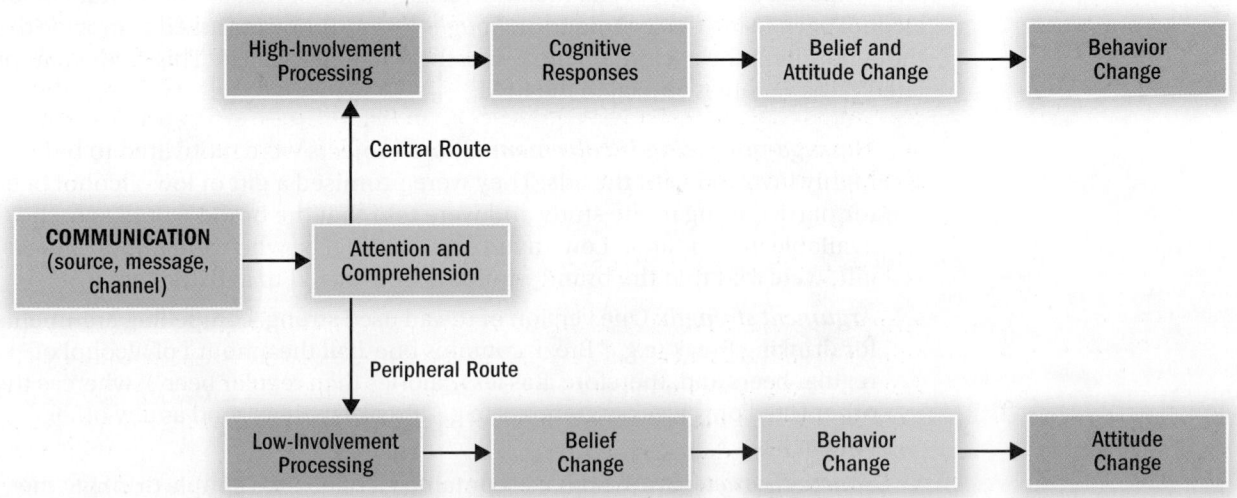

THE CENTRAL ROUTE TO PERSUASION

When the consumer finds the information in a persuasive message to be relevant or somehow interesting, she will carefully attend to the message content. In this case, she's likely to actively think about the arguments the marketer presents and generate *cognitive responses* to these arguments. On hearing a radio message warning about drinking while pregnant, an expectant mother might say to herself, "She's right. I really should stop drinking alcohol now that I'm pregnant." Or she might offer counterarguments, such as "That's a bunch of baloney. My mother had a cocktail every night when she was pregnant with me, and I turned out fine." If a person generates counterarguments in response to a message, it is less likely that she will yield to the message, whereas if she generates further supporting arguments, it's most likely she'll comply.[119]

The central route to persuasion involves the traditional hierarchy of effects we discussed in Chapter 7. In this case, we carefully form and evaluate beliefs, and the strong attitudes that result guide our behavior. The implication is that message factors, such as the quality of arguments an ad presents, will determine attitude change. Prior knowledge about a topic results in more thoughts about the message and also increases the number of counterarguments.[120]

THE PERIPHERAL ROUTE TO PERSUASION

In contrast, we take the peripheral route when we're not really motivated to think about the marketer's arguments. Instead, we're likely to use other cues to decide how to react to the message. These cues include the product's package, the attractiveness of the source, or the context in which the message appears. We call sources of information extraneous to the actual message *peripheral cues* because they surround the actual message.

The peripheral route to persuasion highlights the paradox of low involvement we discussed in Chapter 4: When consumers do not care about a product, the style in which it's presented (e.g., who endorses it or the visuals that go with it) may increase in importance. The implication here is that we may buy low-involvement products chiefly because the marketer has done a good job in designing a "sexy" package, choosing a popular spokesperson, or perhaps simply creating a pleasant shopping environment.

SUPPORT FOR THE ELM

The ELM has received a lot of research support.[121] In a typical study, undergraduates were exposed to one of several mock advertisements for Break, a new brand of low-alcohol beer. Using the technique of *thought listing*, they were asked to provide their thoughts about the ads, which the researcher later analyzed.[122] This study manipulated three variables crucial to the ELM:

Message-processing involvement: Some subjects were motivated to be highly involved with the ads. They were promised a gift of low-alcohol beer for participating in the study and were told that the brand would soon be available in their area. Low-involvement subjects, who were not promised a gift, were told that the brand would be introduced in a distant area.

Argument strength: One version of the ad used strong, compelling arguments for drinking Break (e.g., "Break contains one-half the amount of alcohol of regular beers and, therefore, has less calories than regular beer"), whereas the other listed only weak arguments (e.g., "Break is just as good as any other regular beer").

Source characteristics: Both ads contained a photo of a couple drinking the beer, but the researchers varied the relative social attractiveness of the couples by their dress, posture and nonverbal expressions, and the background information they gave subjects about the educational achievements and occupations of the couples.

Consistent with the ELM, high-involvement subjects had more thoughts related to the ad messages than did low-involvement subjects, who devoted more cognitive activity to the sources the ad presented. The attitudes of high-involvement subjects were swayed by powerful arguments, whereas those of low-involvement subjects were influenced by the ad version using attractive sources. The results of this study, along with numerous others, indicate that the relative effectiveness of a strong message and a favorable source depends on consumers' level of involvement with the advertised product.

These results underscore the basic idea that highly involved consumers look for the "steak" (e.g., strong, rational arguments). Those who are less involved are more affected by the "sizzle" (e.g., the colors and images in packaging or famous people's endorsements). It is important to remember, however, that the *same* communications variable can be both a central and a peripheral cue, depending on its relation to the attitude object. The physical attractiveness of a model might serve as a peripheral cue in a car commercial, but her beauty might be a central cue for a product such as shampoo where enhancing attractiveness is a major benefit.[123]

CHAPTER SUMMARY

Now that you have finished reading this chapter you should understand why:

The communications model identifies several important components for marketers when they try to change consumers' attitudes toward products and services.

● Persuasion refers to an attempt to change consumers' attitudes. The communications model specifies the elements marketers need to transmit meaning. These include a source, a message, a medium, a receiver, and feedback.

The consumer who processes such a message is not necessarily the passive receiver of information marketers once believed him to be.

● The traditional view of communications regards the perceiver as a passive element in the process. New developments in interactive communications highlight the need to consider the active roles a consumer plays in obtaining product information and building a relationship with a company. Advocates of permission marketing argue that it's more effective to send messages to consumers who have already indicated an interest in learning about a product than trying to hit people "cold" with these solicitations.

Several factors influence a message source's effectiveness.

● Two important characteristics that determine the effectiveness of a source are its attractiveness and credibility. Although celebrities often serve this purpose, their credibility is not always as strong as marketers hope. Marketing messages that consumers perceive as buzz (those that are authentic and consumer generated) tend to be more effective than those they categorize as hype (those that are inauthentic, biased, and company generated).

The way a marketer structures his message determines how persuasive it will be.

● Some elements of a message that help to determine its effectiveness include the following: The marketer conveys the message in words or pictures; the message employs an emotional or a rational appeal; how often it's repeated; whether it draws a conclusion; whether it presents both sides of the argument; and whether the message includes fear, humor, or sexual references. Advertising messages often incorporate elements from art or literature, such as dramas, lectures, metaphors, allegories, and resonance.

Audience characteristics help to determine whether the nature of the source or the message itself will be relatively more effective.

● The relative influence of the source versus the message depends on the receiver's level of involvement with the communication. The elaboration likelihood model (ELM) specifies that source effects are more likely to sway a less-involved consumer, whereas a more-involved consumer will be more likely to attend to and process components of the actual message.

KEY TERMS

Allegory, 336
Blogging, 317
Buzz, 321
Communications model, 315
Comparative advertising, 330
Corporate paradox, 321
Elaboration likelihood model
    (ELM), 337

Fear appeals, 334
Hype, 322
Match-up hypothesis, 324
M-commerce, 317
Metaphor, 336
Permission marketing, 316
Persuasion, 314
Refutational arguments, 330

Resonance, 336
Simile, 336
Sleeper effect, 319
Source attractiveness, 323
Source credibility, 318
Two-factor theory, 329

REVIEW QUESTIONS

1   List three psychological principles related to persuasion.
2   Describe the elements of the traditional communications model, and tell how the updated model differs.
3   What are blogs and how can marketers use them?
4   What is source credibility, and what are two factors that influence whether we decide a source is credible?
5   What is the difference between buzz and hype? How does this difference relate to the corporate paradox?
6   What is a halo effect, and why does it happen?
7   What is an avatar, and why might an advertiser choose to use one instead of hiring a celebrity endorser?
8   When should a marketer present a message visually versus verbally?
9   How does the two-factor theory explain the effects of message repetition on attitude change?
10   When is it best to present a two-sided message versus a one-sided message?
11   Do humorous ads work, and if so, under what conditions?
12   Should marketers ever try to arouse fear in order to persuade consumers?
13   Why do marketers use metaphors to craft persuasive messages? Give two examples of this technique.
14   What is the difference between a metaphor and resonance?
15   What is the difference between a lecture and a drama?
16   Describe the elaboration likelihood model, and tell how it is related to the relative importance of *what* is said versus *how* it's said.

CONSUMER BEHAVIOR CHALLENGE

■ DISCUSS

1   What are the pros and cons of using rational versus emotional appeals, that is, trying to persuade consumers by focusing on what they know as opposed to what they feel? When should marketers use one type or the other?

2   Marketers who use deceptive advertising "poison the well" for others because they make it harder to convince skeptical consumers that a message is credible. How big a problem is this? What can ethical marketers do to prevent this?

3 A flog is a fake blog a company posts to build buzz around its brand. Is this ethical?

4 The sleeper effect implies that perhaps we shouldn't worry too much about how positively people evaluate a source. Similarly, there's a saying in public relations that "any publicity is good publicity." Do you agree?

5 Discuss some conditions where you would advise a marketer to use a comparative advertising strategy.

6 The American Medical Association encountered a firestorm of controversy when it agreed to sponsor a line of health-care products Sunbeam manufactured (a decision it later reversed). Should trade or professional organizations, journalists, professors, and others endorse specific products at the expense of other offerings?

7 A marketer must decide whether to incorporate rational or emotional appeals in its communications strategy. Describe conditions that are more favorable to using one or the other.

8 Many, many companies rely on celebrity endorsers as communications sources to persuade. Especially when targeting younger people, these spokespeople often are "cool" musicians, athletes, or movie stars. In your opinion, who would be the most effective celebrity endorser today, and why? Who would be the least effective? Why?

9 Swiss Legend, a watch brand, gets famous people to wear its colorful timepieces. One way it does this is to give away its products at awards shows. This common practice is called "gifting the talent." The point is not only to get celebrities to wear Swiss Legend watches, which sell in the $150 to $450 price range, but also to leverage the press coverage that focuses on what celebrities wear. The stars have been getting their Swiss Legends by way of Backstage Creations, one of several companies that oversee what has long since become a standard practice at awards shows and other galas. One method of gifting the talent is through "goody bags," a practice now so widely known that goody-bag contents are listed in the celebrity press. Backstage Creations does gift bags but also offers a more elaborate approach, creating an entire backstage environment—or "retreat"—decorated by a name interior designer and filled with complimentary products.[124] What do you think about the practice of "gifting the talent" in order to accumulate endorsements? Is this a sound strategy? Is it ethical for celebrities to accept these gifts?

■ APPLY

10 A government agency wants to encourage people who have been drinking to use designated drivers. What advice could you give the organization about constructing persuasive communications? Discuss some factors that might be important, including the structure of the communications, where they should appear, and who should deliver them. Should it use fear appeals, and if so, how?

11 Why would a marketer consider saying negative things about her product? When is this strategy feasible? Can you find examples of it?

12 Collect ads that rely on sex appeal to sell products. How often do they communicate benefits of the actual product?

13 Observe the process of counterargumentation by asking a friend to talk out loud while watching a commercial. Ask him or her to respond to each point in the ad or to write down reactions to the claims made. How much skepticism regarding the claims can you detect?

14 Make a log of all the commercials a network television channel shows during a 2-hour period. Assign each to a product category and decide whether they show drama or argument. Describe the types of messages used (e.g., two-sided arguments), and keep track of the types of spokespeople who appear (e.g., TV actors, famous people, animated characters). What can you conclude about the dominant forms of persuasive tactics marketers currently employ?

15 Collect examples of ads that rely on the use of metaphors or resonance. Do you feel these ads are effective? If you were marketing the products, would you feel more comfortable with ads that use a more straightforward, "hard-sell" approach? Why or why not?

16 Create a list of current celebrities whom you feel typify cultural categories (e.g., clown, mother figure, etc.). What specific brands do you feel each could effectively endorse?

17 Conduct an "avatar hunt" by going to e-commerce Web sites, online video game sites, and online communities such as *The Sims* that let people select what they want to look like in cyberspace. What seem to be the dominant figures people are choosing? Are they realistic or fantasy characters? Male or female? What types of avatars do you believe would be most effective for each of these different kinds of Web sites and why?

Case Study

DAVID BECKHAM: PROFESSIONAL ENDORSER

David Beckham may just be the most famous sports personality in the world. Is it because of his performance as a footballer for Manchester United and Real Madrid? Is it because of his recent high-profile move to the United States to play for the Los Angeles Galaxy? Is it because of his long-standing marriage to Victoria Beckham (aka Posh Spice) and their celebrity lifestyle? Or is it because every inch of the man is endorsed by big-name corporate brands?

In reality, it is probably a combination of these things. But the endorsements certainly haven't hurt Beckham's brand recognition. Early in his professional career, Beckham secured a number of lucrative sponsorship deals with Adidas, Vodafone, and Diesel. Since then, he has signed endorsement contracts with such brands as Rage Software, Castrol, Brylcreem, Police sunglasses, Gillette razors, and Pepsi. Beckham now belongs to the elite ranks of superathletes, such as Michael Jordan and Tiger Woods, who are themselves superbrands.

So does the brand make the player, or does the player make the brand? While we can argue that the marketing power of global mega-corporations can propel an athlete to stardom, the reverse may also be true. Marketers often credit Michael Jordan with establishing Nike as one of the world's most powerful brands. With the most recent contract between David Beckham and Adidas that includes plans for a personalized line of merchandise, Adidas executives hope Beckham will do for the German sportswear company what Michael Jordan did for Nike.

And Beckham may well be on his way to doing just that. Already, the Beckham image has sold more than 3 million pairs of Predator soccer cleats. "We think he can sell anything," said Herbert Hainer, Adidas CEO. Hainer goes on to say that Beckham "has a lot of things coming together. He's a very good footballer, he's passionate, good looking, very professional, not arrogant, and the fans believe what he says."

Some would argue that all money aside, Beckham does not need the image of Adidas or the other brands because the man himself is an icon. Married since 1999 to a former teen idol, the Beckhams symbolize a glam celebrity lifestyle. David Beckham's good looks have carried his influence to the realm of teen fashion and hairstyles. Even allegations of extra-marital affairs in 2004 have not scuffed the image of this superstar. "When you ask people about David Beckham's credibility, his family values aren't the main appeal," says Stephen Cheliotis of branding consultancy Superbrands. "Beckham's fashion appeal, his footballing skills and his good looks are what appeal to people. His family is not the primary function of the Beckham brand."

The strength of the Beckham brand reached new heights as the elite couple arrived in the United States in July of 2007, with all the fanfare of an invasion. In a five-year contract rumored to be worth up to $250 million, the Los Angeles Galaxy signed Beckham with the goal of putting the struggling team on top of the relatively new Major League Soccer organization. But perhaps more importantly, people everywhere have the expectation (or perhaps the hope) that Beckham will be able to push Americans' acceptance of professional soccer closer to that of football, basketball, and baseball.

Beckham's recent American inauguration refuels the fire of his celebrity, which was starting to flicker just a bit as he ages. Marketers clearly recognize his lasting brand power. Hainer asserts that just as Beckham's first pair of soccer cleats were Adidas, his last pair will be also: "We can work with him much longer than his playing career but that's up to him." When it comes to extending the life of a brand, no one can "bend it like Beckham."

DISCUSSION QUESTIONS

1 In the context of source effects, discuss why companies such as Adidas are so keen to sign David Beckham to endorse their products.

2 Considering how we form attitudes, what are the potential positive and negative consequences of Beckham's endorsements for both his sponsors and his own brand image?

Sources: Worth Civils, "Beckham Arrives in U.S. But Will His Appeal Last?", *Wall Street Journal* (July 12, 2007), accessed online at www.wsj.com; Rick Broadbent, Asling O'Connor, and Patrick Barkham, "World Brands It Like Beckham," *London Times* (March 4, 2004); Grant Clelland, "Brand It Like the Beckhams," *Business* (April 11, 2004): 14; Jack Ewing, "Can Football Be Saved?" *Business Week,* (July 19, 2004): 46.

NOTES

1. shoppingthetrend.com/Fall2007FashionTrends.php, accessed August 15, 2007.
2. shoppingthetrend.com/Top10GraphicPrints.php, accessed August 15, 2007.
3. Robert B. Cialdini and Kelton V. L. Rhoads, "Human Behavior and the Marketplace," *Marketing Research* (Fall 2001): 13 (3).
4. Gert Assmus, "An Empirical Investigation into the Perception of Vehicle Source Effects," *Journal of Advertising* 7 (Winter 1978): 4–10. For a more thorough discussion of the pros and cons of different media, see Stephen Baker, *Systematic Approach to Advertising Creativity* (New York: McGraw-Hill, 1979).
5. Alladi Venkatesh, Ruby Roy Dholakia, and Nikhilesh Dholakia, "New Visions of Information Technology and Postmodernism: Implications for Advertising and Marketing Communications," in Walter Brenner and Lutz Kolbe, eds., *The Information Superhighway and Private Households: Case Studies of Business Impacts* (Heidelberg: Physical-Verlag, 1996), 319–37; Donna L. Hoffman and Thomas P. Novak, "Marketing in Hypermedia Computer-Mediated Environments: Conceptual Foundations," *Journal of Marketing* 60, no. 3 (July 1996): 50–68. For an early theoretical discussion of interactivity in communications paradigms, see R. Aubrey Fisher, *Perspectives on Human Communication* (New York: Macmillan, 1978).
6. Seth Godin, Permission Marketing: Turning Strangers into Friends, and Friends into Customers (New York: Simon & Schuster, 1999).
7. Brad Stone, "The War for Your TV," *Newsweek* (July 29, 2002): 46–47.
8. Geoffrey A. Fowler, "Asia's Mobile Ads," *Wall Street Journal Online* (April 25, 2005); Brooke Barnes, "Coming to Your Cell: Paris Hilton," *Wall Street Journal Online* (March 17, 2005); Alice Z. Cuneo, "Marketers Dial in to Messaging," *Advertising Age* (November 1, 2004): 18; Stephen Baker and Heather Green, "Blogs Will Change Your Business," *BusinessWeek* (May 2, 2005): 56 (9).
9. Adrienne W. Fawcett, "8 of 10 Americans Know about Blogs; Half Visit Them Regularly," *Marketing Daily* (August 29, 2007), available at www.mediapost.com, accessed August 29, 2007.
10. Baker and Green, "Blogs Will Change Your Business."
11. Rob Walker, "Smooth Move," *New York Times Magazine*, March 27, 2005, available from www.nytimes.com, accessed March 27, 2005; Melanie Wells, "Have It Your Way," *Forbes* (February 14, 2005): 78–86; Ryan Underwood, "Cracking Jones Soda's Secret Formula," *Fast Company* (March 2005): 74–75.
12. Carl I. Hovland and W. Weiss, "The Influence of Source Credibility on Communication Effectiveness," *Public Opinion Quarterly* 15 (1952): 635–50; for a recent treatment, cf. Yong-Soon Kang and Paul M. Herr, "Beauty and the Beholder: Toward an Integrative Model of Communication Source Effects," *Journal of Consumer Research* 33 (June 2006): 123–30.
13. Herbert Kelman, "Processes of Opinion Change," *Public Opinion Quarterly* 25 (Spring 1961): 57–78; Susan M. Petroshius and Kenneth E. Crocker, "An Empirical Analysis of Spokesperson Characteristics on Advertisement and Product Evaluations," *Journal of the Academy of Marketing Science* 17 (Summer 1989): 217–26.
14. Kenneth G. DeBono and Richard J. Harnish, "Source Expertise, Source Attractiveness, and the Processing of Persuasive Information: A Functional Approach," *Journal of Personality and Social Psychology* 55, no. 4 (1988): 541–46.
15. Joseph R. Priester and Richard E. Petty, "The Influence of Spokesperson Trustworthiness on Message Elaboration, Attitude Strength, and Advertising Effectiveness," *Journal of Consumer Psychology* 13, no. 4 (2003): 408–21.
16. Hershey H. Friedman and Linda Friedman, "Endorser Effectiveness by Product Type," *Journal of Advertising Research* 19, no. 5 (1979): 63–71. For a study that looked at nontarget market effects—the effects of advertising intended for other market segments—see Jennifer L. Aaker, Anne M. Brumbaugh, and Sonya A. Grier, "Non-Target Markets and Viewer Distinctiveness: The Impact of Target Marketing on Advertising Attitudes," *Journal of Consumer Psychology* 9, no. 3 (2000): 127–40.
17. Yeosun Yoon, Zeynep Gurhan-Canli, and Norbert Schwarz, "The Effect of Corporate Social Responsibility (CSR) Activities on Companies with Bad Reputations," *Journal of Consumer Psychology* 16, no. 4, (2006): 377–90.
18. Peter R. Darke and Robin J. B. Ritchie, "The Defensive Consumer: Advertising Deception, Defensive Processing, and Distrust," *Journal of Marketing Research* 44 (February 2007): 114–27.
19. S. Ratneshwar and Shelly Chaiken, "Comprehension's Role in Persuasion: The Case of Its Moderating Effect on the Persuasive Impact of Source Cues," *Journal of Consumer Research* 18 (June 1991): 52–62.
20. Jagdish Agrawal and Wagner A. Kamakura, "The Economic Worth of Celebrity Endorsers: An Event Study Analysis," *Journal of Marketing* 59 (July 1995): 56–62.
21. Nat Ives, "Entertaining Web Sites Promote Products Subtly," *New York Times on the Web* (December 22, 2004); www.subservientchicken.com, accessed July 12, 2007; www.comeclean.com, accessed July 12, 2007.
22. Anthony R. Pratkanis, Anthony G. Greenwald, Michael R. Leippe, and Michael H. Baumgardner, "In Search of Reliable Persuasion Effects: III. The Sleeper Effect Is Dead, Long Live the Sleeper Effect," *Journal of Personality and Social Psychology* 54 (1988): 203–18.
23. Herbert C. Kelman and Carl I. Hovland, "Reinstatement of the Communication in Delayed Measurement of Opinion Change," *Journal of Abnormal Psychology* 48, no. 3 (1953): 327–35.
24. Darlene Hannah and Brian Sternthal, "Detecting and Explaining the Sleeper Effect," *Journal of Consumer Research* 11 (September 1984): 632–42.
25. David Mazursky and Yaacov Schul, "The Effects of Advertisement Encoding on the Failure to Discount Information: Implications for the Sleeper Effect," *Journal of Consumer Research* 15 (June 1988): 24–36.
26. "Robber Makes It Biggs in Ad," *Advertising Age* (May 29, 1989): 26.
27. Robert LaFranco, "MTV Conquers Madison Avenue," *Forbes* (June 3, 1996): 138.
28. Alice H. Eagly, Andy Wood, and Shelly Chaiken, "Causal Inferences about Communicators and Their Effect in Opinion Change," *Journal of Personality and Social Psychology* 36, no. 4 (1978): 424–35.
29. William Dowell, "Microsoft Offers Tips to Agreeable Academics," *Time* (June 1, 1998): 22.
30. Suzanne Vranica and Sam Walker, "Tiger Woods Switches Watches; Branding Experts Disapprove," *Wall Street Journal Interactive Edition* (October 7, 2002).
31. Alex Mindlin, "To Sell Goods, the Celebrity Face Matters," *New York Times Online* (May 8, 2006), accessed May 8, 2006.
32. Ann E. Schlosser, "Posting versus Lurking: Communicating in a Multiple Audience Context," *Journal of Consumer Research* 32 (September 2005): 260–65; Ann E. Schlosser, "Source Perceptions and the Persuasiveness of Internet Word-of-Mouth Communication," in Geeta Menon and Akshay R. Rao, eds., *Advances in Consumer Research*, 32 (2005): 202–03.
33. This section is based on a discussion in Michael R. Solomon, *Conquering Consumerspace: Marketing Strategies for a Branded World* (New York: AMACOM, 2003); see also David Lewis and Darren Bridger, *The Soul of the New Consumer: Authenticity—What We Buy and Why in the New Economy* (London: Nicholas Brealey Publishing, 2000).
34. Hillary Chura, "No Bull: Coke Targets Clubs," *Advertising Age* (December 9, 2002): 3(2).
35. Jeff Neff, "Pressure Points at IPG," *Advertising Age* (December 2001): 4.
36. Eilene Zimmerman, "Catch the Bug," *Sales and Marketing Management* (February 2001): 78.
37. Becky Ebenkamp, "Guerrilla Marketers of the Year," *Brandweek* (November 13, 2001): 25–32.
38. Wayne Friedman, "Street Marketing Hits the Internet," *Advertising Age* (May 2000): 32; Erin White, "Online Buzz Helps Album Skyrocket to Top of Charts," *Wall Street Journal Interactive Edition* (October 5, 1999).
39. Richard Sandomir, "A Pitchman with Punch: George Foreman Sells His Name," *New York Times on the Web* (January 21, 2000).
40. Jeremy Mullman, "Look Who's Got His Own Merlot: Da Coach," *Advertising Age,* (November 2006): 12.
41. Michael J. Baker and Gilbert A. Churchill, Jr., "The Impact of Physically Attractive Models on Advertising Evaluations," *Journal of Marketing Research* 14 (November 1977): 538–55; Marjorie J. Caballero and William M. Pride, "Selected Effects of Salesperson Sex and Attractiveness in Direct Mail Advertisements," *Journal of Marketing* 48 (January 1984): 94–100; W. Benoy Joseph, "The Credibility of Physically Attractive Communicators: A Review," *Journal of Advertising* 11, no. 3 (1982): 15–24; Lynn R. Kahle and Pamola M. Homer, "Physical Attractiveness of the Celebrity Endorser: A Social Adaptation Perspective," *Journal of Consumer Research* 11 (March 1985): 954–61; Judson Mills and Eliot Aronson, "Opinion Change as a Function of Communicator's Attractiveness and Desire to Influence," *Journal of Personality and Social Psychology* 1 (1965): 173–77.
42. Leonard N. Reid and Lawrence C. Soley, "Decorative Models and the Readership of Magazine Ads," *Journal of Advertising Research* 23, no. 2 (1983): 27–32.

43. Marjorie J. Caballero, James R. Lumpkin, and Charles S. Madden, "Using Physical Attractiveness as an Advertising Tool: An Empirical Test of the Attraction Phenomenon," *Journal of Advertising Research* (August–September 1989): 16–22.

44. Baker and Churchill, Jr., "The Impact of Physically Attractive Models on Advertising Evaluations"; George E. Belch, Michael A. Belch, and Angelina Villareal, "Effects of Advertising Communications: Review of Research," in *Research in Marketing* no. 9(Greenwich, CT: JAI Press, 1987): 59–117; A. E. Courtney and T. W. Whipple, *Sex Stereotyping in Advertising* (Lexington, MA: Lexington Books, 1983).

45. Kahle and Homer, "Physical Attractiveness of the Celebrity Endorser."

46. Teri Agins, "New Reality with Her Own Line, Pop Star Rides Rise in Celebrity Fashion Upstaging Upscale Designers, Jessica Simpson Prepares for Big Launch in Stores Nixing a 'Cheesy' Touch," *Wall Street Journal* (June 9, 2005): A1; Louise Story, "Seeing Stars," *New York Times Online* (October 12, 2006), accessed October 12, 2006.

47. Brian Steinberg, "Bob Dylan Gets Tangled Up in Pink: Victoria's Secret Campaign Drafts Counterculture Hero; Just Like the Rolling Stones," *Wall Street Journal* (April 2, 2004): B3.

48. Eric Pfanner, "Star Power Backfires, Costing Agency a Client," *New York Times Online* (June 5, 2007), accessed June 5, 2007.

49. Heather Buttle, Jane E. Raymond, and Shai Danziger, "Do Famous Faces Capture Attention?" Paper presented at Association for Consumer Research Conference Columbus, Ohio (October 1999).

50. Michael A. Kamins, "Celebrity and Noncelebrity Advertising in a Two-Sided Context," *Journal of Advertising Research* 29 (June–July 1989): 34; Joseph M. Kamen, A. C. Azhari, and J. R. Kragh, "What a Spokesman Does for a Sponsor," *Journal of Advertising Research* 15, no. 2 (1975): 17–24; Lynn Langmeyer and Mary Walker, "A First Step to Identify the Meaning in Celebrity Endorsers," in Rebecca H. Holman and Michael R. Solomon, eds., *Advances in Consumer Research* 18 (Provo, UT: Association for Consumer Research, 1991): 364–71.

51. Grant McCracken, "Who Is the Celebrity Endorser? Cultural Foundations of the Endorsement Process," *Journal of Consumer Research* 16, no. 3 (December 1989): 310–21.

52. Bonnie Thompson, "Judge of Character," *Advertising Age* (July 31, 2006): 4–29 (2).

53. Michael A. Kamins, "An Investigation into the 'Match-Up' Hypothesis in Celebrity Advertising: When Beauty May Be Only Skin Deep," *Journal of Advertising* 19, no. 1 (1990): 4–13; Kahle and Homer, "Physical Attractiveness of the Celebrity Endorser."

54. Kevin E. Kahle and Lynn R. Kahle, "Sports Celebrities' Image: A Critical Evaluation of the Utility of Q Scores," working paper, University of Oregon, 2005.

55. Nat Ives, "Marketers Run to Pull the Plug When Celebrity Endorsers Say the Darnedest Things," *New York Times on the Web* (July 16, 2004).

56. Judith A. Garretson and Scot Burton, "The Role of Spokescharacters as Advertisement and Package Cues in Integrated Marketing Communications," *Journal of Marketing* 69 (October, 2005): 118–32.

57. Joel Baglole, "Mascots Are Getting Bigger Role in Corporate Advertising Plans," *Wall Street Journal Interactive Edition* (April 9, 2002).

58. Stuart Elliott, "The Media Business: Advertising: As Marketers Revive Familiar Brand Characters, Prepare to See More of a Certain Cat and Bunny," *New York Times on the Web* (August 27, 2004).

59. Stuart Elliott, "The Names Are Vintage, the Touches Modern," *New York Times* (May 1, 2007); "Colonel Sanders Gets a Makeover in New KFC Logo," *Wall Street Journal on the Web* (November 14, 2006); Jack Neff, "Move over Trump, Here Comes the Brawny Man," *Advertising Age*, May 29, 2006: 3-38 (2); Patricia Winters Lauro, "Mr. Peanut, You're Perfect. Now Change," *New York Times Online* (July 11, 2006), accessed July 11, 2006.

60. Tran T. L. Knanh and Regalado Antonio, "Web Sites Bet on Attracting Viewers with Humanlike Presences of Avatars," *Wall Street Journal Interactive Edition* (January 24, 2001); Brian Morrissey, "Taco Bell to Cast User Avatars in TV Spot," *Adweek* (July 10, 2007), available from www.adweek.com, accessed July 12, 2007.

61. David W. Stewart and David H. Furse, "The Effects of Television Advertising Execution on Recall, Comprehension, and Persuasion," *Psychology & Marketing* 2 (Fall 1985): 135–60.

62. R. C. Grass and W. H. Wallace, "Advertising Communication: Print vs. TV," *Journal of Advertising Research* 14 (1974): 19–23.

63. Elizabeth C. Hirschman and Michael R. Solomon, "Utilitarian, Aesthetic, and Familiarity Responses to Verbal versus Visual Advertisements," in Thomas C. Kinnear, ed., *Advances in Consumer Research* 11 (Provo, UT: Association for Consumer Research, 1984): 426–31.

64. Terry L. Childers and Michael J. Houston, "Conditions for a Picture-Superiority Effect on Consumer Memory," *Journal of Consumer Research* 11 (September 1984): 643–54.

65. Andrew A. Mitchell, "The Effect of Verbal and Visual Components of Advertisements on Brand Attitudes and Attitude toward the Advertisement," *Journal of Consumer Research* 13 (June 1986): 12–24.

66. John R. Rossiter and Larry Percy, "Attitude Change through Visual Imagery in Advertising," *Journal of Advertising Research* 9, no. 2 (1980): 10–16.

67. Jolita Kiselius and Brian Sternthal, "Examining the Vividness Controversy: An Availability–Valence Interpretation," *Journal of Consumer Research* 12 (March 1986): 418–31.

68. Scott B. Mackenzie, "The Role of Attention in Mediating the Effect of Advertising on Attribute Importance," *Journal of Consumer Research* 13 (September 1986): 174–95.

69. Robert B. Zajonc, "Attitudinal Effects of Mere Exposure," *Journal of Personality and Social Psychology* 8 (1968): 1–29.

70. Giles D'Souza and Ram C. Rao, "Can Repeating an Advertisement More Frequently Than the Competition Affect Brand Preference in a Mature Market?" *Journal of Marketing* 59 (April 1995): 32–42.

71. George E. Belch, "The Effects of Television Commercial Repetition on Cognitive Response and Message Acceptance," *Journal of Consumer Research* 9 (June 1982): 56–65; Marian Burke and Julie Edell, "Ad Reactions over Time: Capturing Changes in the Real World," *Journal of Consumer Research* 13 (June 1986): 114–18; Herbert Krugman, "Why Three Exposures May Be Enough," *Journal of Advertising Research* 12 (December 1972): 11–14.

72. Robert F. Bornstein, "Exposure and Affect: Overview and Meta-Analysis of Research, 1968–1987," *Psychological Bulletin* 106, no. 2 (1989): 265–89; Arno Rethans, John Swasy, and Lawrence Marks, "Effects of Television Commercial Repetition, Receiver Knowledge, and Commercial Length: A Test of the Two-Factor Model," *Journal of Marketing Research* 23 (February 1986): 50–61.

73. Curtis P. Haugtvedt, David W. Schumann, Wendy L. Schneier, and Wendy L. Warren, "Advertising Repetition and Variation Strategies: Implications for Understanding Attitude Strength," *Journal of Consumer Research* 21 (June 1994): 176–89.

74. Linda L. Golden and Mark I. Alpert, "Comparative Analysis of the Relative Effectiveness of One- and Two-Sided Communication for Contrasting Products," *Journal of Advertising* 16 (1987): 18–25; Kamins, "Celebrity and Noncelebrity Advertising in a Two-Sided Context"; Robert B. Settle and Linda L. Golden, "Attribution Theory and Advertiser Credibility," *Journal of Marketing Research* 11 (May 1974): 181–85.

75. Cf. Alan G. Sawyer, "The Effects of Repetition of Refutational and Supportive Advertising Appeals," *Journal of Marketing Research* 10 (February 1973): 23–33; George J. Szybillo and Richard Heslin, "Resistance to Persuasion: Inoculation Theory in a Marketing Context," *Journal of Marketing Research* 10 (November 1973): 396–403.

76. Golden and Alpert, "Comparative Analysis of the Relative Effectiveness of One- and Two-Sided Communication for Contrasting Products"; Gita Venkataramani Johar and Anne L. Roggeveen, "Changing False Beliefs from Repeated Advertising: The Role of Claim-Refutation Alignment," *Journal of Consumer Psychology* 17, no. 2 (2007): 118–27.

77. Belch et al., "Effects of Advertising Communications."

78. Frank R. Kardes, "Spontaneous Inference Processes in Advertising: The Effects of Conclusion Omission and Involvement on Persuasion," *Journal of Consumer Research* 15 (September 1988): 225–33.

79. Belch et al., "Effects of Advertising Communications"; Cornelia Pechmann and Gabriel Esteban, "Persuasion Processes Associated with Direct Comparative and Noncomparative Advertising and Implications for Advertising Effectiveness," *Journal of Consumer Psychology* 2, no. 4 (1994): 403–32.

80. Cornelia Dröge and Rene Y. Darmon, "Associative Positioning Strategies through Comparative Advertising: Attribute vs. Overall Similarity Approaches," *Journal of Marketing Research* 24 (1987): 377–89; D. Muehling and N. Kangun, "The Multidimensionality of Comparative Advertising: Implications for the FTC," *Journal of Public Policy and Marketing* (1985): 112–28; Beth A. Walker and Helen H. Anderson, "Reconceptualizing Comparative Advertising: A Framework and Theory of Effects," in Rebecca H. Holman and Michael R. Solomon, eds., *Advances in Consumer Research* 18 (Provo, UT: Association for Consumer Research, 1991): 342–47; William L. Wilkie and Paul W. Farris, "Comparison Advertising: Problems and Potential," *Journal of Marketing* 39 (October 1975): 7–15; R. G. Wyckham, "Implied Superiority Claims," *Journal of Advertising Research* (February–March 1987): 54–63.

81. Suzanne Vranica, "Arby's TV Spots Play Game of Fast-Food Chicken," *Wall Street Journal* (July 5, 2006): A16.

82. Stephen A. Goodwin and Michael Etgar, "An Experimental Investigation of Comparative Advertising: Impact of Message Appeal, Information Load, and Utility of Product Class," *Journal of Marketing Research*

17 (May 1980): 187–202; Gerald J. Gorn and Charles B. Weinberg, "The Impact of Comparative Advertising on Perception and Attitude: Some Positive Findings," *Journal of Consumer Research* 11 (September 1984): 719–27; Terence A. Shimp and David C. Dyer, "The Effects of Comparative Advertising Mediated by Market Position of Sponsoring Brand," *Journal of Advertising* 3 (Summer 1978): 13–19; R. Dale Wilson, "An Empirical Evaluation of Comparative Advertising Messages: Subjects' Responses to Perceptual Dimensions," in B. B. Anderson, ed., *Advances in Consumer Research* 3 (Ann Arbor, MI: Association for Consumer Research, 1976): 53–57.

83. Allison Fass, "Attack Ads," *Forbes* (October 28, 2002): 60.

84. Dhruv Grewal, Sukumar Kavanoor, Edward F. Fern, Carolyn Costley, and James Barnes, "Comparative versus Noncomparative Advertising: A Meta-Analysis," *Journal of Marketing* 61 (October 1997): 1–15.

85. Fass, "Attack Ads."

86. Dröge and Darmon, "Associative Positioning Strategies through Comparative Advertising: Attribute vs. Overall Similarity Approaches."

87. Jean Halliday, "Survey: Comparative Ads Can Dent Car's Credibility," *Advertising Age* (May 4, 1998): 26.

88. Louise Kramer, "In a Battle of Toothpastes, It's Information vs. Emotion," *New York Times* (January 17, 2007): C6.

89. Geoffrey A. Fowler, "For P&G in China, It's Wash, Rinse, Don't Repeat: Shampoo Ads Jettison Task of Focusing on Product Use in Favor of Emotional Pitch," *Wall Street Journal* (April 7, 2006): B3.

90. Alec Klein, "The Techies Grumbled, but Polaroid's Pocket Turned into a Huge Hit," *Wall Street Journal* (May 2, 2000): A1.

91. Edward F. Cone, "Image and Reality," *Forbes* (December 14, 1987): 226.

92. H. Zielske, "Does Day-After Recall Penalize 'Feeling' Ads?" *Journal of Advertising Research* 22 (1982): 19–22.

93. Stuart Elliott, "Marketing with Double Entendres," *New York Times on the Web* (October 4, 2004).

94. Alex Berenson, "Minky Viagra? Pfizer Doesn't Want You to Understand It, Just Buy It," *New York Times Online* (April 30, 2007), accessed April 30, 2007.

95. Allessandra Galloni, "Lee's Cheeky Ads Are Central to New European Campaign," *Wall Street Journal Interactive Edition* (March 15, 2002).

96. Belch et al., "Effects of Advertising Communications"; Courtney and Whipple, *Sex Stereotyping in Advertising*; Michael S. LaTour, "Female Nudity in Print Advertising: An Analysis of Gender Differences in Arousal and Ad Response," *Psychology & Marketing* 7, no. 1 (1990): 65–81; B. G. Yovovich, "Sex in Advertising—The Power and the Perils," *Advertising Age* (May 2, 1983): M4–M5. For an interesting interpretive analysis, see Richard Elliott and Mark Ritson, "Practicing Existential Consumption: The Lived Meaning of Sexuality in Advertising," in Frank R. Kardes and Mita Sujan, eds., *Advances in Consumer Behavior* 22 (1995): 740–45.

97. Penny M. Simpson, Steve Horton, and Gene Brown, "Male Nudity in Advertisements: A Modified Replication and Extension of Gender and Product Effects," *Journal of the Academy of Marketing Science* 24, no. 3 (1996): 257–62.

98. Rebecca Gardyn, "Where's the Lovin'?" *American Demographic* (February 2001): 10.

99. Michael S. LaTour and Tony L. Henthorne, "Ethical Judgments of Sexual Appeals in Print Advertising," *Journal of Advertising* 23, no. 3 (September 1994): 81–90.

100. "Does Sex Really Sell?" *Adweek* (October 17, 2005): 17.

101. Katharine Q. Seelye, "Metamucil Ad Featuring Old Faithful Causes a Stir," *New York Times Online* (January 19, 2003).

102. Marc G. Weinberger and Harlan E. Spotts, "Humor in U.S. versus U.K. TV Commercials: A Comparison," *Journal of Advertising* 18, no. 2 (1989): 39–44.

103. Thomas J. Madden, "Humor in Advertising: An Experimental Analysis" (working paper, No. 83-27, University of Massachusetts, 1984); Thomas J. Madden and Marc G. Weinberger, "The Effects of Humor on Attention in Magazine Advertising," *Journal of Advertising* 11, no. 3 (1982): 8–14; Weinberger and Spotts, "Humor in U.S. versus U.K. TV Commercials"; see also Ashesh Mukherjee and Laurette Dubé, "The Use of Humor in Threat-Related Advertising" (unpublished manuscript, McGill University, June 2002).

104. David Gardner, "The Distraction Hypothesis in Marketing," *Journal of Advertising Research* 10 (1970): 25–30.

105. "Funny Ads Provide Welcome Relief during These Gloom and Doom Days," *Marketing News* (April 17, 1981): 3.

106. Brian Steinberg, "VW Uses Shock Treatment to Sell Jetta's Safety, Ads Test a Risky Approach with Graphic Car Crashes; 'Any of the Actors Hurt?'" *Wall Street Journal* (April 19, 2006): B4.

107. Michael L. Ray and William L. Wilkie, "Fear: The Potential of an Appeal Neglected by Marketing," *Journal of Marketing* 34, no. 1 (1970): 54–62.

108. Brian Sternthal and C. Samuel Craig, "Fear Appeals: Revisited and Revised," *Journal of Consumer Research* 1 (December 1974): 22–34.

109. Punam Anand Keller and Lauren Goldberg Block, "Increasing the Effectiveness of Fear Appeals: The Effect of Arousal and Elaboration," *Journal of Consumer Research* 22 (March 1996): 448–59.

110. Ronald Paul Hill, "An Exploration of the Relationship between AIDS-Related Anxiety and the Evaluation of Condom Advertisements," *Journal of Advertising* 17, no. 4 (1988): 35–42.

111. Randall Rothenberg, "Talking Too Tough on Life's Risks?" *New York Times* (February 16, 1990): D1.

112. Denise D. Schoenbachler and Tommy E. Whittler, "Adolescent Processing of Social and Physical Threat Communications," *Journal of Advertising* 25, no. 4 (Winter 1996): 37–54.

113. Herbert J. Rotfeld, Auburn University, personal communication, December 9, 1997; Herbert J. Rotfeld, "Fear Appeals and Persuasion: Assumptions and Errors in Advertising Research," *Current Issues & Research in Advertising* 11, no. 1 (1988): 21–40; Michael S. LaTour and Herbert J. Rotfeld, "There Are Threats and (Maybe) Fear-Caused Arousal: Theory and Confusions of Appeals to Fear and Fear Arousal Itself," *Journal of Advertising* 26, no. 3 (Fall 1997): 45–59; Kirsten Passyn and Mita Sujan, "Self-Accountability Emotions and Fear Appeals: Motivating Behavior," *Journal of Consumer Research* 32 (March 2006): 583–89; Omar Shehryar and David M. Hunt, "A Terror Management Perspective on the Persuasiveness of Fear Appeals," *Journal of Consumer Psychology* 15, no. 4, (2005): 275–87.

114. Barbara B. Stern, "Medieval Allegory: Roots of Advertising Strategy for the Mass Market," *Journal of Marketing* 52 (July 1988): 84–94.

115. Edward F. McQuarrie and David Glen Mick, "On Resonance: A Critical Pluralistic Inquiry into Advertising Rhetoric," *Journal of Consumer Research* 19 (September 1992): 180–97.

116. Cf. Linda M. Scott, "The Troupe: Celebrities as Dramatis Personae in Advertisements," in Rebecca H. Holman and Michael R. Solomon, eds., *Advances in Consumer Research* 18 (Provo, UT: Association for Consumer Research, 1991): 355–63; Barbara Stern, "Literary Criticism and Consumer Research: Overview and Illustrative Analysis," *Journal of Consumer Research* 16 (1989): 322–34; Judith Williamson, *Decoding Advertisements* (Boston: Marion Boyars, 1978).

117. John Deighton, Daniel Romer, and Josh McQueen, "Using Drama to Persuade," *Journal of Consumer Research* 16 (December 1989): 335–43.

118. Richard E. Petty, John T. Cacioppo, and David Schumann, "Central and Peripheral Routes to Advertising Effectiveness: The Moderating Role of Involvement," *Journal of Consumer Research* 10, no. 2 (1983): 135–46.

119. Jerry C. Olson, Daniel R. Toy, and Philip A. Dover, "Do Cognitive Responses Mediate the Effects of Advertising Content on Cognitive Structure?" *Journal of Consumer Research* 9, no. 3 (1982): 245–62.

120. Julie A. Edell and Andrew A. Mitchell, "An Information Processing Approach to Cognitive Responses," in S. C. Jain, ed., *Research Frontiers in Marketing: Dialogues and Directions* (Chicago: American Marketing Association, 1978).

121. Cf. Mary Jo Bitner and Carl Obermiller, "The Elaboration Likelihood Model: Limitations and Extensions in Marketing," in Elizabeth C. Hirschman and Morris B. Holbrook, eds., *Advances in Consumer Research* 12 (Provo, UT: Association for Consumer Research, 1985): 420–25; Meryl P. Gardner, "Does Attitude toward the Ad Affect Brand Attitude under a Brand Evaluation Set?" *Journal of Marketing Research* 22 (1985): 192–98; C. W. Park and S. M. Young, "Consumer Response to Television Commercials: The Impact of Involvement and Background Music on Brand Attitude Formation," *Journal of Marketing Research* 23 (1986): 11–24; Petty, Cacioppo, and Schumann, "Central and Peripheral Routes to Advertising Effectiveness." For a discussion of how different kinds of involvement interact with the ELM, cf. Robin A. Higie, Lawrence F. Feick, and Linda L. Price, "The Importance of Peripheral Cues in Attitude Formation for Enduring and Task-Involved Individuals," in Rebecca H. Holman and Michael R. Solomon, eds., *Advances in Consumer Research* 18 (Provo, UT: Association for Consumer Research, 1991): 187–93.

122. J. Craig Andrews and Terence A. Shimp, "Effects of Involvement, Argument Strength, and Source Characteristics on Central and Peripheral Processing in Advertising," *Psychology & Marketing* 7 (Fall 1990): 195–214.

123. Richard E. Petty, John T. Cacioppo, Constantine Sedikides, and Alan J. Strathman, "Affect and Persuasion: A Contemporary Perspective," *American Behavioral Scientist* 31, no. 3 (1988): 355–71.

124. Rob Walker, "The Gifted Ones," *New York Times Magazine Online* (November 14, 2004), accessed September 29, 2007.

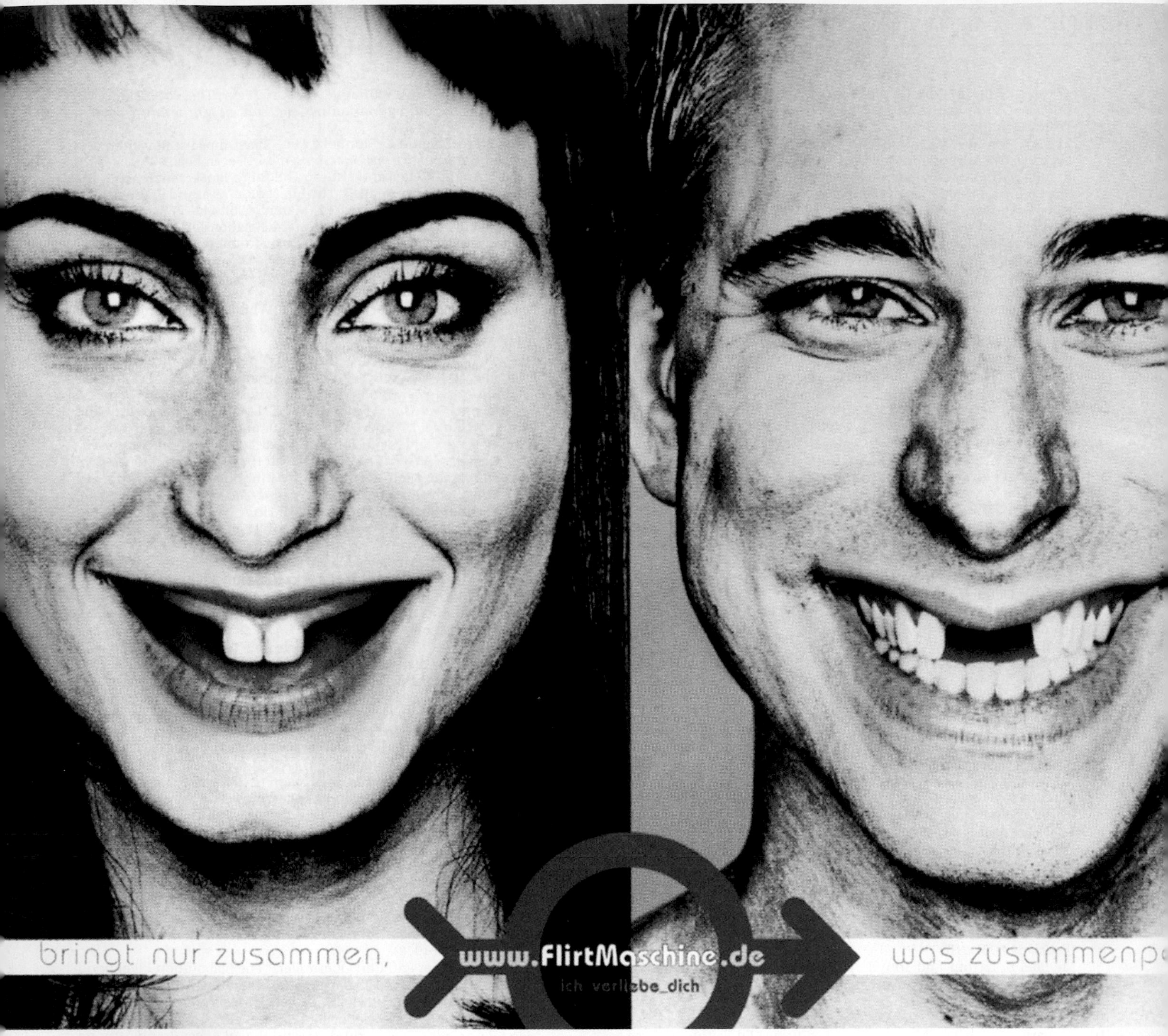
bringt nur zusammen,
www.FlirtMaschine.de
ich verliebe_dich
was zusammenp

CONSUMER BEHAVIOR
1
CONSUMERS IN THE MARKETPLACE
2
CONSUMERS AS INDIVIDUALS
3
CONSUMERS AS DECISION MAKERS
4
CONSUMERS AND SUBCULTURES
5
CONSUMERS AND CULTURES

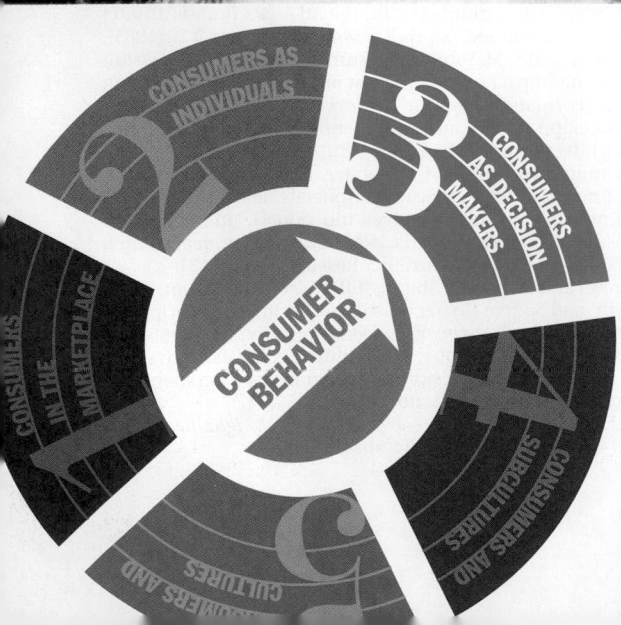

Consumers as Decision Makers

This section explores how we make consumption decisions and discusses the many influences others exert during this process. Chapter 9 focuses on the basic sequence of steps we undergo when we make decisions. Chapter 10 considers how the particular situation in which we find ourselves affects these decisions and how we go about evaluating the results of our choices. Chapter 11 provides an overview of group processes and discusses the reasons we are motivated to conform to the expectations of others when we choose and display our purchases. Chapter 12 goes on to consider the many instances where we make our purchase decisions in conjunction with others, especially co-workers or family members.

■ CHAPTERS AHEAD

CHAPTER 9	CHAPTER 10	CHAPTER 11	CHAPTER 12
Individual Decision Making	Buying and Disposing	Group Influence and Opinion Leadership	Organizational and Household Decision Making

Individual Decision Making

Chapter Objectives

When you finish this chapter you should understand why:

- Consumer decision making is a central part of consumer behavior, but the way we evaluate and choose products (and the amount of thought we put into these choices) varies widely, depending on such dimensions as the degree of novelty or risk in the decision.

- A decision is actually composed of a series of stages that results in the selection of one product over competing options.

- Our access to online sources is changing the way we decide what to buy.

- Decision making is not always rational.

- Consumers rely on different decision rules when evaluating competing options.

- We often fall back on well-learned "rules-of-thumb" to make decisions.

ichard has had it. There's only so much longer he can go on watching TV on his tiny, antiquated black-and-white set. It was bad enough trying to listen to the scratchy music in MTV videos and squinting through *Real World*. The final straw was when he couldn't tell the Titans from the Jaguars during an NFL football game. When he went next door to watch the second half on Mark's home theater setup, he really realized what he had been missing. Budget or not, it was time to act: A man has to have his priorities.

Where to start looking? The Web, naturally. Richard checks out a few comparison-shopping Web sites, including pricegrabber.com and bizrate.com. After narrowing down his options, he ventures out to scope out a few sets in person. He figures he'll probably get a decent selection (and an affordable price) at one of those huge new warehouse stores. Arriving at Zany Zack's Appliance Emporium, Richard heads straight for the Video Zone in the back—barely noticing the rows of toasters, microwave ovens, and stereos on his way. Within minutes, a smiling salesperson in a cheap suit accosts him. Even though he could use some help, Richard tells the salesperson he's only browsing—he figures these guys don't know what they're talking about, and they're simply out to make a sale no matter what.

Richard starts to examine some of the features on the 60-inch color sets. He knew his friend Carol had a set by Prime Wave that she really liked, and his sister Diane had warned him to stay away from the Kamashita. Although Richard finds a Prime Wave model loaded to the max with features such as a sleep timer, on-screen programming menu, cable-compatible tuner, and picture-in-picture, he chooses the less expensive Precision 2000X because it has one feature that really catches his fancy: stereo broadcast reception.

Later that day, Richard is a happy man as he sits in his easy chair, watching Kyndra, Lexie and the others doing their thing on MTV's *Laguna Beach*. If he's going to be a couch potato, he's going in style.

 # Consumers as Problem Solvers

A consumer purchase is a response to a problem, which in Richard's case is the need for a new TV. His situation is similar to those that we encounter virtually every day of our lives (even deciding not to make any decisions on a day off is still a decision!). He realizes that he wants to make a purchase, and he undergoes a series of steps in order to make it. We describe these steps as (1) problem recognition, (2) information search, (3) evaluation of alternatives, and (4) product choice. Of course, after we make a decision, its outcome affects the final step in the process, in which learning occurs based on how well the choice worked out. This learning process, of course, influences the likelihood that we'll make the same choice the next time the need for a similar decision occurs.

Figure 9.1 provides an overview of this decision-making process. This chapter begins by considering various approaches we use when we need to make a purchase decision. We then focus on three of the steps in the decision process: how we recognize the problem, or need for a product; how we search for information about product choices; and how we evaluate alternatives to arrive at a decision. Chapter 10 considers influences in the actual purchase situation, as well as the person's satisfaction with the decision.

Because some purchase decisions are more important than others, the amount of effort we put into each one differs. Sometimes the decision-making process is almost automatic; we seem to make snap judgments based on very little information. At other times, coming to a purchase decision begins to resemble a full-time job. A person may literally spend days or weeks thinking about an important purchase such as a new home, even to the point of obsession. This intensive decision-making process gets even more complicated in today's environment where we have so many options from which to choose. Ironically, for many modern consumers one of the biggest problems they face is not having *too few* choices but having *too many*. We describe this profusion of options as **consumer hyperchoice**, a condition where the large number of available options forces us to make repeated choices that may drain psychological energy while decreasing our abilities to make smart decisions.[1]

PERSPECTIVES ON DECISION MAKING

Traditionally, consumer researchers thought about decision makers from a **rational perspective**. In this view, we calmly and carefully integrate as much information as possible with what we already know about a product, painstakingly weigh the pluses and minuses of each alternative, and make a satisfactory decision. This traditional decision-making perspective incorporates the *economics of information* approach to the search process; it assumes that consumers will gather as much data as they need to make an informed decision. Consumers form expectations of the value of additional information and continue to search to the extent that the rewards of doing so (what economists call the *utility*) exceed the costs. This utilitarian assumption also implies that the person will collect the most valuable units of information first. He will absorb additional pieces only to the extent that he thinks they will add to what he

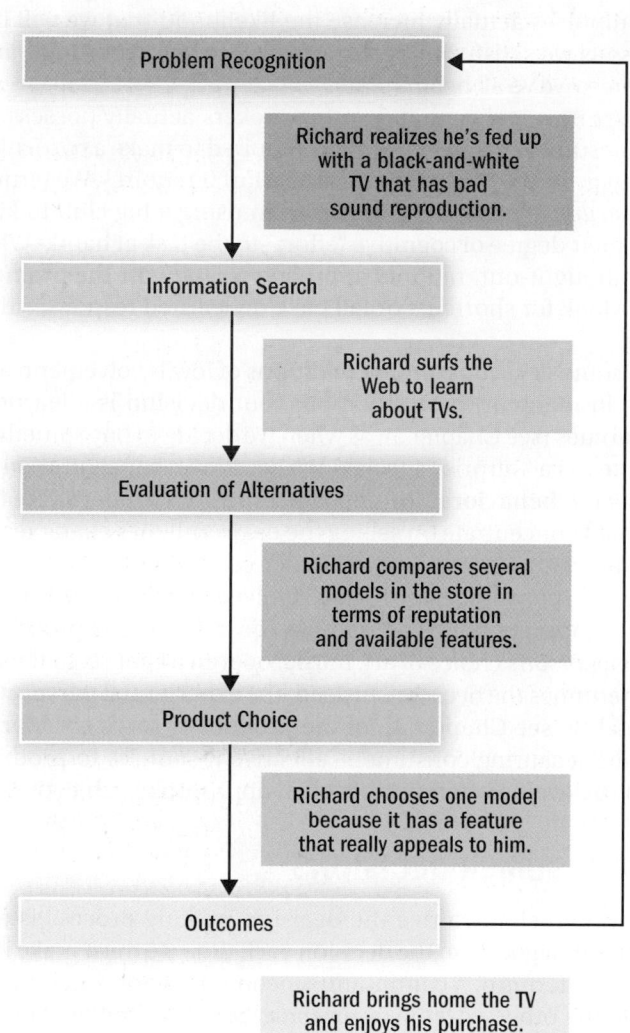

already knows.[2] In other words, people will put themselves out to collect as much information as possible, as long as the process of gathering it is not too onerous or time-consuming.[3]

This process implies that marketing managers should carefully study steps in decision making to understand how consumers obtain information, how they form beliefs, and what criteria they use to make product choices. Then, companies can develop products that emphasize the appropriate attributes, and marketers can tailor promotional strategies to deliver the types of information customers are most likely to desire and in the most effective formats.[4]

It all sounds good, but how valid is this perspective? Sure, consumers do follow these decision-making steps when they make some purchases, but this rational process doesn't accurately portray many of our purchase decisions.[5] We simply don't go through this elaborate sequence every time we buy something. If we did, we'd spend our entire lives making these decisions. This would leave us very little time to enjoy the things we eventually decide to buy. Some of our buying behaviors simply don't seem "rational" because they don't serve a logical purpose (e.g., people in Scotland who break the law to collect the eggs of the osprey, a rare bird, even though they have no monetary value;[6] we purchase some items with virtually no advance planning at all (e.g., when you impulsively grab that tempting candy bar from the rack while you're waiting to pay for groceries). Still other actions actually are contrary to what those rational models predict. For example, **purchase momentum** occurs when these initial impulses actually increase the likelihood that we will buy even more (instead of less as we satisfy our needs); it's like we get "revved up" and plunge into a spending spree (we've all been there!).[7]

Researchers now realize that decision makers actually possess a repertoire of strategies. A consumer evaluates the effort required to make a particular choice, then chooses a strategy best suited to the level of effort it requires. We term this sequence of events *constructive processing*. Rather than using a big club to kill an ant, consumers tailor their degree of cognitive "effort" to the task at hand.[8] When the task requires a well-thought-out, rational approach we'll invest the brainpower to do it. Otherwise, we look for shortcuts or fall back on learned responses that "automate" these choices.

We make some decisions under conditions of low involvement, as we discussed in Chapter 4. In many of these situations, our decision is a learned response to environmental cues (see Chapter 3), as when we decide to buy something on impulse a store promotes as a "surprise special." We describe a concentration on these types of decisions as the **behavioral influence perspective**. Under these circumstances, managers should concentrate on selling the environment's characteristics, such as a store's design or whether a package will entice customers.[9]

In other cases, consumers are highly involved in a decision, but still we can't explain their selections rationally. For example, the traditional approach is hard pressed to account for a person's choice of art, music, or even a spouse. In these cases, no single quality determines the decision. Instead, the **experiential perspective** stresses the *Gestalt*, or totality (see Chapter 2), of the product or service.[10] Marketers in these areas focus on measuring consumers' affective responses to products or services and how best to develop offerings that elicit appropriate subjective reactions.

TYPES OF CONSUMER DECISIONS

One helpful way to characterize the decision-making process is to consider the amount of effort that goes into the decision each time we must make it. Consumer researchers think in terms of a continuum, anchored on one end by *habitual decision making* and at the other extreme by *extended problem solving*. Many decisions fall somewhere in the middle so we describe these as *limited problem solving*. Figure 9.2 presents this continuum.

EXTENDED PROBLEM SOLVING

Decisions involving **extended problem solving** correspond most closely to the traditional decision-making perspective. As Table 9.1 indicates, we usually initiate this

■ FIGURE 9.2 A CONTINUUM OF BUYING DECISION BEHAVIOR

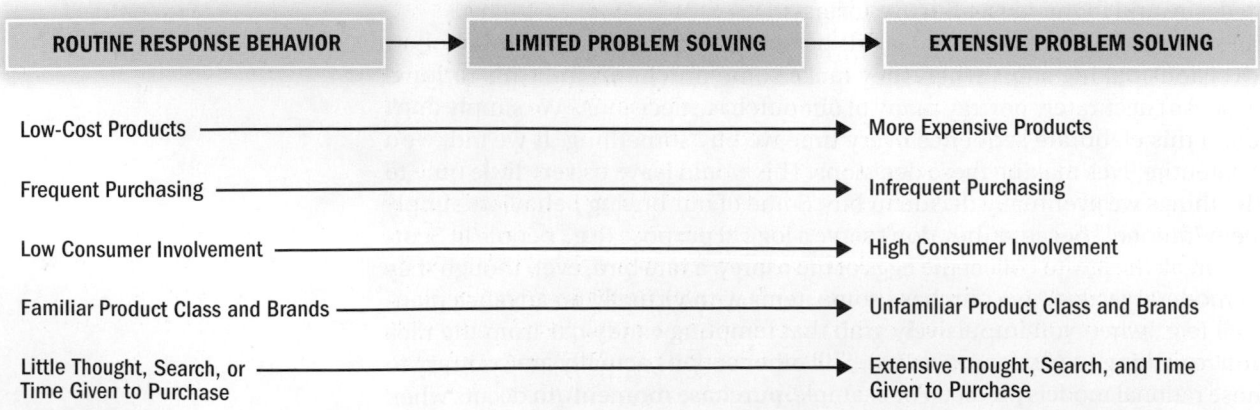

	Limited Problem Solving	**Extended Problem Solving**
TABLE 9.1		
CHARACTERISTICS OF LIMITED VERSUS EXTENDED PROBLEM SOLVING		
Motivation	Low risk and involvement	High risk and involvement
Information Search	Little search	Extensive search
	Information processed passively	Information processed actively
	In-store decision likely	Multiple sources consulted prior to visits
Alternative Evaluation	Weakly held beliefs	Strongly held beliefs
	Only most prominent criteria used	Many criteria used
	Alternatives perceived as basically similar	Significant differences perceived among alternatives
	Noncompensatory strategy used	Compensatory strategy used
Purchase	Limited shopping time; may prefer self-service	Many outlets shopped if needed
	Choice often influenced by store displays	Communication with store personnel often desirable

careful process when the decision we have to make relates to our self-concept (see Chapter 5), and we feel that the outcome may be risky in some way. In that case we try to collect as much information as possible, both from our memory (internal search) and from outside sources such as Google (external search). Then we carefully evaluate each product alternative, often by considering the attributes of one brand at a time and seeing how each brand's attributes shape up to some set of outcomes we hope to get from our choice.

LIMITED PROBLEM SOLVING

Limited problem solving is usually more straightforward and simple. In this case we're not nearly as motivated to search for information or to evaluate each alternative rigorously. Instead, we're likely to use simple *decision rules* to choose among alternatives. These cognitive shortcuts (more about these later) enable us to fall back on general guidelines, instead of having to start from scratch every time we need to decide.

HABITUAL DECISION MAKING

Both extended and limited problem-solving modes involve some degree of information search and deliberation, though they vary in the degree to which we engage in these activities. At the other end of the choice continuum, however, lays **habitual decision making**—choices we make with little to no conscious effort. Many purchase decisions are so routinized that we may not realize we've made them until we look in our shopping carts! We make these choices with minimal effort and without conscious control; researchers call this process *automaticity.*[11]

Although this kind of thoughtless activity may seem dangerous or, at best, stupid, it is actually quite efficient in many cases. By developing these habitual, repetitive behaviors, we minimize the time and energy we spend on mundane purchase decisions. However, habitual decision making poses a problem when a marketer tries to introduce a new way of doing an old task. In this case she must convince us to "unfreeze" our former habit and replace it with a new one—perhaps to use an ATM instead of a live bank teller, or switch to a self-service gas pump instead having an attendant wait on us.

Scotchguard facilitates limited problem solving in this Belgian ad.

Everyday stains* and dirt don't stay long on a carpet treated with Scotchgard™ Protector.

EFFORTLESS CARPET CARE

SCOTCHGARD.
PROTECTOR
3M

 ## Steps in the Decision-Making Process

Richard didn't suddenly wake up and crave a new TV. He went through several steps between feeling the need for a new telly and actually setting one up at home. Let's review the basic steps in this process.

PROBLEM RECOGNITION

Problem recognition occurs whenever we see a significant difference between our current state of affairs and some state. We realize that to get from here to there we need to solve a problem, which may be small or large, simple or complex. A person who unexpectedly runs out of gas on the highway has a problem, as does the person who becomes dissatisfied with the image of his car, even though there is nothing mechanically wrong with it. Although the quality of Richard's TV had not changed, he altered his *standard of comparison,* and as a result he experienced a desire he didn't have before he watched his friend's TV.

This Dutch ad encourages consumers to recognize a problem: They need to get out and go to the movies asap!

Figure 9.3 shows that a problem arises in one of two ways. As in the case of the person who runs out of gas, the quality of an *actual state* sometimes decreases (*need recognition*). However, as in the case of the person who craves a newer, flashier car, we can move our *ideal state* upward (*opportunity recognition*). Either way, there is a gulf between the actual state and the ideal state.[12] Richard perceived a problem as a result of opportunity recognition; he moved his ideal state upward in terms of the quality of TV reception he wanted.

Need recognition occurs in several ways. A person's actual state can decrease if she runs out of a product, or if she buys a product that doesn't adequately satisfy her needs, or if she realizes she has a new need or desire. For example, when you buy a house, this sets off an avalanche of other choices because now we need to buy many new things to fill it—assuming there's any money left over. In contrast, opportunity recognition often occurs when we're exposed to different or better-quality products. This happens because our circumstances have somehow changed, as when we start

■ **FIGURE 9.3**
PROBLEM RECOGNITION: SHIFTS IN ACTUAL OR IDEAL STATES

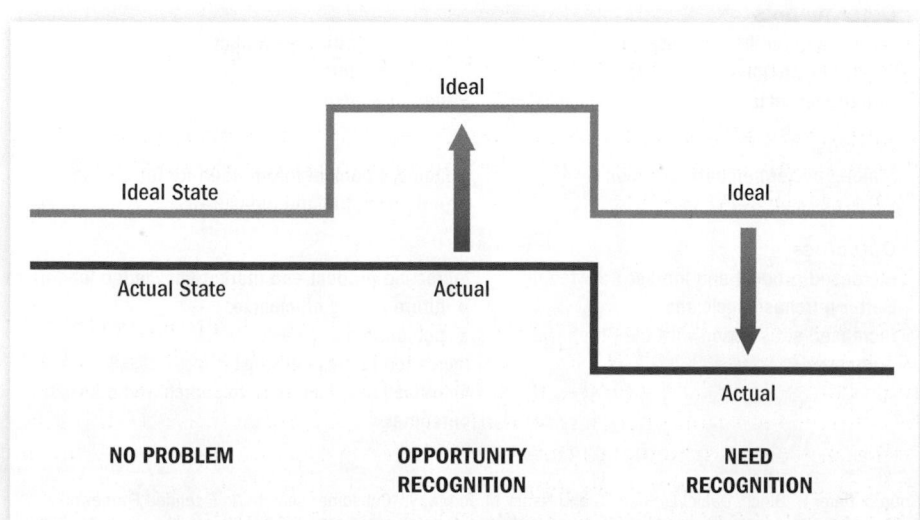

college or land a new job. As our frame of reference shifts, we make purchases to adapt to the new environment. That awesome pair of True Religion jeans you just scored somehow won't make it on a job interview.

INFORMATION SEARCH

Once a consumer recognizes a problem, she needs adequate information to solve it. **Information search** is the process by which we survey the environment for appropriate data to make a reasonable decision. In this section we'll review some of the factors this search involves.[13]

Types of Information Search

You might recognize a need and then search the marketplace for specific information (a process we call *prepurchase search*). However, many of us, especially veteran shoppers, enjoy browsing just for the fun of it or because we like to stay up-to-date on what's happening in the marketplace. Those shopaholics engage in *ongoing search*.[14] Table 9.2 describes some differences between these two search modes.

Internal versus External Search

We break information sources down into two types: internal and external. As a result of prior experience and simply living in a consumer culture, each of us has some degree of knowledge already in memory about many products. When a purchase decision confronts us, we may engage in *internal search* by scanning our own memory banks to assemble information about different product alternatives (see Chapter 3). Usually, though, even those of us who are the most market savvy need to supplement this knowledge with external search, by which we obtain information from advertisements, friends, or just plain people watching. A study in Finland recently demonstrated how what our neighbors buy impacts our own decision making. The researchers discovered that when one of a person's 10 nearest neighbors bought a

TABLE 9.2 A FRAMEWORK FOR CONSUMER INFORMATION SEARCH	
Prepurchase Search	**Ongoing Search**
Determinants	
Involvement in the purchase	Involvement with the product
Market environment	Market environment
Situational factors	Situational factors
Motives	
Making better purchase decisions	Building a bank of information for future use
	Experiencing fun and pleasure
Outcomes	
Increased product and market knowledge	Increased product and market knowledge leading to
Better purchase decisions	● future buying efficiencies
Increased satisfaction with the purchase outcome	● personal influence
	Increased impulse buying
	Increased satisfaction from search and other outcomes

Source: Peter H. Bloch, Daniel L. Sherrell, and Nancy M. Ridgway, "Consumer Search: An Extended Framework," *Journal of Consumer Research* 13 (June 1986): 120. Copyright © 1986 JCR, Inc. Reprinted with permission of the University of Chicago Press.

car, the odds that he would buy a car of the same make during the next week and a half jumped 86 percent. The effect was even stronger for used car purchases—low-income families and those who lived in rural areas were more likely to be influenced by their neighbors than were wealthy Helsinki residents. They explained this finding in terms of the information value of these choices—because used cars are less reliable, a neighbor's endorsement of one kind over others might carry more weight.[16]

Deliberate versus "Accidental" Search

We may know about a product as a result of *directed learning*: On a previous occasion we've already searched for relevant information. A parent who bought a birthday cake for one child last month, for example, probably has a good idea of the best kind to buy for another child this month.

Sometimes we acquire information in a more passive manner. Even though a product may not be of direct interest to us today, we're still exposed to advertising, packaging, and sales promotion activities that result in *incidental learning*. Mere exposure over time to conditioned stimuli and observations of others results in the learning of much material that we may not need for some time if ever. For marketers, this is one of the benefits of steady, "low-dose" advertising, as they establish and maintain product associations until the time we need them.[17]

In some cases, we may be so expert about a product category (or at least believe we are) that we don't undertake any additional search. Frequently, however, our own existing state of knowledge is not sufficient to make an adequate decision, and we must look elsewhere for more information. The sources we consult for advice vary: They may be impersonal and marketer-dominated sources, such as retailers and catalogs; they may be friends and family members; or they may be unbiased third parties, such as *Consumer Reports*.[18]

Of course, Internet search engines (especially Google) are huge players now when it comes to search. In fact, Yahoo! recently found that consumers spend 10 percent more for televisions and digital cameras they buy in stores when they research these purchases online first using a search engine, and people who use these engines consult twice as many information sources as those who don't.[19] When we search online for product information, we're a perfect target for advertisers because we're declaring our desire to make a purchase. Recognizing this, many companies pay **search engines** to show ads to users who have searched for their brand names. However, when DoubleClick (an online marketing company) looked closely at what people search for, it found that searches including brand names account for a small share of our queries. Instead, most prepurchase searches use only generic terms, such as "hard drive." Consumers tend to make these searches early on and then conduct a small flurry of brand-name queries right before buying.[20]

DO CONSUMERS ALWAYS SEARCH RATIONALLY?

As we've seen, consumers don't necessarily engage in a rational search process where they carefully identify every alternative before choosing one they prefer. In fact, the amount of external search we do for most products is surprisingly small, even when we would benefit by having more information. And lower-income shoppers, who have more to lose by making a bad purchase, actually search less prior to buying than more affluent people do.[22]

Like our friend Richard, some consumers typically visit only one or two stores and rarely seek out unbiased information sources prior to making a purchase decision, especially when they have little time available to do so.[23] This pattern is especially prevalent for decisions about durable goods, such as appliances or autos, even when these products represent significant investments. One study of Australian car buyers found that more than a third had made two or fewer trips to inspect cars prior to buying one.[24]

This tendency to avoid external search is less prevalent when consumers consider the purchase of symbolic items, such as clothing. In those cases, not surprisingly,

Marketing Pitfall

When it comes to efficient information search, don't look to American men who are grocery shopping. According to an industry analyst who conducted a study on store behavior, men are ". . . often overwhelmed by the experience." She says they ". . . roam the aisles like lost sheep, and are afraid to make their wives mad by bringing home the wrong brand of cereal bar or toothpaste. . . . They do not want to catch any flak for coming home with the wrong thing. They'd say, 'I'll just tell my wife the store is out of this brand,' rather than admit that they couldn't find it." She notes that grocery stores aren't organized to make life easier for male shoppers. They tend to circle back through aisles multiple times in their searches, become overwhelmed in center-store aisles, and focus their attention within a fairly narrow visual range. But, they're more likely to call their spouses on a cell phone than to ask store employees for help. Kind of like stopping on the road to ask for directions—not happening.[21]

Marketing Pitfall

Labels provide valuable information about the proper way to use products, but sometimes they can be less than clear. Here are some examples of "interesting" labels:[31]

- On a Conair Pro Style 1600 hair dryer: WARNING: Do not use in shower. Never use while sleeping.
- Instructions for folding up a portable baby carriage: Step 1: Remove baby.
- A rest stop on a Wisconsin highway: Do not eat urinal cakes.
- On a bag of Fritos: You could be a winner! No purchase necessary. Details inside.
- On some Swanson frozen dinners: Serving suggestion: Defrost.
- On Tesco's Tiramisu dessert (printed on bottom of box): Do not turn upside down.
- On Marks & Spencer bread pudding: Product will be hot after heating.
- On packaging for a Rowenta iron: Do not iron clothes on body.
- On Nytol sleeping aid: Warning: May cause drowsiness.

people tend to do a fair amount of external search, although most of it involves asking peers' opinions.[25] Although the stakes may be lower financially, people may see these self-expressive decisions as having dire social consequences if they make the wrong choice. The level of risk, a concept we'll discuss shortly, is high.

In addition, consumers often engage in *brand switching*, even if their current brand satisfies their needs. For example, researchers for British brewer Bass Export who were studying the American beer market discovered a consumer trend toward having a repertoire of two to six favorite brands, rather than sticking to only one. This preference for brand switching led the firm to begin exporting its Tennent's 1885 lager to the United States, positioning the brew as an alternative to young drinkers' usual favorite brands.[26]

Sometimes, it seems that people simply like to try new things—we crave variety as a form of stimulation or to reduce boredom. **Variety seeking**, the desire to choose new alternatives over more familiar ones, even influences us to switch from our favorite products to ones we like less! This can occur even before we become *satiated*, or tired, of our favorite. Research supports the idea that we are willing to trade enjoyment for variety because the unpredictability itself is rewarding.[27]

Variety seeking is especially likely to occur when we are in a good mood, or when there isn't a lot of other stuff going on.[28] In the case of foods and beverages, variety seeking can occur as a result of *sensory-specific satiety*. Put simply, this means the pleasantness of a food item we have just eaten drops, whereas the pleasantness of uneaten foods remains unchanged.[29] So even though we have favorites, we still like to sample other possibilities. However, when the decision situation is ambiguous, or when there is little information about competing brands, we tend to opt for the safe choice by selecting familiar brands and maintaining the status quo. Figure 9.4 shows the brand attributes consumers consider most important when choosing among alternatives, according to a survey *Advertising Age* conducted.

BIASES IN THE DECISION-MAKING PROCESS

Consider the following scenario: You've scored a free ticket to a major football game. At the last minute, though, a sudden snowstorm makes getting to the stadium somewhat dangerous. Would you still go? Now, assume the same game and snowstorm, except this time you paid handsomely for the ticket. Would you head out in the storm in this case?

Analyses of people's responses to this situation and to other similar puzzles illustrate principles of **mental accounting**. This process demonstrates that the way we pose a problem (we call this *framing*) and whether it's phrased in terms of gains or losses influences our decisions.[30] In this case, researchers find that people are more likely to risk their personal safety in the storm if they paid for the football ticket than if it's a freebie. Only the most die-hard fan would fail to recognize that this is an irrational choice because the risk is the same regardless of whether you got a great deal on the ticket. Researchers call this decision-making bias the *sunk-cost fallacy*—having paid for something makes us reluctant to waste it.

Loss aversion is another bias. This means that we emphasize our losses more than our gains. For example, for most people losing money is more *unpleasant* than gaining money is *pleasant*. **Prospect theory**, which describes how people make choices, finds that utility is a function of gains and losses. Our sense of risk differs when we face options involving gains versus those involving losses.[32] To illustrate this bias, consider the following choices. For each, would you take the safe bet or choose to gamble?

- **Option 1:** You're given $30 and a chance to flip a coin: Heads you win $9; tails you lose $9.
- **Option 2:** You get $30 outright or you accept a coin flip that will win you either $39 or $21.

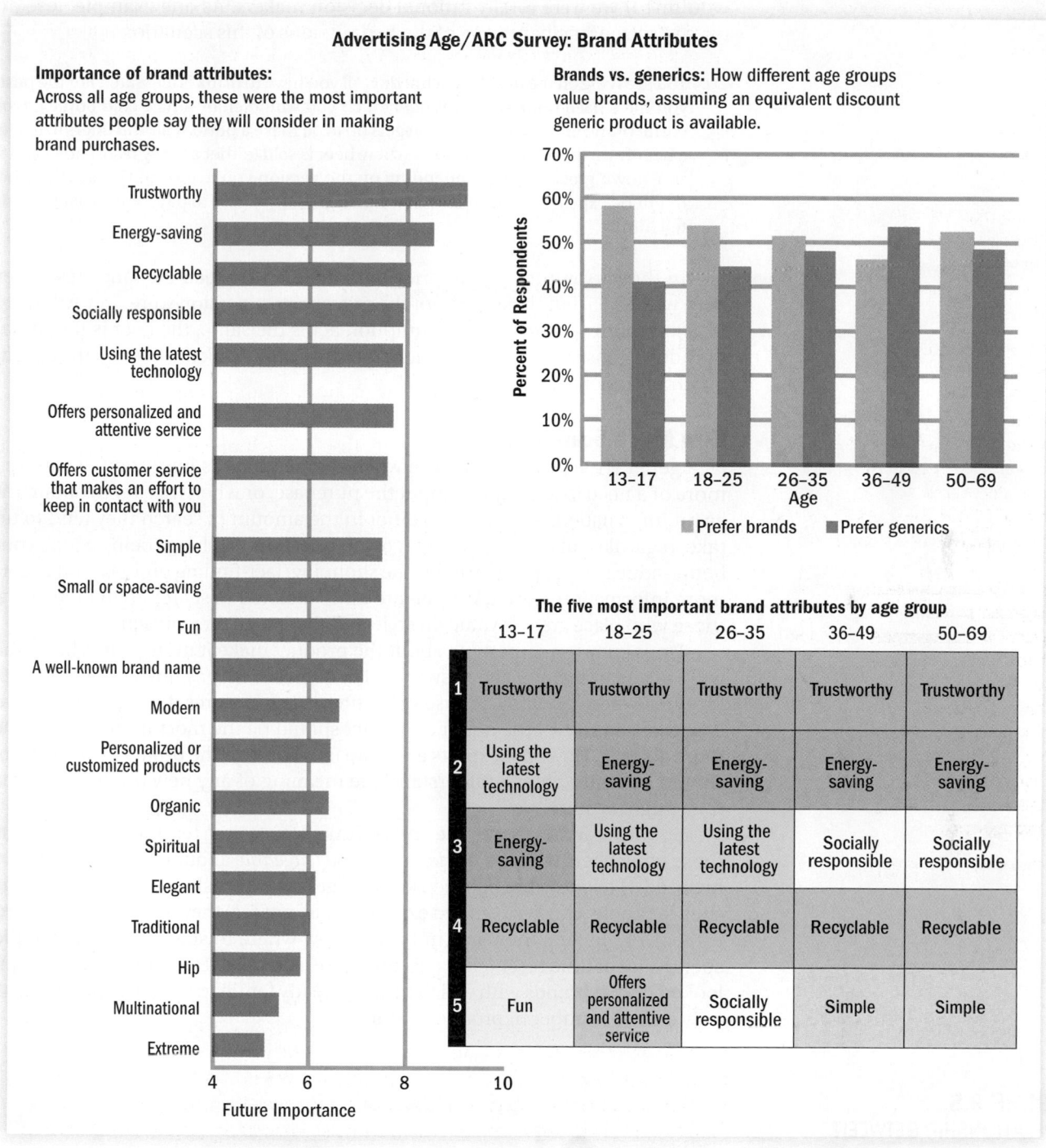

Advertising Age/ARC Survey: Brand Attributes

Importance of brand attributes:
Across all age groups, these were the most important attributes people say they will consider in making brand purchases.

Brands vs. generics: How different age groups value brands, assuming an equivalent discount generic product is available.

The five most important brand attributes by age group

	13–17	18–25	26–35	36–49	50–69
1	Trustworthy	Trustworthy	Trustworthy	Trustworthy	Trustworthy
2	Using the latest technology	Energy-saving	Energy-saving	Energy-saving	Energy-saving
3	Energy-saving	Using the latest technology	Using the latest technology	Socially responsible	Socially responsible
4	Recyclable	Recyclable	Recyclable	Recyclable	Recyclable
5	Fun	Offers personalized and attentive service	Socially responsible	Simple	Simple

In one study, 70 percent of those given option 1 chose to gamble, compared to only 43 percent of those offered option 2. Yet the odds are the same for both options! The difference is that people prefer "playing with the house money"; they are more willing to take risks when they perceive they're using someone else's resources. So, contrary to a rational decision-making perspective, we value money differently depending on its source. This explains, for example, why someone might choose to blow a big bonus on some frivolous purchase but would never consider taking that same amount out of her savings account for this purpose.

Finally, research in mental accounting demonstrates that extraneous characteristics of the choice situation can influence our selections, even though they

■ **FIGURE 9.4**
ADVERTISING AGE POLL: IMPORTANCE OF BRAND ATTRIBUTES

wouldn't *if* we were totally rational decision makers. As one example, researchers gave survey participants one of the two versions of this scenario:

> You are lying on the beach on a hot day. All you have to drink is ice water. For the past hour you have been thinking about how much you would enjoy a nice cold bottle of your favorite brand of beer. A companion gets up to go make a phone call and offers to bring back a beer from the only nearby place where beer is sold (either a fancy resort hotel or a small, run-down grocery store, depending on the version you're given). He says that the beer might be expensive and so asks how much you are willing to pay for it. What price do you tell him?

In the survey, the median price participants who read the fancy resort version gave was $2.65, but those who got the grocery store version were only willing to pay $1.50. In both versions the consumption act is the same, the beer is the same, and they don't consume any "atmosphere" because they drink the beer on the beach.[33] So much for rational decision making!

How Much Search Occurs?

As a general rule, we search more when the purchase is important, when we have more of a need to learn more about the purchase, or when it's easy to obtain the relevant information.[34] Consumers differ in the amount of search they tend to undertake, regardless of the product category in question. All things being equal, younger, better-educated people who enjoy the shopping/fact-finding process tend to conduct more information search. Women are more inclined to search than men are, as are those who place greater value on style and the image they present.[35]

Does knowing something about the product make it more or less likely that we will engage in search? The answer to this question isn't as obvious as first appears: Product experts and novices use very different procedures during decision making. Novices who know little about a product should be the most motivated to find out more about it. However, experts are more familiar with the product category, so they should be better able to understand the meaning of any new product information they might acquire.

So who searches more? The answer is neither: Search tends to be greatest among those consumers who are *moderately knowledgeable* about the product. We find an inverted-U relationship between knowledge and external search effort, as Figure 9.5 shows. People with very limited expertise may not feel they are capable of searching extensively. In fact, they may not even know where to start. Richard, who did not spend a lot of time researching his purchase, is typical. He visited one store, and he looked only at brands with which he was already familiar. In addition, he focused on only a small number of product features.[36]

■ FIGURE 9.5
THE RELATIONSHIP BETWEEN AMOUNT OF INFORMATION SEARCH AND PRODUCT KNOWLEDGE

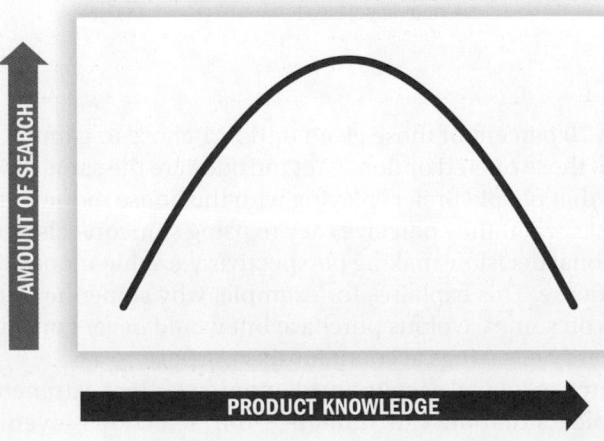

The *type* of search people with varying levels of expertise undertake also differs. Because experts have a better sense of what information is relevant to the decision, they engage in *selective search*, which means their efforts are more focused and efficient. In contrast, novices are more likely to rely on the opinions of others and on "nonfunctional" attributes, such as brand name and price, to distinguish among alternatives. They may also process information in a "top-down" rather than a "bottom-up" manner, focusing less on details than on the big picture. For instance, they may be more impressed by the sheer amount of technical information an ad presents than by the actual significance of the claims it makes.[37]

Perceived Risk

As a rule, purchase decisions that involve extensive search also entail **perceived risk**, or the belief that there may be negative consequences from using or not using a product or service. This may occur when the product is expensive or is complex and hard to understand. Alternatively, perceived risk can be a factor when others

MAYBE THE BEST WAY TO HANDLE RISK IS TO AVOID IT ALTOGETHER.

That's why Minolta created the No-Risk Guarantee. It takes you out of harm's way by letting you decide whether you're happy with the copier's performance.

Even better, it covers our EP 9760 Pro Series Copier, which was recently voted first overall in productivity in the high-volume class.*

Here's how it works: If you're not completely satisfied with our copier within the first three years of normal operation, we will replace it with an identical or comparably equipped model, free of charge. In other

words, it works or it walks. An award-winning copier combined with an iron-clad guarantee? The only risk involved is passing this opportunity up.

For more information, call 1-800-9-MINOLTA.

NO-RISK COPIERS
ONLY FROM THE MIND OF MINOLTA   **MINOLTA**

Minolta features a no-risk guarantee as a way to reduce the perceived risk in buying an office copier.

Marketing Pitfall

In recent years, some researchers have started to focus on the plight of consumers who really have trouble searching—because they have difficulty reading. When we do consumer research, we typically assume that our respondents are fully literate so they are able to find information, identify products, and conduct transactions with few problems. However, it's worth noting that, in fact, more than half of the U.S. population reads at or below a sixth-grade level—and that roughly half are unable to master specific aspects of shopping. This fact reminds us to think more about the **low-literate consumer** who is at a big disadvantage in the marketplace. Some of these people (whom researchers term *social isolates*) cope with the stigma of illiteracy by avoiding situations where they will have to reveal this problem. They may avoid eating at a restaurant with an unfamiliar menu, for example. Low-literate consumers rely heavily on visual cues, including brand logos and store layouts, to navigate in retail settings, but they often make mistakes when they select similarly packaged products (for example, brand line extensions). They also encounter problems with *innumeracy* (understanding numbers); many low-literate people have difficulty knowing, for example, whether they have enough money to purchase the items in their cart and are vulnerable to being cheated out of the correct amount of change due. Not surprisingly, these challenges create an emotional burden for low-literate consumers, who experience stress, anxiety, fear, shame, and other negative emotions before, during, and after they shop.[38]

■ **FIGURE 9.6**
FIVE TYPES OF PERCEIVED RISK

	BUYERS MOST SENSITIVE TO RISK	PURCHASES MOST SUBJECT TO RISK
MONETARY RISK	Risk capital consists of money and property. Those with relatively little income and wealth are most vulnerable.	High-ticket items that require substantial expenditures are most subject to this form of risk.
FUNCTIONAL RISK	Risk capital consists of alternative means of performing the function or meeting the need. Practical consumers are most sensitive.	Products or services whose purchase and use requires the buyer's exclusive commitment are most sensitive.
PHYSICAL RISK	Risk capital consists of physical vigor, health, and vitality. Those who are elderly, frail, or in ill health are most vulnerable.	Mechanical or electrical goods (such as vehicles or flammables), drugs and medical treatment, and food and beverages are most sensitive.
SOCIAL RISK	Risk capital consists of self-esteem and self-confidence. Those who are insecure and uncertain are most sensitive.	Socially visible or symbolic goods, such as clothes, jewelry, cars, homes, or sports equipment are most subject to social risk.
PSYCHO-LOGICAL RISK	Risk capital consists of affiliations and status. Those lacking self-respect or attractiveness to peers are most sensitive.	Expensive personal luxuries that may engender guilt, durables, and services whose use demands self-discipline or sacrifice are most sensitive.

can see what we choose, and we may be embarrassed if we make the wrong choice.[39]

Figure 9.6 lists five kinds of risk—including objective (e.g., physical danger) and subjective (e.g., social embarrassment) factors—as well as the products each type tends to affect. Perceived risk is less of a problem for consumers who have greater "risk capital" because they have less to lose from a poor choice. For example, a highly self-confident person might worry less than a vulnerable, insecure person about choosing a brand that peers think isn't cool.

Evaluating Alternatives

Much of the effort we put into a purchase decision occurs at the stage where we have to put the pedal to the metal and actually choose a product from several alternatives. This may not be easy; modern consumer society abounds with choices. In some cases, there may be literally hundreds of different brands (as in cigarettes) or different variations of the same brand (as in shades of lipstick), each screaming for our attention.

Just for fun, ask a friend to name all of the brands of perfume she can think of. The odds are she will reel off three to five names rather quickly, then stop and think awhile before coming up with a few more. It is likely that she is highly familiar with the first set of brands, and in fact she probably wears one or more of these. Her list may also contain one or two brands that she doesn't like but she thinks of because they smell so nasty. Note also that there are many, many more brands on the market that she did not name at all.

If your friend were to go to the store to buy perfume, it is likely that she would consider buying some or most of the brands she listed initially. She might also consider a few more possibilities if these were forcefully brought to her attention while she was at the store—for example, if an employee "ambushes" her with a scent sample as she's walking through the cosmetics section.

IDENTIFYING ALTERNATIVES

How do we decide which criteria are important, and how do we narrow down product alternatives to an acceptable number and eventually choose one instead of others? The answer varies depending on the decision-making process we are using. A person who is engaging in extended problem solving may carefully evaluate several brands, whereas someone making a habitual decision may not consider any alternatives to his normal brand. Furthermore, some evidence indicates that we do more extended processing in situations that arouse negative emotions because of conflicts among the available choices. This is most likely to occur when there are difficult trade-offs, for example, when a person must choose between the risks involved in having a bypass operation and the potential improvement in his life if the operation succeeds.[40]

We call the alternatives a consumer knows about his evoked set and the ones that he actually considers his **consideration set** (because often we don't seriously consider every single brand in a category because of issues such as price, a prior negative experience, and so on).[41] For example, recall that Richard did not know much about the technical aspects of television sets, and he had only a few major brands in memory. Of these, two were acceptable possibilities and one was not.

Consumers often include a surprisingly small number of alternatives in their evoked sets. One study combined results from several large-scale investigations of consumers' evoked sets. It found that people overall include a small number of products in these sets, although this amount varies by product category and across countries. For example, on average American beer consumers had only three brands in their evoked sets, whereas Canadian consumers typically considered seven brands. In contrast, whereas auto buyers in Norway studied two alternatives, American consumers on average looked at more than eight models before making a decision.[42] We seem to be a lot more picky about our wheels than our brews.

For obvious reasons, a marketer who finds that his brand is not in his target market's evoked set has cause to worry. You often don't get a second chance to make a good first impression; a consumer isn't likely to place a product in his evoked set after he has already considered it and rejected it. Indeed, we're more likely to add a new brand to the evoked set than one that we previously considered but passed over, even after a marketer has provided additional positive information about it.[43] For marketers, consumers' unwillingness to give a rejected product a second chance underscores the importance of ensuring that it performs well from the time it is introduced.

A recent large-scale advertising campaign for Hyundai illustrates how hard a company may need to work to get its brand into consumers' consideration sets. Many people think of Hyundai strictly as a low-cost vehicle, even though it has received high marks for quality in recent years. The carmaker's "Think About It" campaign tries to get consumers to reconsider their long-held beliefs through frank statements like "The logo is there to tell you what the car is, not who you are" and "When a car company charges for roadside assistance, aren't they just helping themselves?" As Hyundai's vice president for marketing in America explained, "Unless we give people a compelling reason to shuffle the brand deck, they'll stand with the brands they know rather than make that switch."[44]

This ad for Sunkist lemon juice attempts to establish a new category for the product by repositioning it as a salt substitute.

CATEGORIZING PRODUCTS

Remember that when consumers process product information, they do not do so in a vacuum. Instead, they evaluate a product stimulus in terms of what they already know about a particular product or other similar ones. A person who thinks about a particular SLR camera will most likely compare it to other SLR cameras rather than to a pocket camera, and it's unlikely she would compare it to a slide projector or a DVD player. Because the category in which a consumer places a product determines the other products she will compare it to, the way we classify a brand in our minds plays a big role in how we evaluate it.

The products in a consumer's evoked set are likely to share some similar features. This process can either help or hurt a product, depending on what people compare it to. For example, in one survey about 25 percent of consumers said they would be less likely to buy a product made of hemp if they know it's derived from the same plant from which marijuana comes (but without any of the latter's effects). When faced with a new product, consumers refer to their already existing knowledge in familiar product categories to form new knowledge.[45]

It is important to understand how consumers cognitively represent this information in a **knowledge structure**, a set of beliefs and the way we organize these beliefs in our minds.[46] We discussed these knowledge structures in Chapter 4. Their make-up matters to marketers because they want to ensure that customers correctly group their products. For example, General Foods brought out a new line of Jell-O flavors, such as Cranberry Orange, that it called Jell-O Gelatin Flavors for Salads. Unfortunately, the company discovered that people would use it only for salad, because the name encouraged them to put the product in their "salad" structure rather than in their "dessert" structure. They wound up dropping the product line.[47]

Levels of Categorization

Typically, we represent a product in a cognitive structure at one of three levels. To understand this idea, consider how someone might respond to these questions about an ice cream cone: What other products share similar characteristics, and which would you consider as alternatives to eating a cone?

These questions may be more complex than they first appear. At one level, a cone is similar to an apple because you could eat both as a dessert. At another level, a cone is similar to a piece of pie because you could eat either for dessert and both are fattening. At still another level, a cone is similar to an ice cream sundae—you could eat either for dessert, both are made of ice cream, and both are fattening. Figure 9.7 depicts these three levels.

It is easy to see that the foods a person associates with, say, the category "fattening dessert" influence his decision about what to eat after dinner. The middle level, or *basic level category*, is typically the most useful to classify products because at this

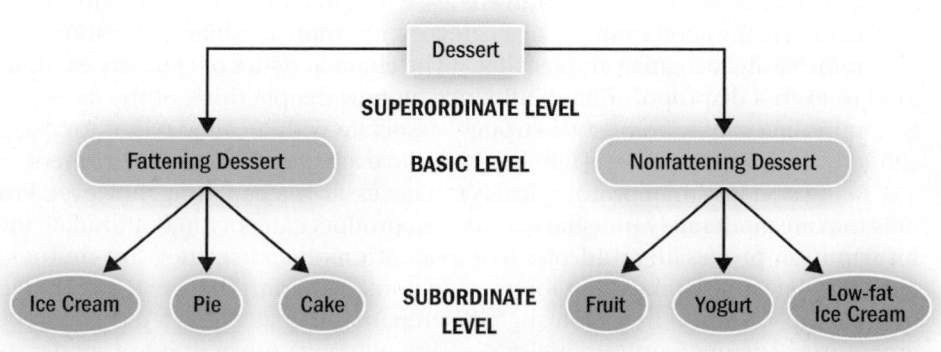

■ FIGURE 9.7
LEVELS OF ABSTRACTION
IN DESSERT CATEGORIES

level the items we group together tend to have a lot in common with each other but still permit us to consider a broad enough range of alternatives. The broader *superordinate category* is more abstract, whereas the more specific *subordinate category* often includes individual brands.[48] Of course, not all items fit equally well into a category. Apple pie is a better example of the subordinate category "pie" than is rhubarb pie, even though both are types of pies. This is because it's more *prototypical*, and most people would think of apple as a pie flavor before they thought of rhubarb. In contrast, true pie experts probably know a lot about both typical and atypical category examples.[49]

Strategic Implications of Product Categorization

The way we categorize products has a lot of strategic implications. This process affects which products consumers will compare to our product and also the criteria they'll use to decide if they like us or the other guys.

Product Positioning. The success of a *positioning strategy* often hinges on the marketer's ability to convince the consumer to consider its product within a given category. For example, the orange juice industry tried to reposition orange juice as a drink that could be enjoyed all day long ("It's not just for breakfast anymore"). However, soft-drink companies attempt the opposite when they portray sodas as suitable for breakfast consumption. They are trying to make their way into consumers' "breakfast drink" category, along with orange juice, grapefruit juice, and coffee. Of course, this strategy can backfire, as Pepsi-Cola discovered when it introduced Pepsi A.M. and positioned it as a coffee substitute. The company did such a good job of categorizing the drink as a morning beverage that customers wouldn't drink it at any other time, and the product failed.[51]

Identifying Competitors. At the abstract, superordinate level, many different product forms compete for membership. The category "entertainment" might comprise both bowling and the ballet, but not many people would consider the substitution of one of these activities for the other. Products and services that on the surface are quite different, however, actually compete with each other at a broad level for consumers' discretionary dollars. Although bowling or ballet may not be a likely trade-off for many people, a symphony might try to lure away season ticket holders to the ballet by positioning itself as an equivalent member of the category "cultural event."[52]

We're often faced with choices between noncomparable categories, where we can't directly relate the attributes in one to those in another (the old problem of comparing apples and oranges). When we can create an overlapping category that encompasses both items (e.g., entertainment, value, usefulness) and then rate each alternative in terms of that superordinate category comparison, the process is easier.[53]

Exemplar Products. As we saw with the case of apple pie versus rhubarb pie, if a product is a really good example of a category, it is more familiar to consumers and they more easily recognize and recall it.[54] The characteristics of category exemplars tend to exert a disproportionate influence on how people think of the category in general.[55] In a sense, brands we strongly associate with a category get to "call the shots" by defining the criteria we should use to evaluate all category members.

Being a bit less than prototypical is not necessarily a bad thing, however. Products that are moderately unusual within their product category may stimulate more information processing and positive evaluations because they are neither so familiar that we will take them for granted nor so different that we won't consider them at all.[56] A brand that is strongly discrepant (such as Zima, a clear malt beverage) may occupy a unique niche position, whereas those that are moderately

Marketing Pitfall

Kimberly-Clark Corp., which makes well-known paper products including Kleenex and Scott tissues, learned the hard way about the perils of product categorization and consumers' resistance to products they find hard to assign to a well-known category. The company announced "the most significant category innovation since toilet paper first appeared in roll form in 1890." Even Jay Leno covered the news of the new product: Cottonelle Fresh Roll-wipes, a roll of moist wipes in a plastic dispenser that clips onto a regular toilet-paper holder. To quiet skeptics who questioned whether Americans would change their bathroom habits so dramatically, Kimberly-Clark unveiled its research showing that 63 percent of U.S. adults were already in the habit of wetting toilet paper or using a wipe.

Although the company spent more than $100 million to develop the roll and dispenser and guards it with more than 30 patents, high hopes for the product have gone down the toilet. Part of the problem is that the company is dealing with a product most Americans don't even want to discuss in the first place, and its advertising failed to show consumers what the wipes even do. Its ad agency tried to create a fun image with TV ads showing shots of people splashing in the water from behind with the slogan, "sometimes wetter is better." A print ad with an extreme close-up of a sumo wrestler's *derriere* was a flop. To make matters worse, the company didn't design a version in small product sizes, so it couldn't pass out free samples. And, the wipes come in a container that is immediately visible in a bathroom—another strike for people already bashful about buying the product.[50]

discrepant (e.g., local microbrews) remain in a distinct position within the general category.[57]

Locating Products. Product categorization also can affect consumers' expectations regarding the places they can locate a desired product. If products do not clearly fit into categories (e.g., is a rug furniture?), this may diminish our ability to find them or figure out what they're supposed to be once we do. For instance, a frozen dog food that pet owners had to thaw and cook before serving to Fido failed in the market, partly because people could not adapt to the idea of buying dog food in the "frozen foods for people" section of their grocery stores.

PRODUCT CHOICE: SELECTING AMONG ALTERNATIVES

Once we assemble and evaluate the relevant options in a category, we have to choose one.[58] Recall that the decision rules guiding our choices can range from very simple and quick strategies to complicated processes requiring much attention and cognitive processing.[59] Our job isn't getting any easier as we often find that there are more and more features to evaluate. We deal with 50-button remote controls, digital cameras with hundreds of mysterious features and book-length manuals, and cars with dashboard systems worthy of the space shuttle. Experts call this spiral of complexity **feature creep**. As evidence that the proliferation of gizmos is counterproductive, Philips Electronics found that at least half of returned products have nothing wrong with them—consumers simply couldn't figure out how to use them! What's worse, on average the person spent only 20 minutes trying to figure out how to use the product before giving up.

Why don't companie avoid this problem? One reason is that when we look at a new product in a store we tend to think that the more features there are, the better. It's only once we get the product home and try to use it that we realize the virtues of simplicity. In one study (see the accompanying *As I See It* box to meet one of the researchers), consumers chose among three models of a digital device that varied in terms of how complex each was. More than 60 percent chose the one with the most features. Then, the participants got the chance to choose from up to 25 features to customize their product—the average person chose 20 of these add-ons. But when they actually used the devices, it turns out that the large number of options only frustrated them—they ended up being much happier with the simpler product. As the saying goes, "Be careful what you wish for . . . ."[60]

EVALUATIVE CRITERIA

When Richard was looking at different television sets, he focused on one or two product features and completely ignored several others. He narrowed down his choices by only considering two specific brand names, and from the Prime Wave and Precision models, he chose one that featured stereo capability.

Evaluative criteria are the dimensions we use to judge the merits of competing options. In comparing alternative products, Richard could have chosen from among many criteria, ranging from very functional attributes ("Does this TV come with remote control?") to experiential ones ("Does this TV's sound reproduction make me imagine I'm in a concert hall?").

Another important point is that criteria on which products *differ* from one another carry more weight in the decision process than do those where the alternatives are *similar*. If all brands a person considers rate equally well on one attribute (e.g., if all TVs come with remote control), he will have to find other reasons to choose one over another. **Determinant attributes** are the features we actually use to differentiate among our choices.

CB AS I SEE IT

Professor Roland Rust
University of Maryland

As information technology advances, it is easy for companies to build products that are increasingly complicated. We see cell phones that do everything but the laundry, and even old-fashioned appliances such as televisions and cars are becoming so complicated that people can't use

them. I recently received a mouse pad that had a radio, calculator, clock, alarm, and even a user's manual. This trend is not going away, so it is important for us to understand how consumers deal with this kind of complexity.

With my co-authors, Debora Thompson and Rebecca Hamilton, I have studied the concept of "feature fatigue." We discovered that consumers actually tend to want and choose products that are too complicated, only to be sorry later. We need to know more about how consumers react to complex products and whether the problem is going away as the generation that grew up with PC's, iPods, and text messages take the lead role in consumption.

Our studies showed that consumers place more weight on

product capabilities than on usability before purchase, leading them to buy products with lots of features. After usage, though, the importance of usability increases a great deal, and consumers prefer a smaller number of features. This can have an important impact on customer retention because customers who buy a product with too many features may become frustrated and not repurchase. So the firm is actually better off putting fewer features in the product and counting on better customer retention rates and better word-of-mouth to counteract the perhaps somewhat lower initial sales. This strategy can be phenomenally successful, as we have seen from the success of the Apple iPod.

Reflecting consumers' renewed interest in ethical and sustainable marketing (see Chapter 4), it makes sense that a company's reputation for social responsibility is emerging as one of the most important determinant attributes when people choose among brands. Each year Harris Interactive/*The Wall Street Journal* conducts a survey and ranks corporate reputations on 20 attributes in 6 categories: financial performance, social responsibility, workplace environment, quality of products and services, vision and leadership, and emotional appeal.[61]

Although Microsoft has its share of critics, in 2007 it achieved the number one ranking—helped to a large extent by founder Bill Gates' philanthropy. The company beat out number two Johnson & Johnson, whose emotionally appealing baby products business had kept it in first place for 7 consecutive years. Other high scorers included Whole Foods, Merck (favorable publicity about its assistance programs for the needy helped to offset the flak it got after pulling the painkiller Vioxx from the market following studies linking the medication to increased risk of strokes and heart attacks), General Mills, and the United Parcel Service. Still, there is a lot of room for improvement; the corporate world's overall reputation remains dismal as new scandals, such as the improper dating of stock-option grants to business executives, continue to emerge. About 69 percent of respondents graded corporate America's reputation as either "not good" or "terrible."

Marketers help to educate consumers about which criteria they should use as determinant attributes. For example, consumer research from Church & Dwight indicated that many consumers view the use of natural ingredients as a determinant attribute. As a result, the company promoted its toothpaste made from baking soda, which the company already manufactured for Church & Dwight's Arm & Hammer brand.[62]

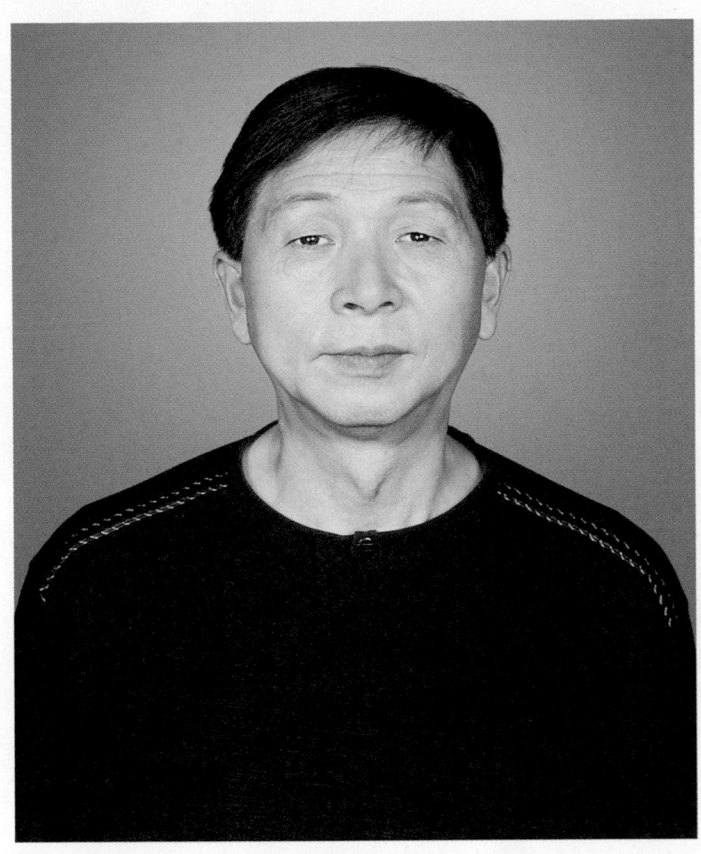
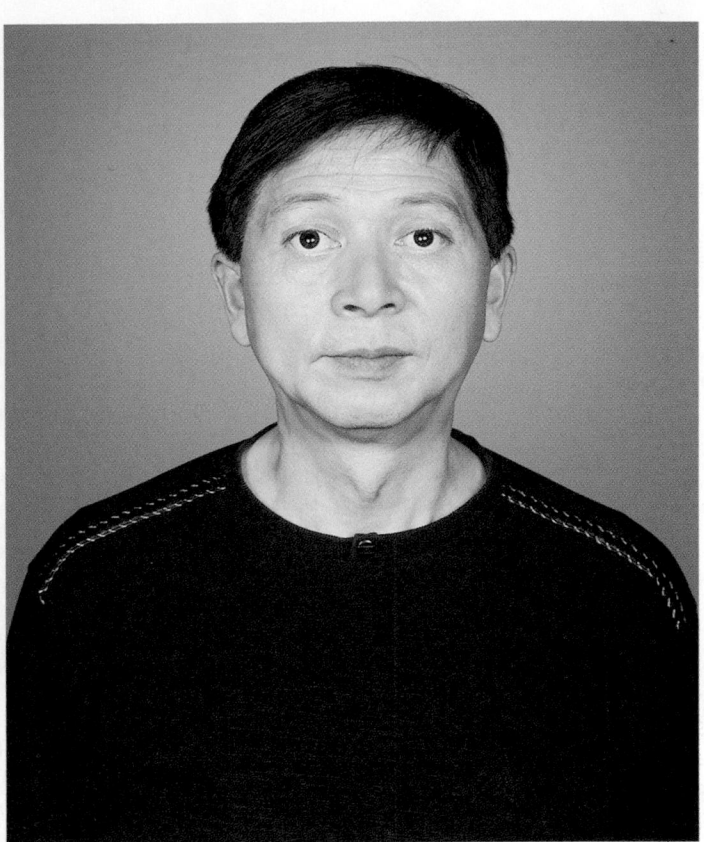

EXTRA STRONG COFFEE FROM ASIA: SUMATRA BOLD.

This Turkish ad for a coffee bar encourages customers to think of coffee's stimulating property as an evaluative criterion.

And sometimes, the company can even invent a determinant attribute: Pepsi-Cola accomplished this by stamping freshness dates on soda cans. It spent about $25 million on an advertising and promotional campaign to convince consumers that there's nothing quite as horrible as a stale can of soda—even though people in the industry estimate that drinkers consume 98 percent of all cans well before this could be a problem. Six months after it introduced the campaign, lo and behold an independent survey found that 61 percent of respondents felt that freshness dating is an important attribute for a soft drink![63] In order for a marketer to effectively recommend a new decision criterion, it should convey three pieces of information:[64]

1 It should point out that there are significant differences among brands on the attribute.
2 It should supply the consumer with a decision-making rule, such as *if* . . . (deciding among competing brands), *then* . . . (use the attribute as a criterion).
3 It should convey a rule that is consistent with how the person made the decision on prior occasions. Otherwise, she is likely to ignore the recommendation because it requires too much mental work.

NEUROMARKETING: HOW YOUR BRAIN REACTS TO ALTERNATIVES

Is there a "buy button" in your brain? Some corporations are teaming up with neuroscientists to find out.[65] **Neuromarketing** uses *functional magnetic resonance imaging* (or *fMRI*), a brain-scanning device that tracks blood flow as we perform mental tasks.

This Indonesian ad shows us one of bubblegum's determinant attributes.

In recent years, researchers have discovered that regions in the brain, such as the amygdala, the hippocampus, and the hypothalamus, are dynamic switchboards that blend memory, emotions, and biochemical triggers. These interconnected neurons shape the ways that fear, panic, exhilaration, and social pressure influence our choices.

Scientists know that specific regions of the brain light up in these scans to show increased blood flow when a person recognizes a face, hears a song, makes a decision, or senses deception. Now they are trying to harness this technology to measure consumers' reactions to movie trailers, choices about automobiles, the appeal of a pretty face, and loyalty to specific brands. British researchers recorded brain activity as shoppers toured a virtual store. They claim to have identified the neural region that becomes active when a shopper decides which product to pluck from a supermarket shelf. DaimlerChrysler took brain scans of men as they looked at photos of cars and confirmed that sports cars activated their reward centers. The company's scientists found that the most popular vehicles—the Porsche- and Ferrari-style sports cars—triggered activity in a section of the brain they call the *fusiform face area*, which governs facial recognition. A psychiatrist who ran the study commented, "They were reminded of faces when they looked at the cars. The lights of the cars look a little like eyes."

A study that took brain scans of people as they drank competing soft-drink brands illustrates how loyalty to a brand affects our reactions, even at a very basic, physiological level. When the researchers monitored brain scans of 67 people who took a blind taste test of Coca-Cola and Pepsi, each soft drink lit up the brain's reward system, and the participants were evenly split as to which drink they preferred—even though three out of four participants *said* they preferred Coke. When told they were drinking Coke, the regions of the brain that control memory lit up, and this activation drowned out the area that simply reacts to taste cues. In this case, Coke's strong brand identity trumped the sensations coming from respondents' taste receptors.

In another study, researchers reported that pictures of celebrities triggered many of the same brain circuits as images of shoes, cars, chairs, wristwatches, sunglasses, handbags, and water bottles. All of these objects set off a rush of activity in a part of the cortex that neuroscientists know links to a sense of identity and social image. The scientists also identified types of consumers based on their responses. At one extreme were people whose brains responded intensely to "cool" products and celebrities with bursts of activity but who didn't respond at all to "uncool" images. They dubbed these participants "cool fools," likely to be impulsive or compulsive shoppers. At the other extreme were people whose brains reacted only to the unstylish items, a pattern that fits well with people who tend to be anxious, apprehensive, or neurotic. Many researchers remain skeptical about how helpful this technology will be for consumer research. If indeed researchers can reliably track consumers' brand preferences by seeing how their brains react, there may be many interesting potential opportunities for new research techniques that rely on what we (at least our brains) do rather than what we say.

CYBERMEDIARIES

As anyone who's ever typed a phrase such as "home theaters" into a search engine such as Google knows, the Web delivers enormous amounts of product and retailer information in seconds. In fact (recall our earlier discussion of the problem of *hyperchoice*), the biggest problem Web surfers face these days is narrowing down their choices, not beefing them up. In cyberspace, simplification is key.

With the tremendous number of Web sites available and the huge number of people surfing the Web each day, how can people organize information and decide where to click? A **cybermediary** often is the answer. This is an intermediary that helps to filter and organize online market information so that customers can identify and evaluate alternatives more efficiently.[66] Many consumers regularly link to comparison-shopping sites, such as Bizrate.com or Pricegrabbers.com, for example, that list many online retailers that sell a given item along with the price each charges.[67]

Cybermediaries take different forms:[68]

- *Directories* and *portals* such as Yahoo! or The Knot are general services that tie together a large variety of different sites.
- *Web site evaluators* reduce the risk to consumers by reviewing sites and recommending the best ones. For example, Point Communications selects sites that it designates as in the top 5 percent of the Web.
- *Forums, fan clubs,* and *user groups* offer product-related discussions to help customers sift through options (more on these in Chapter 11). It's becoming clear that customer product reviews are a key driver of satisfaction and loyalty. In one large survey, about half of the respondents who bought an item from a major Web site remembered seeing customer product reviews. This group's satisfaction with the online shopping experience was 5 percent higher than for shoppers who didn't recall customer reviews.[69] Another advantage is that consumers get to experience a much wider array of options—and at the same time products such as movies, books, and CDs that aren't "blockbusters" are more likely to sell. At NetFlix, the online DVD rental company, for example, fellow subscribers recommend about two-thirds of the films that people order. In fact, between 70 and 80 percent of NetFlix rentals come from the company's back catalog of 38,000 films rather than recent releases.[70]

  Incidentally, this aspect of online customer review is one important factor that's fueling a new way of thinking one writer calls the *long tail*. The basic idea is that we need no longer rely solely on big hits (such as blockbuster movies or bestselling books) to find profits. Companies can also make money by selling small amounts of items that only a few people want—if they sell enough different items. For example, Amazon.com maintains an inventory of 3.7 million books compared to the 100,000 or so you'll find in a Barnes & Noble retail store. Most of these will sell only a few thousand copies (if that), but the 3.6 million books that Barnes & Noble doesn't carry make up a quarter of Amazon's revenues! Other examples of the long tail include successful microbreweries and TV networks that make money on reruns of old shows on channels such as the Game Show Network.[71]

- *Financial intermediaries* authorize payments from buyers to sellers. Payment systems include the electronic equivalents to credit card charges (PayPal), writing checks (Checkfree), paying in cash (Digicash), and sending secure electronic mail authorizing a payment (First Virtual).

Marketing Pitfall

As consumers increasingly choose products and services based on reviews that fellow users post, the potential for abuse is growing as some marketers try to influence the content of these evaluations. For example, some hotels are trying to ensure that their properties get glowing ratings. They encourage guests to write flattering reviews, and in some cases they submit fake recommendations.[75] Across industries, many companies now are hiring college students (maybe even you?) to post fake reviews on Web sites and blogs. Unfortunately, the old saying, "Don't believe everything you read" has never been truer.

Indeed, a few bloggers started a chain reaction to make a statement about the proliferation of customer reviews when they started a movement on the Amazon review site to evaluate a $3.99 gallon of Tuscan-brand whole milk. One user wrote, "I give this Tuscan milk four stars simply because I found the consistency a little too 'milk-like' for my tastes." Another commented, "One word of caution—milk, even when frozen into a baseball-bat shape, is nigh worthless as a baseball bat, merely shattering into cloudy fragments at the first strike of a baseball." The joke snowballed into several hundred bogus reviews. The two guys who started it all posted the story at ytmnd.com, a site that breeds send-ups of pop culture.[76]

Intelligent agents are sophisticated software programs that use *collaborative filtering* technologies to learn from past user behavior in order to recommend new purchases. For example, when you let Amazon.com suggest a new book, it's using an intelligent agent to propose novels based on what you and others like you have bought in the past. Collaborative filtering is still in its infancy. In the next few years, expect to see many new Web-based methods to simplify the consumer decision-making process. Now if only someone could come up with an easier way to pay for all the great stuff you find courtesy of shopping bots!

Researchers are working hard to understand how consumers go about finding information online, and in particular how they react to and integrate recommendations they receive from different kinds of online agents into their own product choices. An **electronic recommendation agent** is a software tool that tries to understand a human decision maker's multiattribute preferences for a product category by asking the user to communicate his preferences. Based on that data, the software then recommends a list of alternatives sorted by the degree that they fit these criteria. Some findings now emerging include the following:[72]

- Consumers who consult recommendation agents select the recommended products twice as often as those who do not.
- The extent to which a consumer has agreed with the agent on past recommendations influences the likelihood he will accept the advice.
- Recommendation agents have a greater impact on decisions when consumers feel the decision is risky, for example, if the consequences of making a poor decision are high or if the item is expensive.
- When a recommendation agent asks the consumer about his preferences for a particular product attribute, the consumer will weigh that attribute more when making an actual product choice.

The Music Genome Project is one of the newest technologies that enable music fans to discover new artists. At Pandora.com, you type in the name of a band or song and immediately begin hearing similar tunes that the site's recommender system has determined you'll enjoy. By rating songs and artists, you can refine the suggestions, allowing Pandora to create a truly personalized station. The service employs 45 analysts, many with music degrees, who rank 15,000 songs a month on 400 characteristics.[73] Similarly Liveplasma.com graphically "maps" consumers' interests in movies and music. If you search for music by The Decemberists, for example, you'll get a graphical representation of what previous Decemberists customers have purchased, presented in clusters of circles of various sizes. The bigger the circle, the greater the popularity of that band.[74]

Heuristics: Mental Shortcuts

Do we actually perform complex mental calculations every time we make a purchase decision? Get a life! When we're not relying on a Web site to steer us to the right place, we often use other decision rules to simplify our choices. For example, Richard relied on certain assumptions as substitutes for a prolonged information search. In particular, he assumed the selection at Zany Zack's was more than sufficient, so he did not bother to shop at any of Zack's competitors. This assumption was a shortcut to more extended information processing.[77]

Especially when limited problem solving occurs prior to making a choice, we often fall back on **heuristics**, or mental rules-of-thumb that lead to a speedy decision. These rules range from the very general ("higher-priced products are higher-quality products" or "buy the same brand I bought last time") to the very specific ("buy Domino, the brand of sugar my mother always bought").[78] Sometimes these shortcuts may not be in our best interests. A car shopper who personally knows one or two people who have had problems with a particular vehicle, for example, might assume he would have similar trouble with it rather than taking the time to find out it has an excellent repair record.[79]

Consumers often simplify choices by using heuristics such as automatically choosing a favorite color or brand.

RELYING ON A PRODUCT SIGNAL

One shortcut we often use is to *infer* hidden dimensions of products from attributes we can observe. In these cases the visible element is a **product signal** that communicates some underlying quality. This explains why someone trying to sell a used car makes sure the car's exterior is clean and shiny: Potential buyers often judge the vehicle's mechanical condition by its appearance, even though this means they may drive away in a clean, shiny clunker.[80]

When we only have incomplete product information, we often base our judgments on our beliefs about *covariation*; the associations we have among events that may or may not actually influence one another.[81] For example, a shopper may judge product quality by the length of time a manufacturer has been in business. Other signals or attributes consumers tend to believe coexist with good or bad products include well-known brand names, country of origin, price, and the retail outlets that carry the product.

Unfortunately, many of us estimate covariation quite poorly. And, our erroneous beliefs persist despite evidence to the contrary. In a process similar to the consistency principle we discussed in Chapter 7, we tend to see what we're looking for. In other

★★★★★ **Saved My Baby's Life**, July 20, 2006
Reviewer: <u>N. Strassner "Dairy Connaisseur"</u> (Bermuda Triangle) - <u>See all my reviews</u>
REAL NAME™

The exact minute I got my milk, my baby's new face burst into flames. I used the gallon to extinguish my baby. Next time, I'll order 2 gallons. Thank you, milk. Thank YOU!

Was this review helpful to you? (Yes) (No) (<u>Report this</u>)

This is one of the bogus reviews of Tuscan milk a blogger posted.

words, we'll look for product information that confirms our guesses and ignore or explain away information that contradicts what we already think. In one experiment, consumers sampled four sets of products to determine their price related to their quality. Those who believed prior to the study that a higher price means higher quality elected to sample higher-priced products, thus creating a self-fulfilling prophecy.[82]

Market Beliefs: Is It Better if I Pay More for It?

We constantly are forming assumptions about companies, products, and stores. These **market beliefs** then become the shortcuts that guide our decisions—regardless of whether these beliefs are accurate.[83] Recall, for instance, that Richard chose to shop at a large "electronics warehouse store" because he *assumed* the selection would be better there than at a specialty store. Researchers have identified a large number of market beliefs. Table 9.3 lists some of these—how many do you share?

Do higher prices mean higher quality? This *price–quality relationship* is one of the most pervasive market beliefs.[84] Novice consumers, in fact, may consider price as the only relevant product attribute. Experts also consider this information, although they tend to use price for its informational value, especially for products (e.g., virgin wool) that they know vary widely in quality. When this quality level is more standard or strictly regulated (e.g., Harris Tweed sport coats), experts do not weigh price in their decisions. For the most part, this belief is justified; you do tend to get what you pay for. However, let the buyer beware: The price–quality relationship is not always justified.[85]

Country-of-Origin as a Product Signal

Does a shrimp have a personality? As cheap imports flood the market, U.S. shrimpers hope they do. They know that consumers prefer coffee from exotic places such as Kenya and salmon from Alaska, so they are trying to persuade American consumers to prefer American shrimp. Some restaurants already are taking up the cause. At Lark in Seattle, diners can read on the menu whether the prawns come from Georgia, Florida, or Alaska. Other places get even more specific about the home address of their crustaceans. The Silverado Resort and Spa in Napa, California, now serves "local West Texas white shrimp."[86]

TABLE 9.3
COMMON MARKET BELIEFS

Brand	All brands are basically the same.
	Generic products are just name brands sold under a different label at a lower price.
	The best brands are the ones that are purchased the most.
	When in doubt, a national brand is always a safe bet.
Store	Specialty stores are great places to familiarize yourself with the best brands; but once you figure out what you want, it's cheaper to buy it at a discount outlet.
	A store's character is reflected in its window displays.
	Salespeople in specialty stores are more knowledgeable than other sales personnel.
	Larger stores offer better prices than small stores.
	Locally owned stores give the best service.
	A store that offers a good value on one of its products probably offers good values on all of its items.
	Credit and return policies are most lenient at large department stores.
	Stores that have just opened usually charge attractive prices.
Prices/Discounts/Sales	Sales are typically run to get rid of slow-moving merchandise.
	Stores that are constantly having sales don't really save you money.
	Within a given store, higher prices generally indicate higher quality.
Advertising and Sales Promotion	"Hard-sell" advertising is associated with low-quality products.
	Items tied to "giveaways" are not a good value (even with the freebie).
	Coupons represent real savings for customers because they are not offered by the store.
	When you buy heavily advertised products, you are paying for the label, not for higher quality.
Product/Packaging	Largest-sized containers are almost always cheaper per unit than smaller sizes.
	New products are more expensive when they're first introduced; prices tend to settle down as time goes by.
	When you are not sure what you need in a product, it's a good idea to invest in the extra features, because you'll probably wish you had them later.
	In general, synthetic goods are lower in quality than goods made of natural materials.
	It's advisable to stay away from products when they are new to the market; it usually takes the manufacturer a little time to work the bugs out.

Source: Adapted from Calvin P. Duncan, "Consumer Market Beliefs: A Review of the Literature and an Agenda for Future Research," in Marvin E. Goldberg, Gerald Gorn, and Edward A. Pollay, eds., *Advances in Consumer Research* 17 (Provo, UT: Association for Consumer Research, 1990): 729–35.

A product's "address" matters. Americans like to buy Italian shoes, Japanese cars, clothing imported from Taiwan, and microwave ovens built in South Korea. A product's **country of origin** often is a determinant attribute in the decision-making process.[87] Consumers strongly associate certain items with specific countries, and products from those countries often attempt to benefit from these linkages. In addition, the consumer's own expertise with the product category moderates the effects of this attribute. When other information is available, experts tend to ignore country-of-origin information, whereas novices continue to rely on it. However, when other information is unavailable or ambiguous, both experts and novices will rely on a product's birthplace to make a decision.

Ethnocentrism is the tendency to prefer products or people of one's own culture to those of other countries. Ethnocentric consumers are likely to feel it is wrong to buy products made elsewhere, particularly because this may have a negative effect on the domestic economy. In the United States, marketing campaigns that stress the desirability of "buying American" obviously appeal to ethnocentric consumers. The Consumer Ethnocentric Scale (CETSCALE) measures this trait: Ethnocentric consumers agree with statements such as the following:

- Purchasing imported products is un-American.
- Curbs should be put on all imports.

A product's country-of-origin in some cases is an important piece of information in the decision-making process. Certain items are strongly associated with specific countries, and products from those countries often attempt to benefit from these linkages.

Marketing Pitfall

Right or wrong, American foreign policy is having a big impact on how consumers in other countries perceive American brands. Surveys consistently show that people in many countries say they are less likely to buy U.S. products because of our actions in Iraq and elsewhere. In several cases, protestors have vented their negative feelings violently by attacking or burning down symbols of U.S. commerce, such as McDonald's and KFC restaurants in Pakistan and Afghanistan— even though local citizens own the franchises. As one young Pakistani explained after rioters destroyed a KFC, "It's not important who owns it. This is just because of American policies. People hate America."[91] The more American people perceive a brand to be, the more they dislike it. In one survey, almost half of the respondents (including 1,000 people from each of the G-8 nations, excluding the United States) associated Mattel's Barbie with America, whereas 10 percent made the same link with Kleenex. Correspondingly, 33 percent of respondents said they would avoid buying Barbie dolls, but only 10 percent won't touch the tissues.[92]

● American consumers who purchase products made in other countries are responsible for putting their fellow Americans out of work.[88]

Of course, Americans are not the only people who display ethnocentrism. Citizens of many countries tend to feel that their native products are superior (just ask a person from France to choose between French and California wines!). Many Canadians are concerned about the dilution of their culture because of a strong U.S. influence. In one poll, 25 percent of the country's citizens identified "life, liberty, and the pursuit of happiness" as a Canadian constitutional slogan rather than a U.S. one![89] Canadian nationalism was stoked by a commercial for Molson Canadian beer called "The Rant" that almost overnight became an unofficial anthem in Canada. A flannel-shirted young Canadian walks onto a stage and calmly begins explaining away Canadian stereotypes: "I'm not a lumberjack or a fur trader. I don't live in an igloo or eat blubber or own a dog sled. . . . My name is Joe and I . . . AM . . . CANADIAN!" In the 6 weeks after the ad started airing, the Molson brand gained almost two points in market share.[90]

CHOOSING FAMILIAR BRAND NAMES: LOYALTY OR HABIT?

When you fall in love with a brand, it may be your favorite for a lifetime. In a study the Boston Consulting Group conducted of the market leaders in 30 product categories, 27 of the brands that were number one in 1930 (such as Ivory Soap and Campbell's Soup) still were at the top more than 50 years later.[94] Clearly "choose a well-known brand name" is a powerful heuristic. As this study demonstrates, some brands in a sense are well known because they are well known; we assume that if so many people choose a product it must be good.

Indeed, our tendency to prefer a number one brand to the competition is so strong that it seems to mimic a pattern scientists find in other domains from earthquakes to linguistics. **Zipf's Law** describes this pattern. In the 1930s, a linguist named George Kingsley Zipf found that *the*—the most-used English word—occurs about twice as often as *of* (second place), about three times as often as *and* (third), and so on. Since then, scientists have found similar relationships between the size and frequency of earthquakes and a variety of other natural and artificial phenomena.

A marketing researcher decided to apply Zipf's Law to consumer behavior. His firm asked Australian consumers to identify the brands of toilet paper and instant coffee they use and to rank them in order of preference. As the model predicted, people spend roughly twice as much of their toilet paper budget on the top choice than on the second-ranked brand, about twice on the number two brand as on the third-ranked brand, and about twice on the number three brand as on the number four brand. One ramification is that a brand that moves from number two to number one in a category will see a much greater jump in sales than will, say, a brand that moves from number four to number three. Brands that dominate their markets are as much as 50 percent more profitable than their nearest competitors.[95]

Inertia: The Lazy Customer

Many people tend to buy the same brand just about every time they go to the store. Often this is because of **inertia**—we buy a brand out of habit merely because it requires less effort (see Chapter 4). If another product comes along that is cheaper (or if the original product is out of stock), we won't hesitate to change our minds. A competitor who is trying to encourage this switch often can do so rather easily because the shopper won't hesitate to jump to the new brand if it offers the right incentive.

When we have little to no underlying commitment to a particular brand, marketers find it easy to "unfreeze" our habit when they use promotional tools such as point-of-purchase displays, extensive couponing, or noticeable price reductions. Some analysts predict that we're going to observe this kind of fickle behavior more and more as consumers flit from one brand to the next. Indeed, one industry observer labels this variety-seeking consumer a *brand slut*; she points out that from 2004 to 2007 the number of women who say a manufacturer's brand name is very influential in their decision to buy a beauty product decreased by 21 percentage points to stand at 19 percent.[96]

Brand Loyalty: A "Friend," Tried-and-True

This kind of "promiscuity" will not occur if true brand loyalty exists. In contrast to inertia, **brand loyalty** describes repeat purchasing behavior that reflects a conscious decision to continue buying the same brand.[97] This definition implies that the consumer not only buys the brand on a regular basis but she also has a strong positive attitude toward it rather than simply buying it out of habit. In fact we often find that a brand-loyal consumer has more than simply a positive attitude; she is passionate about the product. Because of these emotional bonds "true-blue" users react more vehemently when a company alters, redesigns, or (God forbid) eliminates a favorite brand.[98] In one classic example (that you probably learned about in Marketing 101), when Coca-Cola replaced its tried-and-true formula with New Coke in the 1980s, loyal Coke fans besieged the company with a firestorm of national call-in campaigns, boycotts, and other protests until Coke gave in and restored the original formula.

Coke's American origins have helped upstart rivals such as Cola Turka in Turkey, which now sells about 20 percent of the colas Turkish shoppers buy. In one spot for Cola Turka, an American businessperson (played by comedian Chevy Chase) returns home to the suburbs, where his wife has prepared dinner for the family. He watches as his wife and family eat, drink, and break into song. But after starting "Take Me Out to the Ball Game," they switch to a traditional Turkish number. The husband takes a sip of cola and joins in. By the end of the spot, he has sprouted a Turkish-style mustache. A radio spot running in Britain for Opodo, an Internet travel site owned by a group of European airlines, is more vicious: It provides "language lessons" for Britons preparing to visit America. A British voice politely provides useful phrases such as "I would like a cup of coffee, please." An American with a grating, exaggerated Brooklyn accent provides the translation: "Can I get a regular semi-latte with 2 percent milk to go?" The spot concludes with the British phrase, "You've really annoyed me," which the caption translates as "Have a nice day."[93]

Marketers sometimes resort to online games to combat the inertia of online consumers. PopCap Games lets players have the fancy version of the Zuma videogame for free if they are willing to put up with ads.

A decade ago, marketers struggled with the problem of *brand parity*, which refers to consumers' beliefs that there are no significant differences among brands. For example, one survey at that time found that more than 70 percent of consumers worldwide believed that all paper towels, soaps, and snack chips are alike.[99] Some analysts even proclaimed the death of brand names, predicting that private label or generic products that offer the same value for less money would kill off the tried-and-true products.

However, these gloomy predictions turned out to be wrong as major brands made a dramatic comeback. Brand sluts aside, today branding is king! Some attribute this renaissance to information overload—with too many alternatives (many of them unfamiliar names) to choose from, people seem to be looking for clear signals of quality. That's the reason that some Chinese companies that already manufacture many products that are sold under well-known American brand names now are trying to buy the names as well, so that they can cash in on the added brand equity and sell their goods at a higher price. In some cases, they acquire the company, as with Nakamichi stereo gear; in others they get an exclusive licensing deal, as with Benetton cycglass frames.[100]

DECISION RULES WE USE WHEN WE CARE

We've seen that we use different rules to choose among competing products depending on the decision's complexity and how important the choice is to us. Sometimes we use a simple heuristic, but at other times we carefully weigh alternatives in

some systematic fashion. We can describe the processes we use when we're giving more thought to these decisions by dividing the types of rules we use into two categories: *compensatory* and *noncompensatory*. To aid in the discussion of some of these rules, Table 9.4 summarizes the attributes of the TV sets that Richard considered. Now, let's see how some of these rules result in different brand choices.

Noncompensatory Decision Rules

We use **noncompensatory decision rules** when we feel that a product with a low standing on one attribute can't compensate for this flaw by doing better on another attribute. In other words, we simply eliminate all options that do not meet some basic standards. A consumer such as Richard who uses the decision rule, "Only buy well-known brand names," would not consider a new brand, even if it were equal or superior to existing ones. When people are less familiar with a product category or are not very motivated to process complex information, they tend to use simple, noncompensatory rules such as the ones we summarize below.[101]

The Lexicographic Rule. When a person uses the *lexicographic rule*, he selects the brand that is the best on the most important attribute. If he feels two or more brands are equally good on that attribute, he then compares them on the second most important attribute. This selection process goes on until the tie is broken. In Richard's case, because both the Prime Wave and Precision models were tied on his most important attribute (a 60-inch screen), he chose the Precision because of its rating on this second most important attribute—its stereo capability.

TABLE 9.4
HYPOTHETICAL ALTERNATIVES FOR A TV SET

Attribute	Importance Ranking	Brand Ratings		
		Prime Wave	Precision	Kamashita
Size of screen	1	Excellent	Excellent	Excellent
Stereo broadcast capability	2	Poor	Excellent	Good
Brand reputation	3	Excellent	Excellent	Poor
Onscreen programming	4	Excellent	Poor	Poor
Cable-ready capability	5	Good	Good	Good
Sleep timer	6	Excellent	Poor	Good

The Elimination-by-Aspects Rule. Using the *elimination-by-aspects rule*, the buyer also evaluates brands on the most important attribute. In this case, though, he imposes specific cutoffs. For example, if Richard had been more interested in having a sleep timer on his TV (i.e., if it had a higher importance ranking), he might have stipulated that his choice "must have a sleep timer." Because the Prime Wave model had one and the Precision did not, he would have chosen the Prime Wave.

The Conjunctive Rule. Whereas the two former rules involve processing by attribute, the *conjunctive rule* entails processing by brand. As with the elimination-by-aspects procedure, the decision maker establishes cutoffs for each attribute. He chooses a brand if it meets all of the cutoffs, but failure to meet any one cutoff means he will reject it. If none of the brands meet all of the cutoffs, he may delay the choice, change the decision rule, or modify the cutoffs he chooses to apply.

If Richard had stipulated that all attributes had to be rated "good" or better, he would not have been able to choose any of the options. He might then have modified his decision rule, conceding that it was not possible to attain these high standards in the price range he was considering. In this case, perhaps Richard could decide that he could live without on-screen programming, so he would once again consider the Precision model.

Compensatory Decision Rules
Unlike noncompensatory rules, **compensatory decision rules** give a product a chance to make up for its shortcomings. Consumers who employ these rules tend to be more involved in the purchase, so they're willing to exert the effort to consider the entire picture in a more exacting way. The willingness to let good and bad product qualities balance out can result in quite different choices. For example, if Richard were not concerned about having stereo reception, he might have chosen the Prime Wave model. But because this brand doesn't feature this highly ranked attribute, it doesn't stand a chance when he uses a noncompensatory rule.

Researchers identify two basic types of compensatory rules. When he uses a *simple additive rule*, the consumer merely chooses the alternative that has the largest number of positive attributes. This is most likely to occur when his ability or motivation to process information is limited. One drawback to this approach for the consumer is that some of these attributes may not be very meaningful or important. An ad containing a long list of product benefits may be persuasive, despite the fact that many of the benefits included are actually standard within the product class and aren't determinant attributes at all.

The *weighted additive rule* is a more complex version.[102] When using this rule, the consumer also takes into account the relative importance of positively rated attributes, essentially multiplying brand ratings by importance weights. If this process sounds familiar, it should. The calculation process strongly resembles the multiattribute attitude model we described in Chapter 7.

CHAPTER SUMMARY

Now that you have finished reading this chapter you should understand why:

Consumer decision making is a central part of consumer behavior, but the way we evaluate and choose products (and the amount of thought they put into these choices) varies widely, depending on such dimensions as the degree of novelty or risk related to the decision.

- We almost constantly need to make decisions about products. Some of these decisions are very important and entail great effort, whereas we make others on a virtually automatic basis. The decision-making task is further complicated because of the sheer number of decisions we need to make in a marketplace environment characterized by consumer hyperchoice.

  Perspectives on decision making range from a focus on habits that people develop over time to novel situations involving a great deal of risk in which consumers must carefully collect and analyze information prior to making a choice. Many of our decisions are highly automated and we make them largely by habit. This trend is accelerating as marketers begin to introduce smart products that enable silent commerce, where the products literally make their own purchase decisions (e.g., a malfunctioning appliance that contacts the repairperson directly).

A decision is actually composed of a series of stages that results in the selection of one product over competing options.

- A typical decision process involves several steps. The first is problem recognition, where we realize we must take some action. This recognition may occur because a current possession malfunctions or perhaps because we have a desire for something new.

- Once the consumer recognizes a problem and sees it as sufficiently important to warrant some action, he begins the process of information search. This search may range from simply scanning his memory to determine what he's done before to resolve the same problem to extensive fieldwork where he consults a variety of sources to amass as much information as possible. In many cases, people engage in surprisingly little search. Instead, they rely on various mental shortcuts, such as brand names or price, or they may simply imitate others' choices.

- In the evaluation of alternatives stage, the product alternatives a person considers comprise his evoked set. Members of the evoked set usually share some characteristics; we categorize them similarly. The way the person mentally groups products influences which alternatives she will consider, and usually we associate some brands more strongly with these categories (i.e., they are more prototypical).

Our access to online sources is changing the way we decide what to buy.

- The World Wide Web has changed the way many of us search for information. Today, our problem is more likely to involve weeding out excess detail rather than searching for more information. Comparative search sites and intelligent agents help to filter and guide the search process. We may rely on cybermediaries, such as Web portals, to sort through massive amounts of information as a way to simplify the decision-making process.

Decision making is not always rational.

● Research in the field of behavioral economics illustrates that decision making is not always strictly rational. Principles of mental accounting demonstrate that the way a problem is posed (called framing) and whether it is put in terms of gains or losses influences what we decide.

Consumers rely on different decision rules when evaluating competing options.

● When the consumer eventually must make a product choice from among alternatives, he uses one of several decision rules. Noncompensatory rules eliminate alternatives that are deficient on any of the criteria we've chosen. Compensatory rules, which are more likely to be applied in high-involvement situations, allow us to consider each alternative's good and bad points more carefully to arrive at the overall best choice.

We often fall back on well-learned "rules-of-thumb" to make decisions.

● Very often, we use heuristics, or mental rules-of-thumb, to simplify decision making. In particular, we develop many market beliefs over time. One of the most common beliefs is that we can determine quality by looking at the price. Other heuristics rely on well-known brand names or a product's country of origin as signals of product quality. When we consistently purchase a brand over time, this pattern may be the result of true brand loyalty or simply to inertia because it's the easiest thing to do.

KEY TERMS

Behavioral influence perspective, 352
Brand loyalty, 377
Compensatory decision rules, 380
Consideration set, 363
Consumer hyperchoice, 350
Country of origin, 375
Cybermediary, 371
Determinant attributes, 367
Electronic recommendation agent, 372
Ethnocentrism, 375
Evaluative criteria, 367
Experiential perspective, 352

Extended problem solving, 352
Feature creep, 367
Habitual decision making, 353
Heuristics, 372
Inertia, 377
Information search, 356
Intelligent agents, 372
Knowledge structure, 365
Limited problem solving, 353
Low-literate consumer, 361
Market beliefs, 374
Mental accounting, 358
Neuromarketing, 369

Noncompensatory decision rules, 379
Perceived risk, 361
Problem recognition, 354
Product signal, 373
Prospect theory, 358
Purchase momentum, 351
Rational perspective, 350
Search engines, 357
Silent commerce, 356
Variety seeking, 358
Zipf's Law, 377

REVIEW QUESTIONS

1 Why do we say that "mindless" decision making can actually be more efficient?
2 List the steps in the model of rational decision making.
3 What is purchase momentum, and how does it relate (or not) to the model of rational decision making?
4 What is the difference between the behavioral influence and experiential perspectives on decision making? Give an example of the type of purchase that each perspective would most likely explain.
5 Name two ways a consumer problem arises.

6 Give an example of the sunk-cost fallacy.
7 What is prospect theory? Does it support the argument that we are rational decision makers?
8 Describe the relationship between a consumer's level of expertise and how much he is likely to search for information about a product.
9 List three types of perceived risk, and give an example of each.
10 "Marketers need to be extra sure their product works as promised when they first introduce it." How does this

John Smith & Son Bookshop
Thames Valley University
Tel: +44 208 840 7394
Fax: +44 208 840 6453
Email: tv@johnsmith.co.uk

Description	Qty	Cost
80135153369		
nsumer Behavior	1	49.99
tal To Pay:		49.99
yment: Credit / Debit Car		49.99

A credit note will be issued
for any goods returned within 14 days
if stock is in perfect condition with
receipt. Thank you for your custom
VAT: GB 887 1365 84
eceipt No:39,812:16/10/08:1406:0007:01

statement relate to what we know about consumers' evoked sets?

11 Describe the difference between a superordinate category, a basic level category, and a subordinate category.

12 What is an example of an exemplar product?

13 List three product attributes that consumers use as product quality signals and provide an example of each.

14 How does a brand function as a heuristic?

15 Describe the difference between inertia and brand loyalty.

16 What is the difference between a noncompensatory and a compensatory decision rule? Give one example of each.

CONSUMER BEHAVIOR CHALLENGE

■ DISCUSS

1 This chapter argues that in our society having too many choices is a bigger problem than not having enough choices. Do you agree? Is it possible to have too much of a good thing?

2 Silent commerce has the potential to automate many of our decisions. Is there a downside to this trend?

3 The U.S. government's foreign policy affects what consumers around the world think of major American companies. Should these organizations have a say in our foreign policy?

4 How can retailers compete if people believe they can get the same items everywhere?

5 Commercial Alert, a consumer group, is highly critical of neuromarketing. The group's executive director wrote, "What would happen in this country if corporate marketers and political consultants could literally peer inside our brains and chart the neural activity that leads to our selections in the supermarket and voting booth? What if they then could trigger this neural activity by various means, so as to modify our behavior to serve their own ends?"[103] What do you think? Is neuromarketing dangerous?

6 If people are not always rational decision makers, is it worth the effort to study how they make purchasing decisions? What techniques might marketers employ to understand experiential consumption and to translate this knowledge into marketing strategy?

7 Why is it difficult to place a product in a consumer's evoked set after it has already been rejected? What strategies might a marketer use to accomplish this goal?

8 Discuss two different noncompensatory decision rules and highlight the difference(s) between them. How might the use of one rule versus another result in a different product choice?

9 Technology has the potential to make our lives easier by reducing the amount of clutter we need to work through in order to access the information on the Internet that really interests us. However, perhaps intelligent agents that make recommendations based only on what we and others like us have chosen in the past limit us—they reduce the chance that we will stumble on something (e.g., a book on a topic we've never heard of or a music group that's different from the style we usually listen to). Will the proliferation of "shopping bots" make our lives too predictable by only giving us more of the same? If so, is this a problem?

10 It's increasingly clear that many postings on blogs and product reviews on Web sites are fake or are posted there to manipulate consumers' opinions. For example a miniscandal erupted in 2007 when the press learned that the CEO of Whole Foods had regularly been blasting competitor Wild Oats on blogs under a pseudonym.[104] How big a problem is this if consumers increasingly are looking to consumer-generated product reviews to guide their purchase decisions? What steps if any can marketers take to nip this problem in the bud?

■ APPLY

11 This chapter discusses the expensive failure of the Cottonelle Fresh Rollwipes. If the company hired you as a consultant to revamp this effort, what recommendations would you make to persuade consumers to try such a sensitive product?

12 Find examples of electronic recommendation agents on the Web. Evaluate these—are they helpful? What characteristics of the sites you locate are likely to make you buy products you wouldn't have bought on your own?

13 Conduct a poll based on the list of market beliefs you'll find in Table 9.3. Do people agree with these beliefs, and how much do they influence their decisions?

14 Pepsi invented freshness dating and managed to persuade consumers that this was an important product attribute. Devise a similar strategy for another product category by coming up with a brand new product attribute. Using the steps in procedural learning that this chapter describes, how would you communicate this attribute to your customers?

15 Define the three levels of product categorization described in this chapter. Diagram these levels for a health club.

16 Choose a friend or parent who grocery shops on a regular basis and keep a log of his or her purchases of common consumer products during the term. Can you detect any evidence of brand loyalty in any categories based on consistency of purchases? If so, talk to the person about these purchases. Try to determine if his or her choices are based on true brand loyalty or on inertia. What techniques might you use to differentiate between the two?

17 Form a group of three. Pick a product and develop a marketing plan based on each of the three approaches to consumer decision making: rational, experiential, and behavioral influence. What are the major differences in emphasis among the three perspectives? Which is the most likely type of problem-solving activity for the product you have selected? What characteristics of the product make this so?

18 Locate a person who is about to make a major purchase. Ask that person to make a chronological list of all the information sources they consult prior to making a decision. How would you characterize the types of sources he or she uses (i.e., internal versus external, media versus personal, etc.)? Which sources appeared to have the most impact on the person's decision?

19 Perform a survey of country-of-origin stereotypes. Compile a list of five countries and ask people what products they associate with each. What are their evaluations of the products and likely attributes of these different products? The power of a country stereotype can also be demonstrated in another way. Prepare a brief description of a product, including a list of features, and ask people to rate it in terms of quality, likelihood of purchase, and so on. Make several versions of the description, varying only the country from which it comes. Do ratings change as a function of the country of origin?

20 Ask a friend to "talk through" the process he or she used to choose one brand rather than others during a recent purchase. Based on this description, can you identify the decision rule that was most likely employed?

21 Give one of the scenarios described in the section on biases in decision making to 10 to 20 people. How do the results you obtain compare with those reported in this chapter?

22 Think of a product you recently shopped for online. Describe your search process. How did you become aware that you wanted or needed the product? How did you evaluate alternatives? Did you wind up buying online? Why or why not? What factors would make it more or less likely that you would buy something online versus in a traditional store?

Case Study

THE TABLET PC: REVOLUTIONIZING THE PC LANDSCAPE?

Tablet PCs have been around in some form or another since the late 1990s. They were designed from the beginning to meet the needs of users who regularly use standard pads of paper and pen, but who simultaneously need computing power. The advent of an electronic pen-type stylus and a screen that covers the top surface of the computer were original features that made this product attractive. Today, people who work in fields that require them to be away from an office are the most likely users; key target markets include health care, insurance, real estate, law enforcement, and emergency response workers.

While the current tablet PC offerings show tremendous improvements over the original versions, sales in this market niche have yet to increase any faster than sales of the mobile computer market as a whole. Indeed, tablet PC sales have been hovering at about 1 to 2 percent of the total PC market for many years. As long ago as the fall of 2002, Microsoft introduced the Windows Tablet PC operating system. Having the blessing of this software giant certainly

didn't hurt. But it also has not helped nearly as much as tablet manufacturers had hoped.

What is it that potential tablet PC customers want? To begin with, they do not want to sacrifice the necessary features they find in notebooks. This includes processor speed, memory, hard drive capacity, screen resolution, battery life, and audio and video processing capability. Most all tablets makers provide these features. Many have even improved upon some items, such as offering extended battery life options.

The computer industry now classifies tablets as "convertibles;" they have swivel screens that enable the computer to be used either tablet style or as a standard laptop. Design elements have reduced the weight of most tablets so that they are significantly lighter than comparable notebooks. Lenovo's new ThinkPad X41 weighs just 3.5 pounds. Fujitsu's P1500 series starts at a mere 2.2 pounds. This makes these machines far easier to handle as a tablet. Other state-of-the-art tablet features include fingerprint scanning security devices, airbag hard drive protection, more durable cases, Bluetooth compatibility, GPS receivers, and handwriting recognition that really works. So why aren't customers flocking to these amazing machines?

The most likely reason is price: Consumers want to have their cake and eat it too. Most tablet PCs are priced competitively with each other, but they typically run about $300 more than comparable portable notebooks. In spite of technical improvements, experts cite other reasons for the slow growth of this mobile computing category. Specifically, there is still a scarcity of tablet software as well as the need for more hardware features that will better meet this market's specialized needs. And some experts predict that over time the tablet function will become just another standard laptop feature, like WiFi connectivity or double-layer DVD burners. For now though, consumers need to weigh the attributes of tablets versus notebooks carefully before they commit to one format or another.

DISCUSSION QUESTIONS

1 What is the most likely problem-solving process that a potential tablet user will undergo as she decides between a tablet and a traditional notebook computer?

What are the primary obstacles a tablet maker needs to address during this process?

2 Generate a list of potential "problem" situations that would motivate computer customers to consider buying a tablet PC.

3 Based on the problem situations you listed in question 1, trace the path through the stages of the consumer decision-making process for each situation.

Sources: Ian Harvey, "Once Dismissed As 'The Coolest Product No One Could Use,' Tablet PCs Finally Find a Niche," *Globe and Mail* (September 11, 2007): 34; Rhonda Ascierto, "Lenovo Launches Lightweight IBM Tablet PC, Price Still Steep," *ComputerWire* (June 6, 2005); Walter S. Mossberg, "Fujitsu's Tablet PC Feels Like a Paper Pad, So Why is it Clumsy?" *Wall Street Journal* (August 18, 2005): B1; Carmen Nobel, "Lenovo Launches Tablet PC," *eWeek* (June 13, 2005): 30.

NOTES

1. David Glen Mick, Susan M. Broniarczyk, and Jonathan Haidt, "Choose, Choose, Choose, Choose, Choose, Choose, Choose: Emerging and Prospective Research on the Deleterious Effects of Living in Consumer Hyperchoice," *Journal of Business Ethics* 52 (2004): 207–11; see also Barry Schwartz, *The Paradox of Choice: Why More Is Less* (New York: Ecco, 2005).

2. Itamar Simonson, Joel Huber, and John Payne, "The Relationship between Prior Brand Knowledge and Information Acquisition Order," *Journal of Consumer Research* 14 (March 1988): 566–78.

3. John R. Hauser, Glenn L. Urban, and Bruce D. Weinberg, "How Consumers Allocate Their Time When Searching for Information," *Journal of Marketing Research* 30 (November 1993): 452–66; George J. Stigler, "The Economics of Information," *Journal of Political Economy* 69 (June 1961): 213–25. For a set of studies focusing on online search costs, see John G. Lynch, Jr., and Dan Ariely, "Wine Online: Search Costs and Competition on Price, Quality, and Distribution," *Marketing Science* 19, no. 1 (2000): 83–103.

4. John C. Mowen, "Beyond Consumer Decision Making," *Journal of Consumer Marketing* 5, no. 1 (1988): 15–25.

5. Richard W. Olshavsky and Donald H. Granbois, "Consumer Decision Making—Fact or Fiction," *Journal of Consumer Research* 6 (September 1989): 93–100.

6. Chris Marks, "As Two Osprey Nests Are Raided, Fears That Thieves See Scotland as a Soft Option," *Daily Mail* (May 14, 2002).

7. Ravi Dhar, Joel Huber, and Uzma Khan, "The Shopping Momentum Effect," paper presented at the Association for Consumer Research, Atlanta, Georgia, October 2002.

8. James R. Bettman, "The Decision Maker Who Came in from the Cold" (presidential address), in Leigh McAllister and Michael Rothschild, eds., *Advances in Consumer Research* 20 (Provo, UT: Association for Consumer Research (1993): 7–11; John W. Payne, James R. Bettman, and Eric J. Johnson, "Behavioral Decision Research: A Constructive Processing Perspective," *Annual Review of Psychology* 4 (1992): 87–131. For an overview of recent developments in individual choice models, see Robert J. Meyers and Barbara E. Kahn, "Probabilistic Models of Consumer Choice Behavior," in Thomas S. Robertson and Harold H. Kassarjian, eds., *Handbook of Consumer Behavior* (Upper Saddle River, NJ: Prentice Hall, 1991): 85–123.

9. Mowen, "Beyond Consumer Decision Making."

10. The Fits-Like-a-Glove (FLAG) framework is a decision-making perspective that views consumer decisions as a holistic process shaped by the person's unique context; cf. Douglas E. Allen, "Toward a Theory of Consumer Choice as Sociohistorically Shaped Practical Experience: The Fits-Like-a-Glove (FLAG) Framework," *Journal of Consumer Research* 28 (March 2002): 515–32.

11. Joseph W. Alba and J. Wesley Hutchinson, "Dimensions of Consumer Expertise," *Journal of Consumer Research* 13 (March 1988): 411–54.

12. Gordon C. Bruner, III, and Richard J. Pomazal, "Problem Recognition: The Crucial First Stage of the Consumer Decision Process," *Journal of Consumer Marketing* 5, no. 1 (1988): 53–63.

13. For a study that examined trade-offs in search behavior among different channels, cf. Judi Strebel, Tulin Erdem, and Joffre Swait, "Consumer Search in High Technology Markets: Exploring the Use of Traditional Information Channels," *Journal of Consumer Psychology* 14, nos. 1 & 2 (2004): 96–104.

14. Peter H. Bloch, Daniel L. Sherrell, and Nancy M. Ridgway, "Consumer Search: An Extended Framework," *Journal of Consumer Research* 13 (June 1986): 119–26.

15. Kevin Maney, "Tag It: Tiny Wireless Wonders Improve Convenience," *Montgomery Advertiser* (May 6, 2002): D1.

16. David Leonhardt, "The Neighbors as Marketing Powerhouses," *New York Times Online* (June 13, 2005), accessed June 13, 2005.

17. Girish Punj, "Presearch Decision Making in Consumer Durable Purchases," *Journal of Consumer Marketing* 4 (Winter 1987): 71–82.

18. Beales, M. B. Jagis, S. C. Salop, and R. Staelin, "Consumer Search and Public Policy," *Journal of Consumer Research* 8 (June 1981): 11–22.

19. Laurie Peterson, "Study Places Value on Marketing at Consumer Research Stage," *Marketing Daily* (June 27, 2007), available from www.mediapost.com, accessed June 27, 2007.

20. Alex Mindlin, "Buyers Search Online, but Not by Brand," *New York Times Online* (March 13, 2006), accessed March 13, 2006.

21. Sarah Mahoney, "Study Finds Men Bamboozled by Choices in Supermarkets," *Marketing Daily* (May 31, 2007), available from www.mediapost.com, accessed May 31, 2007.

22. Cathy J. Cobb and Wayne D. Hoyer, "Direct Observation of Search Behavior," *Psychology & Marketing* 2 (Fall 1985): 161–79.

23. Sharon E. Beatty and Scott M. Smith, "External Search Effort: An Investigation across Several Product Categories," *Journal of Consumer Research* 14 (June 1987): 83–95; William L. Moore and Donald R. Lehmann, "Individual Differences in Search Behavior for a Nondurable," *Journal of Consumer Research* 7 (December 1980): 296–307.

24. Geoffrey C. Kiel and Roger A. Layton, "Dimensions of Consumer Information Seeking Behavior," *Journal of Marketing Research* 28 (May 1981): 233–39; see also Narasimhan Srinivasan and Brian T. Ratchford, "An Empirical Test of a Model of External Search for Automobiles," *Journal of Consumer Research* 18 (September 1991): 233–42.

25. David F. Midgley, "Patterns of Interpersonal Information Seeking for the Purchase of a Symbolic Product," *Journal of Marketing Research* 20 (February 1983): 74–83.

26. Cyndee Miller, "Scotland to U.S.: 'This Tennent's for You,'" *Marketing News* (August 29, 1994): 26.

27. Rebecca K. Ratner, Barbara E. Kahn, and Daniel Kahneman, "Choosing Less-Preferred Experiences for the Sake of Variety," *Journal of Consumer Research* 26 (June 1999): 1–15.

28. Harper A. Roehm and Michelle L. Roehm, "Revisiting the Effect of Positive Mood on Variety Seeking," *Journal of Consumer Research* 32 (September 2005): 330–336; Satya Menon and Barbara E. Kahn, "The Impact of Context on Variety Seeking in Product Choices," *Journal of Consumer Research* 22 (December 1995): 285–95; Barbara E. Kahn and Alice M. Isen, "The Influence of Positive Affect on Variety Seeking among Safe, Enjoyable Products," *Journal of Consumer Research* 20 (September 1993): 257–70.

29. J. Jeffrey Inman, "The Role of Sensory-Specific Satiety in Consumer Variety Seeking among Flavors" (unpublished manuscript, A. C. Nielsen Center for Marketing Research, University of Wisconsin–Madison, July 1999).

30. Gary Belsky, "Why Smart People Make Major Money Mistakes," *Money* (July 1995): 76; Richard Thaler and Eric J. Johnson, "Gambling with the House Money or Trying to Break Even: The Effects of Prior Outcomes on Risky Choice," *Management Science* 36 (June 1990): 643–60; Richard Thaler, "Mental Accounting and Consumer Choice," *Marketing Science* 4 (Summer 1985): 199–214.

31. Examples provided by Dr. William Cohen, personal communication, October 1999.

32. Daniel Kahneman and Amos Tversky, "Prospect Theory: An Analysis of Decision under Risk," *Econometrica* 47 (March 1979): 263–91; Timothy B. Heath, Subimal Chatterjee, and Karen Russo France, "Mental Accounting and Changes in Price: The Frame Dependence of Reference Dependence," *Journal of Consumer Research* 22, no. 1 (June 1995): 90–97.

33. Richard Thaler, "Mental Accounting and Consumer Choice," *Marketing Science* 4 (Summer 1985): 199–214, quoted on p. 206.

34. Girish N. Punj and Richard Staelin, "A Model of Consumer Search Behavior for New Automobiles," *Journal of Consumer Research* 9 (March 1983): 366–80.

35. Cobb and Hoyer, "Direct Observation of Search Behavior"; Moore and Lehmann, "Individual Differences in Search Behavior for a Nondurable"; Punj and Staelin, "A Model of Consumer Search Behavior for New Automobiles"; Brian T. Ratchford, M. S. Lee, and D. Toluca, "The Impact of the Internet on Information Search for Automobiles," *Journal of Marketing Research* 40, no. 2 (2003): 193–209.

36. James R. Bettman and C. Whan Park, "Effects of Prior Knowledge and Experience and Phase of the Choice Process on Consumer Decision Processes: A Protocol Analysis," *Journal of Consumer Research* 7 (December 1980): 234–48.

37. Alba and Hutchinson, "Dimensions of Consumer Expertise"; Bettman and Park, "Effects of Prior Knowledge and Experience and Phase of the Choice Process on Consumer Decision Processes"; Merrie Brucks, "The Effects of Product Class Knowledge on Information Search Behavior," *Journal of Consumer Research* 12 (June 1985): 1–16; Joel E. Urbany, Peter R. Dickson, and William L. Wilkie, "Buyer Uncertainty and Information Search," *Journal of Consumer Research* 16 (September 1989): 208–15.

38. Natalie Ross Adkins and Julie L. Ozanne, "The Low Literate Consumer," *Journal of Consumer Research* 32, no. 1 (2005): 93; Madhubalan Viswanathan, , Jose Antonio Rosa, and James Edwin Harris "Decision Making and Coping of Functionally Illiterate Consumers and Some Implications for Marketing Management," *Journal of Marketing* 69, no. 1 (2005): 15.

39. For an interpretive treatment of risk, cf. Craig J. Thompson, "Consumer Risk Perceptions in a Community of Reflexive Doubt," *Journal of Consumer Research* 32, no. 2 (2005): 235.

40. Mary Frances Luce, James R. Bettman, and John W. Payne, "Choice Processing in Emotionally Difficult Decisions," *Journal of Experimental Psychology: Learning, Memory, and Cognition* 23 (March 1997): 384–405; example provided by Professor James Bettman, personal communication (December 17, 1997).

41. Some research suggests that structural elements of the information available, such as the number and distribution of attribute levels, will influence how items in a consideration set are processed; cf. Nicholas

H. Lurie, "Decision Making in Information-Rich Environments: The Role of Information Structure," *Journal of Consumer Research* 30 (March 2004): 473–86.

42. John R. Hauser and Birger Wernerfelt, "An Evaluation Cost Model of Consideration Sets," *Journal of Consumer Research* 16 (March 1990): 393–408.

43. Robert J. Sutton, "Using Empirical Data to Investigate the Likelihood of Brands Being Admitted or Readmitted into an Established Evoked Set," *Journal of the Academy of Marketing Science* 15 (Fall 1987): 82.

44. Quoted in Stuart Elliott, "A Brand Tries to Invite Thought," *New York Times Online* (September 7, 2007), accessed September 7, 2007.

45. Cyndee Miller, "Hemp Is Latest Buzzword," *Marketing News* (March 17, 1997): 1.

46. Alba and Hutchison, "Dimensions of Consumer Expertise"; Joel B. Cohen and Kunal Basu, "Alternative Models of Categorization: Toward a Contingent Processing Framework," *Journal of Consumer Research* 13 (March 1987): 455–72.

47. Robert M. McMath, "The Perils of Typecasting," *American Demographics* (February 1997): 60.

48. Eleanor Rosch, "Principles of Categorization," in E. Rosch and B. B. Lloyd, eds., *Recognition and Categorization* (Hillsdale, NJ: Erlbaum, 1978).

49. Michael R. Solomon, "Mapping Product Constellations: A Social Categorization Approach to Symbolic Consumption," *Psychology & Marketing* 5, no. 3 (1988): 233–58.

50. Emily Nelson, "Moistened Toilet Paper Wipes Out after Launch for Kimberly-Clark," *Wall Street Journal Interactive Edition* (April 15, 2002).

51. McMath, "The Perils of Typecasting"

52. Elizabeth C. Hirschman and Michael R. Solomon, "Competition and Cooperation among Culture Production Systems," in Ronald F. Bush and Shelby D. Hunt, eds., *Marketing Theory: Philosophy of Science Perspectives* (Chicago: American Marketing Association, 1982), 269–72.

53. Michael D. Johnson, "The Differential Processing of Product Category and Noncomparable Choice Alternatives," *Journal of Consumer Research* 16 (December 1989): 300–39.

54. Mita Sujan, "Consumer Knowledge: Effects on Evaluation Strategies Mediating Consumer Judgments," *Journal of Consumer Research* 12 (June 1985): 31–46.

55. Rosch, "Principles of Categorization."

56. Joan Meyers-Levy and Alice M. Tybout, "Schema Congruity as a Basis for Product Evaluation," *Journal of Consumer Research* 16 (June 1989): 39–55.

57. Mita Sujan and James R. Bettman, "The Effects of Brand Positioning Strategies on Consumers' Brand and Category Perceptions: Some Insights from Schema Research," *Journal of Marketing Research* 26 (November 1989): 454–67.

58. See William P. Putsis, Jr., and Narasimhan Srinivasan, "Buying or Just Browsing? The Duration of Purchase Deliberation," *Journal of Marketing Research* 31 (August 1994): 393–402.

59. Robert E. Smith, "Integrating Information from Advertising and Trial: Processes and Effects on Consumer Response to Product Information," *Journal of Marketing Research* 30 (May 1993): 204–19.

60. James Surowiecki, "Feature Presentation," *The New Yorker* (May 28, 2007), accessed May 23, 2007. www.NewYorker.com

61. Ronald Alsop, "How Boss's Deeds Buff a Firm's Reputation," *Wall Street Journal* (January 31, 2007): B1.

62. Jack Trout, "Marketing in Tough Times," *Boardroom Reports* 2 (October 1992): 8.

63. Stuart Elliott, "Pepsi-Cola to Stamp Dates for Freshness on Soda Cans," *New York Times* (March 31, 1994): D1; Emily DeNitto, "Pepsi's Gamble Hits Freshness Dating Jackpot," *Advertising Age* (September 19, 1994): 50.

64. Amna Kirmani and Peter Wright, "Procedural Learning, Consumer Decision Making and Marketing Communication," *Marketing Letters* 4, no. 1 (1993): 39–48.

65. Robert Lee Hotz, "Searching for the Why of Buy," *Los Angeles Times Online* (February 27, 2005) www.latimes.com/news/science/la-sci-brain27feb27, 0,3899978.story?coll=la-home-headlines Sandra Blakeslee, "If You Have a 'Buy Button' in Your Brain, What Pushes It?" *New York Times on the Web* (October 19, 2004); Clive Thompson, "There's a Sucker Born in Every Medial Prefrontal Cortex," *New York Times Online* (October 26, 2003), accessed September 29, 2007

66. Michael Porter, *Competitive Advantage* (New York: Free Press, 1985).

67. Linda Stern, "Wanna Deal? Click Here," *Newsweek* (March 22, 2004): 65.

68. Material in this section adapted from Michael R. Solomon and Elnora W. Stuart, *Welcome to Marketing.com: The Brave New World of E-Commerce* (Upper Saddle River, NJ: Prentice Hall, 2001).

69. "Customer Product Reviews Drive Online Satisfaction and Conversion," available from www.mediapost.com, accessed January 24, 2007.

70. Jeffrey M. O'Brien, "You're Sooooooo Predictable," *Fortune* (November 27, 2006): 230.

71. Chris Anderson, *The Long Tail: Why the Future of Business Is Selling Less of More* (New York: Hyperion, 2006).

72. Kristin Diehl, "When Two Rights Make a Wrong: Searching Too Much in Ordered Environments," *Journal of Marketing Research* 42 (August 2005): 313–22; Andrew D. Gershoff, Ashesh Mukherjee, and Anirban Mukhopadhyay, "Consumer Acceptance of Online Agent Advice: Extremity and Positivity Effects," *Journal of Consumer Psychology* 12, nos. 1 & 2 (2003): 161–70; Vanitha Swaminathan, "The Impact of Recommendation Agents on Consumer Evaluation and Choice: The Moderating Role of Category Risk, Product Complexity, and Consumer Knowledge," *Journal of Consumer Psychology* 12, nos. 1 & 2 (2003): 93–101; Gerald Haubl and Kyle B. Murray, "Preference Construction and Persistence in Digital Marketplaces: The Role of Electronic Recommendation Agents," *Journal of Consumer Psychology* 13, nos. 1 & 2 (2003): 75–91; Dan Ariely, John G. Lynch, Jr., and Manuel Aparicio IV, "Learning by Collaborative and Individual-Based Recommendation Agents," *Journal of Consumer Psychology* 14, nos. 1 & 2 (2004): 81–95; Sylvain Senecal and Jacques Nantel, "The Influence of Online Product Recommendations on Consumers' Online Choices," *Journal of Retailing* 80 (2004): 159–69.

73. Jeffrey M O'Brien, "You're Sooooooo Predictable" *Fortune* (November 27, 2006): 230.

74. Laurie J. Flynn, "Like This? You'll Hate That (Not All Web Recommendations Are Welcome)" *New York Times Online* (January 23, 2006), accessed January 23, 2006.

75. Christopher Elliott, "Hotel Reviews Online: In Bed with Hope, Half-Truths and Hype," *New York Times Online* (February 7, 2006), accessed February 7, 2006.

76. Tom Zeller Jr., "On Amazon, All of a Sudden Everyone's a Milk Critic," *New York Times Online* (August 9, 2006), accessed August 9, 2006.

77. Robert A. Baron, *Psychology: The Essential Science* (Boston: Allyn & Bacon, 1989); Valerie S. Folkes, "The Availability Heuristic and Perceived Risk," *Journal of Consumer Research* 15 (June 1989): 13–23; Kahneman and Tversky, "Prospect Theory: An Analysis of Decision under Risk."

78. Wayne D. Hoyer, "An Examination of Consumer Decision Making for a Common Repeat Purchase Product," *Journal of Consumer Research* 11 (December 1984): 822–29; Calvin P. Duncan, "Consumer Market Beliefs: A Review of the Literature and an Agenda for Future Research," in Marvin E. Goldberg, Gerald Gorn, and Richard W. Pollay, eds., *Advances in Consumer Research* 17 (Provo, UT: Association for Consumer Research, 1990): 729–35; Frank Alpert, "Consumer Market Beliefs and Their Managerial Implications: An Empirical Examination," *Journal of Consumer Marketing* 10, no. 2 (1993): 56–70.

79. Michael R. Solomon, Sarah Drenan, and Chester A. Insko, "Popular Induction: When Is Consensus Information Informative?" *Journal of Personality* 49, no. 2 (1981): 212–24.

80. Beales et al., "Consumer Search and Public Policy."

81. Gary T. Ford and Ruth Ann Smith, "Inferential Beliefs in Consumer Evaluations: An Assessment of Alternative Processing Strategies," *Journal of Consumer Research* 14 (December 1987): 363–71; Deborah Roedder John, Carol A. Scott, and James R. Bettman, "Sampling Data for Covariation Assessment: The Effects of Prior Beliefs on Search Patterns," *Journal of Consumer Research* 13 (June 1986): 38–47; Gary L. Sullivan and Kenneth J. Berger, "An Investigation of the Determinants of Cue Utilization," *Psychology & Marketing* 4 (Spring 1987): 63–74.

82. John et al., "Sampling Data for Covariation Assessment."

83. Duncan, "Consumer Market Beliefs."

84. Chr. Hjorth-Andersen, "Price as a Risk Indicator," *Journal of Consumer Policy* 10 (1987): 267–81; David M. Gardner, "Is There a Generalized Price–Quality Relationship?" *Journal of Marketing Research* 8 (May 1971): 241–43; Kent B. Monroe, "Buyers' Subjective Perceptions of Price," *Journal of Marketing Research* 10 (1973): 70–80.

85. David M. Gardner, "Is There a Generalized Price–Quality Relationship?" *Journal of Marketing Research* 8 (May 1971): 241–43; Kent B. Monroe, "Buyers' Subjective Perceptions of Price," *Journal of Marketing Research* 10 (1973): 70–80.

86. Katy McLaughlin, "Shrimp Gets a Makeover, As Foreign Imports Rise U.S. Fishermen Try Giving Prawns Regional Identities; The 'Iodine-y Aftertaste'," *Wall Street Journal* (August 19, 2004): D1.

87. See Sung-Tai Hong and Dong Kyoon Kang, "Country-of-Origin Influences on Product Evaluations: The Impact of Animosity and Perceptions of Industriousness Brutality on Judgments of Typical and Atypical Products," *Journal of Consumer Psychology* 16, no. 3, (2006): 232-39; Richard Jackson Harris, Bettina Garner-Earl, Sara J. Sprick, and Collette Carroll, "Effects of Foreign Product Names and Country-of-Origin Attributions on Advertisement Evaluations," *Psychology & Marketing* 11 (March–April 1994): 129–45; Terence A. Shimp, Saeed Samiee, and Thomas J. Madden, "Countries and Their Products: A Cognitive Structure Perspective," *Journal of the Academy of Marketing Science* 21 (Fall 1993): 323–30; Durairaj Maheswaran, "Country of Origin as a Stereotype: Effects of Consumer Expertise and Attribute Strength on Product Evaluations," *Journal of Consumer Research* 21 (September 1994): 354–65; Ingrid M. Martin and Sevgin Eroglu, "Measuring a Multi-Dimensional Construct: Country Image," *Journal of Business Research* 28 (1993): 191–210; Richard Ettenson, Janet Wagner, and Gary Gaeth, "Evaluating the Effect of Country of Origin and the 'Made in the U.S.A.' Campaign: A Conjoint Approach," *Journal of Retailing* 64 (Spring 1988): 85–100; C. Min Han and Vern Terpstra, "Country-of-Origin Effects for Uni-National and Bi-National Products," *Journal of International Business* 19 (Summer 1988): 235–55; Michelle A. Morganosky and Michelle M. Lazarde, "Foreign-Made Apparel: Influences on Consumers' Perceptions of Brand and Store Quality," *International Journal of Advertising* 6 (Fall 1987): 339–48.

88. Items excerpted from Terence A. Shimp and Subhash Sharma, "Consumer Ethnocentrism: Construction and Validation of the CETSCALE," *Journal of Marketing Research* 24 (August 1987): 282.

89. Roger Ricklefs, "Canada Fights to Fend Off American Tastes and Tunes," *Wall Street Journal Interactive Edition* (September 24, 1998).

90. Adam Bryant, "Message in a Beer Bottle," *Newsweek* (May 29, 2000): 43.

91. Somni Sengupta, "Colonel Sanders Finds Himself under Fiery Siege in Pakistan," *New York Times Online* (June 8, 2005).

92. Sean Gregory, "Anti-U.S. Backlash," *Time* (January 2005): A3.

93. Eric Pfanner, "Foreign Policy and Marketing," *New York Times on the Web* (January 20, 2004).

94. Richard W. Stevenson, "The Brands with Billion-Dollar Names," *New York Times* (October 28, 1988): A1.

95. Eric Pfanner, "Zipf's Law, or the Considerable Value of Being Top Dog, as Applied to Branding," *New York Times Online* (May 21, 2007), accessed May 21, 2007; Ronald Alsop, "Enduring Brands Hold Their Allure by Sticking Close to Their Roots," *Wall Street Journal*, centennial ed. (1989): B4.

96. Greg Morago, "Envy: The Brand Sluts—Many Who Covet Their Retailers' Garb No Longer Look at the Logo," *Hartford Courant on the Web* (January 1, 2007).

97. Jacob Jacoby and Robert Chestnut, *Brand Loyalty: Measurement and Management* (New York: Wiley, 1978).

98. Ibid.

99. Ronald Alsop, "Brand Loyalty Is Rarely Blind Loyalty," *Wall Street Journal* (October 19, 1989): B1.

100. Gabriel Kahn, "After Years behind the Scenes, Chinese Join the Name Game: Manufacturers Buy Rights to Famous Trademarks, Hoping for Fatter Margins," *Wall Street Journal Online* (December 26, 2003), accessed December 26, 2003.

101. C. Whan Park, "The Effect of Individual and Situation-Related Factors on Consumer Selection of Judgmental Models," *Journal of Marketing Research* 13 (May 1976): 144–51.

102. Joseph W. Alba and Howard Marmorstein, "The Effects of Frequency Knowledge on Consumer Decision Making," *Journal of Consumer Research* 14 (June 1987): 14–25.

103. Sandra Blakeslee, "If You Have a 'Buy Button' in Your Brain, What Pushes It?" *New York Times on the Web* (October 19, 2004).

104. David Kesmodel and John R. Wilke, "Whole Foods Is Hot, Wild Oats a Dud—So Said 'Rahodeb' Then Again, Yahoo Poster Was a Whole Foods Staffer, the CEO to Be Precise," *Wall Street Journal* (July 12, 2007): A1.

Buying and Disposing

When you finish this chapter you should understand why:

- Many factors over and above the qualities of the product or service influence the outcome of a transaction. Factors at the time of purchase dramatically influence the consumer decision-making process.

- In addition to what a shopper already knows or believes about a product, information a store or Web site provides can strongly influence a purchase decision.

- A salesperson can be the crucial link between interest in a product and its actual purchase.

- Marketers need to be concerned about a consumer's evaluations of a product after he buys it as well as before.

- Getting rid of products when consumers no longer need or want them is a major concern both to marketers and to public policy makers.

kyle is really psyched. The big day has actually arrived: He's going to buy a car! He's had his eye on that silver 2002 Mustang parked in the lot of Jon's Auto-Rama for weeks now. Although the sticker says $2,999, Kyle figures he can probably get this baby for a cool $2,000—with its dilapidated showroom and somewhat seedy lot, Jon's looks like just the kind of place where they're hungry to move some cars. Besides, he's already done his homework on the Web. First he found out the wholesale value of similar used Mustangs from the Kelley Blue Book (kbb.com), and then he scouted out some cars for sale in his area at autobytel.com. So, Kyle figures he's coming in loaded for bear—he's going to show these guys they're not dealing with some rube.

Unlike some of the newer, flashy car showrooms he's been in lately, this place is a real nuts-and-bolts operation—it's so dingy and depressing he can't wait to get out of there and take a shower. Kyle dreads the prospect of haggling over the price, but he hopes to convince the salesperson to take his offer because he knows the real market value of the car he wants. At the Auto-Rama lot, big signs on all the cars proclaim that today is Jon's Auto-Rama Rip Us Off Day! Things look better than Kyle expected—maybe he can get the Mustang for even less than he had planned. He's a bit surprised when a salesperson comes over to him and introduces herself as Rhoda. He had expected to be dealing with a middle-aged man in a loud sport coat (a stereotype he has about used-car salespeople), but this is more good luck: He figures he won't have to be so tough when dealing with a woman who looks to be about his age.

Rhoda laughs when he offers her $1,800 for the Mustang; she points out that she can't take such a low bid for such a sweet car to her boss or she'll lose her job. Rhoda's enthusiasm for the car convinces him all the more that he has to have it. When he finally writes a check for $2,700, he's exhausted from all the haggling. What an ordeal! In any case, Kyle reminds himself that he at least convinced Rhoda to sell him the car for less than the sticker price—and maybe he can fix it up and sell it for even more in a year or two. That Web surfing really paid off—he's a tougher negotiator than he thought.

Situational Effects on Consumer Behavior

Many consumers dread the act of buying a car. In fact, a survey by Yankelovich Partners found that buying a car is the most anxiety-provoking and least satisfying of any retail experience.[1] But change is in the wind because dealers are transforming the car showroom. Car shoppers like Kyle are logging onto Internet buying services, calling auto brokers who negotiate for them, buying cars at warehouse clubs, and visiting giant auto malls where they can easily comparison shop.

Kyle's experience in buying a car illustrates some of the concepts we'll discuss in this chapter. Making a purchase is often not a simple, routine matter of going to a store and quickly choosing something. As Figure 10.1 illustrates, many personal factors affect our choice, such as our mood, whether we feel time pressure to make the purchase, and the particular situation or context for which we need the product. In some situations, such as when we buy a car or a home, the salesperson or realtor plays a pivotal role in our final selection. And today people are using the Web to arm themselves with product and price information before they even enter a dealership or a store, which puts added pressure on retailers to deliver the value their customers expect.

But the sale doesn't end at the time of purchase. A lot of important consumer activity occurs after we bring a product home. After we use a product, we have to decide whether we're satisfied with it. The satisfaction process is especially important to savvy marketers who realize that the key to success is not selling a product one time, but rather forging a relationship with the consumer so that he will keep coming back. Finally, just as Kyle thought about the resale value of his car, we must also consider how consumers go about disposing of products and how we often rely on secondary markets (e.g., used-car dealers) to obtain what we want. We'll consider these issues in this chapter.

The Denny's chain hopes to motivate college students to drop in for a munch between 10 P.M. and 5 A.M. It introduced a "Pick 3" appetizer promotion for $9.99 on

■ FIGURE 10.1
ISSUES RELATED TO PURCHASE
AND POSTPURCHASE ACTIVITIES

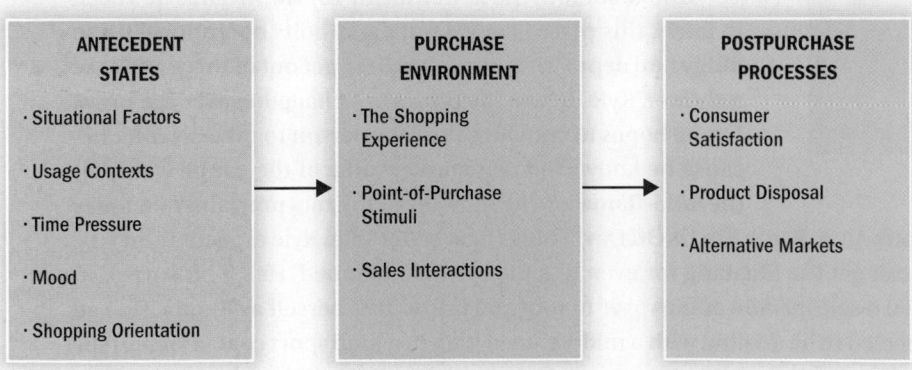

weekdays and gives a 20 percent discount with a college ID on Saturday nights. A company executive explains, ". . . [We] treat each day-part as a specific business. Late-night is one. We wanted to create a marketing and promotions program that targets what we know are our predominate late-night visitors—college kids."[2] Even online advertising is starting to tailor content to time of day. McDonald's advertises breakfast meals in the morning hours on Yahoo! whereas Sanofi-Aventis runs ads for its sleep-aid drug Ambien CR in the middle of the night on CBSNews.com.[3]

These companies understand that a *consumption situation* includes a buyer, a seller, a product or service—but also many other factors, such as the reason we want to make a purchase and how the physical environment makes us feel.[4] Common sense tells us that we tailor our purchases to specific occasions and that the way we feel at a specific point in time affects what we feel like buying or doing. Smart marketers understand these patterns and plan their efforts to coincide with situations in we are most prone to buy. For example, book clubs invest heavily in promotional campaigns in June because many people are looking to stock up on "beach books" to read during the summer.[5] Our moods even change radically during the day, so at different times we might be more or less interested in what a marketer has to offer.

A study used a technique researchers call the *day reconstruction method* to track these changes. More than 900 U.S. workingwomen kept diaries of everything they did

Clothing choices often are heavily influenced by the situation in which they need to be worn.

during the day, from reading the paper in the morning to falling asleep in front of the TV at night. The next day they relived each diary entry and rated how they felt at the time (annoyed, happy, etc.). Overall, researchers found the study participants woke up a little grumpy but soon entered a state of mild pleasure that increased by degrees through the day, punctuated by occasional bouts of anxiety, frustration, and anger. Not surprisingly the subjects were least happy when doing activities such as commuting to work and doing housework, whereas they rated sex, socializing with friends, and relaxing as most enjoyable. Contrary to prior findings, however, the women reported being happier when watching television than when shopping or talking on the phone, and they ranked taking care of children low, below cooking and not far above housework. The good news: Overall, people seem to be pretty happy and these ratings aren't influenced very much by factors such as household income or job security. By far, the two factors that most upset daily moods were a poor night's sleep and tight work deadlines.[6]

In addition to the functional relationships between products and usage situation, another reason to take environmental circumstances seriously is that a person's *situational self-image*—the role she plays at any one time—helps to determine what she wants to buy or consume (see Chapter 5).[7] A guy trying to impress his date by playing the role of "man-about-town" may spend more lavishly, order champagne instead of beer, and buy flowers—purchases he would never consider when he is hanging out with his friends, slurping beer, and playing the role of "one of the boys." Let's see how these dynamics affect the way people think about what they buy.

By systematically identifying important usage situations, market segmentation strategies can position products in such a way as to meet the specific needs these situations create. We can apply this kind of segmentation to many kinds of product categories. For example, we often tailor our furniture choices to specific settings. We prefer different styles for a city apartment, a beach house, or an executive suite. Similarly, we distinguish motorcycles in terms of how riders use them, including commuting, riding them as dirt bikes, or using them on a farm versus highway travel.[8]

Coach, the maker of luxury leather goods, decided to overhaul its marketing strategy in order to convince women that they need more than simply a bag for everyday use and one for dressy occasions. Now, they're helping women to update their wardrobes by offering them weekend bags, evening bags, backpacks, satchels, clutches, totes, briefcases, diaper bags, coin purses, duffels, and a minihandbag that doubles as a bag-within-a-bag it calls a wristlet. The company even makes new bags to fill what it calls "usage voids," activities that range from weekend getaways to trips to the grocery store. Coach introduced its Hamptons Weekend collection by displaying bags stuffed with beach towels and colorful flip-flops. Have bag, will travel.[9]

Table 10.1 gives one example of how situations can fine-tune a segmentation strategy. By listing the major contexts in which a people use a product (e.g., snow skiing and sunbathing for a suntan lotion) and the different product users of the product, we can construct a matrix that identifies specific product features we should emphasize for each situation. For example, during the summer, a lotion manufacturer might promote the fact that the bottle floats and is hard to lose, but it should tout its nonfreezing formula during the winter season.

SOCIAL AND PHYSICAL SURROUNDINGS

A consumer's physical and social environment affects her motives for product usage and how she evaluates products. Important cues include the person's physical surroundings as well as the amount and type of other consumers also present in that situation. Dimensions of the physical environment, such as decor, odors, and even temperature can significantly influence consumption. One study even found that pumping certain odors into a Las Vegas casino actually increased the amount of money patrons fed into

TABLE 10.1
A PERSON-SITUATION SEGMENTATION MATRIX FOR SUNTAN LOTION

Situation	Young Children Fair Skin	Young Children Dark Skin	Teenagers Fair Skin	Teenagers Dark Skin	Adult Women Fair Skin	Adult Women Dark Skin	Adult Men Fair Skin	Adult Men Dark Skin	Benefits/Features
Beach/boat sunbathing	Combined insect repellent				Summer perfume				a. Product serves as windburn protection b. Fomula and container can stand heat c. Container floats and is distinctive (not easily lost)
Home-poolside sunbathing					Combined moisturizer				a. Product has large pump dispenser b. Product won't stain wood, concrete, furnishings
Sunlamp bathing					Combined moisturizer and massage oil				a. Product is designed specifically for type of lamp b. Product has an artificial tanning ingredient
Snow skiing					Winter perfume				a. Product provides special protection from special light rays and weather b. Product has antifreeze formula
Person benefit/features	Special protection a. Protection is critical b. Formula is non-poisonous		Special protection a. Product fits in jean pocket b. Product used by opinion leaders		Special protection Female perfume		Special protection Male perfume		

Source: Adapted from Peter R. Dickson, "Person-Situation: Segmentation's Missing Link," *Journal of Marketing* 46 (Fall 1982): 62. Copyright © 1982 American Marketing Association. By permission of American Marketing Association.

slot machines![10] We'll take a closer look at some of these factors a bit later in this chapter when we consider how important store design is to consumer behavior.

In addition to physical cues, though, groups or social settings significantly affect many of our purchase decisions. In some cases, the sheer presence or absence of **co-consumers**, the other patrons in a setting, actually is a product attribute—think about an exclusive resort or boutique that promises to provide privacy to privileged customers. At other times, the presence of others can have positive value. A sparsely attended ball game or an empty bar can be a depressing sight.

The presence of large numbers of people in a consumer environment increases arousal levels, so our subjective experience of a setting tends to be more intense. This boost, however, can be positive or negative—the experience depends on how we interpret this arousal. It is important to distinguish between *density* and *crowding* for this reason. The former term refers to the actual number of people who occupy a space, whereas the psychological state of crowding exists only if a negative affective state occurs as a result of this density.[11] For example, 100 students packed into a classroom designed for 75 may result in an unpleasant situation for all, but the same number of people jammed together at a party—and occupying a room of the same size—might just make for a great rave.

In addition, the *type* of consumers who patronize a store or service or who use a product affects our evaluations. We often infer something about a store by examining its customers. For this reason, some restaurants require men to wear jackets for dinner (and supply rather tacky ones if they don't), and bouncers at some "hot" nightspots handpick people waiting in line based on whether they have the right "look" for the club. To paraphrase the comedian Groucho Marx, "I would never join a club that would have me as a member!"

TEMPORAL FACTORS

Time is one of consumers' most precious resources. We talk about "making time" or "spending time" and we frequently remind others that "time is money." Common sense tells us that we think more about what we want to buy when we have the luxury to take our time. We might find a meticulous shopper who normally prices an item at three different stores before buying sprinting through the mall at 9:00 P.M. on Christmas Eve, furiously scooping up anything left on the shelves to serve as last-minute gifts.

Time poverty is creating opportunities for many new products (like portable soups) that let people multitask.

Too busy to eat? Help is at hand.

Introducing Campbell's® Soup at Hand.™
A whole new way to eat right when you're on the run.

Now you can enjoy sippable soup, anytime, anywhere, with new Campbell's Soup at Hand. Four deliciously satisfying soups in sippable, heat-and-go microwavable cups. Sure your hands are full, but it's amazing what you can do with new Soup at Hand from Campbell's.

M'm! M'm! Good!®

© 2002 Campbell Soup Company

Economic Time

Time is an economic variable; it is a resource that we must divide among our activities.[12] We try to maximize satisfaction by allocating our time to the appropriate combination of tasks. Of course, people's allocation decisions differ; we all know people who seem to play all of the time, and others who are workaholics. An individual's priorities determine his *timestyle*.[13] People in different countries also "spend" this resource at different rates. A social scientist compared the pace of life in 31 cities around the world as part of a study on timestyles.[14] He and his assistants timed how long it takes pedestrians to walk 60 feet and the time postal clerks take to sell a stamp. Based on these responses, he claims that the fastest and slowest countries are:

Fastest countries: (1) Switzerland, (2) Ireland, (3) Germany, (4) Japan, (5) Italy

Slowest countries: (31) Mexico, (30) Indonesia, (29) Brazil, (28) El Salvador, (27) Syria

Many consumers believe they are more pressed for time than ever before, a feeling marketers call **time poverty**. This feeling appears to be more perception than fact. The reality is we simply have more options for spending our time, so we feel pressured by the weight of all of these choices. The average U.S. working day at the turn of the twentieth century was 10 hours (6 days per week), and women did 27 hours of housework per week, compared to less than 5 hours weekly now. Of course, there are plenty of husbands who share these burdens more, and in some families it's not as important as it used to be to maintain an absolutely spotless home as values change (see Chapter 4).[15] Still, about a third of Americans report always feeling rushed—up from 25 percent of the population in 1964.[16]

This sense of time poverty makes us responsive to marketing innovations that allow us to save time. For example, rush-hour commuters in Hong Kong no longer need to stand in line to buy subway tokens. Instead, a scanner automatically reads an Octopus card and automatically deducts the fare from their accounts. The card doesn't even require contact with the scanner, so women can simply pass their entire handbag over it and race to catch their trains.[17] In the United States, a hospital vending machine called InstyMeds even dispenses prescription drugs after a patient enters a security code and swipes his credit card.[18]

Psychological Time

"Time flies when you're having fun," but other situations (like some classes?) seem to last forever. Our experience of time is very subjective; our immediate priorities and needs determine how quickly time flies. The fluidity of time is important for marketers to understand because we're more likely to be in a consuming mood at some times than at others.

A recent study examined how the timestyles of a group of American women influence their consumption choices.[22] The researchers identified four dimensions of time: (1) the *social dimension* refers to individuals' categorization of time as either "time for me" or "time with/for others"; (2) the *temporal orientation dimension* depicts the relative significance individuals attach to past, present, or future; (3) the *planning orientation dimension* alludes to different time management styles varying on a continuum from analytic to spontaneous; and (4) the *polychronic orientation dimension* distinguishes between people who prefer to do one thing at a time from those who have multitasking timestyles. After interviewing and observing these women, the researchers identified a set of five metaphors that they say capture the participants' perspectives on time:

1 Time is a pressure cooker: Women who personify this metaphor are usually analytical in their planning, other-oriented, and monochronic in their timestyles.

Net Profit

Along with the increase in time poverty, researchers also note a rise in *polychronic activity*, or *multitasking*, where consumers do more than one thing at a time.[19] We're especially likely to multitask when we eat. Consumers often do not allocate a specific time for dining but instead eat on the run. In a poll, 64 percent of respondents said they usually do something else while eating. As one food industry executive commented, "We've moved beyond grazing and into gulping."[20] The food industry is racing to meet consumers' desires to eat on the run. Here are a few on-the-go products:

- General Mills is turning its Yoplait yogurt into a meal with Nouriche, a nonfat yogurt smoothie fortified with 20 vitamins and minerals. A television commercial proclaims, "No time for a meal? Nouriche yourself."
- Kraft Foods launched Nabisco Go-Paks, cupholder-ready contour packages featuring mini versions of its cookies and crackers, similar to the Frito-Lay Go Snacks already on the market.
- Tubes to squeeze on the run are the next big things: Look for Hershey's Portable Pudding in tubes as well as Jolly Rancher Gel Snacks.[21]

They treat shopping in a methodical manner and they often feel under pressure and in conflict.

2 **Time is a map:** Women who exemplify this metaphor are usually analytical planners and have a future temporal orientation and a polychronic timestyle. They often engage in extensive information search and in comparison shopping.

3 **Time is a mirror:** Women in this group are also analytic planners and have a polychronic orientation. However, they have a past temporal orientation. Because of their risk averseness in time use, these women are usually loyal to products and services they know and trust. They prefer convenience-oriented products.

4 **Time is a river:** Women whose timestyles this metaphor describes are usually spontaneous in their planning orientation and have a present focus. They go on unplanned, short, and frequent shopping trips they undertake on impulse.

5 **Time is a feast:** These women are analytical planners who have a present temporal orientation. They view time as something to be consumed in the pursuit of sensory pleasure and gratification, and for this reason hedonic and variety-seeking desires motivate their consumption behavior.

Our experience of time is largely a result of our culture because different societies have varying perspectives on this experience. To most Western consumers, time is a neatly compartmentalized thing: We wake up in the morning, go to school or work, come home, eat dinner, go out, go to sleep, wake up, and do it all over again. We call this perspective *linear separable time*; events proceed in an orderly sequence and "There's a time and a place for everything." There is a clear sense of past, present, and future. We perform many activities as the means to some end that will occur later, as when we "save for a rainy day."

This perspective seems "natural" to us, but not all others share it. Some cultures run on *procedural time* and ignore the clock completely—people simply decide to do something "when the time is right." For example, in Burundi, people might arrange to meet when the cows return from the watering hole. If you ask someone in Madagascar how long it takes to get to the market, you will get an answer such as, "in the time it takes to cook rice."

Alternatively, in *circular*, or *cyclic*, time, natural cycles, such as the regular occurrence of the seasons, govern people's sense of time (a perspective many Hispanic cultures share). To these consumers, the notion of the future does not make sense—that time will be much like the present. Because the concept of future value does not exist, these consumers often prefer to buy an inferior product that is available now rather than wait for a better one that may be available later. Also, it is hard to convince people who function on circular time to buy insurance or save for a rainy day when they don't think in terms of a linear future.

To appreciate all the different ways people think about time, consider those who speak Aymara, an Indian language of the high Andes. They actually see the future as behind them and the past ahead of them! Aymara call the future *qhipa pacha/timpu*, meaning back or behind time, and the past *nayra pacha/timpu*, meaning front time. And they gesture ahead of them when remembering things past and backward when talking about the future. Anthropologists explain that people in this culture distinguish primarily between what they know and what they don't—and they know what they see in front of them with their own eyes. So, because they know the past, it lies ahead of them. The future is unknown, so it lies behind them where they can't see it.[23] Just imagine trying to sell them life insurance!

The sketches in Figure 10.2 illustrate what happened when a researcher asked college students to draw pictures of time. The drawing at the top left represents procedural time; there is lack of direction from left to right and little sense of past, present, and future. The three drawings in the middle denote cyclical time, with

■ FIGURE 10.2
DRAWINGS OF TIME
Source: Esther S. Page-Wood, Carol J. Kaufman, and Paul M. Lane, (1990) "The Art of Time." *Proceedings of the 1990 Academy of Marketing Science* conference, ed B.J. Dunlap, Vol. xiii, Cullowhee, NC: Academy of Marketing Science, 56–61. Copyright © 1990 Academy of Marketing Science. Used with permission.

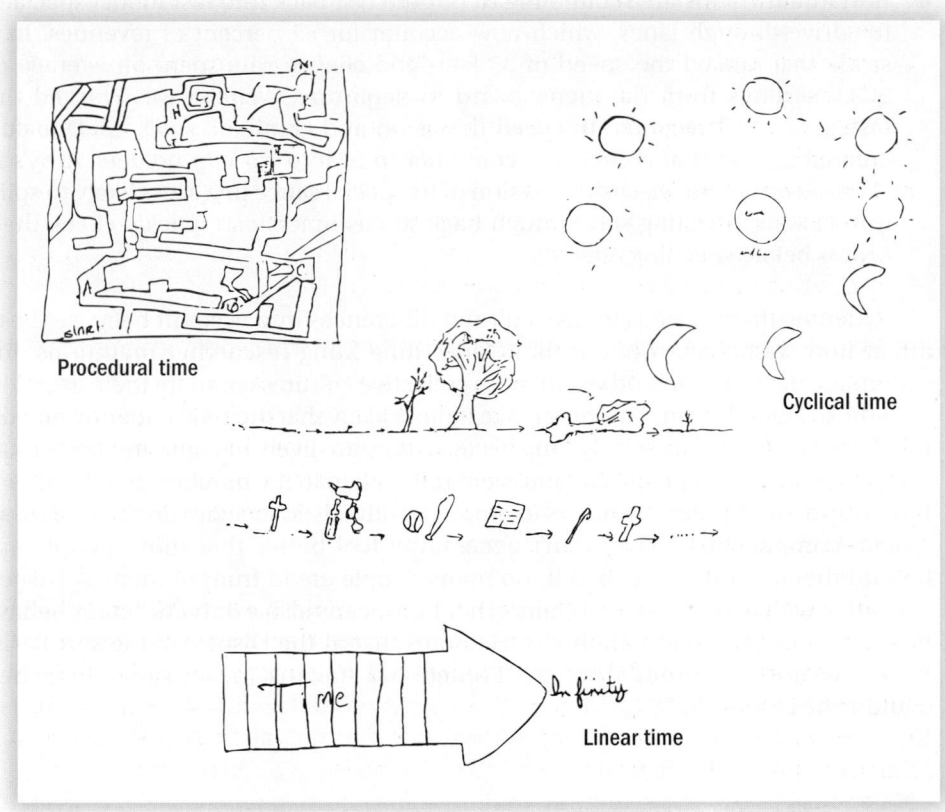

markers that designate regular cycles. The bottom drawing represents linear time, with a segmented time line moving from left to right in a well-defined sequence.[24]

The psychological dimension of time—how we actually experience it—is an important factor in **queuing theory**, the mathematical study of waiting lines. As we all know, our experience while waiting for something has a big effect on our evaluations of what we get at the end of the wait. Although we assume that something must be pretty good if we have to wait for it, the negative feelings that long waits arouse can quickly turn people off.[25] In a recent survey, NCR Corp. found that standing around the local Department for Transport is the most dreaded wait of all. Waiting in line at retail outlets came in a close second, followed by registering at clinics or hospitals, checking in at airports, and ordering at fast-food restaurants or deli counters. On average, American consumers, for example, estimate that they spend more than 2 days per year waiting in line for service, and half believe they waste between 30 minutes and 2 hours each week waiting for service.[26]

Marketers use "tricks" to minimize psychological waiting time. These techniques range from altering customers' perceptions of a line's length to providing distractions that divert attention away from waiting:[27]

● One hotel chain, after receiving excessive complaints about the wait for elevators, installed mirrors near the elevator banks. People's natural tendency to check their appearance reduced complaints, even though the actual waiting time was unchanged.

● Airline passengers often complain about waiting to claim their baggage. In one airport, they would walk 1 minute from the plane to the baggage carousel and then wait 7 minutes for their luggage. By changing the layout so that the walk to the carousel took 6 minutes and bags arrived 2 minutes after that, complaints were almost entirely eliminated.[28]

● Restaurant chains are scrambling to put the fast back into fast food, especially for drive-through lanes, which now account for 65 percent of revenues. In a study that ranked the speed of 25 fast-food chains, cars spent an average of 203.6 seconds from the menu board to departure. Wendy's was clocked the fastest at 150.3 seconds. To speed things up and eliminate spills, McDonald's created a salad that comes in a container to fit into car cup holders. Arby's is working on a "high viscosity" version of its special sauce that's less likely to spill. Burger King is testing see-through bags so customers can quickly check their orders before speeding off.[29]

Queuing theory needs to take cultural differences into account because these affect how we behave while in line. One Hong Kong researcher maintains, for example, that Asians and others in more collective cultures compare their situation with those around them. This may make it more likely that they will patiently remain in a line even if it is excessively long because they are likely to compare their situation to the number of people behind them rather than to the number ahead of them. By contrast, Americans and others in more individualistic societies don't make these "social comparisons." They don't necessarily feel better that more people are behind them, but they feel bad if too many people are in front of them. A Disney executive with reason to know claims that Europeans also exhibit different behaviors depending on their nationality. He notes that at the Disneyland Resort Paris, British visitors are orderly but the French and Italians "never saw a line they couldn't be in front of."[30]

 # The Shopping Environment

Whole Foods Markets wants you to feel really, really mellow before you cruise its grocery aisles. The natural U.S. supermarket chain is testing a spa-within-a-food-store concept. You'll find its Refresh—The Everyday Spa at Whole Foods Market prototype in Dallas enclosed with a soundproof lounge complete with fountains, several treatment rooms, and a private balcony where clients can order lunch.[31] After a Shiatsu massage, it's unlikely you'll care too much if those exotic guavas are on sale before you throw them in your cart.

Our mood at the time of purchase can really impact what we feel like buying.[32] Recall that in Chapter 4 we talked about directing our behavior to satisfy certain goal states and this will make sense. If you don't believe it, try grocery shopping on an empty stomach! Or make a decision when you're stressed and you'll understand how a physiological state impairs information-processing and problem-solving abilities.[33]

Two basic dimensions, *pleasure* and *arousal*, determine whether we will react positively or negatively to a consumption environment.[34] What it boils down to is that you can either enjoy or not enjoy a situation, and you can feel stimulated or not. As Figure 10.3 indicates, different combinations of pleasure and arousal levels result in a variety of emotional states. For example, an arousing situation can be either distressing or exciting, depending on whether the context is positive or negative (e.g., a street riot versus a street festival). Maintaining an "up" feeling in a pleasant context is one factor behind the success of theme parks such as Disney World that try to provide consistent doses of carefully calculated stimulation to visitors.[35] So, a specific mood is some combination of pleasure and arousal. For example, the state of happiness is high in pleasantness and moderate in arousal, whereas elation is high on both dimensions.[36] A mood state (either positive or negative) biases our judgments of products and services in that direction.[37] Put simply, we give more positive evaluations when we're in a good mood (this explains the popularity of the business lunch!).

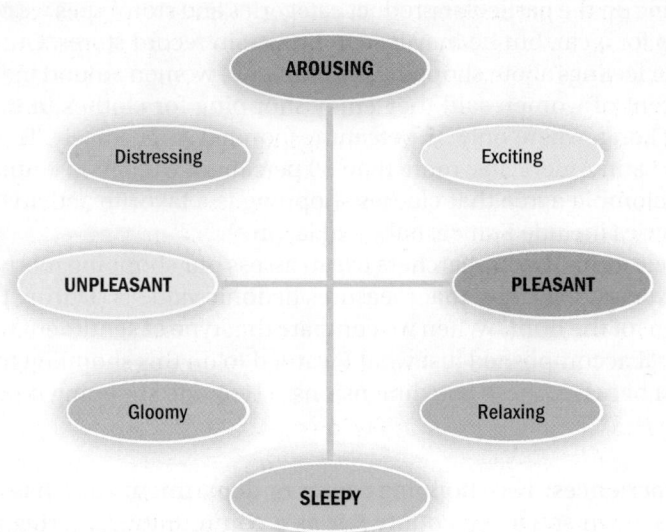

Many factors ranging from store design, the weather, or whether you just had a fight with your significant other affect your mood. Music and television programming do as well.[38] When consumers hear happy music or watch happy programs, they have more positive reactions to commercials and products.[39] And when we're in a good mood, we process ads with less elaboration. We pay less attention to specifics of the message and we rely more on heuristics (see Chapter 9).[40] Our emotional reactions to marketing cues are so powerful that some high-tech companies are developing techniques to study mood in very small doses (in 1/30 of a second increments) by analyzing people's facial reactions when they see ads or new products. They measure happiness by looking for differences between, for example, a true smile (which includes a relaxation of the upper eyelid) and a social smile (which occurs only around the mouth). Whirlpool used this technique to test consumers' emotional reactions to a yet-to-be-launched generation of its Duet washers and dryers. The company's goal: To design an appliance that will actually make people happy. Researchers discovered that even though test subjects said they weren't thrilled with some out-of-the-box design options, such as unusual color combinations, their facial expressions said otherwise.[41]

WHEN THE GOING GETS TOUGH, THE TOUGH GO SHOPPING

We all know some people who shop simply for the sport of it and others whom we have to drag to a mall. Shopping is a way to acquire needed products and services, but social motives for shopping also are important. Thus, shopping is an activity that we can perform for either utilitarian (functional or tangible) or hedonic (pleasurable or intangible) reasons.[42] Judging by the clusters of bored-looking men we often see napping on shopping center benches while their wives hit the stores—in sharp contrast to the "weekend warriors" who gleefully make their way through the aisles of Home Depot—can we equate this preference to the sex roles we discussed in Chapter 5? Some researchers suggest that most women "shop to love," whereas most men "shop to win." In this view, women find emotional fulfillment in the act of buying, whereas men shop to demonstrate their expertise.[43] Obviously, there are many exceptions to this viewpoint, but nonetheless it's clear that the reasons we shop are more complex than may appear on the surface.

Our Reasons for Shopping

Do people hate to shop or love it? It depends. We can segment consumers in terms of their **shopping orientation**, or general attitudes about shopping. These orientations vary depending on the particular product categories and store types we consider. Rob hates to shop for a car, but he may love to browse in record stores. Our culture also influences our feelings about shopping. In a survey of women around the world, more than 60 percent of women said they enjoy shopping for clothes in every country except Hong Kong, where only 39 percent responded so positively. The "shopping" prize goes to Latin Americans; more than 80 percent of women in countries such as Brazil and Colombia agree that clothes shopping is a favorite activity. Other high-scoring countries include France, Italy, and Japan.[44]

Some scale items that researchers use to assess our shopping motivations illustrates this diversity. One item that measures hedonic value is "During the trip, I felt the excitement of the hunt." When we compare that type of sentiment to a functional statement, "I accomplished just what I wanted to on this shopping trip," there's a clear contrast between these two dimensions.[45] Hedonic shopping motives include the following:[46]

- **Social experiences:** The shopping center or department store has replaced the traditional town square or county fair as a community gathering place. Many people (especially in suburban or rural areas) have no place else to spend their leisure time. That probably explains the popularity of late-night games American college students in some rural areas play at their local Wal-Mart. In addition to sports such as scavenger hunts, aisle football, and a relay race limbo under the shopping-cart stand, "10 in 10" is a big attraction. To play this game, students form into teams; each team has 10 minutes to put 10 items from anywhere in the store in a shopping cart. Then they turn their cart over to the opposing team, which has to figure out where the items came from and return them to the shelves where they belong (not so easy in a store stocked with more than 100,000 different items). The first team back to the checkout counters with an empty cart wins.[47] Note: If you get busted for playing this game, you did NOT learn about it here.
- **Sharing of common interests:** Stores frequently offer specialized goods that allow people with shared interests to communicate.
- **Interpersonal attraction:** Shopping centers are a natural place to congregate. The shopping mall is a favorite "hangout" for teenagers. It also represents a controlled, secure environment for the elderly, and many malls now feature "mall walkers' clubs" for early morning workouts.
- **Instant status:** As every salesperson knows, some people savor the experience of being waited on, even though they may not necessarily buy anything. One men's clothing salesman offered this advice: "Remember their size, remember what you sold them last time. Make them feel important! If you can make people feel important, they are going to come back. Everybody likes to feel important!"[48] When a team of researchers conducted in-depth interviews with women to understand what makes shopping a pleasurable experience, they found one motivation was role-playing. For example, one respondent dressed up for shopping excursions to upscale boutiques because she likes to pretend she is wealthy and have salespeople fall all over her.[49]
- **The thrill of the hunt:** Some people pride themselves on their knowledge of the marketplace. Unlike our car-buying friend Rob, they may relish the process of haggling and bargaining, viewing it almost as a sport.

E-COMMERCE: CLICKS VERSUS BRICKS

As more and more Web sites pop up to sell everything from refrigerator magnets to Mack trucks, marketers continue to debate how the online world affects their business.[50] In particular, many are losing sleep wondering whether e-commerce is destined to replace traditional retailing, work in concert with it, or perhaps even fade away to become another fad your kids will laugh about someday.

For marketers, the growth of online commerce is a sword that cuts both ways: On the one hand, they can reach customers around the world even if they're physically located 100 miles from nowhere. On the other hand, their competition now comes not only from the store across the street but also from thousands of Web sites spanning the globe. Also, when consumers obtain products directly from the manufacturer or wholesaler, the intermediary gets eliminated—the loyal, store-based retailers who carry the firm's products and who sell them at a marked-up price.[51] The clicks-versus-bricks dilemma is raging in the marketing world.

So what makes e-commerce sites successful? In a survey NPD Online conducted, 75 percent of online shoppers said that good customer service would make them shop at the site again.[52] And many successful e-tailers are learning that when they take advantage of technology to provide extra value they will attract and keep more customers. For example, Lands' End (www.LandsEnd.com) offers men and women

tuesday, 11:15 p.m.
buying a new dress.

bluefly℠

www.bluefly.com℠
the outlet store in your home℠

Women's, men's and kid's designer fashions.
Save up to 75%.   90-day money back guarantee.

E-commerce sites like Bluefly give shoppers the option of shopping without leaving home.

When is fast food even faster? When we can click for a Coke or text for a taco to go. The restaurant industry is investing in technology to attract on-the-go consumers who live or die by their BlackBerrys or mobile phones. The average American 18 years old and older buys a snack or a meal from a restaurant five times a week on average, and the industry finds that most people are unwilling to wait more than 5 minutes in a drive-through line. According to the National Restaurant Association, about 13 percent of Americans placed online food orders in 2006 and industry experts expect this number to mushroom as more eateries offer this service. As one busy salesperson who orders both breakfast and lunch online observed, "I'm saving time. I'm so adept at it now that I can actually do business on the phone while I'm placing my food order."[55]

a Virtual Model™ that lets them design a model matching their own body type so they can then "try on" the clothing they're looking at on the Web site. At the Cover Girl makeup site (covergirl.com), women build their own "beauty profile" that recommends colors to match their skin and hair types. Soon MTV viewers will be able to use their remote controls to purchase the CDs that go with the music videos they are seeing.

However, all is not perfect in the virtual world. E-commerce does have its limitations. Security is one important concern. We hear horror stories of consumers whose credit cards and other identity information is stolen. Although an individual's financial liability in most theft cases is limited to $50, the damage to his credit rating can last for years. Some shady companies are making money by prying and then selling personal information to others—one company promotes itself as "an amazing new tool that allows you to find out EVERYTHING you ever wanted to know about your friends, family, neighbors, employees, and even your boss!"[53] Of course, you can also find out a lot for free simply by checking out someone's Facebook page. Almost daily we hear of hackers getting into a business or even a government Web site and causing havoc. Businesses risk the loss of trade secrets and other proprietary information. Many must spend significant amounts to maintain security and conduct regular audits to ensure their site's integrity.

The actual shopping experience also puts e-commerce at a disadvantage. Although we may not mind buying a computer or a book on the Internet, it's not nearly as easy to try on a pair of shoes online as in a store. Even though most companies have very liberal return policies, consumers can still get stuck with large delivery and return shipping charges for items that don't fit or simply aren't the right color. E-commerce sales continue to grow, but they still account for a very small percentage of overall sales. Results from a recent survey point to frustrating experiences as a major factor standing in the way of more robust online shopping—59 percent of respondents said that when they have a bad encounter on a retailer's Web site this reduces their opinion of the company, and a whopping 82 percent said they're less likely to shop at the retailer's physical store. However, there is hope—IF retailers offer more engaging and interactive features on their Web sites. Shoppers are most interested in the following:

- The ability to click on an item to create a popup window with more details about the product including price, size, colors, and inventory availability.
- The ability to click on an item and add it to your cart without leaving the page you're on.
- The ability to "feel" merchandise through better imagery, more product descriptions, and details.
- The ability to enter all data related to your purchase on one page, rather than going through several checkout pages.
- The ability to mix and match product images on one page to determine whether they look good together.[54]

Table 10.2 summarizes some of the pros and cons of e-commerce. It's clear that traditional shopping isn't quite dead yet—but bricks-and-mortar retailers do need to work harder to give shoppers something they can't get (yet anyway) in the virtual world—a stimulating or pleasant environment. Now let's check out how they're doing that.

Retailing as Theater

The competition for customers is becoming even more intense as nonstore alternatives, from Web sites and print catalogs to TV shopping networks and home shopping parties, continue to multiply. With all of these shopping alternatives available, how can a traditional store compete? Shopping malls have tried to gain the loyalty of shoppers by appealing to their social motives as well as by providing access to desired

TABLE 10.2
PROS AND CONS OF E-COMMERCE

Benefits of E-Commerce	Limitations of E-Commerce
For the Consumer	**For the Consumer**
Shop 24 hours a day	Lack of security
Less traveling	Fraud
Can receive relevant information in seconds from any location	Can't touch items
	Exact colors may not reproduce on computer monitors
More choices of products	Expensive to order and then return
More products available to less-developed countries	Potential breakdown of human relationships
Greater price information	
Lower prices so that less affluent can purchase	
Participate in virtual auctions	
Fast delivery	
Electronic communities	
For the Marketer	**For the Marketer**
The world is the marketplace	Lack of security
Decreases costs of doing business	Must maintain site to reap benefits
Very specialized business can be successful	Fierce price competition
	Conflicts with conventional retailers
Real-time pricing	Legal issues not resolved

Source: Adapted from Michael R. Solomon and Elnora W. Stuart, *Welcome to Marketing.Com: The Brave New World of E-Commerce* (Upper Saddle River, NJ: Prentice Hall, 2001).

goods. Many malls are becoming giant entertainment centers, almost to the point that their traditional retail occupants seem like an afterthought. As one retailing executive put it, "Malls are becoming the new mini-amusement parks."[56] In the United States, it's commonplace to find carousels, miniature golf, skating rinks, or batting cages in a suburban mall. Hershey opened a make-believe factory smack in the middle of New York's Times Square. It features four steam machines, 380 feet of neon lighting, plus a moving message board that can be programmed for consumers who want to flash messages to surprise their loved ones.[57] The quest to entertain means that many stores are going all out to create imaginative environments that transport shoppers to fantasy worlds or provide other kinds of stimulation. We call this strategy **retail theming**. Innovative merchants today use four basic kinds of theming techniques:

1 *Landscape themes* rely on associations with images of nature, Earth, animals, and the physical body. American sporting goods retailer, Bass Pro Shops, for example, creates a simulated outdoor environment including pools stocked with fish.

2 *Marketscape themes* build on associations with man-made places. An example is The Venetian hotel in Las Vegas that lavishly recreates parts of the Italian city.

3 *Cyberspace themes* are built around images of information and communications technology. eBay's retail interface instills a sense of community among its vendors and traders.

4 *Mindscape themes* draw on abstract ideas and concepts, introspection and fantasy, and often possess spiritual overtones. The Kiva day spa in downtown Chicago offers health treatments based on a theme of Native American healing ceremonies and religious practices.[58]

Wired magazine opened its own temporary pop-up store. By permission of the New York Sun ©.

Cutting-edge retailers are figuring out that they need to convert a store into a **being space** that resembles a commercial living room where we can go to relax, be entertained, hang out with friends, escape the everyday, or even learn. When you think of being spaces, Starbucks will probably come to mind. The coffee chain's stated goal is to become our "third place," where we spend the bulk of our time in addition to home and work. Starbucks led the way when it outfitted its stores with comfy chairs and WiFi. But there are many other marketers who are meeting our needs for exciting commercial spaces—no matter what those needs are. In Asia, venues such as Manboo and Fujiyama Land provide havens where gamers can do their thing 24/7—and even take a shower on-site during a break. Other spaces cater to the needs of **minipreneurs** (one-person businesses) by offering work-centered being spaces. At New York's Paragraph, writers who need a quiet place to ruminate can hang out in a loft that's divided into a writing room and a lounge area. TwoRooms ("You Work, They Play") provides office space and childcare for home-based workers.

Reflecting the ever-quickening pace of our culture, many of these being spaces are deliberately temporary. **Pop-up stores** are appearing in many forms around the world. Typically, these are makeshift installations that do business only for a few days or weeks and then disappear before they get old. Some interesting examples from around the world include these:

- American Apparel opened a 45-day pop-up store in New York featuring daily spontaneous events such as karaoke, dreidel spinning, and mariachi performances.
- The Swatch Instant Store appeared in London, Paris, Barcelona, Amsterdam, and Berlin. The stores sold limited edition watches; as soon as the masses discovered a store, it closed.
- Caravan is a fashion boutique on wheels that turns up unannounced in different New York locations to offer a mix of hip clothing, accessories, gift items, and art.

- In The Netherlands, Dommelsch Beer organized pop-up concerts featuring well-known performers. Fans could enter barcodes they found on cans, beer bottles, and coasters on the brewer's Web site to discover dates and locations.
- Nintendo set up a Pokémon theme park for 6 months in Nagoya, Japan. From there it moved on to other cities for 3-month stints.
- Choice Hotels International built a full-size pop-up guest suite at the Boise International Airport to plug its Cambria Suites. The 13-foot by 30-foot model included two working flat-panel televisions, in-room CD/DVD players, and a spalike bathroom.
- At the LG Wash Bar in Paris, visitors could enjoy music and a drink while doing their laundry. Staff helped customers with their laundry, demonstrating the equipment as needed. Every Tuesday customers who dressed from head to toe in white got free "Whiter than white" (Plus Blanc que Blanc) cocktails.
- The Kodak One Gallery was a month-long interactive space in New York and San Francisco. In addition to exhibits of its latest products, there were artists' exhibits, and professional photographers offered master classes.[59]

Store Image

With so many stores competing for customers, how do we ever pick one over another? As with products (see Chapter 6), stores have "personalities." Some shops have very clearly defined images (either good or bad). Others tend to blend into the crowd. They may not have anything distinctive about them and we may just overlook them. Many different factors determine this personality, or **store image**. Store features, coupled with such consumer characteristics as shopping orientation, help to predict which shopping outlets we prefer.[60] Some of the important dimensions of a store's profile are location, merchandise suitability, and the knowledge and congeniality of the sales staff.[61]

Store image is a crucial part of the shopping experience for all kinds of products and services. Today, even automobile dealers are ramping up their efforts to craft a distinctive retail presence (recall how Kyle made inferences about a car dealership from its physical appearance). Hummer's showrooms feature exposed concrete, metal rafters, and helicopter-like ceiling fans. With arched roofs and 20-foot-high front windows that lean outward, the newly designed Audi dealerships look a little like airport hangars. They replicate the company's German factory, where customers often go to pick up new cars as they roll off the line.[62]

These design features typically work together to create an overall impression. When we think about stores, we don't usually say, "Well, that place is fairly good in terms of convenience, the salespeople are acceptable, and services are good." We're

A recent makeover of FedEx retail outlets illustrates the crucial role design can play in communicating a desirable store image. As shown in the before-and-after shots, consumer research conducted by Ziba Design for FedEx indicated that compared to its main competitors, the firm's brand personality was more innovative, leading-edge, and outgoing—but this impression was certainly not reinforced by its cluttered storefront locations where customers go to drop off packages for delivery. The designers used colors and shapes associated with these attributes to make-over the stores.

more likely to proclaim, "That place gives me the creeps," or "It's a rush to shop there." We quickly get an overall impression of a store, and the feeling we get may have more to do with intangibles, such as interior design and the types of people we find there, than with the store's return policies or credit availability. As a result, some stores routinely pop up in our consideration sets (see Chapter 9), whereas we never consider others. ("Only geeks shop there!")[63]

 ## Atmospherics

Because marketers recognize that a store's image is a very important part of the retailing mix, store designers pay a lot of attention to **atmospherics**, the "conscious designing of space and its various dimensions to evoke certain effects in buyers."[64] These dimensions include colors, scents, and sounds. For example, stores with red interiors tend to make people tense, whereas a blue decor imparts a calmer feeling.[65] As Chapter 2 noted, some preliminary evidence also indicates that odors (olfactory cues) influence our evaluations of a store's environment.[66]

A store's atmosphere in turn affects what we buy. In one study, researchers who asked shoppers how much pleasure they were feeling 5 minutes after they entered a store predicted the amount of time and money they spent there.[67] To boost the entertainment value of shopping (and to lure online shoppers back to bricks-and-mortar stores), some retailers now offer **activity stores** that let consumers participate in the production of the products or services they buy there:

● The Build-A-Bear Workshop chain provides customers with a selection of empty bear bodies that they stuff, fluff, and dress in costumes ranging from bridal veils to baseball gloves. Customers use an in-store computer to print each bear's "birth certificate" and special wish.

● At a chain of stores catering to preteen girls called Club Libby Lu, girls enter a fantasyland environment where they dress as princesses and mix their own fragrances.

● Viking Range Corp. has combined its kitchen appliances with cooking lessons through almost a dozen stores in two chains, Viking Home Chef and Viking

Expo-Xplore, part of a new shopping complex near Durban, South Africa, is the next wave in retail and entertainment design. The courtyard, lined with retailers selling clothes and gear for a variety of outdoor adventure sports, leads to Planet Blue, the ocean-themed heart of the project, with stores oriented around scuba diving, boating, surfing, and other water sports.

CB AS I SEE IT

Professor Cele Otnes
*University of Illinois
at Urbana-Champaign*

How can retailers make consumers' in-store experiences more meaningful in order to positively influence key attitudinal and behavioral measures, such as brand loyalty and likelihood of repeat purchasing? One research topic that relates to this question is how retailers use in-store rituals to shape consumers' experiences. *Rituals* are expressive, dramatic events that can be repeated over time with the same or different consumers that make experiences more meaningful (for more on rituals, see Chapter 16). As the opening vignette of this chapter indicates, many consumers find the car-buying experience exhausting and discouraging. But when GM created the Saturn brand in 1990, it positioned the car-buying experience as more customer friendly than that of its competitors. One innovative tactic for communicating this message is the Saturn "delivery ceremony." When customers buy a car at Saturn, every available salesperson surrounds the customer's new car, meets and thanks the customer, and performs the "Saturn cheer." The salesperson in charge of the transaction then takes a picture of the customer in his or her new car and offers up a small Saturn-related gift. The customer then drives away, and the Saturn team waves goodbye. Participation for salespeople is mandatory, and this ceremony could be repeated dozens of times a week during a busy selling time.

Sound corny? It's worth remembering that love it or hate it, customers talk about the Saturn delivery ceremony long after they have left the dealership. Our research explores whether and how these types of rituals actually impact customers' experience with a brand. We have interviewed more than 20 retailers and service providers who identify themselves as using rituals designed for their employees or customers in order to try and enhance their relationships with these stakeholders, to improve efficiency, and to differentiate themselves for their competitors. We're exploring such issues as how consumers resist rituals (as in, "Please don't make me go through the Saturn delivery ceremony again!"), how consumers help co-create rituals with other shoppers and with retailers (as is the case at Build-A-Bear, when consumers engage in grooming rituals with the toys they've just created), and whether and how these rituals actually enhance consumers' retail experiences. From a strategic perspective, we will also explore whether ritualizing the shopping experience allows retailers to charge premium prices, to be forgiven more easily if they make mistakes with consumers, and to allocate less of their money to marketing communications. So next time you buy a Saturn, stand in line at Marble Slab Creamery, or wear a "birthday sombrero" on your head at your favorite Mexican restaurant, remember—you've been ritualized!

Culinary Academy. The stores have built-in classrooms offering lessons in a full spectrum of cuisine from gingerbread-house building to Indian cuisine. Products in the store change to match the lessons.[68]

Retailers can cleverly engineer their store designs to attract customers. Light colors impart a feeling of spaciousness and serenity, and signs in bright colors create excitement. In one subtle but effective application, fashion designer Norma Kamali replaced fluorescent lights with pink ones in department store dressing rooms. The light flattered shoppers' faces and banished wrinkles, so women were more willing to try on (and buy) the company's bathing suits.[69] Wal-Mart found that sales were higher in areas of a prototype store lit in natural daylight compared to the artificial light in its regular stores.[70] One study found that shoppers in stores with brighter in-store lighting examined and handled more merchandise.[71]

In addition to visual stimuli, all sorts of cues can influence behaviors.[72] For example, patrons of country-and-western bars drink more when the jukebox music is slower. According to a researcher, "Hard drinkers prefer listening to slower-paced, wailing, lonesome, self-pitying music."[73] Music also can affect eating habits. Another study found that diners who listened to loud, fast music ate more food. In contrast, those who listened to Mozart or Brahms ate less and more slowly. The researchers concluded that diners who choose soothing music at mealtimes can increase weight loss by at least 5 pounds a month![74]

IN-STORE DECISION MAKING

Despite all their efforts to "pre-sell" consumers through advertising, marketers increasingly recognize that the store environment exerts a strong influence on many purchases. Women tell researchers, for example, that store displays are one of the major information sources they use to decide what clothing to buy.[75] This influence is even stronger when we shop for food—analysts estimate that shoppers decide on about two out of every three supermarket purchases while walking through the aisles. And people with shopping lists are just as likely to make spontaneous purchases as those without them.[76]

Marketers are scrambling to engineer purchasing environments in order to increase the likelihood they connect with consumers at the exact time they make a decision. This strategy even applies to drinking behavior: Diageo, the world's largest liquor company, discovered that 60 percent of bar customers don't know what they will drink until seconds before they place their orders. To make it more likely that the customer's order will include Smirnoff vodka, Johnnie Walker Scotch, or one of its other brands, Diageo launched its Drinks Invigoration Team to increase what it calls its "share of throat." The Dublin-based team experiments with bar "environments" and bottle-display techniques, and comes up with drinks to match customers' moods. For example, the company researchers discovered that bubbles stimulate the desire for spirits, so it's developing bubble machines to put in back of bars. Diageo has even categorized bars into types and identifies types of drinkers—and the drinks they prefer—who frequent each. These include "style bars," where cutting-edge patrons like to sip fancy fresh-fruit martinis, and "buzz bars," where the clientele likes to drink Smirnoff mixed with energy brew Red Bull.[77]

Spontaneous Shopping

When a shopper suddenly decides to buy something in the store, one of two different processes explains this:

1 She engages in *unplanned buying* when she's unfamiliar with a store's layout or perhaps she's under some time pressure. Or, seeing an item on a store shelf might remind her she needs it. About one-third of all unplanned buying occurs because a shopper recognizes a new need while she's in the store.[78]
2 Or she engages in **impulse buying** when she experiences a sudden urge she simply can't resist. The tendency to buy spontaneously is most likely to result in a purchase when she believes acting on impulse is appropriate, such as purchasing a gift for a sick friend or picking up the tab for a meal.[79] A consumer who researchers asked to sketch a typical impulse purchaser during a study on consumers' shopping experiences drew Figure 10.4.

To cater to these urges, retailers conveniently place so-called *impulse items*, such as candy and gum, near the checkout. Similarly, many supermarkets install wider aisles to encourage browsing, and the widest tend to contain products with the highest profit margins. They stack low markup items that shoppers purchase regularly in narrower aisles to allow shopping carts to speed through.[80] And some retailers have added a high-tech tool to encourage impulse buying: The Portable Shopper is a personal scanning gun that allows customers to ring up their own purchases as they shop. Albert Hejin, the Netherlands' largest grocery chain, initially developed the gun to move customers through the store more quickly.[81] Sony devised a unique way to cash in on impulse buying in the online world. Gamers who are playing its

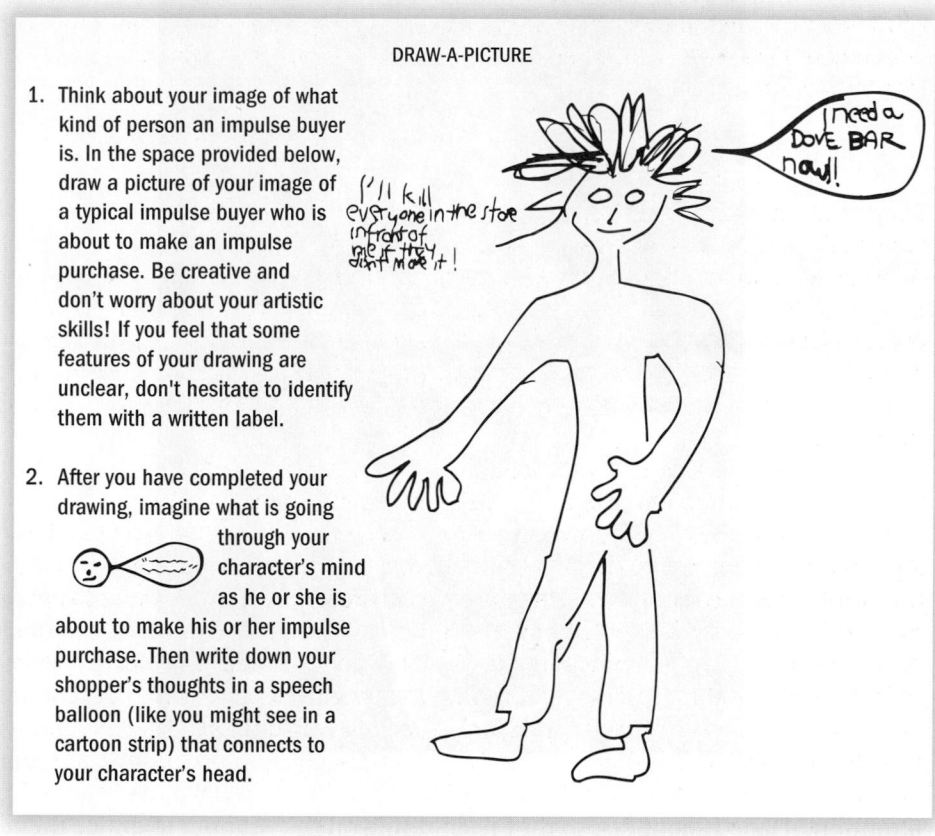

Source: Dennis Rock, "Is Impulse Buying (Yet) a Useful Marketing Concept?" (unpublished manuscript, University of Southern California, Los Angeles, 1990): Fig. 7-A.

popular multiplayer game Everquest II don't have to take a munchie break: They can just type the command "/ pizza" and jump directly to the Pizza Hut Web site, where they place a delivery order without interrupting their game.[82] Now, Starbucks is getting in on the action of impulse purchasing. The chain recently introduced a service in some of its outlets that lets a person with an iPhone or iTunes software loaded onto a laptop download the songs they hear over the store's speakers directly onto those devices at 99 cents a pop.[83]

Point-of-Purchase Stimuli

A well-designed in-store display can boost impulse purchases by as much as 10 percent. That explains why U.S. companies spend more than $13 billion each year on **point-of-purchase (POP) stimuli**. A POP can be an elaborate product display or demonstration, a coupon-dispensing machine, or even someone giving out free samples of a new cookie in the grocery aisle. Now the pace of POP spending will probably pick up even more—an alliance of major marketers including Procter & Gamble, Coca-Cola, 3M, Kellogg, Miller Brewing, and Wal-Mart is using infrared sensors to measure the reach of in-store marketing efforts. Retailers have long counted the number of shoppers who enter and exit their stores, and they use product barcode data to track what shoppers buy. But big consumer-products companies also need to know how many people actually walk by their promotional displays so they can evaluate how effective these are. Although it's possible to fool these sensors (they still can't tell if someone is simply cutting through to reach the other end of the store), this sophisticated measurement system is a valuable first step that many advertisers eagerly await.[85]

The increasing importance of POP also explains why product packages are morphing from functional to fantastic. Marketers are desperate to grab the

Net Profit

The ShopText company introduced a system that's an impulse buyer's dream (or nightmare). It lets you buy a product instantly by sending a text message; you don't even have to visit a store or a Web site. A woman who spies an ad for a pocketbook in a magazine can order it on the spot simply by using her cell phone to send the code she finds printed next to the item. This type of system is already in limited use. Ads for a CD by singer Tim McGraw carry a texting code, as did magazine write-ups for the final Harry Potter novel. Some charities now accept donations via text messages. To use the system, a consumer must first call ShopText to set up an account and specify a shipping address and credit card number. After that, she can buy everything by thumb.[84]

Smart retailers recognize that many purchase decisions are made at the time the shopper is in the store. That's one reason why grocery carts sometimes resemble billboards on wheels.

attention of jaded shoppers, so they're counting on the wrapper to entice them to stop and look:

- In the last 100 years, Pepsi had changed the look of its can, and before that its bottles, only 10 times. Now the company switches designs every few weeks. And, it's experimenting with cans that spray an aroma when you open one to match the flavor of the drink—such as a wild cherry scent misting from a Wild Cherry Pepsi can.
- Coors Light beer bottles sport labels that turn blue when the beer is chilled to the right temperature.
- Huggies' Henry the Hippo hand soap bottles have a light that flashes for 20 seconds to show children how long they should wash their hands.
- Evian's new "palace bottle" is being sold in restaurants and luxury hotels. The bottle has an elegant swanlike neck and sits on a small silver tray.
- Unilever North America sells Axe shower gel bottles shaped like video-game joysticks.
- Some companies are even playing around with the idea of putting a computer chip and tiny speaker inside a package. This gimmick might be useful for cross-promotion. For example, a package of cheese could say "I go well with Triscuit crackers" when a shopper takes it off the shelf. Of course, this attention-getting trick could backfire if everyone starts to do it. As one ad executive commented, "If you're walking down a row in a supermarket and every package is screaming at you, it sounds like a terrifying, disgusting experience." Everything in moderation . . .[86]

The Salesperson: A Lead Role in the Play

The salesperson is one of the most important players in the retailing drama—as Rob learned in his interaction with Rhoda.[87] We can understand this influence in terms of exchange theory, which stresses that every interaction involves an exchange of

Dynamic store displays play an increasingly important sales function.

value. Each participant gives something to the other and hopes to receive something in return.[88] A (competent) salesperson offers a lot of value because his expert advice makes the shopper's choice easier. The Central Market in Austin employs a team of "foodies" who wander through the store talking to customers about cooking and suggesting ways they can master their kitchen domain.[89]

It's no coincidence that Rhoda was an effective salesperson. In fact, a long stream of research attests to the impact of a salesperson's appearance on sales effectiveness. In sales, as in much of life, attractive people appear to hold the upper hand (see Chapter 5).[90] In addition, it's not unusual for service personnel and customers to form fairly warm personal relationships; researchers call these *commercial friendships* (think of all those patient bartenders who double as therapists for many people). Commercial friendships are similar to other friendships in that they can involve affection, intimacy, social support, loyalty, and reciprocal gift giving. They also work to support marketing objectives such as satisfaction, loyalty, and positive word of mouth.[91]

Marketing Pitfall

Not all sales interactions are positive, but some *really* stand out. Here are a few incidents that make the rest of them easier to swallow:

- A woman sued a car dealer in Iowa, claiming that a salesperson persuaded her to climb into the trunk of a Chrysler Concorde to check out its spaciousness. He then slammed the trunk shut and bounced the car several times, apparently to the delight of his co-workers. This bizarre act apparently came about because the manager offered a prize of $100 to the salesperson who could get a customer to climb in.[92]

- A Detroit couple filed a $100 million lawsuit against McDonald's, alleging three McDonald's employees beat them after they tried to return a watery milkshake.

- In Alabama, a McDonald's employee was arrested on second-degree assault charges after stabbing a customer in the forehead with a ballpoint pen.[93]

Music samplers that allow shoppers to check out the latest music tunes before buying have become a fixture in many stores. New versions allow listeners to select files, record them onto a CD, and even select the cover and clip art to personalize it.

A buyer–seller situation is like many other *dyadic encounters* (two-person groups); it is a relationship where both parties must reach some agreement about the roles of each participant during a process of *identity negotiation*.[94] For example, if Rhoda immediately establishes herself as an expert (and Rob accepts this position), she is likely to have more influence over him through the course of the relationship. Some of the factors that help to define a salesperson's role (and effectiveness) are her age, appearance, educational level, and motivation to sell.[95]

In addition, more effective salespersons usually know their customers' traits and preferences better than do ineffective salespersons, and they adapt their approach to meet the needs of each specific customer.[96] The ability to be adaptable is especially vital when customers and salespeople have different *interaction styles*.[97] We each vary in the degree of assertiveness we bring to interactions. At one extreme, nonassertive people believe that complaining is not socially acceptable and they may be intimidated in sales situations. Assertive people are more likely to stand up for themselves in a firm but nonthreatening way. Aggressives may resort to rudeness and threats if they do not get their way.[98] Some recent research also finds that salespeople's degree of confidence determines how happy they will be in their jobs. David's Bridal, America's biggest bridal-store chain, sponsored research to understand the dynamics of selling wedding dresses to anxious brides-to-be (often a stressful encounter). The researcher who conducted the work trained the staff to focus on things that bring them joy when they deal with an indecisive customer.[99]

POSTPURCHASE SATISFACTION

Our overall feelings about a product after we've purchased it—what researchers call **consumer satisfaction/dissatisfaction (CS/D)**—obviously play a big role in our future behavior. It's a lot easier to sell something once than to sell it again if it bombed the first time. We all evaluate the things we buy as we use them and integrate them into our daily consumption activities.[100] In a sense, each of us is a product reviewer regardless of whether we write down these thoughts. Companies that provide satisfaction do more than good deeds, delivering good service also provides a competitive advantage. In Chapter 9 we saw how satisfying customers is a determinant attribute that leads them to choose one company over others. A recent 5-year study of customer satisfaction in the Canadian banking industry provides typical results—banks that provided better service commanded a larger "share of wallet" than did others (i.e., their customers entrusted them with a larger proportion of their money).[101]

Good marketers are constantly on the lookout for reasons why their customers might be dissatisfied so they can try to improve their experiences.[102] For example, United Airlines' advertising agency set out to identify specific aspects of air travel that ticked people off. It gave frequent fliers crayons and a map showing different stages in a long distance trip. Then they had to color in these stages, using hot hues to symbolize areas that cause stress and anger and cool colors for parts of the trip they associate with satisfaction and calm feelings. Although these passengers tended to color jet cabins with a serene aqua color, lo and behold, they colored the ticket counters orange and terminal waiting areas fire-red. As a result, United focused more on improving its overall operations instead of only the in-flight experience, and this change in turn resulted in the "United Rising" campaign.[103]

 # What Is Quality?

Just what do consumers look for in products? That's easy: They want quality and value. Especially because of international competition, claims of product quality have become strategically crucial to maintain a competitive advantage.[104] We infer quality by relying on cues as diverse as brand name, price, product warranties and even our estimate of how much money a company invested in a new product's advertising campaign.[105]

Although everyone wants quality, it is not clear exactly what it means. Certainly, many manufacturers claim to provide it. The Ford Motor Company emphasizes, "Quality is Job 1." But virtually every other carmaker also makes quality claims.[106]

- **Lincoln Mercury:** "the highest quality cars of any major American car company"
- **Chrysler:** "quality engineered to be the best"
- **GMC Trucks:** "quality built yet economical"
- **Oldsmobile:** "fulfilling the quality needs of American drivers"
- **Audi:** "quality backed by our outstanding new warranty"

QUALITY IS WHAT WE EXPECT IT TO BE

In the book *Zen and the Art of Motorcycle Maintenance*, a cult hero of college students in an earlier generation literally went crazy trying to figure out the meaning of quality.[107] Marketers appear to use the word "quality" as a catchall term for "good." Because of its wide and imprecise usage, the attribute of *quality* threatens to become a meaningless claim. If everyone has it, what good is it?

To muddy the waters a bit more, satisfaction or dissatisfaction is more than a reaction to the actual performance quality of a product or service. Our prior expectations strongly influence what we think quality is. According to the **expectancy disconfirmation model**, we form beliefs about product performance based on prior experience with the product or communications about the product that imply a certain level of quality.[108] When something performs the way we thought it would, we may not think much about it. If it fails to live up to expectations, this may create negative feelings. However, if performance happens to exceed our expectations, we are satisfied and pleased.

To understand this perspective, think about different types of restaurants. Diners expect sparkling clear glassware at fancy restaurants, and they won't be happy if they discover a grimy glass. However, they may not be surprised to find fingerprints on a beer mug at a local greasy spoon; they may even shrug it off because it

This ad for Ford relies on a common claim about quality.

Marketing Pitfall

Consumers aren't the only ones who get angry about service interactions. Many employees have an axe to grind as well. At a Web site a disgruntled former employee of a certain fast-food franchise put up, we share the pain of this ex-burger flipper: "I have seen the creatures that live at the bottom of the dumpster. I have seen the rat by the soda machine. I have seen dead frogs in the fresh salad lettuce."[111] Fries with that?

At the customerssuck.com Web site, restaurant and store workers who have to grin and bear it all day go to vent. Once off the clock, they can share their frustrations about the idiocy, slovenliness, and insensitivity of their customers. Some contributors to the Web site share stupid questions their customers ask, such as "How much is a 99-cent cheeseburger?" whereas others complain about working

contributes to the place's "charm." An important lesson for marketers: Don't over-promise if you can't deliver.[109]

This perspective underscores the importance of *managing expectations*—in fact we can often trace a customer's dissatisfaction to his erroneous expectations of the company's ability to deliver a product or service. NO company is perfect so it's just not realistic to think that everything will always turn out perfectly (although some firms don't even come close!). Figure 10.5 illustrates the alternative strategies a firm can choose in these situations. When it's confronted with unrealistic expectations about what it can do, the firm can either accommodate these demands by improving the range or quality of products it offers, alter these expectations, or perhaps even choose to abandon the customer if it is not feasible to meet his needs.[110] How can a marketer alter expectations? For example, a waiter can tell a diner in advance that the portion size she ordered isn't very big, or a car salesperson can warn a buyer that he may smell some strange odors during the break-in period. A firm also can underpromise, as Xerox routinely does when it inflates the time it will take for a service rep to visit. When the rep arrives a day earlier, this simply impresses the customer.

■ **FIGURE 10.5** CUSTOMER EXPECTATION ZONES

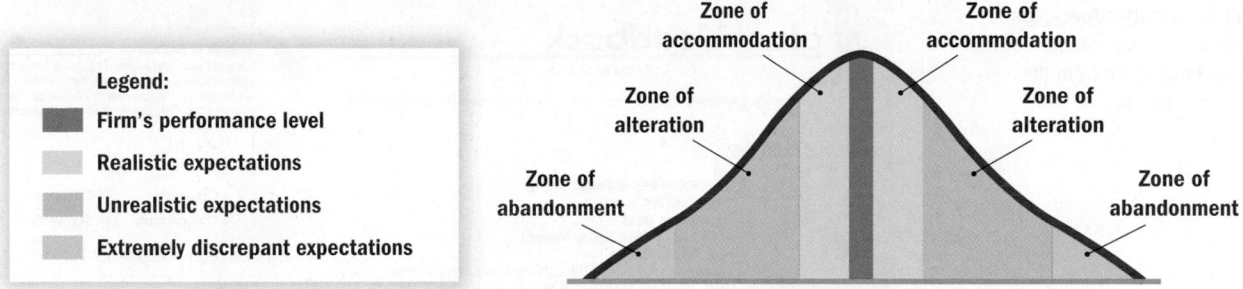

Legend:
- Firm's performance level
- Realistic expectations
- Unrealistic expectations
- Extremely discrepant expectations

Zone of accommodation
Zone of alteration
Zone of abandonment

Source: Dennis Rook, "Is Impulse Buying (Yet) a Useful Marketing Concept?" (unpublished manuscript, University of Southern California, Los Angeles, 1990): Fig 7-A. Copyright © 1990 Dennis Rook. Used with permission.

When a product doesn't work as we expect or turns out to be unsafe (like the recent spate of hazardous products from China, ranging from toothpaste to dog food), it's the understatement of the year to say we're not happy campers. In these situations, marketers must immediately take steps to reassure us or risk losing a customer for life. When the company confronts the problem truthfully, we are often willing to forgive and forget, as was the case for Tylenol (product tampering), Chrysler (disconnecting odometers on executives' cars and reselling them as new), or Perrier (traces of benzene found in the water). But if the firm seems to be dragging its heels or covering up, our resentment grows. This is what happened during Union Carbide's chemical disaster in India, the massive Alaskan oil spill the tanker *Exxon Valdez* caused, and recent corporate scandals such as the collapse of Enron.

Acting on Dissatisfaction

Fifty-four million dollars for a pair of missing pants? A judge in Washington, DC, made the headlines when he filed a $54 million lawsuit against his neighborhood dry cleaner that he accused of losing a pair of his pinstriped suit paints. He claimed that a D.C. consumer protection law entitled him to thousands of dollars for each day over nearly 4 years in which signs at the shop promised "same day service" and "satisfaction guaranteed." The suit dragged on for several months, but at the end of the day the plaintiff went home with empty pockets.[116]

If you're not happy with a product or service, what can you do about it? You have three possible courses of action (though sometimes you can take more than one):[117]

1   **Voice response:** You can appeal directly to the retailer for redress (e.g., a refund).
2   **Private response:** You can express your dissatisfaction to friends and boycott the product or the store where you bought it.
3   **Third-party response:** Like the pantsless judge, you can take legal action against the merchant, register a complaint with the Better Business Bureau, or perhaps write a letter to the newspaper.

In one study, business majors wrote complaint letters to companies. When the company sent a free sample in response, this significantly improved their feelings about the company. This didn't happen, however, when they only received a letter of apology but no swag. Even worse, students who got no response reported an even more negative image than before, indicating that *any* kind of response is better than none.[118]

A number of factors influence which route to dealing with dissatisfaction we will choose. People are more likely to take action for expensive products such as household durables, cars, and clothing than for inexpensive products.[119] Ironically, consumers who are satisfied with a store in general are more likely to complain if they experience something bad; they take the time to complain because they feel connected to the store. Older people are more likely to complain, and they are much

conditions and having to be nice to not-so-nice people. The slogan of the site is "the customer is never right."[112]

Indeed, many dissatisfied customers and disgruntled former employees have created their own Web sites simply to share their tales of woe with others. A Web site for people to complain about the Dunkin' Donuts chain got to be so popular the company bought it in order to control the bad press it was getting. A customer initially created the site to express his outrage over the fact that he was unable to get skim milk for his coffee.[113] As a media lawyer observed, "The person who, 20 years ago, was confined to walking up and down outside Chase Bank with a placard can now publish to millions of people with the click of a button."[114] And, a single individual can do a lot of damage in cyberspace. One famous hacker who went by the *nom de guerre* of Pimpshiz hacked into more than 200 Web sites before he was finally arrested.[115]

The Internet lets customers "vent." In addition to blogging about bad experiences, they can tell it all on planetfeedback.com, which in turn shares these complaints with companies so they can benefit from the (sometimes harsh) feedback.

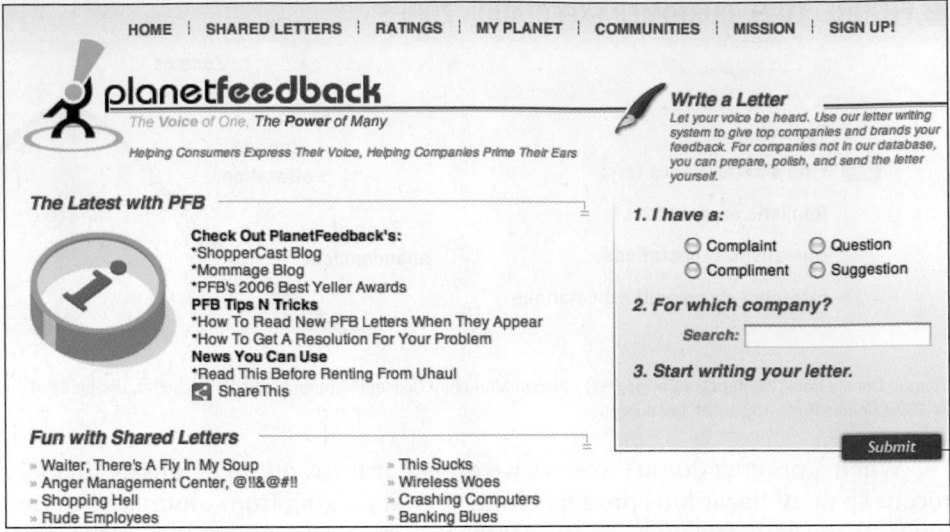

more likely to believe the store will actually resolve the problem. Shoppers who get their problems resolved feel even *better* about the store than if nothing had gone wrong.[120] However, if the consumer does not believe that the store will respond well to a complaint, the person will be more likely to simply switch than fight.[121] The moral: Marketers should actually *encourage* consumers to complain to them: People are more likely to spread the word about unresolved negative experiences to their friends than they are to boast about positive occurrences.[122]

TQM: Going to the Gemba

Many analysts who study consumer satisfaction, or who are trying to design new products or services to increase it, recognize that it is crucial to understand how people actually interact with their environment in order to identify potential problems. They typically conduct these investigations in focus groups where a small set of consumers comes into a facility to try a new item while company personnel observe them from behind a mirror. However, some researchers advocate a more up-close-and-personal approach that allows them to watch people in the actual environment where they consume the product. This perspective grew out of the Japanese approach to **total quality management (TQM)**, a complex set of management and engineering procedures aimed at reducing errors and increasing quality.

To help them achieve more insight, researchers go to the ***gemba***, which to the Japanese means the one true source of information. According to this philosophy, it's essential to send marketers and designers to the precise place where consumers use the product or service rather than asking laboratory subjects to interact with it in a simulated environment. Figure 10.6 illustrates this idea in practice. Host Foods, which operates food concessions in major U.S. airports, sent a team to the gemba—in this case, an airport cafeteria—to identify problem areas. Employees watched as customers chose to (or didn't) enter the facility, then followed them as they inspected the menu, procured silverware, paid, and found a table. The findings were crucial to Host's redesign of the facility to make it easier to use. For example, the team identified a common problem many people traveling solo experience: the need to put down one's luggage to enter the food line and the feeling of panic you get because you're not able to keep an eye on your valuables while you're getting your meal.[124]

PRODUCT DISPOSAL

Because people often do form strong attachments to products, when we decide to dispose of something, this can be a painful decision. Our possessions serve as anchors

Net Profit

To be more responsive to its' customers, Dell created a social networking community it calls *Idea Storm*. This is an online forum for users to submit suggestions about its products; people have deluged the site with thousands of recommendations and comments. Increasingly, companies are figuring out that they're better off revealing their flaws to their customers than pretending to be foolproof—and having to explain away failures later. For example, Delta Airlines (an established player in an industry notorious for low customer satisfaction) recently created its own Web site, Change.Delta.com that hosts suggestions from consumers—"Bigger blankets, please"—as well as polls about features and offerings.[123]

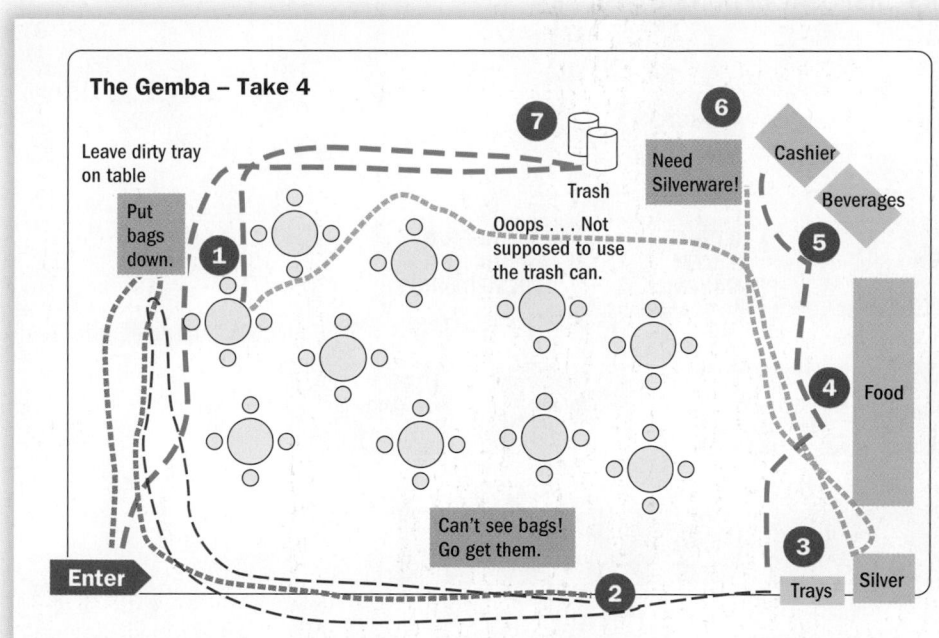

■ **FIGURE 10.6**
GOING TO THE GEMBA
Source: © Quality Function Deployment Institute. Used with permission.

for our identities because our past lives on in our things.[125] Some Japanese ritually "retire" worn-out sewing needles, chopsticks, and even computer chips by burning them to thank them for years of good service.[126]

Although some people have more trouble than others in discarding things, even a "pack rat" does not keep everything. We all have to get rid of our "stuff" at some point, either because it's served its purpose or perhaps because it no longer fits with our view of ourselves (like when newlyweds "upgrade" to a real place). Concern about the environment coupled with a need for convenience makes ease of product disposal a key attribute in categories from razors to diapers. And our demand for sustainable products that don't strain the environment when we're done with them is creating new markets (such as carbon offsets) and new opportunities for entrepreneurs who find a better alternative in an existing category.

For example, America's Terra Cycle is a start-up brand that's found success selling an "exotic" product: a key ingredient on its label is "liquefied worm poop." A 25-year-old college dropout founded the company—company literature confesses that he was trying to grow "certain plants" in a worm bin inside his college apartment in order to "harvest the buds" when he stumbled on the idea. Inspiration comes from many sources! Terra Cycle makes fertilizer products it packages in used plastic bottles, many of which the company itself collects through a nationwide recycling program it organized. Terra Cycle claims that waste packaged in waste makes it the "ultimate ecofriendly" product. The fertilizer comes from containers filled with shredded newspaper, food scraps—and worms who eat this waste and digest it. The resulting "poop" happens to make great plant food.[127]

Disposal Options

When a consumer decides that a product is no longer of use, he has several choices: (1) keep the item, (2) temporarily dispose of it, or (3) permanently dispose of it. In many cases, the person acquires a new product even though the old one still functions. Some reasons for replacing an item include a desire for new features, a change in the person's environment (e.g., a refrigerator is the wrong color for a freshly painted kitchen), or a change in the person's role or self-image.[128] Figure 10.7 provides an overview of consumers' disposal options.

■ **FIGURE 10.7**   CONSUMERS' DISPOSAL OPTIONS

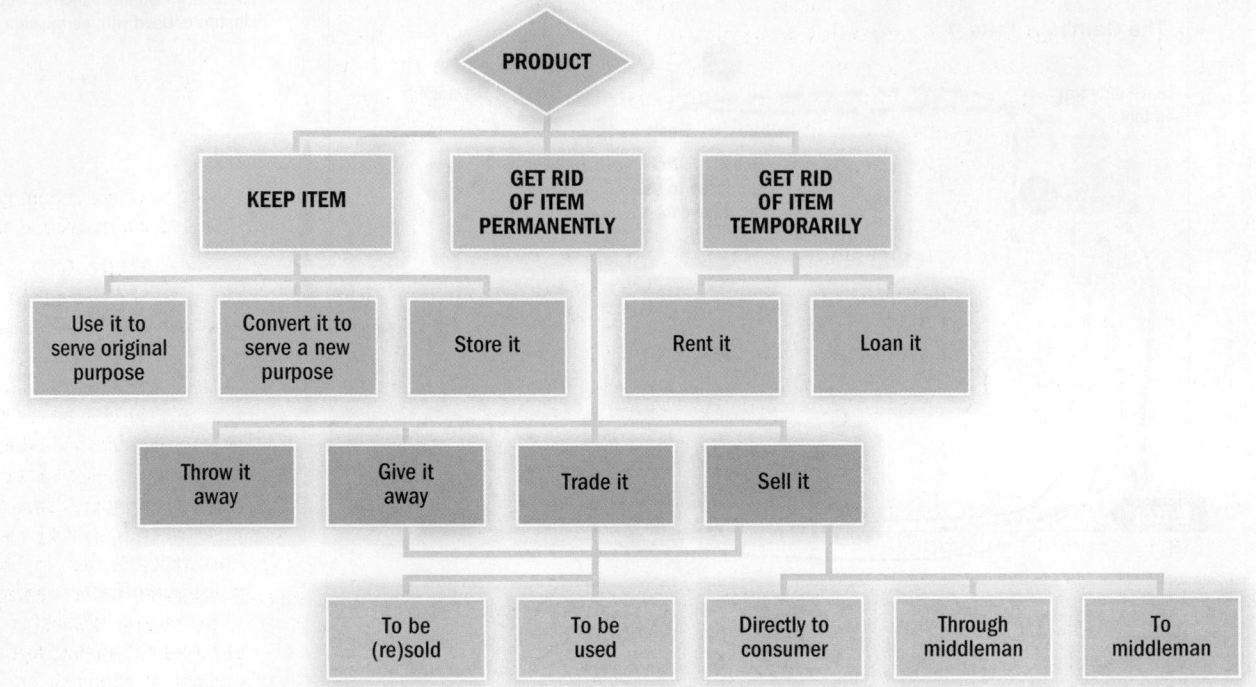

Source: Jacob Jacoby, Carol K. Berning, and Thomas S. Dietvorst, "What about Disposition?" *Journal of Marketing* 41 (April 1977): 23. Reprinted with permission from Journal of Marketing, published by the American Marketing Association. Used with permission.

The issue of product disposition is doubly vital because of its enormous public policy implications. We live in a throwaway society, which creates problems for the environment and also results in a great deal of unfortunate waste. One study reported that we never use as much as 12 percent of the grocery products we buy; nearly two-thirds of these *abandoned products* were bought for a specific purpose, such as a recipe that did not materialize. Because the items were not used immediately, they were slowly pushed to the back of the cupboard and forgotten.[129] Some of those "science projects" growing in the back of your refrigerator might qualify. In another survey, 15 percent of U.S. adults admitted they are pack rats and another 64 percent said they are selective savers. In contrast, 20 percent say they throw out as much garbage as they can. The consumers most likely to save things are older people and single households.[130]

Training consumers to recycle has become a priority in many countries. In Japan, residents sort their garbage into as many as 44 different categories; for example, if they are discarding one sock it goes into a bin for burnables, but if they are throwing out a pair it goes into used cloth, though only if the socks "are not torn, and the left and right sock match."[131] Companies continue to search for ways to use resources more efficiently, often at the prompting of activist consumer groups. McDonald's restaurants bowed to pressure by eliminating the use of Styrofoam packages, and its outlets in Europe are experimenting with edible breakfast platters made of maize.[132]

In the United States, lateral cycling is literally a lifestyle for some people with an anticonsumerist bent who call themselves **freegans** (this label is a takeoff on *vegans*, who shun all animal products). Freegans are modern-day scavengers who live off discards as a political statement against corporations and consumerism. They forage through supermarket trash and eat the slightly bruised produce or just-expired canned goods that we routinely throw out, and negotiate gifts of surplus food from sympathetic stores and restaurants. Freegans dress in castoff clothes and furnish their homes with items they find on the street. They get the word on locations where people are throwing out a lot of stuff (end-of-semester dorm cleanouts are a prime target) by checking out postings at freecycle.org where users post unwanted items and at so-called *freemeets* (flea markets where no one exchanges money).[133]

A study examined the relevant goals consumers have when they recycle. It used a means–end chain analysis of the type we described in Chapter 4 to identify how consumers link specific instrumental goals to more abstract terminal values. Researchers identified the most important lower-order goals to be "avoid filling up land-fills," "reduce waste," "reuse materials," and "save the environment." They linked these to the terminal values of "promote health/avoid sickness," "achieve life-sustaining ends," and "provide for future generations." Another study reported that the perceived effort involved in recycling was the best predictor of whether people would go to the trouble—this pragmatic dimension outweighed general attitudes toward recycling and the environment in predicting intention to recycle.[134] By applying such techniques to study recycling and other product disposal behaviors, it will be easier for social marketers to design advertising copy and other messages that tap into the underlying values that will motivate people to increase environmentally responsible behavior.[135]

Lateral Cycling: Junk versus "Junque"

During **lateral cycling**, one consumer exchanges something she owns with someone else for something she owns. Reusing other people's things is especially important in our throwaway society because, as one researcher put it, "there is no longer an 'away' to throw things to."[141] Although traditional marketers don't pay much attention to used-product sellers, factors such as concern about the environment, demands for quality, and cost and fashion consciousness are conspiring to make these "secondary" markets more important.[142] In fact, economic estimates of this **underground economy** range from 3 to 30 percent of the gross national product of the United States and up to 70 percent of the gross domestic product of other countries. Trade publications such as *Yesteryear, Swap Meet Merchandising, Collectors Journal, The Vendor Newsletter*, and *The Antique Trader* offer reams of practical advice to consumers who want to bypass formal retailers and swap merchandise.

In the United States alone, there are more than 3,500 flea markets—including at least a dozen huge operations such as the 60-acre Orange County Marketplace in California—that operate nationwide to produce upwards of $10 billion in gross sales.[143] Other growth areas include student markets for used computers and text-books, as well as ski swaps, at which consumers exchange millions of dollars worth of used ski equipment. A new generation of secondhand storeowners is developing markets for everything from used office equipment to cast-off kitchen sinks. Many are nonprofit ventures started with government funding. A U.S. trade association called the Reuse Development Organization (www.redo.org) encourages them. The Internet has revolutionized the lateral cycling process, as millions of people flock to eBay to buy and sell their "treasures." This phenomenally successful online auction site started as a trading post for Beanie Babies and other collectibles. Now two-thirds of the site's sales are for practical goods; eBay expects to sell $2 billion worth of used cars and $1 billion worth of computers a year. Coming next are event tickets, food, industrial equipment, and real estate.[144] And entrepreneurs keep coming up with new ways to facilitate online bartering. At Peerflix 250,000 members post titles of DVDs they are willing to trade; the company helps out by providing printable forms that include postage and the recipient's address. PaperBackSwap's members trade 30,000 books weekly for $1.59 apiece.[145]

If our possessions do indeed come to be a part of us, how do we bring ourselves to part with these precious items? The way we divest ourselves of our things may make a statement (think about throwing out things an ex-partner gave you). In one new twist on this process, a current trend among some newlyweds is to stage a "trash the dress" photo shoot where, after the wedding (maybe as a sign of relief after all the

Marketing Opportunity

Entrepreneurs are finding gold in cast-offs of all kinds, including these:

- America's $700 billion supermarket industry discards more than $2.6 billion of what it calls *unsalables*—mostly food, but also such items as bleach and razor blades. Manufacturers and supermarkets ship the discards to warehouses, which sell them to individuals and organizations such as Second Harvest (secondharvest.org). They donate what they don't sell to food banks.[136]

- **Freecycling** is the practice of giving away useful but unwanted goods to keep them out of landfills and maybe to help someone less fortunate in the process. At freecycle.org, roughly 3 million people from more than 70 countries exchange unwanted items.[137]

- Hawaii's Pacific Biodiesel opened for business in 1996 with the explicit goal of helping the environment. That company collects used restaurant cooking oil—the stuff used to fry French fries and doughnuts—and converts it to diesel fuel. The company now produces about 4 million gallons of oil per year.[138]

- In a backlash against the mounting costs of pull-out-all-the-stops weddings, some brides are selling their dresses right after the honeymoon or buying secondhand ones at a discount (top-tier gowns can start at $3,000 to $4,000). In order to keep their stock fresh with the latest styles most bridal consignment shops have age limits on dresses, ranging from 1 to 3 years, with unusual sizes or styles the exception. They typically reduce the gowns by 25 percent or more from the retail price and the bride receives half of the sale proceeds.[139]

- A Denver company called Thought Equity even recycles old ("pre-aired") commercials. Small companies with tight promotional budgets can select from Thought Equity's online library of snippets from ready-to-recycle commercials, collected from more than 300 ad agencies.[140]

Marketing Pitfall

As if other kinds of waste weren't bad enough, one consequence of our infatuation with new technology is figuring out what to do with the stuff that quickly becomes obsolete. People simply don't know where to take their *e-trash*; so much of it sits in drawers. The toxic materials many electronics contain, such as lead and mercury, present more obstacles. About 2 million tons of e-trash was generated in 2001, the last year for which numbers are available, according to estimates by the Environmental Protection Agency. That's 400 million pounds of broken BlackBerrys, old monitors, and burned-out cell phones. One popular solution seems to be to ship unwanted electronic waste, such as old computer monitors and circuit boards, to the Third World. As much as 50 to 80 percent of electronics waste collected for recycling in the United States is placed on container ships and sent to China, India, Pakistan, or other developing countries, where it is reused or recycled under largely unregulated conditions. Recycling industries in these places often use young children to handle cathode ray tubes filled with lead and other toxic substances. The European Union is so concerned about the problem that it is moving toward requiring manufacturers to take cradle-to-grave responsibility for their products.[148]

buildup?), the bride models her gown while romping in the ocean, climbing up a fire escape, washing a car, or rolling in the mud (check out some examples at TrashtheDress.com).[146]

Some researchers recently examined how consumers practice **divestment rituals**, where they take steps to gradually distance themselves from things they treasure so that they can sell them or give them away (more on rituals in Chapter 16). As they observed people getting items ready to be sold at garage sales, the researchers identified these rituals:

- **Iconic transfer ritual:** Taking pictures and videos of objects before selling them.
- **Transition-place ritual:** Putting items in an out-of-the way location such as a garage or attic before disposing of them.
- **Ritual cleansing:** Washing, ironing, and/or meticulously wrapping the item.[147]

SUMMARY

Now that you have finished reading this chapter you should understand why:

Many factors over and above the qualities of the product or service influence the outcome of a transaction. Factors at the time of purchase dramatically influence the consumer decision-making process.

- The act of purchase is affected by many factors. These include the consumer's antecedent state (e.g., his or her mood, time pressure, or disposition toward shopping). Time is an important resource that often determines how much effort and search will go into a decision. Our moods are influenced by the degree of pleasure and arousal a store environment creates.

- The usage context of a product can be a basis for segmentation; consumers look for different product attributes, depending on the use to which they intend to put their purchase. The presence or absence of other people (co-consumers)—and the types of people they are—can also affect a consumer's decisions.

- The shopping experience is a pivotal part of the purchase decision. In many cases, retailing is like theater—the consumer's evaluation of stores and products may depend on the type of "performance" he witnesses. The actors (e.g., salespeople), the setting (the store environment), and props (e.g., store displays) influence this evaluation. Like a brand personality, a number of factors, such as perceived convenience, sophistication, and expertise of salespeople, determine store image. With increasing competition from nonstore alternatives, creating a positive shopping experience has never been more important. Online shopping is growing in importance, and this new way to acquire products has both good (e.g., convenience) and bad (e.g., security) aspects.

In addition to what a shopper already knows or believes about a product, information a store or Web site provides can strongly influence a purchase decision.

- Because we don't make many purchase decisions until we're actually in the store, point-of-purchase (POP) stimuli are very important sales tools. These include product samples, elaborate package displays, place-based media, and in-store promotional materials such as "shelf talkers." POP stimuli are particularly useful in promoting impulse buying, which happens when a consumer yields to a sudden urge for a product.

A salesperson can be the crucial link between interest in a product and its actual purchase.

● The consumer's encounter with a salesperson is a complex and important process. The outcome can be affected by such factors as the salesperson's similarity to the customer and his or her perceived credibility.

Marketers need to be concerned about a consumer's evaluations of a product after he buys it as well as before.

● A person's overall feelings about the product after he buys determine consumer satisfaction/dissatisfaction. Many factors influence our perceptions of product quality, including price, brand name, and product performance. Our degree of satisfaction often depends on the extent to which a product's performance is consistent with our prior expectations of how well it will function.

Getting rid of products when consumers no longer need or want them is a major concern both to marketers and to public policy makers.

● Product disposal is an increasingly important problem. Recycling is one option that will become more crucial as consumers' environmental awareness grows. Lateral cycling occurs when we buy, sell, or barter secondhand objects.

KEY TERMS

Activity stores, 406
Atmospherics, 406
Being space, 404
Co-consumers, 393
Consumer satisfaction/
  dissatisfaction (CS/D), 412
Divestment rituals, 420
Expectancy disconfirmation
  model, 413

Freecycling, 419
Freegans, 418
Gemba, 416
Impulse buying, 408
Lateral cycling, 419
Minipreneurs, 404
Point-of-purchase (POP)
  stimuli, 409
Pop-up stores, 404

Queuing theory, 397
Retail theming, 403
Shopping orientation, 399
Store image, 405
Time poverty, 395
Total quality management
  (TQM), 416
Underground economy, 419

REVIEW QUESTIONS

1 What do we mean by situational self-image? Give an example of this phenomenon.

2 Describe the difference between density and crowding. Why is this difference relevant in purchase environments?

3 What is time poverty, and how can it influence our purchase decisions?

4 What are the two dimensions that determine whether we will react positively or negatively to a purchase environment?

5 List three separate motivations for shopping, and give an example of each.

6 What are some important pros and cons of e-commerce?

7 List three factors that help to determine store image.

8 What is the difference between unplanned buying and impulse buying?

9 Describe what we mean by a commercial friendship, and provide an example.

10 How do a consumer's prior expectations about product quality influence his satisfaction with the product after he buys it?

11 List three actions a consumer can take if he is dissatisfied with a purchase.

12 What is the underground economy?

CONSUMER BEHAVIOR CHALLENGE

■ DISCUSS

1 Is the customer always right? Why or why not?

2 Are pop-up stores simply a fad or a retailing concept that's here to stay?

3 Discuss some of the shopping motivations the chapter describes. How might a retailer adjust its strategy to accommodate these motivations?

4 What are some positive and negative aspects of requiring employees who interact with customers to wear some kind of uniform or of mandating a dress code in the office?

5 Think about exceptionally good and bad salespeople you have encountered in the past. What qualities seem to differentiate them?

6 Discuss the concept of "timestyle." Based on your own experiences, how might we segment consumers in terms of their timestyles?

7 Compare and contrast different cultures' conceptions of time. What are some implications for marketing strategy within each of these frameworks?

8 The movement away from a "disposable consumer society" toward one that emphasizes creative recycling creates many opportunities for marketers. Can you identify some?

9 Some retailers work hard to cultivate a certain look or image, and they may even choose employees who fit this look. Abercrombie & Fitch, for example, seems to link itself to a clean-cut, all-American image. A U.S. federal lawsuit filed in 2003 claimed that Abercrombie & Fitch systematically "refuses to hire qualified minority applicants as brand representatives to work on the sales floor and discourages applications from minority applicants." Abercrombie has said the complaints are without merit, and that the company has "zero tolerance for discrimination."[149] Americans know the Hooters restaurant chain for its attractive female waitresses. Should a retailer have the right to recruit employees who are consistent with its image even if this means excluding certain types of people (e.g., non-Caucasians, men) from the sales floor?

10 The mall of the future will most likely be less about purchasing products than about exploring them in a physical setting. This means that retail environments will have to become places to build brand images, rather than simply places to sell products. What are some strategies stores can use to enhance the emotional/sensory experiences they give to shoppers?

11 The store environment is heating up as more and more companies put their promotional dollars into point-of-purchase efforts. Some stores confront shoppers with videos at the checkout counter, computer monitors attached to their shopping carts, and ads stenciled on the floors. And we're increasingly exposed to ads in non-shopping environments. Recently, a health club in New York was forced to remove TV monitors that showed advertising on the Health Club Media Networks; exercisers claimed they interfered with their workouts. Do you feel that these innovations are overly intrusive? At what point might shoppers "rebel" and demand some peace and quiet while shopping? Do you see any market potential in the future for stores that "countermarket" by promising a "hands-off" shopping environment?

12 Courts often prohibit special interest groups from distributing literature in shopping malls. Mall managements claim that these centers are private property. However, these groups argue that the mall is the modern-day version of the town square and as such is a public forum. Find some recent court cases involving this free-speech issue, and examine the arguments pro and con. What is the current status of the mall as a public forum? Do you agree with this concept?

■ APPLY

13 Conduct naturalistic observation at a local mall. Sit in a central location and observe the activities of mall employees and patrons. Keep a log of the nonretailing activity you observe (e.g., special performances, exhibits, socializing, etc.). Does this activity enhance or detract from business the mall conducts? As malls become more like high-tech game rooms, how valid is the criticism that shopping areas are only encouraging more loitering by teenage boys, who don't spend a lot in stores and simply scare away other customers?

14 Select three competing clothing stores in your area and conduct a store image study for them. Ask a group of consumers to rate each store on a set of attributes and plot these ratings on the same graph. Based on your findings, are there any areas of competitive advantage or disadvantage you could bring to the attention of store management?

15 Using Table 10.1 as a model, construct a person–situation segmentation matrix for a brand of perfume.

16 What applications of queuing theory can you find that local services use? Interview consumers who are waiting in lines to determine how their experience affects their satisfaction with the service.

17 Interactive tools allow surfers on sites such as landsend.com to view apparel product selections on virtual models in full, 360-degree rotational view. In

some cases, the viewer can modify the bodies, face, skin coloring, and the hairstyles of these models. In others, the consumer can project his *own* likeness into the space by scanning a photo into a "makeover" program. Visit landsend.com or another site that offers a personalized mannequin. Surf around. Try on some clothes. How was your experience? How helpful was this mannequin? When you shop for clothes online, would you rather see how they look on a body with dimensions the same as yours or on a different body? What advice can you give Web site designers who are trying to personalize these shopping environments by creating lifelike models to guide you through the site?

18 Interview people who are selling items at a flea market or garage sale. Ask them to identify some items to which they had a strong attachment. Then, see if you can prompt them to describe one or more divestment rituals they went through as they prepared to offer these items for sale.

19 Identify three people who own electric coffeemakers. Then, "go to the gemba" by observing them as they actually prepare coffee in the appliance at home. Based on these experiences, what recommendations might you make to the designer of a new coffeemaker model that would improve customers' experiences with the product?

Case Study

GIVING AND RECEIVING ON FREECYCLE.ORG

Like it or not, we live in a disposable society. And it isn't just paper products and fast food containers we're throwing away. We use our televisions, computers, cell phones, furniture, clothing, and other products until something better comes along, and then we toss them. Landfills everywhere are reeling under the onslaught of trash we create.

But what if people could find someone to take their old junk off their hands? Or what if individuals could find a needed item that someone just so happens to be throwing away? As we saw in the chapter, Freecycle.org meets this need. This Web site came into being as a recycling concept to reduce the strain on landfills and cut down on consumer wastefulness. Freecycle, which uses a bulletin board structure, works so well because it's so simple. It connects people who have items to give away with others who need them, and *vice versa*. It's basically like an "eBay for free." Indeed, many users call the site by its nickname of "Freebay."

From its small beginning in the Tucson, Arizona, area in 2003, today there are millions of members who comprise thousands of user-communities in over 75 countries; they say they are "changing the world one gift at a time." Freecycle.org is one of the most popular nonprofit destinations in cyberspace; *Time* dubbed it "one of the 50 coolest" Web sites. This notoriety comes within a few short years and with no promotion other than word-of-mouth and plenty of free publicity.

Anyone can join this 24/7 virtual garage sale, and membership is free. In fact, the principle rule of Freecycle.org is that you can only offer free items. Givers and receivers contact each other via email and then arrange for delivery. The site's founder estimates that the average freecycled item

weighs 1 pound. That means that the Freecycle movement keeps 300 tons of "garbage" out of landfills every day.

This is certainly a sign of success. But other measures of success have become apparent as well, like the satisfaction of all those involved. What one person doesn't want, someone else will take away from them. Both get something for free and everyone wins. "It's become a huge gift economy and very life affirming for everyone who has given away something. You can't help but get a good feeling when you've helped another person," the founder said.

Jinnie Parsley is a San Antonio, Texas, stay-at-home mother who clearly appreciates the benefits of Freecycle. "There were things I needed but couldn't go out and buy just yet," Parsley said. "The best thing about Freecycle is that it helped me clean out my house and get more organized. Now, I don't know what I'd do without this Web site."

As long as there are people looking to get rid of or acquire an old couch, a six-year-old husky, a storm door, a van that needs a transmission, or even horse manure, Freecycle has a bright future. "When it comes to the Internet and connecting with one another, there are no limitations," Beal said. "We'll continue growing and experiencing the goodness that comes from giving."

DISCUSSION QUESTIONS

1 Why do you think Freecycle.org has achieved such high levels of growth in such a short period of time?

2 Freecycle created an alternative disposal option that is rapidly growing. Discuss ways that freecycling might affect the purchase habits of consumers.

3 Can, or should, for-profit businesses like eBay get into the freecycling business? Should companies motivate more consumers to give things away that they might otherwise be able to sell or auction? Can they still make a profit while helping to eliminate waste?

Sources: Tamsin Kelly, "Multi-Bargain Swap Shop," *Daily Telegraph* (July 7, 2007): 13; "A Brief History," accessed at www.freecycle.org (September 2007). Rosemary Barnes, "What Goes Around . . . Looking For a Used Couch or a Hundred Baby Food Jars? Freecycle.org is for you," *San Antonio Express* (October 30, 2004): 6H; Patty Day, "For Free? Secondhand Stuff Online; Freecycle Keeps Stuff Out of Landfills," *Salt Lake Tribune* (February 18, 2005): N1.

NOTES

1. Keith Naughton, "Revolution in the Showroom," *BusinessWeek* (February 19, 1996): 70.
2. Quoted in "Denny's Targets College Kids with Late-Night Campaign," available from www.Promo.Com, accessed April 9, 2007.
3. David Kesmodel, "More Marketers Place Web Ads by Time of Day," *Wall Street Journal* (June 23, 2006): B1.
4. Pradeep Kakkar and Richard J. Lutz, "Situational Influence on Consumer Behavior: A Review," in Harold H. Kassarjian and Thomas S. Robertson, eds., *Perspectives in Consumer Behavior*, 3rd ed. (Glenview, IL: Scott, Foresman, 1981): 204–14.
5. Ibid.
6. Benedict Carey, "TV Time, Unlike Child Care, Ranks High in Mood Study," *New York Times on the Web* (December 3, 2004).
7. Carolyn Turner Schenk and Rebecca H. Holman, "A Sociological Approach to Brand Choice: The Concept of Situational Self-Image," in Jerry C. Olson, ed., *Advances in Consumer Research* 7 (Ann Arbor, MI: Association for Consumer Research, 1980): 610–14.
8. Peter R. Dickson, "Person–Situation: Segmentation's Missing Link," *Journal of Marketing* 46 (Fall 1982): 56–64.
9. Ellen Byron, "How Coach Won a Rich Purse by Inventing New Uses for Bags: What Was a Semiannual Buy Is Now a Regular Ritual; Wristlets, Clutches, Totes, Fresh Competition from Gap," *Wall Street Journal on the Web* (November 17, 2004): A1.
10. Alan R. Hirsch, "Effects of Ambient Odors on Slot-Machine Usage in a Las Vegas Casino," *Psychology & Marketing* 12 (October 1995): 585–94.
11. Daniel Stokols, "On the Distinction between Density and Crowding: Some Implications for Future Research," *Psychological Review* 79 (1972): 275–77.
12. Carol Felker Kaufman, Paul M. Lane, and Jay D. Lindquist, "Exploring More Than 24 Hours a Day: A Preliminary Investigation of Polychronic Time Use," *Journal of Consumer Research* 18 (December 1991): 392–401.
13. Laurence P. Feldman and Jacob Hornik, "The Use of Time: An Integrated Conceptual Model," *Journal of Consumer Research* 7 (March 1981): 407–19; see also Michelle M. Bergadaa, "The Role of Time in the Action of the Consumer," *Journal of Consumer Research* 17 (December 1990): 289–302.
14. Alan Zarembo, "What If There Weren't Any Clocks to Watch?" *Newsweek* (June 30, 1997): 14; based on research reported in Robert Levine, *A Geography of Time: The Temporal Misadventures of a Social Psychologist, or How Every Culture Keeps Time Just a Little Bit Differently* (New York: Basic Books, 1997).
15. Robert J. Samuelson, "Rediscovering the Rat Race," *Newsweek* (May 15, 1989): 57.
16. John P. Robinson, "Time Squeeze," *Advertising Age* (February 1990): 30–33.
17. "Plugged In: Hong Kong Embraces the Octopus Card," *New York Times on the Web* (June 8, 2002).
18. "Instant Refills," *Wired* (June 2002): 36.
19. Kaufman, Lane, and Lindquist, "Exploring More Than 24 Hours a Day."
20. Dena Kleiman, "Fast Food? It Just Isn't Fast Enough Anymore," *New York Times* (December 6, 1989): C12.
21. Stephanie Thompson, "'To Go' Becoming the Way to Go," *Advertising Age* (May 13, 2002): 73.
22. June S. Cotte, S. Ratneshwar, and David Glen Mick, "The Times of Their Lives: Phenomenological and Metaphorical Characteristics of Consumer Timestyles," *Journal of Consumer Research* 31 (September 2004): 333–45.
23. James Gorman, "Does This Mean People Turned Off, Tuned Out and Dropped In?" *New York Times Online* (June 27, 2006), accessed June 27, 2006.
24. Robert J. Graham, "The Role of Perception of Time in Consumer Research," *Journal of Consumer Research* 7 (March 1981): 335–42; Esther S. Page-Wood, Paul M. Lane, and Carol J. Kaufman, "The Art of Time," *Proceedings of the 1990 Academy of Marketing Science Conference*, ed. B. J. Dunlap, Vol. XIII, Cullowhee, NC: Academy of Marketing Science (1990): 56–61.
25. Dhruv Grewal, Julie Baker, Michael Levy, and Glenn B. Voss, "The Effects of Wait Expectations and Store Atmosphere Evaluations on Patronage Intentions in Service-Intensive Retail Store," *Journal of Retailing* 79 (2003): 259–68; cf. also Shirley Taylor, "Waiting for Service: The Relationship between Delays and Evaluations of Service," *Journal of Marketing* 58 (April 1994): 56–69.
26. "We're Hating the Waiting; 43% Prefer Self-Service," *Marketing Daily* (January 23, 2007), available from www.mediapost.com, accessed January 23, 2007.
27. David H. Maister, "The Psychology of Waiting Lines," in John A. Czepiel, Michael R. Solomon, and Carol F. Surprenant, eds., *The Service Encounter: Managing Employee/Customer Interaction in Service Businesses* (Lexington, MA: Lexington Books, 1985): 113–24.
28. David Leonhardt, "Airlines Using Technology in a Push for Shorter Lines," *New York Times on the Web* (May 8, 2002).
29. Jennifer Ordonez, "An Efficiency Drive: Fast-Food Lanes, Equipped with Timers, Get Even Faster," *Wall Street Journal Interactive Edition* (May 18, 2000).
30. Henry Fountain, quoted in "The Ultimate Body Language: How You Line Up for Mickey," *New York Times Online* (September 18, 2005), accessed September 18, 2005.
31. Christine Bittar, "Massage in Aisle 7: Whole Foods Opens Spa," *Marketing Daily* (December 13, 2006), available from www.mediapost.com, accessed December 13, 2006.
32. Laurette Dube and Bernd H. Schmitt, "The Processing of Emotional and Cognitive Aspects of Product Usage in Satisfaction Judgments," in Rebecca H. Holman and Michael R. Solomon, eds., *Advances in Consumer Research* 18 (Provo, UT: Association for Consumer Research, 1991): 52–56; Lalita A. Manrai and Meryl P. Gardner, "The Influence of Affect on Attributions for Product Failure," in Rebecca H. Holman and Michael R. Solomon, eds., *Advances in Consumer Research* 18 (Provo, UT: Association for Consumer Research, 1991): 249–54.
33. Kevin G. Celuch and Linda S. Showers, "It's Time to Stress Stress: The Stress–Purchase/Consumption Relationship," in Rebecca H. Holman and Michael R. Solomon, eds., *Advances in Consumer Research* 18 (Provo, UT: Association for Consumer Research, 1991): 284–89; Lawrence R. Lepisto, J. Kathleen Stuenkel, and Linda K. Anglin, "Stress: An Ignored Situational Influence," in Rebecca H. Holman and Michael R. Solomon, eds., *Advances in Consumer Research* 18 (Provo, UT: Association for Consumer Research, 1991): 296–302.
34. Velitchka D. Kaltcheva and Barton A. Weitz, "When Should a Retailer Create an Exciting Store Environment?" *Journal of Marketing* 70 (January 2006): 107–118.
35. See Eben Shapiro, "Need a Little Fantasy? A Bevy of New Companies Can Help," *New York Times* (March 10, 1991): F4.
36. John D. Mayer and Yvonne N. Gaschke, "The Experience and Meta-Experience of Mood," *Journal of Personality and Social Psychology* 55 (July 1988): 102–11.
37. Meryl Paula Gardner, "Mood States and Consumer Behavior: A Critical Review," *Journal of Consumer Research* 12 (December 1985): 281–300; Scott Dawson, Peter H. Bloch, and Nancy M. Ridgway, "Shopping Motives, Emotional States, and Retail Outcomes," *Journal of Retailing* 66 (Winter 1990): 408–27; Patricia A. Knowles, Stephen J. Grove, and W. Jeffrey Burroughs, "An Experimental Examination of Mood States on Retrieval and Evaluation of Advertisement and Brand Information," *Journal of the Academy of Marketing Science* 21 (April 1993): 135–43; Paul W. Miniard, Sunil Bhatla, and Deepak Sirdeskmukh, "Mood as a Determinant of Postconsumption Product Evaluations: Mood Effects

and Their Dependency on the Affective Intensity of the Consumption Experience," *Journal of Consumer Psychology* 1, no. 2 (1992): 173–95; Mary T. Curren and Katrin R. Harich, "Consumers' Mood States: The Mitigating Influence of Personal Relevance on Product Evaluations," *Psychology & Marketing* 11 (March–April 1994): 91–107; Gerald J. Gorn, Marvin E. Goldberg, and Kunal Basu, "Mood, Awareness, and Product Evaluation," *Journal of Consumer Psychology* 2, no. 3 (1993): 237–56.

38. Gordon C. Bruner, "Music, Mood, and Marketing," *Journal of Marketing* 54 (October 1990): 94–104; Basil G. Englis, "Music Television and its Influences on Consumers, Consumer Culture, and the Transmission of Consumption Messages," in Rebecca H. Holman and Michael R. Solomon, eds., *Advances in Consumer Research* 18 (Provo, UT: Association for Consumer Research, 1991): 111–14.

39. Marvin E. Goldberg and Gerald J. Gorn, "Happy and Sad TV Programs: How They Affect Reactions to Commercials," *Journal of Consumer Research* 14 (December 1987): 387–403; Gorn, Goldberg, and Basu, "Mood, Awareness, and Product Evaluation"; Curren and Harich, "Consumers' Mood States."

40. Rajeev Batra and Douglas M. Stayman, "The Role of Mood in Advertising Effectiveness," *Journal of Consumer Research* 17 (September 1990): 203; John P. Murry, Jr., and Peter A. Dacin, "Cognitive Moderators of Negative-Emotion Effects: Implications for Understanding Media Context," *Journal of Consumer Research* 22 (March 1996): 439–47; see also Curren and Harich, "Consumers' Mood States"; Gorn, Goldbergand Basu, "Mood, Awareness, and Product Evaluation."

41. Jeffrey Zaslow, "Happiness Inc.," *Wall Street Journal* (March 18, 2006): P1.

42. For a scale to assess these dimensions of the shopping experience, see Barry J. Babin, William R. Darden, and Mitch Griffin, "Work and/or Fun: Measuring Hedonic and Utilitarian Shopping Value," *Journal of Consumer Research* 20 (March 1994): 644–56.

43. Cele Otnes and Mary Ann McGrath, "Perceptions and Realities of Male Shopping Behavior," *Journal of Retailing* 77 (Spring 2001): 111–37.

44. "A Global Perspective . . . on Women and Women's Wear," *Lifestyle Monitor* 14 (Winter 1999–2000): 8–11.

45. Babin, Darden, and Griffin, "Work and/or Fun."

46. Edward M. Tauber, "Why Do People Shop?" *Journal of Marketing* 36 (October 1972): 47–48.

47. Ann Zimmerman and Laura Stevens, "Attention, Shoppers: Bored College Kids Competing in Aisle 6," *Wall Street Journal Online* (February 23, 2005).

48. Robert C. Prus, *Making Sales: Influence as Interpersonal Accomplishment* (Newbury Park, CA: Sage Publications, 1989), 225.

49. Micael-Lee Johnstone and Denise M Conroy, "Dressing for the Thrill: An Exploration of Why Women Dress Up to Go Shopping," *Journal of Consumer Behaviour* 4, no. 4 (2005): 234.

50. Some material in this section was adapted from Michael R. Solomon and Elnora W. Stuart, *Welcome to Marketing.com: The Brave New World of E-Commerce* (Upper Saddle River, NJ: Prentice Hall, 2001).

51. Rebecca K. Ratner, Barbara E. Kahn, and Daniel Kahneman, "Choosing Less-Preferred Experiences for the Sake of Variety," *Journal of Consumer Research* 26 (June 1999): 1–15.

52. Jennifer Gilbert, "Customer Service Crucial to Online Buyers," *Advertising Age* (September 13, 1999): 52.

53. Timothy L. O'Brien, "Aided by Internet, Identity Theft Soars," *New York Times on the Web* (April 3, 2000).

54. www.allurent.com/newsDetail.php?newsid=20, accessed January 29, 2007.

55. Quoted in Stephanie Rosenbloom, "www.FriesWithThat?.com," *New York Times Online* (August 5, 2007).

56. Jacquelyn Bivins, "Fun and Mall Games," *Stores* (August 1989): 35.

57. Vanessa O'Connell, "Fictional Hershey Factory Will Send Kisses to Broadway," *Wall Street Journal Interactive Edition* (August 5, 2002).

58. Millie Creighton, "The Seed of Creative Lifestyle Shopping: Wrapping Consumerism in Japanese Store Layouts," in John F. Sherry Jr., ed., *Servicescapes: The Concept of Place in Contemporary Markets* (Lincolnwood, IL: NTC Business Books, 1998), 199–228; also cf. Robert V. Kozinets, John F. Sherry, Diana Storm, Adam Duhachek, Krittinee Nuttavuthisit, and Benet DeBerry-Spence, "Ludic Agency and Retail Spectacle," *Journal of Consumer Research* 31 (December 2004): 658–72.

59. March 2007 Trend Briefing, available from www.trendwatching.com/briefing/, accessed March 30, 2007; Amy Johannes, "Choice Hotels Launches Upscale Brand Via Pop-Up Hotel Suite," *PROMO Xtra* (January 8, 2007).

60. Susan Spiggle and Murphy A. Sewall, "A Choice Sets Model of Retail Selection," *Journal of Marketing* 51 (April 1987): 97–111; William R. Darden and Barry J. Babin, "The Role of Emotions in Expanding the Concept of Retail Personality," *Stores* 76, no. 4 (April 1994): RR7–RR8.

61. Most measures of store image are quite similar to other attitude measures, as discussed in Chapter 7. For an excellent bibliography of store image studies, see Mary R. Zimmer and Linda L. Golden, "Impressions of Retail Stores: A Content Analysis of Consumer Images," *Journal of Retailing* 64 (Fall 1988): 265–93.

62. David Wethe, "Car Dealerships Face the Great Homogenization," *New York Times on the Web* (January 11, 2004).

63. Spiggle and Sewall, "A Choice Sets Model of Retail Selection."

64. Philip Kotler, "Atmospherics as a Marketing Tool," *Journal of Retailing* (Winter 1973–74): 10; Anna Mattila and Jochen Wirtz, "Congruency of Scent and Music as a Driver of In-Store Evaluations and Behavior," *Journal of Retailing* 77, no. 2 (2001): 273–89; J. Duncan Herrington, "An Integrative Path Model of the Effects of Retail Environments on Shopper Behavior," in Robert L. King, ed., *Marketing: Toward the Twenty-First Century* (Richmond, VA: Southern Marketing Association, 1991), 58–62; see also Ann E. Schlosser, "Applying the Functional Theory of Attitudes to Understanding the Influence of Store Atmosphere on Store Inferences," *Journal of Consumer Psychology* 7, no. 4 (1998): 345–69.

65. Joseph A. Bellizzi and Robert E. Hite, "Environmental Color, Consumer Feelings, and Purchase Likelihood," *Psychology & Marketing* 9 (September–October 1992): 347–63.

66. See Eric R. Spangenberg, Ayn E. Crowley, and Pamela W. Henderson, "Improving the Store Environment: Do Olfactory Cues Affect Evaluations and Behaviors?" *Journal of Marketing* 60 (April 1996): 67–80, for a study that assessed olfaction in a controlled, simulated store environment.

67. Robert J. Donovan, John R. Rossiter, Gilian Marcoolyn, and Andrew Nesdale, "Store Atmosphere and Purchasing Behavior," *Journal of Retailing* 70, no. 3 (1994): 283–94.

68. Alice Z. Cuneo, "Malls Seek Boost with 'Activity' Stores," *Advertising Age* (July 21, 2003): 6.

69. Deborah Blumenthal, "Scenic Design for In-Store Try-ons," *New York Times* (April 9, 1988): N9.

70. John Pierson, "If Sun Shines in, Workers Work Better, Buyers Buy More," *Wall Street Journal* (November 20, 1995): B1.

71. Charles S. Areni and David Kim, "The Influence of In-Store Lighting on Consumers' Examination of Merchandise in a Wine Store," *International Journal of Research in Marketing* 11, no. 2 (March 1994): 117–25.

72. Jean-Charles Chebat, Claire Gelinas Chebat, and Dominique Vaillant, "Environmental Background Music and In-Store Selling," *Journal of Business Research* 54 (2001): 115–23; Judy I. Alpert and Mark I. Alpert, "Music Influences on Mood and Purchase Intentions," *Psychology & Marketing* 7 (Summer 1990): 109–34.

73. "Slow Music Makes Fast Drinkers," *Psychology Today* (March 1989): 18.

74. Brad Edmondson, "Pass the Meat Loaf," *American Demographics* (January 1989): 19.

75. "Through the Looking Glass," *Lifestyle Monitor* 16 (Fall–Winter 2002).

76. Jennifer Lach, "Meet You in Aisle Three," *American Demographics* (April 1999): 41.

77. Ernest Beck, "Diageo Attempts to Reinvent the Bar in an Effort to Increase Spirits Sales," *Wall Street Journal Online* (February 23, 2001), accessed October 1, 2007.

78. Easwar S. Iyer, "Unplanned Purchasing: Knowledge of Shopping Environment and Time Pressure," *Journal of Retailing* 65 (Spring 1989): 40–57; C. Whan Park, Easwar S. Iyer, and Daniel C. Smith, "The Effects of Situational Factors on In-Store Grocery Shopping," *Journal of Consumer Research* 15 (March 1989): 422–33.

79. Kathleen D. Vohs and Ronald J. Faber, "Spent Resources: Self-Regulatory Resource Availability Affects Impulse Buying, *Journal of Consumer Research* 33 (March 2007): 537–47; Dennis W. Rook and Robert J. Fisher, "Normative Influences on Impulsive Buying Behavior," *Journal of Consumer Research* 22 (December 1995): 305–13; Francis Piron, "Defining Impulse Purchasing," in Rebecca H. Holman and Michael R. Solomon, eds., *Advances in Consumer Research* 18 (Provo, UT: Association for Consumer Research, 1991): 509–14; Dennis W. Rook, "The Buying Impulse," *Journal of Consumer Research* 14 (September 1987): 189–99.

80. Michael Wahl, "Eye POPping Persuasion," *Marketing Insights* (June 1989): 130.

81. "Zipping Down the Aisles," *New York Times Magazine* (April 6, 1997): 30.

82. The Associated Press, "Sony Game Delivers Pizza Option," *Montgomery Advertiser* (February 28, 2005).

83. Matt Richtel, "At Starbucks, Songs of Instant Gratification," *New York Times Online* (October 1, 2007), accessed October 1, 2007.

84. Louise Story, "New Form of Impulse: Shopping via Text Message," *New York Times Online* (April 16, 2007), accessed April 16, 2007.

85. Ellen Byron and Suzanne Vranica, "Scanners Check Out Who's Browsing Marketers, Retailers Test Sensors to Weigh Reach of In-Store Promotions," *Wall Street Journal* (September 27, 2006): B2.

86. Quoted in Louise Story, "Product Packages Now Shout to Get Your Attention," *New York Times Online* (August 10, 2007), accessed August 10, 2007.

87. See Robert B. Cialdini, *Influence: Science and Practice*, 2nd ed. (Glenview, IL: Scott, Foresman, 1988).

88. Richard P. Bagozzi, "Marketing as Exchange," *Journal of Marketing* 39 (October 1975): 32–39; Peter M. Blau, *Exchange and Power in Social Life* (New York: Wiley, 1964); Marjorie Caballero and Alan J. Resnik, "The Attraction Paradigm in Dyadic Exchange," *Psychology & Marketing* 3, no. 1 (1986): 17–34; George C. Homans, "Social Behavior as Exchange," *American Journal of Sociology* 63 (1958): 597–606; Paul H. Schurr and Julie L. Ozanne, "Influences on Exchange Processes: Buyers' Preconceptions of a Seller's Trustworthiness and Bargaining Toughness," *Journal of Consumer Research* 11 (March 1985): 939–53; Arch G. Woodside and J. W. Davenport, "The Effect of Salesman Similarity and Expertise on Consumer Purchasing Behavior," *Journal of Marketing Research* 8 (1974): 433–36.

89. Marc Gobé, *Emotional Branding: The New Paradigm for Connecting Brands to People* (New York: Allworth Press, 2001); Paul Busch and David T. Wilson, "An Experimental Analysis of a Salesman's Expert and Referent Bases of Social Power in the Buyer-Seller Dyad," *Journal of Marketing Research* 13 (February 1976): 3–11; John E. Swan, Fred Trawick, Jr., David R. Rink, and Jenny J. Roberts, "Measuring Dimensions of Purchaser Trust of Industrial Salespeople," *Journal of Personal Selling and Sales Management* 8 (May 1988): 1.

90. For a study in this area, see Peter H. Reingen and Jerome B. Kernan, "Social Perception and Interpersonal Influence: Some Consequences of the Physical Attractiveness Stereotype in a Personal Selling Setting," *Journal of Consumer Psychology* 2 (1993): 25–38.

91. Linda L. Price and Eric J. Arnould, "Commercial Friendships: Service Provider–Client Relationships in Context," *Journal of Marketing* 63 (October 1999): 38–56.

92. Calmetta Y. Coleman, "A Car Salesman's Bizarre Prank May End up Backfiring in Court," *Wall Street Journal* (May 2, 1995): B1.

93. "Woman Stabbed over McDonald's Meal Dispute," *Opelika/Auburn News* (April 13, 2002).

94. Mary Jo Bitner, Bernard H. Booms, and Mary Stansfield Tetreault, "The Service Encounter: Diagnosing Favorable and Unfavorable Incidents," *Journal of Marketing* 54 (January 1990): 7–84; Robert C. Prus, *Making Sales* (Newbury Park, CA: Sage Publications, 1989); Arch G. Woodside and James L. Taylor, "Identity Negotiations in Buyer–Seller Interactions," in Elizabeth C. Hirschman and Morris B. Holbrook, eds., *Advances in Consumer Research* 12 (Provo, UT: Association for Consumer Research, 1985): 443–49.

95. Barry J. Babin, James S. Boles, and William R. Darden, "Salesperson Stereotypes, Consumer Emotions, and Their Impact on Information Processing," *Journal of the Academy of Marketing Science* 23, no. 2 (1995): 94–105; Gilbert A. Churchill, Jr., Neil M. Ford, Steven W. Hartley, and Orville C. Walker, Jr., "The Determinants of Salesperson Performance: A Meta-Analysis," *Journal of Marketing Research* 22 (May 1985): 103–18.

96. Siew Meng Leong, Paul S. Busch, and Deborah Roedder John, "Knowledge Bases and Salesperson Effectiveness: A Script-Theoretic Analysis," *Journal of Marketing Research* 26 (May 1989): 164; Harish Sujan, Mita Sujan, and James R. Bettman, "Knowledge Structure Differences between More Effective and Less Effective Salespeople," *Journal of Marketing Research* 25 (February 1988): 81–86; Robert Saxe and Barton Weitz, "The SOCCO Scale: A Measure of the Customer Orientation of Salespeople," *Journal of Marketing Research* 19 (August 1982): 343–51; David M. Szymanski, "Determinants of Selling Effectiveness: The Importance of Declarative Knowledge to the Personal Selling Concept," *Journal of Marketing* 52 (January 1988): 64–77; Barton A. Weitz, "Effectiveness in Sales Interactions: A Contingency Framework," *Journal of Marketing* 45 (Winter 1981): 85–103.

97. Jagdish M. Sheth, "Buyer-Seller Interaction: A Conceptual Framework," in *Advances in Consumer Research* 3 (Cincinnati, OH: Association for Consumer Research, 1976): 382–86; Kaylene C. Williams and Rosann L. Spiro, "Communication Style in the Salesperson-Customer Dyad," *Journal of Marketing Research* 22 (November 1985): 434–42.

98. Marsha L. Richins, "An Analysis of Consumer Interaction Styles in the Marketplace," *Journal of Consumer Research* 10 (June 1983): 73–82.

99. Jeffrey Zaslow, "Happiness Inc.," *Wall Street Journal* (March 18, 2006): P1.

100. Rama Jayanti and Anita Jackson, "Service Satisfaction: Investigation of Three Models," in Rebecca H. Holman and Michael R. Solomon, eds., *Advances in Consumer Research* 18 (Provo, UT: Association for Consumer Research, 1991): 603–10; David K. Tse, Franco M. Nicosia, and Peter C. Wilton, "Consumer Satisfaction as a Process," *Psychology & Marketing* 7 (Fall 1990): 177–93. For a recent treatment of satisfaction issues from a more interpretive perspective, see Susan Fournier and David Mick, "Rediscovering Satisfaction," *Journal of Marketing* 63 (October 1999): 5–23.

101. Bruce Cooil, Timothy L. Keiningham, Lerzan Aksoy, and Michael Hsu, "A Longitudinal Analysis of Customer Satisfaction and Share of Wallet: Investigating the Moderating Effect of Customer Characteristics," *Journal of Marketing* 71 (January 2007): 67-83. For a study that looks at consumer variables moderating this relationship, cf. Kathleen Seiders, Glenn B. Voss, Dhruv Grewal, and Andrea L. Godfrey, "Do Satisfied Customers Buy More? Examining Moderating Influences in a Retailing Context," *Journal of Marketing* 69 (October 2005): 26–43.

102. Constance L. Hayes, "Service Takes a Holiday," *New York Times* (December 23, 1998): C1.

103. Leslie Kaufman, "Enough Talk," *Newsweek* (August 18, 1997): 48–49.

104. Robert Jacobson and David A. Aaker, "The Strategic Role of Product Quality," *Journal of Marketing* 51 (October 1987): 31–44. For a review of issues regarding the measurement of service quality, see J. Joseph Cronin, Jr., and Steven A. Taylor, "Measuring Service Quality: A Reexamination and Extension," *Journal of Marketing* 56 (July 1992): 55–68.

105. Amna Kirmani and Peter Wright, "Money Talks: Perceived Advertising Expense and Expected Product Quality," *Journal of Consumer Research* 16 (December 1989): 344–53; Donald R. Lichtenstein and Scot Burton, "The Relationship between Perceived and Objective Price-Quality," *Journal of Marketing Research* 26 (November 1989): 429–43; Akshay R. Rao and Kent B. Monroe, "The Effect of Price, Brand Name, and Store Name on Buyers' Perceptions of Product Quality: An Integrative Review," *Journal of Marketing Research* 26 (August 1989): 351–57; Shelby Hunt, "Post-Transactional Communication and Dissonance Reduction," *Journal of Marketing* 34 (January 1970): 46–51; Daniel E. Innis and H. Rao Unnava, "The Usefulness of Product Warranties for Reputable and New Brands," in Rebecca H. Holman and Michael R. Solomon, eds., *Advances in Consumer Research* 18 (Provo, UT: Association for Consumer Research, 1991): 317–22; Terence A. Shimp and William O. Bearden, "Warranty and Other Extrinsic Cue Effects on Consumers' Risk Perceptions," *Journal of Consumer Research* 9 (June 1982): 38–46.

106. Morris B. Holbrook and Kim P. Corfman, "Quality and Value in the Consumption Experience: Phaedrus Rides Again," in Jacob Jacoby and Jerry C. Olson, eds., *Perceived Quality: How Consumers View Stores and Merchandise* (Lexington, MA: Lexington Books, 1985): 31–58.

107. Holbrook and Corfman, "Quality and Value in the Consumption Experience"; Robert M. Pirsig, *Zen and the Art of Motorcycle Maintenance: An Inquiry into Values* (New York: Bantam Books, 1974).

108. Gilbert A. Churchill, Jr., and Carol F. Surprenant, "An Investigation into the Determinants of Customer Satisfaction," *Journal of Marketing Research* 19 (November 1983): 491–504; John E. Swan and I. Frederick Trawick, "Disconfirmation of Expectations and Satisfaction with a Retail Service," *Journal of Retailing* 57 (Fall 1981): 49–67; Peter C. Wilton and David K. Tse, "Models of Consumer Satisfaction Formation: An Extension," *Journal of Marketing Research* 25 (May 1988): 204–12. For a discussion of what may occur when customers evaluate a new service for which comparison standards do not yet exist, see Ann L. McGill and Dawn Iacobucci, "The Role of Post-Experience Comparison Standards in the Evaluation of Unfamiliar Services," in John F. Sherry, Jr., and Brian Sternthal, eds., *Advances in Consumer Research* 19 (Provo, UT: Association for Consumer Research, 1992): 570–78; William Boulding, Ajay Kalra, Richard Staelin, and Valarie A. Zeithaml, "A Dynamic Process Model of Service Quality: From Expectations to Behavioral Intentions," *Journal of Marketing Research* 30 (February 1993): 7–27.

109. John W. Gamble, "The Expectations Paradox: The More You Offer Customers, the Closer You Are to Failure," *Marketing News* (March 14, 1988): 38.

110. Jagdish N. Sheth and Banwari Mittal, "A Framework for Managing Customer Expectations," *Journal of Market Focused Management* 1 (1996): 137–58.

111. www.protest.net, accessed June 17, 2000.

112. Keith Naughton, "Tired of Smile-Free Service," *Newsweek* (March 6, 2000): 44–45.

113. "Dunkin' Donuts Buys Out Critical Web Site," *New York Times on the Web* (August 27, 1999).

114. Jan McCallum, "I Hate You, and Millions Know It," *BRW* (July 7, 2000): 84.

115. S. McManis, "An Internet Outlaw Goes on Record: Pleasant Hill Student Tells of His 'Hacktivism'," *San Francisco Chronicle* (February 24, 2002): A21.

116. Ariel Sabar, "In Case of Missing Trousers, Aggrieved Party Loses Again," available from www.nytimes.com, accessed June 26, 2007.

117. Mary C. Gilly and Betsy D. Gelb, "Post-Purchase Consumer Processes and the Complaining Consumer," *Journal of Consumer Research* 9 (December 1982): 323–28; Diane Halstead and Cornelia Droge, "Consumer Attitudes toward Complaining and the Prediction of Multiple Complaint Responses," in Rebecca H. Holman and Michael R. Solomon, eds., *Advances in Consumer Research* 18 (Provo, UT: Association for Consumer Research, 1991): 210–16; Jagdip Singh, "Consumer

Complaint Intentions and Behavior: Definitional and Taxonomical Issues," *Journal of Marketing* 52 (January 1988): 93–107.

118. Gary L. Clark, Peter F. Kaminski, and David R. Rink, "Consumer Complaints: Advice on How Companies Should Respond Based on an Empirical Study," *Journal of Services Marketing* 6 (Winter 1992): 41–50.

119. Alan Andreasen and Arthur Best, "Consumers Complain—Does Business Respond?" *Harvard Business Review* 55 (July–August 1977): 93–101.

120. Tibbett L. Speer, "They Complain Because They Care," *American Demographics* (May 1996): 13–14.

121. Ingrid Martin, "Expert-Novice Differences in Complaint Scripts," in Rebecca H. Holman and Michael R. Solomon, eds., *Advances in Consumer Research* 18 (Provo, UT: Association for Consumer Research, 1991): 225–31; Marsha L. Richins, "A Multivariate Analysis of Responses to Dissatisfaction," *Journal of the Academy of Marketing Science* 15 (Fall 1987): 24–31.

122. John A. Schibrowsky and Richard S. Lapidus, "Gaining a Competitive Advantage by Analyzing Aggregate Complaints," *Journal of Consumer Marketing* 11 (1994): 15–26; Clay M. Voorhees, Michael K. Brady, and David M. Horowitz, "A Voice from the Silent Masses: An Exploratory and Comparative Analysis of Noncomplainers," *Journal of the Academy of Marketing Science* 34 (Fall 2006): 514–527.

123. Matthew Creamer, "Dell Quells Critics with Web 2.0, Tack Social Media Has Turned Customer Service Inside-out for All to See," available from www.Advertisingage.com, accessed June 11, 2007.

124. Material adapted from a presentation by Glenn H. Mazur, QFD Institute, 2002.

125. Russell W. Belk, "The Role of Possessions in Constructing and Maintaining a Sense of Past," in Marvin E. Goldberg, Gerald Gorn, and Richard W. Pollay, eds., *Advances in Consumer Research* 17 (Provo, UT: Association for Consumer Research, 1989): 669–76.

126. David E. Sanger, "For a Job Well Done, Japanese Enshrine the Chip," *New York Times* (December 11, 1990): A4.

127. Rob Walker, "The Worm Turns," *New York Times Magazine Online* (May 20, 2007), accessed May 20, 2007.

128. Jacob Jacoby, Carol K. Berning, and Thomas F. Dietvorst, "What about Disposition?" *Journal of Marketing* 41 (April 1977): 22–28.

129. Brian Wansink, S. Adam Brasel, and Steven Amjad, "The Mystery of the Cabinet Castaway: Why We Buy Products We Never Use," *Journal of Family and Consumer Sciences* 92, no. 1 (2000): 104–7.

130. Jennifer Lach, "Welcome to the Hoard Fest," *American Demographics* (April 2000): 8–9.

131. Norimitsu Onishi, "How Do Japanese Dump Trash? Let Us Count the Myriad Ways," *New York Times Online* (May 12, 2005).

132. "Finally, Something at McDonald's You Can Actually Eat," *UTNE Reader* (May–June 1997): 12.

133. Steven Kurutz, "Not Buying It," available from www.nytimes.com, accessed June 21, 2007.

134. Debra J. Dahab, James W. Gentry, and Wanru Su, "New Ways to Reach Non-Recyclers: An Extension of the Model of Reasoned Action to Recycling Behaviors," paper presented at the meetings of the Association for Consumer Research, 1994.

135. Bagozzi and Dabholkar, "Consumer Recycling Goals and Their Effect on Decisions to Recycle," *Psychology & Marketing* 1994, *11(4)*, 313–340 ; see also L. J. Shrum, Tina M. Lowrey, and John A. McCarty, "Recycling as a Marketing Problem: A Framework for Strategy Development," *Psychology & Marketing* 11 (July–August 1994): 393–416; Dahab, Gentry, and Su, "New Ways to Reach Non-Recyclers."

136. Ira Dreyfuss, "Cast-Off Food Lures Shoppers," *Montgomery Advertiser* (April 25, 2004): 6A.

137. Rob Walker, "Unconsumption," *New York Times Magazine* (January 7, 2007): 19; Tina Kelley, "Socks? With Holes? I'll Take It," *New York Times on the Web* (March 16, 2004).

138. Laura Blue, "Let's Talk Trash," *Times* Bonus Section, (November 2006): A37–A38 (2).

139. Heather Won Tesoriero, "Something Old, Something Used to Quietly Cut Costs; Brides Wear Preowned," *Wall Street Journal on the Web* (August 22, 2003).

140. Geoffrey James, "New Life for Old Ads," *BusinessWeek* (June 2004): 50.

141. John F. Sherry, Jr., "A Sociocultural Analysis of a Midwestern American Flea Market," *Journal of Consumer Research* 17 (June 1990): 13–30.

142. Allan J. Magrath, "If Used Product Sellers Ever Get Organized, Watch Out," *Marketing News* (June 25, 1990): 9; Kevin McCrohan and James D. Smith, "Consumer Participation in the Informal Economy," *Journal of the Academy of Marketing Science* 15 (Winter 1990): 62.

143. John F. Sherry, Jr., "Dealers and Dealing in a Periodic Market: Informal Retailing in Ethnographic Perspective," *Journal of Retailing* 66 (Summer 1990): 174.

144. Saul Hansell, "Meg Whitman and eBay, Net Survivors," *New York Times on the Web* (May 5, 2002).

145. Bob Tedeschi, "I'll Trade You My 'Titanic' for Your 'Spider-Man'," *New York Times* E-MailPrint Reprints Save (October 16, 2006).

146. Izzy Grinspan, "Wedding Trashers," *Salon Life* (July 1, 2007), available from www.Salon.com, accessed July 1, 2007.

147. John L. Lastovicka and Karen V. Fernandez, "Three Paths to Disposition: The Movement of Meaningful Possessions to Strangers," *Journal of Consumer Research* 31 (March 2005): 813–23.

148. Ellen Simon, "E-Junk Litters Nation's Homes," *Montgomery Advertiser* (December 6, 2004): 8A; John Markoff, "Technology's Toxic Trash Is Sent to Poor Nations," *New York Times on the Web* (February 25, 2002); "Recycling Phones to Charities, Not Landfills," *New York Times on the Web* (October 26, 2002).

149. Shelly Branch, "Maybe Sex Doesn't Sell, A&F Is Discovering," *Wall Street Journal on the Web* (December 12, 2003).

Group Influence
and Opinion Leadership

Chapter Objectives

When you finish this chapter you should understand why:

● Others, especially those who possess some kind of social power, often influence us.

● We seek out others who share our interests in products or services.

● We are motivated to buy or use products in order to be consistent with what other people do.

● The things that other consumers tell us about products (good and bad) are often more influential than the advertising we see.

● Online technologies are accelerating the impact of word-of-mouth communication.

● Social networking is changing the way companies and consumers interact.

● Certain people are particularly likely to influence others' product choices.

Zachary leads a secret life. During the week, he is a strait-laced stock analyst for a major investment firm. The weekend is another story. Come Friday evening, it's off with the Brooks Brothers suit and on with the black leather, as he trades in his BMW for his treasured Harley-Davidson motorcycle. A dedicated member of HOG (Harley Owners Group), Zachary belongs to the "RUBs" (rich urban bikers) faction of Harley riders. Everyone in his group wears expensive leather vests with Harley insignias and owns customized "Low Riders." Just this week, Zach finally got his new Harley belt buckle when he logged onto The Genuine Harley-Davidson Road-store at Harley-Davidson.com.[1] Surfing around the site makes him realize the lengths to which some of his fellow enthusiasts go to make sure others know they are HOG riders. As one of the Harley Web pages observed, "It's one thing to have people buy your products. It's another thing to have them tattoo your name on their bodies." Zach had to restrain himself from buying more Harley stuff; there were jackets, vests, eyewear, belts, buckles, scarves, watches, jewelry, even housewares ("home is the road") for sale. He settled for a set of Harley salt-and-pepper shakers that would be perfect for his buddy Dan's new crib.

Zach has spent a lot of money on his bike and on outfitting himself to be like the rest of the group. But it's worth it. He feels a real sense of brotherhood with his fellow RUBs. The group rides together in two-column formation to bike rallies that sometimes attract up to 300,000 cycle enthusiasts. What a sense of power he feels when they're all cruising together—it's them against the world!

Of course, an added benefit is the business networking he's been able to accomplish during his weekend jaunts with his fellow professionals who also wait for the weekend to "ride on the wild side."[2] Sometimes sharing a secret can pay off in more ways than one.

 # Reference Groups

Humans are social animals. We all belong to groups, try to please others, and look to others' behavior for cues about what we should do. In fact, our desire to "fit in" or to identify with desirable individuals or groups is the primary motivation for many of our consumption behaviors. We may go to great lengths to please the members of a group whose acceptance we covet.[3]

Zachary's biker group is an important part of his identity, and this membership influences many of his buying decisions. He has spent many thousands of dollars on parts and accessories since acquiring his identity as a RUB. His fellow riders bond via their consumption choices, so total strangers feel an immediate connection with one another when they meet. The publisher of *American Iron*, an industry magazine, observed, "You don't buy a Harley because it's a superior bike, you buy a Harley to be a part of a family."[4]

Zachary doesn't model himself after just *any* biker—only the people with whom he really identifies can exert that kind of influence on him. For example, Zachary's group doesn't have much to do with outlaw clubs whose blue-collar riders sport big Harley tattoos. The members of his group also have only polite contact with "Ma and Pa" bikers, whose rides are the epitome of comfort and feature such niceties as radios, heated handgrips, and floorboards. Essentially, only the RUBs comprise Zachary's *reference group*.

A **reference group** is "an actual or imaginary individual or group conceived of having significant relevance upon an individual's evaluations, aspirations, or behavior."[5] Reference groups influence us in three ways: *informational, utilitarian,* and *value-expressive*. Table 11.1 describes these influences. In this chapter we'll focus on how other people, whether fellow bikers, co-workers, friends, family, or simply casual acquaintances, influence our purchase decisions. We'll consider how our group memberships shape our preferences because we want others to accept us or even because we mimic the actions of famous people we've never met. Finally, we'll explore why some people especially affect our product preferences and how marketers go about finding those people and enlisting their support in persuading consumers to jump on the bandwagon.

WHEN ARE REFERENCE GROUPS IMPORTANT?

Reference group influences are not equally powerful for all types of products and consumption activities. For example, we are not as likely to take others' preferences into account when we choose products that are not very complex, that are low in perceived risk (see Chapter 9), or that we can try before we buy.[6] In addition, knowing what others prefer may influence us at a general level (e.g., owning or not owning a computer, eating junk food versus health food), whereas at other times this knowledge may affect the specific brands we desire within a product category (e.g., wearing Levi's jeans versus Diesel jeans, or smoking Marlboro cigarettes rather than Player's Light).

Two dimensions that influence the degree to which reference groups are important are whether we will consume the item publicly or privately and whether it is a luxury or a necessity. As a rule, reference group effects are more robust for purchases that are (1) luxuries rather than necessities (e.g., sailboats) because products that we buy using discretionary income are subject to individual tastes and preferences, whereas necessities do not offer this range of choices, and (2) socially conspicuous or visible to others (e.g., living room furniture or clothing) because we don't tend to

TABLE 11.1
THREE FORMS OF REFERENCE GROUP INFLUENCE

Information Influence	• The individual seeks information about various brands from an association of professionals or independent group of experts. • The individual seeks information from those who work with the product as a profession. • The individual seeks brand-related knowledge and experience (such as how Brand A's performance compares to Brand B's) from those friends, neighbors, relatives, or work associates who have reliable information about the brands. • The brand the individual selects is influenced by observing a seal of approval of an independent testing agency (such as *Good Housekeeping*). • The individual's observation of what experts do (such as observing the type of car that police drive or the brand of television that repairmen buy) influences his or her choice of a brand.
Utilitarian Influence	• So that he or she satisfies the expectations of fellow work associates, the individual's decision to purchase a particular brand is influenced by their preferences. • The individual's decision to purchase a particular brand is influenced by the preferences of people with whom he or she has social interaction. • The individual's decision to purchase a particular brand is influenced by the preferences of family members. • The desire to satisfy the expectations that others have of him or her has an impact on the individual's brand choice.
Value-Expressive Influence	• The individual feels that the purchase or use of a particular brand will enhance the image others have of him or her. • The individual feels that those who purchase or use a particular brand possess the characteristics that he or she would like to have. • The individual sometimes feels that it would be nice to be like the type of person that advertisements show using a particular brand. • The individual feels that the people who purchase a particular brand are admired or respected by others. • The individual feels that the purchase of a particular brand would help show others what he or she is or would like to be (such as an athlete, successful business person, good parent, etc.).

Source: Adapted from C. Whan Park and V. Parker Lessig, "Students and Housewives: Differences in Susceptibility to Reference Group Influence," *Journal of Consumer Research* 4 September 1977): 102. Copyright © 1977 JCR, Inc. Reprinted with permission of The University of Chicago Press.

be swayed as much by the opinions of others if no one but ourselves will ever see what we buy. (Note: In the old days this used to be true of underwear, but some of today's styles have changed all that!)[7] Figure 11.1 shows the relative effects of reference group influences on some specific product classes.

Why are reference groups so persuasive? The answer lies in the potential power they wield over us. **Social power** is "the capacity to alter the actions of others."[8] To the degree to which you are able to make someone else do something, regardless of whether they do it willingly, you have power over that person. The following classification of power bases helps us to distinguish among the reasons a person exerts power over another, the degree to which the influence is voluntary, and whether this influence will continue to have an effect even when the source of the power isn't around.[9]

● **Referent power:** If a person admires the qualities of a person or a group, he tries to imitate them by copying the referent's behaviors (e.g., choice of clothing, cars, leisure activities)—just as Zack's fellow bikers affected his preferences. Prominent people in all walks of life can affect our consumption behaviors by virtue of product endorsements (e.g., 50 Cent for Reebok), distinctive fashion statements (e.g., Fergie's displays of high-end designer clothing), or championing causes (e.g., Lance Armstrong's work for cancer). Referent power is important to many marketing strategies because consumers voluntarily modify what they do and buy to identify with a referent.

■ **FIGURE 11.1**
RELATIVE REFERENCE GROUPS'
INFLUENCE ON PURCHASE
INTENTION

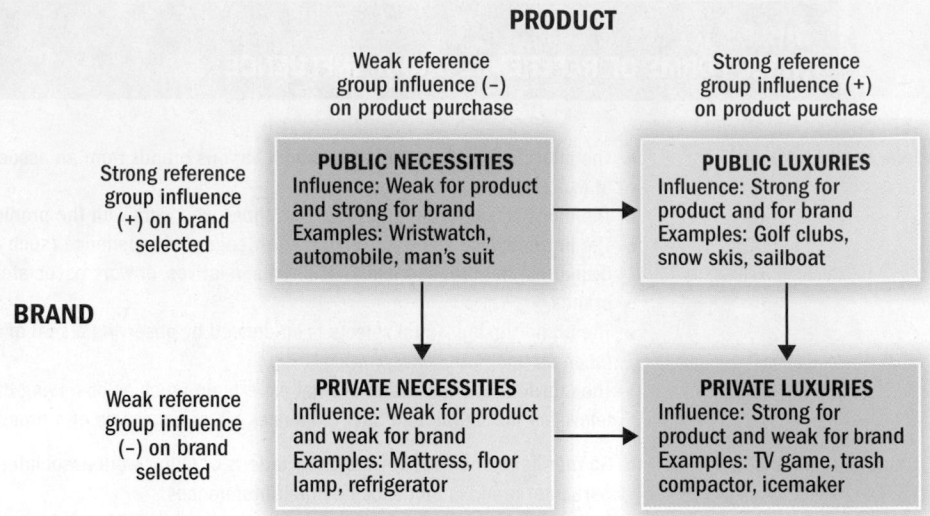

- **Information power:** A person can have power simply because she knows something others would like to know. Editors of trade publications such as *Women's Wear Daily* often possess tremendous power because of their ability to compile and disseminate information that can make or break individual designers or companies. People with information power are able to influence consumer opinion by virtue of their (assumed) access to the "truth."
- **Legitimate power:** Sometimes we grant power by virtue of social agreements, such as the authority we give to police officers, soldiers, and yes, sometimes even professors. The legitimate power a uniform confers wields authority in consumer contexts including teaching hospitals where medical students don white coats to enhance their standing with patients.[10] Marketers may "borrow" this form of power to influence consumers. For example, an ad featuring a model wearing a white doctor's coat can add an aura of legitimacy or authority to the presentation of the product ("I'm not a doctor, but I play one on TV").
- **Expert power:** To attract the casual Internet user, U.S. Robotics signed up British physicist Stephen Hawking to endorse its modems. A company executive commented, "We wanted to generate trust. So we found visionaries who use U.S. Robotics technology, and we let them tell the consumer how it makes their lives more productive." Hawking, who has Lou Gehrig's disease and speaks via a synthesizer, said in one TV spot, "My body may be stuck in this chair, but with the Internet my mind can go to the end of the universe."[11] Hawking's expert power derives from the knowledge he possess about a content area. This helps to explain the weight many of us assign to professional critics' reviews of restaurants, books, movies, and cars—even though with the advent of blogs and open-source references such as Wikipedia it's getting a lot harder to tell just who is really an expert![12]
- **Reward power:** A person or group with the means to provide positive reinforcement (see Chapter 3) has **reward power**. The reward may be the tangible kind such as the contestants on *Survivor* experience when they get voted off the island. Or it can be more intangible, such as the approval the judges on *American Idol* (except Simon) deliver to contestants.
- **Coercive power:** We exert coercive power when we influence someone because of social or physical intimidation. A threat is often effective in the short term, but it doesn't tend to stick because we tend to revert back to our original behavior as soon as the bully leaves the scene. Fortunately, marketers rarely try to use this type of power unless you count those annoying calls from telemarketers!

A physician has expert power, and a white coat reinforces this expertise by conferring legitimate power.

However, we can see elements of this power base in the fear appeals we talked about in Chapter 8 as well as in intimidating salespeople who try to succeed with a "hard sell."

TYPES OF REFERENCE GROUPS

Although two or more people normally form a group, we often use the term *reference group* a bit more loosely to describe *any* external influence that provides social cues.[13] The referent may be a cultural figure who has an impact on many people (e.g., Osama bin Laden) or a person or group whose influence only operates in the consumer's immediate environment (e.g., Zachary's biker club). Reference groups that affect consumption can include parents, fellow motorcycle enthusiasts, the Labor Party, or even the Albicelestes, the Dave Matthews Band, or Luc Besson.

Obviously, some groups and individuals are more powerful than others and affect a broader range of our consumption decisions. For example, our parents may play a pivotal role in forming our values on many important issues, such as attitudes about marriage or where to go to college. We call this **normative influence**—that is, the reference group helps to set and enforce fundamental standards of conduct. In contrast, a Harley-Davidson club exerts **comparative influence** because it affects members' decisions about specific motorcycle purchases.[14]

BRAND COMMUNITIES AND CONSUMER TRIBES

Before it released the popular Xbox game *Halo 2*, the company put up a Web site to explain the story line. However, there was a catch: The story was written from the point of view of the Covenant (the aliens who are preparing to attack Earth in the game)—and in *their* language. Within 48 hours, avid gamers around the world worked together by sharing information in gaming chat rooms to crack the code

Fellow college students may act as a reference group.

and translate the text. More than 1.5 million people preordered the game before its release.[15] This cooperative effort illustrates a major trend in consumer behavior.

A **brand community** is a group of consumers who share a set of social relationships based upon usage or interest in a product. Unlike other kinds of communities, these members typically don't live near each other—except when they may meet for brief periods at organized events or **brandfests** that community-oriented companies such as Jeep or Harley-Davidson sponsor. These events help owners to "bond" with fellow enthusiasts and strengthen their identification with the product as well as with others they meet who share their passion. Researchers find that people who participate in these events feel more positive about the products as a result and this enhances brand loyalty. They are more forgiving than others of product failures or lapses in service quality, and less likely to switch brands even if they learn that competing products are as good or better. Furthermore, these community members become emotionally involved in the company's welfare, and they often serve as brand missionaries by carrying its marketing message to others.[16]

The notion of a **consumer tribe** is similar to a brand community; it is a group of people who share a lifestyle and who can identify with each other because of a shared allegiance to an activity or a product. Although these tribes are often unstable and short-lived, at least for a time members identify with others through shared emotions, moral beliefs, styles of life, and of course the products they jointly consume as part of their tribal affiliation. Some companies, especially those that are more youth oriented, are using a **tribal marketing strategy** that links their product to, say, a group of shredders (more on this in Chapter 5). However, there also are plenty of tribes with older members, such as car enthusiasts who gather to celebrate such cult products (see Chapter 4) as the Citroën in Europe and the Ford Mustang in the United States, or "foodies" who share their passion for cooking with other Jacques Pépin wannabees around the world.[17] Pontiac opened a community hub on Yahoo! it calls Pontiac Underground (pontiacunderground.com), "Where Passion for Pontiac Is Driven By You." The carmaker does no overt marketing on the site; the idea is to let drivers find it and spread the word themselves. Users share photos and videos of cars using Flickr and Yahoo! Video. A Yahoo! Answers zone enables knowledge sharing. Meanwhile, a list of Pontiac clubs in the physical world and on Yahoo! Groups allows users to connect offline and online.[18]

bringt nur zusammen, www.FlirtMaschine.de was zusammenpasst.

Online dating sites (like this German one) are one type of brand community (where the people are the brands!).

MEMBERSHIP VERSUS ASPIRATIONAL REFERENCE GROUPS

A **membership reference group** consists of people we actually know, whereas we don't know those in an **aspirational reference group** but we admire them anyway. These people are likely to be successful businesspeople, athletes, performers, or whomever rocks our world. Not surprisingly, many marketing efforts that specifically adopt a reference group appeal concentrate on highly visible, widely admired figures (such as well-known athletes or performers) and link these people to brands so that the products they use or endorse also take on this aspirational quality. For example an amateur basketball player who idolizes Allen Iverson might strongly identify with Reebok because Iverson endorses these shoes.[19] One study of business students who aspired to the "executive" role found a strong relationship between products they associated with their *ideal selves* (see Chapter 5) and those they assumed real executives own.[20]

Because we tend to compare ourselves to similar others, many promotional strategies include "ordinary" people whose consumption activities provide informational social influence. How can we predict which people you know will be part of your membership reference group? Several factors make it more likely:

● **Propinquity:** As physical distance between people decreases and opportunities for interaction increase, relationships are more likely to form. We call this physical nearness *propinquity*. An early study on friendship patterns in a housing

Brandfests sponsored by companies like Harley-Davidson help to create strong brand communities.

Marketing Opportunity

Most consumers only admire their aspirational reference groups from afar, but more and more of them are shelling out big bucks to get up close and personal with their heroes. *Fantasy camps* today are a $1 billion industry as people pay for the chance to hang out—and play with—their idols. Baseball camps that mix retired players with fans have been around for many years, but now other types are springing up to let people mingle with their favorite hockey players, poker players, even members of the U.S. women's national football team. At one camp, 80 people each paid about $8,000 to jam with rock stars including Nils Lofgren, Dickey Betts, and Roger Daltrey. One enthusiastic novice gushed afterward, "We all grow up with heroes and never get to share a moment with them. But I got to live out my fantasy."[21]

complex showed this factor's strong effects: All things equal, residents were much more likely to be friends with the people next door than with those who lived only two doors away. Furthermore, people who lived next to a staircase had more friends than those at the ends of a hall (presumably, they were more likely to "bump into" people using the stairs).[22]

● **Mere exposure:** We come to like persons or things simply as a result of seeing them more often, which social scientists call the *mere exposure phenomenon*.[23] Greater frequency of contact, even if unintentional, may help to determine one's set of local referents. The same effect holds when evaluating works of art or even political candidates.[24] One study predicted 83 percent of the winners of political primaries solely by the amount of media exposure candidates got.[25]

● **Group cohesiveness:** Cohesiveness refers to the degree to which members of a group are attracted to each other and how much each values their membership in this group. As the value of the group to the individual increases, so too does the likelihood that the group will influence his consumption decisions. Smaller groups tend to be more cohesive because in larger groups the contributions of each member are usually less important or noticeable. By the same token, groups often try to restrict membership to a select few, which increases the value of membership to those who do get in.

POSITIVE VERSUS NEGATIVE REFERENCE GROUPS

Reference groups impact our buying decisions both positively and negatively. In most cases, we model our behavior to be in line with what we think the group expects us to do. Sometimes however we also deliberately do the opposite if we want to distance

This recruiting ad presents a compelling role model for young people contemplating a career in the armed forces.

ourselves from *avoidance groups*. You may carefully study the dress or mannerisms of a group you dislike (e.g., "nerds," "druggies," or "preppies") and scrupulously avoid buying anything that might identify you with that group. For example, rebellious adolescents often resent parental influence and may deliberately do the opposite of what their parents would like to make a statement about their independence.

The motivation to distance oneself from a negative reference group can be as or more powerful than the desire to please a positive group.[26] That's why advertisements occasionally show an undesirable person using a competitor's product. This approach subtly makes the point that you can avoid winding up like *that* kind of person by staying away from the products he buys. As a once-popular book reminded us, "Real men *don't* eat quiche!"[27] Today, a T-shirt for sale on a computer-oriented Web site proudly proclaims, "Real Men Don't Click Help."

The Web encourages the rise of a new kind of group—**antibrand communities**. These groups also coalesce around a celebrity, store, or brand—but in this case they're united by their disdain for it. The Rachael Ray Sucks Community on the blogging

An avoidance group appeal.

and social-networking site *LiveJournal* claims more than 1,000 members who don't hesitate to post their latest thoughts about the various shortcomings, flaws, and disagreeable traits of the (otherwise popular) American television food personality. They criticize Ray's overuse of chicken stock, her kitchen hygiene, her smile (posters like to compare it to The Joker's of Batman fame), her penchant for saying "Yum-o!" and so on. The community has a basic rule for membership: "You must be anti-Rachael!"[28]

One team of researchers that study these communities observes that they tend to attract social idealists who advocate nonmaterialistic lifestyles. After they interviewed members of online communities who oppose Wal-Mart, Starbucks, and McDonald's, they concluded that these antibrand communities provide a meeting place for those who share a moral stance; a support network to achieve common goals; a means for coping with workplace frustrations (many members actually work for the companies they are bashing!); and a hub for information, activities, and related resources.[29] Another study chronicles the level of opposition the Hummer inspires. For example, whereas brand enthusiasts celebrate the Hummer's road safety because of its size and weight, antibranders who drive smaller cars slam the vehicle's bulk. One driver posted this message: "The H2 is a death machine. You'd better hope that you don't collide with an H2 in your economy car. You can kiss your ass goodbye thanks to the H2's massive weight and raised bumpers. Too bad you couldn't afford an urban assault vehicle of your own."[30]

Consumers Do It in Groups

With more people in a group, it becomes less likely that they will single out a member for attention. People in larger groups or those in situations where other are less likely

Costumes hide our true identities and encourage deindividuation.

to identify them have fewer restraints on their behavior. For example, people sometimes behave more wildly at costume parties or on Halloween than they do normally. We call this phenomenon **deindividuation,** a process where individual identities become submerged within a group.

Social loafing happens when we don't devote as much to task because our contribution is part of a larger group effort.[31] You may have experienced this if you've worked on a group project for a class! Waitpersons are painfully aware of social loafing: People who eat in groups tend to tip less per person than when they are eating alone.[32] For this reason, many restaurants automatically tack on a fixed gratuity for groups of six or more.

There is some evidence that decisions groups make differ from those each individual would choose on his own. The **risky shift** refers to the observation that in many cases, group members show a greater willingness to consider riskier alternatives following group discussion than they would if members made individual decisions with no discussion.[34] Psychologists propose several explanations for this increased riskiness. One possibility is that something similar to social loafing occurs. As more people are involved in a decision, each individual is less accountable for the outcome, resulting in *diffusion of responsibility*.[35] The practice of placing blanks in at least one of the rifles a firing squad uses diffuses each soldier's responsibility for the death of a prisoner because it's never certain who actually shot him. Another explanation is the *value hypothesis*, which states that our culture values risky behavior, so when people make decisions in groups they conform to this expectation.[36]

Research evidence for the risky shift is mixed. A more general finding is that group discussion tends to increase **decision polarization**. Therefore, whichever direction the group members were leaning before discussion began (whether a risky choice or a conservative choice) becomes even more extreme in that direction after discussion. Group discussions regarding product purchases tend to create a risky shift for low-risk items, but they yield even more conservative group decisions for high-risk products.[37]

Even shopping behavior changes when people do it in groups. For example, people who shop with at least one other person tend to make more unplanned purchases, buy more, and cover more areas of a store than those who go alone.[38] Both normative and informational social influence explains this. Group members may buy something to gain the approval of the others, or the group may simply expose them to more products and stores. Either way, retailers are well advised to encourage group-shopping activities.

Marketing Pitfall

College parties sometimes illustrate the dark side of deindividuation when revelers encourage their friends to consume almost superhuman volumes of alcohol in group settings. Researchers estimate that about 4.5 million young people are alcohol dependent or problem drinkers. Binge drinking among college students is reaching epidemic proportions. In a 2-week period, 42 percent of all college students engage in binge drinking (more than five drinks at a time) versus 33 percent of their noncollege counterparts. One in three students drinks primarily to get drunk, including 35 percent of college women. For most, social pressure to throw inhibitions aside is the culprit.[33]

Women at a home Tupperware party.

Home shopping parties, as the Tupperware party epitomizes, capitalize on group pressures to boost sales.[39] A company representative makes a sales presentation to a group of people gathered at the home of a friend or acquaintance. This format is effective because of informational social influence: Participants model the behavior of others who can provide them with information about how to use certain products, especially because a relatively homogeneous group (e.g., neighborhood homemakers) attends the party. Normative social influence also operates because others can easily observe our actions. Pressures to conform may be particularly intense and may escalate as more and more group members begin to "cave in" (we call this process the *bandwagon effect*).

In addition, these parties may activate deindividuation or the risky shift. As consumers get caught up in the group, they may find themselves willing to try new products they would not normally consider. These same dynamics underlie the latest wrinkle on the Tupperware home selling technique: the Botox party. The craze for Botox injections that paralyze facial nerves to reduce wrinkles (for 3 to 6 months anyway) is fueled by gatherings where dermatologists or plastic surgeons redefine the definition of house calls. For patients, mixing cocktail hour with cosmetic injections takes some of the anxiety out of the procedure. Egged on by the others at the party, a doctor can dewrinkle as many as 10 patients in an hour. An advertising executive who worked on the Botox marketing strategy explained that the membership reference group appeal is more effective than the traditional route of using a celebrity spokesperson to tout the injections in advertising: "We think it's more persuasive to think of your next-door neighbor using it."[40] The only hitch is that after you get the injections your face is so rigid your friends can't tell if you're smiling!

Conformity

The early Bohemians who lived in Paris around 1830 made a point of behaving, well, differently from others. One flamboyant figure of the time became famous for walking a lobster on a leash through the gardens of the Royal Palace. His friends drank

Group pressure often influences our clothing choices.

wine from human skulls, cut their beards in strange shapes, and slept in tents on the floors of their garrets.[41] Sounds a bit like some frats we've visited.

Although in every age there certainly are those who "march to their own drummers," most people tend to follow society's expectations regarding how they should act and look (with a little improvisation here and there, of course). **Conformity** is a change in beliefs or actions as a reaction to real or imagined group pressure. In order for a society to function, its members develop **norms**, or informal rules that govern behavior. Without these rules, we would have chaos. Imagine the confusion if a simple norm such as stopping for a red traffic light did not exist.

We conform in many small ways everyday—even though we don't always realize it. Unspoken rules govern many aspects of consumption. In addition to norms regarding appropriate use of clothing and other personal items, we conform to rules that include gift-giving (we expect birthday presents from loved ones and get upset if they do not materialize), sex roles (men often pick up the check on a first date), and personal hygiene (our friends expect us to shower regularly).

We don't mimic others' behaviors all the time, so what makes it more likely we'll conform? These are some common culprits:[42]

- **Cultural pressures:** Different cultures encourage conformity to a greater or lesser degree. The American slogan "Do your own thing" in the 1960s reflected a movement away from conformity and toward individualism. In contrast, Japanese society emphasizes collective well-being and group loyalty over individuals' needs.
- **Fear of deviance:** The individual may have reason to believe that the group will apply *sanctions* to punish noncomforming behaviors. It's not unusual to observe adolescents shunning a peer who is "different" or a corporation or university passing over a person for promotion because she is not a "team player."
- **Commitment:** The more people are dedicated to a group and value their membership in it, the more motivated they are to do what the group wants. Rock groupies and followers of TV evangelists may do anything their idols ask of them, and terrorists are willing to die for their cause. According to the *principle of least interest*, the person that is *least* committed to staying in a relationship

The Tangled Web

There is a long tradition of inventing fake stories to see who will swallow them—like the one in 1824 when a man convinced 300 New Yorkers to sign up for a construction project. He claimed all the new building in the lower part of Manhattan (what is now the Wall Street area) was making the island bottom-heavy. So, they needed to saw off this section of town and tow it out to sea to prevent New York City from tipping over!

The Web is a perfect medium for spreading rumors and hoaxes, and we can only guess how much damage this "project" would cause today if the perpetrator recruited construction crews via e-mail! Modern-day hoaxes abound; many of these are in the form of e-mail chain letters promising instant riches if you pass the message on to 10 friends. Your professor will love one variation of this hoax: In a scam called "Win Tenure Fast," academics were told to add their names to a document and then cite it in their own research papers. The idea is that everyone who gets the letter cites the professor's name and with so many citations you're guaranteed to get tenure! If only it were that easy.

Other hoaxes involve major corporations. A popular one promised that if you try Microsoft products you would win a free trip to Disneyland. Nike received several hundred pairs of old sneakers a day after the rumor spread that you would get a free pair of new shoes in exchange for your old, smelly ones (pity the delivery people who had to cart these packages to the company!). Procter & Gamble received more than 10,000 irate calls after a rumor began spreading on newsgroups that its Febreze fabric deodorant kills dogs. In a preemptive strike, the company registered numerous Web site names such as febrezekillspet.com, febrezesucks.com, and ihateprocterandgamble.com to be sure angry consumers didn't use them. The moral: Don't believe everything you click on.

has the most power because that party doesn't care as much if the other person rejects him.[43]

- **Group unanimity, size, and expertise:**—As groups gain in power, compliance increases. It is often harder to resist the demands of a large number of people than only a few—especially when a "mob mentality" rules.

- **Susceptibility to interpersonal influence:**—This trait refers to an individual's need to have others think highly of him. Consumers who don't possess this trait are *role-relaxed*; they tend to be older, affluent, and to have high self-confidence. Subaru created a communications strategy to reach role-relaxed consumers. In one of its commercials, a man proclaims, "I want a car. . . . Don't tell me about wood paneling, about winning the respect of my neighbors. They're my neighbors. They're not my heroes."[44]

WORD-OF-MOUTH COMMUNICATION

Altoids breath mints have been around for 200 years but it's only recently they've been a big hit. How did this happen? The revival began when the mint began to attract a devoted following among smokers and coffee drinkers who hung out in the blossoming Seattle club scene during the 1980s. Until 1993, when Kraft bought manufacturer Callard & Bowers, only those "in the know" sucked the mints. The brand's marketing manager persuaded Kraft to hire advertising agency Leo Burnett to develop a modest promotional campaign. The agency decided to publicize the candy with subway posters sporting retro imagery and other "low-tech" media to avoid making the product seem mainstream—that would turn off the original audience.[45] As young people started to tune into this "retro" treat, its popularity rocketed.

As the Altoids success story illustrates, "buzz" makes a hit product. **Word-of-mouth (WOM)** is product information individuals transmit to other individuals. Because we get the word from people we know, WOM tends to be more reliable and trustworthy than messages from more formal marketing channels. And unlike advertising, WOM often comes with social pressure to conform to these recommendations.[46] Ironically, despite all of the money marketers pump into lavish ads, WOM is far more powerful: It influences two-thirds of all consumer-goods sales.[47] In one recent survey, 69 percent of interviewees said they relied on a personal referral at least once over the course of a year to help them choose a restaurant, 36 percent reported they used referrals to decide on computer hardware and software, and 22 percent got help from friends and associates to decide where to travel.[48]

If you think carefully about the content of your own conversations in the course of a normal day, you will probably agree that much of what you discuss with friends, family members, or co-workers is product related: Whether you compliment someone on her dress and ask her where she bought it, recommend a new restaurant to a friend, or complain to your neighbor about the shoddy treatment you got at the bank, you are engaging in WOM. Recall, for example, that comments and suggestions his fellow RUBs made drove many of Zachary's biker purchases. Marketers have been aware of the power of WOM for many years, but recently they've been more aggressive about trying to promote and control it instead of sitting back and hoping people will like their products enough to talk them up. Companies like BzzAgent enlist as many as hundreds of thousands of "agents" who try new products and spread the word about those they like.[49]

As far back as the Stone Age (well, the 1950s, anyway), communications theorists challenged the assumption that advertising primarily determines what we buy. As a rule, advertising is more effective when it reinforces our existing product preferences than when it tries to create new ones.[50] Studies in both industrial and consumer purchase settings underscore the idea that, although information from impersonal sources is important to create brand awareness, consumers rely on word of mouth

Hoaxkill.com is a Web site dedicated to tracking hoaxes and debunking product rumors.

in the later stages of evaluation and adoption.[51] Quite simply, the more positive information consumers get about a product from peers, the more likely they will be to adopt the product.[52]

The influence of others' opinions is at times even more powerful than our own perceptions. In one study of furniture choices, consumers' estimates of how much their friends would like the furniture was a better predictor of purchase than what they thought of it. [53] In addition, consumers may find their own reasons to push a brand that take the manufacturer by surprise: That's what happened with Mountain Dew; we can trace its popularity among younger consumers to the "buzz" about the soda's high caffeine content. As an advertising executive explained, "The caffeine thing was not in any of Mountain Dew's television ads. This drink is hot by word-of-mouth."[54]

WOM is especially powerful when the consumer is relatively unfamiliar with the product category. We would expect such a situation in the case of new products (e.g., medications to prevent hair loss) or those that are technologically complex (e.g., CD players). One way to reduce uncertainty about the wisdom of a purchase is to talk about it. Talking gives the consumer an opportunity to generate more supporting arguments for the purchase and to garner support for this decision from others. As one example, one study reported that the strongest predictor of a person's intention to buy a residential solar water-heating system is the number of solar-heat users the person knows.[55]

You talk about products for several reasons:[56]

- You might be highly involved with a type of product or activity and enjoy talking about it. Computer hackers, avid football fans, and "fashion plates" seem to share the ability to steer a conversation toward their particular interests.

As its name suggests, BzzAgent recruits consumers to create a "buzz" for clients. You can sign up at bzzagent.com.

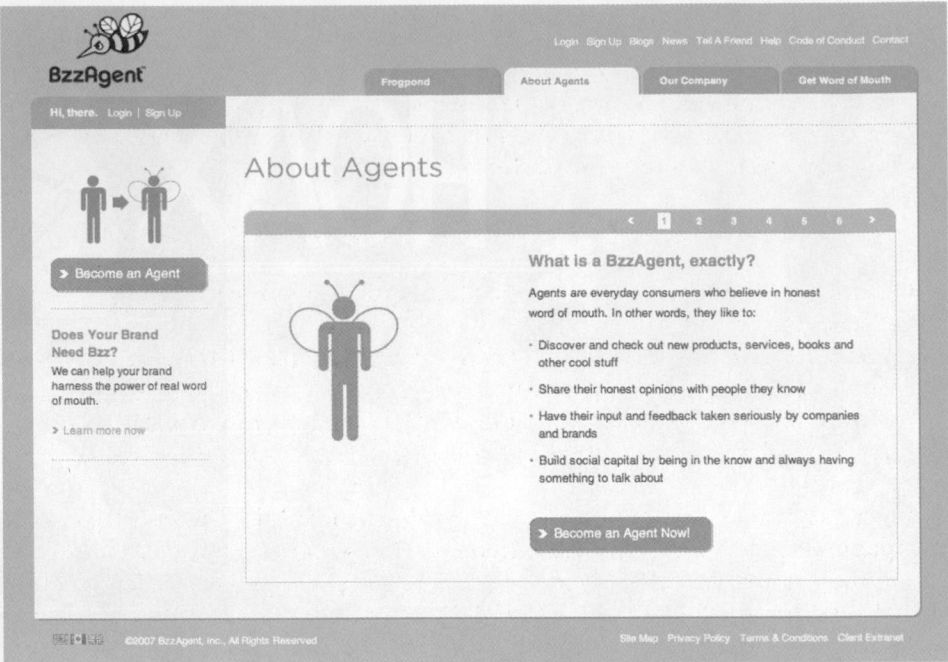

- You might be knowledgeable about a product and use conversations as a way to let others know it. Thus, word-of-mouth communication sometimes enhances the ego of the individual who wants to impress others with her expertise.
- You might initiate a discussion out of genuine concern for someone else. We like to ensure that people we care about buy what is good for them or that they do not waste their money.

NEGATIVE WOM AND THE POWER OF RUMORS

Word of mouth is a two-edged sword that cuts both ways for marketers. Informal discussions among consumers can make or break a product or store. Furthermore, consumers weigh **negative word-of-mouth** more heavily than they do positive comments. According to a study the White House Office of Consumer Affairs did, 90 percent of unhappy customers will not do business with a company again. Each of these people is likely to share his grievance with at least nine other people, and 13 percent of these disgruntled customers will go on to tell more than 30 people of their negative experience.[57]

Especially when we're considering a new product or service, we're likely to pay more attention to negative information than to positive information and to tell others about our nasty experience.[58] Research shows that negative WOM reduces the credibility of a firm's advertising and influences consumers' attitudes toward a product as well as their intention to buy it.[59] Dell found this out the hard way when bloggers started to denounce the computer maker's quality and service levels and the popular media picked up this discontent and magnified it.[60]

As Dell discovered, it's incredibly easy to spread negative WOM online. Many dissatisfied customers and disgruntled former employees are "inspired" to create Web sites simply to share their tales of woe with others. For example, a Web site for people to complain about the Dunkin' Donuts chain got to be so popular the company bought it in order to control the bad press it was getting. It grew out of a complaint by the original owner because he could not get skim milk for his coffee.[61] As it tries to prevent additional negative word of mouth about its Ortho Evra birth control patch that has been linked to blood clots and strokes, Johnson & Johnson is buying the rights to negative domain names including <u>Deathbypatch.com</u> and <u>Orthoevrakills.com</u>.[62]

In an in-depth study of 40 complaint Web sites such as <u>walmartsucks.com</u>, the authors use *protest-framing theory* that sociologists developed to understand how people define a social situation to others in order to influence their behavior.[63] They identify three basic subframes, or themes:

1 **Injustice:** Consumer protestors frequently talk about their repeated attempts to contact the company only to be ignored.
2 **Identity:** Posters characterize the violator (often top management) as evil, rather than simply wrong.
3 **Agency:** Individual Web site creators try to create a collective identity for those who share their anger with a company. They evoke themes of crusade and heroism to rally others to believe that they have the power to change the *status quo* in which companies can wrong consumers without retribution.

A rumor can be very dangerous, especially when it's false. In the 1930s, some companies hired "professional rumormongers" to organize word-of-mouth campaigns that pushed their clients' products and criticized competitors.[64] More recently, Bio Business International, a small Canadian company that markets 100 percent cotton non-chlorine-bleached tampons under the name Terra Femme, encouraged women to spread a message that tampons made by its American competitors contain dioxin. There is very little evidence to support the claim that these products are dangerous, but as a result of this rumor, Procter & Gamble received thousands of complaints about its feminine hygiene products.[65]

As we transmit information to one another, it tends to change. The resulting message usually does not at all resemble the original. The British psychologist Frederic Bartlett used the method of *serial reproduction* to examine how content mutates. Like the game of "Telephone" many of us played as kids, he asked a subject to reproduce a stimulus, such as a drawing or a story. He then gave another subject this reproduction and asked him to copy it, and repeated this process several times. Figure 11.2 illustrates how a message changes as it's reproduced. Bartlett found that distortions almost inevitably follow a pattern: They tend to change from ambiguous forms to more conventional ones as subjects try to make them consistent with their preexisting schemas (see Chapter 2). He called this process *assimilation* and he noted that it often occurs as people engage in *leveling* when they omit details to simplify the structure, or *sharpening* when they exaggerate prominent details.

CUTTING-EDGE WOM STRATEGIES

In the "old days" (i.e., a few years ago), here's how a toy company would launch a new product: Unveil a hot holiday toy during a spring trade fair, run a November–December saturation television ad campaign during cartoon prime time to sell the toy to kids, then sit back and watch as desperate parents scramble through the aisles at Toys-R-Us as you wait for the resulting media coverage to drive still more sales. In today's so-called *New Media/Web2.0 market*, a toy marketer is more likely to encourage buzz from bloggers; instant messaging; subtle product placement in targeted TV shows, movies, and videos "gone viral" on YouTube and hundreds of smaller Web sites dedicated to highly involved hobbyists.

Here's a real example: the Picoo Z helicopter, a $30 toy helicopter Silverlit Toys makes in Hong Kong.[66] In March 2007, a Google search for the Picoo produced more than 109,000 URLs, whereas the URLs for Silverlit Toys was more than 597,000, with many of those links pointing to major online global gift retailers, such as Hammacher-Schlemmer and Toys-R-Us. Do you think this huge exposure was the result of a meticulously planned promotional strategy? Think again. By most

■ FIGURE 11.2
THE TRANSMISSION OF MISINFORMATION

Original Drawing

Net Profit

The emergence of gaming as an online, shared experience opens new vistas to marketers. Consider this: Toyota's digital racing game *Tundra Madness* on MSN's Gaming Zone attracted 2.5 million visitors per month who spent an average of 8 minutes on the site daily. The company's research showed that the campaign raised brand awareness by 28 percent and intent to purchase by 5 percent.[70]

The secret behind the appeal of this format is the huge chunks of time people spend immersed in these games. The average online player logs 17 hours per week, and firms such as Sony, Microsoft, and Sega are building their own virtual worlds to get a piece of the action. As one game company executive put it, "This is not a genre of game but a break-through new medium. It provides a completely new social, collaborative shared experience. We're basically in the Internet community business."[71]

Sony Online's *EverQuest* is among the most successful of the new breed of Massively Multiplayer Online Role-Player Games that allow people to live shadow lives as members of "guilds" who participate in a never-ending journey to slay monsters and earn points. *EverQuest* combines the stunning graphics of advanced gaming with the social scene of a chat room. Like *The Sims*, players create a character

accounts, a 28-year-old tech worker in Chicago started the Picoo Z buzz when he bought his helicopter after reading about it on a hobbyist message board. A few months later he uploaded his homemade video of the toy on YouTube. Within 2 weeks, 15 of his friends bought the toy and they in turn posted their own videos and pointed viewers to the original video. Internet retailers who troll online conversations for fresh and exciting buzz identified the toy and started adding their own links to the clips. Within a few short months there were hundreds of Picoo Z videos and more than a million people viewed them (find one at: youtube.com/watch?v=y6t1R3yB-cs).

As marketers increasingly recognize the power of WOM to make or break a new product, they are coming up with new ways to get consumers to help them sell. Let's review some successful strategies.

Virtual Communities

In ancient times (that is, before the Web was widely accessible), most membership reference groups consisted of people who had face-to-face contact. Now, it's possible to share interests with people you've never met—and probably never will. Consider the case of Widespread Panic. The band has never had a music video on MTV or cracked the Billboard Top 200. But it's one of the top 40 touring bands in the United States. How did it get to be so successful? Simple—the group built a virtual community of fans and opened itself up to them. It enlisted listeners to help promote the group in exchange for free tickets and backstage passes. Then, it went virtual: The band lets fans send messages to its recording studio, and hard-core

Role-playing computer games involve thousands of players worldwide in interactive, online communities.

followers can find out vital information such as what band members ate for lunch via regular updates on their Web sites.[67]

A **virtual community of consumption** is a collection of people who interact online to share their enthusiasm for and knowledge about a specific consumption activity. Like the brand communities we discussed earlier, these groups form around common love for a product, whether it's Barbie dolls or BlackBerry PDAs. However, members remain anonymous because they only interact with each other in cyberspace. Still, these groups can and do make their voices heard. In one recent effort, nearly 14,000 people banded together on Facebook to beg Cadbury Schweppes to bring back Wispa, a chocolate bar the company discontinued in 2003. Sure enough, Cadbury announced in late 2007 that it is reintroducing the candy bar. [68]

Virtual communities come in many different forms:[69]

- **Multiuser dungeons (MUD):** Originally, these were environments in which players of fantasy games met. Now they refer to any computer-generated environment in which people socially interact through the structured format of role- and game-playing.
- **Rooms, rings, and lists:** These include Internet relay chat (IRC), otherwise known as *chat rooms*. *Rings* are organizations of related home pages, and *lists* are groups of people on a single mailing list who share information.
- **Boards:** Online communities organized around interest-specific electronic bulletin boards. Active members read and post messages sorted by date and subject. There are boards devoted to musical groups, movies, wine, cigars, cars, comic strips, and even fast-food restaurants.
- **Blogs:** The **weblog**, or *blog*, is the fastest-growing form of online community. As we saw in Chapter 8, these online personal journals are building an avid following among Internet users who like to dash off a few random thoughts, post them on a Web site, and read similar musings by others. Although these sites are similar to Web pages Geocities and other free services offer, they employ a different technology that lets people upload a few sentences without going through the process of updating a Web site they build with conventional home page software. Bloggers can fire off thoughts on a whim, click a button, and quickly have them appear on a site. Weblogs frequently look like online diaries, with brief musings about the days' events, and perhaps a link or two of interest.

as a virtual alter ego, which may be a wise elf or a backstabbing rogue. Some players sell powerful characters on eBay for $1,000 or more.

The game is also the center of an active social scene. Players can travel around in groups of six. In many cases, they settle into a regular group and spend 2 to 3 hours each night online with the same people.[72] They may also mingle offline; *Fan Faires* attracts several thousand people who often dress as their game characters.[73] The average *EverQuest* subscriber spends about 20 hours a week living in this virtual world. Some view it as an addiction; "EverCrack" is a popular nickname for the game. One factor that makes it hard to kick the habit may be peer pressure because when a player logs off this may hurt his guild's chances of advancing in the game.[74]

But don't be fooled into thinking these sites are "only games." Today, they are more like parallel economies with their own currencies where some players are logging six-figure incomes. An early study of *EverQuest*'s economy showed it to be the seventy-seventh richest "country" in the world, sandwiched between Russia and Bulgaria. In a typical 24 hour period, *Second Life* residents spend almost $2 million in the equivalent of U.S. dollars.[75] Entropia Universe, a Sweden-based virtual world, recently signed a deal with Beijing's municipal government to develop a Chinese virtual economy that it projects will add a billion real dollars to the country's economy.

Traditionally, the only women in video games were digital. Think busty, bare-bellied, pistol-packing Lara Croft of *Tomb Raider*, or the scantily clad walking pin-ups in *Grand Theft Auto*. Beyond these stereotypical male fantasies, women were all but absent from the billion-dollar gaming industry. But that's all changing, thanks to a new generation of hard-core female gamers who are increasing women's visibility and influence in the high-tech, male-dominated video game world.

This burgeoning **blogosphere** (the universe of active weblogs) is a force to be reckoned with. Many blogs are the pet projects of individuals such as Eric Naka-gawa who started I Can Has Cheezburger? (icanhascheezburger.com) in January 2007 and has already made enough money to quit his day job as a software developer (the site consists of pictures of animals with funny captions, surrounded by advertising). Other popular blogs range from those that cover technology (boingboing.net), politics (talkingpointsmemo.com), and celebrity gossip (PerezHilton.com).[76]

How do people get drawn into consumption communities? Internet users tend to progress from asocial information gathering ("lurkers" are surfers who like to watch but don't participate) to increasingly affiliative social activities. At first they will merely browse the site, but later they may well be drawn into active participation. The intensity of identification with a virtual community depends on two factors. The first is that the more central the activity is to a person's self-concept, the more likely he will actively participate in a community. The second is that the intensity of the social relationships the person forms with other members of the virtual community helps to determine the extent of involvement. As Figure 11.3 shows, combining these two factors creates four distinct member types:

1 *Tourists* lack strong social ties to the group, and maintain only a passing interest in the activity.
2 *Minglers* maintain strong social ties, but are not very interested in the central consumption activity.

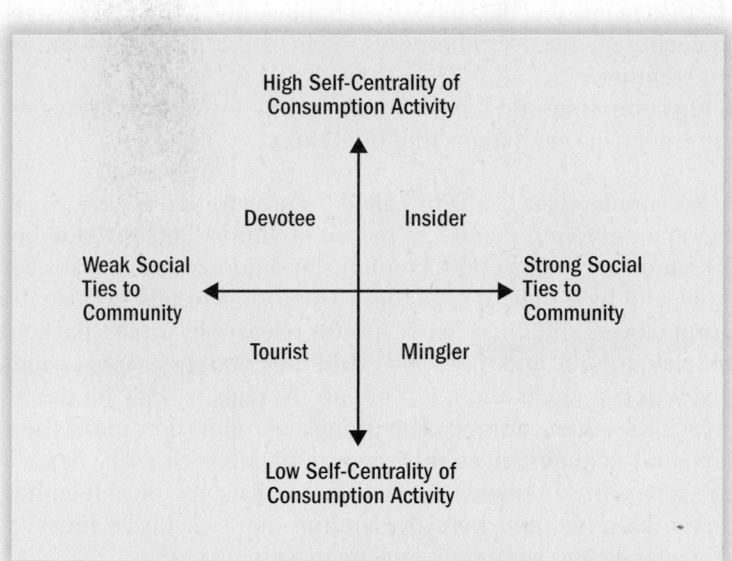

Source: Adapted from Robert V. Kozinets, "E-Tribalized Marketing: The Strategic Implications of Virtual Communities of Consumption," *European Management Journal* 17, 3 (June 1999): 252–264.

3 *Devotees* express strong interest in the activity, but have few social attachments to the group.

4 *Insiders* exhibit both strong social ties and strong interest in the activity.

Devotees and insiders are the most important targets for marketers who wish to leverage communities for promotional purposes. They are the heavy users of virtual communities. And by reinforcing usage, the community may upgrade tourists and minglers to insiders and devotees.[77] Marketers have only scratched the surface of this intriguing new virtual world, but intrepid consumer researchers are working on techniques to help them understand what's going down in cyberspace. Some use a technique they call **netnography**, which adapts ethnographic techniques anthropologists use to study RL cultures when they "live with the natives" to virtual communities.[78] For example, a team of Chinese researchers did a netnography of beauty product enthusiasts to understand how Chinese consumers interact with each other to share their passion for cosmetics.[79]

GUERRILLA MARKETING

In the United States, to promote their hip-hop albums, Def Jam and other labels start building a buzz months before a release, leaking advance copies to deejays who put together "mix tapes" to sell on the street. If the kids seem to like a song, *street teams* then push it to club deejays. As the official release date nears, these groups of fans start slapping up posters around the inner city. They plaster telephone poles, sides of buildings, and car windshields with promotions announcing the release of new albums.[81] These streetwise strategies started in the mid-1970s, when pioneering deejays like Kool DJ Herc and Afrika Bambaataa promoted their parties through graffiti-style flyers. As Ice Cube observed, "Even though I'm an established artist, I still like to leak my music to a kid on the street and let him duplicate it for his homies before it hits radio."[82]

This type of grassroots effort epitomizes **guerrilla marketing**: promotional strategies that use unconventional locations and intensive word-of-mouth campaigns to push products. These campaigns often recruit legions of real consumers who agree to engage in some kind of street theater or other activity in order to convince others to use the product or service. Scion for example often reaches out to its young

The Tangled Web

Virtual consumption communities hold great promise, but there is also great potential for abuse if members can't trust that other visitors are behaving ethically. Many hard-core community members are sensitive to interference from companies and react negatively when they suspect that another member may in fact be a shill of a marketer who wants to influence evaluations of products on the site. One of the reasons for the success of the eBay auction site is that buyers rate the quality and trustworthiness of sellers, so a potential bidder can get a pretty good idea of what he or she is dealing with before participating. In some cases even this system has fallen flat as unscrupulous people find ways to violate the bond of trust.

More generally, e-commerce sites know that consumers give more weight to the opinions of real people, so they are finding ways to include these opinions on their Web sites. Amazon.com started this trend of posting customer reviews way back in 1995. Now, Web sites that sell computers and other high-priced products often post customer reviews. A great idea—but a highly publicized lawsuit accused Amazon of charging publishers to post positive reviews on its site. The company had to offer refunds for all books it recommended and now Amazon tells customers when a publisher has paid for a prominent display on its site. Similarly, some online investment forums have had to hire patrols to keep an eye out for stock promoters whom companies have hired to create a buzz about their stocks.[80]

Marketing Pitfall

Is any publicity good publicity? One of the most widely publicized guerrilla marketing stunts in recent years illustrates the potential for a good idea to go bad in a hurry. To promote its *Aqua Teen Hunger Force* show on the Adult Swim segment of its Cartoon Network, a company Turner Broadcasting hired planted flashing light boards in public areas such as bridges around several cities. Observers in Boston thought they saw terrorist bombs instead and the city essentially shut down as officials dealt with what they thought was a national security issue. Turner had to pay hefty fines and endure a lot of criticism for this stunt. However, the Adult Swim Web site boosted its traffic by 77 percent on the day after the story broke.[88]

buyers with street teams that distribute merchandise and hang wild posters wherever they can to encourage twentysomethings to check out the videos and multiplayer games on its Web site. [83]

Today, big companies are buying into guerrilla marketing strategies big-time. Here are some guerrilla campaigns that built buzz:

● Procter & Gamble started a unit called Tremor to spread the word about its products among young people. It recruited almost 300,000 kids between the ages of 13 and 19 to deliver endorsements in school cafeterias, at sleepovers, by cell phone, and by e-mail. It taps these Tremorites to talk up just about everything, from movies and music (such as new releases by artists like Lenny Kravitz and Coldplay) to milk and motor oil—and they do it free. Tremor looks for kids with a wide social circle and a gift of gab. To register, kids fill out a questionnaire, which asks them, among other things, to report how many friends, family members, and acquaintances they communicate with every day. (Tremorites have an average of 170 names on their buddy lists; a typical teen has 30.) P&G rewards the kids for their help by sending them exclusive music mixes and other trinkets, such as shampoo and cheap watches.[84]

● Kayem Foods, which makes Al Fresco chicken sausage in the U.S., hired a company to organize a guerrilla campaign called the Great Sausage Fanout. On a summer holiday weekend, legions of people showed up at cookouts to which they had been invited up and down the East Coast and in the Midwest bearing packages of Al Fresco chicken sausage for their hosts to throw on the grill. The company sent the "agents" coupons for free sausage and a set of instructions for the best ways to talk up the product.[85]

● The American train line CSX launched a safety-awareness campaign by hiring people to throw eggs at the company's outdoor billboards. The billboards carry the stark black-on-white words "Cars hitting trains." Eggs smashing against the billboard are intended to demonstrate the impact of a car hitting a train. The idea is to get people to be careful when crossing railroad tracks.[86]

● *Brand ambassadors* pop up in eye-catching outfits to announce a new brand or service. AT&T sent its ambassadors to high-traffic areas of California and New Jersey, doing random favors such as handing dog biscuits to people walking their dogs and providing binoculars to concertgoers to promote its new AT&T Local Service. Hyatt Hotels unleashed 100 bellhops in Manhattan, who spent the day opening doors, carrying packages, and handing out pillow mints to thousands of consumers. Dewar's is training a squad of men in the Scotch brand's lore and traditions so they can play the role of the "Dewar's Highlander," who roams bars and restaurants teaching patrons and bartenders how to enjoy whiskey and mix cocktails with Dewar's.[87]

VIRAL MARKETING

Many students are big fans of Hotmail, a free e-mail service. But there's no such thing as a free lunch: Hotmail inserts a small ad on every message sent, making each user a salesperson. The company had 5 million subscribers in its first year and it continues to grow exponentially.[89] **Viral marketing** refers to the strategy of getting visitors to a Web site to forward information on the site to their friends in order to make still more consumers aware of the product—usually by creating online content that is entertaining or just plain weird. To promote a use for a razor that it could never discuss on TV, Philips launched a Norelco Web site, shaveeverywhere.com. The ad features a guy in a bathrobe explaining how to use the shaver in places, well, not on your head. The site uses pictures of fruit and vegetables to refer to male body parts.[90]

CB AS I SEE IT

Professor Albert Muñiz
DePaul University

One way group influence spreads is via word-of-mouth (WOM). WOM is typically revealed in conversations. Consumers tell others about their consumption experiences and disclose, implicitly or explicitly, their preferences for different products and brands. This process is as old as the practice of consumption.

Now, however, group influence is spreading in a different way. Consumers are crafting impressive looking things that strongly resemble advertisements. Consumers are creating images and texts that strongly resemble print ads and videos that resemble broadcast advertisements. Group influence is getting a lot sexier.

George Master's unsolicited and unpaid iPod ad from a few years ago is a great (and beautiful) example. Do a Google search on "george masters' ipod ad" and you'll find it. (Trust me, it's worth it.) George is a high school teacher who spent 5 months crafting a computer animation set to pop music in order to capture the beauty of all that is the iPod. This adlike video was an early instance of what ad agencies have come to call consumer-generated content (CGC). It spread virally and rapidly. (Several links were sent to me in the first few weeks.)

Recently, the advertising industry has been abuzz with talk of CGC. A big deal was made out of the fact that four ads run during the 2007 Super Bowl were crafted by consumers. Critical reaction was lukewarm, with a few analysts going so far as to say that the entire phenomenon of CGC was completely overblown. Perhaps, but I'm not so sure.

The way I see it, the use of CGC in broadcast media is only part of the story. Advertisers may or may not migrate to using consumer-authored ads for official campaigns. That doesn't matter. What is more interesting (and likely to be more influential at the group level) is CGC that spreads among consumers, particularly those in online consumption and brand communities, but just as easily to those outside of such settings. Think about it. How many viral videos do you receive via e-mail in any given week?

Consumers ensconced in brand and consumption communities have long been creating advertising-like content to share with one another and to attract new members. Brand evangelism is the order of the day in these collectives. This content gets distributed widely among (and beyond) the members of these communities and becomes an important part of group influence.

In my research, I've seen that consumers engage in a variety of advertising mimicking activities. They create print and video ads, drawing on the advertising for their brand and competing brands, as well as movies, popular music, and television. In other words, they borrow and use styles and ideas from the wider culture, just like advertising agencies.

My research also demonstrates that consumers can use a lot of the tropes, logics, grammar, and conventions of advertising quite skillfully. In other words, consumers in brand and consumption collectives, indeed most consumers today, have a well-developed literacy of the language and style of advertising, and they use this literacy when writing and creating CGC.

Group influence now spreads in much more stylish and creative ways than simple talk about the product. In some cases, it is spread via CGC that rivals professionally produced advertising content.

SOCIAL NETWORKING AND CROWD POWER

Odds are you've already logged in some serious time on Facebook or MySpace before you started reading this paragraph today. **Social networking**, where members post information about themselves and make contact with others who share similar interests and opinions, may well be the biggest development in consumer behavior since the TV dinner! Almost daily we hear about yet another social networking site where users can set up a home page with photos, a profile, and links to others in their

A campaign to create a buzz for the Mini Cooper was disguised as a debate over whether a British engineer built robots out of Mini car parts. It extended across Web sites, postings in chat rooms, and booklets inserted in magazines like *Motor Trend* and *Rolling Stone*. The 40-page booklets pretended to be excerpts from a book, *Men of Metal: Eyewitness Accounts of Humanoid Robots*, from a fake London publisher specializing in conspiracy-theory literature covering the likes of Bigfoot, the Loch Ness monster, and UFOs. One goal of the campaign was to appeal to mechanical-minded male drivers who may be put off by women's praise of the Mini as "cute."

social networks. They can browse for friends, dates, partners for activities, or contacts of all kinds and invite them to join the users' personal networks as "friends."

Fun aside, social networking has some really serious marketing implications. Indeed, it's fair to say that aspects of this technology revolution are fundamentally changing business models in many industries—especially because they empower end consumers to literally become partners and shape markets. It's hard to overstate the impact this change will have on how we create, distribute, promote, and consume products and services.

Social networking is an integral part of what many call Web 2.0, which is like the Internet on steroids. The key change is the interactivity among producers and users, but these are some other characteristics of a Web 2.0 site:[91]

- It improves as the number of users increases. For example, Amazon's ability to recommend books to you based on what other people with similar interests have bought gets better as it tracks more and more people who are entering search queries.
- Its currency is eyeballs. Google makes its money by charging advertisers according to the number of people who see their ads after typing in a search term.
- It's version-free and in perpetual beta. *Wikipedia*, the online encyclopedia, gets updated constantly by users who "correct" others' errors.
- It categorizes entries according to "folksonomy" rather than "taxonomy." In other words, sites rely on users rather than preestablished systems to sort contents. Listeners at Pandora.com create their own "radio stations" that play songs by artists they choose as well as other similar artists.

This last point highlights a key change in the way some new media companies approach their businesses: Think of it as marketing strategy by committee. The **wisdom of crowds** perspective (from a book by that name) argues that under the right circumstances, groups are smarter than the smartest people in them. If this is true, it implies that large numbers of (nonexpert) consumers can predict successful products.[92]

In a sense a lot of social networking sites let their members dictate purchase decisions. For example, at Threadless.com, customers rank T-shirt designs ahead of time and the company prints the winning ideas. Every week, contestants upload T-shirts designs to the site, where about 700 compete to be among the six that it will print during that time. Threadless visitors score designs on a scale of 0 to 5, and the staff selects winners from the most popular entrants. The six lucky artists each get $2,000 in cash and merchandise. Threadless sells out of every shirt it offers. This business model has made a small fortune for a few designers "the crowd" particularly likes. One pair of Chicago-based artists sold $16 million worth of T-shirts. To keep the judges and buyers coming back, the owners offer rewards—upload a photo of yourself wearing a Threadless T-shirt and you get a store credit of $1.50. Refer a friend who buys a T-shirt and you get $3. The site sells more than 1,500 T-shirts in a typical day.[93]

At threadless.com, users vote on which t-shirt designs the company will print and sell.

FROM **$10** ENDS DEC. 16!

threadless™

HOLIDAY SALE!

Shop Participate Info Login/Join

Join Threadless? Click here!

Username: _____
Password: _____

Log in

Forgot Your Password?

a threadless™ carol

Please sing me a song!

Act **3** of **4**

Tees of Threadless Future

Be Square
by Justin White

Really Exist
by Chow Hon Lam

Puppet In Love
by Lim Heng Swee

Over 1,000 buyers of this T-shirt design called The Communist Party from the Threadless Web site uploaded photos of themselves wearing it.

Here are some more crowd-based sites to watch:

- At the French <u>CrowdSpirit.com</u> site, participants submit ideas for consumer electronics products and the community votes for the best ones. Those go to the site's R&D partners and investors who then decide which to finance for further development. Community members test and fine-tune a prototype and then they can buy the products that go to market. The community handles product support and recommends the new products to retailers.[94]

- <u>Sermo.com</u> is a social network for physicians. It has no advertising, job listings, or membership fees. It makes its money (about $500,000 a year so far) by charging institutional investors for the opportunity to listen in as approximately 15,000 doctors chat among themselves. Say, for example, a young patient breaks out in hives after taking a new prescription. A doctor might post whether she thinks this is because of a rare symptom or perhaps the drug's side-effect. If other doctors feel it's the latter, this negative news could affect the drug manufacturer's stock so their opinions have value to analysts. Doctors who ask or answer a question that paying observers deem especially valuable receive bonuses of $5 to $25 per post.[95]

- How about social networking sites that "create" a concert by persuading an artist to perform in a certain city or country? At <u>Eventful.com</u>, fans can demand events and performances in their town and spread the word to make them happen. Or how about actually buying a piece of the bands you like? Go to <u>SellaBand.com</u> where fans ("believers") buy "parts" in a band for $10 per share. Once the band sells 5,000 parts, SellaBand arranges a professional recording, including top studios, A&R (Artists & Repertoire) managers (industry talent scouts), and producers. Believers receive a limited edition CD of the recording. Believers get a piece of the profits, so they're likely to promote the band wherever they can.

- Individual consumers gain crowd clout by **shopmobbing** with strangers. So far this is most popular in China where the *tuangou* ("team purchase") phenomenon

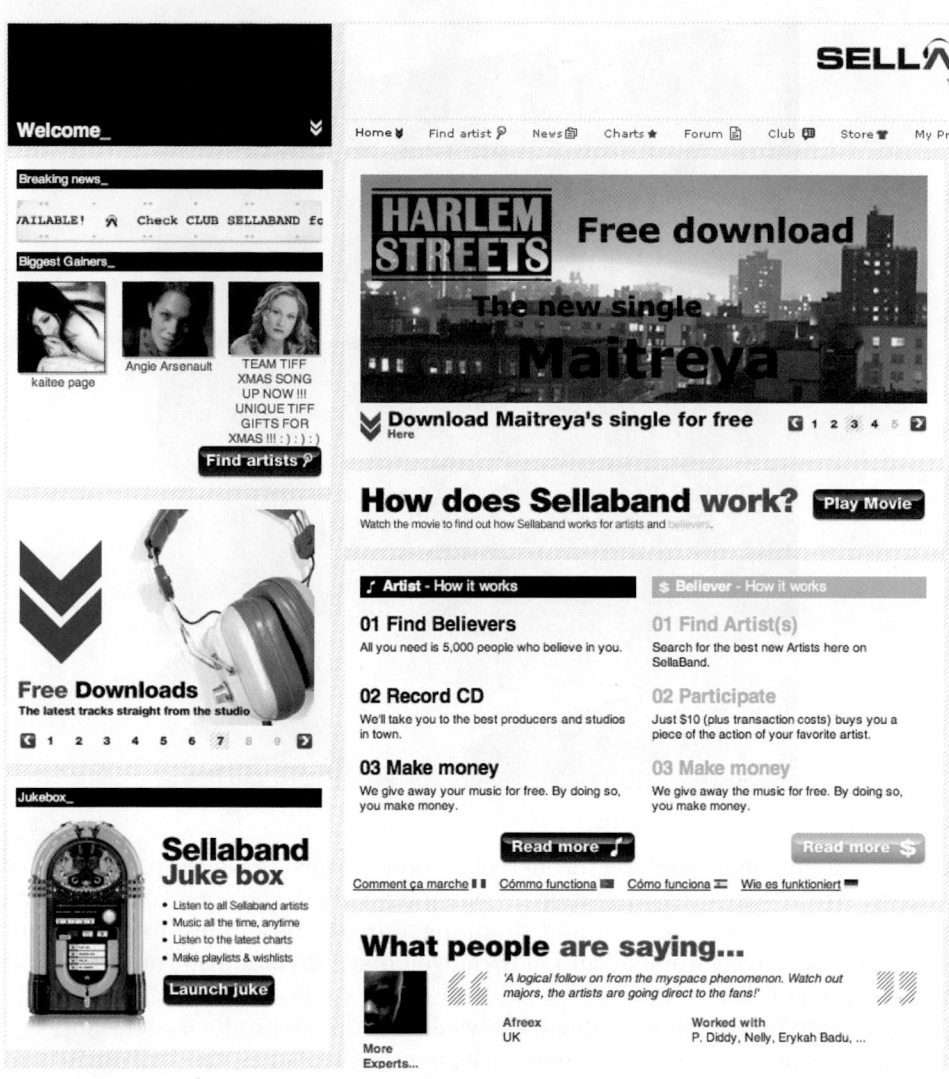

SellaBand.com fans buy "parts" in a band. If a band is popular enough to sell 5,000 parts, SellaBand arranges a professional recording session for the artists.

involves strangers organizing themselves around a specific product or service. Members who meet online at sites such as TeamBuy.com, Taobao.com, and Liba.com arrange to meet at a certain date and time in a real-world store and literally mob the unsuspecting retailer—the bargain-hungry crowd negotiates a group discount on the spot.[96]

OPINION LEADERSHIP

As Cold Stone Creamery expands to Japan, the ice cream store projects a somewhat different image than it has in the United States. The chain wants to be ultracool by generating a buzz among fashion-conscious "office ladies"—as the Japanese call young, single, female professionals. These women are very influential in Japan; their reactions to a new product can make or break it. To woo this group, Cold Stone sponsored a fashion show for young women (assuming the models can fit into the dresses after sampling a few of the chain's caloric creations), and fashion magazines staged photo shoots at the stores.[97]

Although consumers get information from personal sources, they do not usually ask just *anyone* for advice about purchases. If you decide to buy a new stereo, you will most likely seek advice from a friend who knows a lot about sound systems. This friend may own a sophisticated system, or may subscribe to specialized magazines

Opinion leadership is a big factor in the marketing of athletic shoes. Many styles first become popular in the inner city and then spread by word-of-mouth.

and spend free time browsing through electronics stores. However, you may have another friend who has a reputation for being stylish and who spends his free time reading *Gentleman's Quarterly* and shopping at trendy boutiques. You might not bring up your stereo problem with him, but you may take him with you to shop for a new fall wardrobe.

Everyone knows people who are knowledgeable about products and whose advice others take seriously. Like one of the Japanese office ladies, this individual is an **opinion leader**, a person who is frequently able to influence others' attitudes or behaviors.[98] Clearly, some people's recommendations carry more weight than others. Opinion leaders are extremely valuable information sources because they have the social power we discussed earlier in the chapter:

- They are technically competent so they possess expert power.[99]
- They prescreen, evaluate, and synthesize product information in an unbiased way, so they possess knowledge power.[100]
- They are socially active and highly interconnected in their communities.[101]
- They are likely to hold offices in community groups and clubs and to be active outside of the home. As a result, opinion leaders often have legitimate power by virtue of their social standing.
- They tend to be similar to the consumer in terms of their values and beliefs, so they possess referent power. Note that although opinion leaders are set apart by their interest or expertise in a product category, they are more convincing to the extent that they are *homophilous* rather than *heterophilous*. **Homophily** refers to the degree to which a pair of individuals is similar in terms of education, social status, and beliefs.[102]
- Effective opinion leaders tend to be slightly higher in terms of status and educational attainment than those they influence but not so high as to be in a different social class.
- Opinion leaders are often among the first to buy new products, so they absorb much of the risk. This experience reduces uncertainty for others who are not as

courageous. Furthermore, whereas company-sponsored communications tend to focus exclusively on the positive aspects of a product, the hands-on experience of opinion leaders makes them more likely to impart *both* positive and negative information about product performance. Thus, they are more credible because they have no "axe to grind."

How Influential Is an Opinion Leader?

When social scientists initially developed the concept of the opinion leader, they assumed that certain influential people in a community would exert an overall impact on group members' attitudes. Later work, however, began to question the assumption that there is such a thing as a *generalized opinion leader*, somebody whose recommendations we seek for all types of purchases. Very few people are capable of being expert in a number of fields. Sociologists distinguish between those who are *monomorphic*, or expert in a limited field, and those who are *polymorphic*, or expert in several fields.[103] Even opinion leaders who are polymorphic, however, tend to concentrate on one broad domain, such as electronics or fashion.

Research on opinion leadership generally indicates that although opinion leaders do exist for multiple product categories, expertise tends to overlap across similar categories. It is rare to find a generalized opinion leader. An opinion leader for home appliances is likely to serve a similar function for home cleaners but not for cosmetics. In contrast, we may consult a fashion opinion leader whose primary influence is on clothing choices for recommendations on cosmetics purchases but not necessarily for her opinions on microwave ovens.[104]

Types of Opinion Leaders

Early conceptions of the opinion leader role also assumed a static process: The opinion leader absorbs information from the mass media and in turn transmits data to opinion receivers. This view has turned out to be overly simplified; it confuses the functions of several different types of consumers.

Opinion leaders may or may not be purchasers of the products they recommend. As we will see in Chapter 7, early purchasers also tend to be *innovators*. Researchers have termed opinion leaders who also are early purchasers *innovative communicators*. One study identified characteristics of college men who were innovative communicators for fashion products. These men were among the first to buy new fashions, and other students were likely to follow their lead when they made their own purchases. Other characteristics of the men included the following:[105]

- They were socially active.
- They were appearance conscious and narcissistic (i.e., they were quite fond of themselves and self-centered).
- They were involved in rock culture.
- They were intense magazine readers, reading, for example, *Sports Illustrated*.
- They were likely to own more clothing, and a broader range of styles, than other students.

Opinion leaders also are likely to be *opinion seekers*. They are generally more involved in a product category and actively search for information. As a result, they are more likely to talk about products with others and to solicit others' opinions as well.[106] Contrary to the static view of opinion leadership, most product-related conversation does not take place in a "lecture" format in which one person does all of the talking. A lot of product-related conversation occurs in the context of a casual interaction rather than as formal instruction.[107] One study, which found that opinion seeking is especially high for food products, revealed that two-thirds of opinion seekers also view themselves as opinion leaders.[108] Figure 11.4 contrasts this updated view of interpersonal product communication with the traditional view.

■ **FIGURE 11.4**
PERSPECTIVES ON THE
COMMUNICATIONS PROCESS

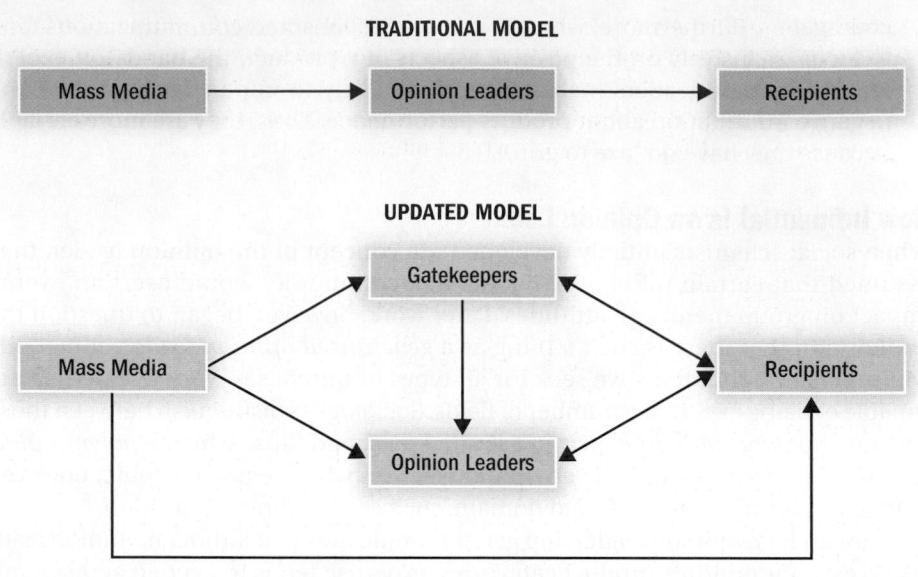

THE MARKET MAVEN

Consumers who are expert in a product category may not actively communicate with others, whereas other consumers may have a more general interest in talking about all sorts of purchases. A **market maven** is a person who likes to transmit marketplace information of all types. These shopaholics are not necessarily interested in certain products and they may not necessarily be early purchasers; they're simply into staying on top of what's happening in the marketplace. They come closer to the function of a generalized opinion leader because they tend to have a solid overall knowledge of how and where to procure products. Researchers use the following scale items, to which respondents indicate how much they agree or disagree, to identify market mavens:[109]

1 I like introducing new brands and products to my friends.
2 I like helping people by providing them with information about many kinds of products.
3 People ask me for information about products, places to shop, or sales.
4 If someone asked me where to get the best buy on several types of products, I could tell him or her where to shop.
5 My friends think of me as a good source of information when it comes to new products or sales.

THE SURROGATE CONSUMER

In addition to everyday consumers who are instrumental in influencing others' purchase decisions, a class of marketing intermediary we call the **surrogate consumer** often influences what we buy. A surrogate consumer is a person whom we hire to provide input into our purchase decisions. Unlike the opinion leader or market maven, the surrogate is usually compensated for his advice. Interior decorators, stockbrokers, professional shoppers, and college consultants are surrogate consumers.

Regardless of whether they actually make the purchase on behalf of the consumer, their recommendations can be enormously influential. The consumer, in essence, relinquishes control over several or all decision-making functions, such as the information search, the evaluation of alternatives, or the actual purchase. For example, a client may commission an interior decorator to redo her house, and we

Net Profit

Surrogate consumers are finding a home in Second Life (SL). The realtor Coldwell Banker set up shop inside the virtual world, where it sells virtual homes to avatars. The firm's SL inventory includes more than 500 homes in 550,000 square meters in the Ranchero section of Second Life. Like real-world homes, the homes are available in many different styles including southwestern, colonial, and contemporary. For those seeking luxury on Second Life, ocean front homes are also available.[111]

Second Life residents can meet with an avatar sales associate. Instead of applying for a mortgage, the sales associate will verify their qualification status with the v-commerce function, which is a virtual palm scanner. Homebuyers who purchase a home in Second Life will receive "virtual furniture" as a gift from Coldwell Banker.[112]

may entrust a broker to make crucial buy/sell decisions on our behalf. Marketers tend to overlook surrogates when they try to convince consumers to buy their goods or services. This can be a big mistake because they may mistarget their communications to end consumers instead of to the surrogates who actually sift through product information and decide among product alternatives.[110]

HOW DO WE FIND OPINION LEADERS?

Companies that want to connect with U.S. teens are mysteriously turning up on the cheerleading circuit. They recognize that cheerleaders often are among the most popular kids in American high schools, and they're able to influence their classmates' opinions about which personal care products or beverages are the coolest. That's why makeup artists affiliated with P&G's CoverGirl line of cosmetics show up at cheerleading clinics to offer makeup tips to some of the 350,000 people per year who attend these training sessions. PepsiCo promotes its Propel by holding workshops at cheerleader events to teach teens about nutrition and the value of drinking water.[113]

Because opinion leaders are so central to consumer decision making, it's not surprising that marketers at P&G and Pepsi work hard to identify the influential people in a product category. In fact, many of their ads are intended to reach these influentials rather than the average consumer, especially if the ads contain a lot of technical information. For example, CBS sent a CD-ROM to 10,000 critics, affiliates, advertising agencies, and others it identified as "influencers" in order to plug the network's prime-time shows.[114]

Unfortunately, because most opinion leaders are everyday consumers and are not formally included in marketing efforts, they are harder to find. A celebrity or an influential industry executive is by definition easy to locate. That person has national or at least regional visibility or is listed in published directories. In contrast, opinion leaders tend to operate at the local level and may influence five to ten consumers rather than an entire market segment.

In some cases, companies have tried to identify influentials and involve them directly in their marketing efforts, hoping to create a "ripple effect" as these consumers sing the company's praises to their friends. To promote the film *Crouching Tiger, Hidden Dragon*, the producers enlisted a core group of celebrities ranging from rapper Ghostface Killah to feminist author Naomi Wolf to attend early screenings, hoping they would fan out and create a sort of party-circuit dialogue about the film.[115] Similarly, Walt Disney Co. set up screenings for orchestra leaders, music teacher associations, and instrument makers to get expert WOM going about the movie *Mr. Holland's Opus,* where actor Richard Dreyfuss plays a music teacher.

Because of the difficulties involved in identifying specific opinion leaders in a large market, most attempts to do so focus instead on exploratory studies. Researchers aim to identify the profile of a representative opinion leader and then generalize these insights to a larger market. For example, one company that went looking for financial opinion leaders found that these consumers were more likely to be involved in managing their own finances and tended to use a computer to do so. They also were more likely to follow their investments on a daily basis and to read books and watch television shows devoted to financial issues.[116]

The Self-Designating Method

The most commonly used technique to identify opinion leaders is simply to ask individual consumers whether they consider themselves to be opinion leaders. Although respondents who report a greater degree of interest in a product category are more likely to be opinion leaders, we must view the results of surveys that hope to identify *self-designated opinion leaders* with some skepticism. Some people have a tendency to inflate their own importance and influence, whereas others who really are influential might not admit to this quality or be conscious of it if they are.[117]

■ FIGURE 11.5 REVISED AND UPDATED VERSION OF THE OPINION LEADERSHIP SCALE

Please rate yourself on the following scales relating to your interactions with friends and neighbors regarding _____.

1. In general, do you talk to your friends and neighbors about _____:

very often				never
5	4	3	2	1

2. When you talk to your friends and neighbors about _____ do you:

give a great deal of information				give very little information
5	4	3	2	1

3. During the past six months, how many people have you told about a new _____?

told a number of people				told no one
5	4	3	2	1

4. Compared with your circle of friends, how likely are you to be asked about new _____?

very likely to be asked				not at all likely to be asked
5	4	3	2	1

5. In discussion of new _____, which of the following happens most?

you tell your friends about _____			your friends tell you about _____	
5	4	3	2	1

6. Overall in all of your discussions with friends and neighbors are you:

often used as a source of advice				not used as a source of advice
5	4	3	2	1

The fact that we transmit advice about products does not mean other people *take* that advice. For someone to be considered a *bona fide* opinion leader, opinion seekers must actually heed his advice. An alternative is to select certain group members (*key informants*) whom we ask to identify opinion leaders. The success of this approach hinges on locating those who have accurate knowledge of the group and on minimizing their response biases (e.g., the tendency to inflate one's own influence on the choices of others).

The self-designating method is not as reliable as a more systematic analysis (in which we can verify individual claims of influence by asking others whether the person is really influential), but it does have the advantage of being easy to apply to a large group of potential opinion leaders. Figure 11.5 shows one of the measurement scales researchers use for this kind of self-designation.

Sociometry

The popular play *Six Degrees of Separation* is based on the premise that everyone on the planet indirectly knows everyone else—or at least knows people who in turn know them. Indeed, social scientists estimate that the average person has 1,500 acquaintances and that five to six intermediaries could connect any two people in the United States.[118] A popular game challenges players to link the actor Kevin Bacon with other actors in much the same way.

Sociometric methods trace communication patterns among members of a group. These techniques allow researchers to systematically map out the interactions among group members. By interviewing participants and asking them to whom they go for product information, researchers identify those who tend to be sources of product-related information. This method is the most precise, but it is very difficult and expensive to implement because it involves very close study of interaction patterns in small groups. For this reason, sociometric techniques are best applied in a closed, self-contained social setting, such as in hospitals, in prisons, and on army bases, where members are largely isolated from other social networks.

A recent sociometric study on obesity provides a striking example of how our social networks influence our consumption behaviors. The researchers analyzed a sample of more than 12,000 Americans who participated in the Framingham Heart Study, which closely documented their health from 1971 to 2003. They discovered that obesity can spread from person to person, much like a virus (we'll talk more about how consumer trends spread in this fashion in Chapter 17). The investigators knew who was friends with whom as well as who was a spouse or sibling or neighbor, and they knew how much each person weighed at various times over 3 decades so they could reconstruct what happened over the years if study participants became obese. Guess what? When one person gains weight, close friends tend to gain weight, too—a person's chances of being obese if a close friend put on the pounds increased by 57 percent! The friend's influence remained even if he lived hundreds of miles away. The researchers explained this "social contagion" effect by speculating that when our best buds get fat, this alters our perception of normal body weight so we aren't as concerned when we put on a few pounds as well. The moral of the story: Hang out with thin people![119]

Many professionals, such as doctors, accountants, and lawyers, as well as services marketers, such as lawn-care companies and cleaning services, depend primarily on word of mouth to generate business. In many cases, consumers recommend a service provider to a friend or co-worker, and in other cases businesspeople make recommendations to their customers. For example, only 0.2 percent of respondents in one study reported choosing a physician based on advertising. Advice from family and friends was the most widely used criterion.[120]

We use sociometric analyses to better understand *referral behavior* and to locate strengths and weaknesses in terms of how one's reputation flows through a community.[121] *Network analysis* focuses on communication in social systems, considers the relations among people in a *referral network*, and measures the *tie strength* among them. Tie strength refers to the nature of the bond between people. It can range from strong primary (e.g., one's spouse) to weak secondary (e.g., an acquaintance that one rarely sees). We can think of a strong tie relationship as a primary reference group; interactions are frequent and important to the individual.

Although strong ties are important, weak ties perform a *bridging function*. This type of connection allows a consumer access between subgroups. For example, you might have a regular group of friends that is a primary reference group (strong ties). If you have an interest in tennis, say, one of these friends might introduce you to a group of people in her dorm who play on the tennis team. As a result, you gain access to their valuable expertise through this bridging function. This referral process demonstrates the *strength of weak ties*. One study using this method examined similarities in brand choice among members of a college sorority. The researchers found evidence that subgroups, or *cliques*, within the sorority were likely to share preferences for various products. In some cases, the sisters even shared their choices of "private" (i.e., socially inconspicuous) products (probably because of shared bathrooms in the sorority house).[122]

CHAPTER SUMMARY

Now that you have finished reading this chapter you should understand why:

Others, especially those who possess some kind of social power, often influence us.

● We belong to or admire many different groups and a desire for them to accept us often drives our purchase decisions. Individuals or groups whose opinions or behavior are particularly important to consumers are reference groups. Both formal and informal groups influence the individual's purchase decisions, although such factors as the conspicuousness of the product and the relevance of the reference group for a particular purchase determine how influential the reference group is.

● Individuals have influence in a group to the extent that they possess social power; types of social power include information power, referent power, legitimate power, expert power, reward power, and coercive power.

We seek out others who share our interests in products or services.

● Brand communities unite consumers who share a common passion for a product. Brandfests, when companies organize to encourage this kind of community, can build brand loyalty and reinforce group membership.

We are motivated to buy or use products in order to be consistent with what other people do.

● We conform to the desires of others for two basic reasons: (1) People who model their behavior after others because they take others' behavior as evidence of the correct way to act are conforming because of informational social influence, and (2) those who conform to satisfy the expectations of others or to be accepted by the group are affected by normative social influence. Group members often do things they would not do as individuals because their identities become merged with the group; they become deindividuated.

The things that other consumers tell us about products (good and bad) are often more influential than the advertising we see.

● Much of what we know about products we learn through word-of-mouth (WOM) communication rather than formal advertising. We tend to exchange product-related information in casual conversations. Guerrilla marketing strategies try to accelerate the WOM process by enlisting consumers to help spread the word.

● Although WOM often is helpful for making consumers aware of products, it can also hurt companies when damaging product rumors or negative WOM occurs.

Online technologies are accelerating the impact of word-of-mouth communication.

● The Web has greatly amplified consumers' abilities to be exposed to numerous reference groups. Virtual consumption communities are composed of people who are united by a common bond—enthusiasm about or knowledge of a specific product or service. Emerging marketing strategies try to leverage the potential of the Web to spread information from consumer to consumer extremely quickly. Viral marketing techniques enlist individuals to tout products, services, Web sites, and so on to others on behalf of companies. A new mode of online communication called blogging allows consumers to easily post their thoughts about products for others to see.

Social networking is changing the way companies and consumers interact.

● Social networking, where members post information about themselves and make contact with others who share similar interests and opinions, represents a change in the way we think about marketing. As Web 2.0 continues to develop, companies and consumers increasingly interact directly. The wisdom of crowds perspective argues that under the right circumstances, groups are smarter than the smartest people in them. If this is true, it implies that large numbers of consumers can predict successful products.[123] In a sense, a lot of social networking sites let their members dictate purchase decisions.

Certain people are particularly likely to influence others' product choices.

● Opinion leaders who are knowledgeable about a product and whose opinions are highly regarded tend to influence others' choices. Specific opinion leaders are somewhat hard to identify, but marketers who know their general characteristics can try to target them in their media and promotional strategies. Other influencers include market mavens, who have a general interest in marketplace activities, and surrogate consumers, who are compensated for their advice about purchases.

KEY TERMS

Antibrand communities, 437
Aspirational reference group, 435
Blogosphere, 448
Brand community, 434
Brandfests, 434
Coercive power, 432
Comparative influence, 433
Conformity, 441
Consumer tribe, 434
Decision polarization, 439
Deindividuation, 439
Expert power, 432
Guerrilla marketing, 449
Home shopping parties, 440

Homophily, 456
Information power, 432
Legitimate power, 432
Market maven, 458
Membership reference group, 435
Negative word-of-mouth, 444
Netnography, 449
Normative influence, 433
Norms, 441
Opinion leader, 456
Reference group, 430
Referent power, 431
Reward power, 432
Risky shift, 439

Shopmobbing, 454
Social loafing, 439
Social networking, 451
Social power, 431
Sociometric methods, 460
Surrogate consumer, 458
Tribal marketing strategy, 434
Viral marketing, 450
Virtual community of consumption, 447
Weblog, 447
Wisdom of crowds, 452
Word-of-mouth (WOM), 442

REVIEW QUESTIONS

1 Name two dimensions that influence whether reference groups impact an individual's purchase decisions.
2 List three types of social power, and give an example of each.
3 Which tend to be more powerful influences on behavior: large formal groups or small informal groups? Why?
4 What is a brand community, and why is it of interest to marketers?
5 Tell the difference between a membership and an aspirational reference group and give an example of each kind.
6 Name one factor that makes it more likely a person will become part of a consumer's membership reference group.
7 Define *deindividuation* and give an example of this effect.
8 What is the risky shift, and how does it relate to going shopping with friends?
9 What is the difference between normative and informational social influence?
10 Define *conformity* and give three examples of it. Name three reasons why people conform.
11 How does the principle of least interest relate to your success in a romantic relationship?
12 What is social comparison? What type of person do we usually choose to compare ourselves to?
13 What is the difference between independence and anti-conformity?
14 What is word of mouth, and why is it more powerful than advertising?
15 Which is more powerful: positive or negative word of mouth?
16 Describe some ways in which marketers are using the Internet to encourage positive WOM.
17 What is viral marketing? Guerrilla marketing? Give an example of each.
18 What is an opinion leader? Give three reasons why they are powerful influences on consumers' opinions. What are some characteristics of opinion leaders?
19 Is there such a thing as a generalized opinion leader? Why or why not?
20 What is the relationship between an opinion leader and an opinion seeker?
21 What is the difference between a market maven and a surrogate consumer?
22 How can marketers use opinion leaders to help them promote their products or services?
23 What are sociometric techniques? Under what conditions does it make sense to use them?

CONSUMER BEHAVIOR CHALLENGE

■ DISCUSS

1 This chapter describes four types of virtual community members. Which are you?
2 The average Internet user in the United States spends 3 hours a day online, with much of that time devoted to work and more than half of it to communications. Researchers report that the Internet has displaced television watching and a range of other activities. Internet users watch television for 1 hour and 42 minutes a day, compared with the national average of 2 hours. One study reported increasing physical isolation among Internet users; it created a controversy and drew angry complaints from some users who insisted that time they spent online did not detract from their social relationships. However, the researchers said they had now gathered further evidence showing that Internet use has lowered the amount of time people spend socializing with friends and even sleeping. According to the study, an hour of time spent using the Internet reduces face-to-face contact with friends, co-workers, and family by 23.5 minutes; lowers the amount of time spent watching television by 10 minutes, and reduces sleep time by 8.5 minutes.[124] What's your perspective on this issue—does increasing use of the Internet have positive or negative implications for interpersonal relationships in our society?
3 The Word-of-Mouth Marketing Association announced a new set of rules and guidelines for word-of-mouth advertising. The trade group maintains that marketers must make sure that people talking up products or services disclose for whom they are working. They also must use real consumers, not actors, who discuss what they really believe about a product.[125] The rules were prompted by several controversial incidents, such as a campaign the U.S. arm of Sony Ericsson Mobile Communications created for a camera phone. The company hired 60 actors to hang out at tourist attractions and ask unsuspecting passersby to take their pictures with the Sony Ericsson devices. It told the actors to identify

themselves only when asked directly. What do you think about "stealth" campaigns such as this? Should marketers be required to disclose their true intentions when they try to initiate positive word-of-mouth?

4 Do you agree that deindividuation encourages binge drinking on campus? What can or should a college do to discourage this behavior?

5 The adoption of a certain brand of shoe or apparel by athletes can be a powerful influence on students and other fans. Should high school and college coaches be paid to determine what brand of athletic equipment their players wear?

6 The strategy of *viral marketing* gets customers to sell a product to other customers on behalf of the company. That often means convincing your friends to climb on the bandwagon, and sometimes you get a cut if they wind up buying something.[126] Some might argue that that means you're selling out your friends (or at least selling to your friends) in exchange for a piece of the action. Others might say you're simply sharing the wealth with those about whom you care. Have you been involved in viral marketing by passing along names of your friends or sending them to a Web site such as hotmail.com? If so, what happened? How do you feel about this practice?

7 Are home shopping parties that put pressure on friends and neighbors to buy merchandise ethical?

8 What is the best way for a company to deal with determined detractors?

9 The high-profile stunt to publicize *Aqua Teen Hunger Force* created a massive public disruption. When does a guerrilla marketing tactic go too far—or is anything fair game in the heated competition to capture jaded consumers' attention?

■ APPLY

10 The power of unspoken social norms often becomes obvious only when we violate them. To witness this result firsthand, try one of the following: Stand facing the back wall in an elevator; serve dessert before the main course; offer to pay cash for dinner at a friend's home; wear pajamas to class; or tell someone *not* to have a nice day.

11 Identify a set of avoidance groups for your peers. Can you identify any consumption decisions that are made with these groups in mind?

12 Identify fashion opinion leaders on your campus. Do they fit the profile the chapter describes?

13 Conduct a sociometric analysis within your dormitory or neighborhood. For a product category such as music or cars, ask each individual to identify other individuals with whom they share information. Systematically trace all of these avenues of communication, and identify opinion leaders by locating individuals who are repeatedly named as providing helpful information.

14 See if you can demonstrate the risky shift. Get a group of friends together and ask each to privately rate the likelihood on a scale from 1 to 7 that they would try a controversial new product (e.g., a credit card that works with a chip implanted in a person's wrist). Then ask the group to discuss the product and rate the idea again. If the average rating changes from the first, you've just observed a risky shift.

15 Trace a referral pattern for a service provider such as a hair stylist by tracking how clients came to choose him or her. See if you can identify opinion leaders who are responsible for referring several clients to the businessperson. How might the service provider take advantage of this process to grow his or her business?

Case Study

JIMMY BUFFETT FANS UNITE

Are you a Parrothead? If you don't know what that is, then you definitely are not. Jimmy Buffett fans all over the world are known by this name. And in many respects, they represent one of the most dedicated fan-bases anywhere.

By some measures, it could be considered that Jimmy Buffett's career peaked in the late 1970s when the singer/songwriter had achieved his highest level of hit songs. And yet even after the music stopped coming, the fans lingered. With the advent of the Internet, these fans had a medium by which to connect. Now, Buffett has more fans and plays more concerts than he ever did in the 1970s. And while he toured on the popularity of old favorites for years, in 2004, he once again achieved a top-selling album of new music that provided the title for his "License to Chill" tour.

Buffett fans gather by the thousands at concerts. A Buffett concert is like a beach party, with fans in Hawaiian shirts, or wearing parrot hats on their heads (hence the name). But the concert itself is only part of the event. Fans get to know each other year after year at tailgate parties. So many people party before Buffett concerts, in fact, that many venues charge admission now just to get into the tailgating area, plus an admission to the concert. A 2004 concert at Boston's lot-less Fenway Park prompted fans to profess that a concert at that venue would never happen again.

How die-hard are Buffett fans? Consider that many plan regular vacations around a Buffett concert (some have racked up dozens) or special trips to visit Buffett-themed restaurants in Caribbean destinations. Houses, boats, and RVs decked out in tropical Buffet décor are not uncommon. Buffett-style weddings, parrot or palm-tree tattoos, and chartering tour busses to take a group of friends to a concert are also not unheard of.

Buffett fans come from all walks of life, age groups, and occupations, typically citing "escapism" as a reason for being a fan. "We can relate to Buffett," said Laura Tarket of Vancouver, Washington. "We like that lifestyle. His songs create feelings of peace and serenity, ocean breezes, tropical sunsets and sunny days. He provides us with sort of a getaway. The music has a calming effect, especially once you've been to the islands. It takes me back to lying on the beach. It reminds me of being in those locations and having fun."

But the "escapism" factor of being a Buffett fan has come to mean much more than just listening to Buffett tunes and "wasting away again in Margaritaville." Buffett's biggest fans spend their free time volunteering at blood drives, raising thousands of dollars to grant the wishes of sick kids, or building houses for the needy. "I think the common bond is that Jimmy's music is an escape for many of us, and we enjoy giving back, which is Jimmy's philosophy," said Johannah

Galgovitch, a corporate event planner and co-founder of the Parrot Head Club of Maine.

And Buffett's management recognizes the charitable efforts of the Buffett community. Parrot Head Clubs get a certain amount of tickets allocated to them. Members still have to pay for them, but they get first dibs on the best seats depending on how many Parrot Points (doled out to members when they participate in charitable or volunteer efforts) they have. As tickets have become harder and harder to obtain, this is indeed a welcome bonus.

DISCUSSION QUESTIONS

1 How can Jimmy Buffett fans be considered as members of a reference group? A brand community? A consumer tribe?

2 Consider your responses to question 1. What kind of opportunities does the existence of the Buffett community present to marketers? Develop a list of specific marketing and promotional tactics.

Sources: Jules Crittenden, "Fan Partying Brings Fun to Fenway," *Boston Herald* (September 11, 2004): 4; Brett Oppegaard, "Parrot Heads Par Excellence: In Hard-Fought Competition, Battle Ground Couple Emerge as the County's Top Jimmy Buffett Fans," *The Columbian* (September 16, 2003): D1; Ray Routhier, "Maine Parrot Heads Prove They're Charity-Minded," *Portland Press Herald* (April 24, 2005): G1.

NOTES

1. www.harley-davidson.com/wcm/Content/Pages/Accessories_and_Apparel/Accessories_and_Apparel.jsp?locale=en_US, accessed August 15, 2007.
2. Details adapted from John W. Schouten and James H. McAlexander, "Market Impact of a Consumption Subculture: The Harley-Davidson Mystique," in Fred van Raaij and Gary Bamossy, eds., *Proceedings of the 1992 European Conference of the Association for Consumer Research* (Amsterdam, 1992); John W. Schouten and James H. McAlexander, "Subcultures of Consumption: An Ethnography of the New Bikers," *Journal of Consumer Research* 22 (June 1995): 43–61. See also Kelly Barron, "Not So Easy Riders," *Forbes* (May 15, 2000).
3. Joel B. Cohen and Ellen Golden, "Informational Social Influence and Product Evaluation," *Journal of Applied Psychology* 56 (February 1972): 54–59; Robert E. Burnkrant and Alain Cousineau, "Informational and Normative Social Influence in Buyer Behavior," *Journal of Consumer Research* 2 (December 1975): 206–15; Peter H. Reingen, "Test of a List Procedure for Inducing Compliance with a Request to Donate Money," *Journal of Applied Psychology* 67 (1982): 110–18.
4. Dyan Machan, "Is the Hog Going Soft?" *Forbes* (March 10, 1997): 114–19.
5. C. Whan Park and V. Parker Lessig, "Students and Housewives: Differences in Susceptibility to Reference Group Influence," *Journal of Consumer Research* 4 (September 1977): 102–10.
6. Jeffrey D. Ford and Elwood A. Ellis, "A Re-examination of Group Influence on Member Brand Preference," *Journal of Marketing Research* 17 (February 1980): 125–32; Thomas S. Robertson, *Innovative Behavior and Communication* (New York: Holt, Rinehart and Winston, 1980), chapter 8.
7. William O. Bearden and Michael J. Etzel, "Reference Group Influence on Product and Brand Purchase Decisions," *Journal of Consumer Research* 9 (1982): 183–94; also cf. A. E. Schlosser and S. Shavitt, "Anticipating Discussion about a Product: Rehearsing What to Say

Can Affect Your Judgments," *Journal of Consumer Research* 29, no. 1 (2002): 101–15.
8. Kenneth J. Gergen and Mary Gergen, *Social Psychology* (New York: Harcourt Brace Jovanovich, 1981), 312.
9. J. R. P. French, Jr., and B. Raven, "The Bases of Social Power," in D. Cartwright, ed., *Studies in Social Power* (Ann Arbor, MI: Institute for Social Research, 1959), 150–67.
10. Michael R. Solomon, "Packaging the Service Provider," *The Service Industries Journal* 5 (March 1985): 64–72.
11. Tamar Charry, "Advertising: Hawking, Wozniak Pitch Modems for U.S. Robotics," *New York Times News Service* (February 5, 1997).
12. Patricia M. West and Susan M. Broniarczyk, "Integrating Multiple Opinions: The Role of Aspiration Level on Consumer Response to Critic Consensus," *Journal of Consumer Research* 25 (June 1998): 38–51.
13. Gergen and Gergen, *Social Psychology*.
14. Harold H. Kelley, "Two Functions of Reference Groups," in Harold Proshansky and Bernard Siedenberg, eds., *Basic Studies in Social Psychology* (New York: Holt, Rinehart and Winston, 1965), 210–14.
15. Kris Oser, "Microsoft's Halo 2 Soars on Viral Push," *Advertising Age* (Octeber 25, 2004): 46.
16. James H. McAlexander, John W. Schouten, and Harold F. Koenig, "Building Brand Community," *Journal of Marketing* 66 (January 2002): 38–54; Albert Muñiz and Thomas O'Guinn, "Brand Community," *Journal of Consumer Research* (March 2001): 412–32.
17. Veronique Cova and Bernard Cova, "Tribal Aspects of Postmodern Consumption Research: The Case of French In-Line Roller Skaters," *Journal of Consumer Behavior* 1 (June 2001): 67–76.
18. Laurie Petersen, "Pontiac Goes Underground to Tap Fans," *Marketing Daily* (February 8, 2007), available from www.mediapost.com, accessed February 8, 2007.

19. Jennifer Edson Escalas and James R. Bettman, "You Are What You Eat: The Influence of Reference Groups on Consumers' Connections to Brands," *Journal of Consumer Psychology* 13 (3) (2003): 339–48.

20. A. Benton Cocanougher and Grady D. Bruce, "Socially Distant Reference Groups and Consumer Aspirations," *Journal of Marketing Research* 8 (August 1971): 79–81.

21. Barry Rehfeld, "At These Camps, Everybody Is a Star (If Only for a Day)," *New York Times Online* (June 12, 2005).

22. L. Festinger, S. Schachter, and K. Back, *Social Pressures in Informal Groups: A Study of Human Factors in Housing* (New York: Harper, 1950).

23. R. B. Zajonc, H. M. Markus, and W. Wilson, "Exposure Effects and Associative Learning," *Journal of Experimental Social Psychology* 10 (1974): 248–63.

24. D. J. Stang, "Methodological Factors in Mere Exposure Research," *Psychological Bulletin* 81 (1974): 1014–25; R. B. Zajonc, P. Shaver, C. Tavris, and D. Van Kreveid, "Exposure, Satiation and Stimulus Discriminability," *Journal of Personality and Social Psychology* 21 (1972): 270–80.

25. J. E. Grush, K. L. McKeogh, and R. F. Ahlering, "Extrapolating Laboratory Exposure Research to Actual Political Elections," *Journal of Personality and Social Psychology* 36 (1978): 257–70.

26. Basil G. Englis and Michael R. Solomon, "To Be and Not to Be: Reference Group Stereotyping and the Clustering of America," *Journal of Advertising* 24 (Spring 1995): 13–28; Michael R. Solomon and Basil G. Englis, "I Am Not, Therefore I Am: The Role of Anti-Consumption in the Process of Self-Definition" (special session at the Association for Consumer Research meetings, October 1996, Tucson, Arizona); cf. also Brendan Richardson and Darach Turley, "Support Your Local Team: Resistance, Subculture and the Desire for Distinction," *Advances in Consumer Research*, 33 (1) (2006): 175–180.

27. Bruce Feirstein, *Real Men Don't Eat Quiche* (New York: Pocket Books, 1982); www.auntiefashions.com, accessed December 31, 2002.

28. Rob Walker, "Anti-Fan Club," *New York Times Online* (November 26, 2006), accessed November 26, 2006.

29. Candice R. Hollenbeck and George M. Zinkhan, "Consumer Activism on the Internet: The Role of Anti-brand Communities," *Advances in Consumer Research* 33 (1) (2006):479–485.

30. Marius K. Luedicke, "Brand Community under Fire: The Role of Social Environments for the Hummer Brand Community," *Advances in Consumer Research* 33 (1) (2006): 486–493.

31. B. Latane, K. Williams, and S. Harkins, "Many Hands Make Light the Work: The Causes and Consequences of Social Loafing," *Journal of Personality and Social Psychology* 37 (1979): 822–32.

32. S. Freeman, M. Walker, R. Borden, and B. Latane, "Diffusion of Responsibility and Restaurant Tipping: Cheaper by the Bunch," *Personality and Social Psychology Bulletin* 1 (1978): 584–87.

33. J. Craig Andrews and Richard G. Netemeyer, "Alcohol Warning Label Effects: Socialization, Addiction, and Public Policy Issues," in Ronald P. Hill, ed., *Marketing and Consumer Research in the Public Interest* (Thousand Oaks, CA: Sage, 1996), 153–75; "National Study Finds Increase in College Binge Drinking," *Alcoholism & Drug Abuse Weekly* (March 27, 2000): 12–13.

34. Nathan Kogan and Michael A. Wallach, "Risky Shift Phenomenon in Small Decision-Making Groups: A Test of the Information Exchange Hypothesis," *Journal of Experimental Social Psychology* 3 (January 1967): 75–84; Nathan Kogan and Michael A. Wallach, *Risk Taking* (New York: Holt, Rinehart and Winston, 1964); Arch G. Woodside and M. Wayne DeLozier, "Effects of Word-of-Mouth Advertising on Consumer Risk Taking," *Journal of Advertising* (Fall 1976): 12–19.

35. Kogan and Wallach, *Risk Taking*.

36. Roger Brown, *Social Psychology* (New York: The Free Press, 1965).

37. David L. Johnson and I. R. Andrews, "Risky Shift Phenomenon Tested with Consumer Product Stimuli," *Journal of Personality and Social Psychology* 20 (1971): 382–85; see also Vithala R. Rao and Joel H. Steckel, "A Polarization Model for Describing Group Preferences," *Journal of Consumer Research* 18 (June 1991): 108–18.

38. Donald H. Granbois, "Improving the Study of Customer In-Store Behavior," *Journal of Marketing* 32 (October 1968): 28–32; Tamara F. Mangleburg, Patricia M. Doney, and Terry Bristol, "Shopping with Friends and Teens' Susceptibility to Peer Influence," *Journal of Retailing* 80 (2004): 101–16.

39. Len Strazewski, "Tupperware Locks in New Strategy," *Advertising Age* (February 8, 1988): 30.

40. Melanie Wells, "Smooth Operator," Forbes (May 13, 2002): 167–68.

41. Luc Sante, "Be Different! (Like Everyone Else!)," *New York Times Magazine Online* (October 17, 1999), accessed October 3, 2007.

42. For a study attempting to measure individual differences in proclivity to conformity, see William O. Bearden, Richard G. Netemeyer, and Jesse E. Teel, "Measurement of Consumer Susceptibility to Interpersonal Influence," *Journal of Consumer Research* 15 (March 1989): 473–81.

43. John W. Thibaut and Harold H. Kelley, *The Social Psychology of Groups* (New York: Wiley, 1959); W. W. Waller and R. Hill, *The Family, a Dynamic Interpretation* (New York: Dryden, 1951).

44. Bearden, Netemeyer, and Teel, "Measurement of Consumer Susceptibility to Interpersonal Influence"; Lynn R. Kahle, "Observations: Role-Relaxed Consumers: A Trend of the Nineties," *Journal of Advertising Research* (March–April 1995): 66–71; Lynn R. Kahle and Aviv Shoham, "Observations: Role-Relaxed Consumers: Empirical Evidence," *Journal of Advertising Research* (May–June 1995): 59–62.

45. Pat Wechsler, "A Curiously Strong Campaign," *BusinessWeek* (April 21, 1997): 134.

46. Johan Arndt, "Role of Product-Related Conversations in the Diffusion of a New Product," *Journal of Marketing Research* 4 (August 1967): 291–95.

47. John Gaffney, "Enterprise: Marketing: The Cool Kids Are Doing It. Should You?" *Asiaweek* (November 23, 2001): 1.

48. Douglas R. Pruden and Terry G. Vavra, "Controlling the Grapevine," *MM* (July–August 2004): 23–30.

49. www.bzzagent.com, accessed July 20, 2007.

50. Elihu Katz and Paul F. Lazarsfeld, *Personal Influence* (Glencoe, IL: Free Press, 1955).

51. John A. Martilla, "Word-of-Mouth Communication in the Industrial Adoption Process," *Journal of Marketing Research* 8 (March 1971): 173–78; see also Marsha L. Richins, "Negative Word-of-Mouth by Dissatisfied Consumers: A Pilot Study," *Journal of Marketing* 47 (Winter 1983): 68–78.

52. Arndt, "Role of Product-Related Conversations in the Diffusion of a New Product."

53. James H. Myers and Thomas S. Robertson, "Dimensions of Opinion Leadership," *Journal of Marketing Research* 9 (February 1972): 41–46.

54. Ellen Neuborne, "Generation Y," *BusinessWeek* (February 15, 1999): 86.

55. Dorothy Leonard-Barton, "Experts as Negative Opinion Leaders in the Diffusion of a Technological Innovation," *Journal of Consumer Research* 11 (March 1985): 914–26.

56. James F. Engel, Robert J. Kegerreis, and Roger D. Blackwell, "Word-of-Mouth Communication by the Innovator," *Journal of Marketing* 33 (July 1969): 15–19; cf. also, Rajdeep Growl, Thomas W. Cline, and Anthony Davies, "Early-Entrant Advantage, Word-of-Mouth Communication, Brand Similarity, and the Consumer Decision Making Process," *Journal of Consumer Psychology* 13, no. 3 (2003): 187–97.

57. Chip Walker, "Word-of-Mouth," *American Demographics* (July 1995): 38–44; Albert M Muñiz, Jr., Thomas O'Guinn, and Gary Alan Fine, "Rumor in Brand Community," in Donald A. Hantula, ed., *Advances in Theory and Methodology in Social and Organizational Psychology" A Tribute to Ralph Rosnow*, (Mahwah, NJ: Erlbaum, 2005).

58. Richard J. Lutz, "Changing Brand Attitudes through Modification of Cognitive Structure," *Journal of Consumer Research* 1 (March 1975): 49–59. For some suggested remedies to bad publicity, see Mitch Griffin, Barry J. Babin, and Jill S. Attaway, "An Empirical Investigation of the Impact of Negative Public Publicity on Consumer Attitudes and Intentions," in Rebecca H. Holman and Michael R. Solomon, eds., *Advances in Consumer Research* 18 (Provo, UT: Association for Consumer Research, 1991): 334–41; Alice M. Tybout, Bobby J. Calder, and Brian Sternthal, "Using Information Processing Theory to Design Marketing Strategies," *Journal of Marketing Research* 18 (1981): 73–79; see also Russell N. Laczniak, Thomas E. DeCarlo, and Sridhar N. Ramaswami, "Consumers' Responses to Negative Word-of-Mouth Communication: An Attribution Theory Perspective," *Journal of Consumer Psychology*, 11, no. 1 (2001): 57–73.

59. Robert E. Smith and Christine A. Vogt, "The Effects of Integrating Advertising and Negative Word-of-Mouth Communications on Message Processing and Response," *Journal of Consumer Psychology* 4, no. 2 (1995): 133–51; Paula Fitzgerald Bone, "Word-of-Mouth Effects on Short-Term and Long-Term Product Judgments," *Journal of Business Research* 32 (1995): 213–23.

60. Keith Schneider, "Brands for the Chattering Masses," available from www.nytimes.com (December 17, 2006), accessed October 3, 2007.

61. "Dunkin' Donuts Buys Out Critical Web Site," *New York Times on the Web* (August 27, 1999). For a discussion of ways to assess negative WOM online, cf. David M. Boush and Lynn R. Kahle, "Evaluating Negative Information in Online Consumer Discussions: From Qualitative Analysis to Signal Detection," *Journal of EuroMarketing* 11, no. 2 (2001): 89–105.

62. Christine Bittar, "Johnson & Johnson Tries Online Damage Prevention," Marketing Daily (April 5, 2007), available from www.mediapost.com, accessed April 5, 2007.

63. James C. Ward and Amy L. Ostrom, "Complaining to the Masses: The Role of Protest Framing in Customer-Created Complaint Web Sites," *Journal of Consumer Research* 33, no. 2 (2006): 220.

64. Charles W. King and John O. Summers, "Overlap of Opinion Leadership across Consumer Product Categories," *Journal of Marketing Research* 7 (February 1970): 43–50.

65. Michael Fumento, "Tampon Terrorism," *Forbes* (May 17, 1999): 170.

66. Adapted from multiple sources, but primarily Jennifer Alsever, "Flying Off the Shelves," *Business 2.0* (December 2006): 47–49; cf. also http://en.wikipedia.org/wiki/Picoo_Z , accessed July 20, 2007.

67. Greg Jaffe, "No MTV for Widespread Panic, Just Loads of Worshipful Fans," *Wall Street Journal Interactive Edition* (February 17, 1999).

68. Eric Pfanner, "Taste of Victory: Online Outcry Revives a Chocolate Bar," *New York Times Online* (August 27, 2007), accessed August 27, 2007.

69. This typology is adapted from Robert V. Kozinets, "E-Tribalized Marketing: The Strategic Implications of Virtual Communities of Consumption," *European Management Journal* 17 (June 1999): 252–64.

70. http://advertising.microsoft.com/advertising-case-studies?Adv_Case StudyID=837, accessed July 20, 2007. See also Miriam Catterall and Pauline Maclaran, "Researching Consumers in Virtual Worlds: A Cyberspace Odyssey," *Journal of Consumer Behavior* 1, no. 3 (February 2000): 228–37.

71. Marc Gunther, "The Newest Addiction," *Fortune* (August 2, 1999): 123.

72. Tom Weber, "Net's Hottest Game Brings People Closer," *Wall Street Journal Interactive Edition* (March 20, 2000).

73. David Kushner, "Where Warriors and Ogres Lock Arms Instead of Swords," *New York Times on the Web* (August 9, 2002).

74. Martha Irvine, "Mother Blames Internet Game for Son's Suicide," *Montgomery Advertiser* (May 26, 2002): 6(A).

75. Edward Castronova, "Virtual Worlds: A First-Hand Account of Market and Society on the Cyberian Frontier," CESifo Working Paper Series No. 618, Indiana University (December 2001); Ania Lichtarowicz, "Virtual Kingdom Richer Than Bulgaria," *BBC News*, http://news.bbc.co.uk/2/hi/science/nature/1899420.stm, March 29, 2002, accessed October 3, 2007; www.secondlife.com, accessed July 20, 2007; Nick Gonzalez, "Entropia's Virtual World Comes to China," *TechCrunch*, www.techcrunch.com/2007/05/30/entropias-virtual-world-comes-to-china/, May 30, 2007.

76. Dan Mitchell, "What's Online," *New York Times* (July 20, 2007): C5.

77. Kozinets, "E-Tribalized Marketing: The Strategic Implications of Virtual Communities of Consumption."

78. Robert V. Kozinets, "Click to Connect: Netnography and Tribal Advertising," *Journal of Advertising Research*, 46, no. 3 (2006): 279–288.

79. Stella Yiyan Li and Kineta H. Hung, "Netnographic Study of a Community of Beauty Product Enthusiasts in China," *Advances in Consumer Research* 33, no. 1 (2006).

80. Glyn Moody, "Gold in Amazon's Box of Tricks," *Computer Weekly* (July 18, 2002): 27; "Shopping (online consumer ratings)," *Yahoo! Internet Life* (July 1, 2002); Bob Tedeschi, "Online Retailers Find That Customer Reviews Build Loyalty," *New York Times on the Web* (September 6, 1999); "Bookseller Offers Refunds for Advertised Books," *Opelika-Auburn [Alabama] News* (February 11, 1999): A11; Jason Anders, "When It Comes to Promoters, Boards Say, 'Reader Beware,'" *Wall Street Journal Interactive Edition* (July 25, 1998).

81. Sonia Murray, "Street Marketing Does the Trick," *Advertising Age* (March 20, 2000): S12.

82. "Taking to the Streets," *Newsweek* (November 2, 1998): 70–73.

83. Karl Greenberg, "Scion's Web-Based Pre-Launch Scorns Tradition," *Marketing Daily* (March 6, 2007), available from www.mediapost.com, accessed March 6, 2007.

84. Melanie Wells, "Wabbing," *Forbes* (February 2, 2004): 84–88; Jeff Leeds, "The Next Hit Song? Ask P&G," *New York Times on the Web* (November 8, 2004).

85. Rob Walker, "The Hidden (in Plain Sight) Persuaders," *New York Times on the Web* (December 5, 2004).

86. Suzanne Vranica, "Guerrilla Marketing Takes a Soft-Boiled Approach: Public-Service Campaigns Are Now Using the Tactic; Smashing Eggs for Safety," *Wall Street Journal on the Web* (July 8, 2004): B4.

87. Kate Fitzgerald, "Branding Face to Face," *Advertising Age* (October 21, 2002): 47.

88. David Goetzl, "Boston Bomb Stunt Drove Online Traffic to Cartoon Network," *Marketing Daily* (February 5, 2007) available from www.mediapost.com, accessed February 5, 2007.

89. Jared Sandberg, "The Friendly Virus," *Newsweek* (April 12, 1999): 65–66.

90. Brian Steinberg, "Marketing the Unmentionable? Talk to the Web Mainstream Advertisers with Sensitive Pitches Narrow in on Their Targets," *Wall Street Journal* (May 11, 2006): B2.

91. Some material adapted from a presentation by Matt Leavey, Prentice Hall Business Publishing, July 18, 2007.

92. Jeff Surowiecki, *The Wisdom of Crowds* (New York: Anchor, 2005); Jeff Howe, "The Rise of Crowdsourcing," *Wired* (June 2006): www.wired.com/wired/archive/14.06/crowds.html, accessed October 3, 2007.

93. Mark Weingarten, "Designed to Grow," *Business 2.0* (June 2007): 35–37.

94. "April 2007 Trend Briefing," available from www.trendwatching.com/briefing/, accessed March 13, 2007.

95. Susanna Hamner, "Cashing in on Doctor's, Thinking," *Business 2.0* (June 2006): 40.

96. "Shopmobbing," *Fast Company* (April 2007): 31.

97. Amy Chozick, "Cold Stone Aims to Be Hip in Japan Ice-Cream Chain, Uses Word of Mouth as Part of Bid for an Urban Image," *Wall Street Journal* (December 14, 2006): B10.

98. Everett M. Rogers, *Diffusion of Innovations*, 3rd ed. (New York: Free Press, 1983).

99. Leonard-Barton, "Experts as Negative Opinion Leaders in the Diffusion of a Technological Innovation;" Rogers, *Diffusion of Innovations*.

100. Herbert Menzel, "Interpersonal and Unplanned Communications: Indispensable or Obsolete?" in Edward B. Roberts, ed., *Biomedical Innovation* (Cambridge, MA: MIT Press, 1981), 155–63.

101. Meera P. Venkatraman, "Opinion Leaders, Adopters, and Communicative Adopters: A Role Analysis," *Psychology & Marketing* 6 (Spring 1989): 51–68.

102. Rogers, *Diffusion of Innovations*.

103. Robert Merton, *Social Theory and Social Structure* (Glencoe, IL: Free Press, 1957).

104. King and Summers, "Overlap of Opinion Leadership across Consumer Product Categories"; see also Ronald E. Goldsmith, Jeanne R. Heitmeyer, and Jon B. Freiden, "Social Values and Fashion Leadership," *Clothing and Textiles Research Journal* 10 (Fall 1991): 37–45; J. O. Summers, "Identity of Women's Clothing Fashion Opinion Leaders," *Journal of Marketing Research* 7 (1970): 178–85.

105. Steven A. Baumgarten, "The Innovative Communicator in the Diffusion Process," *Journal of Marketing Research* 12 (February 1975): 12–18.

106. Laura J. Yale and Mary C. Gilly, "Dyadic Perceptions in Personal Source Information Search," *Journal of Business Research* 32 (1995): 225–37.

107. Russell W. Belk, "Occurrence of Word-of-Mouth Buyer Behavior as a Function of Situation and Advertising Stimuli," in Fred C. Allvine, ed., *Combined Proceedings of the American Marketing Association*, series no. 33 (Chicago: American Marketing Association, 1971): 419–22.

108. Lawrence F. Feick, Linda L. Price, and Robin A. Higie, "People Who Use People: The Other Side of Opinion Leadership," in Richard J. Lutz, ed., *Advances in Consumer Research* 13 (Provo, UT: Association for Consumer Research, 1986): 301–5.

109. For discussion of the market maven construct, see Lawrence F. Feick and Linda L. Price, "The Market Maven," *Managing* (July 1985): 10; scale items adapted from Lawrence F. Feick and Linda L. Price, "The Market Maven: A Diffuser of Marketplace Information," *Journal of Marketing* 51 (January 1987): 83–87.

110. Michael R. Solomon, "The Missing Link: Surrogate Consumers in the Marketing Chain," *Journal of Marketing* 50 (October 1986): 208–18.

111. "Coldwell Banker Selling Second Life Homes," *Digital Trends* (March 23, 2007), available from http://news.digitaltrends.com/news_printer friendly12534.html, accessed March 23, 2007.

112. Ibid.

113. Brian Steinberg, "Gimme an Ad! Brands Lure Cheerleaders Marketers Try to Rally Influential Teen Girls Behind New Products," *Wall Street Journal* (April 19, 2007): B4.

114. "CBS Extends Its High-Tech Reach: CD-ROM Goes to 'Influencers'", *PROMO: The International Magazine for Promotion Marketing* (October 1994): 59.

115. John Lippman, "Sony's Word-of-Mouth Campaign Creates Buzz for 'Crouching Tiger'", *Wall Street Journal Online* (January 11, 2001), accessed January 11, 2001.

116. B. Stern and S. J. Gould, "The Consumer as Financial Opinion Leader." *Journal of Retail Banking* 10 (1988) 47–49.

117. William R. Darden and Fred D. Reynolds, "Predicting Opinion Leadership for Men's Apparel Fashions," *Journal of Marketing Research* 1 (August 1972): 324–28. A modified version of the opinion leadership scale with improved reliability and validity can be found in Terry L. Childers, "Assessment of the Psychometric Properties of an Opinion Leadership Scale," *Journal of Marketing Research* 23 (May 1986): 184–88.

118. Dan Seligman, "Me and Monica," *Forbes* (March 23, 1998): 76.

119. Gina Kolata, "Find Yourself Packing It On? Blame Friends," *New York Times Online Edition* (July 26, 2007).

120. "Referrals Top Ads as Influence on Patients' Doctor Selections," *Marketing News* (January 30, 1987): 22.

121. Peter H. Reingen and Jerome B. Kernan, "Analysis of Referral Networks in Marketing: Methods and Illustration," *Journal of Marketing Research* 23 (November 1986): 370–78.

122. Peter H. Reingen, Brian L. Foster, Jacqueline Johnson Brown, and Stephen B. Seidman, "Brand Congruence in Interpersonal Relations: A Social Network Analysis," *Journal of Consumer Research* 11 (December 1984): 771–83; see also James C. Ward and Peter H. Reingen, "Sociocognitive Analysis of Group Decision-making among Consumers," *Journal of Consumer Research* 17 (December 1990): 245–62.

123. Jeff Surowiecki, *The Wisdom of Crowds*, (New York: Anchor, 2005); Jeff Howe, "The Rise of Crowdsourcing," *Wired* (June 2006): 176(8).

124. John Markoff, "Internet Use Said to Cut into TV Viewing and Socializing," *New York Times on the Web* (December 30, 2004).

125. Suzanne Vranica, "Getting Buzz Marketers to Fess Up," *Wall Street Journal on the Web* (February 9, 2005): B9.

126. Thomas E. Weber, "Viral Marketing: Web's Newest Ploy May Make You an Unpopular Friend," *Wall Street Journal Interactive Edition* (September 13, 1999).

Organizational and Household Decision Making

Chapter Objectives

When you finish this chapter you should understand why:

- Marketers often need to understand *consumers'* behavior rather than consumer behavior because in many cases more than one person decides what to buy.

- Companies as well as individuals make purchase decisions. The decision-making process differs when people choose what to buy on behalf of a company versus a personal purchase.

- Many important demographic dimensions of a population relate to family and household structure.

- Our traditional notions about families are outdated.

- Members of a family unit play different roles and have different amounts of influence when the family makes purchase decisions.

- Children learn over time what and how to consume.

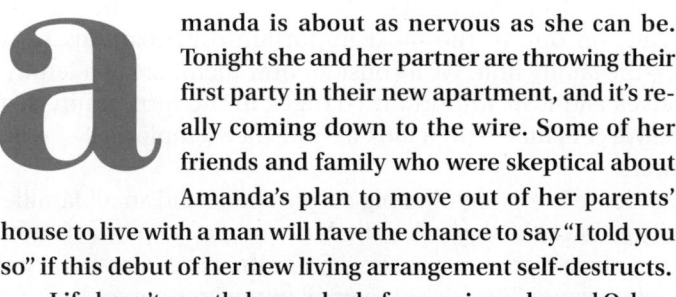

amanda is about as nervous as she can be. Tonight she and her partner are throwing their first party in their new apartment, and it's really coming down to the wire. Some of her friends and family who were skeptical about Amanda's plan to move out of her parents' house to live with a man will have the chance to say "I told you so" if this debut of her new living arrangement self-destructs.

Life hasn't exactly been a bed of roses since she and Orlando moved in together. It's a bit of a mystery—although his desk is tidy and organized at the publishing company where they both work, his personal habits are another story. Orlando's really been making an effort to clean up his act, but Amanda has still been forced to take on more than her share of cleaning duties—partly out of self-defense because they have to share a bathroom! And she's learned the hard way not to trust Orlando to do the grocery shopping—he goes to the store with a big list of staples and returns with beer and junk food. You would think that a man who is responsible for buying the firm's multimillion-dollar computer network would have a bit more sense when it comes to sticking to a budget and picking out the right household supplies. What's even more frustrating is that although Orlando can easily spend a week digging up information about the new big-screen TV they're buying (with her bonus!), she has to virtually drag him by the ear to look at dining room furniture. Then, to add insult to injury, he's quick to criticize her choices—especially if they cost too much.

So, how likely is it that while she's at work Orlando has been home cleaning up the apartment and making some hors d'oeuvres as he promised? Amanda did her part by downloading a recipe for crabmeat salad and wasabi caviar from the entertaining section on <u>epicurious.com</u>. She even jotted down some adorable table setting ideas such as napkin holders made out of homegrown bamboo at <u>marthastewart.com</u>. The rest is up to him—at this point she'd be happy if Orlando remembers to pick up his underwear from the living room couch. This soiree could turn out to be a real proving ground for their relationship. Amanda sighs as she walks into an editors' meeting. She sure has learned a lot about relationships since setting up a new household; living together is going to be a lot bumpier than it's made out to be in romance novels.

 # Organizational Decision Making

Amanda's trials and tribulations with Orlando illustrate the joint nature of many consumer decisions. The individual decision-making process we described in detail in Chapter 9 is, in many cases, overly simplistic. This is because more than one person often participates in the problem-solving sequence, from initial problem recognition and information search to evaluation of alternatives and product choice. To further complicate matters, these decisions often include two or more people who may not have the same level of investment in the outcome, the same tastes and preferences, or the same consumption priorities.

In this chapter we examine *collective decision making*, situations where more than one person chooses the products or services that multiple consumers use. In the first part of the chapter we look at organizational decision making, where one person or a group decides on behalf of a larger group. We then move on to focus more specifically on one of the most important organizations to which most of us belong—the family unit. We'll consider how members of a family negotiate among themselves and how important changes in modern family structure affect this process. We conclude with a look at how "new employees"—children—learn to be consumers.

Why do we lump together big corporations and small families? One important similarity is that in both cases individuals or groups play a number of specific roles when they choose products or services for their organizational unit.[1] Depending on the decision, it may include some or all of the group members, and different group members play important roles in what can be a complicated process. These roles include the following:

● **Initiator**: The person who brings up the idea or identifies a need.
● **Gatekeeper:** The person who conducts the information search and controls the flow of information available to the group. In organizational contexts the gatekeeper identifies possible vendors and products for the rest of the group to consider.
● **Influencer:** The person who tries to sway the outcome of the decision. Some people may be more motivated than others to get involved, and participants also differ in terms of the amount of power they have to convince others of their choice. In organizations, engineers are often influencers for product information, whereas purchasing agents play a similar role when the group evaluates the vendors that supply these items.
● **Buyer:** The person who actually makes the purchase. The buyer may or may not actually use the product. This person may pay for the item, actually procure it, or both.
● **User:** The person who winds up using the product or service.

ORGANIZATIONAL DECISION MAKING

Many employees of corporations or other organizations make purchase decisions on a daily basis. **Organizational buyers** are people like Orlando who purchase goods and services on behalf of companies for use in manufacturing, distribution, or resale. These individuals buy from **business-to-business (B2B) marketers** who specialize in meeting the needs of organizations such as corporations, government agencies, hospitals, and retailers. In terms of sheer volume, *B2B marketing* is where the action is: Roughly $2 trillion worth of products and services change hands among organizations, which is actually *more* than end consumers purchase.

Organizational buyers have a lot of responsibility. They must decide on the vendors with whom they want to do business and what specific items they require from these suppliers. The items they consider range in price and significance from paper clips to that multimillion-dollar computer system about which Orlando worries. Obviously, there is a lot at stake for marketers to understand how they make these important decisions.

A number of factors influence the organizational buyer's perception of the purchase situation. These include his *expectations* of the supplier (e.g., product quality, the competence and behavior of the firm's employees, and prior experiences in dealing with that supplier), the *organizational climate* of his own company (i.e., how the company rewards performance and what it values), and the buyer's *assessment* of his own performance (e.g., whether he believes in taking risks).[2]

Like other consumers, organizational buyers engage in a learning process where employees share information with one another and develop an "organizational memory" that consists of shared beliefs and assumptions about the best choices to make.[3] Just as our "market beliefs" influence him when he goes shopping with the family on the weekend (see Chapter 9), the same thing happens at the office. He (perhaps with fellow employees) solves problems by searching for information, evaluating alternatives, and making decisions.[4] There are, of course, some important differences between the two situations.

HOW DOES ORGANIZATIONAL DECISION MAKING COMPARE TO CONSUMER DECISION MAKING?

Many factors distinguish organizational and industrial purchase decisions from individual consumer decisions. Let's summarize the differences here:[5]

- Purchase decisions companies make frequently involve many people, including those who do the actual buying, those who directly or indirectly influence this decision, and the employees who will actually use the product or service.
- Organizations and companies often use precise technical specifications that require a lot of knowledge about the product category.
- Impulse buying is rare (industrial buyers do not suddenly get an "urge to splurge" on lead pipe or silicon chips). Because buyers are professionals, they base their decisions on past experience and by carefully weighing alternatives.
- Decisions often are risky, especially in the sense that a buyer's career may be riding on his judgment.
- The dollar volume of purchases is often substantial, dwarfing most individual consumers' grocery bills or mortgage payments. One hundred to 250 organizational customers often account for more than half of a supplier's sales volume, which gives the buyers a lot of influence over the supplier.
- Business-to-business marketing often involves more of an emphasis on personal selling than on advertising or other forms of promotion. Dealing with organizational buyers typically requires more face-to-face contact than when marketers sell to end consumers.

Industrial marketers can be creative when they want to be, as this European ad for heavy equipment manufacturer demonstrates.

Call the experts© for more power at high reach.

Reach further with Komatsu's telescopic handlers. With lifting heights from 9 to over 16 metres and lifting capacities from 3500 to 4500 kg, the range includes machines to suit every application. The state-of-the-art hydraulic system and single PPC joystick let you get the most from the huge power available and deliver precise control of the working equipment even during simultaneous operations. To complete the package, each of these highly versatile machines offers exceptional stability, high travel speed, superb manoeuvrability and best-in-class all-round visibility. Not bad for a telescopic.

KOMATSU

Komatsu Europe International nv - Mechelsesteenweg 586 - B-1800 Vilvoorde - Belgium

We must consider these important features when we try to understand the purchasing decisions organizations make. Still, there are actually more similarities between organizational buyers and ordinary consumers than many people realize. True, organizational purchase decisions do tend to have a higher economic or functional component compared to individual consumer choices, but emotional aspects enter the scene as well. For example, although organizational buyers may appear to the outsider to be models of rationality, still at times they base their decisions on brand loyalty, on long-term relationships with particular suppliers or salespeople, or even on aesthetic preferences.

How Do Organizational Buyers Operate?

Like end consumers, both internal and external stimuli influence organizational buyers. Internal stimuli include the buyer's unique psychological characteristics, such as his willingness to make risky decisions, job experience, and training. External stimuli include the nature of the organization for which he works as well as the overall economic and technological environment in which the industry operates. Another set of factors is cultural; we find vastly different norms for doing business in different countries. For example, Americans tend to be less formal in their interactions than are many of their European or Asian counterparts.

Type of Purchase

As you'd expect, the organizational buyer's decision-making process depends on just what he needs to buy. As with consumer purchases, the more complex, novel, or risky the decision, the more effort he devotes to the information search and the evaluation of alternatives. However, relying on a fixed set of suppliers for routine purchases is one strategy that greatly reduces his information search and effort to evaluate competing alternatives.[6] Typically, a group of people (members of a **buying center**) play different roles in more complex organizational decisions. As we will see later on, this joint involvement is somewhat similar to family decision making, where more family members are likely to participate in more important purchases.

The Buyclass Framework

Using the **buyclass theory of purchasing**, we divide organizational buying decisions into three types, which range from the most to the least complex. These three decision-making dimensions describe the purchasing strategies of an organizational buyer:[7]

1 The level of information he must gather prior to making a decision.
2 The seriousness with which he must consider all possible alternatives.
3 The degree to which he is familiar with the purchase.

In practice these three dimensions relate to how much cognitive effort the buyer expends when he decides. Three types of "buyclasses," or strategies these dimensions determine, encompass most organizational decision situations.[8] Each type of purchase corresponds to one of the three types of decisions we discussed in Chapter 9: habitual decision making, limited problem solving, and extensive problem solving. Table 12.1 summarizes these strategies.

A **straight rebuy** is a habitual decision. It's an automatic choice, as when an inventory level reaches a preestablished reorder point. Most organizations maintain an approved vendor list, and as long as experience with the vendor is satisfactory there is little or no ongoing information search or evaluation.

A **modified rebuy** situation involves limited decision making. It occurs when an organization wants to repurchase a product or service but with some minor modifications. This decision might involve a limited search for information, most likely by speaking to a few vendors. One or a few people will probably make the final decision.

A **new task** involves extensive problem solving. Because the company hasn't made a similar decision already, there is often a serious risk that the product won't perform as it should or that it will be too costly. The organization designates a buying center with assorted specialists to evaluate the purchase, and they typically gather a lot of information before coming to a decision.

TABLE 12.1
TYPES OF ORGANIZATIONAL BUYING DECISIONS

Buying Situation	Extent of Effort	Risk	Buyer's Involvement
Straight rebuy	Habitual decision making	Low	Automatic reorder
Modified rebuy	Limited problem solving	Low to moderate	One or a few
New task	Extensive problem solving	High	Many

Source: Adapted from Patrick J. Robinson, Charles W. Faris, and Yoram Wind, *Industrial Buying and Creative Marketing* (Boston: Allyn & Bacon, 1967).

Crowd Power in Organizations

Are all of us smarter than each of us? A **prediction market** is one of the hottest new trends in organizational decision-making techniques; it's one outgrowth of the *wisdom of crowds* phenomenon we discussed in Chapter 11. This approach asserts that groups of people with knowledge about an industry are jointly better predictors of the future than are any individuals—especially when each person stands to benefit from picking winners, just as they would if they were choosing companies to invest in on the New York Stock Exchange.

Companies from Microsoft to Eli Lilly and Hewlett-Packard empower their employees as "traders" who place bets on what they think will happen regarding future sales, the success of new products, or how other firms in a distribution channel will behave. For example, the pharmaceutical giant Eli Lilly routinely places multimillion-dollar bets on drug candidates that face overwhelming odds of failure—the relatively few new compounds that do succeed need to make enough money to cover the losses the others incur. Obviously, the company will benefit if it can do a better job of separating the winners from the losers earlier in the process. Lilly ran an experiment where about 50 of its employees involved in drug development, including chemists, biologists, and project managers, traded six mock drug candidates through an internal market. The group correctly predicted the three most successful drugs.[9]

In another emerging application, many companies are finding that it's both cost efficient and productive to call on outsiders from around the world to solve problems their own scientists can't handle. Just as a firm might outsource production to a subcontractor, they are **crowdsourcing.** For example, InnoCentive is a network of more than 90,000 "solvers" whose member companies, such as Boeing, DuPont, Procter & Gamble, and Eli Lilly, are invited to tackle problems they are wrestling with internally. If a "solver" finds a solution, he or she gets a $10,000 to $100,000 reward.[10]

B2B E-Commerce

The Web is radically changing the way organizational buyers learn about and select products for their companies. **Business-to-business (B2B) e-commerce** refers to Internet interactions between two or more businesses or organizations. This includes exchanges of information, products, services, or payments. A majority of U.S. firms plan to transact business on the Web, if they're not doing so already.

The Web is revolutionizing the way companies communicate with other firms and even the way they share information with their own people. Roughly half of B2B e-commerce transactions take the form of auctions, bids, and exchanges where numerous suppliers and purchasers interact.[11] For example, the 62 major retailers that belong to the Worldwide Retail Exchange use this online resource to cut costs as they develop new products and identify suppliers.[12] Working in cyberspace facilitates the creative process as well: Product designers at apparel manufacturers such as VF Corp. can log into the firm's intranet and play with product samples and colors in a database as they come up with new clothing ideas. Don't like that color or the way that button looks? A click of a button gives you a new one. In the old days, a new sample would have to be physically produced and evaluated, but now designers can create new styles and specify the materials they will need to produce them right on their desktops.[13] That's business at light speed.

In the simplest form of B2B e-commerce, the Internet provides an online catalog of products and services businesses need. Companies such as Dell Computer use their Internet site to deliver online technical support, product information, order status information, and customer service to corporate customers. Early on, Dell discovered that it could serve the needs of its customers more effectively by tailoring its Internet presence to different customer segments. Dell's Internet site allows shoppers to get recommendations based on their customer segment (home, home office, government, small business, and education). The company saves millions of dollars a year by replacing hard-copy manuals with electronic downloads. For its larger customers, Dell provides customer-specific, password-protected pages that allow business customers to obtain technical support or to place an order.

As social networking technologies proliferate (see Chapter 11), businesses are adopting these approaches also. They are introducing **wikis** that let several people change a document on a Web page and then track those changes (of course the most famous wiki is Wikipedia). High-tech companies, such as Intel, SAP, and IBM, are experimenting with recording meetings that get downloaded to iPods, blogs where employees can talk back to their bosses, and internal Web pages that allow people to read their colleagues' meeting notes and add their own.[14]

The Family Unit

Sometimes we read in newspapers and magazines about the death of the family unit. Although it is true that the proportion of people living in a traditional family structure consisting of a married couple with children living at home continues to decline, the reality is that many other types of families are growing rapidly. Indeed, some experts have argued that as traditional family living arrangements wane, we place even greater emphasis on siblings, close friends, and other relatives in providing companionship and social support.[16] Some people join "intentional families": groups of unrelated people who meet regularly for meals and who spend holidays together.[17] Indeed, for some, the act of meeting together to consume homemade food plays a central role in defining family—it is a symbolic way to separate a family unit from other social groups by allowing the cook(s) to personalize the meal and express affection via the effort that went into preparing the feast.[18]

THE MODERN FAMILY

The **extended family** used to be the most common family unit. It consists of three generations living together and it often includes grandparents, aunts, uncles, and cousins. Like the Cleavers of American television's *Leave It to Beaver* and other TV families of the 1950s, the **nuclear family**—a mother, a father, and one or more children (perhaps with a sheepdog thrown in for good measure)—replaced the extended family in many Western countries. However, we've witnessed many changes since the days of Beaver Cleaver. Although many people continue to base their image of the typical American family on old TV shows, demographic data tell us this ideal image of the family is no longer realistic. The U.S. Census Bureau regards any occupied housing unit as a household, regardless of the relationships among people living there. Thus in the United States one person living alone, three roommates, or two lovers (whether straight or gay) constitute a household.

Indeed, in 2005, America hit a watershed event: the U.S. Census Bureau announced that married couples officially make up a minority (49.7 percent) of American households. What's more, for the first time a majority (51 percent) of American women now live without a spouse (up from 35 percent in 1950). The survey estimated that about 5 percent of U.S. households consist of unmarried opposite-sex partners the government euphemistically calls **POSSLQ**, which stands for Persons of Opposite Sex Sharing Living Quarters. Like Amanda and Orlando, this situation is increasingly common. Nearly half of Americans aged 25 to 40 have at some point lived with a person of the opposite sex.[19] These changes are part of a broader shift toward nonfamily and childless households. There are also sizeable numbers of same-sex couples living together. Some of these changes came from unexpected places; for example, in the rural Midwest the number of households made up of male partners rose 77 percent since 2000.[20] As we saw previously, same-sex households are increasingly common and as a result more marketers target them as a family unit. Gayweddings.com and twobrides.com offer wedding decorations and gifts.[21]

Net Profit

Some innovative companies—most notably IBM—are migrating to *Second Life* to explore the potential of improving organizational decision making in virtual worlds. IBM owns more than 24 islands on *Second Life* and about 10 percent of its employees routinely go in-world in avatar form to conduct company business. The company believes that *Second Life* stimulates collaboration among a diverse workforce and it encourages its employees spread across several continents to forge bonds just as they would in RL by lingering in-world before and after meetings—something they can't easily do on impersonal conference calls. IBM's CEO is squarely behind this effort. He got the company buzzing when, as 5,000 employees around the globe observed, he attended a meeting in China in avatar form and toured a virtual version of Beijing's Forbidden City.[15]

This ad for *Family Circle* magazine humorously emphasizes that some traditional family values persist among young people today.

Another 5 percent of U.S. households are people who live alone. A large number of these singles appear to have two things in common: financial success and the willingness to spend to satisfy their desires. Single-person U.S. households spend 153 percent more per person on rent than those who live in households of two people or more. They also spend more on alcohol ($314 per year compared with $181). And they shell out more per person for reading materials, health care, and tobacco products and smoking supplies.[22]

Family Size

Family size depends on such factors as educational level, the availability of birth control, and religion.[23] Demographers define the **fertility rate** as the number of births per year per 1,000 women of childbearing age. Marketers keep a close eye on the population's birthrate to gauge how the pattern of births will affect demand for products in the future. The U.S. fertility rate increased dramatically in the late 1950s and early 1960s, when the parents of so-called baby boomers began to reach childbearing age. It declined in the 1970s and began to climb again in the 1980s as baby boomers began to have their own children in a new "baby boomlet."

Worldwide, surveys show that almost all women want smaller families today. This trend is a problem for European countries whose fertility rates have plummeted during past decades. Ironically, whereas populations boom in many underdeveloped parts of the world, industrialized countries face future crises because there will be relatively fewer young people to support their elders. In order for population levels to remain constant, this rate needs to be 2.0 so that the two children can replace their parents. That's not happening in places such as Spain,

Freshly brewed coffee for ten. For one.

Aroma-fresh pouch.

Contains ground roast coffee in its own filter.

Folgers Coffee Singles
THE ULTIMATE ONE CUP COFFEE MACHINE.

Folger's Coffee addresses an important need by allowing single people to brew one cup of coffee at a time.

Sweden, Germany, and Greece, where the fertility rate is 1.4 or lower. As a benchmark, the U.S. rate is almost exactly 2.0.

Some countries are weighing measures to encourage people to have more children. For example, Spain is looking at cheaper utility bills for large families, assisting young couples trying to afford homes, and creating hundreds of thousands of new preschools and nursery schools. The Italian government provides mothers with nearly full salary compensation for about a half year of maternity leave, but women are stubbornly refusing to have more kids. There are many reasons for this shift from past eras where heavily Catholic countries tended to have large families: Contraception and abortion are more readily available, divorce is more common, and older people who used to look after grandchildren now are pursuing other activities such as travel. And some experts cite the fact that many Italian men live with their mothers into their 30s so when they do get married they're not prepared to help out at home. One analyst commented, "Even the most open-minded guy—if you scratch with the nail a little bit, there's the mother who did everything for him."[24]

In the United States, The National Center of Health Statistics confirms that the percentage of women of childbearing age who define themselves as *voluntarily childless* is rising. Childless couples are an attractive market segment for some companies (but obviously not for others, such as Gerber Baby Food). So-called **DINKS** (double income, no kids) couples are better educated than two-income couples with children. According to the U.S. Census Bureau, 30 percent of childless couples consist of two college graduates, compared with 17 percent of those with kids. The childless are more likely to have professional or managerial occupations (24 percent versus 16 percent of dual-employed couples with children). Dave and Buster's, a Dallas-based restaurant chain, caters to this group by enforcing strict policies to deter families with small children. However, many childless couples feel they are snubbed by a child-oriented society. In recent years, they have formed several networking organizations such as Child-Free by Choice (childfreebychoice.com) and No Kidding! (nokidding.net) to support this lifestyle choice.[25]

The Sandwich Generation

Although traditional families are shrinking, ironically in other cases the traditional extended family is very much a reality. Many adults care for their own parents as well as for their children. In fact, Americans on average spend 17 years caring for children, but 18 years assisting aged parents.[26] Some label middle-aged people "the sandwich generation" because they must attend to those above and below them in age. In addition to dealing with live-in parents, many adults find to their surprise that their children are living with them longer or are moving back in well after their "lease" has expired.[27] As an Argentinean jeans ad asked, "If you are over 20 and still live with your parents, this is wrong. Isn't it high time you started looking for an apartment for them?"

Demographers call these returnees **boomerang kids**. The number of children between 18 and 34 years old living at home is growing dramatically, and today more than one-fifth of 25-year-old Americans still live with their parents. Young adults who do leave the nest to live by themselves are relatively unlikely to return, whereas those who move in with roommates are more likely to come back. And young people who move in with a romantic partner are more likely than average to end up back home if the relationship fails![28] If this trend continues, it will affect a variety of markets as boomerang kids spend less on housing and staples and more on discretionary purchases such as entertainment.

Animals Are People Too! Nonhuman Family Members

Almost one-third of all U.S. households have at least one pet, and 92 percent of pet owners consider their furry friends members of the family—83 percent call themselves "Mommy" or "Daddy" when they talk to their pets.[29] Many of us assume pets share our emotions—perhaps that helps to explain why more than three-quarters of domestic cats and dogs receive presents on holidays and birthdays.[30] We've doubled our spending on our pets in the past decade, and today the pet industry pulls in more revenue (almost $40 billion annually) than either the toy or candy industries. Here are some recent examples of pet-smart marketing:[31]

- Kennels are looking a lot more like spas for the furry. At some of them, dogs can hike, swim, listen to music, watch TV, and even get a pedicure—complete with nail polish. Heated tile floors and high-tech ventilation systems are common. When a day dog stays in the "ambassador suite" at Club Bow-Wow, a staff member sleeps overnight in the room. PetSmart, the largest U.S. pet-store chain, is opening 435 PetsHotels, where guests will lounge on hypoallergenic lambskin blankets and snack on lactose-free, fat-free ice cream. The suites have raised dog beds and a television that plays videos, such as *Lady and the Tramp* and *101 Dalmatians*.
- Companies that make human products, such as Gucci, Juicy Couture, Harley-Davidson, IKEA, Lands' End, Paul Mitchell, and Ralph Lauren, also sell products

for pets—from shampoos to nail polish to gold-plated bowls. Harley-Davidson started its pet collection after it noticed that customers at rallies and other events were bringing along their dogs—some riding shotgun in the motorcycles' saddle bags or side cars. Customers can buy denim and leather jackets for their pets, as well as riding goggles, bandanas, spiked leather collars, and even squeaky toys shaped like oil cans.

● Designer water for dogs? A California company started things off by introducing a vitamin-enriched water for dogs. A Florida company sells "DogWater" in containers that double as throwing toys. Then there's K9 Water Inc., a new company whose catalog lists products such as "Gutter Water" and chicken-flavored "Toilet Water."

● Car manufacturers find that people like to travel with their animals in tow. Saab offers a full line of pet-friendly accessories including seat-belt restraints

This Spanish public service ad promotes pet sterilization via a fake ad for dog condoms.

The author's pug, Kelbie Rae.

Net Profit

It started back in the 1990s, when a Japanese company created a craze for Tamagotchi pets, virtual critters that inhabited small, egg-shaped electronic gadgets. Then Neopets ramped up the fad when it created an online world where users become custodians of colorful, cartoonlike critters in Neopia, an imaginary world with its own currency (Neopoints), stock market (the Neodaq), and weather system. Users also get a dose of product plugs from companies such as General Mills Inc. and McDonald's Corp.

The site is so popular among young people that MTV bought it for $160 million in the summer of 2005 in order to take advantage of the merchandising opportunities because users have created more than 140 million different Neopets. Unlike many online game sites, the audience of approximately 25 million pet caretakers is mostly female. Users select a Neopet to adopt, give their creations names, and designate their behavior profiles (such as "making friends" or "bullying others"). Pet owners can play games with their Neopets, or even battle other Neopets inside the Battledome. When they engage in activities on the Web site, they can earn Neopoints, a virtual currency they can use to buy food for their Neopets.[32] Good luck with that virtual potty training.

What's next? Webkinz, of course. The $11 you shell out for the stuffed animal includes a secret code on its tag that allows children to log on to the Webkinz Web site to adopt the animal. Then they can chat with friends and play games to earn "Kinzcash," an online currency they can spend on prizes.

and a travel bowl that prevents spilling. General Motors is developing its Pet Pro concept for the GMC Envoy. The SUV will feature rear storage units customized for pet supplies and an integrated vacuum cleaner and dog ramp that slides out of the rear cargo area to help older dogs who may have difficulty climbing aboard.

● And what happens when that companion goes to the great kennel in the sky? One trend is to freeze-dry the departed pet rather than bury it or cremate it. The bereaved say turning furry friends into perma-pets helps them deal with loss and maintain a connection to their former companions. Once dried, the animal's body doesn't decay, so it can continue to occupy that special place on the couch.

The Family Life Cycle

Many factors affect what a family spends, including the number of people (children and adults) in the family, their ages, and whether one, two, or more adults work outside of the home. Two especially important factors that determine how a couple spends time and money are (1) whether they have children and (2) whether the woman works.

Recognizing that family needs and expenditures change over time, marketers apply the **family life cycle (FLC)** concept to segment households. The FLC combines trends in income and family composition with the changes these demands place on this income. As we age, our preferences and needs for products and activities tend to change. Twentysomethings spend less than average on most products and services because their households are small and their incomes are low. Income levels tend to rise (at least until retirement), so that people can afford more over time. Older consumers spend more *per capita* on luxury items such as gourmet foods and upscale home furnishings.[33] In addition, many purchases we have to make when we're first starting out don't have to be repeated very often. For example, we tend to accumulate durable goods such as large appliances and only replace them as necessary.

As Amanda and Orlando discovered when they moved in together, a life-cycle approach to the study of the family assumes that pivotal events alter role relationships and trigger new stages of life that alter our priorities. Carvel ice cream, for example,

Dodge appeals to both macho men and soccer moms with its Durango SUV.

is partnering with a company that publishes a pregnancy living guide, as it recognizes expecting women's "reputation" for craving ice cream. In August, which boasts both the highest birthrate and the highest daily temperatures nationwide, it posts descriptions of 10 new flavors where pregnant women vote on their favorite.[34] In addition to the birth of a first child, other pivotal events include the departure of the last child from the house, the death of a spouse, retirement of the principal wage earner, and divorce.[35] As people move through these life stages, we observe significant changes in expenditures in leisure, food, durables, and services, even after we adjust the figures to reflect changes in income.[36]

FLC Models

Getting a handle on long longitudinal changes in priorities is particularly valuable when we want to predict demand for specific product categories over time. For example, the money a couple with no children spends on dinners out and vacations will go to quite different purchases after the birth of a child. Ironically, although the entertainment industry focuses on winning the hearts and wallets of young consumers, it's the senior citizens who have become America's true party animals. The average household a 65- to 74-year-old heads spends more on entertainment than does the average household where the primary wage earner is under age 25. (more on this in Chapter 15).[37]

Researchers have proposed a number of models to describe family life-cycle stages, but with limited effect because most failed to take into account such important social trends as the changing role of women, the acceleration of alternative lifestyles, childless and delayed-child marriages, and single-parent households. We need to focus on four variables to adequately describe these changes: (1) age; (2) marital status; (3) the presence or absence of children in the home; and (4) the ages of children, if present. In addition, we must relax our definition of marital status to include any couple living together in a long-term relationship. Thus, although we might not consider roommates "married," for marketing purposes a man and woman who have established a household would be, as would two homosexual men who have a similar understanding.

When we update our outlook, we identify a set of categories that includes many more types of family situations.[38]

LIFE-CYCLE EFFECTS ON BUYING

Consumers we classify into these categories show marked differences in consumption patterns:

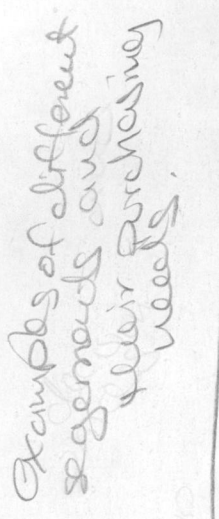

- Young bachelors and newlyweds are the most likely to exercise; to go out to bars, concerts, movies, and restaurants; and to drink alcohol. Although people in their twenties account for less than 4 percent of all household spending in the United States, their expenditures are well above average in such categories as apparel, electronics, and gasoline.[39]
- Families with young children are more likely to consume health foods such as fruit, juice, and yogurt; those made up of single parents and older children buy more junk foods. The dollar value of homes, cars, and other durables is lowest for bachelors and single parents but increases as people go through the full nest and childless couple stages.
- Perhaps helped by the bounty of wedding gifts, newlyweds are the most likely to own appliances such as toaster ovens and electric coffee grinders. Babysitter and day-care usage is, of course, highest among single-parent and full-nest households, whereas older couples and bachelors are most likely to employ home maintenance services (e.g., lawn mowing).

THE INTIMATE CORPORATION: FAMILY DECISION MAKING

The decision process within a household unit resembles a business conference. Certain matters go on the table for discussion, different members have different priorities and agendas, and there may be power struggles to rival any tale of corporate intrigue. In just about every living situation, whether a conventional family, students sharing a sorority house or apartment, or some other nontraditional arrangement, group members seem to take on different roles just as purchasing agents, engineers, account executives, and others do within a company.

Household Decisions

When Chevrolet wanted to win drivers over to its new Venture minivan, the company sent teams of anthropologists to observe families in their natural habitats. Conventional wisdom says that minivan buyers are practical; they care about affordability, lots of features, and plenty of room. But these researchers discovered a different story: People see the vehicles as part of the family. When they asked consumers to identify the best metaphor for a minivan, many picked a photo of a hang glider because it represents freedom and families on the go. The advertising slogan for the Venture became, "Let's go."[40]

Families make two basic types of decisions:[41]

1. In a **consensual purchase decision**, members agree on the desired purchase, differing only in terms of how it will be achieved. In these circumstances, the family will most likely engage in problem solving and consider alternatives until the means for satisfying the group's goal is found. For example, a household considering adding a dog to the family but concerned about who will take care of it might draw up a chart assigning individuals to specific duties.

In the **female** the ability to match colors comes at an early age. In the **male** it comes when he marries a female.

The City Casuals three-button, crepe jacket. 100% cotton, French-yarn shirt, Bedford cord pants, and a touch of color.

HAGGAR
Stuff you can work with.

2 In an **accommodative purchase decision**, group members have different preferences or priorities and they cannot agree on a purchase to satisfy the minimum expectations of all involved. It is here that they are likely to use bargaining, coercion, and compromise to achieve agreement on what to buy or who gets to use it. Conflict occurs when there is not complete correspondence in family members' needs and preferences. Although money is the most common source of conflict between marriage partners, TV-viewing choices come in a close second![42]

In general, decisions will involve conflict among family members to the extent that they are somehow important or novel, or if individuals have strong opinions about good and bad alternatives. The degree to which these factors generate conflict determines the type of decision the family will make.[43] Some specific factors that determine how much family decision conflict there will be include the following:[44]

- **Interpersonal need:** (a person's level of investment in the group): A teenager may care more about what her family buys for the house than will a college student who is temporarily living in a dorm.
- **Product involvement and utility:** (the degree to which a person will use the product to satisfy a need): A mother who is an avid coffee drinker will obviously be more interested in the purchase of a new coffeemaker than will her teenage son who swigs Coke by the gallon.
- **Responsibility:** (for procurement, maintenance, payment, and so on): People are more likely to have disagreements about a decision if it entails long-term

Although many men still wear the pants in the family, it's women who buy them. Haggar is redirecting $8 million worth of advertising to target women who shop for and with men. The apparel manufacturer placed menswear ads in about a dozen women's magazines after its research found that women exert tremendous influence over men's clothing choices. In a survey, nearly half of the females polled had purchased men's pants without the man present, and 41 percent said they accompanied the man when he bought pants. Female influence is strongest for decisions involving the matching of colors and the mixing/matching of separates.

consequences and commitments. For example, a family decision about getting a dog may involve conflict regarding who will be responsible for walking it and feeding it.

- **Power:** (or the degree to which one family member exerts influence over the others in making decisions): In traditional families, the husband tends to have more power than the wife, who in turn has more than the oldest child, and so on. In family decisions, conflict can arise when one person continually uses the power he has within the group to satisfy his priorities. For example, if a child believed that his life would end if he did not receive a Wii for his birthday, he might be more willing to "cash in some chips" and throw a tantrum.

Sex Roles and Decision Making Responsibilities

Who "wears the pants" in the family? Sometimes it's not obvious which spouse makes the decisions. Indeed, although many men still wear the pants, it's women who buy them. When Haggar's research showed that nearly half of married women bought pants for their husbands without them being present, the firm started advertising its menswear products in women's magazines.[45] When one family member chooses a product, we call this an **autonomic decision**. In traditional households, for example, men often have sole responsibility for selecting a car, whereas decorating choices fall to women. **Syncretic decisions**, such as choosing a vacation destination, might involve both partners.

According to a study Roper Starch Worldwide conducted, wives still tend to have the most say when buying groceries, children's toys, clothes, and medicines. Syncretic decisions are common for vacations, homes, appliances, furniture, home electronics and long-distance phone services. As the couple's education increases, they are more likely to make decisions together.[46]

Roper sees signs of a shift in marital decision making toward more compromise and turn-taking. For example, the survey finds that wives tend to win out in arguments about how the house is kept, whereas husbands get control of the remote![47]

To what degree are traditional sex roles changing? Recent evidence says quite a bit; men and women increasingly express similar attitudes about balancing home life and work. Some experts argue that the gender revolution is developing into **gender convergence**. A comprehensive view of current research reported more similarities than differences between American men and women; most people recognize that mothers are working more and doing less housework, and men are working less and doing more housework and childcare than a generation ago— although still significantly less than women.[48]

In any case, spouses typically exert significant influence on decision making— even after one of them has died. An Irish study found that many widows claim to sense the continued presence of their dead husbands and to conduct "conversations" with them about household matters![49] Comments from married women who participated in focus groups *Redbook* magazine conducted illustrate some of the dynamics of autonomic versus syncretic decision making:

- "We just got our steps done and that was a big project. The contractor would talk (to my husband) and not talk to me. And I said, 'Excuse me, I'm here, too.'"
- "We are looking for a house now, and we're making decisions on which side of town we want it on, what size house do we want, and it's a together decision. That's never how my mother did it."
- "My husband did not want a van, because we have just one child, but I said, 'I want a van. And it's not because everyone else has a van. I want comfort.' He wanted a convertible. And we got a van."[50]

Identifying the Decision Maker

Figuring out who makes buying decisions is an important issue for marketers because this information tells them who to target and whether they need to reach both spouses to influence a choice. For example, marketing research in the 1950s indicated that women were beginning to play a larger role in household purchasing decisions. In response, lawn mower manufacturers began to emphasize the rotary mower over other power mowers to downplay women's fears of injury. Rotary models, which conceal the cutting blades and engine, began to pop up in ads featuring young women and smiling grandmothers cutting the grass.[51]

Researchers pay special attention to which spouse plays the role of the **family financial officer (FFO)**, the individual who keeps track of the family's bills and decides how to spend any surplus funds. Newlyweds tend to share this role, and then over time one spouse or the other takes over these responsibilities.[52] In traditional families (and especially those with low educational levels), women are primarily responsible for family financial management—the man makes it, and the woman spends it. Each spouse "specializes" in certain activities.[53]

The pattern is different among families where more modern sex-role norms operate. These couples believe both people should participate in family maintenance activities. In these cases, husbands assume more responsibility for laundering, housecleaning, grocery shopping, and so on, in addition to such traditionally "male" tasks as home maintenance and garbage removal.[54] Shared decision making is becoming the norm for most American couples today—a recent Roper poll reported that 94 percent of partnered women say they make the decision or share equally in home furnishings selections (not a huge surprise), but in addition, 81 percent said the same for financial savings/investments and 74 percent participate in deciding what car to buy.[55]

Working mothers often struggle with what one researcher calls the "juggling lifestyle," a frenzied, guilt-ridden compromise between conflicting cultural ideals of motherhood and professionalism.[56] This frantic way of life isn't surprising in light of a recent survey by the U.S. Department of Labor that shows that the average working woman spends about twice as much time as the average working man on household chores and the care of children. And she also gets about an hour less sleep each night than the average stay-at-home mom.[57]

Figure 12.1 shows four distinct mother types LeoShe, a unit of the Leo Burnett advertising agency, identified in a study on marketing to women:[58]

- **June Cleaver, the Sequel:** Women who maintain the traditional roles of stay-at-home moms. They are mostly white, highly educated, and upscale.
- **Tug of War:** Women who are forced to work but who aren't happy about it. They tend to be strapped for time, so they buy well-known brand names to make shopping easier.
- **Strong Shoulders:** Women who are in lower-income levels but who have a positive view of themselves and their future. More than one-third of the women in this segment are single moms. LeoShe concludes that they are good candidates to try new brands that will help them express themselves.
- **Mothers of Invention:** These women enjoy motherhood and also work out of the home. One reason for their contentment is that their husbands pitch in a lot.

Cultural background plays a big role in determining whether husbands or wives control purchase decisions. For example, husbands tend to dominate decision making among couples with a strong Hispanic ethnic identification. Vietnamese Americans also are more likely to adhere to the traditional model: The man makes the decision for any large purchase, whereas the woman gets a budget to manage the home. In a study comparing marital decision making in the United States and China, American women reported more "wife decides" situations than did the Chinese.

■ **FIGURE 12.1**
LEOSHE MOTHER TYPES

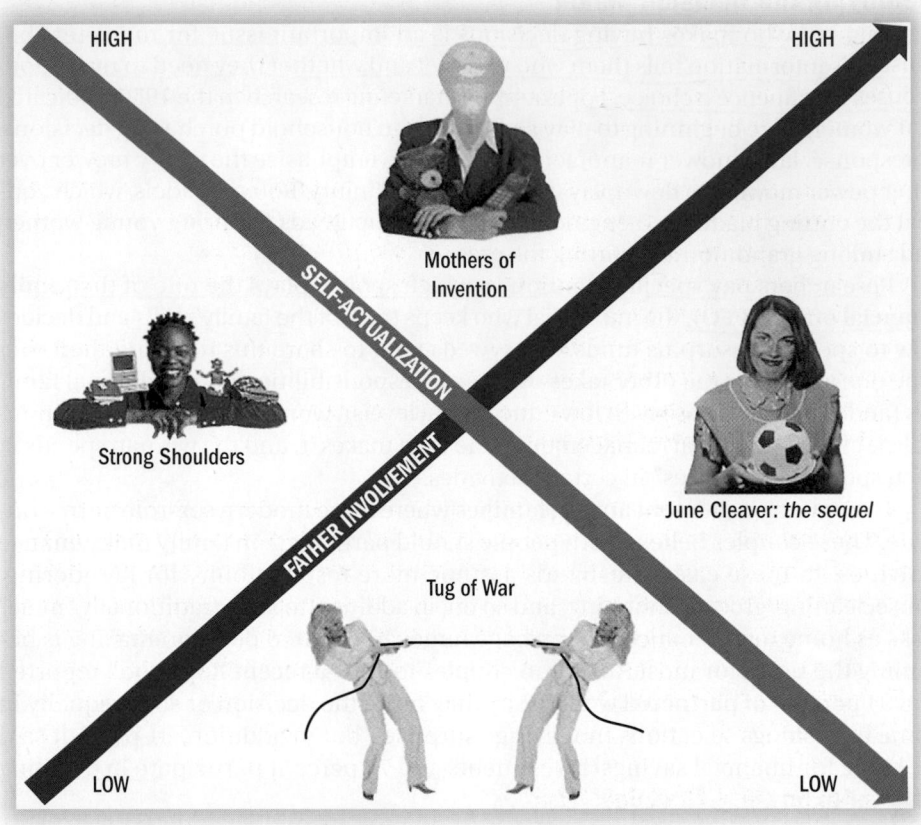

Advertising and marketing strategies often reflect assumptions about "who's the boss." These examples illustrate some cross-cultural differences:[59]

● The Coca-Cola Company developed a campaign to appeal to Latin American women based on a big research project the company conducted in Brazil. It found that a motherly female kangaroo was most likely to appeal to women shopping for their families—who happen to account for 80 percent of Coke's $3.5 billion in Brazilian sales. Coke used the theme "Mom knows everything," after women in focus groups said they felt the media neglected them even though they were responsible for purchasing all the products in their households.

● Butterfly, an Indian program, enlists village medicine men to convince local women to take birth control pills. A big obstacle is that women are not accustomed to making these decisions for themselves. The response of one village resident is typical: "I have never taken contraceptives. My husband is my master—he will decide."

● Traditional sex-role norms also influenced a commercial Procter & Gamble produced for its Ariel laundry detergent in India. It shows a man named Ravi doing the laundry, which is highly unusual there. A female voice questions, "Where's the wife? Are you actually going to wash them? . . . a man should not wash clothes . . . [he is] sure to fail."

● Ads showing men doing housework are risky in Asia as well, even though more Asian women are working outside the home. A South Korean vacuum cleaner ad showed a woman lying on the floor giving herself a facial with slices of cucumber while her husband vacuums around her. Women there didn't appreciate this ad. As a local ad executive put it, they regarded the ad as a challenge to "the leadership of women in the home."

In general, four factors appear to determine the degree to which one or the other spouse or both jointly will decide what to buy:[60]

1 **Sex-role stereotypes:** Couples who believe in traditional sex-role stereotypes tend to make individual decisions for sex-typed products (i.e., those they consider "masculine" or "feminine," as we discussed in Chapter 5).
2 **Spousal resources:** The spouse who contributes more resources to the family has the greater influence.
3 **Experience:** Couples who have gained experience as a decision-making unit make individual decisions more frequently.
4 **Socioeconomic status:** Middle-class families make more joint decisions than do either higher- or lower-class families.

Despite recent changes in decision-making responsibilities, women are still primarily responsible for the continuation of the family's **kin-network system**: They perform the rituals that maintain ties among family members, both immediate and extended. Women are more likely to coordinate visits among relatives, stay in touch with family members, send greeting cards, and arrange social engagements.[61] This organizing role means that women often make important decisions about the family's leisure activities, and they are more likely to decide with whom the family will socialize.

Heuristics in Joint Decision Making

The **synoptic idea** calls for the husband and wife to take a common view and to act as joint decision makers. According to this view, they would very thoughtfully weigh alternatives, assign one another well-defined roles, and calmly make mutually beneficial consumer decisions. The couple would act rationally, analytically, and use as much information as possible to maximize joint utility. In reality, however, spousal decision making may be more about choosing whatever option will result in less conflict. A couple "reaches" rather than "makes" a decision. Researchers simply describe this process as "muddling through."[62]

One common technique for simplifying the decision-making process is to use *heuristics* (see Chapter 9). Some decision-making patterns realtors frequently observe when a couple decides on a new house illustrate the use of heuristics:

- The couple defines their areas of common preference on obvious, objective dimensions rather than subtler, hard-to-define cues. For example, they may easily agree on the number of bedrooms they need in the new home, but they will have a harder time agreeing on how the home should look.
- The couple agrees on a system of *task specialization* in which each is responsible for certain duties or decision areas and does not intrude on the other's "turf." For many couples, sex roles often dictate just what these territories are. For example, the wife may scout out houses that meet their requirements in advance, and the husband determines whether the couple can obtain a mortgage.
- Concessions relate to the intensity of each spouse's preferences. One spouse will yield to the influence of the other in many cases simply because his level of preference for a certain attribute is not particularly intense, whereas in other situations he is more willing to fight for what he wants (in other words, "choose your battles").[63] In cases where intense preferences for different attributes exist, rather than attempt to influence each other, spouses will "trade off" a less-intense preference for a more strongly felt one. For example, a husband who is

CB AS I SEE IT

Professor Greg Rose
The University of Washington at Tacoma

Changes in family and household decision making are dynamic, evolving, and complex. Global shifts in gender roles, household structure, and idealized visions of the family make this a fascinating area for conducting research. My own research has concentrated primarily on cross-cultural differences in parental practices and beliefs.

More specifically, my colleagues and I have found several major parental styles that vary in their level of nurturance, strictness, and dependence. Parents from collectivist nations, such as India, Greece, or Japan, tend to expect children to develop consumer skills slowly, foster high levels of dependence in their children, and restrict their children's levels of independent consumption (their ability to buy things on their own). Parents from individualistic nations, such as Australia and the United States, generally foster independence and provide their children with greater opportunities for independent consumption. Differences also occur between parents within any nation, with each nation having its own unique pattern of predominate parental types. Thus, research in this area has only begun to scratch the surface in explaining global differences in family decision making.

Additional research could further assess global family processes and consumer socialization. The development of traditionally masculine (agentic) and traditionally feminine (communal) attitudes in children as they mature, children's navigation and learning of Web content, and differences in these processes across nations are currently being examined by me and my colleagues. Previous research indicates that younger children (about 5 to 6 years of age) tend to have more rigid sex role orientations than older children (aged 8 to 10) and we test the extent to which girls and boys in these different age groups prefer more agentic or communal ads. Younger children also tend to be more perceptual and less directed in their search processes than older children. We examine these differences in the context of Web site content and find that younger children prefer the use of a visual point-and-click map, whereas older children are better able to use a content list (similar to a menu in a computer application). Other areas of interest include changes in idealized images of masculinity and femininity among adults in various societies; the role of siblings and peers in consumer socialization; and purchasing patterns, social support, and life satisfaction among adults living alone. Overall, dramatic societal and global changes have occurred in recent years and additional research is needed in this area.[64]

somewhat indifferent about kitchen design may give in to his wife, in exchange for the license to design his own garage workshop.

CHILDREN AS DECISION MAKERS: CONSUMERS-IN-TRAINING

Carmakers are wooing a new kind of consumer: One who's too young to drive. Many are advertising in child-oriented areas such as gyms that cater to kids, social networking sites where young people hang out, and the Saturday morning cartoons. In Whyville.net, a virtual world where nearly 2 million children aged 8 to 15 hang out, kids can buy virtual Scion xBs if they have enough "clams" (Whyville's monetary unit). If not, they can meet with Eric, a virtual Toyota Financial Services adviser, to finance an xB replica they can use to tool around while in-world. Hummer is talking directly to kids with a special Web site (HUMMERkids.com) and toy cars it gives out in McDonald's Happy Meals. Small wonder: About one-third of parents say their kids "actively participate" in car-buying decisions.[65]

Anyone who has had the "delightful" experience of grocery shopping with children in tow knows that kids often have a say (sometimes a loud, whiney one) in what their parents buy. Children make up three distinct markets:[66]

Primary Market. Kids spend a lot on their own wants and needs that include toys, apparel, movies, and games. When marketers at M&Ms candy figured out who was actually buying a lot of their products, they redesigned vending machines with coin slots lower to the ground to accommodate shorter people, and sales rose dramatically.[67] Most children choose their own brands of toothpaste, shampoo, and adhesive bandage. A large 2006 survey of kids aged 6 to 11 also revealed these tidbits:[68]

- Seven percent have visited or used <u>MySpace.com</u> in the past month.
- Ten percent have downloaded music online in the past month.
- Six percent have written or read an online journal or blog in the past month.
- Fifty-four percent have televisions in their rooms.
- Twenty-six percent have stereos in their rooms.
- Nineteen percent have computers in their rooms.

Influence Market. **Parental yielding** occurs when a parental decision maker "surrenders" to a child's request.[69] Yielding drives many product selections because about 90 percent of requests to a parent are by brand name. Researchers estimate that children directly influence about $453 billion worth of family purchases in a year. They report that on average children weigh in with a purchase request every 2 minutes when they shop with parents.[70] In recognition of this influence, Mrs. Butterworth's Syrup created a $6 million campaign to target kids directly with humorous ads that show the lengths to which adults will go to get the syrup bottle to talk to them. An executive who worked on the campaign explained, "We needed to create the *nag factor* [where kids demand their parents buy the product]."[71]

The likelihood of yielding depends partly on the dynamics within a particular family. As we all know, parental styles range from permissive to strict, and they also vary in terms of the amount of responsibility parents give to their children.[72] Income level also comes into play, with kids at the lower end of the spectrum having a greater say in brand purchases than those whose families have higher incomes. Parents whom children can most easily influence also tend to be highly receptive to advertising; according to a major research firm, these "child influenced shoppers" are twice as likely as the average U.S. adult to agree that if they see a brand name product on a TV show, they are reassured it is a good product. They're also twice as likely to say that if they see a character in a movie use a brand-name product they have never tried before, they are likely to try it.

One study documented the strategies kids use to request purchases. Although most children simply asked for things, some other common tactics included saying they had seen it on TV, saying that a sibling or friend has it, or doing chores in exchange. Other actions were less innocuous; they included directly placing the object in the cart and continuous pleading—often a "persuasive" behavior![73] In addition, the amount of influence children have over consumption is culturally determined. Children who live in individualistic cultures such as the United States have more direct influence, whereas kids in collective cultures such as Japan get their way more indirectly.[74] Table 12.2 documents kids' influence in 10 different product categories.

Future Market. Kids have a way of growing up to be adults and savvy marketers try to lock in brand loyalty at an early age. That explains why Kodak encourages kids to become photographers. Currently, only 20 percent of children aged 5 to 12 own

Marketing Pitfall

Bowing to pressure, The Kellogg Company is phasing out advertising its products to children under age 12 unless the foods meet specific nutrition guidelines for calories, sugar, fat, and sodium. It also no longer uses licensed characters or branded toys to promote foods unless the products meet these guidelines. These changes affect about half of the products that Kellogg currently markets to children worldwide, including Froot Loops and Apple Jacks cereals and some varieties of Pop-Tarts.

Does advertising encourage unhealthy eating—and childhood obesity? In two studies, British researchers compared the effects of television advertising on the eating habits of 152 kids between the ages of 5 and 11. In both studies, the kids watched 10 ads followed by a cartoon. In one session, the kids saw ads for toys before they watched a video. But in another session, they replaced the toy ads with food ads that commonly run during children's programs. After both viewings, held 2 weeks apart, the kids were allowed to snack as much as they wanted from a table of low-fat and high-fat snacks, including grapes, cheese-flavored rice cakes, chocolate buttons, and potato chips. The 5-to-7-year-old kids who saw the food ads ate 14 to 17 percent more calories than those who saw the toy ads. The results were even more dramatic among 9-to-11-year-olds. Those in the food ad condition ate from 84 to 134 percent more calories than did those in the TV ad condition.[75]

TABLE 12.2
KIDS' INFLUENCE ON HOUSEHOLD PURCHASES

Top 10 Selected Products	Industry Sales (Billions)	Influence Factor (%)	Sales Influence (Billions)
Fruit snacks	0.30	80	0.24
Frozen novelties	1.40	75	1.05
Kids' beauty aids	1.20	70	0.84
Kids' fragrances	0.30	70	0.21
Toys	13.40	70	9.38
Canned pasta	0.57	60	0.34
Kids' clothing	18.40	60	11.04
Video games	3.50	60	2.10
Hot cereals	0.74	50	0.37
Kids' shoes	2.00	50	1.00

Source: "Charting the Children's Market," *Adweek* (February 10, 1992): 42.

cameras, and they shoot an average of only one roll of film a year. The company produces ads that portray photography as a cool pursuit and as a form of rebellion. It packages cameras with an envelope to mail the film directly back so parents can't see the photos.

Consumer Socialization

We've seen that kids are responsible for a lot of marketplace activity, but how do they know what they like and want? Children do not spring from the womb with consumer skills already in memory. **Consumer socialization** is the process "by which young people acquire skills, knowledge, and attitudes relevant to their functioning in the marketplace."[76] From where does this knowledge come? Friends and teachers certainly participate in this process. For instance, children talk to one another about consumer products, and this tendency increases with age.[77] Especially for young children, though, the two primary socialization sources are the family and the media.

Parents' Influence

Parents influence consumer socialization both directly and indirectly. They deliberately try to instill their own values about consumption in their children ("You're going to learn the value of money!"). Parents also determine the degree to which their children come into contact with other information sources such as television, salespeople, and peers.[78] Cultural expectations regarding the involvement of children in purchase decisions influence when and how parents socialize their kids as consumers. For example, parents in traditional cultures such as Greece and India rely on later development timetables for consumer-related skills and understanding advertising practices than do American and Australian parents.[79]

Grown-ups also serve as significant models for observational learning (see Chapter 3). Children learn about consumption as they watch their parents' behaviors and imitate them. Marketers encourage this process by packaging adult products

A CONSUMER IS BORN

Children start accompanying parents to the marketplace as early as one month old
and begin to make independent purchases as early as four years old.

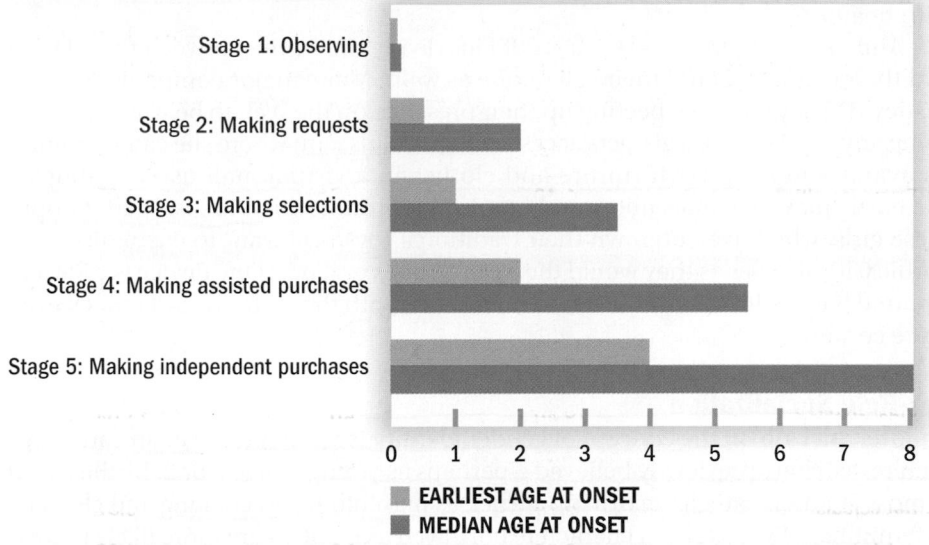

■ **FIGURE 12.2**

FIVE STAGES OF CONSUMER
DEVELOPMENT BY EARLIEST AGE AT
ONSET AND MEDIAN AGE AT ONSET

in child versions. This "passing down" of product preferences helps to create brand
loyalty; researchers find evidence of intergenerational influence when they study the
product choices of mothers and their daughters.[80]

The process of consumer socialization begins with infants, who accompany their
parents to stores and get exposed to marketing stimuli. Within the first 2 years, children begin to make requests for desired objects. As kids learn to walk, they also begin
to make their own selections while visiting stores. By about age 5, most kids are making purchases with the help of parents and grandparents, and by 8 most are making
independent purchases and have become full-fledged consumers.[81] Figure 12.2 summarizes the sequence of stages involved in turning kids into consumers.

Parents exhibit different styles when they socialize their children.[82] For example, "authoritarian parents" are hostile, restrictive, and emotionally uninvolved.
They do not have warm relationships with their children, they censor the types of
media their children see, and they tend to have negative views about advertising.
"Neglecting parents" also are detached from their children and the parents don't
exercise much control over what their children do. In contrast, "indulgent parents"
communicate more with their children about consumption-related matters and are
less restrictive. They believe that children should be allowed to learn about the marketplace without much interference.

Television and the Web: Electric Babysitters

Advertising's influence over us begins at a very early age. As we've seen, many marketers start to push their products on kids to encourage them to build a habit at an
early age. One controversial exception occurred in France. An ad McDonald's placed
in the magazine *Femme Actuelle* actually encouraged parents to limit kids' visits to
its outlets by proclaiming, "There is no reason to eat excessive amounts of junk food,
nor go more than once a week to McDonald's." A spokesperson for McDonald's in
the United States said the company did not agree with the views the ad expressed.[83]

This anticonsumption message is certainly unique in the barrage of messages
marketers aim at kids, especially on television. Because the media teach people
about a culture's values, the more a child watches television, whether the show is
MTV's *Laguna Beach* or *SpongeBob SquarePants*, the more he will accept the images

it depicts as real.[84] Kids also see idealized images of what it is like to be an adult. Because children over the age of 6 do about a quarter of their television viewing during prime time, adult programs and commercials have a big affect on them. For example, young girls who see adult lipstick commercials come to associate lipstick with beauty.[85]

And, as we've already seen, a lot of kids divide their time between their TV set and their computer (and their cell phone as well). Many major companies such as Disney (Disney.com) are beefing up their presence on the Web to be where kids are going anyway. For $60, a girl gets access to BarbieGirls.com where she can customize an avatar and shop for furniture and clothes in a virtual mall using "B-bucks" she earns playing games and watching product promotion videos. Mattel hopes these girls, who have outgrown their traditional toys, will want to customize their Barbie Girls devices as they would their cell phones or iPods. One device is a Barbie-inspired handheld MP3 music device to interact with the Web site and unlock even more content.[86]

Sex-Role Socialization

Children pick up on the concept of gender identity (see Chapter 5) at an earlier age than researchers previously believed—perhaps as young as age 1 or 2. By the age of 3, most children categorize driving a truck as masculine and cooking and cleaning as feminine.[87] Even cartoon characters portrayed as helpless are more likely to wear frilly or ruffled dresses.[88] Toy companies perpetuate these stereotypes by promoting gender-linked toys with commercials that reinforce sex-role expectations through their casting, emotional tone, and copy.[89]

One function of child's play is to rehearse for adulthood. Children "act out" different roles they might assume later in life and learn about the expectations others have of them. The toy industry provides the props children use to perform these roles.[90] Depending on which side of the debate you're on, these toys either reflect or teach children about what society expects of males and females. Preschool boys and girls do not exhibit many differences in toy preferences, but after the age of 5 they part company: Girls tend to stick with dolls, whereas boys gravitate toward "action figures" and high-tech diversions.

Industry critics charge this is because males dominate the toy industry, but toy company executives counter that they are simply responding to kids' natural preferences.[91] Indeed, after 2 decades of working to avoid boy-versus-girl stereotypes, many companies seem to have decided that differences are inevitable. Toys-R-Us unveiled a new store design after it interviewed 10,000 kids; the chain now has separate sections it calls Girls' World and Boys' World. According to the president of Fox Family Channel, "Boys and girls are different, and it's great to celebrate what's special about each."[92] Boys tend to be more interested in battle and competition; girls are more interested in creativity and relationships. This is what experts refer to as "male and female play patterns."[93]

Recognizing the powerful role toys play in consumer socialization, doll manufacturers are creating characters they hope will teach little girls about the real world—not the fantasy "bimbo" world that many dolls represent. Recently, a group of California entrepreneurs brought out a line of dolls they call Smartees. These characters include Ashley the attorney, Emily the entrepreneur, and Destiny the doctor. A paperback tells each doll's story and includes a sample résumé for a person who might have that job in real life.

Not to be outdone, Barbie's rebirth as a career woman illustrates how a firm can take concerns about socialization to heart. Although Mattel introduced a Barbie doll astronaut in 1964 and an airline pilot in 1999, it never provided much detail about the careers themselves. Now a Working Woman Barbie is on the market as the result of a partnership between Mattel and *Working Woman* magazine. She comes with a miniature computer and cell phone as well as a CD-ROM about understanding finances.

She dresses in a gray suit, but the skirt reverses to a red dress for her to wear with red platform shoes for her after-work adventures with Ken.[94]

Cognitive Development

Children's abilities to make mature, "adult" consumer decisions obviously increases with age (not that grown-ups always make mature decisions). Marketers segment kids by age in terms of their **stage of cognitive development**, or their ability to comprehend concepts of increasing complexity. Some evidence indicates that very young children are able to learn consumption-related information surprisingly well.[95]

The Swiss psychologist Jean Piaget was the foremost proponent of the idea that children pass through distinct stages of cognitive development. He believed that a certain cognitive structure characterizes each stage as the child learns to process information.[96] In one classic demonstration of cognitive development, Piaget poured the contents of a short, squat glass of lemonade into a taller, thinner glass that actually held the same amount of liquid. Five-year-olds, who still believed that the shape of the glass determined its contents, thought this glass held more liquid than the first glass. They are in what Piaget termed a *preoperational stage of development*. In contrast, 6-year-olds tended to be unsure, but 7-year-olds knew the amount of lemonade had not changed.

Many developmental specialists no longer believe that children necessarily pass through these fixed stages at the same time. An alternative view proposes that they differ in information-processing capability, or ability to store and retrieve information from memory (see Chapter 3). Researchers who advocate this approach identified these three segments:[97]

1 **Limited:** Children who are younger than age 6 do not employ storage and retrieval strategies.
2 **Cued:** Children between the ages of 6 and 12 employ these strategies but only when prompted.
3 **Strategic:** Children 12 and older spontaneously employ storage and retrieval strategies.

Marketing Pitfall

Do marketers rob kids of their childhood? A spokesperson for designer Donna Karan observed, "These 7-year-olds are going on 30. A lot of them have their own sense of style." Maybe so, but perhaps one of the consequences is that they are forced to adopt adult values earlier than they should. One author of a book about kids complains, "We are seeing the deliberate teening of childhood. Parents are giving their kids a lot more choices on what to wear at ever-younger ages. The advertisers know this, and they are exploiting the kids' longing to seem sophisticated and grown-up. One of the great things about childhood in the United States used to be that kids were protected by the market and allowed to grow their own ideas. Now, there is no time to be a kid separate from those pressures. You may have always had kids who are little princesses, but now there are 8-year-old boys who are extremely uptight if they don't get the right Abercrombie & Fitch sweatshirt." Maybe that explains why preteens now account for $200 million of the $3 billion mass-market sales of makeup; a survey of 8- to 12-year-old girls found that two-thirds regularly used cosmetics. So much for the age of innocence.[98]

LEGO did research to learn how boys and girls play with it's building toys. When executives watched girls play with the toys they noticed they were more likely to build living areas while boys tended to build cars. The company introduced a new version of it's product called Paradisa to entice girls to buy more LEGOs. This set emphasizes the ability to build "socially oriented structures" such as homes, swimming pools, and stables. Sales to girls picked up, though the company still sells most of it's sets to boys.

This sequence of development underscores the notion that children do not think in the same way adults do, and we can't expect them to use information the same way either. It also reminds us that they do not necessarily form the same conclusions as adults do when they absorb product information. For example, kids are not as likely to realize that something they see on TV is not "real," and as a result they are more vulnerable to persuasive messages.

Recent research underscores the idea that children's understanding of brand names evolves as they age. Kids learn to relate to brand names at an early age; they recognize brand names in stores, develop preferences for some brands over others, and request branded items by name. However, brand names function as simple perceptual cues for these children that lets them identify a familiar object with particular features. Conceptual brand meanings, which specify the nonobservable abstract features of the product, enter into the picture in middle childhood (about age 8), and children incorporate them into their thinking and judgments a few years later. By the time children reach 12 years of age, they are able to think about brands on a conceptual or symbolic level and they are also likely to incorporate these meanings into many types of brand-related judgments.[99]

Several new business ventures illustrate that using sound principles of consumer psychology can also make good financial sense. The trend started a long time ago with public television's *Sesame Street*, but today the for-profit networks are getting into the game as well. The first successful foray into the preschool market was *Blue's Clues* in 1996, which turned into a huge hit as viewers abandoned the smarmy *Barney & Friends* to share in the learning experiences.

Now, when millions of preschoolers tune in to Nickelodeon's hit show *Dora the Explorer*, they don't realize that they are responding to content based upon "multiple-intelligence theory." This influential perspective argues for other types of intelligence, such as athletic prowess or musical ability, beyond the traditional math and verbal skills psychologists use to measure IQ. Thus, when Dora consults her map, she is promoting "spatial" skills. And when Dora asks her young viewers to help her count planks to build a bridge, she is building "interpersonal intelligence." And Dora is bilingual and she teaches a Spanish word or phrase in every episode. Latin American consultants helped to develop her character—in an early stage of development, they changed her eye color from green to brown to reflect a more common Latino look.[100]

Marketing Research and Children

Compared to adults, kids are difficult subjects for market researchers. They tend to be unreliable reporters of their own behavior, they have poor recall, and they often do not understand abstract questions.[101] Some European countries restrict marketers' ability to interview children so it's even harder to collect this kind of data there. Still, market research can pay off, and many companies, as well as a number of specialized firms, have successfully researched some of the issues that matter to kids.[102]

Product Testing

A particularly helpful type of research with children is product testing. Young subjects can provide a valuable perspective on what products will succeed with other kids. Marketers obtain these insights either by watching kids play with toys or by talking to them in focus groups. For example, the Fisher-Price Company maintains a nursery it calls the Playlab. Children it chooses from a waiting list of 4,000 play with new toys while staff members watch from behind a one-way mirror.[103]

Message Comprehension

Because children differ in their abilities to process product-related information, when advertisers try to appeal directly to them this raises many serious ethical issues.[104]

Children's advocacy groups argue that kids younger than age 7 do not understand the persuasive intent of commercials and younger children cannot readily distinguish between a commercial and programming. Kids' cognitive defenses are not yet sufficiently developed to filter out commercial appeals, so in a sense, altering their brand preferences may be likened to "shooting fish in a barrel," as one critic put it.[105] Figure 12.3 shows one attempt to assess whether kids can tell that a commercial is trying to persuade them.

Beginning in the 1970s, the U.S. Federal Trade Commission (FTC) took some action to protect children, such as limiting commercials during "children's" programming (most often Saturday morning television) and requiring "separators" to help children discern when a program ended and a commercial began (e.g., "We'll be right back after these commercial messages"). The FTC reversed itself in the early 1980s during the deregulatory, probusiness climate of the Reagan administration. The 1990 Children's Television Act restored some of these restrictions. Still, critics argue that rather than sheltering children from marketplace influences, the dominant way that marketers view them is as what one calls "kid customer."[106]

CHAPTER SUMMARY

Now that you have finished reading this chapter you should understand why:

Marketers often need to understand *consumers'* behavior rather than consumer behavior because in many cases more than one person decides what to buy.

● More than one person actually makes many purchasing decisions. Collective decision making occurs whenever two or more people evaluate, select, or use a product or service. In organizations and in families, members play several different roles during the decision-making process. These roles include the gatekeeper, influencer, buyer, and user.

Companies as well as individuals make purchase decisions. The decision-making process differs when people choose what to buy on behalf of a company versus a personal purchase.

● Organizational buyers are people who make purchasing decisions on behalf of a company or other group. Although many of the same factors that affect how they make decisions in their personal lives influence these buyers, their organizational choices tend to be more rational. They are also likely to involve more financial risk, and as they become more complex, it is probable that a greater number of people will be involved in making the decision. The amount of cognitive effort that goes into organizational decisions relates to internal factors, such as the individuals' psychological characteristics, and external factors, such as the company's willingness to tolerate risk. One of the most important determinants is the type of purchase the company wants to make: The extent of problem solving required depends on whether the product or service it procures is simply a reorder (a straight rebuy), a reorder with minor modifications (modified rebuy), or something it never bought before or something complex and risky (new task). Online purchasing sites are revolutionizing the way organizational decision makers collect and evaluate product information in business-to-business (B2B) e-commerce.

Many important demographic dimensions of a population relate to family and household structure.

● Demographics are statistics that measure a population's characteristics. Some of the most important of these relate to family structure (e.g., the birthrate, the marriage rate, and the divorce rate). A household is an occupied housing unit.

Our traditional notions about families are outdated.

● The number and type of U.S. households is changing in many ways, including delays in getting married and having children, and in the composition of family households, which a single parent increasingly heads. New perspectives on the family life cycle, which focuses on how people's needs change as they move through different stages in their lives, are forcing marketers to more seriously consider consumer segments such as gays and lesbians, divorced persons, and childless couples when they develop targeting strategies.

Members of a family unit play different roles and have different amounts of influence when the family makes purchase decisions.

● Marketers have to understand how families make decisions. Spouses in particular have different priorities and exert varying amounts of influence in terms of effort and power. Children are also increasingly influential during a widening range of purchase decisions.

Children learn over time what and how to consume.

● Children undergo a process of socialization, where they learn how to be consumers. Parents and friends instill some of this knowledge, but a lot of it comes from exposure to mass media and advertising. Because it's so easy to persuade children, consumers, academics, and marketing practitioners hotly debate the ethical aspects of marketing to them.

KEY TERMS

Accommodative purchase
  decision, 485
Autonomic decision, 486
Boomerang kids, 480
Business-to-business (B2B)
  e-commerce, 476
Business-to-business (B2B)
  marketers, 473
Buyclass theory of purchasing, 475
Buying center, 475
Consensual purchase decision, 484

Consumer socialization, 492
Crowdsourcing, 476
DINKS, 480
Extended family, 477
Family financial officer (FFO), 487
Family life cycle (FLC), 482
Fertility rate, 478
Gender convergence, 486
Kin-network system, 489
Modified rebuy, 475
New task, 475

Nuclear family, 477
Organizational buyers, 473
Parental yielding, 491
POSSLQ, 477
Prediction market, 476
Stage of cognitive development, 495
Straight rebuy, 475
Syncretic decision, 486
Synoptic ideal, 489
Wiki, 477

REVIEW QUESTIONS

1   What are some factors that influence how an organizational buyer evaluates a purchase decision?
2   What is a prediction market?
3   Summarize the buyclass model of purchasing. How do decisions differ within each class?
4   What are some of the ways organizational decisions differ from individual consumer decisions? How are they similar?
5   List at least three roles people play in the organizational decision-making process.
6   What is a nuclear family, and how is it different from an extended family?
7   How do we calculate a nation's fertility rate? What fertility rate is required to ensure that population size does not decline?
8   What are boomerang kids?
9   What is the FLC, and why is it important to marketers?
10 List some variables we must consider when trying to understand different stages in the FLC.
11 What is the difference between a consensual and an accommodative purchase decision? What are some factors that help to determine how much conflict the family will experience when making a decision?
12 Summarize the difference between an autonomic and a syncretic decision.
13 What are some diferences between "traditional" and "modern" couples in terms of how they allocate household responsibilities?
14 What factors help to determine if decisions will be made jointly or by one spouse or the other?
15 What is a kin-network system?
16 Describe a heuristic a couple might use when making a decision, and provide an example of it.
17 What are three reasons why children are an important segment to marketers?
18 What is consumer socialization? Who are some important players in this process? How do toys contribute?
19 Discuss stages of cognitive development and how these relate to the comprehension of marketing messages.
20 Why is it difficult to conduct marketing research with children?

CONSUMER BEHAVIOR CHALLENGE

■ DISCUSS

1   Is the family unit dead?
2   Discuss the pros and cons of the voluntarily childless movement. Are followers of this philosophy selfish?
3   Are marketers robbing kids of their childhood?
4   The Defense Department shut down a controversial research program following a public outcry. Its intent was to create a prediction market to try to forecast terrorist activities. Was the decision to terminate the program warranted? Why or why not?
5   Do you think market research should be performed with children? Give the reasons for your answer.
6   What do you think of the practice of companies and survey firms collecting public data (e.g., from marriage licenses, birth records, or even death announcements) to compile targeted mailing lists? State your opinion from both a consumer's and a marketer's perspective.
7   Marketers have been criticized for donating products and services to educational institutions in exchange for free promotion. Is this a fair exchange, in your opinion, or should corporations be prohibited from attempting to influence youngsters in school?
8   For each of the following five product categories— groceries, automobiles, vacations, furniture, and appliances—describe the ways in which you believe having children or not affects a married couple's choices.
9   In identifying and targeting newly divorced couples, do you think marketers are exploiting these couples' situations? Are there instances in which you think marketers may actually be helpful to them? Support your answers with examples.
10 Industrial purchase decisions are totally rational. Aesthetic or subjective factors don't—and shouldn't—play a role in this process. Do you agree?
11 We can think of college students living away from home as having a substitute "family." Whether you live with your parents, with a spouse, or with other students, how are decisions made in your college residence "family"? Do some people take on the role of mother or father or child? Give a specific example of a decision that had to be made and the roles that were played.

Stanford University Medical Center prohibits its physicians from accepting even small gifts such as pens and mugs from pharmaceutical sales representatives under a new policy it hopes will limit industry influence on patient care and doctor education. The new policy is part of a small but growing movement among centers (Yale and the University of Pennsylvania have similar policies). The policy also prohibits doctors from accepting free drug samples and from publishing articles in medical journals that industry contractors ghost-write (a fairly common practice). These changes come at a time when many of us are concerned about the safety and rising cost of drugs and medical devices. About 90 percent of the pharmaceutical industry's $21 billion marketing budget targets physicians. Some studies have shown that even small gifts create a sense of obligation;

one critical study charged that free drug samples are "... a powerful inducement for physicians and patients to rely on medications that are expensive but not more effective." Indeed, some industry documents from a civil lawsuit show that big pharmaceutical companies sometimes calculate to the penny the profits that doctors could make from their drugs. Sales representatives shared those profit estimates with doctors and their staffs, the documents show.[107] Where is the line between legitimately promoting one's products and unethical practice? Should professionals engage in organizational decision making that has such far-reaching medical and financial ramifications?

■ APPLY

12 Arrange to interview two married couples, one younger and one older. Prepare a response form listing five product categories—groceries, furniture, appliances, vacations, and automobiles—and ask each spouse to indicate, without consulting the other, whether purchases in each category are made by joint or unilateral decisions, and to indicate whether the unilateral decisions are made by the husband or the wife. Compare each couple's responses for agreement between husbands and wives relative to who makes the decisions, and compare both couples' overall responses for differences relative to the number of joint versus unilateral decisions. Report your findings and conclusions.

13 Collect ads for three different product categories that target families. Find another set of ads for different brands of the same items that don't feature families. Prepare a report comparing the probable effectiveness of the two approaches. Which specific categories would most likely benefit from a family emphasis?

14 Pick three married couples and ask each husband and wife to list the names of all cousins, second cousins, and so on for both sides of the family. Based on the results, what can you conclude about the relative role of men and women in maintaining the kin-network system?

15 Observe the interactions between parents and children in the cereal section of a local grocery store (remember to bring earplugs). Prepare a report on the number of children who expressed preferences, how they expressed their preferences, and how parents responded, including the number who purchased the child's choice.

16 Watch 3 hours of children's programming on commercial television stations. Evaluate the marketing techniques used in the commercials in terms of the ethical issues raised in the final section of this chapter. Report your findings and conclusions.

17 Select a product category, and using the life-cycle stages the chapter describes, list the variables likely to affect a purchase decision for the product by consumers in each stage of the cycle.

18 Consider three important changes in the modern family structure. For each, find an example of a marketer who seems to be conscious of this change in its product communications, retailing innovations, or other aspects of the marketing mix. If possible, also try to find examples of marketers who have failed to keep up with these developments.

Case Study

CHILDREN: THE FINAL FRONTIER . . . FOR CELL PHONES

What do Nokia, Samsung, Motorola, and Walt Disney Co. have in common? They all market cell phones to children worldwide. With the adult and even teen markets for cell phones quickly saturating (over 65 percent of U.S. teens have cell phones), the industry is looking to other segments. The growth market for the cell phone industry in the near future is children, ages 8 to 12—or even younger. Many in the industry see grade school children as the final frontier if phone manufacturers are to continue to grow. Already, parents are giving children as young as 5 years old their own cell phones.

In early 2005, a host of companies released phones aimed at the younger market. Disney, Hasbro, Mattel, and Firefly Mobile all released models in bright colors, often featuring graphics of favorite characters such as Sponge Bob SquarePants or Barbie. They designed these phones for smaller hands, and many lack traditional keypads. Parents could program what the phones do, control incoming and outgoing calls, and prepay minutes.

But do children really need a cell phone? There are many child advocates, including Ralph Nader, Canadian kids' entertainer Raffi, and various politicians, who say that they do not. Some critics claim that cell phone makers have declared "open season" on children with their aggressive marketing tactics. Many are even petitioning the U.S. Congress to investigate this hot marketing trend.

The cell phone companies defend their actions. Many have released statements saying that they don't market their products (even the kid-friendly ones) to children, but rather to their parents. Disney said it developed the Disney Mobile as a service to address the needs of a family audience, and that its products and services will be available for all members of the family including adults. Marketers claim that they are simply answering the demands of consumers for services such as the five-key, parent-programmable Firefly. Of course, children want the phones because they're cool, because their friends have them, and because they want to be more grown-up. In fact, many tweens reject the kiddie versions and demand real adult-style cell phones. In reference to phones like the Firefly, one young customer proclaimed, "It's for kids in third grade. By the end of the fifth grade, you should get a real phone."

Coolness and prestige alone are usually not good enough for parents to give in and buy one of the gadgets for their kids. However, marketers position the phones to Mom and Dad on a different basis: The phones provide an extra layer of security to anxious parents who want to be able to locate their kids at all times. Many of the children's phones offer GPS tracking as well as all the parental control features. When parents are convinced that the increased ability to stay connected with their children enhances safety, the purchase decision is simple. "Suddenly, you're not an overindulgent parent. You're a caring parent," says Margaret C. Campbell, a marketing professor at the University of Colorado.

Whether due to safety concerns or simply because parents are giving in to their kids' demands, the efforts of cell phone marketers appear to be paying off. Already, 46 percent of children ages 9 to 11 and 20 percent of children ages 6 to 8 carry cell phones. If companies can get younger children in the habit of using phones, the kids will probably be consumers for life. Whether or not this is a good thing is still open to debate.

DISCUSSION QUESTIONS

1 When it comes to cell phones for kids, who is the customer? Discuss the dynamics of the decision to buy a cell phone for a young child.

2 How do current trends in the family life cycle affect the marketing of cell phones to children?

Sources: Madhusmita Bora, "Must-Have For Tweens: Cell Phone," *St. Petersburg Times* (August 26, 2007): 1A; Alice Z. Cuneo, "Cell Phone Marketing Fraught with Hang-ups," *Advertising Age* (March 14, 2005): 3; Jenny Deam, "'I'm on My Cell:' Kids Are the Latest Wireless Market, But Do They Really Need a Phone?" *Denver Post* (August 25, 2005): F1.

NOTES

1. Fred E. Webster and Yoram Wind, *Organizational Buying Behavior* (Upper Saddle River, NJ: Prentice Hall, 1972).

2. See J. Joseph Cronin, Jr., and Michael H. Morris, "Satisfying Customer Expectations; the Effect on Conflict and Repurchase Intentions in Industrial Marketing Channels," *Journal of the Academy of Marketing Science* 17 (Winter 1989): 41–49; Thomas W. Leigh and Patrick F. McGraw, "Mapping the Procedural Knowledge of Industrial Sales Personnel: A Script-Theoretic Investigation," *Journal of Marketing* 53 (January 1989): 16–34; William J. Qualls and Christopher P. Puto, "Organizational Climate and Decision Framing: An Integrated Approach to Analyzing Industrial Buying," *Journal of Marketing Research* 26 (May 1989): 179–92.

3. James M. Sinkula, "Market Information Processing and Organizational Learning," *Journal of Marketing* 58 (January 1994): 35–45.

4. Allen M. Weiss and Jan B. Heide, "The Nature of Organizational Search in High Technology Markets," *Journal of Marketing Research* 30 (May 1993): 220–33; Jennifer K. Glazing and Paul N. Bloom, "Buying Group Information Source Reliance," *Proceedings of the American Marketing Association Educators' Conference* (Summer 1994): 454.

5. B. Charles Ames and James D. Hlaracek, *Managerial Marketing for Industrial Firms* (New York: Random House Business Division, 1984); Edward F. Fern and James R. Brown, "The Industrial/Consumer Marketing Dichotomy: A Case of Insufficient Justification," *Journal of Marketing* 48 (Spring 1984): 68–77.

6. Daniel H. McQuiston, "Novelty, Complexity, and Importance as Causal Determinants of Industrial Buyer Behavior," *Journal of Marketing* 53 (April 1989): 66–79.

7. Patrick J. Robinson, Charles W. Faris, and Yoram Wind, *Industrial Buying and Creative Marketing* (Boston: Allyn & Bacon, 1967).

8. Erin Anderson, Wujin Chu, and Barton Weitz, "Industrial Purchasing: An Empirical Examination of the Buyclass Framework," *Journal of Marketing* 51 (July 1987): 71–86.

9. Barbara Kiviat, "The End of Management," *Time Inside Business* (July 12, 2004), www.time.com/time/magazine/article/0,9171,994658,00.html, accessed October 5, 2007.

10. Jeff Howe, "The Rise of Crowdsourcing," *Wired* (June 2006): 176 (8).

11. Steven J. Kafka, Bruce D. Temkin, Matthew R. Sanders, Jeremy Sharrard, and Tobias O. Brown, "eMarketplaces Boost B2B Trade," *The Forrester Report* (Cambridge, MA: Forrester Research, Inc., February 2000).

12. www.worldwideretailexchange.org, accessed January 8, 2003.

13. Alison Hardy, "Designing Time and Sampling Money," *Apparel Industry Magazine* (May 2000): 22.

14. Vauhini Vara, "Offices Co-Opt Consumer Web Tools Like 'Wikis' and Social Networking," *Wall Street Journal on the Web* (September 12, 2006).

15. David Kirkpatrick, "It's Not a Game" *CNNMoney.com* (February 5, 2007) http://money.cnn.com/magazines/fortune/fortune_archive/2007/02/05/8399120/index.htm, accessed October 5, 2007.

16. Robert Boutilier, "Targeting Families: Marketing to and through the New Family," in *American Demographics Marketing Tools* (Ithaca, NY: 1993): 4–6; W. Bradford Fay, "Families in the 1990s: Universal Values, Uncommon Experiences," *Marketing Research: A Magazine of Management & Applications* 5 (Winter 1993): 47.

17. Ellen Graham, "Craving Closer Ties, Strangers Come Together as Family," *Wall Street Journal* (March 4, 1996): B1.

18. Risto Moisio, Eric J. Arnould, and Linda L. Price, "Between Mothers and Markets: Constructing Family Identity through Homemade Food," *Journal of Consumer Culture* 4, no. 3 (2004): 361–84.

19. Brad Edmondson, "Inside the New Household Projections," *The Number News* (July 1996).

20. Sam Roberts, "It's Official: To Be Married Means to Be Outnumbered," *New York Times Online* (October 15, 2006), accessed October 15, 2006; Sam Roberts, "51% of Women Are Now Living without Spouse," *New York Times Online* (January 16, 2007), accessed January 16, 2007.

21. Ronald Alsop, "Businesses Market to Gay Couples as Same Sex Households Increase," *Wall Street Journal Interactive Edition* (August 8, 2002).

22. James Morrow, "A Place for One," *American Demographics* (November, 2003): 25–30; Michelle Conlin, "Unmarried America," *BusinessWeek* (October 20, 2003): 106–16.

23. Karen Hardee-Cleaveland, "Is Eight Enough?" *American Demographics* (June 1989): 60.

24. Frank Bruni, "Persistent Drop in Fertility Reshapes Europe's Future," *New York Times on the Web* (December 26, 2002).

25. P. Paul, "Childless by Choice," *American Demographics* (November 2001): 45–48, 50; www.childfreebychoice.com, accessed July 22, 2007; www.nokidding.net, accessed July 22, 2007.

26. "Mothers Bearing a Second Burden," *New York Times* (May 14, 1989): 26.

27. Thomas Exter, "Disappearing Act," *American Demographics* (January 1989): 78; see also Kerenami Johnson and Scott D. Roberts, "Incompletely-Launched and Returning Young Adults: Social Change, Consumption, and Family Environment," in Robert P. Leone and V. Kumar, eds., *Enhancing Knowledge Development in Marketing* (Chicago: American Marketing Association), 249–54; John Burnett and Denise Smart, "Returning Young Adults: Implications for Marketers," *Psychology & Marketing* 11 (May–June 1994): 253–69.

28. Marcia Mogelonsky, "The Rocky Road to Adulthood," *American Demographics* (May 1996): 26.

29. Rebecca Gardyn, "Animal Magnetism," *American Demographics* (May 2002): 31–37.

30. For a review cf. Russell W. Belk, "Metaphoric Relationships with Pets," *Society and Animals* 4, no. 2 (1996): 121–46.

31. Carla Baranauckas, "A Dog's Life, Upgraded," *New York Times Online* (September 24, 2006), accessed September 24, 2006; Thom Forbes, "PetSmart's Hotels Offer Doggies the Lap of Luxury," *Miami Herald/Bloomberg News Online* (December 28, 2006), accessed December 28, 2006; Stephanie Thompson, "What's Next, Pup Tents in Bryant Park?" *Advertising Age* (January 29, 2007): 4; Maryann Mott, "Catering to the Consumers with Animal Appetites," *New York Times on the Web* (November 14, 2004); Jim Carlton, "For Finicky Drinkers, Water from the Tap Isn't Tasty Enough," *Wall Street Journal Online* (March 11, 2005).

32. Nick Wingfield, "Web's Addictive Neopets Are Ready for Big Career Leap," *Wall Street Journal Online* (February 22, 2005); Bloomberg News, "MTV Paying $160 Million for a 'Virtual Pets' Site," *New York Times Online* (June 21, 2005); Ann Pleshette Murphy and Laura Lacy, "Is the Webkinz Craze Bad for Kids? Interactive Toys Are Hugely Popular but Keep Kids Glued to the Computer," available from www.abcnews.go.com/GMA/print?id=3033380, accessed April 12, 2007.

33. Brad Edmondson, "Do the Math," *American Demographics* (October 1999): 50–56.

34. "The Bump Partnership Targets Expectant Women," *Marketing Daily* (May 14, 2007), available from www.mediapost.com, accessed May 14, 2007.

35. Rex Y. Du and Wagner A. Kamakura, "Household Life Cycles and Lifestyles in the United States," *Journal of Marketing Research* 43 (February 2006): 121–132; Mary C. Gilly and Ben M. Enis, "Recycling the Family Life Cycle: A Proposal for Redefinition," in Andrew A. Mitchell, ed., *Advances in Consumer Research* 9 (Ann Arbor, MI: Association for Consumer Research, 1982): 271–76.

36. Charles M. Schaninger and William D. Danko, "A Conceptual and Empirical Comparison of Alternative Household Life Cycle Models," *Journal of Consumer Research* 19 (March 1993): 580–94; Robert E. Wilkes, "Household Life-Cycle Stages, Transitions, and Product Expenditures," *Journal of Consumer Research* 22 (June 1995): 27–42.

37. Cheryl Russell, "The New Consumer Paradigm," *American Demographics* (April 1999): 50.

38. These categories are an adapted version of an FLC model proposed by Gilly and Enis (1982). Based on a recent empirical comparison of several competing models, Schaninger and Danko found that this framework outperformed others, especially in terms of its treatment of nonconventional households, though they recommend several improvements to this model as well. See Gilly and Enis, "Recycling the Family Life Cycle"; Schaninger and Danko, "A Conceptual and Empirical Comparison of Alternate Household Life Cycle Models"; Scott D. Roberts, Patricia K. Voli, and Kerenami Johnson, "Beyond the Family Life Cycle: An Inventory of Variables for Defining the Family as a Consumption Unit," in Victoria L. Crittenden, ed., *Developments in Marketing Science* 15 (Coral Gables, FL: Academy of Marketing Science, 1992): 71–75.

39. Edmondson, "Do the Math."

40. Jennifer Lach, "Intelligence Agents," *American Demographics* (March 1999): 52–60; for a detailed ethnographic study of how households assimilate products, cf. Jennifer Chang Coupland, "Invisible Brands: An Ethnography of Households and the Brands in Their Kitchen Pantries," *Journal of Consumer Research* 33, no. 2 (2005): 106.

41. Harry L. Davis, "Decision Making within the Household," *Journal of Consumer Research* 2 (March 1972): 241–60; Michael B. Menasco and David J. Curry, "Utility and Choice: An Empirical Study of Wife/Husband Decision Making," *Journal of Consumer Research* 16 (June 1989): 87–97; Conway Lackman and John M. Lanasa, "Family Decision

Making Theory: An Overview and Assessment," *Psychology & Marketing* 10 (March–April 1993): 81–94.

42. Shannon Dortch, "Money and Marital Discord," *American Demographics* (October 1994): 11.

43. For research on factors affecting how much influence adolescents exert in family decision making, see Ellen Foxman, Patriya Tansuhaj, and Karin M. Ekstrom, "Family Members' Perceptions of Adolescents' Influence in Family Decision Making," *Journal of Consumer Research* 15 (March 1989): 482–91; Sharon E. Beatty and Salil Talpade, "Adolescent Influence in Family Decision Making: A Replication with Extension," *Journal of Consumer Research* 21 (September 1994): 332–41; for a recent study that compared the influence of parents versus siblings, cf. June Cotte and S. L. Wood, "Families and Innovative Consumer Behavior: A Triadic Analysis of Sibling and Parental Influence," *Journal of Consumer Research* 31, no. 1 (2004): 78–86.

44. Daniel Seymour and Greg Lessne, "Spousal Conflict Arousal: Scale Development," *Journal of Consumer Research* 11 (December 1984): 810–21.

45. Robert Lohrer, "Haggar Targets Women with $8M Media Campaign," *Daily News Record* (January 8, 1997): 1.

46. Diane Crispell, "Dual-Earner Diversity," *American Demographics* (July 1995): 32–37.

47. "Marriage: The Art of Compromise," *American Demographics* (February 1998): 41.

48. Patricia Cohen, "Signs of Détente in the Battle between Venus and Mars," *New York Times Online* (May 31, 2007), accessed May 31, 2007; for a detailed look at couples' goal-setting with regarding to artifical reproductive technologies, cf. Eileen Fisher, Cele C. Otnes, and Linda Tuncay, "Pursuing Parenthood: Integrating Cultural and Cognitive Perspectives on Persistent Goal Striving," *Journal of Consumer Research* 34, in press.

49. Darach Turley, "Dialogue with the Departed," *European Advances in Consumer Research* 2 (1995): 10–13.

50. "Wives and Money," *American Demographics* (December 1997): 34; for a recent study of decision making among lesbian couples, cf. Robert Wilkes and Debra A. Laverie, "Purchasing Decisions in Non-Traditional Households: The Case of Lesbian Couples," *Journal of Consumer Behaviour*, 6 (1), in press.

51. Thomas Hine, *Populuxe* (New York: Knopf, 1986).

52. Robert Boutilier, "Targeting Families: Marketing to and through the New Family."

53. Dennis L. Rosen and Donald H. Granbois, "Determinants of Role Structure in Family Financial Management," *Journal of Consumer Research* 10 (September 1983): 253–58; Robert F. Bales, *Interaction Process Analysis: A Method for the Study of Small Groups* (Reading, MA: Addison-Wesley, 1950). For a cross-gender comparison of food shopping strategies, see Rosemary Polegato and Judith L. Zaichkowsky, "Family Food Shopping: Strategies Used by Husbands and Wives," *Journal of Consumer Affairs* 28, no. 2 (1994): 278–99.

54. Alma S. Baron, "Working Parents: Shifting Traditional Roles," *Business* 37 (January–March 1987): 36; William J. Qualls, "Household Decision Behavior: The Impact of Husbands' and Wives' Sex Role Orientation," *Journal of Consumer Research* 14 (September 1987): 264–79; Charles M. Schaninger and W. Christian Buss, "The Relationship of Sex-Role Norms to Household Task Allocation," *Psychology & Marketing* 2 (Summer 1985): 93–104.

55. Jennifer Steinhauer, "Mars and Venus: Who Is 'the Decider'?" *New York Times Online* (April 26, 2006), accessed April 26, 2006; "Tailor-Made," *Advertising Age* (September 23, 2002): 14.

56. Craig J. Thompson, "Caring Consumers: Gendered Consumption Meanings and the Juggling Lifestyle," *Journal of Consumer Research* 22 (March 1996): 388–407.

57. Edmund L. Andrews, "Survey Confirms It: Women Outjuggle Men," *New York Times on the Web* (September 15, 2004).

58. Cristina Merrill, "Mother's Work Is Never Done," *American Demographics* (September 1999): 29–32.

59. Miriam Jordan, "India's Medicine Men Market an Array of Contraceptives," *Wall Street Journal Interactive Edition* (September 21, 1999); Patricia Winters Lauro, "Sports Geared to Parents Replace Stodgy with Cool," *New York Times on the Web* (January 3, 2000); Cynthia Webster, "Effects of Hispanic Ethnic Identification on Marital Roles in the Purchase Decision Process," *Journal of Consumer Research* 21 (September 1994): 319–31. For a recent study that examined the effects of family depictions in advertising among Hispanic consumers, see Gary D. Gregory and James M. Munch, "Cultural Values in International Advertising: An Examination of Familial Norms and Roles in Mexico," *Psychology & Marketing* 14 (March 1997): 99–120; John Steere, "How Asian-Americans Make Purchase Decisions," *Marketing News* (March 13, 1995): 9; John B. Ford, Michael S. LaTour, and Tony L. Henthorne,

"Perception of Marital Roles in Purchase Decision Processes: A Cross-Cultural Study," *Journal of the Academy of Marketing Science* 23 (Spring 1995): 120–31; Chankon Kim and Hanjoon Lee, "A Taxonomy of Couples Based on Influence Strategies: The Case of Home Purchase," *Journal of Business Research* 36 (June 1996): 157–68; Claudia Penteado, "Coke Taps Maternal Instinct with New Latin American Ads," *Advertising Age International* (January 1997): 15.

60. Gary L. Sullivan and P. J. O'Connor, "The Family Purchase Decision Process: A Cross-Cultural Review and Framework for Research," *Southwest Journal of Business & Economics* (Fall 1988): 43; Marilyn Lavin, "Husband-Dominant, Wife-Dominant, Joint," *Journal of Consumer Marketing* 10, no. 3 (1993): 33–42.

61. Micaela DiLeonardo, "The Female World of Cards and Holidays: Women, Families, and the Work of Kinship," *Signs* 12 (Spring 1942): 440–53.

62. C. Whan Park, "Joint Decisions in Home Purchasing: A Muddling-Through Process," *Journal of Consumer Research* 9 (September 1982): 151–62; see also William J. Qualls and Francoise Jaffe, "Measuring Conflict in Household Decision Behavior: Read My Lips and Read My Mind," in John F. Sherry Jr. and Brian Sternthal, eds., *Advances in Consumer Research* 19 (Provo, UT: Association for Consumer Research, 1992): 522–31.

63. Kim P. Corfman and Donald R. Lehmann, "Models of Cooperative Group Decision Making and Relative Influence: An Experimental Investigation of Family Purchase Decisions," *Journal of Consumer Research* 14 (June 1987): 1–13.

64. For further reading on see: Gregory M. Rose, "Consumer Socialization, Parental Style, and Developmental Timetables in the U.S. and Japan," *Journal of Marketing* 63 no. 3 (1999): 105–19; Gregory M. Rose, Vassilis Dalakas, and Fredric Kropp, "Consumer Socialization and Parental Style across Cultures: Findings from Australia, Greece, and India," *Journal of Consumer Psychology* 13 no. 4, (2003): 366–76; Gregory M. Rose, Victoria D. Bush, and Lynn Kahle, "The Influence of Family Communication Patterns on Parental Reactions toward Advertising: A Cross-National Examination," *Journal of Advertising* 27, no. 4 (1998): 71–85; Aysen Bakir, Gregory M. Rose, Aviv Shoham, "Family Communication and Parental Control of Children's Television Viewing: A Multi-Rater Approach, *Journal of Marketing Theory and Practice* 13, no. 2, (2005): 47-58; Aysen Bakir, Jeff Blodgett, and Gregory M. Rose, "Children's Sex Role Orientation and Advertising Preference," working paper, conditionally accepted, *Journal of Advertising Research*; Mei C. Rose, Gregory M. Rose, and Jeff Blodgett. "Children's Learning and Navigation of Web Sites," working paper.

65. Jennifer Saranow, "'This Is the Car We Want, Mommy'—Car Makers Direct More Ads at Kids (and Their Parents); A 5-Year-Old's Toy Hummer," *Wall Street Journal* (November 9, 2006): D1.

66. James U. McNeal, "Tapping the Three Kids' Markets," *American Demographics* (April 1998): 3, 737–41.

67. Harris Curtis, "Making Kids Street Smart," *Newsweek* (September 16, 2002): 10.

68. "Kids Strongly Influence Brand Decisions," available from www.marketingpower.com, accessed February 22, 2007.

69. Kay L. Palan and Robert E. Wilkes, "Adolescent-Parent Interaction in Family Decision Making," *Journal of Consumer Research* 24 (September 1997): 159–69; cf. also Tiffany Meyers, "Kids Gaining Voice in How Home Looks," *Advertising Age* (March 29, 2004): S4.

70. Russell N. Laczniak and Kay M. Palan, "Under the Influence," *Marketing Research* (Spring 2004): 34–39.

71. Stephanie Thompson, "Mrs. Butterworth's Changes Her Target," *Advertising Age* (December 20, 1999): 44.

72. Adrienne W. Fawcett, "Kids Sway One In Three Parents to Buy Stuff (Duh)," available from http://publications.mediapost.com, accessed February 15, 2007; Les Carlson, Ann Walsh, Russell N. Laczniak, and Sanford Grossbart, "Family Communication Patterns and Marketplace Motivations, Attitudes, and Behaviors of Children and Mothers," *Journal of Consumer Affairs* 28, no. 1 (1994): 25–53; see also Roy L. Moore and George P. Moschis, "The Role of Family Communication in Consumer Learning," *Journal of Communication* 31 (Autumn 1981): 42–51.

73. Leslie Isler, Edward T. Popper, and Scott Ward, "Children's Purchase Requests and Parental Responses: Results from a Diary Study," *Journal of Advertising Research* 27 (October–November 1987): 28–39.

74. Gregory M. Rose, "Consumer Socialization, Parental Style, and Development Timetables in the United States and Japan," *Journal of Marketing* 63, no. 3 (1999): 105–19; Gregory M. Rose, Vassilis Dalakis, and Fredric Kropp, "Consumer Socialization and Parental Style across Cultures: Findings from Australia, Greece, and India." *Journal of Consumer Psychology* 13, no. 4 (2003): 366–76.

75. Andrew Martin, "Kellogg to Curb Marketing of Foods to Children," available from www.ytimes.com, accessed June 14, 2007; Tara Parker-Pope,

"Watching Food Ads on TV May Program Kids to Overeat," *Wall Street Journal* (July 10, 2007): D1.

76. Scott Ward, "Consumer Socialization," in Harold H. Kassarjian and Thomas S. Robertson, eds., *Perspectives in Consumer Behavior* (Glenview, IL: Scott, Foresman, 1980), 380; cf. also Patricia Robinson, and Steven Maxwell Kates, "Children and Their Brand Relationships," *Advances in Consumer Research* 32, no. 1, (2005); Terry O'Sullivan, "Advertising and Children: What Do the Kids Think?" *Qualitative Market Research* 8, no. 4 (2005): 371.

77. Thomas Lipscomb, "Indicators of Materialism in Children's Free Speech: Age and Gender Comparisons," *Journal of Consumer Marketing* (Fall 1988): 41–46.

78. George P. Moschis, "The Role of Family Communication in Consumer Socialization of Children and Adolescents," *Journal of Consumer Research* 11 (March 1985): 898–913.

79. Gregory M. Rose, Vassilis Dalakas, and Fredric Kropp, "A Five-Nation Study of Developmental Timetables, Reciprocal Communication and Consumer Socialization," *Journal of Business Research* 55 (2002): 943–49.

80. Elizabeth S. Moore, William L. Wilkie, and Richard J. Lutz, "Passing the Torch: Intergenerational Influences as a Source of Brand Equity," *Journal of Marketing* 66 (April 2002): 17–37.

81. James U. McNeal and Chyon-Hwa Yeh, "Born to Shop," *American Demographics* (June 1993): 34–39.

82. See Les Carlson, Sanford Grossbart, and J. Kathleen Stuenkel, "The Role of Parental Socialization Types on Differential Family Communication Patterns Regarding Consumption," *Journal of Consumer Psychology* 1, no. 1 (1992): 31–52.

83. Marian Burros, "McDonald's France Puts Its Mouth Where Its Money Is," *New York Times on the Web* (October 30, 2002).

84. Cf. Patricia M. Greenfield, Emily Yut, Mabel Chung, Deborah Land, Holly Kreider, Maurice Pantoja, and Kris Horsley, "The Program-Length Commercial: A Study of the Effects of Television/Toy Tie-Ins on Imaginative Play," *Psychology & Marketing* 7 (Winter 1990): 237–56 for a study on the effects of commercial programming on creative play.

85. Gerald J. Gorn and Renee Florsheim, "The Effects of Commercials for Adult Products on Children," *Journal of Consumer Research* 11 (March 1985): 962–67. For a recent study that assessed the impact of violent commercials on children, see V. Kanti Prasad and Lois J. Smith, "Television Commercials in Violent Programming: An Experimental Evaluation of Their Effects on Children," *Journal of the Academy of Marketing Science* 22, no. 4 (1994): 340–51.

86. "Mattel Aims at Preteens with Barbie Web Brand: Toymaker Turns to Tech as Sales Slump for Iconic Fashion Doll," *The Associated Press* (April 26, 2007), available from www.msnbc.com, accessed April 26, 2007.

87. Glenn Collins, "New Studies on 'Girl Toys' and 'Boy Toys'," *New York Times* (February 13, 1984): D1.

88. Susan B. Kaiser, "Clothing and the Social Organization of Gender Perception: A Developmental Approach," *Clothing and Textiles Research Journal* 7 (Winter 1989): 46–56.

89. D. W. Rajecki, Jill Ann Dame, Kelly Jo Creek, P. J. Barrickman, Catherine A. Reid, and Drew C. Appleby, "Gender Casting in Television Toy Advertisements: Distributions, Message Content Analysis, and Evaluations," *Journal of Consumer Psychology* 2, no. 3 (1993): 307–27.

90. Lori Schwartz and William Markham, "Sex Stereotyping in Children's Toy Advertisements," *Sex Roles* 12 (January 1985): 157–70.

91. Joseph Pereira, "Oh Boy! In Toyland, You Get More If You're Male," *Wall Street Journal* (September 23, 1994): B1; Joseph Pereira, "Girls' Favorite Playthings: Dolls, Dolls, and Dolls," *Wall Street Journal* (September 23, 1994): B1.

92. Lisa Bannon, "More Kids' Marketers Pitch Number of Single-Sex Products," *Wall Street Journal Interactive Edition* (February 14, 2000).

93. Ibid.

94. Constance L. Hayes, "A Role Model's Clothes: Barbie Goes Professional," *New York Times on the Web* (April 1, 2000).

95. Laura A. Peracchio, "How Do Young Children Learn to Be Consumers? A Script-Processing Approach," *Journal of Consumer Research* 18 (March 1992): 425–40; Laura A. Peracchio, "Young Children's Processing of a Televised Narrative: Is a Picture Really Worth a Thousand Words?" *Journal of Consumer Research* 20 (September 1993): 281–93; see also M. Carole Macklin, "The Effects of an Advertising Retrieval Cue on Young Children's Memory and Brand Evaluations," *Psychology & Marketing* 11 (May–June 1994): 291–311.

96. Jean Piaget, "The Child and Modern Physics," *Scientific American* 196, no. 3 (1957): 46–51; see also Kenneth D. Bahn, "How and When Do Brand Perceptions and Preferences First Form? A Cognitive Developmental Investigation," *Journal of Consumer Research* 13 (December 1986): 382–93.

97. Deborah L. Roedder, "Age Differences in Children's Responses to Television Advertising: An Information-Processing Approach," *Journal of Consumer Research* 8 (September 1981): 144–53; see also Deborah Roedder John and Ramnath Lakshmi-Ratan, "Age Differences in Children's Choice Behavior: The Impact of Available Alternatives," *Journal of Marketing Research* 29 (May 1992): 216–26; Jennifer Gregan-Paxton and Deborah Roedder John, "Are Young Children Adaptive Decision Makers? A Study of Age Differences in Information Search Behavior," *Journal of Consumer Research* 21, no. 4 (1995): 567–80.

98. Kay Hymovitz, quoted in Leslie Kaufman, "New Style Maven: Six Years Old and Picky," *New York Times on the Web* (September 7, 1999); Tara Parker-Pope, "Cosmetics Industry Takes Look at the Growing Preteen Market," *Wall Street Journal Interactive Edition* (December 4, 1998).

99. Gwen Bachmannn Achenreiner and Deborah Roedder John, "The Meaning of Brand Names to Children: A Developmental Investigation," *Journal of Consumer Psychology* 13, no. 3 (2003): 205–19.

100. Paula Lyon Andruss, "'Dora' Translates Well," *Marketing News* (October 13, 2003): 8.

101. Janet Simons, "Youth Marketing: Children's Clothes Follow the Latest Fashion," *Advertising Age* (February 14, 1985): 16.

102. see Laura A. Peracchio, "Designing Research to Reveal the Young Child's Emerging Competence," *Psychology & Marketing* 7 (Winter 1990): 257–76 for details regarding the design of research on children.

103. Laura Shapiro, "Where Little Boys Can Play with Nail Polish," *Newsweek* (May 28, 1990): 62.

104. Gary Armstrong and Merrie Brucks, "Dealing with Children's Advertising: Public Policy Issues and Alternatives," *Journal of Public Policy and Marketing* 7 (1988): 98–113.

105. Bonnie Reece, "Children and Shopping: Some Public Policy Questions," *Journal of Public Policy and Marketing* (1986): 185–94.

106. Daniel Cook, University of Illinois, personal communication, December 2002; Daniel Cook, "Contradictions and Conundrums of the Child Consumer: The Emergent Centrality of an Enigma in the 1990s," paper presented at the Association for Consumer Research, October 2002.

107. Alex Berenson, "Cancer Drug Representatives Spelled Out the Way to Profit," *New York Times Online* (June 12, 2007), accessed June 12, 2007; Andrew Pollack, "Stanford to Ban Drug Makers' Gifts to Doctors, Even Pens," *New York Times Online* (September 12, 2006), accessed September 12, 2006.

CONSUMERS AS DECISION MAKERS 3

CONSUMERS AND SUBCULTURES 4

CONSUMER BEHAVIOR

CONSUMERS AS INDIVIDUALS 2

CONSUMERS IN THE MARKETPLACE 1

CONSUMERS AND CULTURES 5

Chapter Objectives

When you finish this chapter you should understand why:

- Both personal and social conditions influence how we spend our money.

- We group consumers into social classes that say a lot about where they stand in society.

- A person's desire to make a statement about his social class, or the class to which he hopes to belong, influences the products he likes and dislikes.

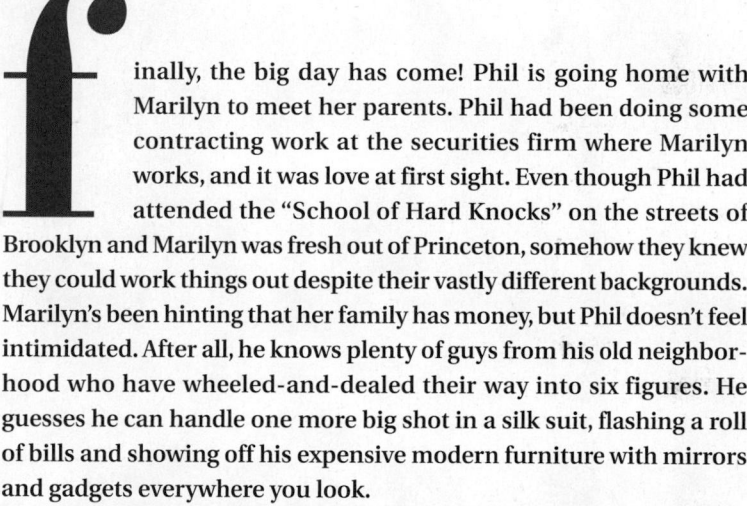

finally, the big day has come! Phil is going home with Marilyn to meet her parents. Phil had been doing some contracting work at the securities firm where Marilyn works, and it was love at first sight. Even though Phil had attended the "School of Hard Knocks" on the streets of Brooklyn and Marilyn was fresh out of Princeton, somehow they knew they could work things out despite their vastly different backgrounds. Marilyn's been hinting that her family has money, but Phil doesn't feel intimidated. After all, he knows plenty of guys from his old neighborhood who have wheeled-and-dealed their way into six figures. He guesses he can handle one more big shot in a silk suit, flashing a roll of bills and showing off his expensive modern furniture with mirrors and gadgets everywhere you look.

When they arrive at the family estate in Connecticut, Phil looks for a Rolls-Royce parked in the circular driveway, but he only sees a beat-up Jeep Cherokee, which must belong to one of the servants. Once inside, Phil is surprised by how simply the house is decorated and by how shabby everything seems. The hall entryway is covered with a faded Oriental rug, and all of the furniture looks really old.

Phil is even more surprised when he meets Marilyn's father, Mr. Caldwell. He had half expected him to be wearing a tuxedo and holding a large brandy snifter like the rich people he's seen in the movies. In fact, Phil had put on his best shiny Italian suit in anticipation, and he wore his large cubic zirconium pinky ring so this guy would know that he had some money too. When Marilyn's father emerges from his study wearing an old rumpled cardigan sweater and tennis sneakers, Phil realizes he's definitely not one of those guys from the old neighborhood.

Consumer Spending and Economic Behavior

As Phil's eye-opening experience at the Caldwells' house suggests, there are many ways to spend money and there's also a wide gulf between those who have it and those who don't. Perhaps an equally wide gap exists between those who have it had it for a long time and those who "made it the hard way—by earning it!" This chapter begins by briefly considering how general economic conditions affect the way consumers allocate their money. Then, reflecting the adage that says "The rich are different," we'll explore how people who occupy different positions in society consume in very different ways.

Whether a skilled worker like Phil or a child of privilege like Marilyn, a person's social class has a profound impact on what he does with money and on how consumption choices reflect his "place" in society. As this chapter illustrates, these

Luxury items like diamond engagement rings are valued as status symbols the world over, as this Brazilian ad for a jeweler reminds us.

choices also serve another purpose. We often deliberately use the specific products and services we buy to lets others know of our social standing—or what we would like it to be. Consumers frequently buy and display products as markers of social class; they value these items as **status symbols**. This is especially true in large, modern societies where we can no longer count on our behavior and reputation to convey our position to others whom we meet.

INCOME PATTERNS

A popular saying goes, "You can never be too thin or too rich." Many Americans feel they don't make enough money, but in reality the average American's standard of living continues to improve. We link these income shifts to two key factors: a shift in women's roles and increases in educational attainment.[1]

Woman's Work

One reason for this increase in U.S. income is the larger proportion of people of working age who participate in the labor force. Mothers with preschool children are the fastest-growing segment of working people. Furthermore, many of them work in high-paying occupations, such as medicine and architecture, which men used to dominate. Although women are still a minority in most professional occupations, their ranks continue to swell. The steady increase in the numbers of working women is a primary cause of the rapid growth of middle- and upper-income families.

Yes, It Pays to Go to School!

Education also determines who gets a bigger piece of the economic pie. Although picking up the tab for college often entails great sacrifice, it still pays off in the long run. In the United States, college graduates earn about 50 percent more than those who have only gone through high school during the course of their lives. Women without high school diplomas earn only 40 percent as much as women who have a college degree.[2] So, hang in there!

To Spend or Not to Spend, That Is the Question

Consumer demand for goods and services depends both on our ability and our willingness to buy. Whereas demand for necessities tends to be stable over time, we postpone or eliminate other expenditures if we don't feel that now is a good time to

Education is strongly linked to a higher standard of living. People who earn a college degree are likely to earn much more during their lives than those who do not.

spend money.[3] For example, you may decide to "make do" with your current clunker for another year rather than buy a new car right away.

Discretionary income is the money available to a household over and above what it requires to have a comfortable standard of living. Economists estimate that American consumers wield about $400 billion a year in discretionary spending power. People aged 35 to 55, whose incomes are at a peak, account for about half of this amount. As the population ages and income levels rise, the way a typical U.S. household spends its money changes. The most noticeable shift is to allocate a much larger share of its budget to shelter and transportation, and less to food and apparel (note: this doesn't mean that higher income households buy less food and clothing; the *proportion* of dollars that goes toward these categories decreases). We can explain this shift by noting the large rise in home ownership (the number of homeowners rose by more than 80 percent during the past 3 decades) and also the commuting costs that working wives need to pay. On a more cheerful note, U.S. households spend more now on entertainment and education than they used to.

Individual Attitudes toward Money

Especially in the wake of 9/11, many consumers experience doubts about their individual and collective futures, and they are anxious to hold on to what they have. Of course, not everyone has the same attitudes about money and its importance. Table 13.1 summarizes seven distinct types of money personalities.

TABLE 13.1
MONEY PERSONALITIES

	Types						
	The Hunter	**The Gatherer**	**The Protector**	**The Splurger**	**The Striver**	**The Nester**	**The Idealist**
Percent of population	13	19	16	14	13	14	10
Mean income	$44,000	$35,000	$36,000	$33,000	$29,000	$31,000	$30,000
Exemplar	Bill Gates (CEO Microsoft)	Warren Buffet (Nebraska-based investor)	Paul Newman (actor and entrepreneur)	Elizabeth Taylor (movie star)	Tonya Harding (disgraced figure skater)	Roseanne (comedienne/ actress)	Allen Ginsberg (deceased poet)
Profile	Takes risks to get ahead	Is better safe than sorry	Puts others first	Travels first class or not at all	Is controlled by money	Needs just enough to take care of self	Believes there's more to life than money
Characteristics	Is aggressive and equates money with happiness and achievement; is likely to have unstable personal life	Is a conservative investor with traditional values; tends to be thrifty and tries to minimize borrowing	Believes money is a means of protecting loved ones; tends to be predominantly women; is most likely married	Is self-indulgent; prefers to buy luxury items rather than practical items; is self-centered and not a good planner	Believes money makes the world go round; equates money with power; tends not to be well educated and most likely is divorced	Is not very interested in money; mostly concerned about meeting immediate needs	Mostly believes that money is the root of all evil; is not very interested in material things

Source: Adapted from Robert Sullivan, "Americans and Their Money," *Worth* (June 1994): 60, based on a survey of approximately 2,000 American consumers conducted by Roper Starch Worldwide. Reprinted by permission of *Worth* magazine.

Wal-Mart did a year of intensive research to group its customers in terms of how they think about money and brand names. The company is organizing its products around these groups, which Wal-Mart says represent the majority of its business. A separate team will service each group across five so-called "power" product categories: food, entertainment, apparel, home goods and pharmacy.[4] The three groups are

1 **Brand aspirationals:** People with low incomes who are obsessed with names such as KitchenAid
2 **Price-sensitive affluents:** Wealthier shoppers who love deals
3 **Value-price shoppers:** Those who like low prices and cannot afford much more

A consumer's anxieties about money don't necessarily relate to how much he actually has: Acquiring and managing money is more a state of mind than of wallet. For example, we all know people who are "tightwads" with their money and others whose cash seems to burn a hole in their wallets until they part with it. In recent years, being frugal has become a passion for some people who consider it a point of honor not to pay more than they have to for anything. *The Tightwad Gazette* is one of numerous publications that offers advice on buying in bulk, buying used goods, reusing products, and timing showers to save on water bills.[5]

Money has many complex psychological meanings; we equate it with success or failure, social acceptability, security, love, or freedom.[6] There are therapists who specialize in treating money-related disorders, and they report that some people even feel guilty about their success and deliberately make bad investments to reduce this feeling! Some other clinical conditions include *atephobia* (fear of being ruined), *harpaxophobia* (fear of becoming a victim of robbers), *peniaphobia* (fear of poverty), and *aurophobia* (fear of gold).[7]

CONSUMER CONFIDENCE

The field of **behavioral economics**, or *economic psychology*, studies the "human" side of economic decisions (including the decision-making biases we learned about in Chapter 9). Beginning with the pioneering work of psychologist George Katona, this discipline studies how consumers' motives and their expectations about the future affect their current spending, and how these individual decisions add up to affect a society's economic well-being.[8]

Consumers' beliefs about what the future holds are an indicator of **consumer confidence**, which reflects the extent to which people are optimistic or pessimistic about the future health of the economy and how they will fare down the road. These beliefs influence how much money they will pump into the economy when they make discretionary purchases.

Many businesses take forecasts about anticipated spending very seriously, and periodic surveys "take the pulse" of the American consumer. The Conference Board conducts a survey of consumer confidence, as does the Survey Research Center at the University of Michigan. The following are the types of questions they pose to consumers:[9]

● Would you say that you and your family are better off or worse off financially than a year ago?
● Will you be better off or worse off a year from now?
● Is now a good time or a bad time for people to buy major household items, such as furniture or a refrigerator?
● Do you plan to buy a car in the next year?

When people are pessimistic about their prospects and about the state of the economy, they tend to cut back their spending and take on less debt. However, when they are optimistic about the future, they tend to reduce the amount they save, take on more debt, and buy discretionary items. These factors influence the overall savings rate:

1   Individual consumers' pessimism or optimism about their personal circumstances such as a sudden increase in personal wealth as the result of an inheritance
2   World events such as the conflict in Iraq
3   Cultural differences in attitudes toward saving (e.g., the Japanese have a much higher savings rate than do Americans)[10]

SOCIAL CLASS

We divide all societies into the "haves" and the "have-nots" (though sometimes the amount people "have" is relative). The United States is a place where "all men are created equal," but even so some people seem to be more equal than others. As Phil's encounter with the Caldwells suggests, a complex set of variables, including income, family background, and occupation determines his standing in society.

The place you occupy in the social structure helps to determine not only how much money you spend but also how you spend it. Phil was surprised that the Caldwells, who clearly had a lot of money, did not seem to flaunt it. This understated way of living is a hallmark of so-called "old money." People who have had it for a long time don't need to prove they've got it. In contrast, consumers who are relative newcomers to affluence might allocate their booty very differently.

Picking a Pecking Order

In many animal species, a social organization develops whereby the most assertive or aggressive animals exert control over the others and have the first pick of food, living space, and even mating partners. Chickens, for example, exhibit a clearly defined *dominance–submission hierarchy*. Within this hierarchy, each hen has a position in which she is submissive to all of the hens above her and dominates all of the ones below her (hence the origin of the term *pecking order*).[11]

People are not much different. They also develop a pecking order, which ranks them in terms of their relative standing in society. This standing determines their access to such resources as education, housing, and consumer goods. People try to improve their ranking by moving up in the social order. This desire to improve one's lot in life, and often to let others know that one has done so, is at the core of many marketing strategies.

Just as marketers try to carve society into groups for segmentation purposes, sociologists describe meaningful divisions of society in terms of people's relative social and economic resources. Some of these divisions involve political power, whereas others revolve around purely economic distinctions. Karl Marx, the nineteenth-century economic theorist, argued that a person's relationship to the *means of production* determined his position in a society. The "haves" control resources, and they use the labor of others to preserve their privileged positions. The "have-nots" depend on their own labor for survival, so these people have the most to gain by changing the system. The German sociologist Max Weber showed that the rankings people develop are not one dimensional. Some involve prestige or "social honor" (he called these *status groups*), some rankings focus on power (or *party*), and some revolve around wealth and property (*class*).[12]

We use the term **social class** more generally to describe the overall rank of people in a society. People who belong to the same social class have approximately equal social standing in the community. They work in roughly similar occupations, and they tend to have similar lifestyles by virtue of their income levels and common tastes. These people tend to socialize with one another and share many ideas and values regarding the way life should be lived.[13]

Whatever your customers love to do for fun, Libbey refreshes them along the way. Libbey offers glasses to fit any lifestyle and specific taste. □ You can satisfy your customers' preferences and reflect your store's distinctiveness, too. □ Contact your Libbey representative today for a personal viewing. We will come out to see you with so many choices, we know it will be very refreshing indeed. **Libbey** America's Glassmaker™

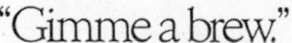

"Peach cooler, please."

"Gimme a brew."

This ad implies that there are social class differences in leisure activities and preferred beverages.

Indeed, "birds of a feather do flock together." We tend to marry people in a similar social class to ours, a tendency sociologists call **homogamy**, or "assortative mating." Well over 90 percent of married high school dropouts marry someone who also dropped out or who has only a high school diploma. On the other side of the spectrum, less than 1 percent of the most highly educated Americans have a spouse who did not complete high school.[14]

Social class is as much a state of being as it is of having: As Phil saw, class is also a matter of what you do with your money and how you define your role in society. Although we may not like the idea that some members of society are better off or "different" from others, most consumers do acknowledge the existence of different classes and the effect of class membership on consumption. As one wealthy woman observed when researchers asked her to define social class:

> I would suppose social class means where you went to school and how far. Your intelligence. Where you live. . . . Where you send your children to school. The hobbies you have. Skiing, for example, is higher than the snowmobile. . . . It can't be [just] money, because nobody ever knows that about you for sure.[15]

In school, some kids seem to get all the breaks. They have access to many resources, such as special privileges, fancy cars, large allowances, or dates with other popular classmates. At work, some co-workers get promoted to high-prestige jobs with higher salaries and perks such as a parking space, a large office, or the keys to the executive washroom.

In virtually every context, some people rank higher than others. Patterns of social arrangements evolve whereby some members get more resources than others by

Some people still inherit wealth,
the rest of us have no choice but to earn it.

The good news is, a lot of us know how. But then
what? Phoenix has been showing people
innovative new directions for 150 years.
We understand that making
money—and knowing what to
do with it—are two different
skills. It's one reason high-
net-worth people and
their advisors turn to
Phoenix for help. To
learn more about
how Phoenix could
be helping you, con-
tact your financial
advisor or visit
www.phoenixwm.com.

Money.

It's just not what it used to be.

PHOENIX
WEALTH MANAGEMENT

In industrialized countries, wealth is more
likely to be earned than inherited.

virtue of their relative standing, power, or control in the group.[16] The process of **social stratification** refers to this creation of artificial divisions: "those processes in a social system by which scarce and valuable resources are distributed unequally to status positions that become more or less permanently ranked in terms of the share of valuable resources each receives."[17]

Achieved versus Ascribed Status

Think back to groups to which you've belonged. You'll probably agree that in many instances some members seem to get more than their fair share of goodies, whereas other individuals are not so lucky. Some of these resources probably went to people who earned them through hard work or diligent study, or *achieved status*. But someone may have gotten the goodies because she was lucky enough to be born with "a silver spoon in her mouth." Such good fortune reflects *ascribed status*.

Whether rewards go to the "best and the brightest" or to someone who happens to be related to the boss, allocations are rarely equal within a social group. Most groups exhibit a structure, or **status hierarchy**, where some members are somehow better off than others. They may have more authority or power, or other members simply like or respect them.

CLASS STRUCTURE IN THE UNITED STATES

The United States in theory does not have a rigid, objectively defined class system. Nevertheless, Americans tend to maintain a stable class structure in terms of income distribution. Unlike some other countries, however, what *do* change are the groups (ethnic, racial, and religious) that occupy different positions within this structure

INCOME

UPPER AMERICANS
Upper-Upper (0.3%): The "capital S society" world of inherited wealth
Lower-Upper (1.2%): The newer social elite, drawn from current professionals
Upper-Middle (12.5%): The rest of college graduate managers and professionals; lifestyle
centers on private clubs, causes, and the arts

MIDDLE AMERICANS
Middle Class (32%): Average pay white-collar workers and their blue-collar friends; live on
"the better side of town;" try to "do the proper things"
Working Class (38%): Average pay blue-collar workers; lead "working class lifestyle"
whatever the income, school, background, and job

LOWER AMERICANS
"A lower group of people, but not the lowest" (9%): Working, not on welfare; living standard
is just above poverty; behavior judged "crude," "trashy"
"Real Lower-Lower" (7%): On welfare, visibly poverty-stricken, usually out of work (or have
"the dirtiest jobs"); "bums," "common criminals"

at different times.[18] A sociologist named W. Lloyd Warner proposed the most influential classification of American class structure in 1941. Warner identified six social classes:[19]

1 Upper upper   4 Lower middle
2 Lower upper   5 Upper lower
3 Upper middle   6 Lower lower

These classifications imply that access to resources, such as money, education, and luxury goods increases as you move up the ladder from lower lower to upper upper. Other social scientists have proposed variations on this system over the years, but these six levels summarize fairly well the way Americans still think about class—although the proportion of consumers who fall into each category fluctuates over time. Figure 13.1 provides one view of the American status structure.

CLASS STRUCTURE AROUND THE WORLD

Every society has some type of hierarchical class structure that determines people's access to products and services. Let's take a quick look at a few important ones.

China. In China, an economic boom is rapidly creating a middle class of more than 130 million people that analysts project to grow to more than 400 million in 10 years. During the cultural revolution, Mao's Red Guards seized on even the smallest possessions—a pocket watch or silk scarf—as evidence of "bourgeois consciousness." Change came rapidly in the early 1990s, after Mao's successor Deng Xiaoping uttered the phrase that quickly became the credo of the new China: "To get rich is glorious." Because costs are low, a family with an annual income below the U.S. poverty threshold of about $14,000 can enjoy middle-class comforts, including stylish clothes, Chinese-made color televisions, DVD players, and cell phones. Wealthier Chinese entrepreneurs can indulge in Cuban Cohiba cigars that sell for $25 each, a quarter of the average Chinese laborer's monthly wage. In bustling Shanghai, newly minted "yuppies" drop their kids off for golf lessons; visit Maserati and Ferrari showrooms; buy some luxury items from Louis Vuitton, Hugo Boss, or Prada; then pick up some Häagen-Dazs ice cream before heading to an Evian spa to unwind.

Nike, which consumers in a recent survey named China's coolest brand, profits mightily from the rise of the Chinese middle class. Nike shoes are a symbol of success, and the company opens an average of 1.5 new stores a day there. The company worked for a long time to attain this status; it started by outfitting top Chinese athletes and sponsoring all the teams in China's pro basketball league. Still, becoming a fashion icon (and persuading consumers to spend twice the average monthly salary for a pair of shoes) is no mean feat in a country that's not exactly sports-crazy. So Nike affiliated with the NBA (which had begun televising games in China), bringing over players such as Michael Jordan for visits. Slowly but surely, in-the-know Chinese came to call sneakers "Nai-ke."[20]

Japan. Japan is a highly status conscious society where upscale, designer labels are incredibly popular. The Japanese love affair with top brands started in the 1970s when the local economy was booming and many Japanese could buy Western luxury accessories for the first time. Some analysts say Japan's long slump may be fostering a psychological need to splurge on small luxuries to give them the illusion of wealth and to forget their anxieties about the future. Single, working women are largely responsible for fueling Japan's luxury-goods spending—about three-quarters of Japanese women aged 25 to 29 work outside the home. As we saw in Chapter 11, these "office ladies" save money by living with their parents so this leaves them with cash on hand to spend on clothes, accessories, and vacations.[21]

The Middle East. In contrast to the Japanese, few Arab women work, so searching for the latest in Western luxury brands is a major leisure activity. Dressing rooms are large, with antechambers to accommodate friends and family members who often come along on shopping sprees. A major expansion of Western luxury brands is under way across the Middle East, home to some of the fashion industry's best customers. High-end retailers such as Saks Fifth Avenue and Giorgio Armani operate opulent stores to cater to this growing market. However, fashion retailers must take cultural and religious considerations into account. Missoni makes sure that collections include longer pants and skirts, and evening gowns with light shawls to cover heads or bare shoulders. And advertising and display options are more

Golf is a high-status game in Japan, where land is scarce and greens fees are extremely high.

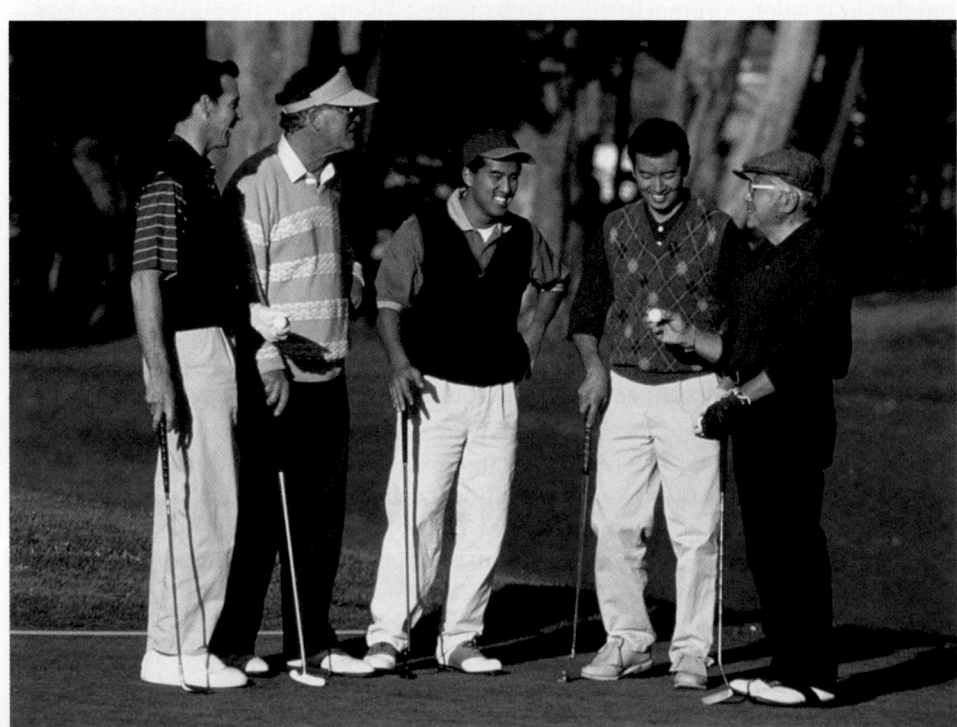

limited: Erotic images don't work. In the strict religious culture of Saudi Arabia, mannequins can't reveal a gender or human shape. At Saks' Riyadh store, models are headless and don't have fingers. Half of the two-level store is off-limits to men.[22]

The United Kingdom. England is an extremely class conscious country, and at least until recently, inherited position and family background largely predetermined consumption patterns. Members of the upper class were educated at schools such as Eton and Oxford and they spoke like Henry Higgins in *My Fair Lady*. We can still find remnants of this rigid class structure. "Hooray Henrys" (wealthy young men) play polo at Windsor and hereditary peers still dominate the House of Lords.

However, the supremacy of inherited wealth appears to be fading in Britain's traditionally aristocratic society. Today, 86 of the 200 wealthiest people in England made their money the old-fashioned way: They earned it. Extensive tabloid exposure and the antics of younger family members whom people regard more as rock stars than royalty dilute the sanctity of the royal family. As one observer put it, "the royal family has gone down-market . . . to the point that it sometimes resembles soap opera as much as grand opera."[23]

Now, some big marketers such as Unilever and Groupe Danone have set their sights on a more lower-class group the British call **chavs**. This label refers to young, lower-class men and women who mix flashy brands and accessories from big names such as Burberry with track suits. Their style icons include football star David Beckham and his wife, Victoria aka Posh Spice (both of whom made a huge splash when they moved to the United States in 2007). Despite their (alleged) tackiness, marketers like chavs because they spend a lot of their disposable income on fashion, food, and gadgets. France's Danone, which makes HP Sauce, a condiment the British have poured over bacon sandwiches and fries for a century, launched a series of ads playing up to the chav culture. One features a brawl over the sauce at a wedding buffet; another includes glammy football players' wives mingling cattily at a party.[24] Danone found "chavvy" people on the streets of Liverpool to star in the ads.

India. Like China, India's economy is booming and many higher-end global brands are catching on. One of Bollywood's biggest stars, Shahrukh Khan, is "brand ambassador" for Tag Heuer watches, which cost thousands of dollars. He gives them away on the Indian version of *Who Wants to Be a Millionaire?* India's ascendancy is fairly recent; for decades after the country became independent from Britain, its economy was socialistic and traditional. Today, young consumers watch MTV, read international fashion magazines, and are embracing the power of plastic; credit-card spending in India has risen by 30 percent a year for the past 5 years.[25]

THE RISE OF MASS CLASS

It's getting more difficult in many countries to clearly link certain brands or stores with a specific class, and changes in the marketplace make it more difficult for the casual observer to accurately place a consumer in a certain class by looking at the products he buys. That's because a lot of "affordable luxuries" now are within reach of many consumers who could not have acquired them in the past. The driver of this global change is income distribution. Traditionally, it's common to find a huge gulf between the rich and the poor—you were either one or the other. Today, rising incomes in many economically developing countries, such as South Korea and China, coupled with decreasing prices for quality consumer goods and services, level the playing field so that there are many more opportunities for people making modest incomes to get a taste of the good life.

Similar things go on in the United States. Rising incomes, flattening prices, and easily available credit give many Americans access to high-end goods so that these traditional status markers don't mean what they used to. College women buy pricey bags from Louis Vuitton or Coach, and then eat cheap Ramen noodles for dinner. To make matters even more confusing, a wealthy family may well buy its wine at Costco and its bath towels at a discount retailer, like Target.[26]

This change is fueling demand for mass-consumed products that still offer some degree of *panache*. Companies such as H&M, Zara, EasyJet, and L'Oréal provide creature comforts to a consumer segment analysts label **mass class**. This refers to the hundreds of millions of global consumers who now enjoy a level of purchasing power that's sufficient to let them afford high-quality products—except for big-ticket items such as college educations, housing, or luxury cars. The mass-class market, for example, spawned several versions of affordable cars: Latin Americans have their Volkswagen Beetle (they affectionately call it *el huevito*, the little egg); Indian consumers have their Maruti 800 (it sells for as little as U.S. $4,860); and the Fiat Palio, the company's "world car," targets people in emerging countries such as Brazil, Argentina, India, China, and Turkey.[27]

SOCIAL MOBILITY

To what degree do people tend to change their social classes? In some societies such as India it's difficult to change one's social class, but Americans like to say "Any man (or woman?) can grow up to be president" (though being related to a former president doesn't hurt your chances). **Social mobility** refers to the "passage of individuals from one social class to another."[28]

Horizontal mobility occurs when a person moves from one position to another that's roughly equivalent in social status, for instance, a nurse who becomes an elementary school teacher. *Downward mobility* is, of course, movement none of us wants, but unfortunately we observe this pattern fairly often as farmers and other displaced workers go on welfare rolls or join the ranks of the homeless. A conservative estimate is that 2 million Americans are homeless on any given day.[29]

Despite that discouraging trend, demographics, in fact, decree that overall there must be *upward mobility* in society. The middle and upper classes reproduce less (i.e., have fewer children per family) than the lower classes (an effect demographers call *differential fertility*), and they tend to restrict family size to below replacement level (i.e., often having only one child). Therefore, so the reasoning goes, over time those of lower status must fill positions of higher status.[30]

Overall, though, the offspring of blue-collar consumers are blue-collar, and the offspring of white-collar consumers are white-collar.[31] People do improve their positions over time, but these increases are not usually dramatic enough to catapult them from one social class to another. The exception is when a person marries someone considerably richer. This "Cinderella fantasy" is a popular theme in our society; we see it in movies (*Pretty Woman* or *Maid in Manhattan*) and popular TV shows such as *The Bachelor*.

Components of Social Class

When we think about a person's social class, we may consider a number of pieces of information. Two major ones are occupation and income. Let's take a quick look at both.

Occupational Prestige

In a system in which (like it or not) we define people to a great extent by what they do for a living, *occupational prestige* is one way we evaluate their "worth." Hierarchies of occupational prestige tend to be quite stable over time, and they also are similar across different societies. Researchers find similarities in occupational prestige in countries as diverse as Brazil, Ghana, Guam, Japan, and Turkey.[32]

A typical ranking includes a variety of professional and business occupations at the top (e.g., CEO of a large corporation, physician, and college professor), whereas jobs that hover near the bottom include shoe shiner, ditchdigger, and garbage collector. Because a person's occupation is strongly linked to his use of leisure time, allocation of family resources, aesthetic preferences, and political orientation, many social scientists consider it the single best indicator of social class.

Income

The distribution of wealth is of great interest to social scientists and to marketers because it determines which groups have the greatest buying power and market potential. Wealth is by no means distributed evenly across the classes. The top fifth of the population controls about 75 percent of all assets.[33] As we have seen, income per se is not often a very good indicator of social class because the way we spend our money is more telling than how much we spend. Still, people need money to obtain goods and services to express their tastes, so obviously income is still very important. American consumers are getting both wealthier and older, and these changes will continue to influence consumption preferences.

How Income Relates to Social Class

Although we equate money with class, the precise relationship between other aspects of social class and income is not clear and social scientists debate it.[34] The two are by no means synonymous, which is why many people with a lot of money try to buy their way into a higher social class. One problem is that even if a family adds one or more wage earners and increases its household income, each additional job is likely to be lower in status than the primary wage earner's job. In addition, these members don't necessarily pool their earnings toward the common good of the family.[35]

So which is a better predictor of consumer behavior? The answer partly depends on the type of product we sell—do people buy it largely for its functional value (what it does) or for its symbolic value (the impression it conveys to others)?

- Social class is a better predictor of purchases that have symbolic aspects, but low to moderate prices (e.g., cosmetics, liquor).
- Income is a better predictor of major expenditures that do not have status or symbolic aspects (e.g., major appliances).
- We need both social class and income data to predict purchases of expensive, symbolic products (e.g., cars, homes).

How Do We Measure Social Class?

Because social class is a complex concept that depends on a number of factors, it is not surprising that social scientists have trouble measuring it. Early measures included the Index of Status Characteristics from the 1940s and the Index of Social Position from the 1950s.[36] These indices used various combinations of individual characteristics (e.g., income, type of housing) to arrive at a label of class standing. The accuracy of these composites is still a subject of debate among researchers; a study claimed that for segmentation purposes, raw education and income measures work as well as composite status measures.[37] Figure 13.2 shows one commonly used measurement instrument.

American consumers generally have little difficulty placing themselves in either the working class (lower-middle class) or middle class. Also the number of people who reject the idea that such categories exist is rather small.[38] The proportion of consumers who identify themselves as working class tended to rise until about 1960, but it has been declining since then. Blue-collar workers with relatively high-prestige jobs still tend to view themselves as working class, even though their income levels may be equivalent to many white-collar workers.[39] This fact reinforces the idea that the labels of "working class" or "middle class" are very subjective. Their meanings say at least as much about self-identity as they do about economic well-being.

Problems with Measures of Social Class

Market researchers were among the first to propose that we can distinguish people from different social classes from one another in important ways. Some of these class

■ FIGURE 13.2 EXAMPLE OF A COMPUTERIZED STATUS INDEX

Interviewer circles code numbers (for the computer) that in his/her judgment best fit the respondent and family. Interviewer asks for detail on occupation, then makes rating. Interviewer often asks the respondent to describe neighborhood in own words. Interviewer asks respondent to specify income—a card is presented to the respondent showing the eight brackets—and records R's response. If interviewer feels this is overstatement or understatement, a "better judgment" estimate should be given, along with an explanation.

EDUCATION:	Respondent	Respondent's Spouse
Grammar school (8 yrs or less)	–1	–1
Some high school (9 to 11 yrs)	–2	–2
Graduated high school (12 yrs)	–3	–3
Some post high school (business, nursing, technical, 1 yr college)	–4	–4
Two, three years of college—possibly Associate of Arts degree	–5	–5
Graduated four-year college (B.A./B.S.)	–7	–7
Master's or five-year professional degree	–8	–8
Ph.D. or six/seven-year professional degree	–9	–9

R's Age ____   Spouse's Age ____

OCCUPATION PRESTIGE LEVEL OF HOUSEHOLD HEAD: Interviewer's judgment of how head of household rates in occupational status.

(Respondent's description—asks for previous occupation if retired, or if R is widow, asks husband's: _____)

Chronically unemployed—"day" laborers, unskilled; on welfare	–0
Steadily employed but in marginal semiskilled jobs; custodians, minimum pay factory help, service workers (gas attendants, etc.)	–1
Average-skill assembly-line workers, bus and truck drivers, police and firefighters, route deliverymen, carpenters, brickmasons	–2
Skilled craftsmen (electricians), small contractors, factory foremen, low-pay salesclerks, office workers, postal employees	–3
Owners of very small firms (2–4 employees), technicians, salespeople, office workers, civil servants with average-level salaries	–4
Middle management, teachers, social workers, lesser professionals	–5
Lesser corporate officials, owners of middle-sized businesses (10–20 employees), moderate-success professionals (dentists, engineers, etc.)	–7
Top corporate executives, "big successes" in the professional world (leading doctors and lawyers), "rich" business owners	–9

AREA OF RESIDENCE: Interviewer's impressions of the immediate neighborhood in terms of its reputation in the eyes of the community.

Slum area: people on relief, common laborers	–1
Strictly working class: not slummy but some very poor housing	–2
Predominantly blue-collar with some office workers	–3
Predominantly white-collar with some well-paid blue-collar	–4
Better white-collar area: not many executives, but hardly any blue-collar either	–5
Excellent area: professionals and well-paid managers	–7
"Wealthy" or "society"-type neighborhood	–9

TOTAL SCORE _____

TOTAL FAMILY INCOME PER YEAR:

Under $5,000	–1	$20,000 to $24,999	–5
$5,000 to $9,999	–2	$25,000 to $34,999	–6
$10,000 to $14,999	–3	$35,000 to $49,999	–7
$15,000 to $19,999	–4	$50,000 and over	–8

Estimated Status _____

(Interviewer's estimate: _____ and explanation _____)

R's MARITAL STATUS: Married ____ Divorced/Separated ____ Widowed ____ Single ____ (CODE: ____)

distinctions still exist, but others have changed.[40] Unfortunately, many of these measures are badly dated and are not as valid today.[41]

One reason is that social scientists designed most measures of social class with the traditional nuclear family in mind that included a male wage earner in the middle of his career and a female full-time homemaker. These measures have trouble accounting for two-income families; young singles living alone; or households women head, which, as we saw in Chapter 12, are so prevalent in Western countries today.

Another problem with measuring social class is the increasing anonymity of our society. Earlier studies relied on the *reputational method*, where researchers conducted extensive interviews within an area to determine the reputations and backgrounds of individuals (see the discussion of sociometry in Chapter 11). When they used information and also traced people's interaction patterns, they could generate a very comprehensive view of social standing within a community. However, this approach is virtually impossible to implement in most communities today. One compromise is to interview individuals to obtain demographic data and to combine these data with the interviewer's subjective impressions of each person's possessions and standard of living.

As an example, refer to the items in Figure 13.2. Note that the accuracy of this questionnaire relies largely on the interviewer's judgment, especially regarding the quality of the respondent's neighborhood. The interviewer's own circumstances can bias these impressions because they can affect her standard of comparison. Furthermore, the instrument uses highly subjective terms: "Slummy" and "excellent" are not objective measures. These potential problems highlight the need to adequately train interviewers, as well as for some attempt to cross-validate such data, possibly by employing multiple judges to rate the same area.

One problem with assigning any group of people to a social class is that they may not be equal in their standing on all of the relevant dimensions. A person might come from a low-status ethnic group but have a high-status job, whereas another may live in a fancy part of town but he may not have finished high school. Social scientists use the concept of **status crystallization** to assess the impact of inconsistency on the self and social behavior.[42] The logic behind this idea is that stress occurs because the rewards from each part of such an "unbalanced" person's life are variable and unpredictable. People who exhibit such inconsistencies tend to be more receptive to social change than are those whose identities are more firmly rooted.

Lottery winners who experience sudden wealth may have trouble adapting to their new social status.

A related problem occurs when a person's social-class standing creates expectations that he can't meet. Some people find themselves in the not-unhappy position of making more money than we expect of those in their social class. This means they are *overprivileged,* a condition we define as an income that is at least 25 to 30 percent greater than the median for one's class.[43] In contrast, *underprivileged* consumers, who earn at least 15 percent less than the median, must often allocate a big chunk of their income toward maintaining the impression that they occupy a certain status. For example, some people talk about being "house-poor" where they pay so much for a lavish home that they can't afford to furnish it.

We traditionally assume that husbands define a family's social class, whereas wives must live it. Women achieve their social status through their husbands.[44] Indeed, the evidence indicates that physically attractive women do tend to "marry up" (*hierogamy*) in social class to a greater extent than attractive men do. Women trade the resource of sexual appeal, which historically has been one of the few assets they were allowed to possess, for the economic resources of men.[45]

We must strongly question the accuracy of this assumption in today's world. Many women now contribute equally to the family's well-being, and they work in positions of comparable or even greater status than their spouses. Employed women tend to average both their own and their husband's positions when they estimate their own subjective status.[46] Nevertheless, a prospective spouse's social class is often an important "product attribute" when someone in the "marriage market" evaluates their options (as Phil and Marilyn found out).

PROBLEMS WITH SOCIAL CLASS SEGMENTATION: A SUMMARY

Social class remains an important way to categorize consumers. Many marketing strategies do target different social classes. However, for the most part marketers fail to use social-class information as effectively as they could because

- They ignore status inconsistency.
- They ignore intergenerational mobility.
- They ignore subjective social class (i.e., the class with which a consumer identifies rather than the one to which he actually belongs).
- They ignore consumers' aspirations to change their class standing.
- They ignore the social status of working wives.

HOW SOCIAL CLASS INFLUENCES PURCHASE DECISIONS

Many of us feel that certain products and stores are appropriate for certain social classes.[47] Working-class consumers tend to evaluate products in more utilitarian terms such as sturdiness or comfort rather than style or fashionability. They are less likely to experiment with new products or styles, such as modern furniture or colored appliances.[48] In contrast, more affluent people who live in the suburbs think more about appearance and body image, so they are more avid consumers of diet foods and drinks compared to people in more downscale small towns. These differences mean that marketers can use class standing to segment markets for soft drinks and other similar products.[49]

CLASS DIFFERENCES IN WORLDVIEW

A *worldview* is one way to differentiate among social classes. To generalize, the world of the working class (i.e., the lower-middle class) is more intimate and constricted. For example, working-class men are likely to name local sports figures as heroes and are less likely to take long vacation trips to out-of-the-way places.[50] Immediate needs, such as a new refrigerator or TV, tend to dictate buying behavior, whereas the higher classes focus on more long-term goals, such as saving for college tuition or retirement.[51] Working-class consumers depend heavily on relatives for emotional support and tend to orient themselves in terms of the local community rather than the world at large. They are more likely to be conservative and family oriented. Maintaining the appearance of one's home and property is a priority, regardless of the size of the house.

One recent study that looked at social class and how it relates to consumers' feelings of *empowerment* reported that lower-class men aren't as likely to feel they have the power to affect their outcomes. Respondents varied from those who were what the researcher calls *potent actors* (those who believe they have the ability to take actions that affect their world) to *impotent reactors* (those who feel they are at the mercy of their economic situations). This orientation influenced consumption behaviors; for example, the professionals in the study who were likely to be potent actors set themselves up for financial opportunity and growth. They took very broad perspectives on investing and planned their budgets strategically.[52]

Although they would like to have more in the way of material goods, working-class people do not necessarily envy those who rank above them in social standing.[53] They may not view the maintenance of a high-status lifestyle as worth the effort. As one blue-collar consumer commented, "Life is very hectic for those people. There are more breakdowns and alcoholism. It must be very hard to sustain the status, the clothes, and the parties that are expected. I don't think I'd want to take their place."[54]

This person may be right. Although good things appear to go hand-in-hand with higher status and wealth, the picture is not that clear. The social scientist Émile Durkheim observed that suicide rates are much higher among the wealthy; he wrote in 1897, "The possessors of most comfort suffer most."[55] Durkheim's wisdom may still be accurate today. Many well-off consumers seem to be stressed or unhappy despite or even because of their wealth, a condition some call *affluenza*.[56] A *New York Times*/CBS News poll asked kids aged 13 to 17 to compare their lives with what their parents experienced growing up. Forty-three percent said they were having a harder time, and upper-income teenagers were the most likely to say that their lives are harder and subject to more stress. Apparently, they feel the pressure to get into elite schools and to maintain the family's status.[57]

"WHAT DO YOU USE THAT FORK FOR?" TASTE CULTURES, CODES, AND CULTURAL CAPITAL

A **taste culture** describes consumers in terms of their aesthetic and intellectual preferences. This concept helps to illuminate the important, yet sometimes-subtle, distinctions in consumption choices among the social classes.[59] For example, a comprehensive analysis of social-class differences using data from 675,000 U.S. households supports the mass-class phenomenon we discussed before: Differences in consumption patterns between the upper and upper-middle classes and between the middle and working classes are disappearing. However, strong differences still emerge in terms of how consumers spend their discretionary income and leisure time. Upper- and upper-middle-class people are more likely to visit museums and attend live theater, and middle-class consumers are more likely to go camping and fishing. The upper classes are more likely to listen to all-news programs, whereas the middle classes are more likely to tune in to country music.[60]

Some social critics don't like the taste culture perspective because they charge it's elitist. Judgments of the relative artistic value of Beethoven versus The Beastie Boys aside, it is very helpful to recognize that we segment ourselves in terms of our shared tastes in literature, art, music, leisure activities, and home decoration. Indeed, all of the thousands of online brand communities we discussed in Chapter 11 are living evidence that we do this all the time!

Net Profit

Affluent Americans spend more time on the Internet, and they're also more likely to use this time to search for products rather than simply to surf around. According to Jupiter Research, in 2007 Americans with annual household incomes of more than $100,000 spent a median of 17 hours a week online, compared with 14 hours for everyone else. They devoted a good chunk of their online time to online banking, paying bills, and trading stocks. The study found that 20 percent of affluent people visit business Web sites, compared with 11 percent of everyone else. They may not be hanging out much on MySpace, but they're certainly stimulating the economy.[58]

People in the upper classes are more likely to share tastes in the arts as well. They spend relatively more of their leisure time attending the symphony, museums, the theater, and so on.

In one of the classic studies of social differences in taste, researchers cataloged homeowners' possessions as they were sitting in their living rooms and asking them about their income and occupation. They identified clusters of furnishings and decorative items that seemed to appear together with some regularity, and they found different clusters depending on the consumer's social status (see Figure 13.3). For example, they tended to find a cluster consisting of religious objects, artificial flowers, and still-life portraits in relatively lower-status living rooms, whereas they were likely to catalog a cluster of abstract paintings, sculptures, and modern furniture in a higher-status home.[61]

Another approach to social class focuses on the *codes* (the ways consumers express and interpret meanings) people within different social strata use. It's valuable for marketers to discover these codes because they can use this knowledge to communicate to target customers with concepts and terms they are most likely to understand and appreciate. Marketing appeals we construct with class differences in mind result in quite different messages. For example, a life insurance ad a company targets to a lower-class person might depict in simple, straightforward terms a hard-working family man who feels good immediately after he buys a policy. A more upscale appeal might depict a more affluent older couple surrounded by photos of their children and grandchildren. It might include extensive copy that plugs the satisfaction of planning for the future and highlights the benefits of a whole-life insurance policy.

Social classes use different codes. We find restricted codes among the working class, whereas the middle and upper classes use elaborated codes. **Restricted codes** focus on the content of objects, not on relationships among objects. **Elaborated codes**, in contrast, are more complex and depend on a more sophisticated worldview. These code differences extend to the way consumers approach basic concepts such as time, social relationships, and objects. Table 13.2 summarizes some differences between these two code types.

Clearly, not all taste cultures are created equal. The upper classes have access to resources that enable them to perpetuate their privileged position in society. Pierre Bourdieu was a French theorist who wrote at length about how people compete for

■ **FIGURE 13.3** LIVING ROOM CLUSTERS AND SOCIAL CLASS

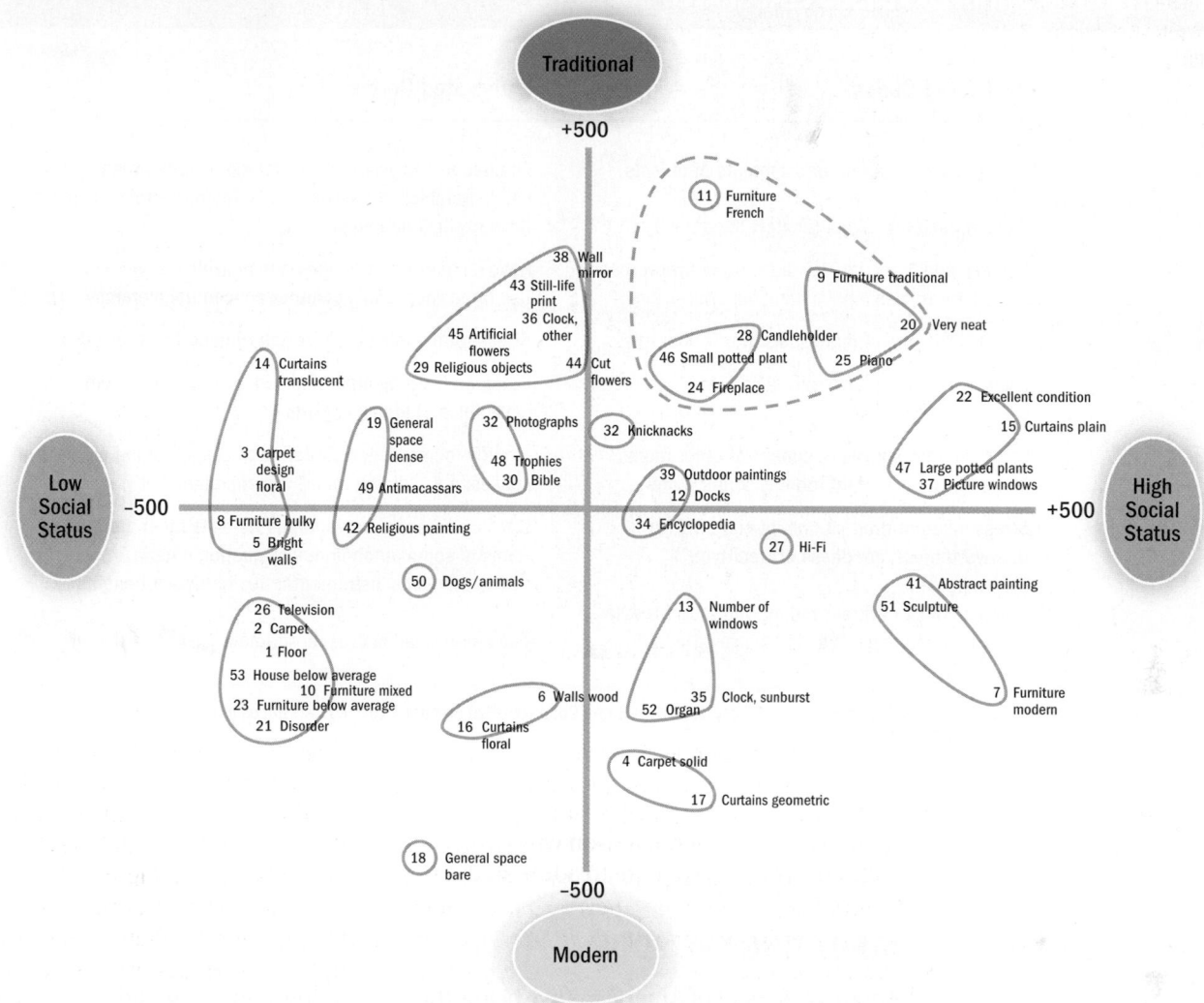

resources, or *capital*. Bourdieu did large-scale surveys to track people's wealth and he related this "economic capital" to patterns of taste in entertainment and the arts. He concluded that "taste" is a status-marking force, or **habitus**, that causes consumption preferences to cluster together. Later analyses of American consumers largely confirm these relationships; for example, higher-income people are more likely than the average consumer to attend the theater, whereas lower-income people are more likely to attend a wrestling match.[62]

Capital takes forms other than simply money. In addition to *economic capital* (financial resources), Bourdieu pointed to the significance of *social capital* (organizational affiliations and networks). The legions of aspiring professionals who take up golf because they conduct so much business on the greens demonstrate how social capital operates.

More importantly, Bourdieu reminds us of the consequences of **cultural capital**. This refers to a set of distinctive and socially rare tastes and practices—knowledge of "refined" behavior that admits a person into the realm of the upper class.[64] The elites in a society collect a set of skills that enable them to hold positions of power and authority, and they pass these on to their children (think etiquette lessons and debutante balls). These resources gain in value because class members restrict access to

TABLE 13.2
EFFECTS OF RESTRICTED VERSUS ELABORATED CODES

	Restricted Codes	Elaborated Codes
General characteristics	Emphasize description and contents of objects Have implicit meanings (context dependent)	Emphasize analysis and interrelationship between objects; i.e., hierarchical organization and instrumental connections Have explicit meanings
Language	Use few qualifiers, i.e., few adjectives or adverbs Use concrete, descriptive, tangible symbolism	Have language rich in personal, individual qualifiers Use large vocabulary, complex conceptual hierarchy
Social relationships	Stress attributes of individuals over formal roles	Stress formal role structure, instrumental relationships
Time	Focus on present; have only general notion of future	Focus on instrumental relationship between present activities and future rewards
Physical space	Locate rooms, spaces in context of other rooms and places: e.g., "front room," "corner store"	Identify rooms, spaces in terms of usage; formal ordering of spaces; e.g., "dining room," "financial district"
Implications for marketers	Stress inherent product quality, contents (or trustworthiness, goodness of "real-type"), spokesperson Stress implicit of fit of product with total lifestyle Use simple adjectives, descriptions	Stress differences, advantages vis-à-vis other products in terms of some autonomous evaluation criteria Stress product's instrumental ties to distant benefits Use complex adjectives, descriptors

Source: Adapted from Jeffrey F. Durgee, "How Consumer Sub-Cultures Code Reality: A Look at Some Code Types," in Richard J. Lutz, ed., *Advances in Consumer Research*, 13 (Provo, UT: Association of Consumer Research, 1986): 332.

them. That's part of the reason why people compete so fiercely for admission to elite colleges. Much as we hate to admit it, the rich *are* different.

TARGETING THE POOR

About 14 percent of Americans live below the poverty line, and most marketers largely ignore this segment. Still, although poor people obviously have less to spend than do rich ones, they have the same basic needs as everyone else. Low-income families purchase staples, such as milk, orange juice, and tea, at the same rates as average-income families. Minimum wage–level households spend more than average on out-of-pocket health-care costs, rent, and food they eat at home.[65] Unfortunately, they find it harder to obtain these resources because many businesses are reluctant to locate in lower-income areas. On average, residents of poor neighborhoods must travel more than 2 miles to have the same access to supermarkets, large drug stores, and banks as do residents of more affluent areas.[66]

Still, a lot of companies are taking a second look at marketing to the poor because of their large numbers. The economist C. K. Pralahad added fuel to this fire with his book *The Fortune at the Bottom of the Pyramid*, which argued big companies could profit and help the world's 4 billion poor or low-income people by finding innovative ways to sell them soap and refrigerators.[67]

Some companies are getting into these vast markets by revamping their distribution systems or making their products simpler and less expensive. When Nestlé Brazil shrank the package size of its Bono cookies (no relation to the U2 singer) from 200 grams to 140 grams and dropped the price, sales jumped 40 percent. Unilever called a new soap brand Ala so that illiterate peple in Latin America could easily recognize it. In Mexico, cement company Cemex improved housing in poor areas after it introduced a pay-as-you-go system for buying building supplies.[68]

CB AS I SEE IT

Professor Morris B. Holbrook
Columbia University

According to many liberal American sociologists, the influence of class distinctions in the United States has dwindled during the past century as mobility among the echelons of society has increased and as differences in consumption styles have decreased. Nonetheless, the role of the status hierarchy based on income, education, occupation, living accommodations, and so forth remains an important source of differences in consumption behavior among various groups. For example, the French sociologist Pierre Bourdieu has called attention to hierarchically organized patterns of consumption-based homologies that reflect bipolar oppositions related to *economic capital* (wealth) and *cultural capital* (education): Wealthy/Poor :: Educated/Uneducated :: Rolex/Timex :: Saks Fifth Avenue/K-Mart :: Mercedes/Chevy :: Opera/Grand Ol' Opry :: PBS/CBS :: *The New Yorker/Field & Stream*.

One consistent finding—also reported by American researchers such as Paul DiMaggio—concerns the ubiquitous tendency for patronage of the arts and entertainment to reflect differences in income and *especially* in education. Better-/less-educated audiences enjoy Thelonious Monk/Clay Aiken or Pablo Picasso/Norman Rockwell. Beyond that, higher-status folks tend to be *cultural omnivores*, showing a tendency to participate in *all* sorts of cultural activities.

Further, within a particular *cultural field*—say, motion pictures, jazz, cooking, or professional wrestling—tastes vary hierarchically in accord with socially sanctioned claims to legitimacy based on education, training, and other sources of relevant expertise. For example, professional film critics (experts) honor different criteria in evaluating cinematic excellence from those determining audience popularity with ordinary consumers (nonexperts).

Thus, across numerous studies, the correlation between expert judgments and popular appeal tends to be about .30 or less—in other words, an explained variance or r^2 of less than 10 percent. More recent research suggests that this significant-but-weak association rises considerably—to a correlation of about .55 or 30 percent explained variance—when controlling for market- and marketing-related factors that might contaminate the relationship between excellence and popularity (promotional budgets, production budgets, theatrical box office, video rentals, and so forth). Apparently, when measured correctly, even the mass audience does display aspects of "good taste."

Muhammad Yunus, a Bangladeshi economist, won the 2006 Nobel Prize in Economics for pioneering the concept of **microloans**. His Grameen Bank loans small sums—typically less than $100—to entrepreneurs in developing countries. Many of these go to "cell-phone women," who rent time on the phones to others in their remote villages. The bank has issued about 6 million loans to date, and almost 99 percent of recipients repay them (compared to a 50 percent repayment rate for a typical bank in a developing country).[69]

The success of La Curacao, a chain of department stores in southern California with an Hispanic focus, comes from the company's desire to serve the needs of lower-income consumers. The stores are the brainchild of two Israeli brothers who share a similar experience with many of their customers: They were once illegal immigrants searching for a better life in the United States. They realized that poor people can be good credit risks, *if* the retailer gives them reason to be grateful someone has taken a chance on them. This trust seems to be working: Shoppers use store credit cards for 95 percent of purchases, and for 8 out of 10 of these customers, the La Curacao credit card is the first one they've ever had. The chain's slogan is *Un Poco de Su Pais* or "A Little Bit of Your Country." Everything about the stores—from the exterior emblazoned with Mayan and Aztec statues to the piped-in salsa music, Spanish-speaking sales staff, and Spanish-language sale signs inside—strives to make the customers feel as if they're back home. And because many of the immigrant families who shop there can't afford to take their kids to places such as Disneyland, every store also has a stage that features mariachi bands, clowns, and other family entertainment.[70]

TARGETING THE RICH

If you've got enough money, you can buy a Pink Splendor Barbie complete with crystal jewelry and a bouffant gown sewn with 24-karat threads. To dress a "living doll," Victoria's Secret offers its Million Dollar Miracle Bra, with more than 100 carats of real diamonds. When Neiman Marcus's limited edition Maserati Quattroporte went on sale, all 60 of the $125,000 customized sedans sold out in 4 minutes. The company reported that other extravagant gifts featured in its annual Christmas catalog sold at an unusually brisk pace, including hand-encrusted crystal versions of Mr. and Mrs. Potato Head, for $8,000 each, and a $20,000 customized suit of armor.[71]

Even the way we pay for these lavish items can become a statement about wealth—especially if you're 1 of the only 5,000 people American Express invited to hold its black Centurion credit card. The mysterious card is blank except for a black-on-black pattern. To be card-worthy, you have to charge more than $150,000 a year and pay an annual fee of $2,500.

Many marketers try to target affluent, upscale markets. This often makes sense because these consumers obviously have the resources to spend on costly products (often with higher profit margins). However, it is a mistake to assume that we should place everyone with a high income into the same market segment. As we noted earlier, social class involves more than absolute income. It is also a way of life, and

Many companies, like this Austrian bank, agressively pursue the upper class consumer.

Bank Austria
Creditanstalt

Banking for success.

It's not our job to tell you the best thing to do with your inheritance,
but it is our job to advise you the best way of going about it.

factors including where they got their money, how they got it, and how long they have had it significantly affect affluents' interests and spending priorities.[72]

Despite our stereotype of rich people living it up, one study found the typical millionaire is a 57-year-old man who is self-employed, earns a median household income of $131,000, has been married to the same wife for most of his adult life, has children, has never spent more than $399 on a suit or more than $140 for a pair of shoes, and drives a Ford Explorer (the humble billionaire investor Warren Buffett comes to mind). Interestingly, many affluent people don't consider themselves to be rich. One tendency researchers notice is that they indulge in luxury goods while pinching pennies on everyday items—buying shoes at Neiman Marcus and deodorant at Wal-Mart, for example.[73]

SRI Consulting Business Intelligence (the research firm that developed VALS2™, discussed in Chapter 6) divides consumers into three groups based on their attitudes toward luxury:

1 **Luxury is functional:** These consumers use their money to buy things that will last and have enduring value. They conduct extensive prepurchase research and make logical decisions rather than emotional or impulsive choices.

2 **Luxury is a reward:** These consumers tend to be younger than the first group but older than the third group. They often use luxury goods to say, "I've made it." The desire to be successful and to demonstrate their success to others motivates these consumers to purchase conspicuous luxury items, such as high-end automobiles and homes in exclusive communities.

3 **Luxury is indulgence:** This group is the smallest of the three and tends to include younger consumers and slightly more males than the other two groups. To these consumers, the purpose of owning luxury is to be extremely lavish and self-indulgent. This group is willing to pay a premium for goods that express their individuality and make others take notice. They have a more emotional approach to luxury spending and are more likely than the other two groups to make impulse purchases.[74]

As Phil discovered, people who are used to having money for a long time use their fortunes a lot differently. *Old money* families (e.g., the Rockefellers, DuPonts, Fords, etc.) live primarily on inherited funds.[75] One commentator called this group "the class in hiding."[76] Following the Great Depression of the 1930s, monied families became more discreet about exhibiting their wealth. Many fled from mansions such as those we still find in Manhattan (the renovated Vanderbilt mansion now is Ralph Lauren's flagship store) to hideaways in Virginia, Connecticut, and New Jersey.

Merely having wealth is not sufficient to achieve social prominence in these circles. You also need to demonstrate a family history of public service and philanthropy, and tangible markers of these contributions often enable donors to achieve a kind of immortality (e.g., Rockefeller University, Carnegie Hall or the Whitney Museum).[77] "Old money" consumers distinguish among themselves in terms of ancestry and lineage rather than wealth.[78] And (like the Caldwells) they're secure in their status. In a sense, they have trained their whole lives to be rich.

In contrast to people with old money, today there are many people—including high-profile billionaires such as Bill Gates, Steve Jobs, and Richard Branson—who are "the working wealthy."[79] The Horatio Alger myth, where a person goes from "rags to riches" through hard work and a bit of luck, is still a powerful force in U.S. society. That's why a commercial showing the actual garage where the two cofounders of Hewlett-Packard first worked strikes a chord in so many.

Although many people do in fact become "self-made millionaires," they often encounter a problem (although not the worst problem one could think of!) after they have become wealthy and change their social status. The label *nouveau riche* describes consumers who recently achieved their wealth and who don't have the benefit of years of training to learn how to spend it.

Pity the poor *nouveau riches;* many suffer from *status anxiety*. They monitor the cultural environment to ensure that they do the "right" thing, wear the "right" clothes, get seen at the "right" places, use the "right" caterer, and so on.[80] Their flamboyant consumption is an example of *symbolic self-completion* because they try to display symbols they believe have "class" to make up for an internal lack of assurance about the "correct" way to behave.[81] In major Chinese cities such as Shanghai, some people have taken to wearing pajamas in public as a way to flaunt their newfound wealth. As one consumer explained, "Only people in cities can afford clothes like this. In farming villages, they still have to wear old work clothes to bed."[82]

Advertising directed to this group often plays on these insecurities. Clever merchandising supplies these consumers with the props they need to pass as old money people. For example, ads for *Colonial Homes* magazine feature consumers who "have worked very hard to make it look like they never had to." A housing development near Santa Monica, California, epitomizes the demand for ready-made affluent lifestyles. It features completely furnished "McMansions" (complete with linens, dishes, and even artwork), and each residence also includes four-car garages, hot tubs, fake boulders that double as outdoor speaker enclosures, and a built-in computer network. IBM Home Director software controls the lighting and the coffeemaker and even phones you anywhere in the world if the temperature gets too high in the wine cellar (don't you just *hate* when that happens?). Buyers choose from one of four different prefab lifestyle fantasies: English Country Estate, Tuscan Villa, French Regency, or New York Penthouse.[83]

Status Symbols

We all have a deep-seated tendency to evaluate ourselves, our professional accomplishments, our appearance, and our material well-being relative to others. The popular phrase "keeping up with the Joneses" (in Japan it's "keeping up with the Satos") refers to a desire to compare your standard of living with your neighbors—and exceed it if you can. In one poll, 81 percent of respondents agreed they felt social pressure to buy high-priced goods.[84]

Often it's not enough to have wealth or fame—what matters is that you have more of it than others. A major motivation to buy and display what we buy is not to enjoy these items but rather to let others know that we can afford them. In other words, these products are *status symbols* like those we discussed at the beginning of this chapter. The popular bumper sticker slogan, "He who dies with the most toys, wins" summarizes the desire to accumulate these "badges of achievement." Status-seeking is a significant source of motivation to procure appropriate products and services that we hope will let others know we've "made it."

As we discussed earlier in the chapter, the rise in the United States and elsewhere of a *mass-class* market means that many luxury products have gone down-market. Does this mean Americans no longer yearn for status symbols? Hardly. The market continues to roll out ever-pricier goods and services, from $130,000 Hummers and $12,000 mother–baby diamond tennis bracelet sets to $600 jeans, $800 haircuts, and $400 bottles of wine. Although it seems that almost everyone can flout a designer handbag (or at least a counterfeit version with a convincing logo), the wealthiest U.S. consumers employ 9,000 personal chefs, visit plastic surgeons, and send their children to $400-an-hour math tutors. A sociologist explained, "Whether or not someone has a flat-screen TV is going to tell you less than if you look at the services they use, where they live and the control they have over other people's labor, those who are serving them."[85]

Of course, the particular products that count as status symbols vary across cultures and locales:

● To own a private helicopter is a must for well-to-do Brazilians, who have to contend both with traffic snarls and kidnappers. There are more than 400 of these choppers prowling the skies of São Paulo.[86]

Armored cars are a status symbol in Brazil. This ad for an armored car maker uses an egg carton metaphor to illustrate the security it offers.

- In China, children are status symbols (partly because the government strongly discourages couples from having more than one baby). Parents want to show off their pampered child and are eager to surround their "little emperors" with luxury goods. Chinese families spend one-third to one-half of their disposable income on their children.[87]

- Largely because of an oil boom, there are at least 25 billionaires and 88,000 millionaires in Russia. Muscovites are craving luxury goods to show off their newfound wealth. Some buy the GoldVish cell phone that glitters with 120 carats of diamonds encrusting a case of white gold. The desire to spend as much as possible on indulgences fuels a popular joke in Moscow: A wealthy businessman tells a friend he bought a tie for $100. He responds, "You fool. You can get the same tie for $200 just across the street."[88]

- In Indonesia as in Russia, a cell phone is a status symbol (see Marketing Pitfall box)—but instead of a sleek iPhone, a decade-old Nokia model users call "the Brick" is the one to have. This "smart phone" never took off in the West; its bulky design makes it look dated. But in Jakarta, its heft is what people like about it. At a whopping half-pound, it doesn't fit into a pocket so it's very visible when models, politicians, and other celebrities cart it around with them. Nokia even sells a gold-plated version for $2,500. In the world of status symbols, anything goes as long as others don't have it.[89]

The social analyst Thorstein Veblen first discussed the motivation to consume for the sake of consuming at the turn of the twentieth century. For Veblen, we buy things to create **invidious distinction**; this means we use them to inspire envy in others

Status symbols are always in flux. At one time, having very pale skin was the mark of an upper social class because it indicated that the person did not have to work in the fields. Today, a suntan is equated with leisure time and consumers go to great lengths to get one naturally or with "help."

through our display of wealth or power. Veblen coined the term **conspicuous consumption** to refer to people's desires to provide prominent visible evidence of their ability to afford luxury goods. The material excesses of his time motivated Veblen's outlook. Veblen wrote in the era of the "robber barons," where the likes of J. P. Morgan, Henry Clay Frick, and William Vanderbilt built massive financial empires and flaunted their wealth as they competed to throw the most lavish party. Some of these events were legendary, as this account describes:

> There were tales, repeated in the newspapers, of dinners on horseback; of banquets for pet dogs; of hundred-dollar bills folded into guests' dinner napkins; of a hostess who attracted attention by seating a chimpanzee at her table; of centerpieces in which lightly clad living maidens swam in glass tanks, or emerged from huge pies; of parties at which cigars were ceremoniously lighted with flaming banknotes of large denominations.[92]

Sounds like they really lived it up back in the old days, right? Well, maybe the more things change, the more they stay the same: The recent wave of corporate scandals involving companies such as Enron, WorldCom, and Tyco infuriated many consumers when they discovered that some top executives lived it up even as other employees were laid off. One account of a $1 million birthday party the chief executive of Tyco threw for his wife is eerily similar to a robber baron shindig: The party reportedly had a gladiator theme and featured an ice sculpture of Michelangelo's David with vodka streaming provocatively from the sculpture into crystal glasses. The company also furnished the executive's New York apartment with such essentials as a $6,000 shower curtain, a $2,200 gilt wastebasket, and a $17,100 "traveling toilette box."[93]

This phenomenon of conspicuous consumption was, for Veblen, most evident among what he termed the *leisure class,* people for whom productive work is taboo. In Marxist terms, such an attitude reflects a desire to link oneself to ownership or control of the means of production, rather than to the production itself. Those who control these resources, therefore, avoid any evidence they actually have to work for a living, as the term the *idle rich* suggests.

To Veblen, wives are an economic resource. He criticized the "decorative" role of women as rich men showered them with expensive clothes, pretentious homes, and a life of leisure as a way to advertise their own wealth (note that today he might have argued the same for a smaller number of husbands). Fashions such as high-heeled shoes, tight corsets, billowing trains on dresses, and elaborate hairstyles all conspired to ensure that wealthy women could barely move without assistance, much less perform manual labor. Similarly, the Chinese practice of foot-binding prevented female members of the aristocracy from walking, and servants carried them from place to place.

Veblen's inspiration came from anthropological studies he read of the Kwakiutl Indians, who lived in the Pacific Northwest. At a *potlatch* ceremony, the host showed off his wealth and gave extravagant presents to the guests. The more he gave away, the greater his status. Sometimes, the host employed an even more radical strategy to flaunt his wealth. He would publicly *destroy* some of his property just to demonstrate how much he had.

And the plot thickens: Because guests had to reciprocate by giving a gift of equal value, the host could humiliate a poorer rival with an invitation to a lavish potlatch. The hapless guest would eventually be forced into bankruptcy because he needed to give away as much as the host, even though he could not afford it. If this practice sounds "primitive," think for a moment about many modern weddings. Parents commonly invest huge sums of money to throw a lavish party and compete with others for the distinction of giving their daughter the "best" or most extravagant wedding, even if they have to dip into their retirement savings to do it.

Like the *potlatch* ritual, in modern times our desire to convince others we have a surplus of resources creates the need for us to exhibit the evidence that we do. Accordingly, we may prioritize consumption activities that use up as many resources as possible in nonconstructive pursuits. This *conspicuous waste,* in turn, shows others that we have the assets to spare. Veblen wrote, "We are told of certain Polynesian chiefs, who, under the stress of good form, preferred to starve rather than carry their food to their mouths with their own hands."[94]

As the competition to accumulate status symbols escalates, sometimes the best tactic is to switch gears and go in reverse. One way to do this is to deliberately *avoid* status symbols—that is, to seek status by mocking it. Social scientists call this sophisticated form of conspicuous consumption **parody display**.[95] Hence, the popularity of old, ripped blue jeans (or more likely the ones companies stonewash so they look old and ripped) and "utility" vehicles such as Jeeps among the upper classes (like the Caldwells).

Today, brands with a strong blue-collar heritage, such as Von Dutch truckers' hats and Red Wing boots, are in vogue among trendy young people. To capitalize on its newfound popularity, Red Wing is sprucing up many of its 430 stores with new

Marketing Pitfall

Think about those of us who suffer from cell phone envy: Did *you* stake out your place in line when Apple first released its coveted iPhone? British researchers observed how men in clubs used their phones as part of "the mating ritual." Wherease female patrons generally kept their phones in their purses and retrieved them only when they needed them, most men took their phones out of their jacket pockets or briefcases when they sat down and placed them on the bar counter or table for all to see.

The authors propose that men use their mobile phones just as peacocks use their plumage or male bullfrogs use their croaks—to advertise their status to available mates. They noted that the amount of time the men spent toying with and displaying their phones increased significantly as the number of men relative to women increased—just as male peacocks fan open their feathers more vigorously as the number of competing suitors increases.[90]

Today, the average cell phone user replaces his phone in less than 2 years, and many aficionados pant for a new model much sooner than that. It's not about function; it's about fashion and the next best thing. Motorola learned about the status value of phones when its fortunes plunged along with the price of its Razr model (a 30 percent drop in stock price in 6 months). Although the Razr was a big hit when Motorola launched it, the company sat on its laurels and didn't realize that customers soon would crave the latest and greatest. As one industry analyst stated, "Phone manufacturers are only as hot as their last major hit—if they haven't smacked it over the fence in a while, they're in trouble. Motorola failed to follow it up with something similarly as big as the Razr." Motorola hoped that its newer Krzr model would lure back style-conscious consumers because it's got better functionality than the Razr. But the Krzr also looks a lot like a Razr and analysts doubt that phoneaholics are going to buy into a product that looks like it's *so* yesterday.[91]

Ripped jeans (especially the pricey kind that come that way when you buy them) are an example of parody display.

lighting and displays, and relocating some of its key stores to upscale strip malls. Red Wing also hired more designers to help push into new markets, such as women's shoes and motorcycle boots.[96]

CHAPTER SUMMARY

Now that you have finished reading this chapter you should understand why:

Both personal and social conditions influence how we spend our money.

● The field of behavioral economics studies how consumers decide what to do with their money. Consumer confidence—the state of mind consumers have about their own personal situation, as well as their feelings about their overall economic prospects—helps to determine whether they will purchase goods and services, take on debt, or save their money.

We group consumers into social classes that say a lot about where they stand in society.

● A consumer's social class refers to his standing in society. Factors including education, occupation, and income determine the class to which we belong.

● Virtually all groups make distinctions among members in terms of relative superiority, power, and access to valued resources. This social stratification creates a status hierarchy where consumers prefer some goods over others.

● Although income is an important indicator of social class, the relationship is far from perfect. Factors such as place of residence, cultural interests, and worldview also determine social class. As income distributions change around the world, it is getting more difficult to distinguish among members of social classes—many products succeed because they appeal to a newly emerging group marketers call the mass class (people with incomes high enough to purchase luxury items, at least on a small scale).

A person's desire to make a statement about his social class, or the class to which he hopes to belong, influences the products he likes and dislikes.

● Conspicuous consumption, where a person flaunts his status by deliberately using up valuable resources, is one way to "buy up" to a higher social class. *Nouveau riches,* whose relatively recent acquisition of income rather than ancestry or breeding accounts for their enhanced social mobility, are the most likely to do this.

● We use status symbols (usually scarce goods or services) to communicate our standing to others. Parody display occurs when we seek status by deliberately avoiding fashionable products.

KEY TERMS

Behavioral economics, 513
Chavs, 519
Conspicuous consumption, 534
Consumer confidence, 513
Cultural capital, 527
Discretionary income, 512
Elaborated codes, 526

Habitus, 527
Homogamy, 515
Invidious distinction, 533
Mass class, 520
Microloans, 529
Parody display, 535
Restricted codes, 526

Social class, 514
Social mobility, 520
Social stratification, 516
Status crystallization, 523
Status hierarchy, 520
Status symbol, 510
Taste culture, 525

REVIEW QUESTIONS

1 How have women contributed to the overall rise in income in Western society?
2 Define discretionary income.
3 How does consumer confidence influence consumer behavior?
4 What is a pecking order?
5 What is social class? Is it different from income and if so how?
6 What is the difference between achieved and ascribed status?
7 What is a chav?
8 Describe what we mean by the term *mass class* and tell what is causing this phenomenon.
9 Define social mobility and what different forms it can take.
10 What one variable is the best indicator of social class? What are some other important indicators?

11 Why does earning more money often *not* result in a corresponding change in social class?
12 What are some of the problems we encounter when we try to measure social class?
13 Define status crystallization and give an example.
14 How does the *worldview* of blue-collar and white-collar consumers differ?
15 What is a taste culture?
16 Describe the difference between a restricted and an elaborated code, giving an example of each.
17 What is cultural capital and why is enrolling in an etiquette class a way to accumulate it?
18 How do you differentiate between "old money" versus "*nouveau riche*" consumers?
19 What is conspicuous consumption? Give a current example.
20 What is a current example of parody display?

CONSUMER BEHAVIOR CHALLENGE

■ DISCUSS

1 Sears, JCPenney, and Wal-Mart made concerted efforts in recent years to upgrade their images and appeal to higher-class consumers. How successful have these efforts been? Do you believe this strategy is wise?

2 What are some of the obstacles to measuring social class in today's society? Discuss some ways to get around these obstacles.

3 Do you believe "affluenza" is a problem among people your age? Why or why not?

4 What consumption differences might you expect to observe between a family we characterize as underprivileged and one whose income is average for its social class?

5 How do you assign people to social classes, or do you at all? What consumption cues do you use (e.g., clothing, speech, cars, etc.) to determine social standing?

6 Thorstein Veblen argued that men used women as "trophy wives" to display their wealth. Is this argument still valid today?

7 Given present environmental conditions and dwindling resources, what is the future of "conspicuous waste"? Can we ever eliminate the desire to impress others with our affluence?

8 This chapter observes that some marketers find "greener pastures" by targeting low-income people. How ethical is it to single out consumers who cannot afford to waste their precious resources on discretionary items? Under what circumstances should we encourage or discourage this segmentation strategy?

9 Status symbols are products we value because they show others how much money or prestige we have, such as Rolex watches or expensive sports cars. Do you believe that your peer group values status symbols? Why or why not? If yes, what are the products that you think are status symbols for consumers your age? Do you agree with the assertion in this chapter that a cell phone is a status symbol for many young people?

■ APPLY

10 Using the status index in Figure 13.3, compute a social-class score for people you know, including their parents, if possible. Ask several friends (preferably from different places) to compile similar information for people they know. How closely do your answers compare? If you find differences, how can you explain them?

11 Compile a list of occupations and ask a sample of students in a variety of majors (both business and nonbusiness) to rank the prestige of these jobs. Can you detect any differences in these rankings as a function of students' majors?

12 Compile a collection of ads that depict consumers of different social classes. What generalizations can you make about the reality of these ads and about the media in which they appear?

Case Study

NO SUCH THING AS FREE TIME?

When you think of really nice watches, what brands come to mind? Tissot? Tag Heuer? Movado? And how much does a really nice watch cost? $300? $600? You might think that buying a watch like this is extravagant, maybe even out of reach. If so you'll be surprised to learn that to people who really know watches, these prices are pocket change. In fact, high-end watches start at around $3,000 and command prices up to $500,000 or more!

Who would buy such a watch? Wealthy people who are fascinated by *horology* (the study of the measurement of time). Melvyn Teillol-Foo, a pharmaceutical executive from Singapore, is one such individual. For him, a fine watch is even more of a status symbol than an exotic car. It costs just as much, but it never has to be left behind. "There's more to life than just Ferraris and Maseratis," he says. The big difference between an exotic watch and an exotic car is that very few people can tell the difference between a $3,000 watch and one costing 10 times as much. The distinctions are subtle.

Unlike most status symbols, fine watches are much more about craftsmanship and mechanical details than they are about the glitzy embellishments. To even qualify as a superior timepiece, battery power is a no-no. A fine watch must be mechanical, either winding or automatic. For serious collectors, a watch must be handmade in Switzerland or possibly Germany. Beyond these qualifiers, some commonly sought-after features (known as "complications") include perpetual calendars, minute repeaters, moon phase calendars, and even ultra-miniature chimes that sound off hours and minutes. One particular pricey feature is known as a "tourbillon," which counters the effects of gravity and movement on a watch's accuracy.

Some high-end limited edition watches are made in batches of as few as 30 pieces. The more limited the watch, the more expensive it gets. With countries such as India, China, and Russia experiencing high economic growth, global demand for such watches is growing. But manufacturers have not significantly increased production.

This scarcity means that even long-time authorized dealers for prestigious brands can only get access to few if any of the more coveted and valuable watches. The scarcity factor trickles down to buyers like Mr. Teillot-Foo, who says the biggest cost of collecting watches isn't measured in money, but in time and energy. He remembers when dealers pursued him. Now, he frequently criss-crosses Asia to keep tabs on the dealers. He plans his vacations to Europe around trips to watch factories to see new models. His avocation has become so consuming, it has led him to state, "It's about how much you have to sacrifice in terms of family life."

Watch makers maintain a delicate balance between meeting customer needs and exclusivity. In the end, if anyone can get a watch, it isn't worth much. So the well-heeled are willing to pay their dues in order to procure the trophies they seek.

DISCUSSION QUESTIONS

1 Discuss the ways that social class affects the purchase of a watch.

2 What factors help to make a watch a status symbol?

3 How do watch companies promote their products to play on this status element?

Sources: Michael Clerizo, "Customize It: The Luxury of Personalized Design," *Wall Street Journal* (June 8, 2007), accessed online at www.wsj.com; Stacy Meichtry, "What Your Time Is Really Worth," *Wall Street Journal* (April 7, 2007), accessed online at www.wsj.com.

NOTES

1. Data in this section adapted from Fabian Linden, *Consumer Affluence: The Next Wave* (New York: The Conference Board, 1994). For additional information about U.S. income statistics, access Occupational Employment and Wage Estimates at www.bls.gov/oes/oes_data.htm.
2. Mary Bowler, "Women's Earnings: An Overview," *Monthly Labor Review* 122 (December 1999): 13–22.
3. Christopher D. Carroll, "How Does Future Income Affect Current Consumption?" *Quarterly Journal of Economics* 109 (February 1994): 111–47.
4. Michael Barbaro, "It's Not Only about Price at Wal-Mart," *New York Times Online* (March 2, 2007), accessed March 2, 2007.
5. For a scale that measures consumer frugality, see John L. Lastovicka, Lance A. Bettencourt, Renee Shaw Hughner, and Ronald J. Kuntze, "Lifestyle of the Tight and Frugal: Theory and Measurement," *Journal of Consumer Research* 26 (June 1999): 85–98.
6. José F. Medina, Joel Saegert, and Alicia Gresham, "Comparison of Mexican-American and Anglo-American Attitudes toward Money," *Journal of Consumer Affairs* 30, no. 1 (1996): 124–45.
7. Kirk Johnson, "Sit Down. Breathe Deeply. This Is Really Scary Stuff," *New York Times* (April 16, 1995): F5; cf. also Matthew J. Bernthal, David Crockett, and Randall L. Rose, "Credit Cards As Lifestyle Facilitators," *Journal of Consumer Research* 32 (June 2005): 130–45.
8. Fred van Raaij, "Economic Psychology," *Journal of Economic Psychology* 1 (1981): 1–24.
9. Richard T. Curtin, "Indicators of Consumer Behavior: The University of Michigan Surveys of Consumers," *Public Opinion Quarterly* (1982): 340–52.
10. George Katona, "Consumer Saving Patterns," *Journal of Consumer Research* 1 (June 1974): 1–12.
11. Floyd L. Ruch and Philip G. Zimbardo, *Psychology and Life*, 8th ed. (Glenview, IL: Scott, Foresman, 1971).
12. Jonathan H. Turner, *Sociology: Studying the Human System*, 2nd ed. (Santa Monica, CA: Goodyear, 1981).
13. Richard P. Coleman, "The Continuing Significance of Social Class to Marketing," *Journal of Consumer Research* 10 (December 1983): 265–80; Turner, *Sociology: Studying the Human System*.
14. Rebecca Gardyn, "The Mating Game," *American Demographics* (July–August 2002): 33–34.
15. Richard P. Coleman and Lee Rainwater, *Standing in America: New Dimensions of Class* (New York: Basic Books, 1978), 89.
16. Ibid.
17. Turner, *Sociology: Studying the Human System.*
18. James Fallows, "A Talent for Disorder (Class Structure)," *U.S. News & World Report* (February 1, 1988): 83.
19. Coleman, "The Continuing Significance of Social Class to Marketing"; W. Lloyd Warner and Paul S. Lunt, eds., *The Social Life of a Modern Community* (New Haven, CT: Yale University Press, 1941).
20. Howard W. French, "Chinese Children Learn Class, Minus the Struggle," *New York Times Online* (September 22, 2006), accessed September 22, 2006; Bay Fang, "The Shanghai High Life," *U.S. News & World Report* (June 20, 2005), www.usnews.com/usnews/biztech/articles/050620/20china.b2.htm, accessed June 20, 2005 http://travel.guardian.co.uk/cities/story/0,7450,489488,00.html, accessed June 20, 2005; Russell Flannery, "Long Live the $25 Cigar," *Forbes* (December 27, 2004): 51; Clay Chandler, "China Deluxe," *Fortune* (July 26, 2004): 149–56; Matthew Forney, "How Nike Figured Out China," *Time* (November 2004): A10–A14; J. David Lynch, "Emerging Middle Class Reshaping China," *USA Today* (November 12, 2002): 13A.
21. Sebastian Moffett, "The Japanese Paradox: Pinched by Economic Slump, Women Buy More Handbags from Vuitton, Prada, Hermes," *Wall Street Journal on the Web* (September 23, 2003).
22. Cecilie Rohwedder, "Design Houses Build Stores, Pamper Demanding Shoppers in Fashion-Industry Hot Spot," *Wall Street Journal on the Web* (January 21, 2004).
23. Robin Knight, "Just You Move Over, 'Enry 'Iggins; A New Regard for Profits and Talent Cracks Britain's Old Class System," *U.S. News & World Report* 106 (April 24, 1989): 40.
24. Robert Guy Matthews, "Bawdy British Ads Target Hot Youth," *Wall Street Journal* (April 20, 2005): B9.
25. Eric Bellman, "Name Game: As Economy Grows, India Goes for Designer Goods," *Wall Street Journal* (March 27, 2007): A1.
26. Jennifer Steinhauer, "When the Joneses Wear Jeans," *New York Times Online* (May 29, 2005), accessed May 29, 2005.
27. Steinhauer, "When the Joneses Wear Jeans"; Paul F. Nunes, Brian A. Johnson, and R. Timothy S. Breene, "Moneyed Masses," *Harvard*

Business Review (July–August 2004): 94–104; *Trend Update: Massclusivity*, report from Reinier Evers and Trendwatching.com, available from Zyman Institute of Brand Science, Emory University, http://www.zibs.com/, accessed February 25, 2005.

28. Turner, *Sociology: Studying the Human System*, 260.

29. See Ronald Paul Hill and Mark Stamey, "The Homeless in America: An Examination of Possessions and Consumption Behaviors," *Journal of Consumer Research* 17 (December 1990): 303–21; estimate provided by Dr. Ronald Hill, personal communication, December 1997.

30. Joseph Kahl, *The American Class Structure* (New York: Holt, Rinehart and Winston, 1961).

31. Leonard Beeghley, *Social Stratification in America: A Critical Analysis of Theory and Research* (Santa Monica, CA: Goodyear, 1978).

32. Coleman and Rainwater, *Standing in America: New Dimensions of Class*.

33. Turner, *Sociology: Studying the Human System*.

34. See Coleman, "The Continuing Significance of Social Class to Marketing"; Charles M. Schaninger, "Social Class versus Income Revisited: An Empirical Investigation," *Journal of Marketing Research* 18 (May 1981): 192–208.

35. Coleman, "The Continuing Significance of Social Class to Marketing."

36. August B. Hollingshead and Fredrick C. Redlich, *Social Class and Mental Illness: A Community Study* (New York: Wiley, 1958).

37. John Mager and Lynn R. Kahle, "Is the Whole More than the Sum of the Parts? Re-evaluating Social Status in Marketing," *Journal of Business Psychology* 10 (Fall 1995): 3–18.

38. Beeghley, *Social Stratification in America: A Critical Analysis of Theory and Research*.

39. R. Vanneman and F. C. Pampel, "The American Perception of Class and Status," *American Sociological Review* 42 (June 1977): 422–37.

40. Donald W. Hendon, Emelda L. Williams, and Douglas E. Huffman, "Social Class System Revisited," *Journal of Business Research* 17 (November 1988): 259.

41. Coleman, "The Continuing Significance of Social Class to Marketing."

42. Gerhard E. Lenski, "Status Crystallization: A Non-Vertical Dimension of Social Status," *American Sociological Review* 19 (August 1954): 405–12.

43. Richard P. Coleman, "The Significance of Social Stratification in Selling," in Martin L. Bell, ed., *Marketing: A Maturing Discipline: Proceedings of the American Marketing Association 43rd National Conference* (Chicago: American Marketing Association, 1960), 171–84.

44. E. Barth and W. Watson, "Questionable Assumptions in the Theory of Social Stratification," *Pacific Sociological Review* 7 (Spring 1964): 10–16.

45. Zick Rubin, "Do American Women Marry Up?" *American Sociological Review* 33 (1968): 750–60.

46. K. U. Ritter and L. L. Hargens, "Occupational Positions and Class Identifications of Married Working Women: A Test of the Asymmetry Hypothesis," *American Journal of Sociology* 80 (January 1975): 934–48.

47. J. Michael Munson and W. Austin Spivey, "Product and Brand-User Stereotypes among Social Classes: Implications for Advertising Strategy," *Journal of Advertising Research* 21 (August 1981): 37–45.

48. Stuart U. Rich and Subhash C. Jain, "Social Class and Life Cycle as Predictors of Shopping Behavior," *Journal of Marketing Research* 5 (February 1968): 41–49.

49. Thomas W. Osborn, "Analytic Techniques for Opportunity Marketing," *Marketing Communications* (September 1987): 49–63.

50. Coleman, "The Continuing Significance of Social Class to Marketing."

51. Jeffrey F. Durgee, "How Consumer Sub-Cultures Code Reality: A Look at Some Code Types," in Richard J. Lutz, ed., *Advances in Consumer Research* 13 (Provo, UT: Association for Consumer Research, 1986): 332–37.

52. Paul C. Henry, "Social Class, Market Situation, and Consumers' Metaphors of (Dis)Empowerment," *Journal of Consumer Research* 31 (March 2005): 766–78.

53. David Halle, *America's Working Man: Work, Home, and Politics among Blue-Collar Owners* (Chicago: University of Chicago Press, 1984); David Montgomery, "America's Working Man," *Monthly Review* (1985): 1.

54. Coleman and Rainwater, *Standing in America: New Dimensions of Class*, 139.

55. Roger Brown, *Social Psychology* (New York: Free Press, 1965).

56. Kit R. Roane, "Affluenza Strikes Kids," *U.S. News & World Report* (March 20, 2000): 55.

57. Ibid.

58. Adrienne W. Fawcett, "Another Way the Rich Differ: They're Online Longer," *Marketing Daily*, www.mediapost.com.

59. Herbert J. Gans, "Popular Culture in America: Social Problem in a Mass Society or Social Asset in a Pluralist Society?" in Howard S. Becker, ed., *Social Problems: A Modern Approach* (New York: Wiley, 1966).

60. Eugene Sivadas, George Mathew, and David J. Curry, "A Preliminary Examination of the Continuing Significance of Social Class to Marketing: A Geodemographic Replication," *Journal of Consumer Marketing* 41, no. 6 (1997): 463–79.

61. Edward O. Laumann and James S. House, "Living Room Styles and Social Attributes: The Patterning of Material Artifacts in a Modern Urban Community," *Sociology and Social Research* 54 (April 1970): 321–42; see also Stephen S. Bell, Morris B. Holbrook, and Michael R. Solomon, "Combining Esthetic and Social Value to Explain Preferences for Product Styles with the Incorporation of Personality and Ensemble Effects," *Journal of Social Behavior and Personality* 6 (1991): 243–74.

62. Morris B. Holbrook, Michael J. Weiss, and John Habich, "Class-Related Distinctions in American Cultural Tastes," *Empirical Studies of the Arts* 22, no. 1 (2004): 91–115.

63. Ruth LaFerla, "A Facebook for the Few," *New York Times Online* (September 6, 2007), accessed September 6, 2007.

64. Pierre Bourdieu, *Distinction: A Social Critique of the Judgment of Taste* (Cambridge, UK: Cambridge University Press, 1984); see also Douglas B. Holt, "Does Cultural Capital Structure American Consumption?" *Journal of Consumer Research* 1 (June 1998): 1–25.

65. Paula Mergenhagen, "What Can Minimum Wage Buy?" *American Demographics* (January 1996): 32–36.

66. Linda F. Alwitt and Thomas D. Donley, "Retail Stores in Poor Urban Neighborhoods," *Journal of Consumer Affairs* 31, no. 1 (1997): 108–27.

67. C. K. Pralahad, *The Fortune at the Bottom of the Pyramid: Eradicating Poverty Through Profits* (Philadelphia: Wharton School Publishing, 2004).

68. Antonio Regalado, "Marketers Pursue the Shallow-Pocketed," *Wall Street Journal* (January 26, 2007): B3.

69. www.radicalcongruency.com/20061014-microfinance-wins-the-nobel-prize (July 22, 2007), accessed July 24, 2007.

70. Miriam Jordan, "Credito Hispano: Trust in Poor Built Consumer Empire for Israeli Brothers," *Wall Street Journal on the Web* (August 20, 2004): A1.

71. Ellen Byron, "Retailing's Velvet Rope: How Neiman Marcus's Tansky Stays above the Wannabes," *Wall Street Journal* (December 9, 2004): B1; Cyndee Miller, "Baubles Are Back," *Marketing News* (April 14, 1997): 1; Cyndee Miller, "New Line of Barbie Dolls Targets Big, Rich Kids," *Marketing News* (June 17, 1996): 6; David Carr, "No Name for Hush-Hush Magazine," *New York Times on the Web* (September 13, 2004).

72. "Reading the Buyer's Mind," *U.S. News & World Report* (March 16, 1987): 59.

73. Shelly Reese, "The Many Faces of Affluence," *Marketing Tools* (November–December 1997): 44–48.

74. Rebecca Gardyn, "Oh, the Good Life," *American Demographics* (November 2002): 34.

75. Paul Fussell, *Class: A Guide through the American Status System* (New York: Summit Books, 1983), 29.

76. Ibid.

77. Elizabeth C. Hirschman, "Secular Immortality and the American Ideology of Affluence," *Journal of Consumer Research* 17 (June 1990): 31–42.

78. Coleman and Rainwater, *Standing in America: New Dimensions of Class*, 150.

79. Kerry A. Dolan, "The World's Working Rich," *Forbes* (July 3, 2000): 162.

80. Jason DeParle, "Spy Anxiety: The Smart Magazine That Makes Smart People Nervous about Their Standing," *Washingtonian Monthly* (February 1989): 10.

81. For an examination of retailing issues related to the need for status, cf. Jacqueline Kilsheimer Eastman, Leisa Reinecke Flynn, and Ronald E. Goldsmith, "Shopping for Status: The Retail Managerial Implications," *Association of Marketing Theory and Practice* (Spring 1994): 125–30; also cf. Wilfred Amaldoss and Sanjay Jain, "Pricing of Conspicuous Goods: A Competitive Analysis of Social Effects," *Journal of Marketing Research* 42 (February 2005): 30–42.

82. Martin Fackler, "Pajamas: Not Just for Sleep Anymore," *Opelika-Auburn News* (September 13, 2002): 7A.

83. Jerry Adler and Tara Weingarten, "Mansions off the Rack," *Newsweek* (February 14, 2000): 60.

84. Steinhauer, "When the Joneses Wear Jeans."

85. Quoted in Steinhauer, "When the Joneses Wear Jeans."

86. Seth Lubove, "Copter Crazy," *Forbes* (May 13, 2002): 50.

87. "Western Companies Compete to Win Business of Chinese Babies," *Wall Street Journal Interactive Edition* (May 15, 1998).

88. Andrew E. Kramer, "New Czars of Conspicuous Consumption," *New York Times Online* (November 1, 2006), accessed November 1, 2006.

89. Tom Wright, "Ringing Up Sales in Indonesia Nokia's Bulky Smart Phones Find Niche Following There as Business Status Symbol," *Wall Street Journal* (May 22, 2007): B1.

90. Natalie Angier, "Cell Phone or Pheromone? New Props for Mating Game," *New York Times on the Web* (November 7, 2000).

91. Brad Stone, "Cellphone Envy Lays Motorola Low," *New York Times Online* (February 3, 2007), accessed February 3, 2007.

92. John Brooks, *Showing Off in America* (Boston: Little, Brown, 1981), 13.

93. Naughton Keith, "The Perk Wars," *Newsweek* (September 30, 2002): 42–46.

94. Thorstein Veblen, *The Theory of the Leisure Class* (1899; reprint, New York: New American Library, 1953): 45.

95. Brooks, *Showing Off in America.*

96. Timothy Aeppel, "Red Wing Digs in Its Heels to Fight Chains and Imports, Bootmaker Updates Its Look, but Is Still 'Made in the USA,'" *Wall Street Journal* (September 28, 2004): B1.

Ethnic, Racial, and Religious Subcultures

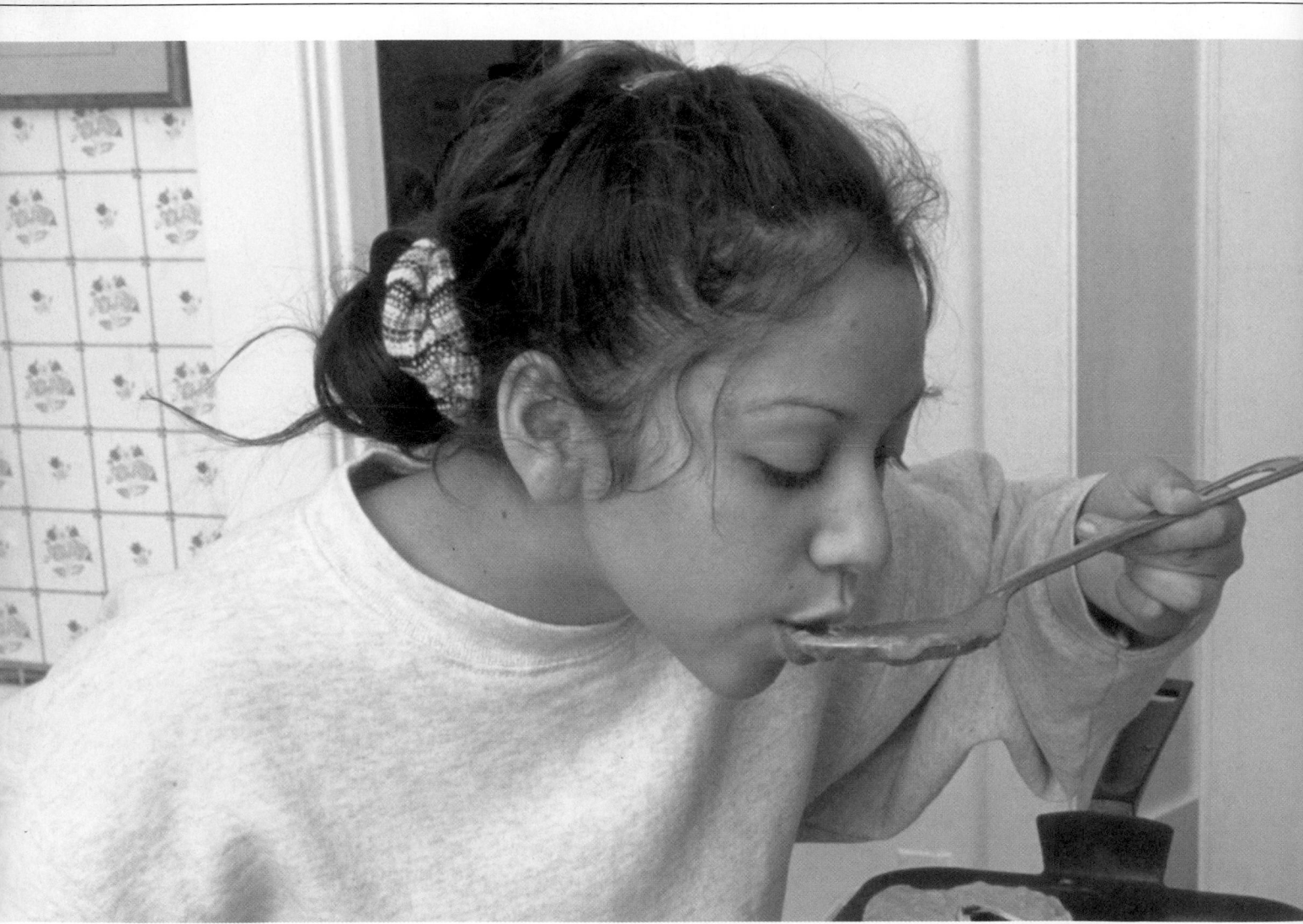

Chapter Objectives

When you finish this chapter you should understand why:

- Our memberships in ethnic, racial, and religious subcultures often play a big role in guiding our consumption behaviors.

- Additional influences come from our identification with microcultures that reflect a shared interest in some organization or activity.

- Many marketing messages appeal to ethnic and racial identity.

- African Americans, Hispanic Americans, and Asian Americans are the three most important ethnic/racial subcultures in the United States.

- Marketers increasingly use religious and spiritual themes when they talk to consumers.

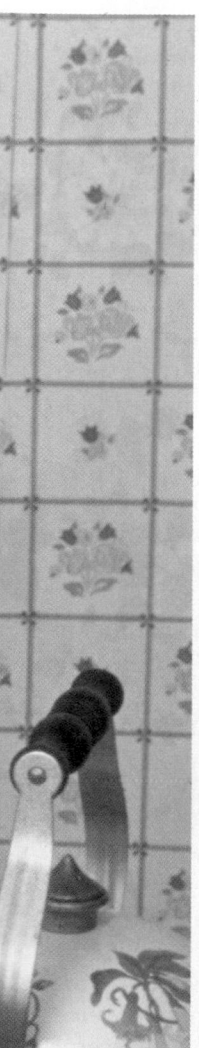

maria wakes up early on Saturday morning and braces herself for a long day of errands and chores. As usual, her mother is at work and expects Maria to do the shopping and help prepare dinner for the big family gathering tonight. Of course, her older brother José would never be asked to do the grocery shopping or help out in the kitchen—these are women's jobs.

Family gatherings make a lot of work, and Maria wishes that her mother would use prepared foods once in a while, especially on a Saturday when Maria has an errand or two of her own to do. But no, her mother insists on preparing most of her food from scratch. She rarely uses any convenience products, to ensure that the meals she serves are of the highest quality.

Resigned, Maria watches a *telenovela* (soap opera) on Univision while she's getting dressed, and then she heads down to the *carnicería* (small grocery store) to buy a newspaper—there are almost 40 different Spanish newspapers published in her area, and she likes to pick up new ones occasionally. Then Maria buys the grocery items her mother wants; the list is full of well-known brand names that she gets all the time, such as Casera and Goya, so she's able to finish quickly. With any luck, she'll have a few minutes to go to the *mercado* (shopping center) to pick up that new Latin hip-hop CD by Los Rhythm Kings that Quepasa.com raved about.[1] She'll listen to it in the kitchen while she chops, peels, and stirs.

Maria smiles to herself: Los Angeles is a great place to live and what could be better than spending a lively, fun evening with *la familia*.

Subcultures, Microcultures, and Consumer Identity

Yes, Maria lives in Los Angeles, not Mexico City. More than one in four Californians are Hispanic, and overall the state has more nonwhite than white residents. In fact, more people watch Spanish-language Univision in L.A. than any other network.[2] If current trends continue, demographers say the entire United States will have a non-white majority by the year 2050.[3]

Maria and other Hispanic Americans have much in common with members of other racial and ethnic groups who live in the United States. They observe the same national holidays, the country's economic health affects what they spend, and they may root for Team USA in the Olympics. Nonetheless, American citizenship may provide the raw material for some consumption decisions, but the enormous variations in the social fabric of the country profoundly affect many others. The United States truly is a "melting pot" of hundreds of diverse and interesting groups, from Italian and Irish Americans to Mormons and Seventh-Day Adventists.

Our group memberships *within* our society-at-large help to define us. A **subculture** is a group whose members share beliefs and common experiences that set them apart from others. Every one of us belongs to many subcultures, depending on our age, race, ethnic background, or place of residence. Maria's Hispanic heritage exerts a huge influence on her everyday experience and consumption preferences.

In contrast to larger, demographically based subcultures (that Nature usually determines), people who are part of a **microculture** freely choose to identify with a lifestyle or aesthetic preference. A good example is the microculture automobile hobbyists call "Tuners." These are single men in their late teens and early 20s, usually in Latino or Asian communities, who share a passion for fast cars, high-tech auto upgrades, and specialized car parts. This microculture started with late-night meets among illegal street racers in New York and L.A. Now, Tuners are more mainstream; magazines including *Import Tuner* and *Sport Compact Car* and major companies such as Pioneer eagerly court these high-tech hot-rodders. A commercial the Honda Civic targeted to Hispanic American consumers showed a fleet of cars in different colors with customized features such as chrome rims and tinted windows.[4]

Whether Tuners, Dead Heads, or skinheads, each microculture exhibits its own unique set of norms, vocabulary, and product insignias (for example, the Grateful Dead subculture's distinctive skulls and roses). A study of contemporary "mountain men" in the western United States illustrates the binding influence of a microculture on its members. Researchers found that group members shared a strong sense of identity they expressed in weekend retreats, where they reinforced these ties by using authentic items like *tipis*, buffalo robes, buckskin leggings, and beaded moccasins to create a sense of community among fellow mountain men.[5]

These microcultures can even gel around fictional characters and events, and they often play a key role in defining the extended self (see Chapter 5). Many devotees of *Star Trek,* for example, immerse themselves in a make-believe world of starships, phasers, and Vulcan mind melds. Our microcultures typically command fierce loyalty: *Star Trek* fans are notorious for their devotion to the cause, as this excerpt from a fan's e-mail illustrates:

> I have to admit to keeping pretty quiet about my devotion to the show for many years simply because people do tend to view a *Trek* fan as weird or crazy.... [after attending her first convention she says] Since then I have proudly worn my Bajoran earring and not cared about the looks I get from others.... I have also met ... other *Trek* fans and some

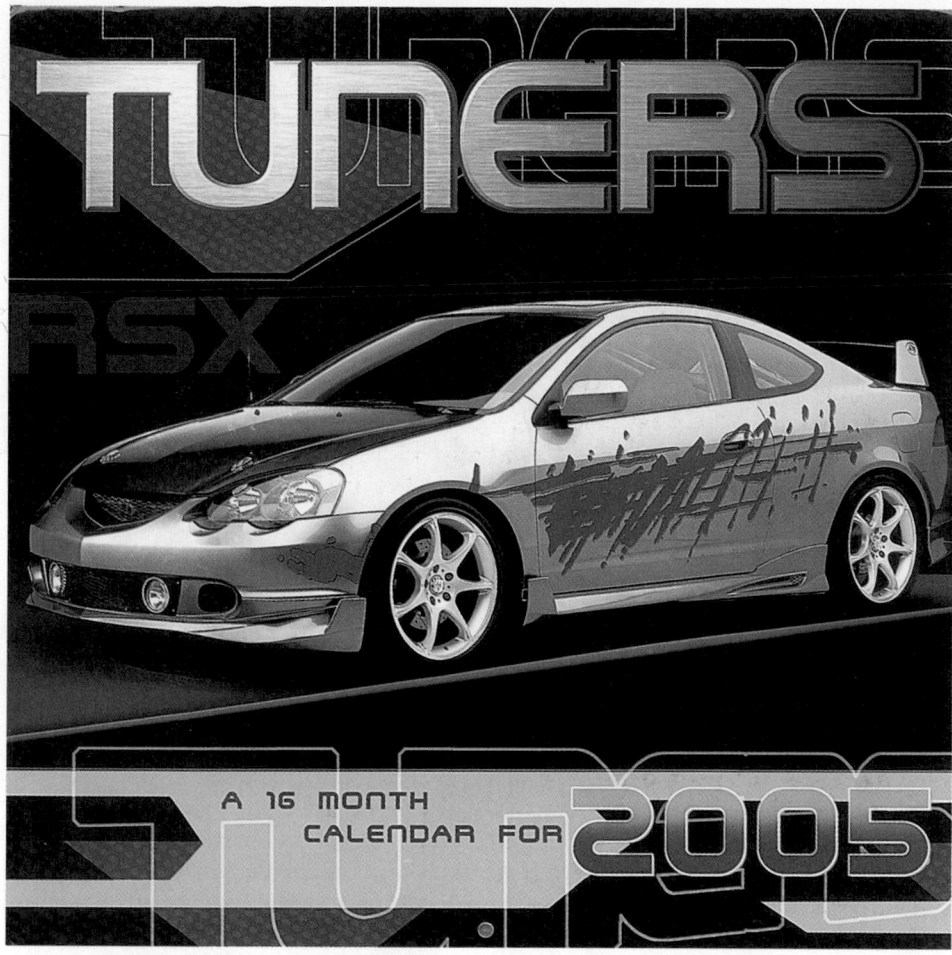

Many specialized products appeal specifically to the Tuner microculture.

of these people have become very close friends. We have a lot in common and have had some of the same experiences as concerns our love of *Trek*.[6]

Star Trek is a merchandising empire that continues to beam up millions of dollars in revenues. Needless to say, it's not alone in this regard. Numerous other microcultures are out there, thriving on their collective worship of mythical and not-so-mythical worlds and characters ranging from the music group Phish to Hello Kitty.

Trend trackers find some of the most interesting—and rapidly changing— microcultures in Japan, where young women start many trends that eventually make their way around the world (more on this in Chapter 17). One emerging microculture to watch is *Onna Otaku* (she-nerds), girls who get their geek on by stocking up on femme-friendly comics, gadgets, and action figures instead of makeup and clothes. According to one insider, these are some ways to identify an *Onna Otaku*:

- Generic jeans, shirts, and sneakers (with price tag left on)
- Virtual puppies on her Nintendo DS that she feeds and walks every hour
- Phone worn clipped on pocket to look "technical"; it features high-tech add-ons including a 3-megapixel camera, built-in smartcard purchasing, TV tuner, MP3 player, and browser
- Eats beef bowls and habanero snack chips she buys at 7-Eleven
- A laptop that holds a script for the Sailor Moon/Anakin Skywalker *doujinshi* (fan comic), links to manga release schedules and <u>2ch.net</u> (think Slashdot)
- Under her mattress: *Boy's Love* comics[7]

Net Profit

King for a day? Sure, the Internet allows people to form their own microcultures— but how about your own nation? Numerous "micronations" exist in cyberspace, some complete with their own monarchs and constitutions. Here's a sampler of these cybermicrocultures:[8]

- **The Kingdom of Talossa** (<u>kingdom oftalossa.net</u>): The King of Talossa lives with his father and sister near the University of Wisconsin–Milwaukee campus. At age 14 (more than 20 years ago), he proclaimed his bedroom a sovereign nation. The name of the country comes from a Finnish word meaning "inside the house." The roughly 60 citizens of Talossa have a body of law, four political parties, an online journal, local holidays, and even a flag. They also have their own language and maintain a dictionary with 28,000 entries.
- **The Principality of Freedonia** (<u>free donia.org</u>): This micronation is a Boston-based collective of libertarians. Its monarch is a former Babson College student who goes by the name of Prince John I. Members have minted their own line of currency, but for now the capital of the country is Prince John's house.
- **The Principality of New Utopia** (<u>new-utopia.com</u>): This micronation proposes to build a chain of islands in international waters and sells citizenship bonds over the Web for $1,500. The country's founder goes by the name of Prince Lazarus Long. Buyer beware: The Prince does not have the best of diplomatic relations with the Securities Exchange Commission because of these sales.

Want to start your own micronation? Visit <u>www.geocities.com/micronations/</u> for instructions.

Some microcultures exist on the fringes of mainstream society. Piaggio SpA, the Italian firm that manufacturers Vespa scooters, lets each of the 85 merchants that sell its product in the United States decide how to sell the brand here.

ETHNIC AND RACIAL SUBCULTURES

An **ethnic subculture** is a self-perpetuating group of consumers who share common cultural or genetic ties, where both its members and others recognize it as a distinct category.[9] In some countries like Japan, ethnicity is virtually synonymous with the dominant culture because most citizens claim the same homogenous cultural ties (although even Japan has sizable minority populations, most notably people of Korean ancestry). In a heterogeneous society such as the United States, which incorporates many different cultures, consumers expend great effort to keep their subcultural identification from being submerged into the mainstream of the dominant society.

Ethnic and racial Subcultural

The Kingdom of Talossa home page.

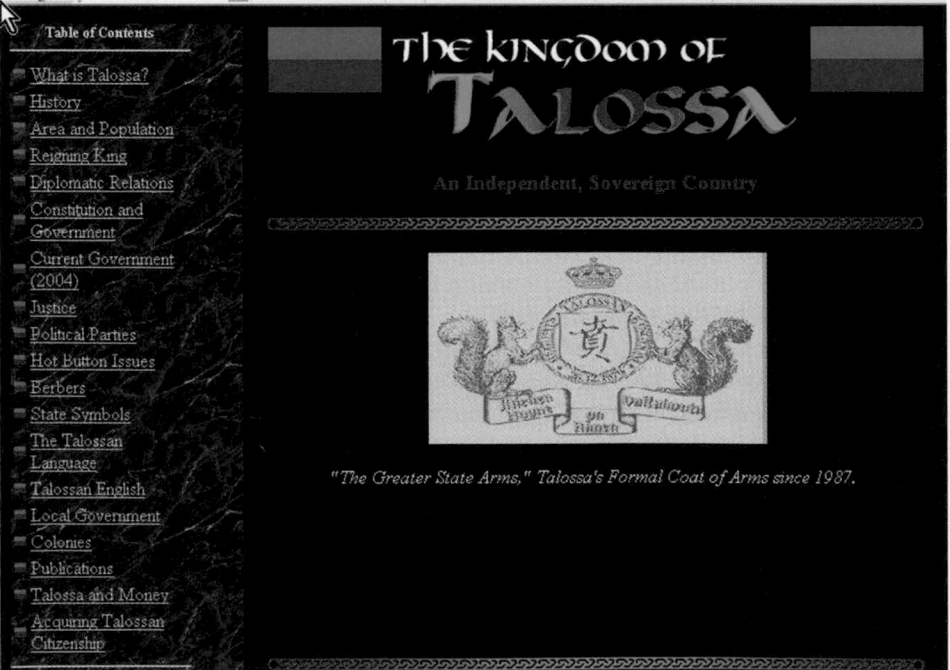

"The Greater State Arms," Talossa's Formal Coat of Arms since 1987.

Marketers cannot ignore the stunning diversity of cultures that are reshaping many mainstream societies. Ethnic minorities in the United States spend more than $600 billion a year on products and services, so firms must tailor products and communications strategies to their unique needs. And this vast market is growing all the time: Immigrants now make up 10 percent of the U.S. population and will account for 13 percent by 2050.[10] This important change encourages advertisers to rethink their old strategies, which assumed that virtually all of their customers were Caucasians hailing from Western Europe. For example, as part of Crest toothpaste's fiftieth-anniversary celebration, Procter & Gamble revived its "Crest Kid," who first appeared as an apple-cheeked urchin Norman Rockwell illustrated in 1956. Now, a Cuban-born girl plays the character. An independent panel chose her because of her sparkling smile, but it's significant that this mainstream American figure now is Hispanic.[11]

Almost half of all *Fortune* 1000 companies have an ethnic marketing program up and running. For example, AT&T sponsors Chinese Dragon Boat Festival races and Cuban folk festivals; it also airs advertisements it aims at 30 different cultures, including messages in languages such as Tagalog, which Filipinos speak, and Twi, a West African dialect. As AT&T's director of multicultural marketing observed, "Marketing today is part anthropology."[12] It makes good business sense to cater to these segments by (literally) speaking their language when promoting products and services: Surveys repeatedly show that members of ethnic groups get much of their product information from specialized ethnic media; one found that 63 percent of ethnic Californians watch native-language TV daily and a third of them also read an ethnic newspaper at least once a week.[13] The advertisements that people who view these media see ideally should match up with the way they communicate in daily life.

One important subcultural difference is how abstract or literal the group is. Sociologists make a basic distinction: In a **high-context culture,** group members tend to be tightly knit, and they infer meanings that go beyond the spoken word. Symbols and gestures, rather than words, carry much of the weight of the message. In contrast, people in a **low-context culture** are more literal. Compared to Anglos (who tend to be low-context), many minority cultures are high-context and have strong oral traditions, so consumers are more sensitive to nuances in advertisements that go beyond the message copy.[14]

Ethnicity and Marketing Strategies

Although some people feel uncomfortable with the notion that marketers should explicitly take into account people's racial and ethnic differences when they formulate their strategies, the reality is that these subcultural memberships do shape many consumers' needs and wants. Research indicates, for example, that members of minority groups find an advertising spokesperson from their own group more trustworthy, and this enhanced credibility in turn translates into more positive brand attitudes.[15] However, marketers need to avoid the pitfall of painting all members of an ethnic or racial group with the same brush; these generalizations not only are inaccurate but they also are likely to turn off the very people a company wants to reach.[16]

Is Ethnicity a Moving Target?

Although ethnic marketing is in vogue with many firms, to actually define and target members of a distinct ethnic group is not always so easy in our "melting pot" society. In the 2000 U.S. Census, some 7 million people identified with two or more races, refusing to describe themselves as only white, black, Asian, Korean, Samoan, or one of the other racial categories.[17]

The popularity of golfer Tiger Woods illuminates the complexity of ethnic identity in the United States. Although we laud Tiger as an African American role model, in reality he is a model of multiracialism. His mother is Thai, and he also has Caucasian and Indian ancestry. Other popular multiracial celebrities include actor Keanu Reeves (Hawaiian, Chinese, and Caucasian), singer Mariah Carey (black Venezuelan and white), and Dean Cain of Superman fame (Japanese and Caucasian).[18]

Bagels have been deethnicized and are now part of mainstream culture.

Marketing Pitfall

The mass merchandising of ethnic products is a growing practice. Native American Aztec designs appear on sweaters, gym shoes come in *kente* cloth from an African tribe, and greeting cards bear likenesses of Native American sand paintings. However, some worry about the borrowing—and in some cases, misinterpretation—of distinctive symbolism. Consider, for example, the storm of protest from the international Islamic community over a dress in a House of Chanel fashion show. Supermodel Claudia Schiffer wore a strapless evening gown (with a price tag of almost $23,000) that Karl Lagerfeld designed. The dress included Arabic letters that the designer believed spelled out a love poem. Instead, the message was a verse from the Koran, the Muslim holy book. To add insult to injury, the word "God" happened to appear over the model's right breast. Both the designer and the model received death threats, and the controversy subsided only after the company burned the dress. More recently, Nike caught flak from activists when in late 2007 it introduced an athletic shoe specially designed for Native Americans. Along with its trademark swoosh, the Nike Air Native N7 features feathers and arrowheads. One young Spokane/Coeur d'Alene Indian commented, "The day it was announced, I thought: 'Are they going to have dream catchers on them? Are they going to be beaded? Will they have native bumper stickers on them that say, 'Custer had it coming'?"[21, 22]

Products that companies market with an ethnic appeal don't always intend that only people from that subculture will use the product. **Deethnicization** occurs when a product we associate with a specific ethnic group detaches itself from its roots and appeals to other groups as well. Think about the popularity of bagels, a staple of Jewish cuisine that's mass marketed. Recent variations include jalapeño bagels, blueberry bagels, and even a green bagel for St. Patrick's Day.[19] Bagels now account for 3 to 6 percent of all American breakfasts, and bagel franchisers such as Bruegger's Corporation and the Einstein/Noah Bagel Corporation operate hundreds of stores in cities that had never heard of a bagel just a few years ago.[20]

NEW ETHNIC GROUPS

The dominant American culture historically exerted pressure on immigrants to divest themselves of their origins and integrate with mainstream society. As President Theodore Roosevelt put it in the early part of the twentieth century, "We welcome the German or the Irishman who becomes an American. We have no use for the German or the Irishman who remains such."[23]

Indeed, there is a tendency for ethnic groups with a relatively longer history of settling in the United States to view themselves as more mainstream and relax their identification with their country of origin. When the 2000 U.S. Census asked respondents to write up to two ancestries that defined their background, the results showed a clear decline in the number of people who identified themselves as of Irish, German, or other European origin. Compared to other subcultures, more people from these countries simply choose to call themselves "American."[24]

The bulk of American immigrants historically came from Europe, but immigration patterns have shifted dramatically. New immigrants are much more likely to be Asian or Hispanic. As these new waves of immigrants settle in the United States, marketers try to track their consumption patterns and adjust their strategies accordingly. It's best to market to these new arrivals—whether Arabs, Asians,

■ FIGURE 14.1 AMERICA'S NEWEST MARKETS

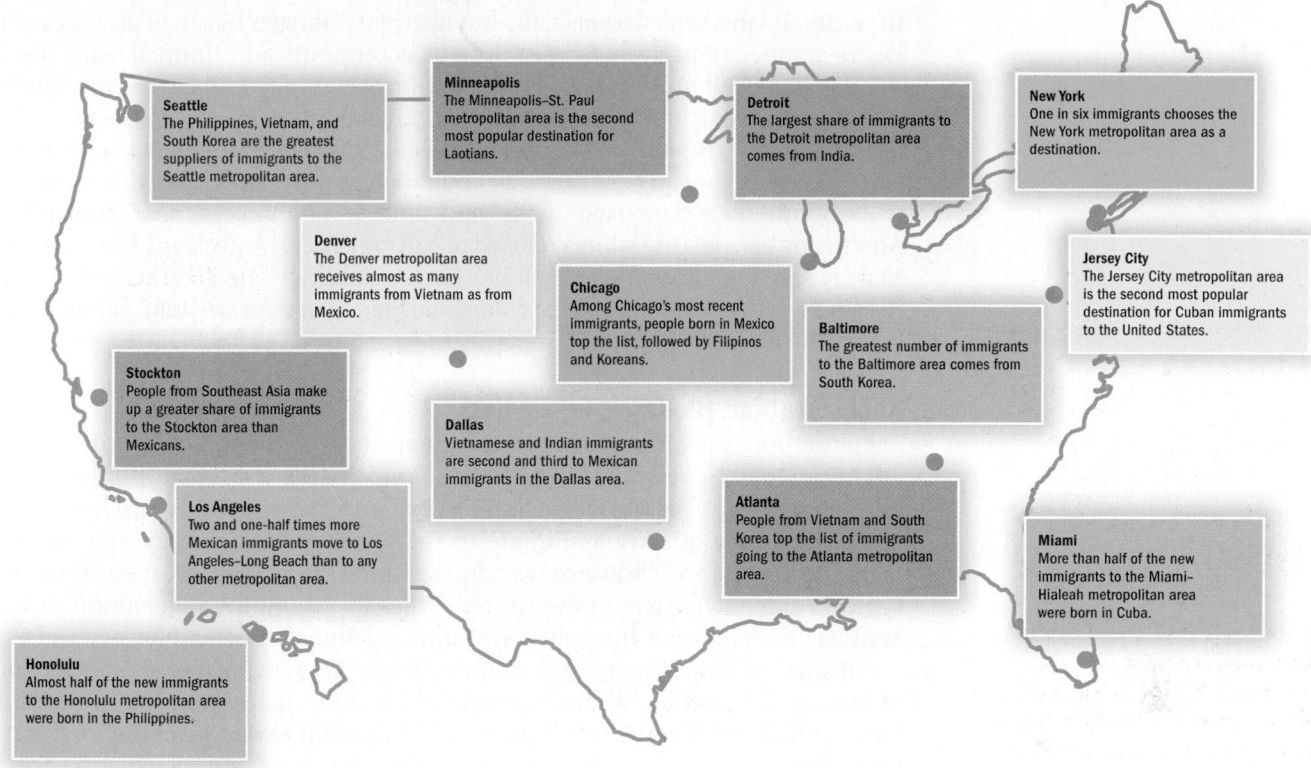

Seattle
The Philippines, Vietnam, and South Korea are the greatest suppliers of immigrants to the Seattle metropolitan area.

Minneapolis
The Minneapolis–St. Paul metropolitan area is the second most popular destination for Laotians.

Detroit
The largest share of immigrants to the Detroit metropolitan area comes from India.

New York
One in six immigrants chooses the New York metropolitan area as a destination.

Denver
The Denver metropolitan area receives almost as many immigrants from Vietnam as from Mexico.

Chicago
Among Chicago's most recent immigrants, people born in Mexico top the list, followed by Filipinos and Koreans.

Baltimore
The greatest number of immigrants to the Baltimore area comes from South Korea.

Jersey City
The Jersey City metropolitan area is the second most popular destination for Cuban immigrants to the United States.

Stockton
People from Southeast Asia make up a greater share of immigrants to the Stockton area than Mexicans.

Dallas
Vietnamese and Indian immigrants are second and third to Mexican immigrants in the Dallas area.

Los Angeles
Two and one-half times more Mexican immigrants move to Los Angeles–Long Beach than to any other metropolitan area.

Atlanta
People from Vietnam and South Korea top the list of immigrants going to the Atlanta metropolitan area.

Miami
More than half of the new immigrants to the Miami–Hialeah metropolitan area were born in Cuba.

Honolulu
Almost half of the new immigrants to the Honolulu metropolitan area were born in the Philippines.

Russians, or people of Caribbean descent—in their native languages. They tend to cluster together geographically, which makes them easy to reach. The local community is the primary source for information and advice, so word of mouth is especially important (see Chapter 11). Figure 14.1 shows how new waves of immigrants are changing the ethnic composition of major American cities.

ETHNIC AND RACIAL STEREOTYPES

A controversial Taco Bell television commercial illustrates how marketers (intentionally or not) use ethnic and racial stereotypes to craft promotional communications. The spot for the restaurant's Wild Burrito featured dark-skinned "natives" with painted faces who danced around in loincloths. Following an uproar in the African American community, Taco Bell withdrew the ad.[25]

Many subcultures have powerful stereotypes the general public associates with them. In these cases outsiders assume that group members possess certain traits. Unfortunately, a communicator can cast the same trait as either positive or negative, depending on his biases or intentions. For example, the Scottish stereotype in the United States is largely positive, so we tend to look favorably on their (supposed) frugality. 3M uses Scottish imagery to denote value (e.g., Scotch tape), as does the Scotch Inns, a motel chain that offers inexpensive lodging. However, invoking the Scottish "personality" might carry quite different connotations to the British or Irish. One person's "thrifty" is another's "stingy."

In the past, American marketers used ethnic symbolism as shorthand to convey certain product attributes. They often employed crude and unflattering images when they depicted African Americans as subservient or Mexicans as bandits.[26] Aunt Jemima sold pancake mix and Rastus was a grinning black chef who pitched Cream of Wheat hot cereal. The Gold Dust Twins were black urchins who peddled a soap powder for Lever Brothers and Pillsbury hawked powdered drink mixes using characters such as

Injun Orange and Chinese Cherry—who had buck teeth.[27] As the U.S. Civil Rights Movement gave more power to minority groups and their rising economic status began to command marketers' respect, these negative stereotypes began to disappear. Frito-Lay responded to protests by the Hispanic community and stopped using the Frito Bandito character in 1971, and Quaker Foods gave Aunt Jemima a makeover in 1989.

Now, the Mars company is taking an interesting risk with its Uncle Ben's rice brand. For more than 60 years, packages featured the black Uncle Ben character. He wore a bow tie evocative of servants and Pullman porters, and his title reflects how white Southerners once used "uncle" and "aunt" as honorary names for older African Americans because the whites refused to call the African Americans "Mr." and "Mrs." Mars is reviving the character, but he's been remade as Ben, an accomplished businessman with an opulent office who shares his "grains of wisdom" about rice and life on the brand's Web site.[28]

Acculturation: Blending In (or Not)

Acculturation is the process of movement and adaptation to one country's cultural environment by a person from another country.[29] This is a very important issue for marketers because of our increasingly global society. As people move from place to place, they may quickly assimilate to their new homes or they may resist this blending process and choose to insulate themselves from the mainstream culture. It's typical for a new arrival in the United States for example to feel ambivalence or conflict about relinquishing old ways (and consumer behaviors) for new ones.

A study of Mexican immigrants to the United States using the research technique of *ethnography* probed their acculturation as they adapted to life in the United States.[30] Indeed, after the researchers interviewed these people in their natural settings they reported a lot of ambivalence. On the one hand, they are happy about the improvements in the quality of their lives because of greater job availability and educational opportunities for their children. On the other hand, they report bittersweet feelings about leaving Mexico. They miss their friends, their holidays, their food, and the comfort that comes from living in familiar surroundings.

As Figure 14.2 shows, many factors affect the nature of the transition process. Individual differences, such as whether the person speaks English, influence how rocky the adjustment will be. The person's contact with **acculturation agents**—people

■ FIGURE 14.2
A MODEL OF CONSUMER ACCULTURATION
Source: Lisa Peñaloza, "*Atravesando Fronteras*/Border Crossings: A Critical Ethnographic Exploration of the Consumer Acculturation of Mexican Immigrants," *Journal of Consumer Research* (June 1994): 32–54. Copyright © 1994 JCR, Inc. Used by permission of University of Chicago Press.

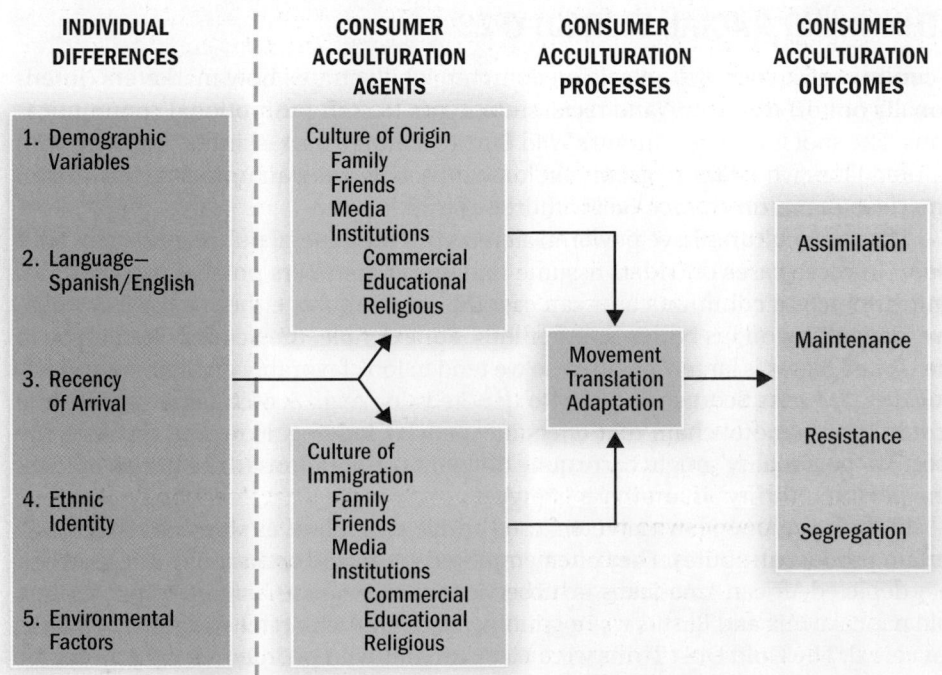

and institutions that teach the ways of a culture—are also crucial. Some of these agents come from the *culture of origin* (in this case, Mexico), including family, friends, the church, local businesses, and Spanish-language media that keep the consumer in touch with his country of origin. Other agents come from the *culture of immigration* (in this case, America), and help the consumer to learn how to navigate in the new environment. These include public schools, English-language media, and government agencies.

Several processes come into play as immigrants adapt to their new surroundings. *Movement* refers to the factors that motivate people to physically uproot themselves from one location and go to another. In this case, people leave Mexico because of the scarcity of jobs and the desire to provide a good education for their children. On arrival, immigrants encounter a need for *translation*. This means the attempt to master a set of rules for operating in the new environment, whether learning how to decipher a different currency or figuring out the social meanings of unfamiliar clothing styles. This cultural learning leads to a process of *adaptation,* by which people form new consumption patterns. For example, some of the Mexican women in the study started to wear shorts and pants once they settled in the United States, although people in Mexico frown on this practice.

During the acculturation process, many immigrants undergo *assimilation,* where they adopt products, habits, and values they identify with the mainstream culture. At the same time, there is an attempt at *maintenance* of practices they associate with the culture of origin. Immigrants stay in touch with people in their country and, like Maria, many continue to eat Spanish foods and read Spanish newspapers. Their continued identification with Mexican culture may cause *resistance,* as they resent the pressure to submerge their Mexican identities and take on new roles. Finally, immigrants (voluntarily or not) tend to exhibit *segregation*; they are likely to live and shop in places physically separated from mainstream Anglo consumers. These processes illustrate that ethnicity is a fluid concept and that members of a subculture are constantly recreating its boundaries.

The **progressive learning model** helps us to understand the acculturation process. This perspective assumes that people gradually learn a new culture as they increasingly come in contact with it. Thus, we expect that when people acculturate they will mix the practices of their original culture with those of their new or **host culture.**[31] Research generally supports this pattern when it examines such factors as shopping orientation, the importance people place on various product attributes, media preference, and brand loyalty.[32] When researchers take into account the intensity of ethnic identification, they find that consumers who retain a strong ethnic identification differ from their more assimilated counterparts in these ways:[33]

- They have a more negative attitude toward business in general (probably caused by frustration as a result of relatively low income levels).
- They are higher users of media that's in their native language.
- They are more brand loyal.
- They are more likely to prefer brands with prestige labels.
- They are more likely to buy brands that specifically advertise to their ethnic group.

The acculturation process embraces all kinds of moves, including those that involve relocating from one place to another within the same country. If you have ever moved (and it's likely you have), you no doubt remember how difficult it was to give up old habits and friends and adapt to what people in your new location do. A recent study of Turkish people who move from the countryside to an urban environment illustrates how people cope with change and unfamiliar circumstances. The authors describe a process of **warming,** which they describe as transforming objects and places into those that feel cozy, hospitable, and authentic. The study's informants described the process of turning a cold and unfamiliar house into a home as *güzel* ("beautiful and good," "modern and warm"). In this context that means incorporating symbols of village life into their new homes by blanketing them with the embroidered, crocheted, and lace textiles that people traditionally make by hand for brides' dowries in the villages. The researchers reported that migrants' homes contained far more of these pieces than they would have in their village homes because they used them to adorn the modern appliances they acquired. The dowry textiles symbolize traditional norms and social networks composed of friends and family in the villages, so they link the "cold" modern objects with the owner's past. Thus, the unfamiliar becomes familiar.[34]

Another group of researchers examined the plight of people who were forced to leave their homes and settle in a foreign country with little planning and few possessions.[35] As "strangers in a strange land," they must essentially start over and completely resocialize. The authors did an in-depth study of refugees from a number of countries who lived in an Austrian refugee shelter. They found, for example, that teenagers are traumatized by their experience and turn to adaptive consumption strategies to cope. For example, the adolescents all have stuffed animals (including the boys) they use to comfort themselves. And all of the teenage boys wore earrings as a way to create their own community.

THE "BIG THREE" AMERICAN SUBCULTURES

African Americans, Hispanic Americans, and Asian Americans account for much of America's current growth. According to the 2000 U.S. Census, the Hispanic population is now the largest ethnic subculture, with 12.5 percent of Americans.[36] Asian Americans, though much smaller in absolute numbers with only 3.6 percent of the population, are the fastest-growing racial group.[37]

African Americans

African Americans comprise a significant racial subculture; they were 12.3 percent of the U.S. population in the 2000 Census.[38] Although African American consumers do differ in important ways from Caucasians, the African American market is hardly as homogenous as many marketers seem to believe. Indeed, some commentators argue that black–white differences are largely illusory. With some exceptions, both groups have the same overall spending patterns; they allocate about two-thirds of their incomes to housing, transportation, and food.[39]

The differences we do observe more likely are the result of differences in income, the relatively high concentration of African Americans in urban areas, and other dimensions of social class we discussed in Chapter 13. And these differences continue to diminish as African American consumers move up the economic ladder. Although it is still lower than the white majority, their median household income is at an historic high. We can trace this improvement directly to a steady increase in educational attainment. African Americans had a median household income of $30,439 in 2000, up from $18,676 in 1990, and more than 51 percent of married African Americans make $50,000 or more.[40]

Nonetheless, there clearly are some differences between American blacks and whites in consumption priorities and marketplace behaviors that demand marketers' attention.[41] In late 2007, Procter & Gamble launched a new program it calls "My Black Is Beautiful" for African American women after the company's research told it that these women think they are represented poorly in the mainstream media. The campaign includes a discussion guide booklet to encourage women to facilitate dialogue in their local communities and a supporting Web site at myblackisbeautiful.com. P&G found that almost three-quarters of these consumers say they are portrayed worse than other racial groups and that these messages have a negative impact on teens.[42]

Sometimes these differences are subtle but they still can be important. When Coffee-Mate discovered that African Americans tend to drink their coffee with sugar and cream much more than do Caucasians, the company mounted a promotional blitz in the African American media and in return benefited from double-digit increases in sales volume and market share for this segment.[43] Volvo North America created its first advertising campaign targeting African Americans after research showed that car crashes are the leading cause of death among African American children, who are half as likely to use seat belts as other children.[44]

New research by Unilever illustrates how *body cathexis* dynamics (see Chapter 5) vary across subcultures; it finds that skin takes on a deeper meaning for African Americans. In a poll it ran in *Essence* magazine, the company asked more than 1,400 African American women aged 18 to 64 to describe their skin, and the most common response was "beautiful" (59 percent). Another 30 percent described their skin as "strong." The survey also found that African American women rank skin as "most important to them" (49 percent) above their hair, figure, makeup, and clothes. About one-third say their skin is a source of their heritage, one-fourth say it's a source of pride, and "almost half of African American women say their skin tells a story of who they are and identifies them," the company says. The survey is part of Unilever's Skinvoice campaign, where the company invites women to talk about their skin at skinvoice.com. This deep attachment is clear in posted comments such as "My skin is my life's historian," and "My skin represents the blending of my parents, an outward expression of their love."[45]

Hispanic Americans

The umbrella term *Hispanic* describes people of many different backgrounds. According to the 2000 U.S. Census, nearly 60 percent of Hispanic Americans are of Mexican descent. The next largest group, Puerto Ricans, make up just fewer than 10 percent of Hispanics. Other groups the Census includes in this category are Central Americans, Dominicans, South Americans, and Cubans.

One of AOL's Web sites for Hispanics.

The Tangled Web

The release of several popular video games underscores the concern of some critics who argue that these games play on racial stereotypes, including images of African American youths committing and reveling in violent street crime:

- *Grand Theft Auto:* San Andreas is set in a city resembling gang-ridden stretches of Los Angeles of the 1990s. It features a digital cast of African American and Hispanic men, some wearing braided hair and scarves over their faces and aiming Uzis from low-riding cars.

- *Def Jam Fight for NY* features hip-hop-style characters (one with the voice of the rapper Snoop Dogg) who slap, kick, and pummel one another in locations such as the 125th Street train station in Harlem.

- *25 to Life* is an "urban action game" that includes a hip-hop soundtrack. It lets gamers play the role of police officers or criminals, and includes lots of images of young gun-toting African American gangsters.

- *Notorious: Die to Drive* features "gangsta-style car combat" with players seeking to "rule the streets of four West Coast neighborhoods." The game's Web site proclaims, "High-priced honeys, the finest bling, and millionaire cribs are just some of the rewards for the notorious few who can survive this most dangerous game. Once you go Notorious, there's no going back."[46]

The Hispanic subculture is a sleeping giant that many U.S. marketers ignored until recently. The growth and increasing affluence of this group has now made it impossible to overlook, and major corporations avidly court Hispanic consumers such as Maria and her family. From 1990 to 2006, Hispanics' disposable income rose by 832 percent, to $798 billion, compared with 154 percent for the rest of the population.

In addition, the Hispanic population is young: Thirty-four percent were younger than age 18 in 2004, compared with 25 percent for the total population. Marketers especially like the fact that Hispanics tend to be brand loyal. In one study, about 45 percent reported that they always buy their usual brand, whereas only one in five said they frequently switch brands.[47] Another study found that Hispanics who strongly identify with their ethnic origin are more likely to seek Hispanic vendors, to be loyal to brands used by family and friends, and to be influenced by Hispanic media.[48]

This segment also concentrates geographically by country of origin, which makes them relatively easy to reach. More than 50 percent of all Hispanic Americans live in the Los Angeles, New York, Miami, San Antonio, San Francisco, and Chicago metropolitan areas.[49]

One roadblock for mainstream marketers is the relatively low degree of acculturation among some Hispanic consumers who don't choose to assimilate. About 38 percent of all Hispanics live in *barrios*, or predominantly Hispanic neighborhoods, which tend to be somewhat insulated from mainstream society.[50]

For this reason, native language and culture are important components of Hispanic identity and self-esteem (about three-quarters of Hispanics still speak Spanish at home), and many Hispanic Americans appreciate marketing efforts that acknowledge their cultural heritage.[51] More than 40 percent say they deliberately attempt to buy products that show an interest in the Hispanic consumer, and this number jumps to more than two-thirds for Cuban Americans.[52] Still, the acculturation process inevitably means that over time these differences will probably narrow. Whereas 73 percent of Hispanic immigrants prefer the Spanish language to English, the number falls to 25 percent of their children and only 1 percent of their grandchildren. With a larger proportion of Hispanics being born in the United States,

Tide detergent targets Hispanic consumers.

TABLE 14.1 SEGMENTING THE HISPANIC AMERICAN SUBCULTURE BY DEGREE OF ACCULTURATION				
Segment	**Size**	**Status**	**Description**	**Characteristics**
Established adapters	17%	Upwardly mobile	Older, U.S.-born; assimilated into U.S. culture	Relatively low identification with Hispanic culture
Young strivers	16%	Increasingly important	Younger, born in U.S.; highly motivated to succeed; adaptable to U.S. culture	Movement to reconnect with Hispanic roots
Hopeful loyalists	40%	Largest but shrinking	Working class; attached to traditional values	Slow to adapt to U.S. culture; Spanish is dominant language
Recent seekers	27%	Growing	Newest; very conservative with high aspirations	Strongest identification with Hispanic background; little use of non-Hispanic media

Source: Adapted from a report by Yankelovich Clancy Shulman, described in "A Subculture with Very Different Needs," *Adweek* (May 11, 1992): 44. By permission of Yankelovich Partners, Inc.

experts predict that English will increasingly supplant Spanish as the most effective language for marketing messages.

However, third-generation Hispanics, born in the United States, still retain a strong sense of Hispanic identity and heritage that creates demand for publications such as *Urban Latino* that cater to the "new generation Latino." This demand also fuels the emergence of a new, mostly English-language radio genre, "hurban" ("Hispanic Urban").[53] Table 14.1 describes one attempt to segment Hispanic consumers in terms of their degree of acculturation.

Many initial efforts to market to Hispanic Americans were, to say the least, counterproductive. Companies bumbled in their efforts to translate advertising adequately or to compose copy that captured the nuances advertisers intended. These mistakes do not occur so much anymore because marketers are more sophisticated in dealing with this segment and tend to involve Hispanics in advertising production to ensure they are getting it right. These translation mishaps slipped through before Anglos got their acts together:[56]

- The Perdue slogan, "It takes a tough man to make a tender chicken," translated as "It takes a sexually excited man to make a chick affectionate."
- Budweiser was the "queen of beers."
- Braniff (now defunct), promoting the comfortable leather seats on its airplanes, used the headline, *Sentado en cuero,* which translates as "Sit naked."
- Coors beer's slogan to "get loose with Coors" appeared in Spanish as "get the runs with Coors."

Even today, confused meanings create problems for some well-intentioned marketers. In 2007, a division of Macy's department stores pulled a T-shirt it intended to sell to Hispanic shoppers in Georgia and Texas that proclaimed "Brown is the New White."[57] In another gaffe, Volkswagen caught flak when it tried to attract Hispanic drivers to its GTI 2006 model with a word they would recognize. Americans use the Spanish word "cojones" to describe a gutsy person, but literally it means testicles. Billboards in huge black letters proclaimed "Turbo-Cojones." VW removed the boards in Cuban-dominated Miami following an outcry. As one local commented, "In English, Turbo-Balls might not sound so offensive. But in the Spanish-speaking community, it will always have a vulgar connotation." It replaced the ads with others that say "Here Today. Gone Tamale" and "Kick a Little Gracias."[58]

The Tangled Web

A 2007 report finds that Hispanic Americans are less likely to use the Internet—overall 56 percent of adults are online as opposed to 71 percent of non-Hispanic whites and 60 percent of non-Hispanic blacks. Lower levels of education and limited English ability largely explain the gap in Internet use. One in three Latinos who speak only Spanish go online, compared to 78 percent of Latinos who are English-dominant and 76 percent of bilingual Latinos. And although 89 percent of Latinos who have college degrees are active online users, this proportion drops to 31 percent for those who did not complete high school. Even holding other factors including age, language, and income constant, Mexicans are least likely to use the Internet.[54] Hopefully, these numbers will shift upward over time. MySpace recently launched a version of its site specifically for U.S. Spanish speakers at latino.myspace.com as well as la.myspace.com, a pan-regional site for Latin American Spanish speakers.[55]

Marketing Pitfall

Mexico has a new tourist attraction: Guests make believe they are illegally crossing the Rio Grande from Mexico into the United States. The four-hour *caminata nocturna* (nighttime hike) traverses desert, hills, brambles, and riverbeds in an eco-park in the state of Hidalgo, about 3 hours northwest of Mexico City (and roughly 700 miles from the U.S. border). The park's owners say they offer tourists a taste of life as an illegal immigrant.[60]

Music crossovers like Shakira are giving mainstream music an Hispanic flavor.

In perhaps a more sophisticated effort, Unilever in 2007 launched *ViveMejor*, a major digital, print, TV, and retail Hispanic marketing program that combines all of its food and personal care brands together in a single marketing platform for Hispanic consumers. The campaign includes a bilingual Web site (ViveMejor.com), a free bilingual magazine Unilever will distribute in stores, and TV segments to run on Spanish-language television. *ViveMejor* was the result of a major research program where Unilever looked in depth at the shopping habits of more than 800 Hispanic consumers. It found these consumers shop more often because they prepare more meals at home, but they enjoy their shopping experiences less than general-market shoppers. They also are more receptive to in-store meal suggestions and recipes than the general population.[59]

Some successful advertising campaigns simply don't work in Hispanic subcultures. For example, the California Milk Processor Board discovered that its hugely successful "Got Milk?" campaign was not well received by Hispanics because biting, sarcastic humor is not part of their culture. In addition, the notion of milk deprivation is not funny to the Hispanic homemaker because running out of milk means she has failed her family. To make matters worse, "Got Milk?" translates as "Are you lactating?" so the organization revised Spanish-language ads as, "And you, have you given them enough milk today?" with tender scenes centered on cooking flan in the family kitchen.[61]

However, there are aspects of U.S. Hispanic culture that make some products popular for reasons Anglos may not understand. This is the case with Clamato, a clam-flavored tomato juice that has gotten a new lease on life thanks to its popularity among Latino consumers. Many Latinos consider the clam to be an aphrodisiac, and the drink is popular among young people who use it as a base for the seafood cocktail *ceviche* or mix it with beer because they believe it arouses passion.[62]

As we saw earlier, one of the most notable characteristics of the Hispanic market is its youth: The median age of Hispanic Americans is 23.6, compared with the U.S. average of 32. Many of these consumers are "young biculturals" who bounce back and forth between hip-hop and *Rock en Español*, blend Mexican rice with

spaghetti sauce, and spread peanut butter and jelly on tortillas.[63] Latino youth are changing mainstream culture. The U.S. Census Bureau estimates that by the year 2020 the number of Hispanic teens will grow by 62 percent compared with 10 percent growth in teens overall. They are looking for spirituality, stronger family ties, and more color in their lives—three hallmarks of Latino culture. Music crossovers are leading the trend, including musicians such as Shakira and Big Pun, the first Latino hip-hop artist to go platinum.

A second notable characteristic of this market is that family size tends to be large. The average U.S. Hispanic household contains 3.5 people, compared to only 2.7 for other U.S. households. These differences obviously affect the overall allocation of income to various product categories. For example, U.S. Hispanic households spend 15 to 20 percent more of their disposable income than the U.S. average on groceries.[64] That helps to explain why General Mills developed a breakfast cereal called Buñuelitos specifically for this market. The brand name is an adaptation of *buñuelos,* a traditional Mexican pastry served on holidays.[65]

We can't overstate the importance of the family to Hispanics such as Maria. Preferences to spend time with family influence the structure of many consumption activities. For this subculture, that's why shopping is a family affair. More than a third (36 percent) of Hispanics say they prefer shopping with their families and 30 percent report that they like shopping with their children.[66] Hispanic parents gravitate to purchases that underscore their ability to provide well for the family. They regard clothing their children well as a matter of pride.

In contrast, convenience and a product's ability to save time are not terribly important to the Hispanic homemaker. Women like Maria's mother are willing to purchase labor-intensive products if it means that their families will benefit. For this reason, a time-saving appeal short-circuited for Quaker Foods when the company discovered that Hispanic women tend to cook Instant Quaker Oats on the stove as if it were regular oatmeal, refrigerate it, and serve it later as a pudding.[67] Similarly, telephone company promotions that emphasize cheaper rates for calling family members offend many Hispanic consumers, who would view deferring a phone call home simply to save money as an insult![68] This orientation also explains why generic products do not tend to do well in the Hispanic market; these consumers value the quality well-known brand names promise.

Asian Americans

Realtors who do business in areas with a high concentration of Asian American buyers adapt to some unique cultural traditions. Asians are very sensitive to the design and location of a home, especially as these affect the home's *chi*—an invisible energy current they believe brings good or bad luck. Asian homebuyers are concerned about whether a prospective house offers a good *feng shui* environment (translated literally as "the wind and the water"). One home developer in San Francisco sold up to 80 percent of its homes to Asian customers after he made a few minor design changes, such as reducing the number of "T" intersections in the houses and adding rounded rocks to the garden—harmful *chi* travels in a straight line, whereas gentle *chi* travels on a curved path.[69]

Marketers are just beginning to recognize Asian Americans' potential as a unique market segment, and some now tailor their products and messages to them. The problems American marketers encountered when they first tried to reach the Hispanic market also occurred when they initially went after Asian Americans:[70]

- The Coca-Cola slogan "Coke Adds Life" was translated as "Coke brings your ancestors back from the dead" in Japanese.
- Kentucky Fried Chicken described its chicken as "finger-lickin' good" to the Chinese, who don't think licking your fingers is very polite.
- A footwear ad depicted Japanese women performing foot-binding, which only the Chinese do.

CB AS I SEE IT

Professor Lisa Peñaloza
*University of Utah and École De
Hautes Études Commerciales du Nord
(EDHEC), Lille and Nice, France*

The Latino/a market is one of the
fastest growing in the United States.
Numbering almost 45 million persons
and with annual spending of just
under $800 billion by 2006, it has
certainly come into its own during the
past 2 decades. No longer do
advertisers have to convince
marketers to target this group; the list
of firms targeting Latinos/as with
products and services includes most
major U.S. and other multinational
producers and distributors of
consumer products and services
across the spectrum, including
appliances, fast foods and beverages,
entertainment, finance, health care,
and communications devices and
media. Yet although it is gratifying to
see Latinos/as in more and more ad
campaigns, films, music, and so on,
is it possible to use this marketing
and media activity to encourage the
development of Latino/a

communities, where the median
family income for Hispanics is
$34,968, compared to $55,885 for
whites, and rates of poverty follow a
similar pattern, with almost 40
percent of Hispanic families living in
poverty compared to 20 percent of
white families?

Many scholars assert that we live
in a consumer society. Although
consumption is increasingly a major
part of our lives, I suggest that our
understanding remains in its infancy,
roughly comparable to the way we
regarded labor at the beginning of the
Industrial Revolution. Like workers
then, most people now don't look at
themselves primarily as consumers;
nor do they think a lot about the ways
consumption behavior influences
social relations. Instead, most of us
tend to think of consumption as just
satisfying our functional needs
without considering how these
choices impact on the rest of our lives
as well as fulfilling the needs and
desires of *individuals*.

At the time of the Industrial
Revolution, workers organized
themselves according to their
interests, raising consciousness only
for more increases in the distribution
of resources. So today, consumers
appeal to firms for fair trade, decent

working conditions, and healthy
environmental protections across the
world, yet all too often their causes
are isolated and geographically
dispersed. Although there has been
some attention to increasing
demands on consumers in self-
service kiosks at airports, grocery
stores, and banks, and marketers'
capitalization of consumers' cultural
meanings, we as academics,
practitioners, and students have
much more work to do to fully develop
consumer consciousness.

Consider tourism. Consumers
spend billions every day in places
such as San Antonio or Albuquerque
consuming culture, which serves to
reaffirm and legitimate Latino/a
people. A tourist tax is often part of
the solution to siphon money back to
the community, yet it often goes to
the "squeaky wheels," those best
able to advance their causes through
city government. Might there be
additional ways of encouraging
community organizations, artists,
musicians, and theater groups to use
city facilities in providing consumers
more culturally authentic experiences
that at the same time develop
Latino/a communities in more
organically connected tourist
markets?

Now, the American advertising industry spends between $200 million and $300
million to court these consumers.[71] Ford set up a toll-free consumer hotline it staffs
with operators fluent in three Asian languages, and JCPenney holds one-day sales
in stores in Asian communities during certain holidays such as the moon festival.[72]
Wonder Bra even launched a special line it sized for the slimmer Asian body.[73]

Why all the interest? Asians not only make up the fastest-growing population
group but they are also generally the most affluent, best educated, and most likely to
hold technology jobs of any ethnic subculture. Indeed, Asian Americans are much
more likely than average Americans to buy high-tech gadgets. They are almost three
times as likely to own a digital camcorder and twice as likely to have an MP3 player.[74]
About 32 percent of Asian households have incomes of more than $50,000 compared
to 29 percent in the entire U.S. population. Estimates put this segment's buying power

at $253 billion annually. That explains why the brokerage firm Charles Schwab now employs more than 300 people who speak Chinese, Korean, and Vietnamese at its call centers.[75]

Despite its potential, this group is hard to market to because it actually is composed of subgroups that are culturally diverse and speak many different languages and dialects. The term *Asian* refers to 20 ethnic groups, with Chinese being the largest and Filipino and Japanese second and third, respectively. Filipinos are the only Asians who speak English predominantly among themselves; like Hispanics most Asians prefer media in their own languages. The languages Asian Americans speak most frequently are Mandarin Chinese, Korean, Japanese, and Vietnamese.

Not only are Asian consumers the most frequent shoppers of all racial and ethnic groups but they are also the most brand conscious. Almost half (43 percent) of these consumers say that they always look for a brand name when they shop. Yet, interestingly, they are also the least brand loyal. Fully a quarter of Asians say they change brands often, compared with 22 percent of Hispanics, 20 percent of African Americans, and 17 percent of whites. Asian consumers are also the most concerned about keeping up appearances. More than a quarter (26 percent) say they buy what they think their neighbors will approve of, compared with 12 percent each of Hispanics and African Americans and only 10 percent of whites. As one Asian American advertising executive noted, "Prosperous Asians tend to be very status-conscious and will spend their money on premium brands, such as BMW and Mercedes-Benz, and the best French cognac and Scotch whiskey."[76] Advertising with Asian celebrities can be particularly effective. When Reebok used tennis star Michael Chang in one advertisement, shoe sales among Asian Americans soared.

Net Profit

The affluent Asian immigrant population in the United States is creating a new market for Asian products. For example, the Chinese music industry is benefiting from the demand in the Asian American community for the mix of syrupy ballads known as Mandarin pop. Music idols such as Andy Lau and Jacky Cheung tour the United States, and Chinese record companies are using the Web to build a bigger following overseas. Two of the most popular Web sites that expose fans to Asian music are RockaCola.com and YesAsia.com.[77]

 ## Religious Subcultures

In recent years, the United States has witnessed an explosion of religion and spirituality in popular culture including the box office success of actor-director Mel Gibson's movie *The Passion of the Christ* and the tremendous popularity and controversy surrounding the book *The Da Vinci Code*.[78] Mainstream marketers that used to avoid religion like the plague (pardon the pun) now actively court church members. For example, DaimlerChrysler (now just Chrysler) rolled out a marketing campaign to target worshipers at African American churches across the United States. The carmaker hosted one-day test-drives at churches in several large cities in connection with gospel singer Patti LaBelle's concert tour.[79]

And, mainstream churches are marketing themselves much more aggressively. In the United States there are approximately 400 **megachurches,** each serving 2,000 or more congregants per week (some actually attract more than 20,000 to Sunday services!), with a combined annual income of $1.85 billion.[80] As a church marketing consultant observes, "Baby boomers think of churches like they think of supermarkets. They want options, choices, and convenience. Imagine if Safeway was open only one hour a week, had only one product, and didn't explain it in English."[81] Clearly, religion is big business.

And you don't have to be active in an organized religion to "worship" products. A study of a brand community centered on the Apple Newton illustrates how religious themes can spill over into everyday consumption, particularly in the case of "cult products." Apple abandoned the Newton PDA years ago, but many avid users still keep the faith. The researchers examined postings in chat rooms devoted to the product. They found that many of the messages have supernatural, religious, and magical themes, including the miraculous performance and survival of the brand, as well as the return of the brand creator. The most common postings

Some U.S. megachurches have more than 20,000 members.

concerned instances where dead Newton batteries magically come back to life. Here is an excerpt from one story, posted on a listserv under the heading "Another Battery Miracle":

> The battery that came with the 2100 that I just received seemed dead. . . . I figured that the battery was fried and I have nothing to lose. While "charging," I unplugged the adapter until the indicator said it was running on batteries again, and then plugged it back in until it said "charging" . . . after a few times, the battery charge indicator started moving from the left to right and was full within 10 minutes! . . . I've been using the Newt for about 4 hours straight without any problems. Strange. It looks like there has been yet another Newton battery miracle! Keep the faith.[82]

OLD AND NEW RELIGIONS

What are the dominant religions worldwide? The Barna Research Group estimates that there are 2 billion Christians, 1.2 billion people practicing Islam, 900 million Hindus, 315 million Buddhists, 15 million Jews, and a category it calls Primal Indigenous makes up another 190 million. In addition, there are 750,000 practicing Scientologists and 700,000 Rastafarians. Among Americans, the majority (57 percent) is Protestant; one-quarter is Catholic. Muslims, Hindus, and Buddhists make up 5 percent of the population, and Jews are another 2 percent. About 12 percent of Americans have no religious preference.[84] Figure 14.3 summarizes some of the demographic characteristics of many different religious subcultures.

In addition to these established practices, a major survey of 113,000 people on religious attitudes reminds us of how many new religious subcultures exist. For example, it found that there are more Scientologists than Fundamentalists and also sizable numbers of followers of Wicca (witchcraft) and New Age faiths.[85] Something for everybody.[86]

Net Profit

Do avatars worship digital deities? Religion has arrived in *Second Life*, where residents attend virtual Easter and Passover celebrations and Muslim prayer meetings. An in-world synagogue combined a traditional Passover Seder with lessons on essential SL skills such as flying. Some pious residents offer animated "pray-ables" that pop an avatar into a prayer position— it may bow on a carpet, kneel in a cathedral, or land in the lotus position at a Buddhist spiritual center. In addition to accommodating RL religions, some new ones are popping up: Avatars of Change, for example, claims about 180 members from Christians to Jedi to Rastafarians.[83]

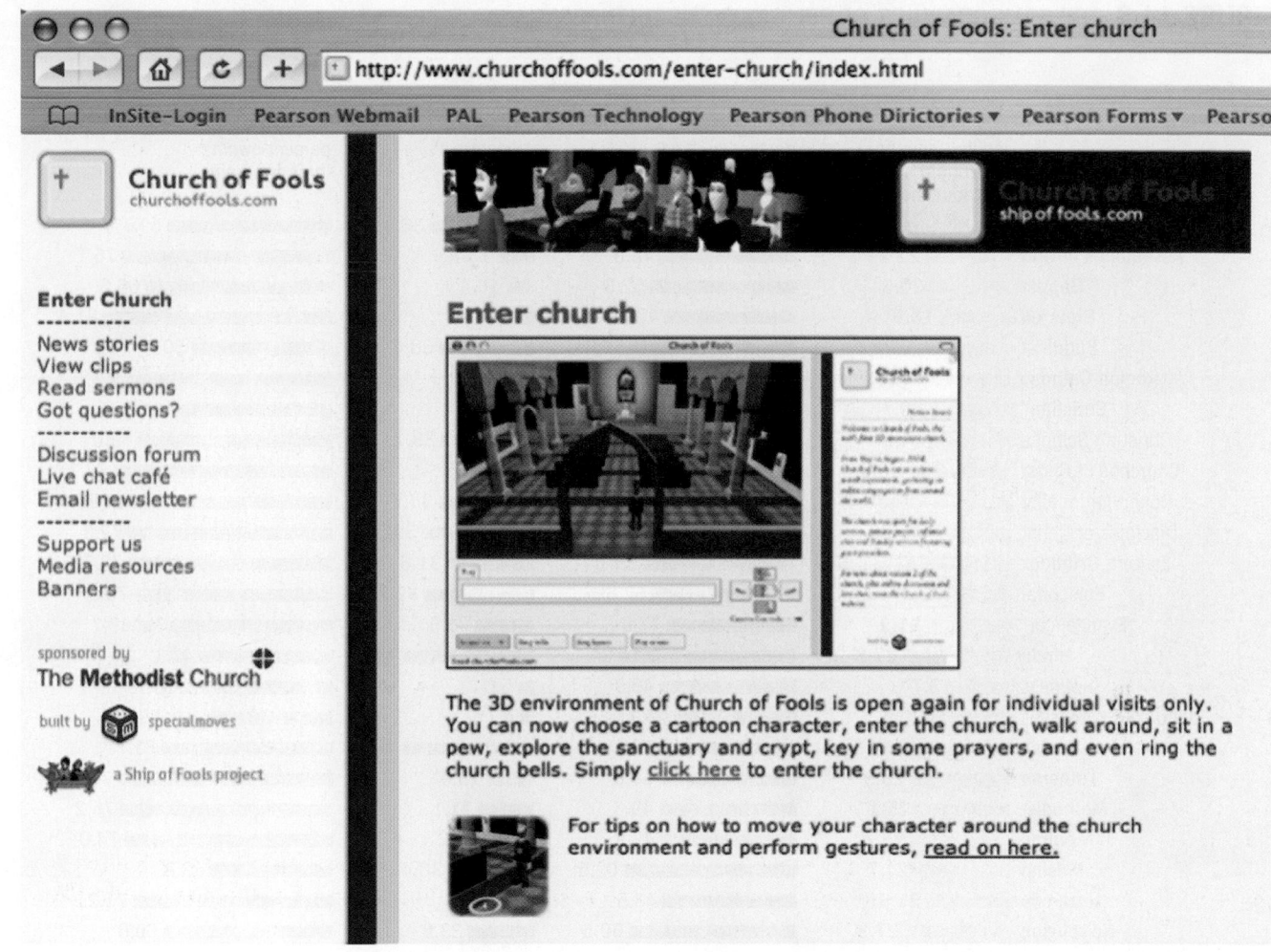

The Church of Fools home page.

HOW RELIGION INFLUENCES CONSUMPTION

Marketing scholars have not studied religion extensively, possibly because many view it as a taboo subject.[87] In some cases dietary or dress requirements create demand for certain products, and these items then may gain in popularity among other groups. For example, less than a third of the 6 million consumers who buy the 86,000 kosher products now on the market are Jewish. Seventh-Day Adventists and Muslims have very similar dietary requirements, and other people simply believe that kosher food is of higher quality. That's why some of the nation's largest manufacturers get involved. About two-thirds of Pepperidge Farm's products, for example, are kosher.[88]

Mindful of the success of kosher certification, some Muslims recognize that *halal* foods also may appeal to mainstream consumers. The Islamic Food and Nutrition Council of America certifies halal products with a "crescent M," much like the circled "O" of the Orthodox Union, the largest kosher certifier. Both kosher and halal followers forbid pork, and both require similar rituals for butchering meat. Religious Jews don't mix milk and meat, nor do they eat shellfish, whereas religious Muslims don't drink alcohol. Neither group eats birds of prey or blood.[89]

In addition to food products, religious subcultures have an impact on consumer variables such as personality, attitudes toward sexuality, birthrates and household formation, income, and political attitudes. Church leaders can encourage consumption, but more importantly, they can *discourage* it—sometimes with powerful effects. The Disney Corporation discovered how effective these movements could be

■ FIGURE 14.3 THE DEMOGRAPHICS OF RELIGIOUS SUBCULTURES

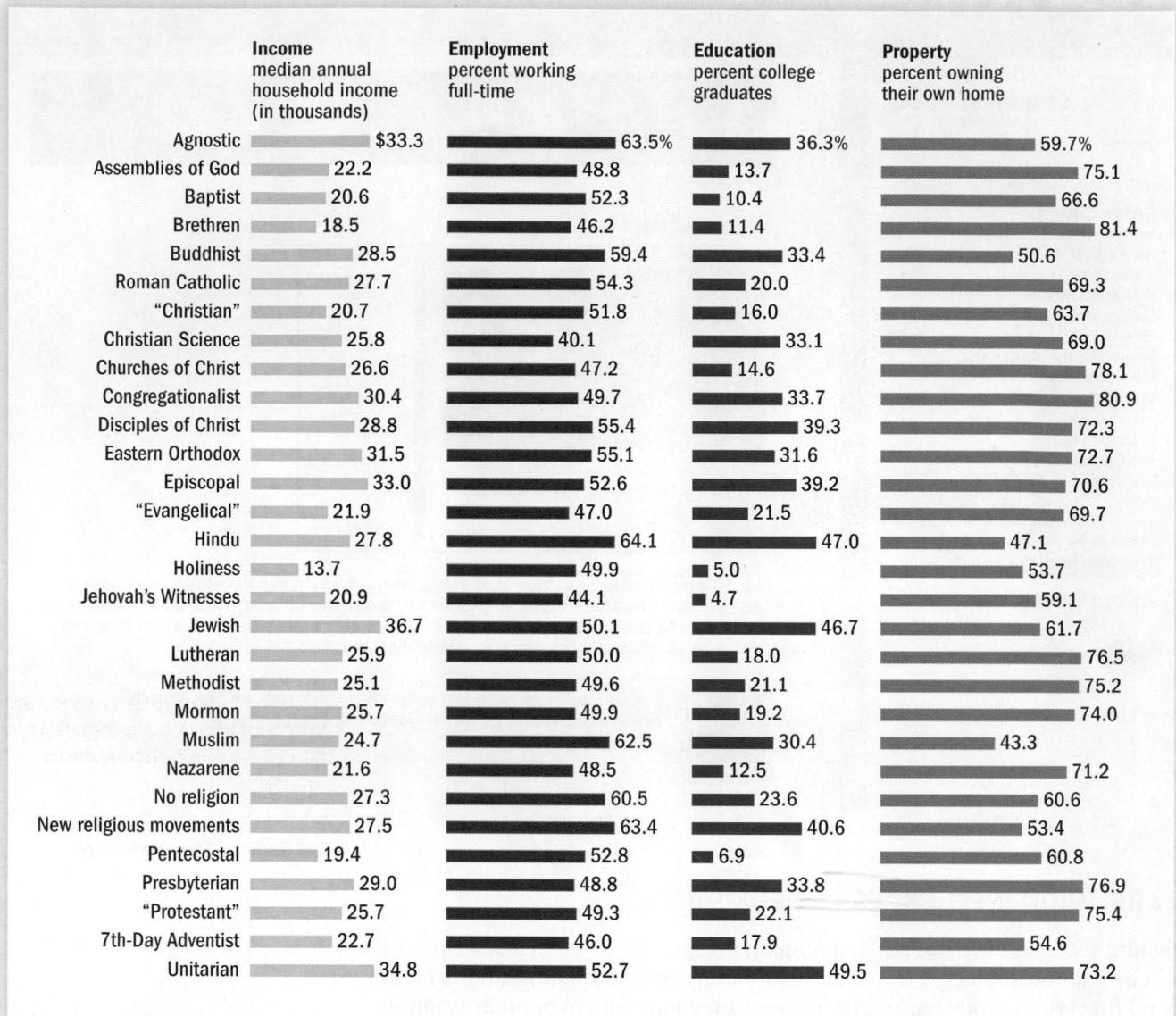

	Income median annual household income (in thousands)	Employment percent working full-time	Education percent college graduates	Property percent owning their own home
Agnostic	$33.3	63.5%	36.3%	59.7%
Assemblies of God	22.2	48.8	13.7	75.1
Baptist	20.6	52.3	10.4	66.6
Brethren	18.5	46.2	11.4	81.4
Buddhist	28.5	59.4	33.4	50.6
Roman Catholic	27.7	54.3	20.0	69.3
"Christian"	20.7	51.8	16.0	63.7
Christian Science	25.8	40.1	33.1	69.0
Churches of Christ	26.6	47.2	14.6	78.1
Congregationalist	30.4	49.7	33.7	80.9
Disciples of Christ	28.8	55.4	39.3	72.3
Eastern Orthodox	31.5	55.1	31.6	72.7
Episcopal	33.0	52.6	39.2	70.6
"Evangelical"	21.9	47.0	21.5	69.7
Hindu	27.8	64.1	47.0	47.1
Holiness	13.7	49.9	5.0	53.7
Jehovah's Witnesses	20.9	44.1	4.7	59.1
Jewish	36.7	50.1	46.7	61.7
Lutheran	25.9	50.0	18.0	76.5
Methodist	25.1	49.6	21.1	75.2
Mormon	25.7	49.9	19.2	74.0
Muslim	24.7	62.5	30.4	43.3
Nazarene	21.6	48.5	12.5	71.2
No religion	27.3	60.5	23.6	60.6
New religious movements	27.5	63.4	40.6	53.4
Pentecostal	19.4	52.8	6.9	60.8
Presbyterian	29.0	48.8	33.8	76.9
"Protestant"	25.7	49.3	22.1	75.4
7th-Day Adventist	22.7	46.0	17.9	54.6
Unitarian	34.8	52.7	49.5	73.2

when the U.S. Southern Baptist Convention voted to persuade all its members to boycott its operations.[90] The church instituted its anti-Mickey rebellion to protest the "Gay Days" at the theme parks and a view that Disney had a radical homosexual agenda that it promoted through its broadcasts. Soon other organizations joined the cause, including the American Family Association, the General Council of the Assemblies of God, the Congregational Holiness Church, the Catholic League for Religious and Civil Rights, and the Free Will Baptists. The fallout from the boycott was significant, resulting in a layoff of 4,000 employees.[91]

The Born-Again Boom

In the United States, we trace most religion-oriented marketing activity to Born-Again Christians, those who follow literal interpretations of the Bible and who acknowledge being born again through belief in Jesus. Theirs is among the fastest-growing religious affiliations in the United States. One research company reported

Religious symbols often show up in popular culture.

Specialized ethnic media, like this magazine for Muslim women, are springing up to meet the needs of underserved American subcultures.

Religious groups can influence companies' decisions by encouraging their members to boycott products or stage protests.

Marketing Pitfall

Religious sensibilities vary around the world, and big trouble can result if marketers violate taboo subjects in other cultures. Here are some examples:[94]

- A Lipton ad won the prestigious Gold Lion award in Cannes, but the company had to decline the honor in the face of objections. The ad mocked the Catholic Church by showing a man standing in the communion line with a bowl of onion dip in his hand.

- In Salt Lake City, a proposed billboard for a beer called Polygamy Porter aroused the ire of Mormons worldwide. The billboard company under contract with the brewery refused to erect the ad. The board, which was going to show a picture of a scantily clad man, cherubs, and a six-pack of spouses, advises drinkers to "take some home for the wives."

- An ad for Levi's jeans produced in London shows a young man buying condoms from a pharmacist and hiding them in the small side pocket of his jeans. When he goes to pick up his date, he discovers that her father is the same pharmacist. The commercial was a hit in the United Kingdom, but people in strongly Catholic Italy and Spain didn't appreciate it at all.

that about 72 million of the 235 million Christians in the United States say they are born-again.[92]

This growing movement in the United States is fueling a spike in Christian-related marketing and merchandise. Christian bookstores bring in revenues of well over $2 billion per year, and the proliferation of born-agains (especially younger evangelicals) is propelling religiously oriented products into more mainstream stores as vendors update their messages for a younger generation (one T-shirt for sale shows a hand with a nail through it along with the caption, "Body Piercing Saved My Life"). C28, a chain of California stores, takes its names from the Bible verse Colossians 2:8, "See to it that no one takes you captive through hollow and deceptive philosophy, which depends on human tradition and the basic principles of this world rather than on Christ." C28 has its own house brand, Not of This World, featuring modern designs coupled with biblical verses. The owner claims that hundreds of people have converted to Born-Again Christianity in his stores: "Our mission is to share the grace, the truth and the love of Jesus. And what better place to do it than a mall?"[93]

C28, a chain of California stores, takes its name from the Bible verse Colossians 2:8.

- A Brazilian ad for Pirelli tires drew heat from religious leaders. The ad shows a soccer superstar with his arms spread and a tire tread on the sole of his foot standing in place of the Christ the Redeemer statue that overlooks Rio de Janeiro.
- The French car manufacturer Renault withdrew an ad in a Danish campaign in response to protests from the local Catholic community. It depicted a dialogue during confession between a Catholic priest and a repenting man. The man atones for his sins by praying *Ave Marias* until he confesses to having scratched the paint of the priest's new Renault—then the priest shouts "heathen" and orders the man to pay a substantial penalty to the church.
- Burger King had to modify a commercial it aired on U.S. African American radio stations in which a coffeehouse poet reads an ode to a Whopper with bacon. In the original spot the person's name is Rasheed and he uses a common Islamic greeting. The Council on American–Islamic Relations issued a press release noting that Islam prohibits the consumption of pork products. In the new version the poet was renamed Willie.

CHAPTER SUMMARY

Now that you have finished reading this chapter you should understand why:

Our memberships in ethnic, racial, and religious subcultures often play a big role in guiding our consumption behaviors.

- Consumers identify with many groups that share common characteristics and identities. Subcultures are large groups that exist within a society and membership in them often gives marketers a valuable clue about individuals' consumption decisions. A person's ethnic origins, racial identity, and religious background often are major components of his identity.

Additional influences come from our identification with microcultures that reflect a shared interest in some organization or activity.

- Microcultures are communities of consumers who participate in or otherwise identify with specific art forms, popular culture movements, and hobbies.

Many marketing messages appeal to ethnic and racial identity.

- The three largest ethnic and racial subcultures are African Americans, Hispanic Americans, and Asian Americans, but marketers are beginning to focus on consumers with many diverse backgrounds as well. Indeed, the growing numbers of people who claim multiethnic backgrounds is beginning to blur the traditional distinctions we draw among these subcultures.

African Americans, Hispanic Americans, and Asian Americans are the three most important ethnic/racial subcultures in the United States.

- African Americans are a very important market segment. In some respects, the market expenditures of these consumers do not differ that much from whites, but African Americans are above-average consumers in such categories as personal care products.

- Hispanic Americans and Asian Americans are other ethnic subcultures that marketers are courting actively. Both groups are growing rapidly, though numerically Hispanics are the nation's single largest ethnic segment. Asian Americans on the whole are extremely well educated, and the socioeconomic status of Hispanics is increasing as well.

- Key issues for reaching the Hispanic market are consumers' degree of acculturation into mainstream American society and the recognition of important cultural differences among Hispanic subgroups (e.g., Puerto Ricans, Cubans, and Mexicans).

- Both Asian Americans and Hispanic Americans tend to be extremely family oriented and are receptive to advertising that understands their heritage and reinforces traditional family values.

Marketers increasingly use religious and spiritual themes when they talk to consumers.

- The quest for spirituality influences demand in product categories including books, music, and cinema. Although the impact of religious identification on consumer behavior is not clear, some differences among religious subcultures do emerge. Marketers need to consider the sensibilities of believers carefully when they use religious symbolism to appeal to members of different denominations.

KEY TERMS

Acculturation agents, 550
Deethnicization, 548
Ethnic subculture, 546
High-context culture, 547

Host culture, 551
Low-context culture, 547
Megachurches, 559
Microculture, 544

Progressive learning model, 551
Subculture, 544
Warming, 551

REVIEW QUESTIONS

1 What is a subculture? How does it differ from a microculture?

2 What is the difference between a high-context and a low-context culture? What is an example of this difference?

3 Why is it difficult to identify consumers in terms of their ethnic subculture membership?

4 What is deethnicization? Give an example.

5 Why are Hispanic American consumers attractive to marketers?

6 What is acculturation? How does it differ from enculturation?

7 Who are acculturation agents? Give two examples.

8 Describe the processes involved when a person assimilates into a new host culture.

9 Why are Asian Americans an attractive market segment? Why can they be difficult for marketers to reach?

10 How can we equate consumers' allegiance to some products as a form of religious observance?

11 How do religious subcultures affect consumption decisions?

CONSUMER BEHAVIOR CHALLENGE

■ DISCUSS

1 Some industry experts feel that it's acceptable to appropriate symbols from another culture even if the buyer does not know their original meaning. They argue that even in the host society there is often disagreement about these meanings. What do you think?

2 The prominence of African American characters in video games containing violent story lines is all the more striking because of the narrow range of video games in which African Americans have been present over the years. One study found that of 1,500 video game characters surveyed, 288 were African American males, and 83 percent of those were athletes.[95] Do you think this is a problem, and if so how would you address it?

3 Should members of a religious group adapt marketing techniques that manufacturers customarily use to increase market share for their products? Why or why not?

4 Several years ago R. J. Reynolds announced plans to test market a menthol cigarette called Uptown specifically to African American consumers. According to the company, about 70 percent of African American smokers prefer menthol, more than twice the average rate. After market research showed that blacks tend to open cigarette packs from the bottom, the company decided to pack Uptowns with the filters facing down. Reynolds cancelled its plans after private health groups and government officials protested. Does a company have the right to exploit a subculture's special characteristics, especially to increase sales of a harmful product such as cigarettes? What about the argument that virtually every business that follows the marketing concept designs a product to meet the needs and tastes of a preselected segment?

5 The Uncle Ben campaign described in the chapter gives an attractive "makeover" to a character many found objectionable. What do you think of this action?

6 Describe the progressive learning model and discuss why this perspective is important when marketing to subcultures.

7 In 2007 General Motors' GMC Division launched an advertising campaign it aimed at the African American market to promote its new Sierra Crew Cab and Sierra Denali pickup trucks. Pickup ads almost always show the vehicles being used for blue-collar work, charging down rutted back roads, and hauling bales of hay or boats. In this campaign, however, the trucks cruise in urban settings with a hip-hop soundtrack. As onlookers turn to admire the pickup, it veers off the road and climbs the vertical face of a skyscraper, leaping into the air at the top before shooting down the other side.[96] How credible is an advertisement that upends such a strongly held stereotype (i.e., "blue-collar" rural men drive pickups)?

8 Like the simulated Rio Grande river crossing described in the chapter, the humanitarian group Doctors without Borders set up a camp of tents, medical stations, and latrines in New York's Central Park to recreate the setting of a refugee camp.[97] What are the pros and cons of subjecting consumers to degrading experiences like these?

9 Born-Again Christian groups have been instrumental in organizing boycotts of products advertised on shows they find objectionable, especially those that they feel undermine family values. Do religious groups have a right or a responsibility to dictate what advertising a network should carry?

10 Religious symbolism appears in advertising, even though some people object to this practice. For example, a French Volkswagen ad for the relaunch of the Golf showed a modern version of *The Last Supper* with the tagline, "Let us rejoice, my friends, for a new Golf has been born."[98] A group of clergy in France sued the company and the ad had to be removed from 10,000 billboards. One of the bishops involved in the suit said, "Advertising experts have told us that ads aim for the sacred in order to shock, because using sex does not work anymore." Do you agree? Should religion be used to market products? Do you find this strategy effective or offensive? When and where is this appropriate, if at all?

■ APPLY

11 Locate current examples of marketing stimuli that depend on an ethnic or religious stereotype to communicate a message. How effective are these appeals?

12 To understand the power of ethnic stereotypes, conduct your own poll. For a set of ethnic groups, ask people to anonymously provide attributes (including personality traits and products) most likely to characterize each group, using the technique of free association where they simply say what comes to mind when you mention each group. How much agreement do you obtain across respondents? To what extent do the characteristics derive from or reflect negative stereotypes? Compare the associations for an ethnic group between actual members of that group and nonmembers.

13 Locate one or more consumers (perhaps family members) who have emigrated from another country. Interview them about how they adapted to their host culture. In particular, what changes did they make in their consumption practices over time?

Case Study

ROLLIN' IN A 'SCLADE

When Cadillac introduced its first Escalade in 1998, it was little more than a gussied up GMC Yukon Denali. In 2001, the company unveiled an all-new version with unique styling. The big brass at GM's luxury division were merely responding to the growing market for full-size, luxury SUVs when they targeted this model toward their traditional customers. They had no idea what was to follow.

The overwhelming success of the second-generation Escalade in America was not so much due to aging, upper-middle class, Caucasian drivers. The vehicle received a tremendous boost from American pop-culture. Specifically, hip-hop culture. This has changed the demographics of Cadillac buyers to include buyers that are younger as well as African American.

Why did professional athletes and rap artists wrap their arms around the Escalade? Was it the in-your-face styling? The mammoth size? The bling-bling look of the Cadillac crest? It may have been all of these things. But as the Escalade brand found its way into the hip-hop media, Cadillac's sales of this model steadily rose.

Lucian James, a San Francisco marketing consultant, takes the relationship between brand success and hip-hop popularity very seriously. He has taken to counting the number of times that the Billboard charts mention brand names. Most of these connections come from hip-hop songs that refer to luxury brands. When the 2006 winners of James's count were announced, top honors went to Mercedes, Nikes, then Cadillac. Bentley and Rolls-Royce rounded out the top five. Mr. James says the Billboard chart "represents a key barometer, albeit an unscientific one, of brand relevance in hip-hop and youth culture."

GM executives still wonder at the popularity of Cadillac among young, urban African Americans. Bob Lutz, General Motors's 70-year-old-plus design chief, knows a bunch of aging whites guys in Detroit can't intentionally make vehicles so cool that they're hot. "I don't think you can market your way into the cool culture," Mr. Lutz has admitted.

But even if Cadillac can't understand how it got there, it took its new customer base very seriously as it completely redesigned the Escalade for the 2007 year. Cadillac invited 35 of the biggest names in entertainment to a sneak preview of the new model. The list included NBA stars, TV actors, movie producers, and hip-hop artists. Most of the people on the list owned at least one Escalade.

Cadillac may have been caught by surprise the first time around, having done nothing special to cultivate buyers in this market segment. But this time, it sought out the trend-setters to catalog their likes and dislikes—and generate buzz. "We wanted to put the Escalade out in front of the people recognized as understanding 'cool,'" said Cadillac Marketing Director Jay Spenchian. "We wanted to see if they thought we were headed in the right direction. That way we still had time to make some modifications if we needed to."

DISCUSSION QUESTIONS

1 Describe Cadillac's "new customer" as a subculture.
2 Discuss the features and attributes (tangible and intangible) of the Escalade that have made it a hip-hop hit. Do you think that Cadillac can extend this appeal to its other models? Why or why not?
3 What lessons can other companies learn from Cadillac's good fortune with its Escalade model?

Sources: Russ Heaps, "The SUV World's Yin and Yang Prove To Be Intriguing," *Washington Times* (August 3, 2007): G7; Michael Paoletta, "The Name Game," *Billboard* (February 18, 2006); Paul Brent, "Caddy's Your Daddy in Bling Appeal," *National Post* (February 6, 2004): D7. Jason Stein, "Star-Studded Sneak Preview; General Motors Enlists Celebrities to Critique New Cadillac Escalade," *Automotive News* (February 28, 2005) 1.

NOTES

1. www.rdsmarketing.com/LosRhythmKings.html, accessed August 15, 2007.

2. Jaime Mejia and Gabriel Sama, "Media Players Say 'Si' to Latino Magazines," *Wall Street Journal Interactive Edition* (May 15, 2002).

3. Pui-Wing Tam, "The Growth in Ethnic Media Usage Poses Important Business Decisions," *Wall Street Journal Interactive Edition* (April 23, 2002).

4. Brian Steinberg, "Pioneer's Hot-Rod Ads Too Cool for Mainstream," *Wall Street Journal Interactive Edition* (March 14, 2003); Mireya Navarro, "Advertisers Carve Out a New Segment," *New York Times on the Web* (May 22, 2003).

5. Russell W. Belk and Janeen Arnold Costa, "The Mountain Man Myth: A Contemporary Consuming Fantasy," *Journal of Consumer Research* 25 (1998): 218–40.

6. Robert V. Kozinets, "Utopian Enterprise: Articulating the Meanings of *Star Trek*'s Culture of Consumption," *Journal of Consumer Research* 28 (June 2001): 74.

7. Lisa Katayama, "Anatomy of a Nerd; Japanese Schoolgirl Watch," *Wired* (March 2006), www.wired.com/wired/archive/14.03/play. html?pg=3, accessed October 6, 2007.

8. www.geocities.com/micronations, accessed July 24, 2007; Alex Blumberg, "It's Good to Be King," *Wired* (March 2000): 132–49; www.kingdomoft alossa.net/index.cgi, accessed July 24, 2007; www.freedonia.org, accessed July 24, 2007; www.new-utopia.com, accessed July 24, 2007.

9. See Frederik Barth, *Ethnic Groups and Boundaries: The Social Organization of Culture Difference* (London: Allen and Unwin, 1969); Janeen A. Costa and Gary J. Bamossy, "Perspectives on Ethnicity, Nationalism, and Cultural Identity," in J. A. Costa and G. J. Bamossy, eds., *Marketing in a Multicultural World: Ethnicity, Nationalism, and Cultural Identity* (Thousand Oaks, CA: Sage, 1995): 3–26; Michel Laroche, Annamma Joy, Michael Hui, and Chankon Kim, "An Examination of Ethnicity Measures: Convergent Validity and Cross-Cultural Equivalence," in Rebecca H. Holman and Michael R. Solomon, eds., *Advances in Consumer Research* 18 (Provo, Utah: Association for Consumer Research, 1991): 150–57; Melanie Wallendorf and Michael Reilly, "Ethnic Migration, Assimilation, and Consumption," *Journal of Consumer Research* 10 (December 1983): 292–302; Milton J. Yinger, "Ethnicity," *Annual Review of Sociology* 11 (1985): 151–80.

10. D'Vera Cohn, "2100 Census Forecast: Minorities Expected to Account for 60% of U.S. Population," *Washington Post* (January 13, 2000): A5.

11. Brian Sternberg, "P&G Brushes Up Iconic Image of 'Crest Kid' in New Campaign," *Wall Street Journal Online* (March 29, 2005).

12. Thomas McCarroll, "It's a Mass Market No More," *Time* (Fall 1993): 80–81.

13. Pui-Wing Tam, "The Growth in Ethnic Media Usage Poses Important Business Decisions," *Wall Street Journal Interactive Edition* (April 23, 2002).

14. Steve Rabin, "How to Sell across Cultures," *American Demographics* (March 1994): 56–57.

15. Rohit Deshpandé and Douglas M. Stayman, "A Tale of Two Cities: Distinctiveness Theory and Advertising Effectiveness," *Journal of Marketing Research* 31 (February 1994): 57–64.

16. Warren Brown, "The Potholes of Multicultural Marketing," www.washingtonpost.com (June 10, 2007): G02, accessed June 10, 2007.

17. J. Raymond, "The Multicultural Report," *American Demographics* (November 2001): S3, S4, S6.

18. Ibid.

19. Eils Lotozo, "The Jalapeño Bagel and Other Artifacts," *New York Times* (June 26, 1990): C1.

20. Dana Canedy, "The Shmeering of America," *New York Times* (December 26, 1996): D1.

21. Andrew Adam Newman, "Nike Adds Indian Artifacts to Its Swoosh," *New York Times Online* (October 3, 2007), accessed October 3, 2007.

22. Karyn D. Collins, "Culture Clash," *Asbury Park Press* (October 16, 1994): D1.

23. Peter Schrag, *The Decline of the WASP* (New York: Simon & Schuster, 1971): 20.

24. "Nation's European Identity Falls by the Wayside," *Montgomery Advertiser* (June 8, 2002): A5.

25. McCarroll, "It's a Mass Market No More."

26. Marty Westerman, "Death of the Frito Bandito," *American Demographics* (March 1989): 28.

27. Stuart Elliott, "Uncle Ben, Board Chairman," *New York Times Online* (March 30, 2007), accessed March 30, 2007.

28. Ibid.

29. See Lisa Peñaloza, "Atravesando Fronteras/Border Crossings: A Critical Ethnographic Exploration of the Consumer Acculturation of Mexican Immigrants," *Journal of Consumer Research* 21 (June 1994): 32–54; Lisa Peñaloza and Mary C. Gilly, "Marketer Acculturation: The Changer and the Changed," *Journal of Marketing* 63 (July 1999): 84–104; Carol Kaufman-Scarborough, "Eat Bitter Food and Give Birth to a Girl; Eat Sweet Things and Give Birth to a Cavalryman: Multicultural Health Care Issues for Consumer Behavior," *Advances in Consumer Research* 32, no.1 (2005): 226–269; Søren Askegaard, Eric J. Arnould, and Dannie Kjeldgaard, "Postassimilationist Ethnic Consumer Research: Qualifications and Extensions," *Journal of Consumer Research* 32, no. 1 (2005): 160.

30. Peñaloza, "Atravesando Fronteras/Border Crossings."

31. Wallendorf and Reilly, "Ethnic Migration, Assimilation, and Consumption."

32. Ronald J. Faber, Thomas C. O'Guinn, and John A. McCarty, "Ethnicity, Acculturation and the Importance of Product Attributes," *Psychology & Marketing* 4 (Summer 1987): 121–34; Humberto Valencia, "Developing an Index to Measure Hispanicness," in Elizabeth C. Hirschman and Morris B. Holbrook, eds., *Advances in Consumer Research* 12 (Provo, Utah: Association for Consumer Research, 1985): 118–21.

33. Rohit Deshpande, Wayne D. Hoyer, and Naveen Donthu, "The Intensity of Ethnic Affiliation: A Study of the Sociology of Hispanic Consumption," *Journal of Consumer Research* 13 (September 1986): 214–20.

34. Ger, Güliz, "Warming: Making the New Familiar and Moral," *Journal of European Ethnology* (special issue of the journal *Ethnologia Europea*), Richard Wilk and Orvar Lofgren, eds. (forthcoming).

35. Elisabeth Kriechbaum-Vitellozzi and Robert Kreuzbauer, "Poverty Consumption: Consumer Behavior of Refugees in Industrialized Countries," *Advances in Consumer Research* 33, no. 1 (2006); cf. also L. Wamwara-Mbugua, T. Wakiuru, Bettina Cornwell, and Gregory Boller, "Triple Acculturation: The Role of African Americans in the Consumer Acculturation of Kenyan Immigrants," *Advances in Consumer Research* 33 no. 1 (2006).

36. U.S. Census Bureau, *Census 2000 Brief: Overview of Race and Hispanic Origin* (U.S. Department of Commerce, Economics and Statistics Administration, March 2001).

37. Robert Pear, "New Look at the U.S. in 2050: Bigger, Older and Less White," *New York Times* (December 4, 1992): A1.

38. U.S. Census Bureau, *Census 2000 Brief: Overview of Race and Hispanic Origin.*

39. William O'Hare, "Blacks and Whites: One Market or Two?" *American Demographics* (March 1987): 44–48.

40. For an article that examines the impact of political ideologies on the African American community, cf. David Crockett and Melanie Wallendorf, "The Role of Normative Political Ideology in Consumer Behavior," *Journal of Consumer Research* 31 (December 2004): 511–28.

41. For studies on racial differences in consumption, see Robert E. Pitts, D. Joel Whalen, Robert O'Keefe, and Vernon Murray, "Black and White

Response to Culturally Targeted Television Commercials: A Values-Based Approach," *Psychology & Marketing* 6 (Winter 1989): 311–28; Melvin T. Stith and Ronald E. Goldsmith, "Race, Sex, and Fashion Innovativeness: A Replication," *Psychology & Marketing* 6 (Winter 1989): 249–62.

42. Karl Greenberg, "P&G Borrows 'Black Power' Phrase for Campaign," *Marketing Daily*, available from www.mediapost.com, accessed August 10, 2007.

43. Bob Jones, "Black Gold," *Entrepreneur* (July 1994): 62–65.

44. Jean Halliday, "Volvo to Buckle Up African-Americans," *Advertising Age* (February 14, 2000): 28.

45. Sarah Mahoney, "Unilever Finds Skin Takes on Deep Meaning among Black Women," *Marketing Daily*, available from www.mediapost.com accessed May 23, 2007.

46. Michel Marriott, "The Color of Mayhem, in a Wave of 'Urban' Games," *New York Times on the Web* (August 12, 2004).

47. Joe Schwartz, "Hispanic Opportunities," *American Demographics* (May 1987): 56–59.

48. Naveen Donthu and Joseph Cherian, "Impact of Strength of Ethnic Identification on Hispanic Shopping Behavior," *Journal of Retailing* 70, no. 4 (1994): 383–93. For another study that compared shopping behavior and ethnicity influences among six ethnic groups, see Joel Herce and Siva Balasubramanian, "Ethnicity and Shopping Behavior," *Journal of Shopping Center Research* 1 (Fall 1994): 65–80.

49. Amy Cortese, "At the Mall, Mariachi Instead of Muzak," *New York Times Online* (May 20, 2007), accessed May 20, 2007.

50. Sigfredo A. Hernandez and Carol J. Kaufman, "Marketing Research in Hispanic Barrios: A Guide to Survey Research," *Marketing Research* (March 1990): 11–27.

51. "Dispel Myths before Trying to Penetrate Hispanic Market," *Marketing News* (April 16, 1982): 1.

52. Schwartz, "Hispanic Opportunities."

53. Erik Sass, "Long-Term Hispanic Trend: Spanish Less Important in Future?" *Marketing Daily*, available from www.mediapost.com, accessed May 23, 2007.

54. "Education and English Proficiency Preclude Wider Hispanic Internet Use Center for Media Research," available from www.mediapost.com, accessed April 9, 2007.

55. "Do You Want to Be My Amigo? MySpace Launches En Espanol," *Marketing Daily*, available from www.mediapost.com accessed April 26, 2007.

56. Schwartz, "Hispanic Opportunities."

57. Macy's Yanks T-Shirt in Georgia and Texas, *Marketing Daily*, available from www.mediapost.com, accessed July 25, 2007.

58. Miriam Jordan, "VW Rethinks Its High-Testosterone Ads," *Wall Street Journal* (March 17, 2006): B1.

59. Jack Neff, "Unilever Launches Major Hispanic-Aimed Marketing Program *ViveMejor* Brings Together All Food, Personal-Care Brands," *Advertising Age* (May 21, 2007), accessed May 21, 2007.

60. Patrick O'Gilfoil Healy, "Heads Up Hidalgo, Mexico: Run! Hide! The Illegal Border Crossing Experience," *New York Times Online* (February 4, 2007), accessed February 4, 2007.

61. Rick Wartzman, "When You Translate 'Got Milk' for Latinos, What Do You Get?" *Wall Street Journal Interactive Edition* (June 3, 1999).

62. Gabriel Sama, "Appeal of Clamato Isn't Just Its Taste," *Wall Street Journal* (October 23, 2003).

63. Wartzman, "When You Translate 'Got Milk' for Latinos, What Do You Get?"

64. Cheryl Russell, *Racial Ethnic Diversity: Asians, Blacks, Hispanics, Native Americans, and Whites,* 2nd ed. (Ithaca, NY: American Demographics, 1998).

65. Beth Enslow, "General Mills: Baking New Ground," *Forecast* (November–December 1993): 18.

66. Rebecca Gardyn and John Fetto, "Race, Ethnicity and the Way We Shop," *American Demographics* (February 2003): 30–33.

67. Westerman, "Death of the Frito Bandito."

68. Stacy Vollmers and Ronald E. Goldsmith, "Hispanic-American Consumers and Ethnic Marketing," *Proceedings of the Atlantic Marketing Association* (1993): 46–50.

69. Dan Fost, "Asian Homebuyers Seek Wind and Water," *American Demographics* (June 1993): 23–25.

70. Marty Westerman, "Fare East: Targeting the Asian-American Market," *Prepared Foods* (January 1989): 48–51; Eleanor Yu, "Asian-American Market Often Misunderstood," *Marketing News* (December 4, 1989): 11.

71. Greg Johnson and Edgar Sandoval, "Advertisers Court Growing Asian Population: Marketing, Wide Range of Promotions Tied to New Year Typify Corporate Interest in Ethnic Community," *Los Angeles Times* (February 4, 2000): C1.

72. Alice Z. Cuneo and Jean Halliday Ford, "Penney's Targeting California's Asian Populations," *Advertising Age* (January 4, 1999): 28.

73. Dorinda Elliott, "Objects of Desire," *Newsweek* (February 12, 1996): 41.

74. "Made in Japan," *American Demographics* (November 2002): 48.

75. Hassan Fattah, "Asia Rising," *American Demographics* (July–August 2002), www.findarticles.com/p/articles/mi_m4021/is_2002_July_1/ai 89374125 , accessed October 6, 2007.

76. Donald Dougherty, "The Orient Express," *The Marketer* (July/August 1990):14.

77. Pui-Wing Tam, "Mandarin Pop Is Looking to Penetrate U.S. Markets," *Wall Street Journal Interactive Edition* (March 31, 2000); http://us.YesAsia.com, accessed July 25, 2007; www.RockaCola.com, accessed July 25, 2007.

78. Dan Brown, *The Da Vinci Code* (New York: Doubleday, 2003).

79. Stephen Power, "Chrysler to Take Its Cars to Church Deal with Patti LaBelle Offers Tickets, Test Drives to Sunday Worshipers," *Wall Street Journal* (October 19, 2006): B4.

80. Patricia Leigh Brown, "Megachurches as Minitowns: Full-Service Havens from Family Stress Compete with Communities," *New York Times* (May 9, 2002): D1; Edward Gilbreath, "The New Capital of Evangelicalism: Move Over, Wheaton and Colorado Springs—Dallas, Texas, Has More Megachurches, Megaseminaries, and Mega-Christian Activity Than Any Other American City," *Christianity Today* (May 21, 2002): 38; Tim W. Ferguson, "Spiritual Reality: Mainstream Media Are Awakening to the Avid and Expanding Interest in Religion in the U.S.," *Forbes* (January 27, 1997): 70.

81. Richard Cimino and Don Lattin, *Shopping for Faith: American Religion in the New Millennium,* New York: Jossey-Bass, 2002.

82. Albert M. Muñiz Jr. and Hope Jensen Schau, "Religiosity in the Abandoned Apple Newton Brand Community," *Journal of Consumer Research* 31 (March 2005): 737–747.

83. Cathy Grossman, "Faithful Build a Second Life for Religion Online," *USA Today* (April 3, 2007), available from www.usatoday.com , accessed April 3, 2007; Lillian Kwon, "Christians Bring Jesus into Virtual 'Second Life,'" *Christian Post* (April 5, 2007), available from www.christianpost.com/pages/print.htm?aid=26727, accessed April 5, 2007.

84. Susan Mitchell, *American Attitudes,* 2nd ed. (Ithaca, NY: New Strategist Publications, 1998). (Taken from a sample page off the New Strategist Publications Web page, www.newstrategist.com.)

85. Kenneth L. Woodward, "The Rites of Americans," *Newsweek* (November 29, 1993): 80.

86. "Somebody Say Amen!" *American Demographics* (April 2000): 72.

87. For a couple of exceptions, see Michael J. Dotson and Eva M. Hyatt, "Religious Symbols as Peripheral Cues in Advertising: A Replication of

the Elaboration Likelihood Model," *Journal of Business Research* 48 (2000): 63–68; Elizabeth C. Hirschman, "Religious Affiliation and Consumption Processes: An Initial Paradigm," *Research in Marketing* (Greenwich, CT: JAI Press, 1983), 131–70.

88. Yochi Dreazen, "Kosher-Food Marketers Aim More Messages at Non-Jews," *Wall Street Journal Interactive Edition* (July 30, 1999).

89. Barry Newman, "Halal Meets Kosher in Health-Food Aisle," *Wall Street Journal* (May 5, 2006): B1; Louise Story, "Rewriting the Ad Rules for Muslim-Americans," *New York Times Online* (April 28, 2007), accessed April 28, 2007.

90. www.religioustolerance.org/new1_966.htm , accessed October 6, 2007. www.erlc.com/WhoSBC/Resolutions/1997/97Disney.htm.

91. Alex Johnson, "Southern Baptists End 8-year Disney Boycott," www.msnbc.com (June 22, 2005), accessed October 6, 2007.

92. Michael Fielding, "The Halo," *Marketing News* (February 1, 2005): 18–20.

93. Rob Walker, "Cross Selling," *New York Times Magazine Online* (March 6, 2005); John Leland, "At Festivals, Faith, Rock and T-Shirts Take Center Stage," *New York Times on the Web* (July 5, 2004).

94. Jack Neff, "Dip Ad Stirs Church Ire," *Advertising Age* (July 2, 2001): 8; G. Burton, "Oh, My Heck! Beer Billboard Gets the Boot," *Salt Lake Tribune* (November 6, 2001); n.a. "Religion Reshapes Realities for U.S. Restaurants in Middle East," *Nation's Restaurant News* 32 (February 16, 1998); Sarah Ellison, "Sexy-Ad Reel Shows What Tickles in Tokyo Can Fade Fast in France," *Wall Street Journal Interactive Edition* (March 31, 2000); Claudia Penteado, "Brazilian Ad Irks Church," *Advertising Age* (March 23, 2000): 11; "Burger King Will Alter Ad That Has Offended Muslims," *Wall Street Journal Interactive Edition* (March 15, 2000).

95. Michel Marriott, "The Color of Mayhem, in a Wave of 'Urban' Games," *New York Times on the Web* (August 12, 2004).

96. Karl Greenberg, "GM Truck Ads Aim at Urban African-American Market," *Marketing Daily,* available from www.mediapost.com , accessed May 25, 2007.

97. Patrick O'Gilfoil Healy, "Heads Up Hidalgo, Mexico: Run! Hide! The Illegal Border Crossing Experience."

98. Penteado, "Brazilian Ad Irks Church."

Age Subcultures

Chapter Objectives

When you finish this chapter you should understand why:

- People have many things in common with others because they are about the same age.

- Teens are an important age segment for marketers.

- Baby boomers continue to be the most powerful age segment economically.

- Seniors will increase in importance as a market segment.

i t's the last week of summer vacation, and Kurt is looking forward to going back to college. It's been a tough summer. He had trouble finding a summer job and seems to be out of touch with his old friends—and with so much time on his hands just hanging around the house, he and his mother aren't getting along too well. Kurt plops on the couch and aimlessly flips channels—from *The Real Housewives of Orange County* to *Avatars* on Nickelodeon, to a Sony sponsored beach volleyball tournament on ESPN, back to Bravo. Suddenly, his mother marches in, grabs the remote, and switches the channel to public television. Yet another documentary is on about Woodstock (the original one, way back in 1969). When Kurt protests, "Come on Pam, get a life. . . ." his mom snaps back, "Keep your cool. You might actually learn about what it was like to be in college when it really meant something. And what's with the first name stuff? In my day I would never have dreamed of calling my mom or dad by their first name!"

That's when Kurt loses it. He's tired of hearing about the "good old days" of Woodstock, Berkeley, and 20 other places he doesn't care about. Besides, most of his mom's ex-hippie friends now work for the very corporations they used to protest about—who are they to preach to him about doing something meaningful with his life? In disgust, Kurt storms into his room, cranks up Korn on his iPod, and pulls the covers up over his head. So much for a constructive use of time. What's the difference, anyway—they'll probably all be dead from global warming by the time he graduates.

Age and Consumer Identity

The era in which you grow up bonds you with the millions of others who come of age during the same time period. Obviously, your needs and preferences change as you grow older, often in concert with others of your own age (even though some of us don't really believe we'll ever get older). For this reason, our age is a big part of our identity. All things being equal, we are more likely to have things in common with others of our own age than with those younger or older. As Kurt found out, this identity may become even stronger when the actions and goals of one generation conflict with those of others—an age-old battle.

A marketer needs to communicate with members of an age group in their own language. For example, Sony finally figured out that it had to sponsor events such as beach volleyball to get young people's attention. When the electronics giant first entered the U.S. car stereo market, it hammered on its usual themes of technical prowess and quality. This got nothing but yawns from the 16- to 24-year-olds who make up half of the consumers who buy these products, and Sony ranked a pitiful seventh in the market after 10 years. Finally, the company got the picture—it totally revamped its approach and eventually doubled its car stereo revenues.[1]

Now, Sony Electronics has reorganized its entire internal marketing organization so that it can target products to consumers' different life stages. Instead of assigning managers to products, the company assigns them to age-related segments such as gen Y (younger than age 25), young professionals/DINKs (double income no kids, aged 25 to 34), families (35- to 54-year-olds), and zoomers (those older than age 55).[2] In this chapter, we'll explore some of the important characteristics of some key age groups and consider how marketers must modify their strategies to appeal to diverse age subcultures.

An **age cohort** consists of people of similar ages who have similar experiences. They share many common memories about cultural heroes (e.g., John Wayne versus Brad Pitt), important historical events (e.g., World War II versus the 2001 terrorist attacks), and so on. Although there is no universally accepted way to divide up people into age cohorts, each of us seems to have a pretty good idea what we mean when we refer to "my generation."

Marketers often target products and services to a specific age cohort; our possessions help us identify with others of a certain age and express the priorities and needs we encounter at each life stage.[3] An ad campaign for Saturn featured a set of commercials that represent stages in life from childhood and high school to college and marriage. As four friends drive around in the Saturn Ion, they see kids playing on swing sets, students on prom night, partying fraternity members, and young marrieds in tuxedos and wedding gowns. The campaign communicates the idea that the car takes its owner through each life stage.[4]

The same offering probably won't appeal to people of different ages, nor will the language and images marketers use to reach them. In some cases companies develop separate campaigns for age cohorts. For example, Norelco found that younger men are far less likely to use electric shavers than are its core customer base of older men. The firm launched a two-pronged effort, on the one hand, to convince younger men to switch from wet shaving to electric, and on the other hand, to maintain loyalty among its older following. Ads for Norelco's Speedrazor it aimed at males aged 18 to 35 ran on late-night TV and in *GQ* and *Details*. Messages about the company's triple-head razors, geared to men older than age 35, ran instead in publications that attract older readers, such as *Time* and *Newsweek*.

Because consumers within an age group confront crucial life changes at roughly the same time, the values and symbolism marketers use to appeal to them can evoke powerful feelings of nostalgia (see Chapter 3). Adults older than age 30 are particularly susceptible to this phenomenon.[5] However, references to the past

NISSAN X-TRAIL. THE SUV FOR EVOLVING LIVES.

This Canadian ad for Nissan underscores the need for marketers to adapt to their customers' changing priorities as they age.

influence young people as well as old. In fact, research indicates that some people are more disposed to be nostalgic than others, regardless of age. Table 15.1 shows a scale researchers use to measure the impact of nostalgia on individual consumers.

Although most products appeal to one age cohort or another, some marketers of late are trying to woo people of different ages with a **multigenerational marketing strategy** where they use imagery from an older generation that also turns on younger consumers. These companies recognize that older baby boomers (more on these guys later) have a youthful attitude and many are quite comfortable with new technology. However, a lot of young people are very sophisticated consumers who don't want companies to talk down to them.

When Honda launched its boxy Element SUV it was going after young men—but to the company's surprise a lot of middle-aged women also bought the vehicle. Based on that experience, Honda is deliberately going after two age groups at once with its new Fit subcompact. It places ads in youth-oriented niche publications such as *Filter* music magazine while running others in *Time* magazine. TV commercials include cartoon characters such as a "speedy demon" monster that appeal to youth but also resemble creatures you might find in 1970s comic books. Similarly, the Scion tC screams youth—but in reality its buyers' median age is 49. It turns out people in their 50s and 60s like the car's low floor height because it's easy to step into!

In one interesting crossover experiment, *DUB* magazine (which targets Tuner car fanatics like the ones we've discussed) pimped out a few Buick Lucernes. Although the average age of the Buick buyer is 65, the cars took on a whole new image after hitting the road with tinted windows and 22-inch chrome wheels. Buick parks the cars outside nightclubs to attract younger drivers. So why did *DUB* initiate this partnership? It turns out that the model is popular among young African Americans in the

Marketing Opportunity

People who were not necessarily fond of each other in high school or college come together at a reunion to celebrate the common experience of having been in school at the same time and place. Groups hold more than 150,000 reunions in the United States each year, and 22 million people attend them (the 10-year high school reunion gets the biggest turnout on average). In addition to the boon this nostalgia provides to caterers and professional reunion organizers, some marketers realize that the people who attend reunions represent a valuable customer base. They self-select to be fairly successful because the "failures" tend not to show up! Some companies use reunion-goers to test new products, and travel-related businesses interview attendees about their trips or provide special promotional packages for the event. So, rent that limo, drop those unwanted extra pounds, print up some impressive business cards, and have a great time.[6]

TABLE 15.1
THE NOSTALGIA SCALE

Scale Items

They don't make 'em like they used to.

Things used to be better in the good old days.

Products are getting shoddier and shoddier.

Technological change will ensure a brighter future (reverse coded).

History involves a steady improvement in human welfare (reverse coded).

We are experiencing a decline in the quality of life.

Steady growth in GNP has brought increased human happiness (reverse coded).

Modern business constantly builds a better tomorrow (reverse coded).

Note: Items are presented on a nine-point scale ranging from strong disagreement (1) to strong agreement (9), and responses are summed.
Source: Morris B. Holbrook and Robert M. Schindler, "Age, Sex, and Attitude toward the Past as Predictors of Consumers' Aesthetic Tastes for Cultural Products," *Journal of Marketing Research* 31 (August 1994): 416. Copyright © 1994 American Marketing Association. Reprinted by permission of the Journal of Marketing Research Published by the American Marketing Association.

Oakland area who customize it to make "scrapers." These tricked-out rides feature wheels so big the tires scrape the inside of the car's fender.[7]

 # The Youth Market

In 1956, the label "teenage" entered the general American vocabulary when Frankie Lymon and the Teenagers became the first pop group to identify themselves with this new subculture. Believe it or not, the concept of a teenager is a fairly new idea. Throughout most of history a person simply made the transition from child to adult, and many cultures marked this abrupt change in status with some sort of ritual or ceremony, as we'll see in the next chapter.

The magazine *Seventeen* was first published in America in 1944 when its founders realized that modern young women didn't want to be little clones of Mom. Following World War II, the teenage conflict between rebellion and conformity began to unfold, pitting Elvis Presley with his slicked hair and suggestive pelvis swivels against the wholesome Pat Boone with his white bucks (see Figure 15.1). Today, this rebellion continues to play out as American pubescent consumers forsake their Barbies for the likes of Paris Hilton, Lindsay Lohan (when they're not in jail or rehab), or the teen heartthrob *de jour*.[8]

A major reason for the overwhelming size and future potential of this market is simple: Because of high birthrates (see Chapter 13) in many countries, a large proportion of the population is very young. For example, consider that while 21 percent of U.S. residents are 14 or younger, these are the corresponding percentages in some other countries:[9]

- China: 25 percent
- Argentina: 27 percent
- Brazil: 29 percent
- India: 33 percent

■ **FIGURE 15.1** THE U.S. TEEN POPULATION

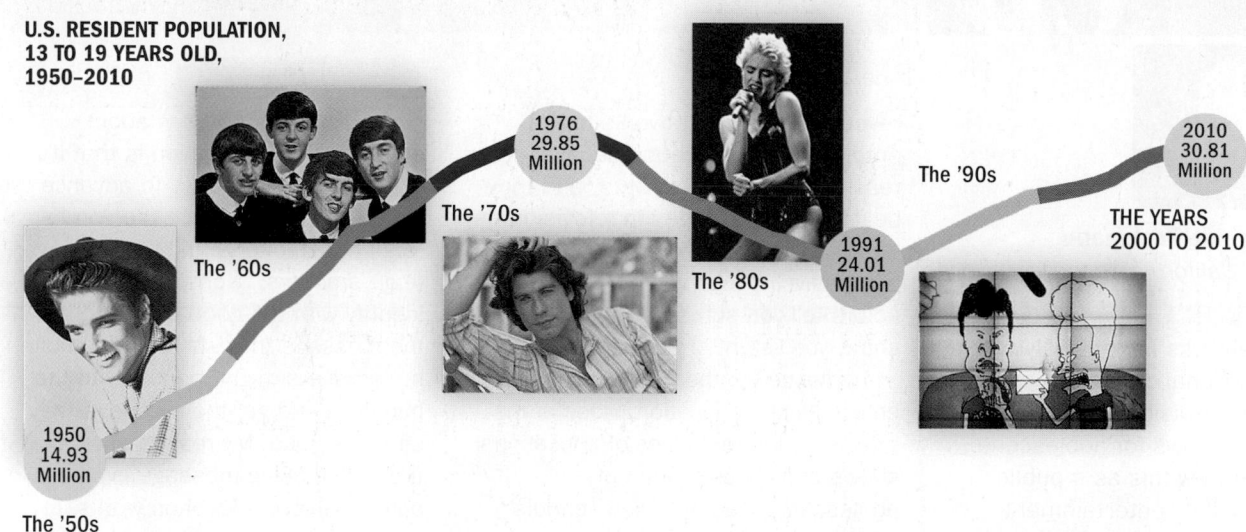

U.S. RESIDENT POPULATION,
13 TO 19 YEARS OLD,
1950–2010

The '60s

The '70s

1976
29.85
Million

The '80s

The '90s

1991
24.01
Million

2010
30.81
Million

THE YEARS
2000 TO 2010

1950
14.93
Million

The '50s

- Iran: 33 percent
- Malaysia: 35 percent
- Philippines: 37 percent

TEEN VALUES, CONFLICTS, AND DESIRES

As anyone who has been there knows, puberty and adolescence can be both the best of times and the worst of times. Many exciting changes happen as we leave the role of child and prepare to assume the role of adult. These changes create a lot of uncertainty about the self, and the need to belong and to find one's unique identity as a person becomes extremely important. At this age, our choices of activities, friends, and clothes are crucial. Teens actively search for cues for the "right" way to look and behave from their peers and from advertising. Advertising to teens is typically action oriented and depicts a group of "in" teens using the product.

Consumers in this age subculture have a number of needs, including experimentation, belonging, independence, responsibility, and approval from others. Product usage is a significant medium that lets them express these needs. For example, many kids view smoking cigarettes as a status activity because of the numerous movies they've seen that glorify this practice. In one study, ninth graders watched original movie footage with either smoking scenes or control footage with the smoking edited out. Sure enough, when the young viewers saw the actors smoking, this enhanced their perceptions of smokers' social stature and increased their own intent to smoke. (The good news: When kids see an antismoking advertisement before the film these effects cancel out.)[10]

Teenagers in every culture grapple with fundamental developmental issues when they transition from childhood to adult. Throughout history young people have coped with insecurity, parental authority, and peer pressure (although each generation has trouble believing it's not the first!). According to Teenage Research Unlimited, the five most important social issues for teens are AIDS, race relations, child abuse, abortion, and the environment. Today's teens often have to cope with additional family responsibilities as well, especially if they live in nontraditional families where they have significant responsibility for shopping, cooking, and housework. It's hard work

CB AS I SEE IT

Professor Connie Pechmann
University of California, Irvine

Television networks increasingly try to include educational content in the plots of their television shows, particularly in shows for adolescents. The networks view this as a public service and call it "entertainment education." Previously the networks aired educational public service announcements at commercial breaks, typically late at night to minimize the loss in paid advertising revenue. Now the networks prefer entertainment education because it reaches prime-time viewers, and they believe that messages in television shows are more credible and persuasive. If your favorite television actors tell you something within their show, you listen, or so they believe.

I am studying the effectiveness of entertainment education. I look at the effects of different types of educational shows on various groups of adolescents. I go into high schools and arrange for students to be released from a class, watch one type of educational show, and then complete a survey. I study television shows that tell adolescents not to smoke. A major concern about entertainment education is that it might polarize viewers. To advance the plot, shows depict both the good guys (e.g., nonsmokers) and the bad guys (e.g., smokers). Nonsmokers might identify with the good guys and get the message they should not smoke, but smokers might identify with the bad guys and get the message they should smoke. My results show that if the antismoking message is clear, entertainment education works. In effect, everyone listens to the good guys. However, if the message is mixed, the show is counterproductive and actually encourages smokers to light up.

being a teen in the modern world. The Saatchi & Saatchi advertising agency identified four basic conflicts common to all teens:

- **Autonomy versus belonging:** Teens need to acquire independence, so they try to break away from their families. However, they need to attach themselves to a support structure, such as peers, to avoid being alone. One survey of teens found that only 11 percent view themselves as "popular."[11]
- **Rebellion versus conformity:** Teens need to rebel against social standards of appearance and behavior, yet they still need to fit in and be accepted by others. They prize "in-your-face" products that cultivate a rebellious image, such as those the retail chain Hot Topic sells, for this reason.
- **Idealism versus pragmatism:** Teens tend to view adults as hypocrites, whereas they see themselves as being sincere. They have to struggle to reconcile their view of how the world should be with the realities they perceive around them.
- **Narcissism versus intimacy:** Teens are often obsessed with their own appearance and needs. However, they also feel the desire to connect with others on a meaningful level.[12]

These needs often collide, sometimes in unpleasant ways. One researcher recently explored the role of *ridicule* as a mechanism through which Western adolescents exchange information about consumption norms and values. He found that often beginning in middle school, adolescents use ridicule to ostracize, haze, or admonish peers who violate consumption norms. One result of this painful process is that kids internalize their peers' stereotypes about aspirational and avoidance groups (remember Chapter 11) and often significantly alter their consumption patterns to try to align themselves with the former and distance themselves from the latter. For example, one of the kids in the study quickly exchanged a pair of white sneakers for more stylish black ones after his peers ridiculed him.

Car manufacturers are developing new models that appeal to youth subcultures.

The author identifies three primary types of ridicule; he labels these *ostracism, hazing,* and *admonishment.* These types vary along a continuum of four dimensions: the ridicule's primary message, the relationship between teaser and target, the emotional response of the target, and the target's behavioral reaction. For example, in hazing the teaser's relationship to the target is like that of mentor to apprentice: The group accepts the target if he corrects his violation of its norms. The target's emotion is usually one of embarrassment because of the unwanted attention, rather than because of the transgression itself. As one informant recalled, ". . . in middle school the basketball jersey was the style. They were wearing them. I didn't have one at the time. . . . You would start hearing the whispers behind your back. And then they would start talking about your shirt. Saying 'What kind of shirt is that?' Then they will say something like it is a Payless shirt or Kmart . . . looking, pointing, and laughing . . . when there is a group laughing, I mean, you are in the middle of attention, but you aren't getting the attention that you want."[13]

Although teens have the "rep" of always questioning authority, it's also important to keep in mind that one person's rebellion is another's disobedience—there are strong cultural differences when it comes to the desirability of revolting against the establishment.[14] Teen rebellion is a new phenomenon in Japan, a country with a tradition of rigid conformity and constant pressure to achieve. Now, more and more teenagers seem to be making up for lost time. The dropout rate among Japanese students in junior and senior high school increased by 20 percent in a 2-year period. More than 50 percent of girls have had intercourse by their senior year of high school.[15]

Elsewhere in Asia, however, things are different: Many Asian teens don't necessarily value rebellion against a middle class that they are just now starting to join. An MTV executive commented, "Asian youth are schizophrenic. They lead double lives, almost. On one hand, they've got their earrings, belly-button rings and pony-tails, but on the other hand, they're completely conformist." In Singapore, Coca-Cola discovered that teen-oriented ads it used successfully elsewhere, such as a shirtless guy bodysurfing at a rock concert or recklessly riding a grocery cart down a store aisle, simply didn't make it with local kids who thought the ads were too unruly. One 18-year-old Singaporean's reactions to a scene showing kids head-banging sums up this feeling: "They look like they're on drugs constantly. And if they're on drugs, then how can they be performing at school?"

TWEENS

Marketers invented the term **tweens** to describe the 27 million children aged 8 to 14 who spend $14 billion a year on clothes, CDs, movies, and other "feel good" products. Tweens are "between" childhood and adolescence and they exhibit characteristics of both age groups. As one tween commented, "When we're alone we get weird and crazy and still act like kids. But in public we act cool, like teenagers."[16]

One of the biggest tween success stories is the meteoric rise of Mary-Kate and Ashley Olsen, who made their acting debut as little girls on the TV series *Full House*. Today, the Olsen twins are a formidable marketing machine. They are the most financially successful child stars in history; the twins generated more than $500 million in retail sales in only 1 year. They have been television, video, and film stars, editors-in-chief of their own magazine, fashion designers, recording artists, executive producers, authors, and even video game heroines.[17]

A recent marketing campaign in the United States by Victoria's Secret illustrates the fine line marketers must walk when they deal with consumers who are not children but not yet adults, or even full-fledged teens. When the retail chain developed Pink, a lingerie line for younger girls, it wanted to avoid the heat that Abercrombie & Fitch attracted when it sold child-size thong underwear. The company recruited about 2 dozen (female) students at colleges such as Ohio State, UCLA, and Penn State as brand ambassadors. These older girls became role models for the tween set. Members of Team Pink hand out free gift fliers, give away tickets to special screenings of the popular TV show *The OC*, and orchestrate stunts such as hiding a thousand pink stuffed animals around campus. "All they are really asking me to do is support another cause," one ambassador explained to her school newspaper, "and the cause happens to be underwear instead of the homeless, child poverty or hunger." Pink offers a way for Victoria's Secret to make its stores a little less intimidating to a younger customer, with a whole section of relatively innocuous apparel for her to explore.[18] Another marketer took a different tack: Hoping to get Barbie back on the cultural radar screen, Mattel Inc. hired the teen actress and singer Hilary Duff to give her blessing to a line of Barbie clothing for flesh-and-blood girls.[19]

GEN Y

Generation Y kids go by several names, including "Echo Boomers" and "Millennials." They already make up nearly one-third of the U.S. population, and they spend $170 billion a year of their own and their parents' money. They love brands such as Sony, Patagonia, Gap, Aveda, and Apple. Echo Boomers are a reflection of the sweeping changes in American life during the past 20 years. They are also the most diverse generation ever: Thirty-five percent are nonwhite, and, as we saw in Chapter 12, they often grow up in nontraditional families: Today one in four 21-year-olds was raised by a single parent and three out of four have a working mother.

Unlike their parents or older siblings, American Gen Y-ers tend to hold relatively traditional values and they believe in the value of fitting in rather than rebelling. Their acculturation agents (see Chapter 14) stress teamwork—team teaching, team grading, collaborative sports, community service, service learning, and student juries. Violent crime among teenagers is down 60 to 70 percent. The use of tobacco and alcohol is at an all-time low, as is teen pregnancy. Five out of ten Echo Boomers say they trust the government, and virtually all of them trust Mom and Dad.[20]

The global youth market is massive, representing about $100 billion in spending power! Much of this money goes toward "feel-good" products: cosmetics, posters, and fast food—with the occasional nose ring thrown in. Because they are so interested in many different products and have the resources to obtain them, many marketers avidly court the teen market—often by engaging them on multiple media platforms. For example, McDonald's is going where the action is to retain its young customers who grew up on Happy Meals. They are using iPods and blogs to talk to them, as well as the <u>mcdonaldslatenight.com</u> Web site, which includes popular music artists as well as a feature that lets you record your own voice. The chain also rolled out a bar mirror that shows an ad when you activate it with a motion sensor. In Seattle, franchisees give bar patrons free rides home—perhaps stopping en route at a McDonald's drive-through. Drink coasters offer morning wake-up calls; one shows a Double Quarter Pounder hamburger and asks how many patties the person sees. If he answers incorrectly, the coaster's backside suggests "Take a cab."[21]

Digital Natives

Millennials are the first generation to grow up with computers at home, in a 500-channel TV universe. They are multitaskers with cell phones, music downloads, and instant messaging on the Internet. They are totally at home in a *thumb culture* that communicates online and by cell phone (more likely via text and IM than by voice). These consumers truly are **digital natives**. Many young people prefer to use the Internet to communicate because its anonymity makes it easier to talk to people of the opposite sex or of different ethnic and racial groups.[22]

Young consumers think wired phones or computers are antiques. They're jugglers who value being both footloose and connected to their "peeps" 24/7. The advertising agency Saatchi & Saatchi labels this new kind of lifestyle **connexity**. To help **Gen Y-ers** feel connected with one another, companies including Apple and Philips developed miniature devices such as the iPod and MP3 key ring that store music and images for kids on the run—and they plug directly into a USB port for up- and downloading. When Toyota was developing its youth-oriented Scion model, its researchers learned that Echo Boomers practically live in their cars; one-quarter of Gen Y-ers, for example, keep a full change of clothes in their vehicles. So Toyota's designers made the Scion resemble a home on wheels: It has fully reclining front seats so drivers can nap between classes and a 15-volt outlet so they can plug in their computers.[23]

The Web also provides a forum for experimentation that appeals to teens grappling with identity issues. Researchers report that teens value privacy when they surf the Web because they view it as a way to express their individuality—that's why it's common for them to have multiple e-mail accounts, each with a different "personality."[24] Nearly a quarter of them keep at least one name secret so they can go online without friends recognizing them. And 24 percent of teens who use e-mail, IM, or chat rooms pretend to be someone else.[25]

One pair of researchers took an in-depth look at how 13- and 14-year-olds integrate the computer into their lives and how they use it express their *cyberidentities*. These tweens have limited mobility in RL (too young to drive), so they use the computer to transport themselves to other places and modes of being. The researchers explored the metaphors these kids use when they think about their computers. For some, the PC is a "fraternity house" where they can socialize; it also can be a "carnival" where they play games and an "external brain" that helps with homework.[26] Clearly young people are forging intimate relationships with these portals to online spaces we are only beginning to understand. Here's how some marketers meet these challenges:

- <u>Flip.com</u> is a new Web site for teenage girls. The digital division of publisher Condé Nast sees it as its answer to MySpace. Developers enlist girls to join a "flip squad" that gives them feedback on the site. It offers a forum to create "flip books": multimedia scrapbooks of photographs, homemade music videos, and other postings. CondéNet hopes to tap into the same creative flair that girls show when they decorate their school lockers or textbooks. Girls can choose which marketers they want to appear on their individual sites.[27]
- HP is pitching its PCs to teens with a viral campaign it calls the Society for Parental Mind Control that lets them into their parents' minds to orchestrate the purchase of a new PC. At <u>controltheirminds.com</u>, the teen chooses a PC and fills in the names of the "target" and his or her e-mail address. The unsuspecting

Marketing Pitfall

A new study the U.S. National Institutes of Health funded reports that young people tend to drink more in areas with more alcohol advertising compared to areas with less advertising. The study looked at alcohol advertising in 24 media markets across the United States and the researchers collected data on the amount of alcohol people aged 15 to 26 in those markets consume.

On average, young people reported consuming about 38.5 drinks per month and they reported seeing an average of 23 ads per month. Respondents who said they saw more ads and who lived in areas with higher-per-capita populations also said they drank more than those who saw fewer ads. The authors estimate that each $1 per-capita increase in alcohol spending boosts drinking by 3 percent in a month. All things being equal, a 20-year-old male who lives in a media market with the highest per capita advertising consumes about 26 drinks per month, compared to his counterpart in an area with less alcohol ads.[31]

parent gets an e-mail that links to the site, where a young, female voice intones instructions for complying with the teen's wishes.[28]

● A visitor to MTV's Virtual Laguna Beach can create an avatar of herself, choose a hot outfit and car, and buy DVDs and T-shirts using MTV bucks. The virtual high school includes cliques and catty students, and you can even vote for prom queen. Real brands abound; you can skin your IM window as a Cingular cell phone and buy a can of virtual Pepsi.[29]

● Heavy.com, a large Web host of short films and animation, is giving away many of its clips that are specially formatted for Sony's handheld game system PlayStation Portable. The company hopes advertisers will support the free content by paying for quick commercials before or after the downloads.

● Unilever hopes to lure young customers for its Axe body spray with its series of branded shorts about Evan and Gareth, two guys who roam the United States and film their efforts to meet women. Although consumers can access the same content on the evanandgareth.com Web site, Axe's marketers recognize their fractured media habits. As one manager explains, "He is still watching television, but even when he's doing that, he's online or might have his PSP on in front of him. The more pieces you can reach, the better."[30]

Speaking to Teens in Their Language

Because modern teens were raised on TV and tend to be more "savvy" than older generations, marketers must tread lightly in attempts to reach them. In particular, gen Y-ers must see the messages as authentic and not condescending. As one researcher observed, "they have a B.S. alarm that goes off quick and fast. . . . They walk in and usually make up their minds very quickly about whether it's phat or not phat, and whether they want it or don't want it. They know a lot of advertising is based on lies and hype."[32]

So what are the rules of engagement for young consumers?[33]

Rule 1: Don't Talk Down. Younger consumers want to feel they are drawing their own conclusions about products. In the words of one teen: "I don't like it when someone tells me what to do. Those drugs and sex commercials preach. What do they know? Also, I don't like it when they show a big party and say come on and fit in with this product. That's not how it works."

Rule 2: Don't Try to Be What You're Not. Stay True to Your Brand Image. Kids value straight talk. Firms that back up what they say impress them. Procter & Gamble appealed to this value with a money-back guarantee on its Old Spice High Endurance deodorant with an invitation to phone 1–800–PROVEIT.

Rule 3: Entertain Them. Make It Interactive and Keep the Sell Short. Gen Y kids like to find brands in unexpected places. The prospect of catching appealing ads is part of the reason they're watching that TV show in the first place. If they want to learn more, they'll check out your Web site.

Rule 4: Show That You Know What They're Going Through, but Keep It Light. A commercial for Hershey's Ice Breakers mints subtly points out its benefit by when it highlights the stress a guy feels as he's psyching himself up to approach a strange girl at a club. "I'm wearing my lucky boxers," he reassures himself. "Don't trip. Don't drool. Relax. How's my breath?"

Youth Tribes

We talked about the emergence of consumer tribes in Chapter 11. Brands with a tribal appeal reinforce belonging by letting the person display tribal trappings.[34] In-line roller skaters in France are a great example of the tribal phenomenon at

Marketers often influence public policy by creating messages to influence behaviors like smoking and drug use. This mosaic was used to promote Lorillard Tobacco's Youth Smoking Prevention Program.

work. There are about 2 million in-line skaters in France today, divided equally by gender. This group has its "in-groups" and "out-groups" within the tribe, but all connect via their shared skating experience. These urban skaters hold national gatherings in Paris that can attract 15,000 people, many of whom belong to associations such as Roller et Coquillages and Paris Roller. Specialized Web sites for members of the skating tribe let them meet to chat and to exchange information. Small tribal divisions exist (e.g., fitness skaters versus stunt skaters), but all identify with the broader skating tribe.

Tribal gatherings provide manufacturers with an opportunity to strengthen the group bond when they offer accessories such as shoes, key chains, belts and hats, backpacks, sunglasses, T-shirts, and other goodies that reinforce membership. For example, although skaters can choose from many brands K2, Razors, Oxygen, Tecnica, and Nike, the original Rollerblade product still holds cult status within the tribe. A company such as Tatoo, the pager arm of France Telecom, builds on tribal bonds with in-line skaters when it sponsors Tatoo Roller Skating in Paris and similar events around the country. Specialized magazines such as *Crazy Roller, Urban,* and *Roller Saga* carry informational articles as well as celebrity spots.

The American athletic shoe company And 1 appeals to members of a basketball tribe that admits members who can blow by a defender on the court. The company carefully cultivates a trash-talking street image (it distributes shirts with slogans such as "I'm sorry. I thought you could play") and it recruits street players to match its renegade brand image.[35]

The tribal phenomenon is very strong in Japan, where teenagers invent, adopt, and discard fads with lightning speed. Teenage girls in Japan exhibit what science fiction writer William Gibson (who invented the term *cyberspace*) calls "techno-cultural suppleness"—a willingness to grab something new and use it for their own ends—matched by no other group on earth. According to one estimate, cell phones sit in the purses and pockets of about 95 percent of all Japanese teenage girls. Unlike American phones, these devices connect constantly to the Internet and plug these girls into a massive network. Index, a Tokyo software start-up company, offers a Net-phone service called God of Love. For about $1.40 per month, users can tap the birth date of a potential mate into their phones and receive a computerized prediction of the relationship's future.[36]

RESEARCHING THE YOUTH MARKET

Research firms that specialize in the youth market have to be innovative because many millennials don't respond well to traditional survey techniques. Pizza Hut invites teens into its boardroom to eat lunch with company executives and share their opinions about the perfect pie.[37] Some research companies give teens video cameras and ask them to record a "typical" day at school—along with play-by-play commentary to help interpret what's going on. Other marketers pay $2,500 a head to spend a day at Trend School, a monthly one-day forum in New York and Los Angeles. The "students" hang out with über-cool kids to learn about the latest tech, music, and fashion trends.[38]

When the Leo Burnett advertising agency revamped Heinz ketchup's image to make it cool, the account research team took teens to dinner to see how they actually use ketchup. These meals opened their eyes; new ads focus on teens' need for control when they show ketchup smothering fries "until they can't breathe" and tout new uses for the condiment on pizza, grilled cheese, and potato chips.[39] Procter & Gamble goes to the Web to learn what kids are thinking. The company built two teen community Web sites to identify emerging trends. One of them, <u>tremor.com</u>, recruits teen members and rewards them with merchandise for spreading the word about products, whereas <u>toejam.com</u> (which stands for Teens Openly Expressing Just About Me) lets members preview new products and critique ads before they are widely distributed.[40]

All of these techniques are about defining what is cool to teens—the Holy Grail of youth marketing. One study asked young people in the United States and the Netherlands to write essays about what is "cool" and "uncool" and to create visual collages representing things that embody what it means to cool.[41] The researchers found that being cool has several meanings, though there were a lot of similarities between the two cultures. Some of the common dimensions include having charisma, being in control, and being a bit aloof. And many of the respondents agreed that being cool is a moving target: The harder you try to be cool, the more uncool you are! Some of their actual responses are as follows:

- "Cool means being relaxed, to nonchalantly be the boss of every situation, and to radiate that" (Dutch female).
- "Cool is the perception from others that you've got 'something' which is macho, trendy, hip, etc." (Dutch male).
- "Cool has something standoffish, and at the same time, attractive" (Dutch male).
- "Being different, but not too different. Doing your own thing, and standing out, without looking desperate while you're doing it" (American male).

- "When you are sitting on a terrace in summer, you see those machos walk by, you know, with their mobile [phones] and their sunglasses. I always think, 'Oh please, come back to earth!' These guys only want to impress. That is just so uncool" (Dutch female).
- "When a person thinks he is cool, he is absolutely uncool" (Dutch female).
- "To be cool we have to make sure we measure up to it. We have to create an identity for ourselves that mirrors what we see in magazines, on TV, and with what we hear on our stereos" (American male).

Marketers view teens as "consumers-in-training" because we often develop strong brand loyalty during adolescence. A teenager who is committed to a brand may continue to purchase it for many years to come. Such loyalty creates a barrier-to-entry for other brands he didn't choose during these pivotal years. Thus, advertisers sometimes try to "lock in" consumers so that in the future they will buy their brands more or less automatically. As one teen magazine ad director observed, "We . . . always say it's easier to start a habit than stop it."[42]

Teens also exert a big influence on the purchase decisions of their parents (see Chapter 12).[43] In addition to providing "helpful" advice to parents, teens often buy on behalf of the family. The majority of mothers in Europe and the United States today work outside the home so they have less time to shop for the family. This fundamental change in family structure changes how marketers need to think about teenage consumers. Although teens are still a good market for discretionary items, now they actually spend more on "basics" such as groceries than for nonessentials. Marketers are beginning to respond to these changes—the next time you are leafing through a magazine such as *Seventeen*, notice the large number of ads for food products.

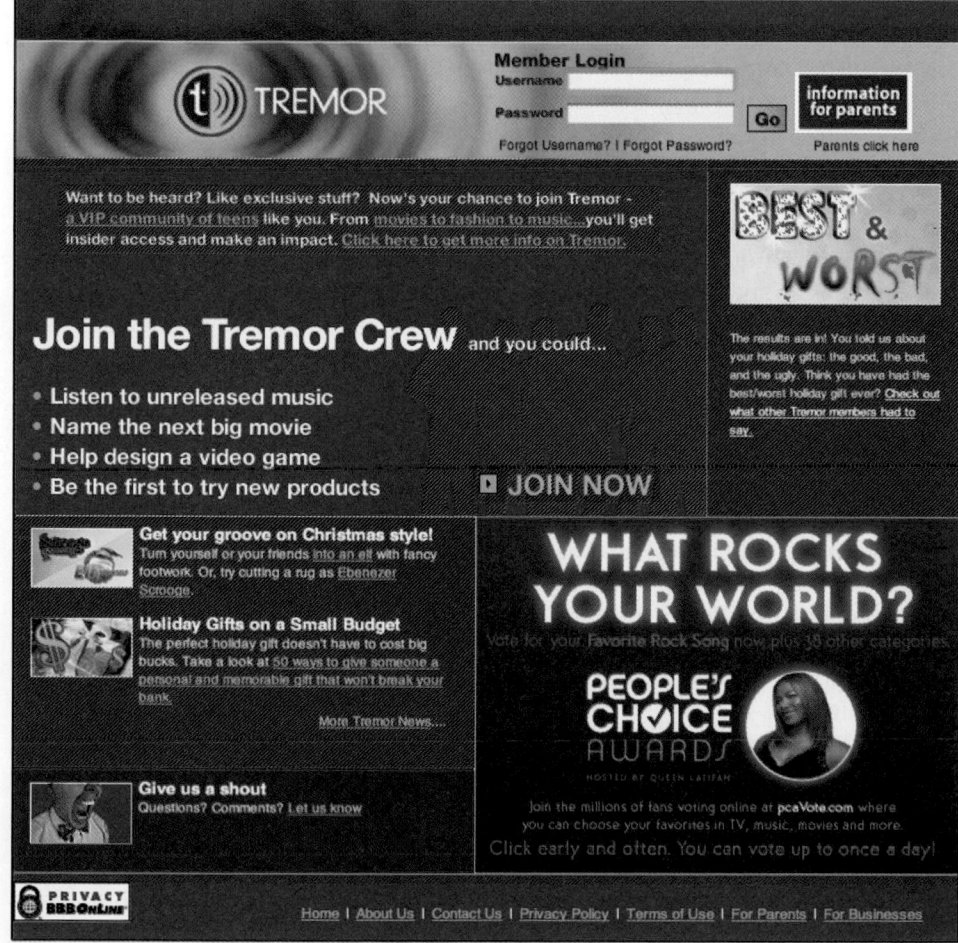

Tremor (owned by Procter & Gamble) provides teens with information about cool new products, shows, music, and so on that they can share with their friends if they choose.

A growing number of marketers are capitalizing on the ritual of Spring Break to reach college students.

Big (Wo)Man on Campus

U.S. advertisers spend approximately $100 million a year on campuses to woo college students, and with good reason: Overall, students spend more than $11 billion a year on snacks and beverages, $4 billion on personal care products, and $3 billion on CDs and tapes.[44] Many students have plenty of extra cash and free time (not you, of course. . .): On an average day the average student spends 1.7 hours in class and another 1.6 hours studying. This "average" student (or are all students above average?) has about $287 to spend on discretionary items per month. As one marketing executive observed, "This is the time of life where they're willing to try new products. . . . This is the time to get them in your franchise."[45] The college market is also attractive to many companies because these novice consumers are away from home for the first time, so they have yet to form unshakeable brand loyalty in some product categories such as cleaning supplies (bummer!).

Nevertheless, college students pose a special challenge for marketers because they are hard to reach via conventional media such as newspapers. Of course, online advertising is very effective: Fully 99 percent of college students go online at least a few times per week and 90 percent do so daily. Web sites such as mtvU.com and collegehumor.com blossom because they reach students where they live and play."[46] These specialized networks provide college students with irreverent programming that appeals to their sense of humor with shows such as *Bridget the Midget*, which follows the life of a 3-foot-tall former porn star who is now an aspiring rock singer, and an anti–Martha Stewart cooking show called *Half Baked*, which features celebrities such as Shaquille O'Neal and Lisa Loeb sharing recipes.[47] To acknowledge the power of this market, Nielsen Media Research recently began to include college students living away from home in its television ratings. Nielsen reports that American students watch an average of 24.3 hours of television a week. For the first time, the ratings will reflect viewing habits in dorm rooms, fraternity and sorority houses, and off-campus apartments.[48]

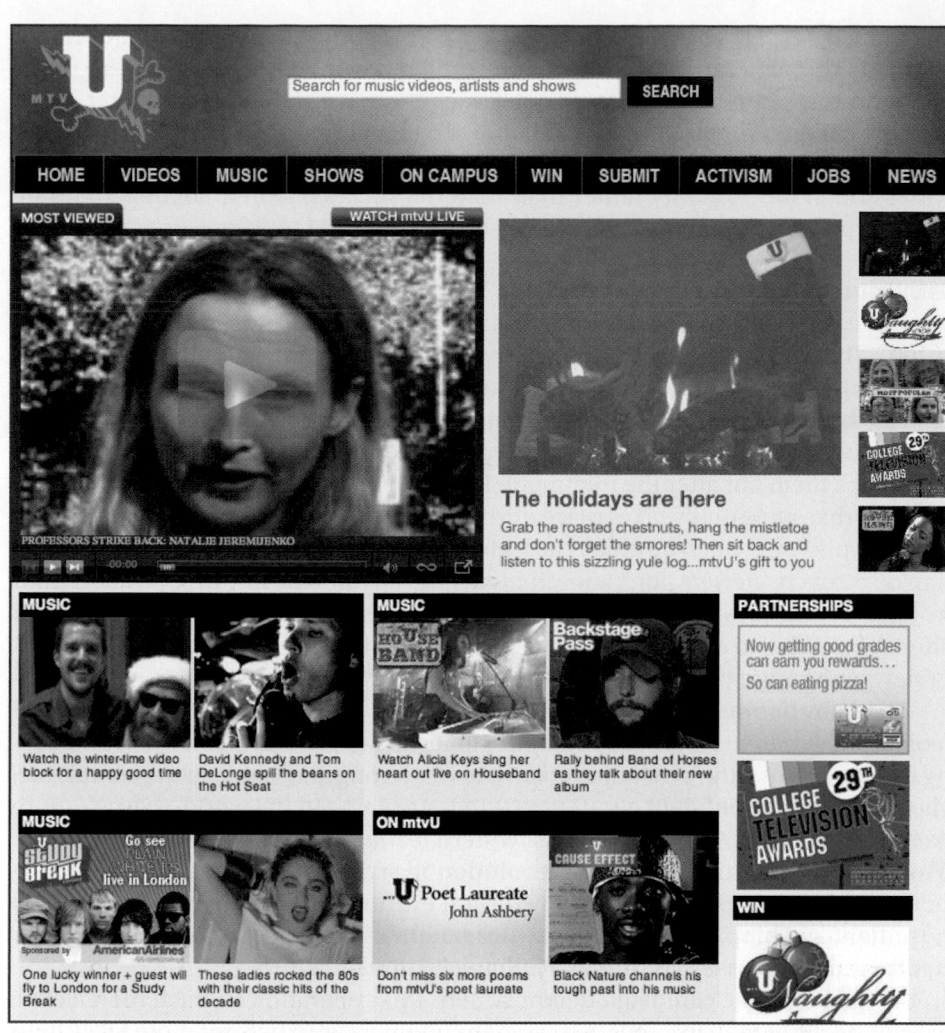

Baby Busters: "Generation X"

The cohort of U.S. consumers born between 1966 and 1976 consists of 46 million people. This group got the label **"Generation X"** following the bestselling 1991 novel of that name. Some called them "slackers" or "baby busters" because of their supposed alienation and laziness, and these stereotypes live on in movies such as *Clueless* and in music groups such as Marilyn Manson.[49]

Advertisers fell all over themselves trying to create messages that would not turn off the worldly Generation X cohort. Many of them referenced old TV shows such as *Gilligan's Island* or vignettes featuring disheveled actors in turned-around baseball caps doing their best to appear blasé. This approach actually turned off a lot of busters because it implies that they have nothing else to do but sit around and watch old television reruns. Subaru sponsored one of the first commercials of this genre. It showed a sloppily dressed young man who described the Impreza model as "like punk rock" while denouncing the competition as "boring and corporate." The commercial did not play well with its intended audience, and Subaru eventually switched advertising agencies.

Perhaps one reason marketing appeals to Gen X-ers with messages of alienation, cynicism, and despair didn't succeed is that many busters turned out not to be so depressed after all! Generation X-ers actually are quite a diverse group—they don't all wear reversed baseball caps and work as burger flippers. A CNN/*Time* study found that 60 percent want to be their own bosses, and another study revealed that X-ers are already responsible for 70 percent of new start-up businesses in the United States.

Marketing Opportunity

At least according to the popular stereotype, a frustrated man deals with a "midlife crisis" when he sports a toupee (probably a bad one) and cruises around in a red sports car. Today many women join the club when they buy a car to mark their freedom from hauling kids around to football games. Sales of "reward cars" (as the industry calls them) among women older than age 45 are skyrocketing. The number who purchase cars in the "mid-sized sporty" niche that includes two-door models such as the Mazda RX-8 and the Chrysler Crossfire is up 277 percent since 2000. Among women 45 and older earning at least $100,000, smaller luxury cars such as the BMW 3 Series and the Audi A4 are up 93 percent. As one woman who had just splurged on a snazzy Mercedes explained, "I'm just celebrating my life."[53]

One industry expert observed, "Today's Gen X-er is both values-oriented and value-oriented. This generation is really about settling down." As they have aged, many people in this segment seem to be determined to have stable families after being latchkey children themselves. Seven out of ten regularly save some portion of their income, a rate comparable to their parents'. X-ers tend to view the home as an expression of individuality rather than material success. More than half do home improvement and repair projects.[50] They don't sound all that lazy.

Baby Boomers

Restylane is the top-selling dermal injection to reduce the appearance of wrinkles. In 2007, the company decided to pitch it directly to consumers for the first time, so in keeping with new media trends it launched a multipronged campaign that recognizes the technical prowess of many middle-aged people. A conventional TV spot features before-and-after results along with women who talk about how frequently men check them out after the treatment. But a second component is a video skit on YouTube that supposedly takes place during a woman's fiftieth birthday party. While her son works on a video birthday card, Mom gets caught smooching with a younger man on a couch. Viewers don't know the skit is an ad until the last 15 seconds. A third prong is a contest to name the "Hottest Mom in America"; contestants will submit videos to a Web site and the winner gets cash, free treatments for a year, and an interview with a modeling agency.[51]

The **baby boomer** age cohort (people born between 1946 and 1964) consists of people whose parents established families following the end of World War II and during the 1950s when the peacetime economy was strong and stable (as a general rule, when people feel confident about how things are going in the world, they are more likely to decide to have children).[52] As Western teenagers in the 1960s and 1970s, the "Woodstock generation" created a revolution in style, politics, and consumer attitudes. As they age, they have fueled cultural events as diverse as the Free Speech movement and hippies in the 1960s to Reaganomics and yuppies in the 1980s. Now that they are older, they continue to influence popular culture.

As the Restalyne campaign demonstrates, this generation is much more active and physically fit than its predecessors; baby boomers are 6 percent more likely than the national average to engage in some kind of sports activity.[54] And Boomers are now in their peak earning years. As one commercial for VH1, the music video network that caters to those who are a bit too old for MTV, pointed out, "The generation that dropped acid to escape reality. . . is the generation that drops antacid to cope with it."

Levi Strauss is a good example of a company that built its core business on the backs (or backsides) of Boomers. More recently, though, the apparel maker faced the challenge of keeping aging customers in its franchise as former jeans-wearing hippies lost interest in traditional styles. Levi Strauss answered this challenge when it created its "New Casuals" product category with pants that are more formal than jeans but more casual than dress slacks. The target audience is men aged 25 to 49 with higher-than-average education and income, who work in white-collar jobs in major metropolitan areas. The Dockers line was born.[55]

Western consumers aged 35 to 44 spend the most on housing, cars, and entertainment. Baby boomers are busy "feathering their nests"; they account for roughly 40 percent of all the money consumers spend on household furnishings and equipment.[56] In addition, consumers aged 45 to 54 spend the most of any age category on food (30 percent above average), apparel (38 percent above average), and retirement programs (57 percent above average).[57] To appreciate the impact middle-aged consumers have and will have on our economy, consider this: At current spending levels, a 1 percent increase in the population of householders aged 35 to 54 results in an additional $8.9 billion in consumer spending.

In addition to the direct demand for products and services this age group creates, these consumers have also fostered a new baby boom of their own to keep marketers busy in the future. Because fertility rates have dropped, this new boom is not

now it's Pepsi-for those who think young
Thinking young is a wholesome attitude, an enthusiastic outlook. It means getting the most out of life, and everyone can join in. This is the life for Pepsi —light, bracing, clean-tasting Pepsi. Think young. Say "Pepsi, please!"

ENJOY THE STEVE ALLEN SHOW PRESENTED BY PEPSI WEEKLY ON ABC-TV

This 1962 Pepsi ad highlights the emphasis on youth power that began to shape our culture as baby boomers came of age in the 1960s.

as big as the one that created the baby boom generation; we can best describe the new upsurge in the number of U.S. children as a *baby boomlet*. Many boomer couples postponed getting married and having children because of the new opportunities and options for women. They began having babies in their late 20s and early 30s, resulting in fewer (but perhaps more pampered) children per family. This new emphasis on children and the family creates opportunities for products such as cars (e.g., the success of the SUV concept among "soccer Moms"), services (e.g., the day-care industry and big chains such as KinderCare), and media (e.g., magazines such as *Working Mother*).

Although advertisers are always lured by youth, many are reconsidering this fixation in light of boomers' huge spending power. An ad for the Toyota Highlander which shows boomers whose nests are emptying declares, "For your newfound freedom, it's about how you are going to reinvent yourself for what could be 30 or 40 years of retirement, which is very different from your parents and grandparents."[58] Even mobile marketers who typically blast messages to kids on their cell phones are

Many baby boomers are interested in maintaining a youthful appearance and will go to great lengths to preserve it. Botox injections are the newest craze.

beginning to target the middle-aged. For example, *Redbook* readers can bid on a year's worth of movie tickets via text messaging.[59]

THE GRAY MARKET

The old woman sits alone in her dark apartment while the television blares out a soap opera. Once every couple of days, her arthritic hands slowly and painfully open her triple-locked door and she ventures out to the corner store to buy essentials such as tea, milk, and cereal, always picking the least expensive brand. Most of the time she sits in her rocking chair, thinking sadly of her dead husband and the good times they used to have together.

Is this the image you have of a typical elderly U.S. consumer? Until recently, many marketers did. They neglected the elderly in their feverish pursuit of the youth market. But as our population ages and we live longer and healthier lives, the game is rapidly changing. A lot of businesses are updating their old stereotype of the poor recluse. The newer, more accurate image is of an active person interested in what life has to offer, and who is an enthusiastic consumer with the means and willingness to buy many goods and services. For example, as we saw earlier in this chapter, Sony targeted zoomers after the company discovered that about a third of its sales come from consumers aged 50 and older. And this market is growing even as we speak: An American turns 50 every 7 seconds.[60]

Gray Power: Seniors' Economic Clout

Think about this: By the year 2010, one of every seven Americans will be 65 or older. And by 2100 there will be 5 million of us who are at least 100 years old.[61] Few of us may be around then, but we can already see the effects of the **gray market** today. Older adults control more than 50 percent of discretionary income and worldwide, consumers over age 50 spend nearly $400 billion a year.[62] The mature market is the second-fastest-growing market segment in the United States, lagging only behind boomers. We're living longer and healthier because of more wholesome lifestyles (at least some of us), improved medical diagnoses and treatment, and changing cultural expectations about appropriate behaviors for the elderly.

Given the economic clout of senior consumers, it's often surprising how many marketers ignore them in favor of younger buyers—even though they are among the most brand loyal of any group. Older U.S. consumers repurchase a brand more frequently, consider fewer brands and dealers, and choose long-established brands more often.[63] Still, most contemporary advertising campaigns don't recognize these buyers. Even though people over the age of 50 account for half of all the discretionary spending in the United States, watch more television, go to more movies, and buy more CDs than do the young, Americans over age 50 are the focus of less than 10 percent of the advertising![64]

And the economic health of older consumers is good and getting better. Some of the important areas that stand to benefit from the surging gray market include exercise facilities, cruises and tourism, cosmetic surgery and skin treatments, and "how-to" books and university courses that offer enhanced learning opportunities. In many product categories seniors spend their money at an even greater rate than other age groups: Householders aged 55 to 64 spend 15 percent more than average per capita. They shell out 56 percent more than the average consumer on women's clothing, and as new grandparents they actually spring for more toys and playground equipment than people aged 25 to 44.[65] In fact, the average U.S. grandparent spends an average of about $500 per year on gifts for grandchildren—have you called yours today?[66]

How Should Marketers Talk to Seniors?

Hallmark's marketing group thought it stumbled on a gold mine. When it realized that about 78 million baby boomers are hitting age 50, the company created "Time of Your Life" cards to subtly flatter the aging ego. They depicted youthful-looking oldsters frolicking on beaches and diving into pools. But Hallmark missed one tiny yet crucial psychological detail: No self-respecting senior wants others to catch him shopping in the "old-people's card" section. It had to scrap the line.[67]

This debacle underscores how important it is to understand the psyche of older people. Researchers point to a set of key values relevant to mature consumers. For marketing strategies to succeed, they should link to one or more of these factors:[68]

- **Autonomy:** Mature consumers want to lead active lives and to be self-sufficient. The advertising strategy for Depends, undergarments for incontinent women made by Kimberly-Clark, centers on senior celebrities such as actress June Allyson, who plays golf and goes to parties without worrying about her condition.
- **Connectedness:** Mature consumers value the bonds they have with friends and family. Quaker Oats successfully tapped into this value with its ads featuring actor Wilford Brimley, who dispenses grandfatherly advice to the younger generation about eating right.
- **Altruism:** Mature consumers want to give something back to the world. Thrifty Car Rental found in a survey that more than 40 percent of older consumers would select a rental car company if it sponsors a program that gives van discounts to senior citizens' centers. Based on this research, the company launched its highly successful program, "Give a Friend a Lift."

PERCEIVED AGE: YOU'RE ONLY AS OLD AS YOU FEEL

Market researchers who work with older consumers often comment that people think of themselves as 10 to 15 years younger than they actually are. In fact, research confirms the popular wisdom that age is more a state of mind than of body. A person's mental

Echoing the saying, "You're only as old as you feel," this ad reminds us that a person's perceived age often does not correspond to his or her chronological age.

A ROCKING CHAIR IS A PIECE OF FURNITURE.

NOT A STATE OF MIND.

We know people whose lust for life has not and will not diminish because it's the morning after their 65th birthday. They're too busy putting the finishing touches on a book of poems. Tutoring underprivileged kids with their math. Learning the tango. Or taking acting classes. It's an outlook that works rather well with ours. Whether it's annuities, 401(k)s, IRAs, mutual funds or life insurance for your family, we've packaged a unique set of tools to help you realize your life's next great exploit. Which comes naturally when retirement isn't viewed as merely an end. But rather the way you've been living all along: passionately. For a free brochure, call 1-800-AETNA-60 or visit us at http://www.aetna.com.

Build for Retirement. Manage for Life.

Aetna Retirement Services.

outlook and activity level have a lot more to do with his longevity and quality of life than does *chronological age*, the actual number of years he has actually been alive.

That's why **perceived age**, or how old a person *feels*, is a better yardstick to use. Researchers measure perceived age on several dimensions, including "feel-age" (i.e., how old a person feels) and "look-age" (i.e., how old a person looks). [69] The older consumers get, the younger they feel relative to their actual age. For this reason, many marketers emphasize product benefits rather than age-appropriateness in marketing campaigns because many consumers will not relate to products that target their chronological age.[70]

Segmenting Seniors

The senior subculture is an extremely large market: The number of Americans aged 65 and older exceeds the entire population of Canada.[71] Senior consumers are particularly well suited for segmentation because they're easy to identify by age and stage in the family life cycle. Most receive Social Security benefits, so marketers can locate them and many belong to organizations such as the American Association of Retired Persons (aarp.org), which boasts more than 12 million dues-paying members. *AARP Magazine* (formerly *Modern Maturity*) segments its customers when it prints three outwardly similar but distinct editions: one for readers in their 50s, one for readers in their 60s, and one for those 70 years old or older.[72]

In addition to chronological age, marketers segment the elderly in terms of the particular years a person came of age (his age cohort), current marital status (e.g., widowed versus married), and his health and outlook on life.[73] For example, one ad

☐ wrinkled?
☐ wonderful?

Will society ever accept old can be beautiful?

agency devised a segmentation scheme for American women over the age of 65 that used two dimensions: self-sufficiency and perceived opinion leadership.[74] It discovered many important differences among the groups. For example, the self-sufficient group was more independent, cosmopolitan, and outgoing. Compared to the other seniors, these women were more likely to read a book, attend concerts and sporting events, and dine out.

Several segmentation approaches begin with the premise that a major determinant of elderly marketplace behavior is the way a person deals with being old.[75] **Social aging theories** try to understand how society assigns people to different roles across the life span. For example, when people retire they may reflect society's expectations for someone at this life stage—this is a major transition point when we exit from many relationships.[76] Some people become depressed, withdrawn, and apathetic as they age; some get angry and resist the thought of aging; and others accept the new challenges and opportunities this period of life offers. Table 15.2 summarizes some selected findings from **gerontographics**, a segmentation scheme that classifies mature consumers in terms of their physical well-being and social conditions such as becoming a grandparent or losing a spouse.

Selling to Seniors

<u>Match.com</u> is the largest online subscription dating service in the United States. One big reason is that it aggressively reaches out to 50+ singles and divorcées. The company

TABLE 15.2
GERONTOGRAPHICS: SELECTED CHARACTERISTICS

Segment	% of 55+ Population	Profile	Marketing Ramifications
Healthy Indulgers	18%	Have experienced the fewest events related to aging, such as retirement or widowhood, and are most likely to behave like younger consumers. Main focus is on enjoying life.	Looking for independent living and are good customers for discretionary services like home cleaning and answering machines.
Healthy Hermits	36%	React to life events like the death of a spouse by becoming withdrawn. Resent that they are expected to behave like old people.	Emphasize conformity. They want to know their appearance is socially acceptable, and tend to be comfortable with well-known brands.
Ailing Outgoers	29%	Maintain positive self-esteem despite adverse life events. They accept limitations but are still determined to get the most out of life.	Have health problems that may require a special diet. Special menus and promotions will bring these people into restaurants seen as catering to their needs.
Frail Recluses	17%	Have adjusted their lifestyles to accept old age, but have chosen to cope with negative events by becoming spiritually stronger.	Like to stay put in the same house where they raised their families. Good candidates for remodeling, also for emergency-response systems.

Source: Adapted from George P. Moschis, "Life Stages of the Mature Market," *American Demographics* (September 1996): 44–50.

made its site easier to navigate for people who are not Internet savvy. Its TV commercials feature a 71-year-old with the user name DanishBeauty22.[77]

Most older people lead more active, multidimensional lives than we assume. Nearly 60 percent engage in volunteer activities, one in four seniors aged 65 to 72 still works, and more than 14 million provide care for their grandchildren.[78] And it is crucial to remember that income alone does not express seniors' spending power. Older U.S. consumers are finished with many of the financial obligations that siphon off the income of younger consumers. Eighty percent of consumers older than age 65 own their own homes. In addition, childrearing costs are over. As the popular American bumper sticker proudly proclaims, "We're Spending Our Children's Inheritance!"

Still, outdated images of mature consumers persist. The editors of *AARP Magazine* reject about a third of the ads companies submit to them because they portray older people in a negative light. In one survey, one-third of consumers older than age 55 reported that they deliberately did not buy a product because of the way its ads stereotype older people.[79] To address these negative depictions, some marketers provide more welcoming environments for seniors:

- Wal-Mart hires older people as greeters to be sure their senior customers feel at home.
- Home Savings of America is a California bank with branches that cater to seniors. The bank supplies coffee and donuts and encourages its older customers to think of the locations as places to meet up with friends.[80]
- The Adeg Aktiv Markt 50+ in Salzburg, Austria, is Europe's first supermarket for shoppers older than age 50. The labels are big; the aisles are wide; the floors are nonskid, even when wet; and there are plenty of places to sit down. The lights are specially calibrated to reduce glare on elderly customers' more sensitive eyes. The shelves are lower so products are within easy reach. And in addition to regular shopping carts, there are carts that hook onto wheelchairs and carts

that double as seats for the weary—as soon as a shopper sits down, the wheels lock.[81]

● Japan's population is graying rapidly (21 percent of all Japanese are older than 65 years old), and businesses need to shift gears to keep up with this reality. Like the Austrian market previously mentioned, the popular Lawson convenience store chain recently embarked on a plan to eventually convert 20 percent of its nearly 8,400 stores to senior-friendly centers. These will feature broader aisles to accommodate wheelchairs, lower shelves for easier access, and price tags with enlarged print. The stores will stock instant meals that shoppers can consume without chewing and hearing aid batteries.[82]

Senior-Friendly Products

Products get a more sympathetic reception from seniors when their designers make them sensitive to physical limitations. Packages often are awkward and difficult to manage, especially for those who are frail or arthritic. Also, many serving sizes are too big for people who live alone, and coupons tend to be good for family-sized products rather than for single servings.

Some seniors have difficulty with pull-tab cans and push-open milk cartons. Ziploc packages and clear plastic wrap also can be difficult to handle. Packages need to be easier to read and they need to be lighter and smaller. Finally, designers need to pay attention to contrasting colors. A slight yellowing of the eye's lens as one ages can make it harder to see background colors on packages. Discerning between blues, greens, and violets becomes especially difficult. The closer identifying type colors are to the package or ad background color, the less visibility and attention they will command.

Carmakers are working hard to adapt their products to the aged drivers. GM redesigned some Oldsmobile models to include bigger buttons and clearer dashboard displays, and Cadillac's rearview mirrors automatically dim when headlights hit them. The Lincoln Town Car (the average age of a Lincoln driver is 67) features two sets of radio and air conditioning controls, one on the dashboard and one on the steering wheel because some older drivers have trouble shifting attention from controls to the road. Chrysler engineers are experimenting with collision-control systems that sound an alarm when a driver is too close to another car.[83]

CHAPTER SUMMARY

Now that you have finished reading this chapter you should understand why:

People have many things in common with others because they are about the same age.

● Consumers who grew up at the same time share many cultural memories because they belong to a common age cohort, so they may respond well to marketers' nostalgia appeals that remind them of these experiences.

Teens are an important age segment for marketers.

● Teenagers are in the middle of a transition from childhood to adulthood, and their self-concepts tend to be unstable. They are receptive to products that help them to be accepted and enable them to assert their independence. Because many teens earn money but have few financial obligations, they are a particularly important segment for many nonessential or expressive products, ranging from chewing gum to clothing fashions and music. Because of changes in family structure, many teens also are taking more responsibility for their families' day-to-day shopping. College students are an important but hard-to-reach market. In many cases, they are living alone for the first time, so they are making important decisions about setting up a household. Tweens are kids aged 8 to 14; they are influential purchasers of clothing, CDs, and other "feel-good" products. Many young people belong to youth tribes that influence their lifestyles and product preferences.

Baby boomers continue to be the most powerful age segment economically.

● Baby boomers are the most powerful age segment because of their size and economic clout. Boomers continue to affect demands for housing, childcare, automobiles, clothing, and many other products.

Seniors will increase in importance as a market segment.

● As the population ages, the needs of older consumers will become increasingly important. Many marketers ignore seniors because of the stereotype that they are too inactive and spend too little. This stereotype is no longer accurate. Many older adults are healthy, vigorous, and interested in new products and experiences—and they have the income to purchase them. Marketing appeals to this age subculture should focus on consumers' perceived ages, which tend to be more youthful than their chronological ages. Marketers also should emphasize concrete benefits of products because this group tends to be skeptical of vague, image-related promotions.

KEY TERMS

Age cohort, 574
Baby Boomer, 588
Connexity, 581
Digital native, 581
Generation X, 587

Gen Y, 581
Gerontographics, 593
Gray market, 590
Multigenerational marketing
   strategy, 575

Perceived age, 592
Social aging theories, 593
Tweens, 580

REVIEW QUESTIONS

1 What is an age cohort, and why is it of interest to marketers?
2 List three basic conflicts that teens face, and give an example of each.
3 How are Gen Y kids different from their older brothers and sisters?
4 What are tweens, and why are so many marketers interested in them?
5 How do tribal gatherings represent a marketing opportunity?

6 What are some of the most efficient ways for marketers to connect with college students?
7 What is a "reward car" and who buys this type of vehicle?
8 What are some industries that stand to benefit most from the increasing affluence and vitality of the senior market?
9 What are some effective ways to segment the senior market?

CONSUMER BEHAVIOR CHALLENGE

■ DISCUSS

1 What are some possible marketing opportunities at reunions? What effects might attending such an event have on consumers' self-esteem, body image, and so on?

2 This chapter describes members of Gen Y as much more traditional and team oriented than their older brothers and sisters. Do you agree?

3 What are some of the positives and negatives of targeting college students? Identify some specific marketing strategies you feel have either been successful or unsuccessful. What characteristics distinguish the successes from the failures?

4 Why have Baby Boomers had such an important impact on consumer culture?

5 How has the baby boomlet changed attitudes toward childrearing practices and created demand for different products and services?

6 "Kids these days seem content to just hang out, surf the Net, IM with their friends, and watch mindless TV shows all day." How accurate is this statement?

7 Is it practical to assume that people age 55 and older constitute one large consumer market? How can marketers segment this age subculture? What are some important variables to keep in mind when we tailor marketing strategies to older adults?

■ APPLY

8 Find good and bad examples of advertising that targets older consumers. To what degree does advertising stereotype the elderly? What elements of ads or other promotions appear to determine their effectiveness in reaching and persuading this group?

9 If you were a marketing researcher assigned to study what products are "cool," how would you do this? Do you agree with the definitions of "cool" the young people provided in the chapter?

10 Marketers of entrenched brands like Nike, Pepsi, and Levi Strauss are tearing their hair out over gen Y consumers. Image-building campaigns (e.g., 50 Cent endorsing Reebok) are not as effective as they once were. What advice would you give to a marketer who wants to appeal to Gen Y? What are major dos and don'ts? Can you provide some examples of specific marketing attempts that work or don't work?

Case Study

SCION'S QUEST TO CRACK GEN Y

How can a big company capture the attention of Gen Y? To do so, Toyota created an entirely new division to go after young drivers. After various attempts to sell vehicles to people born between 1977 and 1994, the giant Japanese carmaker decided that if it was going to seriously go after this age segment, it needed an entirely new approach and image.

Scion (pronounced *sigh-on*) launched in early 2004 with only two models; the small, wedgy four-door xA hatchback, and the odd-looking four-door xB hatchback that looks more like the shipping crate that a real car would come in. Since then, the company added the more stylish tC coupe and the xD hatchback. All are packed with standard features and retail for less than $18,000.

Scion is more than just another car company, however. Jim Farley, vice president of the division, calls Scion a "laboratory for understanding the quirks and demands of Generation Y." Scion's marketers have discovered some core

characteristics of this group that have influenced their marketing strategy. These include:

● **Gen Y-ers are impervious to traditional advertising:** Like so many other companies, Scion has found that Gen Y consumers resent the common mass media tactics of big brands. For this reason, Scion spends most of its promotional dollars on advertising in obscure lifestyle magazines that target small youth culture niches. In addition, Scion uses grassroots efforts to take the brand to the target market through staged events that seem to just make the vehicle appear in natural situations (i.e., traveling art and music shows).

● **Gen Y-ers are individualistic:** Young drivers want more than transportation. They want a customized fashion statement. Because of this, Scion's big allure is the huge list of dealer options. This includes everything from spoilers and LED interior lights to custom graphics, leather interiors, engine-performance parts, and custom wheels. Eighty percent of Scion buyers purchase at least one accessory to make their car their own.

- **Gen Y-ers are relatively well-off:** This age group has more money (and more credit cards) than did previous generations at the same age. While they are still somewhat limited by their beer level budgets, they have champagne appetites. That's why Scions come well-equipped with standard features. That's also why Scion has priced its vehicles low. This way, customers can spend their money on custom accessories. And that they do. The average buyer spends $800 to $1,000 on accessories up front. Many continue to treat their vehicles as works in progress; they add goodies as they can afford them.

- **Gen Y-ers are Web savvy:** For this reason, Scion has a strong Web-presence, including a very well-developed Web site that allows prospective buyers to customize online. Two-thirds of buyers do so prior to visiting the showroom. Scion owners often gather at community Internet sites like Scionlife.com, which gets hundreds of thousands of hits a day.

Have Toyota's efforts to reach America's youth paid off? Sales exceeded expectations from the beginning, with 173,000 Scions flying out of U.S. showrooms in 2006. Scion customers are among the youngest in the industry; the average owner ranges in age from 26 to 38 (the average age for the industry is well over 40). What's more, 80 percent of Gen Y

shoppers now recognize the Scion brand. Moreover, 85 percent of buyers are new to Toyota, with most coming from the company's number one competitor, Honda.

Scion's long-term objective is to reach unit sales of 300,000. By 2010, 63 million gen Y members reach driving age. At this time they will replace their Boomer parents as the largest and most influential population in the United States. If Scion stays on its current course, it's in good shape to command the loyalty of a fickle generation.

DISCUSSION QUESTIONS

1 Is Toyota wasting its time by paying so much attention to age as a segmentation variable? Explain.

2 Considering the characteristics of Generation Y, what do you see as some of the challenges that Scion faces in the future as their brand grows?

3 If Gen Y-ers indeed are "impervious to advertising," how can Scion continue to grow without reaching young people through traditional media outlets?

Sources: Mark Rechtin, "Scion Marketing To Stay Outside Mainstream," *Automotive News* (May 7, 2007): 8; Terry Box, "Toyota's Scion Sales Soar with Young Buyers," *Dallas Morning News* (April 22, 2005); Lillie Guyer, "Scion Chases Cool Kids in Cool Mags," *Automotive News* (March 21, 2005): 50; Chris Woodyard, "Outside-the-Box Scion Scores with Young Drivers," *USA Today* (May 2, 2005), 1B.

NOTES

1. Shelly Reese, "The Lost Generation," *Marketing Tools* (April 1997): 50.
2. Toby Elkin, "Sony Marketing Aims at Lifestyle Segments," *Advertising Age* (March 18, 2002): 3.
3. Anil Mathur, George P. Moschis, and Euehun Lee, "Life Events and Brand Preference Changes," *Journal of Consumer Behavior* 3, no. 2 (December 2003): 129–41; James W. Gentry, Stacey Menzel Baker, and Frederic B. Kraft, "The Role of Possessions in Creating, Maintaining, and Preserving Identity: Variations over the Life Course," in Frank Kardes and Mita Sujan, eds., *Advances in Consumer Research* 22 (1995): 413–18.
4. Stuart Elliot, "Saturn Tries Alternate Worlds to Change Its Image," *New York Times on the Web* (January 8, 2003).
5. Bickley Townsend, "*Ou Sont les Reiges Díantan?* (Where Are the Snows of Yesteryear?)" *American Demographics* (October 1988): 2.
6. Paula Mergenhagen, "The Reunion Market," *American Demographics* (April 1996): 30–34.
7. Gina Chon and Jennifer Saranow, "Bling-Bling Buick Seeking Younger Buyers, General Motors' Staid Brand Uses Customized Cars, Celebrities to Reach the Hip Hop Crowd," (January 11, 2007): B1; Gina Chon, "Car Makers Court Two Generations," *Wall Street Journal* (May 9, 2006): B1.
8. Stephen Holden, "After the War the Time of the Teen-Ager," *New York Times* (May 7, 1995): E4.
9. Arundhati Parmar, "Global Youth United," *Marketing News* (October 28, 2002): 1–49.
10. Cornelia Pechmann and Chuan-Fong Shih, "Smoking Scenes in Movies and Antismoking Advertisements before Movies: Effects on Youth," *Journal of Marketing* 63 (July 1999): 1–13.
11. Maureen Tkacik, "Alternative Teens Are Hip to Hot Topics Mall Stores," *Wall Street Journal Interactive Edition* (February 12, 2002).
12. Junu Bryan Kim, "For Savvy Teens: Real Life, Real Solutions," *New York Times* (August 23, 1993): S1.
13. Excerpted from David B. Wooten, "From Labeling Possessions to Possessing Labels: Ridicule and Socialization among Adolescents," *Journal of Consumer Research* 33 (September 2006): 188–98.
14. For a look at localized versus global youth culture dynamics in Scandinavia, cf. Dannie Kjeldgaard, and Søren Askegaard, "The Glocalization of Youth Culture: The Global Youth Segment as Structures of Common Difference," *Journal of Consumer Research* 33, no. 2 (2006): 231.
15. Howard W. French, "Vocation for Dropouts Is Painting Tokyo Red," *New York Times on the Web* (March 5, 2000).
16. Karen Springen, Ana Figueroa, and Nicole Joseph-Goteiner, "The Truth about Tweens," *Newsweek* (October 18, 1999): 62–72.
17. "The Human Truman Show," *Fortune* (July 8, 2002): 96–98.
18. Rob Walker, "Training Brand," *New York Times Magazine Online* (February 27, 2005), accessed February 27, 2005.
19. Queena Sook Kim and Suzanne Vranica, "Tween Queen Comes to Fashion Doll's Aid," *Wall Street Journal* (August 23, 2004): B1.
20. Steve Kroft, "The Echo Boomers," available from www.CBSNews.com (October 3, 2004), accessed October 3, 2004.
21. Richard Gibson, "McDonald's Seeks Young Adults in Their Realm [Podcasts]," *Wall Street Journal Online* (August 2, 2006), accessed August 2, 2006.
22. Scott McCartney, "Society's Subcultures Meet by Modem," *Wall Street Journal* (December 8, 1994): B1.
23. Michael J. Weiss, "To Be about to Be," *American Demographics* (September 2003): 29–48.
24. Ellen Neuborne, "Generation Y," *BusinessWeek* (February 15, 1999): 83.
25. A. A. Nolan, "Me, Myself, and IM," *Brandweek* (August 13, 2001): 24.
26. Laurel Anderson and Julie L. Ozanne, "The Cyborg Teen: Identity Play and Deception on the Internet," *Advances in Consumer Research* 33, no. 1 (2006).
27. Sarah Ellison and Emily Steel, "To Lure Teens to Its Latest Web Site, Condé Nast Turns to the 'Flip Squad,'" (December 19, 2006): B1; www.flip.com, accessed July 26, 2007.
28. Nina M. Lentini, "HP Ads Help Teens Take Control of Parents' Minds," *Marketing Daily* (July 26, 2007), www.mediapost.com, accessed July 26, 2007.

29. Alex Vieiga, "Virtual Design Wizards Kept Busy by Online Worlds Like Second Life," *USAToday.com* (February 24, 2007), accessed February 24, 2007.

30. Nat Ives, "Latest Promotion Vehicle Is a Hand-Held Media Device. Will Anyone Watch?" *New York Times Online* (May 3, 2005), accessed May 3, 2005.

31. Jennifer Corbett Dooren, "Alcohol Ads Impact Consumption among the Young, Study Shows," *Wall Street Journal Online* (January 2, 2006), accessed January 2, 2006; cf. also Maria G. Piacentini and Emma N. Banister, "Getting Hammered? Students Coping with Alcohol," *Journal of Consumer Behaviour* 5, no. 2 (2006): 145.

32. Cyndee Miller, "Phat Is Where It's at for Today's Teen Market," *Marketing News* (August 15, 1994): 6; see also Tamara F. Mangleburg and Terry Bristol, "Socialization and Adolescents' Skepticism toward Advertising," *Journal of Advertising* 27 (Fall 1998): 11; see also Gil McWilliam and John Deighton, "Alloy.com: Marketing to Generation Y," *Journal of Interactive Marketing* 14 (Spring 2000): 74–83.

33. Adapted from Gerry Khermouch, "Didja C That Kewl Ad?" *BusinessWeek* (August 26, 2002): 158–60.

34. Veronique Cova and Bernard Cova, "Tribal Aspects of Postmodern Consumption Research: The Case of French In-Line Roller Skaters," *Journal of Consumer Behavior* 1 (June 2001): 67–76.

35. Terry Lefton, "Feet on the Street," *Brandweek* (March 2000): 36–40.

36. C. C. Mann, "Why 14-Year-Old Japanese Girls Rule the World," *Yahoo! Internet Life* (August 2001): 98–105.

37. Dave Carpenter, "Tuning in Teens: Marketers Intensify Pitch for 'Most Savvy' Generation Ever," *Canadian Press* (November 19, 2000).

38. Beth Synder Bulik, "Want to Build a Hipper Brand? Take a Trip to Trend School: Intelligence Group Endeavor Gives Marketers a Crash Course in Cool," *AdAge.com* (February 19, 2007), accessed February 19, 2007.

39. Daniel McGinn, "Pour on the Pitch," *Newsweek* (May 31, 1999): 50–51.

40. Jack Neff, "P&G Targets Teens via Tremor, Toejam Site," *Advertising Age* (March 5, 2001): 12.

41. Gary J. Bamossy, Michael R. Solomon, Basil G. Englis, and Trinske Antonidis, "You're Not Cool If You Have to Ask: Gender in the Social Construction of Coolness," paper presented at the Association for Consumer Research Gender Conference, Chicago, June 2000; see also Clive Nancarrow, Pamela Nancarrow, and Julie Page, "An Analysis of the Concept of Cool and Its Marketing Implications," *Journal of Consumer Behavior* 1 (June 2002): 311–22.

42. Ellen Goodman, "The Selling of Teenage Anxiety," *Washington Post* (November 24, 1979).

43. Ellen R. Foxman, Patriya S. Tansuhaj, and Karin M. Ekstrom, "Family Members' Perceptions of Adolescents' Influence in Family Decision-making," *Journal of Consumer Research* 15 (March 1989): 482–91.

44. Rebecca Gardyn, "Educated Consumers," *Demographics* (November 2002): 18.

45. Tibbett L. Speer, "College Come-Ons," *American Demographics* (March 1998): 40–46; Fannie Weinstein, "Time to Get Them in Your Franchise," *Advertising Age* (February 1, 1988): S6.

46. www.mtvU.com, accessed July 26, 2007; www.collegehumor.com, accessed July 26, 2007.

47. Laura Randall, "Battle of the Campus TV Networks," *New York Times on the Web* (January 12, 2003).

48. Maria Aspan, "Nielsen Will Start to Measure TV Habits of College Students," *New York Times on the Web* (February 20, 2006).

49. Laura Zinn, "Move Over, Boomers," *BusinessWeek* (December 14, 1992): 7.

50. Robert Scally, "The Customer Connection: Gen X Grows Up, They're in Their 30s Now," *Discount Store News* 38, no. 20 (1999).

51. Angel Jennings, "Contests, YouTube and Commercials Converge for Skin Product," *New York Times Online* (July 26, 2007), accessed July 26, 2007; cf. also Isabelle Szmigin and Marylyn Carrigan, "Consumption and Community: Choices for Women over Forty," *Journal of Consumer Behaviour* 5, no. 4 (2006): 292.

52. Brad Edmondson, "Do the Math," *American Demographics* (October 1999): 50–56.

53. Alex Williams, "What Women Want: More Horses," *New York Times Online* (June 12, 2005).

54. John Fetto, "The Wild Ones," *American Demographics* (February 2000): 72.

55. Kevin Keller, *Strategic Marketing Management* (Upper Saddle River, NJ: Prentice Hall, 1998).

56. Edmondson, "Do the Math."

57. Amy Merrick, "Gap Plans Five Forth & Towne Stores for Fall," *Wall Street Journal* (April 22, 2005): B1.

58. Stuart Eliot, "Flower Power in Ad Land," *New York Times Online* (April 11, 2006), accessed April 11, 2006.

59. Emily Steel, "Grabbing Older Consumers via Cellphone Mobile Marketing Finds Success in Sweepstakes; Teaching How to Text," *Wall Street Journal* (January 31, 2007): B3.

60. Elkin Tobi, "Sony Ad Campaign Targets Boomers-Turned-Zoomers," *Advertising Age* (October 21, 2002): 6.

61. D'Vera Cohn, "2100 Census Forecast: Minorities Expected to Account for 60% of U.S. Population," *Washington Post* (January 13, 2000): A5.

62. Catherine A. Cole and Nadine N. Castellano, "Consumer Behavior," in James E. Binnen, ed., *Encyclopedia of Gerontology*, Vol. 1 (San Diego, CA: Academic Press, 1996), 329–39.

63. Raphaël Lambert-Pandraud, Gilles Laurent, and Eric Lapersonne, "Repeat Purchasing of New Automobiles by Older Consumers: Empirical Evidence and Interpretations," *Journal of Marketing* 69 (April 2005): 97–113.

64. Jonathan Dee, "The Myth of '18 to 34,'" *New York Times Magazine Online* (October 13, 2002), accessed October 11, 2007; Hillary Chura, "Ripe Old Age," *Advertising Age* (May 13, 2002): 16.

65. Cheryl Russell, "The Ungraying of America," *American Demographics* (July 1997): 12.

66. Jeff Brazil, "You Talkin' to Me?" *American Demographics* (December 1998): 55–59.

67. Pamela Paul, "Sell It to the Psyche," *Time* (September 15, 2003): Bonus Section inside Business.

68. David B. Wolfe, "Targeting the Mature Mind," *American Demographics* (March 1994): 32–36.

69. Benny Barak and Leon G. Schiffman, "Cognitive Age: A Nonchronological Age Variable," in Kent B. Monroe, ed., *Advances in Consumer Research* 8 (Provo, UT: Association for Consumer Research, 1981): 602–6.

70. David B. Wolfe, "An Ageless Market," *American Demographics* (July 1987): 27–55.

71. Lenore Skenazy, "These Days, It's Hip to Be Old," *Advertising Age* (February 15, 1988): 8.

72. Nat Ives, "AARP Aims to Deliver Message to Marketers," *New York Times on The Web* (January 12, 2004).

73. L. A. Winokur, "Targeting Consumers," *Wall Street Journal Interactive Edition* (March 6, 2000).

74. Ellen Day, Brian Davis, Rhonda Dove, and Warren A. French, "Reaching the Senior Citizen Market(s)," *Journal of Advertising Research* (December 1987–January 1988): 23–30.

75. Day et al., "Reaching the Senior Citizen Market(s)"; Warren A. French and Richard Fox, "Segmenting the Senior Citizen Market," *Journal of Consumer Marketing* 2 (1985): 61–74; Jeffrey G. Towle and Claude R. Martin, Jr., "The Elderly Consumer: One Segment or Many?" in Beverlee B. Anderson, ed., *Advances in Consumer Research* 3 (Provo, UT: Association for Consumer Research, 1976): 463.

76. Catherine A. Cole and Nadine N. Castellano, "Consumer Behavior," *Encyclopedia of Gerontology*, vol. 1 (1996): 329–39.

77. Sara Silver, "How Match.com Found Love among Boomers; Dating Site Prospers Targeting Older Singles; The Body Art Question," *Wall Street Journal* (January 27, 2007): A1.

78. Rick Adler, "Stereotypes Won't Work with Seniors Anymore," *Advertising Age* (November 11, 1996): 32.

79. Melinda Beck, "Going for the Gold," *Newsweek* (April 23, 1990): 74.

80. Paco Underhill, "Seniors & Stores," *American Demographics* (April 1996): 44–48.

81. Tania Ralli, "As Europe Ages, a Grocery Chain Extends a Hand," *New York Times Online* (December 27, 2003).

82. Norimitsu Onishi, "In a Graying Japan, Lower Shelves and Wider Aisles," *New York Times Online* (September 4, 2006), accessed September 4, 2006.

83. Michelle Krebs, "50-Plus and King of the Road," *Advertising Age* (May 1, 2000): S18; Daniel McGinn and Julie Edelson Halpert, "Driving Miss Daisy—and Selling Her the Car," *Newsweek* (February 3, 1997): 14.

FEELING LUCKY?

Consumers and Culture

OK, we're coming up to the finish line. In the final section of the book, we'll look at ourselves as members of a broad cultural system. We'll focus on the "profound" idea that everyday, mundane consumption activities often have deeper meanings. In Chapter 16, we explore some of the basic building blocks of culture and the impact that myths and rituals exert on "modern" consumers. Chapter 17 focuses on the ways products spread throughout the members of a culture, and across cultures as well. This final chapter talks about why some consumer products succeed while others don't, and it also examines how successful Western products influence consumer behavior around the world.

■ CHAPTERS AHEAD

CHAPTER 16	CHAPTER 17
Cultural Influences on Consumer Behavior	Global Consumer Culture

Cultural Influences on Consumer Behavior

Chapter Objectives

When you finish this chapter you should understand why:

- A culture is a society's personality; it shapes our identities as individuals.

- Myths are stories that express a culture's values, and in modern times marketing messages convey these values.

- Many of our consumption activities including holiday observances, grooming, and gift-giving are rituals.

- We describe products as either sacred or profane, and it's not unusual for some products to move back and forth between the two categories.

Christine is at her wits' end. It's bad enough that she has a deadline looming on that new Christmas promotion for her gift shop. Now, there's trouble on the home front as well: Her son Ken had to go and flunk his driver's license road exam, and he's just about suicidal because he feels he can't be a "real man" without successfully obtaining his license. To top things off, now her much-anticipated vacation to Disney World with her younger stepchildren will have to be postponed because she simply can't find the time to get away.

When Christine meets up with her buddy Melissa at their local Starbucks for their daily "retreat," her mood starts to brighten. Somehow the calm of the café rubs off as she savors her *grande cappuccino*. Melissa consoles her with her usual assurances, and then she prescribes the ultimate remedy to defeat the blues: Go home, take a nice long bath, and then consume a quart of Starbucks Espresso Swirl ice cream. Yes, that's the ticket. It's amazing how the little things in life can make such a big difference. As she strolls out the door, Christine makes a mental note to get Melissa a really nice Christmas gift this year. She's earned it.

Understanding Culture

People around the globe mimic Christine's daily coffee "fix" as they take a break from the daily grind and affirm their relationships with others. Of course, the products they consume in the process range from black Turkish coffee to Indian tea, or from lager beer to hashish. Starbucks turns the coffee break into a cultural event that for many is almost like a cult. The average Starbucks customer visits 18 times a month, and 10 percent of the clientele stops by twice a day.[1] Even a simple cup of coffee is more than a simple cup of coffee.

Culture is a society's personality. It includes both abstract ideas, such as values and ethics, and material objects and services, such as the automobiles, clothing, food, art, and sports, that a society produces and values. Put another way, **culture** is the accumulation of shared meanings, rituals, norms, and traditions among the members of an organization or society.

We simply can't understand consumption unless we consider its cultural context: Culture is the "lens" through which people view products. Ironically, the effects of culture on consumer behavior are so powerful and far-reaching that it's sometimes difficult to grasp their importance. Like a fish immersed in water, we don't always appreciate this power until we encounter a different culture. Suddenly, many of the assumptions we take for granted about the clothes we wear, the food we eat, or the way we address others no longer seem to apply. The effect of encountering such differences can be so great that the term "culture shock" is not an exaggeration.

We often discover these cultural expectations only when we violate them. For example, while on tour in New Zealand, the Spice Girls (remember them?) created a stir among New Zealand's indigenous Maoris when they performed a war dance that only men can do. A tribal official indignantly stated, "It is not acceptable in our culture, and especially by girlie pop stars from another culture."[2] Americans had a somewhat similar reaction when Posh Spice came to the United States with her husband David Beckham to teach Americans about the joys of football! Sensitivity to cultural issues, whether among rock stars or brand managers, can only occur when we understand these underlying dimensions—and that's this chapter's goal.

Our culture determines the overall priorities we attach to different activities and products, and it also helps to decide whether specific products will make it. A product that provides benefits to members of a culture at any point in time has a much better chance of attaining marketplace acceptance. For example, American culture began to emphasize the concept of a fit, trim body as an ideal of appearance in the mid-1970s. The premium consumers put on thinness, which stemmed from underlying values such as mobility, wealth, and a focus on the self, greatly contributed to Miller's success when the brewer launched its Lite beer. However, when Gablinger's introduced a similar low-cal beer in the 1960s the product failed. This beverage was "ahead of its time" because American beer drinkers at that time (who were almost all men) weren't worried about cutting down on calories.

The relationship between consumer behavior and culture is a two-way street. On the one hand, consumers are more likely to embrace products and services that resonate with a culture's priorities at any given time. On the other hand, it's worthwhile for us to understand which products do get accepted because this knowledge provides a window into the dominant cultural ideals of that period. Consider, for example, some American products that successfully reflected dominant values during their time:

- The TV dinner reflected changes in U.S. family structure and the onset of a new informality in American home life.
- Cosmetics made from natural materials without animal testing reflected consumers' apprehensions about pollution, waste, and animal rights.

This ad for a line of veggie foods borrows the look of World War II propaganda art to imply that eating our broccoli is an heroic act.

- Condoms marketed in pastel carrying cases for female buyers signaled changes in attitudes toward sexual responsibility and openness in the West.

Culture is not static. It is continually evolving, synthesizing old ideas with new ones. A *cultural system* consists of these functional areas:[3]

- **Ecology:** The way a system adapts to its habitat. The technology a culture uses to obtain and distribute resources shapes its ecology. The Japanese, for example, greatly value products that make efficient use of space because of the cramped conditions in their urban centers.[4]

- **Social structure:** The way people maintain an orderly social life. This includes the domestic and political groups dominant within the culture (e.g., the nuclear family versus the extended family; representative government versus dictatorship).
- **Ideology:** The mental characteristics of a people and the way they relate to their environment and social groups. This relates to the idea of a common *worldview* (discussed in Chapter 13). Members of a culture tend to share ideas about principles of order and fairness. They also share an *ethos*, or a set of moral and aesthetic principles. A theme park in Bombay called Water Kingdom that caters to India's emerging middle class illustrates how distinctive a culture's worldview can be. Many consumers there are unfamiliar with mixed-sex swimming in public, so the park rents swimsuits to women who have never worn them before. No thongs here, though: The suits cover the women from wrists to ankles.[5]

Although every culture is different, four dimensions account for much of this variability:[6]

1 **Power distance:** The way members perceive differences in power when they form interpersonal relationships. Some cultures emphasize strict, vertical relationships (e.g., Japan), whereas others, such as the United States, stress a greater degree of equality and informality.
2 **Uncertainty avoidance:** The degree to which people feel threatened by ambiguous situations and have beliefs and institutions that help them to avoid this uncertainty (e.g., organized religion).
3 **Masculinity/femininity:** The degree to which a culture clearly defines sex roles (see Chapter 5). Traditional societies are more likely to possess very explicit rules about the acceptable behaviors of men and women, such as who is responsible for certain tasks within the family unit.
4 **Individualism:** The extent to which the culture values the welfare of the individual versus that of the group (see Chapter 11). Cultures differ in their emphasis on individualism versus collectivism. In **collectivist cultures**, people subordinate their personal goals to those of a stable in-group. In contrast, consumers in **individualist cultures** attach more importance to personal goals, and people are more likely to change memberships when the demands of the group (e.g., workplace, church, etc.) become too costly. Whereas a collectivist society will stress values (see Chapter 4), such as self-discipline and accepting one's position in life, people in individualist cultures emphasize personal enjoyment, excitement, equality, and freedom. Some strongly individualist cultures include the United States, Australia, Great Britain, Canada, and the Netherlands. Venezuela, Pakistan, Taiwan, Thailand, Turkey, Greece, and Portugal are some examples of strongly collectivist cultures.[7]

As we saw in Chapter 4, values are very general ideas about good and bad goals. From these flow norms, or rules that dictate what is right or wrong, acceptable or unacceptable. We explicitly decide on *enacted norms*, such as the rule that a green traffic light means "go" and a red one means "stop." Many norms, however, are much more subtle. We discover these *crescive norms* as we interact with others. These are all types of crescive norms:[8]

- A *custom* is a norm people handed down that controls basic behaviors, such as division of labor in a household or how we practice particular ceremonies.
- A *more* ("mor-ay") is a custom with a strong moral overtone. It often involves a *taboo*, or forbidden behavior, such as incest or cannibalism. Violation of a more often meets with strong sanctions. In Islamic countries such as Saudi Arabia, people consider it sacrilege to display underwear on store mannequins or to feature a woman's body in advertising, so retailers have to tread lightly—one

lingerie store designed special headless and legless mannequins with only the slightest hint of curves to display its products.[9]

- *Conventions* are norms regarding the conduct of everyday life. These rules often deal with the subtleties of consumer behavior, including the "correct" way to furnish one's house, wear one's clothes, host a dinner party, and so on. The Chinese are grappling with a cultural problem as they prepare for the 2008 Olympics in Beijing: Local habits are at odds with what foreign visitors expect to encounter. For one, it's common to spit on the sidewalk—the sinus-clearing, phlegmy pre-spit hawking sound is so common that one visitor dubbed it "the national anthem of China." The government already is imposing a hefty fine for public spitting to get people accustomed to holding in their saliva before hordes of fans descend on the city.[10]

All three types of crescive norms at times operate to completely define a culturally appropriate behavior. For example, a more may tell us what kind of food it's OK to eat. These norms vary across cultures, so a meal of dog is taboo in the United States, Hindus shun steak, and Muslims avoid pork products. A custom dictates the appropriate hour at which we should serve the meal. Conventions tell us how to eat the meal, including such details as the utensils we use, table etiquette, and even the appropriate apparel to wear at dinnertime. We often take these conventions for granted, assuming that they are the "right" things to do (again, until we travel to a foreign country!). It is good to remember that much of what we know about these norms we learn *vicariously* (see Chapter 3) as we observe the behaviors of actors in television commercials, sitcoms, print ads, and other media.

Cultural differences show up in all kinds of daily activities. For example, a Big Boy restaurant in Thailand was having trouble attracting customers. After interviewing hundreds of people, the company found out why. Some said the restaurant's "room energy" was bad and that the food was unfamiliar. Others said the Big Boy statue (like the one Dr. Evil rode in the *Austin Powers* movies) made them nervous. One of the restaurant's executives commented, "It suddenly dawned on me that, here I was, trying to get a 3,500-year-old culture to eat 64-year-old food." Now, since the company put some Thai items on the menu, business is picking up.[11] No word yet on the fate of the statue.

MYTHS AND RITUALS

Every culture develops stories and ceremonies that help us make sense of the world. When we hear about some strange practice that goes on in another place, it may be hard to figure out what these people are thinking. Yet, our own cultural practices seem quite normal—even though a visitor may find them equally bizarre! Just take a European to a NASCAR event and you'll see how this works.

To appreciate how "primitive" belief systems influence our supposedly "modern" rational society, consider the avid interest many of us have in magic and luck. Marketers of health foods, antiaging cosmetics, exercise programs, and gambling casinos often imply that their offerings have "magical" properties that ward off sickness, old age, poverty, or just plain bad luck. People by the millions play their "lucky numbers" in the lottery, carry rabbits' feet and other amulets to ward off "the evil eye," and own "lucky" clothing.

When the calendar hit July 7, 2007—7/7/07—many people scrambled to take advantage of its link to lucky 777. Western culture associates the number seven with good fortune (like the seven sacraments in Roman Catholicism) and marketers from Wal-Mart to Las Vegas casinos jumped on the bandwagon. The Mandalay Bay Casino hosted a group wedding for more than 100 couples. The New York City Ritz-Carlton even offered a Lucky Number 7 wedding package with a reception for 77, a seven-tier wedding cake, and a seven-night honeymoon at any Ritz in the world for $77,777.[13] Keep in mind that these beliefs are culturecentric so they take on different forms

Marketing Pitfall

Marketers continue to push the envelope as they challenge society's norms regarding what topics are appropriate to discuss in public. Products that people only used to whisper about now are popping up in ads and billboards, including feminine hygiene products, condoms, lubricants, grooming aids, and pregnancy tests. A recent set of commercials for a digital home-pregnancy test kit even broke a taboo on showing urination. As a stream of liquid flows onto the device, a voice-over says, "Introducing the most sophisticated piece of technology . . . you will ever pee on." Ads for feminine hygiene products used to barely hint at their function (often by depicting a smiling woman wearing white to signal how well the item worked). Today, Procter & Gamble's Always line of menstrual pads advertises with the cheerful theme, "Have a happy period."[12]

CB AS I SEE IT

Professor Russell Belk
York University

In a 1979 movie called *The China Syndrome*, a meltdown in an American nuclear reactor threatened to bore a hole through the earth to China. Today, there are much faster ways to reach China by e-mail, text messaging, satellite television, podcasts, and other such technologies. The year before *The China Syndrome* opened in theaters, China opened its doors to the world through a group of strategically positioned special economic zones. Deng Xiaoping had replaced Mao Zedong and "market socialism" was beginning to replace the centralized planning of communism. Deng came to the special economic zone city of Shenzhen, across the border from Hong Kong, and pronounced a revolutionary new slogan. In sharp contrast to the old mottos urging Chinese people to sacrifice and carry the revolution forward by hard work and austere consumption, the new slogan read "To Get Rich Is Glorious."

This was the beginning of an outward-looking China that initiated a still-continuing period of remarkable economic growth toward becoming the world's largest economy (something it should achieve by 2026 given its current rates of growth). It was also the start of an equally profound consumer revolution in China as the market-directed economy took hold. Especially in China's large cities, a prosperous new middle class arose along with a number of millionaires and a few billionaires. From drab stores, identical Sun Yat-Sen ("Mao") jackets, and advertising-free public spaces, Chinese consumer culture burst on the scene in these cities in a spectacular way. China quickly became a natural laboratory in which we might observe the effects of consumerism, materialism, and dramatic changes in material lifestyles.

What sorts of effects are we seeing from these changes in Chinese consumption? One effect that seems apparent is that besides its *nouveau riche* consumers, China as a nation might be regarded as a *nouveau riche* country, with all the reckless and brash spending this implies. Shanghai now has more skyscrapers than New York City. Beijing totally revamped itself for the 2008 Olympics. And Shenzhen is now virtually indistinguishable from Hong Kong, except for its three large amusement parks, including Window on the World with its replica of the Eiffel Tower, an indoor ski mountain,

around the world. For example, in China eight is the luckiest number. The Chinese word for eight is *ba*, which rhymes with *fa*, the Chinese character for wealth. It's no coincidence that the Summer Olympics in Beijing opens on 8/8/08 at 8 P.M.[14]

Even scientists and astronauts, those most rational of folks, have their own defenses against bad karma. In a custom that dates from the first U.S. space shuttle mission in 1981, shuttle crews won't leave the suit-up room until the commander loses in a card game where they repeatedly draw poker hands until he ends up with the lowest. During the Apollo era, one of the program managers always wore the same sport coat and he shredded the coat and distributed pieces to his co-workers when the program ended. Russian cosmonauts by tradition don't watch their spacecraft roll to the landing pad before liftoff and they also repeat a tradition that Yuri Gagarin, the first man in space, started in 1961: They urinate against a tire of the bus that takes them to the spacecraft prior to launch.[15]

Interest in the occult tends to spike when members of a society feel overwhelmed or powerless—magical remedies simplify our lives by giving us "easy" answers. Many consumers even regard the computer with awe as a sort of "electronic magician" with the ability to solve our problems (or in other cases to cause data to magically disappear!).[16] Software developers even supply "wizards" that help guide the uninitiated and the reconstructions of many famous world monuments and icons. It is said that the national bird of China is the construction crane. Whereas Japan remains the world's largest market for luxury brands such as Luis Vuitton, Prada, and Chanel, Chinese consumption of such brands is not far behind and is growing rapidly. And for those who can't yet afford such brands, there is an array of counterfeits that are graded "A," "B," and "C" according to how perfectly they replicate the originals. In an eight-country study posing consumer "ethical dilemmas" that included buying counterfeit goods, Giana Eckhardt, Tim Devinney, and I found that Chinese consumers stood out by failing to see any ethical problem with such behavior. They instead insisted that the famous brands were unethical because their prices were so outrageous. If the clever Chinese could find a way to right the balances with copies, then good for them our Chinese interviewees said.

Something else that has changed in China is advertising. When advertising returned to China in the late 1970s, it was initially unemotional, informational, and utilitarian in its appeals. But 30 years later, Nan Zhou and I found that Chinese advertising has become much more similar to Western advertising, including its use of many Caucasian models. This prompted a study that is currently underway examining portrayals of beauty and skin color in several Asian countries. Early results suggest that although lighter skin color is held to be extremely important in these countries, this is not entirely because of a desire to look more Western or to attain a globalized standard of beauty. There are also distinctly Asian traditions of whiteness such as those of Japanese geishas and Chinese opera. But the study also raises important questions about globalism, race, and nationalism.

In studies I have done with Güliz Ger, we found that consumer materialism (believing that consumer goods are the major source of happiness in life) tends to increase during periods of sudden economic growth. Such growth appears to upset the status quo with regard to social prestige, and consumer goods increase in importance as a way to shore up or increase social status. The current China syndrome involving conspicuous consumption, luxury goods, counterfeit goods, and volatile standards of beauty seems to be a key example of such a status scramble. At the same time, the formerly flat Chinese income distribution is becoming more polarized through extremes of wealth and poverty that differ between urban and rural areas, coastal and non-coastal areas, dominant and minority ethnic groups, and Eastern and Western China. Thirty years is enough to see some of the effects of the consumer revolution in China, but the natural experiment is far from over. And we have only to contrast the consumer boom in pre-communist Shanghai of the 1930s versus the Chinese cultural revolution of the 1960s to realize that conditions can change dramatically in an equally short period of time.

through their programs! Or, we may even believe a person's soul possesses an object; kids (and maybe some adults as well) believe that when they put on their Air Nikes they magically absorb some of the athletic ability of Michael Jordan. Sound preposterous? The movie *Like Mike* (2002) had this storyline. In this section, we'll discuss myths and rituals, two aspects of culture common to all societies from the ancients to the modern world.

MYTHS

A **myth** is a story with symbolic elements that represents a culture's ideals. The story often focuses on some kind of conflict between two opposing forces, and its outcome serves as a moral guide for listeners. In this way, a myth reduces anxiety because it provides consumers with guidelines about their world.

Most members of a culture learn these stories, but usually we don't really think about their origins. Consider, for example, a familiar story in our culture: *Little Red Riding Hood*. This myth started as a peasant's tale in sixteenth-century France, where a girl meets a werewolf on her way to granny's house (there is historical evidence for a plague of wolf attacks during this time, including several incidents where men were

LuckySurf.com, a free lottery site, puts an interesting twist on the common practice of keeping a lucky rabbit's foot.

FEELING LUCKY?

LuckySurf.com

tried for allegedly transforming themselves into the deadly animals). The werewolf has already killed granny, stored her flesh in the pantry, and poured her blood in a bottle. Contrary to the version we know however, when the girl arrives at the house she snacks on granny, strips naked, and climbs into bed with the wolf! To make the story even more scandalous, some versions refer to the wolf as a "gaffer" (a contraction of "grandfather") implying incest as well.

This story first appeared in print in 1697; it was a warning to the loose ladies of Louis XIV's court (the author puts her in red in this version because this color symbolizes harlots). Eventually, the Brothers Grimm wrote their own version in 1812, but they substituted violence for sex in order to scare kids into behaving. And to reinforce the sex-role standards of that time, in the Grimm version a man rescues the girl from the wolf.[17] So, this myth sends vivid messages about such cultural no-nos as cannibalism, incest, and promiscuity.

An understanding of cultural myths is important to marketers, who in some cases (most likely unconsciously) pattern their messages along a mythic structure. Consider, for example, the way that McDonald's takes on "mythical" qualities.[18] The "golden arches" are a symbol consumers everywhere recognize as virtually synonymous with American culture. They offer sanctuary to Americans around the world who know exactly what to expect once they enter. Basic struggles involving good versus evil play out in the fantasy world McDonald's advertising creates, for example, when Ronald McDonald confounds the Hamburglar. McDonald's even has a "seminary" (Hamburger University) where inductees go to learn the ways of The Golden Arches.

Corporations often have myths and legends in their history, and some make a deliberate effort to be sure newcomers to the organization learn these. Nike designates senior executives as "corporate storytellers" who explain the company's heritage to the hourly workers at Nike stores. They recount tales about the coach of the Oregon track team who poured rubber into his family waffle iron to make better shoes for his team—the origin of the Nike waffle sole. The stories emphasize the dedication of runners and coaches to reinforce the importance of teamwork. Rookies even visit the track where the coach worked to be sure they grasp the importance of the Nike legends. And rumor has it that senior Nike executives (including the CEO) have a "swoosh" tattoo on their backsides.[19]

The Functions and Structure of Myths

Myths serve four interrelated functions in a culture:[20]

1 **Metaphysical:** They help to explain the origins of existence.
2 **Cosmological:** They emphasize that all components of the universe are part of a single picture.
3 **Sociological:** They maintain social order by authorizing a social code for members of a culture to follow.
4 **Psychological:** They provide models for personal conduct.

We analyze myths by examining their underlying structures, a technique the French anthropologist Claude Lévi-Strauss (no relation to the blue jeans company) pioneered. Lévi-Strauss noted that many stories involve **binary opposition**, which represents two opposing ends of some dimension (e.g., good versus evil, nature versus technology).[21] Advertisers sometimes define products in terms of what they are *not* rather than what they *are* (e.g., "This is *not* your father's Oldsmobile," "I can't believe it's *not* butter").

Recall from our discussion of Freudian theory in Chapter 6 that the ego functions as a kind of "referee" between the opposing needs of the id and the superego. In a similar fashion, a *mediating figure* may resolve the conflict between mythical opposing forces; this links the opposites by sharing characteristics of each. For example, many myths are about animals that have human abilities (e.g., a talking snake) to bridge the gap between humanity and nature, just as marketers often give cars (technology) animal names (nature) such as Cougar, Cobra, or Mustang.

Myths Abound in Modern Popular Culture

We associate myths with the ancient Greeks or Romans, but in reality comic books, movies, holidays, and yes, even commercials embody our own cultural myths. And researchers report that some people create their own *consumer fairy tales* where they tell stories that include magical agents, donors, and helpers to overcome villains and obstacles as they seek out goods and services in their quest for happy endings.[22]

Some companies are more than happy to help us in these efforts. Consider the popularity of the elaborate weddings Disney stages for couples who want to reenact their own version of a popular fairy tale: At Disney World in Florida, the princess bride wears a tiara and rides to the park's lakeside wedding pavilion in a horse-drawn coach, complete with two footmen in gray wigs and gold lamé pants. At the exchange of vows, trumpets blare as Major Domo (he helped the Duke in his quest for Cinderella) walks up the aisle with two wedding bands gently placed in a glass slipper on a velvet pillow. Disney stages about 2,000 of these extravaganzas each year. Disney is expanding

Disney stages about 2,000 fairy-tale weddings a year.
Source: Ting-Li Wang/*The New York Times*

the appeal of this myth as it moves into the bridal gown business. It sells a line of billowing princess gowns complete with crystal tiaras. Fairy-tale brides can walk down the aisle posing as Cinderella, Snow White, Belle, Sleeping Beauty, Jasmine, or Ariel.[23]

Comic book superheroes demonstrate how a culture communicates myths to consumers of all ages. Marvel Comics' Spiderman character tells stories about balancing the obligations of being a superhero with the need of his alter ego, Peter Parker, to succeed in school and have a normal love life.[24] Indeed, some of these fictional figures embody such fundamental properties that they become a **monomyth**, a myth that is common to many cultures.[25] Consider Superman; a father (Jor-el) gives his only son to save a world with his supernatural powers. Sound familiar?

Many "blockbuster" movies and hit TV shows draw directly on mythic themes. Although dramatic special effects or attractive stars certainly don't hurt, a number of these movies also owe their success to their presentation of characters and plot structures that follow mythic patterns. Here are three examples of mythic blockbusters:[26]

● *Gone with the Wind* (1939). Myths are often set in times of upheaval such as wars. In this story, the North (which represents technology and democracy) battles the South (which represents nature and aristocracy). The movie depicts a romantic era (the antebellum South) when love and honor were virtues. Following the war, newer values of materialism and industrialization (i.e., modern consumer culture) replace these priorities. The movie depicts a lost era where man and nature existed in harmony.

● *E.T.: The Extraterrestrial* (1982). E.T. represents a familiar myth involving messianic visitation. The gentle creature from another world visits Earth and

The popular *Star Trek* saga is based on myths, including the quest for paradise.

performs miracles (e.g., reviving a dying flower). His "disciples" are neighborhood children, who help him combat the forces of modern technology and an unbelieving secular society. The myth teaches that the humans God chooses are pure and unselfish.

● *Star Trek:* The television series and movies documenting the adventures of the starship *Enterprise* also link to myths, such as the story of the New England Puritans exploring and conquering a new continent—"the final frontier." Encounters with the Klingons mirror skirmishes with Native Americans. In addition, at least 13 out of the original 79 episodes employed the theme of a quest for paradise.[27]

Advertisements sometimes represent mythic themes. For example, commercials for Pepperidge Farm ask consumers to "remember" the good old days (lost paradise) when products were wholesome and natural. Both Chrysler and Avis use the theme of the underdog prevailing over the stronger foe (i.e., David and Goliath).[28] A commercial that encourages Hispanic consumers to buy more milk features a female phantom that wails as she walks through a home. She is *La Llorona* (the crying one), a character in a Hispanic myth who murders her children, commits suicide, and roams for all eternity looking for her lost family. In this version, however, the moaning phantom makes her way to the refrigerator, only to find an empty milk carton.[29]

Even packages can mythologize a brand, as researchers who analyzed the messages on some "natural" products report. The authors found that many of the packages present a narrative about a romantic past, where values of family, tradition, authenticity, peace, and simplicity reigned. For example, the label on a box of Celestial Seasoning's tea reads: "When you find a quiet moment, ease into a cup of contentment with Honey Vanilla Chamomile Herb Tea." The brand name itself, note the authors, conjures the transcendent possibilities of tea consumption (celestial). The package includes a personally signed guarantee of satisfaction from the company's founder. These elements subtly invoke the binary opposition to large, impersonal corporations where the founder would never take the time to write a message. Other "natural" product packaging often includes origin myths such as: "It began very simply. In 1960 in the back of a small health food store. . . ."[30]

RITUALS

A **ritual** is a set of multiple, symbolic behaviors that occurs in a fixed sequence and is repeated periodically.[31] Bizarre tribal ceremonies, perhaps involving animal or human sacrifice, may come to mind when you think of rituals, but in reality many contemporary consumer activities are ritualistic. Just think of Christine's daily "mental health" trip to Starbucks.

Or consider a ritual that many beer drinkers in the United Kingdom and Ireland hold near and dear to their hearts—the spectacle of a pub bartender "pulling" the perfect pint of Guinness. According to tradition, the slow pour takes exactly 119.5 seconds as the bartender holds the glass at a 45-degree angle, fills it three-quarters full, lets it settle, and tops it off with its signature creamy head. Guinness wanted to make the pull faster so the bar could serve more drinks on a busy night so it introduced FastPour, an ultrasound technology that dispenses the dark brew in only 25 seconds. You probably guessed the outcome: The brewer had to scrap the system when drinkers resisted the innovation. Note: Diageo (which owns Guinness) hasn't given up and is experimenting with other techniques in markets where this ritual isn't so inbred. A system called Guinness Surger is being tested in Tokyo. It is for bars that are too small to accommodate kegs: The bartender pours a pint from a bottle, places the glass on a special plate, and zaps it with ultrasound waves that generate the characteristic head.[32]

A recent study the BBDO Worldwide advertising agency conducted illustrates just how crucial rituals are to many brands.[33] It labels brands that we closely link to our rituals **fortress brands** because once they become embedded in our rituals—whether brushing our teeth, drinking a beer, or shaving—we're unlikely to replace them. The study ran in 26 countries, and the researchers found that overall people worldwide practice roughly the same consumer rituals. The study claims that 89 percent of people use the same brands for these sequenced rituals, and three out of four are disappointed or irritated when something disrupts their ritual or their brand of choice isn't available. For example, the report identifies one common ritual category it calls *preparing for battle*. For most of us this means getting ready for work. Relevant rituals include brushing the teeth, taking a shower or bath, having something to eat or drink, talking to a family member or partner, checking e-mail, shaving, putting on makeup, watching TV or listening to the radio, and reading a newspaper.

Many colleges boast unique rituals in which students engage in some scripted group activity, but in recent years some institutions abolished these because of safety concerns or because they encourage underage drinking. Recent casualties included spring couch burning at the University of Vermont and Princeton's Nude Winter Olympics. The death of 12 people from collapsing logs in 1999 brought to an end the tradition of Texas A&M's bonfire on the eve of the annual football game against the University of Texas (the bonfire ritual has since been revived off campus). Some campus rituals that survive include the following:

- MIT: Each spring students haul a steer into a dorm courtyard, put it on a spit, and light a fire under it with a flaming roll of toilet paper lowered from the roof.
- Wesleyan College (Connecticut): Students honor the pot-smoking Doonesbury character Zonker Harris each spring with a day of live music, face painting, and plenty of open marijuana use.
- Simon Fraser University (British Columbia): Costumed engineering students throw one another in the reflection pond during February's Polar Plunge.
- Wellesley: Seniors toss the winner of the annual spring hoop roll into chilly Lake Waban. This ritual has changed to keep up with the times—the winner used to be declared the first to marry; now she's proclaimed the most likely to succeed.

TABLE 16.1
TYPES OF RITUAL EXPERIENCE

Primary Behavior Source	Ritual Type	Examples
Cosmology	Religious	Baptism, meditation, mass
Cultural values	Rites of passage	Graduation, marriage festivals, holidays
	Cultural	(Valentine's Day), Super Bowl
Group learning	Civic	Parades, elections, trials
	Group	Fraternity initiation, business negotiations, office luncheons
	Family	Mealtimes, bedtimes, birthdays, Mother's Day, Christmas
Individual aims and emotions	Personal	Grooming, household rituals

Source: Dennis W. Rook, "The Ritual Dimension of Consumer Behavior," *Journal of Consumer Research* 12 (December 1985): 251–64. Copyright © 1985 JCR, Inc. Reprinted with permission of the University of Chicago Press.

- University of California at Santa Barbara: Students run naked across campus on the first rainy day of the year. Princeton and the University of Michigan have banned nude sprints, but at Yale seniors still run naked through two campus libraries at the end of each semester and toss candy at underclass students cramming for finals.[34]

Table 16.1 notes that rituals can occur at several levels. Some affirm broad cultural or religious values. Public rituals such as the Super Bowl, presidential inaugurations, and graduation ceremonies are communal activities that affirm our membership in the larger group and reassure us that we are reading from the same script as everyone else.[36] Other rituals occur in small groups or even in isolation. Market researchers discovered that for many people (such as Christine) the act of late-night ice cream eating has ritualistic elements, often involving a favorite spoon and bowl![37] And rituals are not always set in stone; they change with the times. For example, throwing rice at a Western wedding expresses a desire for the couple to be fertile. In recent years, many newlyweds substitute soap bubbles, jingling bells, or butterflies because birds eat the rice, which expands inside their bodies with nasty results.[38]

Many businesses owe their livelihoods to their ability to supply **ritual artifacts** to consumers. These are items we need to perform rituals, such as wedding rice, birthday candles, diplomas, specialized foods and beverages (e.g., wedding cakes, ceremonial wine, or even hot dogs at the ball park), trophies and plaques, band uniforms, greeting cards, and retirement watches.[39] In addition, we often follow a *ritual script* to identify the artifacts we need, the sequence in which we should use them, and who uses them. Examples include graduation programs, fraternity manuals, and etiquette books.

Whether you brush your hair 100 strokes a day or give yourself a pep talk in the mirror before a big date, virtually all of us practice private **grooming rituals**. These are sequences of behaviors that aid in the transition from the private self to the public self or back again. These rituals serve various purposes that range from inspiring confidence before confronting the world to cleansing the body of dirt and other impure materials. When consumers talk about their grooming rituals, some of the dominant themes that emerge from these stories reflect the almost mystical qualities we attribute to grooming products and behaviors. Many people emphasize a before-and-after phenomenon, whereby the person feels magically transformed after using certain products (similar to the Cinderella myth).[40]

Some companies that make personal care products understand the power of these rituals and they try to tailor their offerings to help consumers enact them. Nair, the depilatory maker, recently decided to expand its customer base by targeting younger girls with its new Nair Pretty product—a market the industry calls "first-time hair removers." Researchers conducted focus groups with mothers and their daughters, where they found that as one senior marketing executive described it, "When a girl removes hair for the first time, it's a life-changing moment." Some of the respondents were actually having hair removal slumber parties, where the moms were going out and buying the products for the teens to remove their hair. So, instead of focusing on boys or romance, ads for Nair Pretty suggest that the depilatory is a stubble-free path to empowerment. "I am a citizen of the world," reads the ad copy. "I am a dreamer. I am fresh. I am so not going to have stubs sticking out of my legs."[41]

Two sets of binary oppositions personal rituals express are *private/public* and *work/leisure*. Many beauty rituals, for instance, reflect a transformation from a natural state to the social world (as when a woman "puts on her face") or vice versa. To her, a bath may be cleansing time, a way to wash away the "sins" of the profane world.[42] In these daily rituals, women reaffirm the value their culture places on personal beauty and the quest for eternal youth.[43] This cleansing ritual is clear in ads for Oil of Olay Beauty Cleanser that proclaim, "And so your day begins. The Ritual of Oil of Olay."

Gift-Giving Rituals

The promotion of appropriate gifts for every conceivable holiday and occasion provides an excellent example of the strong relationship between rituals and consumer behavior. In a **gift-giving ritual**, we procure the perfect object, meticulously remove the price tag, carefully wrap the object (this symbolically changes the item from a commodity to a unique good), and deliver it to the recipient.[44] Gifts can be store-bought objects, homemade items, or services. Some recent research even argues that music file-sharing systems such as Napster, KaZaa, or Morpheus really are all about gifting. This work finds, for example, clear evidence of the gift-giving norm of reciprocity; people who download files without leaving their own files available to others get labeled as "leeches."[45]

Researchers view gift-giving as a form of *economic exchange* where the giver transfers an item of value to a recipient, who in turn must reciprocate. However, gift-giving also involves *symbolic exchange*, for example, when a giver such as Christine wants to acknowledge her friend Melissa's intangible support and companionship. In fact, researchers who analyzed the personal memoirs of World War II concentration camp inmates found that even in such a brutal environment where people had to focus on their survival a need to express humanity through generosity prevailed. The authors find that gift-giving, which symbolized recognition of others' plight as well as one's own, was an act of defiance against the dehumanizing existence the camps forced on their prisoners.[46]

Some research indicates that gift-giving evolves as a form of social expression. It is more exchange oriented (instrumental) in the early stages of a relationship (where we keep track of exactly what we give and receive to be sure we're not getting ripped off), but it becomes more altruistic as the relationship develops.[47] Table 16.2 lists the ways giving a gift affects a relationship.

Every culture prescribes certain occasions and ceremonies for giving gifts, whether for personal or professional reasons. Giving birthday presents alone is a major undertaking. Each American on average buys about six birthday gifts a year—about 1 billion gifts in total.[48] Business gifts are an important way to define and maintain professional relationships. Expenditures on business gifts exceed $1.5 billion

TABLE 16.2
GIFT GIVING AND RELATIONSHIPS

Relational Effect	Description	Example
Strengthening	Gift-giving improves the quality of a relationship	An unexpected gift such as one given in a romantic situation
Affirmation	Gift-giving validates the positive quality of a relationship	Usually occurs on ritualized occasions such as birthdays
Negligible Effect	Gift-giving has a minimal effect on perceptions of relationship quality	Informal gift occasions and those in which the gift may be perceived as charity or too good for the current state of the relationship
Negative Confirmation	Gift-giving validates a negative quality of a relationship between the gift giver and receiver	The selection of gift is inappropriate indicating a lack of knowledge of the receiver; alternatively, the gift is viewed as a method of controlling the receiver
Weakening	Gift-giving harms the quality of the relationship between giver and receiver	When there are "strings attached" or the gift is perceived as a bribe, a sign of disrespect, or offensive
Severing	Gift-giving harms the relationship between the giver and receiver to the extent that the relationship is dissolved	When the gift forms part of a larger problem, such as in a threatening relationship; also when a relationship is severed through the receipt of a "parting" gift

Source: Adapted from Julie A. Ruth, Cele C. Otnes, and Frederic F. Brunel, "Gift Receipt and the Reformulation of Interpersonal Relationships," *Journal of Consumer Research* 25 (March 1999): 385–402, Table 1, 389.

per year, and givers take great care to ensure that they purchase the appropriate gifts (sometimes with the aid of professional gift consultants). Most executives believe that corporate gift-giving provides both tangible and intangible results, including improved employee morale and higher sales.[49]

The gift-giving ritual has three distinct stages:[50]

1 During *gestation*, the first stage, the giver procures an item to mark some event. This event may be either *structural* (i.e., prescribed by the culture, as when people buy Christmas presents) or *emergent* (i.e., the decision is more personal and idiosyncratic).

2 The second stage is *presentation*, or the process of gift exchange. The recipient responds to the gift (either appropriately or not), and the donor evaluates this response.

3 In the third stage, *reformulation*, the giver and receiver adjust the bond between them (either looser or tighter) to reflect their new relationship after the exchange. Negativity can arise if the recipient feels the gift is inappropriate or of inferior quality. For example, the hapless husband who gives his wife a vacuum cleaner as an anniversary present is asking to sleep on the couch, and the new suitor who gives his girlfriend intimate apparel won't score many points. The donor may feel the response to the gift was inadequate or insincere or a violation of the **reciprocity norm**, which obliges people to return the gesture of a gift with one of equal value.[51] Both participants may resent having to participate in the ritual.[52]

Japanese gift-giving rituals show how tremendously important these acts are in that culture, where the wrapping is as important (if not more so) than the gift itself. The Japanese view gifts as an important aspect of one's duty to others in one's social group. Giving is a moral imperative (*giri*). Highly ritualized acts occur during the giving of both household/personal gifts and company/professional gifts.

Each person has a well-defined set of relatives and friends with which he shares reciprocal gift-giving obligations (*kosai*). People give personal gifts on social occasions, such as at funerals, for a hospitalization, to mark movements from one life stage to another (e.g., weddings, birthdays), and as greetings (e.g., when one meets a visitor). They give company gifts to commemorate the anniversary of a corporation's founding, the opening of a new building, or the announcement of new products. In keeping with the Japanese emphasis on saving face, the recipient doesn't open the present in front of the giver so that he won't have to hide any disappointment with what he gets.[53]

Holiday Rituals

On holidays, we step back from our everyday lives and perform ritualistic behaviors unique to those occasions.[54] These special events require tons of ritual artifacts and scripts and increasingly enterprising marketers find ways to fill these needs. American's Thanksgiving holiday script, for example, includes serving (in gluttonous portions) foods such as turkey and cranberry sauce that many consume only on that day, complaining about how much they've eaten (yet rising to the occasion to find room for dessert), and (for many) a postmeal trip to the couch for the obligatory American-style football game.

In addition to established holidays, businesses invent new occasions to capitalize on the need for cards and other ritual artifacts that people have to acquire.[55] The greeting card industry originates many of these cultural events to conveniently stimulate demand for more of its products. Some of its creations include Secretaries' Day and Grandparents' Day (as your parents will tell you, *everyday* is Kids' Day!).

In other cases retailers elevate relatively minor holidays to major ones to provide more merchandising opportunities. Most recently the Mexican holiday of Cinco de Mayo is an excuse for Caucasians to drink a lot of margaritas. True, the day marks a May 5, 1862, victory by a small army over stronger French forces, but contrary to what many Americans believe, it is *not* Mexican Independence Day. As the president of an Hispanic American marketing firm notes, "When Mexicans first come to the United States and somebody mentions that they're all excited about some Cinco de Mayo festival, they say, 'What?' It would be like Canadians making a big deal out of the Boston Tea Party." On Cinco de Mayo, Americans eat 17 million pounds of avocados (in the form of guacamole) and sales jump for tequila and other ethnic

This McDonald's ad from Hong Kong celebrates a holiday. The literal translation is "April Fool's Day: The best day to take the piss out of your friends."

products as restaurants and bars catch the fever. Tequila maker Jose Cuervo even dropped a "margarita bar" into the water off Miami to commemorate "Sink-O de Mayo."[56]

Most holidays commemorate a cultural myth, often with an historical (e.g., St. Patrick on St. Patrick's Day) or imaginary (e.g., Cupid on Valentine's Day) character as the story's hero. These holidays persist because their basic elements appeal to our deep-seated needs.[57] Christmas and Halloween do an especially good job of this.

Christmas. Myths and rituals fill the Christmas holiday, from Santa's adventures at the North Pole to others' adventures under the mistletoe. The meaning of Christmas evolved quite dramatically during the past few hundred years. In colonial times, Christmas celebrations resembled carnivals and public rowdiness was the norm. Most notable was the tradition of "wassailing" where packs of poor young men would lay siege to the rich, demanding food and drink. By the end of the 1800s, the mobs were so unruly that Protestant America invented a tradition of families having Christmas gatherings around a tree, a practice they "borrowed" from early pagan rites.

In an 1822 poem, Clement Clarke Moore, the wealthy son of a New York Episcopal bishop, invented the modern-day myth of Santa Claus. The Christmas ritual slowly changed to a focus on children and gift-giving.[58] One of the most important holiday rituals of course stars Santa, a mythical figure for whose arrival children eagerly await (even if their house doesn't have a fireplace). Indeed, an Australian study that analyzed the letters children write to Santa found they specify their brand preferences quite carefully and often employ sophisticated request strategies to be sure they get what they want from the Big Guy.[59] In opposition to Christ, Santa is a champion of materialism. Perhaps it is no coincidence, then, that he appears in stores and shopping malls—secular temples of consumption. Whatever his origins, the Santa Claus myth socializes children as it teaches them to expect a reward when they are good and that people get what they deserve (which may be a lump of coal).

Halloween. Halloween began as a pagan religious ceremony but it's clearly a secular event today. However, in contrast to Christmas, the rituals of Halloween (e.g., trick-or-treating and costume parties) primarily involve nonfamily members. Halloween is an unusual holiday because its rituals are the opposite of many other cultural occasions. In contrast to Christmas, it celebrates evil instead of good and death rather than birth. It encourages revelers to extort treats with veiled threats of "tricks" rather than rewarding only the good.

Because of these oppositions, Halloween is an **antifestival**, an event that distorts the symbols we associate with other holidays. For example, the Halloween witch is an inverted mother figure. The holiday also parodies the meaning of Easter as it stresses the resurrection of ghosts and of Thanksgiving as it transforms the wholesome symbolism of the pumpkin pie into the evil jack-o-lantern.[60] Furthermore, Halloween provides a ritualized, and therefore socially sanctioned, context that allows people to act out uncharacteristic behaviors and try on new roles: Children can go outside after dark, stay up late, and eat all the candy they like for a night. The otherwise geeky guy who always sits in the back of class dresses as Elvis and turns out to be the life of the party (a great example of the deindividuation concept we discussed in Chapter 11).

Halloween observances among adults are booming—and changing the character of this holiday. Halloween is now the second most popular party night for adults (after New Year's Eve), and one in four grown-ups wears a costume.[61] The holiday is trendy in Europe as well, where the French in particular use it as an excuse to hold parties and show off new fashions.[62]

Valentine's Day. On Valentine's Day, people in different countries relax their standards regarding love and express feelings they may have hidden during the rest of the year

Halloween is evolving from a children's festival to an opportunity for adults to experiment with fantasy roles—and party.

(in Japan, it's the women who send gifts to the men). A recent study looked at Valentine's Day rituals to identify how marketing communications help to shape the holiday. The authors identify five familiar classes of rituals:

● Exchanging gifts and cards
● Showing affection
● Going out
● Preparing and consuming food and drink
● Grooming and clothing

Many of their informants (primarily men) understood the holiday as an obligatory occasion for them to buy their partners expensive, "romantic" gifts. One guy posted this warning: "if you want her happy always remember: the gift has to shine or smell [good] or she should be able to wear it! Otherwise, you're doomed." Some informants expressed negative associations with the holiday, including painful emotions because of broken or a lack of relationships and aversion to the "forced" consumption and artificial displays of affection the day requires.[63] But, as much as some of us may grumble about it, this holiday ritual is too powerful to ignore (unless you like sleeping on the couch).

Rites of Passage

What does a dance for recently divorced people have in common with a fraternity Hell Week? Both are modern **rites of passage**, rituals we perform to mark a change in social status. Every society, both primitive and modern, sets aside times for these changes. Some may occur as a natural part of our life cycles (e.g., puberty or death), whereas others are more individual (e.g., getting divorced and reentering the dating market). As Christine's son discovered when he bombed his driving test, the importance

Marketing Opportunity

The Jewish ritual of the *bar mitzvah* (for boys) or *bat mitzvah* (for girls) is a long-standing rite of passage for 13-year-olds who symbolically become adults in the eyes of the religion. A lavish party often celebrates the event. Apparently, a lot of non-Jewish kids feel left out. In some affluent communities, they are bugging their parents for parties like their Jewish friends get—although they may substitute a dance such as the *tarantella* or an Irish jig for the traditional Jewish *hora*. In the words of a Catholic girl who told her parents she also deserves a ceremony to mark her coming of age, "Some of those things apply to me. I'm growing up and becoming a teenager. I should have a party to celebrate."[64]

of a rite of passage becomes more obvious when you fail to undergo it at the prescribed time.

Much like the metamorphosis of a caterpillar into a butterfly, a rite of passage consists of three phases. Let's see how this works for a young person who changes his social status to become a college student:[65]

1 In the first stage, *separation*, he detaches from his original group or status as a high school kid and leaves home for campus.
2 *Liminality* is the middle stage, where he is in limbo between statuses. Think of those bewildered new first-year students who try to find their way around campus during orientation.
3 In the *aggregation* stage, he returns to society with his new status. Our hero returns home for Thanksgiving break as a cocky college "veteran."

Many types of people undergo rites of passage, including fraternity pledges, recruits at boot camp, or novitiates at a convent. We observe a similar transitional state when people prepare for occupational roles. For example, athletes and fashion models typically undergo a "seasoning" process. They leave their normal surroundings (athletes go to training camps, young models move to Paris or New York); they get indoctrinated into a new subculture, and then return to the real world in their new roles (if they successfully pass the trials of their initiation and don't "get cut").

Death also involves rites of passage. Funeral ceremonies help the living organize their relationships with the deceased. Action is tightly scripted, down to the costumes (e.g., the ritual black attire, black ribbons for mourners, the body laid out in its best clothes) and specific behaviors (e.g., sending condolence cards or holding a wake). Passing motorists award special status to the *cortege* (the funeral motorcade) when they recognize its separate, sacred nature by not cutting in as the line of cars proceeds to the cemetery.[66]

Forward-thinking funeral directors recognize that they really are in the business of staging a ritual, so some redefine themselves as party planners. One entrepreneur opened the first nationwide funeral concierge service; for a fee he coordinates tasks from writing the obituary to negotiating prices with undertakers. Some wealthy people seize the opportunity to go out with a bang: Robert Tisch, who ran the Loews Corporation, had a marching band at his memorial service, and mourners at perfume magnate Estée Lauder's funeral consoled themselves with chocolate-covered marshmallows that waiters passed on silver trays. Other ordinary folks arrange their own special send-offs: At a funeral for a former ice cream vendor the deceased's old ice cream truck led the cortege and then it dispensed Popsicles to guests after the ceremony.[67]

Funeral practices vary across cultures, but they're always rich in symbolism. For cxample, a recent study of funeral rituals in Ghana found that the community there determines a person's social value after he has died; this status depends on the type of funeral his family gives him. One of the main purposes of death rituals is to negotiate the social identities of deceased persons. This occurs as mourners treat the corpse with a level of respect that indicates what they think of him. The Asante people who were the subjects of the study don't view death as something to fear but rather as a part of a broader, ongoing process of identity negotiation.[68]

 ## Sacred and Profane Consumption

As we saw when we discussed the structure of myths, many types of consumer activities involve the demarcation, or binary opposition, of categories, such as good versus bad, male versus female—or even regular cola versus diet. One of the most important distinctions we find is between the sacred and the profane. **Sacred**

Marketing Opportunity

Wedding rituals are going green, at least for some brides and grooms who want to rewrite the script to embrace sustainable practices. Some coupes calculate the mileage their guests travel to attend the event and offset their carbon dioxide emissions with donations to programs that plant trees or preserve rain forests. Others substitute hydrangeas, berries, and other local and seasonal flowers for the bride's bouquet and table centerpieces instead of burning up fuel to transport flowers from faraway farms. A bride might choose a vintage dress to avoid the waste of a wedding gown she will never wear again. You can even select a caterer who serves organic food on biodegradable plates made of sugar cane fiber. At Protovert.com you can find even more advice for "ecosavvy brides and grooms."[69]

consumption occurs when we "set apart" objects and events from normal activities and treat them with respect or awe. Note that in this context the term *sacred* does not necessarily carry a religious meaning, although we do tend to think of religious artifacts and ceremonies as "sacred." **Profane consumption** in contrast describes objects and events that are ordinary or everyday; they don't share the "specialness" of sacred ones. Again, note that in this context we don't equate the word *profane* with obscenity although the two meanings do share some similarities.

Again, often we're unaware of the distinction between these two domains—until they conflict with one another. Then, the sparks fly—sort of like the collision between matter and antimatter on *Star Trek*. A recent example of this clash occurred in Thailand. It seems that several Bangkok nightclubs, inspired by the film *Coyote Ugly* about women who dance seductively on a New York bar, began to feature their own "Coyote Girls" dancers. The trend caught on and soon the dancers were showing up at auto shows, in shopping malls, and at outdoor festivals. That's when the trouble started: Thailand's queen learned of one performance the girls put on near a Buddhist temple on a holy day that marks the end of a 3-month period where Buddhists try to refrain from impure thoughts and deeds (sort of like the Christian season of Lent). When the queen saw TV news reports about a motorcycle shop that hired Coyote Girls to promote its wares, she was outraged by the intrusion of profane activity into a sacred domain. Coyote Girls are now banned from dancing in public places.[70]

DOMAINS OF SACRED CONSUMPTION

Sacred consumption events permeate many aspects of our lives. We find ways to "set apart" all sorts of places, people, and events. In this section, we'll look at ways that "ordinary" consumption is sometimes *not* so ordinary after all.

Sacred Places

A society "sets apart" sacred places because they have religious or mystical significance (e.g., Bethlehem, Mecca, Stonehenge) or because they commemorate some aspect of a country's heritage (e.g., the Kremlin, the Emperor's Palace in Tokyo, the Statue of Liberty or, more recently, Ground Zero in Manhattan). **Contamination** makes these places sacred—that is, something sacred happened on that spot, so the place itself takes on sacred qualities.

Still other places originate from the profane world but we endow them with sacred qualities. Graumann's Chinese Theater in Hollywood, where movie stars leave their footprints in concrete for posterity, is one such place. Theme parks are a form of mass-produced fantasy that takes on aspects of sacredness. In particular, Disney World and Disneyland (and their outposts in Europe and Japan) are destinations for "pilgrimages" by consumers around the globe. Disney World displays many characteristics of more traditional sacred places. Some even believe it has healing powers, which helps to explain why a trip to the park is the most common "last wish" for terminally ill children.[71]

As the saying goes, "Home is where the heart is."[72] In many cultures, the home is a particularly sacred place. It's a barrier between the harsh, external world and consumers' "inner space." Americans spend more than $50 billion a year on interior decorators and home furnishings, and our home is a central part of our identity. People all over the world go to great lengths to create a feeling of "homeyness." They personalize the dwelling with door wreaths, mantle arrangements, and a "memory wall" for family photos.[73] Even public places such as Starbucks cafés strive for a home-like atmosphere to shelter customers from the harshness of the outside world.

Sacred People

Some people are sacred; we idolize them, set them apart from the masses, and sometimes we believe they have "superhuman" abilities. Souvenirs, memorabilia, and even mundane items these celebrities touch acquire special meanings (the celebrities "contaminate" the items). Newspapers pay *paparazzi* hundreds of thousands of dollars for candid shots of stars or royalty. Indeed, many businesses thrive on our desire for products we associate with the famous. There is a flourishing market for celebrity autographs, and objects celebrities own such as Princess Diana's gowns or John Lennon's guitars sell on eBay for astronomical prices.

Sacred Events

Sometimes public events resemble sacred, religious ceremonies—think about Americans who hold their hands over their hearts and solemnly sing their national anthems before a ballgame, or how others reverently light matches (or hold up illuminated cell phones) during a rock concert.[74]

The world of sports is sacred to many of us (recent doping and gambling scandals aside). We find the roots of modern sports events in ancient religious rites, such as fertility festivals (e.g., the original Olympics).[75] And it's not uncommon for teams to join in prayer prior to a game. The sports pages are like the scriptures (and we all know ardent fans who read them "religiously"), the stadium is a house of worship, and the fans are members of the congregation. Devotees engage in group activities, such as tailgate parties and the "Wave," where sections of the stadium take turns standing up. The athletes and coaches that fans come to see are godlike; they believe they have almost superhuman powers—a set of researchers recently documented more than 600 children whose parents named them after the legendary University of Alabama coach Paul "Bear" Bryant![76]

Athletes are central figures in a common cultural myth, the *hero tale*. In these stories, the player must prove himself under strenuous circumstances, and he achieves victory only through sheer force of will. On a more mundane level, devotees consume certain ritual artifacts during these ceremonies (such as hot dogs at the ballpark). Sales of certain foods and beverages spike around the time of the World Cup; people spend $10 million more on tortilla chips than during a normal 2-week period and more than $15 million extra on beer in the weeks surrounding the big game.[77]

Tourism is another example of a sacred, nonordinary experience. People occupy sacred time and space when they travel on vacation (though you may not think so if you get stuck sleeping on an airport floor because of a plane delay). The tourist searches for "authentic" experiences that differ from his normal world (think of Club Med's motto, "The antidote to civilization").[78] This traveling experience involves binary oppositions between work and leisure and being "at home" versus "away." Often, we relax everyday (profane) norms regarding appropriate behavior as tourists we scramble after illicit or adventurous experiences they would not dream of engaging in at home ("What happens in Vegas, stays in Vegas").

The desire of travelers to capture these sacred experiences in objects forms the bedrock of the souvenir industry, which really sells sacred memories. Whether a personalized matchbook from a wedding or New York City salt-and-pepper shakers, souvenirs represent a tangible piece of the consumer's sacred experience.[79] In addition to personal mementos, such as ticket stubs saved from a favorite concert, these are some other sacred souvenir icons:[80]

- Local products (e.g., wine from California)
- Pictorial images (e.g., postcards)
- "Piece of the rock" (e.g., seashells, pine cones)
- Symbolic shorthand in the form of literal representations of the site (e.g., a miniature Statue of Liberty)
- Markers (e.g., Hard Rock Cafe T-shirts)

Souvenirs, tacky or otherwise, allow consumers to tangibilize sacred (i.e., out of the ordinary) experiences they accumulate as tourists.

FROM SACRED TO PROFANE, AND BACK AGAIN

Just to make life interesting, some consumer activities move from one sphere to the other.[81] A recent study of tea preparation in Turkey illustrates this movement. Although we are more likely to think of thick Turkish coffee, in reality Turks consume more tea per capita than any other country. In this culture people drink tea continuously, like (or instead of) water. Tea is an integral part of daily life; many households and offices boil water for tea in the traditional *çaydanlik* (double teapot) first thing in the morning, and keep it steaming all day so that the beverage is ready at any time. The tea drinking process links to many symbolic meanings—including the traditional glasses, clear to appreciate the tea's color, and hourglass-shaped like a woman's body—and rituals, such as blending one's own tea, knowing how finely to grind the tea leaves, and how long to steep the tea for optimal flavor. When Lipton introduced the modern tea bag in 1984, Turkey was intent on modernization and soon consumers were buying electric *çaydanlik,* and mugs instead of small, shapely tea glasses. Tea became a symbol of the quick and convenient and the drinking act became more of a fashion statement—it was desacralized. Now, the authors report that many Turkish consumers opt to return to the sacred, traditional rituals as a way to preserve authenticity in the face of rapid societal changes.[82]

Desacralization

Desacralization occurs when we remove a sacred item or symbol from its special place or duplicate it in mass quantities so that it loses its "specialness" and becomes profane. For example, souvenir reproductions of sacred monuments such as the Washington Monument or the Eiffel Tower, artworks such as the *Mona Lisa* or Michelangelo's *David*, or reproductions of sacred symbols such as the American flag on T-shirts eliminate their special aspects; they become inauthentic commodities with relatively little value.

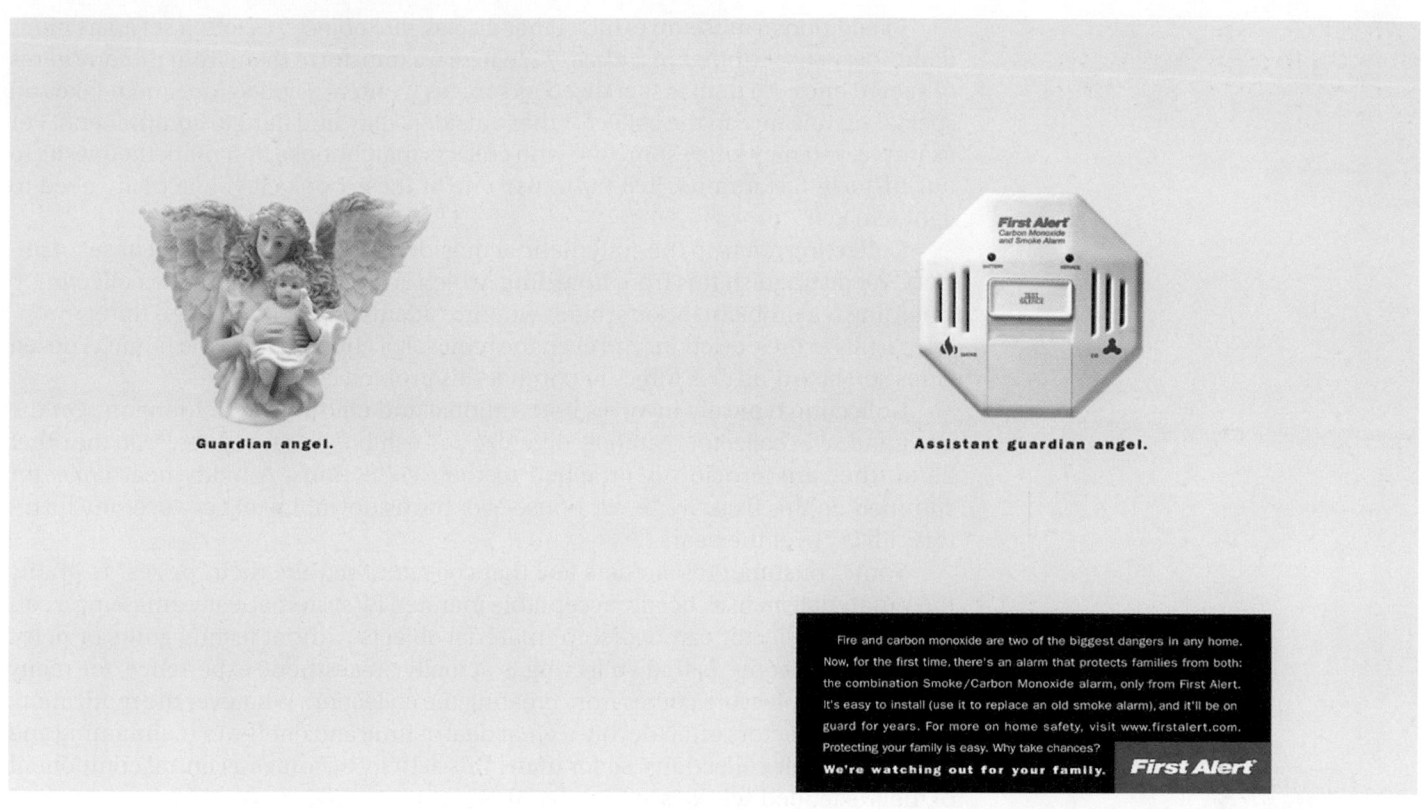

Guardian angel.   Assistant guardian angel.

This ad for an alarm system uses sacred imagery to sell a profane product.

Religion itself has to some extent been desacralized. Religious symbols like stylized crosses or New Age crystals often pop up on fashion jewelry.[83] Critics often charge that Christmas has turned into a secular, materialistic occasion devoid of its original sacred significance. A similar process occurs in relatively Westernized parts of the Islamic Middle East, where the holy month of Ramadan (that people traditionally observe by fasting and prayer) is starting to look like Christmas: People buy lights in the shape of an Islamic crescent moon, send Ramadan cards to one another, and attend lavish fast-breaking feasts at hotels.[84]

Sacralization

Sacralization occurs when ordinary objects, events, and even people take on sacred meaning. As we've seen, many consumers regard events such as the World Cup and people such as singer Elvis Presley as sacred. Indeed, virtually anything can become sacred. Skeptical? Consider the thriving Web site that sells *unlaundered* athletic wear that members of the Dallas Cowboys football team have worn. Quarterback Troy Aikman's shoes sell for $1,999, and an unwashed practice jersey that retains the sweat of an unknown player goes for $99. Used socks fly out the door at $19.99 a pair. Says the owner, "Fans who have never been able to touch the Cowboys before now have an opportunity."[85]

Objectification occurs when we attribute sacred qualities to mundane items (such as smelly socks). One way that this process occurs is via contamination, where, as we've already seen, objects we associate with sacred events or people become sacred in their own right. This explains the desire by many fans for items that belonged to (or were even touched by) famous people. Even the Smithsonian Institution in Washington, D.C. maintains a display featuring such "sacred items" as the ruby slippers from the movie *The Wizard of Oz*, a phaser from TV show *Star Trek*, and Archie Bunker's chair from the television show *All in the Family*—all reverently protected behind sturdy display glass.

In addition to museum exhibits that display rare objects, we often set apart mundane, inexpensive things in *collections*, where we transform them from profane items to sacred ones. An item is sacralized as soon as it enters a collection, and it takes on special significance to the collector that outsiders may find hard to comprehend. For example, you may know someone who collects matchbooks that mark their visits to out-of-town restaurants: Just try to use one of these books if you actually need to light a match.

Collecting refers to the systematic acquisition of a particular object or set of objects. We distinguish this from **hoarding**, which is merely unsystematic collecting.[86] Hoarding is a problem in some cities where residents' refusal to discard things properly results in fires, eviction, and even the removal of children from the home. A dozen cities run hoarding task forces to combat this problem.[87]

Collecting typically involves both rational and emotional components. On the one hand, avid collectors carefully organize and exhibit their treasures.[88] On the other hand, they are ferociously attached to their collections. A teddy bear collector summed up this fixation: "If my house ever burns down, I won't cry over my furniture, I'll cry over the bears."[89]

Some consumer researchers feel that collectors acquire their "prizes" to gratify their materialism in a socially acceptable manner. By systematically amassing a collection, the collector can "worship" material objects without feeling guilty or petty. Another perspective is that collecting is actually an aesthetic experience; for many collectors the pleasure comes from creating the collection. Whatever the motivation, hard-core collectors often devote a great deal of time and energy to maintaining and expanding their collections, so for many this activity becomes a central component of their extended selves (see Chapter 5).[90]

Name an item, and the odds are that a collector lusts after it. You can find collections of just about anything, from movie posters, rare books, and autographs to *Star Wars* dolls, Elvis memorabilia, old computers, and even junk mail.[91] The 1,200 members of the McDonald's collectors' club trade "prizes" such as sandwich wrappers and Happy Meal trinkets—rare ones like the 1987 Potato Head Kids Toys sell for $25.[92] And other consumers collect experiences rather than products: Consider the man who visited more than 10,000 McDonald's restaurants. He keeps a list of unusual menu items and decor, and he defends his hobby this way: "I'm not an oddball or weirdo. I'm a collector of the McDonald's dining experience. So many issues from the last half of the twentieth century can be understood, at least partially, from a seat inside a McDonald's. What could be more quintessentially American?"[93] Supersize that?

CHAPTER SUMMARY

Now that you have finished reading this chapter you should understand why:

A culture is a society's personality; it shapes our identities as individuals.

● A society's culture includes its values, ethics, and the material objects its members produce. It is the accumulation of shared meanings and traditions among members of a society. We describe a culture in terms of ecology (the way people adapt to their habitat), its social structure, and its ideology (including moral and aesthetic principles).

Myths are stories that express a culture's values, and in modern times marketing messages convey these values.

● Myths are stories containing symbolic elements that express the shared ideals of a culture. Many myths involve a binary opposition; they define values in terms of what they are and what they are not (e.g., nature versus technology). Advertising, movies, and other media transmit modern myths.

Many of our consumption activities including holiday observances, grooming, and gift-giving are rituals.

● A ritual is a set of multiple, symbolic behaviors that occur in a fixed sequence and that we repeat periodically. Ritual is related to many consumption activities that occur in popular culture. These include holiday observances, gift-giving, and grooming.

● A rite of passage is a special kind of ritual that marks the transition from one role to another. These passages typically entail the need to acquire ritual artifacts to facilitate the transition. Modern rites of passage include graduations, fraternity initiations, weddings, debutante balls, and funerals.

We describe products as either sacred or profane, and it's not unusual for some products to move back and forth between the two categories.

● We divide consumer activities into *sacred* and *profane* domains. Sacred phenomena are "set apart" from everyday activities or products. *Sacralization* occurs when we set apart everyday people, events, or objects from the ordinary. *Objectification* occurs when we ascribe sacred qualities to products or items that sacred people once owned. *Desacralization* occurs when formerly sacred objects or activities become part of the everyday, as when companies reproduce "one-of-a-kind" works of art in large quantities.

KEY TERMS

Antifestival, 619
Binary opposition, 611
Collecting, 626
Collectivist culture, 606
Contamination, 622
Culture, 604
Desacralization, 624

Fortress brands, 614
Gift-giving ritual, 616
Grooming rituals, 615
Hoarding, 626
Individualist culture, 606
Monomyth, 612
Myth, 609

Profane consumption, 622
Reciprocity norm, 617
Rites of passage, 620
Ritual, 614
Ritual artifacts, 615
Sacralization, 625
Sacred consumption, 621

REVIEW QUESTIONS

1 What is culture? List three dimensions social scientists use to describe a culture and give an example of each.
2 A myth is a special kind of story. What makes it special? What is an example of a modern myth?
3 Give an example of a marketer who uses binary opposition.
4 What is a ritual? Describe three kinds of rituals, providing an example of each.

5 List the three stages of a ritual.
6 What is the difference between sacred and profane consumption? Provide one example of each.
7 In what way is a collection sacred? What is the difference between collecting and hoarding?

CONSUMER BEHAVIOR CHALLENGE

■ DISCUSS

1 A culture is a society's personality. If your culture were a person, how would you describe its personality traits?

2 This chapter argues that not all gift-giving is positive. In what ways can this ritual be unpleasant or negative?

3 For many, Disney is a sacred place. Do you agree? Why or why not?

4 Describe the three stages of the rite of passage associated with graduating from college.

5 Have you ever given yourself a gift? If so, why did you do it and how did you decide what to get?

6 "Fraternity hazing is simply a natural rite of passage that universities should not try to regulate." Do you agree?

7 Identify the ritualized aspects of football that advertising uses.

8 "Christmas has become simply another opportunity to exchange gifts and stimulate the economy." Do you agree? Why or why not?

9 Bridal registries lay out very clearly the gifts that the couple wants. How do you feel about this practice—should people actually specify what you should buy for them, or should a gift be a more personal expression from you?

10 Rituals provide us with a sense of order and security. In a study of the drinking rituals of college students, the researchers found that drinking imposed order in students' daily lives—from the completion of assignments to what and when to eat. In addition, ritualizing an activity such as drinking provides security and fellowship at a time fraught with confusion and turbulent change. Obviously, though, there's a dark side to drinking rituals. Consider the highly publicized death of a MIT student who died 3 days after falling into an alcohol-induced coma as the result of a fraternity pledge.[94] Indeed, while binge drinking is a ritual many college students practice, critics have described it as the most significant health hazard on college campuses today.[95] What role does drinking play in the social life on your campus? Based on your experience, how does it fit into rituals of college life? Should these practices be changed? If so, how?

11 The chapter describes a new wave of commercials that give voice to products and practices people didn't use to discuss in polite conversation. Are any products out-of-bounds to advertising? Can these messages boomerang if they turn off consumers?

■ APPLY

12 When you go out on a first date, identify the crescive norms that you follow. Write a report (preferably when the date is over) describing specific behaviors each person performed that made it clear you were on a first date. What products and services do those norms affect?

13 Interview people you know about any "magic" items they own (e.g., How many of your friends have a lucky charm or keep a St. Christopher's medal or some other object hanging from their rearview mirrors?). Get them to describe their feelings about these objects and tell how they acquired their magical properties. How would they feel if they lost these special items?

14 Identify modern-day myths that corporations create. How do they communicate these stories to consumers?

15 Interview people you know who collect some kind of object. How do they organize and describe their collections? Do you see any evidence of sacred versus profane distinctions?

16 Ask friends to describe an incident where they received a gift they thought was inappropriate. Why did they feel this way, and how did this event influence the relationship between them and the gift-giver?

Case Study

CAMERA PHONES INVADE THE MIDDLE EAST

The camera-equipped cell phone: another marvel of modern technology. And consumers all over the world certainly welcome this high-tech accessory. While only 200,000 camera cell phones sold in 2002, by now sales have mushroomed worldwide to number in the tens of millions every year.

As the popularity of these compact and covert picture-taking phones has increased, so too have concerns about privacy. "With this kind of device, you're going to see the best and the worst," said Philippe Kahn, considered by many to be the inventor of the camera cell phone. Public figures learned this the hard way; the U.K.'s Prince Harry got snapped wearing a Nazi uniform to a costume party and the comedian Michael Richards (Kramer of *Seinfeld* fame) saw his career self-destruct after he was captured on-stage delivering a series of racist epithets to audience members. Everyday people also have been the victims of practices like "happy slapping" (youth filming their friends making random assaults on unsuspecting citizens) and upskirting.

It is for reasons like these that several U.S. states have forbidden people to use their cameras in public places. In the U.K. there has been a call for a ban on the devices in schools. And in Japan men have been prosecuted for taking voyeuristic photos of women without their consent. Donald Rumsfeld, the former U.S. defense secretary, even prohibited the use of phones in military installations in Iraq when officials suspected that the damming Abu Ghraib prison photos had been taken with camera-fitted phones.

But only Arab countries have imposed strict penalties for the use of camera phones in public. In Kuwait, the punishments range from 2 years in prison for taking pictures without consent of the subject, to 10 years for using such pictures as part of practices the government classifies as "immoral." Police sources in the United Arab Emirates have said that people who use cell phones to send pornographic images will face imprisonment.

In Saudi Arabia, regulation and prosecution of cell camera usage occurs at a level that surpasses anywhere else. Considered to be the birthplace of Islam, Saudi Arabia is one of the most conservative societies in the world. The country practices strict segregation of the sexes in public places. Women must also be covered head-to-toe in public with veils and robes. It should not be surprising then that Saudi women are sensitive about being photographed, especially without their veils. Such cultural norms have led to laws that prohibit photography in public places.

As Saudi consumers started to snap up camera phones in 2003 and 2004, reports of public unrest stemming from their use emerged. In one incident, a woman was expelled from her university for taking pictures of female friends and distributing them over the Internet. At a high school in Riyadh, a student's cell phone was destroyed with a mallet because he had been using it to take pictures of other students. And in another incident, a melee broke out at a wedding after a female guest was caught taking pictures of other guests in the women-only section of the celebration.

Such incidents led the Saudi government to ban the import and sale of camera-equipped phones. Spawning tension and heated debate between conservatives and reformists, the ban was rescinded some months later, to the dismay of religious leaders. However, while the government backed off, the country's grand mufti and highest religious authority issued an edict prohibiting the products that remains in place.

Cell phone marketers and less-religious consumers alike embraced the lifted ban, and sales grew rapidly. But in this country that is struggling to find a balance between maintaining traditional values and embracing progress, efforts by the religious establishment to regulate the use of camera phones continue.

DISCUSSION QUESTIONS

1 Why do you think that Saudi Arabia and other Middle Eastern countries have taken a stronger stance on regulating the use of camera phones? Discuss this question in the context of sacred and profane consumption.

2 Consumer acceptance of camera cell phones in Saudi Arabia has obviously been strong. What do you think that this says about the culture in this country?

Sources: Michael Agger, "Launching a Thousand Jackasses," *National Post* (January 20, 2007): A22; Samiran Chakrawertti, "Camera Phones Could Click Privacy Away," *Times of India* (December 17, 2004); Kim Ghattas, "Saudi Ministries Picture the Future as Embargo on Mobiles Draws in King Fahd," *Financial Times* (November 23, 2004): 7; Abdullah Shihri, "Camera-Equipped Cell Phones Banned by Religious Edict in Saudi Arabia," *Associated Press* (September 29, 2004).

NOTES

1. Bill McDowell, "Starbucks Is Ground Zero in Today's Coffee Culture," *Advertising Age* (December 9, 1996): 1. For a discussion of the act of coffee drinking as ritual, cf. Susan Fournier and Julie L. Yao, "Reviving Brand Loyalty: A Reconceptualization within the Framework of Consumer–Brand Relationships" (working paper 96-039, Harvard Business School, 1996).

2. "Spice Girls Dance into Culture Clash," *Montgomery Advertiser* (April 29, 1997): 2A.

3. Clifford Geertz, *The Interpretation of Cultures* (New York: Basic Books, 1973); Marvin Harris, *Culture, People and Nature* (New York: Crowell, 1971); John F. Sherry, Jr., "The Cultural Perspective in Consumer Research," in Richard J. Lutz, ed., *Advances in Consumer Research* 13 (Provo, UT: Association for Consumer Research, 1985): 573–75.

4. William Lazer, Shoji Murata, and Hiroshi Kosaka, "Japanese Marketing: Towards a Better Understanding," *Journal of Marketing* 49 (Spring 1985): 69–81.

5. Celia W. Dugger, "Modestly, India Goes for a Public Swim," *New York Times on the Web* (March 5, 2000).

6. Geert Hofstede, *Culture's Consequences* (Beverly Hills, CA: Sage, 1980); see also Laura M. Milner, Dale Fodness, and Mark W. Speece, "Hofstede's Research on Cross-Cultural Work-Related Values: Implications for Consumer Behavior," in W. Fred van Raaij and Gary J. Bamossy, eds., *European Advances in Consumer Research* (Amsterdam: Association for Consumer Research, 1993): 70–76.

7. Daniel Goleman, "The Group and the Self: New Focus on a Cultural Rift," *New York Times* (December 25, 1990): 37; Harry C. Triandis, "The Self and Social Behavior in Differing Cultural Contexts," *Psychological Review* 96 (July 1989): 506; Harry C. Triandis, Robert Bontempo, Marcelo J. Villareal, Masaaki Asai, and Nydia Lucca, "Individualism and Collectivism: Cross-Cultural Perspectives on Self–Ingroup Relationships," *Journal of Personality and Social Psychology* 54 (February 1988): 323.

8. George J. McCall and J. L. Simmons, *Social Psychology: A Sociological Approach* (New York: The Free Press, 1982).

9. Arundhati Parmar, "Out from Under," *Marketing News* (July 21, 2003): 9–10.

10. Jim Yardley, "No Spitting on the Road to Olympic Glory, Beijing Says," *New York Times Online* (April 17, 2007), accessed April 17, 2007.

11. Robert Frank, "When Small Chains Go Abroad, Culture Clashes Require Ingenuity," *Wall Street Journal Interactive Edition* (April 12, 2000).

12. Nina M. Lentini, "Products No Longer So Personal," *Marketing Daily* (February 9, 2007), available from www.mediapost.com, accessed February 9, 2007; Christine Bittar, "'Pee Ship' Enterprise for Clearblue Pregnancy Test," *Marketing Daily* (December 20, 2006), available from www.mediapost.com, accessed December 20, 2006.

13. Laura Petrecca, "Ad Track: Marketers Bet on lucky 777; That's July 7, 2007," *USA Today Online* (May 29, 2007), accessed May 29, 2007.

14. Jim Yardley, "First Comes the Car, Then the $10,000 License Plate," *New York Times Online* (April 16, 2006), accessed April 16, 2006.

15. Stefano S. Coledan, "Turning to Lady Luck to Bless Launchings," *New York Times Online* (September 7, 2006), accessed September 7, 2006.

16. Molly O'Neill, "As Life Gets More Complex, Magic Casts a Wider Spell," *New York Times* (June 13, 1994): A1.

17. Susannah Meadows, "Who's Afraid of the Big Bad Werewolf?" *Newsweek* (August 26, 2002): 57.

18. Conrad Phillip Kottak, "Anthropological Analysis of Mass Enculturation," in Conrad P. Kottak, ed., *Researching American Culture* (Ann Arbor: University of Michigan Press, 1982), 40–74; cf. also Teresa Davis and Olga Kravets, "Bridges to Displaced Meaning: The Reinforcing Roles of Myth and Marketing in Russian Vodka Labels," *Advances in Consumer Research* 32, no. 1 (2005): 480

19. Eric Ransdell, "The Nike Story? Just Tell It!" *Fast Company* (January–February 2000): 44.

20. Joseph Campbell, *Myths, Dreams, and Religion* (New York: E. P. Dutton, 1970).

21. Claude Lévi-Strauss, *Structural Anthropology* (Harmondsworth, England: Peregrine, 1977).

22. Tina Lowrey and Cele C. Otnes, "Consumer Fairy Tales and the Perfect Christmas," in Cele C. Otnes and Tina M. Lowrey, eds., *Contemporary Consumption Rituals: A Research Anthology* (Mahwah NJ: Lawrence Erlbaum, 2003).

23. Merissa Marr, "Fairy-Tale Wedding? Disney Can Supply the Gown," *Wall Street Journal* (February 22, 2007). B1; Lauram M. Holson, "For $38,000, Get the Cake, and Mickey, Too," *New York Times on the Web* (May 24, 2003).

24. Jeff Jensen, "Comic Heroes Return to Roots as Marvel Is Cast as Hip Brand," *Advertising Age* (June 8, 1998): 3.

25. Jeffrey S. Lang and Patrick Trimble, "Whatever Happened to the Man of Tomorrow? An Examination of the American Monomyth and the Comic Book Superhero," *Journal of Popular Culture* 22 (Winter 1988): 157.

26. Elizabeth C. Hirschman, "Movies as Myths: An Interpretation of Motion Picture Mythology," in Jean Umiker-Sebeok, ed., *Marketing and Semiotics: New Directions in the Study of Signs for Sale* (Berlin: Mouton de Gruyter, 1987), 335–74.

27. See William Blake Tyrrell, "Star Trek as Myth and Television as Mythmaker," in Jack Nachbar, Deborah Weiser, and John L. Wright, eds., *The Popular Culture Reader* (Bowling Green, OH: Bowling Green University Press, 1978): 79–88.

28. Bernie Whalen, "Semiotics: An Art or Powerful Marketing Research Tool?" *Marketing News* (May 13, 1983): 8.

29. Eduardo Porter, "New 'Got Milk?' TV Commercials Try to Entice Hispanic Teenagers," *Wall Street Journal Interactive Edition* (December 28, 2001).

30. Maria Kniazeva and Russell W. Belk, "Packaging as a Vehicle for Mythologizing the Brand," *Consumption, Markets and Culture* 10, no. 1 (2007): 51.

31. See Dennis W. Rook, "The Ritual Dimension of Consumer Behavior," *Journal of Consumer Research* 12 (December 1985): 251–64; Mary A. Stansfield Tetreault and Robert E. Kleine, III, "Ritual, Ritualized Behavior, and Habit: Refinements and Extensions of the Consumption Ritual Construct," in Marvin Goldberg, Gerald Gorn, and Richard W. Pollay, eds., *Advances in Consumer Research* 17 (Provo, UT: Association for Consumer Research, 1990): 31–38.

32. Deborah Ball, "British Drinkers of Guinness Say They'd Rather Take It Slow," *Wall Street Journal on the Web* (May 22, 2003).

33. Karl Greenberg, "BBDO: Successful Brands Become Hard Habit for Consumers to Break," *Marketing Daily* (May 14, 2007), available from www.mediapost.com, accessed May 14, 2007.

34. Laura Randall, "Things You Do at College," *New York Times* (August 1, 2004): 24.

35. Nancy Keates and Charles Passy, "Tailgating, Inc.," *Wall Street Journal on the Web* (August 29, 2003).

36. Virginia Postrel, "From Weddings to Football, the Value of Communal Activities," *New York Times on the Web* (April 25, 2002).

37. Kim Foltz, "New Species for Study: Consumers in Action," *New York Times* (December 18, 1989): A1.

38. For a study that looked at updated wedding rituals in Turkey, see Tuba Ustuner, Güliz Ger, and Douglas B. Holt, "Consuming Ritual: Reframing the Turkish Henna-Night Ceremony," in Stephen J. Hoch and Robert J. Meyers, eds., *Advances in Consumer Research* 27 (Provo, UT: Association for Consumer Research, 2000): 209–14.

39. For a study that looked specifically at rituals pertaining to birthday parties, see Cele Otnes and Mary Ann McGrath, "Ritual Socialization and the Children's Birthday Party: The Early Emergence of Gender Differences," *Journal of Ritual Studies* 8 (Winter 1994): 73–93.

40. Dennis W. Rook and Sidney J. Levy, "Psychosocial Themes in Consumer Grooming Rituals," in Richard P. Bagozzi and Alice M. Tybout, eds., *Advances in Consumer Research* 10 (Provo, UT: Association for Consumer Research, 1983): 329–33.

41. Quoted in Andrew Adam Newman, "Depilatory Market Moves Far Beyond the Short-Shorts Wearers," *New York Times Online* (September 14, 2007), accessed September 14, 2007.

42. Diane Barthel, *Putting on Appearances: Gender and Advertising* (Philadelphia: Temple University Press, 1988).

43. Ibid.

44. Russell W. Belk, Melanie Wallendorf, and John F. Sherry, Jr., "The Sacred and the Profane in Consumer Behavior: Theodicy on the Odyssey," *Journal of Consumer Research* 16 (June 1989): 1–38.

45. Markus Giesler and Mali Pohlmann, "The Anthropology of File Sharing: Consuming Napster as a Gift," in Punam Anand Keller and Dennis W. Rook, eds., *Advances in Consumer Research* 30 (Provo, UT: Association for Consumer Research 2003); Markus Giesler, "Consumer Gift Systems," *Journal of Consumer Research* 33 no. 2 (2006): 283.

46. Jill G. Klein and Tina M. Lowrey, "Giving and Receiving Humanity: Gifts among Prisoners in Nazi Concentration Camps" *Advances in Consumer Research* 33, no. 1 (2006): 659

47. Tina M. Lowrey, Cele C. Otnes, and Julie A. Ruth, "Social Influences on Dyadic Giving over Time: A Taxonomy from the Giver's Perspective," *Journal of Consumer Research* 30 (March 2004): 547–58; Russell W. Belk and Gregory S. Coon, "Gift Giving as Agapic Love: An Alternative to the Exchange Paradigm Based on Dating Experiences," *Journal of Consumer Research* 20 (December 1993): 393–417. See also Cele Otnes,

Tina M. Lowrey, and Young Chan Kim, "Gift Selection for Easy and Difficult Recipients: A Social Roles Interpretation," *Journal of Consumer Research* 20 (September 1993): 229–44; Burcak Ertimur and Ozlem Sandikci, "Giving Gold Jewelry and Coins as Gifts: The Interplay of Utilitarianism and Symbolism," *Advances in Consumer Research* 32, no. 1 (2005).

48. Monica Gonzales, "Before Mourning," *American Demographics* (April 1988): 19.

49. Alf Nucifora, "Tis the Season to Gift One's Best Clients," *Triangle Business Journal* (December 3, 1999): 14.

50. John F. Sherry, Jr., "Gift Giving in Anthropological Perspective," *Journal of Consumer Research* 10 (September 1983): 157–68.

51. Daniel Goleman, "What's under the Tree? Clues to a Relationship," *New York Times* (December 19, 1989): C1.

52. John F. Sherry, Jr., Mary Ann McGrath, and Sidney J. Levy, "The Dark Side of the Gift," *Journal of Business Research* (1993): 225–44.

53. Colin Camerer, "Gifts as Economics Signals and Social Symbols," *American Journal of Sociology* 94 (Supplement 1988): 5, 180–214; Robert T. Green and Dana L. Alden, "Functional Equivalence in Cross-Cultural Consumer Behavior: Gift Giving in Japan and the United States," *Psychology & Marketing* 5 (Summer 1988): 155–68; Hiroshi Tanaka and Miki Iwamura, "Gift Selection Strategy of Japanese Seasonal Gift Purchasers: An Explorative Study," paper presented at the Association for Consumer Research, Boston, October 1994.

54. See, for example, Russell W. Belk, "Halloween: An Evolving American Consumption Ritual," in Richard Pollay, Jerry Gorn, and Marvin Goldberg, eds., *Advances in Consumer Research* 17 (Provo, UT: Association for Consumer Research, 1990): 508–17; Melanie Wallendorf and Eric J. Arnould, "We Gather Together: The Consumption Rituals of Thanksgiving Day," *Journal of Consumer Research* 18 (June 1991): 13–31.

55. Rick Lyte, "Holidays, Ethnic Themes Provide Built-in F&B Festivals," *Hotel & Motel Management* (December 14, 1987): 56; Megan Rowe, "Holidays and Special Occasions: Restaurants Are Fast Replacing 'Grandma's House' as the Site of Choice for Special Meals," *Restaurant Management* (November 1987): 69; Judith Waldrop, "Funny Valentines," *American Demographics* (February 1989): 7.

56. "Cinco de Mayo, a Yawn for Mexicans, Gives Americans a License to Party," *Wall Street Journal Interactive Edition* (May 5, 2000).

57. Bruno Bettelheim, *The Uses of Enchantment: The Meaning and Importance of Fairy Tales* (New York: Alfred A. Knopf, 1976).

58. Kenneth L. Woodward, "Christmas Wasn't Born Here, Just Invented," *Newsweek* (December 16, 1996): 71.

59. Aron O'Cass and Peter Clarke, "Dear Santa, Do You Have My Brand? A Study of the Brand Requests, Awareness and Request Styles at Christmas Time," *Journal of Consumer Behavior* 2 (September 2002): 37–53.

60. Theodore Caplow, Howard M. Bahr, Bruce A. Chadwick, Reuben Hill, and Margaret M. Williams, *Middletown Families: Fifty Years of Change and Continuity* (Minneapolis: University of Minnesota Press, 1982).

61. Andrea Adelson, "A New Spirit for Sales of Halloween Merchandise," *New York Times* (October 31, 1994): D1.

62. Anne Swardson, "Trick or Treat: In Paris, It's Dress, Dance, Eat," *International Herald Tribune* (October 31, 1996): 2.

63. Angeline Close and George M. Zinkhan, "A Holiday Loved and Loathed: A Consumer Perspective of Valentine's Day," *Advances in Consumer Research*, 33, no. 1 (2006). 356–365

64. Elizabeth Bernstein, "More Kids on Cusp of 13 Get Faux Post-Rite Parties," *Wall Street Journal on the Web* (January 14, 2004).

65. Arnold Van Gennep, *The Rites of Passage*, trans. Maika B. Vizedom and Shannon L. Caffee (London: Routledge and Kegan Paul, 1960; orig. published 1908); Michael R. Solomon and Punam Anand, "Ritual Costumes and Status Transition: The Female Business Suit as Totemic Emblem," in Elizabeth C. Hirschman and Morris Holbrook, eds., *Advances in Consumer Research* 12 (Washington, DC: Association for Consumer Research, 1995): 315–18.

66. Walter W. Whitaker, III, "The Contemporary American Funeral Ritual," in Ray B. Browne, ed., *Rites and Ceremonies in Popular Culture* (Bowling Green, OH: Bowling Green University Popular Press, 1980): 316–25. For a recent examination of funeral rituals, see Larry D. Compeau and Carolyn Nicholson, "Funerals: Emotional Rituals or Ritualistic Emotions," paper presented at the Association of Consumer Research, Boston, October 1994.

67. John Leland, "It's My Funeral and I'll Serve Ice Cream If I Want To," *New York Times Online* (July 20, 2006), accessed July 20, 2006.

68. Samuel K. Bonsu and Russell W. Belk, "Do Not Go Cheaply into That Good Night: Death-Ritual Consumption in Asante, Ghana," *Journal of Consumer Research* 30 (June 2003): 41–55; cf also Stephanie O'Donohoe and Darach Turley, "Till Death Do Us Part? Consumption and the Negotiation of Relationships Following a Bereavement," *Advances in Consumer Research* 32, no. 1 (2005): 625–626.

69. Mireya Navarro, "How Green Was My Wedding," *New York Times Online* (February 11, 2007), accessed February 11, 2007.

70. "Queen Prompts Thailand to Restrict 'Coyote Ugly' Dance Troupes," *New York Times on the Web* (December 28, 2006).

71. Kottak, "Anthropological Analysis of Mass Enculturation."

72. Joan Kron, *Home-Psych: The Social Psychology of Home and Decoration* (New York: Clarkson N. Potter, 1983); Gerry Pratt, "The House as an Expression of Social Worlds," in James S. Duncan, ed., *Housing and Identity: Cross-Cultural Perspectives* (London: Croom Helm, 1981): 135–79; Michael R. Solomon, "The Role of the Surrogate Consumer in Service Delivery," *The Service Industries Journal* 7 (July 1987): 292–307.

73. Grant McCracken, "'Homeyness': A Cultural Account of One Constellation of Goods and Meanings," in Elizabeth C. Hirschman, ed., *Interpretive Consumer Research* (Provo, UT: Association for Consumer Research, 1989): 168–84.

74. Emile Durkheim, *The Elementary Forms of the Religious Life* (New York: Free Press, 1915).

75. Susan Birrell, "Sports as Ritual: Interpretations from Durkheim to Goffman," *Social Forces* 60, no. 2 (1981): 354–76; Daniel Q. Voigt, "American Sporting Rituals," in Browne, ed., *Rites and Ceremonies in Popular Culture.*

76. Ronald W. Pimentel and Kristy E. Reynolds, "A Model for Consumer Devotion: Affective Commitment with Proactive Sustaining Behaviors," *Academy of Marketing Science Review* 5 (2004): 1.

77. Mark A. Stein, "Block That Snack," *New York Times* (February 2007): 2.

78. Dean MacCannell, *The Tourist: A New Theory of the Leisure Class* (New York: Shocken Books, 1976).

79. Belk et al., "The Sacred and the Profane in Consumer Behavior."

80. Beverly Gordon, "The Souvenir: Messenger of the Extraordinary," *Journal of Popular Culture* 20, no. 3 (1986): 135–46.

81. Belk et al., "The Sacred and the Profane in Consumer Behavior."

82. Güliz Ger and Olga Kravets (2007), "Rediscovering Sacred Times in the Mundane: Tea Drinking in Turkey," Consuming Routines: Rhythms, Ruptures, and the Temporalities of Consumption, International Workshop, European University Institute, Florence, Italy, May 3–5.; cf. also Güliz Ger "Religion and Consumption: The Profane Sacred," *Advances in Consumer Research* 32, no. 1 (2005): 79–81.

83. Deborah Hofmann, "In Jewelry, Choices Sacred and Profane, Ancient and New," *New York Times Online* (May 7, 1989), accessed October 11, 2007.

84. Lee Gomes, "Ramadan, a Month of Prayer, Takes on a Whole New Look," *Wall Street Journal Interactive Edition* (December 4, 2002).

85. J. C. Conklin, "Web Site Caters to Cowboy Fans by Selling Sweaty, Used Socks," *Wall Street Journal Interactive Edition* (April 21, 2000).

86. Dan L. Sherrell, Alvin C. Burns, and Melodie R. Phillips, "Fixed Consumption Behavior: The Case of Enduring Acquisition in a Product Category," in Robert L. King, ed., *Developments in Marketing Science* 14 (1991): 36–40.

87. Anne Underwood, "Hoarders Pack It In," *Newsweek* (July 26, 2004): 12.

88. Belk, "Acquiring, Possessing, and Collecting: Fundamental Processes in Consumer Behavior," in Ronald F. Bush and Shelby D. Hunt, eds., *Marketing Theory: Philosophy of Science Perspectives* (Chicago: American Marketing Association, 1982): 85–90; cf. 74.

89. Ruth Ann Smith, "Collecting as Consumption: A Grounded Theory of Collecting Behavior" (unpublished manuscript, Virginia Polytechnic Institute and State University, 1994): 14.

90. For a discussion of these perspectives, see Smith, "Collecting as Consumption."

91. For an extensive bibliography on collecting, see Russell W. Belk, Melanie Wallendorf, John F. Sherry, Jr., and Morris B. Holbrook, "Collecting in a Consumer Culture," in Russell W. Belk, ed., *Highways and Buyways* (Provo, UT: Association for Consumer Research, 1991): 178–215. See also Russell W. Belk, "Acquiring, Possessing, and Collecting: Fundamental Processes in Consumer Behavior"; Werner Muensterberg, *Collecting: An Unruly Passion* (Princeton, NJ: Princeton University Press, 1994); Melanie Wallendorf and Eric J. Arnould, "'My Favorite Things': A Cross-Cultural Inquiry into Object Attachment, Possessiveness, and Social Linkage," *Journal of Consumer Research* 14 (March 1988): 531–47.

92. Calmetta Y. Coleman, "Just Any Old Thing from McDonald's Can Be a Collectible," *Wall Street Journal* (March 29, 1995): B1; Ken Bensinger, "Recent Boom in Toy Collecting Leads Retailers to Limit Sales," *Wall Street Journal Interactive Edition* (September 25, 1998); "PC Lovers Loyal to Classics," *Montgomery Advertiser* (April 2, 2000): 1.

93. Philip Connors, "Like Fine Wine, a 'Collector' Visits McDonald's for Subtle Differences," *Wall Street Journal Interactive Edition* (August 16, 1999).

94. Debbie Treise, Joyce M. Wolburg, and Cele C. Otnes, "Understanding the 'Social Gifts' of Drinking Rituals: An Alternative Framework for PSA Developers," *Journal of Advertising* 28 (Summer 1999): 17–31.

95. Ibid.

Global Consumer Culture

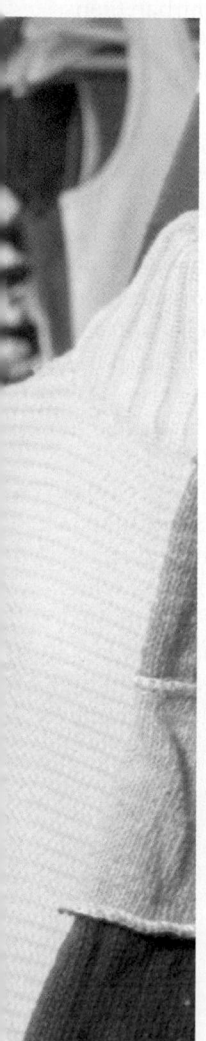

Chapter Objectives

When you finish this chapter you should understand why:

- Styles act as a mirror to reflect underlying cultural conditions.
- We distinguish between high and low culture.
- Many modern marketers are reality engineers.
- New products, services, and ideas spread through a population. Different types of people are more or less likely to adopt them.
- Many people and organizations play a role in the fashion system that creates and communicates symbolic meaning to consumers.
- Fashions follow cycles.
- Products that succeed in one culture may fail in another if marketers fail to understand the differences among consumers in each place.
- Western (and particularly American) culture has a huge impact around the world, although people in other countries don't necessarily ascribe the same meanings to products as we do.

a s Alexandra is browsing through the racks at her local Abercrombie & Fitch store in Wichita, Kansas, her friend Chloe yells to her, "Alex, check this out! This pencil skirt and animal print blouse outfit is, like, so tight!"[1] From watching MTV, Alex knows tight means *cool*, and she agrees. As she takes the pants to the cash register, she's looking forward to wearing them to school the next day. All of her girlfriends in junior high compete with each other to dress just like the women in the Pussycat Dolls and other hot groups—her friends just won't believe their eyes when they see her tomorrow. Maybe some of the younger kids in her school will even think she was fresh off the mean streets of New York City! Even though she has never been east of the Mississippi, Alex just knows she would fit right in with all of the Bronx "sistahs" she reads about in her magazines.

Creating Culture

Even though U.S. inner-city teens represent only 8 percent of all people in that age group and have incomes significantly lower than their white suburban counterparts, their influence on young American's musical and fashion tastes is much greater than these numbers suggest. Turn on MTV, and it won't be long before a rap video fills the screen. Go to the newsstand, and magazines such as *Vibe* await you. Numerous Web sites such as vibe.com and templeofhiphop.org pay homage to hip-hop culture.

"Urban" fashion now is a mainstay in the U.S. heartland as major retail chains pick up on the craze and try to lure legions of young middle-class shoppers. Macy's and JCPenney carry FUBU ("for us by us"); although this urban clothing company sells a lot of shiny satin baseball jackets, baggy jeans with loops, and fleece tops in the inner city, 40 percent of its customers are white American suburbanites. Big names such as Versace, Tommy Hilfiger, Polo by Ralph Lauren, Nautica, Sean Jean, and Guess now are standard issue for junior high kids who are into hip-hop. Web sites such as www.hiphopcapital.com sell other emblems of hip-hop such as "pimp cups," gold plated "grillz," and Bellagio spoke rims.[2] Why does this subculture influence the mass market so strongly?

Outsider heroes—whether John Dillinger, James Dean, or Dr. Dre—who achieve money and fame without being hemmed in by societal constraints have always fascinated Americans. That helps to explain the devotion of many white suburban teens to the urban music scene. As one executive of a firm that researches U.S. urban youth noted, "People resonate with the strong anti-oppression messages of rap, and the alienation of blacks."[3]

Ironically, Alex's only experience of "oppression" was when her parents grounded her after her mom found a half-smoked cigarette in her room. She lives in a white middle-class area in the Midwest but "connects" symbolically with millions of other young consumers when she wears styles from "the hood"—even though the original meanings of those styles have little relevance to her. As a privileged member of "white bread" society, her hip-hop clothes have a very different meaning in her suburban world than they would to street kids in New York City or LA. In fact, these "cutting-edge" types might even interpret the fact that Alex is wearing a style as a sign that this item is no longer in fashion and decide it's time to move on to something else.

Big corporations are working hard to capture the next killer fashion "or flavor" in African American urban culture. For example, Fila, which started as an Italian underwear maker in 1926, first broke into sportswear with a focus on "lily-white" activities such as skiing and tennis. The company made a splash when it signed Swedish tennis sensation Bjorn Borg to endorse its tennis clothes. Ten years later, the tennis fad faded, but company executives noticed that rap stars such as Heavy D wore Fila sweat suits to symbolize their idealized vision of life in white country clubs. Fila switched gears and went with the flow; its share of the sneaker market grew dramatically.[4]

How did hip-hop music and fashions, which began as forms of expression in the African American urban subculture, make it to mainstream America? Here's a brief chronology:

● 1968: Bronx DJ Kool Herc invents hip-hop.
● 1973–1978: Urban block parties feature break-dancing and graffiti.
● 1979: Sugar Hill becomes the first rap label.
● 1980: Manhattan art galleries feature graffiti artists.
● 1981: Blondie's song "Rapture" hits number one on the charts.
● 1985: Columbia Records buys the Def Jam label.
● 1988: MTV begins *Yo! MTV Raps*, featuring Fab 5 Freddy.
● 1990: Hollywood produces the hip-hop film *House Party*; Ice-T's rap album is a big hit on college radio stations; amid controversy, white rapper Vanilla Ice hits the big time; NBC launches a new sitcom, *Fresh Prince of Bel Air*.

- 1991: Mattel introduces its Hammer doll (a likeness of the rap star Hammer, formerly known as M. C. Hammer); designer Karl Lagerfeld shows shiny vinyl raincoats and chain belts in his Chanel collection; designer Charlotte Neuville sells gold vinyl suits with matching baseball caps for $800; Isaac Mizrahi features wide-brimmed caps and takeoffs on African medallions; Bloomingdale's launches Anne Klein's rap-inspired clothing line with a rap performance in its Manhattan store.

- 1992: Rappers turn to low-fitting baggy jeans, sometimes worn backwards; white rapper Marky Mark appears in a national campaign wearing Calvin Klein underwear, exposed above his hip-hugging pants; composer Quincy Jones launches *Vibe* magazine and it wins over many white readers.[5]

- 1993: Hip-hop fashions and slang continue to cross over into mainstream consumer culture. An outdoor ad for Coca-Cola proclaims, "Get Yours 24–7." The company is confident that many viewers in its target market will know that the phrase is urban slang for "always" (24 hours a day, 7 days a week).[6]

- 1994: The (late) Italian designer Versace pushes oversized overalls. In one ad, he asks, "Overalls with an oversize look, something like what rappers and homeboys wear. Why not a sophisticated version?"[7]

- 1996: Tommy Hilfiger, a designer who was the darling of the preppie set, turns hip-hop. He gives free wardrobes to rap artists such as Grand Puba and Chef Raekwon, and in return they mention his name in rap songs—the ultimate endorsement. The September 1996 issue of *Rolling Stone* features the Fugees; several band members prominently display the Hilfiger logo. In the same year, the designer uses rap stars Method Man and Treach of Naughty by Nature as runway models. Hilfiger's new Tommy Girl perfume plays on his name but also is a reference to the New York hip-hop record label Tommy Boy.[8]

- 1997: Coca-Cola features rapper LL Cool J in a commercial that debuts in the middle of the sitcom *In the House*, a TV show starring the singer.[9]

- 1998: In its battle with Dockers for an increased share of the khaki market, GAP launches its first global ad campaign. One of the commercials, "Khakis Groove," includes a hip-hop dance performance set to music by Bill Mason.[10]

- 1999: Rapper turned entrepreneur Sean (Puffy) Combs introduces an upscale line of menswear he calls "urban high fashion." New companies FUBU, Mecca, and Enyce attain financial success in the multibillion-dollar industry.[11] Lauryn Hill and the Fugees sing at a party upscale Italian clothier Emporio Armani sponsors and she proclaims, "We just wanna thank Armani for giving a few kids from the ghetto some great suits."[12]

- 2000: 360hip-hop.com, a Web-based community dedicated to the hip-hop culture, launches. The site lets consumers purchase clothing and music online while they watch video interviews with artists such as Will Smith and Busta Rymes.[13]

- 2001: Hip-hop dancing becomes the rage among China's youth, who refer to it as *jiew*, or street dancing.[14]

- 2002–2003: Toy manufacturers mimic the hip-hop practice of using the letter "Z" instead of the letter "S" in names. This trend started with the 1991 film *Boyz N the Hood* (a title the movie borrowed from a 1989 song by the rap group N.W.A.). It caught on with other hip-hop terms such as "skillz," "gangstaz," and "playaz." Musical artists including 504 Boyz, Kidz Bop Kidz, Xzibit, the Youngbloodz, and Smilez incorporate the popular "Z" into their names. During the 2002 Christmas season, Target creates its "Kool Toyz," kids' section where parents buy dolls with names such as Bratz (Girlz and Boyz), Diva Starz, and Trophy Tailz—and a Dinky Digz dollhouse to store them. There is a "Scannerz" toy; a Loud Lipz karaoke machine; Marble Moovz, a toddlers' marble set, as well as Rescue Rigz, ControlBotz, 4Wheelerz, and American Patriotz action figures.[15]

- 2005–2006: Successful artists begin to expand their empires into other categories. Jay-Z uses his hip-hop fortune to become part owner of the New Jersey

Nets basketball team; Nelly buys into the Charlotte Bobcats; and Usher does the same with the Cleveland Cavaliers.[16] Nelly branches out into the beverage business with Pimp Juice, a hip-hop inspired energy drink, and 50 Cent invests in Vitamin Water. Trina and Usher each create their own fragrances and Gwen Stefani starts her own clothing line. *Esquire* names Andre 3000 of Outkast the world's best-dressed man.

● 2007–2008: Hip-hop disengages from its American roots as artists around the world develop their own localized interpretations. An aboriginal Australian hip-hop dancer tells a crowd the FUBU brand shirt he is wearing means "full blood."[17] Home-grown European artists are popular, such as Jokeren and Den Gale Pose in Denmark, Static and NATiLL in Germany, and Sway in the United Kingdom. Central and eastern European countries develop their own hip-hop subculture with acts such as Parazitii in Romania and Bad Balance/Bad.B in Russia.[18]

It's common for mainstream culture to modify symbols from "cutting-edge" subcultures for a larger audience to consume. As this occurs, these cultural products undergo a process of **co-optation**, where outsiders transform their original meanings. This happened to rap music, which is divorced to a large extent from its original connection with the struggles of young African Americans and is now a mainstream entertainment format.[19] One writer sees the white part of the "hip-hop nation" as a series of concentric rings. In the center are those who actually know African Americans and understand their culture. The next ring consists of those who have indirect knowledge of this subculture via friends or relatives but who don't actually rap, spray-paint, or break-dance. Then, there are those a bit further out who simply play hip-hop between other types of music. Finally come the more suburban "wiggers," who simply try to catch on to the next popular craze.[20] The spread of hip-hop fashions and music is only one example of what happens when the marketing system takes a set of subcultural meanings, reinterprets them, and produces them for mass consumption.

In this chapter we'll look at how our culture creates these meanings—which often reside in everyday products—and how these meanings move through a society. As Figure 17.1 shows, the advertising and fashion industries are a key part of this process as they associate functional products with symbolic qualities such as sexiness, sophistication, or just plain "cool." These goods, in turn, impart their meanings to us, as we use these products to create and express our identities.[21] Recall that in Chapter 1 we learned that "one of the fundamental premises of the modern field of consumer behavior [is that] people often buy products not for what they *do* but for what they *mean*." This closing chapter brings us full circle as we explore how product symbolism evolves and spreads through our culture.

■ **FIGURE 17.1**
THE MOVEMENT OF MEANING

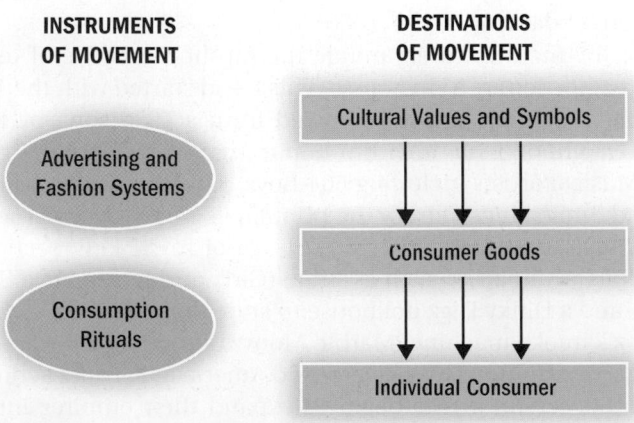

Cultural Selection

Nipple rings. Vuitton handbags. Sushi. High-tech furniture. Postmodern architecture. Twittering. Double decaf cappuccino with a hint of cinnamon. We inhabit a world brimming with different styles and possibilities. The food we eat, the cars we drive, the clothes we wear, the places we live and work, the music we listen to—the ebb and flow of popular culture and fashion influences all of them.

At times we may feel overwhelmed by the sheer number of choices in the marketplace. A person trying to decide on something as routine as a necktie or a color of lipstick has to choose from hundreds of alternatives! Despite this seeming abundance, however, the options available to us at any point in time actually represent only a small fraction of the total set of possibilities. Figure 17.2 shows that our selection of certain alternatives over others—whether automobiles, dresses, computers, recording artists, political candidates, religions, or even scientific methodologies—is the culmination of a complex filtration process that resembles a funnel. Many possibilities initially compete for adoption, and these steadily get winnowed out as they make their way down the path from conception to consumption in a process of **cultural selection**.

We don't form our tastes and product preferences in a vacuum. The many images mass media presents to us drive our choices, as well as our observations of those around us, and even our desires to live in the fantasy worlds marketers create. These options constantly evolve and change. A clothing style or type of cuisine that is "hot" one year may be "out" the next.

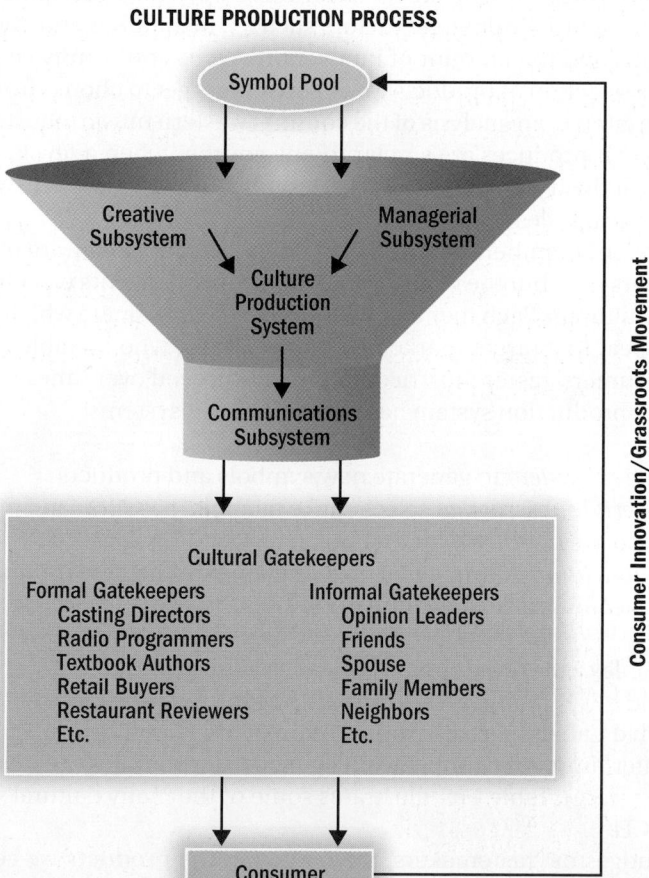

CULTURE PRODUCTION PROCESS

■ FIGURE 17.2
THE CULTURE PRODUCTION PROCESS

Alex's emulation of hip-hop style illustrates some of the characteristics of fashion and popular culture:

● Styles are a reflection of more fundamental societal trends (e.g., politics and social conditions).
● A style begins as a risky or unique statement by a relatively small group of people and then spreads as others increasingly become aware of the style and feel confident about trying it.
● Styles usually originate as an interplay between the deliberate inventions of designers and businesspeople and spontaneous actions by ordinary consumers who modify styles to suit their own needs. Designers, manufacturers, and merchandisers who can anticipate what consumers want will succeed in the marketplace. In the process, they help to fuel the fire when they encourage distribution of the item.
● These cultural products travel widely, often across countries and even continents.
● Influential people in the media play a significant role in deciding which will succeed.
● Most styles eventually wear out as people continually search for new ways to express themselves and marketers scramble to keep up with these desires.

CULTURE PRODUCTION SYSTEMS

No single designer, company, or advertising agency creates popular culture. Instead, many parties contribute to every hit CD, hot car, or new clothing style. A **culture production system (CPS)** is the set of individuals and organizations that create and market a cultural product.[22] The structure of these systems determines the types of products that eventually emerge. Factors such as the number and diversity of competing systems and the amount of innovation versus conformity each encourages influence the selection of products we as consumers get to choose from at any point in time. For example, an analysis of the country/western music industry showed that the hit records it produces are similar to one another when a few large companies dominate the industry, but when a greater number of labels compete we see more diversity in musical styles.[23]

The different members of a CPS may not necessarily be aware of or appreciate the roles others play, but the reality is that many diverse agents work together to create popular culture.[24] Each member does his best to anticipate which particular images will appeal to a target market. Of course, those who are able to consistently forecast consumers' tastes most accurately will succeed over time.[25]

A culture production system has three major subsystems:

1 A *creative subsystem* to generate new symbols and products
2 A *managerial subsystem* to select, make tangible, produce, and manage the distribution of new symbols and products
3 A *communications subsystem* to give meaning to the new product and provide it with a symbolic set of attributes

An example of the three components of a culture production system for a music release would be (1) a singer (e.g., rapper Akon, a creative subsystem); (2) a company (e.g., Umvd Labels that distributes Akon's CDs, a managerial subsystem); and (3) NYLA Entertainment Group, the PR agency that promotes the CDs (a communications subsystem). Table 17.1 illustrates some of the many cultural specialists that create a hit CD.

Many judges or "tastemakers" have a say in the products we consider. These **cultural gatekeepers** filter the overflow of information and materials that makes it way down the "funnel." Gatekeepers include movie, restaurant, and car reviewers;

There's one thing AT&T international long distance customers will never have to worry about.

8 TRACK

DISCO FEVER VOL. II

These days, things seem to go obsolete before you can get them out of the box.

Not so with AT&T International Long Distance.

We're continually upgrading our Worldwide Intelligent Network, before you have time to even think about it.

When we saw that global events were affecting telephone traffic, we expanded our Network Operations Center. Now events are continually monitored 24 hours a day, and traffic is routed accordingly.

We also anticipated the growing demand for international voice, data and fax transmission, by developing the first transpacific and transatlantic fiber-optic cable systems.

© 1989 AT&T

So you'll enjoy fast international connections with unsurpassed clarity.

We could list other examples of advances you'll never have to think about.

But why not call 1 800 222-0400 ext. 1277, and let the innovations speak for themselves.

AT&T
The right choice.

As this AT&T ad demonstrates, many styles and products are destined to become obsolete.

interior designers; disc jockeys; retail buyers; and magazine editors. Collectively, social scientists call this set of agents the *throughput sector*.[26] These people play a role in decision making similar to the *surrogate consumers* we discussed in Chapter 9.

We've already encountered numerous examples of the minirevolution we call consumer-generated content; companies today pay attention to everyday people's opinions when they design new products, create advertising messages, or improve upon shopping experiences. The rise of social networking changes the basic process of innovation, as the consumer feedback loop in Figure 17.1 grows stronger and stronger. This shift from a top-down to a bottom-up process is a symptom of the transition from *marketerspace* where companies exert total control over the market.

Instead, we now live in **consumerspace**, where customers act as partners with companies to decide what the marketplace will offer.[27] Innovative companies understand the value of involving their most forward-thinking customers in business decisions before they introduce the final product. More than 650,000 customers tested a beta version of Microsoft Windows 2000. Many were even prepared to pay Microsoft a fee to do this because working with the program would help them understand how it could create value for their own businesses. The value of the

TABLE 17.1
CULTURAL SPECIALISTS IN THE MUSIC INDUSTRY

Specialist	Functions
Songwriter(s)	Compose music and lyrics; must reconcile artistic preferences with estimates of what will succeed in the marketplace
Performer(s)	Interpret music and lyrics; may be formed spontaneously, or may be packaged by an agent to appeal to a predetermined market (e.g., The Monkees, Menudo, and New Kids on the Block)
Teachers and coaches	Develop and refine performers' talents
Agents	Represent performers to record companies
A&R (artist & repertoire) executives	Acquire artists for the record label
Publicists, image consultants, designers, stylists	Create an image for the group that is transmitted to the buying public
Recording technicians, producers	Create a recording to be sold
Marketing executives	Make strategic decisions regarding performer's appearances, ticket pricing, promotional strategies, and so on
Video directors	Interpret the song visually to create a music video that will help to promote the record
Music reviewers	Evaluate the merits of a recording for listeners
Disc jockeys, radio program directors	Decide which records will be given airplay and/or placed in the radio stations' regular rotations
Record store owners	Decide which of the many records produced will be stocked and/or promoted heavily in the retail environment

research and development investment by customers to Microsoft was more than $500 million. Similarly, Cisco gives its customers open access to its resources and systems so that they can solve the problems other customers encounter.

This approach is more prevalent in high-tech industries that consult their **lead users** about ideas; these are very experienced and knowledgeable customers. Indeed, it's common for these people to propose product improvements—because they have to live with the consequences. According to one estimate, users rather than manufacturers developed 70 percent of the innovations in the chemical industry![28]

Xerox is a traditional company that's now leading the charge toward consumer-space. It's intent on using **voice of the consumer** data in its R&D process, which means that it solicits feedback from end customers well before it puts a new product on the market. The company's standard development process is to design and build a prototype and *then* get customer feedback. Now Xerox is shifting to what it calls "customer-led innovation," which encourages engineers to "dream with the customer." Xerox encourages the engineers to meet face to face with some of the 1,500 to 2,000 customers who visit showrooms at the company's four global research facilities each year. Others work on-site for a week or two with a customer, observing how they behave with the product. A team of ethnographers also observes people in real situations to see how they actually use the company's products.[29] Welcome to consumerspace.

HIGH CULTURE AND POPULAR CULTURE

Question: What do Beethoven and T-Pain have in common? Although we associate both the famous composer and the rap singer with music, many would argue that the similarity stops there. Culture production systems create many kinds of products, but we can make some basic distinctions.

Arts and Crafts

An **art product** is an object we admire strictly for its beauty or because it inspires an emotional reaction in us (perhaps bliss, or perhaps disgust). In contrast, we admire a **craft product** because of the beauty with which it performs some function (e.g., a ceramic ashtray or hand-carved fishing lures).[30] A piece of art is original, subtle, and valuable, and typically we associate it with society's elite (see Chapter 13). A craft tends to follow a formula that permits rapid production.[31]

To appreciate this distinction, consider the phenomenal success of artist Thomas Kinkade. This painter has sold 10 million digital reproductions of his work. He manufactures the pictures at a factory in California, where workers reproduce a digital photograph of each original thousands of times onto thin plastic film they glue to canvasses. Then "high-lighters" sit along an assembly line where they dab oil paint onto set spots. Each of the 10,000 pieces the factory produces each month is signed in ink containing drops of the artist's blood, although he never actually touches most of these works. Kinkade also has licensed images to appear on coffee mugs, La-Z-Boy recliners, and even a romance-novel cover.[32]

HIGH ART VERSUS LOW ART

As Kinkade's "formula for success" demonstrates, the distinction between high and low culture is not as clear as it used to be. In addition to the possible class bias that

As this British ad illustrates, high art merges with popular art in interesting ways.

At home in the world's great landscapes. ⊞Elddis

drives such a distinction (i.e., we assume that the rich have culture but the poor do not), today high and low culture blend together in interesting ways. In addition to selling appliances, tires, and cereals by the case, the warehouse club Costco now stocks fine art, including limited-edition lithographs by Pablo Picasso, Marc Chagall, and Joan Miró.[33]

Marketers often invoke high art imagery to promote products. They may feature works of art on shopping bags or sponsor artistic events to build public goodwill.[34] When observers from Toyota watched customers in luxury car showrooms, the company found that these consumers view a car as an art object. The company then used this theme in an ad for the Lexus with the caption, "Until now, the only fine arts we supported were sculpture, painting, and music."[35]

CULTURAL FORMULAE

Mass culture, in contrast, churns out products specifically for a mass market. These products aim to please the average taste of an undifferentiated audience. Rather than being unique, they are predictable because they follow a well-defined pattern. As Table 17.2 illustrates, many popular art forms, such as detective stories or science fiction, follow a **cultural formula**, where familiar roles and props occur consistently.[36] Romance novels are an extreme case of a cultural formula. Computer programs even allow users to "write" their own romances by systematically varying certain set elements of the story.

Reliance on these formulae also leads to a *recycling* of images, as members of the creative subsystem reach back through time for inspiration. Thus, young people watch retro shows such as *Gilligan's Island* as well as remakes such as *The Real Gilligan's Island*; designers modify styles from Victorian England or colonial Africa; hip-hop deejays sample sound bits from old songs and combine them in new ways; and GAP runs ads featuring now-dead celebrities including Humphrey Bogart, Gene Kelly, and Pablo Picasso who wear khaki pants. With easy access to VCRs, CD burners, digital cameras, and imaging software, virtually anyone can "remix" the past.[37]

TABLE 17.2
CULTURAL FORMULAE IN PUBLIC ART FORMS

Art Form/Genre	Classic Western	Science Fiction	Hard-Boiled Detective	Family Sitcom
Time	1800s	Future	Present	Anytime
Location	Edge of civilization	Space	City	Suburbs
Protagonist	Cowboy (lone individual)	Astronaut	Detective	Father (figure)
Heroine	Schoolmarm	Spacegal	Damsel in distress	Mother (figure)
Villain	Outlaws, killers	Aliens	Killer	Boss, neighbor
Secondary characters	Townfolk, Indians	Technicians in spacecraft	Cops, underworld	Kids, dogs
Plot	Restore law and order	Repel aliens	Find killer	Solve problem
Theme	Justice	Triumph of humanity	Pursuit and discovery	Chaos and confusion
Costume	Cowboy hat, boots, etc.	High-tech uniforms	Raincoat	Regular clothes
Locomotion	Horse	Spaceship	Beat-up car	Station wagon
Weaponry	Sixgun, rifle	Rayguns	Pistol, fists	Insults

Source: Arthur A. Berger, *Signs in Contemporary Culture: An Introduction to Semiotics,* 2/e, p.118. Copyright © 1984 by Sheffield Publishing Company, Salem, Wisconsin. Reprinted with permission of the publisher.

This ad mimics the cultural formula of a tabloid to attract visitors to a zoo.

REALITY ENGINEERING

People love the Geico caveman. He appears in commercials as a throwback dressed in "yuppie" clothing who struggles against the insurance company's insensitivity when its ads claim, "It's so easy even a caveman can do it." How much do viewers love him? The ABC network decided to develop a sitcom about a group of caveman roommates who battle prejudice in modern-day America. Geico receives hundreds of letters and e-mails about the characters, and fans at college sporting events hold up signs that say "Beating [team name] is so easy, even a caveman can do it." Burger King's creepy "King" mascot shows up in a series of video games and the fast-food chain is arranging for him to star in a feature film. And the mythical Simpsons family debuted in real life as 7-Eleven transformed many of its stores into Kwik-E-Marts to promote the cartoon series' movie. During the promotion customers snapped up KrustyO's cereal, Buzz Cola, and ice Squishees, all products from the show.[38]

Reality engineering occurs when marketers appropriate elements of popular culture and use them as promotional vehicles.[39] It's hard to know what's real anymore; specialists even create "used jeans" when they apply chemical washes, sandpaper, and other techniques to make a new pair of jeans look like they're ready for retirement. The industry even has a term for this practice that sums up the contradiction: *new vintage*![40]

Reality engineers have many tools at their disposal; they plant products in movies, pump scents into offices and stores, attach video monitors in the backs of taxicabs, buy ad space on police patrol cars, or film faked "documentaries" such as *The Blair Witch Project*.[41] This process is accelerating; historical analyses of Broadway plays, bestselling novels, and the lyrics of hit songs, for example, clearly show large increases in the use of real brand names over time.[42] Here are some recent examples of reality engineering:

- A Japanese company lets philandering dating partners or spouses doctor snapshots with its "Alibi Buddy" service. For 105 yen (about $1) a month, users can retouch and crop images on a mobile phone. They simply insert their photo into an office background and send their partner proof that they're working late. To add more realism, they can dial in a Tokyo cable radio station that plays the sound of a busy city street in the background.[43]
- Actress Demi Moore and her fiancé heartthrob Ashton Kutcher appeared on the cover of *Star* magazine, under the headline "$1 Million Wedding of the Year!" She's wearing a sexy white fitted dress, and he's decked out in a white suit. But wait—it turns out Ms. Moore's dress was really chocolate brown and Mr. Kutcher's suit was really pink. The magazine digitally altered the colors before it went to press.[44]
- In homage to the famous movie *Casablanca*, a former U.S. diplomat opened a Rick's Café in that Moroccan city. The new Rick's has the same warm atmosphere as the Hollywood original (which was created on a sound stage in Hollywood). Waiters in traditional fez caps and wide-legged pants serve customers at candlelit tables. The owner commented, "Because there has never been a Rick's Café here, I could be reasonably assured that it would succeed. It was already an institution, and it never even existed. It's not often you get a chance to turn myth into reality."[45]
- A father named his baby boy ChamberMaster after a software company won the naming rights in a charitable auction his father held.
- Well-known authors including Stephen King and John Grisham similarly participate in fund-raisers that offer naming opportunities to the highest bidder; lucky readers pay up to $25,000 to be immortalized in a new novel.
- A New York couple funded their $80,000 wedding by selling corporate plugs; they inserted coupons in their programs and tossed 25 bouquets from 1-800-FLOWERS.
- Internet casino GoldenPalace.com paid people a total of $100,000 to tattoo the company name on their foreheads, cleavage, and pregnant bellies.
- In one survey, about half of the respondents said they would consider accepting money from corporations in exchange for naming rights to their babies. Others do it for free: In 2000, the latest year for which data are available, 571 babies in the United States were named Armani, 55 were named Chevy, and 21 were named L'Oreal.[46] Perhaps a related fact: The top 20 songs of 2005 specifically mentioned Mercedes-Benz 100 times, Nike 63, Cadillac 62, Bentley 51, and Rolls-Royce 46.[47]

PRODUCT PLACEMENT

Traditionally, TV networks demanded that producers "geek" (alter) brand names before they could appear in a show, as when *Melrose Place* changed a Nokia cell phone to a "Nokio." [48] Nowadays, though, real products pop up everywhere. In many cases,

Art imitates life imitates art: ABC distributed laundry bags to promote the TV show *Desperate Housewives*. The idea became part of the plot in a later episode of the show.

these "plugs" are no accident. **Product placement** is the insertion of real products in fictional movies, TV shows, books, and plays. Many types of products play starring (or at least supporting) roles in our culture; in 2007 for example the most visible brands ranged from Coca-Cola and Nike apparel to the Chicago Bears football team and the Pussycat Dolls band.[49] This practice is so commonplace (and profitable) now that it's evolving into a new form of promotion we call **branded entertainment**, where advertisers showcase their products in longer-form narrative films instead of brief commercials. For example, *SportsCenter* on ESPN showed installments of "The Scout presented by Craftsman at Sears," a 6-minute story about a washed-up baseball scout who discovers a stunningly talented stadium groundskeeper.[50]

Today most major releases brim with real products, even though a majority of consumers believe the line between advertising and programming is becoming too fuzzy and distracting (though as we might expect, concerns about this blurring of boundaries are more pronounced among older people than younger).[51] A 2006 study reported that U.S. consumers respond well to placements when the show's plot makes the product's benefit clear. It found that the year's most effective brand integration occurred on U.S. television on ABC's now-cancelled *Miracle Workers* reality show, where physicians performed novel, life-changing surgeries. Audiences reacted strongly to CVS Pharmacy's role in covering the costs of medications that patients needed after the procedures. Similarly, audiences had a favorable impression of when the retailer provided furniture, clothes, appliances, and other staples for struggling families who get help on ABC's *Extreme Makeover: Home Edition*.[52]

Although we hear a lot of buzz today about product placement, in reality it's a long-standing cinematic tradition. The difference is that today the placements are more blatant and financially lucrative. In the heyday of the major Hollywood studios, brands such as Bell telephone, Buick, Chesterfield cigarettes, Coca-Cola,

Marketing Pitfall

One of the most controversial intersections between marketing and society occurs when companies provide "educational materials" to schools.[66] Many firms including Nike, Hershey, Crayola, Nintendo, and Foot Locker provide free book covers swathed in ads. Standard art supplies, blocks, trucks, and dolls get supplemented with Milton Bradley and Care Bears worksheets, Purell hand-cleaning activities, and Pizza Hut reading programs. Walt Disney advertised its "Little Einsteins" DVDs for preschoolers on the paper liners of examination tables in 2,000 pediatricians' offices, whereas Hasbro introduced the Play-Doh McDonald's Restaurant Playset (with which kids can "extrude Play-Doh shakes and fries") and the Play-Doh George Foreman Grill. Clearasil provides sample packets of its acne medication along with brochures to educate high school students about proper skin care; the handouts also direct students to the Clearasil.com site, where they can also register for music downloads and iPods.

Other companies contract with schools to run focus groups with their students during the schoolday in order to get reactions

De Beers diamonds, and White Owl cigars regularly appeared in films. For example, in a scene in the classic *Double Indemnity* (1944) that takes place in a grocery store, the director Billy Wilder made some products such as Green Giant vegetables face the camera whereas others "mysteriously" were turned around to hide their labels. Indeed, the practice dates at least as far back as 1896, when an early movie shows a cart bearing the brand name Sunlight (a Lever Brothers brand) parked on a street.[53] Perhaps the greatest product placement success story was Reese's Pieces; sales jumped by 65 percent after the candy appeared in the film *E.T.*[54]

Directors like to incorporate branded props because they contribute to the film's realism. When Stephen Spielberg directed the movie *Minority Report* (2002) he used brands such as Nokia, Lexus, Pepsi, Guinness, Reebok, and American Express to lend familiarity to the plot's futuristic settings. Lexus even created a new sports car model just for the film.[55] And new technologies even let Hollywood studios dub product placements into films so they can substitute one product plug for another in the domestic and overseas versions of the same movie. This first occurred in the futuristic police drama *Demolition Man* (1993). In the U.S. release, PepsiCo Inc. bought a major role for its Taco Bell brand, which a character in the movie described as "the only restaurant to survive the franchise wars." The overseas version of the movie featured Pizza Hut instead.[56]

Some researchers claim that product placement aids consumer decision making because the familiarity of these props creates a sense of cultural belonging while generating feelings of emotional security. Another study found that placements consistent with a show's plot do enhance brand attitudes, but incongruent placements that aren't consistent with the plot affect brand attitudes *negatively* because they seem out of place.[57]

For better or worse, products are popping up everywhere. Worldwide product placement in all media was worth $3.5 billion in 2004, a 200 percent increase from 1994. In 2005, there were 108,000 instances of product placement in television programming, up 30 percent from the year before.[58] Here are a few recent placements:

● During the first 4 months of 2006, TV shows mentioned or showed Apple products at least 250 times.
● Entire episodes of NBC's *The Apprentice* revolve around one brand: Instead of selling lemonade or giving rickshaw rides, the aspiring business tycoons now sell Mars's newest candy bar, hawk Crest toothpaste, and construct a new toy for Mattel. Pontiac sold 1,000 Solstices in less than an hour following an episode that featured the car.[59]
● In *Shrek 2*, the ogre and his bride-to-be drive through a town that has a Baskin-Robbins storefront. Out in the real world, the ice cream retailer created three flavors—Fiona's Fairytale, Puss in Boots Chocolate Mousse, and Shrek's Swirl—named for characters in the film.
● A script for ABC's soap opera *All My Children* was reworked so that one of the characters would plug a new Wal-Mart perfume called Enchantment. Daytime TV stars eat Butterball turkeys, wear NASCAR shirts, and use Kleenex tissue. And the characters on *All My Children* have been drinking a lot of Florida orange juice—not only because they're thirsty.[60]
● The Chinese talent program *Lycra My Show* is partly funded by Invista, the maker of Lycra fabric, so contestants sing while wearing stretchy Lycra-based clothing. Ford produced a *Survivor* clone called *Ford Maverick Beyond Infinity* where 12 contestants on a tropical island hunt for treasure in a Ford Maverick sport utility vehicle, leap onto rafts while wearing Nike clothing, and cool off with Nestlé drinks. Ford's marketing director in China noted, "We really built the show around the product."[61]
● In an episode on Spain's top-rated television show, *Aqui no hay Quien Viva* (No One Can Live Here), two characters stage a wedding as a ruse to get gifts from

their friends. Instead of having a fancy reception, they drive their Hummer up to a McDonald's drive-through window.[62]

- Colleges are selling advertising space on everything from basketball nets (State Farm) to student apartments. One company throws parties for prospective tenants at two buildings adjacent to Marquette and DePaul Universities. The apartments feature Herman Miller furniture and the company stocks them with Vitamin Water and Bliss and Kiehl's cosmetics.[63]

- DC Comics' "Rush City" miniseries includes visible promotional support from Pontiac. "The Rush," a new hero, drives a Pontiac Solstice in the comic book. Meanwhile, Marvel Entertainment Inc. puts Nike's "swoosh" logo in the scenes of some titles, such as "New X-Men."[64]

- New advances in technology are taking product placement to the next level, as producers can insert brands into shows after filming them. Virtual product placement put a box of Club Crackers into an episode of *Yes, Dear* producers also inserted Cheez-Its, a can of Star-Kist tuna, and Nutri-Grain bars into the show. This new procedure means that a brand doesn't have to be written into the script and it can't be deleted by late editing changes.[65]

Advergaming

If you roar down the streets in the *Need for Speed Underground 2* video racing game, you'll pass a Best Buy store as well as billboards hawking Old Spice and Burger King. Chrysler devotes 10 percent of its overall marketing budget to planting Chrysler, Jeep, and Dodge cars in more than a dozen video games.[67] *America's Army*, produced by the U.S. government as a recruitment tool, is one of the most successful advergames. Twenty-eight percent of those who visit the *America's Army* Web page click through to the recruitment page.

As gaming goes mass market, marketers turn to **advergaming**, where online games merge with interactive advertisements that let companies target specific types of consumers. And, the mushrooming popularity of user-generated videos on YouTube and other sites creates a growing market for linking ads to these sources as well. At Starstyle.com, for example, you can buy the fashions you see on TV shows and in music videos. This strategy is growing so rapidly that there's even a new (trademarked) term for it. **Plinking™** is the act of embedding a product or service link in a video.

Clearly, computer gaming isn't what it used to be. Not long ago, the typical players were scruffy teenage boys shooting at TV screens in their basements. But with the online gaming explosion of recent years (the industry rakes in $16 billion per year in global revenue), gamers have become a more sophisticated lot and are now more representative of the general population. There are about 36 million people in the United States playing personal computer or console games at least five hours a week. More women are participating, as well as older people and professionals. About half a percent of people older than age 30 play online games.

Why is this new medium so hot? For one thing, compared to a 30-second TV spot, advertisers can get viewers' attention for a much longer time: Players spend an average of 5 to 7 minutes on an advergame site. Also, they can tailor the nature of the game and the products in it to the profiles of different users. For example, they can direct strategy games to upscale, educated users, while at the same time gearing action games to younger users. In addition, the format gives advertisers great flexibility because gamemakers now are shipping PC video games with blank spaces in them to insert virtual ads. This allows advertisers to change ads on the fly and pay only for the number of game players that actually see them. Finally, there's great potential to track usage and conduct marketing research. For example, an inaudible audio signal coded into Activision's *Tony Hawk's Underground 2* skating game on PCs alerts a Nielsen monitoring system each time the test game players view Jeep product placements within the game.

to new product ideas. Some schools encourage kids to practice their math by counting Tootsie Rolls, and the kids use reading software sporting the logos of Kmart, Coke, Pepsi, and Cap'n Crunch cereal. Entire schools are being branded; one in Brooklawn Center, New Jersey, sold naming rights for its gym to the local ShopRite grocery store, whereas several high schools in Texas sold naming rights to their football stadiums for more than a million dollars. At Vernon Hills High outside Chicago, fans watch their players run up and down Rust-Oleum Field.

Corporate involvement with schools is hardly new—in the 1920s Ivory Soap sponsored soap-carving competitions for students. But the level of intrusion is sharply increasing as companies scramble to compensate for the decrease in children's viewership of television on Saturday mornings and weekday afternoons and try to compete with videos and computer games for kids' attention. Many educators argue that these materials are a godsend for resource-poor schools that otherwise could not provide computers and other goodies to their students. However, a California law bans the use of textbooks with brand names and company logos. This legislation was prompted by complaints from parents about a middle school math book that uses names such as Barbie, Oreos, Nike, and Sony PlayStation in word problems.

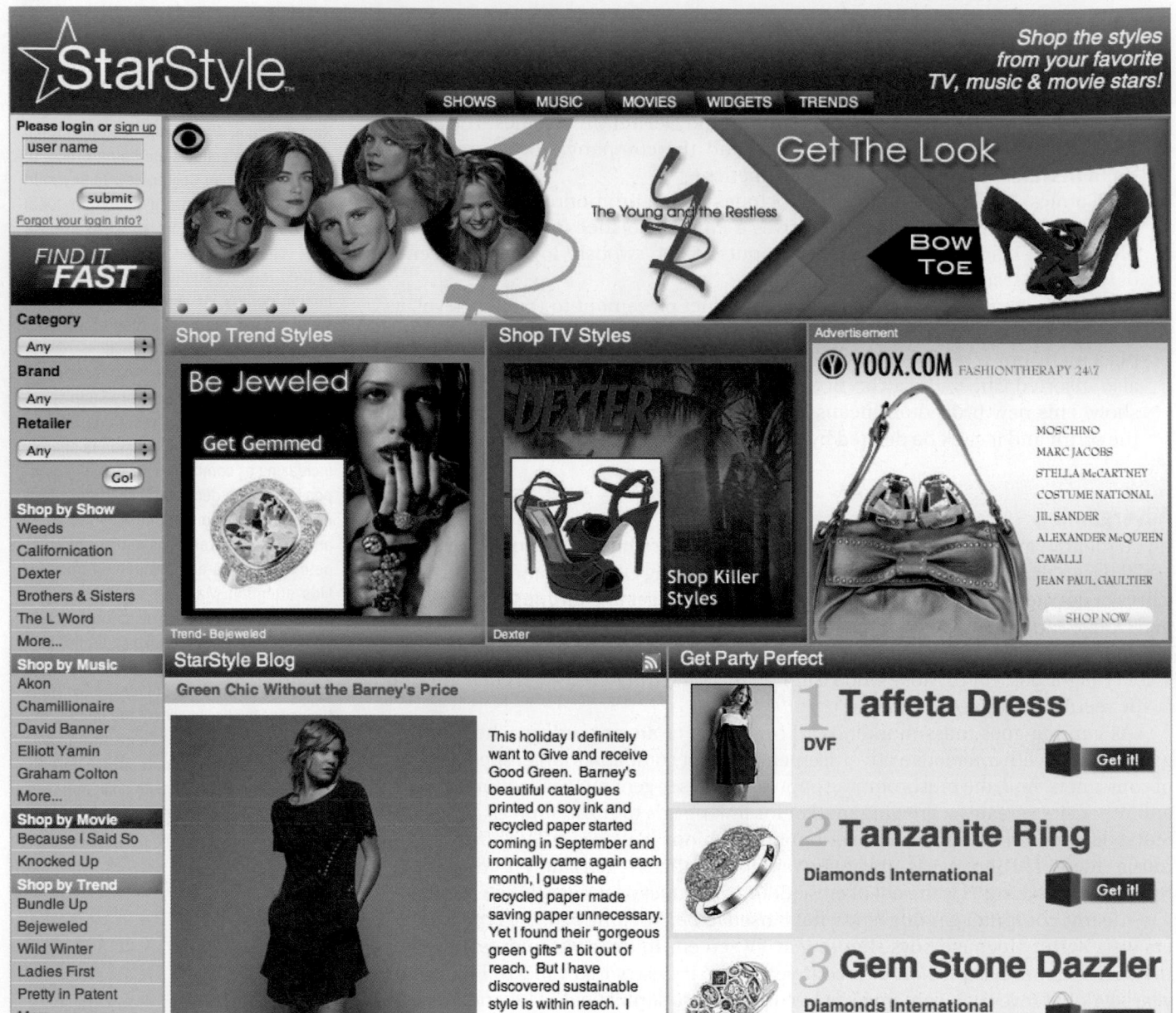

When life imitates art: At the Starstyle Web site, you can buy the fashions you see on TV shows and in music videos.

THE DIFFUSION OF INNOVATIONS

The originators of skateboarding in 1970s Southern California (and portrayed in the popular documentary *Dogtown and Z-Boys*) wouldn't recognize the sport today. At that time boarders were outlaws; as one of the main characters in the film says, "We get the beat-down from all over. Everywhere we go, man, people hate us."

Now skateboarding is about as countercultural as *The Simpsons*. More kids ride skateboards than play basketball, and many of them snap up pricey T-shirts, skate shoes, helmets, and other accessories. In fact, boarders spend almost six times as much on "soft goods" such as T-shirts, shorts, and sunglasses (about $4.4 billion in a year) than on hard-core equipment including the boards themselves.[71]

The progression of skateboarding from a cultlike activity with rebellious undertones to a mainstream hobby mirrors the journey many products and services take through a culture. An **innovation** is any product or service that consumers perceive to be new. It may take the form of an activity (skateboarding), a clothing style (e.g., skirts for men), a new manufacturing technique (such as the ability to design

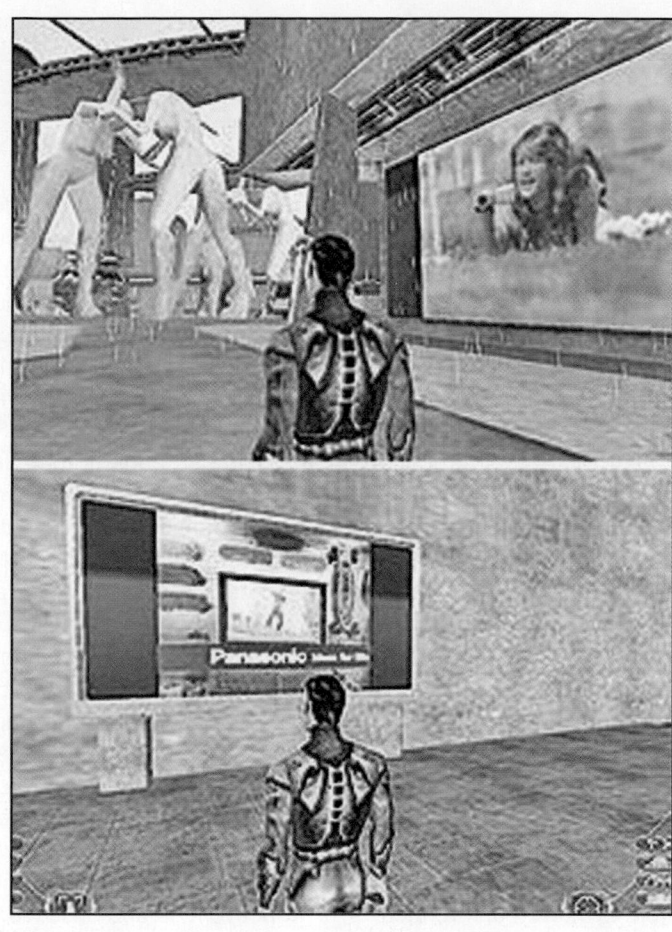

your own running shoe at <u>nike.com</u>), a new variation on an existing product (such as Parkay Fun Squeeze Colored Margarine that now comes in electric blue and shocking pink), a new way to deliver a product (such as ordering groceries online and having Peapod deliver them to your home), or a new way to package a current product (such as Campbell's Soup at Hand Microwaveable Soup that comes in a travel mug).[72]

If an innovation is successful (most are not!), it spreads through the population. First only a trickle of people decides to try it. Then, more and more consumers decide to adopt it, until sometimes it seems that almost everyone is buying it—if it's a "hit." **Diffusion of innovations** refers to the process whereby a new product, service, or idea spreads through a population. The rate at which a product diffuses varies. For example, within 10 years after introduction, 40 percent of U.S. households watched cable TV, 35 percent listened to compact disks, 25 percent used answering machines, and 20 percent bought color TVs. It took radio 30 years to reach 60 million users and TV 15 years to reach this number. In contrast, within 3 years 90 million of us were surfing the Web.[73]

Adopting Innovations

Our adoption of an innovation resembles the decision-making sequence we discussed in Chapter 9. We move through the stages of awareness, information search, evaluation, trial, and adoption. The relative importance of each stage differs, however, depending on how much we already know about a product, as well as on cultural factors that affect our willingness to try new things.[74]

A study of 11 European countries found that consumers in individualistic cultures are more innovative than consumers in collective cultures (see Chapter 16).[75]

CB AS I SEE IT

Professor L. J. Shrum
The University of Texas at San Antonio

Television has always fascinated me. It remains a powerful medium despite worries that its influence would be reduced or even replaced by new media such as the Internet. It is still the primary promotional outlet for most major advertisers. However, the extent of its influence is often underestimated. Rather than being merely carriers for the ads within and between the programs, the programs themselves convey important information through their narrative structure, that is, the stories they tell. This is one reason (among many) why advertisers are so keen to get *inside* the program through techniques such as product placement and immersion.[68]

The stories conveyed in the television programs exert an influence on viewers in at least two important ways. One is as an agent of consumer socialization. That is, the stories tell us about other people, what they think, what they want, what they have, and what they do. This is one reason why both films and television programs often become trendsetters in fashion and yet another reason why advertisers want to get their products onto the (popular!) stars (think Tom Cruise and Ray-Ban sunglasses; James Bond and Omega watches). A second important way in which the stories exert influence is through the lessons that they teach us about life. Thus, television programs become a vehicle for the transmission of personal and cultural values that are important to a society.

Although such transmission of information may seem quite normal and even innocuous, as with anything, there are often unintended consequences, and this has been the focus of my research. One consequence is that the judgments we form based on television information may not be accurate. For example, we know from analyzing the content of television programs that the demographics of the television world are quite different from those of the real world. Perhaps in an effort to generate maximum appeal, the characters on television shows tend to be richer, younger, and more attractive than the norm. The unintended consequence of this misrepresentation is that viewers tend to infer that the *real* world is richer, younger, and more attractive than it really is, and this effect becomes greater the more people watch.[69]

A second unintended consequence pertains to the lessons that we may learn from television. Perhaps because we live in a materialistic society, television programs not only focus on the trappings of wealth (e.g., mansions, limos, servants) but also associate such trappings with attractiveness and success. One unintended consequence of this is that viewers may come to covet these signs of wealth and success themselves, which may explain why those who watch more television have been found to be more materialistic than those who watch less.[70]

However, even within the same culture, not all people adopt an innovation at the same rate. Some do so quite rapidly, and others never do at all. We place consumers into approximate categories based on their likelihood of adopting an innovation.

As Figure 17.3 shows, roughly one-sixth of the population (innovators and early adopters) are very quick to adopt new products, and one-sixth of the people (**laggards**) are very slow. The other two-thirds, so-called **late adopters**, are somewhere in the middle. These consumers are the mainstream public. They are interested in new things, but they do not want them to be *too* new. In some cases, people deliberately wait to adopt an innovation because they assume that the company will improve its technology or that its price will fall after it has been on the market awhile.[76] Keep in mind that the proportion of consumers who fall into each category is an estimate; the actual size of each depends on such factors as the complexity of the product, its cost, and how much risk people associate with it.

Even though **innovators** represent only about 2.5 percent of the population, marketers are eager to identify them. These are the brave souls who are always on the lookout for novel products or services and who are first to try something new. Just as generalized opinion leaders do not appear to exist (see Chapter 11), innovators tend

■ FIGURE 17.3 TYPES OF ADOPTERS

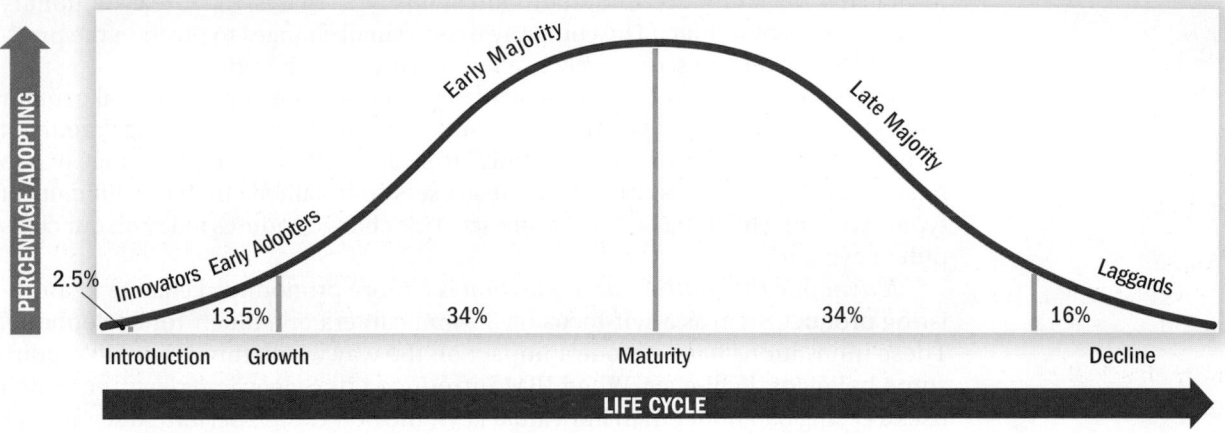

to be category specific as well. A person who is an innovator in one area may be a laggard in another. A clotheshorse who prides himself as being on the cutting edge of fashion may have no conception of new developments in recording technology—he may still stubbornly cling to his antique phonograph albums even as he searches for the latest *avant-garde* clothing styles in trendy boutiques. Despite this qualification, we can summarize the profile of someone who's a good candidate to be an innovator.[77] Not surprisingly, for example, she tends to be a risk-taker. She's also likely to have a relatively high educational and income level and to be socially active.

How do we locate innovators? Ad agencies and market research companies are always on the prowl for people who are on top of developing trends. One ad agency surveys taxi drivers about what they see on the streets everyday. Others get more sophisticated and use the Internet and their global networks to monitor what "people in the know" do. The agency DDB runs a service it calls SignBank, which collects thousands of snippets of information from its 13,000 employees around the world about cultural change in order to advise their clients on what it all means for them. For example, sign spotters in several markets noticed that dinner party guests were bringing their hosts flowers instead of chocolate because of concerns about health and obesity—that's valuable information for a client that makes chocolate as it develops new products. Lowe Worldwide sends questionnaires to dozens of global opinion leaders, including magazine editors, to try to figure out what the *avant-garde* think.[78]

Early adopters share many of the same characteristics as innovators. But an important difference is their high degree of concern for social acceptance, especially with regard to expressive products, such as clothing, cosmetics, and so on. Generally speaking, an early adopter is receptive to new styles because she is involved in the product category and values being in fashion. What appears on the surface to be a fairly high-risk adoption (e.g., wearing a skirt 3 inches above the knee when most people are wearing them below the knee) is actually not *that* risky. Innovators who truly took the fashion risk have already "field-tested" the style change. We're likely to find early adopters in "fashion-forward" stores that feature the latest "hot" designer brands. In contrast, we're more likely to find true innovators in small boutiques that carry merchandise from as-yet-unknown designers.

Behavioral Demands of Innovations

We categorize innovations by the degree to which they demand adopters to change their behavior. Researchers identify three major types of innovations, though these three categories are not absolutes. They refer, in a relative sense, to the amount of disruption or change they bring to people's lives.

A *continuous innovation* is a modification of an existing product, such as when General Mills introduces a Honey Nut version of Cheerios or Levi's promotes shrink-to-fit jeans. Most product innovations are of this type; that is, they are evolutionary rather than revolutionary. The company makes small changes to position the product, add line extensions, or merely to alleviate consumer boredom.

When a consumer adopts this kind of new product, she only has to make minor changes in her habits. A typewriter company, for example, many years ago modified its product to make it more "user friendly" to secretaries. One simple change was to make the tops of the keys concave because users complained about the difficulty of typing with long fingernails on a flat surface. This change endures today on our computer keyboards.

A *dynamically continuous innovation* is a more pronounced change in an existing product, such as a self-focusing 35-mm camera or a touch-tone telephone. These innovations have a modest impact on the way we do things and do require some behavioral changes. When IBM introduced its Selectric typewriter, which uses a typing ball rather than individual keys, the new design permitted secretaries to instantly change the typeface of manuscripts by replacing one Selectric ball with another.

A *discontinuous innovation* creates major changes in the way we live. Major inventions, such as the airplane, the car, the computer, and the television radically changed modern lifestyles. The personal computer replaced the typewriter, and it also allows some of us to "telecommute" from our homes. Of course, the cycle continues, as new continuous innovations (e.g., new versions of software) constantly update our computers. Dynamically continuous innovations such as the "mouse" and trackballs compete for adoption, and discontinuous innovations such as streaming video transmitted on cell phones start to appear in stores.

Prerequisites for Successful Adoption

Regardless of how much we have to change what we do if we adopt an innovation, if it's going to succeed, it should possess these attributes:[79]

Compatibility. The innovation should be compatible with consumers' lifestyles. A manufacturer of personal care products tried unsuccessfully several years ago to introduce a cream hair remover for men as a substitute for razors and shaving cream. This formulation was similar to what many women use to remove hair from their legs. Although the product was simple and convenient to use, it failed because men were not interested in a product they perceived to be too feminine and thus a threat to their masculine self-concepts.

Trialability. Because we think an unknown product is risky, we're more likely to adopt an innovation if we can experiment with it prior to making a commitment. To reduce this risk, companies often choose the expensive strategy of distributing free "trial-size" samples of new products.

Complexity. The product should be low in complexity. All things being equal, we will choose a product that's easier to understand and use rather than a more complex one. This strategy requires less effort from us and it also lowers our perceived risk. Manufacturers of VCRs and DVD recorders, for example, put a lot of effort into simplifying usage (e.g., on-screen programming) to encourage nontechies to adopt them.

Observability. Innovations that are readily apparent are more likely to spread because we can learn about them more easily. The rapid proliferation of fanny packs (pouches people wear around the waist in lieu of wallets or purses) was a result of their high visibility. It was easy for others to see the convenience this alternative offered (even if they were a bit nerdy).

Relative Advantage. Most importantly, the product should offer relative advantage over other alternatives. The consumer must believe that using it will provide a benefit other products cannot offer. For example, the Bugchaser is a wristband containing insect repellent. Mothers with young children like it because it's nontoxic and nonstaining—these are clear advantages over alternatives. In contrast, the Crazy Blue Air Freshener, which you add to windshield wiper fluid and it emits a fragrance when you turn on your car wipers, fizzled: People didn't see the need for the product and felt there were simpler ways to freshen their cars.

The Fashion System

The **fashion system** includes all the people and organizations that create symbolic meanings and transfer those meanings to cultural goods. Although we often equate fashion with clothing, it's important to keep in mind that fashion processes affect *all* types of cultural phenomena, including music, art, architecture, and even science (i.e., certain research topics and scientists are "hot" at any point in time). Even business practices are subject to the fashion process; they evolve and change depending on which management techniques are in vogue, such as total quality management, just-in-time inventory control, or "managing by walking around."

We think of fashion as a *code*, or a language, that helps us to decipher these meanings.[80] Unlike a language, however, fashion is *context-dependent*. Different consumers interpret the same style differently.[81] In semiotic terms (see Chapter 2), fashion products are *undercoded*. There is no one precise meaning but rather plenty of room for interpretation among perceivers.

At the outset, let's distinguish among some confusing terms. **Fashion** is the process of social diffusion by which some group(s) of consumers adopts a new style. In contrast, *a fashion* (or style) is a particular combination of attributes (say, stovepipe jeans women wear with a tunic top). And to be *in fashion* means that some reference group positively evaluates this combination (i.e., *Vogue* endorses this look as "in" for this season). Thus, the term *Danish Modern* refers to particular characteristics of furniture design (i.e., a fashion in interior design); it does not necessarily imply that Danish Modern is a fashion that consumers currently desire.[82]

CULTURAL CATEGORIES

The meanings we give to products reflect underlying **cultural categories** that correspond to the basic ways we characterize the world.[83] Our culture distinguishes between different times, between leisure and work, and between genders. The fashion system provides us with products that signify these categories. For example, the apparel industry gives us clothing to denote certain times (e.g., evening wear, resort wear); it differentiates between leisure clothes and work clothes, and it promotes masculine versus feminine styles.

These cultural categories affect many different kinds of products. As we saw in Chapter 16, the way that companies design and market their products reflects the dominant values of a culture at a point in time. This concept is a bit hard to grasp because on the surface a clothing style, say, has little in common with a piece of furniture or a car. However, an overriding concern with a value such as achievement or environmentalism determines the types of products consumers look for at any point in time. These underlying themes then surface in the design of many different products. A few examples of this interdependence demonstrate how a dominant fashion *motif* reverberates across industries.

• Costumes that politicians or movie and rock stars wear affect the fortunes of the apparel and accessory industries. A movie appearance by actor Clark Gable without a T-shirt (unusual at that time) dealt a severe setback to the men's apparel industry, whereas Jackie Kennedy's famous pillbox hat prompted a rush for hats by women in the 1960s. Other cross-category effects include the craze for ripped sweatshirts the movie *Flashdance* (1983) instigated, a boost for cowboy boots from the movie *Urban Cowboy* (1980), and singer Madonna's legitimation of lingerie as a garment women wear outside of the boudoir.

- The architect I. M. Pei's remodeling of The Louvre in Paris included a controversial glass pyramid at the entrance. Shortly thereafter, several designers unveiled pyramid-shaped clothing at Paris fashion shows.[84]

- In the 1950s and 1960s, America was preoccupied with science and technology. The Russians' launching of the *Sputnik* satellite fueled a sense of urgency as people feared that the United States was falling behind in the technology race (and also losing the Cold War). The theme of technical mastery of nature and of futuristic design became a motif that cropped up in many aspects of American popular culture—from car designs with prominent tail fins to high-tech kitchen styles.

- At any point in time a small number of colors dominate in the design world. Many companies actually buy color forecasts from specialists, such as Pantone, that rank the top 10 fashion colors for each season. These charts influence mass-market fashion companies, as well as other industries such as automotive, home furnishings, and home appliances. A dominant color often takes years to emerge. For example, when black was prominent during the 1980s and 1990s, designers snubbed brown as a "dirty" color. Then, Starbucks began to take off and espresso, latte, and other coffee colors began to seep into mass culture. In addition, consumers rediscovered gourmet chocolates such as Godiva and (at least in some circles) fur regained its popularity. Color forecasts put brown back on the fast track. Sure enough, now the United Parcel Service asks, "What can Brown do for You?"[85]

Remember that creative subsystems within a culture production system attempt to anticipate the tastes of the buying public. Despite their unique talents, members of this subsystem are also members of mass culture. Cultural gatekeepers draw from a common set of cultural categories, so it's not that surprising that their choices often

A cultural emphasis on science in the 1950s and 1960s affected product designs, as seen in the design of automobiles with large tail fins (to resemble rockets).

converge—even though they compete against one another to offer the consumer something new or different. **Collective selection** is the process by which CPS members choose some symbolic alternatives over others.[86] Although rivals within each category compete for acceptance, we can usually group them because they follow a dominant theme or motif—be it "The Western Look," "New Wave," "Danish Modern," or "Nouvelle Cuisine."

BEHAVIORAL SCIENCE PERSPECTIVES ON FASHION

Fashion is a very complex process that operates on many levels. At one extreme, it's a societal phenomenon that affects many of us simultaneously. At the other, it exerts a very personal effect on individual behavior. Many of us desire to be in fashion, and this motivates us as to what we buy. Fashion products also are aesthetic objects, their origins deriving from art and history. For this reason, there are many perspectives on the origin and diffusion of fashion. Let's summarize some major approaches.[87]

Psychological Models of Fashion

Many psychological factors help explain what motivates us to be fashionable. These include conformity, desires for variety seeking, the need to express personal creativity, and sexual attraction. For example, many consumers seem to have a "need for uniqueness": They want to be different (though not necessarily *too* different!).[88] For this reason, people often conform to the basic outlines of a fashion, but they still improvise to make a personal statement within these general guidelines.

One of the earliest theories of fashion argued that "shifting *erogenous zones*" (sexually arousing areas of the body) accounted for fashion changes and that different zones become the object of interest because they reflect societal trends. J. C. Flugel, a disciple of Freud, proposed in the 1920s that sexually charged areas wax and wane as we grow bored with them; clothing styles change to highlight or hide the parts that currently are the focus of attention. For example, it was common for Renaissance-era women to drape their abdomens in fabrics in order to give a swollen appearance— successful childbearing was a priority in the disease-ridden fourteenth and fifteenth centuries. Now, some suggest that the current prevalence of the exposed midriff reflects the premium our society places on fitness.[89]

It's important to note, by the way, that until very recently the study of fashion focused almost exclusively on women. Some researchers today also probe the meanings of the fashion system for men.[90]

Economic Models of Fashion

Economists approach fashion in terms of the model of supply and demand. Items in limited supply have high value, whereas our desire decreases for readily available products. Rare items command respect and prestige. As we discussed in Chapter 13, Veblen argued that the wealthy practice conspicuous consumption to display their prosperity. As we also noted, this approach is somewhat outdated; upscale consumers today engage in *parody display* where they deliberately buy inexpensive products. Other factors also influence the demand curve for fashion-related products. These include a *prestige–exclusivity effect*, where high prices still create high demand, and a *snob effect*, whereby lower prices actually reduce demand ("If it's that cheap, it can't be any good").[91]

Sociological Models of Fashion

The collective selection model we discussed previously is a sociological approach to fashion. This perspective focuses on a subculture's adoption of a fashion (idea, style, etc.) and its subsequent diffusion into society as a whole. This process often begins with youth subcultures such as the hip-hop segment. Another current example is the integration of Goth culture into the mainstream. This fashion started as an expression of rebellion by young outcasts who admired nineteenth-century romantics and

This ad for Maidenform illustrates that fashions have accentuated different parts of the female anatomy throughout history.

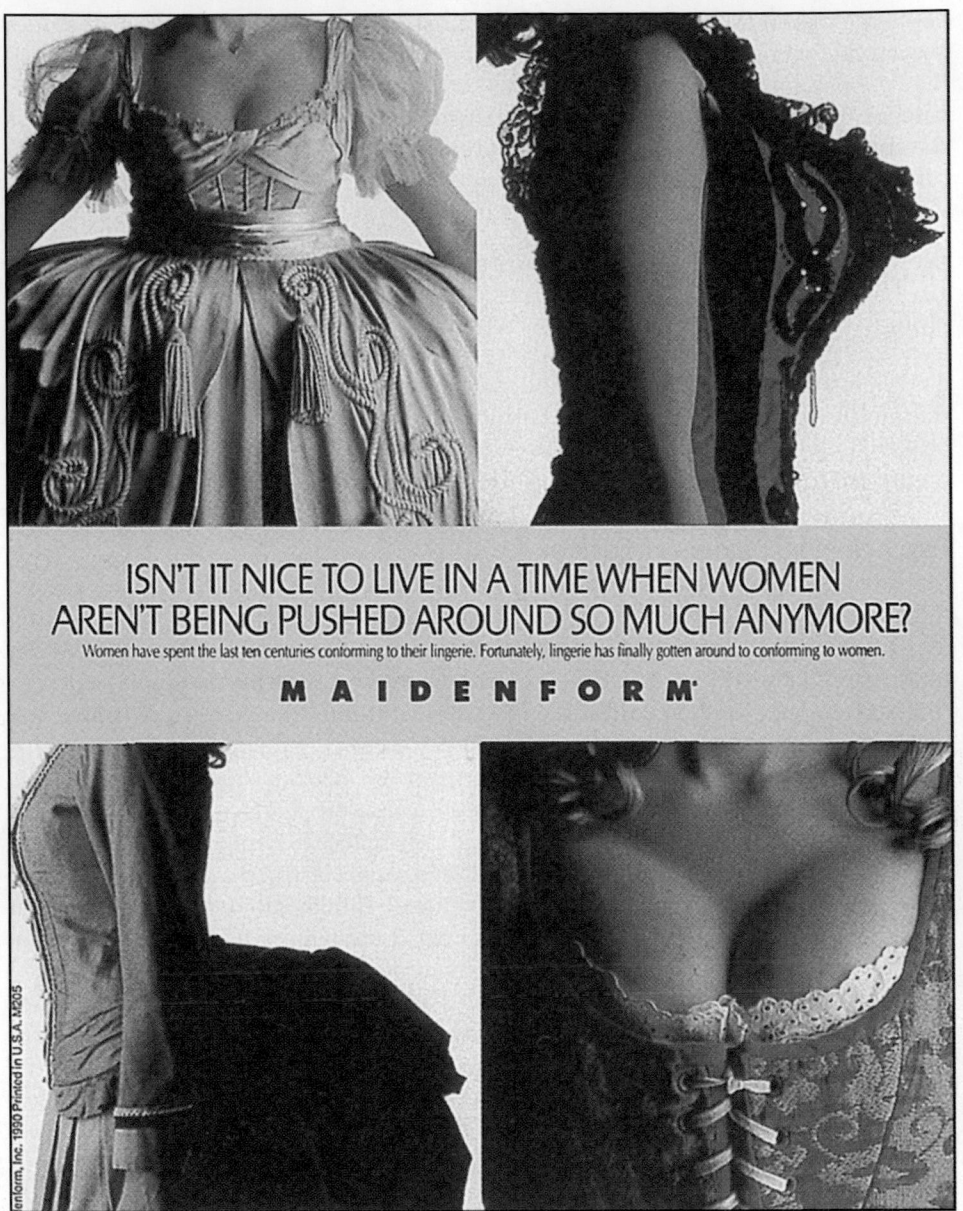

who defied conventional styles with their black clothing (often including over-the-top fashion statements such as Count Dracula capes, fishnet stockings, studded collars, and black lipstick) and punk music from bands such as Siouxsie & the Banshees and Bauhaus. Today, Virgin Megastores sells vampire-girl lunchboxes, and mall outlets sell tons of clunky cross jewelry and black lace. You can find a T-shirt that looks like a corset at Kmart. At the Hot Topic Web site, teen surfers can buy a "multiring choker." Hard-core Goths are not amused, but hey, that's fashion for you.[92]

Trickle-down theory, which the sociologist Georg Simmel first proposed in 1904, is one of the most influential fashion perspectives. It states that there are two conflicting forces that drive fashion change. First, subordinate groups adopt the status symbols of the groups above them as they attempt to climb up the ladder of social mobility. Dominant styles thus originate with the upper classes and *trickle down* to those below.

However, this is where the second force kicks in: Those people in the superordinate groups keep a wary eye on the ladder below them to be sure they're not imitated. When lower-class consumers "impersonate" them, they adopt new fashions to distance themselves. These two processes create a self-perpetuating cycle of change—the machine that drives fashion.[93]

The integration of hip-hop phrases into our vocabulary illustrates how people who set fashions resist mainstream adoption by the broader society. The street elite shunned some slang terms such as *bad*, *fresh*, and *jiggy* once they became too mainstream. The rap community even held a funeral (with a eulogy by Reverend Al Sharpton) for the word *Def* once the *Oxford English Dictionary* included it in its new edition.[94]

Trickle-down theory applies to a society with a stable class structure that allows us to easily identify lower- versus upper-class consumers. This task is no longer so easy. In contemporary Western society, we have to modify this theory to account for new developments in mass culture:[95]

● A perspective we base on class structure can't account for the wide range of styles we now have available to us. We have many more choices today because of technological advances that let manufacturers drastically speed up production times and real-time media that keep us informed of style changes in minutes. Stores such as Zara and H&M can replenish their inventories in weeks rather than months. An adolescent like Alex simply watches MTV or chats on Facebook or Stardoll.com to stay on top of the latest trends; *mass fashion* thus replaces elite fashion because our media lets many market segments learn about a style simultaneously.

● Consumers today are more influenced by opinion leaders who are similar to them—even if these innovators don't live in the same town or even country. As a result each social group has its own fashion innovators who determine fashion trends. It's more accurate to speak of a *trickle-across effect*, where fashions diffuse horizontally among members of the same social group.[96]

● Finally, current fashions often originate with the lower classes and *trickle up*. Grassroots innovators typically are people who lack prestige in the dominant culture (e.g., urban youth). Because they are less concerned with maintaining the status quo, they are free to innovate and take risks.[97]

A "Medical" Model of Fashion

For years and years, the lowly Hush Puppy was a shoe for nerds. Suddenly—almost overnight—the shoe became a chic fashion statement even though its manufacturer

Grassroots innovators typically are people who lack prestige in the dominant culture such as urban youth who are the drivers behind the hip-hop craze.

did nothing to promote this image. Why did this style diffuse through the population so quickly? **Meme theory** explains this process with a medical metaphor. A *meme* is an idea or product that enters the consciousness of people over time—examples include tunes, catch-phrases ("You're fired!"), or styles such as the Hush Puppy. In this view, memes spread among consumers in a geometric progression just as a virus starts off small and steadily infects increasing numbers of people until it becomes an epidemic. Memes "leap" from brain to brain via a process of imitation.

The memes that survive tend to be distinctive and memorable, and the hardiest ones often combine aspects of prior memes. For example, the *Star Wars* movies evoked prior memes relating to the legend of King Arthur, religion, heroic youth, and 1930s adventure serials. Indeed, George Lucas studied comparative religion and mythology as he prepared his first draft of the *Star Wars* saga, "The Story of Mace Windu."[98]

The diffusion of many products in addition to Hush Puppies seems to follow the same basic path. A few people initially use the product, but change happens in a hurry when the process reaches the moment of critical mass—what one author calls

The cell phone has become a fashion statement.
Source: Absolut® Vodka. Absolut Country of Sweden Vodka & Logo, Absolut, Absolut Calligraphy are trademarks owned by V&S Vin S Sprit AB (publ). © 2005 V&S Vin & Sprit AB (publ). Photographer: Shu Akashi. Under permission by V&S Vin & Sprit AB (publ.).

the **tipping point**. For example, Sharp introduced the first low-priced fax machine in 1984 and sold about 80,000 in that year. There was a slow climb in the number of users for the next 3 years. Then, suddenly in 1987 enough people had fax machines that it made sense for everyone to have one—suddenly Sharp sold a million units. Cell phones followed a similar trajectory.[99]

CYCLES OF FASHION ADOPTION

In the early 1980s, Cabbage Patch dolls were all the rage among American children. Faced with a limited supply of the product, some retailers reported near-riots among adults as they tried desperately to buy the dolls for their children. A Milwaukee deejay jokingly announced that people should bring catcher's mitts to a local stadium because an airplane was going to fly overhead and drop 2,000 dolls. He told his listeners to hold up their American Express cards so their numbers could be photographed from the plane. More than two dozen anxious parents apparently didn't get the joke; they showed up in subzero weather, mitts in hand.[100]

The Cabbage Patch craze lasted for a couple of seasons before it eventually died out, and consumers moved on to other things, such as Teenage Mutant Ninja Turtles, which grossed more than $600 million in 1989.[101] The Mighty Morphin Power Rangers eventually replaced the Turtles, and Beanie Babies and Giga Pets in turn deposed them before the invasion of Pokémon followed by Yu-Gi-Oh! Cards and now Webkinz.[102] What will be next?

Fashion Life Cycles

Although the longevity of a particular style can range from a month to a century, fashions tend to flow in a predictable sequence. The fashion life cycle is quite similar to the product life cycle you probably learned about in your basic marketing course. As Figure 17.4 shows, an item or idea progresses through basic stages from birth to death.

The diffusion process we discussed earlier in this chapter applies to the popularity of fashion-related items. To illustrate how this process works, consider how the **fashion acceptance cycle** works in the popular music business. In the *introduction stage*, a small number of music innovators hear a song. Clubs or college radio stations may play it—which is how "grunge rock" groups such as Nirvana got their start. During the *acceptance stage*, the song enjoys increased social visibility as large segments of the population start to check it out. Top 40 stations may start to give it wide airplay as it climbs the charts "like a bullet." In the *regression stage*, the song reaches a state

■ FIGURE 17.4 A NORMAL FASHION CYCLE

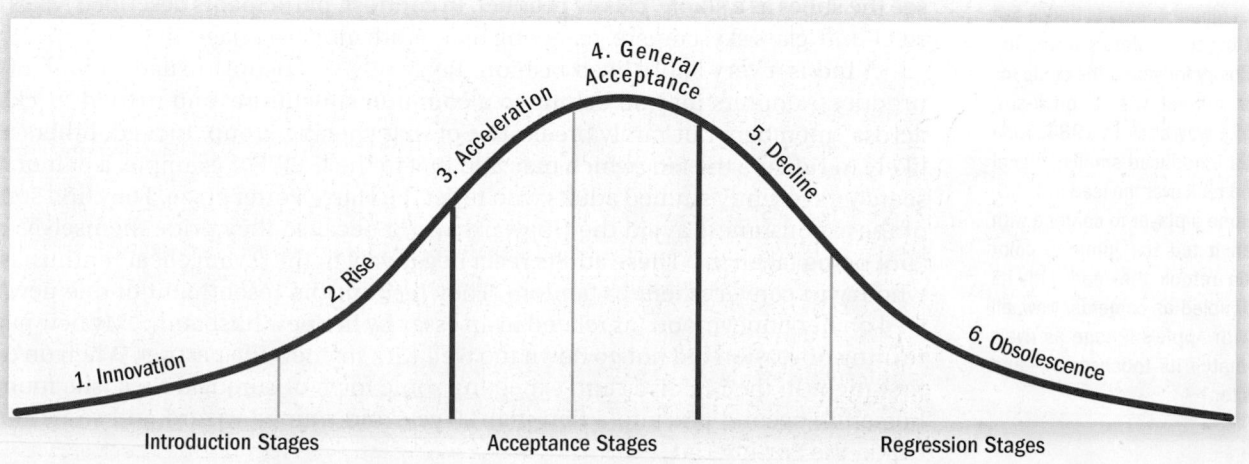

■ **FIGURE 17.5**

COMPARISON OF THE ACCEPTANCE
CYCLES OF FADS, FASHIONS,
AND CLASSICS

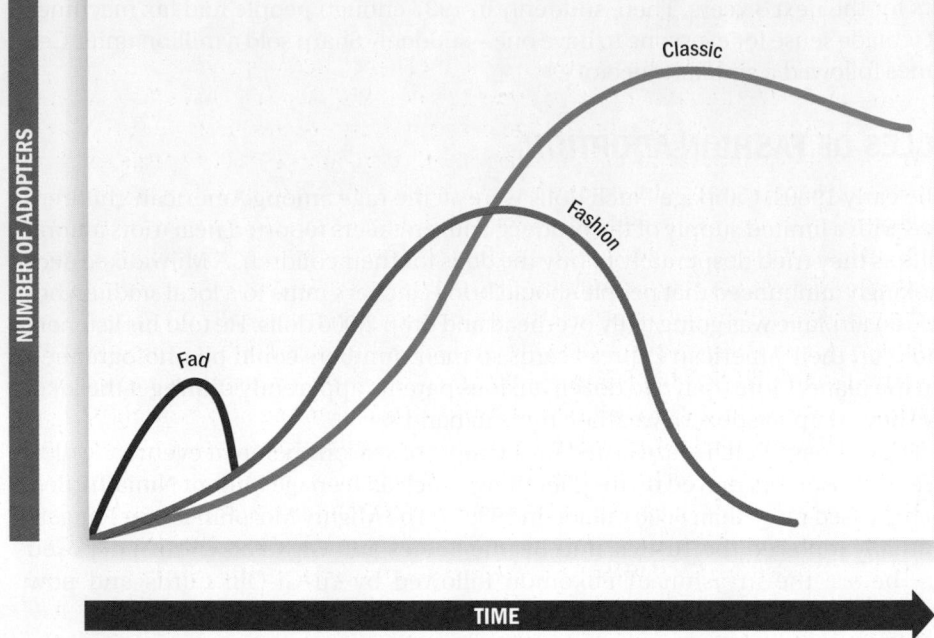

Marketing Pitfall

Change travels at lightning speed in our global economy. The downside: Companies have to work harder than ever to continually innovate rather than simply introduce a great product and rest on their laurels. Product development cycles accelerate in many industries from apparel (which used to have four seasons but now has six per year) to computers. Players in the $60 billion cell phones industry have to be especially nimble; major new styles or technological advances in cell phones now appear somewhere in the world almost annually. Some Chinese manufacturers, such as Ningbo Bird and TCL, replace their equipment every 6 months. That's good news for manufacturers that jump on an emerging trend early—they can be first-to-market with an innovation and command a higher price. However, companies that ignore emerging trends can also miss out big time. Motorola was the king of the industry for years; the company pioneered the market with a brick-size $4,000 handset way back in 1984. Then Finland's Nokia introduced smaller, digital cell phones and took over the lead in 1998. Samsung became a player to contend with in 2002 when it led the jump to color screens. Nokia retook the lead with its phones that doubled as cameras. Now, all bets are off with Apple's iPhone as rivals scramble to match its touchscreen—and "coolness" factor.[103]

of social saturation as Top 40 stations play it once an hour for several weeks. At some point listeners tire of it and focus their attention on newer releases. The former hit record eventually winds up in the discount rack at the local record store.

Figure 17.5 illustrates that fashions begin slowly, but if they "make it," they diffuse rapidly through a market, peak, and then retreat into obscurity. We identify different classes of fashion when we look at the relative length of their acceptance cycle. Many fashions have a moderate cycle; they take several months or even years to work their way through the stages of acceptance and decline; others are extremely long lived or short lived.

A **classic** is a fashion with an extremely long acceptance cycle. It is in a sense "antifashion" because it guarantees stability and low risk to the purchaser for a long period of time. Keds sneakers, introduced in 1917, appeal to those who are turned off by the high fashion, trendy appeal of Nike or Reebok. When researchers asked consumers in focus groups to imagine what kind of building Keds would be, a common response was a country house with a white picket fence. In other words, consumers see the shoes as a stable, classic product. In contrast, participants described Nikes as steel-and-glass skyscrapers, reflecting their more modern image.[104]

A **fad** is a very short-lived fashion. Relatively few people usually adopt a fad product. Adopters may all belong to a common subculture, and the fad "trickles across" members but rarely breaks out of that specific group. Indeed, others are likely to ridicule the fad (which may add fuel to the fire). For example, a pair of researchers recently studied adults who resist the Harry Potter craze. They find some of these consumers avoid the Hogwarts world because they pride themselves on "not being taken in." These adults react negatively to the "evangelical" enthusiasts who try to convert them to fandom. They recount the resentment of one newlywed on her honeymoon (as related in an essay by her new husband): "My new page turning obsession did not go down too well with my new life partner. When on our first night in the Maldives and expecting some form of conjugal rites [she found] herself in second place to a fictional 11-year-old trainee wizard and something called the Sorting Hat."[105]

Some notable past fad products include hula hoops, snap bracelets, and pet rocks; to learn more about these and other "must have" products, visit badfads.com. Here are some more recent fads:

- Rubik's Cube, a puzzle that first was a fad hit in the 1980s, is back.[106] In a pivotal scene from *The Pursuit of Happyness* (2006), Will Smith's character solves a Rubik's Cube in front of a brokerage executive who is stumped by the puzzle. The feat lands him an internship despite his less-than-stellar resume. A Hungarian teacher invented the cube and when Ideal Toys brought the puzzle to the United States in 1980 it sold 100 million of them in 3 years. Now, there's a Yahoo Speedcubing group where cubers share techniques and solutions online. Major cities worldwide host speedcubing competitions where contestants try to solve the puzzle blindfolded, one-handed, and underwater.

- Johnny Earle turned his nickname—"Cupcake"—into a booming business. He started selling his T-shirts featuring cupcakes in unlikely places (for example, one with a cupcake and crossbones) out of the trunk of his car. He wound up with two retail stores, including one on upscale Newbury Street in Boston. Customers walk away with the shirts wrapped in doughnut boxes rather than bags.[107]

- The Japanese love fads, but a recent one is a bit troublesome. Chihuahuas became a hot breed after one starred in some popular TV ads. In the early 1990s, a TV drama featuring a Siberian husky sent annual sales rocketing from only a few hundred dogs to 60,000, even though the dogs are way too large for most of Japan's cramped homes. Now, "designer dogs" are a new status symbol, such as a teacup poodle so tiny it will fit into a purse. The problem with these inbred dogs is that they often arrive with genetically defective littermates that lack paws, eyes, or a nose. There have been dogs with brain disorders so severe that they spent all day running in circles, and others with bones so frail they dissolved in their bodies.[108]

Johnny Cupcake created a hit fad.
Courtesy of Johnnycupcakes.com.

■ FIGURE 17.6
THE BEHAVIOR OF FADS

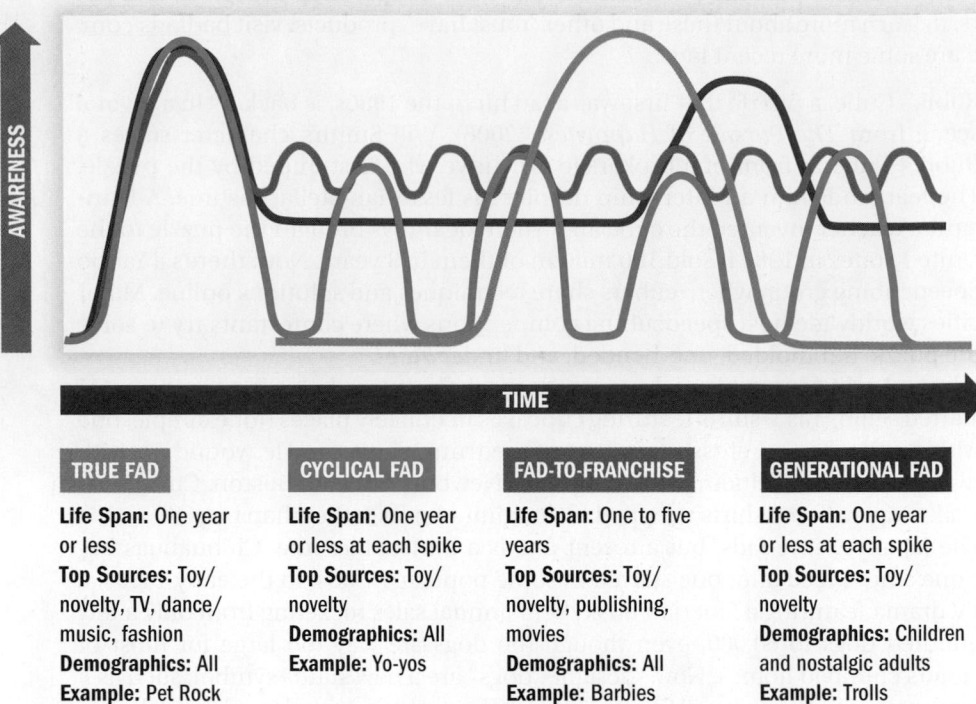

TRUE FAD	CYCLICAL FAD	FAD-TO-FRANCHISE	GENERATIONAL FAD
Life Span: One year or less	**Life Span:** One year or less at each spike	**Life Span:** One to five years	**Life Span:** One year or less at each spike
Top Sources: Toy/novelty, TV, dance/music, fashion	**Top Sources:** Toy/novelty	**Top Sources:** Toy/novelty, publishing, movies	**Top Sources:** Toy/novelty
Demographics: All	**Demographics:** All	**Demographics:** All	**Demographics:** Children and nostalgic adults
Example: Pet Rock	**Example:** Yo-yos	**Example:** Barbies	**Example:** Trolls

The *streaking* fad hit U.S. college campuses in the mid-1970s. This term described students running nude through classrooms, cafeterias, dorms, and sports venues. Although the practice quickly spread across many campuses, it was primarily restricted to college settings. Streaking highlights several of a fad's "naked truths:"[109]

● The fad is nonutilitarian; it does not perform any meaningful function.
● The fad often spreads impulsively; people do not undergo stages of rational decision making before they join in.
● The fad diffuses rapidly, gains quick acceptance, and dies.

Figure 17.6 illustrates some types of fads have longer life spans than others.

Fad or Trend?

Chrysler's PT Cruiser was the talk of the town when it came out in the U.S. in 2000. With its 1930s-gangster getaway-car looks, cutely compact size, and innovative features—such as a panel in the back that you can use as a picnic table—the PT was hot. Chrysler sold 145,000 of them in 2001. By 2003, PT Cruiser sales slumped to 107,759 cars, and Chrysler offered discounts to keep the miniwagon moving. In the fall of 2005, Chrysler launched a revamped version; the grille and front end now look more like other new Chrysler models, and it upgraded the interior. The PT Cruiser's sales curve—a 25 percent fall from peak to trough—suggests the market for funky, retro three-quarter-sized wagons generated a lot of excitement at the beginning. But instead of being a hot new model for young trendsetters, the car wound up appealing to graying baby boomers—the median age of owners is 50 years old. Are retro cars a fad or a trend? The jury is still out—especially because General Motors also launched its Chevy HHR—a retro car that according to GM executives was inspired by a 1949 Chevrolet Suburban, *not* the PT Cruiser.[110]

The first company to identify a trend and act on it has an advantage, whether the firm is Starbucks (gourmet coffee), Nabisco (Snackwells low-fat cookies and crackers), Taco Bell (value pricing), or Chrysler (retro cars). Nothing is certain, but some guidelines help to predict whether the innovation will endure as a long-term trend

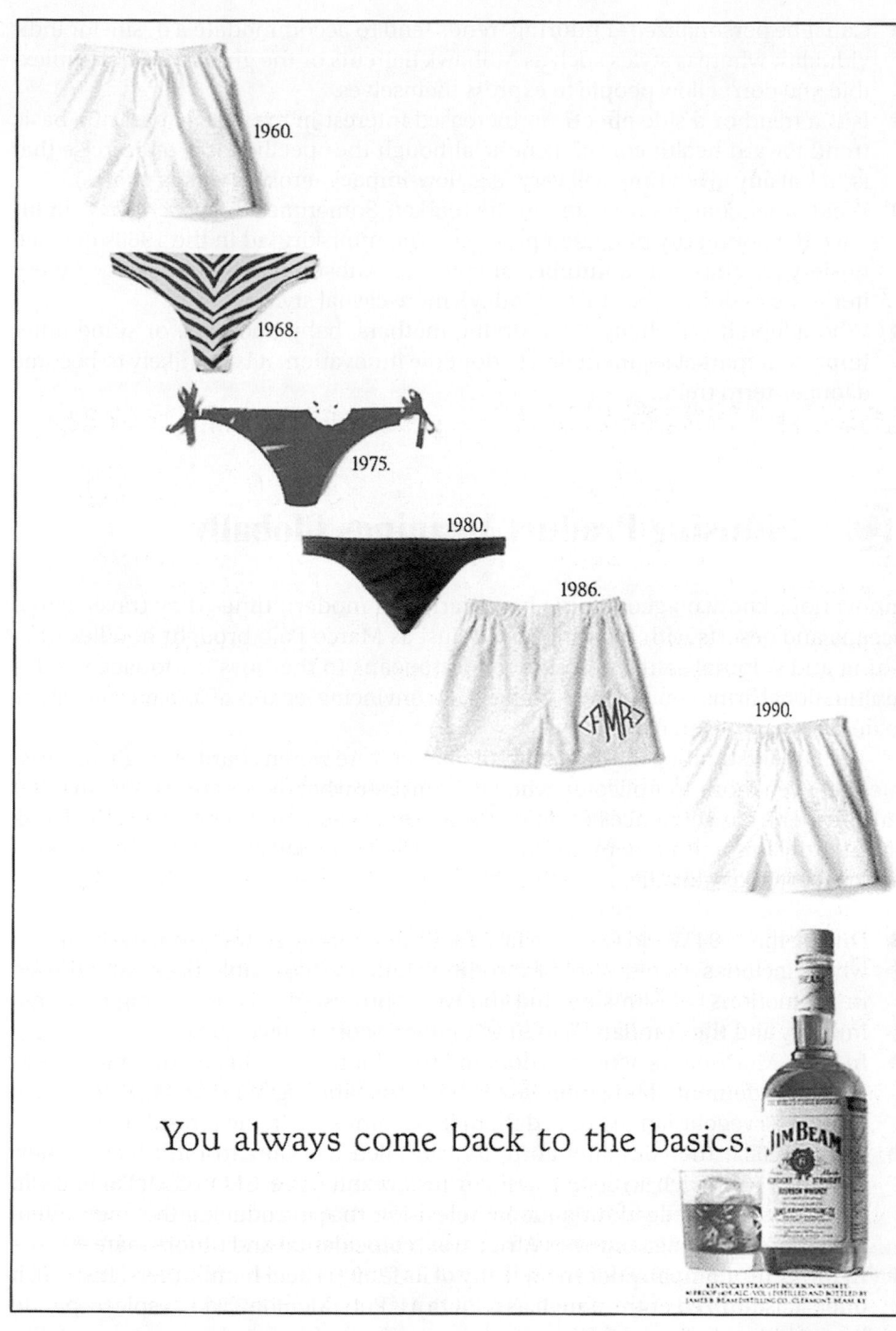

You always come back to the basics.

or if it's just a fad destined to go the way of hula-hoops, pet rocks, and little rubber spiders called Wally Wallwalkers that slowly crawled down walls instead of just dropping to the ground:[111]

- Does it fit with basic lifestyle changes? If a new hairstyle is hard to care for, this innovation isn't consistent with women's increasing time demands. However, the movement to shorter-term vacations is more likely to last because this innovation makes trip planning easier for harried consumers who want to get away for a few days at a time.
- What are the benefits? The switch to poultry and fish from beef came about because these meats are healthier.

- Can it be personalized? Enduring trends tend to accommodate a desire for individuality, whereas styles such as Mohawk haircuts or the grunge look are inflexible and don't allow people to express themselves.
- Is it a trend or a side effect? An increased interest in exercise is part of a basic trend toward health consciousness, although the specific form of exercise that is "in" at any given time will vary (e.g., low-impact aerobics versus pilates).
- What other changes occurred in the market? Sometimes *carryover effects* influence the popularity of related products. The miniskirt fad in the 1960s boosted hosiery purchases in a number of countries substantially. Now, sales of these items are in decline because of today's more casual styles.
- Who adopted the change? If working mothers, baby boomers, or some other important market segment don't adopt the innovation, it is not likely to become a longer-term trend.

 # Diffusing Product Meanings Globally

Innovations know no geographic boundaries; in modern times they travel across oceans and deserts with blinding speed. Just as Marco Polo brought noodles from China and colonial settlers introduced Europeans to the "joys" of tobacco, today multinational firms conquer new markets by convincing legions of foreign consumers to desire what they make.

As if understanding the dynamics of one's culture weren't hard enough, these issues get even more complicated when we consider what drives consumers in other cultures. The consequences of ignoring cultural sensitivities can be costly. Think about problems a prominent multinational company such as McDonald's encounters as it expands globally:

- During the 1994 World Cup, the fast-food giant reprinted the Saudi Arabian flag, which includes sacred words from the Koran, on disposable packaging it used in promotions. Muslims around the world protested this borrowing of sacred imagery and the company had to scramble to correct its mistake.[112]
- In 2002, McDonald's agreed to donate $10 million to Hindu and other groups as partial settlement of litigation involving its mislabeling of French fries and hash browns as vegetarian (it cooked them in oil tainted with meat residue).[113]
- Also in 2002, the company abruptly cancelled its plans to introduce its new McAfrika sandwich in its Norwegian restaurants. The CEO of McDonald's in Norway acknowledged on national television that introducing this menu item at a time of growing famine in Africa was "coincidental and unfortunate."[114]
- In India, the company doesn't sell any of its famous beef hamburgers. Instead, it offers customized entrees such as a Pizza McPuff, McAloo Tikki (a spiced-potato burger), Paneer Salsa McWrap, and even a Crispy Chinese burger, to capitalize on the great popularity of Chinese food in India. It makes its mayonnaise without eggs, and all stores maintain separate kitchen sections for vegetarian and nonvegetarian dishes. Workers from the nonvegetarian section must shower before they cross over to the other area.[115]
- In 2005, McDonald's introduced the spicy Prosperity Burger in nine countries from South Korea to Indonesia in recognition of the Lunar New Year.[116]

In the next section, we'll consider some of the issues that confront marketers who seek to understand the cultural dynamics of other countries. We'll also consider the consequences of the "Americanization" of global culture. As U.S. (and to some extent, Western European) marketers continue to export Western popular culture to a globe full of increasingly affluent consumers, many customer eagerly replace their

Venus:
one of the markets
Electrolux
doesn't dominate.

Electrolux
The world leader in home appliances.
PROSDÓCIMO

Globalization has become an integral part of the marketing strategy of many, if not most, major corporations.

traditional products with the likes of McDonald's, Levi's, and MTV. But, as we'll also see, there are plenty of obstacles to success for multinational firms.

Rather than ignore the global characteristics of their brands, firms have to manage them strategically. That's critical because future growth for most companies will come from foreign markets. In 2002, developed countries in North America, Europe, and East Asia accounted for 15 percent of the world's population of 6.3 billion. By 2030, according to the World Bank, the planet's population will rise to 9 billion—and 90 percent of these people will live in developing countries.

THINK GLOBALLY, ACT LOCALLY

As corporations compete in many markets around the world, the debate intensifies regarding the need to develop separate marketing plans for each culture versus crafting a single plan a firm implements everywhere. Let's briefly consider each viewpoint.

Adopt a Standardized Strategy

Starbucks is becoming a household name in Japan (where it is pronounced *STAH-buks-zu*). Like their American counterparts, local outlets feature comfortable sofas, and hip-hop and reggae tunes play in the background. The idea of hanging out in a coffee shop knocking back an oversized gourmet coffee is new to most Japanese; who typically sip tea from tiny cups in dimly lit shops. Until Starbucks arrived, locals who did drink coffee associated it with a weak "American blend," which U.S. soldiers introduced after World War II. Starbucks became an instant hit, and now there are well over 300 outlets buzzing with Japanese customers. In addition to the Western cachet they associate with the chain, unlike most Japanese coffee shops (*kisaten*), Starbucks does not allow smoking. This policy attracts young women who do not smoke nearly as much as Japanese men.[117]

Starbucks exports its recipe for success around the world. The company continues to confound local experts as it brings its version of the coffee experience to local cultures that (unlike Japan) have a long history of coffee snobbery. It runs stores in San Juan and Mexico as part of a push into Latin America, where *cafe con leche* is part of the culture.[118] And talk about a brash move: Now Starbucks is doing business in Austria, which already boasts one coffeehouse for every 530 citizens. These people take their coffee seriously. Again, although some *aficionados* who are used to ordering their coffee from waiters and drinking it out of china cups turned up their noses at this American intrusion, so far the new Starbucks stores are thriving.

The company's latest foray is into China, where it hopes one day to have its largest presence outside of the United States. But it still has a way to go: Coffee is so unpopular in China's tea-drinking culture that until recently many Starbucks didn't brew regular drip coffee unless a customer ordered it. But the chain bets that a new generation of Chinese with an appetite for status will learn to love java. The cafés distribute brochures titled "Coffee Brewing Wisdom" and others that answer questions such as "What is espresso?" Workers pass out small cups of pumpkin-spice latte and other samples. And the brew certainly has one ingredient to make it a status symbol: A 16-ounce latte costs about $3.50 in Shanghai, where the average annual wage is about $3,800.[119]

Critics of the cultural consequences of standardization often point to Starbucks as an example of a company that succeeds by obliterating local customs and driving small competitors out of business. An in-depth study of patrons of local coffee shops in one U.S. city examined the effect of the Starbucks phenomenon specifically as it looked at how consumers react to the influence of global brands on local culture. Many of the customers voiced strong negative feelings about Starbucks (note that these respondents are not Starbucks customers, who we would expect to have a different opinion). The authors identify two distinct types of consumers who choose to give their business to local shops rather than to Starbucks:

- *Café flaneurs* view local coffeeshops as dynamic public spaces and enjoy them primarily for the social spectacle of the crowd and for the feeling of artistic inspiration they gain from the ambiance.
- *Oppositional localists* view their choice of local coffeeshops as a way to express solidarity with the local community.[120]

Proponents of a standardized marketing strategy argue that many cultures, especially those of industrialized countries, have become so homogenized that the same approach will work throughout the world. By developing one approach for multiple markets, a company can benefit from economies of scale because it does not have to incur the substantial time and expense to develop a separate strategy for each culture.[121] This viewpoint represents an **etic perspective**, which focuses on commonalities across cultures. An etic approach to a culture is objective and analytical; it reflects impressions of a culture as outsiders view it.

Adopt a Localized Strategy

Unlike Disney World in Florida, visitors to the Walt Disney Studios theme park at Disneyland Paris don't hear the voices of American movie stars narrating their guided tours. Instead, European actors such as Jeremy Irons, Isabella Rossellini, and Nastassja Kinski provide commentary in their native tongues.

Disney learned the hard way about the importance of being sensitive to local cultures after it opened its Euro Disney Park in 1992. The company got slammed for creating an entertainment venue that recreated its American locations without catering to local customs (such as serving wine with meals). Visitors to Euro Disney from many countries took offense, even at what seem to be small slights. For example, initially the park only sold a French sausage, which drew complaints from Germans, Italians, and others who believed their own local version to be superior. Euro Disney's CEO explains, "When we first launched there was the belief that it was enough to be Disney. Now we realize that our guests need to be welcomed on the basis of their own culture and travel habits."[122]

Disney applies the lessons it learned in cultural sensitivity to its newer Hong Kong Disneyland. Executives shifted the angle of the front gate by 12 degrees after they consulted a *feng shui* specialist, who said the change would ensure prosperity for the park (see Chapter 14). Disney also put a bend in the walkway from the train station to the gate to make sure the flow of positive energy, or *chi*, did not slip past the entrance and out to the China Sea. Cash registers are close to corners or along walls to increase prosperity. The company burned incense as it finished each building, and it picked a lucky day (September 12) for the opening. One of the park's main ballrooms measures 888 square meters because eight is a lucky number in Chinese culture.

And because the Chinese consider the number four bad luck, you won't find any fourth-floor buttons in hotel elevators. Disney also recognizes that Chinese family dynamics are different so it's revamping its' advertising: Print ads show a grandmother, mother, and daughter all wearing tiaras at the park. In China, bonding between parents and children is difficult because of the culture's hierarchical nature so an executive explains, "We want to say it's OK to let your hair down." Camping out with stopwatches, the company's designers discovered that Chinese people take an average of 10 minutes longer to eat than Americans. So they've added 700 extra seats to dining areas.

Ironically, some locals feel Disney tries *too* hard to cater to local customs—activists raised a ruckus when the company announced it would serve the traditional Chinese dish of shark's fin soup at wedding banquets held in the park. The species is endangered, and one group distributed T-shirts showing Mickey Mouse and Donald Duck holding knives and leering over three bleeding sharks. Nonetheless, Disney forges ahead with localized products. One of its latest ventures is in India, where it's making animated films with the voices of Bollywood stars. It's also making a Hindi version of the U.S. TV hit *High School Musical*—set against a backdrop of cricket instead of basketball.

Disney's experience supports the view of marketers who endorse an **emic perspective**, which stresses variations across cultures. They feel that each culture is unique, with its own value system, conventions, and regulations. This perspective argues that each country has a *national character*, a distinctive set of behavior and personality characteristics.[123] A marketer must therefore tailor its strategy to the sensibilities of each specific culture. An emic approach to a culture is subjective and experiential; it attempts to explain a culture as insiders experience it.

Sometimes this strategy involves modifying a product or the way a marketer positions it to make it acceptable to local tastes. When Wal-Mart started to open stores abroad in the early 1990s, it offered a little piece of America to foreign consumers—and that was the problem. It promoted golf clubs in football-mad Brazil and pushed ice skates in Mexico. It trained its German clerks to smile at customers—who thought they were flirting. Now Wal-Mart is adapting (though not in Germany where it had to give up). Its Chinese stores sell live turtles and snakes and lure shoppers who come on foot or bicycle with free shuttle buses and home delivery for refrigerators and other large items.[124]

In some cases, consumers in one place simply do not like some products that are popular elsewhere, or their different lifestyles require companies to adapt the way they make their products. IKEA finally realized that Americans use a lot of ice in their drinks so they weren't buying smaller European glasses. The Swedish furniture chain also figured out that compared to Europeans, Americans sleep in bigger beds, need bigger bookshelves, and like to curl up on sofas rather than sit on them.[126] Snapple failed in Japan because the drink's cloudy appearance and the pulp floating in the

Marketing Pitfall

Insensitivity to local norms and cultural pride can cause embarrassing consequences. In China, an ad for Nippon Paint caused an uproar when it showed a sculptured dragon unable to keep its grip on a pillar coated in smooth wood-coating paint. Dragons are potent symbols in China, and seeing one easily defeated by a Japanese product proved too much. In another incident, Chinese broadcast authorities banned from the airwaves a Nike television commercial showing U.S. basketball star LeBron James battling an animated cartoon *kung fu* master, saying the ad insults Chinese national dignity.[125]

bottles were a turnoff. Similarly, Frito-Lay stopped selling Ruffles potato chips (too salty) and Cheetos (the Japanese didn't appreciate having orange fingers after they ate a handful).[127] The company still makes Cheetos in China, but the local version doesn't contain any cheese, which is not a staple of the Chinese diet. Instead, local flavors come in varieties such as Savory American Cream and Japanese Steak.[128]

CULTURAL DIFFERENCES RELEVANT TO MARKETERS

So, which perspective is correct—the emic or the etic? As you might guess, the best bet probably is a combination of both. Some researchers argue that the relevant dimension to consider is **consumer style**, which is a pattern of behaviors, attitudes, and opinions that influences all of a person's consumption activities—including attitudes toward advertising, preferred channels of information and purchase, brand loyalty, and price consciousness. These researchers identified four major clusters of consumer styles when they looked at data from the United States, the United Kingdom, France, and Germany: *price-sensitive consumers, variety seekers, brand-loyal consumers,* and *information seekers.* They found that consumers in the United States and Europe do differ from one another on these dimensions but at the same time cluster membership is not independent of country. For example, the authors note that price-sensitive consumers are overrepresented among Germans and underrepresented among Americans and British. Brand-loyal consumers are overrepresented among the British respondents and underrepresented among the consumers from Germany and the United States. American respondents were over-represented in the information-seeking cluster (the largest cluster in the United States). The largest segment in the United Kingdom was the brand-loyal group.[129]

Given the sizeable variations in tastes within the United States alone, it is hardly surprising that people around the world have developed their own unique preferences. Panasonic touted the fact that its rice cooker kept the food from getting too crisp—until the company learned that consumers in the Middle East like to eat their rice this way. Unlike Americans, Europeans favor dark chocolate over milk chocolate, which they think of as a children's food. Sara Lee sells its pound cake with chocolate chips in the United States, raisins in Australia, and coconuts in Hong Kong. Crocodile handbags are popular in Asia and Europe but not in the United States.[130] When Marvel Comics launched "Spiderman India," the first ethnic adaptation of the popular comic book series, the writers turned Peter Parker of New York City into Pavitr Prabhakar of Mumbai. Mary Jane became Meera Jain, and the villainous Norman Osbourne (a.k.a. the Green Goblin) is Nalin Oberoi. Spider-Man changed from a semitragic figure representing the dangers of scientific experimentation into a hero trying to navigate a modern India still steeped in Hindu mysticism.[131]

The language barrier is one obvious problem that marketers who wish to break into foreign markets must navigate. Travelers abroad commonly encounter signs in tortured English such as a note to guests at a Tokyo hotel saying, "You are invited to take advantage of the chambermaid," a notice at a hotel in Acapulco to reassure people that "The manager has personally passed all the water served here," or a dry cleaner in Majorca who urges passing customers to "drop your pants here for best results." And local product names often raise eyebrows to visiting Americans who might stumble on a Japanese coffee creamer called Creap; a Mexican bread named Bimbo; or even Super Piss, a Scandinavian product to unfreeze car locks.

Chapter 14 noted some gaffes U.S. marketers made when they advertised to ethnic groups in their own country. Imagine how these mistakes multiply outside of the United States! One technique marketers use to avoid this problem is *back-translation*, where a different interpreter retranslates a translated ad back into its original language to catch errors. Here are some errors that could have used a bit of back-translation:[132]

● The Scandinavian company that makes Electrolux vacuum cleaners sold them in the United States with this slogan: "Nothing sucks like an Electrolux."

- Colgate introduced Cue toothpaste in France—this also happens to be the name of a well-known porn magazine.
- When Parker marketed a ballpoint pen in Mexico, its ads were supposed to say, "It won't leak in your pocket and embarrass you." The translation actually said "It won't leak in your pocket and make you pregnant."
- Fresca (a soft drink) is Mexican slang for lesbian.
- Ford had several problems in Spanish markets. The company discovered that a truck model it called Fiera means "ugly old woman" in Spanish. Its Caliente model is slang for a streetwalker. In Brazil, Pinto is a slang term for "small male appendage."
- When Rolls-Royce introduced its Silver Mist model in Germany, it found that the word *mist* translates as excrement. Similarly, Sunbeam's hair-curling iron, called the Mist-Stick, translates as manure wand. To add insult to injury, Vicks is German slang for sexual intercourse, so the company had to change its name to Wicks in that country.
- Toyota encountered a similar problem in France, where its MR2 roadster sounds like "M-R-deux," which sounds a lot like *merde*, which means crap.
- Recently, Buick had to scramble to rename its new LaCrosse sedan the Allure in Canada after discovering that the name comes awfully close to a Québécois word for masturbation.
- IKEA had to explain that the Gutvik children's bunk bed is named "for a tiny town in Sweden" after German shoppers noted that the name sounded a lot like a phrase that means "good f***." IKEA has yet to issue an explanation for a workbench called Fartfull and a computer table dubbed Jerker.[133]

DOES GLOBAL MARKETING WORK?

So, what's the verdict? Does global marketing work? Perhaps the more appropriate question is, "*When* does it work?" Although the argument for a homogenous world culture is appealing in principle, in practice it hasn't worked out too well. One reason for the failure of global marketing is that consumers in different countries have varying conventions and customs, so they simply do not use products the same way. Kellogg, for example, discovered that in Brazil people don't typically eat a big breakfast—they're more likely to eat cereal as a dry snack.

In fact, significant cultural differences even show up within the same country—we certainly feel that we've traveled to a different place as we move around the United States. Advertisers in Canada know that when they target consumers in French-speaking Quebec their messages must be much different from those they address to those in English-speaking regions. Ads in Montreal tend to be a lot racier than those in Toronto, reflecting differences in attitudes toward sexuality between consumers with French versus British roots.[134]

Some large corporations such as Coca-Cola have been successful in crafting a single, international image. Still, even the soft drink giant must make minor modifications to the way it presents itself in each culture. Although Coke commercials are largely standardized, the company permits local agencies to edit them so they highlight close-ups of local faces.[135] To maximize the chances of success for these multicultural efforts, marketers must locate consumers in different countries who nonetheless share a common worldview. This is more likely to be the case among people whose frame of reference is relatively more international or cosmopolitan, or who receive much of their information about the world from sources that incorporate a worldwide perspective.

Who is likely to fall into this category? Two consumer segments are particularly good candidates: (1) affluent people who are "global citizens" and who come into contact with ideas from around the world through their travels, business contacts, and media experiences; and (2) young people whose tastes in music and fashion are strongly influenced by MTV and other media that broadcast many of the same images to multiple countries. For example, viewers of MTV Europe in Rome or Zurich can check out the same "buzz clips" as their counterparts in London or Luxembourg.[136]

A large-scale study with consumers in 41 countries identified the characteristics people associate with global brands, and it also measured the relative importance of those dimensions when consumers buy products.[137] The researchers grouped consumers who evaluate global brands in the same way and they identified four major segments:

1 **Global citizens:** The largest segment (55 percent of consumers) uses the global success of a company as a signal of quality and innovation. At the same time, they are concerned whether companies behave responsibly on issues such as consumer health, the environment, and worker rights.

2 **Global dreamers:** The second-largest segment, at 23 percent, consists of consumers who see global brands as quality products and readily buy into the myths they author. They aren't nearly as concerned with social responsibility as are the global citizens.

3 **Antiglobals:** Thirteen percent of consumers are skeptical that transnational companies deliver higher-quality goods. They dislike brands that preach American values and they don't trust global companies to behave responsibly. They try to avoid doing business with transnational firms.

4 **Global agnostics:** The remaining 9 percent of consumers don't base purchase decisions on a brand's global attributes. Instead, they evaluate a global product by the same criteria they use to judge local brands and don't regard its global nature as meriting special consideration.

 # The Diffusion of Consumer Culture

Coca-Cola is the drink of choice among young people in Asian countries, and McDonald's is the favorite restaurant.[138] The U.S. National Basketball Association sells $500 million of licensed merchandise every year *outside* of the United States.[139] Walk the streets of Lisbon or Buenos Aires, and the sight of Nike hats, GAP T-shirts, and Levi's jeans will accost you at every turn. The allure of American consumer culture has spread throughout the world.

However, it's not simply about exporting American culture. In a global society, people are quick to borrow from any culture they admire. For example, the cultural scene in Japan influences many Koreans because they believe the Japanese are sophisticated consumers. Japanese rock bands are more popular in Korea than Korean bands, and shoppers eagerly snap up other exports such as comic books, fashion magazines, and game shows. A Korean researcher explains, "Culture is like water. It flows from stronger nations to weaker ones. People tend to idolize countries that are wealthier, freer, and more advanced, and in Asia that country is Japan."[140]

I'D LIKE TO BUY THE WORLD A COKE . . .

The West (and especially the United States) is a net exporter of popular culture. Many consumers equate Western lifestyles in general and the English language in particular with modernization and sophistication, and many American brands slowly but surely insinuate themselves into local cultures. A survey in Beijing found that nearly half of all children under 12 think McDonald's is a domestic Chinese brand![141] Indeed, some global brands are so widespread that many are only vaguely aware of their countries of origin. In surveys, consumers routinely guess that Heineken is German (it's really Dutch) and that Nokia is Japanese (it's Finnish).[142]

American television inspires knockoffs around the world. Some local shows "borrow" from American programs; the German hit *Das Traumschiff* (the "Dream Ship") is a remake of the old American hit *Love Boat*. In fairness, American reality show hits such as *Big Brother* and *American Idol* started out as European concepts that U.S. producers imported.[143] The *Big Brother* format, which films contestants locked together in a house, is repeated around the world—but not without problems. The U.K. version briefly went off the air after a fight broke out and housemates threatened to kill each other.[144] The German version attracted accusations of "shameless voyeurism" after a female contestant had her nipple pierced on live TV—without anesthetic.

And of course the hit U.S. show *The Apprentice* is reproduced all over the globe. As local versions spread rapidly across Europe, Latin America, and Asia, such disparate taskmasters as a German football-team manager, a billionaire Arab entrepreneur, and a Brazilian ad agency CEO assume "The Donald's" role. Each local "Apprentice" reflects the country's culture; contestants sell flowers in London, hot dogs in Frankfurt, and rolled fish in Finland.[145] Not everyone is treated quite as harshly as the American losers either—in Finland contestants are told, "You're free to leave."

Despite the allure of American popular culture, in many areas the U.S. government is extremely unpopular. According to one poll, nearly 20 percent of consumers abroad say they avoid U.S. companies and products such as McDonald's, Starbucks, American Airlines, and Barbie dolls because of America's unilateral foreign policies. And the more American people overseas perceive a brand to be, the more they resist it. For instance, almost half the survey respondents (including 1,000 people from each of the G-8 nations, excluding the United States) associate Mattel's Barbie with America, whereas 10 percent make the same link with Kleenex. So 33 percent of respondents say they avoid Barbie, but only 10 percent won't touch the tissues.[146] Coca-Cola estimates that it lost 40 million to 50 million cases of soft drink sales in the Persian Gulf, Egypt, and Saudi Arabia in one year alone as a result of an anti-U.S. backlash.[147]

Critics in other countries deplore the creeping Americanization of their cultures because of what they view as excessive materialism. City officials in Oaxaca, Mexico, successfully fought to bar McDonald's from installing its arches in the town's central plaza.[148] The French have been the most outspoken opponents of American influence on their culture. They tried to ban the use of such "Franglish" terms as *le drugstore, le fast food*, and even *le marketing*.[149] One French critic summarized this resistance to the diffusion of American culture; he described the Euro Disney theme park as "a horror made of cardboard, plastic, and appalling colors—a construction of hardened chewing gum and idiotic folklore taken straight out of a comic book written for obese Americans."[150]

Perhaps it's fair to say that at this point the world has a love–hate relationship with the United States. A recent billboard in the U.K. reflects this ambivalence. It reads, "Nothing good ever came out of America." But the ad turned out to be a teaser to promote a new TV channel, Five US, that features only American programming. The boards were replaced with new ones that showed actors such as Brad Pitt, Susan Sarandon, and William H. Macy countering, "Who says nothing good ever came out of America?" American shows including *CSI: Miami, House, Monk, Law & Order, Desperate Housewives,* and *Grey's Anatomy* screen regularly on European television.[151] Hate American politicians, but love American celebrities.

EMERGING CONSUMER CULTURES IN TRANSITIONAL ECONOMIES

In the early 1980s the Romanian Communist government broadcast the American TV show *Dallas* to point out the decadence of Western capitalism. This strategy backfired, as the devious (but rich!) J. R. Ewing became a revered icon in parts of Eastern Europe and the Middle East. A popular tourist attraction outside of Bucharest includes a big

Marketing Opportunity

The huge popularity of a humble local product that Brazilian peasants traditionally wear—*Havaianas*, or flip-flops—illustrates the diffusion of global consumer culture as consumers hunger for fresh ideas and styles from around the globe. Brazilians associate the lowly shoes, which sell for $2 a pair, so strongly with poor people that the expression *pe de chinelo*, or "slipper foot," is a popular slang term for the downtrodden. The main buyers in Brazil continue to be blue-collar workers, but now fashionable men and women in cities from Paris to Sydney wear the peasant shoes to trendy clubs and in some cases even to work.

How did these flip-flops make the leap to fashion statement? In an attempt to boost profit margins, a company named Alpargatas introduced new models in colors such as lime green and fuchsia that cost twice as much as the original black- or blue-strapped sandal with a cream-colored sole. Then, it launched newer styles, including a masculine surf model. Middle-class Brazilians started to adopt the shoes and even the country's president wore them in public. The fashion spread as a few celebrities, including supermodels Naomi Campbell, Kate Moss, and Brazil's own Gisele Bundchen, discovered the flip-flops. Company representatives helped fuel the fire by giving out free sandals to stars at the Cannes Film Festival. The result: Alpargatas's international sales zoomed from virtually zero to more than 5 million sandals sold around the world.[157]

white log gate that announces (in English) the name, "South Fork Ranch."[152] Western "decadence" appears to be infectious.[153]

More than 60 countries have a gross national product of less than $10 billion, and there are at least 135 transnational companies with revenues greater than that. The dominance of these marketing powerhouses creates a **globalized consumption ethic**. Tempting images of luxury cars, glam rock stars on MTV, and modern appliances that make life easier surround us wherever we turn. People the world over begin to share the ideal of a material lifestyle and value well-known brands that symbolize prosperity. Shopping evolves from a wearying, task-oriented struggle to locate even basic necessities to a leisure activity. Possessing these coveted items becomes a mechanism to display one's status (see Chapter 13)—often at great personal sacrifice.

After the downfall of communism, Eastern Europeans emerged from a long winter of deprivation into a springtime of abundance. The picture is not all rosy, however, because attaining consumer goods is not easy for many in **transitional economies**, which are countries (examples include China, Portugal, and Romania) that struggle with the difficult adaptation from a controlled, centralized economy to a free-market system. In these situations rapid changes occur on social, political, and economic dimensions as the populace suddenly is exposed to global communications and external market pressures.[154]

Some of the consequences of the transition to capitalism include a loss of confidence and pride in the local culture, as well as alienation, frustration, and increased stress as citizens sacrifice their leisure time to work ever harder to buy consumer goods. The yearning for the trappings of Western material culture is perhaps most evident in parts of Eastern Europe, where citizens who threw off the shackles of communism now have direct access to coveted consumer goods from the United States and Western Europe—if they can afford them. One analyst observed, "As former subjects of the Soviet empire dream it, the American dream has very little to do with liberty and justice for all and a great deal to do with soap operas and the Sears Catalogue."[155]

As the global consumption ethic spreads, rituals and product preferences in different cultures become homogenized. For example, some urbanites in Muslim Turkey now celebrate Christmas even though gift-giving is not customary in many parts of the country—even on birthdays. In China, Christmas fever is gripping China's newly rising urban middle class as an excuse to shop, eat, and party. People there snap up Christmas trees, ornaments, and Christian religious objects (even though the street vendors peddling photos of Jesus and Mary can't always identify who they are). Chinese consumers embrace Christmas because to them the holiday is international and modern not because it's a traditional Christian celebration. The government encourages this practice because it stimulates consumer spending. To make the holiday even merrier, China exports about $1 billion worth of Christmas products every year and its factories churn out $7.5 billion of the toys people worldwide put under their trees.[156]

Does this homogenization mean that in time consumers who live in Nairobi, New Guinea, or the Netherlands will all be indistinguishable from those in New York or Nashville? Probably not, because the meanings of consumer goods mutate to blend with local customs and values. For example, in Turkey some urban women use ovens to dry clothes and dishwashers to wash muddy spinach. Or a person in Papua New Guinea may combine a traditional clothing style such as a *bilum* with Western items such as Mickey Mouse shirts or baseball caps.[158] These processes make it unlikely that global homogenization will overwhelm local cultures, but it is likely that there will be multiple consumer cultures, each blending global icons such as Nike's pervasive "swoosh" with indigenous products and meanings.

Creolization occurs when foreign influences integrate with local meanings. Modern Christianity adapted the pagan Christmas tree into its own rituals. In India handicapped beggars sell bottles of Coke from tricycles, and Indipop, a popular music hybrid, mixes traditional styles with rock, rap, and reggae.[159] As we saw in Chapter 14, young Hispanic Americans bounce between hip-hop and *Rock en Español*, blend

Mexican rice with spaghetti sauce, and spread peanut butter and jelly on tortillas.[160] In Argentina, Coca-Cola launched Nativa, a soft drink flavored with the country's traditional yerba mate herbal tea, as part of a strategy to broaden its portfolio with products it makes from indigenous ingredients.[161]

The creolization process sometimes results in bizarre permutations of products and services when locals modify them to be compatible with their customs. Consider these creolized adaptations, for example:[162]

- In Peru, Indian boys carry rocks they paint to look like transistor radios.
- In highland Papua New Guinea, tribespeople put Chivas Regal wrappers on their drums and wear Pentel pens instead of nosebones.
- Bana tribespeople in the remote highlands of Kako, Ethiopia, pay to watch *Pluto the Circus Dog* on a Viewmaster.
- When an African Swazi princess marries a Zulu king, she wears a traditional costume of red touraco wing feathers around her forehead and a cape of windowbird feathers and oxtails. But guests record the ceremony on a Kodak movie camera while the band plays "The Sound of Music."
- The Japanese use Western words as a shorthand for anything new and exciting, even if they do not understand what they mean. They give cars names such as Fairlady, Gloria, and Bongo Wagon. Consumers buy *deodoranto* (deodorant) and *appuru pai* (apple pie). Ads urge shoppers to *stoppu rukku* (stop and look), and products claim to be *yuniku* (unique).[163] Coca-Cola cans say, "I feel Coke & sound special," and a company called Cream Soda sells products with the slogan, "Too old to die, too young to happy."[164] Other Japanese products with English names include Mouth Pet (breath freshener), Pocari Sweat ("refreshment water"), Armpit (electric razor), Brown Gross Foam (hair-coloring mousse), Virgin Pink Special (skin cream), Cow Brand (beauty soap), and Mymorning Water (canned water).[165]

CHAPTER SUMMARY

Now that you have finished reading this chapter you should understand why:

Styles act as a mirror to reflect underlying cultural conditions

- The styles prevalent in a culture at any point in time reflect underlying political and social conditions. We term the set of agents responsible for creating stylistic alternatives a culture production system (CPS). Factors such as the types of people involved in this system and the amount of competition by alternative product forms influence the choices that eventually make their way to the marketplace for consideration by end consumers.

We distinguish between high and low culture.

- Social scientists distinguish between high (or elite) forms and low (or popular) forms of culture. Products of popular culture tend to follow a cultural formula and contain predictable components. However, these distinctions blur in modern society as marketers increasingly incorporate imagery from "high art" to sell everyday products.

Many modern marketers are reality engineers.

- Reality engineering occurs when marketers appropriate elements of popular culture to use in their promotional strategies. These elements include sensory and spatial aspects of everyday existence, whether in the form of products that appear in movies, scents pumped into offices and stores, billboards, theme parks, or video monitors they attach to shopping carts.

New products, services, and ideas spread through a population. Different types of people are more or less likely to adopt them.

● Diffusion of innovations refers to the process whereby a new product, service, or idea spreads through a population. Innovators and early adopters are quick to adopt new products, and laggards are very slow. A consumer's decision to adopt a new product depends on his personal characteristics as well as on characteristics of the innovation itself. We are more likely to adopt a new product if it demands relatively little behavioral change, is easy to understand, and provides a relative advantage compared to existing products.

Many people and organizations play a role in the fashion system that creates and communicates symbolic meanings to consumers.

● The fashion system includes everyone involved in creating and transferring symbolic meanings. Many different products express common cultural categories (e.g., gender distinctions). Many people tend to adopt a new style simultaneously in a process of collective selection. According to meme theory, ideas spread through a population in a geometric progression much as a virus infects many people until it reaches epidemic proportions. Other perspectives on motivations for adopting new styles include psychological, economic, and sociological models of fashion.

Fashions follow cycles.

● Fashions follow cycles that resemble the product life cycle. We distinguish the two extremes of fashion adoption, classics and fads, in terms of the length of this cycle.

Products that succeed in one culture may fail in another if marketers fail to understand the differences among consumers in each place.

● Because a consumer's culture exerts such a big influence on his lifestyle choices, marketers must learn as much as possible about differences in cultural norms and preferences when they do business in more than one country. One important issue is the extent to which we need to tailor our marketing strategies to each culture. Followers of an etic perspective believe people in many cultures appreciate the same universal messages. Believers in an emic perspective argue that individual cultures are too unique to permit such standardization; marketers must instead adapt their approaches to local values and practices. Attempts at global marketing have met with mixed success; in many cases this approach is more likely to work if the messages appeal to basic values or if the target markets consist of consumers who are internationally rather than locally oriented.

Western (and particularly American) culture has a huge impact around the world, although people in other countries don't necessarily ascribe the same meanings to products as we do.

● The United States is a net exporter of popular culture. Consumers around the world eagerly adopt American products, especially entertainment vehicles and items they link to an American lifestyle (e.g., Marlboro cigarettes, Levi's jeans). Despite the continuing "Americanization" of world culture, some consumers reject American products because of dissatisfaction with our foreign policies. Some people resist globalization because they fear it will dilute their own local cultures. In other cases, they practice creolization as they integrate these products with existing cultural practices.

KEY TERMS

REVIEW QUESTIONS

1 What is collective selection? Give an example.
2 Describe a culture production system (CPS) and list its three components. What is an example of a CPS with these three components?
3 Define a cultural gatekeeper, and give three examples.
4 Describe the difference between arts and crafts.
5 What is a cultural formula? Give an example.
6 What is "new vintage?" How is this an example of reality engineering?
7 Define product placement and list three examples of it. How is this practice the same or different from branded entertainment?
8 What is advergaming? Give an example.
9 What is the diffusion of innovations?
10 Who are innovators? Early adopters? Laggards?
11 Describe the differences among continuous innovations, dynamically continuous innovations, and discontinuous innovations, and provide an example of each. Which type are consumers least likely to adopt an innovation?

12 What are the differences among *fashion, a fashion*, and *in fashion*?
13 What are cultural categories and how do they influence product designs?
14 Summarize some of the major approaches we can use to understand fashion from the perspectives of psychologists, economists, and sociologists.
15 What is an example of a meme?
16 What is the trickle-down effect? List some reasons why it is no longer as valid as it used to be.
17 What is the difference between a fad, a fashion, and a classic fashion life cycle?
18 What is the difference between an emic and an etic perspective on globalization?
19 Why is the United States a net exporter of popular culture?
20 What country provides an example of a transitional economy?
21 Define creolization and provide an example.

CONSUMER BEHAVIOR CHALLENGE

■ DISCUSS

1 Watchdog groups have long decried product placements for blurring the line between content and advertising without adequately informing viewers. And the networks themselves appear to be divided on how far they want to open the gate. "You've got to wonder when it starts to destroy the entertainment value," declares one former television executive. In some instances, placements are extremely subtle. For example, Polaroid handed out cameras to the band Outkast, whose hit song "Hey Ya" includes the lyric, "Take it like a Polaroid picture."[166] How do you see the future of product placement—will it get out of hand and create a consumer backlash, or is it a valuable alternative to traditional advertising?

2 The chapter described a few instances where consumers sold their kids' "naming rights" to corporations—mostly for charitable purposes. Would you do this—and why or why not?

3 Is advertising an art or a craft? Which should it be?

4 Movie companies routinely conduct market research when they produce big-budget films. If necessary they will reshoot part of a movie when viewers say they don't like it. Some people oppose this practice; they claim that movies, or books, songs, plays, or other artistic endeavors should not conform to what the market wants lest they sacrifice their integrity. What do you think?

5 Because of higher competition and market saturation, marketers in industrialized countries try to develop Third World markets. Asian consumers alone spend $90 billion a year on cigarettes, and U.S. tobacco manufacturers push relentlessly into these markets. We find cigarette advertising, often depicting glamorous Western models and settings, just about everywhere—on billboards, buses, storefronts, and clothing—and tobacco companies sponsor many major sports and cultural events. Some companies even hand out cigarettes and gifts in amusement areas, often to preteens. Should governments allow these practices, even if the products may be harmful to their citizens or divert money poor people should be spending on essentials? If you were a trade or health official in a Third World country, what guidelines, if any, might you suggest to regulate the import of luxury goods from advanced economies?

6 Comment on the growing practice of reality engineering. Do marketers "own" our culture? Should they?

7 If you worked in marketing research for a cosmetics firm, how might you apply the lead user concept to help you identify new product opportunities?

8 Boots with 6-inch heels were a fashion rage among young Japanese women a few years ago. Several teens died after they tripped over their shoes and fractured their skulls. However, followers of the style claim they are willing to risk twisted ankles, broken bones, bruised faces, and other dangers the platform shoes cause. One teenager said, "I've fallen and twisted my ankle many times, but they are so cute that I won't give them up until they go out of fashion."[167] Many consumers around the world seem willing to suffer for the sake of fashion. Others argue that we are merely pawns in the hands of designers, who conspire to force unwieldy fashions down our throats. What do you think? What is and what should be the role of fashion in our society? How important is it for people to be in style? What are the pros and cons of keeping up with the latest fashions? Do you believe that we are at the mercy of designers?

■ APPLY

9 The chapter talks about the Cupcake T-shirt fad. Clearly, it's a matter of time before consumers tire of these designs and move on. What can the company's owner do to prolong the life of his brand?

10 If you were a consultant to a toy company, what would you forecast as the next big trend in this market? Survey toy stores and watch what kids play with to help you with your prediction.

11 How might the rise of peer-to-peer music sharing influence the structure of the music CPS? One guess is that this method erodes the dominance of the big labels because listeners are more likely to access music from lesser-known groups. Survey your friends to determine whether this in fact is happening—are they listening to a wider variety of artists or simply downloading more from the big-time groups?

12 Read several romance or action novels to see if you can identify a cultural formula at work. Do you see parallels among the roles different characters play (e.g., the hero, the evildoer, the temptress, etc.)?

13 Watch 12 hours of TV and keep a log of all product placements you see. What are the dominant products shows are inserting?

Case Study

STARBUCKS: PURVEYOR OF COFFEE—OR CULTURE?

Starbucks originally opened in 1971 to sell gourmet whole coffee beans and equipment in the Seattle area. The current chairman, Howard Schultz, joined the company in 1982. A year later, Schultz visited Milan where he fell in love with the classic Italian espresso bar culture. Convinced that there was money to be made in the United States selling coffee drinks based on that model, he assumed ownership of the Starbucks chain and began to replicate this experience in the U.S.A. The rest, as they say, is history.

Starbucks operates in 39 countries, but it first established its identify by selling Italian culture to on-the-go consumers in the United States. Schultz's hunch was right. In just over 20 years, Starbucks has grown from a handful of stores to over 13,000 company-owned and licensed coffeehouses, employing over 150,000 people. In the past five years alone, the company has tripled its revenues to approximately $8 billion. Recently, Schultz announced that his coffee empire has no intention of slowing down. Starbucks plans to open 10,000 new stores in the next four years, and ultimately the company wants to see 40,000 outlets scattered all over the world.

Like many multinational corporations, Starbucks started with a standardized product, then tweaked it to appeal to the cultural tastes of individual countries. Aside from minor menu variations however (for example, cinnamon-flavored drinks are more popular among Russians), Starbucks uses basically the same menu and the same "third place" model around the world that it does in America. That is, the chain intends for customers to make it one of the three places, in addition to work and home, where they spend their time. Starbucks designs its stores with creative lighting, overstuffed chairs, mood music, and free WiFi to encourage people to hang out there for a long time each day.

But after years of rapid expansion, the CEO recently acknowledged a problem that many outside observers had been noticing for some time. The Starbucks experience has become sterile and unromantic; a diluted version of the Italian espresso bar culture that was core to the company's brand image in the late 1980s and early 1990s. "We have had to make a series of decisions," Schultz wrote, "that, in retrospect, have led to the watering down of the Starbucks experience, and what some might call the commoditization of our brand."

In an effort to regain its soul, Starbucks is launching a series of in-store promotions, each focusing on a particular region of the world. The first campaign focuses not on Italy, but on Costa Rica. A year ago, a team of Starbucks marketers and designers spent five days touring Costa Rica in search of an authentic vibe. The result is a campaign that includes in-store posters featuring Costa Rican farmers, artists, and regular folks, accompanied by the tagline, "I am Starbucks." Authentic paintings and colorful mugs by Costa Rican artisans will be available for sale. And perhaps most importantly, this effort has produced two new premium beverages, Dulce de Leche Latte and Frappuccino.

Perhaps partly due to this watered-down, homogenized experience, the coffeehouse chain's expansion around the world has not been totally smooth. On a practical level, the company has had to deal with issues such as antiwar protesters in Lebanon and possible terrorist attacks in Israel. But more importantly it has also faced some pushback by those who simply do not find the Starbucks version of a coffeehouse to be appealing. In some cases this is because local consumers resent what they view as the company's attempt to "hijack" their local culture and standardize it—some critics refer to this as the "McDonaldization" of local culture. In France, for example, many older consumers who cling to memories of the French café culture reject Starbucks and still flock to their local establishments. Time will tell if Starbucks is able to incorporate local flavors into its global brew

DISCUSSION QUESTIONS

1 How has Starbucks influenced culture throughout the world? Have local cultures also influenced the way Starbucks does business? What do you think the future holds for the relationship between the Starbucks experience and the cultures of the world?
2 Discuss the spread of Starbucks in the context of the concept of "diffusion of innovations."
3 How can Starbucks handle its rapid expansion by ensuring consistent quality in all of its stores while customizing the experience it delivers to customers in each local market?

Sources: Burt Helm, "Saving Starbucks' Soul," *BusinessWeek* (April 9, 2007): 56; Janet Adamy, "From Seattle, With Lattes," *Wall Street Journal* (August 31, 2007): B1; Daniel Workman, "Starbucks Global Sales," Suite101.com (August 29, 2006).

NOTES

1. www.abcnews.go.com/GMA/AmericanFamily/Story?id=3397793&page=2, accessed August 15, 2007.
2. www.pbs.org/newshour/infocus/fashion/hiphop.html, accessed July 30, 2007.
3. Marc Spiegler, "Marketing Street Culture: Bringing Hip-Hop Style to the Mainstream," *American Demographics* (November 1996): 29–34.
4. Joshua Levine, "Badass Sells," *Forbes* (April 21, 1997): 142.
5. Nina Darnton, "Where the Homegirls Are," *Newsweek* (June 17, 1991): 60; "The Idea Chain," *Newsweek* (October 5, 1992): 32.
6. Cyndee Miller, "X Marks the Lucrative Spot, but Some Advertisers Can't Hit Target," *Marketing News* (August 2, 1993): 1.
7. Ad appeared in *Elle* (September 1994).
8. Spiegler, "Marketing Street Culture: Bringing Hip-Hop Style to the Mainstream"; Levine, "Badass Sells."
9. Jeff Jensen, "Hip, Wholesome Image Makes a Marketing Star of Rap's LL Cool J," *Advertising Age* (August 25, 1997): 1.
10. Alice Z. Cuneo, "GAP's 1st Global Ads Confront Dockers on a Khaki Battlefield," *Advertising Age* (April 20, 1998): 3–5.
11. Jancee Dunn, "How Hip-Hop Style Bum-Rushed the Mall," *Rolling Stone* (March 18, 1999): 54–59.
12. Teri Agins, "The Rare Art of 'Gilt by Association': How Armani Got Stars to Be Billboards," *Wall Street Journal Interactive Edition* (September 14, 1999).
13. Eryn Brown, "From Rap to Retail: Wiring the Hip-Hop Nation," *Fortune* (April 17, 2000): 530
14. Martin Fackler, "Hip Hop Invading China," *Birmingham News* (February 15, 2002): D1.
15. Maureen Tkacik, "'Z' Zips into the Zeitgeist, Subbing for 'S' in Hot Slang," *Wall Street Journal Interactive Edition* (January 4, 2003); Maureen Tkacik, "Slang from the 'Hood Now Sells Toyz in Target," *Wall Street Journal Interactive Edition* (December 30, 2002).
16. www.hiphop-elements.com/article/read/4/6319/1, accessed July 9, 2005; www.bevnet.com/reviews/pimpjuice, accessed July 9, 2005; www.sohh.com/thewire/read.php?contentID=6893, accessed July 9, 2005; www.undercover.com.au/news/2005/mar05/20050324_usher.html, accessed July 9, 2005.
17. Arthur, Damien, "Authenticity and Consumption in the Australian Hip Hop Culture," *Qualitative Market Research* 9 no. 2 (2005): 140.
18. "European Hip Hop," Wikipedia.com, available from http://en.wikipedia.org/wiki/European_hip_hop, accessed July 30, 2007.
19. Elizabeth M. Blair, "Commercialization of the Rap Music Youth Subculture," *Journal of Popular Culture* 27 (Winter 1993): 21–34; Basil G. Englis, Michael R. Solomon, and Anna Olofsson, "Consumption Imagery in Music Television: A Bi-Cultural Perspective," *Journal of Advertising* 22 (December 1993): 21–34.
20. Spiegler, "Marketing Street Culture: Bringing Hip-Hop Style to the Mainstream."
21. Grant McCracken, "Culture and Consumption: A Theoretical Account of the Structure and Movement of the Cultural Meaning of Consumer Goods," *Journal of Consumer Research* 13 (June 1986): 71–84.
22. Richard A. Peterson, "The Production of Culture: A Prolegomenon," in Richard A. Peterson, ed., *The Production of Culture, Sage Contemporary Social Science Issues* 33 (Beverly Hills, CA: Sage, 1976), 7–22. For a study that looked at ways consumers interact with marketers to create cultural meanings, cf. Lisa Peñaloza, "Consuming the American West: Animating Cultural Meaning and Memory at a Stock Show and Rodeo," *Journal of Consumer Research* 28 (December 2001): 369–98.
23. Richard A. Peterson and D. G. Berger, "Entrepreneurship in Organizations: Evidence from the Popular Music Industry," *Administrative Science Quarterly* 16 (1971): 97–107.
24. Elizabeth C. Hirschman, "Resource Exchange in the Production and Distribution of a Motion Picture," *Empirical Studies of the Arts* 8, no. 1 (1990): 31–51; Michael R. Solomon, "Building Up and Breaking Down: The Impact of Cultural Sorting on Symbolic Consumption," in J. Sheth and E. C. Hirschman, eds., *Research in Consumer Behavior* (Greenwich, CT: JAI Press, 1988), 325–51.
25. For a new perspective on market changes, cf. Markus Giesler, "Conflict and Compromise: Drama in Marketplace Evolution," *Journal of Consumer Research*, forthcoming.
26. See Paul M. Hirsch, "Processing Fads and Fashions: An Organizational Set Analysis of Cultural Industry Systems," *American Journal of Sociology* 77, no. 4 (1972): 639–59; Russell Lynes, *The Tastemakers* (New York: Harper and Brothers, 1954); Michael R. Solomon, "The Missing Link: Surrogate Consumers in the Marketing Chain," *Journal of Marketing* 50 (October 1986): 208–19.
27. Michael R. Solomon, *Conquering Consumerspace: Marketing Strategies for a Branded World*, (New York: AMACOM, 2003).
28. C. K. Prahalad and Venkatram Ramaswamy, "Co-Opting Customer Competence," *Harvard Business Review* (January–February 2000): 79–87; Eric von Hipple, "Users as Innovators," *Technology Review* 80 (January 1978): 3–11; Jakki Mohr, *Marketing of High-Technology Products and Services* (Upper Saddle River, NJ: Prentice Hall, 2001).
29. Byrnes, Nanette, "Xeroxs' New Design Team: Customers," *Business Week* (May 7, 2007): 72.
30. Howard S. Becker, "Arts and Crafts," *American Journal of Sociology* 83 (January 1987): 862–89.
31. Herbert J. Gans, "Popular Culture in America: Social Problem in a Mass Society or Social Asset in a Pluralist Society?" in Howard S. Becker, ed., *Social Problems: A Modern Approach* (New York: Wiley, 1966).
32. Karen Breslau, "Paint by Numbers," *Newsweek* (May 13, 2002): 48.
33. Martin Forstenzer, "In Search of Fine Art amid the Paper Towels," *New York Times on the Web* (February 22, 2004).
34. Annetta Miller, "Shopping Bags Imitate Art: Seen the Sacks? Now Visit the Museum Exhibit," *Newsweek* (January 23, 1989): 44.
35. Kim Foltz, "New Species for Study: Consumers in Action," *New York Times* (December 18, 1989): A1.
36. Arthur A. Berger, *Signs in Contemporary Culture: An Introduction to Semiotics* (New York: Longman, 1984).
37. Michiko Kakutani, "Art Is Easier the 2d Time Around," *New York Times* (October 30, 1994): E4.
38. Brooks Barnes and Suzanne Vranica, "Why Advertising's Cavemen Are Going Totally Hollyrock," *Wall Street Journal* (March 5, 2007): B1; Nina M. Lentini, "Doh! Looks Like 7-Eleven Stores May Get Homered," *Marketing Daily* (March 30, 2007), available from www.mediapost.com, accessed March 30, 2007.
39. Michael R. Solomon and Basil G. Englis, "Reality Engineering: Blurring the Boundaries between Marketing and Popular Culture," *Journal of Current Issues and Research in Advertising* 16, no. 2 (Fall 1994): 1–17.
40. Austin Bunn, "Not Fade Away," *New York Times on the Web* (December 2, 2002).
41. Marc Santora, "Circle the Block, Cabby, My Show's On," *New York Times on the Web* (January 16, 2003); Wayne Parry, "Police May Sell Ad Space," *Montgomery Advertiser* (November 20, 2002): A4.
42. This process is described more fully in Michael R. Solomon, *Conquering Consumerspace: Marketing Strategies for a Branded World* (New York: AMACOM, 2003); cf. also T. Bettina Cornwell and Bruce Keillor, "Contemporary Literature and the Embedded Consumer Culture: The Case of Updike's Rabbit," in Roger J. Kruez and Mary Sue MacNealy, eds., *Empirical Approaches to Literature and Aesthetics: Advances in Discourse Processes* 52 (Norwood, NJ: Ablex, 1996), 559–72; Monroe Friedman, "The Changing Language of a Consumer Society: Brand Name Usage in Popular American Novels in the Postwar Era," *Journal of Consumer Research* 11 (March 1985): 927–37; Monroe Friedman, "Commercial Influences in the Lyrics of Popular American Music of the Postwar Era," *Journal of Consumer Affairs* 20 (Winter 1986): 193.
43. Brian Ashcraft, "For an Airtight Alibi, Press 1 Now," *Wired* (April 2004): 74.
44. James Bandler, "Only in the *Star!* Demi Moore's Brown Dress Turns White!" *Wall Street Journal Online Edition* (April 14, 2004): B1.
45. Nicolas Marmie, "Casablanca Gets a Rick's," *Montgomery Advertiser* (May 9, 2004): 3AA.
46. Jeff Zaslow, "Meet John 'Your Ad Here' Smith," *Wall Street Journal* (March 16, 2006): D3.
47. Louise Story, "Add This to the Endangered List: Blank Spaces," *New York Times Online* (January 15, 2007), accessed January 15, 2007.
48. Fara Warner, "Why It's Getting Harder to Tell the Shows from the Ads," *Wall Street Journal* (June 15, 1995): B1.
49. "Top 10 Product Placements in First Half of '07," *Marketing Daily* (September 26, 2007), www.mediapost.com, accessed September 26, 2007.
50. Nat Ives, "'Advertainment' Gains Momentum," *New York Times on the Web* (April 21, 2004).
51. Claire Atkinson, "Ad Intrusion Up, Say Consumers," *Advertising Age* (January 6, 2003): 1.
52. Motoko Rich, "Product Placement Deals Make Leap from Film to Books," *New York Times Online* (June 12, 2006), accessed June 12, 2006.
53. Stuart Elliott, "Greatest Hits of Product Placement," *New York Times Online* (February 28, 2005).
54. Benjamin M. Cole, "Products That Want to Be in Pictures," *Los Angeles Herald Examiner* (March 5, 1985): 36; see also Stacy M. Vollmers and Richard W. Mizerski, "A Review and Investigation into the Effectiveness

of Product Placements in Films," in Karen Whitehill King, ed., *Proceedings of the 1994 Conference of the American Academy of Advertising*, 97–102; Solomon and Englis, "Reality Engineering: Blurring the Boundaries between Marketing and Popular Culture."

55. Wayne Friedman, "'Minority Report' Stars Lexus, Nokia," *Advertising Age* (June 17, 2002): 41.

56. Charles Goldsmith, "Dubbing in Product Plugs: How 'Spider-Man 2' Made Dr. Pepper a Star in the U.S. and Mirinda a Star Overseas," *Wall Street Journal Online Edition* (December 6, 2004): B1.

57. Cristel Antonia Russell, "Investigating the Effectiveness of Product Placements in Television Shows: The Role of Modality and Plot Connection Congruence on Brand Memory and Attitude," *Journal of Consumer Research* 29 (December 2002): 306–18; Denise E. DeLorme and Leonard N. Reid, "Moviegoers' Experiences and Interpretations of Brands in Films Revisited," *Journal of Advertising* 28, no. 2 (1999): 71–90; Barbara B. Stern, and Cristel A. Russell "Consumer Responses to Product Placement in Television Sitcoms: Genre, Sex and Consumption," *Consumption, Markets and Culture* 7 (December 2004): 371–94.

58. Louise Story, "Add This to the Endangered List: Blank Spaces," *New York Times Online* (January 15, 2007), accessed January 15, 2007.

59. Evelyn Nussenbaum, "Products Slide into More TV Shows, with Help from New Middlemen," *New York Times* (September 6, 2004).

60. Brooks Barnes, "Good Soap Script Includes Love, Tears and Frosted Flakes as Ratings Slip, Daytime TV Gets Generous with Plugs; A Kiss before Using OnStar," *Wall Street Journal Online Edition* (January 17, 2005): A1.

61. Geoffrey A. Fowler, "New Star on Chinese TV: Product Placements," *Wall Street Journal Online Edition* (June 2, 2004): B1.

62. Aaron O. Patrick and Keith Johnson, "Spanish Television Reigns as King of Product Plugs It's Hard to Tell Where Shows Stop and Ads Begin; In 3 Hours, 105 Mentions," *Wall Street Journal* (February 2, 2007): A1.

63. Stuart Elliott, "State Farm Is There, Right by the Backboard," *New York Times Online* (January 31, 2007), accessed January 31, 2007; Max Chafkin, "School Ties," *Inc.* (May 2006): 38.

64. Brian Steinberg, "Look—Up in the Sky! Product Placement!" *Wall Street Journal*, (April 18, 2006): B1.

65. Sam Lubell, "Advertising's Twilight Zone: That Signpost Up Ahead May Be a Virtual Product," *New York Times Online* (January 2, 2006), accessed January 2, 2006.

66. Jack Neff, "Clearasil Marches into Middle-School Classes, *Advertising Age*, November 2006: 8; Bill Pennington, "Reading, Writing and Corporate Sponsorships," *New York Times on the Web* (October 18, 2004); Caroline E. Mayer, "Nurturing Brand Loyalty: With Preschool Supplies, Firms Woo Future Customers and Current Parents," *Washington Post* (October 12, 2003): F1.

67. Louise Story, "More Marketers Are Grabbing the Attention of Players During Online Games," *New York Times Online* (January 24, 2007), accessed January 24, 2007; Shankar Gupta, "King of the Advergames," available from www.mediapost.com, accessed December 22, 2006; "Plinking," *Fast Company* (April 2007): 31; Sarah Sennott, "Gaming the Ad," *Newsweek* (January 31, 2005): E2; "Advertisements Insinuated into Video Games," *New York Times on the Web* (October 18, 2004).

68. Tina M. Lowrey, L. J. Shrum, and John A. McCarty, "The Future of Television Advertising," in Allan J. Kimmel ed., *Marketing Communication: Emerging Trends and Developments*, ed. (New York: Oxford University Press, 2005): 113-132.

69. L. J. Shrum, Robert S. Wyer, and Thomas C. O'Guinn, "The Effects of Television Consumption on Social Perceptions: The Use of Priming Procedures to Investigate Psychological Processes," *Journal of Consumer Research* 24, no. 4 (1998): 447–58; Thomas C, O'Guinn and L. J. Shrum, "The Role of Television in the Construction of Consumer Social Reality," *Journal of Consumer Research* 23 no. 4 (1997): 278–94.

70. L. J. Shrum, James E. Burroughs, and Aric Rindfleisch, "Television's Cultivation of Material Values," *Journal of Consumer Research* 32, (December 2005): 473–79.

71. Damien Cave, "Dogtown, U.S.A.," *New York Times Online* (June 12, 2005), accessed June 12, 2005.

72. Emily Nelson, "Moistened Toilet Paper Wipes Out after Launch for Kimberly-Clark," *Wall Street Journal Interactive Edition* (April 15, 2002).

73. Robert Hof, "The Click Here Economy," *BusinessWeek* (June 22, 1998): 122–28.

74. Eric J. Arnould, "Toward a Broadened Theory of Preference Formation and the Diffusion of Innovations: Cases from Zinder Province, Niger Republic," *Journal of Consumer Research* 16 (September 1989): 239–67; Susan B. Kaiser, *The Social Psychology of Clothing* (New York: Macmillan, 1985); Thomas S. Robertson, *Innovative Behavior and Communication* (New York: Holt, Rinehart and Winston, 1971).

75. Jan-Benedict E. M. Steenkamp, Frenkel ter Hofstede, and Michel Wedel, "A Cross-National Investigation into the Individual and National Cultural Antecedents of Consumer Innovativeness," *Journal of Marketing* 63, no. 7 (1999): 55–69.

76. Susan L. Holak, Donald R. Lehmann, and Fareena Sultan, "The Role of Expectations in the Adoption of Innovative Consumer Durables: Some Preliminary Evidence," *Journal of Retailing* 63 (Fall 1987): 243–59.

77. Hubert Gatignon and Thomas S. Robertson, "A Propositional Inventory for New Diffusion Research," *Journal of Consumer Research* 11 (March 1985): 849–67.

78. Eric Pfanner, "Agencies Look beyond Focus Groups to Spot Trends," *New York Times Online* (January 2, 2006), accessed January 2, 2006.

79. Everett M. Rogers, *Diffusion of Innovations*, 3rd ed. (New York: The Free Press, 1983).

80. Umberto Eco, *A Theory of Semiotics* (Bloomington: Indiana University Press, 1979).

81. Fred Davis, "Clothing and Fashion as Communication," in Michael R. Solomon, ed., *The Psychology of Fashion* (Lexington, MA: Lexington Books, 1985): 15–28.

82. Melanie Wallendorf, "The Formation of Aesthetic Criteria through Social Structures and Social Institutions," in Jerry C. Olson, ed., *Advances in Consumer Research* 7 (Ann Arbor, MI: Association for Consumer Research, 1980): 3–6.

83. Grant McCracken, "Culture and Consumption: A Theoretical Account of the Structure and Movement of the Cultural Meaning of Consumer Goods," *Journal of Consumer Research* 13 (June 1986): 71–84.

84. "The Eternal Triangle," *Art in America* (February 1989): 23.

85. Sally Beatty, "Fashion's 'It' Colors: How Runway Dresses, Cars—Even Washer-Dryers—Turned Shades of Blue, Brown," *Wall Street Journal Online Edition* (February 4, 2005).

86. Herbert Blumer, *Symbolic Interactionism: Perspective and Method* (Upper Saddle River, NJ: Prentice Hall, 1969); Howard S. Becker, "Art as Collective Action," *American Sociological Review* 39 (December 1974): 767–776; Richard A. Peterson, "Revitalizing the Culture Concept," *Annual Review of Sociology* 5 (1979): 137–66.

87. For more details, see Kaiser, *The Social Psychology of Clothing*; George B. Sproles, "Behavioral Science Theories of Fashion," in Michael R. Solomon, ed., *The Psychology of Fashion* (Lexington, MA: Lexington Books, 1985): 55–70.

88. C. R. Snyder and Howard L. Fromkin, *Uniqueness: The Human Pursuit of Difference* (New York: Plenum Press, 1980).

89. Linda Dyett, "Desperately Seeking Skin," *Psychology Today* (May–June 1996): 14; Alison Lurie, *The Language of Clothes* (New York: Random House, 1981).

90. Susan Kaiser, Michael Solomon, Janet Hethorn, Basil Englis, Van Dyk Lewis, and Wi-Suk Kwon, "Menswear, Fashion, and Subjectivity," paper presented in Special Session: Susan Kaiser, Michael Solomon, Janet Hethorn, and Basil Englis (Chairs), "What Do Men Want? Media Representations, Subjectivity, and Consumption," at the ACR Gender Conference, Edinburgh, Scotland, June 2006.

91. Harvey Leibenstein, *Beyond Economic Man: A New Foundation for Microeconomics* (Cambridge, MA: Harvard University Press, 1976).

92. Nara Schoenberg, "Goth Culture Moves into Mainstream," *Montgomery Advertiser* (January 19, 2003): 1G.

93. Georg Simmel, "Fashion," *International Quarterly* 10 (1904): 130–55.

94. Maureen Tkacik, "'Z' Zips into the Zeitgeist, Subbing for 'S' in Hot Slang," *Wall Street Journal Interactive Edition* (January 4, 2003); Maureen Tkacik, "Slang from the 'Hood Now Sells Toyz in Target," *Wall Street Journal Interactive Edition* (December 30, 2002).

95. Grant D. McCracken, "The Trickle-Down Theory Rehabilitated," in Michael R. Solomon, ed., *The Psychology of Fashion* (Lexington, MA: Lexington Books, 1985): 39–54.

96. Charles W. King, "Fashion Adoption: A Rebuttal to the 'Trickle-Down' Theory," in Stephen A. Greyser, ed., *Toward Scientific Marketing* (Chicago: American Marketing Association, 1963): 108–25.

97. Alf H. Walle, "Grassroots Innovation," *Marketing Insights* (Summer 1990): 44–51.

98. Robert V. Kozinets, "Fandoms' Menace/Pop Flows: Exploring the Metaphor of Entertainment as Recombinant/Memetic Engineering," *Association for Consumer Research* (October 1999). The new science of memetics, which tries to explain how beliefs gain acceptance and predict their progress, was spurred by Richard Dawkins who in the 1970s proposed culture as a Darwinian struggle among "memes" or mind viruses. See Geoffrey Cowley: "Viruses of the Mind: How Odd Ideas Survive," *Newsweek* (April 14, 1997): 14.

99. Malcolm Gladwell, *The Tipping Point* (New York: Little, Brown and Co., 2000).

100. "Cabbage-Hatched Plot Sucks in 24 Doll Fans," *New York Daily News* (December 1, 1983).

101. "Turtlemania," *The Economist* (April 21, 1990): 32.

102. John Lippman, "Creating the Craze for Pokémon: Licensing Agent Bet on U.S. Kids," *Wall Street Journal Interactive Edition* (August 16, 1999).

103. David Pringle, Jesse Drucker, and Evan Ramstad, "Cellphone Makers Pay a Heavy Toll for Missing Fads," *Wall Street Journal Online Edition* (October 30, 2003).

104. Anthony Ramirez, "The Pedestrian Sneaker Makes a Comeback," *New York Times* (October 14, 1990): F17.

105. Quoted in Stephen Brown and Anthony Patterson, "You're a Wizard, Harry!" Consumer Responses to the Harry Potter Phenomenon," *Advances in Consumer Research* 33, no. 1 (2006): 155–160

106. Kurt Badenhausen, "Rubik Redux Outfront," *Forbes* (December 2006): 48.

107. Elizabeth Holmes, "Turning a Fad Product into a Brand of Apparel Johnny Cupcakes Extends and Expands Product Line to Keep Customers Coming,"*Wall Street Journal* (September 26, 2006): B5.

108. Martin Fackler, "Japan, Home of the Cute and Inbred Dog," *New York Times Online* (December 28, 2006), accessed December 28, 2006.

109. B. E. Aguirre, E. L. Quarantelli, and Jorge L. Mendoza, "The Collective Behavior of Fads: The Characteristics, Effects, and Career of Streaking," *American Sociological Review* (August 1989): 569.

110. Joseph B. White, "From Fad to Trend," *Wall Street Journal Online* (June 21, 2005).

111. Martin G. Letscher, "How to Tell Fads from Trends," *American Demographics* (December 1994): 38–45.

112. "Packaging Draws Protest," *Marketing News* (July 4, 1994): 1.

113. "McDonald's to Give $10 Million to Settle Vegetarian Lawsuit," *Wall Street Journal Interactive Edition* (June 4, 2002).

114. Gerard O'Dwyer, "McD's Cancels McAfrika Rollout," *Advertising Age* (September 9, 2002): 14.

115. Saritha Rai, "Tastes of India in U.S. Wrappers," *New York Times on the Web* (April 29, 2003).

116. Geoffrey A. Fowler, "For Prosperity Burger, McDonald's Tailors Ads to Asian Tastes," *Wall Street Journal Online Edition* (January 24, 2005).

117. K. Belson, "As Starbucks Grows, Japan, Too, Is Awash," *New York Times on the Web* (October 21, 2001).

118. Ariane Bernard, "New American Beachhead in France: Starbucks," *New York Times on the Web* (January 16, 2004): 122; "Starbucks Plans 24 Stores in Puerto Rico, Mexico: Will Consumers Buy $5 Coffee in the Land of 50 Cent Cafe?" *Wall Street Journal Interactive Edition* (August 29, 2002); Steven Erlanger, "An American Coffeehouse (or 4) in Vienna," *New York Times on the Web* (June 1, 2002).

119. Janet Adamy, "Different Brew Eyeing a Billion Tea Drinkers, Starbucks Pours It on in China Its Big Challenge: Creating a New Taste for Coffee, and Charging Top Prices Wooing the 'Little Emperors,'" *Wall Street Journal* (November 29, 2006): A1.

120. Craig J. Thompson and Zeynep Arsel, "The Starbucks Brandscape and Consumers' (Anticorporate) Experiences of Glocalization," *Journal of Consumer Research* 31 (December 2004): 631–42.

121. Theodore Levitt, *The Marketing Imagination* (New York: The Free Press, 1983).

122. Merissa Marr, "Small World: Disney Rewrites Script to Win Fans in India; China, Latin America Are also in Turnaround; A 'Princess' in Mumbai," *Wall Street Journal* (June 11, 2007): A1; Laura M. Holson, "The Feng Shui Kingdom," *New York Times on the Web* (April 25, 2005); Keith Bradsher, "Disneyland for Chinese Offers a Soup and Lands in a Stew," *New York Times* (June 17, 2005): A1; Paulo Prada and Bruce Orwall, "Disney's New French Theme Park Serves Wine—and Better Sausage," *Wall Street Journal Interactive Edition* (March 12, 2002).

123. Terry Clark, "International Marketing and National Character: A Review and Proposal for an Integrative Theory," *Journal of Marketing* 54 (October 1990): 66–79.

124. Geraldo Samor, Cecilie Rohwedder, and Ann Zimmerman, "Innocents Abroad? Wal-Mart's Global Sales Rise as It Learns from Mistakes; No More Ice Skates in Mexico, *Wall Street Jounal* (May 16, 2006): B1.

125. "China Bans Nike Ad, Citing Assault on National Dignity," *Wall Street Journal Online Edition* (December 6, 2004).

126. Marc Gobé, *Emotional Branding: The New Paradigm for Connecting Brands to People* (New York: Allworth Press, 2001).

127. Norihiko Shirouzu, "Snapple in Japan: How a Splash Dried Up," *Wall Street Journal* (April 15, 1996): B1.

128. Glenn Collins, "Chinese to Get a Taste of Cheese-Less Cheetos," *New York Times* (September 2, 1994): D4.

129. Martin McCarty, Martin I. Horn, Mary Kate Szenasy, and Jocelyn Feintuch, "An Exploratory Study of Consumer Style: Country Differences and International Segments," *Journal of Consumer Behaviour* 6, no. 1 (2007): 48.

130. Julie Skur Hill and Joseph M. Winski, "Goodbye Global Ads: Global Village Is Fantasy Land for Marketers," *Advertising Age* (November 16, 1987): 22.

131. Jason Overdorf, "Comics: Off to Save Mumbai," *Newsweek* (August, 2, 2004): 15.

132. Shelly Reese, "Culture Shock," *Marketing Tools* (May 1998): 44–49; Steve Rivkin, "The Name Game Heats Up," *Marketing News* (April 22, 1996): 8; David A. Ricks, "Products That Crashed into the Language Barrier," *Business and Society Review* (Spring 1983): 46–50.

133. Mark Lasswell, "Lost in Translation," *Business* (August 2004): 68–70.

134. Clyde H. Farnsworth, "Yoked in Twin Solitudes: Canada's Two Cultures," *New York Times* (September 18, 1994): E4.

135. Hill and Winski, "Goodbye Global Ads."

136. MTV Europe, personal communication, 1994; see also Teresa J. Domzal and Jerome B. Kernan, "Mirror, Mirror: Some Postmodern Reflections on Global Advertising," *Journal of Advertising* 22 (December 1993): 1–20; Douglas P. Holt, "Consumers' Cultural Differences as Local Systems of Tastes: A Critique of the Personality-Values Approach and an Alternative Framework," *Asia Pacific Advances in Consumer Research* 1 (1994): 1–7.

137. Douglas B. Holt, John A. Quelch, and Earl L. Taylor, "How Global Brands Compete," *Harvard Business Review* (September 2004): 68–75.

138. Normandy Madden, "New GenerAsians Survey Gets Personal with Asia-Pacific Kids," *Advertising Age International* (July 13, 1998): 2.

139. Adam Thompson and Shai Oster, "NBA in China Gets Milk to Sell Hoops," *Wall Street Journal* (January 22, 2007): B1; "They All Want to Be Like Mike," *Fortune* (July 21, 1997): 51–53.

140. Calvin Sims, "Japan Beckons, and East Asia's Youth Fall in Love," *New York Times* (December 5, 1999): 3.

141. Elisabeth Rosenthal, "Buicks, Starbucks and Fried Chicken, Still China?" *New York Times on the Web* (February 25, 2002).

142. Special Report, "Brands in an Age of Anti-Americanism," *BusinessWeek* (August 4, 2003): 69–76.

143. Suzanne Kapner, "U.S. TV Shows Losing Potency around World," *New York Times on the Web* (January 2, 2003).

144. "Big Brother Nipple Sparks Outrage," BBCNews.com (September 10, 2004).

145. Laurel Wentz and Claire Atkinson, "Apprentice Translators Hope for Hits All over Globe," *Advertising Age* (February 14, 2005): 3(2).

146. Sean Gregory, "Anti-U.S. Backlash," *Time* (January 2005): A3.

147. Kevin J. Delaney, "U.S. Brands Could Suffer Even Before War Begins," *Wall Street Journal Interactive Edition* (January 28, 2003).

148. Julie Watson, "City Keeps McDonald's from Opening in Plaza," *Montgomery Advertiser* (December 15, 2002): 5AA.

149. "French Council Eases Language Ban," *New York Times* (July 31, 1994): 12.

150. Alan Riding, "Only the French Elite Scorn Mickey's Debut," *New York Times* (1992): A1.

151. Eric Pfanner, "As U.S. Is Reviled Abroad, American TV Charms," *New York Times* (October 16, 2006).

152. Professor Russell Belk, University of Utah, personal communication, July 25, 1997.

153. Material in this section adapted from Güliz Ger and Russell W. Belk, "I'd Like to Buy the World a Coke: Consumptionscapes of the 'Less Affluent World,'" *Journal of Consumer Policy* 19, no. 3 (1996): 271–304; Russell W. Belk, "Romanian Consumer Desires and Feelings of Deservingness," in Lavinia Stan, ed., *Romania in Transition* (Hanover, NH: Dartmouth Press, 1997): 191–208; see also Güliz Ger, "Human Development and Humane Consumption: Well Being Beyond the Good Life," *Journal of Public Policy and Marketing* 16 (1997): 110–25.

154. Professor Güliz Ger, Bilkent University, Turkey, personal communication, July 25, 1997.

155. Erazim Kohák, "Ashes, Ashes . . . Central Europe after Forty Years," *Daedalus* 121 (Spring 1992): 197–215; Belk, "Romanian Consumer Desires and Feelings of Deservingness."

156. David Murphy, "Christmas's Commercial Side Makes Yuletide a Hit in China," *Wall Street Journal Interactive Edition* (December 24, 2002).

157. Miriam Jordan and Teri Agins, "Fashion Flip-Flop: Sandal Leaves the Shower Behind," *Wall Street Journal Interactive Edition* (August 8, 2002).

158. This example courtesy of Professor Russell Belk, University of Utah, personal communication, July 25, 1997.

159. Miriam Jordan, "India Decides to Put Its Own Spin on Popular Rock, Rap and Reggae," *Wall Street Journal Interactive Edition* (January 5, 2000); Rasul Bailay, "Coca-Cola Recruits Paraplegics for 'Cola War' in India," *Wall Street Journal Interactive Edition* (June 10, 1997).

160. Rick Wartzman, "When You Translate 'Got Milk' for Latinos, What Do You Get?" *Wall Street Journal Interactive Edition* (June 3, 1999).

161. Charles Newbery, "Coke Goes Native with New Soft Drink," *Advertising Age* (December 1, 2003): 34

162. Eric J. Arnould and Richard R. Wilk, "Why Do the Natives Wear Adidas: Anthropological Approaches to Consumer Research," *Advances in Consumer Research* 12 (Provo, UT: Association for Consumer Research, 1985): 748–52.

163. John F. Sherry, Jr. and Eduardo G. Camargo, "May Your Life Be Marvelous: English Language Labelling and the Semiotics of Japanese Promotion," *Journal of Consumer Research* 14 (1987): 174–188.

164. Bill Bryson, "A Taste for Scrambled English," *New York Times* (July 22, 1990): 10; Rose A. Horowitz, "California Beach Culture Rides Wave of Popularity in Japan," *Journal of Commerce* (August 3, 1989): 17; Elaine Lafferty, "American Casual Seizes Japan: Teen-agers Go for N.F.L. Hats, Batman and the California Look," *Time* (November 13, 1989): 106.

165. Lucy Howard and Gregory Cerio, "Goofy Goods," *Newsweek* (August 15, 1994): 8.

166. Brian Steinberg and Suzanne Vranica, "Prime-Time TV's New Guest Stars: Products," *Wall Street Journal Online* (January 12, 2004), accessed January 12, 2004.

167. Calvin Sims, "For Chic's Sake, Japanese Women Parade to the Orthopedist," *New York Times on the Web* (November 26, 1999).

Glossary

ABC model of attitudes a multidimensional perspective stating that attitudes are jointly defined by affect, behavior, and cognition

Absolute threshold the minimum amount of stimulation that can be detected on a given sensory channel

Accommodative purchase decision the process of using bargaining, coercion, compromise, and the wielding of power to achieve agreement among group members who have different preferences or priorities

Acculturation the process of learning the beliefs and behaviors endorsed by another culture

Acculturation agents friends, family, local businesses, and other reference groups that facilitate the learning of cultural norms

Activation models of memory approaches to memory stressing different levels of processing that occur and activate some aspects of memory rather than others, depending on the nature of the processing task

Activity stores a retailing concept that lets consumers participate in the production of the products or services being sold in the store

Actual self a person's realistic appraisal of his or her qualities

Adaptation the process that occurs when a sensation becomes so familiar that it no longer commands attention

Advergaming online games merged with interactive advertisements that let companies target specific types of consumers

Advertising wear-out the condition that occurs when consumers become so used to hearing or seeing a marketing stimulus that they no longer pay attention to it

Affect the way a consumer feels about an attitude object

Age cohort a group of consumers of approximately the same age who have undergone similar experiences

Agentic goals an emphasis on self-assertion and mastery, often associated with traditional male gender roles

AIOs (activities, interests, and opinions) the psychographic variables researchers use to group consumers

Allegory a story told about an abstract trait or concept that has been personified as a person, animal, or vegetable

Allocentric person who has a group orientation

Animism cultural practices whereby inanimate objects are given qualities that make them somehow alive

Antibrand communities groups of consumers who share a common disdain for a celebrity, store, or brand

Anticonsumption the actions taken by consumers involving the deliberate defacement or mutilation of products

Antifestival an event that distorts the symbols associated with other holidays

Approach–approach conflict a person must choose between two desirable alternatives

Approach–avoidance conflict a person desires a goal but wishes to avoid it at the same time

Avoidance–avoidance conflict a person faces a choice between two undesirable alternatives

Archetypes a universally shared idea or behavior pattern, central to Carl Jung's conception of personality; archetypes involve themes—such as birth, death, or the devil—that appear frequently in myths, stories, and dreams

Art product a creation viewed primarily as an object of aesthetic contemplation without any functional value

Aspirational reference group high-profile athletes and celebrities used in marketing efforts to promote a product

Associative network a memory system that organizes individual units of information according to some set of relationships; may include such concepts as brands, manufacturers, and stores

Atmospherics the use of space and physical features in store design to evoke certain effects in buyers

Attention the assignment of processing activity to selected stimuli

Attentional gate a process whereby information retained for further processing is transferred from sensory memory to short-term memory

Attitude a lasting, general evaluation of people (including oneself), objects, or issues

Attitude object (A_o) anything toward which one has an attitude

Attitude toward the act of buying (A_{act}) the perceived consequences of a purchase

Attitude toward the advertisement (A_{ad}) a predisposition to respond favorably or unfavorably to a particular advertising stimulus during a particular exposure occasion

Autonomic decision when one family member chooses a product for the whole family

Avatar manifestation of a Hindu deity in superhuman or animal form. In the computing world it has come to mean a cyberspace presence represented by a character that you can move around inside a visual, graphical world

Avoidance–avoidance conflict when we desire a goal but wish to avoid it at the same time

B2C e-commerce businesses selling to consumers through electronic marketing

Baby boomer a large cohort of people born between the years of 1946 and 1964 who are the source of many important cultural and economic changes

Balance theory a theory that considers relations among elements a person might perceive as belonging together, and people's tendency to change relations among elements in order to make them consistent or "balanced"

Behavior a consumer's actions with regard to an attitude object

Behavioral economics the study of the behavioral determinants of economic decisions

Behavioral influence perspective the view that consumer decisions are learned responses to environmental cues

Behavioral learning theories the perspectives on learning that assume that learning takes place as the result of responses to external events

683

Behavioral targeting the appearance and personality a person takes on as an avatar in a computer-mediated environment like Second Life

Being space a retail environment that resembles a residential living room where customers are encouraged to congregate

Binary opposition a defining structural characteristic of many myths in which two opposing ends of some dimension are represented (e.g., good versus evil, nature versus technology)

Bitcoms a new way to boost viewers' retention of a set of ads inserted within a TV show; the commercials are preceded with a stand-up comedian (perhaps an actor in the show itself) who performs a small set that leads into the actual ads

Blogging a growing practice where people post messages to the Web in diary form

Blogosphere the universe of active weblogs (online diaries)

Body cathexis a person's feelings about aspects of his or her body

Body image a consumer's subjective evaluation of his or her physical self

Boomerang kids grown children who return to their parents' home to live

Brand community a set of consumers who share a set of social relationships based on usage or interest in a product

Brand equity a brand that has strong positive associations in a consumer's memory and commands a lot of loyalty as a result

Brand loyalty repeat purchasing behavior that reflects a conscious decision to continue buying the same brand

Brand personality a set of traits people attribute to a product as if it were a person

Branded entertainment a format where advertisers showcase their products in longer-form narrative films instead of commercials

Brandfests a corporate-sponsored event intended to promote strong brand loyalty among customers

Business ethics rules of conduct that guide actions in the marketplace

Business-to-business (B2B) e-commerce Internet interactions between two or more businesses or organizations

Business-to-business (B2B) marketers specialists in meeting the needs of organizations such as corporations, government agencies, hospitals, and retailers

Buyclass theory of purchasing a framework that characterizes organizational buying decisions in terms of how much cognitive effort is involved in making a decision

Buying center the part of an organization charged with making purchasing decisions

Buzz word of mouth that is viewed as authentic and generated by customers

C2C e-commerce consumer-to-consumer activity through the Internet

Carbon footprint the impact human activities have on the environment in terms of the amount of greenhouse gases they produce; measured in units of carbon dioxide

Chavs British term that refers to young, lower-class men and women who mix flashy brands and accessories from big names such as Burberry with track suits

Chunking a process in which information is stored by combining small pieces of information into larger ones

Classic a fashion with an extremely long acceptance cycle

Classical conditioning the learning that occurs when a stimulus eliciting a response is paired with another stimulus that initially does not elicit a response on its own but will cause a similar response over time because of its association with the first stimulus

Closure principle the *Gestalt* principle that describes a person's tendency to supply missing information in order to perceive a holistic image

Co-branding strategies linking products together to create a more desirable connotation in consumer minds

Co-consumers other patrons in a consumer setting

Coercive power influencing a person by social or physical intimidation

Cognition the beliefs a consumer has about an attitude object

Cognitive learning theory approaches that stress the importance of internal mental processes. This perspective views people as problem solvers who actively use information from the world around them to master their environment

Collecting the systematic acquisition of a particular object or set of objects

Collective selection the process by which certain symbolic alternatives tend to be jointly chosen over others by members of a society

Collectivist culture cultural orientation that encourages people to subordinate their personal goals to those of a stable in-group; values such as self-discipline and group accomplishment are stressed

Communal goals an emphasis on affiliation and the fostering of harmonious relations, often associated with traditional female gender roles

Communications model a framework specifying that a number of elements are necessary for communication to be achieved, including a source, message, medium, receivers, and feedback

Comparative advertising a strategy in which a message compares two or more specifically named or recognizably presented brands and makes a comparison of them in terms of one or more specific attributes

Comparative influence the process whereby a reference group influences decisions about specific brands or activities

Compensatory decision rules a set of rules that allows information about attributes of competing products to be averaged in some way; poor standing on one attribute can potentially be offset by good standing on another

Compulsive consumption the process of repetitive, often excessive, shopping used to relieve tension, anxiety, depression, or boredom

Conditioned response (CR) a response to a conditioned stimulus caused by the learning of an association between a conditioned stimulus (CS) and an unconditioned stimulus (UCS)

Conditioned stimulus (CS) a stimulus that produces a learned reaction through association over time

Conformity a change in beliefs or actions as a reaction to real or imagined group pressure

Connexity a lifestyle term coined by the advertising agency Saatchi & Saatchi to describe young consumers who place high value on being both footloose and connected

Conscientious consumerism a new value that combines a focus on personal health with a concern for global health

Consensual purchase decision a decision in which the group agrees on the desired purchase and differs only in terms of how it will be achieved

Consideration set the products a consumer actually deliberates about choosing

Conspicuous consumption the purchase and prominent display of luxury goods to provide evidence of a consumer's ability to afford them

Consumed consumers those people who are used or exploited, whether willingly or not, for commercial gain in the marketplace

Consumer a person who identifies a need or desire, makes a purchase, and/or disposes of the product

Consumer addiction a physiological and/or psychological dependency on products or services

Consumer behavior the processes involved when individuals or groups select, purchase, use, or dispose of products, services, ideas, or experiences to satisfy needs and desires

Consumer confidence the state of mind of consumers relative to their optimism or pessimism about economic conditions; people tend to make more discretionary purchases when their confidence in the economy is high

Consumer-generated content a hallmark of Web 2.0; everyday people voice their opinions about products, brands, and companies on blogs, podcasts and social networking sites and film their own commercials they post on Web sites

Consumer hyperchoice a condition where the large number of available options forces us to make repeated choices that drain psychological energy and diminish our ability to make smart decisions

Consumer satisfaction/dissatisfaction (CS/D) the overall attitude a person has about a product after it has been purchased

Consumer socialization the process by which people acquire skills that enable them to function in the marketplace

Consumerspace marketing environment where customers act as partners with companies to decide what the marketplace will offer

Consumer style a pattern of behaviors, attitudes, and opinions that influences all of a person's consumption activities—including attitudes towards advertising; preferred channels of information and purchase; brand loyalty; and price consciousness

Consumer tribe group of people who share a lifestyle and who can identify with each other because of a shared allegiance to an activity or a product

Consumption communities Web groups where members share views and product recommendations online

Consumption constellation a set of products and activities used by consumers to define, communicate, and perform social roles

Contamination when a place or object takes on sacred qualities because of its association with another sacred person or event

Contrast stimuli that differ from others around them

Co-optation a cultural process by which the original meanings of a product or other symbol associated with a subculture are modified by members of mainstream culture

Core values common general values held by a culture

Corporate paradox the more involved a company appears to be in the dissemination of news about its products, the less credible it becomes

Country of origin original country from which a product is produced. Can be an important piece of information in the decision-making process

Craft product a creation valued because of the beauty with which it performs some function; this type of product tends to follow a formula that permits rapid production, and it is easier to understand than an art product

Creolization foreign influences are absorbed and integrated with local meanings

Crowdsourcing similar to a firm that outsources production to a subcontractor; companies call upon outsiders from around the world to solve problems their own scientists can't handle

Cult products items that command fierce consumer loyalty and devotion

Cultural capital a set of distinctive and socially rare tastes and practices that admits a person into the realm of the upper class

Cultural categories the grouping of ideas and values that reflect the basic ways members of a society characterize the world

Cultural formula a sequence of media events in which certain roles and props tend to occur consistently

Cultural gatekeepers individuals who are responsible for determining the types of messages and symbolism to which members of mass culture are exposed

Cultural selection the process by which some alternatives are selected over others by cultural gatekeepers

Culture the values, ethics, rituals, traditions, material objects, and services produced or valued by the members of a society

Culture jamming the defacement or alteration of advertising materials as a form of political expression

Culture production system (CPS) the set of individuals and organizations responsible for creating and marketing a cultural product

Cybermediary intermediary that helps to filter and organize online market information so that consumers can identify and evaluate alternatives more efficiently

Database marketing tracking consumers' buying habits very closely, and then crafting products and messages tailored precisely to people's wants and needs based on this information

Decay structural changes in the brain produced by learning decrease over time

Decision polarization the process whereby individuals' choices tend to become more extreme (polarized), in either a conservative or risky direction, following group discussion of alternatives

Deethnicization process whereby a product formerly associated with a specific ethnic group is detached from its roots and marketed to other subcultures

Deindividuation the process whereby individual identities get submerged within a group, reducing inhibitions against socially inappropriate behavior

Demographics the observable measurements of a population's characteristics, such as birthrate, age distribution, and income

Desacralization the process that occurs when a sacred item or symbol is removed from its special place, or is duplicated in mass quantities, and becomes profane as a result

Determinant attributes the attributes actually used to differentiate among choices

Differential threshold the ability of a sensory system to detect changes or differences among stimuli

Diffusion of innovations the process whereby a new product, service, or idea spreads through a population

Digital native young people who have grown up with computers and mobile technology; multitaskers with cell phones, music downloads, and instant messaging on the Internet. Who are comfortable communicating online and by text and IM rather than by voice

DINKS acronym for Double Income, No Kids; a consumer segment with a lot of disposable income

Discretionary income the money available to a household over and above that required for necessities

Divestment rituals the steps people take to gradually distance themselves from things they treasure so that they can sell them or give them away

Doppelgänger brand image A parody of a brand posted on a Web site that looks like the original but is in fact a critique of it

Downshifting reducing reliance on possessions and learning to get by with less

Drive the desire to satisfy a biological need in order to reduce physiological arousal

Drive theory concept that focuses on biological needs that produce unpleasant states of arousal

Early adopters people who are receptive to new products and adopt them relatively soon, though they are motivated more by social acceptance and being in style than by the desire to try risky new things

Economics of information perspective in which advertising is an important source of consumer information emphasizing the economic cost of the time spent searching for products

Ego the system that mediates between the id and the superego

80/20 rule a rule-of-thumb in volume segmentation, which says that about 20 percent of consumers in a product category (the heavy users) account for about 80 percent of sales

Elaborated codes the ways of expressing and interpreting meanings that are more complex and depend on a more sophisticated worldview, which tend to be used by the middle and upper classes

Elaboration likelihood model (ELM) the approach that one of two routes to persuasion (central versus peripheral) will be followed, depending on the personal relevance of a message; the route taken determines the relative importance of the message contents versus other characteristics, such as source attractiveness

Elaborative rehearsal a cognitive process that allows information to move from short-term memory into long-term memory by thinking about the meaning of a stimulus and relating it to other information already in memory

Electronic recommendation agent a software tool that tries to understand a human decision maker's multiattribute preferences for a product category by asking the user to communicate his or her preferences. Based on that data, the software then recommends a list of alternatives sorted by the degree that they fit with the person's preferences

Embeds tiny figures inserted into magazine advertising by using high-speed photography or airbrushing. These hidden figures, usually of a sexual nature, supposedly exert strong but unconscious influences on innocent readers

Emic perspective an approach to studying for (or marketing to) cultures that stresses the unique aspects of each culture

Encoding the process in which information from short-term memory enters into long-term memory in a recognizable form

Enculturation the process of learning the beliefs and behaviors endorsed by one's own culture

Episodic memories memories that relate to personally relevant events; this tends to increase a person's motivation to retain these memories

Ethnic subculture a self-perpetuating group of consumers held together by common cultural ties

Ethnocentrism the belief in the superiority of one's own country's practices and products

Etic perspective an approach to studying (or marketing to) cultures that stresses commonalities across cultures

Evaluative criteria the dimensions used by consumers to compare competing product alternatives

Evoked set those products already in memory plus those prominent in the retail environment that are actively considered during a consumer's choice process

Exchange theory the perspective that every interaction involves an exchange of value

Expectancy disconfirmation model states that we form beliefs about product performance based on prior experience with the product and/or communications about the product that imply a certain level of quality; when something performs the way we thought it would, we may not think much about it. If it fails to live up to expectations, this may create negative feelings. On the other hand, we are satisfied if performance exceeds our initial expectations

Expectancy theory the perspective that behavior is largely "pulled" by expectations of achieving desirable outcomes, or positive incentives, rather than "pushed" from within

Experience the result of acquiring and processing stimulation over time

Experiential perspective an approach stressing the *Gestalt* or totality of the product or service experience, focusing on consumers' affective responses in the marketplace

Expert power authority derived from possessing a specific knowledge or skill

Exposure an initial stage of perception during which some sensations come within range of consumers' sensory receptors

Extended family traditional family structure in which several generations live together

Extended problem solving an elaborate decision-making process, often initiated by a motive that is fairly central to the self-concept and accompanied by perceived risk; the consumer tries to collect as much information as possible, and carefully weighs product alternatives

Extended self the definition of self created by the external objects with which one surrounds oneself

Extinction the process whereby a learned connection between a stimulus and response is eroded so that the response is no longer reinforced

Fad a very short-lived fashion

Family branding an application of stimulus generalization when a product capitalizes on the reputation of its manufacturer's name

Family financial officer (FFO) the individual in the family who is in charge of making financial decisions

Family life cycle (FLC) a classification scheme that segments consumers in terms of changes in income and family composition and the changes in demands placed on this income

Fantasy a self-induced shift in consciousness, often focusing on some unattainable or improbable goal; sometimes fantasy is a way of compensating for a lack of external stimulation or for dissatisfaction with the actual self

Fashion the process of social diffusion by which a new style is adopted by some group(s) of consumers

Fashion acceptance cycle the diffusion process of a style through three stages: introduction, acceptance, and regression

Fashion system those people and organizations involved in creating symbolic meanings and transferring these meanings to cultural goods

Fear appeals an attempt to change attitudes or behavior through the use of threats or by highlighting negative consequences of noncompliance with the request

Feature creep trend toward an increasing number of options a product offers that make it more difficult for consumers to decide among competitors

Fertility rate a rate determined by the number of births per year per 1,000 women of childbearing age

Figure-ground principle the *Gestalt* principle whereby one part of a stimulus configuration dominates a situation whereas other aspects recede into the background

Flow state situation in which consumers are truly involved with a product, an ad, or a Web site

Food culture pattern of food and beverage consumption that reflects the values of a social group

Foot-in-the-door technique based on the observation that a consumer is more likely to comply with a request if he or she has first agreed to comply with a smaller request

Fortress brands brands that consumers closely link to rituals; this makes it unlikely they will be replaced

Freecycling the practice of giving away useful but unwanted goods to keep them out of landfills

Freegans a takeoff on *vegans*, who shun all animal products; anticonsumerists who live off discards as a political statement against corporations and materialism

Frequency marketing a marketing technique that reinforces regular purchasers by giving them prizes with values that increase along with the amount purchased

Gemba Japanese term for the one true source of information

Gender convergence blurring of sex roles in modern society; men and women increasingly express similar attitudes about balancing home life and work

Generation X a widely used term to describe "twentysomething" consumers who are (stereotypically) characterized as being confused, alienated, and depressed

Geodemography techniques that combine consumer demographic information with geographic consumption patterns to permit precise targeting of consumers with specific characteristics

Gerontographics a segmentation approach that divides the mature market into groups based on both level of physical well-being and social conditions such as becoming a grandparent or losing a spouse

Gestalt meaning derived from the totality of a set of stimuli, rather than from any individual stimulus

Gift-giving ritual the events involved in the selection, presentation, acceptance, and interpretation of a gift

Global consumer culture a culture in which people around the world are united through their common devotion to brand name consumer goods, movie stars, celebrities, and leisure activities

Globalized consumption ethic the global sharing of a material lifestyle including the valuing of well-known multinational brands that symbolize prosperity

Goal a consumer's desired end state

Gray market the economic potential created by the increasing numbers of affluent elderly consumers

Green marketing a marketing strategy involving an emphasis on protecting the natural environment

Grooming rituals sequences of behaviors that aid in the transition from the private self to the public self or back again

Group dieting online communities devoted to excessive weight loss

Guerrilla marketing promotional strategies that use unconventional locations and intensive word-of-mouth campaigns

Habitual decision making choices made with little or no conscious effort

Habitus ways in which we classify experiences as a result of our socialization processes

Halo effect a phenomenon that occurs when people react to other, similar stimuli in much the same way they responded to the original stimulus

Heavy users a name companies use to identify their customers who consume their products in large volumes

Hedonic consumption the multisensory, fantasy, and emotional aspects of consumers' interactions with products

Heuristics the mental rules of thumb that lead to a speedy decision

Hierarchical processing model perspective on information processing that proposes we analyze an incoming message in a bottom-up fashion; processing begins at a very basic level and is subject to increasingly complex processing operations that require greater cognitive capacity as needed

Hierarchy of effects a fixed sequence of steps that occurs during attitude formation; this sequence varies depending on such factors as the consumer's level of involvement with the attitude object

High-context culture group members tend to be close-knit and are likely to infer meanings that go beyond the spoken word

Hoarding unsystematic acquisition of objects (in contrast to collecting)

Homeostasis the state of being in which the body is in physiological balance; goal-oriented behavior attempts to reduce or eliminate an unpleasant motivational state and return to a balanced one

Home shopping parties a gathering where a company representative makes a sales presentation to a group of people who have gathered in the home of a friend or acquaintance

Homogamy the tendency for individuals to marry others similar to themselves

Homophily the degree to which a pair of individuals is similar in terms of education, social status, and beliefs

Host culture a new culture to which a person must acculturate

Hype corporate propaganda planted by companies to create product sensation—dismissed as inauthentic by customers

Hyperreality the becoming real of what is initially simulation or "hype"

Icon a sign that resembles the product in some way

Id the system oriented toward immediate gratification

Ideal of beauty a model, or exemplar, of appearance valued by a culture

Ideal self a person's conception of how he or she would like to be

Identity marketing a practice whereby consumers are paid to alter some aspects of their selves to advertise for a branded product

Idiocentric a person who has an individualist orientation

Illusion of truth effect telling people that a consumer claim is false can make them misremember it as true

Impression management our efforts to "manage" what others think of us by strategically choosing clothing and other cues that will put us in a good light

Impulse buying a process that occurs when the consumer experiences a sudden urge to purchase an item that he or she cannot resist

Incidental learning unintentional acquisition of knowledge

Index a sign that is connected to a product because they share some property

Individualist culture cultural orientation that encourages people to attach more importance to personal goals than to group goals; values such as personal enjoyment and freedom are stressed

Inertia the process whereby purchase decisions are made out of habit because the consumer lacks the motivation to consider alternatives

Information search the process by which the consumer surveys his or her environment for appropriate data to make a reasonable decision

Innovation a product or style that is perceived as new by consumers

Innovators people who are always on the lookout for novel developments and will be the first to try a new offering

Instrumental conditioning also known as operant conditioning, occurs as the individual learns to perform behaviors that produce positive outcomes and to avoid those that yield negative outcomes

Instrumental values goals endorsed because they are needed to achieve desired end states, or terminal values

Intelligent agents software programs that learn from past user behavior in order to recommend new purchases

Interactive mobile marketing real-time promotional campaigns targeted to consumers' cell phones

Interference one way that forgetting occurs; as additional information is learned, it displaces the earlier information

Interpretant the meaning derived from a sign or symbol

Interpretation the process whereby meanings are assigned to stimuli

Interpretivism as opposed to the dominant positivist perspective on consumer behavior, instead stresses the importance of symbolic, subjective experience and the idea that meaning is in the mind of the person rather than

existing "out there" in the objective world

Invidious distinction the display of wealth or power to inspire envy in others

Involvement the motivation to process product-related information

j.n.d. (just noticeable difference) the minimum difference between two stimuli that can be detected by a perceiver

Kansei engineering a Japanese philosophy that translates customers' feelings into design elements

Kin-network system the rituals intended to maintain ties among family members, both immediate and extended

Knowledge structure organized system of concepts relating to brands, stores, and other concepts

Laddering a technique for uncovering consumers' associations between specific attributes and general values

Laggards consumers who are exceptionally slow to adopt innovations

Late adopters the majority of consumers who are moderately receptive to adopting innovations

Lateral cycling a process in which already-purchased objects are sold to others or exchanged for other items

Latitudes of acceptance and rejection in the social judgment theory of attitudes, the notion that people differ in terms of the information they will find acceptable or unacceptable. They form latitudes of acceptance and rejection around an attitude standard. Ideas that fall within a latitude will be favorably received, but those falling outside of this zone will not

Lead users involved, experienced customers (usually corporate customers) who are very knowledgeable about the field

Learning a relatively permanent change in a behavior caused by experience

Licensing popular marketing strategy that pays for the right to link a product or service to the name of a well-known brand or designer

Lifestyle a set of shared values or tastes exhibited by a group of consumers, especially as these are reflected in consumption patterns

Limited problem solving a problem-solving process in which consumers are not motivated to search for information or to rigorously evaluate each alternative; instead they use simple decision rules to arrive at a purchase decision

List of Values (LOV) scale identifies consumer segments based on the values

members endorse and relates each value to differences in consumption behaviors

LOHAS an acronym for "lifestyles of health and sustainability"; a consumer segment that worries about the environment, wants products to be produced in a sustainable way, and who spend money to advance what they see as their personal development and potential

Long-term memory (LTM) the system that allows us to retain information for a long period of time

Look-alike packaging putting a generic or private label product in a package that resembles a popular brand to associate the brand with the popular one

Looking-glass self the process of imagining the reaction of others toward oneself

Low-context culture in contrast to high-context cultures that have strong oral traditions and that are more sensitive to nuance, low-context cultures are more literal

Low-literate consumer people who read at a very low level; tend to avoid situations where they will have to reveal their inability to master basic consumption decisions such as ordering from a menu

M-commerce the practice of promoting and selling goods and services via wireless devices including cell phones, PDAs, and iPods

Machinimas short films based on scenes from games or events that occur in virtual worlds

Market beliefs a consumer's specific beliefs or decision rules pertaining to marketplace phenomena

Market maven a person who often serves as a source of information about marketplace activities

Market segmentation strategies targeting a brand only to specific groups rather than to everybody

Masculinism study devoted to the male image and the cultural meanings of masculinity

Masked branding strategy that deliberately hides a product's origin

Mass class a term analysts use to describe the millions of global consumers who now enjoy a level of purchasing power that's sufficient to let them afford many high-quality products

Mass customization the personalization of products and services for individual customers at a mass-production price

Match-up hypothesis a celebrity's image and that of the product he or she endorses should be similar to maximize the credibility and effectiveness of the communication

Materialism the importance consumers attach to worldly possessions

Megachurches very large churches that serve between 2,000 and 20,000 congregants

Membership reference group ordinary people whose consumption activities provide informational social influence

Meme theory a perspective that uses a medical metaphor to explain how an idea or product enters the consciousness of people over time, much like a virus

Memory a process of acquiring information and storing it over time so that it will be available when needed

Mental accounting principle that states that decisions are influenced by the way a problem is posed

Metaphor the use of an explicit comparison ("A" is "B") between a product and some other person, place, or thing

Metrosexual a straight, urban male who exhibits strong interests and knowledge regarding product categories such as fashion, home design, gourmet cooking, and personal care that run counter to the traditional male sex role

Microcultures groups that form around a strong shared identification with an activity or art form

Microloans Small sums—typically less than $100—banks lend to entrepreneurs in developing countries

Minipreneurs one-person businesses

Modeling imitating the behavior of others

Modified rebuy in the context of the buy-class framework, a task that requires a modest amount of information search and evaluation, often focused on identifying the appropriate vendor

Monomyth a myth with basic characteristics that are found in many cultures

Motivation an internal state that activates goal-oriented behavior

Motivational research a qualitative research approach, based on psychoanalytic (Freudian) interpretations, with a heavy emphasis on unconscious motives for consumption

Multiattribute attitude models those models that assume that a consumer's attitude (evaluation) of an attitude object depends on the beliefs he or she has about several or many attributes of the object; the use of a multiattribute model implies that an attitude toward a product or brand can be predicted by identifying these specific beliefs and combining them to derive a measure of the consumer's overall attitude

Multigenerational marketing strategy an appeal to people of different ages with imagery from an older generation that also turns on younger consumers

Multiple pathway anchoring and adjustment (MPAA) model a model that emphasizes multiple pathways to attitude formation

Multitasking processing information from more than one medium at a time

Myth a story containing symbolic elements that expresses the shared emotions and ideals of a culture

Narrative product information in the form of a story

Need a basic biological motive

Negative reinforcement the process whereby the environment weakens responses to stimuli so that inappropriate behavior is avoided

Negative word of mouth the passing on of negative experiences involved with products or services by consumers to other potential customers to influence others' choices

Netnography a research technique that adapts ethnographic techniques anthropologists use to study real-world cultures to understand the social dynamics of virtual communities

Neuromarketing a new technique that uses a brain scanning device called functional magnetic resonance imaging (fMRI), that tracks blood flow as people perform mental tasks. Scientists know that specific regions of the brain light up in these scans to show increased blood flow when a person recognizes a face, hears a song, makes a decision, senses deception, and so on. Now they are trying to harness this technology to measure consumers' reactions to movie trailers, choices about automobiles, the appeal of a pretty face, and loyalty to specific brands

New task in the context of the buyclass framework, a task that requires a great degree of effort and information search

Noncompensatory decision rules decision shortcuts a consumer makes when a product with a low standing on one attribute cannot make up for this position by being better on another attribute

Normative influence the process in which a reference group helps to set and enforce fundamental standards of conduct

Norms the informal rules that govern what is right or wrong

Nostalgia a bittersweet emotion; the past is viewed with sadness and longing; many "classic" products appeal to consumers' memories of their younger days

Nuclear family a contemporary living arrangement composed of a married couple and their children

Object in semiotic terms, the product that is the focus of a message

Observational learning the process in which people learn by watching the actions of others and noting the reinforcements they receive for their behaviors

Opinion leader person who is knowledgeable about products and who frequently is able to influence others' attitudes or behaviors with regard to a product category

Organizational buyers people who purchase goods and services on behalf of companies for use in the process of manufacturing, distribution, or resale

Paradigm a widely accepted view or model of phenomena being studied; the perspective that regards people as rational information processors is currently the dominant paradigm, although this approach is now being challenged by a new wave of research that emphasizes the frequently subjective nature of consumer decision making

Parental yielding the process that occurs when a parental decision maker is influenced by a child's product request

Parody display deliberately avoiding status symbols; to seek status by mocking it

Part-list cueing effect a strategy to utilize the interference process in memory; when a marketer presents only a portion of the items in a category to consumers, they don't recall the omitted items as easily

Pastiche mixture of images

Perceived age how old a person feels as compared to his or her true chronological age

Perceived risk belief that a product has potentially negative consequences

Perception the process by which stimuli are selected, organized, and interpreted

Perceptual defense the tendency for consumers to avoid processing stimuli that are threatening to them

Perceptual filters past experiences that influence what stimuli we decide to process.

Perceptual map a research tool used to understand how a brand is positioned in consumers' minds relative to competitors

Perceptual selection process by which people attend to only a small portion of the stimuli to which they are exposed

Perceptual vigilance the tendency for consumers to be more aware of stimuli that relate to their current needs

Permission marketing popular strategy based on the idea that a marketer will be much more successful in persuading consumers who have agreed to let them try

Personality a person's unique psychological makeup, which consistently influences the way the person responds to his or her environment

Personality traits identifiable characteristics that define a person

Persuasion an active attempt to change attitudes

Pleasure principle the belief that behavior is guided by the desire to maximize pleasure and avoid pain

Plinking act of embedding a product or service link in a video

Point-of-purchase (POP) stimuli the promotional materials that are deployed in stores or other outlets to influence consumers' decisions at the time products are purchased

Popular culture the music, movies, sports, books, celebrities, and other forms of entertainment consumed by the mass market

Pop-up stores temporary locations that allow a company to test new brands without a huge financial commitment

Positioning strategy an organization's use of elements in the marketing mix to influence the consumer's interpretation of a product's meaning vis-à-vis competitors

Positive reinforcement the process whereby rewards provided by the environment strengthen responses to stimuli and appropriate behavior is learned

Positivism a research perspective that relies on principles of the "scientific method" and assumes that a single reality exists; events in the world can be objectively measured; and the causes of behavior can be identified, manipulated, and predicted

POSSLQ (Persons of Opposite Sex Sharing Living Quarters) U.S. Census designation for unmarried couples who cohabitate

Prediction market an approach based on the idea that groups of people with knowledge about an industry are jointly better predictors of the future than are any individuals

Priming properties of a stimulus that evoke a schema that leads us to compare the stimulus to other similar ones we encountered in the past

Principle of cognitive consistency the belief that consumers value harmony among their thoughts, feelings, and behaviors and that they are motivated to maintain uniformity among these elements

Principle of similarity the *Gestalt* principle that describes how consumers tend to group objects that share similar physical characteristics

PRIZM (Potential Rating Index by Zip Market) clustering technique that classifies every zip code in the United States into one of 66 categories, ranging from the most affluent "Blue-Blood Estates" to the least well off "Public Assistance," developed by Claritas, Inc.

Problem recognition the process that occurs whenever the consumer sees a significant difference between his or her current state of affairs and some desired or ideal state; this recognition initiates the decision-making process

Product complementarity the view that products in different functional categories have symbolic meanings that are related to one another

Product line extension related products to an established brand

Product placement the process of obtaining exposure for a product by arranging for it to be inserted into a movie, television show, or some other medium

Product signal communicates an underlying quality of a product through the use of aspects that are only visible in the ad

Profane consumption the process of consuming objects and events that are ordinary or of the everyday world

Progressive learning model the perspective that people gradually learn a new culture as they increasingly come in contact with it; consumers assimilate into a new culture, mixing practices from their old and new environments to create a hybrid culture

Prospect theory a descriptive model of how people make choices

Psychographics the use of psychological, sociological, and anthropological factors to construct market segments

Psychophysics the science that focuses on how the physical environment is integrated into the consumer's subjective experience

Punishment the learning that occurs when a response is followed by unpleasant events

Purchase momentum initial impulses to buy in order to satisfy our needs increase the likelihood that we will buy even more

Queuing theory the mathematical study of waiting lines

Rational perspective a view of the consumer as a careful, analytical decision maker who tries to maximize utility in purchase decisions

Reality engineering the process whereby elements of popular culture are appropriated by marketers and become integrated into marketing strategies

Reality principle principle that the ego seeks ways that will be acceptable to society to gratify the id

Recall the process of retrieving information from memory; in advertising research the extent to which consumers can remember a marketing message without being exposed to it during the study

Reciprocity norm a culturally learned obligation to return the gesture of a gift with one of equal value

Recognition in advertising research the extent to which consumers say they are familiar with an ad the researcher shows them

Reference group an actual or imaginary individual or group that has a significant effect on an individual's evaluations, aspirations, or behavior

Refutational arguments calling attention to a product's negative attributes as a persuasive strategy where a negative issue is raised and then dismissed; this approach can increase source credibility

Relationship marketing the strategic perspective that stresses the long-term, human side of buyer-seller interactions

Resonance a literary device, frequently used in advertising that uses a play on words (a double meaning) to communicate a product benefit

Response bias a form of contamination in survey research in which some factor, such as the desire to make a good impression on the experimenter, leads respondents to modify their true answers

Restricted codes the ways of expressing and interpreting meanings that focus on the content of objects, which tend to be used by the working class

Retail theming strategy where stores create imaginative environments that transport shoppers to fantasy worlds or provide other kinds of stimulation

Retrieval the process whereby desired information is recovered from long-term memory

Retro brand an updated version of a brand from a prior historical period

RFID (response frequency identification device) a small plastic tag that holds a computer chip capable of storing a small amount of information, along with an antenna that lets the device communicate with a computer network. These devices are being implanted in a wide range of products to enable marketers to track inventory more efficiently

Rich media elements of an online ad that employ movement to gain attention

Risky shift the tendency for individuals to consider riskier alternatives after conferring with a group than if members made their own decisions with no discussion

Rites of passage sacred times marked by a change in social status

Ritual a set of multiple, symbolic behaviors that occur in a fixed sequence and that tend to be repeated periodically

Ritual artifacts items (consumer goods) used in the performance of rituals

Role theory the perspective that much of consumer behavior resembles actions in a play

Sacralization a process that occurs when ordinary objects, events, or people take on sacred meaning to a culture or to specific groups within a culture

Sacred consumption the process of consuming objects and events that are set apart from normal life and treated with some degree of respect or awe

Salience the prominence of a brand in memory

Schema an organized collection of beliefs and feelings represented in a cognitive category

Script a learned schema containing a sequence of events an individual expects to occur

Search engines software (such as Google) that helps consumers access information based upon their specific requests

Self-concept the beliefs a person holds about his or her own attributes and how he or she evaluates these qualities

Self-gifts consumers purchase self-gifts as a way to regulate their behavior. The items consumers purchase for themselves are to reward them for good deeds, to console them after negative events, or to motivate them to accomplish some goal

Self-image congruence models the approaches based on the prediction that products will be chosen when their attributes match some aspect of the self

Self-perception theory an alternative (to cognitive dissonance) explanation of dissonance effects; it assumes that people use observations of their own behavior to infer their attitudes toward some object

Semiotics a field of study that examines the correspondence between signs and symbols and the meaning or meanings they convey

Sensation the immediate response of sensory receptors (eyes, ears, nose, mouth, fingers) to such basic stimuli as light, color, sound, odors, and textures

Sensory marketing marketing strategies that focus on the impact of sensations on our product experiences

Sensory memory the temporary storage of information received from the senses

Sensory overload a condition where consumers are exposed to far more information than they can process

Sex-typed traits characteristics that are stereotypically associated with one gender or the other

Shaping the learning of a desired behavior over time by rewarding intermediate actions until the final result is obtained

Shopmobbing new Japanese practice; strangers organize online around a specific product or service and arrange to meet at a certain date and time in a real-world store to negotiate a group discount

Shopping orientation a consumer's general attitudes and motivations regarding the act of shopping

Short-term memory (STM) the mental system that allows us to retain information for a short period of time

Shrinkage the loss of money or inventory from shoplifting and/or employee theft

Sign the sensory imagery that represents the intended meanings of the object

Silent commerce new trend that enables transactions and information gathering to occur in the background without any direct intervention by consumers or managers

Simile comparing two objects that share a similar property

Sleeper effect the process whereby differences in attitude change between positive and negative sources seem to diminish over time

Social aging theories a perspective to understand how society assigns people to different roles across the life span

Social class the overall rank of people in a society; people who are grouped within the same social class are approximately equal in terms of their income, occupations, and lifestyles

Social judgment theory the perspective that people assimilate new information about attitude objects in light of what they already know or feel; the initial attitude acts as a frame of reference, and new information is categorized in terms of this standard

Social loafing the tendency for people not to devote as much to a task when their contribution is part of a larger group effort

Social marketing the promotion of causes and ideas (social products), such as energy conservation, charities, and population control

Social mobility the movement of individuals from one social class to another

Social networking a growing practice whereby Web sites let members post information about themselves and make contact with others who share similar interests and opinions or who want to make business contacts

Social power the capacity of one person to alter the actions or outcome of another

Social stratification the process in a social system by which scarce and valuable resources are distributed unequally to status positions that become more or less permanently ranked in terms of the share of valuable resources each receives

Sociometric methods the techniques for measuring group dynamics that involve tracing communication patterns in and among groups

Source attractiveness the dimensions of a communicator that increase his or her persuasiveness; these include expertise and attractiveness

Source credibility a communications source's perceived expertise, objectivity, or trustworthiness

Spacing effect the tendency to recall printed material to a greater extent when the advertiser repeats the target item periiodically rather than presenting it over and over at the same time

Spontaneous recovery ability of a stimulus to evoke a weakened response even years after the person initially perceived it

Spreading activation meanings in memory are activated indirectly; as a node is activated, other nodes linked to it are also activated so that meanings spread across the network

Stage of cognitive development the ability to comprehend concepts of increasing complexity as a person matures

Starch test widely-used measure of recall for magazine advertisements

State-dependent retrieval people are better able to access information if their internal state is the same at the time of recall as when they learned the information

Status crystallization the extent to which different indicators of a person's status (income, ethnicity, occupation) are consistent with one another

Status hierarchy a ranking of social desirability in terms of consumers' access to resources such as money, education, and luxury goods

Status symbols products that are purchased and displayed to signal membership in a desirable social class

Stimulus discrimination the process that occurs when behaviors caused by two stimuli are different, as when consumers learn to differentiate a brand from its competitors

Stimulus generalization the process that occurs when the behavior caused by a reaction to one stimulus occurs in the presence of other, similar stimuli

Storage the process that occurs when knowledge in long-term memory is integrated with what is already in memory and "warehoused" until needed

Store image a store's "personality," composed of such attributes as location, merchandise suitability, and the knowledge and congeniality of the sales staff

Straight rebuy in the context of the buy-class framework, the type of buying decision that is virtually automatic and requires little deliberation

Subculture a group whose members share beliefs and common experiences that set them apart from other members of a culture

Subjective norm an additional component to the multiattribute attitude model that accounts for the effects of what we believe other people think we should do

Subliminal perception the processing of stimuli presented below the level of the consumer's awareness

Superego the system that internalizes society's rules and that works to prevent the id from seeking selfish gratification

Surrogate consumer a professional who is retained to evaluate and/or make purchases on behalf of a consumer

Symbol a sign that is related to a product through either conventional or agreed-on associations

Symbolic interactionism a sociological approach stressing that relationships with other people play a large part in forming the self; people live in a symbolic environment, and the meaning attached to any situation or object is determined by a person's interpretation of these symbols

Symbolic self-completion theory the perspective that people who have an incomplete self-definition in some context will compensate by acquiring symbols associated with a desired social identity

Syncretic decision purchase decision that is made jointly by both spouses

Synoptic ideal a model of spousal decision making in which the husband and wife take a common view and act as joint decision makers, assigning each other well-defined roles and making mutually beneficial decisions to maximize the couple's joint utility

Taste culture a group of consumers who share aesthetic and intellectual preferences

Terminal values end states desired by members of a culture

Theory of cognitive dissonance theory based on the premise that a state of tension is created when beliefs or behaviors conflict with one another; people are motivated to reduce this inconsistency (or dissonance) and thus eliminate unpleasant tension

Theory of reasoned action an updated version of the Fishbein multiattribute attitude theory that considers factors such as social pressure and A_{act} (the attitude toward the act of buying a product), rather than simply attitudes toward the product itself

Theory of trying states that the criterion of behavior in the reasoned action model of attitude measurement should be replaced with *trying* to reach a goal

The Values and Lifestyles System (VALS™) a psychographic segmentation system used to categorize consumers into clusters, or "VALS types"

Time poverty a feeling of having less time available than is required to meet the demands of everyday living

Tipping point moment of critical mass

Total quality management (TQM) management and engineering procedures aimed at reducing errors and increasing quality; based on Japanese practices

Trade dress color combinations that become strongly associated with a corporation

Transitional economies a country that is adapting from a controlled, centralized economy to a free-market system

Tribal marketing strategy linking a product's identity to an activity-based "tribe" such as basketball players

Trickle-down theory the perspective that fashions spread as the result of status symbols associated with the upper classes "trickling down" to other social classes as these consumers try to emulate those with greater status

Tweens a marketing term used to describe children aged 8 to 14

Two-factor theory the perspective that two separate psychological processes are operating when a person is repeatedly exposed to an ad: repetition increases familiarity and thus reduces uncertainty about the product but over time boredom increases with each exposure, and at some point the amount of boredom incurred begins to exceed the amount of uncertainty reduced, resulting in wear-out

Übersexual male who is similar to a metrosexual but who also has traditional masculine qualities

U-commerce the use of ubiquitous networks that will slowly but surely become a part of us, such as wearable computers or customized advertisements beamed to us on our cell phones

Unconditioned stimulus (UCS) a stimulus that is naturally capable of causing a response

Underground economy secondary markets (such as flea markets) where transactions are not officially recorded

Value a belief that some condition is preferable to its opposite

Value system a culture's ranking of the relative importance of values

Variety seeking the desire to choose new alternatives over more familiar ones

Vigilante marketing a practice where freelancers and fans film their own commercials for favorite products and post them on Web sites

Viral marketing the strategy of getting customers to sell a product on behalf of the company that creates it

Virtual community of consumption a collection of people whose online interactions are based on shared enthusiasm for and knowledge of a specific consumption activity

Virtual identity the appearance and personality a person takes on as an avatar in a computer-mediated environment like Second Life

Voice of the consumer an approach to new product development that solicits feedback from end customers well before the company puts a new product on the market

Voluntary simplifiers people who believe that once basic material needs are satisfied, additional income does not lead to happiness

Von Restorff effect techniques like distinctive packaging that increase the novelty of a stimulus also improve recall

Want the particular form of consumption chosen to satisfy a need

Warming process of transforming new objects and places into those that feel cozy, hospitable and authentic

Web 2.0 rebirth of the Internet as a social, interactive medium from its original roots as a form of one-way transmission from producers to consumers

Weber's Law the principle that the stronger the initial stimulus, the greater its change must be for it to be noticed

Weblog online personal journal

Wiki online program that let several people change a document on a Web page and then track those changes

Wisdom of crowds a perspective that argues under the right circumstances, groups are smarter than the smartest people in them; implies that large numbers of consumers can predict successful products

Word of mouth (WOM) product information transmitted by individual consumers on an informal basis

Zipf's Law pattern that describes the tendency for the most robust effect to be far more powerful than others in its class; applies to consumer behavior in terms of buyers' overwhelming preferences for the market leader in a product category

Credits

Chapter 1
28: Reprinted with the permision of Primedia Enthusiast Media, Inc.; 30: © Steve Chenn/CORBIS; 36: Reprinted with the permision of Primedia Enthusiast Media, Inc.; 37: The Burger King ® trademark and images of the Burger King are used with permission from Burger King Brands, Inc.; 38: with permission of Museum of Bad Art (MOBA); 41: © The Procter & Gamble Company. Used by permission; 41: Alain Le Bot/Getty Images, Inc.; 41: Courtesy of The Pillsbury Company; 42: Courtesy of Samsung Electronics America, Inc. Reprinted by permission; 44: Courtesy of BBDO Singapore; 46: Courtesy of R. Torre and Company; 49: Used with permission of American Association of Advertising Agencies; 50: Courtesy of Almap BBDO Communicacoes Ltda., photographer: Alexandre Ermel; 53: Used with the permission Duval Guillaume Ad Agency; 54: Used Courtesy of Leo Burnett Shanghai Advertising Ltd.; 55: By Alan Andreasen, Georgetown University; 56: Used with permission of Saatchi & Saatchi Singapore; 57: "Tippex" ANTI NUCLEAR CAMPAIGN for GREENPEACE. Created by Tiempo BBDO. Creative General Manager: Siscu Molina, Executive Creative Director: Ferran Blanch, Copywriter: Javi Inglés, Art Director: Manuel Padilla, Account Supervisor: Marta Puig Advertiser's Supervisor: Alberto Zschiesche. Used courtesy of Tiempo BBDO and Greenpeace; 58: © Unknown Artist, 2007; 59: Used with permission of Modern Drunkard Magazine.

Chapter 2
74: Used with permission of Francesco Biasia and D'Adda, Lorenzini, Vigorelli BBDO; 76: © CORBIS SYGMA; 80: Courtesy of Leagas Delaney, Milan; 81: Used with the permission of The City of Helsinki Information office; 83: Used with permission of the San Francisco Ballet; 85: Craig Maxwell Photography Inc.; 85: Courtesy of Grey Worldwide, Indonesia; 86: Courtesy of Tide/Leo Burnett, Mumbai, India; 88: Courtesy of Cashmere/John St., Toronto; 89: Client: PowWow Bar & Restaurant. Agency: Jung von Matt/Spree, Germany. Chief Creative Officer: Burkhart von Scheven. Art Direction: David Mously. Copywriters: Mirko Stolz, Anteje Lichtenberg. Photographer: Karin Stelzer; 90: Source: Tiempo BBDO Barcelona; 92: By Larry D. Compeau, Clarkson University; 93: Campbell Soup Company; 94: © 2005. Molson USA, LLC.; 95: © 2005. Molson USA, LLC.; 100: Courtesy of Saatch & Saatchi, Singapore Frederic Eng; 101: Used with permission TWBA London on behalf of French Connection; 102: © M&C Saatchi, 2007; 104: By Prof. Kent Grayson, Associate Professor of Marketing, Northwestern University; 110: Courtesy of SideTrack Technologies, Inc.

Chapter 3
114: Getty Images, Inc.-Stone Allstock/Bruce Ayres; 117: Used with permission of Sukle Advertising & Design; 119: Used with permission of American Airlines; 120: Courtesy of Chiquita Brands, Inc.; 127: Used with permission of American Airlines and the OneWorld Airline Consortium; 131: Courtesy of The Miller Group Advertising Agency, Los Angeles; 132: By Jennifer Escalas, Vanderbilt University; 134: Courtesy of Grey Worldwide; 140: © Reminisce Magazine, 2007; 142: Used with permission of Fossil Inc. Photography by Thom Jackson and Jon Kirk; 144: © 2007, Merkle Agency.

Chapter 4
152: © Thierry Orban/CORBIS SYGMA; 155: Courtesy of M & C Saatchi, Singapore; 156: Used with the permission of Soloflex; 157: designed & released by Publinet Advertising & Publicity LLC, Dubai, UAE; 158: used with permission of Mazda NA; 163: Courtesy of Dr. Janeen Costa, University of Utah; 165: Courtesy of Swisspatat; 167: © Copyright 2007, Roto-Rooter Inc. Used with permission; 168: Courtesy of Jones Soda Co.; 173: © Doug Kanter/The New York Times; 175: Courtesy of Saatchi & Saatchi, China; 177: Used with permission of Ink! Coffee and Cultivator Advertising & Design; 179: By Lynn Kahle, University of Oregon; 187: © Climate Clean LLC. Used with permission; 188: Courtesy of Prof. Robert Kozinets, York University.

Chapter 5
194: PhotoEdit, Inc./ Robert Brenner; 196: © Michael Seibel, 2007. Used with permission; 199: courtesy of TBWA, Amsterdam, and Joshua Burrows. Photography by Dimitri Daniloff; 200: Robbie Cooper; 201: Robbie Cooper; 201: Robbie Cooper; 202: Hope Jensen Schau; 203: Andrea Mohin/The New York Times; 205: Used with permission of D'Adda, Lorenzini, Vigorelli BBDO; 208: Used with permission of Francesco Biasia and D'Adda, Lorenzini, Vigorelli BBDO; 211: Courtesy of Bijan Fragrances c/o FashionWorld; 213: © Hiroshi Kai, 2007. Wired logo/text © 2007 Wired, Inc. Used with permission; 214: Used with the permission of August, Lang and Husak, Inc.; 215: Agency: Downtown Partners Chicago. Writer: Sean Austin. Art Directors: Joe Stuart and Tom Kim; 217: Courtesy of Bartle Bogle Hegarty New York aka BBH; 218: Used courtesy of KesselsKramer; 220: Copyright © 2006 Philip Greenberg; 222: © 2007 Headblade, Inc.; 228: Courtesy of Unilever Home and Personal Care NA; 232: Used with permission of Tattoo Arts Magazine and Art and Ink Enterprise.

Chapter 6
242: © David Pu'u/CORBIS; 245: Used with permission of United Airlines; 252: © SHAUN CURRY/AFP/Getty Images; 254: Harvard Graduate School of Business Administration; 256: By Susan Fournier, Professor of Marketing; 258: Courtesy of Blue Media, Bliss Beverage; 259: © 2003 General Motors Corporation. Used with permission of HUMMER and General Motors; 259: Courtesy of White Aryan Resistance; 260: Courtesy of Jayco Inc.; 261: Courtesy of General Electric; 263: Ad Agency: SCPF, Photographer: Biel Capllonch; 270: Courtesy of 86 The Onion Ad Agency; 271: Courtesy of Saskatoon Restaurant, Greenville, SC.

Chapter 7
280: Corbis RF/Jose Luis Pelaez, Inc.; 284: AP World Wide Photos; 288: By Joseph Priester, University of Southern California; 289: Courtesy of Energy BBD0, Chicago; 290: Courtesy of Smith & Wollensky Steak House; 291: Bokelberg, US, Inc/Wayne Bokelberg; 292: AP Wide World Photos; 293: © Vizoo, Inc., 2007; 294: PhotoEdit, Inc/David Young-Wolff; 296: PhotoEdit, Inc/Michael Newman; 298: PhotoEdit, Inc./Spencer Grant; 302: PhotoDisc/Getty Images; 303: Client: Asia Injury Prevention Foundation. Greig Craft - President, Asia Injury Prevention Foundation Mirjam Sidik - Vice President of Regional Operations. Agency: Ogilvy & Mather. Tom Notman - Executive Creative Director. Le Cong Ky-Production Manager. Alex Clegg - Planning Director. Alan Couldrey-Regional Director Asia Pacific. Katryna Mojica - Managing Director. Carla Laus - Group Account Director. Huy Bui - Account Director. Dung Tran - Account Executive. NamPhuong Tran - Account Executive. Photographer: Dusit Phongkraphan.

Chapter 8
312: © Jose Luis Pelaez, Inc/ CORBIS; 319: © The Procter & Gamble Company. Used by permission; 320: Ann E. Schlosser; 321: © epinions.com. All rights reserved, 2007; 326: Used with permission of NoDNA c/o Vierte Art; 328: Courtesy of DDB, London; 332: © Procter & Gamble Company, 2007. Used with permission; 334: Courtesy of KesselsKramer, Amsterdam; 335: Courtesy of Saatchi & Saatchi.

Chapter 9
346: Courtesy of Jung von Matt/Basis GmbH; 348: © Gary Houlder/CORBIS; 354: 3M and Scotchgard are registered trademarks of 3M; 355: © KesselsKramer, Amsterdam; 361: Courtesy of Minolta Corporation;

363: © Abbott Mead Vickers BBDO, London. Ad created and produced by Simon Langley, Richard Morgan and John Offenbach; 364: Courtesy of Sunkist Growers; 368: By Roland Rust, University of Maryland; 369: Creative Director/Copywriter: Karpat Polat. Art Director: Ali Bati. Photographer: Ilkay Muratoglu; 370: Courtesy of draft FCB Jakarta Indonesia; 373: Courtesy of iParty Retail Store corp.; 374: © YTMND Inc. 2007; 376: Courtesy of www.frenchwinesfood.com; 378: © PopCap Games, 2007; 379: Photo courtesy of Newscast and MINI, a Division of BMW of North America, LLC.

Chapter 10
388: Getty Images, Inc.; 391: Courtesy of Hart Schaffner Marx/Hartmarx; 394: Courtesy Campbell Soup Company; 401: Courtesy of Bluefly.com; 404: By Permission of The New York Sun ©; 405: Ziba Designs; 405: Ziba Designs; 406: Design Group; 407: By Cele Otnes, University of Illinois at Urbana-Champaign; 410: Photo Researchers, Inc./Peter Byron; 411: AP Wide World Photos/Paul Sakuma; 412: Peter Freed; 414: Courtesy of Ford Motor Co.; 416: Courtesy of Planetfeedback.com c/o Consumer Café LLC.

Chapter 11
428: Getty Images, Inc-Taxi/Ken Ross; 433: PhotoEdit, Inc./Michael Newman; 434: PhotoEdit, Inc./Bill Aron; 436: Courtesy of Jung von Matt/Basis GmbH; 436: AP Wide World Photos; 437: Courtesy of U.S. Marines c/o JWT J. Walter Thompson ad agency; 438: © Michelin North America, Inc., 2007; 439: AP Wide World Photos; 440: PhotoEdit, Inc./Spencer Grant; 441: Corbis/Bettmann/Rob Lewine; 443: Courtesy of Joroen Siking Hoaxkill.com; 444: © 2007 Bzzagent; 447: The Image Works/Susan Goldman; 448: AP Wide World Photos/Kevok Djansezian; 451: By Al Muñiz, DePaul University; 452: Courtesy of MINI Division c/o BMW of North America LLC; 453: © Threadless, 2007; 454: © Tom Burns, 2007. Used with permission; 455: Courtesy of Sellaband; 456: Getty Images, Inc.-Liaison/Carl Scnneider.

Chapter 12
470: Corbis RF; 490: By Greg Rose, University of Washington at Tacoma; 474: used courtesy of Komatsu Europe; 478: Courtesy of Meredith Corp.; 479: © Procter and Gamble. Used with permission; 481: Source: Tiempo BBDO Barcelona; 483: © DaimlerChrysler Company LLC.; 485: Courtesy of Haggar Clothing Co.; 490: By Greg Rose, University of Washington at Tacoma; 495: PhotoEdit, Inc./Tom Prettyman.

Chapter 13
506: Christopher and Sally Gable © Doris Kindersley; 508: Getty Images, Inc./David Hanover; 510: Courtesy of F Nazca Saatchi & Saatchi; 511: Digital Vision; 515: Courtesy of Libbey Glass Co.; 516: Courtesy of The Phoenix Companies, Inc.; 518: Getty Images, Inc.; 523: AP World Wide Photos; 526: © Raymond Reuter/Corbis Sygma; 529: By Morris B. Holbrook, Columbia University; 530: Client: Bank Austria Creditanstalt AG. Agency: Jung von Matt/Donau, Austria. Creative direction: Gerd Schulte-Doeinghaus, Alexander Rabl. Art Direction:

Christian Hummer-Koppendorfer. Copywriters: Christoph Gaunersdorfer. Photographers: Gunter Parth; 533: Courtesy of Jagger Blindados; 534: Courtesy of Johnson & Johnson Health Care; 536: Stock Boston/Bob Kramer.

Chapter 14
532: PhotoEdit, Inc./Michael Newman; 545: © Ron Kimball Stock; 546: Vespa ® Image Courtesy of Piaggio USA, Inc. © the Piaggio Group of Companies 2003. All rights reserved; 546: Courtesy of Kingdom of Talossa; 548: PhotoEdit, Inc/Susan Van Etten; 553: America Online, Inc. AOL and the AOL Triangle logo are registered trademarks of America On-Line, Inc. Screenshot content © 2005 America Online, Inc. Used with Permission. All rights reserved; 554: used with permission of the Procter & Gamble Company; 556: Corbis/Bettmann/Timothy A. Clary; 558: École des Hautes Études Commerciales du Nord (EDHEC) ad; 560: PhotoEdit, Inc./A. Ramey; 561: © shipoffools.com; 563: Used courtesy of I.D. Magazine. Photo copyright © Smoke & Mirros Studio, Inc.; 563: Courtesy of Wow Publishing; 564: © Ted Streshinsky/Corbis; 565: © C28.com.

Chapter 15
572: Corbis/Bettmann/Larry Williams; 575: © TBWA, Toronto, 2007; 578: By Connie Pechmann; 579: American Honda Motor Co. Inc.; 583: Courtesy of Lorilland Tobacco Corp. c/o Lowe Worldwide; 585: © Procter & Gamble, 2007; 586: Stock Boston/Christopher Brown; 587: © Viacom, Inc., 2007; 589: Courtesy of Pepsico; 590: Botox® Cosmetics ad used with permission of Allergan Inc.; 592: Courtesy of Atena US Healthcare; 593: Courtesy of Unilver.

Chapter 16
600: Courtesy of Lucksurf.com; 602: © Peter Hvizdak/The Image Works; 605: Courtesy of Fantastic Foods; 608: By Russell W. Belk, York University; 610: Courtesy of LuckSurf.com; 612: Ting-Li Wang/The New York Times; 613: Corbis/Sygma; 618: Courtesy of DDB Hong Kong; 620: Hugh Rogers; 624: Deborah Denker/Getty Images, Inc.-Liason; 625: Courtesy of First Alert Corp.

Chapter 17
632: © Peter M. Fisher/Corbis; 639: Courtesy of AT & T archives; 641: Courtesy of Eddis Trailers c/o The Explorer Group; 643: Advertising Savants, Inc. St. Louis, MO USA; 645: Campaign by Ambient Planet, New York (Perry Kirk-Cerchio, President).; 648: © Entertainment Media Works, Inc.; 649: Courtesy of Massive Inc., owned by Microsoft; 650: J.L. Shrum; 654: Getty Images, Inc.- Hutton Archive Photos; 656: Courtesy of Maidenform Inc.; 657: Corbis/Sygma; 658: Under permission by V&S Vin & Sprit AB(publ). Absolut® Vodka. Absolut Country of Sweden Vodka & Logo, Absolut, Absolut Bottle Design and Absolute Caligraphy are Trademarks Owned by V&S Vin & Sprit AB(publ). © 2005 V&S Vin & Sprit AB(publ). Photographer: Shu Akashi; 661: Courtesy of Johnny Cupcakes; 663: Courtesy of Jim Beam Brands; 665: Courtesy of Electrolux.

Indexes

Name

Subject

Products/Organizations

Consumer Behavior Is Global

 DON'T MISS THESE EXAMPLES AND CONCEPTS FROM AROUND THE WORLD